SEVENTH EDITION

Australian School Oxford Dictionary

Australia's bestselling dictionaries

Edited by Mark Gwynn and Amanda Laugesen

Grammar and reference guide written by Margaret McKenzie and Susan Leslie

OXFORD
UNIVERSITY PRESS

Oxford University Press is a department of the University of Oxford. It furthers the University's objective of excellence in research, scholarship, and education by publishing worldwide. Oxford is a registered trademark of Oxford University Press in the UK and in certain other countries.

Published in Australia by
Oxford University Press
Level 8, 737 Bourke Street, Docklands, Victoria 3008, Australia.

First published 1994
Second edition 1998
Third edition 2004
Fourth edition 2008
Fifth edition 2012
Sixth edition 2016
Seventh edition 2021
Reprinted 2022, 2023, 2024, 2025 (twice)

A catalogue record for this book is available from the National Library of Australia

ISBN 978 0 19 033068 2

Botanical cover illustrations by Ink and Spindle
Typeset by CBT Typesetting & Design CC
Printed in India by Manipal Technologies Limited

Oxford University Press Australia & New Zealand is committed to sourcing paper responsibly.

Disclaimer
Links to third party websites are provided by Oxford in good faith and for information only. Oxford disclaims any responsibility for the materials contained in any third party website referenced in this work.

Acknowledgement of Country
Oxford University Press acknowledges the Traditional Owners of the many lands on which we create and share our learning resources. We acknowledge the Traditional Owners as the original storytellers, teachers and students of this land we call Australia. We pay our respects to Elders, past and present, for the ways in which they have enabled the teachings of their rich cultures and knowledge systems to be shared for millennia.

Warning to First Nations Australians
Aboriginal and Torres Strait Islander peoples are advised that this publication may include images or names of people now deceased.

Contents

Preface

The *Australian School Oxford Dictionary* has been specially written for students in the middle school years. It should serve as a working tool in the classroom and accustom its users to the style in which most adult dictionaries are written. At the same time, this dictionary is easy for students to use because it avoids abbreviations and similar conventions. Like other Australian dictionaries published by Oxford University Press, it draws on the continually updated database of Australian English at the Australian National Dictionary Centre in Canberra, as well as the vast resources and databases of Oxford Dictionaries in the UK, including the *Oxford English Dictionary*.

The words in this dictionary have been chosen with the needs and interests of its intended audience in mind. The seventh edition includes new and revised usage notes. These notes provide guidance and clarification for words that can present difficulties in regards to pronunciation, spelling, grammar, or their use in Australian society. As well as updates to existing entries, a significant number of new entries have also been included in this edition. Many of these revisions and additions reflect the use of language encountered by students in school resources including workbooks. A revised Grammar and Reference guide by Margaret McKenzie and Susan Leslie is included as an insert.

The *Australian School Oxford Dictionary* gives the origin of words (where the derivation sheds light on the word's meaning) to show the connection between related words, to help with recognising word elements, or for general interest in the history of a word. For words that have been borrowed from Aboriginal languages the etymology section specifies the language from which the word has been borrowed, and the language can be located on the map provided (p. viii). Many words are given pronunciations—a detailed guide is provided (p. vi).

We would like to thank Lauren Sadow for her editorial assistance on this project. Thank you to the team at Oxford University Press (especially Katrina Heydon and Phillip Louw) for their ongoing support and publishing expertise.

Mark Gwynn and Amanda Laugesen

Guide to dictionary entries

amnesia (*say* am-**nee**-zee-uh) *noun* loss of memory. [from Greek *a-* = without, + *-mnesis* = memory]

formal[1] *adjective* strictly following the accepted rules or customs; ceremonious. **formally** *adverb*

kilo *noun* (*plural* **kilos**) a kilogram.

kind[1] *noun* a class of similar things or animals; a sort or type.
payment in kind payment in goods not in money.

> **Usage** Correct use is *this kind of thing* or *these kinds of things* (not 'these kind of things').

kind[2] *adjective* friendly and helpful; considerate. **kind-hearted** *adjective*, **kindness** *noun*

kindy *noun* (*Australian informal*) kindergarten.

king *noun* **1** a man who is the ruler of a country through inheriting the position. **2** a person or thing regarded as supreme, *the lion is the king of beasts*. **3** the most important piece in chess. **4** a playing card with a picture of a king. **kingly** *adjective*

opt *verb* choose.
opt out decide not to join in. [from Latin *optare* = wish for]

weapon *noun* something used to do harm in a battle or fight. **weaponry** *noun*

wear[1] *verb* (**wore, worn, wearing**) **1** have something on your body as clothes, ornaments, etc. **2** damage something by rubbing or using it often; become damaged in this way, *The carpet has worn thin*. **3** last while in use, *It has worn well*. **wearable** *adjective*, **wearer** *noun*
wear off 1 be removed by wear or use. **2** become less intense.
wear on pass gradually, *The night wore on*.
wear out 1 use or be used until it becomes weak or useless. **2** exhaust.

wear[2] *noun* **1** clothes, *formal wear*. **2** damage resulting from ordinary use, *wear and tear*.

weary[1] *adjective* (**wearier, weariest**) **1** tired. **2** tiring, *It's weary work*. **wearily** *adverb*, **weariness** *noun*

weary[2] *verb* (**wearied, wearying**) tire.

worn[1] *past participle* of **wear**[1].

Headword: the word being defined in the entry. Entries are arranged in alphabetical order of headwords.

Plural: the plural form of the headword.

Raised numbers: distinguish words with the same spelling that have separate entries for different parts of speech or unrelated meanings.

Compound: a word formed from the headword plus one or more other words.

Derivative: a word derived from the headword whose meaning can be worked out from the meaning of the headword.

Verb forms: the first form is the past tense, the second the past participle, and the third the present participle.

Phrase: listed and defined under the entry for the main word in the phrase.

Verb forms: the first form is the past tense and past participle; the second is the present participle.

Pronunciation: shows how to say the word. (See also p. vi.)

Etymology: the origin of the headword.

Definition: the meaning of the headword.

Usage note: a note explaining correct usage.

Usage label: indicates the word belongs to Australian English and is normally used informally. (See p. vii for more information on usage labels.)

Part of speech: describes the grammatical use of a word as a *noun, verb, adverb, adjective,* etc.

Numbers: used for different senses of the headword.

Example: shows how the word is used and helps to clarify the meaning.

Adjective forms: the comparative and superlative forms of the headword.

Cross-reference: refers the reader to another entry for more information.

Spelling

Many verbs ending in **-ise** (such as *realise*) and their corresponding nouns ending in **-isation** (such as *realisation*) may also be spelt with *z* instead of *s*. However, only **-ise** should be used in *advertise, advise, apprise, arise, chastise, comprise, compromise, demise, despise, devise, enfranchise, enterprise, excise, exercise, franchise, improvise, incise, merchandise, practise, promise, revise, rise, supervise, surmise, surprise, televise*, and in verbs ending in *-aise*, *-oise*, and *-uise*.

Pronunciation

A guide to pronunciation is given for any word that is difficult to pronounce, or difficult to recognise when read, or spelled the same as another word but pronounced differently. The pronunciation given represents standard Australian speech.

The sounds represented are as follows:

a	as in **a**nd, b**a**t, c**a**t
ah	as in c**al**m, p**a**th, **ar**m
air	as in f**air**, c**are**, th**ere**
aw	as in l**aw**, f**or**, s**ore**
ay	as in pl**ay**, **a**ge, f**a**ce
b	as in **b**ed
ch	as in **ch**in, **ch**ur**ch**, whi**ch**
d	as in **d**ay
e	as in b**e**d, t**e**n, **e**gg
ee	as in m**ee**t, m**ea**t, **ea**ch
eer	as in b**eer**, h**ere**, f**ear**
er	as in h**er**, b**ir**d
f	as in **f**at
g	as in **g**et, wa**g**on, do**g**
h	as in **h**at
i	as in p**i**n, s**i**t, **i**s
j	as in **j**am, **j**ob, en**j**oy
k	as in **k**ing, **c**at, pi**que**
l	as in **l**eg
m	as in **m**e
n	as in **n**ot
ng	as in si**ng**, thi**ng**, a**n**xious
o	as in g**o**t, t**o**p, **o**n
oh	as in m**o**st, b**oa**t, g**o**
oi	as in j**oi**n, v**oi**ce, b**oy**
oo	as in s**oo**n, b**oo**t, **oo**ze
oor	as in t**our**
ow	as in c**ow**, h**ow**, **ou**t
owuh	as in h**our**, p**ower**
p	as in **p**eg
r	as in **r**ed
s	as in **s**it

sh	as in **sh**op, fi**sh**, **ch**arade
t	as in **t**op
th	as in **th**in, me**th**od, bo**th**
th	as in **th**is, ei**th**er, **th**ose
u	as in b**u**n, **u**p
uh	as in **a**bove, c**o**rrect, moth**er**
uu	as in b**oo**k, l**oo**k, p**u**ll
uy	as in cr**y**, l**igh**t
uyuh	as in f**ire**, w**ire**, sp**ire**
v	as in **v**an, ri**v**er
w	as in **w**as, **w**ish
x	as in Scottish lo**ch**
y	as in **y**ard, **y**es, **y**ou
yoo	as in f**ew**, d**ue**, b**eau**ty, t**u**ne
yoor	as in c**ure**, p**ure**, end**ure**
z	as in **z**oo, la**z**y, rai**s**e
zh	as in divi**si**on, vi**si**on, mea**s**ure

Note

1 The pronunciation is shown in brackets, usually directly after the headword e.g. galah (say guh-**lah**).
2 Words are broken up into syllables by means of hyphens, as an aid to correct pronunciation.
3 The main stress of a word of two or more syllables is indicated in bold type, like **this**.

Usage labels

If the use of a word is restricted in any way this is indicated by a label printed in italics. Some words or senses may be restricted to a particular region or subject area, while others may be classed as *informal, formal, derogatory,* and so on. Words labelled *formal* are normally restricted to formal (especially written) English, whereas those labelled *informal* are normally used only in speaking or informal writing. Those marked *derogatory* are normally used to express a low opinion or to be deliberately insulting.

Proprietary terms

This dictionary includes some words which are, or are asserted to be, proprietary names or trademarks. Their inclusion does not imply that they have acquired for legal purposes a non-proprietary or general significance, nor is any other judgement implied concerning their legal status. In cases where the editor has some evidence that a word is used as a proprietary name or trademark this is indicated by the label *trademark*, but no judgement concerning the legal status of such words is made or implied thereby.

Locations of Australian Aboriginal Languages

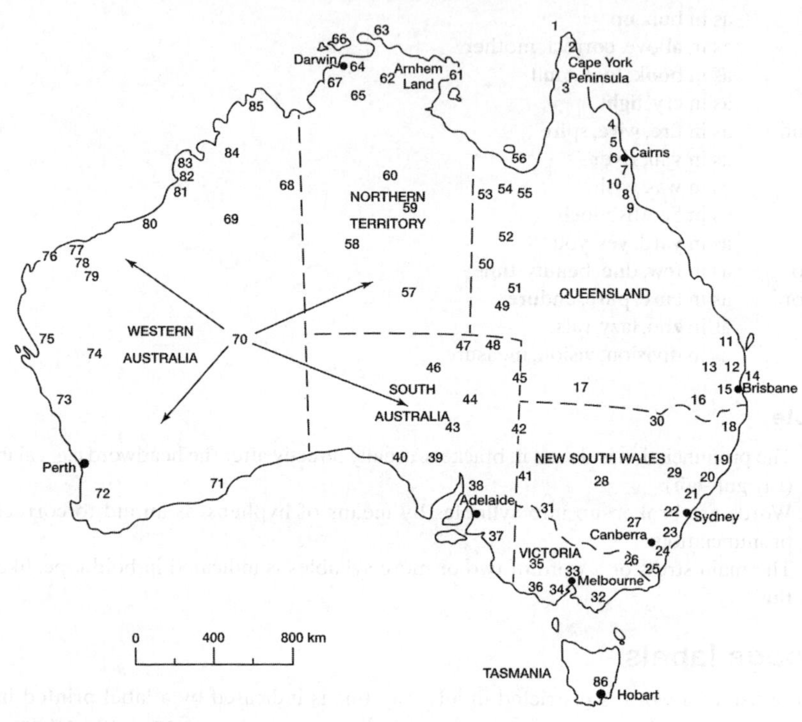

Adnyamathanha	43
Arabana	46
Arrernte	57
Awabakal	21
Bardi	83
Barngarla	39
Batjamal	67
Bigambil	16
Bundjalung	18
Dhanggati	19
Dharawal	23
Dhurga	24

Dieri	44
Djaru	68
Dyirbal	7
Gamilaraay	29
Gathang	20
Gooreng Gooreng	11
Gowar	14
Gubbi Gubbi	12
Gunditjmara	36
Gunnai	32
Gunwinygu	62
Gunya	17
Guugu Yimithirr	4

Aa

a *adjective* (called the *indefinite article* and changing to **an** before most vowel sounds) **1** one (but not any special one), *Can you lend me a book?* **2** each; per, *We can see it once a day or once an hour.*

a-[1] *prefix* **1** on; to; towards (as in *afoot*, *ashore*, *aside*). **2** in the process of (as in *a-hunting*).

a-[2] *prefix* (**an-** is used before a vowel sound) not; without (as in *asymmetrical*, *anarchy*). [from Greek *a-* = not]

aardvark (*say* **ahd**-vahk) *noun* an African animal with a pig-like body and a tubular snout, feeding on termites. [from Afrikaans *aarde* = earth, + *vark* = pig]

ab- *prefix* (changing to **abs-** before *c* and *t*) away; from (as in *abduct*, *abnormal*, *abstract*). [from Latin *ab* = away]

aback *adverb* **taken aback** surprised.

abacus (*say* **ab**-uh-kuhs) *noun* (*plural* **abacuses**) a frame used for counting with beads sliding on wires. [Latin from Greek from Hebrew]

abalone (*say* ab-uh-**loh**-nee) *noun* an edible mollusc with a shell lined with mother-of-pearl.

abandon[1] *verb* **1** give up. **2** leave a person, thing, or place without intending to return, *Abandon ship!* **abandonment** *noun*

abandon[2] *noun* a casual and careless manner, *dancing with great abandon.*

abase *verb* (**abased**, **abasing**) humiliate.

abashed *adjective* embarrassed.

abate *verb* (**abated**, **abating**) make or become less; die down, *The storm had abated.* **abatement** *noun*

abattoir (*say* **ab**-uh-twah) *noun* a place where animals are killed for food. [French]

abbess *noun* the head of an abbey of nuns.

abbey *noun* (*plural* **abbeys**) **1** a monastery or convent. **2** a church that was once part of a monastery, *Westminster Abbey.*

abbot *noun* the head of an abbey of monks.

abbreviate *verb* (**abbreviated**, **abbreviating**) shorten something.

abbreviation *noun* **1** a shortened form of a word or words, such as *maths*, *TV*, *USA.* **2** abbreviating something.

ABC *noun* **1** a name for the alphabet, *We know our ABC.* **2** Australian Broadcasting Corporation.

abdicate *verb* (**abdicated**, **abdicating**) resign from a throne; give up an important responsibility. **abdication** *noun*

abdomen (*say* **ab**-duh-muhn) *noun* **1** the lower front part of a person's or animal's body, containing the stomach, intestines, and other digestive organs. **2** the rear section of an insect's body. **abdominal** (*say* ab-**dom**-uh-nuhl) *adjective*

abduct *verb* take a person away illegally; kidnap. **abduction** *noun*, **abductor** *noun* [from *ab-*, + Latin *ductum* = led]

aberration (*say* ab-uh-**ray**-shuhn) *noun* a deviation from what is normal.

abet *verb* (**abetted**, **abetting**) help or encourage someone to commit a crime. **abetter** or **abettor** *noun*

abeyance (*say* uh-**bay**-uhns) *noun* **in abeyance** suspended or postponed.

abhor *verb* (**abhorred**, **abhorring**) detest. **abhorrence** *noun*, **abhorrent** *adjective* [from Latin *abhorrere* = shrink in fear]

abide *verb* (**abided** (in sense 1 **abode**), **abiding**) **1** (*old use*) remain; dwell. **2** bear; tolerate, *I can't abide flies.*
abide by keep a promise; act in accordance with a rule or decision.

abiding *adjective* lasting; permanent.

ability *noun* (*plural* **abilities**) **1** being able to do something. **2** cleverness; talent.

abiotic *adjective* not having life.

abject (*say* **ab**-jekt) *adjective* **1** wretched; miserable, *living in abject poverty.* **2** humble, *an abject apology.* [from *ab-*, + Latin *-jectum* = thrown]

ablaze *adjective* blazing; on fire.

able *adjective* **1** having the power or skill or opportunity to do something. **2** skilful; clever. **ably** *adverb*

ablution *noun* ceremonial washing of the hands or sacred vessels.

ablutions *plural noun* (*informal*) washing yourself, *perform your ablutions.*

abnormal *adjective* not normal; unusual. **abnormality** *noun*, **abnormally** *adverb*

aboard *adverb & preposition* on or into a ship or aircraft or train.

abode[1] *noun* (*old use*) the place where someone lives.

abode[2] *past tense & past participle* of **abide**.

abolish *verb* put an end to. **abolition** (*say* ab-uh-**lish**-uhn) *noun*

abominable *adjective* very bad; detestable. **abominably** *adverb*

abominate *verb* (**abominated**, **abominating**) detest. **abomination** *noun*

aboriginal[1] *adjective* **1** inhabiting or existing in a land from the earliest times. **2** (usually **Aboriginal**) of Australian Aboriginal people.

aboriginal[2] *noun* **1** an aboriginal inhabitant of a place. **2** (usually **Aboriginal**) a person belonging to one of the indigenous peoples of Australia. **3** (*informal*) (usually **Aboriginal**) any of the numerous Australian Aboriginal languages.

Aboriginality *noun* **1** the quality of being Aboriginal. **2** Aboriginal culture.

aborigine (*say* ab-uh-**rij**-uh-nee) *noun* (*plural* **aborigines**) **1** an original inhabitant of a place. **2** (usually **Aborigine**) an aboriginal inhabitant of Australia. [from Latin *ab origine* = from the beginning]

abort *verb* put an end to something before it has been completed, *They aborted the space flight because of problems.*

abortion *noun* removal of a foetus from the womb before it has developed enough to survive.

abortive *adjective* unsuccessful, *an abortive attempt.*

abound *verb* **1** be plentiful or abundant, *Fish abound in the river.* **2** have something in great quantities, *The river abounds in fish.*

about[1] *preposition* **1** near in amount or size or time; approximately, *It costs about $5; Come about two o'clock.* **2** on the subject of; in connection with, *Tell me about your holiday.* **3** all round; in various parts of, *They ran about the yard.*

about[2] *adverb* **1** approximately. **2** in various directions, *They were running about.* **3** not far away, *He is somewhere about.*
be about to be going to do something.

about-face *noun* (also **about-turn**) a reversal of previous actions or opinions.

above[1] *preposition* **1** higher than. **2** more than.

above[2] *adverb* **1** at or to a higher place. **2** earlier in a book or article, *mentioned above.*

above board *adjective & adverb* honest; without deception.

abrade *verb* (**abraded**, **abrading**) scrape or wear something away by rubbing it. **abrasion** *noun*

abrasive[1] *adjective* **1** that abrades things. **2** harsh, *an abrasive manner.*

abrasive[2] *noun* a rough substance used for rubbing or polishing things.

abreast *adverb* **1** side by side. **2** keeping up with something.

abridge *verb* (**abridged**, **abridging**) shorten, especially by using fewer words, *an abridged edition.* **abridgement** *noun* [from Old French *abregier* = shorten]

abroad *adverb* in or to another country.

abrupt *adjective* **1** sudden; hasty. **2** brief and rude. **abruptly** *adverb*, **abruptness** *noun* [from *ab*-, + Latin *ruptum* = broken]

ABS *abbreviation* **1** anti-lock braking system. **2** Australian Bureau of Statistics.

abs- *prefix* see **ab-**.

abscess (*say* **ab**-suhs) *noun* (*plural* **abscesses**) an inflamed place where pus has formed in the body.

abscond *verb* go away secretly, *The cashier had absconded with the money.*

abseil (*say* **ab**-sayl) *verb* descend a rock face using a doubled rope that is fixed at a higher point.

absence *noun* **1** being away; the period of this. **2** a lack of something.

absent[1] (*say* **ab**-suhnt) *adjective* not here; not present, *absent from school.*

absent[2] (*say* ab-**sent**) *verb* **absent yourself** stay away.

absentee *noun* a person who is absent. **absenteeism** *noun*

absent-minded *adjective* having your mind on other things; forgetful.

absolute *adjective* **1** complete. **2** not restricted. [same origin as *absolve*]

absolutely *adverb* **1** completely. **2** (*informal*) yes, I agree.

absolute majority *noun* a majority over all rivals combined; more than half.

absolution *noun* a priest's formal declaration that people's sins are forgiven.

absolve *verb* (**absolved**, **absolving**) **1** clear a person of blame or guilt. **2** release from a promise or obligation. [from *ab*-, + Latin *solvere* = set free]

absorb *verb* **1** soak up; take in. **2** receive something and reduce its effects, *The buffers absorbed most of the shock.* **3** take up a person's attention or time. **absorbent** *adjective*, **absorption** *noun*

abstain *verb* keep yourself from doing something (e.g. from voting); refrain. **abstainer** *noun*, **abstention** *noun*

abstemious (*say* uhb-**stee**-mee-uhs) *adjective* eating or drinking only small amounts; not greedy. **abstemiously** *adverb*, **abstemiousness** *noun*

abstinence *noun* abstaining, especially from alcohol. **abstinent** *adjective*

abstract[1] (*say* **ab**-strakt) *adjective* **1** concerned with ideas, not with objects, *Truth is abstract.* **2** (of a painting or sculpture) showing the artist's ideas or feelings, not showing a recognisable person or thing.

abstract[2] (*say* **ab**-strakt) *noun* a summary. [from *abs*-, + Latin *tractum* = pulled]

abstracted *adjective* with your mind on other things; not paying attention.

abstract noun *noun* a noun denoting an idea, quality, state, or action.

abstruse (*say* uhb-**stroos**) *adjective* hard to understand; obscure.

absurd *adjective* ridiculous; foolish. **absurdity** *noun*, **absurdly** *adverb* [from Latin *absurdus* = out of tune]

abundance *noun* plenty.

abundant *adjective* plentiful. **abundantly** *adverb*

abuse[1] (*say* uh-**byooz**) *verb* (**abused**, **abusing**) **1** use badly or wrongly; misuse. **2** ill-treat. **3** say unpleasant things to a person or thing.

abuse[2] (*say* uh-**byoos**) *noun* **1** a misuse. **2** ill-treatment. **3** words abusing a person or thing; insults. **abusive** *adjective* [from *ab*- + use]

abut *verb* (**abutted**, **abutting**) end against something, *Their shed abuts against ours.* **abutment** *noun*

abysmal (*say* uh-**biz**-muhl) *adjective* extremely bad, *abysmal ignorance.*

abyss (*say* uh-**bis**) *noun* (*plural* **abysses**) an extremely deep pit.

AC *abbreviation* **1** (also **ac**) alternating current. **2** Companion of the Order of Australia.

ac- *prefix* see **ad-**.

acacia (*say* uh-**kay**-shuh) *noun* any tree or shrub of the genus *Acacia*, to which wattles belong.

academic *adjective* **1** of a school or college or university. **2** scholarly. **3** theoretical; having no practical application.

academy *noun* (*plural* **academies**) **1** a school or college, especially for specialised training. **2** a society of scholars, *The Australian Academy of Science.*

a cappella (*say* ah kuh-**pel**-uh) *adverb* & *adjective* (of choral music) sung without instrumental accompaniment.

accede (*say* ak-**seed**) *verb* **1** agree to what is asked or suggested, *accede to a request.* **2** take office; become king or queen, *accede to the throne.* [from *ac*-, + Latin *cedere* = go]

accelerate *verb* (**accelerated**, **accelerating**) **1** make or become quicker. **2** happen or cause to happen earlier or more quickly. **acceleration** *noun* [from *ac*-, + Latin *celer* = swift]

accelerator *noun* something that speeds things up; the pedal that a driver presses to make a motor vehicle go faster.

accent[1] (*say* **ak**-sent) *noun* **1** the way a person pronounces words, *She has a French accent.* **2** emphasis; pronouncing part of a word more strongly than the rest, *In 'action', the accent is on 'ac-'.* **3** a mark placed over a letter to show its pronunciation, e.g. on *café.*

accent[2] (*say* ak-**sent**) *verb* pronounce part of a word more strongly than the other parts; emphasise.

accentuate (*say* ak-**sen**-choo-ayt) *verb* (**accentuated**, **accentuating**) emphasise; accent. **accentuation** *noun*

accept *verb* **1** take a thing that is offered or presented. **2** say yes to an offer or invitation. **acceptance** *noun*

Usage Do not confuse *accept* with *except.*

acceptable *adjective* worth accepting; pleasing. **acceptability** *noun*, **acceptably** *adverb*

access[1] (*say* **ak**-ses) *noun* a way in; a way to reach something.

access[2] *verb* find information that has been stored in a computer.

Usage Do not confuse *access* with *excess.*

accessible *adjective* able to be reached. **accessibility** *noun*, **accessibly** *adverb*

accession *noun* **1** reaching a rank or position. **2** an addition, *recent accessions to the library.*

accessory (*say* uhk-**ses**-uh-ree) *noun* (*plural* **accessories**) **1** an extra thing that goes with something. **2** a person who helps another with a crime.

accident *noun* an unexpected happening, especially one causing injury or damage. **by accident** by chance; without its being arranged in advance. [from *ac*-, + Latin *cadens* = falling]

accidental *adjective* happening or done by accident. **accidentally** *adverb*

acclaim *verb* welcome or applaud. **acclaim** *noun*, **acclamation** *noun* [from *ac*-, + Latin *clamare* = to shout]

acclimatise *verb* (**acclimatised**, **acclimatising**) make or become used to a new climate or new conditions. **acclimatisation** *noun*

accolade (*say* **ak**-uh-layd) *noun* **1** praise. **2** the ceremonial conferring of a knighthood by tapping a person on the shoulders with a sword.

accommodate *verb* (**accommodated**, **accommodating**) **1** provide room or lodging for somebody. **2** help by providing something, *We can accommodate you with skis.*

accommodation *noun* somewhere to live; lodgings.

accompanist *noun* a person who plays a musical accompaniment.

accompany *verb* (**accompanied**, **accompanying**) **1** go somewhere with somebody. **2** be present with something, *Thunder accompanied the storm.* **3** play music that supports a singer or another player. **accompaniment** *noun*

accomplice (*say* uh-**kum**-pluhs) *noun* a person who helps another in a crime or wrongdoing.

accomplish *verb* do something successfully. **accomplishment** *noun*

accomplished *adjective* skilled.

accord[1] *noun* **1** agreement; consent. **2** a formal agreement or treaty.
of your own accord voluntarily; without being asked or compelled.

accord[2] *verb* **1** be consistent with something. **2** (*formal*) give, *He was accorded this privilege.*

accordance *noun* **in accordance with** in agreement with, *This is done in accordance with the rules.*

according *adverb* **according to 1** as stated by, *According to him, she's a genius.* **2** in a way that suits, *Price the apples according to their size.*

accordingly *adverb* **1** in the way that is required, *It's a formal occasion, so please dress accordingly.* **2** therefore.

accordion *noun* a portable musical instrument like a large concertina with bellows, metal reeds, and keys or buttons. **accordionist** *noun*

accost *verb* approach and speak to a person.

account[1] *noun* **1** a statement of money owed, spent, or received; a bill. **2** an arrangement to keep money in a bank or firm. **3** a description; a report.
on account of because of.
on no account certainly not.
take into account consider.

account[2] *verb* **account for** make it clear why something happens.

accountable *adjective* responsible; having to explain why you have done something. **accountability** *noun*

accountant *noun* a keeper or inspector of financial accounts. **accountancy** *noun*

accounting *noun* keeping financial accounts.

accredited *adjective* officially recognised, *our accredited agent.*

accrue (*say* uh-**kroo**) *verb* (**accrued**, **accruing**) accumulate. **accrual** *noun*

accumulate *verb* (**accumulated**, **accumulating**) **1** collect; pile up. **2** grow numerous; increase. **accumulation** *noun* [from *ac*-, + Latin *cumulus* = heap]

accumulator *noun* a storage battery.

accurate *adjective* correct; exact. **accuracy** *noun*, **accurately** *adverb*

accuse *verb* (**accused**, **accusing**) claim that someone has done something wrong; blame. **accusation** *noun*, **accuser** *noun*

accustom *verb* make a person become used to something. [from *ac*- + custom]

accustomed *adjective* customary; usual.

ace *noun* **1** a playing card with one spot. **2** a very skilful person or thing.

acetylene (*say* uh-**set**-uh-leen) *noun* a gas that burns with a bright flame, used in cutting and welding metal.

ache[1] *noun* **1** a dull continuous pain. **2** mental distress.

ache[2] *verb* (**ached**, **aching**) have an ache.

achieve *verb* (**achieved**, **achieving**) succeed in doing or producing something; accomplish. **achievable** *adjective*, **achievement** *noun* [from Old French *a chief* = to a head]

acid[1] *noun* a chemical substance that contains hydrogen and neutralises alkalis. **acidic** *adjective*, **acidity** *noun*

acid[2] *adjective* **1** sharp-tasting; sour. **2** looking or sounding bitter, *an acid reply.* **acidly** *adverb*

acid rain *noun* rain made acid by mixing with waste gases from industrial processes such as power generation.

acid test *noun* a severe or conclusive test.

acknowledge *verb* (**acknowledged**, **acknowledging**) **1** admit that something is true. **2** state that you have received or noticed something, *Acknowledge this letter.* **3** express thanks or appreciation for something. **acknowledgement** or **acknowledgment** *noun*

acknowledgement of country *noun* (*Australian*) a formal recognition of the traditional Aboriginal owners of the land.

acme (*say* **ak**-mee) *noun* the highest degree of something, *the acme of perfection.* [from Greek *akme* = highest point]

acne (*say* **ak**-nee) *noun* inflamed red pimples on the face and neck.

acorn *noun* the seed of the oak tree.

acoustic (*say* uh-**koo**-stik) *adjective* **1** of sound or hearing. **2** (of a musical instrument) not electronic, *an acoustic guitar.* **acoustically** *adverb* [from Greek *akouein* = hear]

acoustics *plural noun* **1** the qualities of a room or building that make it good or bad for carrying sound. **2** the properties of sound.

acquaint *verb* tell somebody about something, *Acquaint him with the facts.* **be acquainted with** know slightly.

acquaintance *noun* **1** a person you know slightly. **2** being acquainted.

acquiesce (*say* ak-wee-**es**) *verb* (**acquiesced, acquiescing**) agree to something. **acquiescence** *noun*, **acquiescent** *adjective*

acquire *verb* (**acquired, acquiring**) obtain. **acquisition** *noun* [from *ac*-, + Latin *quaerere* = seek]

acquisitive (*say* uh-**kwiz**-uh-tiv) *adjective* eager to acquire things.

acquit *verb* (**acquitted, acquitting**) decide that somebody is not guilty. **acquittal** *noun*

acre (*say* **ay**-kuh) *noun* an area of land measuring 0.405 hectares. **acreage** *noun*

acrid *adjective* bitter, *an acrid smell.*

acrimonious (*say* ak-ruh-**moh**-nee-uhs) *adjective* (of a person's manner or words) sharp and bad-tempered or bitter. **acrimony** (*say* **ak**-ruh-muh-nee) *noun*

acrobat *noun* a person who performs spectacular gymnastic stunts for entertainment. **acrobatic** *adjective*, **acrobatics** *plural noun* [from Greek *akrobatos* = walking on tiptoe]

acronym (*say* **ak**-ruh-nim) *noun* a word or name formed from the initial letters of other words, *ASEAN is an acronym of Association of South East Asian Nations.* [from Greek *akros* = top, + *onyma* = name]

across *preposition & adverb* **1** from one side to the other, *Swim across the river. Are you across yet?* **2** on the opposite side, *the house across the street.* **across the board** applying to all.

acrostic *noun* a word puzzle or poem in which the first or last letters of each line form a word or words.

acrylic (*say* uh-**kril**-ik) *noun* a kind of fibre, plastic, or resin made from an organic acid.

act[1] *noun* **1** an action. **2** a law passed by a parliament. **3** one of the main divisions of a play or opera. **4** a short performance in a program of entertainment, *a juggling act.* **5** (*informal*) a pretence, *She is only putting on an act.*

act[2] *verb* **1** do something; behave; perform actions. **2** perform a part in a play or film. **3** function; have an effect. **4** pretend. [from Latin *actum* = done]

acting *adjective* serving temporarily, especially as a substitute, *the acting principal.*

action *noun* **1** doing something. **2** something done. **3** a battle; fighting, *He was killed in action.* **4** a lawsuit. **5** a series of events in a story or play. **6** exciting activity, *an action-packed holiday.* **7** the mechanism of an instrument. **out of action** not functioning. **take action** do something.

activate *verb* (**activated, activating**) start something working. **activation** *noun*, **activator** *noun*

active *adjective* **1** doing things; moving about; taking part in activities. **2** functioning; in operation, *an active volcano.* **3** radioactive. **4** (of a form of a verb) used when the subject of the verb is performing the action. In 'Tom *washed* the car' the verb is active; in 'The car *was washed by* Tom' the verb is passive. (Compare **passive**.) **actively** *adverb*, **activeness** *noun*

activist *noun* a person who believes in vigorous action, especially in politics.

activity *noun* (*plural* **activities**) **1** an action or occupation, *outdoor activities.* **2** being active or lively.

actor *noun* a performer in a play or film.

actress *noun* a female actor.

actual *adjective* real. **actuality** *noun*, **actually** *adverb*

actuate *verb* (**actuated, actuating**) activate. **actuation** *noun*

acumen (*say* **ak**-yuh-muhn) *noun* sharpness of mind. [Latin, = a point]

acupuncture (*say* **ak**-yuh-pungk-chuh) *noun* pricking parts of the body with needles to relieve pain or cure disease. **acupuncturist** *noun* [from Latin *acu* = with a needle, + *puncture*]

acute *adjective* **1** sharp; strong, *acute pain.* **2** having a sharp mind. **3** (of an illness) coming quickly to a crisis, *acute appendicitis.* **acutely** *adverb*, **acuteness** *noun*

acute accent *noun* a mark over a vowel, as over e in café.

acute angle *noun* an angle of less than 90°.

AD *abbreviation* Anno Domini (Latin = in the year of Our Lord), used in dates counted from the birth of Jesus Christ, *The Roman Emperor Nero died in AD 68.*

ad- *prefix* (changing to **ac-, af-, ag-, al-, an-, ap-, ar-, as-, at-** before certain consonants) to; towards (as in *adapt*, *admit*). [from Latin *ad* = to]

adage (*say* **ad**-ij) *noun* a short saying; a proverb.

adagio (*say* uh-**dah**-zhee-oh) *adverb & adjective* (in music) in slow time. [Italian]

adamant (*say* **ad**-uh-muhnt) *adjective* firm and not giving way to requests.

Adam's apple *noun* the lump at the front of a man's neck.

adapt *verb* make or become suitable for a new purpose or situation. **adaptable** *adjective* [from *ad*-, + Latin *aptus* = fitted]

adaptation *noun* **1** the process of adapting or being adapted. **2** a thing that has been adapted. **3** the process by which an organism or species becomes suited to its environment, *Living in groups is an adaptation to increase the efficiency of hunting.*

adaptor *noun* a device to connect pieces of electrical or other equipment.

ADD *abbreviation* attention deficit disorder.

add *verb* **1** put one thing with another. **2** make another remark.
add to increase.
add up 1 make or find a total. **2** (*informal*) make sense; seem reasonable.

addendum *noun* (*plural* **addenda**) a thing added at the end of a book. [Latin, = thing to be added]

adder *noun* a small poisonous snake. [originally called *a nadder*, which became *an adder*]

addict *noun* a person who does or uses something that they cannot give up. **addicted** *adjective*, **addiction** *noun* [from Latin *addictus* = person given as a servant to someone to whom he owes money]

addictive *adjective* causing people to become addicts, *an addictive drug.*

addition *noun* **1** the process of adding. **2** something added. **additional** *adjective*, **additionally** *adverb*
in addition also; as an extra thing.

additive *noun* a substance added to another in small amounts for a special purpose, e.g. as a flavouring.

addled *adjective* (of eggs) rotted and producing no chick after being brooded.

address[1] *noun* **1** the details of the place where a person lives or an organisation is situated; the place where someone lives or an organisation is situated. **2** a combination of letters or numbers that identifies a destination for email messages or the location of a website. **3** a speech to an audience. **4** (in computing) the location of an item of stored information.

address[2] *verb* **1** write an address on a letter or parcel. **2** make a speech or remark to somebody. **3** give your attention to something.

addressee *noun* the person to whom something is addressed.

adenoids *plural noun* thick spongy flesh at the back of the nose and throat, which may hinder breathing.

adenovirus *noun* any of a group of DNA viruses, most of which cause respiratory diseases.

adept (*say* **ad**-ept or uh-**dept**) *adjective* very skilful.

adequate *adjective* enough; good enough. **adequacy** *noun*, **adequately** *adverb*

ADHD *abbreviation* attention deficit hyperactivity disorder.

adhere *verb* (**adhered, adhering**) **1** stick to something. **2** keep to, *We adhered to the rules.* **adhesion** *noun* [from *ad*-, + Latin *haerere* = to stick]

adherent (*say* uhd-**heer**-uhnt) *noun* a person who supports a certain person, group, or set of ideas. **adherence** *noun*

adhesive[1] *adjective* causing things to stick together, *adhesive tape.*

adhesive[2] *noun* a substance used to stick things together; glue.

ad hoc *adjective & adverb* done or arranged for a particular occasion or purpose, *an ad hoc arrangement.* [Latin, = for this]

adieu (*say* uh-**dyoo**) *interjection* goodbye. [from French *à* = to, + *Dieu* = God]

ad infinitum (*say* ad in-fuh-**nuy**-tuhm) *adverb* without limit; for ever. [Latin, = to infinity]

adjacent *adjective* **1** near; next. **2** (of a pair of angles) formed on the same side of a line when intersected by another line. [from *ad*-, + Latin *jacens* = lying]

adjective *noun* a word that describes a noun or adds to its meaning, e.g. *big, honest.* **adjectival** *adjective*, **adjectivally** *adverb*

adjoin *verb* be next or nearest to something.

adjourn (*say* uh-**jern**) *verb* **1** postpone, break off temporarily. **2** break off and go somewhere else, *They adjourned to the library.* **adjournment** *noun* [from Latin, = to another day]

adjudicate (*say* uh-**joo**-duh-kayt) *verb* (**adjudicated, adjudicating**) act as judge in a competition etc. **adjudication** *noun*, **adjudicator** *noun* [from *ad*-, + Latin *judicare* = to judge]

adjunct (*say* **aj**-ungkt) *noun* something added that is useful but not essential. [from *ad*-, + Latin *junctum* = joined]

adjust *verb* **1** put a thing into its proper position or order. **2** alter so as to fit. **3** make oneself used to new circumstances. **adjustable** *adjective*, **adjustment** *noun*

ad lib[1] *adverb* as you please; freely.

ad lib[2] *verb* (**ad libbed, ad libbing**) say or do something without any rehearsal or preparation. [from Latin *ad libitum* = according to pleasure]

administer *verb* **1** give; provide, *He administered the punishment.* **2** manage business affairs.

administration *noun* **1** administering. **2** the management of public or business affairs. **3** the people who manage an organisation; the government, *the Trump administration.* **administrative** *adjective*, **administrator** *noun*

admirable *adjective* worth admiring; excellent. **admirably** *adverb*

admiral *noun* a naval officer of high rank. [from Arabic *amir* = commander]

admire *verb* (**admired, admiring**) **1** look at something and enjoy it. **2** think that someone or something is very good. **admiration** *noun*, **admirer** *noun* [from *ad-*, + Latin *mirari* = wonder at]

admissible *adjective* able to be admitted or allowed.

admission *noun* **1** admitting. **2** the charge for being allowed to go in. **3** a statement admitting something; a confession.

admit *verb* (**admitted, admitting**) **1** allow someone or something to come in. **2** state reluctantly that something is true; confess, *We admit that the task is difficult; He admitted his crime.* [from *ad-*, + Latin *mittere* = send]

admittance *noun* the process or fact of entering or being allowed to enter a place or institution.

admittedly *adverb* as an agreed fact; without denying it.

admonish *verb* advise or warn firmly but mildly. **admonition** *noun*

ad nauseam (*say* ad **naw**-zee-uhm) *adverb* until people are sick of it. [Latin, = to sickness]

ado *noun* fuss; excitement. [originally in *much ado* = much to do]

adolescence (*say* ad-uh-**les**-uhns) *noun* the time between being a child and being an adult. **adolescent** *adjective & noun* [from Latin *adolesco* = grow up]

adopt *verb* **1** take someone into your family as your own child. **2** accept something; take and use, *They adopted his plan.* **adoption** *noun*, **adoptive** *adjective* [from *ad-*, + Latin *optare* = choose]

adore *verb* (**adored, adoring**) **1** love very much. **2** worship. **adorable** *adjective*, **adoration** *noun* [from *ad-*, + Latin *orare* = pray]

adorn *verb* decorate. **adornment** *noun*

adrenalin (*say* uh-**dren**-uh-luhn) *noun* a hormone that stimulates the nervous system.

adrift *adjective & adverb* drifting.

ADSL *abbreviation* asymmetric digital subscriber line, a technology for transmitting digital information over standard telephone lines.

adulation *noun* very great flattery.

adult *noun* a fully grown or mature person. **adult** *adjective*

adulterate *verb* (**adulterated, adulterating**) make a thing impure or less good by adding something to it. **adulteration** *noun* [from Latin *adulterare* = corrupt]

adultery *noun* being unfaithful to your wife or husband by having sexual intercourse with someone else. **adulterer** *noun*, **adulterous** *adjective*

advance[1] *noun* **1** a forward movement; progress. **2** an increase. **3** a loan; payment made before it is due.
in advance beforehand; ahead.

advance[2] *verb* (**advanced, advancing**) **1** move forward; make progress. **2** lend or pay money ahead of the proper time, *Advance her a month's salary.* **advancement** *noun*

advanced *adjective* **1** far on in progress. **2** not elementary. **3** ahead of the times.

advantage *noun* **1** something useful or helpful. **2** the next point won after deuce in tennis. **advantageous** *adjective*
take advantage of use profitably or unfairly.
to advantage making a good effect, *The painting shows to advantage here.*
to your advantage profitable or helpful to you.

Advent *noun* **1** the period before Christmas, when Christians commemorate the coming of Christ. **2** (**advent**) the arrival of a new person or thing, *the advent of computers.* [from *ad-*, + Latin *ventum* = arrived]

adventure *noun* **1** an exciting or dangerous experience. **2** willingness to take risks. **adventurer** *noun*, **adventurous** *adjective*

adverb *noun* a word that adds to the meaning of a verb, adjective, or other adverb and tells how, when, or where something happens, e.g. *gently*, *soon* and *upstairs*. **adverbially** *adverb* [from *ad-*, + Latin *verbum* = word]

adverbial[1] *adjective* functioning as an adverb or adverbial.

adverbial[2] *noun* a word or phrase that functions as an adverb, usually indicating place (*in the city*), time (*in April*), or manner (*in a funny way*).

adversary (*say* **ad**-vuh-suh-ree) *noun* (*plural* **adversaries**) an opponent or enemy.

adverse *adjective* unfavourable; harmful, *adverse effects.* **adversely** *adverb*, **adversity** *noun* [from Latin *adversus* = opposite (*ad* = to, *versus* = turned)]

advertise *verb* (**advertised, advertising**) **1** make something publicly known, *advertise a meeting.* **2** promote (goods or services) publicly to encourage people to buy or sell them. **3** ask or offer by a public notice, *advertise for a secretary.* **advertisement** *noun*, **advertiser** *noun*

advice *noun* **1** a statement telling a person what you think they should do. **2** a piece of information, *We received advice that the goods had been sent.*

> **Usage** Note the spelling: *advice* is a noun, *advise* is a verb.

advisable *adjective* that is the wise thing to do. **advisability** *noun*

advise *verb* (**advised, advising**) **1** give somebody advice; recommend. **2** inform. **adviser** *noun*, **advisory** *adjective*

advocate[1] (*say* ad-vuh-**kayt**) *verb* (**advocated, advocating**) speak in favour of something; recommend, *We advocate reform.*

advocate[2] (*say* **ad**-vuh-kuht) *noun* **1** a person who advocates a policy or idea, *She is an advocate of reform.* **2** a lawyer presenting someone's case in a lawcourt.

adze *noun* an axe-like tool with a curved blade.

aegis (*say* **ee**-juhs) *noun* protection; sponsorship, *The scheme is under the aegis of the Scout Association.* [from Greek *aigis* = magical shield of the God Zeus]

aeon (*say* **ee**-on) *noun* (also **eon**) an immense time.

aerate (*say* **air**-rayt) *verb* (**aerated, aerating**) **1** add air to something. **2** add carbon dioxide to a liquid, *aerated water.*

aerial[1] *adjective* **1** of or in or from the air. **2** of or by aircraft.

aerial[2] *noun* a wire or rod for receiving or transmitting radio or television signals.

aero- *prefix* of air or aircraft (as in *aeronautics*). [from Greek *aer* = air]

aerobatics *plural noun* spectacular performances by flying aircraft. **aerobatic** *adjective* [from *aero-* + *acrobatics*]

aerobic *adjective* **1** using oxygen from the air. **2** (of exercises) designed to strengthen the heart and lungs. **aerobics** *plural noun*

aerodrome *noun* an airfield. [from *aero-*, + Greek *dromos* = running track]

aerodynamics *noun* the study of the interaction between the air and solid bodies moving through it. **aerodynamic** *adjective* [from *aero-* + *dynamic*]

aeronautics *noun* the study of aircraft and flying. **aeronautic** *adjective*, **aeronautical** *adjective* [from *aero-* + *nautical*]

aeroplane *noun* a flying machine with wings. [from *aero-* + *plane*[1]]

aerosol *noun* a device for producing a fine spray of a substance. [from *aero-* + *solution*]

aerospace *noun* the earth's atmosphere and space beyond it.

aesthetic (*say* ees-**thet**-ik or uhs-**thet**-ik) *adjective* **1** of or showing appreciation of beautiful things. **2** artistic, tasteful. [from Greek, = perceiving]

af- *prefix* see **ad-**.

afar *adverb* far away, *The din was heard from afar.*

affable *adjective* polite and friendly. **affability** *noun*, **affably** *adverb*

affair *noun* **1** a thing; a matter; an event. **2** a temporary sexual relationship between two people who are not married to each other. [from French *à faire* = to do]

affairs *plural noun* public or private business, *He put his affairs in order.*

affect *verb* **1** have an effect on. **2** (of a disease) attack or infect. **3** arouse sympathy or sadness in a person. **4** pretend, *She affected ignorance.*

> **Usage** Do not confuse with *effect* which means 'to cause, to produce', e.g. *The government effected great changes.* Note that *effect* is commonly used as a noun as well as a verb.

affectation *noun* a pretence; behaviour that is put on for show and not natural.

affected *adjective* pretended; unnatural.

affection *noun* love; a liking.

affectionate *adjective* showing affection; loving. **affectionately** *adverb*

affidavit (*say* af-uh-**day**-vuht) *noun* a statement written down and sworn to be true, for use as legal evidence. [Latin, = he or she has stated on oath]

affiliated *adjective* officially connected with a larger organisation. [from Latin *affiliatum* = adopted (from *af-*, + *filius* = son)]

affinity *noun* (*plural* **affinities**) **1** a strong attraction. **2** a relationship or similarity to each other, *There are many affinities between the two languages.*

affirm *verb* state definitely or firmly. **affirmation** *noun*

affirmative *adjective* that says 'yes', *an affirmative reply.* (Compare **negative**[1] 1.)

affix[1] (*say* uh-**fiks**) *verb* **1** attach, *affix a stamp.* **2** add in writing, *affix your signature.*

affix[2] (*say* **af**-iks) *noun* a prefix or suffix.

afflict *verb* cause somebody distress. **affliction** *noun* [from *af*-, + Latin *flictum* = struck]

affluent (*say* **af**-loo-uhnt) *adjective* rich. **affluence** *noun* [from Latin *affluens* = overflowing (see *fluent*)]

afford *verb* **1** have enough money to pay for something. **2** have enough time or resources to do something.

afforestation *noun* the planting of trees to form a forest.

affray *noun* fighting or rioting in public.

affront[1] *verb* insult; offend; embarrass.

affront[2] *noun* an insult.

afield *adverb* at or to a distance; away from home, *travelling far afield.*

aflame *adjective & adverb* in flames; glowing.

afloat *adjective & adverb* floating; on the sea.

afoot *adjective* happening, *Changes are afoot.*

aforesaid *adjective* mentioned previously.

afraid *adjective* frightened; alarmed. **be afraid** regret, *I'm afraid I'm late.*

afresh *adverb* again; in a new way, *We must start afresh.*

African *adjective* of Africa or its people. **African** *noun*

aft *adverb* at or towards the back of a ship or aircraft.

after[1] *preposition* **1** later than, *Come after tea.* **2** behind in place or order, *Which letter comes after H?* **3** trying to catch; pursuing, *Run after him.* **4** in spite of, *We can come after all.* **5** in imitation or honour of, *She is named after her aunt.* **6** about; concerning, *He asked after you.*

after[2] *adverb* **1** behind, *Jill came tumbling after.* **2** later, *It came a week after.*

after[3] *adjective* coming or done afterwards, *in after years*; *the after-effects.*

aftermath *noun* the conditions after something, *the aftermath of war.* [from *after* + *math* = mowing (i.e. new grass that grows after a mowing)]

afternoon *noun* the time from noon or lunchtime to evening.

afterthought *noun* something thought of or added later.

afterwards *adverb* at a later time.

ag- *prefix* see **ad-**.

again *adverb* **1** another time; once more, *try again.* **2** as before, *You will soon be well again.* **3** besides; moreover.

against *preposition* **1** touching; hitting, *He leant against the wall.* **2** in opposition to; not in favour of, *They voted against the proposal.* **3** in preparation for, *Protect them against the cold.*

age[1] *noun* **1** the length of time a person has lived or a thing has existed. **2** a special period of history or geology, *the ice age.* **come of age** reach the age at which you have an adult's legal rights and obligations.

age[2] *verb* (**aged, ageing**) make or become old.

aged *adjective* **1** (*say* ayjd) having the age of, *a girl aged 9.* **2** (*say* **ay**-juhd) very old, *an aged man.*

agency *noun* (*plural* **agencies**) **1** the office or business of an agent, *a travel agency.* **2** the means by which something is done, *Flowers are pollinated by the agency of bees.*

agenda (*say* uh-**jen**-duh) *noun* (*plural* **agendas**) a list of things to be done or discussed, *The agenda is rather long.* [from Latin, = things to be done]

agent *noun* **1** a person who organises things for other people. **2** a spy, *a secret agent.* [from Latin *agens* = doing things]

ages *plural noun* (*informal*) a very long time, *We've been waiting for ages.*

agglomeration *noun* a mass of things collected together. [from *ag*-, + Latin *glomus* = mass]

aggravate *verb* (**aggravated, aggravating**) **1** make a thing worse or more serious. **2** (*informal*) annoy. **aggravation** *noun* [from *ag*-, + Latin *gravare* = load heavily]

aggregate[1] (*say* **ag**-ruh-guht) *noun* a total amount or score. [from *ag*-, + Latin *gregatum* = herded together]

aggregate[2] (*say* **ag**-ruh-guht) *adjective* combined; total, *the aggregate amount.*

aggression *noun* **1** the act or practice of attacking without provocation, especially beginning a fight or war. **2** self-assertiveness; forcefulness. **3** hostile or destructive tendency or behaviour. [from *ag*- = against, + Latin *gressum* = gone]

aggressive *adjective* **1** likely to attack people. **2** forceful. **aggressively** *adverb*, **aggressiveness** *noun*

aggressor *noun* the person or nation that started an attack or war.

aggrieved (*say* uh-**greevd**) *adjective* resentful because of being treated unfairly.

aghast *adjective* horrified.

agile *adjective* moving quickly or easily. **agilely** *adverb*, **agility** *noun*

agist *verb* take in and pasture other people's livestock for a fee. **agistment** *noun*

agitate *verb* (**agitated, agitating**) **1** make someone feel upset or anxious. **2** stir up public interest or concern; campaign, *They agitated for better conditions.* **3** shake something about. **agitation** *noun*, **agitator** *noun* [from Latin *agitare* = shake]

aglow *adjective* glowing.

agnostic (*say* ag-**nos**-tik) *noun* a person who believes that it is impossible to know whether God exists. **agnosticism** *noun* [from *a-* = not, + Greek *gnostikos* = knowing]

ago *adverb* in the past, *long ago.* [from an old word *agone* = gone by]

agog *adjective* eager and excited.

agony *noun* (*plural* **agonies**) extremely great pain or suffering. **agonising** *adjective* [from Greek *agon* = a struggle]

agoraphobia (*say* ag-uh-ruh-**foh**-bee-uh) *noun* abnormal fear of being in open spaces. [from Greek *agora* = market place, + *phobia*]

agrarian (*say* uh-**grair**-ree-uhn) *adjective* of farm land or its cultivation. [from Latin *ager* = field]

agree *verb* (**agreed**, **agreeing**) **1** hold a similar opinion. **2** consent, *She agreed to come*; *She agreed to the plan.* **3** suit a person's health or digestion, *Curry doesn't agree with me.* **4** correspond in grammatical number, gender, or person. In 'They were good teachers', *they* agrees with *teachers* (both are plural forms) and *were* agrees with *they*; *was* would be incorrect because it is singular. **5** be in harmony, *Their answers agree.*

agreeable *adjective* **1** willing, *We shall go if you are agreeable.* **2** pleasant, *an agreeable place.* **agreeably** *adverb*

agreement *noun* **1** agreeing. **2** an arrangement that people have agreed on.

agriculture *noun* the process of cultivating land on a large scale and rearing livestock; farming. **agricultural** *adjective* [from Latin *agric* = of a field, + *culture*]

aground *adverb & adjective* stranded on the bottom in shallow water.

ah *interjection* an exclamation used to express a range of emotions including surprise, pity, and admiration.

ahead *adverb* **1** further forward; in front. **2** forwards, *Full steam ahead!*

ahistorical *adjective* lacking historical perspective or context.

ahoy *interjection* an exclamation used by sailors to call attention.

aid[1] *noun* **1** help. **2** something that helps, *a hearing aid.* **3** financial or material help given to another country or area to help it, *overseas aid.*
in aid of for the purpose of; to help something.

aid[2] *verb* help.

aide *noun* an assistant. [French]

aide-de-camp (*say* ayd-duh-**kon**) *noun* a military officer who is the assistant to a senior officer. [French, = camp helper]

Aids *noun* a disease that greatly weakens a person's ability to resist infections. [from the initials of 'acquired immune deficiency syndrome']

ail *verb* (*old use*) be ill; make a person ill.

ailing *adjective* **1** ill; unwell. **2** in poor condition, *an ailing industry.*

ailment *noun* a slight illness.

aim[1] *verb* **1** point or send towards a target. **2** throw or kick in a particular direction. **3** try or intend to do something.

aim[2] *noun* **1** the act of aiming. **2** purpose; intention.

aimless *adjective* without a purpose. **aimlessly** *adverb*

air[1] *noun* **1** the mixture of gases that surrounds the earth and which everyone breathes. **2** the open space above the earth. **3** a breeze or light wind. **4** a tune; a melody. **5** an appearance or impression of something, *an air of mystery.* **6** an impressive or haughty manner, *He puts on airs.*
by air in or by aircraft.
on (the) air on radio or television.
up in the air uncertain.

air[2] *verb* **1** expose clothes or a room to air. **2** express, *She aired her opinions.*

air bag *noun* a safety device in a car that fills with air in a collision to protect the people sitting in the front.

airborne *adjective* **1** (of an aircraft) in flight. **2** carried by the air or by aircraft.

air conditioning *noun* a system controlling the temperature and humidity of the air in a room, building, or vehicle. **air-conditioned** *adjective*

aircraft *noun* (*plural* **aircraft**) a machine capable of flight such as an aeroplane or helicopter.

aircraft carrier *noun* a large ship with a long deck where aircraft can take off and land.

airfare *noun* the price to be paid by an aircraft passenger for a journey.

airfield *noun* an area equipped with runways and hangars for aircraft.

air force *noun* the part of a country's armed forces that is equipped with aircraft.

airgun *noun* a gun in which compressed air propels a pellet or dart.

airlift *noun* the emergency transport of supplies by air.

airline *noun* a company that provides a regular service of transport by aircraft.

airliner *noun* a large aircraft for carrying passengers.

airlock *noun* **1** a compartment with an airtight door at each end, through which people can go in and out of a pressurised chamber. **2** a bubble of air that stops liquid flowing through a pipe.

airmail *noun* mail carried by air.

airman *noun* (*plural* **airmen**) a man who is a member of an air force or of the crew of an aircraft.

airport *noun* an airfield for aircraft carrying passengers and goods.

air raid *noun* an attack by aircraft.

airship *noun* a large balloon with engines, designed to carry passengers or goods.

airspace *noun* the part of the sky above a country and subject to its control.

airstrip *noun* a strip of ground prepared for aircraft to land and take off.

airtight *adjective* not letting air in or out.

airtime *noun* time during which a broadcast is being transmitted.

airworthy *adjective* (of an aircraft) fit to fly. **airworthiness** *noun*

airy *adjective* **1** with plenty of fresh air. **2** light as air. **3** light-hearted; insincere, *airy promises.* **airily** *adverb*

aisle (*say* uyl) *noun* **1** a passage between or beside rows of seats or pews. **2** a side part of a church.

ajar *adverb & adjective* slightly open, *Leave the door ajar.*

akimbo *adverb* **arms akimbo** with hands on hips and elbows out.

akin *adjective* related; similar.

Akubra *noun* (*trademark*) a wide-brimmed Australian felt hat.

al- *prefix* see **ad-**.

alabaster (*say* **al**-uh-bahs-tuh) *noun* a kind of hard stone, usually white.

à la carte *adjective & adverb* ordered and paid for as separate items from a menu. (Compare **table d'hôte**.) [French, = from the menu]

alacrity *noun* speed and willingness, *She accepted with alacrity.*

alarm[1] *noun* **1** a warning sound or signal; an apparatus for giving this. **2** a feeling of fear or anxiety. **3** an alarm clock.

alarm[2] *verb* make someone frightened or anxious. [from Italian *all'arme!* = to arms!]

alarm clock *noun* a clock that can be set to make a sound at a fixed time to wake a person.

alarmist *noun* a person who raises unnecessary alarm.

alas *interjection* an exclamation of sorrow.

albatross *noun* (*plural* **albatrosses**) a large sea bird with very long wings.

albeit (*say* awl-**bee**-it) *conjunction* (*formal*) although.

albino (*say* al-**bee**-noh) *noun* (*plural* **albinos**) a person or animal with no colour in the skin and hair (which are white). [from Latin *albus* = white]

album *noun* **1** a book with blank pages in which to keep a collection of photographs, stamps, autographs, or pictures. **2** a sound recording containing several items. [Latin, = white piece of stone etc. on which to write things]

albumen (*say* **al**-byuh-muhn) *noun* white of egg. [from Latin *albus* = white]

alchemy (*say* **al**-kuh-mee) *noun* an early form of chemistry, the chief aim of which was to turn ordinary metals into gold. **alchemist** *noun* [from Arabic *alkimiya* = the art of changing metals]

alcheringa (*say* al-chuh-**ring**-guh) *noun* the dreamtime. [from Arrernte *altyerre* = dream, + *-nge* = from, of]

alcohol *noun* **1** a colourless liquid made by fermenting sugar or starch. **2** an intoxicating drink containing this liquid (e.g. wine, beer, whisky). [from Arabic *al-kuhl*]

alcoholic[1] *adjective* of alcohol; containing alcohol.

alcoholic[2] *noun* a person who is seriously addicted to alcohol. **alcoholism** *noun*

alcopop *noun* a ready-mixed soft drink containing alcohol.

alcove *noun* a section of a room or garden that is set back from the main part; a recess. [from Arabic *al-kubba* = the arch]

alderman (*say* **awl**-duh-muhn) *noun* (*plural* **aldermen**) a local government councillor in some Australian states and in England. [from Old English *aldor* = older, + *man*]

ale *noun* beer.

alert[1] *adjective* watching for something; ready to act. **alertly** *adverb*, **alertness** *noun*

alert[2] *noun* a warning signal or alarm. **on the alert** on the lookout; watchful.

alert[3] *verb* warn of danger; make someone aware of something. [from Italian *all'erta!* = to the watchtower!]

alfresco *adjective & adverb* in the open air, *an alfresco meal.* [from Italian *al fresco* = in the fresh air]

alga (*say* **al**-guh) *noun* (*plural* **algae**, *say*

al-jee) a kind of plant that grows in water, with no true stems or leaves.

Usage Although *algae* is the plural form of *alga*, it functions as a collective noun, and can take either a singular or plural verb.

algebra (*say* **al**-juh-bruh) *noun* mathematics in which letters and symbols are used to represent quantities. [from Arabic *al-jabr* = putting together broken parts]

algebraic (*say* al-juh-**bray**-ik) *adjective* **1** relating to or using algebra. **2** (of a mathematical expression or fraction) combining numbers and symbols following the rules of algebra.

algorithm (*say* **al**-guh-ri*th*-uhm) *noun* a process or set of rules to be followed in calculations or other problem-solving operations.

alias[1] (*say* **ay**-lee-uhs) *noun* (*plural* **aliases**) a false or different name.

alias[2] *adverb* also named, *Robert Zimmerman, alias Bob Dylan.* [Latin, = at another time]

alibi (*say* **al**-uh-buy) *noun* (*plural* **alibis**) **1** evidence that a person accused of a crime was somewhere else when it was committed. **2** (*informal*) an excuse of any kind. [Latin, = at another place]

Usage The use of *alibi* in sense 2 is considered incorrect by some people.

alien[1] (*say* **ay**-lee-uhn) *noun* **1** a person who is not a citizen of the country where they are living; a foreigner. **2** a being from another world.

alien[2] *adjective* **1** foreign. **2** unnatural, *Cruelty is alien to her nature.* [from Latin *alius* = another]

alienate (*say* **ay**-lee-uhn-ayt) *verb* (**alienated**, **alienating**) make a person become unfriendly or hostile. **alienation** *noun*

alight[1] *adjective* **1** on fire. **2** lit up. [from *a*-[1] + *light*[1]]

alight[2] *verb* **1** get out of a vehicle or down from a horse. **2** fly down and settle, *The bird alighted on a branch.* [from *a*-[1] + *light*[2]]

align (*say* uh-**luyn**) *verb* **1** arrange in a line. **2** join as an ally, *They aligned themselves with the Germans.* **alignment** *noun* [from French *à ligne* = into line]

alike *adjective & adverb* like one another; in the same way, *The twins are very alike. Treat them alike.*

alimentary canal *noun* the tube along which food passes from the mouth to the anus in the process of being digested and absorbed by the body. [from Latin *alimentum* = food]

alive *adjective* **1** living. **2** alert, *Be alive to the possible dangers.* **3** swarming with; full of, *The place was alive with tourists.*

alkali (*say* al-**kuh**-luy) *noun* (*plural* **alkalis**) a substance that neutralises acids. **alkaline** *adjective* [from Arabic *al-kily* = the ashes]

all[1] *adjective* the whole number or amount of, *All my books are here; all day.*

all[2] *noun* **1** everything, *That is all I know.* **2** everybody, *All are agreed.*

all[3] *adverb* **1** completely, *She was dressed all in white.* **2** is to each team or competitor, *The score is 15 all.*
all right 1 satisfactory. **2** in good condition. **3** as desired. **4** yes, I consent.
all there (*informal*) having an alert mind.
all the same in spite of this; making no difference, *I like him, all the same.*
all together all at once; all in one place.

Allah *noun* the Muslim and Arabic name of God.

allay (*say* uh-**lay**) *verb* (**allayed**, **allaying**) calm, *He allayed their fears.*

all-clear *noun* a signal that a danger has passed.

allegation (*say* al-uh-**gay**-shuhn) *noun* a statement made without proof.

allege (*say* uh-**lej**) *verb* (**alleged**, **alleging**) say something without being able to prove it, *He alleged that I had cheated.*
allegedly *adverb*

allegiance (*say* uh-**lee**-juhns) *noun* loyalty. [compare *liege*]

allegory (*say* **al**-uh-gree) *noun* (*plural* **allegories**) a story in which the characters and events represent or symbolise an underlying meaning. **allegorical** (*say* al-uh-**go**-ri-kuhl) *adjective*

allegro *adverb & adjective* (in music) fast and lively. [Italian]

alleluia *interjection* praise to God. [from Hebrew]

Allen key *noun* (*trademark*) a spanner that fits into and turns an Allen screw.

Allen screw *noun* (*trademark*) a screw with a hexagonal socket in the head.

allergic *adjective* very sensitive to something that may make you ill, *He is allergic to pollen, which gives him hay fever.*
allergy *noun*

alleviate (*say* uh-**lee**-vee-ayt) *verb* (**alleviated**, **alleviating**) make a thing less severe, *alleviate pain.* **alleviation** *noun* [from *al*-, + Latin *levis* = light]

alley *noun* (*plural* **alleys**) **1** a narrow street or passage. **2** a place where you can play skittles or tenpin bowling. [from French *aller* = go]

alliance *noun* an association formed by countries or groups who wish to support each other.

allied *adjective* **1** joined as allies. **2** of the same kind.

alligator *noun* a kind of crocodile. [from Spanish *el lagarto* = the lizard]

all-in *adjective* including or allowing everything, *an all-in price.*

alliteration *noun* having the same letter or sound at the beginning of several words, e.g. in *Sit in solemn silence.* [from *al*-, + Latin *littera* = letter]

allocate *verb* (**allocated**, **allocating**) allot; set aside for a particular purpose. **allocation** *noun* [from *al*-, + Latin *locus* = a place]

allot *verb* (**allotted**, **allotting**) distribute officially; give as a share of things available or tasks to be done.

allotment *noun* **1** a small piece of land; a building block. **2** allotting; the amount allotted.

allow *verb* **1** permit, *Smoking is not allowed.* **2** permit someone to have something; provide with, *She was allowed $20 for books.* **3** agree, *I allow that you have been patient.* **allowable** *adjective*

allowance *noun* **1** allowing something. **2** what is allowed, *an allowance of $20 for books.*
make allowances be considerate; excuse, *Make allowances for his age.*

alloy *noun* a metal formed of a mixture of metals or of metal and another substance.

all-round *adjective* general; not specialist, *an all-round athlete.* **all-rounder** *noun*

allude *verb* (**alluded**, **alluding**) mention something briefly or indirectly, *He alluded to his wealth.*

allure *verb* (**allured**, **alluring**) entice; attract. **allurement** *noun* [from French *à* = to, + *lure*]

allusion (*say* uh-**loo**-*zh*uhn) *noun* (often followed by *to*) an expression designed to call something to mind without mentioning it explicitly; an indirect or passing reference, *an allusion to Shakespeare.*

alluvium (*say* uh-**loo**-vee-uhm) *noun* sand and soil deposited by a river or flood. **alluvial** *adjective*

ally[1] *noun* (*plural* **allies**) **1** a country with an agreement to support another country, especially in war. **2** a person who cooperates with another.

ally[2] *verb* (**allied**, **allying**) form an alliance.

almanac *noun* an annual publication containing a calendar and other information.

almighty *adjective* **1** having complete power. **2** (*informal*) very great, *an almighty din.*

almond (*say* **ah**-muhnd) *noun* an oval edible nut.

almost *adverb* near to being something but not quite, *almost ready.*

alms (*say* ahmz) *noun* (*old use*) money and gifts given to the poor.

aloft *adverb* high up; overhead.

alone *adjective* without any other people or things; without help. [from *all one*]

along[1] *preposition* following the length of something, *Walk along the path.*

along[2] *adverb* **1** on; onwards, *Push it along.* **2** accompanying somebody, *I've brought my brother along.*

alongside *preposition & adverb* next to something; beside.

aloof[1] *adverb* apart; not taking part, *We stayed aloof from their quarrels.*

aloof[2] *adjective* distant and not friendly in manner, *She seemed aloof.*

aloud *adverb* in a voice that can be heard.

alpaca (*say* al-**pak**-uh) *noun* **1** a South American animal, similar to a llama, with long wool. **2** its wool, or fabric made from its wool. [from Aymara, an indigenous South American language]

alpha *noun* the first letter of the Greek alphabet, = a.

alphabet *noun* the letters used in a language, usually arranged in a set order. **alphabetical** *adjective*, **alphabetically** *adverb* [from *alpha*, *beta*, the first two letters of the Greek alphabet]

alpine *adjective* of high mountains. [from the Alps, mountains in Switzerland]

already *adverb* by now; before now.

also *adverb* as an extra person or thing; besides; as well.

altar *noun* a table or similar structure used in religious ceremonies.

alter *verb* make or become different; change. **alteration** *noun* [from Latin *alter* = other]

altercation (*say* awl-tuh-**kay**-shuhn) *noun* a noisy argument or quarrel.

alter ego *noun* another, very different, side of someone's personality. [Latin, = other self]

alternate[1] (*say* awl-**ter**-nuht) *adjective* happening or coming in turns; first the one and then the other. **alternately** *adverb*

> **Usage** See the note at *alternative.*

alternate[2] (*say* **awl**-tuh-nayt) *verb* (**alternated**, **alternating**) use or come alternately. **alternation** *noun*, **alternator** *noun*

alternate angles *plural noun* two angles, not adjoining one another, that are formed on opposite sides of a line that intersects two other lines.

alternating current *noun* electric current that keeps reversing its direction at regular intervals.

alternative[1] *adjective* **1** available instead of something else. **2** unconventional, *alternative medicine.* **alternatively** *adverb*

> **Usage** Do not confuse *alternative* with *alternate*. If there are *alternative colours* it means that there is a choice of two or more colours, but *alternate colours* means that there is first one colour and then the other.

alternative[2] *noun* one of two or more possibilities.
no alternative no choice.

although *conjunction* though.

altimeter *noun* an instrument used in aircraft for showing the height above sea level. [from Latin *altus* = high, + *meter*]

altitude *noun* the height of something, especially above sea level. [from Latin *altus* = high]

alto *noun* (*plural* **altos**) **1** an adult male singer with a very high voice. **2** a contralto. **3** a musical instrument with the second or third highest pitch in its group. [Italian, = high]

altogether *adverb* **1** with all included; in total, *The outfit costs $120 altogether.* **2** completely, *The creek dries up altogether in summer.* **3** on the whole, *Altogether, it was a good concert.*

> **Usage** Note that *altogether* means 'in total', whereas *all together* means 'all at once' or 'all in one place'. The phrases *six rooms altogether* (in total) and *six rooms all together* (in one place) illustrate the difference.

altruistic (*say* al-troo-**is**-tik) *adjective* unselfish; thinking of other people's welfare. **altruism** *noun*, **altruist** *noun* [from Italian *altrui* = somebody else]

aluminium *noun* a lightweight silver-coloured metal.

always *adverb* **1** at all times. **2** often, *You are always crying.* **3** whatever happens, *You can always sleep on the floor.*

Alzheimer's (*say* **alts**-huy-muhz) *noun* a disease, usually found among older people, that results in the gradual loss of memory, speech, movement, and the ability to think clearly. [named after Alois Alzheimer, a German neurologist]

am 1st person singular present tense of **be**, *When I am older I'd like to be an astronaut.*

a.m. *abbreviation* ante meridiem. [Latin, = before noon]

amalgam *noun* **1** an alloy of mercury. **2** a soft mixture.

amalgamate *verb* (**amalgamated**, **amalgamating**) mix; combine. **amalgamation** *noun*

amass *verb* heap up; collect.

amateur (*say* **am**-uh-tuh) *noun* a person who does something as a hobby, not as a professional. **amateurish** *adjective* [from Latin *amator* = lover]

amaze *verb* (**amazed**, **amazing**) surprise somebody greatly; fill with wonder. **amazement** *noun*

amazing *adjective* **1** causing great surprise or wonder; astonishing, *An amazing number of people came to the show.* **2** very impressive; excellent, *Dad makes the most amazing cakes.*

ambassador *noun* **1** a diplomat sent by one country as a permanent representative or on a special mission to another. **2** a representative or promoter of a specified activity, *an ambassador for peace.*

amber *noun* **1** a hard clear yellowish substance used for making ornaments. **2** a yellow traffic light shown as a signal for caution, placed between red (= stop) and green (= go).

ambi- *prefix* both; on both sides (as in *ambidextrous*). [from Latin *ambo* = both]

ambidextrous *adjective* able to use either the left hand or the right hand equally well. [from *ambi-*, + Latin *dexter* = right-handed]

ambience *noun* the atmosphere of a place.

ambient *adjective* surrounding, *ambient temperature.*

ambiguous *adjective* having more than one possible meaning; unclear. **ambiguity** *noun*, **ambiguously** *adverb*

ambit *noun* the bounds, scope, or extent of something.

ambition *noun* **1** a strong desire to achieve something. **2** the thing desired.

ambitious *adjective* **1** full of ambition. **2** showing or requiring ambition, *an ambitious project.*

ambivalent (*say* am-**biv**-uh-luhnt) *adjective* having mixed feelings about something (e.g. liking and disliking it). **ambivalence** *noun* [from *ambi-*, + Latin *valens* = strong]

amble *verb* (**ambled**, **ambling**) walk at a slow easy pace. [from Latin *ambulare* = walk]

ambo *noun* (*Australian informal*) ambulance officer.

ambulance *noun* a vehicle equipped to carry sick or injured people.

ambush[1] *noun* (*plural* **ambushes**) a surprise attack from people who have concealed themselves.

ambush[2] *verb* lie in wait for someone; attack from an ambush.

ameliorate (*say* uh-**mee**-lee-uh-rayt) *verb* (**ameliorated**, **ameliorating**) make or become better; improve. **amelioration** *noun* [from *ad-*, + Latin *melior* = better]

amen *interjection* a word used at the end of a prayer or hymn, meaning 'may it be so'. [from Hebrew, = certainly]

amenable (*say* uh-**mee**-nuh-buhl) *adjective* willing to be guided or controlled by something, *He is not amenable to discipline.* [from French *amener* = to lead]

amend *verb* (**amended**, **amending**) alter something so as to improve it.
amendment *noun*
make amends make up for having done something wrong; atone.

> **Usage** *Amend* is often confused with *emend*, a more technical word used in the context of textual correction.

amenity (*say* uh-**men**-uh-tee) *noun* (*plural* **amenities**) a pleasant or useful feature of a place or building, *The town has many amenities.*

American *adjective* **1** of the continent of America. **2** of the United States of America.
American *noun*

amethyst *noun* a purple precious stone.

amiable *adjective* friendly; good-tempered.
amiably *adverb*

amicable *adjective* friendly. **amicably** *adverb* [from Latin *amicus* = friend]

amid *preposition* (also **amidst**) in the middle of; among.

amino acid (*say* uh-**mee**-noh) *noun* an acid found in proteins.

amir (*say* uh-**meer**) *noun* an emir. [Arabic, = a ruler]

amiss[1] *adjective* wrong; faulty, *There is nothing amiss with the engine.*

amiss[2] *adverb* wrongly; faultily.
take amiss be offended by, *Don't take his criticism amiss.*

ammonia *noun* a colourless gas or liquid with a strong smell.

ammonite *noun* the fossil of a coil-shaped shell.

ammunition *noun* a supply of bullets and shells for use in fighting. [from French *la munition*, wrongly taken as *l'ammunition*]

amnesia (*say* am-**nee**-zee-uh) *noun* loss of memory. [from Greek *a-* = without, + *-mnesis* = memory]

amnesty *noun* (*plural* **amnesties**) a general pardon for people who have committed a crime.

amoeba (*say* uh-**mee**-buh) *noun* (*plural* **amoebas**) a microscopic creature consisting of a single cell which constantly changes shape.

amok *adverb* **run amok** rush about in a destructive or murderous frenzy. [from Malay, = fighting mad]

among *preposition* (also **amongst**) **1** surrounded by; in, *There were weeds among the flowers.* **2** between, *Divide the lollies among the children.* [from Old English *ongemang* = in a crowd]

amoral (*say* ay-**mo**-ruhl) *adjective* not based on moral standards; neither moral nor immoral. [from *a-*[2] = not, + *moral*]

amorous *adjective* showing love, *amorous glances.* [from Latin *amor* = love]

amorphous (*say* uh-**maw**-fuhs) *adjective* shapeless, *an amorphous mass.* [from *a-*[2] = not, + Greek *morphe* = form]

amount[1] *noun* **1** a quantity. **2** a total.

amount[2] *verb* **amount to 1** add up to. **2** be equivalent to, *Their reply amounts to a refusal.* [from Latin *ad montem* = to the mountain, upwards]

amp *noun* **1** an ampere. **2** (*informal*) an amplifier.

ampere (*say* **am**-pair) *noun* a unit for measuring electric current. [named after the French scientist A.M. Ampère]

ampersand *noun* the symbol & (= and).

amphi- *prefix* both; on both sides; in both places (as in *amphibian*). [from Greek *amphi* = around]

amphibian *noun* **1** an amphibious animal; an animal (e.g. a frog) that at first (as a tadpole) has gills and lives in water but later develops lungs and breathes air. **2** an amphibious aircraft or vehicle. [from *amphi-*, + Greek *bios* = life]

amphibious *adjective* able to live or move both on land and in water.

amphitheatre *noun* an oval or circular unroofed building with tiers of seats round a central arena. [from Greek *amphi-* = all round, + *theatre*]

ample *adjective* **1** quite enough, *ample provisions.* **2** large. **amply** *adverb*

amplifier *noun* a device for making sounds louder or signals stronger.

amplify *verb* (**amplified**, **amplifying**) **1** make louder or stronger, *to amplify sound.* **2** give more details about something. [from Latin *amplificare* = make more ample]

amplitude *noun* **1** breadth. **2** largeness; abundance.

amputate *verb* (**amputated**, **amputating**) cut off by a surgical operation. **amputation** *noun*

amputee *noun* a person who has had an arm or leg amputated.

amulet *noun* a thing worn as a charm against bad luck or evil.

amuse *verb* (**amused**, **amusing**) **1** make a person laugh or smile. **2** make time pass pleasantly for someone. **amusing** *adjective* [from French *amuser* = distract]

amusement *noun* **1** being amused. **2** something that amuses.

an *adjective* (called the *indefinite article*) a word used instead of **a** when the next word begins with a vowel sound or a silent **h**, *an apple*; *$5 an hour.*

an-[1] *prefix* see **a-**[2].

an-[2] *prefix* see **ad-**.

ana- *prefix* up; back (as in *analysis*). [from Greek *ana* = up]

anabolic steroid *noun* a synthetic steroid hormone used to increase muscle size.

anabranch *noun* (*Australian*) an arm of a river leaving and later rejoining it.

anachronism (*say* uh-**nak**-ruh-niz-uhm) *noun* something wrongly placed in a particular historical period, or regarded as out of date, *Bows and arrows would be an anachronism in modern warfare.* **anachronistic** *adjective* [from *ana-*, + Greek *chronos* = time]

anaconda (*say* an-uh-**kon**-duh) *noun* a large South American snake. [from Sinhalese]

anaemia (*say* uh-**nee**-mee-uh) *noun* a shortage of red blood cells or their haemoglobin, causing paleness and weakness. **anaemic** *adjective* [from *an-*[1] = without, + Greek *haima* = blood]

anaerobic *adjective* not using oxygen from the air, *anaerobic bacteria.*

anaesthetic (*say* an-uhs-**thet**-ik) *noun* a substance or gas that makes you unable to feel pain. **anaesthesia** *noun* [from *an-*[1] = without, + Greek *aisthesis* = sensation]

anaesthetist (*say* uh-**nees**-thuh-tuhst) *noun* a person trained to give anaesthetics. **anaesthetise** *verb*

anagram *noun* a word or phrase made by rearranging the letters of another, *'Stripe' is an anagram of 'priest'.* [from *ana-*, + Greek *gramma* = letter]

anal (*say* **ay**-nuhl) *adjective* of the anus.

analgesic (*say* an-uhl-**jee**-zik) *noun* a substance that relieves pain. [from *an-*[1] = without, + Greek *algesis* = pain]

analog *adjective* (also **analogue**) **1** of or using signals or information represented by a continuously variable physical quantity such as spatial position, voltage, etc. (Compare **digital** 1.) **2** (of a clock or watch) showing the time by means of hands or a pointer rather than displayed digits. **3** not involving or relating to the use of computer technology, as a contrast to a digital counterpart, *analog skills in reading, writing, and remembering.*

analogy (*say* uh-**nal**-uh-jee) *noun* (*plural* **analogies**) a partial likeness between two things that are compared, *the analogy between the human heart and a pump.* **analogous** *adjective*

analyse *verb* (**analysed**, **analysing**) **1** examine (something) in detail, especially in order to explain and interpret it. **2** identify and measure the chemical constituents of (a substance). **analysis** *noun*, **analyst** *noun*, **analytic** *adjective*, **analytical** *adjective* [from *ana-*, + Greek *lysis* = loosening]

anaphylaxis (*say* an-uh-fuh-**lak**-suhs) *noun* (*plural* **anaphylaxes**) an extreme allergic reaction to something, e.g. peanuts. **anaphylactic** *adjective* [from *ana-* = again, + Greek *phulaxis* = guarding]

anarchist (*say* **an**-uh-kuhst) *noun* a person who believes that all forms of government are bad and should be abolished.

anarchy (*say* **an**-uh-kee) *noun* **1** lack of government or control, resulting in lawlessness. **2** disorder. [from *an-*[1] = without, + Greek *arche* = rule]

anatomy (*say* uh-**nat**-uh-mee) *noun* the study of the structure of the body. **anatomical** *adjective*, **anatomist** *noun* [from *ana-*, + Greek *tome* = cutting]

ancestor *noun* anyone from whom a person is descended. **ancestral** *adjective*, **ancestry** *noun*

anchor[1] *noun* a heavy object joined to a ship by a chain or rope and dropped to the bottom of the sea to stop the ship from moving. **anchorage** *noun*

anchor[2] *verb* **1** fix or be fixed by an anchor. **2** fix firmly.

anchovy *noun* (*plural* **anchovies**) a small fish with a strong flavour.

ancient *adjective* **1** very old. **2** of times long past, *ancient history.*

ancillary (*say* an-**sil**-uh-ree) *adjective* helping people to do something, *ancillary services.* [from Latin *ancilla* = servant]

and *conjunction* **1** together with; in addition to, *We had bacon and eggs.* **2** so that; with this result, *Work hard and you will pass.* **3** to, *Go and buy a pen.*

android *noun* **1** (in science fiction) a robot with a human appearance. **2** (also **Android**) (*trademark*) an open-source operating system used for smartphones and tablet computers.

anecdote *noun* a short amusing or interesting story about a real person or thing. **anecdotal** *adjective*

anemone (*say* uh-**nem**-uh-nee) *noun* **1** a plant with cup-shaped red, purple, or white flowers. **2** a sea anemone. [from Greek, = wind-flower]

anemonefish *noun* a clownfish.

anew *adverb* again; in a new or different way, *begin anew.*

angel (*say* **ayn**-juhl) *noun* **1** an attendant or messenger of God. **2** a very kind or beautiful person. **angelic** (*say* an-**jel**-ik) *adjective* [from Greek *angelos* = messenger]

anger[1] *noun* a strong feeling that makes you want to quarrel or fight.

anger[2] *verb* make a person angry.

angina *noun* (in full **angina pectoris**) severe chest pain brought on by exertion, owing to an inadequate supply of blood to the heart.

angle[1] *noun* **1** the space between two lines or surfaces that meet; the amount by which a line or surface must be turned to make it lie along another. **2** a point of view.

angle[2] *verb* (**angled**, **angling**) **1** put something in a slanting position. **2** present information from a particular point of view.

angler *noun* a person who fishes with a fishing rod and line. **angling** *noun*

angle of depression *noun* the angle a descending line makes with the horizontal.

angle of elevation *noun* the angle an ascending line makes with the horizontal.

Anglican *adjective* of the Church of England or a Church in communion with it, e.g. the Anglican Church of Australia. **Anglican** *noun*

Anglo- *prefix* English or British (as in *Anglo-American*). [from the *Angles*, a Germanic people who came to England in the 5th century and eventually gave their name to it]

Anglo-Celtic *adjective* of or from the British Isles.

Anglo-Saxon *noun* **1** an English person, especially of the time before the Norman conquest in 1066. **2** the Old English language. **Anglo-Saxon** *adjective*

angora *noun* **1** a long-haired variety of cat, goat, or rabbit. **2** a yarn or fabric made from the hair of angora goats or rabbits.

angry *adjective* (**angrier**, **angriest**) feeling or showing anger. **angrily** *adverb*

anguish *noun* severe suffering, great sorrow or pain. **anguished** *adjective*

angular *adjective* **1** having angles or sharp corners. **2** (of a person) bony, not plump.

animal *noun* **1** a living thing that can feel and usually move about, *Horses, birds, fish, bees, and people are all animals.* **2** a brutish person; someone not worthy of being called human. [from Latin *animalis* = having breath]

animate[1] (*say* **an**-uh-muht) *adjective* having life.

animate[2] (*say* **an**-uh-mayt) *verb* (**animated**, **animating**) **1** make a thing lively. **2** make a film by photographing a series of drawings, giving an illusion of movement, *an animated cartoon.* **animator** *noun*

animation *noun* **1** liveliness; being alive. **2** producing a moving picture from a sequence of drawings or the movement of puppets or models. **3** the manipulation of electronic images using a computer to create moving images.

anime (*say* **an**-uh-may) *noun* Japanese animation.

animosity (*say* an-uh-**mos**-uh-tee) *noun* a feeling of hostility.

aniseed *noun* a sweet-smelling seed used for flavouring things.

ankle *noun* the part of the leg where it joins the foot.

anklet *noun* an ornamental chain or band worn round the ankle.

annals *plural noun* a history of events, especially when written year by year. [from Latin *annales* = yearly books]

annex *verb* **1** take possession of something and add it to what you have already. **2** add or join a thing to something else. [from *an*-[2], + Latin *nexum* = tied]

annexe *noun* a building added to a larger or more important building.

annihilate (*say* uh-**nuy**-uh-layt) *verb* (**annihilated**, **annihilating**) destroy completely. **annihilation** *noun* [from *an*-[2], + Latin *nihil* = nothing]

anniversary *noun* (*plural* **anniversaries**) a day when you remember something special that happened on the same day in a previous year. [from Latin *annus* = year, + *versum* = turned]

annotate (*say* **an**-oh-tayt) *verb* (**annotated**, **annotation**) add notes of explanation to something written or printed. **annotation** *noun*

announce *verb* (**announced**, **announcing**) make something known, especially by saying it publicly or to an audience. **announcement** *noun* [from *an*-[2], + Latin *nuntius* = messenger]

announcer *noun* a person who announces items in a broadcast.

annoy *verb* **1** make a person slightly angry. **2** be troublesome to someone. **annoyance** *noun* [from Latin *in odio* = hateful]

annual[1] *adjective* **1** happening or done once a year, *her annual visit.* **2** of one year; reckoned by the year, *our annual income.* **3** living for one year or one season, *an annual plant.* **annually** *adverb*

annual[2] *noun* **1** a book that comes out once a year. **2** an annual plant. [from Latin *annus* = year]

annuity (*say* uh-**nyoo**-uh-tee) *noun* (*plural* **annuities**) a fixed annual allowance of money, especially from a kind of investment. [same origin as *annual*]

annul *verb* (**annulled, annulling**) cancel a law or contract; end something legally, *Their marriage was annulled.* **annulment** *noun* [from *an-*[2], + Latin *nullus* = none]

annular *adjective* ring-shaped.

Annunciation *noun* the Christian festival (on 25 March) commemorating the announcement by the angel to the Virgin Mary that she was to be the mother of Jesus Christ.

anode *noun* the electrode by which electric current enters a device. (Compare **cathode.**) [from *ana-* = up, + Greek *hodos* = way]

anoint *verb* put oil or ointment on something, especially in a religious ceremony.

anomaly (*say* uh-**nom**-uh-lee) *noun* (*plural* **anomalies**) something that does not follow the general rule or that is unlike the usual or normal kind. **anomalous** *adjective* [from *an-*[1] = not, + Greek *homalos* = even]

anon *adverb* (*old use*) soon, *I will say more about this anon.*

anon. *abbreviation* anonymous.

anonymous (*say* uh-**non**-uh-muhs) *adjective* of or by a person whose name is not known or not made public, *an anonymous donor.* , **anonymity** (*say* an-uh-**nim**-uh-tee) *noun*, **anonymously** *adverb* [from *an-*[1] = not, + Greek *onyma* = name]

anorak *noun* a waterproof jacket with a hood. [from an Eskimo word]

anorexia (*say* an-uh-**rek**-see-uh) *noun* an illness that makes a person unwilling to eat. **anorexic** *adjective* [from *an-*[1] = not, + Greek *orexis* = appetite]

another *adjective & pronoun* **1** additional; one more, *Can I have another biscuit? She became another of his stars.* **2** different, *come back another day*; *moving from one place to another.*

answer[1] *noun* **1** a reply. **2** the solution to a problem.

answer[2] *verb* **1** give or find an answer to; reply. **2** respond to a signal, *Answer the telephone.*
answer back reply cheekily.
answer for be responsible for.
answer to correspond to, *This answers to the description of the stolen bag.*

answerable *adjective* **1** able to be answered. **2** having to be responsible for something.

ant *noun* a very small insect that lives as one of an organised group.

ant- *prefix* see **anti-**.

antagonise *verb* (**antagonised, antagonising**) make a person feel hostile or angry.

antagonism (*say* an-**tag**-uh-niz-uhm) *noun* an unfriendly feeling; hostility. **antagonist** *noun*, **antagonistic** *adjective* [from *ant-*, + Greek *agon* = struggle]

Antarctic *adjective* of the regions round the South Pole.

ante- *prefix* before (as in *ante-room*). [from Latin]

anteater *noun* an animal that feeds on ants and termites, in Australia an echidna or numbat.

antecedent (*say* an-tuh-**see**-duhnt) *noun* something that exists or comes before something else, *the war and its antecedents.* [from *ante-*, + Latin *cedere* = go]

antechinus (*say* an-tee-**kuy**-nuhs) *noun* marsupial mouse of Australia and New Guinea. [Latin from Greek, = simulating hedgehog]

antediluvian (*say* an-tee-duh-**loo**-vee-uhn) *adjective* **1** of the time before Noah's Flood in the Old Testament. **2** (*informal*) very old or out of date. [from *ante-*, + Latin *diluvium* = deluge]

antelope *noun* (*plural* **antelope** or **antelopes**) an animal like a deer.

antenatal (*say* an-tee-**nay**-tuhl) *adjective* before birth; during pregnancy.

antenna *noun* **1** (*plural* **antennae**) a feeler on the head of an insect or crustacean. **2** (*plural* **antennas**) an aerial.

anterior *adjective* **1** situated at the front or the head. (The opposite is **posterior**[1].) **2** earlier. [Latin, = further forward]

ante-room *noun* a room leading to a more important room.

anthem *noun* a religious or patriotic song, usually sung by a choir or group of people.

anther *noun* the part of a flower's stamen that bears pollen.

anthill *noun* a mound over an ants' nest.

anthology *noun* a collection of poems, stories, or songs in one book or album. [from Greek *anthos* = flower, + *-logia* = collection]

anthracite *noun* a kind of hard coal.

anthrax *noun* a disease of sheep and cattle that can also infect people.

anthropoid *adjective* resembling a human being, *Gorillas are anthropoid apes.* [from Greek *anthropos* = human being]

anthropology *noun* the study of human beings and their customs. **anthropological** *adjective*, **anthropologist** *noun* [from Greek *anthropos* = human being, + *-logy*]

anti- *prefix* (changing to **ant-** before a vowel) against; preventing (as in *antifreeze*). [from Greek *anti* = against]

anti-aircraft *adjective* used against enemy aircraft.

antibacterial *adjective* active against bacteria.

antibiotic *noun* a substance (e.g. penicillin) that destroys bacteria or prevents them from growing. [from *anti-*, + Greek *bios* = life]

antibody *noun* (*plural* **antibodies**) a protein that forms in the blood as a defence against certain substances which it then attacks and destroys.

anticipate *verb* (**anticipated, anticipating**) **1** do something before the proper time or before someone else, *They anticipated the vote counting by claiming victory even before the polls had closed.* **2** foresee, *They had anticipated our needs.* **3** expect, *We anticipate that it will rain.* **anticipation** *noun*, **anticipatory** *adjective* [from *ante-*, + Latin *capere* = take]

anticlimax *noun* a disappointing ending or result where something exciting had been expected.

anticlockwise *adverb & adjective* moving in the direction opposite to clockwise.

antics *plural noun* comical or foolish actions.

anticyclone *noun* an area where air pressure is high, usually producing fine settled weather.

antidote *noun* something that acts against the effects of a poison or disease. [from *anti-*, + Greek *dotos* = given]

antifreeze *noun* a liquid added to water to make it less likely to freeze.

antigen *noun* a substance (e.g. a toxin) that causes the body to produce antibodies. [from *anti-*, + Greek *genes* = born]

antihistamine *noun* a substance that protects people against unpleasant effects when they are allergic to something.

antimony *noun* a brittle silvery metal.

antioxidant *noun* a substance that slows the rate at which something decays because of its combination with oxygen.

antipasto (*say* an-tee-**pah**-stoh) *noun* (*plural* **antipasti**) an Italian hors d'oeuvre. [from Italian *anti* = before, + *pasto* = food]

antipathy (*say* an-**tip**-uh-thee) *noun* a strong dislike. [from *anti-*, + Greek *pathos* = feeling]

antiperspirant *noun* a substance that prevents or reduces sweating.

antipodes (*say* an-**tip**-uh-deez) *plural noun* **1** places on opposite sides of the earth. **2** (**the Antipodes**) Australia, New Zealand, and the areas near them, in relation to Europe. **antipodean** *adjective* [from Greek, = having the feet opposite (*pod-* = foot)]

antiquarian (*say* an-tuh-**kwair**-ree-uhn) *adjective* of the study of antiques.

antiquated *adjective* old-fashioned.

antique[1] (*say* an-**teek**) *adjective* very old; belonging to the distant past.

antique[2] *noun* something that is valuable because it is very old. [from Latin *antiquus* = ancient]

antiquities *plural noun* objects that were made in ancient times.

antiquity (*say* an-**tik**-wuh-tee) *noun* ancient times.

antiretroviral *adjective* relating to a class of drugs that slow down the activity of retroviruses such as HIV.

anti-Semitic (*say* suh-**mit**-ik) *adjective* unfriendly or hostile towards Jews. **anti-Semitism** (*say* **sem**-uh-tiz-uhm) *noun*

antiseptic[1] *adjective* **1** able to destroy bacteria, especially those that cause things to become septic or to decay. **2** thoroughly clean and free from germs.

antiseptic[2] *noun* a substance with an antiseptic effect.

antisocial *adjective* unfriendly or inconsiderate towards other people.

antistatic *adjective* counteracting the effects of static electricity.

antithesis (*say* an-**tith**-uh-suhs) *noun* (*plural* **antitheses**) **1** the direct opposite of something, *Slavery is the antithesis of freedom.* **2** contrast of ideas. [from *anti-*, + Greek *thesis* = placing]

antitoxin *noun* a substance that neutralises a toxin and prevents it from having a harmful effect. **antitoxic** *adjective*

antivenom *noun* a serum containing antibodies against specific poisons in the venom of animals like snakes and spiders.

antler *noun* the branching horn of a deer.

antonym (*say* **an**-tuh-nim) *noun* a word that is opposite in meaning to another, *'Soft' is an antonym of 'hard'.* [from *ant-*, + Greek *onyma* = name]

anus (*say* **ay**-nuhs) *noun* the opening at the lower end of the alimentary canal, through which solid waste matter is passed out of the body.

anvil *noun* a large block of iron on which a blacksmith hammers metal into shape. [from Old English *an* = on, + *filt-* = beat]

anxious *adjective* **1** worried. **2** eager, *She is anxious to please us.* **anxiety** *noun*, **anxiously** *adverb*

any[1] *adjective & pronoun* **1** one or some, *Have you any wool? There isn't any.* **2** no matter which, *Come any day you like.* **3** every, *Any fool knows that!*

any[2] *adverb* at all; in some degree, *Is that any better?*

anybody *noun & pronoun* any person.

anyhow *adverb* **1** anyway. **2** (*informal*) carelessly, *He does his work anyhow.*

anymore *adverb* to any further extent; any longer, *She refused to listen anymore.*

anyone *pronoun* anybody.

> **Usage** *Anyone* is written as two words to emphasise a numerical sense, as in *any one of us can do it.*

anything *noun & pronoun* any thing.

anyway *adverb* whatever happens; whatever the situation may be.

anywhere[1] *adverb* in or to any place.

anywhere[2] *pronoun* any place, *Anywhere will do.*

Anzac *noun* **1** a soldier in the Australian and New Zealand Army Corps during the First World War (1914–1918). **2** any soldier from Australia or New Zealand.

Anzac biscuit *noun* a biscuit made from rolled oats and golden syrup.

Anzac Day *noun* 25 April, commemorating the landing on Gallipoli, 1915, and all Australian war dead.

AO *abbreviation* Officer of the Order of Australia.

aorta (*say* ay-**aw**-tuh) *noun* the great artery carrying blood away from the left side of the heart.

ap-[1] *prefix* see **ad-**.

ap-[2] *prefix* see **apo-**.

apace *adverb* quickly.

apart *adverb* **1** away from each other; separately, *Keep your desks apart.* **2** into pieces, *It fell apart.* **3** excluded, *Joking apart, what do you think of it?* [from French *à* = to, + *part* = side]

apartheid (*say* uh-**pah**-tuyd) *noun* the policy that used to be practised in South Africa of keeping people of different races apart. [Afrikaans, = being apart]

apartment *noun* **1** a set of rooms. **2** a flat.

apathy (*say* **ap**-uh-thee) *noun* lack of interest or concern. **apathetic** (*say* ap-uh-**thet**-ik) *adjective* [from *a-*[2] = without, + Greek *pathos* = feeling]

apatosaurus *noun* (*plural* **apatosauruses**) a large dinosaur that fed on plants. Also called a *brontosaurus*. [from Greek *apate* = deceit, + *sauros* = lizard]

ape[1] *noun* any of the four kinds of monkey (gorillas, chimpanzees, orang-utans, gibbons) that do not have a tail.

ape[2] *verb* (**aped**, **aping**) imitate; mimic.

aperitif (*say* uh-**pe**-ruh-**teef**) *noun* an alcoholic drink taken before a meal to stimulate the appetite. [French]

aperture *noun* an opening. [from Latin *aperire* = to open]

apex (*say* **ay**-peks) *noun* (*plural* **apexes**) the tip or highest point.

aphid (*say* **ay**-fuhd) *noun* (*plural* **aphids**) a tiny insect that sucks the juices from plants.

aphorism (*say* **af**-uh-riz-uhm) *noun* a short witty saying.

apiary (*say* **ay**-pyuh-ree) *noun* (*plural* **apiaries**) a place with a number of hives where bees are kept. **apiarist** *noun* [from Latin *apis* = bee]

apiece *adverb* to, for, or by each, *They cost 50 cents apiece.*

aplomb (*say* uh-**plom**) *noun* dignity and confidence. [from French, = straight as a plumb-line]

apo- *prefix* (changing to **ap-** before a vowel or *h*) from; out or away (as in *Apostle*). [from Greek *apo* = away from]

apocryphal (*say* uh-**pok**-ruh-fuhl) *adjective* untrue; invented, *This account of his travels is apocryphal.* [from the *Apocrypha*, books of the Old Testament that were not accepted by the Jews as part of the Hebrew Scriptures]

apolitical (*say* ay-puh-**lit**-i-kuhl) *adjective* not political; not interested in politics. [from *a-*[2] = not, + *political*]

apologetic *adjective* saying or feeling sorry for something you have done. **apologetically** *adverb*

apologise *verb* (**apologised**, **apologising**) say that you are sorry for something you have done.

apology *noun* (*plural* **apologies**) **1** a statement saying that you are sorry for having done something wrong or badly. **2** a poor specimen, *this feeble apology for a meal.* [from Greek *apologia* = a speech in your own defence]

apoplexy (*say* **ap**-uh-plek-see) *noun* sudden loss of the ability to feel and move, caused by the blocking or breaking of a blood vessel in the brain. **apoplectic** *adjective* [from Greek, = a stroke]

Apostle *noun* any of the 12 men sent out by Christ to preach the Gospel. [from Greek *apostellein* = send out]

apostrophe (*say* uh-**pos**-truh-fee) *noun* the punctuation mark (') used to show that letters have been missed out (as in *can't* = *cannot*) or to show possession (as in *the boy's book*; *the boys' books*). [from *apo*-, + Greek *strophe* = turning]

apothecary (*say* uh-**poth**-uh-kuh-ree) *noun* (*plural* **apothecaries**) (*old use*) a chemist who prepares medicines.

app *noun* a computer application.

appal *verb* (**appalled, appalling**) fill with horror; shock somebody very much. [from Old French *apalir* = become pale]

apparatus *noun* **1** the equipment used for doing something; the instruments used in scientific experiments. **2** a complex organisation or system, *the apparatus of government.*

apparel *noun* (*formal*) clothing.

apparent *adjective* **1** clear; obvious. **2** seeming; appearing to be true but not really so. **apparently** *adverb* [same origin as *appear*]

apparition *noun* **1** a ghost. **2** something strange or surprising that appears.

appeal[1] *verb* **1** ask for something earnestly or formally, *They appealed for funds.* **2** ask for a decision to be changed, *He appealed against the prison sentence.* **3** seem attractive or interesting, *Cricket doesn't appeal to me.*

appeal[2] *noun* **1** the action of appealing for something or about a decision; an earnest or formal request. **2** attraction; interest.

appear *verb* **1** come into sight. **2** seem. **3** take part in a play, film, or show.

appearance *noun* **1** appearing. **2** what somebody looks like. **3** what something appears to be.

appease *verb* (**appeased, appeasing**) calm or pacify someone, especially by giving in to demands. **appeasement** *noun* [from French *à* = to, + *paix* = peace]

appellation *noun* a name or title.

append *verb* add at the end; attach. [from *ap*-, + Latin *pendere* = hang]

appendage *noun* something added or attached; a thing that forms a natural part of something larger.

appendicitis *noun* inflammation of the appendix.

appendix *noun* **1** (*plural* **appendixes**) a small tube leading off from the intestine. **2** (*plural* **appendices**) a section added at the end of a book. [same origin as *append*]

appetising *adjective* stimulating the appetite. **appetiser** *noun*

appetite *noun* a desire, especially for food. [from *ap*-, + Latin *petere* = seek]

applaud *verb* show that you like something, especially by clapping your hands. **applause** *noun* [from *ap*-, + Latin *plaudere* = clap hands]

apple *noun* a round fruit with a red, yellow, or green skin.
the apple of your eye a person or thing that you love and are proud of.

applet *noun* a small computer application running within a larger program.

appliance *noun* a piece of equipment for a particular purpose, *electrical appliances.*

applicable (*say* uh-**plik**-uh-buhl) *adjective* able to be applied; suitable; relevant.

applicant *noun* a person who applies for something, *a job applicant.*

application *noun* **1** the action of applying. **2** a formal request. **3** the practical use of something. **4** the ability to apply yourself. **5** a computer program designed for a particular purpose.

applicator *noun* a device for applying something.

applied *adjective* put to practical use, *applied science.*

appliqué (*say* **ap**-luh-kay) *noun* needlework in which cut-out pieces of material are sewn or fixed ornamentally on another piece. [French, = put on]

apply *verb* (**applied, applying**) **1** put one thing on another. **2** start using something. **3** concern; be relevant, *This rule does not apply to you.* **4** make a formal request, *apply for a job.*
apply yourself give all your attention to a job; work diligently.

appoint *verb* **1** choose a person for a job. **2** arrange officially, *They appointed a time for the meeting.*

appointment *noun* **1** an arrangement to meet or visit somebody at a particular time. **2** choosing somebody for a job. **3** a job or position.

apportion *verb* divide into shares; allot. **apportionment** *noun*

apposite (*say* **ap**-uh-zuht) *adjective* (of a remark) suitable; relevant.

apposition *noun* placing things together, especially nouns and phrases in a grammatical relationship. In 'We visited Canberra, the capital of Australia' *the capital of Australia* is in apposition to *Canberra.* [from *ap*- + *position*]

appraise *verb* (**appraised, appraising**) estimate the value or quality of a person or thing. **appraisal** *noun*

appreciable *adjective* enough to be noticed or felt; perceptible. **appreciably** *adverb*

appreciate *verb* (**appreciated**, **appreciating**) **1** enjoy; value. **2** understand. **3** increase in value. **appreciative** *adjective* [from *ap*-, + Latin *pretium* = price]

appreciation *noun* **1** favourable or grateful recognition. **2** a written assessment of an artist or piece of work. **3** an understanding of or reaction to, *an appreciation of the problem.* **4** an increase in monetary value, *the appreciation of the dollar against the pound.*

apprehend *verb* **1** seize; arrest. **2** understand. **3** expect something with fear or worry. [from *ap*-, + Latin *prehendere* = to grasp]

apprehension *noun* **1** fear. **2** understanding. **3** arrest. **apprehensive** *adjective*

apprentice[1] *noun* a person who is learning a trade or craft by a legal agreement with an employer. **apprenticeship** *noun*

apprentice[2] *verb* (**apprenticed**, **apprenticing**) place a person as an apprentice. [from French *apprendre* = learn]

approach[1] *verb* **1** come near. **2** go to someone with a request or offer, *They approached me for help.* **3** set about doing something or tackling a problem. **approachable** *adjective*

approach[2] *noun* (*plural* **approaches**) **1** approaching. **2** a way or road. **3** a way of doing or tackling something.

approbation *noun* approval.

appropriate[1] (*say* uh-**proh**-pree-uht) *adjective* suitable. **appropriately** *adverb*

appropriate[2] (*say* uh-**proh**-pree-ayt) *verb* (**appropriated**, **appropriating**) take something and use it as your own.

appropriation *noun* **1** the action of appropriating something. **2** the deliberate reworking of images and styles from earlier, well-known works of art.

approval *noun* **1** approving somebody or something. **2** permission; consent.
on approval received by a customer to examine before deciding to buy.

approve *verb* (**approved**, **approving**) **1** say or think that a person or thing is good or suitable. **2** agree to, *The bank approved the loan.*

approximate[1] (*say* uh-**prok**-suh-muht) *adjective* almost exact or correct but not completely so. **approximately** *adverb*

approximate[2] (*say* uh-**prok**-suh-mayt) *verb* (**approximated**, **approximating**) make or be almost the same as something. [from *ap*-, + Latin *proximus* = very near]

apricot *noun* a juicy orange-coloured fruit with a stone in it.

April *noun* the fourth month of the year. [Latin]

a priori (*say* ay pruy-**aw**-ruy) *adjective* **1** (of reasoning) from cause to effect. **2** (of ideas) not derived from experience. **3** assumed without investigation. [Latin, = from what is before]

apron *noun* **1** a garment worn over the front of the body, especially to protect other clothes. **2** a hard-surfaced area on an airfield where aircraft are loaded and unloaded. [originally *a naperon*, from French *nappe* = tablecloth]

apropos (*say* ap-ruh-**poh**) *adjective* appropriate, *Her comment was very apropos.*
apropos of concerning, *Apropos of tennis, who is the new champion?* [from French *à propos* = to the purpose]

apse *noun* a semicircular part projecting from a church or other building.

apt *adjective* **1** likely, *He is apt to be careless.* **2** suitable, *an apt quotation.* **3** quick at learning, *an apt pupil.* **aptly** *adverb*, **aptness** *noun* [from Latin *aptus* = fitted]

aptitude *noun* a talent or skill.

aqualung *noun* a diver's portable breathing apparatus, with cylinders of compressed air connected to a face mask. [from Latin *aqua* = water, + *lung*]

aquamarine *noun* **1** a bluish-green precious stone. **2** its colour. [from Latin *aqua marina* = seawater]

aquarium *noun* (*plural* **aquariums**) a tank or building in which live fish and other water animals are displayed. [from Latin *aquarius* = of water]

Aquarius *noun* **1** a constellation and the eleventh sign of the zodiac (the Water Carrier). **2** a person born when the sun is in this sign. [Latin, related to aquarium]

aquatic *adjective* of, on, or in water, *aquatic sports.* [from Latin *aqua* = water]

aqueduct *noun* a bridge carrying a water-channel across low ground or a valley. [from Latin *aqua* = water, + *ducere* = to lead]

aquifer *noun* a layer of water-bearing rock or soil. [from Latin *aqua* = water, + *ferre* = bring]

aquiline (*say* **ak**-wuh-luyn) *adjective* hooked like an eagle's beak, *an aquiline nose.* [from Latin *aquila* = eagle]

ar- *prefix* see **ad-**.

Arab *noun* a member of a people living in Arabia and other parts of the Middle East and North Africa. **Arabian** *adjective*

arabesque (*say* a-ruh-**besk**) *noun* **1** (in dancing) a position with one leg stretched backwards in the air. **2** an ornamental design of leaves and branches.

Arabic[1] *adjective* of the Arabs or their language.

Arabic[2] *noun* the language of the Arabs.

Arabic numeral *noun* any of the symbols 0, 1, 2, 3, 4, 5, 6, 7, 8, and 9.

arable *adjective* suitable for ploughing or growing crops on, *arable land.* [from Latin *arare* = to plough]

arachnid (*say* uh-**rak**-nid) *noun* a member of the group of animals that includes spiders and scorpions. [from Greek *arachne* = spider]

arbiter *noun* a person who has the power to decide what shall be done or accepted.

arbitrary (*say* **ah**-buh-truh-ree) *adjective* chosen or done on an impulse, not according to a rule or law, *an arbitrary decision.* **arbitrarily** *adverb*

arbitration *noun* settling a dispute by calling in a person or persons from outside to make a decision. **arbitrate** *verb*, **arbitrator** *noun* [from Latin *arbitrari* = to judge]

Arbitration Court *noun* (*Australian*) a tribunal for settling industrial disputes and making award rates for industry.

arboreal (*say* ah-**baw**-ree-uhl) *adjective* of trees; living in trees. [from Latin *arbor* = tree]

arbour (*say* **ar**-buh) *noun* a shady place among trees, often in a garden with climbing plants growing over a framework.

arc *noun* **1** a curve; part of the circumference of a circle. **2** a luminous electric current passing between two electrodes. [same origin as *archer*]

arcade *noun* a covered passage or area, especially for shopping.

arcane *adjective* secret; mysterious.

arch[1] *noun* (*plural* **arches**) **1** a curved structure that helps to support a bridge or other structure. **2** something shaped like this.

arch[2] *verb* form into an arch; curve. [same origin as *archer*]

arch[3] *adjective* pretending to be playful, *an arch smile.* **archly** *adverb*

arch- *prefix* chief; principal (as in *arch-enemy*).

archaeology (*say* ah-kee-**ol**-uh-jee) *noun* the study of the remains of past people and cultures. **archaeological** *adjective*, **archaeologist** *noun* [from Greek *archaios* = old, + *-logy*]

archaic (*say* ah-**kay**-ik) *adjective* belonging to former or ancient times. [from Greek *arche* = beginning]

archangel *noun* an angel of the highest rank.

archbishop *noun* the chief bishop of a province of the Church.

archdeacon *noun* a senior priest ranking next below a bishop.

arch-enemy *noun* the chief enemy.

archer *noun* a person who shoots with a bow and arrows. **archery** *noun* [from Latin *arcus* = a bow or curve]

archetype (*say* **ah**-kuh-tuyp) *noun* the original form or model from which others are copies. **archetypal** *adjective* [from *arch-* + *type*]

Archimedes' principle (*say* ar-kuh-**mee**-deez) *noun* the law that a body immersed in a fluid is subject to an upward force equal in magnitude to the weight of fluid it displaces. [named after an ancient Greek mathematician]

archipelago (*say* ah-kuh-**pel**-uh-goh) *noun* (*plural* **archipelagos**) a large group of islands, or the sea containing these. [from *arch-*, + Greek *pelagos* = sea]

architect (*say* **ah**-kuh-tekt) *noun* a person who designs buildings. [from *arch-*, + Greek *tekton* = builder]

architecture *noun* **1** the process of designing buildings. **2** a particular style of building. **architectural** *adjective*

archive (*say* **ah**-kuyv) *noun* **1** (often **archives**) a collection of documents or records providing information about a place, institution, or group of people; the place where these are kept. **2** a complete record of the data in part or all of a computer system. **archive** *verb*, **archivist** (*say* **ah**-kuh-vuhst) *noun* [from Greek *archeia* = public records]

archway *noun* an arched passage or entrance.

Arctic *adjective* **1** of the regions round the North Pole. **2** (**arctic**) very cold, *The weather was arctic.*

ardent *adjective* full of ardour; enthusiastic. **ardently** *adverb* [from Latin *ardens* = burning]

ardour *noun* great warmth of feeling.

arduous *adjective* needing much effort; laborious. **arduously** *adverb* [from Latin *arduus* = steep]

are plural and 2nd person singular present tense of **be**, *The police are looking for the escaped prisoner; I'm happy you are coming for dinner.*

area *noun* **1** the extent or measurement of a surface. **2** a particular region. **3** a space set aside for a specific purpose, *a picnic area.*

arena (*say* ah-**ree**-nuh) *noun* the level area in the centre of an amphitheatre or sports stadium. [Latin, = sand]

aren't (*informal*) are not.
aren't I? (*informal*) am I not?

arguable *adjective* **1** able to be asserted; likely to be correct. **2** open to doubt; not certain. **arguably** *adverb*

argue *verb* (**argued, arguing**) **1** say that you disagree; exchange angry comments. **2** state that something is true and give reasons.

argument *noun* **1** a disagreement; a quarrel. **2** a reason put forward; a series of reasons.

argumentative *adjective* fond of arguing.

aria (*say* **ah**-ree-uh) *noun* a solo in an opera or oratorio. [Italian]

arid *adjective* dry and barren.

Aries *noun* (*plural* **Aries**) **1** a constellation and the first sign of the zodiac (the Ram). **2** a person born when the sun is in this sign. [Latin, = ram]

arise *verb* (**arose, arisen, arising**) **1** come into existence; come to people's notice, *Problems arose.* **2** (*old use*) rise; stand up, *Arise, Sir Francis.*

aristocracy (*say* a-ruh-**stok**-ruh-see) *noun* people of the highest social rank; members of the nobility. [from Greek *aristos* = best, + *-cracy*]

aristocrat (*say* **a**-ruh-stuh-krat) *noun* a member of the aristocracy. **aristocratic** *adjective*

arithmetic *noun* the science or study of numbers; calculating with numbers. **arithmetical** *adjective* [from Greek *arithmos* = number]

ark *noun* **1** the ship in which Noah and his family escaped the Flood. **2** a wooden box in which the writings of the Jewish Law were kept. [from Latin *arca* = box]

arm[1] *noun* **1** either of the two upper limbs of the body, between the shoulder and the hand. **2** a sleeve. **3** something shaped like an arm or jutting out from a main part; the raised side part of a chair. **armful** *noun* [Old English]

arm[2] *verb* **1** supply with weapons. **2** prepare for war. [from Latin *arma* = weapons]

armada (*say* ah-**mah**-duh) *noun* a fleet of warships. [Spanish, = navy]

armadillo *noun* (*plural* **armadillos**) a small burrowing South American animal whose body is covered with a shell of bony plates.

armaments *plural noun* military weapons and equipment.

armature *noun* **1** the current-carrying part of a dynamo or electric motor. **2** an iron bar placed in contact with the poles of a magnet to preserve its power. Also called a *keeper*.

armchair *noun* a chair with arms.

armed forces *noun* (also **armed services**) a country's military forces; the army, navy, and air force.

armistice *noun* an agreement to stop fighting in a war or battle. [from Latin *arma* = weapons, + *sistere* = stop]

armour *noun* **1** a protective covering for the body, formerly worn in fighting. **2** a metal covering on a warship, tank, or car to protect it from missiles. **armoured** *adjective* [same origin as *arm*[2]]

armoury *noun* a place where weapons and ammunition are stored.

armpit *noun* the hollow underneath the top of the arm, below the shoulder.

arms *plural noun* **1** weapons. **2** a coat of arms.
up in arms protesting vigorously. [same origin as *arm*[2]]

arms race *noun* competition between nations in building up supplies of weapons.

army *noun* (*plural* **armies**) **1** a large number of people trained to fight on land. **2** a large group, *an army of helpers.*

aroma (*say* uh-**roh**-muh) *noun* a smell, especially a pleasant one. **aromatic** (*say* a-ruh-**mat**-ik) *adjective*

arose *past tense* of **arise**.

around *adverb & preposition* all round; about.

arouse *verb* (**aroused, arousing**) rouse.

arrange *verb* (**arranged, arranging**) **1** put into a certain order; adjust. **2** form plans for something, *We arranged to be there.* **3** prepare music for a particular purpose. **arrangement** *noun*

arrant *adjective* thorough and obvious, *Arrant nonsense!*

array[1] *noun* **1** a display. **2** an orderly arrangement. **3** (in mathematics) an arrangement of quantities or symbols in rows and columns.

array[2] *verb* (**arrayed, arraying**) **1** arrange in order. **2** clothe; adorn. [from *ar-*, + old form of *ready*]

arrears *plural noun* **1** money that is owing and ought to have been paid earlier. **2** work that should have been finished but is still waiting to be dealt with.
in arrears behind with payments.

arrest[1] *verb* **1** seize a person by authority of the law. **2** stop a process or movement.

arrest[2] *noun* **1** arresting somebody. **2** stopping something.

arrhythmia (*say* ah-**rith**-mee-uh) *noun* deviation from the normal rhythm of the heart.

arrive *verb* (**arrived, arriving**) **1** reach the end of a journey or a point on it. **2** come, *The great day arrived.* **arrival** *noun*

arrogant *adjective* proud and overbearing, thinking you are superior to other people. **arrogance** *noun*, **arrogantly** *adverb*

arrow *noun* **1** a pointed stick to be shot from a bow. **2** a sign with an outward-pointing V at the end, used to show direction or position. **arrowhead** *noun*

arsenal *noun* a place where weapons and ammunition are stored or manufactured. [from Arabic, = workshop]

arsenic *noun* a very poisonous metallic substance. [from Persian *zar* = gold]

arson *noun* the crime of deliberately setting fire to property. **arsonist** *noun*

art *noun* **1** producing something beautiful, especially by painting or drawing; things produced in this way. **2** a skill, *the art of sailing.*
the arts creative activities such as painting, music, theatre, and writing.

art deco (*say* aht **dek**-oh) *noun* a style of decorative art and architecture popular in the 1920s and 1930s. [from French *art decoratif* = decorative art]

artefact *noun* an object made by a human being, typically one of cultural or historical interest. [from Latin *arte* = by art, + *factum* = made]

artery *noun* (*plural* **arteries**) **1** any of the tubes that carry blood away from the heart to all parts of the body. (Compare **vein** 1.) **2** an important road or route. **arterial** (*say* ah-**teer**-ree-uhl) *adjective*

artesian bore *noun* (also **artesian well**) a well that is bored straight down into a place where water will rise easily to the surface.

artful *adjective* crafty. **artfully** *adverb*

arthritis (*say* ah-**thruy**-tuhs) *noun* a disease that makes joints in the body stiff and painful. **arthritic** (*say* ah-**thrit**-ik) *adjective* [from Greek *arthron* = joint]

arthropod *noun* an animal of the group that includes insects, spiders, crabs, and centipedes. [from Greek *arthron* = joint, + *podos* = of a foot]

artichoke *noun* a kind of plant with a flower head used as a vegetable.

article *noun* **1** a piece of writing published in a newspaper or magazine. **2** an object.
definite article the word 'the'.
indefinite article the word 'a' or 'an'.

articulate[1] (*say* ah-**tik**-yuh-luht) *adjective* able to express things clearly and fluently.

articulate[2] (*say* ah-**tik**-yuh-layt) *verb* (**articulated**, **articulating**) **1** say or speak clearly. **2** connect by a joint. **articulation** *noun*

articulated vehicle *noun* a vehicle that has sections connected by a flexible joint.

artifice *noun* a piece of trickery; a clever device. [same origin as *artificial*]

artificial *adjective* **1** not natural; made by human beings in imitation of a natural thing. **2** insincere. **artificiality** *noun* **artificially** *adverb* [from Latin *ars* = art, + *facere* = make]

artificial respiration *noun* helping somebody to start breathing again after their breathing has stopped.

artillery *noun* **1** large guns. **2** the part of the army that uses large guns.

artisan[1] (*say* ah-tuh-**zan**) *noun* a worker in a skilled trade, especially one that involves making things by hand.

artisan[2] *adjective* (of food or drink) made in a traditional or non-mechanised way using high-quality ingredients.

artist *noun* **1** a person who produces works of art, especially a painter. **2** an entertainer. **artistry** *noun*

artistic *adjective* **1** of art or artists. **2** showing skill and good taste. **artistically** *adverb*

artless *adjective* simple and natural; not artful. **artlessly** *adverb*

art nouveau (*say* aht noo-**voh**) *noun* a style of art developed in the late 19th century, with ornamental and flowing designs. [French, = new art]

arts *plural noun* subjects (e.g. languages, literature, history) in which opinion and understanding are very important, as opposed to sciences where measurements and calculations are used.

art union *noun* (*Australian*) a lottery.

arvo *noun* (*Australian informal*) afternoon.

as[1] *adverb* equally; similarly, *This is just as easy.*

as[2] *preposition* in the capacity or form of, *Use it as a handle.*

as[3] *conjunction* **1** when; while, *She slipped as she got off the bus.* **2** because, *As he was late, we missed the train.* **3** in the way that, *Leave it as it is.*
as for with regard to, *As for you, I forgive you.*
as it were in some way, *She became, as it were, her own enemy.*
as well also.

as- *prefix* see **ad-**.

ASAP *abbreviation* as soon as possible, *Please call me ASAP.*

asbestos *noun* a soft fireproof material.

ascend *verb* go up.
ascend the throne become king or queen. [from Latin *ascendere* = climb up]

ascendant *adjective* rising.
in the ascendant rising, especially in power or influence.

ascending *adjective* **1** increasing in size or importance. **2** sloping or leading upwards.

ascension *noun* ascending.

Ascension Day *noun* the 40th day after Easter, when Christians commemorate the ascension of Christ into heaven.

ascent *noun* **1** ascending. **2** a way up; an upward path or slope.

ascertain (*say* as-uh-**tayn**) *verb* find out by asking. **ascertainable** *adjective*

ascetic[1] (*say* uh-**set**-ik) *adjective* not allowing yourself pleasure and luxuries. **asceticism** *noun*

ascetic[2] *noun* a person who leads an ascetic life, often for religious reasons. [from Greek *asketes* = hermit]

ascorbic acid (*say* uh-**skaw**-bik) *noun* vitamin C.

ascribe *verb* (**ascribed**, **ascribing**) attribute.

aseptic (*say* ay-**sep**-tik) *adjective* clean and free from bacteria that cause things to become septic. [from *a-*[2] = not, + *septic*]

asexual *adjective* (in biology, of reproduction) by other than sexual methods. [from *a-*[2] = not, + *sexual*]

ash[1] *noun* (*plural* **ashes**) the powder that is left after something has been burned. **ashen** *adjective*, **ashy** *adjective*
the Ashes the trophy for which England and Australia play each other at cricket.

ash[2] *noun* (*plural* **ashes**) a tree with silvery-grey bark.

ashamed *adjective* feeling shame.

ashore *adverb* to or on the shore.

ashram *noun* a place of religious retreat, especially for Hindus. [from Sanskrit *āśrama* = hermitage]

ashrama *noun* (in Hinduism) any of the four stages of an ideal life.

ashtray *noun* a small bowl for tobacco ash.

Ash Wednesday *noun* the first day of Lent.

Asian *adjective* of Asia or its people. **Asian** *noun*

Asiatic *adjective* of Asia.

aside[1] *adverb* **1** to or at one side, *pull it aside.* **2** away; in reserve.
aside from other than.

aside[2] *noun* words spoken so that only certain people will hear.

asinine (*say* **as**-uh-nuyn) *adjective* silly; stupid. [same origin as *ass*]

ask *verb* **1** speak so as to find out something. **2** seek to obtain from someone. **3** invite, *Ask her to the party.*

askance (*say* uh-**skans**) *adverb* **look askance at** regard with distrust or disapproval.

askew *adverb & adjective* crooked; not straight or level.

asleep *adverb & adjective* sleeping.

asp *noun* a small poisonous snake.

asparagus *noun* a plant whose young shoots are eaten as a vegetable.

aspect *noun* **1** one part of a problem or situation, *Violence was the worst aspect of the crime.* **2** a person's or thing's appearance, *The forest had a sinister aspect.* **3** the direction a thing faces, *This room has a southern aspect.* [from *as-*, + Latin *specere* = to look]

aspen *noun* a poplar tree with leaves that move in the slightest wind.

Asperger's syndrome *noun* a mild autistic disorder characterised by awkwardness in social interaction, pedantry in speech, and preoccupation with very narrow interests. [from Austrian psychiatrist Hans Asperger]

asperity *noun* harshness; severity. [from Latin *asper* = rough]

aspersions *plural noun* an attack on someone's reputation, *He cast aspersions on his rivals.*

asphalt (*say* **ash**-felt or **as**-felt) *noun* a sticky black substance like tar, often mixed with gravel to surface roads or footpaths.

asphyxia (*say* as-**fik**-see-uh) *noun* suffocation. [Greek, = stopping of the pulse]

asphyxiate (*say* as-**fik**-see-ayt) *verb* (**asphyxiated**, **asphyxiating**) suffocate. **asphyxiation** *noun*

aspic *noun* a savoury jelly containing meats, eggs, or seafood.

aspidistra *noun* a house plant with broad leaves. [from Greek *aspis* = a shield]

aspirant (*say* **as**-puh-ruhnt) *noun* a person who aspires to something.

aspirate (*say* **as**-puh-ruht) *noun* the sound of 'h'. [same origin as *aspire*]

aspiration *noun* ambition; strong desire.

aspire *verb* (**aspired**, **aspiring**) have an ambition or strong desire, *He aspired to be prime minister.* [from *ad-* = to, + Latin *spirare* = breathe]

aspirin *noun* a medicinal drug used to relieve pain or reduce fever.

ass *noun* (*plural* **asses**) **1** a donkey. **2** (*informal*) a stupid person. [from Latin *asinus* = donkey]

assail *verb* attack. **assailant** *noun* [from Latin *assilire* = leap upon]

assassin *noun* a person who assassinates somebody. [from Arabic, = hashish-takers, fanatics who murdered people during the time of the Crusades]

assassinate *verb* (**assassinated**, **assassinating**) kill an important person deliberately and violently, especially for political reasons. **assassination** *noun*

assault[1] *noun* a violent or illegal attack.

assault[2] *verb* make an assault on someone. [same origin as *assail*]

assay (*say* uh-**say**) *noun* a test made on metal or ore to discover its quality. [from French *essai* = trial]

assemble *verb* (**assembled**, **assembling**) **1** bring or come together. **2** fit or put together. **assemblage** *noun*

assembly *noun* (*plural* **assemblies**) **1** assembling. **2** a regular meeting, such as when everybody in a school meets together. **3** people who regularly meet for a special purpose; a parliament.

assembly line *noun* a series of workers and machines along which a product passes to be assembled part by part.

assent[1] *verb* consent; say you agree.

assent[2] *noun* consent; approval.

assert *verb* state firmly. **assertion** *noun* **assert yourself** use firmness or authority.

assertive *adjective* asserting yourself. **assertively** *adverb*, **assertiveness** *noun*

assess *verb* decide or estimate the value or quality of a person or thing. **assessment** *noun*, **assessor** *noun* [from Latin *assessor* = an assistant judge]

asset *noun* something useful.

assets *plural noun* a person's or company's property, reckoned as having value.

assiduous (*say* uh-**sid**-yoo-uhs) *adjective* working hard; persevering. **assiduity** *noun*, **assiduously** *adverb*

assign *verb* **1** allot; give. **2** appoint a person to perform a task. [from *as*-, + Latin *signare* = mark out]

assignation (*say* as-ig-**nay**-shuhn) *noun* **1** assigning something. **2** an arrangement to meet someone.

assignment *noun* **1** assigning. **2** something assigned; a task given to someone.

assimilate *verb* (**assimilated**, **assimilating**) take in and absorb something, e.g. nourishment into the body or knowledge into the mind. **assimilation** *noun*

assist *verb* help. **assistance** *noun* [from Latin *assistere* = stand by]

assistant[1] *noun* **1** a person who assists another; a helper. **2** a person who serves customers in a shop.

assistant[2] *adjective* assisting; helping and ranking next below a senior person, *the assistant manager.*

associate[1] (*say* uh-**soh**-she-ayt or uh-**soh**-see-ayt) *verb* (**associated**, **associating**) **1** put or go naturally or regularly together. **2** work together; have frequent dealings.

associate[2] (*say* uh-**soh**-she-uht or uh-**soh**-see-uht) *noun* a colleague or companion; a partner. **associate** *adjective* [from *as*-, + Latin *socius* = an ally]

association *noun* **1** an organisation of people; a society. **2** associating. **3** something associated.

associative *noun* **1** of or involving association. **2** (in mathematics) involving the condition that a group of quantities connected by operators gives the same result whatever their grouping, as long as their order remains the same, e.g. $(a \times b) \times c = a \times (b \times c)$.

assonance (*say* **as**-uh-nuhns) *noun* similarity of vowel sounds, e.g. in *vermin* and *furnish.* [from *as*-, + Latin *sonus* = sound]

assorted *adjective* of various sorts put together; mixed. **assortment** *noun*

assuage (*say* uh-**swayj**) *verb* (**assuaged**, **assuaging**) soothe; make less severe, *We drank to assuage our thirst.* [from *as*-, + Latin *suavis* = pleasant]

assume *verb* (**assumed**, **assuming**) **1** accept (without proof or question) that something is true or sure to happen. **2** take on; undertake, *She assumed the extra responsibility.* **3** put on, *He assumed an innocent expression.* **assumption** *noun* [from *as*-, + Latin *sumere* = take]

assurance *noun* **1** a promise or guarantee that something is true or will happen. **2** life insurance. **3** self-confidence.

assure *verb* (**assured**, **assuring**) **1** tell somebody confidently; promise. **2** make certain.

aster *noun* a garden plant with daisy-like flowers in various colours. [from Greek *aster* = star]

asterisk *noun* a star-shaped sign (*) used to draw attention to something. [from Greek *asteriskos* = little star]

astern *adverb* **1** at the back of a ship or aircraft. **2** backwards, *Full speed astern!*

asteroid *noun* one of the small planets found mainly between the orbits of Mars and Jupiter. [same origin as *aster*]

asthma (*say* **as**-muh) *noun* a disease that makes breathing difficult. **asthmatic** *adjective & noun*

astigmatism (*say* uh-**stig**-muh-tiz-uhm) *noun* a defect that prevents an eye or lens from focusing properly. **astigmatic** *adjective* [from *a*-[2] = not, + Greek *stigma* = a point]

astir *adverb & adjective* in motion; moving.

astonish *verb* surprise somebody greatly. **astonishment** *noun*

astound *verb* astonish; shock greatly.

astral *adjective* of the stars. [same origin as *aster*]

astray *adverb & adjective* away from the right path or place or course of action.

astride *adverb & preposition* with one leg on each side of something.

astringent *adjective* **1** causing skin or body tissue to contract. **2** harsh; severe, *astringent criticism.* **astringency** *noun* [from *as-*, + Latin *stringere* = bind tightly]

astrology *noun* the study of how the stars may affect people's lives. **astrologer** *noun*, **astrological** *adjective* [from Greek *astron* = star, + *-logy*]

astronaut *noun* a person who travels in a spacecraft. **astronautics** *noun* [from Greek *astron* = star, + *nautes* = sailor]

astronomical *adjective* **1** of astronomy. **2** enormous in amount, *The cost was astronomical.* **astronomically** *adverb*

astronomy *noun* the study of the stars and planets and their movements. **astronomer** *noun* [from Greek *astron* = star, + *-nomia* = arrangement]

astute *adjective* clever; shrewd. **astutely** *adverb*, **astuteness** *noun*

asunder *adverb* apart; into pieces.

asylum *noun* **1** refuge and safety; a place of refuge, *The defeated rebels sought political asylum in another country.* **2** (*old use*) a mental hospital. [from Greek, = refuge]

asylum seeker *noun* a person seeking refuge, especially political asylum.

asymmetrical (*say* ay-suh-**met**-ri-kuhl) *adjective* not symmetrical. **asymmetrically** *adverb*

asymptote (*say* **as**-uhm-toht) *noun* a line that continuously approaches a curve but never touches it.

asystole (*say* uh-**sis**-tuh-lee) *noun* a condition in which the heart no longer beats.

at *preposition* This word is used to show **1** position (*at the top*), **2** time (*at midnight*), **3** condition (*stand at ease*), **4** direction towards something (*Aim at the target*), **5** level, price or age (*Sell them at $1 each*), **6** cause (*We were annoyed at his failure*).
at all in any way; of any kind.
at it doing or working at something.
at once 1 immediately. **2** at the same time, *It all came out at once.*

at- *prefix* see **ad-**.

ATAR *abbreviation* Australian Tertiary Admission Rank.

ate *past tense* of **eat**, *I ate the rest of the cake for morning tea.*

atheist (*say* **ay**-thee-ist) *noun* a person who believes that there is no God. **atheism** *noun* [from *a-*[2] = not, + Greek *theos* = god]

athlete *noun* a person who is good at athletics.

athletic *adjective* **1** physically strong and active. **2** of athletes. **athletically** *adverb*, **athleticism** *noun*

athletics *plural noun* physical exercises and sports, e.g. running and jumping.

atlas *noun* (*plural* **atlases**) a book of maps. [named after Atlas, a giant in Greek mythology, who was made to support the universe]

ATM *abbreviation* automated (or automatic) teller machine, a machine at which customers can conduct their banking using a plastic card and a personal identification number (PIN).

atmosphere *noun* **1** the air round the earth. **2** a feeling given by surroundings, *the happy atmosphere of the showground.* **atmospheric** *adjective* [from Greek *atmos* = vapour, + *sphere*]

atoll *noun* a ring-shaped coral reef.

atom *noun* the smallest particle of a substance. **atomic** *adjective* [from Greek *atomos* = indivisible]

atomic energy *noun* energy created by splitting the nuclei of certain atoms.

atomiser *noun* a device for making a liquid into a fine spray.

atonal *adjective* (of music) not written in any particular key or scale system.

atone *verb* (**atoned**, **atoning**) make amends; make up for having done something wrong. **atonement** *noun* [from *at one*]

atrium (*say* **ay**-tree-uhm) *noun* (*plural* **atria** or **atriums**) **1** a high open space in the centre of a building. **2** either of the two upper cavities in the heart.

atrocious (*say* uh-**troh**-shuhs) *adjective* extremely bad or wicked. **atrociously** *adverb* [from Latin *atrox* = cruel]

atrocity (*say* uh-**tros**-uh-tee) *noun* (*plural* **atrocities**) something extremely bad or wicked; wickedness.

atrophy (*say* **at**-ruh-fee) *noun* wasting away through undernourishment or lack of use. [from *a-*[2], + Greek *-trophia* = nourishment]

attach *verb* **1** fix or join to something else. **2** regard as belonging to something, *We attach great importance to hygiene.* **attachment** *noun*
attached to fond of.

attaché (*say* uh-**tash**-ay) *noun* a special assistant to an ambassador, *our military attaché.* [French, = attached]

attaché case *noun* a small rectangular case for carrying documents.

attack[1] *noun* **1** a violent attempt to hurt or overcome somebody. **2** a piece of strong criticism. **3** sudden illness or pain, *a heart attack.*

attack[2] *verb* **1** try to hurt or overcome somebody using violence. **2** criticise strongly. **3** act harmfully on, *Rust attacks metals.* **4** begin vigorous work on, *Let's attack the dishes.* **attacker** *noun*

attain *verb* accomplish; succeed in doing or getting something. **attainable** *adjective*, **attainment** *noun*

attempt[1] *verb* make an effort to do something; try.

attempt[2] *noun* an effort to do something; a try. [from *at*-, + Latin *temptare* = try]

attend *verb* **1** give care and thought to something; look and listen, *Why don't you attend to your teacher?* **2** be present somewhere; go regularly to, *She attends school.* **3** look after someone; be an attendant. **4** accompany. **attendance** *noun*

attendant *noun* a person who helps or accompanies someone.

attention *noun* **1** attending to someone or something. **2** a position in which a soldier stands with feet together and arms straight downwards.

attention deficit disorder *noun* (also **attention deficit hyperactivity disorder**) any of a range of behavioural disorders, including such symptoms as poor concentration, hyperactivity, and learning difficulties.

attentive *adjective* giving attention. **attentively** *adverb*, **attentiveness** *noun*

attenuate *verb* (**attenuated**, **attenuating**) make a thing thinner or weaker. **attenuation** *noun*

attest *verb* declare or prove that something is true or genuine. **attestation** *noun* [from *at*-, + Latin *testari* = be a witness]

attic *noun* a room in the roof of a house.

attire[1] *noun* (*formal*) clothes.

attire[2] *verb* (**attired**, **attiring**) (*formal*) clothe.

attitude *noun* **1** the position of the body or its parts; posture. **2** a way of thinking or behaving.

attorney *noun* (*plural* **attorneys**) **1** a person who is appointed to act on behalf of another in business or legal matters. **2** (*American*) a lawyer.

attorney-general *noun* (*plural* **attorneys-general**) the (chief) law minister in an Australian government; the chief legal officer in some countries.

attract *verb* **1** get someone's attention or interest; seem pleasant to someone. **2** pull something by an invisible force, *Magnets attract metal pins.* [from *at*-, + Latin *tractum* = pulled]

attraction *noun* **1** attracting. **2** something that attracts interest.

attractive *adjective* **1** pleasant or good-looking. **2** interesting or appealing, *an attractive offer.* **attractively** *adverb* **attractiveness** *noun*

attribute[1] (*say* uh-**trib**-yoot) *verb* (**attributed**, **attributing**) regard as belonging to or created by, *We attribute his success to hard work.* **attribution** *noun*

attribute[2] (*say* **at**-ruh-byoot) *noun* a quality or characteristic, *Kindness is one of his attributes.* [from *at*-, + Latin *tribuere* = allot]

attributive (*say* uh-**trib**-yuh-tiv) *adjective* expressing an attribute and placed before the word it describes, e.g. *old* in *the old dog.* (Compare **predicative.**) **attributively** *adverb*

attrition (*say* uh-**trish**-uhn) *noun* wearing something away gradually.

attune *verb* (**attuned**, **attuning**) bring into harmony.

aubergine (*say* **oh**-buh-*zh*een) *noun* an eggplant.

auburn *adjective* (of hair) reddish-brown.

auction[1] *noun* a public sale where things are sold to the person who offers the most money for them.

auction[2] *verb* sell by auction. **auctioneer** *noun* [from Latin *auctum* = increased]

audacious (*say* aw-**day**-shuhs) *adjective* bold; daring. **audaciously** *adverb*, **audacity** *noun* [from Latin *audax* = bold]

audible *adjective* loud enough to be heard. **audibility** *noun*, **audibly** *adverb* [from Latin *audire* = hear]

audience *noun* **1** people who have gathered to hear or watch something. **2** the people addressed by a film, book, or play. **3** a formal interview with an eminent person. [from Latin *audire* = hear]

audio *noun* reproduced sounds.

audiobook *noun* a compact disc or tape recording of a reading of a book.

audiovisual *adjective* using both sound and pictures to give information.

audit[1] *noun* an official examination of financial accounts to see that they are correct.

audit[2] *verb* (**audited**, **auditing**) make an audit of accounts. **auditor** *noun*

audition *noun* a test to see if a performer is suitable for a job. **audition** *verb* [same origin as *audience*]

auditorium *noun* (*plural* **auditoriums**) the part of a building where the audience sits.

au fait (*say* oh **fay**) *adjective* knowing a subject or procedure well. [French, = to the point]

augment *verb* increase or add to something. **augmentation** *noun* [from Latin *augere* = increase]

au gratin (*say* oh **grat**-uhn) *adjective* cooked with a crisp topping of breadcrumbs or grated cheese. [French]

augur (*say* **aw**-guh) *verb* be a sign of what is to come, *These exam results augur well.* [from Latin *augur* = prophet]

August (*say* **aw**-guhst) *noun* the eighth month of the year. [Latin *Augustus*, the first Roman emperor]

august (*say* aw-**gust**) *adjective* majestic; imposing. [from Latin *augustus* = majestic]

aunt *noun* the sister of your father or mother; your uncle's wife.

auntie *noun* (also **aunty**) **1** aunt. **2** (*Australian*) (in Aboriginal English) a respectful mode of address to an older woman.

au pair (*say* oh **pair**) *noun* a young person from overseas who helps with childcare and housework and receives board and lodging in return. [French, = on equal terms]

aura (*say* **aw**-ruh) *noun* a general feeling surrounding a person or thing, *an aura of happiness.* [Greek, = breeze]

aural (*say* **aw**-ruhl) *adjective* of the ear; of hearing. **aurally** *adverb* [from Latin *auris* = ear]

Usage Do not confuse *aural* with *oral.*

au revoir (*say* oh ruh-**vwah**) *interjection* goodbye for the moment. [French, = to be seeing again]

aurora (*say* aw-**raw**-ruh) *noun* bands of coloured light appearing in the sky at night, the **aurora australis** (*say* o-**strah**-luhs) in the southern hemisphere and the **aurora borealis** (*say* baw-ree-**ah**-luhs) in the northern hemisphere. [from Latin *aurora* = dawn]

auspices (*say* **aw**-spuh-suhz) *plural noun* protection; sponsorship, *under the auspices of the Red Cross.*

auspicious (*say* aw-**spish**-uhs) *adjective* fortunate; favourable, *an auspicious start.*

Aussie[1] (*say* **oz**-ee) *noun* (*informal*) **1** an Australian, *He's a dinkum Aussie.* **2** Australia.

Aussie[2] *adjective* (*informal*) Australian.

Aussie Rules *plural noun* (*informal*) Australian Rules.

austere (*say* o-**steer**) *adjective* very simple and plain, without luxuries. **austerely** *adverb*, **austerity** *noun* [from Greek, = severe]

Australasian *adjective* of Australasia, a region consisting of Australia, New Zealand, and neighbouring islands in the South Pacific.

Australia Day *noun* a public holiday on 26 January commemorating the beginning of British settlement at Sydney Cove.

Australian[1] *noun* a person from Australia.

Australian[2] *adjective* of Australia or its people, *Australian English.*

Australian Rules *plural noun* a form of football originating in Victoria played with an oval ball by teams of 18.

aut- *prefix* see **auto-**.

authentic *adjective* genuine, *an authentic signature.* **authentically** *adverb*, **authenticity** *noun*

authenticate *verb* (**authenticated**, **authenticating**) confirm something as being authentic. **authentication** *noun*

author *noun* **1** the writer of a book, play, or poem. **2** the originator of a plan, policy, or idea. **authorship** *noun* [from Latin *auctor* = originator]

authorise *verb* (**authorised**, **authorising**) give official permission for something. **authorisation** *noun*

authoritarian *adjective* believing that people should be completely obedient to those in authority.

authoritative *adjective* having proper authority or expert knowledge; official.

authority *noun* (*plural* **authorities**) **1** the right or power to give orders to other people. **2** a person or organisation with the right to give orders. **3** an expert; a book or source that gives reliable information, *an authority on spiders.* [same origin as *author*]

autism (*say* **aw**-tiz-uhm) *noun* a developmental disorder of variable severity that is characterised by difficulty in social interaction and communication and by restricted or repetitive patterns of thought and behaviour. **autistic** *adjective* [from *auto-*]

auto- *prefix* (changing to **aut-** before a vowel) self-; of or by yourself or itself (as in *autograph*, *automatic*). [from Greek *autos* = self]

autobiography *noun* (*plural* **autobiographies**) the story of a person's life written by himself or herself. **autobiographical** *adjective* [from *auto-* + *biography*]

autocracy (*say* aw-**tok**-ruh-see) *noun* (*plural* **autocracies**) despotism; rule by a person with unlimited power. [from *auto-* + *-cracy*]

autocrat *noun* a person with unlimited power; a dictatorial person. **autocratic** *adjective*, **autocratically** *adverb*

autocrine *adjective* denoting or relating to a cell-produced substance that has an effect on the cell that secretes it. [from *auto-*, + Greek *krinein* = to separate]

autograph[1] *noun* a person's signature.

autograph[2] *verb* sign your name on or in something. [from *auto-* + *-graph*]

automate *verb* (**automated**, **automating**) work something by automation.

automatic[1] *adjective* **1** working on its own without continuous attention or control by people. **2** done without thinking. **automatically** *adverb*

automatic[2] *noun* a vehicle whose gears change automatically. [from Greek *automatos* = self-operating]

automation *noun* making processes automatic; using machines instead of people to do jobs.

automaton (*say* aw-**tom**-uh-tuhn) *noun* **1** a robot. **2** a person who seems to act mechanically without thinking.

automobile *noun* a motor car. [from *auto-* + *mobile*]

automotive *adjective* of motor vehicles, *the automotive industry.*

autonomy (*say* aw-**ton**-o-mee) *noun* self-government. **autonomous** *adjective* [from *auto-*, + Greek *-nomia* = arrangement]

autopsy (*say* **aw**-top-see) *noun* (*plural* **autopsies**) a post-mortem. [from Greek *autopsia* = seeing with your own eyes]

autumn *noun* the season between summer and winter. **autumnal** *adjective*

auxiliary[1] (*say* og-**zil**-yuh-ree) *adjective* giving help and support, *auxiliary services.*

auxiliary[2] *noun* (*plural* **auxiliaries**) a helper. [from Latin *auxilium* = help]

auxiliary verb *noun* a verb used in forming the tenses, moods, and voices of other verbs, e.g. *have* in *I have finished.*

avail[1] *noun* usefulness; help, *Their pleas were of no avail.*

avail[2] *verb* be useful or helpful, *Nothing availed against the storm.*
avail yourself of make use of something. [from Latin *valere* = be strong]

available *adjective* ready or able to be used; obtainable. **availability** *noun*

avalanche *noun* a mass of snow or rock falling down the side of a mountain. [French, from *avaler* = descend]

avant-garde (*say* av-on-**gahd**) *noun* people who use a very modern style in art, literature, or fashion. [French, = vanguard]

avarice (*say* **av**-uh-ruhs) *noun* greed for gain. **avaricious** *adjective* [from Latin *avarus* = greedy]

avatar (*say* **av**-uh-tah) *noun* **1** an incarnation or embodiment of a person or idea. **2** (in computing) a movable icon representing a person in computer games and online forums.

avenge *verb* (**avenged**, **avenging**) take vengeance for something done to harm you. **avenger** *noun*

avenue *noun* **1** a street or road, especially a wide one lined with trees. **2** a way of achieving something, *They explored every avenue to try to raise the money.*

average[1] *noun* **1** the value obtained by adding several quantities together and dividing by the number of quantities. **2** the usual or ordinary standard.

average[2] *adjective* **1** worked out as an average, *Their average age is ten.* **2** of the usual or ordinary standard; mediocre.

average[3] *verb* (**averaged**, **averaging**) work out, produce, or amount to as an average.

averse *adjective* unwilling; feeling opposed to something. [same origin as *avert*]

aversion *noun* a strong dislike.

avert *verb* **1** turn something away, *People averted their eyes from the accident.* **2** prevent, *We averted a disaster.* [from *ab-* = away, + Latin *vertere* = turn]

avian *adjective* of or relating to birds.

avian influenza *noun* a type of influenza virus that may be transferred from birds to humans.

aviary (*say* **ay**-vuh-ree) *noun* (*plural* **aviaries**) a large cage or building for keeping birds. [from Latin *avis* = bird]

aviation *noun* the flying of aircraft. **aviator** *noun* [from Latin *avis* = bird]

avid (*say* **av**-uhd) *adjective* eager, *an avid reader.* **avidity** *noun*, **avidly** *adverb*

AVO *abbreviation* apprehended violence order.

avocado (*say* av-uh-**kah**-doh) *noun* (*plural* **avocados**) a pear-shaped tropical fruit with a leathery skin and pale green flesh.

avoid *verb* **1** keep yourself away from someone or something. **2** keep yourself from doing something. **3** refrain from, *Avoid rash promises.* **avoidable** *adjective*, **avoidance** *noun*

avoirdupois (*say* av-uh-duh-**poiz**) *noun* a system of weights using the unit of 16 ounces = 1 pound. [from French, = goods of weight]

avuncular *adjective* like a kindly uncle.

AWA *abbreviation* Australian Workplace Agreement.

await *verb* wait for.

awake[1] *verb* (**awoke, awoken, awaking**) wake up.

awake[2] *adjective* not asleep.

awaken *verb* awake. **awakening** *noun*

award[1] *verb* give something officially as a prize, payment, or penalty.

award[2] *noun* something awarded.

award wage *noun* (*Australian*) a wage settled by an industrial tribunal as the minimum legal payment for work.

aware *adjective* knowing; realising, *She was aware of the danger.* **awareness** *noun*

awash *adjective* with waves or water flooding over it.

away[1] *adverb* **1** to or at a distance; not at the usual place. **2** out of existence, *The water had boiled away.* **3** continuously; persistently, *We worked away at it.*

away[2] *adjective* played on an opponent's ground, *an away match.*

awe *noun* fearful or reverent wonder. **awed** *adjective*, **awe-inspiring** *adjective*, **awestricken** *adjective*, **awestruck** *adjective*

aweigh *adverb* hanging just clear of the sea bottom, *The anchor is aweigh.*

awesome *adjective* **1** very impressive; inspiring awe, *The awesome power of a cyclone is scary.* **2** (*informal*) very good; excellent, *The movie was awesome.*

awful *adjective* **1** very bad, *an awful accident.* **2** (*informal*) very great, *That's an awful lot of money.* **3** causing awe or fear. **awfully** *adverb* [from *awe* + *full*]

awhile *adverb* for a short time.

awkward *adjective* **1** difficult to use or deal with; not convenient. **2** clumsy; not skilful. **3** embarrassed. **awkwardly** *adverb*, **awkwardness** *noun*

awl *noun* a small pointed tool for making holes, especially in leather and wood.

awning *noun* a roof-like shelter made of canvas etc.

awoke *past tense* of **awake**[1].

awoken *past participle* of **awake**[1].

awry (*say* uh-**ruy**) *adverb & adjective* **1** twisted to one side; crooked. **2** wrong, *Plans went awry.*

axe[1] *noun* a tool for chopping things.
get the axe (*informal*) **1** be dismissed from a job. **2** be cancelled, *Their program got the axe.*
have an axe to grind have a personal interest in something and want to take care of it.

axe[2] *verb* (**axed, axing**) (*informal*) **1** dismiss someone from a job. **2** abolish, *The project was axed.*

axiom *noun* an established general truth or principle. **axiomatic** *adjective*

axis *noun* (*plural* **axes**) **1** a line through the centre of a spinning object. **2** a line dividing a thing in half. [Latin, = axle]

axle *noun* the rod through the centre of a wheel, on which the wheel turns.

axolotl (*say* **aks**-uh-lot-uhl) *noun* a newt-like amphibian from Mexico.

ayatollah (*say* uy-uh-**tol**-uh) *noun* a Muslim religious leader in Iran. [Persian, = token of God]

aye (*say* uy) *adverb* yes.

azalea (*say* uh-**zay**-lee-uh) *noun* a kind of flowering shrub.

azan (*say* uh-**zahn**) *noun* Muslim call to prayer.

azure *adjective & noun* sky-blue.

Bb

baa *noun* the cry of a sheep or lamb. **baa** *verb*

baba ganoush (*say* bah-buh **ga**-noosh) *noun* a thick sauce made from puréed eggplants and sesame seeds. [Arabic]

babble *verb* (**babbled**, **babbling**) **1** talk in a meaningless way. **2** make a continuous murmuring sound. **babble** *noun*, **babbler** *noun*

babe *noun* a baby.

baboon *noun* a large African or Arabian monkey.

baby[1] *noun* (*plural* **babies**) **1** a very young child or animal. **2** a timid or childish person **3** (*informal*) something that is one's creation or in one's care. **4** (*informal*) a lover or spouse (often as a form of address). **babyish** *adjective*

baby[2] *verb* (**babied**, **babying**) treat like a baby; pamper.

baby boomer *noun* (*informal*) a person born in the years following the Second World War (ended 1945), when there was a temporary marked increase in the birth rate.

babysit *verb* look after a child or children while the parents are out. **babysitter** *noun*

bachelor *noun* **1** a man who has not married. **2** (usually in titles) a person who has taken a first degree at university, *Bachelor of Arts.*

bacillus (*say* buh-**sil**-uhs) *noun* (*plural* **bacilli**, *say* buh-**sil**-uy) a rod-shaped bacterium.

back[1] *noun* **1** the part furthest from the front. **2** the back part of the body from the shoulders to the buttocks. **3** the part of a chair that your back rests against. **4** a defending player near the goal in some team sports.

back[2] *adjective* **1** placed at or near the back. **2** of the back.

back[3] *adverb* **1** to or towards the back. **2** to the place you have come from, *Go back home.* **3** to an earlier time or condition or position, *Put the clocks back one hour.*

back[4] *verb* **1** move backwards. **2** give support or help to someone. **3** bet on something. **4** cover the back of something, *Back the rug with canvas.* **backer** *noun*
back down withdraw a claim or argument.
back out refuse to do what was agreed.
back up 1 give support or help to a person or thing. **2** make a copy of a computer record to be stored in safety separately from the original.

backbencher *noun* a member of parliament who does not hold a senior office, and is therefore not entitled to sit on the front benches in parliament.

backbiting *noun* spiteful talk.

backblocks *noun* (*Australian*) a settlement far from towns or cities.

backbone *noun* **1** the column of bones down the centre of the back. **2** strength of character.

backdrop *noun* a painted curtain at the back of a stage.

backfire *verb* (**backfired**, **backfiring**) **1** make an explosion when fuel burns too soon in an engine or ignites in the exhaust system. **2** produce an unwanted effect, *Their plans backfired.*

backflip *noun* **1** a backward somersault in the air. **2** a complete change of policy.

backgammon *noun* a game played on a board with draughts and dice. [from *back* + Old English *gamen* = game]

background *noun* **1** the back part of a scene or view. **2** the conditions influencing something. **3** a person's experience, education, and social circumstances.

backhand *noun* a stroke made in tennis etc. with the back of the hand turned outwards. **backhanded** *adjective*

backing *noun* **1** support. **2** material that forms a support or lines the back of something. **3** musical accompaniment.

backlash *noun* (*plural* **backlashes**) a violent reaction to some event or development.

backlog *noun* an amount of work that should have been finished but is still waiting to be done.

backpack *noun* a bag carried on the back. **backpacker** *noun*

backside *noun* (*informal*) the buttocks.

backstroke *noun* a way of swimming on your back. **backstroker** *noun*

backtrack *verb* **1** go back the same way that you came. **2** back down from an argument or policy; reverse a previous action.

backup *noun* **1** support; reserve. **2** (in computing) the making of spare copies of data for safety; a copy so made.

backward[1] *adjective* **1** directed towards the back. **2** having made less than the normal progress. **backwardness** *noun*

backward[2] *adverb* backwards.

backwards *adverb* **1** to or towards the back. **2** with the back end going first. **3** in reverse order, *Count backwards.*
backwards and forwards in each direction alternately; to and fro.

backwater *noun* **1** a branch of a river that comes to a dead end with stagnant water. **2** a place that is not affected by progress or new ideas.

backwoods *noun* a remote or backward area.

backyard *noun* a garden or enclosed area behind a house, *We like to play cricket in the backyard.*

bacon *noun* smoked or salted meat from the back or sides of a pig.

bacterium *noun* (*plural* **bacteria**) a microscopic organism. **bacterial** *adjective*

> **Usage** *Bacteria* is the plural form of *bacterium*. Like any other plural it should be used with the plural form of the verb: 'the bacteria causing salmonella are killed by thorough cooking', not 'the bacteria causing salmonella is killed by thorough cooking'.

bad *adjective* (**worse**, **worst**) **1** not having the right qualities; not good. **2** wicked; evil. **3** serious, *a bad accident.* **4** ill; unhealthy; diseased. **5** harmful, *Sweets are bad for your teeth.* **6** decayed, *The meat went bad.* **badness** *noun*

bade old *past tense* of **bid**[3].

badge *noun* a thing worn to show one's rank, membership of an organisation, or support for a cause.

badger[1] *noun* a grey burrowing animal with a white patch on its head.

badger[2] *verb* pester.

badly *adverb* (**worse**, **worst**) **1** in a bad way; not well. **2** severely; so as to cause much injury, *He was badly wounded.* **3** very much, *She badly wanted to win.*

badminton *noun* a game in which a light object called a *shuttlecock* is hit to and fro with rackets across a high net. [named after Badminton in England, where it was invented in about 1870]

baffle *verb* (**baffled**, **baffling**) **1** puzzle or perplex somebody. **2** frustrate, *We baffled their attempts to capture us.* **bafflement** *noun*

bag[1] *noun* a flexible container for holding or carrying things.

bag[2] *verb* (**bagged**, **bagging**) **1** seize; catch. **2** put into a bag or bags. **3** (*Australian informal*) claim or demand, *I bags the front seat.*

bagatelle *noun* **1** a game played on a board with small balls struck into holes. **2** something small and unimportant. **3** a short light piece of music.

bagel (*say* **bay**-guhl) *noun* a hard bread roll in the shape of a ring. [Yiddish]

baggage *noun* luggage.

baggy *adjective* (**baggier**, **baggiest**) hanging loosely.

bagpipes *plural noun* a musical instrument in which air is squeezed out of a bag into pipes.

bags *plural noun* (*informal*) plenty, *bags of room.*

baht *noun* the unit of money in Thailand.

bail[1] *noun* money paid or promised as a guarantee that a person accused of a crime will return for trial if released temporarily.

bail[2] *verb* provide bail for a person.
bail out rescue a person from a difficulty.

bail[3] *noun* **1** one of the two small pieces of wood placed on top of the stumps in cricket. **2** a framework securing a cow's head during milking.

bail[4] *verb* **bail up** (*Australian*) **1** drive a cow into a stall in a milking shed. **2** hold up and rob a traveller. **3** buttonhole somebody.

bail[5] *verb* scoop out water that has entered a boat. [from French *baille* = bucket]

bailey *noun* the courtyard of a castle; the wall round this courtyard.

bailiff *noun* a law officer who helps a sheriff by serving writs and performing arrests.

Baisakhi (*say* buy-**sah**-kee) *noun* (also **Vaisakhi**) a Sikh festival commemorating the founding of the Khalsa.

bait[1] *noun* food put on a hook or in a trap to catch fish or animals.

bait[2] *verb* **1** put bait on a hook or in a trap. **2** torment or tease by jeering.

baize *noun* thick green woollen cloth used chiefly for covering snooker tables.

bake *verb* (**baked**, **baking**) **1** cook in an oven. **2** make or become very hot. **3** make a thing hard by heating it.

baker *noun* a person who bakes and sells bread or cakes. **bakery** *noun*

baklava (*say* **bak**-luh-vuh or **bahk**-luh-vuh) *noun* a dessert made from flaky pastry, honey, and nuts. [Turkish]

balaclava *noun* a hood covering the head and neck and part of the face. [named after the

Battle of Balaclava (1854) in the Crimean War]

balalaika (*say* bal-uh-**luy**-kuh) *noun* a musical instrument like a guitar with a triangular body. [Russian]

balance[1] *noun* **1** a steady position; having the weight or amount evenly distributed. **2** an apparatus for weighing things, especially one with two containers hanging from a bar. **3** the difference between money paid into an account and money taken out of it. **4** the money left after something has been paid for.

balance[2] *verb* (**balanced, balancing**) make or be steady or equal. [from Latin *bilanx* = having two scale-pans]

balcony *noun* (*plural* **balconies**) **1** a platform projecting from an outside wall of a building. **2** the upstairs part of a theatre or cinema.

bald *adjective* **1** without hair on the top of the head. **2** with no details; blunt, *bald facts.* **baldly** *adverb*, **baldness** *noun*

bale[1] *noun* a large bundle of hay, straw, cotton, or wool, usually tied up tightly.

bale[2] *verb* (**baled, baling**) **bale out** jump out of an aircraft with a parachute.

baleful *adjective* bringing harm or evil; menacing, *a baleful frown.* **balefully** *adverb* [from Old English *balu* = evil]

ball[1] *noun* **1** a round object used in many games. **2** a solid or hollow sphere; a round mass, *a ball of string.* **on the ball** (*informal*) alert, competent.

ball[2] *noun* a grand gathering where people dance. [same origin as *ballet*]

ballad *noun* a simple song or poem telling a story.

ballast (*say* **bal**-uhst) *noun* heavy material carried in a ship to keep it steady.

ball bearings *plural noun* small steel balls rolling in a groove on which parts can move easily in machinery.

ballcock *noun* a floating device controlling the water level in a cistern.

ballerina (*say* bal-uh-**ree**-nuh) *noun* a female ballet dancer.

ballet (*say* **bal**-ay) *noun* a stage entertainment telling a story or expressing an idea in dancing and mime. [from Old French *baler* = to dance]

ballistic (*say* buh-**lis**-tik) *adjective* **1** of projectiles such as bullets and missiles. **2** (*informal*) wildly angry. [from Greek *ballein* = to throw]

balloon *noun* **1** an inflatable rubber pouch with a neck, used as a toy or decoration. **2** a large round bag inflated with hot air or light gases to make it rise in the air. **3** an outline round spoken words in a comic strip or cartoon. **balloon** *verb*, **balloonist** *noun*

ballot[1] *noun* **1** a secret method of voting by means of papers or tokens. **2** a piece of paper on which a vote is made.

ballot[2] *verb* (**balloted, balloting**) vote or allow people to vote by a ballot. [from Italian *ballotta* = little ball (because originally this voting was by dropping balls into a box)]

ballpark *noun* (*American*) a baseball ground.

ballpark figure *noun* (*informal*) a number or amount that is approximately correct.

ballpoint pen *noun* a pen with a tiny ball round which the ink flows.

ballroom *noun* a large room where dances are held.

balm (*say* bahm) *noun* **1** a sweet-scented ointment. **2** a soothing influence.

balmy *adjective* **1** sweet-scented like balm. **2** soft and warm.

balsa *noun* a kind of very lightweight wood.

balsam *noun* **1** a kind of gum produced by certain trees. **2** a tree producing balsam. **3** a kind of flowering plant.

balti (*say* **bawl**-tee) *noun* a type of Pakistani cuisine, usually cooked and served in a dish like a shallow wok.

balustrade *noun* a row of short posts or pillars supporting a rail or strip of stonework round a balcony or terrace.

bamboo *noun* **1** a tall plant with hard hollow stems. **2** a stem of the bamboo plant. [from a Malay word]

bamboozle *verb* (**bamboozled, bamboozling**) (*informal*) cheat or mystify someone.

ban[1] *verb* (**banned, banning**) forbid something officially.

ban[2] *noun* an order that bans something.

banal (*say* buh-**nahl**) *adjective* ordinary and uninteresting. **banality** *noun*

banana *noun* a finger-shaped yellow or green fruit.

band[1] *noun* **1** a strip or loop of something. **2** a range of values, wavelengths, etc.

band[2] *noun* **1** an organised group doing something together, *a band of robbers.* **2** a set of people playing music together.

band[3] *verb* form an organised group.

bandage *noun* a strip of material for binding up a wound. **bandage** *verb*

bandanna *noun* (also **bandana**) a large coloured handkerchief or scarf.

bandicoot *noun* a small nocturnal Australian marsupial with a long pointed head. [from Telugu (a southern Indian language) *pandikokku* = pig-rat]

bandit *noun* a member of a band of robbers. [from Italian *bandito* = outlawed or banned]

bandwidth *noun* **1** a range of frequencies within a given band, in particular that used for transmitting a signal. **2** the transmission capacity of a computer network or other telecommunication system.

B & S *noun* (*Australian*) (in full **bachelor and spinster ball**) a formal dance for unattached young people, especially in a country region.

bandstand *noun* a platform for a band playing music outdoors.

bandwagon *noun* a wagon for a band playing music in a parade.
jump or **climb on the bandwagon** join in something that is successful.

bandwidth *noun* a range of frequencies, especially in telecommunications.

bandy[1] *adjective* having legs that curve outwards at the knees.

bandy[2] *verb* (**bandied**, **bandying**) pass to and fro, *The story was bandied about.*

bane *noun* a cause of trouble or worry, *Exams are the bane of our lives!* **baneful** *adjective*, **banefully** *adverb*

bang[1] *noun* **1** a sudden loud noise like that of an explosion. **2** a sharp blow or knock.

bang[2] *verb* **1** hit or shut noisily. **2** make a sudden loud noise.

bang[3] *adverb* **1** with a bang; suddenly. **2** (*informal*) exactly, *bang in the middle.*

banger *noun* **1** a firework made to explode noisily. **2** (*informal*) a sausage.

bangle *noun* a stiff bracelet. [from Hindi *bangri*]

banish *verb* **1** send a person away from a country or place as an official punishment. **2** get rid of something unwanted.
banishment *noun*

banisters *plural noun* a handrail with upright supports beside a staircase.

banjo *noun* (*plural* **banjos**) an instrument like a guitar with a round body.

bank[1] *noun* **1** a slope. **2** a long piled-up mass of sand, snow, cloud, or other soft material. **3** a row of lights or switches.

bank[2] *verb* **1** build or form a bank. **2** tilt sideways while changing direction, *The plane banked as it prepared to land.*

bank[3] *noun* **1** a business that looks after people's money. **2** a reserve supply, *a blood bank.*

bank[4] *verb* put money in a bank.
bank on rely on.

banker[1] *noun* a person who runs a bank.

banker[2] *noun* (*Australian*) a river flowing as high as its banks, *The river's running a banker.*

banknote *noun* a piece of paper money.

bankrupt *adjective* unable to pay debts.
bankruptcy *noun* [from *bank*[2], + Latin *ruptum* = broken]

banksia *noun* an Australian shrub with yellowish cylindrical heads of flowers. [from Sir Joseph Banks, English naturalist]

banner *noun* **1** a flag. **2** a strip of cloth with a design or slogan, carried in a procession or demonstration, or hung in a public place. **3** an advertisement on a website in the form of a bar, column, or box.

banns *plural noun* an announcement in a church that the two people named are going to marry each other. [from *ban* = proclamation]

banquet *noun* a formal public meal. [from Old French *banquet* = little bench]

bantam *noun* a kind of small fowl. [named after Bantam, in Java]

banter *noun* playful teasing or joking.
banter *verb*

baobab (*say* **bay**-oh-bab) *noun* (also **boab**) a tree with a massive trunk and edible pulpy fruit.

baptise *verb* (**baptised**, **baptising**) receive a person into the Christian Church in a ceremony in which they are sprinkled with or dipped in water, and usually given a name or names. **baptism** *noun* [from Greek *baptisein* = to dip]

baptist *noun* (also **Baptist**) a member of a Protestant denomination believing that a person should not be baptised until old enough to understand what baptism means.

bar[1] *noun* **1** a long piece of hard substance. **2** a counter or room where refreshments, especially alcoholic drinks, are served. **3** a barrier; an obstruction. **4** (**the Bar**) barristers. **5** one of the small equal sections into which music is divided, *three beats to the bar.*

bar[2] *verb* (**barred**, **barring**) **1** fasten with a bar or bars. **2** block; obstruct, *A man with a dog barred the way.* **3** forbid; ban.

barb *noun* the backward-pointing part of a spear, fish hook, arrowhead, or similar object, that makes it difficult to withdraw. [from Latin *barba* = beard]

barbarian *noun* an uncivilised or brutal person. **barbaric** *adjective*, **barbarism** *noun*, **barbarity** *noun*, **barbarous** *adjective* [from Greek *barbaros* = babbling, not speaking Greek]

barbecue *noun* (also **barbeque**) **1** a metal frame for grilling food over an open fire outdoors. **2** a party where food is cooked in this way. **barbecue** *verb* [Spanish from an indigenous South American language]

barbecue stopper *noun* (*Australian informal*) an important topic of public discussion.

barbed *adjective* having a barb or barbs.

barbed wire *noun* wire with small spikes in it, used to make fences.

barber *noun* a men's hairdresser. [from Latin *barba* = beard]

barbie *noun* (*Australian informal*) a barbecue.

bar chart *noun* (also **bar graph**) a column graph.

barcode *noun* a machine-readable code in the form of numbers and a pattern of parallel lines of varying widths, printed on a commodity and used especially for stock control, *She scanned the barcode to see how much the chocolate cost.*

bard *noun* (*formal*) a poet or minstrel.

bardi *noun* (*Australian*) an edible grub found in the bark of some trees. [from Noongar and other languages]

bare[1] *adjective* **1** without clothing or covering. **2** unfurnished; empty, *The cupboard was bare.* **3** plain; without details, *the bare facts.* **4** only just enough, *the bare necessities of life.* **barely** *adverb*, **bareness** *noun*

bare[2] *verb* (**bared**, **baring**) uncover; reveal, *The dog bared its teeth in a snarl.*

bareback *adjective & adverb* riding on a horse without a saddle.

barefaced *adjective* shameless; bold and unconcealed, *It's barefaced robbery!*

bargain[1] *noun* **1** an agreement about buying or selling or exchanging something. **2** something bought cheaply.

bargain[2] *verb* argue over the price to be paid or what you will do in return for something. **bargain for** or **on** be prepared for; expect, *He got more than he bargained for.*

barge[1] *noun* a long flat-bottomed boat.

barge[2] *verb* (**barged**, **barging**) move clumsily or heavily.
barge in intrude.

barista (*say* buh-**ris**-tuh) *noun* (*plural* **baristas** or **baristi**) a person who makes coffee professionally. [Italian]

baritone *noun* a male singer with a voice between a tenor and a bass. [from Greek *barys* = heavy, + *tone*]

barium (*say* **bair**-ree-uhm) *noun* a soft silvery-white metal.

bark[1] *noun* the short harsh sound made by a dog or fox. **bark** *verb*

bark[2] *noun* the outer covering of a tree's branches or trunk.

bark[3] *verb* scrape your shin accidentally.

bark painting *noun* (*Australian*) a picture painted on bark, originally as ceremonial art in Arnhem Land.

barley *noun* a cereal plant from which malt is made.

barley sugar *noun* a sweet made from boiled sugar.

bar mitzvah *noun* a religious ceremony for Jewish boys aged 13. [Hebrew, = son of the commandment]

barmy *adjective* (*informal*) crazy.

barn *noun* a farm building used for storing hay, grain, or straw, or for housing livestock. **barnyard** *noun* [from Old English *bere ern* = barley-house]

barnacle *noun* a shellfish that attaches itself to rocks and the bottoms of ships.

barn dance *noun* a kind of country dance; an informal gathering for dancing.

barney *noun* (*informal*) a noisy dispute.

barometer (*say* buh-**rom**-uh-tuh) *noun* an instrument that measures air pressure, used in forecasting the weather. **barometric** *adjective* [from Greek *baros* = weight, + *meter*]

baron *noun* **1** a member of the lowest rank of noblemen in Britain. **2** an important owner of an industry or business, *a newspaper baron.* **baroness** *noun*, **baronial** *adjective*, **barony** *noun*

baronet *noun* a nobleman ranking below a baron but above a knight. **baronetcy** *noun*

baroque (*say* buh-**rok**) *noun* an elaborately decorated style of architecture used in the 17th and 18th centuries; an ornate style of music from this period.

barrack *verb* (*Australian*) **1** encourage or cheer on, *We were there to barrack for the home team.* **2** tease or jeer at, *The speaker had some barracking to put up with.* [probably from Northern Ireland = to brag]

barracks *noun* a large building or group of buildings for soldiers to live in. [from Spanish *barraca* = a soldier's tent]

barracouta (*say* ba-ruh-**koo**-tuh) *noun* a long narrow fish of southern waters.

barrage (*say* **ba**-rahzh) *noun* **1** an artificial barrier; a dam. **2** heavy gunfire. **3** a rapid fire of questions or comments. [from French *barre* = a bar]

barramundi (*say* ba-ruh-**mun**-dee) *noun* a large freshwater Australian fish. [probably from an indigenous Queensland language]

barre *noun* a horizontal bar used by dancers to steady themselves while exercising. [French]

barrel *noun* **1** a large rounded container with flat ends. **2** the metal tube of a gun, through which the shot is fired.

barrel organ *noun* a musical instrument that you play by turning a handle.

barren *adjective* **1** not producing any fruit or seeds; not fertile, *barren land.* **2** unable to have young, *a barren couple.*
barrenness *noun*

barricade[1] *noun* a barrier, especially one put up hastily across a street or entryway.

barricade[2] *verb* (**barricaded, barricading**) block or defend with a barricade.

barrier *noun* **1** something that prevents people or things from getting past. **2** an obstacle.

barrister *noun* a lawyer who is qualified to represent people in any lawcourt.

barrow *noun* **1** a wheelbarrow. **2** a small cart pushed or pulled by hand. [from Old English *bearwe* = carrying]

barter[1] *verb* trade by exchanging goods for other goods, not for money.

barter[2] *noun* the system of bartering.

basalt (*say* **bas**-awlt or **bas**-olt) *noun* a kind of dark volcanic rock.

base[1] *noun* **1** the lowest part of something; the part on which a thing stands. **2** a basis. **3** a headquarters. **4** a substance that can combine with an acid to form a salt. **5** the number on which a system of counting and calculation is based, e.g. 10 in conventional notation, 2 in the binary system. **6** (in geometry) a line or surface on which a figure is regarded as standing, *the base of the triangle.* **7** each of the four corners that must be reached by a runner in baseball.

base[2] *verb* (**based, basing**) use something as a basis, *The story is based on facts.* [from Greek *basis* = stepping]

base[3] *adjective* **1** dishonourable, *base motives.* **2** not of great value, *base metals.* **basely** *adverb*, **baseness** *noun* [from French *bas* = low]

baseball *noun* **1** a team game in which runs are scored by hitting a ball with a bat and running round a series of four bases. **2** the ball used in this game.

basement *noun* a room or rooms below ground level.

base word *noun* a word that serves as a base form, *Friendless, friendly, and friendship are formed from the base word friend.*

bash[1] *verb* hit hard; attack violently.

bash[2] *noun* (*plural* **bashes**) **1** a hard hit. **2** (*informal*) a try, *Have a bash at it.*

bashful *adjective* shy and self-conscious.
bashfully *adverb* [from *abash*]

basic *adjective* forming a basis or starting point; very important, *Bread is a basic food.* **basically** *adverb* [from *base*[1]]

basil *noun* a sweet-smelling herb.

basilica (*say* ba-**sil**-i-kuh) *noun* a large oblong hall or church with two rows of columns and an apse at one end.

basilisk (*say* **baz**-uh-lisk) *noun* a mythical reptile said to cause death by its glance or breath.

basin *noun* **1** a deep bowl. **2** a washbasin. **3** an enclosed area of water. **4** the area from which water drains into a river, *the Amazon basin.*

basis *noun* (*plural* **bases**) something to start from or add to; the main principle or ingredient. [same origin as *base*[1]]

bask *verb* sit or lie comfortably warming yourself.

basket *noun* a container for holding or carrying things, made of interwoven strips of flexible material or wire.

basketball *noun* **1** a game between two teams of five players in which goals are scored by putting the ball through a high hooped net at each end of a court. **2** the ball used in this game.

basmati (*say* baz-**mah**-tee) *noun* a kind of long-grain rice. [from Hindi, = fragrant]

bass[1] (*say* bays) *adjective* deep-sounding; of the lowest notes in music.

bass[2] *noun* (*plural* **basses**) **1** a male singer with a very deep voice. **2** a bass instrument or part. [from *base*[1]]

basset *noun* a short-legged dog used for hunting hares. [from French *bas* = low]

bassinet *noun* a basket for a baby to lie in.

bassoon *noun* a bass woodwind instrument.
bassoonist *noun*

bastard *noun* (often *offensive*) **1** (*old use*) an illegitimate child. **2** (*informal*) a person; an unpleasant or difficult person or thing.
bastardy *noun*

baste[1] *verb* (**basted, basting**) moisten meat with fat while it is cooking.

baste[2] *verb* (**basted, basting**) tack material or a hem.

bastion *noun* **1** a projecting part of a fortified building. **2** a centre of support for a cause.

bat[1] *noun* **1** an implement used to hit the ball in games such as cricket and baseball. **2** a person batting, especially in cricket, *their opening bat.*
off your own bat without help from other people.

bat[2] *verb* (**batted**, **batting**) **1** (of a sports team or player) take the role of hitting rather than throwing. **2** hit.

bat[3] *noun* a flying animal that looks like a mouse with wings.

bat[3] *verb* (**batted**, **batting**) flutter, *it batted its wings.*
not bat an eyelid show no reaction.

batch[1] *noun* (*plural* **batches**) a set of things or people dealt with together.

batch[2] *verb* (*Australian*) live alone; provide for yourself without the usual conveniences. [from *bachelor*]

bated *adjective* **with bated breath** anxiously; hardly daring to speak. [from *abate*]

bath[1] *noun* **1** washing your whole body while sitting in water. **2** a large container for water in which to wash your whole body; this water, *Your bath is getting cold.* **3** a liquid in which something is placed, *an acid bath.*

bath[2] *verb* wash in a bath.

bathe *verb* (**bathed**, **bathing**) **1** go swimming. **2** wash something gently. **bathe** *noun*, **bather** *noun*

bathers *noun* (*Australian*) a swimming costume.

bathroom *noun* a room containing a bath or shower.

baths *plural noun* **1** a building with rooms where people can bath. **2** a public swimming pool.

batik (*say* buh-**teek**) *noun* a method of dyeing fabric by waxing the parts not to be coloured.

baton *noun* a short stick, e.g. one used to conduct an orchestra.

batsman *noun* (*plural* **batsmen**) a player who uses a bat, especially in cricket.

battalion *noun* an army unit containing two or more companies. [from Italian *battaglia* = battle]

batten[1] *noun* a strip of wood or metal holding something in place.

batten[2] *verb* feed or grow fat on something, *Pigeons battened on the crops.*

batter[1] *verb* hit hard and often.

batter[2] *noun* **1** a beaten mixture of flour, eggs, and milk or water, used for making pancakes or cakes, or for coating before frying. **2** (in sport) a player batting. [from Latin *battuere* = to beat]

battering ram *noun* a heavy pole used to break down walls or gates.

battery *noun* (*plural* **batteries**) **1** a portable device for storing and supplying electricity. **2** a set of similar pieces of equipment; a group of large guns. **3** a series of cages in which poultry or animals are kept close together. [same origin as *batter*]

battle[1] *noun* **1** a fight between large organised forces. **2** a struggle. **battlefield** *noun*, **battleground** *noun*

battle[2] *verb* (**battled**, **battling**) fight; struggle. [same origin as *batter*]

battlements *plural noun* the top of a castle wall, often with gaps from which the defenders could fire at the enemy.

battler *noun* (*Australian*) someone who struggles against difficulties and does not give up.

battleship *noun* a heavily armed warship.

batty *adjective* (*informal*) crazy. [from *bat*[3]]

bauble *noun* a showy but valueless trinket.

baulk *verb* **1** shirk or jib at something; stop and refuse to go on, *The horse baulked at the fence.* **2** frustrate; prevent from doing or getting something.

bauxite (*say* **bawk**-suyt) *noun* the clay-like substance from which aluminium is obtained.

bawdy *adjective* (**bawdier**, **bawdiest**) funny but vulgar. **bawdiness** *noun*

bawl *verb* **1** shout. **2** cry noisily.

bay[1] *noun* **1** a place where the shore curves inwards. **2** an alcove.

bay[2] *noun* a kind of laurel with dark green leaves used for flavouring food.

bay[3] *noun* the long deep cry of a hunting hound or other large dog.
at bay 1 cornered but defiantly facing attackers, *a stag at bay.* **2** prevented from coming near or causing harm, *We need laws to keep poverty at bay.*

bay[4] *adjective* reddish-brown.

bayonet *noun* a stabbing blade attached to a rifle. [named after Bayonne in France, where it was first made]

bay window *noun* a window projecting from the main wall of a house.

bazaar *noun* **1** a set of shops or stalls in a Middle Eastern country. **2** a sale of goods to raise funds. [from Persian *bazar*]

bazooka *noun* a portable weapon for firing anti-tank rockets. [the word originally meant a musical instrument rather like a trombone]

BBQ *abbreviation* barbecue.

BBS *abbreviation* bulletin board system.

BC *abbreviation* before Christ (used of dates reckoned back from the birth of Jesus Christ).

bcc *abbreviation* blind carbon copy (used as an indication that a duplicate email has been or should be sent to another person without the knowledge of the main recipient). **bcc** *verb*

BCE *abbreviation* before the Common Era.

> **Usage** Used to indicate the dates traditionally designated by BC.

be *verb* (**am, are, is; was, were; been, being**) **1** exist. **2** occupy a position, *The shop is on the corner.* **3** happen; take place, *The wedding is tomorrow.* This verb is also used **4** to join subject and predicate (*She is my teacher*), **5** to form parts of other verbs (*It is raining. He was killed*).
have been have gone or come as a visitor, *We have been to Fiji.*

be- *prefix* used to form verbs (as in *befriend, belittle*) or strengthen their meaning (as in *begrudge.*)

beach *noun* (*plural* **beaches**) the part of the seashore nearest to the water.

beachcomber *noun* a person who searches beaches for useful or valuable things washed up by the sea.

beacon *noun* a light or fire used as a signal.

bead *noun* **1** a small piece of a hard substance with a hole in it for threading with others on a string or wire, e.g. to make a necklace. **2** a drop of liquid.

beady *adjective* like beads; small and bright, *beady eyes.*

beagle *noun* a small hound used for hunting.

beak *noun* the hard horny part of a bird's mouth.

beaker *noun* **1** a tall drinking cup, often without a handle. **2** a glass container used for pouring liquids in a laboratory.

beam[1] *noun* **1** a long thick bar of wood or metal. **2** a ray or stream of light or other radiation. **3** a bright look on someone's face; a happy smile.

beam[2] *verb* **1** smile happily. **2** send out a beam of light or other radiation.

bean *noun* **1** a kind of plant with seeds growing in pods. **2** its seed or pod eaten as food. **3** the seed of coffee and some other plants.

beanie *noun* a close-fitting knitted cap.

bear[1] *noun* a large heavy animal with thick fur.

bear[2] *verb* (**bore, borne, bearing**) **1** carry; bring or take. **2** support. **3** have a mark etc., *She still bears the scar.* **4** endure; tolerate, *I can't bear this pain.* **5** produce; give birth to, *She bore him two sons.* **bearer** *noun*
bear out show that something is true.

> **Usage** The past participle *born* is used with reference to birth (*was born in July; he was born lucky; her wisdom was born of experience*), although *borne* is used with reference to the act of giving birth (*she has borne a son*). In all other contexts the past participle is *borne.*

bearable *adjective* able to be borne; tolerable.

beard[1] *noun* hair on and around a man's chin. **bearded** *adjective*

beard[2] *verb* boldly confront or challenge someone formidable.

bearing *noun* **1** the way a person stands, walks, or behaves. **2** relevance, *It has no bearing on this problem.* **3** the direction or position of one thing in relation to another. **4** a device for preventing friction in a machine, *ball bearings.*
get your bearings work out where you are in relation to things.

beast *noun* **1** any large four-footed animal. **2** (*informal*) a cruel person. **beastly** *adjective*

beat[1] *verb* (**beat, beaten, beating**) **1** hit often, especially with a stick. **2** shape or flatten something by hitting it. **3** stir vigorously. **4** make repeated movements, *The heart beats.* **5** do better than somebody; overcome. **beater** *noun*
beat up give a beating to, especially with punches and kicks.

beat[2] *noun* **1** a regular rhythm or stroke, *the beat of your heart*; a sound of this. **2** recurring emphasis marking rhythm in music or poetry. **3** a police officer's regular route.

beatbox[1] *noun* **1** a drum machine. **2** a radio or portable stereo used to play loud music.

beatbox[2] *verb* mimic an instrument, especially a percussion instrument, using one's voice.

beatific (*say* bee-uh-**tif**-ik) *adjective* showing great happiness, *a beatific smile.*

beatify (*say* bee-**at**-uh-fuy) *verb* (**beatified, beatifying**) (in the Roman Catholic Church) honour a person who has died by declaring that they are among the Blessed, as a step towards declaring that person a saint. **beatification** *noun* [from Latin *beatus* = blessed]

beaut[1] *adjective* (*Australian informal*) excellent.

beaut[2] *noun* (*Australian informal*) an excellent person or thing.

beautiful *adjective* having beauty. **beautifully** *adverb*

beautify *verb* (**beautified, beautifying**) make beautiful. **beautification** *noun*

beauty *noun* (*plural* **beauties**) **1** a quality that gives pleasure to your senses or your mind. **2** a person or thing that has beauty.

beaver[1] *noun* an amphibious animal with soft brown fur and strong teeth.

beaver[2] *verb* work hard, *beavering away.*

becalmed *adjective* (in sailing) unable to move because there is no wind.

became *past tense* of **become**.

because *conjunction* for the reason that.
because of for the reason of, *He limped because of his bad leg.*

beck *noun* **at someone's beck and call** always ready and waiting to do what someone asks. [from *beckon*]

beckon *verb* make a gesture with the hand, arm, or head to encourage or instruct someone to approach or follow.

become *verb* (**became**, **become**, **becoming**)
1 come or grow to be; start being, *It became dark.* **2** be suitable for; make a person look attractive.
become of happen to, *What became of that friend you had?*

bed *noun* **1** a thing to sleep or rest on; a piece of furniture with a mattress and coverings, *His bed is too small for him now.* **2** a part of a garden where plants are grown. **3** the bottom of the sea or of a river. **4** a flat base; a foundation. **5** a layer of rock or soil.

bedclothes *plural noun* coverings for a bed, such as sheets and blankets.

bedding *noun* mattresses and bedclothes.

bedlam *noun* uproar. [from 'Bedlam', the popular name of the Hospital of St Mary of Bethlehem, a London mental hospital in the 14th century]

bedpan *noun* a container for use as a toilet by a person confined to bed.

bedraggled (*say* buh-**drag**-uhld) *adjective* very untidy; wet and dirty.

bedridden *adjective* too weak to get out of bed.

bedrock *noun* solid rock beneath soil.

bedroom *noun* a room for sleeping in.

bedsitter *noun* a room used for both living and sleeping in.

bedspread *noun* a covering spread over a bed.

bedstead *noun* the framework of a bed.

bedtime *noun* the time for going to bed.

bee *noun* a stinging insect with four wings that makes honey.

beech *noun* (*plural* **beeches**) a tree with smooth bark and glossy leaves.

beef *noun* **1** meat from an ox, bull, or cow. **2** (*informal*) a complaint.

beefy *adjective* having a solid muscular body.
beefiness *noun*

beehive *noun* a box or other container for bees to live in.

beeline *noun* **make a beeline for** go straight or quickly towards something.

been *past participle* of **be**.

beer *noun* an alcoholic drink made from malt and hops. **beery** *adjective*

beeswax *noun* a yellow substance produced by bees, used for polishing wood.

beet *noun* (*plural* **beet** or **beets**) a plant with a thick root used as a vegetable or for making sugar.

beetle *noun* an insect with hard shiny wing covers.

beetling *adjective* prominent; overhanging, *beetling brows.*

beetroot *noun* (*plural* **beetroot**) the crimson root of beet used as a vegetable.

befall *verb* (**befell**, **befallen**, **befalling**) (*formal*) happen; happen to someone.

befitting *adjective* suitable.

before[1] *adverb* at an earlier time, *Have you been here before?*

before[2] *preposition & conjunction* **1** earlier than, *I was here before you!* **2** ahead of; in front of, *leg before wicket.*

beforehand *adverb* earlier; in readiness.

befriend *verb* act as a friend to someone.

beg *verb* (**begged**, **begging**) **1** ask for food or money as charity. **2** ask earnestly or humbly or formally.
beg the question 1 assume the truth of an argument needing proof, without arguing it or proving it. **2** raise the question.
go begging be available.
I beg your pardon I apologise; I did not hear what you said.

> **Usage** Sense 2 of the expression *beg the question* is considered incorrect by some people.

began *past tense* of **begin**.

begat (*old use*) *past tense* of **beget**.

beget *verb* (**begot** or **begat**, **begotten**, **begetting**) (*literary*) **1** be the father of someone. **2** produce, *War begets misery.*

beggar *noun* **1** a person who lives by begging. **2** (*informal*) a person, *You lucky beggar!*
beggary *noun*

begin *verb* (**began**, **begun**, **beginning**) **1** do the earliest or first part of something; start speaking. **2** come into existence, *The problem began last year.* **3** have something as its first element, *The word begins with B.*

beginner *noun* a person who is just beginning to learn a skill.

beginning *noun* **1** the starting point; a source or origin. **2** the first part.

begone *verb* (*old use*) go away immediately.

begonia (*say* buh-**goh**-nee-uh) *noun* a garden plant with brightly coloured flowers.

begot *past tense* of **beget**.

begotten *past participle* of **beget**.

begrudge *verb* (**begrudged, begrudging**) grudge.

beguile (*say* buh-**guyl**) *verb* (**beguiled, beguiling**) **1** amuse. **2** deceive.

begun *past participle* of **begin**.

behalf *noun* **on behalf of** for someone; as the representative of someone.

behave *verb* (**behaved, behaving**) **1** act or function in a particular way, *They behaved badly.* **2** show good manners, *Behave yourself!* **behaviour** *noun*, **behavioural** *adjective*

behead *verb* cut the head from; execute a person in this way.

beheld *past tense & past participle* of **behold**.

behest *noun* (*formal*) a command.

behind[1] *adverb* **1** at or to the back; at a place people have left, *Don't leave it behind.* **2** not making good progress; late, *I'm behind with my rent.*

behind[2] *preposition* **1** at or to the back of; on the further side of. **2** having made less progress than, *He is behind the others in French.* **3** supporting; causing, *What is behind all this trouble?*
behind a person's back without a person's knowledge and in an unfair way.
behind the times out of date.

behind[3] *noun* **1** (*informal*) a person's bottom. **2** (in Australian Rules) a score of one point when a ball goes over a line between a goalpost and an outer post.

behindhand *adverb & adjective* **1** late. **2** out of date.

behold *verb* (**beheld, beholding**) (*old use*) see. **beholder** *noun*

beholden *adjective* owing thanks; indebted, *We are greatly beholden to you.*

behove *verb* (**behoved, behoving**) be a person's duty, *It behoves you to be loyal.*

beige (*say* bayzh) *noun & adjective* light fawn colour.

being[1] *noun* **1** existence. **2** a creature.

being[2] *present participle* of **be**, *Why are you being so mean?*

belated *adjective* coming very late or too late. **belatedly** *adverb*

belch *verb* **1** send out wind from your stomach through your mouth noisily. **2** send out from an opening, especially smoke or flames. **belch** *noun*

beleaguered (*say* bee-**lee**-guhd) *adjective* besieged; oppressed. [from Dutch *belegeren* = camp round]

belfry *noun* (*plural* **belfries**) a tower or part of a tower in which bells hang.

belie *verb* (**belied, belying**) give a false idea of something, *Its condition belies its age.*

belief *noun* **1** believing. **2** something a person believes.

believe *verb* (**believed, believing**) think that something is true or that someone is telling the truth. **believable** *adjective*, **believer** *noun*
believe in think that something exists or is good or can be relied on.

belittle *verb* (**belittled, belittling**) make something seem of little value, *Do not belittle their success.* **belittlement** *noun*

bell *noun* **1** a cup-shaped metal instrument that makes a ringing sound when struck by the clapper hanging inside it; any device that makes a ringing or buzzing sound to attract attention. **2** a bell-shaped object.

bellbird *noun* a bird with a clear ringing note.

bellicose (*say* **bel**-uh-kohs) *adjective* eager to fight. [from Latin *bellum* = war]

belligerent (*say* buh-**lij**-uh-ruhnt) *adjective* **1** aggressive; eager to fight. **2** fighting; engaged in a war. **belligerence** *noun*, **belligerently** *adverb* [from Latin *bellum* = war, + *gerens* = waging]

bellow[1] *noun* **1** the loud deep sound made by a bull or other large animal. **2** a deep shout.

bellow[2] *verb* give a bellow; shout.

bellows *plural noun* a device for pumping air into or through something, especially a fire or organ pipes.

belly *noun* (*plural* **bellies**) the abdomen; the stomach.

belong *verb* have a proper place, *The pans belong in the kitchen.*
belong to 1 be the property of. **2** be a member of, *We belong to the same club.*

belongings *plural noun* a person's possessions.

beloved *adjective* dearly loved.

below[1] *adverb* at or to a lower position; underneath, *There's fire down below.*

below[2] *preposition* lower than; under, *The temperature was ten degrees below zero.*

belt[1] *noun* **1** a strip of leather or other material worn around the waist. **2** a band of flexible material used in machinery. **3** a long narrow area, *a belt of rain.*

belt[2] *verb* **1** put a belt round something. **2** (*informal*) hit. **3** (*informal*) rush along.

bemused *adjective* **1** bewildered. **2** lost in thought.

bench *noun* (*plural* **benches**) **1** a long seat. **2** a long table for working at. **3** the seat where judges or magistrates sit; the judges or magistrates hearing a lawsuit.

benchtop *noun* a flat working table, especially one on which food is prepared for cooking etc.

bend[1] *verb* (**bent, bending**) **1** change from being straight. **2** turn downwards; stoop, *She bent to pick it up.*

bend[2] *noun* a place where something bends; a curve or turn.

bene- (*say* ben-ee) *prefix* well (as in *benefit, benevolent*). [from Latin *bene* = well]

beneath[1] *preposition* **1** under. **2** unworthy of, *Cheating is beneath you.*

beneath[2] *adverb* underneath.

benediction *noun* a blessing. [from *bene-*, + Latin *dicere* = to say]

benefactor *noun* a person who gives money or other help. [from *bene-*, + Latin *factor* = doer]

beneficial *adjective* having a good or helpful effect; advantageous.

beneficiary (*say* ben-uh-**fish**-uh-ree) *noun* (*plural* **beneficiaries**) a person who receives benefits, especially from a will.

benefit[1] *noun* **1** something that is helpful or profitable. **2** a payment to which a person is entitled from government funds or from an insurance policy.

benefit[2] *verb* (**benefited, benefiting**) **1** do good to a person or thing. **2** receive a benefit. [from *bene-*, + Latin *facere* = do]

benevolent *adjective* **1** kind and helpful. **2** formed for charitable purposes, *a benevolent fund.* **benevolence** *noun*, **benevolently** *adverb* [from *bene-*, + Latin *volens* = wishing]

benign (*say* buh-**nuyn**) *adjective* **1** kindly. **2** favourable. **3** (of a disease) mild, not malignant. **benignly** *adverb* [from Latin *benignus* = kind-hearted]

benignant (*say* buh-**nig**-nuhnt) *adjective* kindly.

bent[1] *adjective* curved; crooked.
bent on intending to do something.

bent[2] *noun* a talent for something.

bento (*say* **ben**-toh) *noun* a Japanese-style packed lunch, consisting of such items as rice, vegetables, and sashimi. [Japanese]

benzene *noun* a substance obtained from coal tar and used as a solvent, motor fuel, and in the manufacture of plastics.

benzine *noun* a spirit obtained from petroleum and used in dry cleaning.

bequeath *verb* leave something to a person, especially in a will.

bequest *noun* something bequeathed.

berate *verb* (**berated, berating**) scold.

bereaved *adjective* deprived of a relative or friend who has died. **bereavement** *noun* [from *reave* = take forcibly]

bereft *adjective* deprived of something.

beret (*say* **be**-ray) *noun* a round flat cap.

beriberi (*say* be-ree-**be**-ree) *noun* a tropical disease caused by a vitamin deficiency. [from a Sinhalese word]

berley *noun* (*Australian*) bait thrown into fishing ground to attract fish.

berry *noun* (*plural* **berries**) any small round juicy fruit without a stone.

berserk (*say* buh-**zerk**) *adjective* **go berserk** become uncontrollably violent. [from Icelandic *berserkr* = wild warrior (*ber-* = bear, *serkr* = coat)]

berth[1] *noun* **1** a sleeping place on a ship or train. **2** a place where a ship can moor.
give a wide berth keep at a safe distance from a person or thing.

berth[2] *verb* moor in a berth.

beryl *noun* a pale green precious stone.

beseech *verb* (**besought, beseeching**) ask earnestly; implore. [from *be-* + *seek*]

beset *verb* (**beset, besetting**) surround, *They are beset with problems.*

beside *preposition* **1** by the side of; near. **2** compared with.
be beside himself or **herself** be very excited or upset.
beside the point not relevant.

besides *preposition & adverb* in addition to; also, *Who came besides you? And besides, it's the wrong colour.*

besiege *verb* (**besieged, besieging**) **1** surround a place with troops in order to capture it. **2** crowd round, *Fans besieged the pop star after the concert.*

besotted *adjective* infatuated.

besought *past tense & past participle* of **beseech.**

bespoke *adjective* (of goods, especially clothing) made to order, *a bespoke suit.*

best[1] *adjective* most excellent.

best[2] *adverb* **1** in the best way; most. **2** most usefully; most wisely, *We had best go.*

bestial (*say* **bes**-tee-uhl) *adjective* of or like a beast; cruel. **bestiality** *noun* [from Latin *bestia* = beast]

bestie *noun* (*informal*) a person's best friend.

best man *noun* the bridegroom's chief attendant at a wedding.

bestow *verb* present as a gift. **bestowal** *noun*

bet[1] *noun* **1** an agreement pledging something that will be forfeited if one's forecast of some event proves wrong. **2** the money that you agree to pay in this way.

bet[2] *verb* (**bet** or **betted**, **betting**) **1** make a bet. **2** (*informal*) think most likely; predict, *I bet he will forget.*

beta (*say* **bee**-tuh) *noun* the second letter of the Greek alphabet, = b.

bête noire (*say* bayt **nwah**) *noun* a person or thing you greatly dislike. [French, = black beast]

betide *verb* **woe betide you** trouble will come to you. [from *be-*, + an old word *tide* = befall]

betoken *verb* be a sign of.

betray *verb* **1** be disloyal to. **2** reveal something that should have been kept secret. **betrayal** *noun*, **betrayer** *noun* [from *be-*, + Latin *tradere* = hand over]

betrothed *adjective* (*formal*) engaged to be married. **betroth** *verb*, **betrothal** *noun*

better[1] *adjective* **1** more excellent; more satisfactory. **2** recovered from illness.

better[2] *adverb* **1** in a better way; more. **2** more usefully; more wisely, *We had better go.*

better[3] *verb* **1** improve something. **2** do better than. **betterment** *noun*

bettong (*say* **bet**-ong) *noun* a very small short-nosed Australian marsupial. Also called a *rat-kangaroo*. [from Sydney language *bidung*]

between *preposition & adverb* **1** within two or more given limits, *between the walls.* **2** connecting two or more people, places, or things, *The train runs between Sydney and Perth.* **3** shared by, *Divide this money between you.* **4** separating; comparing, *Can you tell the difference between them?*

> **Usage** The preposition *between* is followed by the object form of the pronoun (*me, her, him, them,* or *us*). Correct use is *between you and me, between us, between him and her*, etc.

betwixt *preposition & adverb* (*old use*) between.

bevel *verb* (**bevelled**, **bevelling**) give a sloping edge to something.

beverage *noun* any kind of drink.

bevy *noun* (*plural* **bevies**) a large group.

bewail *verb* mourn for something.

beware *verb* be careful, *Beware of pickpockets.* [from *be-*, + *ware* = wary]

bewilder *verb* puzzle someone hopelessly. **bewilderment** *noun* [from *be-*, + an old word *wilder* = lose your way]

bewitch *verb* **1** put a magic spell on someone. **2** delight someone very much.

beyond *preposition & adverb* **1** further than; further on, *Don't go beyond the boundary.* **2** outside the range of; too difficult for, *The problem is beyond me.*

bi- *prefix* two (as in *bicycle*); twice (as in *biannual*). [from Latin *bis* = twice]

biannual *adjective* happening twice a year. **biannually** *adverb*

> **Usage** Do not confuse this word with *biennial.*

bias *noun* (*plural* **biases**) **1** a feeling or influence for or against someone or something; a prejudice. **2** a tendency to swerve. **3** a slanting direction. **biased** *adjective*

bib *noun* **1** a cloth or covering put under a baby's chin during meals. **2** the part of an apron above the waist.

Bible *noun* the sacred book of the Jews (the Old Testament) and of the Christians (the Old and New Testament). [from Greek *biblia* = books (originally = rolls of papyrus from Byblos, a port now in Lebanon)]

biblical *adjective* of or in the Bible.

bibliography (*say* bib-lee-**og**-ruh-fee) *noun* (*plural* **bibliographies**) **1** a list of books about a subject or by a particular author. **2** the study of books and their history. **bibliographical** *adjective* [from Greek *biblion* = book, + *graphy*]

bicentenary (*say* buy-sen-**tee**-nuh-ree) *noun* a 200th anniversary. **bicentennial** (*say* buy-sen-**ten**-ee-uhl) *adjective*

biceps (*say* **buy**-seps) *noun* the large muscle at the front of the arm above the elbow. [Latin, = two-headed (because its end is attached at two points)]

bicker *verb* quarrel over unimportant things; squabble.

bickie *noun* (*informal*) a biscuit. **big bickies** a large sum of money.

bicuspid *noun* a tooth with two points. [from *bi-*, + Latin *cuspis* = sharp point]

bicycle *noun* a two-wheeled vehicle driven by pedals. **bicyclist** *noun*

bid[1] *noun* **1** the offer of an amount you are willing to pay for something, especially at an auction. **2** an attempt.

bid[2] *verb* (**bid**, **bidding**) make a bid. **bidder** *noun*

bid[3] *verb* (**bid** (or *old use* **bade**), **bid** or **bidden**, **bidding**) **1** command, *Do as you are bid or bidden.* **2** say as a greeting or farewell, *bidding them good night.*

biddable *adjective* willing to obey.

bidding *noun* a command.

bide *verb* (**bided**, **biding**) wait.

bidet (*say* **bee**-day) *noun* a low washbasin to sit on for washing the lower part of the body. [from French *bidet* = a pony]

biennial[1] (*say* buy-**en**-ee-uhl) *adjective* **1** lasting for two years. **2** happening every second year. **biennially** *adverb*

biennial[2] *noun* **1** a plant that lives for two years, flowering and dying in the second year. **2** a festival taking place every second year, *Brisbane Biennial.* [from *bi*-, + Latin *annus* = year]

bier (*say* beer) *noun* a movable stand on which a coffin or a dead body is placed before it is buried.

bifocal (*say* buy-**foh**-kuhl) *adjective* (of spectacle lenses) made in two sections, with the upper part for looking at distant objects and the lower part for reading.

bifocals *plural noun* bifocal spectacles.

big *adjective* (**bigger**, **biggest**) **1** large, *Her cat is bigger than the dog next door.* **2** important, *the big match.* **3** more grown-up; elder, *my big sister.*

bigamy (*say* **big**-uh-mee) *noun* the crime of marrying a person when you are already married to someone else. **bigamist** *noun*, **bigamous** *adjective* [from *bi*-, + Greek *gamos* = marriage]

big bang theory *noun* the theory that the universe began with a massive explosion of dense matter.

bight *noun* **1** a long inward curve in a coast. **2** a loop of rope.

big-note *verb* (*Australian informal*) exalt yourself, *He takes every opportunity to big-note himself.*

bigot *noun* a narrow-minded and intolerant person. **bigoted** *adjective*, **bigotry** *noun*

big smoke *noun* a large town or city.

big top *noun* the main tent at a circus.

bike *noun* (*informal*) a bicycle or motorcycle.

biker *noun* a cyclist, especially a motorcyclist.

bikie *noun* (*Australian informal*) a motorcyclist, especially one of a gang.

bikini *noun* (*plural* **bikinis**) a woman's two-piece swimsuit. [named after the Bikini atoll in the Pacific Ocean, which was previously used by the US to test nuclear weapons]

bilateral *adjective* **1** of or on two sides. **2** of two people or groups, *a bilateral agreement.* [from *bi*- + *lateral*]

bilberry *noun* (*plural* **bilberries**) a small dark blue edible berry.

bilby *noun* a small Australian nocturnal burrowing marsupial with blue-grey fur. [from Yuwaalaraay and neighbouring languages *bilba*, *bilbi*]

bile *noun* a bitter liquid produced by the liver, helping to digest fats.

bilge *noun* **1** the bottom of a ship; the water that collects there. **2** (*informal*) nonsense; worthless ideas.

bilingual (*say* buy-**ling**-gwuhl) *adjective* **1** written in two languages. **2** able to speak two languages. [from *bi*-, + Latin *lingua* = language]

bilious *adjective* feeling sick; sickly. **biliousness** *noun* [from *bile*]

bill[1] *noun* **1** a written statement of charges for goods or services that have been supplied. **2** a poster. **3** a list; a program of entertainment. **4** the draft of a proposed law to be discussed by parliament. **5** a banknote.

bill[2] *noun* a bird's beak.

billabong *noun* (*Australian*) a branch of a river forming a backwater. [from Wiradjuri *bilabang*]

billet[1] *noun* a lodging for troops, conference delegates or sports teams, especially in a private house.

billet[2] *verb* (**billeted**, **billeting**) house someone in a billet.

billiards *noun* a game in which three balls are struck with cues on a cloth-covered table. [from French *billard* = cue]

billion *noun* **1** a thousand million (1,000,000,000). **2** (*old use*) a million million. **billionth** *adjective & noun* [from *bi*- + *million*]

billionaire *noun* a person whose assets are worth one billion dollars or more.

bill of fare *noun* a menu.

billow[1] *noun* a huge wave.

billow[2] *verb* rise or roll like waves.

billy *noun* (*plural* **billies**) a pot with a lid, used by campers as a kettle or cooking pot. **billycan** *noun*

billycart *noun* (*Australian*) a home-made children's vehicle like a go-kart. [short for *billy-goat cart*, a small cart drawn by a goat]

billy goat *noun* a male goat. (Compare **nanny goat**.) [from the name *Billy*]

bimodal *adjective* (especially of statistical data) having two modes.

bin *noun* a large or deep container.

binary (*say* **buy**-nuh-ree) *adjective* involving sets of two; consisting of two parts. [from Latin *binarius* = two together]

binary digit *noun* either of the two digits (0 and 1) used in the **binary system** to code information.

bind[1] *verb* (**bound**, **binding**) **1** fasten material round something. **2** fasten the pages of a book into a cover. **3** tie up; tie together. **4** make somebody agree to do something;

oblige. **binder** *noun*
bind a person over make a person agree not to break the law.

bind² *noun* (*informal*) a nuisance; a bore.

bindi-eye *noun* a small Australian plant bearing barbed fruits. [from Gamilaraay and Yuwaalaraay *bindayaa*]

binge¹ *noun* (*informal*) a period of excessive indulgence in an activity, especially drinking alcohol or eating.

binge² *verb* (*informal*) **1** indulge in an activity, *She binged on ice cream.* **2** watch multiple episodes of a television program over a short period of time.

bingo *noun* a game using cards on which numbered squares are covered up as the numbers are called out at random.

binoculars *plural noun* a device with lenses for both eyes, making distant objects seem nearer. [from Latin *bini* = two together, + *oculus* = eye]

bio- *prefix* life (as in *biology*). [from Greek *bios* = life]

biochemistry *noun* the study of the chemical composition and processes of living things. **biochemical** *adjective*, **biochemist** *noun*

biodegradable *adjective* able to be broken down by bacteria in the environment.

biodiversity *noun* diversity of plant and animal life.

biofuel *noun* fuel derived directly from living matter.

biogas *noun* gaseous fuel, especially methane, produced by fermentation of organic matter.

biography (*say* buy-**og**-ruh-fee) *noun* the story of a person's life. **biographer** *noun*, **biographical** *adjective* [from *bio-* + *-graphy*]

biology *noun* the study of the life and structure of living things. **biological** *adjective*, **biologist** *noun* [from *bio-* + *-logy*]

bionic (*say* buy-**on**-ik) *adjective* (of a person or parts of the body) operated by electronic devices. [from *bio-* + *electronic*]

biopsy (*say* **buy**-op-see) *noun* (*plural* **biopsies**) examination of tissue from a living body. [from *bio-* + *autopsy*]

bioterrorism *noun* use of infectious agents or other harmful biological or biochemical substances as weapons of terrorism.

biotic *adjective* **1** relating to life or living things. **2** of biological origin.

bipartisan *adjective* of or involving two political or other parties.

bipartite *adjective* having two parts; involving two groups, *a bipartite agreement.*

biped (*say* **buy**-ped) *noun* a two-footed animal. [from *bi-*, + Latin *pedis* = of a foot]

biplane *noun* an aeroplane with two sets of wings, one above the other.

bipolar *adjective* **1** having two poles or extremities. **2** (of psychiatric illness) alternating periods of elation and depression.

bipolar disorder *noun* a mental condition marked by alternating periods of elation and depression.

birch *noun* (*plural* **birches**) **1** a deciduous tree with slender branches. **2** a bundle of birch branches used for flogging.

bird *noun* **1** an animal with feathers, two wings, and two legs, *Emus and penguins are birds that can't fly.* **2** (*informal*) a young woman.

bird flu *noun* (*informal*) avian influenza.

birdie *noun* **1** (*informal*) a bird. **2** a score of one stroke under par for a hole at golf.

bird's-eye view *noun* a view from above.

biro *noun* (*plural* **biros**) (*trademark*) a kind of ballpoint pen. [named after its Hungarian inventor L. Biro]

birth *noun* **1** the process by which a baby or young animal comes out from its mother's body. **2** origin; beginning. **3** parentage, *She is of noble birth.*

birth control *noun* contraception.

birthday *noun* the anniversary of the day a person was born, *It's my mum's birthday today and she turns 40.*

birthmark *noun* a coloured mark that has been on a person's skin since birth.

birth rate *noun* the number of children born in one year for every 1000 people.

birthright *noun* a right or privilege to which a person is entitled through being born into a particular family (especially as the eldest son) or in a particular country.

biryani (*say* bi-ree-**yah**-nee) *noun* (also **biriyani**) an Indian dish made with highly seasoned rice and meat, fish, or vegetables. [Urdu from Persian *biriyān* = fried, grilled]

biscuit *noun* a small flat piece of pastry baked crisp. [from Latin *bis* = twice, + *coctus* = cooked]

bisect (*say* buy-**sekt**) *verb* divide into two equal parts. **bisection** *noun*, **bisector** *noun* [from *bi-*, + Latin *sectum* = cut]

bisexual¹ *adjective* **1** sexually attracted not exclusively to people of one particular gender; attracted to both men and women. **2** having both male and female sexual organs in one individual.

bisexual² *noun* a person who is sexually attracted not exclusively to people of one particular gender.

bishop *noun* **1** an important member of the clergy in charge of all the churches in a city or district. **2** a chess piece shaped like a bishop's mitre.

bishopric *noun* the position or diocese of a bishop.

bismillah (*say* **bis**-mil-uh) *interjection* in the name of God (an invocation used by Muslims at the beginning of an undertaking). [Arabic]

bismuth *noun* **1** a greyish-white metal. **2** a compound of this used in medicine.

bison (*say* **buy**-suhn) *noun* (*plural* **bison**) a wild ox with shaggy hair.

bistro *noun* a small restaurant.

bit[1] *noun* **1** a small piece or amount of something. **2** the metal part of a horse's bridle that is put into its mouth. **3** the part of a tool that cuts or grips things when twisted. **4** a short distance or time, *Wait a bit.*
bit by bit gradually.

bit[2] *past tense* of **bite**[1].

bit[3] *noun* (in computers) a unit of information expressed as a choice between two possibilities. [from *bi*nary digi*t*]

bitch *noun* (*plural* **bitches**) **1** a female dog, fox, or wolf. **2** (*informal*) a spiteful woman.
bitchy *adjective*

bite[1] *verb* (**bit**, **bitten**, **biting**) **1** cut or take with your teeth. **2** penetrate; sting. **3** accept bait, *The fish are biting.*
bite the dust fall wounded and die.

bite[2] *noun* **1** biting. **2** a mark or spot made by biting, *an insect bite.* **3** a snack.

bitser *noun* (*Australian informal*) a mongrel dog.

bitten *past participle* of **bite**[1].

bitter *adjective* **1** tasting sharp, not sweet. **2** feeling or causing mental pain or resentment, *a bitter disappointment.* **3** very cold. **bitterly** *adverb*, **bitterness** *noun*

bittern *noun* a wading bird of the heron family.

bitumen (*say* **bich**-uh-muhn) *noun* **1** a black substance used especially for covering roads. **2** (*Australian*) a tarred road.
bituminous *adjective*

bivalve *noun* a shellfish (e.g. an oyster) that has a shell with two hinged parts.

bivariate *adjective* (of statistical data) involving two variables.

bivouac[1] (*say* **biv**-oo-ak) *noun* a temporary camp without tents.

bivouac[2] *verb* (**bivouacked**, **bivouacking**) camp in a bivouac.

bizarre (*say* buh-**zah**) *adjective* very odd in appearance or effect.

blab *verb* (**blabbed**, **blabbing**) tell tales; let out a secret.

black[1] *noun* **1** the very darkest colour, like coal or soot. **2** (also **Black**) a member of a dark-skinned people.

black[2] *adjective* **1** of the colour black. **2** very dirty. **3** dismal; not hopeful, *The outlook is black.* **4** hostile; disapproving, *He gave me a black look.* **5** (also **Black**) of the human group with dark skin. **6** (of tea or coffee) without milk. **blackly** *adverb*, **blackness** *noun*

black[3] *verb* make a thing black.
black out 1 cover windows so that no light can penetrate. **2** faint, lose consciousness.

blackberry *noun* (*plural* **blackberries**) a sweet black berry.

blackbird *noun* a European songbird, the male of which is black.

blackboard *noun* a dark board for writing on with chalk.

blacken *verb* **1** make or become black. **2** speak evil of, *blacken someone's character.*

black eye *noun* an eye with a bruise round it.

blackguard (*say* **blag**-ahd) *noun* a scoundrel.

blackhead *noun* a small black spot in the skin.

black hole *noun* a region in outer space with such a strong gravitational field that no matter or radiation can escape from it.

blackleg *noun* a person who works while fellow workers are on strike.

blacklist *verb* put someone on a list of those who are disapproved of.

black magic *noun* evil magic.

blackmail *verb* demand payment or action from someone by threats. **blackmail** *noun*, **blackmailer** *noun*

black market *noun* illegal trading.

blackout *noun* **1** a temporary loss of consciousness. **2** a failure of power supply.

black sheep *noun* one bad character in a well-behaved group.

blacksmith *noun* a person who makes and repairs iron things, especially one who makes and fits horseshoes.

black spot *noun* a dangerous place.

black stump *noun* (*Australian*) an imaginary marker of the limits of settlement, *beyond the black stump.*

bladder *noun* **1** the bag-like part of the body in which urine collects. **2** the inflatable bag inside a football.

blade[1] *noun* **1** the flat cutting part of a knife, sword, axe, or similar object. **2** the flat wide part of an oar, spade, or propeller. **3** a flat narrow leaf, *blades of grass.* **4** a broad flat bone, *shoulder blade.*

blade[2] *verb* (*informal*) skate using rollerblades.

blame[1] *verb* (**blamed**, **blaming**) **1** say that somebody or something has caused what is wrong, *They blamed me.* **2** find fault with someone, *We can't blame them for wanting a holiday.*

blame[2] *noun* blaming; responsibility for what is wrong.

blameless *adjective* deserving no blame; innocent.

blanch *verb* make or become white or pale, *He blanched with fear.*

blancmange (*say* bluh-**monzh**) *noun* a jelly-like pudding made with milk. [from French *blanc* = white, + *mange* = eat]

bland *adjective* **1** having a mild flavour not a strong one. **2** gentle and casual; not irritating or stimulating, *a bland manner.* **blandly** *adverb*, **blandness** *noun* [from Latin *blandus* = soothing]

blank[1] *adjective* **1** not written or printed on; unmarked. **2** without interest or expression, *a blank look.* **3** without an opening, *a blank wall.* **blankly** *adverb*, **blankness** *noun*

blank[2] *noun* **1** an empty space. **2** a blank cartridge. [from French *blanc* = white]

blank cartridge *noun* a cartridge that makes a noise but does not fire a bullet.

blank cheque *noun* a signed cheque with the amount not yet filled in.

blanket[1] *noun* **1** a thick covering made of woollen or other fabric. **2** any thick soft covering, *a blanket of snow.*

blanket[2] *adjective* covering a wide range of conditions, *a blanket agreement.*

blank verse *noun* poetry without rhymes.

blare *verb* (**blared**, **blaring**) make a loud, harsh sound. **blare** *noun*

blasé (*say* **blah**-zay) *adjective* bored or unimpressed by things because you are used to them. [French]

blaspheme (*say* blas-**feem**) *verb* (**blasphemed**, **blaspheming**) talk or write irreverently about sacred things. [from Greek *blasphemos* = evil-speaking]

blasphemy (*say* **blas**-fuh-mee) *noun* (*plural* **blasphemies**) irreverent talk about sacred things. **blasphemous** *adjective*

blast[1] *noun* **1** a strong rush of wind or air. **2** an explosion. **3** a loud noise, *the blast of the trumpets.*

blast[2] *verb* blow up with explosives.
blast off launch by the firing of rockets. **blast-off** *noun*

blast furnace *noun* a furnace for smelting ore, with hot air driven in.

blatant (*say* **blay**-tuhnt) *adjective* very obvious, *a blatant lie.* **blatantly** *adverb* [from an old word meaning 'noisy']

blaze[1] *noun* a very bright flame, fire, or light.

blaze[2] *verb* (**blazed**, **blazing**) **1** burn or shine brightly. **2** show great feeling, *He was blazing with anger.*

blaze[3] *noun* **1** a white mark on an animal's face. **2** a mark chipped in the bark of a tree to show a route.

blaze[4] *verb* (**blazed**, **blazing**) mark a tree or route by cutting blazes.
blaze a trail show the way for others to follow.

blazer *noun* a kind of jacket, often with a badge or in the colours of a school or team. [from *blaze*[2]]

bleach[1] *verb* make or become white.

bleach[2] *noun* (*plural* **bleaches**) a substance used to bleach things.

bleak *adjective* **1** bare and cold, *a bleak hillside.* **2** dreary; miserable, *a bleak future.* **bleakly** *adverb*, **bleakness** *noun*

bleary *adjective* watery and not seeing clearly, *bleary eyes.* **blearily** *adverb*

bleat *noun* the cry of a lamb, goat, or calf. **bleat** *verb*

bleed *verb* (**bled**, **bleeding**) **1** lose blood. **2** draw blood or fluid from.

bleep *noun* a short high sound used as a signal. **bleep** *verb*

blemish *noun* (*plural* **blemishes**) a flaw, a mark that spoils a thing's appearance. **blemish** *verb*

blench *verb* flinch.

blend[1] *verb* mix smoothly or easily. **blender** *noun*

blend[2] *noun* a mixture.

bless *verb* **1** make sacred or holy. **2** bring God's favour on a person or thing.

blessing *noun* **1** a prayer that blesses a person or thing; being blessed. **2** something that people are glad of. **3** approval.

blew *past tense* of **blow**[1].

blight[1] *noun* **1** a disease that withers plants. **2** a bad or evil influence.

blight[2] *verb* **1** affect with blight. **2** spoil something.

blind[1] *adjective* **1** without the ability to see. **2** without any thought or understanding, *blind obedience.* **3** (of a passage, tube, or road) closed at one end. **blindly** *adverb*, **blindness** *noun*

blind[2] *verb* make a person blind.

blind[3] *noun* **1** a screen for a window. **2** a deception; something used to hide the truth, *His journey was a blind.*

blindfold *verb* deprive someone of sight by placing a covering over their eyes. **blindfold** *noun*

bling *noun* (also **bling-bling**) (*informal*) expensive, ostentatious clothing and jewellery.

blink *verb* shut and open your eyes rapidly. **blink** *noun*

blinkers *plural noun* leather pieces fixed on a bridle to prevent a horse from seeing sideways. **blinkered** *adjective*

bliss *noun* perfect happiness. **blissful** *adjective*, **blissfully** *adverb*

blister *noun* a swelling like a bubble, especially on skin. **blister** *verb*

blithe (*say* bluy*th*) *adjective* casual and carefree. **blithely** *adverb*

blitz *noun* (*plural* **blitzes**) a sudden violent attack; the bombing of London in 1940. [short for German *blitzkrieg* (*blitz* = lightning, *krieg* = war)]

blizzard *noun* a severe snowstorm.

bloated *adjective* swollen by fat, gas, or liquid.

blob *noun* a small round mass of something, *blobs of paint.*

bloc *noun* a group of countries uniting to support a common interest.

block[1] *noun* **1** a solid piece of something. **2** an obstruction. **3** a large building divided into flats or offices. **4** a group of buildings. **5** (*Australian*) an area of land divided for settlement. **6** (*Australian*) a plot of land for residential building.

block[2] *verb* obstruct; prevent from moving or being used. **blockage** *noun*

blockade[1] *noun* the blocking of access to a place in order to prevent people and goods from going in or out.

blockade[2] *verb* (**blockaded**, **blockading**) set up a blockade of a place.

block letters *plural noun* plain capital letters.

blog[1] *noun* a regularly updated website or webpage that is written in an informal style [short for *weblog*]

blog[2] *verb* (**blogged**, **blogging**) add new material to or regularly update a blog. **blogger** *noun*

blogosphere *noun* (*informal*) personal websites and weblogs collectively.

bloke *noun* (*informal*) a man.

blond *adjective* (also **blonde**) fair-haired; fair. [from Latin *blondus* = yellow]

blonde *noun* a fair-haired girl or woman.

blood *noun* **1** the red liquid that flows through veins and arteries. **2** family relationship; ancestry, *He is of royal blood.* **in cold blood** deliberately and cruelly.

bloodbath *noun* a massacre.

blood-curdling *adjective* causing or expressing terror or horror.

bloodhound *noun* a large dog used to track people by their scent.

bloodshed *noun* the killing or wounding of people.

bloodshot *adjective* (of eyes) streaked with red.

bloodthirsty *adjective* eager for bloodshed.

blood vessel *noun* a tube carrying blood in the body; an artery, vein, or capillary.

bloody *adjective* (**bloodier**, **bloodiest**) **1** blood-stained. **2** with much bloodshed. **3** (*informal*) annoying, very great, *Don't be a bloody fool.* (This use may offend some people.)

bloody-minded *adjective* deliberately awkward and not helpful. **bloody-mindedness** *noun*

bloom[1] *noun* **1** a flower. **2** the fine powder on certain fresh fruits such as grapes.

bloom[2] *verb* produce flowers.

blossom[1] *noun* a flower or mass of flowers, especially on a fruit tree.

blossom[2] *verb* **1** produce flowers. **2** develop into something, *She blossomed into a fine singer.*

blot[1] *noun* **1** a spot of ink. **2** a flaw or fault; something ugly, *a blot on the landscape.*

blot[2] *verb* (**blotted**, **blotting**) **1** make a blot or blots on something. **2** dry with blotting paper.
blot out 1 cross out thickly. **2** obscure, *Fog blotted out the view.*

blotch *noun* (*plural* **blotches**) an untidy patch of colour. **blotchy** *adjective*

blotting paper *noun* absorbent paper for soaking up ink from writing.

blouse *noun* a garment like a shirt.

blow[1] *verb* (**blew**, **blown**, **blowing**) **1** send out a current of air. **2** (of the wind) move along. **3** move in or with a current of air, *Her hat blew off.* **4** make or sound something by blowing, *blow bubbles*; *blow the whistle.* **5** melt with too strong an electric current, *A fuse has blown.* **6** (*informal*) waste, *He blew his savings on an old bomb.*
blow in (*informal*) arrive unexpectedly. **blow-in** *noun*
blow up 1 inflate. **2** exaggerate. **3** explode; shatter by an explosion.

blow[2] *noun* the action of blowing.

blow[3] *noun* **1** a hard knock or hit. **2** a shock; a disaster.

blowfly *noun* a fly that lays its eggs on meat.

blowtorch *noun* a portable device for directing a very hot flame at something.

blubber[1] *noun* the fat of whales.

blubber[2] *verb* sob noisily.

bludge *verb* (*Australian informal*) **1** avoid work or responsibility. **2** impose on other people. **bludge** *noun*, **bludger** *noun* [from British slang *bludgeoner* = a pimp]

bludgeon (*say* **bluj**-uhn) *noun* a short stick with a thickened end, used as a weapon.

blue[1] *noun* **1** the colour of a cloudless sky. **2** (*Australian informal*) a mistake. **3** (*Australian informal*) an argument, a fight. **out of the blue** unexpectedly.

blue[2] *adjective* **1** of the colour blue. **2** unhappy; depressed. **3** indecent; obscene, *blue films.* **blueness** *noun*

bluebell *noun* a plant with blue bell-shaped flowers.

blue blood *noun* noble birth.

bluebottle *noun* **1** (*Australian*) a jellyfish with a painful sting. **2** a large bluish fly.

blue-collar worker *noun* a manual or industrial worker.

bluefin *noun* a common large tuna found in warm seas.

blue heeler *noun* an Australian cattle dog with a blue or red-flecked coat.

blueprint *noun* a detailed plan.

blues *noun* **1** a melancholic music of African-American origin. **2** a very sad feeling; depression.

blue-screen *adjective* denoting a special-effects technique in which scenes shot against a blue background are superimposed on other scenes.

bluestone *noun* (*Australian*) a building stone.

bluetongue *noun* an Australian lizard with a cobalt-blue tongue.

Bluetooth *noun* (*trademark*) a standard for the short-range interconnection of electronic devices.

bluey *noun* (*Australian*) a bushman's swag.

bluff[1] *verb* deceive someone, especially by pretending to be able to do something.

bluff[2] *noun* bluffing; a threat that you make but do not intend to carry out. [from Dutch *bluffen* = boast]

bluff[3] *adjective* frank and hearty in manner. **bluffness** *noun*

bluff[4] *noun* a cliff with a broad steep front.

bluish *adjective* rather blue.

blunder[1] *noun* a stupid mistake.

blunder[2] *verb* **1** make a blunder. **2** move clumsily and uncertainly.

blunderbuss *noun* an old type of gun that fired many balls in one shot. [from Dutch *donderbus* = thunder gun]

blunt[1] *adjective* **1** not sharp. **2** speaking in plain terms; straightforward, *a blunt refusal.* **bluntly** *adverb*, **bluntness** *noun*

blunt[2] *verb* make a thing blunt.

blur[1] *verb* (**blurred**, **blurring**) make or become indistinct or smeared. **blurry** *adjective*

blur[2] *noun* an indistinct appearance; a smear.

Blu-ray *noun* (*trademark*) a type of DVD used for the storage of high-definition video and data.

blurt *verb* say something suddenly or tactlessly, *He blurted it out.*

blush *verb* become red in the face because you are ashamed or embarrassed. **blush** *noun*

bluster *verb* **1** blow in gusts; be windy. **2** talk threateningly. **blustery** *adjective*

BMI *abbreviation* body mass index.

BMX *abbreviation* a kind of bicycle for use in racing on a dirt track.

boa (*say* **boh**-uh) *noun* (also **boa constrictor**) a large South American snake that squeezes its prey so as to suffocate it.

boab *noun* a baobab.

boar *noun* **1** a wild pig. **2** a male pig.

board[1] *noun* **1** a flat piece of wood. **2** a flat piece of stiff material, e.g. a chessboard. **3** daily meals supplied in return for payment or work, *board and lodging.* **4** a committee. **5** (*Australian*) the part of the floor of a shearing shed where the shearers work. **on board** on or in a ship, aircraft, or other vehicle.

board[2] *verb* **1** go on to a ship, aircraft, or other vehicle. **2** give or get meals and accommodation. **board up** block with fixed boards.

boarder *noun* **1** a pupil who lives at a boarding school during the term. **2** a lodger who receives meals.

boarding house *noun* a house where people obtain board and lodging for payment.

boarding school *noun* a school where pupils live during the term.

boardroom *noun* a room where the meetings of the board of a company are held.

boardshorts *plural noun* long shorts, originally as used by surfboard riders.

boast[1] *verb* **1** speak with great pride and try to impress people. **2** have something to be proud of, *The town boasts a fine park.* **boaster** *noun*, **boastful** *adjective*, **boastfully** *adverb*

boast[2] *noun* a boastful statement.

boat *noun* a hollow structure built to travel on water. **in the same boat** in the same situation; suffering the same difficulties.

boater *noun* a hard flat straw hat.

boatswain (*say* **boh**-suhn) *noun* a ship's officer in charge of equipment and the crew.

bob[1] *verb* (**bobbed**, **bobbing**) **1** move quickly, especially up and down. **2** cut hair in a bob.

bob[2] *noun* **1** a bobbing movement. **2** a short straight hairstyle.

bobbin *noun* a small spool holding thread or wire in a machine.

bobble *noun* a small round ornament, often made of wool.

bobbles *plural noun* small plastic balls attached to elastic, used for fastening girls' hair.

bobcat[1] *noun* a small North American wild cat with a short tail.

bobcat[2] *noun* (*trademark*) a small four-wheeled earth-moving machine.

bobsled *noun* (also **bobsleigh**) a sledge with two sets of runners.

bocconcini (*say* bok-on-**chee**-nee) *noun* a small ball-shaped cheese. [Italian, = small mouthfuls]

bode *verb* (**boded**, **boding**) be a sign or omen of what is to come, *It bodes well.*

bodice *noun* the upper part of a dress.

bodkin *noun* a thick blunt needle for drawing tape or cord through a hem.

body *noun* (*plural* **bodies**) **1** the physical structure, including the bones, flesh, and organs of a person or animal. **2** the main part of this apart from the head and limbs. **3** a corpse. **4** the main part of something, *a car body.* **5** a group or quantity regarded as a unit, *the school's governing body.* **6** a distinct object or piece of matter, *Stars and planets are heavenly bodies.* **bodily** *adjective & adverb*

bodyguard *noun* a guard to protect a person's life.

body language *noun* communication through gestures and poses, *Her anger was clearly expressed in her body language.*

body mass index *noun* a measure of whether someone is over- or underweight, calculated by dividing their weight in kilograms by the square of their height in metres.

body surf *noun* ride waves by streamlining your body and keeping it rigid like a board.

boffin *noun* (*informal*) an expert, especially in science.

bog *noun* an area of wet spongy ground.
boggy *adjective*
bogged down stuck and unable to make any progress.

bogan *noun* (*Australian informal*) a person who is regarded as being uncultured and unsophisticated.

bogey[1] *noun* a score of one stroke over par for a hole at golf.

bogey[2] *noun* (*Australian*) **1** a swim or bathe. **2** (in full **bogey hole**) a swimming hole. [from Sydney language]

boggle *verb* (**boggled**, **boggling**) hesitate in fear or doubt, *Our minds boggled at the idea.* [from dialect *bogle* = bogy]

bogong *noun* a large brown Australian moth. [from Ngarigo *bugung*]

bogus *adjective* not real; sham.

bogy *noun* (*plural* **bogies**) **1** an evil spirit. **2** something that frightens people. **bogyman** *noun* [originally *Old Bogey* = the Devil]

boil[1] *verb* **1** make or become hot enough to bubble and give off steam. **2** cook or wash something in boiling water. **3** be very hot.

boil[2] *noun* **1** an inflamed swelling under the skin. **2** boiling point, *Bring the milk to the boil.* [from Latin *bulla* = a bubble]

boiler *noun* a container in which water is heated.

boisterous *adjective* noisy and lively.

bok choy *noun* a vegetable used in Asian cooking. [Chinese]

bold *adjective* **1** brave; courageous. **2** impudent. **3** (of colours) strong and vivid. **4** (also **boldface**) printed in a thick black typeface. **boldly** *adverb*, **boldness** *noun*

bole *noun* the trunk of a tree.

bollard *noun* **1** a short thick post to which a ship's mooring rope may be tied. **2** a short post for preventing traffic from entering an area.

bolster[1] *noun* a long pillow for placing across a bed under other pillows.

bolster[2] *verb* add extra support.

bolt[1] *noun* **1** a sliding bar for fastening a door. **2** a thick metal pin for fastening things together. **3** a sliding bar that opens and closes the breech of a rifle. **4** a shaft of lightning. **5** an arrow shot from a crossbow. **6** the action of bolting.
a bolt from the blue a surprise, usually an unpleasant one.
bolt upright quite upright.

bolt[2] *verb* **1** fasten with a bolt or bolts. **2** run away; (of a horse) run off out of control. **3** swallow food quickly.

bomb[1] *noun* **1** an explosive device. **2** (**the bomb**) an atomic or hydrogen bomb. **3** (*Australian informal*) a dilapidated old car.

bomb[2] *verb* attack with bombs. **bomber** *noun* [from Greek *bombos* = loud humming]

bombard *verb* **1** attack with gunfire or many missiles. **2** direct a large number of questions or comments at somebody. **bombardment** *noun*

bombastic (*say* bom-**bas**-tik) *adjective* using pompous words.

bombora (*say* bom-**baw**-ruh) *noun* (*Australian*) a dangerous stretch of water where waves break over a submerged reef or rock; the reef or rock itself. [possibly from Sydney language]

bombshell *noun* a great shock.

bona fide (*say* boh-nuh **fuy**-dee) *adjective* genuine; without fraud, *Are they bona fide tourists or spies?* [Latin, = in good faith]

bona fides *noun* honest intention; sincerity, *We do not doubt his bona fides.* [Latin, = good faith]

bonanza (*say* buh-**nan**-zuh) *noun* sudden great wealth or luck.

bond[1] *noun* **1** something that binds, restrains, or unites people or things. **2** a document stating an agreement.

bond[2] *verb* connect or unite with a bond.

bondage *noun* slavery; captivity.

bone[1] *noun* one of the hard parts of a person's or animal's body (excluding teeth, nails, horns, and cartilage).

bone[2] *verb* (**boned**, **boning**) remove the bones from meat or fish.

bone-dry *adjective* quite dry.

bonfire *noun* an outdoor fire to burn rubbish or celebrate something. [originally *bone fire*, = a fire to dispose of people's or animals' bones]

bongo *noun* (*plural* **bongos**) each of a pair of small drums played with the fingers.

bonito *noun* a tuna-like fish. [Spanish]

bonnet *noun* **1** a hat with strings that tie under the chin. **2** a Scottish beret. **3** the hinged cover over a car engine.

bonny *adjective* (**bonnier**, **bonniest**) **1** healthy-looking. **2** (especially *Scottish*) good-looking. [from French *bon* = good]

bonsai (*say* **bon**-suy) *noun* **1** a plant or tree grown as a miniature by artificially restricting its growth. **2** the method of cultivating this. [Japanese]

bonus (*say* **boh**-nuhs) *noun* (*plural* **bonuses**) an extra payment or benefit. [from Latin *bonus* = good]

bon voyage (*say* bon voi-**yahzh**) *interjection* pleasant journey! [French]

bony *adjective* **1** with large bones; having bones with little flesh on them. **2** full of bones. **3** like bones.

bonzer *adjective* (*Australian informal*) excellent. [probably from British dialect *bouncer* = anything very large of its kind]

boo *verb* shout 'boo' in disapproval.

boobook *noun* a small brown Australian owl with a spotted back and wings. [from Sydney language *bug-bug*, an imitation of the bird call]

booby prize *noun* a prize given as a joke to someone who comes last in a contest.

booby trap *noun* something designed to hit or injure someone unexpectedly.

boofhead *noun* (also **boof**) (*Australian informal*) a fool or simpleton. [from *bufflehead* (bullock head) = fool]

boofy (*Australian informal*) *adjective* foolish; big and stupid. [from *boofhead*]

book[1] *noun* **1** a set of sheets of paper, usually with printing or writing on them, fastened together inside a cover. **2** a literary composition that is published or intended for publication as a book, *Her new book about dogs can be found online.* **bookshop** *noun*

book[2] *verb* **1** reserve a place in a theatre, hotel, train, etc. **2** write something down in a book or list; enter in a police record, *The police booked him for speeding.*

bookcase *noun* a piece of furniture with shelves for books.

bookkeeping *noun* the systematic recording of business transactions. **bookkeeper** *noun*

booklet *noun* a small thin book.

bookmaker *noun* a person whose business is taking bets.

bookmark[1] *noun* **1** something to mark a place in a book. **2** (in computing) a record of the address of a file, webpage, or other data, enabling quick access by a user.

bookmark[2] *verb* record the address of a website, file, etc. to enable quick access in future.

bookworm *noun* **1** a grub that eats holes in books. **2** a person who loves reading.

boom[1] *verb* **1** make a deep hollow sound. **2** be growing and prospering, *Business is booming.*

boom[2] *noun* **1** a booming sound. **2** prosperity; growth.

boom[3] *noun* **1** a long pole at the bottom of a sail to keep it stretched. **2** a long pole carrying a microphone. **3** a chain or floating barrier that can be placed across a river or a harbour entrance.

boomer *noun* **1** (*Australian*) a large adult male kangaroo. **2** (*informal*) a baby boomer.

boomerang[1] *noun* a curved wooden missile used traditionally by Aboriginal people, especially one that can be thrown so that it returns to the thrower if it fails to hit anything. [probably from Dharawal]

boomerang[2] *verb* (of a plan) backfire, *The preparations for the picnic boomeranged when the rain started.*

boon *noun* a benefit. [from Old Norse *bon* = prayer]

boor *noun* an ill-mannered person. **boorish** *adjective*

boost[1] *verb* **1** increase the strength, value, or reputation of a person or thing. **2** push something upwards. **booster** *noun*

boost[2] *noun* **1** an increase. **2** an upward push.

boot[1] *noun* **1** a shoe that covers the foot and ankle or leg. **2** the compartment for luggage in a car.

boot[2] *verb* **1** kick. **2** make a computer ready for use.
boot out (*informal*) get rid of forcefully.

boot camp *noun* military training for new recruits, with very harsh discipline; any similar training camp or course.

bootee *noun* a baby's knitted boot.

booth *noun* a small stall or enclosure.

booty *noun* loot.

booze[1] *verb* (**boozed**, **boozing**) (*informal*) drink alcohol.

booze[2] *noun* (*informal*) alcoholic drink.

bora (*say* **baw**-ruh) *noun* (*Australian*) (in traditional Aboriginal culture) an initiation ceremony for boys. [from Gamilaraay *buurra*]

borax *noun* a soluble white powder used in making glass, detergents, and enamels.

border[1] *noun* **1** the boundary of a country; the part near this. **2** an edge. **3** something placed round an edge to strengthen or decorate it. **4** a strip of ground round a garden or part of it.

border[2] *verb* put or be a border to something.

borderline[1] *noun* a boundary.

borderline[2] *adjective* on the boundary between two different groups or kinds of things, *a borderline case.*

bore[1] *verb* (**bored**, **boring**) **1** drill a hole. **2** get through by pushing.

bore[2] *noun* **1** the internal width of a gun barrel. **2** a hole made by boring. **3** (*Australian*) an artesian bore.

bore[3] *verb* (**bored**, **boring**) make somebody feel uninterested by being dull.

bore[4] *noun* a boring person or thing. **boredom** *noun*

bore[5] *noun* a tidal wave with a steep front that moves up some estuaries.

bore[6] *past tense* of **bear**[2].

born *adjective* **1** have come into existence by birth. **2** having a certain natural quality or ability, *a born leader.*

Usage See the note at *bear*[2].

borne[1] see **bear**[2].

borne[2] *adjective* carried or transported by the thing specified, *airborne pollution*; *waterborne bacteria.*

boronia *noun* an aromatic Australian shrub. [from Francesco Borone, Italian botanist]

borough (*say* **bu**-ruh) *noun* an important town or district. [from Old English *burg* = fortress or fortified town]

borrow *verb* **1** get something to use for a time, with a promise to give it back afterwards. **2** obtain money as a loan. **borrower** *noun*

bosom *noun* a person's breast.

boss[1] *noun* (*plural* **bosses**) (*informal*) a manager; a person whose job is to give orders to workers.

boss[2] *verb* (*informal*) order someone about. [from Dutch *baas* = master]

boss[3] *noun* a round raised knob or stud.

bossy *adjective* (*informal*) fond of ordering people about. **bossiness** *noun*

bot[1] *verb* (*Australian informal*) cadge.
bot on impose on.

bot[2] *noun* (in computing) an autonomous program on a network that can interact with systems or users. [from *robot*]

botany *noun* the study of plants. **botanical** *adjective*, **botanist** *noun* [from Greek *botane* = a plant]

botch *verb* spoil something by poor or clumsy work. **botch** *noun*

both[1] *adjective & pronoun* the two; not only one, *Both films are good; Both are old.*

both[2] *adverb* **both ... and** not only ... but also, *The house is both small and ugly.*

bother[1] *verb* **1** cause somebody trouble or worry; pester. **2** take trouble; feel concern, *Don't bother to reply.*

bother[2] *noun* trouble; worry.

Botox *noun* (*trademark*) a drug made from botulin, used medically to treat certain muscular conditions and cosmetically to remove wrinkles.

bottle[1] *noun* **1** a narrow-necked container for liquids. **2** (*informal*) courage.

bottle[2] *verb* (**bottled**, **bottling**) put or store in bottles.
bottle up conceal or restrain, especially a feeling.

bottlebrush *noun* **1** a cylindrical brush for washing bottles. **2** an Australian plant with flowers shaped like a cylindrical brush.

bottleneck *noun* a narrow place where something (especially traffic) cannot flow freely.

bottler *noun* (*Australian informal*) an admirable or unusual person or thing.

bottom[1] *noun* **1** the lowest part; the base. **2** the part furthest away, *the bottom of the garden.* **3** a person's buttocks.

bottom[2] *adjective* lowest, *the bottom shelf.*

bottomless *adjective* extremely deep.

botulin (*say* **bot**-shuh-luhn) *noun* a bacterial toxin involved in botulism.

botulism *noun* poisoning caused by a bacillus in badly preserved food.

boudoir (*say* **boo**-dwah) *noun* a woman's private room. [from French, = place to sulk in]

bough *noun* a large branch coming from the trunk of a tree.

bought *past tense & past participle* of **buy**[1].

boulder *noun* a very large smooth stone.

boulevard (*say* **boo**-luh-vahd) *noun* a wide street, often with trees. [French]

bounce[1] *verb* (**bounced, bouncing**) **1** spring back when thrown against something; cause to do this. **2** (*informal*, of a cheque) be sent back by the bank as worthless. **3** jump suddenly; move in a lively manner. **4** (*informal*, of an email) be returned to its sender after failing to reach its destination. **bouncer** *noun*

bounce[2] *noun* **1** the action or power of bouncing. **2** a lively confident manner, *full of bounce.* **bouncy** *adjective*

bound[1] *verb* jump or spring; run with jumping movements, *bounding along.*

bound[2] *noun* a bounding movement.

bound[3] *past tense & past participle* of **bind**[1].

bound[4] *adjective* obstructed or hindered by something, *We were fog-bound.*
bound to certain to, *He is bound to succeed.*
bound up with closely connected with, *Happiness is bound up with success.*

bound[5] *adjective* going towards something, *We are bound for Paris.*

bound[6] *verb* limit; be the boundary of, *Their land is bounded by the river.*

boundary *noun* (*plural* **boundaries**) **1** a line that marks a limit. **2** a hit to the boundary of a cricket field. [from *bound*[6]]

boundary rider *noun* (*Australian*) a person employed to ride around the fences of a cattle or sheep station and keep them in good order.

bounden *adjective* obligatory, *your bounden duty.* [from *bind*[1]]

boundless *adjective* unlimited.

bounds *plural noun* limits.
out of bounds where you are not allowed to go. [from *bound*[6]]

bountiful *adjective* **1** plentiful; abundant, *bountiful harvest.* **2** giving generously.

bounty *noun* (*plural* **bounties**) **1** a generous gift. **2** generosity in giving things. **3** a reward for doing something. [from Latin *bonitas* = goodness]

bouquet (*say* boo-**kay** or boh-**kay**) *noun* a bunch of flowers. [French, = group of trees]

bout *noun* **1** a boxing or wrestling contest. **2** a period of exercise or work or illness, *a bout of flu.*

boutique (*say* boo-**teek**) *noun* a small shop selling fashionable clothes. [French]

bovine (*say* **boh**-vuyn) *adjective* **1** of or like oxen. **2** dull and stupid. [from Latin *bovis* = of an ox]

bow[1] (*rhymes with* go) *noun* **1** a strip of wood curved by a tight string joining its ends, used for shooting arrows. **2** a wooden rod with horsehair stretched between its ends, used for playing the violin and other stringed instruments. **3** a knot made with loops.

bow[2] (*rhymes with* cow) *verb* **1** bend your body forwards to show respect or as a greeting. **2** bend downwards, *bowed by the weight.*

bow[3] *noun* bowing your body.

bow[4] (*rhymes with* cow) *noun* the front part of a ship.

bowel *noun* the intestine. [from Latin *botellus* = little sausage]

bower *noun* a leafy shelter.

bowerbird *noun* **1** an Australian bird that decorates its nest with feathers, shells, and other objects. **2** someone who collects and hoards things.

bowl[1] *noun* **1** a rounded usually deep container for food or liquid; this with its contents. **2** a rounded, concave part of an object, *a toilet bowl.*

bowl[2] *noun* a heavy ball used in the game of bowls.

bowl[3] *verb* **1** (in cricket) send a ball to be played by a batter; get a batter out by bowling. **2** send a ball rolling.

bow-legged *adjective* having bandy legs.

bowler[1] *noun* a person who bowls.

bowler[2] *noun* (also **bowler hat**) a stiff felt hat with a rounded top.

bowling *noun* the game of tenpin bowling or a similar game using skittles.

bowls *noun* a game played by rolling bowls towards a target (the *jack*).

bowser *noun* (*Australian*) a petrol pump.

bow tie *noun* a man's tie tied into a bow.

bow window *noun* a curved window.

bowyang *noun* (*Australian*) a string or narrow strap tied round a trouser leg below the knee.

box[1] *noun* (*plural* **boxes**) **1** a container with a flat base, usually with a top or lid. **2** a compartment in a theatre or lawcourt, *witness box.* **3** a hut or shelter, *sentry box.* **4** a small evergreen shrub. **5** an Australian tree with hard wood. **6** (*informal*) (**the box**) television.
out of the box (*Australian informal*) excellent.

box[2] *verb* put something into a box.

box[3] *verb* **1** fight with the fists. **2** slap, *box someone's ears.*

boxer *noun* a person who boxes.

Boxing Day *noun* the day after Christmas Day. [from the old custom of giving presents (*Christmas boxes*) to tradesmen and servants on that day]

box office *noun* **1** an office for booking seats at a theatre or cinema. **2** the commercial aspect of the arts and entertainment.

box plot *noun* (also **box-and-whisker plot**) a way of displaying statistical data by using a rectangle to represent quartiles, and usually with a vertical line within the rectangle to indicate the median.

boy *noun* **1** a male child, *There are more boys than girls in her school.* **2** a young man. **boyhood** *noun*, **boyish** *adjective*

boycott *verb* refuse to use or have anything to do with, *They boycotted the buses when the fares went up.* **boycott** *noun* [from the name of Captain Boycott, a harsh landlord in Ireland whose tenants in 1880 refused to deal with him]

boyfriend *noun* a person's regular male companion or lover.

bra *noun* a piece of underwear worn by women to support their breasts. [short for French *brassière*]

brace[1] *noun* **1** a device for holding things in place. **2** a pair, *a brace of pheasants.*

brace[2] *verb* (**braced**, **bracing**) support; make a thing firm against something. [from Latin *bracchia* = arms]

bracelet *noun* an ornament worn round the wrist. [same origin as *brace*]

braces *plural noun* straps to hold trousers up, passing over the shoulders.

bracing *adjective* invigorating.

bracken *noun* **1** a large fern. **2** a mass of ferns.

bracket[1] *noun* **1** a mark used in pairs to enclose words or figures, *There are round brackets ( ), square brackets [ ], and angle brackets < >.* **2** a support attached to a wall for holding a shelf or other object. **3** a group or range between certain limits, *a high income bracket.*

bracket[2] *verb* (**bracketed**, **bracketing**) **1** enclose in brackets. **2** put things together because they are similar.

brackish *adjective* (of water) slightly salty.

bract *noun* a leaf-like part of a plant that is often coloured like a petal.

brag *verb* (**bragged**, **bragging**) boast.

braggart *noun* a person who brags.

brahmin *noun* a member of the highest Hindu class, originally priests. [from Sanskrit *brahman* = priest]

braid[1] *noun* **1** a plait of hair. **2** a strip of cloth with a woven decorative pattern, used as trimming.

braid[2] *verb* **1** plait. **2** trim with braid.

braille *noun* a system of representing letters by raised dots that blind people can read by feeling them. [named after Louis Braille, a blind French teacher who invented it in about 1830]

brain *noun* **1** the organ inside the top of the head that controls the body. **2** the mind; intelligence.

brainwash *verb* force a person to give up one set of ideas or beliefs and accept new ones; indoctrinate.

brainwave *noun* a sudden bright idea.

brainy *adjective* clever; intelligent.

braise *verb* (**braised**, **braising**) cook slowly in a little liquid in a closed container. [from French *braise* = burning coals]

brake[1] *noun* a device for slowing or stopping something.

brake[2] *verb* (**braked**, **braking**) use a brake.

bramble *noun* a blackberry bush or a prickly bush like it.

bran *noun* ground-up husks of grain.

branch[1] *noun* (*plural* **branches**) **1** a woody arm-like part of a tree or shrub. **2** a part of a railway, road, or river etc. that leads off from the main part. **3** a shop or office etc. that belongs to a large organisation.

branch[2] *verb* form a branch.
branch out start something new. [from Latin *branca* = a paw]

branch stacking *noun* (*Australian*) improperly increasing the membership of a local branch of a political party in order to ensure the pre-selection of a particular candidate.

brand[1] *noun* **1** a particular make of goods. **2** a mark made by branding. **3** a piece of burning wood.

brand[2] *verb* **1** mark livestock with a hot iron to identify them. **2** sell goods under a particular trademark.

brandish *verb* wave something about.

brand-new *adjective* completely new.

brandy *noun* (*plural* **brandies**) a strong alcoholic drink. [from Dutch *brandewijn* = burnt (distilled) wine]

brash *adjective* **1** impudent. **2** reckless.

brass *noun* (*plural* **brasses**) **1** a metal that is an alloy of copper and zinc. **2** wind instruments made of brass, e.g. trumpets and trombones. **brass** *adjective*, **brassy** *adjective*

brat *noun* (usually *derogatory*) a child.

bravado (*say* bruh-**vah**-doh) *noun* a display of boldness. [from Spanish *bravata*]

brave[1] *adjective* **1** having or showing courage. **2** spectacular, *a brave show of poppies.* **bravely** *adverb*, **bravery** *noun*

brave[2] *noun* a warrior of a North American indigenous people.

brave[3] *verb* (**braved**, **braving**) face and endure something bravely.

bravo (*say* **brah**-voh) *interjection* well done!

brawl[1] *noun* a noisy quarrel or fight.

brawl[2] *verb* take part in a brawl.

brawn *noun* **1** muscular strength. **2** cold boiled pork or veal pressed in a mould.

brawny *adjective* strong and muscular.

bray *noun* the loud harsh cry of a donkey. **bray** *verb*

brazen[1] *adjective* **1** made of brass. **2** shameless, *brazen impudence.*

brazen[2] *verb* **brazen it out** behave as if there is nothing to be ashamed of when you know you have done wrong.

brazier (*say* **bray**-zee-uh) *noun* a metal framework for holding burning coals.

breach[1] *noun* (*plural* **breaches**) **1** the breaking of an agreement or rule. **2** a broken place; a gap.

breach[2] *verb* **1** break an agreement or rule. **2** break through; make a gap.

bread *noun* a food made by baking flour and water, usually with yeast.

breadth *noun* width; broadness.

breadwinner *noun* the member of a family who earns money to support the others.

break[1] *verb* (**broke**, **broken**, **breaking**) **1** divide or fall into pieces by hitting or pressing. **2** fail to keep a promise or law. **3** stop for a time; end, *She broke her silence.* **4** change, *The weather broke.* **5** damage; stop working properly. **6** (of waves) fall in foam. **7** go suddenly or with force, *They broke through.* **8** appear suddenly, *Dawn has broken.* **9** do better than, *break a record.* **breakage** *noun*
break down 1 stop working properly. **2** collapse.
break in 1 force one's way into a building. **2** accustom to a new routine. **break-in** *noun*
break out 1 begin suddenly. **2** escape.
break the news make something known.
break up 1 break into small parts. **2** separate at the end of a school term. **3** (of a couple) separate. **break-up** *noun*

break[2] *noun* **1** a broken place; a gap. **2** an escape; a sudden dash. **3** a short rest from work. **4** a number of points scored continuously in snooker or billiards. **5** (*informal*) a piece of luck; an opportunity.
break of day dawn.

breakable *adjective* able to be broken.

breakbeat *noun* **1** a sample of a syncopated drum beat. **2** (also **breaks**) dance music featuring breakbeats.

breakdancing *noun* an acrobatic style of street dancing. **breakdance** *noun*, **breakdancer** *noun*

breakdown *noun* **1** breaking down; failure. **2** a collapse of mental or physical health. **3** an analysis of accounts or statistics.

breaker *noun* a large wave breaking on the shore.

breakfast *noun* the first meal of the day. [from *break* + *fast*[3]]

breakneck *adjective* dangerously fast.

breakthrough *noun* an important advance or achievement.

breakwater *noun* a wall built out into the sea to protect a coast from heavy waves.

breakwind *noun* (*Australian*) an Aboriginal shelter; any temporary shelter.

bream (*say* brim) *noun* (*plural* **bream**) a kind of fish with an arched back.

breast *noun* **1** one of the two parts on the upper front of a woman's body that produce milk to feed a baby. **2** a person's or animal's chest.

breastbone *noun* the flat bone down the centre of the chest or breast.

breastplate *noun* a piece of armour covering the chest.

breaststroke *noun* a swimming stroke made by extending both arms forward and sweeping them back. **breaststroker** *noun*

breath (*say* breth) *noun* **1** air drawn into the lungs and sent out again. **2** a gentle blowing, *a breath of wind.*
out of breath panting.
take your breath away surprise or delight you greatly.
under your breath in a whisper.

breathalyser *noun* a device for measuring the amount of alcohol in a person's breath. **breathalyse** *verb* [from *breath* + *analyse*]

breathe (*say* bree*th*) *verb* (**breathed**, **breathing**) **1** take air into the body and send it out again. **2** speak; utter, *Don't breathe a word of this.*

breather (*say* **bree**-*th*uh) *noun* a pause for rest, *Let's take a breather.*

breathless *adjective* out of breath.

breathtaking *adjective* very surprising or delightful.

bred *past tense & past participle* of **breed**[1].

breech *noun* (*plural* **breeches**) the back part of a gun barrel, where the bullets are put in.
breech birth a birth in which the baby's buttocks or feet appear first.

breeches (*say* **brich**-uhz) *plural noun* trousers reaching to just below the knees.

breed[1] *verb* (**bred**, **breeding**) **1** produce young creatures. **2** keep animals so as to produce young ones from them. **3** bring up; train. **4** create; produce, *Poverty breeds illness.* **breeder** *noun*

breed[2] *noun* a variety of animals with qualities inherited from their parents.

breeze *noun* a wind. **breezy** *adjective*

brethren *plural noun* (*old use*) brothers.

breve (*say* breev) *noun* a note in music, equal to two semibreves in length.

brevity *noun* shortness; briefness.

brew[1] *verb* **1** make beer or tea. **2** develop, *Trouble is brewing.*

brew[2] *noun* a brewed drink.

brewer *noun* a person who brews beer for sale.

brewery *noun* (*plural* **breweries**) a place where beer is brewed.

briar *noun* **1** a thorny bush, especially the wild rose. **2** a hard root used especially for making tobacco pipes.

bribe[1] *noun* money or a gift offered to a person to influence them.

bribe[2] *verb* (**bribed**, **bribing**) give someone a bribe. **bribery** *noun*

brick[1] *noun* **1** a small hard block of baked or dried clay or other substance used to build walls. **2** a rectangular block of something.

brick[2] *verb* close something with bricks, *We bricked up the gap in the wall.*

bricklayer *noun* a worker who builds with bricks.

bride *noun* a woman on her wedding day. **bridal** *adjective* [from Old English *bryd*]

bridegroom *noun* a man on his wedding day.

bridesmaid *noun* a girl or unmarried woman who attends the bride at a wedding.

bridge[1] *noun* **1** a structure built over and across a river, railway, road, or other obstacle to allow people to cross it. **2** a high platform above a ship's deck, for the officer in charge. **3** the bony upper part of the nose. **4** something that connects things.

bridge[2] *verb* (**bridged**, **bridging**) make or form a bridge over something.

bridge[3] *noun* a card game for four players.

bridle *noun* the part of a horse's harness that fits over its head.

brie (*say* bree) *noun* a kind of soft cheese, originally from Brie in France.

brief[1] *adjective* short. **briefly** *adverb*, **briefness** *noun*
in brief in a few words.

brief[2] *noun* instructions and information given to someone, especially to a barrister.

brief[3] *verb* **1** give a brief to a barrister. **2** instruct or inform someone concisely in advance. [from Latin *brevis* = short]

briefcase *noun* a flat case for carrying documents.

briefing *noun* a meeting to give someone concise instructions or information.

briefs *plural noun* underpants.

brigade *noun* **1** a large unit of an army. **2** a group of people organised for a special purpose, *the fire brigade.* [from Italian *brigata* = a troop]

brigadier *noun* a brigade commander.

brigand *noun* a member of a band of robbers.

bright *adjective* **1** giving a strong light; shining. **2** (of colour) intense, strong. **3** sunny. **4** clever. **5** cheerful. **brightly** *adverb*, **brightness** *noun*

brighten *verb* **1** make or become brighter. **2** make or become more cheerful.

brilliant *adjective* **1** very bright; sparkling. **2** very clever. **brilliance** *noun*, **brilliantly** *adverb* [from Italian *brillare* = shine]

brim[1] *noun* **1** the edge of a cup, hollow, or channel. **2** the projecting edge of a hat.

brim[2] *verb* (**brimmed**, **brimming**) be full to the brim.
brim over overflow.

brimstone *noun* (*old use*) sulphur.

brine *noun* salt water. **briny** *adjective*

bring *verb* (**brought**, **bringing**) **1** cause a person or thing to come; lead; carry. **2** cause; result in.
bring about cause to happen.
bring off achieve; do something successfully.
bring up 1 look after and train growing children. **2** mention a subject. **3** vomit. **4** cause to stop suddenly.

brink *noun* **1** the edge of a steep place or of a stretch of water. **2** the point beyond which something will happen, *We were on the brink of war.*

bris *noun* a ceremony in which a Jewish baby boy is circumcised.

brisk *adjective* quick and lively. **briskly** *adverb*, **briskness** *noun*

bristle[1] *noun* **1** a short stiff hair. **2** one of the stiff pieces of hair, wire, or plastic in a brush. **bristly** *adjective*

bristle[2] *verb* (**bristled**, **bristling**) **1** (of an animal) raise its bristles in anger or fear. **2** show indignation.
bristle with be full of, *The plan bristled with problems.*

British *adjective* of Britain (the island containing England, Wales, and Scotland).

brittle *adjective* hard but easy to break or snap. **brittleness** *noun*

bro *noun* (*informal*) **1** brother. **2** a friendly greeting or form of address.

broach *verb* **1** make a hole in something and draw out liquid. **2** start a discussion of something, *They broached the subject.*

broad *adjective* **1** large across; wide. **2** full and complete, *broad daylight.* **3** in general terms; not detailed, *We are in broad agreement.* **4** strong and unmistakable, *a broad hint; a broad accent.* **broadly** *adverb*, **broadness** *noun*

broadband[1] *adjective* using signals over a broad range of frequencies, especially in telecommunications.

broadband[2] *noun* a high-speed network for the transmission of a range of frequencies including video and audio.

broad bean *noun* a bean with large flat seeds.

broadcast[1] *noun* a program sent out by radio or television.

broadcast[2] *verb* (**broadcast**, **broadcasting**) send out or take part in a broadcast. **broadcaster** *noun*

broaden *verb* make or become broader.

broad-minded *adjective* tolerant; not easily shocked.

broadside *noun* **1** firing by all guns on one side of a ship. **2** a verbal attack.

brocade *noun* material woven with raised patterns.

broccoli *noun* (*plural* **broccoli**) a kind of cauliflower with greenish flower heads. [Italian, = cabbage heads]

brochure (*say* **broh**-shuh) *noun* a booklet or pamphlet containing information, *travel brochures.* [from French, = stitching]

brogue (*rhymes with* rogue) *noun* **1** a strong kind of shoe. **2** a strong accent, *He spoke with an Irish brogue.*

broil *verb* **1** cook on a fire or gridiron. **2** make or be very hot. [from French *brûler* = to burn]

broke[1] *past tense* of **break**[1].

broke[2] *adjective* (*informal*) having spent all your money; bankrupt.

broken *past participle* of **break**[1].

broken-hearted *adjective* overwhelmed with grief.

broker *noun* a person who buys and sells things for other people. **brokerage** *noun*

brolga *noun* a large grey Australian crane with a red patch on the head. [from Gamilaraay and neighbouring languages *burraalga*]

bronchial (*say* **brong**-kee-uhl) *adjective* of the tubes that lead from the windpipe to the lungs. [from Greek *bronchos* = windpipe]

bronchitis (*say* brong-**kuy**-tuhs) *noun* a disease with inflammation of the bronchial tubes.

brontosaurus (*plural* **brontosauruses**) another name for **apatosaurus**. [from Greek *bronte* = thunder, + *sauros* = lizard]

bronze *noun* **1** a metal that is an alloy of copper and tin. **2** something made of bronze; a bronze medal, usually given as third prize. **3** yellowish-brown. **bronze** *adjective*

Bronze Age *noun* the time when tools and weapons were made of bronze.

bronzewing *noun* an Australian pigeon with bronze markings on the wings.

brooch (*rhymes with* coach) *noun* (*plural* **brooches**) an ornament with a hinged pin for fastening it on to clothes.

brood[1] *noun* young birds that were hatched together.

brood[2] *verb* **1** sit on eggs to hatch them. **2** keep thinking about something, especially with resentment.

broody *adjective* **1** (of a hen) wanting to sit on eggs. **2** thoughtful; brooding.

brook[1] *noun* a small stream.

brook[2] *verb* tolerate, *brook no delay.*

broom *noun* **1** a brush with a long handle, for sweeping. **2** a shrub with yellow, white, or pink flowers.

broomstick *noun* a broom handle.

broth *noun* a kind of thin soup.

brothel *noun* a house in which women work as prostitutes.

brother *noun* **1** a son of the same parents as another person, *She has two older brothers.* **2** a male friend or associate. **3** a man who is a fellow member of a church, trade union, or other organisation. **brotherhood** *noun*, **brotherly** *adjective* [from Old English *brothor*]

brother-in-law *noun* (*plural* **brothers-in-law**) the brother of a married person's spouse; the husband of a person's sibling.

brought *past tense & past participle* of **bring**.

brow *noun* **1** an eyebrow. **2** the forehead. **3** the ridge at the top of a hill; the edge of a cliff.

brown[1] *noun* a colour between orange and black.

brown[2] *adjective* **1** of the colour brown. **2** having a brown skin; suntanned.

brown[3] *verb* make or become brown.

brownie *noun* **1** a small square of chocolate cake with nuts. **2** (**Brownie**) a member of a junior branch of the Guides.

browse *verb* (**browsed**, **browsing**) **1** feed on grass or leaves. **2** read or look at something casually.

browser *noun* **1** a web browser. **2** a person or animal that browses.

bruise[1] *noun* a dark mark made on the skin by hitting it.

bruise[2] *verb* (**bruised**, **bruising**) give or get a bruise or bruises.

brumby *noun* (*Australian*) a wild or partly tamed horse.

brunch *noun* (*informal*) a meal combining breakfast and lunch.

brunette *noun* a woman with dark brown hair. [from French *brun* = brown]

brunt *noun* the chief impact or strain, *They bore the brunt of the attack.*

bruschetta (*say* bruus-**ket**-uh or bruh-**shet**-uh) *noun* toasted Italian bread drenched in olive oil.

brush[1] *noun* (*plural* **brushes**) **1** an implement used for cleaning or painting things or for smoothing the hair, usually with pieces of hair, wire, or plastic set in a solid base. **2** a fox's bushy tail. **3** brushing, *Give it a good brush.* **4** a short fight, *They had a brush with the enemy.* **5** (*Australian*) dense forest; scrub.

brush[2] *verb* **1** use a brush on something. **2** touch gently in passing.
brush aside dismiss a person or idea lightly.
brush up revise a subject.

brusque (*say* bruusk) *adjective* curt and offhand in manner. **brusquely** *adverb* [from Italian *brusco* = sour]

Brussels sprouts *plural noun* the edible buds of a kind of cabbage. [named after Brussels, the capital of Belgium]

brutal *adjective* very cruel. **brutality** *noun*, **brutally** *adverb*

brute *noun* **1** a brutal person. **2** an animal. **brutish** *adjective* [from Latin *brutus* = stupid]

bubble[1] *noun* **1** a thin transparent ball of liquid filled with air or gas. **2** a small ball of air in something.

bubble[2] *verb* (**bubbled**, **bubbling**) **1** send up bubbles; rise in bubbles. **2** show great liveliness.

bubble gum *noun* chewing gum that can be blown into large bubbles.

bubbler *noun* (*Australian*) a drinking fountain.

bubbly *adjective* **1** full of bubbles. **2** lively, *a bubbly personality.*

bubonic plague *noun* a contagious disease with inflamed swellings in the groin or armpit. [from Latin *bubo* = a swelling]

buccaneer *noun* a pirate.

buck[1] *noun* a male deer, rabbit, or hare.

buck[2] *verb* **1** (of a horse) jump with its back arched. **2** oppose, resist.
buck up (*informal*) **1** hurry. **2** cheer up.

buck[3] *noun* an object used in the game of poker to show whose turn it is.
pass the buck (*informal*) pass the responsibility for something to another person.

buck[4] *noun* (*informal*) a dollar.

bucket[1] *noun* **1** a container with a handle, for carrying especially liquids. **2** (*Australian*) a carton for ice cream, chips, etc.
bucketful *noun*

bucket[2] *verb* (*Australian*) condemn, criticise.

buckle[1] *noun* a device through which a belt or strap is threaded to fasten it.

buckle[2] *verb* (**buckled**, **buckling**) **1** fasten with a buckle. **2** bend or crumple.
buckle down to start working hard at.

buckler *noun* a small round shield.

Buckley's *noun* (*Australian*) (in full **Buckley's chance**) no chance at all.

buck's party *noun* (*Australian*) (also **buck's night**) an all-male celebration for a man about to marry.

bucolic (*say* byoo-**kol**-ik) *adjective* of country life. [from Greek *boukolos* = herdsman]

bud *noun* a flower or leaf before it opens.

Buddhism (*say* **buud**-iz-uhm) *noun* a faith that started in Asia and follows the teachings of the Indian philosopher Gautama Buddha, who lived in the 5th century BC. **Buddhist** *noun* [from Sanskrit *Buddha* = enlightened one]

budding *adjective* beginning to develop.

buddy *noun* (*plural* **buddies**) (*informal*) a friend.

budge *verb* (**budged**, **budging**) move slightly.

budgerigar (*say* **buj**-uh-ree-gah) *noun* a small Australian parrot, often kept as a pet in a cage. [probably an alteration of

Gamilaraay (and related languages) *gidjirrigaa*]

budget[1] *noun* **1** an estimate of income and expenditure for a set period of time, *the weekly household budget.* **2** (**the Budget**) the government's annual estimate or plan of revenue and expenditure.

budget[2] *verb* (**budgeted**, **budgeting**) plan a budget.

budgie *noun* (*informal*) a budgerigar.

buff[1] *noun* **1** a dull yellow colour. **2** (*informal*) an enthusiast, *film buffs.*

buff[2] *verb* polish with soft material.

buff[3] *adjective* (*informal*) in good physical shape; muscular.

buffalo *noun* (*plural* **buffalo** or **buffaloes**) a wild ox with long curved horns.

buffer *noun* something that softens a blow, especially a device on a railway engine or wagon or at the end of a track.

buffet[1] (*say* **buf**-ay) *noun* **1** a refreshment counter. **2** a meal where guests serve themselves. **3** a sideboard. [from French, = stool]

buffet[2] (*say* **buf**-uht) *noun* a hit, especially with the hand. [from Old French *buffe* = a blow]

buffet[3] *verb* (**buffeted**, **buffeting**) hit, knock, *Strong winds buffeted the aircraft.*

buffoon *noun* a clown; a person who plays the fool. **buffoonery** *noun* [from Latin *buffo* = clown]

bug[1] *noun* **1** an insect. **2** (*informal*) a germ or microbe. **3** (*informal*) a secret hidden microphone. **4** (*informal*) an error in a computer program or system.

bug[2] *verb* (**bugged**, **bugging**) (*informal*) **1** fit with a secret hidden microphone. **2** annoy.

bugbear *noun* something you fear or dislike. [from an old word *bug* = bogy]

buggy *noun* (*plural* **buggies**) **1** (*old use*) a light horse-drawn carriage. **2** a small strong vehicle.

bugle *noun* a brass instrument like a small trumpet, used for sounding military signals. **bugler** *noun*

build[1] *verb* (**built**, **building**) make something by putting parts together.
build in include. **built-in** *adjective*
build up 1 establish gradually. **2** accumulate. **3** cover an area with buildings. **4** make stronger or more famous, *build up a reputation.* **built-up** *adjective*

build[2] *noun* the shape of someone's body, *of slender build.*

builder *noun* someone who puts up buildings.

building *noun* **1** the process of constructing something. **2** a permanent built structure that people can go into.

building society *noun* an organisation that accepts deposits of money and lends to people who want to buy or make improvements to houses.

bulb *noun* **1** a thick rounded part of a plant from which a stem grows up and roots grow down. **2** a rounded part of something, *the bulb of a thermometer.* **3** a glass globe that produces electric light. **bulbous** *adjective*

bulge[1] *noun* a rounded swelling; an outward curve. **bulgy** *adjective*

bulge[2] *verb* (**bulged**, **bulging**) form or cause to form a bulge.

bulgur *noun* (also **bulghur**) wheat grains that have been partly boiled and dried, so that they only need to be soaked before being eaten.

bulimia (*say* buh-**lim**-ee-uh) *noun* an eating disorder in which a person overeats and then induces vomiting.

bulk[1] *noun* **1** the size of something, especially when it is large. **2** the greater portion; the majority, *The bulk of the population voted for it.*
in bulk in large amounts.

bulk[2] *verb* increase the size or thickness of something, *bulk it out.*

bulky *adjective* (**bulkier**, **bulkiest**) taking up much space. **bulkiness** *noun*

bull *noun* the fully grown male of cattle or of certain other large animals (e.g. elephant, whale, seal). (Compare **cow[1]**.)

bull ant *noun* a large Australian ant with a painful sting.

bullbar *noun* a heavy metal grid on the front of a vehicle to reduce damage in the case of a collision.

bulldog *noun* a dog of a powerful courageous breed with a short thick neck.

bulldoze *verb* (**bulldozed**, **bulldozing**) clear with a bulldozer.

bulldozer *noun* a powerful tractor with a wide metal blade or scoop in front, used for shifting soil or clearing ground.

bulldust *noun* (*Australian*) **1** fine dust on outback roads. **2** (*informal*) nonsense.

bullet *noun* a small lump of metal shot from a rifle or revolver.

bulletin *noun* a public statement giving news.

bulletin board system *noun* an information storage system for computer users to access and add to from a remote terminal.

bulletproof *adjective* able to keep out bullets.

bullfight *noun* a public entertainment in which bulls are tormented and killed in an arena. **bullfighter** *noun*

bullfrog *noun* a large frog with a booming croak.

bullion *noun* bars of gold or silver.

bullock *noun* a castrated bull.

bullocky *noun* (*Australian informal*) a driver of a team of bullocks.

bullroarer *noun* (*Australian*) a flat strip of wood on a string making a whirring sound when whirled around, used especially in traditional Aboriginal ceremony and ritual.

bullseye *noun* the centre of a target.

bully[1] *verb* (**bullied, bullying**) **1** persecute or oppress by force or threats. **2** start play in hockey, when two opponents tap the ground and each other's stick, *bully off.*

bully[2] *noun* (*plural* **bullies**) someone who bullies people.

bulrush *noun* (*plural* **bulrushes**) a tall rush with a thick velvety head.

bulwark *noun* a wall of earth built as a defence; a protection.

bulwarks *plural noun* a ship's side above the level of the deck.

bum *noun* (*informal*) a person's bottom.

bumble *verb* (**bumbled, bumbling**) **1** move or behave clumsily. **2** speak in a rambling way.

bumblebee *noun* a large bee with a loud hum.

bump[1] *verb* **1** knock against something. **2** move along with jolts.
bump into (*informal*) meet by chance.
bump off (*informal*) kill.

bump[2] *noun* **1** the action or sound of bumping. **2** a swelling or lump.
bumpy *adjective*

bumper[1] *noun* **1** (also **bumper bar**) a bar along the front or back of a motor vehicle to protect it in collisions. **2** a ball in cricket that bounces high.

bumper[2] *adjective* unusually large or plentiful, *a bumper crop.*

bumpkin *noun* a country person with awkward manners.

bumptious (*say* **bump**-shuhs) *adjective* conceited, self-assertive.
bumptiousness *noun*

bun *noun* **1** a small round sweet cake. **2** hair twisted into a rounded bunch at the back of the head.

bunch *noun* (*plural* **bunches**) **1** a number of things joined or fastened together. **2** (*informal*) a group; a gang.

bundle[1] *noun* a number of things tied or wrapped together.

bundle[2] *verb* (**bundled, bundling**) **1** make into a bundle. **2** push hurriedly or carelessly, *They bundled him into a taxi.*

bung[1] *noun* a stopper for closing a hole in a barrel or jar.

bung[2] *verb* (*informal*) throw, *Bung it here.*
bunged up (*informal*) blocked.

bung[3] *adjective* (*Australian informal*) broken down, useless.
go bung break down; go bankrupt. [from Yagara *bang* = old, dead]

bungalow *noun* a one-storeyed house. [from Hindi *bangla* = of Bengal]

bungee (*say* **bun**-jee) *noun* an elasticated cord used for securing baggage and in bungee jumping.

bungee jumping *noun* the sport of jumping from a height attached to a bungee.

bungle *verb* (**bungled, bungling**) do something unsuccessfully; spoil by being clumsy. **bungle** *noun*, **bungler** *noun*

bunion *noun* a swelling at the side of the joint where the big toe joins the foot.

bunk[1] *noun* a bed built like a shelf.

bunk[2] *noun* **do a bunk** (*informal*) run away.

bunker *noun* **1** a container for storing fuel. **2** a sandy hollow built as an obstacle on a golf course. **3** an underground shelter.

bunny *noun* (*plural* **bunnies**) (*informal*) a rabbit. [from dialect *bun* = rabbit]

Bunsen burner *noun* a small gas burner used in scientific work as a source of heat. [named after Robert Bunsen, a German chemist]

bunting[1] *noun* a kind of small bird.

bunting[2] *noun* strips of cloth hung up to decorate streets and buildings.

bunyip *noun* a mythical Australian monster living in swamps and billabongs. [from Wathaurong *banyip*]

buoy[1] (*say* boi) *noun* (*plural* **buoys**) a floating object anchored to indicate a navigable channel, showing the position of submerged rocks or other hazards, or for mooring.

buoy[2] *verb* **1** keep something afloat. **2** hearten; cheer, *They were buoyed up with new hope.*

buoyant (*say* **boi**-uhnt) *noun* **1** able to float. **2** light-hearted; cheerful. **buoyancy** *noun*, **buoyantly** *adverb*

burble *verb* (**burbled, burbling**) make a gentle murmuring sound. **burble** *noun*

burden[1] *noun* **1** something carried; a heavy load. **2** something troublesome that you have to bear, *the burden of taxation.*
burdensome *adjective*
burden of proof the obligation to prove one's case.

burden[2] *verb* **1** load; put a burden on. **2** oppress.

bureau (*say* **byoo**-roh) *noun* (*plural* **bureaux**) **1** a writing desk. **2** an office or department, *the weather bureau.* [French, = desk]

bureaucracy (*say* byoo-**rok**-ruh-see) *noun* (*plural* **bureaucracies**) **1** government by officials, not by elected representatives. **2** too much official routine. **bureaucratic** (*say* byoo-ruh-**krat**-ik) *adjective* [from *bureau* + *-cracy*]

bureaucrat (*say* **byoo**-ruh-krat) *noun* an official of a bureaucracy.

burgeon (*say* **ber**-juhn) *verb* grow rapidly.

burger *noun* a hamburger.

burglar *noun* a person who enters a building illegally, especially in order to steal things. **burglary** *noun*

burgle *verb* (**burgled**, **burgling**) rob a place as a burglar.

burgundy *noun* a red or white wine from Burgundy in France.

burial *noun* burying somebody.

burka *noun* (also **burqa**) a garment covering the entire body, worn by some Muslim women.

burlesque (*say* ber-**lesk**) *noun* a comical imitation.

burly *adjective* (**burlier**, **burliest**) with a strong heavy body; sturdy.

burn[1] *verb* (**burned** or **burnt**, **burning**) **1** blaze or glow with fire; produce heat or light by combustion. **2** damage or destroy something by fire, heat, or chemicals. **3** be damaged or destroyed by fire, heat, or chemicals. **4** feel very hot. **5** record data on (a CD or DVD).

> **Usage** The word *burnt* (not *burned*) is always used when an adjective is required, e.g. in *burnt wood*. As parts of the verb, either *burned* or *burnt* may be used, e.g. *the wood had burned* or *had burnt completely*.

burn[2] *noun* **1** a mark or injury made by burning. **2** the firing of a spacecraft's rockets.

burner *noun* the part of a lamp or cooker that gives out the flame.

burning *adjective* **1** intense, *a burning ambition.* **2** very important; hotly discussed, *a burning question.*

burnish *verb* polish by rubbing.

burp *verb* bring up wind from the stomach through the mouth. **burp** *noun*

burr *noun* **1** a plant's seed case or flower that clings to hair or clothes. **2** a whirring sound.

burrito (*say* buh-**ree**-toh) *noun* (*plural* **burritos**) a Mexican dish consisting of a tortilla rolled around a savoury filling. [Latin American Spanish]

burrow[1] *noun* a hole or tunnel dug by an animal such as a rabbit or wombat as a dwelling.

burrow[2] *verb* **1** dig a burrow. **2** push your way through or into something; search deeply, *She burrowed in her handbag.*

bursar *noun* a person who manages the finances and other business of a school or college. [from Latin *bursa* = a bag]

bursary *noun* a grant given to a student.

burst[1] *verb* (**burst, bursting**) **1** break or force apart. **2** come or start suddenly, *It burst into flame. They burst out laughing.* **3** be very full, *bursting with energy.*

burst[2] *noun* **1** bursting; a split. **2** something short and forceful, *a burst of gunfire.*

bury *verb* (**buried, burying**) **1** place a dead body in the earth, a tomb, or the sea. **2** put underground; cover up.
bury the hatchet agree to stop quarrelling or fighting.

bus *noun* (*plural* **buses**) a large vehicle for passengers to travel in. [short for *omnibus*]

bush *noun* (*plural* **bushes**) **1** a shrub. **2** wild uncultivated land, especially in Australia and Africa. **3** (**the bush**) (*Australian*) the country, as opposed to the city.
bushy *adjective*

bushel *noun* a measure for grain and fruit.

bushfire *noun* a dangerous outbreak of fire in uncleared or forest land.

bushfire plan *noun* (also **bushfire survival plan**) (*Australian*) a plan that outlines what you should do if threatened by bushfire.

bushie *noun* (*Australian*) a person who lives in the country.

bushman *noun* (*Australian*) **1** a person who is skilled in travelling and surviving in the bush. **2** a person who lives in the bush.

bushranger *noun* (*Australian*) (in former times) a person who committed armed robbery, escaping into, or living in the bush.

bush telegraph *noun* (*Australian*) unofficial circulation of news; the grapevine.

bushwalk *noun* (*Australian*) a hike in the bush.

bushwalker *noun* (*Australian*) a person hiking in the bush. **bushwalking** *noun*

busily *adverb* in a busy way.

business (*say* **biz**-nuhs) *noun* (*plural* **businesses**) **1** a person's concern or responsibilities, *Mind your own business.* **2** a person's occupation. **3** an affair or subject, *I'm tired of the whole business.* **4** a commercial operation or company; a shop. **5** buying and selling things; trade. **6** (*Australian*) (in Aboriginal English) traditional lore and ritual.

businesslike *adjective* practical; well-organised.

busker *noun* a person who entertains people in the street. **busk** *verb* [from an old word *busk* = be a pedlar]

bust[1] *noun* **1** a sculpture of a person's head, shoulders, and chest. **2** the upper front part of a woman's body.

bust[2] *verb* (**bust, busting**) (*informal*) burst.
go bust (*informal*) become bankrupt.

bustard *noun* a large bird that can run very swiftly.

bustle[1] *verb* (**bustled, bustling**) hurry in a busy or excited way.

bustle[2] *noun* hurried or excited activity.

bustle[3] *noun* padding used to puff out the top of a long skirt at the back.

busy[1] *adjective* (**busier, busiest**) **1** having much to do; occupied. **2** full of activity.
busily *adverb*, **busyness** *noun*

busy[2] *verb* (**busied, busying**) **busy yourself** occupy yourself; keep busy.

busybody *noun* (*plural* **busybodies**) a person who interferes.

but[1] *conjunction* however; nevertheless, *I wanted to go, but I couldn't.*

but[2] *preposition* except, *There is no one here but me.*

but[3] *adverb* only; no more than, *We can but try.*

butane *noun* a flammable gas produced from petroleum, used in liquid form as a fuel.

butch *adjective* (*informal*) tough-looking; masculine.

butcher[1] *noun* **1** a person who cuts up meat and sells it. **2** a person who kills cruelly or needlessly. **butchery** *noun*

butcher[2] *verb* kill cruelly or needlessly.

butler *noun* the chief male servant of a household, in charge of the wine cellar. [from Old French *bouteillier* = bottler]

butt[1] *noun* **1** the thicker end of a weapon or tool. **2** a stub, *cigarette butts.* [from Dutch *bot* = stumpy]

butt[2] *noun* a large cask or barrel. [from Latin *buttis* = cask]

butt[3] *noun* **1** a person or thing that is a target for ridicule or teasing, *He was the butt of their jokes.* **2** a mound of earth behind the targets on a shooting range. [from Old French *but* = goal]

butt[4] *verb* **1** push or hit with the head as a ram or goat does. **2** place the edges of things together.
butt in interrupt; intrude; meddle. [from Old French *buter* = hit]

butter[1] *noun* a soft fatty food made by churning cream. **buttery** *adjective*

butter[2] *verb* spread with butter.
butter up (*informal*) flatter somebody.

buttercup *noun* a wild plant with bright yellow cup-shaped flowers.

butterfingers *noun* a person who often drops things.

butterflies *plural noun* (*informal*) a nervous feeling.

butterfly *noun* (*plural* **butterflies**) **1** an insect with large white or coloured wings. **2** a swimming stroke in which both arms are lifted at the same time.

buttermilk *noun* the liquid that is left after butter has been made.

butternut *noun* a pear-shaped pumpkin.

butterscotch *noun* a kind of hard toffee.

buttock *noun* either of the two fleshy rounded parts at the lower end of the back.

button[1] *noun* **1** a knob or disc sewn on clothes as a fastening or ornament. **2** a small knob, *Press the button.*

button[2] *verb* fasten with a button or buttons.

buttonhole[1] *noun* **1** a slit through which a button passes to fasten clothes. **2** a flower worn on a lapel.

buttonhole[2] *verb* (**buttonholed, buttonholing**) attract the attention of and detain someone in conversation, typically against their will.

buttress *noun* (*plural* **buttresses**) a support built against a wall. **buttress** *verb* [same origin as *butt*[4]]

buxom *adjective* plump and healthy-looking.

buy[1] *verb* (**bought, buying**) get something by paying for it. **buyer** *noun*

buy[2] *noun* something bought; a purchase.

buzz *noun* (*plural* **buzzes**) **1** a vibrating humming sound. **2** (*informal*) a telephone call. **3** (*informal*) a thrill. **buzz** *verb*

buzzard *noun* a kind of hawk.

buzzer *noun* a device that makes a buzzing sound as a signal.

by[1] *preposition* This word is used to show **1** closeness (*Sit by me*), **2** direction or route (*We got here by a short cut*), **3** time (*They came by night*), **4** manner or method (*cooking by gas*), **5** amount (*You missed it by centimetres*).
by the way incidentally.
by yourself alone; without help.

by[2] *adverb* **1** past, *I can't get by.* **2** in reserve; for future use, *Put it by.*
by and by soon; later on.
by and large on the whole.

bye *noun* **1** a run scored in cricket when the ball goes past the batter without being touched. **2** having no opponent for one round in a tournament.

bye-bye *interjection* goodbye.

by-election *noun* an election to replace a Member of Parliament who has died or resigned.

bygone *adjective* belonging to the past.
let bygones be bygones forgive and forget.

by-law *noun* a regulation made by a local government authority.

bypass[1] *noun* (*plural* **bypasses**) **1** a main road taking traffic past a town or its centre. **2** a channel that allows something to flow when the main route is blocked. **3** a surgical operation to redirect the flow of blood away from a damaged part of the heart.

bypass[2] *verb* avoid by means of a bypass.

by-product *noun* something produced while something else is being made.

bystander *noun* a person standing near but not taking part in something.

byte *noun* a fixed number of bits (= binary digits) in a computer, often representing a single character.

byway *noun* a minor road.

byword *noun* **1** a person or thing spoken of as a famous example, *Their firm became a byword for quality.* **2** a proverb.

C c

C *abbreviation* Celsius; centigrade.

c *abbreviation* (also **c.**) **1** century. **2** circa. **3** cent(s).

cab *noun* **1** a taxi. **2** a compartment for the driver of a truck, train, bus, or crane. **first cab off the rank** (*Australian informal*) the first person to do or get something.

cabaret (*say* **kab**-uh-ray) *noun* an entertainment, especially one provided for the customers in a restaurant or nightclub. [French, = tavern]

cabbage *noun* a vegetable with green or purple leaves.

cabbage tree *noun* an Australian palm with large fan-shaped leaves.

cabbala alternative spelling of **kabbala**.

cabernet sauvignon (*say* kab-uh-nay **soh**-vin-yon) *noun* a variety of black grape; the red wine made from this. [French]

cabin *noun* **1** a hut or shelter. **2** a compartment in a ship, aircraft, or spacecraft. **3** a driver's cab.

cabinet *noun* **1** a cupboard or container with drawers or shelves. **2** (**Cabinet**) the group of chief ministers, chosen by the prime minister, who meet to decide government policy.

cable *noun* **1** a thick rope of fibre or wire; a thick chain. **2** a set of insulated wires for carrying electricity or electronic signals. **3** a telegram sent overseas.

cable television *noun* pay television.

cacao (*say* kuh-**kay**-oh) *noun* (*plural* **cacaos**) a tropical tree with a seed from which cocoa and chocolate are made.

cache (*say* kash) *noun* **1** hidden stores of treasure. **2** a hiding place for treasure or stores. **3** (*say* kaysh) an area of fast memory in a computer where copies of data are stored so that they can be retrieved quickly. [from French *cacher* = hide]

cackle *noun* **1** the loud clucking noise a hen makes. **2** a loud silly laugh. **3** noisy chatter. **cackle** *verb*

cacophony (*say* kuh-**kof**-uh-nee) *noun* a loud harsh unpleasant sound. **cacophonous** *adjective* [from Greek *kakos* = bad, + *phone* = sound]

cactus *noun* (*plural* **cacti**) a fleshy plant, usually with prickles, from a hot dry climate.

cad *noun* a dishonourable person.

cadaverous (*say* kuh-**dav**-uh-ruhs) *adjective* pale and gaunt. [from Latin *cadaver* = corpse]

caddie *noun* (also **caddy**) a person who carries a golfer's clubs during a game.

caddy *noun* (*plural* **caddies**) a small box or tin for holding tea.

cadence (*say* **kay**-duhns) *noun* **1** rhythm; the rise and fall of the voice in speaking. **2** the final notes of a musical phrase.

cadenza (*say* kuh-**den**-zuh) *noun* an elaborate passage for a solo instrument or singer, to show the performer's skill.

cadet *noun* a young person being trained for the armed forces, the police, or journalism. **cadetship** *noun*

cadge *verb* (**cadged**, **cadging**) get something by begging for it. **cadger** *noun*

cadmium *noun* a metal that looks like tin.

Caesarean section (*say* suh-**zair**-ree-uhn) *noun* a surgical operation for taking a baby alive out of the mother's womb. [so called because Julius Caesar is said to have been born in this way]

café (*say* **kaf**-ay) *noun* (also **cafe**) a small restaurant. [French, = coffee]

cafeteria (*say* kaf-uh-**teer**-ree-uh) *noun* a self-service restaurant.

caffeine (*say* **kaf**-een) *noun* a stimulant substance found in tea and coffee.

caffe latte (*say* kaf-ay **lah**-tay) see **latte**.

caftan *noun* a long loose coat or dress.

cage *noun* **1** a container with bars or wires, in which birds or animals are kept. **2** the enclosed platform of a lift. **caged** *adjective*

cagey *adjective* (**cagier**, **cagiest**) (*informal*) cautious about giving information, secretive. **cagily** *adverb*

cairn *noun* a pile of loose stones set up as a landmark or monument.

cajole *verb* (**cajoled**, **cajoling**) coax. **cajolery** *noun*

cake[1] *noun* **1** a baked food typically made from a mixture of flour, fat, eggs, sugar, and other ingredients, *I like chocolate cake more than orange cake.* **2** a shaped or hardened mass, *a cake of soap; fish cakes.*

cake² *verb* **1** harden into a compact mass. **2** encrust with a hardened mass.

calamari *noun* (*plural* **calamari**) a squid used as food.

calamine *noun* a pink powder used to make a soothing lotion for the skin.

calamity *noun* (*plural* **calamities**) a disaster. **calamitous** *adjective*

calcium *noun* a chemical substance found in teeth, bones, and lime. [from Latin *calcis* = of lime]

calculate *verb* (**calculated, calculating**) **1** find out by using mathematics; count. **2** plan something deliberately; intend. **calculable** *adjective*, **calculating** *adjective*, **calculation** *noun*

calculator *noun* a small electronic device for making calculations.

calculus *noun* mathematics for working out problems about rates of change. [from Latin *calculus* = small stone (used on an abacus)]

calendar *noun* a chart or series of pages showing the days, weeks, and months of a particular year, or giving particular seasonal information.

calf¹ *noun* (*plural* **calves**) the young of cattle, also of the elephant, whale, and certain other animals.

calf² *noun* (*plural* **calves**) the fleshy back part of the leg below the knee.

calibre (*say* **kal**-uh-buh) *noun* **1** the diameter of a tube or gun barrel, or of a bullet or shell. **2** ability; importance, *someone of your calibre.* [from Arabic *kalib* = mould]

calicivirus (*say* kuh-**lee**-see-vuy-ruhs) *noun* a virus that causes influenza in cats, and can kill rabbits.

calico *noun* a kind of cotton cloth. [from Calicut, a town in India]

caliph (*say* **kay**-luhf) *noun* the former title of the ruler in certain Muslim countries. [from Arabic *khalifa* = successor of Muhammad]

call¹ *noun* **1** a shout or cry. **2** a visit. **3** a summons. **4** telephoning somebody. **5** a need; reason, *no call for you to worry.*

call² *verb* **1** shout or speak loudly, e.g. to attract someone's attention; utter a call, *I called goodbye as I ran out of the house.* **2** tell somebody to come to you; summon. **3** wake a person up. **4** telephone somebody, *I'll call you at the weekend.* **5** make a short visit. **6** name a person or thing. **7** (*Australian*) describe a race for a broadcast. **caller** *noun*

call a person's bluff challenge a person to do what was threatened, and expose the fact that it was a bluff.

call for 1 come and collect. **2** require, *The scandal calls for investigation.*

call up summon to join the armed forces.

call centre *noun* an office in which a large number of telephone calls are handled.

calligraphy (*say* kuh-**lig**-ruh-fee) *noun* beautiful handwriting. [from Greek *kalos* = beautiful, + *-graphy*]

calling *noun* an occupation; a profession or trade.

calliper *noun* a support for a weak or injured leg.

callipers *plural noun* compasses for measuring the width of tubes or of round objects.

callous (*say* **kal**-uhs) *adjective* hard-hearted; unsympathetic. **callously** *adverb*, **callousness** *noun*

callow *adjective* immature and inexperienced. **callowly** *adverb*, **callowness** *noun*

callus *noun* (*plural* **calluses**) a small patch of skin that has become thick and hard through being continually pressed or rubbed.

calm¹ *adjective* **1** quiet and still; not windy. **2** not excited or agitated. **calm** *noun*, **calmly** *adverb*, **calmness** *noun*

calm² *verb* make or become calm.

calorie *noun* a unit for measuring an amount of heat or the energy produced by food. **calorific** *adjective* [from Latin *calor* = heat]

calumny (*say* **kal**-uhm-nee) *noun* (*plural* **calumnies**) slander.

calve *verb* (**calved, calving**) give birth to a calf.

calypso *noun* (*plural* **calypsos**) a West Indian song about current happenings.

calyx (*say* **kay**-liks) *noun* (*plural* **calyces**) a ring of leaves (**sepals**) forming the outer case of a bud.

calzone (*say* kal-**zoh**-nee) *noun* (*plural* **calzoni** or **calzones**) a type of pizza that is folded in half before cooking.

camaraderie (*say* kam-uh-**rah**-duh-ree) *noun* comradeship. [French]

camber *noun* a slight upward curve or arch, e.g. on a road to allow drainage.

cambric *noun* thin linen or cotton cloth.

came *past tense* of **come**.

camel *noun* a large animal with a long neck and either one or two humps on its back, used in desert countries for riding and for carrying goods.

camellia *noun* a kind of evergreen flowering shrub.

camembert (*say* **cam**-uhm-bair) *noun* a soft cheese originally made near Camembert in Normandy, France.

cameo (*say* **kam**-ee-oh) *noun* (*plural* **cameos**) **1** a small hard piece of stone carved with a raised design in its upper layer. **2** something small but well executed, especially a small character part in a play or film, played by a distinguished actor.

camera *noun* a device for taking photographs, films, or television pictures.
cameraman *noun*
in camera 1 in a judge's private room. **2** in private. [from Latin]

camisole *noun* a woman's undergarment or top, usually having narrow shoulder straps.

camomile *noun* a plant with sweet-smelling daisy-like flowers.

camouflage[1] (*say* **kam**-uh-flah*zh*) *noun* a way of hiding things by making them look like part of their surroundings.

camouflage[2] *verb* (**camouflaged**, **camouflaging**) hide by camouflage. [from French *camoufler* = disguise]

camp[1] *noun* a place where people live temporarily in tents, huts, or similar shelters. **campsite** *noun*

camp[2] *verb* make a camp; live in a camp.
camper *noun* [same origin as *campus*]

campaign *noun* **1** a series of battles in one area or with one purpose. **2** a planned series of actions, *an advertising campaign.*
campaign *verb*, **campaigner** *noun*

camp draft *noun* (*Australian*) a competitive equestrian event in which a steer is driven around a set course.

camphor *noun* a strong-smelling white substance used in medicine and mothballs and in making plastics.

campus *noun* (*plural* **campuses**) the grounds of a university or college. [Latin, = field]

can[1] *noun* **1** a metal or plastic container for liquids, *a can of tomato soup.* **2** a sealed tin in which food or drink is preserved.

can[2] *verb* (**canned**, **canning**) preserve in a sealed can. **canner** *noun*, **cannery** *noun*

can[3] *auxiliary verb* (*past tense* **could**) **1** be able to, *He can play the violin.* **2** have the right or permission to, *You can go.* [from an old word meaning 'know']

> **Usage** In sense 2 it is more formal to say *You may go*.

canal *noun* **1** an artificial river cut through land so that boats can sail along it or so that it can drain or irrigate an area. **2** a tube through which something passes in the body, *the alimentary canal.* [same origin as *channel*]

canary *noun* (*plural* **canaries**) a small yellow bird that sings.

cancan *noun* a lively dance in which the legs are kicked very high.

cancel *verb* (**cancelled**, **cancelling**) **1** say that something planned will not be done or will not take place. **2** stop an order or instruction for something. **3** mark a stamp or ticket so that it cannot be used again.
cancellation *noun*
cancel out stop each other's effect, *The good and harm cancel each other out.*

Cancer *noun* **1** a constellation and the fourth sign of the zodiac (the Crab). **2** a person born when the sun is in this sign.

cancer *noun* **1** a disease in which harmful growths form in the body. **2** a tumour, especially a harmful one. **cancerous** *adjective* [from Latin *cancer* = crab]

candelabrum (*say* kan-duh-**lah**-bruhm) *noun* (*plural* **candelabra**) a candlestick with several branches for holding candles. [from Latin *candela* = candle]

candid *adjective* frank. **candidly** *adverb*, **candidness** *noun* [from Latin *candidus* = white]

candidate *noun* **1** a person who wants to be elected or chosen for a particular job or position. **2** a person taking an examination.
candidacy *noun*, **candidature** *noun* [from Latin *candidus* = white (because Roman candidates for office had to wear a pure white toga)]

candied *adjective* coated or preserved in sugar.

candle *noun* a stick of wax with a wick through it, giving light when burning.
candlelight *noun*

candlestick *noun* a holder for a candle or candles.

candour (*say* **kan**-duh) *noun* frankness.

candy *noun* (*plural* **candies**) (*especially American*) sweets; a sweet. [from Arabic *kand* = sugar]

cane[1] *noun* **1** the stem of a reed or tall grass. **2** a thin stick.

cane[2] *verb* (**caned**, **caning**) beat with a cane.

cane toad *noun* a large toad introduced into Queensland to control insects in sugar cane plantations but spreading more widely.

canine[1] (*say* **kay**-nuyn) *adjective* of dogs.

canine[2] *noun* **1** a dog. **2** (in full **canine tooth**) a pointed tooth between the incisors and molars. [from Latin *canis* = dog]

canister *noun* a metal container.

canker *noun* a disease that rots the wood of trees and plants or causes ulcers and sores on animals.

cannabis *noun* hemp, especially when smoked as a drug. [from *Cannabis*, the Latin name of the hemp plant]

cannibal *noun* **1** a person who eats human flesh. **2** an animal that eats animals of its own kind. **cannibalise** *verb*, **cannibalism** *noun* [named after the Caribs, a West Indian people reputed to have eaten humans]

cannon[1] *noun* **1** (*plural* **cannon**) a large heavy gun. **2** the hitting of two balls in billiards by the third ball.

cannon[2] *verb* (**cannoned, cannoning**) bump into something heavily.

cannonball *noun* a large solid ball fired from a cannon.

cannot can not.

canny *adjective* (**cannier, canniest**) shrewd. **cannily** *adverb*, **canniness** *noun*

canoe[1] *noun* a narrow lightweight boat.

canoe[2] *verb* (**canoed, canoeing**) travel in a canoe. **canoeist** *noun*

canola *noun* plant grown for its oil-rich seeds.

canon *noun* **1** a general principle; a rule. **2** a set of writings by a particular author; a set of writings considered to be of the highest quality, *the English canon.* **3** a passage or piece of music in which a theme is taken up by several parts in succession. **4** a member of the clergy who is part of a cathedral chapter.

canonise *verb* (**canonised, canonising**) declare officially that someone is a saint. **canonisation** *noun*

canopy *noun* (*plural* **canopies**) **1** a hanging cover forming a shelter above a throne, bed, or person. **2** the part of a parachute that spreads in the air. **3** the uppermost layers of leaves in a forest.

cant[1] *verb* slope; tilt. [from a Dutch word meaning 'edge']

cant[2] *noun* **1** insincere talk. **2** jargon. [from Latin *cantare* = sing]

can't cannot, *I can't go to school tomorrow.*

cantaloupe *noun* a small round orange-coloured melon; a rockmelon.

cantankerous *adjective* bad-tempered.

cantata (*say* kan-**tah**-tuh) *noun* a musical composition for singers, like an oratorio but shorter. [from Italian *cantare* = sing]

canteen *noun* **1** a restaurant for workers in a factory or office. **2** a school shop selling food for snacks and lunches; a tuckshop. **3** a case or box containing a set of cutlery. **4** a soldier's or camper's water flask.

canter[1] *noun* a gentle gallop.

canter[2] *verb* go or ride at a canter. [short for 'Canterbury gallop', the gentle pace at which pilgrims were said to travel to Canterbury in the Middle Ages]

canticle *noun* a religious song with words taken from the Bible, e.g. the Magnificat. [from Latin, = little song]

cantilever *noun* a projecting beam or girder supporting a bridge, balcony, or similar structure.

canton *noun* each of the districts into which Switzerland is divided.

canvas *noun* (*plural* **canvases**) **1** a kind of strong coarse cloth. **2** a piece of canvas for painting on; a painting. [from Latin *Cannabis* = hemp, from whose fibres cloth was made]

canvass *verb* visit people to ask for votes, orders for goods, or opinions. **canvasser** *noun*

canyon *noun* a deep valley, usually with a river running through it. [from Spanish *cañon* = tube]

cap[1] *noun* **1** a soft hat without a brim but often with a peak. **2** a special headdress, e.g. that worn by a nurse; that showing membership of a sports team; an academic mortarboard. **3** a cap-like cover or top. **4** something that makes a bang when fired in a toy pistol.

cap[2] *verb* (**capped, capping**) **1** put a cap or cover on something; cover. **2** award a sports cap to a person chosen as a member of a team. **3** do better than something, *Can you cap that joke?*

capable *adjective* able to do something. **capability** *noun*, **capably** *adverb*

capacious (*say* kuh-**pay**-shuhs) *adjective* roomy; able to hold a large amount.

capacity *noun* (*plural* **capacities**) **1** the amount that something can hold. **2** ability; capability. **3** the position that someone occupies, *In my capacity as your guardian I am responsible for you.*

cape[1] *noun* a cloak.

cape[2] *noun* a promontory on the coast.

caper[1] *verb* jump or run about playfully.

caper[2] *noun* **1** capering. **2** (*informal*) an activity; an adventure.

caper[3] *noun* a bud of a prickly shrub, pickled for use as a flavouring.

capillary[1] (*say* kuh-**pil**-uh-ree) *noun* (*plural* **capillaries**) any of the very fine blood vessels that connect veins and arteries.

capillary[2] *adjective* of or occurring in a very narrow tube; of a capillary. [from Latin *capillus* = hair]

capital[1] *adjective* **1** important. **2** (*informal*) excellent.

capital[2] *noun* **1** a capital city. **2** a capital letter. **3** the top part of a pillar. **4** money or property that can be used to produce more wealth. [from Latin *caput* = head]

capital city *noun* the most important city in a country or state.

capitalise (*say* **kap**-uh-tuh-luyz) *verb* (**capitalised**, **capitalising**) **1** write or print as a capital letter. **2** change something into capital; provide with capital (= money). **capitalisation** *noun*
capitalise on profit by something; use it to your own advantage, *You could capitalise on your skill at drawing.*

capitalism (*say* **kap**-uh-tuh-liz-uhm) *noun* a system in which trade and industry are controlled by private owners for profit. (Compare **communism.**)

capitalist (*say* **kap**-uh-tuh-luhst) *noun* **1** a person who has much money or property being used to make more wealth; a very rich person. **2** a person who is in favour of capitalism.

capital letter *noun* a large letter of the kind used at the start of a name or sentence.

capital punishment *noun* punishing criminals by putting them to death.

capitulate *verb* (**capitulated**, **capitulating**) admit that you are defeated and surrender. **capitulation** *noun*

cappuccino (*say* kap-uh-**chee**-noh) *noun* (*plural* **cappuccinos**) coffee topped with milk made frothy with pressurised steam. [Italian]

caprice (*say* kuh-**prees**) *noun* a capricious action or impulse; a whim.

capricious (*say* kuh-**prish**-uhs) *adjective* deciding or changing your mind in an impulsive way. **capriciously** *adverb*, **capriciousness** *noun*

Capricorn *noun* **1** a constellation and the tenth sign of the zodiac. **2** a person born when the sun is in this sign. [from Latin *caper* 'goat' + *cornu* 'horn']

capsicum *noun* a type of pepper plant with red, green, or yellow hollow fruits.

capsicum spray *noun* an oil spray extracted from cayenne pepper used especially by police to ward off attackers or disarm violent offenders.

capsize *verb* (**capsized**, **capsizing**) overturn, *The boat capsized.*

capstan *noun* a thick post that can be turned to pull in a rope or cable that winds round it as it turns.

capsule *noun* **1** a hollow pill containing medicine. **2** a plant's seed case that splits open when ripe. **3** a compartment that can be separated from the rest of a spacecraft.

captain[1] *noun* **1** a person given authority over a group or team. **2** an army officer ranking next below a major; a naval officer ranking next below a commodore. **captaincy** *noun*

captain[2] *verb* act as captain of; lead. [same origin as *capital*]

captcha *noun* (also **CAPTCHA**) a computer program or system intended to distinguish human from machine input. [from the initials of 'Completely Automated Public Turing (test to tell) Computers (and) Humans Apart']

caption *noun* **1** the words printed with a picture to describe it. **2** a short title or heading in a newspaper or magazine.

captious (*say* **kap**-shuhs) *adjective* pointing out small mistakes or faults.

captivate *verb* (**captivated**, **captivating**) charm or delight someone. **captivation** *noun*

captive[1] *noun* someone taken prisoner.

captive[2] *adjective* taken prisoner; unable to escape. **captivity** *noun*

captor *noun* someone who has captured a person or animal.

capture[1] *verb* (**captured**, **capturing**) **1** seize; make a prisoner of someone. **2** take or obtain by force, trickery, skill, or attraction, *He captured her heart.*

capture[2] *noun* **1** capturing. **2** a person or thing captured. [from Latin *capere* = take]

car *noun* **1** a motor vehicle for a driver and small number of passengers, *When it's raining dad drives me to school in his car.* **2** a carriage, *cable car.* [from Latin *carrus* = wagon]

carafe (*say* kuh-**rahf**) *noun* a glass bottle holding wine or water for pouring out at the table. [from Arabic *gharrafa*]

caramel *noun* **1** a kind of toffee tasting like burnt sugar. **2** burnt sugar used for colouring and flavouring food.

carapace (*say* **ka**-ruh-pays) *noun* the shell on the back of a tortoise or crustacean.

carat *noun* **1** a measure of weight for precious stones. **2** a measure of the purity of gold, *Pure gold is 24 carats.*

caravan *noun* **1** an enclosed carriage equipped for living in, usually towed by a car. **2** a group of people travelling together across desert country. [from Persian *karwan*]

caraway *noun* a plant with spicy seeds that are used for flavouring food.

carb *noun* dietary carbohydrate, *A diet low in carbs can help you maintain a healthy weight.* [short for *carbohydrate*]

carbohydrate *noun* **1** a compound of carbon, oxygen, and hydrogen (e.g. sugar). **2** food consisting of or containing a lot of carbohydrates, *They ate fewer carbohydrates while dieting.*

carbolic *noun* a kind of disinfectant.

carbon *noun* a substance that is present in all living things and that occurs in its pure form as diamond and graphite.

carbonara *adjective* denoting a pasta sauce made with bacon or ham, egg, and cream. [Italian]

carbonate *noun* a compound that gives off carbon dioxide when mixed with acid.

carbonated *adjective* with carbon dioxide added, *Carbonated drinks are fizzy.*

carbon copy *noun* **1** a copy made with carbon paper. **2** an exact copy.

carbon credit *noun* a credit for something (such as the planting of a forest) that reduces or absorbs carbon dioxide.

carbon dating *noun* a method of deciding the age of prehistoric objects by measuring the decay of radiocarbon in them.

carbon dioxide *noun* a gas formed by the burning of carbon or breathed out by animals in respiration.

carbon footprint *noun* the amount of carbon dioxide produced by a particular person or group.

carboniferous *adjective* producing coal. [from *carbon*, + Latin *ferre* = to bear]

carbon monoxide *noun* a poisonous gas formed when carbon burns incompletely.

carbon neutral *adjective* balancing carbon emissions by the purchase of carbon offsets.

carbon offset *noun* a process (such as tree planting) that helps to balance the production of carbon emissions.

carbon paper *noun* thin carbon-coated paper, placed between sheets of paper to make copies of what is written on the top sheet.

carbon sequestration *noun* a process by which carbon dioxide is removed from the atmosphere and stored in solid or liquid form.

carbon sink *noun* an area (such as a forest) that stores carbon dioxide.

carbon tax *noun* a tax on petrol, heavy industry, etc., intended to reduce carbon dioxide emissions.

carbon trading *noun* the process of offsetting emissions of carbon dioxide by buying carbon credits.

carbuncle *noun* **1** a bad abscess in the skin. **2** a bright red gem.

carburettor *noun* a device for mixing fuel and air in an engine.

carcass *noun* (*plural* **carcasses**) **1** the dead body of an animal. **2** the bony part of a bird's body before or after it is cooked.

carcinogenic (*say* kah-sin-uh-**jen**-ik) *adjective* producing cancer.

card[1] *noun* **1** a small usually oblong piece of stiff paper or of plastic, *business card; credit card.* **2** (also **playing card**) each of a set of cards (usually 52) with shapes or pictures on them, used for playing games. **3** cardboard.
on the cards likely; possible.

card[2] *verb* clean and disentangle wool fibres with a wire brush or toothed instrument called a **card**.

cardboard *noun* stiff paper or pasteboard.

cardiac (*say* **kah**-dee-ak) *adjective* of the heart.

cardigan *noun* a knitted jacket. [named after the Earl of Cardigan, who led the Charge of the Light Brigade in the Crimean War]

cardinal[1] *noun* a senior priest in the Roman Catholic Church.

cardinal[2] *adjective* **1** chief; most important, *the cardinal features of our plan.* **2** deep scarlet (like a cardinal's cassock).

cardinal number *noun* a whole number, e.g. 1, 2, 3, etc. (Compare **ordinal number**.)

cardinal point *noun* any of the four main points of the compass (North, East, South, West).

cardio- *prefix* heart. [from Greek *kardia* = heart]

cardiology *noun* the study of the structure and diseases of the heart. **cardiological** *adjective*, **cardiologist** *noun* [from *cardio-*, + *-logy*]

cardiothoracic *adjective* of or relating to the heart and the organs of the chest.

cards *plural noun* a game played with cards.

care[1] *noun* **1** serious attention and thought, *Plan your holiday with care.* **2** caution to avoid damage or loss, *Handle with care.* **3** protection; supervision, *Leave the child in my care.* **4** worry; anxiety, *freedom from care.* [from Old English *caru* = sorrow]

care[2] *verb* (**cared, caring**) **1** feel interested or concerned. **2** feel affection.
care for 1 have in your care. **2** be fond of.

career[1] *noun* **1** progress through life, especially in work. **2** an occupation with opportunities for promotion.

career[2] *verb* rush along wildly.

carefree *adjective* without worries or responsibilities.

careful *adjective* **1** giving serious thought and attention to something. **2** avoiding damage or danger; cautious. **carefully** *adverb*, **carefulness** *noun*

careless *adjective* **1** not taking care or paying attention. **2** done without care. **3** unthinking, insensitive. **carelessly** *adverb*, **carelessness** *noun*

carer *noun* a person looking after a sick or disabled person.

caress[1] *noun* a gentle loving touch.

caress[2] *verb* touch lovingly.

caret *noun* a mark (^ or ⁁) showing where something is to be inserted in writing or printing. [Latin, = it is lacking]

caretaker *noun* a person employed to look after a house or building.

cargo *noun* (*plural* **cargoes**) goods carried in a ship or aircraft.

Caribbean *adjective* of or from the Caribbean Sea, a part of the Atlantic Ocean east of Central America.

caribou (*say* **ka**-ruh-boo) *noun* (*plural* **caribou**) a North American reindeer.

caricature *noun* an amusing or exaggerated picture of someone. **caricature** *verb* [from Italian *caricare* = exaggerate]

caries (*say* **kair**-reez) *noun* (*plural* **caries**) decay in teeth or bones. [Latin]

carillon (*say* kuh-**ril**-yuhn) *noun* a set of bells sounded from a keyboard or mechanically.

carmine *adjective & noun* deep red.

carnage *noun* the killing of many people.

carnal *adjective* of the body as opposed to the spirit; not spiritual. [from Latin *carnis* = of flesh]

carnation *noun* a garden flower with a sweet smell.

carnival *noun* **1** a festival, often with a procession in fancy dress. **2** a series of sporting events. [originally this meant the festivities before Lent when meat (Latin *carnis* = of flesh) was given up until Easter]

carnivorous (*say* kah-**niv**-uh-ruhs) *adjective* meat-eating. (Compare **herbivorous**.) **carnivore** *noun* [from Latin *carnis* = of flesh, + *vorare* = devour]

carob (*say* **ka**-ruhb) *noun* the edible pod of a Mediterranean tree, sometimes used as a substitute for chocolate.

carol *noun* a joyful song; a Christmas hymn.

carousel (*say* ka-ruh-**sel**) *noun* **1** a merry-go-round. **2** a rotating conveyor, e.g. for baggage at an airport.

carp[1] *noun* an edible freshwater fish.

carp[2] *verb* keep finding fault.

carpal[1] *adjective* of the wrist joint.

carpal[2] *noun* a wrist bone.

carpenter *noun* a person who makes things out of wood. **carpentry** *noun*

carpet *noun* a thick soft covering for a floor. **carpeted** *adjective*, **carpeting** *noun*

carport *noun* a shelter for a car.

carpus *noun* (*plural* **carpi**) the group of small bones between the main part of the forelimb and the metacarpus. [from Greek *karpos* = wrist]

carrel *noun* a small reading cubicle in a library.

carriage *noun* **1** one of the separate parts of a train, where passengers sit. **2** a passenger vehicle pulled by horses. **3** carrying goods from one place to another; the cost of carrying goods, *Carriage is extra.* **4** a moving part carrying or holding something in a machine.

carriageway *noun* the part of a road on which vehicles travel.

carrier *noun* a person or thing that carries something.

carrion *noun* dead and decaying flesh. [same origin as *carnal*]

carrot *noun* a plant with a thick orange-coloured root used as a vegetable.

carry *verb* (**carried, carrying**) **1** take something from one place to another. **2** support the weight of something. **3** travel clearly, *Sound carries in the mountains.* **4** win; approve, *The motion was carried by ten votes to six.*
be carried away be very excited.
carry on 1 continue. **2** manage or conduct. **3** (*informal*) behave excitedly. **4** (*informal*) complain.
carry out put into practice. [same origin as *car*]

cart[1] *noun* **1** an open vehicle for carrying loads. **2** a shallow open container on wheels that may be pulled or pushed by hand. **3** a facility on a website that records items selected by a customer for purchase until the transaction is completed.

cart[2] *verb* **1** carry in a cart. **2** (*informal*) carry something heavy or tiring, *I've carted these books all round the school.*

carte blanche (*say* kaht **blonsh**) *noun* freedom to act as you think best. [French, = blank paper]

Cartesian coordinates *plural noun* a system for locating a point by reference to its distance from two or three axes intersecting at right angles. [named after René Descartes, a French philosopher and mathematician]

carthorse *noun* a large strong horse used for pulling heavy loads.

cartilage *noun* tough white flexible tissue attached to a bone.

cartography *noun* drawing maps. **cartographer** *noun*, **cartographic** *adjective* [from French *carte* = map, + *-graphy*]

carton *noun* a cardboard or plastic container.

cartoon *noun* **1** an amusing drawing. **2** a comic strip (see **comic**[1]). **3** an animated film. **cartoonist** *noun*

cartridge *noun* **1** a case containing the explosive for a bullet or shell. **2** a container holding film for a camera, ink for a pen, etc. **3** the device that holds the stylus of a record player.

cartwheel *noun* **1** the wheel of a cart. **2** a handstand balancing on each hand in turn with arms and legs spread like spokes of a wheel.

carve *verb* (**carved**, **carving**) **1** make by cutting wood or stone. **2** cut designs or letters in wood or stone. **3** cut cooked meat into slices. **carver** *noun*

cascade[1] *noun* a waterfall.

cascade[2] *verb* (**cascaded**, **cascading**) fall like a cascade.

case[1] *noun* **1** a container. **2** a suitcase. [from Latin *capsa* = box]

case[2] *noun* **1** an example of something existing or occurring; a situation, *In every case we found that someone had cheated.* **2** something investigated, especially by police or a lawcourt, *a murder case.* **3** a set of facts or arguments to support something, *She put forward a good case for equality.* **4** the form of a word that shows how it is related to other words. *Fred's* is the possessive case of *Fred*; *him* is the objective case of *he*.
in any case anyway.
in case because something may happen; lest. [from Latin *casus* = occasion]

casement *noun* a window that opens on hinges at its side.

case-sensitive *adjective* differentiating between upper and lower case letters.

cash[1] *noun* **1** money in coin or notes. **2** immediate payment for goods.

cash[2] *verb* give or get cash for, *cashed a cheque.*
cash in on (*informal*) profit from something.

cashew *noun* a small edible kidney-shaped nut.

cashier *noun* a person who takes in and pays out money in a bank or takes payments in a shop.

cashmere *noun* very fine soft wool. [first made from the hair of goats from Kashmir in Asia]

cash register *noun* a device that records the amount of money put in, used in a shop.

casing *noun* a protective covering.

casino *noun* (*plural* **casinos**) a public building or room for gambling.

cask *noun* **1** a barrel. **2** (*Australian*) a box with plastic or foil lining for storing and serving wine or juice.

casket *noun* **1** a small box for jewellery or valuables. **2** a coffin.

Cassandra *noun* a prophet of disaster, especially one who is disregarded. [from the name of a prophetess in Greek mythology]

cassava *noun* a tropical plant with starchy roots that are an important source of food in tropical countries.

casserole *noun* **1** a covered dish in which food is cooked and served. **2** food cooked in a casserole. [from Greek, = little cup]

cassette *noun* a small sealed case containing a reel of film or magnetic tape. [French, = little case]

cassock *noun* a long garment worn by clergy.

cassowary *noun* (*plural* **cassowaries**) a large flightless Australasian bird with a heavy body, stout legs, and a bony crest on its forehead. [from Malay *kasuari*]

cast[1] *verb* (**cast**, **casting**) **1** throw. **2** shed or throw off. **3** make a vote. **4** make something of metal or plaster in a mould. **5** choose performers for a play or film.

cast[2] *noun* **1** a shape made by pouring liquid metal or plaster into a mould. **2** all the performers in a play or film.

castanets *plural noun* two pieces of wood, ivory, or plastic held in one hand and clapped together to make a clicking sound, usually for dancing. [from Spanish *castañetas* = little chestnuts]

castaway *noun* a shipwrecked person.

caste *noun* (in India) one of the social classes into which Hindus are born. [from Spanish *casta* = descent from ancestors]

caster sugar *noun* finely ground white sugar.

castigate *verb* (**castigated**, **castigating**) punish or rebuke severely. **castigation** *noun* [from Latin *castigare* = punish]

casting vote *noun* the vote that decides which group wins when the votes on each side are equal.

cast iron *noun* a hard alloy of iron made by casting it in a mould.

castle *noun* **1** a large old fortified building. **2** a piece in chess. Also called a *rook*.
castles in the air daydreams. [from Latin *castellum* = fort]

castor *noun* (also **caster**) a small wheel on the leg of a table, chair, or other piece of furniture.

castor oil *noun* oil from the seeds of a tropical plant, used as a laxative.

castrate *verb* (**castrated**, **castrating**) remove the testicles of a male animal; geld. (Compare **spay**.) **castration** *noun*

casual *adjective* **1** happening by chance; not planned. **2** not careful; not methodical. **3** informal; suitable for informal occasions, *casual clothes.* **4** not permanent, *casual work.* **casually** *adverb*, **casualness** *noun*

casualty *noun* (*plural* **casualties**) a person who is killed or injured in war or in an accident.

casuarina *noun* an Australian tree or shrub with jointed branches that resemble gigantic horsetails. Also called a *she-oak.*

cat *noun* **1** a small furry domestic animal. **2** an animal of the same family as the domestic cat, *Lions and tigers are cats.* **3** (*informal*) a spiteful girl or woman.
let the cat out of the bag reveal a secret.

cata- *prefix* (becoming **cat-** before a vowel; combining with an *h* to become **cath-**) **1** down (as in *catapult*). **2** thoroughly (as in *catalogue*). [from Greek *kata* = down]

cataclysm (*say* **kat**-uh-kliz-uhm) *noun* a violent upheaval or disaster.

catacombs (*say* **kat**-uh-kohmz) *plural noun* underground passages with compartments for tombs.

catalogue[1] *noun* **1** a list of things (e.g. of books in a library), usually arranged in order. **2** a book containing a list of things available, *Christmas catalogue.*

catalogue[2] *verb* (**catalogued, cataloguing**) enter something in a catalogue. [from Greek *katalogos* = list]

catalyst (*say* **kat**-uh-luhst) *noun* something that starts or speeds up a change or reaction. **catalytic** *adjective* [from *cata-*, + Greek *lysis* = loosening]

catamaran *noun* a boat with twin hulls. [from Tamil *kattumaram* = tied wood]

catapult[1] *noun* **1** a device with elastic for shooting small stones. **2** an ancient military device for hurling stones or other missiles.

catapult[2] *verb* hurl or rush violently. [from *cata-*, + Greek *pellein* = throw]

cataract *noun* **1** a large waterfall or rush of water. **2** a cloudy area that forms in the eye and prevents a person from seeing clearly.

catarrh (*say* kuh-**tah**) *noun* inflammation in your nose that makes it drip a watery fluid. [from Greek, = flow down]

catastrophe (*say* kuh-**tas**-truh-fee) *noun* a sudden great disaster. **catastrophic** (*say* kat-uh-**strof**-ik) *adjective,* **catastrophically** *adverb*

catcall *noun* a disapproving whistle.

catch[1] *verb* (**caught, catching**) **1** take and hold something. **2** capture. **3** overtake. **4** be in time to get on a bus, train, or aircraft. **5** become infected with an illness. **6** hear, *I didn't catch what he said.* **7** surprise or detect somebody, *caught in the act.* **8** trick somebody. **9** make or become fixed or unable to move; snag; entangle, *I caught my dress on a nail.* **10** hit; strike, *The blow caught him on the nose.*
catch fire start burning.
catch it (*informal*) be scolded or punished.
catch on (*informal*) **1** become popular. **2** understand.

catch[2] *noun* (*plural* **catches**) **1** catching something. **2** something caught or worth catching. **3** a hidden difficulty. **4** a device for fastening something.

catching *adjective* infectious.

catchment area *noun* **1** the whole area from which water drains into a river or reservoir. **2** the area from which a school takes pupils or a hospital takes patients.

catchphrase *noun* a popular phrase.

catch-22 *noun* (*informal*) a dilemma where the victim is bound to suffer, no matter which course of action is chosen. [from the title of a novel by J. Heller (1961), set in the Second World War, in which the hero wishes to avoid flying any more missions and decides to go crazy, only to be told that anyone who wants to get out of combat duty is not really crazy]

catchy *adjective* easy to remember, soon becoming popular, *a catchy tune.*

catechism (*say* **kat**-uh-kiz-uhm) *noun* a set of questions and answers that give the basic beliefs of a religion.

categorical (*say* kat-uh-**go**-ri-kuhl) *adjective* definite and absolute, *a categorical refusal.* **categorically** *adverb*

category *noun* (*plural* **categories**) a set of people or things classified as being similar to each other. **categorise** *verb*

cater *verb* provide what is needed or wanted, especially food or entertainment.
caterer *noun*
cater to try to satisfy (a need or demand).

caterpillar *noun* the creeping worm-like creature (*larva*) that will turn into a butterfly or moth. [from Old French *chatepelose* = hairy cat]

caterwaul *verb* make a cat's howling cry.

catfish *noun* a freshwater or sea fish that has fleshy filaments around its mouth that look like the whiskers of a cat.

cath- *prefix* see **cata-**.

cat head *noun* a small Australian plant with spiny fruits.

cathedral *noun* the most important church of a diocese. [from Greek *kathedra* = seat]

catheter *noun* a tube for insertion into a body cavity for introducing or removing fluid. [from Greek *kathienai* = send down]

cathode *noun* the electrode by which electric current leaves a device. (Compare **anode**.) [from *cata-* = down, + Greek *hodos* = way]

catholic *adjective* **1** including a wide variety of things; all-embracing, *Her taste in movies is catholic.* **2** (**Catholic** or **Roman Catholic**) of the section of the Christian Church that has the pope as its head. **Catholic** *noun,*

Catholicism *noun* [from Greek *katholikos* = universal]

catkin *noun* a spike of small soft flowers on trees such as hazel and willow. [from Dutch *katteken* = kitten]

catnap *noun* a short sleep.

CAT scan *noun* (in full **computerised axial tomography scan**) an X-ray image of internal organs, used for detecting medical problems like disease.

cattle *plural noun* animals with horns and hoofs, kept by farmers for their milk and beef.

cattle dog *noun* (*Australian*) a dog trained to work with cattle.

catty *adjective* (**cattier**, **cattiest**) speaking or spoken spitefully.

catwalk *noun* a raised narrow pathway.

Caucasian (*say* kaw-**kay**-*zh*uhn) *adjective* of a white or light-skinned race.
Caucasian *noun*

caucus *noun* (*plural* **caucuses**) (in Australia) the parliamentary members of a political party; a meeting of these.

caudal *adjective* of or at the tail. [from Latin *cauda* = tail]

caught *past tense & past participle* of **catch**[1].

cauldron *noun* a large deep pot for boiling things in. [from Latin *caldarium* = hot bath]

cauliflower *noun* a cabbage with a large head of white flowers. [from French *chou fleuri* = flowered cabbage]

causal *adjective* of or forming a cause.
causally *adverb*

cause[1] *noun* **1** a person or thing that makes something happen or produces an effect. **2** a reason, *There is no cause for worry.* **3** a purpose for which people work; an organisation or charity.

cause[2] *verb* (**caused**, **causing**) be the cause of; make something happen.

causeway *noun* a raised road across low or marshy ground.

caustic *adjective* **1** able to burn or wear things away by chemical action. **2** sarcastic.
caustically *adverb* [from Greek *kaustikos* = capable of burning]

cauterise *verb* (**cauterised**, **cauterising**) burn the surface of flesh to destroy infection or stop bleeding. **cauterisation** *noun* [from Greek *kauterion* = branding iron]

caution[1] *noun* **1** care taken so as to avoid danger; attention to safety. **2** a warning.

caution[2] *verb* warn someone.

cautionary *adjective* giving a warning.

cautious *adjective* showing caution. **cautiously** *adverb*, **cautiousness** *noun*

cavalcade *noun* a procession. [from Italian *cavalcare* = ride]

cavalry *noun* soldiers who fight on horseback or in armoured vehicles. (Compare **infantry**.) [from Latin *caballus* = horse]

cave[1] *noun* a large hollow place in the side of a hill or cliff, or underground.

cave[2] *verb* (**caved**, **caving**) **cave in 1** fall inwards. **2** give way in an argument. [from Latin *cavus* = hollow]

caveat (*say* **kav**-ee-uht) *noun* a warning. [Latin, = let a person beware]

caveman *noun* (*plural* **cavemen**) a person living in a cave in ancient times.

cavern *noun* a large cave. **cavernous** *adjective*

caviar (*say* **kav**-ee-ah) *noun* the pickled roe of sturgeon or other large fish.

cavil *verb* (**cavilled**, **cavilling**) raise petty objections.

caving *noun* exploring caves.

cavity *noun* (*plural* **cavities**) a hollow or hole. [same origin as *cave*]

cavort (*say* kuh-**vawt**) *verb* jump or run about excitedly.

cavy (*say* **kay**-vee) *noun* a guinea pig.

caw *noun* the harsh cry of a crow or similar bird. **caw** *verb*

cc[1] *abbreviation* (also **c.c.**) **1** carbon copy. **2** cubic centimetre(s).

cc[2] *verb* send a copy of an email, document, etc. to (a third party).

CCTV *abbreviation* closed circuit television.

CD *noun* a compact disc.

CD-R *noun* a CD that can be recorded on only once. [from the initials of 'compact disc recordable']

CD-ROM *noun* a compact disc storing data that can be read but not altered by a computer. [from the initials of 'compact disc read-only memory']

CD-RW *noun* a CD on which recordings can be made and erased a number of times. [from the initials of 'compact disc rewritable']

CE *abbreviation* Common Era.

> **Usage** Used to indicate the dates traditionally designated by AD.

cease[1] *verb* (**ceased, ceasing**) stop; end.

cease[2] *noun* **without cease** not ceasing.

ceasefire *noun* a signal to stop firing; an agreement to stop fighting.

ceaseless *adjective* not ceasing.

cedar *noun* an evergreen tree with hard fragrant wood.

cede (*say* seed) *verb* (**ceded**, **ceding**) give up your rights to something; surrender, *They* *had to cede some of their territory.* [from Latin *cedere* = yield]

cedilla (*say* suh-**dil**-uh) *noun* a mark under *c* in certain languages to show that it is pronounced as *s*, e.g. in *façade*. [from Spanish, = a little *z*]

ceiling *noun* **1** the flat surface under the top of a room. **2** the highest limit that something can reach.

celebrate *verb* (**celebrated**, **celebrating**) **1** do something special or enjoyable to show that a day or event is important. **2** make merry. **3** perform a religious ceremony. **celebrant** *noun*, **celebration** *noun*

celebrated *adjective* famous.

celebrity *noun* (*plural* **celebrities**) **1** a famous person. **2** fame; being famous.

celeriac (*say* suh-**le**-ree-ak) *noun* a kind of celery with a turnip-like root.

celerity (*say* suh-**le**-ruh-tee) *noun* swiftness.

celery *noun* a vegetable with crisp white or green stems.

celestial (*say* suh-**les**-tee-uhl) *adjective* **1** positioned in or relating to the sky, or outer space as observed in astronomy, *celestial bodies.* **2** of heaven; divine.

celibate (*say* **sel**-uh-buht) *adjective* remaining unmarried, especially for religious reasons. **celibacy** *noun*

cell *noun* **1** a very small room, e.g. in a monastery or a prison. **2** a microscopic unit of living matter. **3** a compartment of a honeycomb. **4** a device for producing electric current chemically. **5** a small group or unit in an organisation. [from Latin *cella* = storeroom]

cellar *noun* an underground room. [same origin as *cell*]

cello (*say* **chel**-oh) *noun* (*plural* **cellos**) a musical instrument like a large violin, placed between the knees of the player. **cellist** *noun* [short for *violoncello*]

cellular *adjective* **1** of or containing cells. **2** with an open mesh, *cellular blankets.*

cellulite *noun* a lumpy form of fat, especially on the hips and thighs.

celluloid *noun* a kind of plastic.

cellulose *noun* **1** tissue that forms the main part of all plants and trees. **2** paint made from cellulose.

Celsius (*say* **sel**-see-uhs) *adjective* (of a temperature scale) measuring temperature on a scale using 100 degrees, where water freezes at 0° and boils at 100°. [named after A. Celsius, a Swedish astronomer]

Celtic *adjective* of the languages or inhabitants of ancient Britain and France before the Romans came, or of their descendants, e.g. Irish, Welsh, Gaelic.

cement[1] *noun* **1** a mixture of lime and clay used in building and to join bricks together. **2** a strong glue.

cement[2] *verb* **1** put cement on something. **2** join firmly; strengthen.

cemetery (*say* **sem**-uh-tree) *noun* (*plural* **cemeteries**) a place where people are buried. [from Greek *koimeterion* = dormitory]

cenotaph (*say* **sen**-uh-tahf) *noun* a monument, especially as a war memorial, to people who are buried elsewhere. [from Greek *kenos* = empty, + *taphos* = tomb]

censer *noun* a container in which incense is burnt. [same origin as *incense*]

censor *noun* a person who examines films, books, letters, etc. and removes or bans anything that seems harmful. **censor** *verb*, **censorship** *noun* [Latin, = a magistrate with power to ban unsuitable people from ceremonies]

censorious (*say* sen-**saw**-ree-uhs) *adjective* criticising something strongly.

censure (*say* **sen**-shuh) *noun* strong criticism or disapproval of something. **censure** *verb*

census *noun* (*plural* **censuses**) an official count or survey of the population or things (e.g. traffic). [Latin, from *censere* = estimate]

cent *noun* a coin worth one hundredth of a dollar. [from Latin *centum* = 100]

centenarian (*say* sen-tuh-**nair**-ree-uhn) *noun* a person who is 100 years old or more.

centenary (*say* sen-**tee**-nuh-ree) *noun* a 100th anniversary. **centennial** (*say* sen-**ten**-ee-uhl) *adjective*

centi- *prefix* **1** one hundred (as in *centipede*). **2** one hundredth (as in *centimetre*). [from Latin *centum* = 100]

centigrade *adjective* Celsius. [from *centi-*, + Latin *gradus* = step]

centimetre *noun* one hundredth of a metre, about four tenths of an inch, *Her pencil is ten centimetres long.*

centipede *noun* a small crawling creature with a long body and many legs. [from *centi-*, + Latin *pedes* = feet]

central *adjective* **1** of or at the centre. **2** most important. **centrally** *adverb*

central heating *noun* a system of heating a building from one source by circulating hot water or hot air or steam in pipes or by linked radiators.

centralise *verb* (**centralised**, **centralising**) bring under a central authority's control. **centralisation** *noun*

central processing unit *noun* the principal operating part of a computer.

centre[1] *noun* **1** the middle point or part. **2** an important place, e.g. from which things are organised; a place where certain things happen, *shopping centre.*

centre[2] *verb* (**centred, centring**) place something in or at the centre. [from Greek *kentron* = sharp point]

centrifugal *adjective* moving away from the centre. [from Latin *centrum* = centre, + *fugere* = flee]

centrifugal force *noun* a force that makes a thing that is travelling round a central point fly outwards off its circular path.

centripetal *adjective* moving towards the centre. [from Latin *centrum* = centre, + *petere* = seek]

centurion (*say* sen-**tyoo**-ree-uhn) *noun* an officer in the ancient Roman army. [originally he was in charge of 100 men (Latin *centum* = 100)]

century *noun* (*plural* **centuries**) **1** a period of 100 years. **2** 100 runs scored by a batter in an innings at cricket. [from Latin *centum* = 100]

CEO *noun* the highest-ranking person in a company or other institution, ultimately responsible for taking managerial decisions. [from the initials of 'chief executive officer']

cephalopod (*say* **sef**-uh-luh-pod) *noun* a mollusc (such as an octopus) that has a head with a ring of tentacles round the mouth. [from Greek *kephale* = head, + *podos* = of a foot]

ceramic *adjective* of pottery.

ceramics *plural noun* pottery-making.

cereal *noun* **1** a grass producing seeds which are used as food, e.g. wheat, barley, rice. **2** a breakfast food made from these seeds. [from the name of Ceres, Roman goddess of the corn]

cerebral (*say* **se**-ruh-bruhl) *adjective* of the brain. [from Latin *cerebrum* = brain]

cerebral palsy *noun* a condition involving muscle spasms and involuntary movements.

ceremonial *adjective* of or used in a ceremony; formal. **ceremonially** *adverb*

ceremonious *adjective* full of ceremony; elaborately performed.

ceremony *noun* (*plural* **ceremonies**) **1** a formal religious or public occasion, *a wedding ceremony; an opening ceremony.* **2** the formal actions carried out on an important occasion.

ceroc (*say* suh-**rok**) *noun* a type of dance having elements of rock and roll, jive, and salsa. [from French *c'est roc* = this is rock]

certain *adjective* **1** feeling sure, convinced. **2** known for sure; without doubt. **3** able to be relied on to happen, *Victory was certain; It is certain to rain.* **4** unfailing, reliable, *a certain cure.* **5** particular but not named, *a certain person.*

certainly *adverb* **1** for certain. **2** yes.

certainty *noun* (*plural* **certainties**) **1** something that is sure to happen. **2** being sure.

certificate *noun* an official written or printed statement giving certain facts, *a birth certificate.*

certify *verb* (**certified, certifying**) declare something formally; show on a certificate. **certification** *noun*, **certified** *adjective*

certitude *noun* a feeling of certainty.

cervix *noun* **1** the neck. **2** the neck of the womb. **cervical** *adjective* [Latin, = neck]

cessation *noun* ceasing.

cession *noun* ceding something.

cesspit *noun* (also **cesspool**) a covered pit where liquid waste or sewage is stored temporarily.

c'est la vie (*say* say **luh** vee) *interjection* life is like that. [French, = that is life]

CFC *abbreviation* chlorofluorocarbon.

CFO *noun* a senior executive with responsibility for the financial affairs of a company or other institution. [from the initials of 'chief financial officer']

CGI *abbreviation* computer-generated imagery.

cha-cha *noun* a Latin-American dance.

chafe *verb* (**chafed, chafing**) **1** rub a person's skin to make it warm again. **2** make or become sore by rubbing. **3** become irritated or impatient, *We chafed at the delay.* [from French *chauffer* = make warm]

chaff[1] *noun* **1** husks of grain, separated from the seed. **2** teasing; joking.

chaff[2] *verb* tease; joke.

chaffinch *noun* (*plural* **chaffinches**) a kind of finch.

chagrin (*say* **shag**-ruhn or shuh-**green**) *noun* a feeling of being annoyed and embarrassed or disappointed. [French]

chain[1] *noun* **1** a row of metal rings linked together. **2** a connected series of things, *a chain of mountains; a chain of events.* **3** a number of shops, hotels, or restaurants owned by the same company.

chain[2] *verb* fasten with a chain or chains.

chain letter *noun* a letter that you are asked to copy and send to several other people.

chain reaction *noun* a series of happenings in which each causes the next.

chair[1] *noun* **1** a movable seat, with a back, for one person. **2** a position of authority at a meeting, *Dr Jones was in the chair.* **3** a chairperson.

chair[2] *verb* act as a chairperson or preside over a meeting, organisation, or public event, *Who will chair this meeting?*

chairman *noun* (*plural* **chairmen**) the person who is in control of a meeting.
chairmanship *noun*

chairperson *noun* a chairman or chairwoman.

chairwoman *noun* (*plural* **chairwomen**) the woman who is in control of a meeting.

chalet (*say* **shal**-ay) *noun* a usually wooden house with a steeply sloping roof, especially one built in a mountain area.

chalice *noun* a large goblet for holding wine, especially one used at Mass or Communion. [from Latin *calix* = cup]

chalk *noun* **1** a soft white or coloured stick used for writing on blackboards or for drawing. **2** soft white limestone.
chalky *adjective*

chalkie *noun* (*Australian informal*) a schoolteacher.

challenge[1] *noun* a demand to have a contest, do something difficult, say who you are, etc.

challenge[2] *verb* (**challenged, challenging**) **1** make a challenge to someone. **2** question whether something is true or correct.
challenger *noun*

challenged *adjective* lacking a physical or mental attribute.

challenging *adjective* demanding, testing, *challenging work.*

chamber *noun* **1** an assembly hall; the hall used for meetings of a parliament; the members of the group using it. **2** a cavity or compartment in the body of an animal or plant, or in machinery. **3** (*old use*) a room.

chamberlain *noun* an official who manages the household of a sovereign or great noble.

chamber music *noun* music for a small group of players.

chamber pot *noun* a receptacle for urine etc., used in a bedroom.

chambers *plural noun* rooms used by a barrister or a judge; a set of rooms.

chameleon (*say* kuh-**mee**-lee-uhn) *noun* a small lizard that can change its colour to that of its surroundings.

chamois *noun* (*plural* **chamois**) **1** (*say* **sham**-wah) a small wild antelope living in the mountains. **2** (*say* **sham**-ee) a piece of soft yellow leather used for washing and polishing things. [French]

champ *verb* munch or bite something noisily.

champagne (*say* sham-**payn**) *noun* **1** a bubbly white wine from Champagne in France. **2** (loosely) a similar wine from elsewhere.

champion[1] *noun* **1** a person or thing that has defeated all the others in a sport or competition. **2** someone who supports a cause by fighting, speaking, or arguing.
championship *noun*

champion[2] *verb* support a cause by fighting or speaking for it.

chance[1] *noun* **1** a possibility. **2** an opportunity, *Now is your chance to escape.* **3** the way things happen without being planned, *I met her by chance.*
take a chance take a risk.

chance[2] *verb* (**chanced, chancing**) **1** happen by chance, *I chanced to meet her.* **2** (*informal*) risk, *Let's chance it.*

chance[3] *adjective* happening by chance; accidental.

chancel *noun* the part of a church nearest to the altar.

chancellor *noun* **1** the honorary head of a university. **2** the head of government in some countries. **3** (chiefly *British*) a government or legal official.

chancy *adjective* risky.

chandelier (*say* shan-duh-**leer**) *noun* a hanging support for several lights. [from French *chandelle* = candle]

change[1] *verb* (**changed, changing**) **1** make or become different. **2** exchange. **3** put on fresh clothes or coverings. **4** go from one to another, *change trains.*

change[2] *noun* **1** changing; alteration. **2** coins or notes of small values. **3** money given back to the payer when the price is less than the amount handed over. **4** a fresh set of clothes. **5** a variation in routine, *Let's walk home for a change.* **6** an exchange.

changeable *adjective* likely to change; changing frequently.

changeling *noun* a child believed to have been substituted secretly for another, especially by fairies.

channel[1] *noun* **1** a stretch of water connecting two seas. **2** a way for water to flow along. **3** the navigable part of a waterway, deeper than the parts on either side. **4** a broadcasting wavelength.

channel[2] *verb* (**channelled, channelling**) **1** make a channel in something. **2** direct something through a channel or other route. [from Latin *canalis* = canal]

channel surf *verb* flip rapidly between television channels using a remote control.

chant[1] *noun* **1** a tune to which words with no regular rhythm are fitted, e.g. one used in singing psalms. **2** a rhythmic call or shout.

chant[2] *verb* **1** sing. **2** call out words in a rhythm. [from Latin *cantare* = sing]

chaos (*say* **kay**-os) *noun* great disorder. **chaotic** *adjective*, **chaotically** *adverb* [Greek, = bottomless pit]

chap *noun* (*informal*) a man. [short for *chapman*, an old word for a pedlar]

chapel *noun* **1** a place used for Christian worship, other than a cathedral or parish church; a religious service in this. **2** a section of a large church, with its own altar.

chaperone (*say* **shap**-uh-rohn) *noun* a person, especially an older woman, in charge of a young one on social occasions. **chaperone** *verb*

chaplain *noun* a member of the clergy who looks after a college, school, hospital, regiment, etc.

chapped *adjective* with skin split or cracked.

chapter *noun* **1** a division of a book. **2** the clergy of a cathedral or members of a monastery.

char *verb* (**charred**, **charring**) make or become black by burning. [from *charcoal*]

character *noun* **1** a person in a novel, play, or film. **2** all the qualities that make a person or thing what he, she, or it is. **3** (*informal*) a person. **4** (*informal*) an eccentric or interesting person. **5** a letter of the alphabet; a symbol or digit.

characterise *verb* (**characterised**, **characterising**) **1** be a characteristic of. **2** describe the character of. **characterisation** *noun*

characteristic[1] *noun* a quality that forms part of a person's or thing's character.

characteristic[2] *adjective* typical of a person or thing. **characteristically** *adverb*

charade (*say* shuh-**rahd**) *noun* a pretence.

charades *plural noun* a game in which people try to guess a word from other people's acting.

charcoal *noun* a black substance made by burning wood slowly.

chardonnay (*say* **shar**-duh-nay) *noun* a variety of white grape; the white wine made from this. [French]

charge[1] *noun* **1** the price asked for something. **2** a rushing attack. **3** the amount of explosive needed for one explosion. **4** electricity in something. **5** an accusation of having committed a crime. **6** care, custody. **7** a person or thing in someone's care.
in charge in control; deciding what shall happen to a person or thing.

charge[2] *verb* (**charged**, **charging**) **1** ask a particular price. **2** rush forward in an attack. **3** give an electric charge to something. **4** accuse someone of committing a crime. **5** entrust someone with a responsibility or task.

charger *noun* (*old use*) a cavalry horse.

chargrill *verb* grill quickly at a very high heat.

chariot *noun* a horse-drawn vehicle with two wheels, used in ancient times for fighting or racing. **charioteer** *noun*

charisma (*say* kuh-**riz**-muh) *noun* the special quality that makes a person popular or influential. [Greek, = divine favour]

charismatic (*say* ka-ruhz-**mat**-ik) *adjective* having charisma.

charity *noun* (*plural* **charities**) **1** an organisation set up to help people who are poor or have suffered a disaster. **2** giving money or help to the needy. **3** loving kindness towards others; being unwilling to think badly of people. **charitable** *adjective*, **charitably** *adverb* [from Latin *caritas* = love]

charlatan (*say* **shah**-luh-tuhn) *noun* a person who falsely claims to be an expert. [from Italian, = babbler]

charm[1] *noun* **1** the power to please or delight people; attractiveness. **2** a magic spell; a small object believed to bring good luck. **3** an ornament worn on a bracelet or chain.

charm[2] *verb* **1** give pleasure or delight to people. **2** put a spell on; bewitch. **charmer** *noun* [from Latin *carmen* = song or spell]

chart[1] *noun* **1** a map for people sailing ships or flying aircraft. **2** an outline map showing special information, *a weather chart.* **3** a diagram or list giving information in an orderly way.
the charts a list of the music albums or songs that are most popular.

chart[2] *verb* make a chart of something; map. [from Latin *charta* = card]

charter[1] *noun* **1** an official document giving somebody certain rights. **2** chartering an aircraft, ship, or vehicle.

charter[2] *verb* **1** hire an aircraft, ship, or vehicle. **2** give a charter to someone.

chartered accountant *noun* an accountant who is qualified according to the rules of an association that has a royal charter.

chary (*say* **chair**-ree) *adjective* cautious about doing or giving something.

chase *verb* (**chased**, **chasing**) go quickly after a person or thing in order to capture or catch them up or drive them away. **chase** *noun*

chasm (*say* **kaz**-uhm) *noun* a deep opening in the ground. [Greek, = wide hollow]

chassis (*say* **shaz**-ee) *noun* (*plural* **chassis**) the framework under a vehicle, on which other parts are mounted.

chaste *adjective* not having sexual intercourse at all, or only with the person to whom you are married. **chastity** *noun* [from Latin *castus* = pure]

chasten (*say* **chay**-suhn) *verb* discipline a person by punishing them; make someone feel subdued.

chastise *verb* (**chastised**, **chastising**) punish severely. **chastisement** *noun*

chat[1] *noun* **1** a friendly conversation. **2** the online exchange of messages in real time with one or more simultaneous users of a computer network.

chat[2] *verb* (**chatted**, **chatting**) have a chat. [from *chatter*]

château (*say* **sha**-toh) *noun* (*plural* **châteaux**) a large country house in France. [French]

chat room *noun* an area on the Internet where users can communicate.

chattel *noun* something you own that can be moved from place to place (distinguished from a house or land).

chatter[1] *verb* **1** talk quickly about unimportant things; keep on talking. **2** make a rattling sound, *He was so cold that his teeth chattered.* **chatterer** *noun*

chatter[2] *noun* chattering talk or sound.

chatterbox *noun* a talkative person.

chatty *adjective* (**chattier**, **chattiest**) fond of chatting.

chauffeur (*say* **shoh**-fuh) *noun* a person employed to drive a car. [French, = stoker]

chauvinism (*say* **shoh**-vuh-niz-uhm) *noun* prejudiced belief that your own group or country is superior to others. **chauvinist** *noun*, **chauvinistic** *adjective* [from the name of Nicolas Chauvin, a French soldier under Napoleon, noted for his extreme patriotism]

cheap *adjective* **1** low in price; not expensive. **2** of poor quality; of low value. **cheaply** *adverb*, **cheapness** *noun* [from Old English *ceap* = a bargain]

cheapen *verb* make or become cheap.

cheat[1] *verb* **1** trick or deceive somebody. **2** try to do well in an examination or game etc. by breaking the rules.

cheat[2] *noun* a person who cheats.

check[1] *verb* **1** make sure that something is correct or in good condition. **2** make something stop or go slower.

check[2] *noun* **1** checking something. **2** stopping or slowing; a pause. **3** the situation in chess when a king may be captured. [from Persian *shah* = king]

check[3] *noun* a pattern of squares. **checked** *adjective* [from *chequered*]

checkmate *noun* the winning situation in chess. **checkmate** *verb* [from Persian *shah mat* = the king is dead]

checkout *noun* a place where goods are paid for in a shop, especially a supermarket.

cheddar *noun* a firm cheese of a kind originally made in Cheddar in England.

cheek *noun* **1** the side of the face below the eye. **2** impudence.

cheeky *adjective* impudent. **cheekily** *adverb*, **cheekiness** *noun*

cheer[1] *noun* **1** a shout of praise or pleasure or encouragement, especially 'hurray'. **2** cheerfulness, *full of good cheer.*

cheer[2] *verb* **1** give a cheer. **2** gladden or encourage somebody.
cheer up make or become cheerful.

cheerful *adjective* **1** looking or sounding happy. **2** pleasantly bright. **cheerfully** *adverb*, **cheerfulness** *noun*

cheerio *interjection* (*informal*) goodbye.

cheerless *adjective* gloomy; dreary.

cheery *adjective* bright and cheerful.

cheese *noun* a solid food made from milk.

cheesy *adjective* **1** like cheese in taste, smell, or appearance. **2** (*informal*) smelly. **3** (*informal*) hackneyed and overly or obviously sentimental.

cheetah *noun* a very swift wild cat with leopard-like spots. [from Hindi *cītā*]

chef (*say* shef) *noun* the cook in a hotel or restaurant. [French, = chief]

chemical[1] *adjective* of or produced by chemistry.

chemical[2] *noun* a substance obtained by or used in chemistry.

chemist *noun* **1** a person who makes or sells medicines. **2** an expert in chemistry.

chemistry *noun* **1** the way that substances combine and react with one another. **2** the study of substances and their reactions etc. [same origin as *alchemy*]

cheque *noun* a printed form on which you write instructions to a bank to pay out money from your account.

chequered *adjective* marked with a pattern of squares.

cherish *verb* **1** look after a person or thing lovingly. **2** be fond of. [from French *cher* = dear]

cherry *noun* (*plural* **cherries**) a small soft round fruit with a stone.

cherry picker *noun* a crane for raising and lowering people.

cherub *noun* (*plural* **cherubim** or **cherubs**) an angel, often pictured as a chubby child with wings. **cherubic** (*say* chuh-**roo**-bik) *adjective* [from Hebrew]

chess *noun* a game for two players with 16 pieces each (called **chessmen**) on a board of 64 squares (a **chessboard**). [same origin as *check*[2]]

chest *noun* **1** the front part of the body between the neck and the waist. **2** a large strong box for storing things in.

chestnut[1] *noun* **1** a tree that produces hard brown nuts. **2** the nut of this tree. **3** an old joke or story.

chestnut[2] *adjective* reddish-brown.

chest of drawers *noun* a piece of furniture with drawers for storing clothes.

chevron (*say* **shev**-ruhn) *noun* a V-shaped stripe.

chew *verb* grind food between the teeth. **chewy** *adjective*

chewing gum *noun* a sticky flavoured substance for chewing.

chiack (*say* **chuy**-ak) *verb* (*Australian informal*) tease, jeer at. [from British slang]

chic (*say* sheek) *adjective* stylish and elegant. [French]

chicanery (*say* shuh-**kay**-nuh-ree) *noun* trickery. [from French *chicaner* = quibble]

chick *noun* a very young bird.

chicken[1] *noun* **1** a young bird, especially of the domestic fowl. **2** the flesh of a domestic fowl as food. **3** (*informal*) a coward.

chicken[2] *adjective* (*informal*) afraid to do something; cowardly.

chicken[3] *verb* **chicken out** (*informal*) withdraw because you are afraid.

chickenpox *noun* a disease that produces red spots on the skin.

chide *verb* (**chided**, **chidden**, **chiding**) (*old use*) scold.

chief[1] *noun* a person with the highest rank or authority.

chief[2] *adjective* most important; main. **chiefly** *adverb*

chieftain *noun* the chief of a people, clan, or other group.

chiffon (*say* **shif**-on) *noun* a very thin almost transparent fabric. [French]

chihuahua (*say* chuh-**wah**-wuh) *noun* a very small smooth-haired dog. [from the name of a city and state in Mexico]

chilblain *noun* a sore swollen place, usually on a hand or foot, caused by cold weather. [from *chill* + *blain* = a sore]

child *noun* (*plural* **children**) **1** a young person; a boy or girl. **2** someone's son or daughter.

childhood *noun* the time when a person is a child.

childish *adjective* like a child; unsuitable for a grown person. **childishly** *adverb*

childless *adjective* having no children.

childlike *adjective* innocent, frank, etc., like a child.

chill[1] *noun* **1** unpleasant coldness. **2** an illness that makes you shiver.

chill[2] *verb* make a person or thing cold.

chilli *noun* (*plural* **chillies**) the hot-tasting pod of a red pepper.

chilly *adjective* **1** rather cold. **2** unfriendly. **chilliness** *noun*

chime[1] *noun* a series of notes sounded by a set of bells each making a different musical sound.

chime[2] *verb* (**chimed**, **chiming**) make a chime.

chimney *noun* (*plural* **chimneys**) a tall pipe or structure that carries away smoke from a fire.

chimney sweep *noun* a person who cleans soot from inside chimneys.

chimpanzee *noun* an African ape, smaller than a gorilla.

chin *noun* the lower part of the face below the mouth.

china *noun* thin delicate pottery.

chink[1] *noun* **1** a narrow opening, *a chink in the curtains.* **2** a chinking sound.

chink[2] *verb* make a sound like glasses or coins being struck together.

chintz *noun* a shiny cotton cloth used for making curtains and upholstery. [from Hindi]

chip[1] *noun* **1** a thin piece cut or broken off something hard. **2** a fried oblong strip of potato; a potato crisp. **3** a place where a small piece has been knocked off something. **4** a small counter used in games. **5** a microchip.
a chip off the old block a child who resembles a parent.
have a chip on your shoulder have a grievance and feel bitter or resentful.

chip[2] *verb* (**chipped**, **chipping**) knock small pieces off something.
chip in 1 interrupt. **2** contribute money.

chipboard *noun* board made from chips of wood pressed and stuck together.

chipmunk *noun* a small striped squirrel-like animal of North America.

chipolata (*say* chip-uh-**lah**-tuh) *noun* a small thin sausage. [French, from Italian *cipollata* = a dish of onions]

chiropody (*say* kuh-**rop**-uh-dee) *noun* the treatment of ailments of the feet, e.g. corns. **chiropodist** *noun* [from Greek *cheir* = hand, + *pod-* = foot]

chiropractor (*say* **kuy**-ruh-prak-tuh) *noun* a person who treats certain disorders by manipulating the joints, especially those of the spine. [from Greek *cheir* = hand, + *prattein* = to do]

chirp *verb* make short sharp sounds like a small bird. **chirp** *noun*

chirpy *adjective* lively and cheerful.

chisel[1] *noun* a tool with a sharp end for shaping wood, stone, or metal.

chisel[2] *verb* (**chiselled**, **chiselling**) shape or cut with a chisel.

chitterlings *plural noun* the small intestines of a pig, cooked as food.

chivalrous (*say* **shiv**-uhl-ruhs) *adjective* being considerate and helpful towards people less strong than yourself. **chivalry** *noun* [from French *chevalier* = knight, from Latin *caballus* = horse]

chive *noun* a small herb with leaves that taste like onions.

chlamydia (*say* kluh-**mid**-ee-uh) *noun* (*plural* **chlamydiae**) a parasitic bacterium that can cause diseases such as trachoma, and can be sexually transmitted. [modern Latin, from Greek *khlamud* = cloak]

chlorinate *verb* (**chlorinated**, **chlorinating**) put chlorine into something. **chlorination** *noun*

chlorine (*say* **klaw**-reen) *noun* a greenish-yellow gas used especially to disinfect water and in industry. [from Greek *chloros* = green]

chlorofluorocarbon *noun* a gaseous compound of carbon, hydrogen, chlorine, and fluorine, formerly used in refrigerators and aerosols, and harmful to the ozone layer.

chloroform (*say* **klo**-ruh-fawm) *noun* a liquid that gives off a vapour that makes people unconscious.

chlorophyll (*say* **klo**-ruh-fil) *noun* the substance that makes plants green. [from Greek *chloros* = green, + *phyllon* = leaf]

chock *noun* a block or wedge used to prevent something from moving.

chock-a-block *adjective* crammed or crowded together.

chocker *adjective* (also **chockers**) (*Australian informal*) very full.

chock-full *adjective* crammed full.

chocolate *noun* **1** a solid brown food or powder made from roasted cacao seeds. **2** a drink made with this powder. **3** a sweet made of or covered with chocolate. [from Nahuatl *chocolatl*]

choice[1] *noun* **1** choosing; the power to choose between things. **2** a variety from which someone can choose, *There is a wide choice of holidays.* **3** a person or thing chosen, *This is my choice.*

choice[2] *adjective* of the best quality, *choice bananas.*

choir *noun* a group of people trained to sing together, especially in a church. [from Latin *chorus* = choir]

choke[1] *verb* (**choked**, **choking**) **1** cause somebody to stop breathing properly. **2** be unable to breathe properly. **3** clog.

choke[2] *noun* a device controlling the flow of air into the engine of a motor vehicle.

choko *noun* a green pear-shaped vegetable.

cholera (*say* **kol**-uh-ruh) *noun* an infectious disease that is often fatal. [from Greek *chole* = bile]

cholesterol (*say* kuh-**les**-tuh-rol) *noun* a fatty substance that can clog the arteries. [from Greek *chole* = bile, + *stereos* = stiff]

chook *noun* (*Australian informal*) a chicken or a fowl. [from British dialect *chuck* = chicken]

choose *verb* (**chose**, **chosen**, **choosing**) take one or more from among a number of people or things; select.

choosy *adjective* (**choosier**, **choosiest**) (*informal*) choosing carefully; hard to please.

chop[1] *verb* (**chopped**, **chopping**) cut or hit something with a heavy blow.

chop[2] *noun* **1** a chopping blow. **2** a small thick slice of meat, usually on a rib.

chopper *noun* **1** a chopping tool; a small axe. **2** (*informal*) a helicopter.

choppy *adjective* (**choppier**, **choppiest**) not smooth; full of small waves, *choppy seas.* **choppiness** *noun*

chopsticks *plural noun* a pair of thin sticks used for eating Chinese, Vietnamese, Japanese, etc. food.

choral *adjective* of or for or sung by a choir or chorus.

chorale (*say* kuh-**rahl**) *noun* a choral composition using the words of a hymn.

chord[1] (*say* kawd) *noun* a number of musical notes sounded together. [from *accord*]

chord[2] (*say* kawd) *noun* a straight line joining two points on a curve. [from *cord*]

chore (*say* chaw) *noun* a regular or dull task.

choreography (*say* ko-ree-**og**-ruh-fee) *noun* the composition of ballets or stage dances. **choreographer** *noun* [from Greek *choreia* = dance, + *-graphy*]

chorister (*say* **ko**-ruh-stuh) *noun* a member of a choir.

chortle *noun* a loud chuckle. **chortle** *verb* [a mixture of *chuckle* and *snort*]

chorus[1] *noun* (*plural* **choruses**) **1** the words repeated after each verse of a song or poem. **2** music sung by a group of people. **3** a group singing together.

chorus[2] *verb* (**chorused**, **chorusing**) sing or speak in chorus. [from Greek]

chose *past tense* of **choose**.

chosen *past participle* of **choose**.

chow (*rhymes with* cow) *noun* a long-haired dog of a Chinese breed.

chowder *noun* a rich soup typically containing fish, clams, or corn with potatoes and onions.

chow mein (*say* chow **min**) *noun* a Chinese dish of fried noodles with shredded meat and vegetables. [from Chinese *chao mian* = stir-fried noodles]

christen *verb* **1** baptise. **2** give a name or nickname to a person or thing. **christening** *noun*

Christian[1] *noun* a person who believes in Jesus Christ and his teachings.

Christian[2] *adjective* of Christians or their beliefs. **Christianity** *noun*

Christian name *noun* a name given at a christening; a person's given name.

Christmas *noun* (*plural* **Christmases**) the day (25 December) when Christians commemorate the birth of Jesus Christ; the days round it. [from *Christ* + *Mass*]

Christmas tree *noun* an evergreen or artificial tree decorated at Christmas.

chromatic (*say* kruh-**mat**-ik) *adjective* of colours. [from Greek *chroma* = colour]

chromatic scale *noun* a musical scale going up or down in semitones.

chrome (*say* krohm) *noun* chromium. [from Greek *chroma* = colour (because its compounds have brilliant colours)]

chroming *noun* (*Australian informal*) the inhaling of chrome-based spray-paint.

chromium (*say* **kroh**-mee-uhm) *noun* a shiny silvery metal. [from *chrome*]

chromosome (*say* **kroh**-muh-sohm) *noun* a tiny thread-like part of an animal cell or plant cell, carrying genes. [from Greek *chroma* = colour, + *soma* = body]

chronic *adjective* lasting for a long time, *a chronic illness.* **chronically** *adverb* [from Greek *chronikos* = of time]

chronicle *noun* a record of events in the order of their happening. [same origin as *chronic*]

chronological *adjective* arranged in the order of happening. **chronologically** *adverb*

chronology (*say* kruh-**nol**-uh-jee) *noun* the arrangement of events in the order in which they happened, e.g. in history or geology. [from Greek *chronos* = time, + *-logy*]

chronometer (*say* kruh-**nom**-uh-tuh) *noun* a very exact device for measuring time. [from Greek *chronos* = time, + *meter*]

chrysalis *noun* (*plural* **chrysalises**) a caterpillar that is changing into a butterfly or moth. [from Greek *chrysos* = gold (the colour of its covering)]

chrysanthemum *noun* a garden flower that blooms in autumn. [from Greek *chrysos* = gold, + *anthemon* = flower]

chubby *adjective* (**chubbier**, **chubbiest**) plump. **chubbiness** *noun*

chuck[1] *verb* (*informal*) **1** throw. **2** vomit. **chuck in** give up, *He chucked in his job.* **chuck out 1** throw away. **2** force a person to leave a place.

chuck[2] *noun* **1** the gripping-part of a lathe. **2** the part of a drill that holds the bit.

chuckle *verb* (**chuckled**, **chuckling**) laugh quietly. **chuckle** *noun*

chug *verb* (**chugged**, **chugging**) make the sound of an engine.

chum *noun* (*informal*) a friend. **chummy** *adjective*

chunk *noun* a thick piece of something. **chunky** *adjective*

church *noun* (*plural* **churches**) **1** a public building for Christian worship. **2** a religious service in a church, *I will see you after church.* **3** (**the Church**) all Christians; a group of these. [from Greek *kuriakon* = Lord's house]

churinga *noun* (*Australian*) an Aboriginal sacred object, normally carved or painted. [from Arrernte *tywerrenge* = object from the dreaming]

churlish *adjective* ill-mannered; surly.

churn[1] *noun* **1** a large can in which milk is carried from a farm. **2** a machine in which milk is beaten to make butter.

churn[2] *verb* **1** make butter in a churn. **2** stir or swirl vigorously. **churn out** produce in large quantities.

chute (*say* shoot) *noun* a steep channel for people or things to slide down. [French, = a fall]

chutney *noun* a thick sauce made from fruit or vegetables, vinegar, sugar, and spices. [from Hindi *catni*]

chutzpah (*say* **huuts**-puh or **xuuts**-puh) *noun* extreme self-confidence or audacity. [from Yiddish]

ciabatta (*say* chuh-**bah**-tuh) *noun* an Italian bread with a floury crust. [Italian]

cicada (*say* suh-**kah**-duh or suh-**kay**-duh) *noun* a large insect that makes a shrill chirping sound.

cider *noun* an alcoholic or non-alcoholic drink made from apples.

cigar *noun* a roll of compressed tobacco leaves for smoking. [from Spanish *cigarro*]

cigarette *noun* a small roll of shredded tobacco in thin paper for smoking. [French, = little cigar]

cinch *noun* (*informal*) an easy task; a certainty.

cinder *noun* a small piece of partly burnt coal or wood.

cinema *noun* **1** a place where films are shown. **2** films in general. **cinematic** *adjective* [from Greek *kinema* = movement]

cinnamon (*say* **sin**-uh-muhn) *noun* a yellowish-brown spice.

cipher (*say* **suy**-fuh) *noun* **1** the symbol 0, representing nought or zero. **2** a kind of code. [from Arabic *sifr* = nought]

circa *preposition* (often preceding a date) approximately, *The school was built circa 1875.* [Latin]

circle[1] *noun* **1** a perfectly round flat shape or thing. **2** a circular route. **3** a number of people with similar interests. **4** the balcony of a cinema or theatre.

circle[2] *verb* (**circled**, **circling**) move in a circle; go round something.

circuit (*say* **ser**-kuht) *noun* **1** a circular line or journey. **2** a motor-racing track. **3** the path of an electric current. [from Latin *circum* = round, + *itum* = gone]

circuitous (*say* ser-**kyoo**-uh-tuhs) *adjective* going a long way round; not direct.

circular[1] *adjective* **1** shaped like a circle; round. **2** moving round a circle. **circularity** *noun*

circular[2] *noun* a letter or advertisement sent to a number of people.

circulate *verb* (**circulated**, **circulating**) **1** go round something continuously, *Blood circulates in the body.* **2** pass from place to place. **3** send round; send to a number of people. **circulation** *noun*

circum- *prefix* around (as in *circumference*). [from Latin *circum* = around]

circumcise *verb* (**circumcised**, **circumcising**) **1** cut off the foreskin of (a young boy or man, especially a baby) as a religious rite or as a medical treatment. **2** (as a practice traditional in some cultures) partially or totally remove the external genitalia of (a girl or young woman) for non-medical reasons. **circumcision** *noun* [from *circum*-, + Latin *caedere* = cut]

circumference *noun* the distance round something, especially round a circle. [from *circum*-, + Latin *ferens* = carrying]

circumflex accent *noun* a mark over a vowel, as over *e* in *fête*.

circumlocution *noun* a roundabout expression, using many words where a few would do, e.g. 'at this moment in time' for 'now'.

circumnavigate *verb* (**circumnavigated**, **circumnavigating**) **1** sail or travel all the way around (something, especially the world). **2** go around or avoid something, *I had to circumnavigate the busy road to get to school.* **circumnavigation** *noun* [from *circum-* + *navigate*]

circumscribe *verb* (**circumscribed**, **circumscribing**) **1** draw a line round something. **2** limit; restrict, *Her powers are circumscribed by many regulations.* [from *circum*-, + Latin *scribere* = write]

circumspect *adjective* cautious and watchful. **circumspection** *noun* [from *circum*-, + Latin *specere* = to look]

circumstance *noun* a fact or condition connected with an event or person or action. [from *circum*-, + Latin *stans* = standing]

circumstantial (*say* ser-kuhm-**stan**-shuhl) *adjective* **1** giving full details, *a circumstantial account of her journey.* **2** consisting of facts that strongly suggest something but do not actually prove it, *circumstantial evidence.*

circumvent *verb* find a way of avoiding, *We managed to circumvent the rules.* **circumvention** *noun* [from *circum*-, + Latin *ventum* = come]

circus *noun* (*plural* **circuses**) a travelling show with clowns, acrobats, animals, etc. [Latin, = ring]

cisgender *adjective* (also **cisgendered**) denoting or relating to someone whose sense of personal identity and gender corresponds with their birth sex. [from Latin *cis* = on this side of, + *gender*]

cistern *noun* a tank for storing water.

citadel *noun* a fortress protecting a city.

cite (*say* suyt) *verb* (**cited**, **citing**) quote as an example. **citation** *noun*

citizen *noun* a person belonging to a particular city or country and having certain rights and duties because of this. **citizenship** *noun* [same origin as *city*]

citric acid (*say* **sit**-rik) *noun* the acid in the juice of lemons, limes, and other citrus fruits.

citrus fruit *noun* a lemon, orange, grapefruit, mandarin, etc.

city *noun* (*plural* **cities**) a large important town. [from Latin *civitas* = city]

civet *noun* (also **civet cat**) a cat-like animal of central Africa.

civic *adjective* of a city or town; of citizens. [from Latin *civis* = citizen]

civics *noun* the study of the way citizens and towns are governed and of the rights and duties of citizens.

civil *adjective* **1** of citizens. **2** of civilians; not military, *civil aviation.* **3** polite. **civilly** *adverb*

civil engineering *noun* the design and building of roads, bridges, and similar structures.

civilian *noun* a person who is not serving in the armed forces.

civilisation *noun* **1** a civilised condition or society. **2** making or becoming civilised.

civilise *verb* (**civilised, civilising**) **1** bring a place or people to a stage of social development considered to be more advanced. **2** enlighten; refine and educate. **civilised** *adjective*

civility *noun* (*plural* **civilities**) politeness; a polite act.

civil rights *plural noun* the rights of citizens, especially to have freedom, equality, and the right to vote.

civil servant *noun* a public servant.

civil war *noun* war between groups of people of the same country.

clad *adjective* clothed.

claim[1] *verb* **1** ask for something to which you believe you have a right. **2** declare; state something without being able to prove it. **claimant** *noun*

claim[2] *noun* **1** claiming. **2** something claimed. **3** a piece of ground claimed or assigned to someone for mining. **4** a right or title to something. [same origin as *clamour*[2]]

clairvoyant *noun* a person who is said to be able to perceive future events or things that are happening out of sight. **clairvoyance** *noun* [from French *clair* = clear, + *voyant* = seeing]

clam *noun* a large shellfish.

clamber *verb* climb with difficulty.

clammy *adjective* damp and sticky.

clamour[1] *noun* **1** a loud confused noise. **2** an outcry; a loud protest or demand. **clamorous** *adjective*

clamour[2] *verb* make a loud protest or demand. [from Latin *clamare* = call out]

clamp[1] *noun* a device for holding things tightly.

clamp[2] *verb* fix with a clamp; fix firmly. **clamp down on** become stricter about something; put a stop to it.

clan *noun* a group sharing the same ancestor, especially among Aboriginal groups and in Scotland. **clannish** *adjective*

clandestine (*say* klan-**des**-tuhn) *adjective* done secretly; kept secret.

clang *noun* a loud ringing sound. **clang** *verb*

clangour *noun* a clanging noise.

clank *noun* a sound like heavy pieces of metal banging together. **clank** *verb*

clap[1] *verb* (**clapped, clapping**) **1** strike the palms of the hands together loudly, especially as applause. **2** put quickly, *They clapped him into gaol.*

clap[2] *noun* **1** a sudden sharp noise, *a clap of thunder.* **2** clapping; applause.

clapper *noun* the tongue or hanging piece inside a bell that strikes against the bell to make it sound.

claptrap *noun* insincere talk.

claret *noun* a kind of red wine.

clarify *verb* (**clarified, clarifying**) make or become clear or easier to understand. **clarification** *noun* [from Latin *clarus* = clear]

clarinet *noun* a woodwind instrument. **clarinettist** *noun*

clarion *noun* an old type of trumpet.

clarity *noun* clearness.

clash *verb* **1** make a loud sound like that of cymbals banging together. **2** conflict. **3** happen inconveniently at the same time. **4** (of colours) look unpleasant together. **clash** *noun*

clasp[1] *noun* **1** a device for fastening things, with interlocking parts. **2** a grasp.

clasp[2] *verb* **1** grasp or hold tightly. **2** fasten with a clasp.

class[1] *noun* (*plural* **classes**) **1** a group of students who are taught together; a session when they are taught. **2** a group of similar people, animals, or things. **3** people of the same social or economic level. **4** level of quality, *first class.*

class[2] *verb* **1** classify. **2** (*Australian*) grade fleeces in a shearing shed. **classer** *noun* [from Latin *classis* = a social division of the Roman people]

class action *noun* legal action brought against a company etc. by a group of people, each with the same complaint.

classic[1] *adjective* **1** generally agreed to be excellent or important. **2** very typical, *a classic case.* **3** having enduring worth.

classic[2] *noun* **1** a work of art of recognised and established value. **2** a thing that is memorable and a very good example of its kind, *My grandmother's chocolate cake is a classic.* [from Latin *classicus* = of the highest class]

classical *adjective* **1** of ancient Greek or Roman literature, art, and culture. **2** of traditional and long-established form or style, *classical music.*

classics *noun* the study of ancient Greek and Latin languages, literature, and culture.

classified *adjective* **1** put into classes or groups. **2** (of information) declared officially to be secret and available only to certain people.

classify *verb* (**classified, classifying**) arrange things in classes or groups. **classification** *noun*, **classificatory** *adjective*

classmate *noun* someone in the same class at school.

classroom *noun* a room where a class of children or students is taught.

clatter *verb & noun* rattle.

clause *noun* **1** a single part of a treaty, law, or contract. **2** part of a complex sentence, with its own verb, *There are two clauses in 'We choose what we want'.*

claustrophobia *noun* fear of being inside something. [from Latin *claustrum* = enclosed space, + *phobia*]

claves *plural noun* a pair of sticks that make a hollow sound when struck together, used as a musical instrument.

clavichord (*say* **klav**-uh-kord) *noun* a stringed keyboard instrument with a very soft tone.

clavicle (*say* **klav**-i-kuhl) *noun* the collarbone. [from Latin *clavicula* = small key]

claw[1] *noun* **1** a sharp nail on a bird's or animal's foot. **2** a claw-like part or device used for grasping things.

claw[2] *verb* grasp, pull, or scratch with a claw or hand.

clay *noun* a kind of stiff sticky earth that becomes hard when baked, used for making bricks and pottery. **clayey** *adjective*

claymation *noun* the technique of filming successive positions of clay figures to create an illusion of movement when the film is shown as a sequence.

claypan *noun* (*Australian*) a natural hollow in clay soil, retaining water after rain.

clean[1] *adjective* **1** without any dirt or marks or stains. **2** fresh; not yet used. **3** honourable; not unfair, *a clean fight.* **4** not indecent, *a clean joke.* **cleanly** *adverb*, **cleanness** *noun*

clean[2] *verb* make a thing clean.

clean[3] *adverb* completely, *I clean forgot.*

cleaner *noun* **1** a person who cleans things, especially rooms. **2** something used for cleaning things.

cleanliness (*say* **klen**-lee-nuhs) *noun* being clean.

cleanse (*say* klenz) *verb* (**cleansed**, **cleansing**) **1** clean. **2** make pure. **cleanser** *noun*

clean-shaven *adjective* without a beard or moustache.

cleanskin *noun* (*Australian*) **1** an unbranded animal. **2** (*informal*) an unlabelled bottle of wine.

clear[1] *adjective* **1** transparent; not muddy or cloudy. **2** easy to see or hear or understand; distinct. **3** free from obstacles or unwanted things. **4** free from guilt, *a clear conscience.* **5** complete, *Give three clear days' notice.* **clearly** *adverb*, **clearness** *noun* [from Latin *clarus* = clear]

clear[2] *adverb* **1** distinctly; clearly, *We heard you loud and clear.* **2** completely, *He got clear away.* **3** apart; not in contact, *Stand clear of the doors.*

clear[3] *verb* **1** make or become clear. **2** show that someone is innocent or reliable. **3** jump over something without touching it. **4** get approval or authorisation for something, *Clear this with the teacher.*
clear away remove an obstruction or unwanted item from somewhere.
clear off (*informal*) go away.
clear up 1 make things tidy. **2** become better or brighter. **3** solve, *clear up the mystery.*

clearance *noun* **1** clearing something. **2** getting rid of unwanted goods. **3** the space between two things.

clearing *noun* an open space in a forest.

clearway *noun* a road on which vehicles must not stop between certain hours.

cleave[1] *verb* (*past tense* **cleaved**, **clove**, or **cleft**; *past participle* **cleft** or **cloven**; *present participle* **cleaving**) **1** divide by chopping; split. **2** make a way through, *cleaving the waves.* **cleavage** *noun*

cleave[2] *verb* (**cleaved**, **cleaving**) (*old use*) cling to something.

cleaver *noun* a butcher's chopper.

clef *noun* a symbol on a stave in music, showing the pitch of the notes, *treble clef; bass clef.* [French, = key]

cleft[1] *past tense & past participle* of **cleave**[1].

cleft[2] *noun* a split; a separation.

cleft palate *noun* a defect in the roof of the mouth where two sides of the palate failed to join before birth.

clemency *noun* mildness; mercy.

clench *verb* close teeth or fingers tightly.

clergy *noun* the people who have been ordained as priests or ministers of the Christian Church.

cleric *noun* a member of the clergy.

clerical *adjective* **1** of clerks or their work. **2** of the clergy.

clerk (*say* klahk) *noun* a person employed to keep records or accounts, deal with papers in an office, and undertake other routine administrative duties.

clever *adjective* quick at learning and understanding things; skilful. **cleverly** *adverb*, **cleverness** *noun*

cliché (*say* **klee**-shay) *noun* a phrase or idea that is used too often. [French, = stereotyped]

click *noun* **1** a short sharp sound. **2** (in computing) an act of pressing a button on a mouse or similar device. **click** *verb*

client *noun* a person who gets help from a lawyer, architect, or professional person other than a doctor; a customer.

clientele (*say* kluy-uhn-**tel** or klee-uhn-**tel**) *noun* clients.

cliff *noun* a steep rock face, especially on a coast.

climate *noun* **1** the weather conditions prevailing in an area in general or over a long period. **2** a region with a particular climate, *She lived in a cold climate.* **3** the prevailing trend of public opinion or of another aspect of life. **climatic** *adjective*

climate change *noun* a change in global or regional climate patterns, in particular a change apparent from the mid to late 20th century onwards and attributed largely to the increased levels of atmospheric carbon dioxide produced by the use of fossil fuels.

climax *noun* (*plural* **climaxes**) the event or point of greatest interest or intensity; a culmination. **climactic** *adjective* [from Greek *klimax* = ladder]

climb *verb* **1** go up or over or down something. **2** grow upwards. **3** go higher. **climb** *noun*, **climber** *noun*

clinch *verb* **1** fasten securely. **2** settle definitely, *clinch the deal.* **3** (in boxing) be clasping each other. **clinch** *noun* [from *clench*]

clincher *noun* a fact, argument, or event that settles a matter conclusively.

cling *verb* (**clung**, **clinging**) hold on tightly.

clinic *noun* a place or session at which specialised treatment or advice is given to visiting persons, *a medical clinic.* [from Greek *klinikos* = of a bed]

clinical *adjective* **1** of a clinic. **2** of or used in the treatment of patients. **3** unemotional; cool and detached.

clink *noun* a thin sharp sound like glasses being struck together. **clink** *verb*

clinker *noun* a piece of rough stony material left after coal has burned.

clip[1] *noun* a fastener for keeping things together, usually worked by a spring.

clip[2] *verb* (**clipped**, **clipping**) fasten with a clip.

clip[3] *verb* (**clipped**, **clipping**) **1** cut with shears or scissors. **2** (*informal*) hit.

clip[4] *noun* **1** clipping something; a piece clipped off or out. **2** an extract from a film or video. **3** the wool cut from a sheep or flock at one shearing. **4** (*informal*) a sharp blow.

clipboard *noun* **1** a small board with a clip for holding papers. **2** (in computing) a temporary storage area where material cut or copied from a file is kept until pasted into another file.

clipper *noun* an old type of fast sailing ship.

clippers *plural noun* an instrument for cutting hair.

clique (*say* kleek) *noun* a small group of people who stick together and keep others out.

cloak[1] *noun* a sleeveless garment that hangs loosely from the shoulders.

cloak[2] *verb* cover; conceal.

cloakroom *noun* a place where people can leave outdoor clothes or luggage.

clobber *verb* (*informal*) **1** hit hard again and again. **2** defeat completely.

clock[1] *noun* **1** a device (other than a watch) that shows what the time is. **2** a measuring device with a dial or showing figures. [from Latin *clocca* = bell]

clock[2] *verb* time a race or a competitor.
clock in or **on** record the time you arrive at work.
clock off or **out** record the time you leave work.
clock up achieve a certain speed or distance.

clockwise *adverb & adjective* moving round a circle in the same direction as a clock's hands. [from *clock* + *wise*[2]]

clockwork *noun* a mechanism with a spring that has to be wound up.
like clockwork very regularly.

clod *noun* a lump of earth or clay.

clog[1] *noun* a shoe with a wooden sole.

clog[2] *verb* (**clogged**, **clogging**) block up.

cloister *noun* a covered path around a quadrangle, especially in a convent, monastery, or college. [from Latin *claustrum* = enclosed place]

cloistered *adjective* sheltered, secluded.

clone *noun* an animal or plant made from the cells of another animal or plant and therefore exactly like it. **clone** *verb*

close[1] (*say* klohs) *adjective* **1** near. **2** dear to each other, *close friends.* **3** detailed; concentrated, *close examination.* **4** tight; with little empty space, *a close fit.* **5** in which competitors are nearly equal, *a close contest.* **6** stuffy. **closely** *adverb*, **closeness** *noun*

close[2] *adverb* closely, *close behind.*

close[3] *noun* a street closed at one end.

close[4] (*say* klohz) *verb* (**closed**, **closing**) **1** shut. **2** end.
close in get nearer.

close[5] *noun* end, *the close of play.* [from Latin *clausum* = shut]

closet[1] *noun* a cupboard; a small room; a storeroom.

closet[2] *verb* (**closeted**, **closeting**) shut away in a private room.

closure *noun* closing.

clot[1] *noun* **1** a small thickened mass of blood or other liquid. **2** (*informal*) a stupid person.

clot[2] *verb* (**clotted**, **clotting**) form clots.

cloth *noun* **1** woven material or felt. **2** a piece of this material. **3** a tablecloth.

clothe *verb* (**clothed**, **clothing**) put clothes on someone.

clothes *plural noun* things worn to cover the body. [originally the plural of *cloth*]

clothing *noun* clothes.

clotted cream *noun* cream thickened by being scalded.

cloud[1] *noun* **1** a mass of condensed water vapour floating in the sky. **2** an indistinct or billowing mass, especially of smoke or dust. **3** a state of gloom, trouble, or suspicion, *casting a cloud over the festivities.* **4** (usually **the cloud**) a network of remote servers hosted on the Internet and used to store, manage, and process data in place of local servers or personal computers.

cloud[2] *verb* fill or obscure with clouds.

cloudburst *noun* a sudden violent rainstorm.

cloudless *adjective* without clouds.

cloudy *adjective* (**cloudier**, **cloudiest**) **1** full of clouds. **2** not transparent, *The liquid became cloudy.* **cloudiness** *noun*

clout[1] *verb* (*informal*) hit.

clout[2] *noun* **1** (*informal*) a hard blow. **2** influence; power.

clove[1] *noun* the dried bud of a tropical tree, used as a spice.

clove[2] *noun* one of the small bulbs in a compound bulb, *a clove of garlic.*

clove[3] *past tense* of **cleave**[1].

clove hitch *noun* a kind of knot.

cloven *past participle* of **cleave**[1].

cloven hoof *noun* a hoof that is divided, like those of cows and sheep.

clover *noun* a small plant usually with three leaves on each stalk.
in clover in ease and luxury.

clown[1] *noun* **1** a performer who does comical tricks and actions, especially in a circus. **2** a person who clowns.

clown[2] *verb* behave comically.

clownfish *noun* a brightly coloured tropical fish that lives in close association with sea anemones.

cloying *adjective* sickeningly sweet.

club[1] *noun* **1** a heavy stick used as a weapon. **2** a stick with a shaped head used to hit the ball in golf. **3** a group of people who meet because they are interested in the same thing; the premises where they meet. **4** a playing card with black shapes like clover leaves on it.

club[2] *verb* (**clubbed**, **clubbing**) hit with a heavy stick.
club together join with other people in doing something, *club together to buy a boat.*

cluck *verb* make a hen's throaty cry.
cluck *noun*

clucky *adjective* (*Australian informal*) (of a woman) wanting to have a baby. [from the noise made by a broody hen]

clue *noun* something that helps a person to solve a puzzle or a mystery.
not have a clue (*informal*) be stupid or helpless.

clump[1] *noun* **1** a cluster or mass of things. **2** a clumping sound.

clump[2] *verb* **1** form a cluster or mass. **2** walk with a heavy tread.

clumsy *adjective* (**clumsier**, **clumsiest**) **1** heavy and ungraceful; likely to knock things over or drop things. **2** not skilful; not tactful, *a clumsy apology.* **clumsily** *adverb*, **clumsiness** *noun*

clung *past tense & past participle* of **cling**.

cluster[1] *noun* a small close group.

cluster[2] *verb* form a cluster.

clutch[1] *verb* grasp tightly.

clutch[2] *noun* (*plural* **clutches**) **1** a tight grasp. **2** a device for connecting and disconnecting the engine of a motor vehicle from its gears.

clutch[3] *noun* (*plural* **clutches**) a set of eggs for hatching.

clutter[1] *noun* things lying about untidily.

clutter[2] *verb* fill with clutter.

cm *abbreviation* centimetre(s).

Co. *abbreviation* Company.

c/o *abbreviation* (also **c/-**) care of.

co- *prefix* together, jointly (as in *coexistence, cooperate*); joint (as in *co-pilot*). [from *com-*]

coach[1] *noun* (*plural* **coaches**) **1** a bus used for long journeys. **2** a carriage of a railway train. **3** a large horse-drawn carriage with four wheels. **4** an instructor in sports. **5** a teacher giving private specialised tuition.

coach[2] *verb* instruct or train somebody, especially in sports.

coagulate *verb* (**coagulated**, **coagulating**) change from liquid to semi-solid; clot.
coagulant *noun*, **coagulation** *noun*

coal *noun* a hard black mineral substance used for burning to supply heat; a piece of this. **coalfield** *noun*, **coalmine** *noun*

coalesce (*say* koh-uh-**les**) *verb* (**coalesced**, **coalescing**) combine and form one whole thing. **coalescence** *noun*, **coalescent** *adjective*

coalition *noun* **1** an alliance. **2** (**the Coalition**) (*Australian*) the alliance between the Liberal Party and the National Party.

coal seam gas *noun* a form of natural gas, especially methane, found in coal deposits.

coarse *adjective* **1** not smooth, not delicate; rough. **2** composed of large particles; not fine. **3** not refined; vulgar, *a coarse joke.* **coarsely** *adverb*, **coarseness** *noun*

coarsen *verb* make or become coarse.

coast[1] *noun* the seashore; the land close to it. **coastal** *adjective*, **coastline** *noun*
the coast is clear there is no chance of being seen or hindered.

coast[2] *verb* ride without using power.

coaster *noun* a small mat or tray for a glass or bottle.

coastguard *noun* an organisation that polices the coast in order to assist people or ships in danger and to prevent smuggling; a member of this organisation.

coat[1] *noun* **1** an outdoor garment with sleeves. **2** the hair or fur on an animal's body. **3** a coating, *a coat of paint.*

coat[2] *verb* cover with a coating.

coating *noun* a covering layer.

coat of arms *noun* a design on a shield, used as an emblem by a family, city, country, institution, etc.

coax *verb* persuade gently or patiently.

cob *noun* **1** the central part of an ear of maize, on which the corn grows. **2** a sturdy horse for riding. **3** a male swan. (The female is a *pen.*)

cobalt *noun* a hard silvery-white metal.

cobber *noun* (*Australian informal*) a friend; a mate. [probably from Yiddish *chaber* = comrade]

cobble[1] *noun* a rounded stone used for paving. **cobbled** *adjective*

cobble[2] *verb* (**cobbled**, **cobbling**) make or mend roughly.

cobbler *noun* a shoe repairer.

cobra (*say* **kob**-ruh or **koh**-bruh) *noun* a poisonous snake that can rear up.

cobweb *noun* the thin sticky net made by a spider to trap insects. [from an old word *coppe* = spider, + *web*]

cocaine *noun* a drug made from the leaves of a tropical plant called *coca.*

coccyx (*say* **kok**-siks) *noun* (*plural* **coccyges** or **coccyxes**) a small triangular bone at the base of the spine. [from Greek *kokkux* = cuckoo (the bone looks like a cuckoo's beak)]

cock[1] *noun* **1** a male bird; a male fowl. **2** a stopcock. **3** a lever in a gun.

cock[2] *verb* **1** make a gun ready to fire by raising the cock. **2** turn something upwards or in a particular direction, *The dog cocked its ears.*

cockatoo *noun* a crested parrot.

cockerel *noun* a young male fowl.

cocker spaniel *noun* a kind of small spaniel.

cock-eyed *adjective* (*informal*) **1** crooked; not straight. **2** absurd.

cockle *noun* an edible shellfish.

cockney *noun* (*plural* **cockneys**) **1** a person born in the East End of London. **2** the dialect or accent of cockneys.

cockpit *noun* the compartment where the pilot of an aircraft sits.

cockroach *noun* (*plural* **cockroaches**) a dark brown beetle-like insect.

cocksure *adjective* very sure; too confident.

cocktail *noun* **1** a mixed alcoholic drink. **2** a food containing shellfish or fruit.

cocky[1] *adjective* (**cockier**, **cockiest**) (*informal*) conceited; cheeky. **cockiness** *noun*

cocky[2] *noun* (*plural* **cockies**) (*Australian informal*) **1** a cockatoo. **2** a farmer with a small property.

cocoa *noun* **1** a hot drink made from a powder of crushed cacao seeds. **2** this powder. [an alteration of *cacao*]

coconut *noun* **1** a large round nut that grows on a kind of palm tree. **2** its white lining, used in sweets and cookery. [from Spanish *coco* = grinning face (the base of the nut looks like a monkey's face)]

cocoon[1] *noun* **1** the covering round a chrysalis. **2** a protective wrapping.

cocoon[2] *verb* protect by wrapping.

cod *noun* (*plural* **cod**) any of several sea or freshwater fish, used as food.

coda (*say* **koh**-duh) *noun* the final passage of a piece of music. [Italian]

coddle *verb* (**coddled**, **coddling**) **1** cherish and protect carefully. **2** cook in water just below boiling point, *coddled eggs.*

code[1] *noun* **1** a word or phrase used to represent a message in order to keep its meaning secret. **2** a set of laws or rules, *a code of practice.* **3** (in computing) program instructions. **4** a set of signs used in sending messages by machine, *Morse code.*

code[2] *verb* (**coded**, **coding**) **1** put into code. **2** write code for a computer program.

codicil *noun* an addition to a will.

codify *verb* (**codified**, **codifying**) arrange laws or rules into a code or system. **codification** *noun*

coeducation *noun* educating boys and girls together. **coeducational** *adjective*

coefficient *noun* a number by which another number is multiplied; a factor.

coelacanth (*say* **see**-luh-kanth) *noun* a large sea fish formerly thought to be extinct.

coeliac disease (*say* **see**-lee-ak) *noun* a disease in which the small intestine is hypersensitive to gluten.

coerce (*say* koh-**ers**) *verb* (**coerced, coercing**) compel someone by using threats or force. **coercion** *noun*

coexist *verb* exist together. **coexistence** *noun*, **coexistent** *adjective*

coffee *noun* **1** a hot drink made from the roasted ground seeds (*coffee beans*) of a tropical plant. **2** these seeds. [from Arabic *kahwa*]

coffer *noun* a large strong box for holding money and valuables.

coffin *noun* a long box in which a body is buried or cremated.

cog *noun* one of a number of projections round the edge of a wheel, fitting into and pushing those on another wheel.

cogent (*say* **koh**-juhnt) *adjective* convincing, *a cogent argument.*

cogitate *verb* (**cogitated, cogitating**) think deeply. **cogitation** *noun*

cogwheel *noun* a wheel with cogs.

cohere *verb* (**cohered, cohering**) **1** stick to each other in a mass. **2** be logical or consistent. **cohesive** *adjective* [from *co-*, + Latin *haerere* = to stick]

coherent (*say* koh-**heer**-ruhnt) *adjective* **1** cohering. **2** clear and reasonable; not incoherent. **coherently** *adverb*

cohesion *noun* **1** cohering, a tendency to stick together. **2** the action or fact of forming a united whole.

coil[1] *noun* something wound into a spiral.

coil[2] *verb* wind into rings or a spiral.

coin[1] *noun* a shaped piece of metal used to buy things.

coin[2] *verb* **1** manufacture coins. **2** (*informal*) make a lot of money as profit. **3** invent a word or phrase.

coinage *noun* **1** coining. **2** coins; a system of money. **3** a new word or phrase.

coincide *verb* (**coincided, coinciding**) **1** happen at the same time as something else. **2** be in the same place. **3** be the same, *My opinion coincided with hers.* [from *co-*, + Latin *incidere* = fall on]

coincidence *noun* the happening of similar events at the same time by chance. **coincidental** *adjective*

coke *noun* the solid fuel left when gas and tar have been extracted from coal.

col- *prefix* see **com-**.

colander *noun* a bowl-shaped container with holes for straining water from food after cooking.

colby *noun* a firm cheese of a kind originally made in Colby in the US.

cold[1] *adjective* **1** having or at a low temperature; not warm. **2** not friendly or loving; not enthusiastic. **coldly** *adverb*, **coldness** *noun*
get cold feet feel afraid or reluctant to do something.
give someone the cold shoulder be deliberately unfriendly to someone.

cold[2] *noun* **1** lack of warmth; low temperature; cold weather. **2** an infectious illness, typically causing running at the nose, sneezing, and a sore throat.

cold-blooded *adjective* **1** having a body temperature that changes according to the surroundings. **2** callous; deliberately cruel.

cold case *noun* an unsolved criminal investigation that remains open pending the discovery of new evidence.

cold war *noun* a situation where nations are enemies without actually fighting.

coleslaw *noun* a salad of shredded raw cabbage, carrot, and other vegetables mixed with mayonnaise.

colic *noun* severe spasmodic abdominal pain. **colicky** *adjective*

colitis (*say* kuh-**luy**-tuhs) *noun* inflammation of the lining of the colon.

collaborate *verb* (**collaborated, collaborating**) work together on a job. **collaboration** *noun*, **collaborator** *noun* [from *col-*, + Latin *laborare* = to work]

collage (*say* kuh-**lahzh**) *noun* **1** a picture made by fixing bits of paper, cloth, string, and other materials to a surface. **2** a collection of unrelated things. [French, = gluing]

collagen *noun* a protein substance found in bone and tissue.

collapse *verb* (**collapsed, collapsing**) **1** fall down or inwards suddenly; break. **2** become very weak or ill. **3** break down; fail. **4** fold up. **collapse** *noun* [from *col-*, + Latin *lapsum* = slipped]

collapsible *adjective* able to be folded up.

collar[1] *noun* **1** an upright or turned-over band round the neck of a garment. **2** a band that goes round the neck of an animal to control or restrain it.

collar[2] *verb* (*informal*) seize. [from Latin *collum* = neck]

collarbone *noun* the bone joining the breastbone and shoulder blade; the clavicle.

collate *verb* (**collated, collating**) **1** compare in detail. **2** collect and arrange systematically. **collation** *noun*

collateral *adjective* **1** parallel to something. **2** additional but less important.

colleague *noun* a person you work with.

collect[1] (*say* kuh-**lekt**) *verb* **1** bring people or things together from various places. **2** obtain examples of things as a hobby, *She collects stamps.* **3** come together. **4** ask for money or contributions from people. **5** fetch, *Collect your coat from the cleaners.* **collector** *noun*

collect[2] (*say* **kol**-ekt) *noun* a short prayer.

collection *noun* **1** collecting. **2** things collected. **3** money collected for a charity or at a church service.

collective *adjective* of a group taken as a whole, *our collective opinion.*

collective *noun* a noun that is singular in form but refers to many individuals taken as a unit, e.g. *army, herd.*

college *noun* **1** a place where people can continue learning something after they have left school. **2** a school. **3** a residential part of a university.

collide *verb* (**collided**, **colliding**) crash into something. **collision** *noun*

collie *noun* a dog with a long pointed face.

colliery *noun* (*plural* **collieries**) a coalmine and its buildings. [from *coal*]

collocate *verb* **1** to place together or side by side. **2** to bring together for purposes of comparison.

collocation *noun* **1** collocating. **2** the customary association of words with other particular words.

colloquial (*say* kuh-**loh**-kwee-uhl) *adjective* suitable for conversation but not for formal speech or writing. **colloquialism** *noun*, **colloquially** *adverb* [from *col-* + Latin *loqui* = speak]

collusion *noun* a secret agreement between two or more people who are trying to deceive or cheat someone. [from *col-*, + Latin *ludere* = to play]

cologne (*say* kuh-**lohn**) *noun* eau de Cologne or a similar liquid.

colon[1] *noun* a punctuation mark (:), often used to introduce lists and quotations.

colon[2] *noun* the largest part of the intestine.

colonel (*say* **ker**-nuhl) *noun* an army officer in charge of a regiment. [from French]

colonial *adjective* of a colony.

colonialism *noun* the policy of acquiring and keeping colonies.

colonise *verb* (**colonised**, **colonising**) establish a colony in a country. **colonisation** *noun*, **colonist** *noun*

colonnade *noun* a row of columns.

colonoscopy *noun* the examination of the colon and rectum, using a video-camera instrument.

colony *noun* (*plural* **colonies**) **1** an area of land that the people of another country settle in and control. **2** the people of a colony. **3** a group of people or animals of the same kind living close together.

coloration *noun* colouring.

colossal *adjective* immense; enormous.

colossus *noun* (*plural* **colossi**) **1** a huge statue. **2** a person of immense importance. [from the bronze statue of Apollo at Rhodes, the *Colossus of Rhodes*]

colour[1] *noun* **1** the effect produced by waves of light of a particular wavelength. **2** the use of various colours, not only black and white. **3** the colour of someone's skin. **4** a substance used to colour things. **5** the special flag of a ship or regiment.

colour[2] *verb* **1** put colour on; paint or stain. **2** blush. **3** influence what someone says or believes. **colouring** *noun*

colour-blind *adjective* unable to see the difference between certain colours.

coloured *adjective* **1** having colour. **2** having a dark skin.

colourful *adjective* **1** full of colour. **2** lively; with vivid details.

colourless *adjective* **1** without colour. **2** lacking interest.

colt *noun* a young male horse.

column *noun* **1** a pillar. **2** something long or tall and narrow, *a column of smoke; a column of trucks.* **3** a vertical section of a page, *There are two columns on this page.* **4** a vertical arrangement of figures or other information. **5** a regular article in a newspaper. **columnist** *noun*

column graph *noun* a chart using bars to represent quantity.

com- *prefix* (becoming **col-** before *l*, **cor-** before *r*, **con-** before many other consonants) with; together (as in *combine*, *connect*). [from Latin *cum* = with]

coma (*say* **koh**-muh) *noun* a state of deep unconsciousness, especially in someone who is ill or injured. **comatose** *adjective* [from Greek, = deep sleep]

comb[1] *noun* **1** a strip of rigid material with teeth, used to tidy hair or hold it in place. **2** something used like this, e.g. to separate strands of wool. **3** the red crest on a fowl's head. **4** a honeycomb.

comb[2] *verb* **1** tidy with a comb. **2** search thoroughly.

combat *noun & verb* (**combated**, **combating**) fight. **combatant** (*say* **kom**-buh-tuhnt) *noun*

combination *noun* **1** combining. **2** a number of people or things that are combined. **3** a series of numbers or letters used to open a combination lock.

combination lock *noun* a lock that can be opened only by setting a dial or dials to positions shown by numbers or letters.

combine[1] (*say* kuhm-**buyn**) *verb* (**combined, combining**) join or mix together.

combine[2] (*say* **kom**-buyn) *noun* a group of people or companies combining in business. [from *com-*, + Latin *bini* = pair]

combine harvester *noun* a machine that both reaps and threshes grain.

combustible *adjective* able to be set on fire and burn.

combustion *noun* the process of burning, a chemical process (accompanied by heat) in which substances combine with oxygen in air.

come *verb* (**came, come, coming**) **1** move towards somewhere, *Come here!* **2** arrive; reach a place or condition or result, *They came to a city; We came to a decision.* **3** happen, *How did you come to lose it?* **4** occur, *It comes on the next page.* **5** result, *That's what comes of being careless.*
come about happen.
come across find or meet by chance.
come back return.
come by obtain.
come down come to a place or position regarded as lower.
come in for receive a share of.
come out 1 become known; be published. **2** (of stains) be removed. **3** (of a problem) be solved.
come round become conscious again.
come to 1 amount to. **2** become conscious again.
come to pass happen.
come up 1 come to a higher position. **2** arise, *A problem came up.*
come up with produce an idea.

comeback *noun* **1** a return to an earlier successful position. **2** (*informal*) a retaliation or retort.

comedian *noun* someone who entertains people by making them laugh.

comedown *noun* **1** a loss of status. **2** an anticlimax; a disappointment.

comedy *noun* (*plural* **comedies**) **1** a play, film, or broadcast program intended to make people laugh. **2** humour. [from Greek *komos* = merrymaking, + *oide* = song]

comely *adjective* good-looking.

comet *noun* an object moving across the sky with a bright tail of light. [from Greek *kometes* = long-haired]

comfort[1] *noun* **1** a state of ease and contentment. **2** soothing somebody who is unhappy or in pain. **3** a person or thing that gives comfort.

comfort[2] *verb* make a person less unhappy; soothe.

comfortable *adjective* **1** free from worry or pain. **2** making someone feel at ease; not tight or harsh. **comfortably** *adverb*

comfy *adjective* (*informal*) comfortable.

comic[1] *adjective* making people laugh. **comical** *adjective*, **comically** *adverb*

comic[2] *noun* **1** a paper or magazine full of comic strips. **2** a comedian.

comic strip *noun* a series of drawings telling a funny story or a serial.

comma *noun* a punctuation mark (,) used to mark a pause in a sentence or to separate items in a list. [from Greek *komma* = clause]

command[1] *noun* **1** a statement telling somebody to do something; an order. **2** authority; control. **3** ability to use something; mastery, *She has a good command of Spanish.*

command[2] *verb* **1** give a command to somebody; order. **2** have authority over. **3** deserve and get, *They command our respect.* **commander** *noun*

commandant (*say* **kom**-uhn-dant) *noun* the officer in command, especially of a military academy.

commandeer *verb* take or seize something for military purposes or for your own use.

commandment *noun* a sacred command, especially one of the Ten Commandments given to Moses.

commando *noun* (*plural* **commandos**) a soldier trained for making dangerous raids.

commemorate *verb* (**commemorated, commemorating**) be a celebration or reminder of some past event or person. **commemoration** *noun*, **commemorative** *adjective* [compare *memory*]

commence *verb* (**commenced, commencing**) begin. **commencement** *noun*

commend *verb* **1** praise, *He was commended for bravery.* **2** entrust, *We commend him to your care.* **commendation** *noun*

commendable *adjective* deserving praise.

comment[1] *noun* an opinion given briefly about an event or in explanation or criticism.

comment[2] *verb* make a comment.

commentary *verb* (*plural* **commentaries**) a set of comments, especially describing an event while it is happening. **commentate** *verb*, **commentator** *noun*

commerce *noun* trade and the services that assist it, e.g. banking and insurance. [from *com-*, + Latin *merx* = merchandise]

commercial[1] *adjective* **1** of commerce. **2** paid for by businesses whose advertisements are included, *commercial radio.* **3** profitable. **commercially** *adverb*

commercial[2] *noun* a broadcast advertisement.

commercialised *adjective* altered in order to become profitable, *a commercialised resort.* **commercialisation** *noun*

commiserate *verb* (**commiserated, commiserating**) sympathise. **commiseration** *noun* [from *com-*, + Latin *miserari* = to pity]

commission[1] *noun* **1** committing something. **2** authorisation to do something; the task authorised, *a commission to paint a portrait.* **3** an appointment to be an officer in the armed forces. **4** a group of people given authority to do or investigate something. **5** payment to someone for selling your goods or services.

commission[2] *verb* **1** give a commission to. **2** place an order for, *commissioned a portrait.*

commissionaire *noun* a uniformed door attendant at a theatre, hotel, or other building.

commissioner *noun* **1** an official appointed by commission. **2** a member of a commission.

commit *verb* (**committed, committing**) **1** do; perform, *commit a crime.* **2** place in someone's care or custody; consign, *He was committed to prison.* **3** pledge; assign, *Don't commit all your spare time to helping him.*

commitment *noun* **1** an engagement or obligation. **2** a pledge or promise. **3** dedication; loyalty.

committal *noun* **1** the act of sending a person to an institution, especially a prison or psychiatric hospital. **2** the burial of a dead body.

committee *noun* a group of people appointed to deal with something.

commode *noun* a box or chair into which a chamber pot is fitted. [same origin as *commodity*]

commodious *adjective* roomy.

commodity *noun* (*plural* **commodities**) a useful thing; a product. [from Latin *commodus* = convenient]

commodore *noun* **1** a naval officer ranking next below a rear admiral. **2** the commander of part of a fleet.

common[1] *adjective* **1** ordinary; usual; occurring frequently, *a common weed.* **2** of all or most people, *They worked for the common good.* **3** shared, *Music is their common interest.* **4** vulgar. **commonly** *adverb*, **commonness** *noun*

in common shared by two or more people or things.

common[2] *noun* (chiefly *British*) a piece of land that everyone can use. [from Latin *communis* = common]

common denominator *noun* **1** (in mathematics) a common multiple of the denominators of several fractions. **2** a feature shared by all members of a group.

commoner *noun* a member of the ordinary people, not of the nobility.

common factor *noun* a factor that is common to two or more numbers, e.g. the common factors of 8 and 12 are 1, 2 and 4.

common law *noun* law based on custom and judicial precedent rather than statutes.

common noun see **noun**.

commonplace *adjective* ordinary; usual.

common sense *noun* normal good sense in thinking or behaviour.

Commonwealth *noun* **1** an association of countries, *The Commonwealth consists of Britain and various other countries, including Canada, Australia, and New Zealand.* **2** a federal association of states, *the Commonwealth of Australia.*

commotion *noun* an uproar; a fuss.

communal (*say* **kom**-yuh-nuhl) *adjective* shared by several people. **communally** *adverb* [same origin as *common*]

commune[1] (*say* **kom**-yoon) *noun* **1** a group of people living together and sharing possessions and responsibilities. **2** a district of local government in France and some other countries.

commune[2] (*say* kuh-**myoon**) *verb* (**communed, communing**) talk together.

communicate *verb* (**communicated, communicating**) **1** share or exchange information, news, or ideas. **2** have social dealings. **3** transfer or transmit. **4** (of rooms) open into each other; connect.

communication *noun* **1** communicating. **2** something communicated; a message.

communications *plural noun* links between places (e.g. roads, railways, telephones, radio).

communicative *adjective* willing to talk.

communion *noun* **1** religious fellowship. **2** social dealings between people. **3** (**Communion** or **Holy Communion**) the Christian ceremony in which consecrated bread and wine are given to worshippers.

communiqué (*say* kuh-**myoo**-nuh-kay) *noun* an official message giving a report. [French, = communicated]

communism *noun* **1** a system where property is shared by the community. **2** a political system where the state controls property, production, trade, etc. (Compare **capitalism**.)

communist *noun* [from French *commun* = common]

community *noun* (*plural* **communities**) **1** the people living in one area. **2** a group with similar interests or origins.

commutative *adjective* (of a mathematical operation) producing the same result regardless of the order in which the quantities are taken, e.g. 3 + 4 = 7, 4 + 3 = 7.

commute *verb* (**commuted, commuting**) **1** travel a fairly long way by train, bus, or car to and from your daily work. **2** exchange; alter a punishment to something less severe. [from *com-*, + Latin *mutare* = change]

commuter *noun* a person who commutes to and from work.

compact[1] *noun* an agreement; a contract. [from *com-* + *pact*]

compact[2] *adjective* **1** closely or neatly packed together. **2** concise. **compactly** *adverb*, **compactness** *noun*

compact[3] *noun* a small flat container for face powder.

compact[4] *verb* join or press firmly together or into a small space. [from Latin *compactum* = put together]

compact disc *noun* a small round flat object on which sound or information is recorded digitally and read by means of a laser beam.

companion *noun* **1** a person who accompanies another. **2** one of a matching pair of things. **3** a handbook or reference book, *A Companion to Music.* **companionship** *noun* [from *com-*, + Latin *panis* = bread, = 'person who eats bread with another']

companionable *adjective* sociable.

company *noun* (*plural* **companies**) **1** a number of people together. **2** a business organisation. **3** having people with you; companionship. **4** visitors, *We've got company.* **5** a section of a battalion.

comparable (*say* **kom**-puh-ruh-buhl) *adjective* similar. **comparably** *adverb*

comparative[1] *adjective* **1** measured or judged by estimating the similarity or dissimilarity between one thing and another; relative. **2** of comparisons; comparing a thing with something else, *They live in comparative comfort.* **comparatively** *adverb*

comparative[2] *noun* the form of an adjective or adverb that expresses 'more', *The comparative of 'big' is 'bigger'.* (Compare **positive**[1] 7, **superlative**[2].)

compare *verb* (**compared, comparing**) **1** put things together so as to tell in what ways they are similar or different. **2** liken. **compare notes** share information. **compare with 1** be similar to. **2** be as good as, *Our football oval cannot compare with the Melbourne Cricket Ground.* [from Latin *comparare* = match with each other]

comparison *noun* **1** comparing. **2** similarity.

compartment *noun* one of the spaces into which something is divided; a separate room or enclosed space. [from *com-*, + Latin *partiri* = to share]

compass *noun* (*plural* **compasses**) a device with a pointer that points north.

compasses *plural noun* a device for drawing circles, usually with two rods hinged together at one end.

compassion *noun* pity; mercy. **compassionate** *adjective*, **compassionately** *adverb* [from *com-*, + Latin *passum* = suffered]

compatible *adjective* **1** able to live or exist or be used together. **2** consistent. **compatibility** *noun*, **compatibly** *adverb*

compatriot *noun* someone who comes from the same country as you.

compel *verb* (**compelled, compelling**) force somebody to do something. [from *com-*, + Latin *pellere* = to drive]

compendious *adjective* giving much information concisely.

compendium *noun* a package of notepaper and envelopes, or of games. [Latin, = a saving]

compensate *verb* (**compensated, compensating**) **1** make a suitable payment in return for (loss or damage). **2** have a balancing effect, *This victory compensates for our earlier defeats.* **compensation** *noun*, **compensatory** *adjective*

compère (*say* **kom**-pair) *noun* a person who introduces the performers in a show or broadcast. **compère** *verb* [French, = godfather]

compete *verb* (**competed, competing**) **1** take part in a competition. **2** try to win or gain something.

competent *adjective* able to do a particular thing. **competence** *noun*, **competently** *adverb*

competition *noun* **1** a game or race or other contest in which people try to win. **2** competing. **3** the people competing with you. **competitive** *adjective*

competitor *noun* someone who competes; a rival.

compile *verb* (**compiled, compiling**) put things together into a list or collection, e.g. to form a book. **compilation** *noun*, **compiler** *noun*

complacent *adjective* self-satisfied. **complacency** *noun*, **complacently** *adverb* [from *com-*, + Latin *placens* = pleasing]

complain *verb* say that you are annoyed or unhappy about something. **complainer** *noun*

complaint *noun* **1** a statement complaining about something. **2** an illness.

complement[1] *noun* **1** the quantity needed to fill or complete something, *The ship had its full complement of sailors.* **2** the word or words used after verbs such as *be* and *become* to complete the sense. In *He was brave* and *She became prime minister*, the complements are *brave* and *prime minister*.

complement[2] *verb* make a thing complete, *The hat complements the outfit.* [same origin as *complete*]

> **Usage** Do not confuse with *compliment*.

complementary *adjective* completing; forming a complement.

> **Usage** Do not confuse with *complimentary*.

complementary angle *noun* either of two angles whose sum is 90°.

complete[1] *adjective* **1** having all its parts. **2** finished. **3** thorough; in every way, *a complete stranger.* **completely** *adverb*, **completeness** *noun*

complete[2] *verb* (**completed**, **completing**) make a thing complete; add what is needed. **completion** *noun* [from Latin *completum* = filled up]

complex[1] *adjective* **1** made up of parts. **2** complicated. **complexity** *noun*

complex[2] *noun* **1** a group of related things, especially a set of buildings. **2** a group of feelings or ideas that influence a person's behaviour, *an inferiority complex.* [from Latin *complexum* = embraced, plaited]

complexion *noun* **1** the natural colour and appearance of the skin of the face. **2** the way things seem, *That puts a different complexion on the matter.*

complex sentence *noun* a sentence containing a subordinate clause or clauses.

compliant *adjective* complying; obedient. **compliance** *noun*

complicate *verb* (**complicated**, **complicating**) make a thing complex or complicated. [from *com-*, + Latin *plicare* = to fold]

complicated *adjective* **1** made up of many parts. **2** difficult through being complex.

complication *noun* **1** something that complicates things or adds difficulties. **2** a complicated condition.

complicity *noun* being involved in a crime or wrongdoing.

compliment[1] *noun* something said or done to show that you approve of a person or thing, *pay a compliment.*

compliment[2] *verb* pay someone a compliment; congratulate.

> **Usage** Do not confuse with *complement*.

complimentary *adjective* **1** expressing a compliment. **2** given free of charge.

> **Usage** Do not confuse with *complementary*.

compliments *plural noun* formal greetings given in a message.

comply *verb* (**complied**, **complying**) obey laws or rules.

compo *noun* (*Australian informal*) a payment made under a workers' compensation scheme, *Dad was on compo after his injury last year.*

component *noun* each of the parts of which a thing is composed.

compose *verb* (**composed**, **composing**) **1** form; make up, *The class is composed of 20 students.* **2** create in music or literature. **3** arrange in good order. **4** make calm, *compose yourself.* [from Latin *compositum* = put together]

composed *adjective* calm, *a composed manner.* **composedly** *adverb*

composer *noun* a person who writes music.

composite (*say* **kom**-puh-zuht) *adjective* **1** made up of a number of parts or different styles. **2** (of a number) able to be divided exactly by one or more whole numbers as well as by itself; not prime. [same origin as *compose*]

composite number *noun* a number that can be divided exactly by one or more whole numbers as well as by itself and one.

composition *noun* **1** composing. **2** something composed, especially a piece of music. **3** an essay or story written as a school exercise. **4** the parts that make up something, *the composition of the soil.*

compos mentis *adjective* in your right mind; sane. (The opposite is **non compos mentis.**) [Latin, = having control of the mind]

compost *noun* decayed leaves, grass, vegetables, and other organic matter used for enriching soil. [same origin as *compose*]

composure *noun* calmness of manner.

compound[1] *adjective* made of two or more parts or ingredients.

compound[2] *noun* **1** a thing or substance made up of two or more parts or ingredients. **2** (in chemistry) a substance formed from two or more elements chemically united in fixed proportions.

compound[3] *verb* **1** put together; combine. **2** increase or add to, *Bad weather compounded the problem.* [from Latin *componere* = put together]

compound[4] *noun* a fenced area containing buildings. [from Malay *kampong* = enclosure]

compound interest *noun* interest paid on the original capital and on the interest that has been added to it. (Compare **simple interest.**)

compound sentence *noun* a sentence with more than one subject or predicate.

comprehend *verb* **1** understand. **2** include.

comprehensible *adjective* understandable.

comprehension *noun* the act or capability of understanding, especially writing or speech.

comprehensive *adjective* including all or many kinds of people or things.

compress[1] (*say* kuhm-**pres**) *verb* **1** press together or into a smaller space. **2** (in computing) alter the form of data to reduce the amount of storage necessary. **compression** *noun*, **compressor** *noun*

compress[2] (*say* **kom**-pres) *noun* a soft pad or cloth pressed on the body to stop bleeding or cool inflammation.

comprise *verb* (**comprised, comprising**) include; consist of, *The pentathlon comprises five events.*

compromise[1] (*say* **kom**-pruh-muyz) *noun* settling a dispute by each side accepting less than it asked for.

compromise[2] *verb* (**compromised, compromising**) **1** settle a dispute by each side accepting less than it asked for. **2** expose to danger or suspicion, *His confession compromised his sister.*

compulsion *noun* compelling.

compulsive *adjective* having or resulting from an uncontrollable urge, *a compulsive gambler; a compulsive desire.*

compulsory *adjective* that must be done; not optional.

compunction *noun* a guilty feeling, *She felt no compunction about hitting the burglar.* [from *com-*, + Latin *punctum* = pricked (by conscience)]

compute *verb* (**computed, computing**) calculate. **computation** *noun*

computer *noun* an electronic machine for making calculations, storing and analysing information put into it, or controlling machinery automatically.

computerise *verb* (**computerised, computerising**) equip with computers; perform or produce by computer. **computerisation** *noun*

computing *noun* the use of computers.

comrade *noun* a companion who shares in your activities. **comradeship** *noun* [from Spanish *camarada* = room-mate]

con[1] *noun* (*informal*) a confidence trick.

con[2] *verb* (**conned, conning**) (*informal*) swindle.

con[3] *noun* a reason against something, *There are pros and cons.* [from Latin *contra* = against]

con- *prefix* see **com-**.

concave *adjective* curved like the inside of a ball or circle. (The opposite is **convex.**) **concavity** *noun* [from *con-*, + Latin *cavus* = hollow]

conceal *verb* hide; keep something secret. **concealment** *noun*

concede *verb* (**conceded, conceding**) **1** admit that something is true. **2** grant; allow, *They conceded us the right to cross their land.* **3** admit that you have been defeated.

conceit *noun* being too proud of yourself; vanity. **conceited** *adjective*

conceivable *adjective* able to be imagined or believed. **conceivably** *adverb*

conceive *verb* (**conceived, conceiving**) **1** become pregnant; form a baby in the womb. **2** form an idea or plan; imagine, *I can't conceive why you want to come.*

concentrate *verb* (**concentrated, concentrating**) **1** give your full attention or effort to something. **2** bring or come together in one place. **3** make less dilute. [from *con-* + *centre*]

concentration *noun* concentrating.

concentration camp *noun* a place where political prisoners or members of persecuted minorities are brought together and confined.

concentric *adjective* having the same centre, *concentric circles.*

concept *noun* an idea.

conception *noun* **1** conceiving. **2** an idea.

concern[1] *verb* **1** be important to or affect somebody. **2** worry somebody. **3** be about; have as its subject, *The story concerns a group of rabbits.*

concern[2] *noun* **1** something that concerns you; a responsibility. **2** worry. **3** a business.

concerned *adjective* **1** worried. **2** involved in or affected by something.

concerning *preposition* on the subject of; about, *laws concerning food handling.*

concert *noun* a musical entertainment.

concerted *adjective* done in cooperation with others, *We made a concerted effort.*

concertina *noun* a portable musical instrument with bellows, played by squeezing.

concerto (*say* kuhn-**sher**-toh) *noun* (*plural* **concertos** or **concerti**) a piece of music for a solo instrument and an orchestra. [Italian]

concession *noun* **1** conceding. **2** something conceded. **3** a reduction in price for certain categories of person. **concessionary** *adjective*

conch *noun* the spiral shell of a kind of shellfish.

conciliate *verb* (**conciliated**, **conciliating**) **1** win over an angry or hostile person by friendliness. **2** help people who disagree to come to an agreement. **conciliation** *noun*

concise *adjective* brief; giving much information in a few words. **concisely** *adverb*, **conciseness** *noun*

conclude *verb* (**concluded**, **concluding**) **1** bring or come to an end. **2** decide; form an opinion by reasoning, *The jury concluded that he was guilty.* [from *con-*, + Latin *claudere* = shut]

conclusion *noun* **1** the end or finish of an event, process, or text; the summing-up of an argument or text. **2** a judgement or decision reached by reasoning; a proposition that is reached by given premises.

conclusive *adjective* putting an end to all doubt. **conclusively** *adverb*

concoct *verb* **1** make something by putting ingredients together. **2** invent, *concoct an excuse.* **concoction** *noun* [from *con-*, + Latin *coctum* = cooked]

concord *noun* friendly agreement or harmony. [from *con-*, + Latin *cor* = heart]

concordance *noun* **1** agreement. **2** an index of the words used in a book or an author's works.

concourse *noun* **1** a crowd. **2** an open area through which people pass, e.g. at an airport. [same origin as *concur*]

concrete[1] *noun* cement mixed with sand and gravel, used in building.

concrete[2] *adjective* **1** able to be touched and felt; not abstract. **2** definite, *We need concrete evidence, not theories.*

concrete noun *noun* a noun denoting a material object as opposed to an abstract quality, state, or action.

concur *verb* (**concurred**, **concurring**) **1** agree. **2** happen together; coincide. **concurrence** *noun*, **concurrent** *adjective* [from *con-*, + Latin *currere* = run]

concussion *noun* a temporary injury to the brain caused by a hard knock. **concussed** *adjective* [from Latin *concussum* = shaken violently]

condemn *verb* **1** say that you strongly disapprove of something. **2** convict or sentence a criminal. **3** destine to something unhappy, *condemned to a lonely life.* **4** declare unfit for use or uninhabitable, *condemned buildings.* **condemnation** *noun* [from *con-*, + Latin *damnare* = damn]

condense *verb* (**condensed**, **condensing**) **1** make a liquid denser or more compact. **2** put something into fewer words. **3** change from gas or vapour to liquid, *Steam condenses on windows.* **condensation** *noun*, **condenser** *noun*

condescend *verb* behave in a way which shows that you feel superior. **condescending** *adjective*, **condescension** *noun*

condiment *noun* a seasoning, sauce, or relish used to add flavour to food.

condition[1] *noun* **1** the state or fitness of a person or thing, *This bicycle is in good condition.* **2** the situation or surroundings that affect something, *working conditions.* **3** something required as part of an agreement. **4** an illness or abnormality, *a heart condition.*

on condition that only if; on the understanding that something will be done.

condition[2] *verb* **1** put something into a proper condition. **2** train; accustom.

conditional *adjective* dependent; containing a condition, *a conditional offer.* **conditionally** *adverb*

conditioner *noun* an agent that brings something into good condition, especially an agent applied to the hair.

condole *verb* (**condoled**, **condoling**) express sympathy. **condolence** *noun* [from *con-*, + Latin *dolere* = grieve]

condom *noun* a sheath worn on the penis during sexual intercourse either as a contraceptive or to prevent infection.

condone *verb* (**condoned**, **condoning**) forgive or ignore wrongdoing, *Do not condone violence.* **condonation** *noun*

condor *noun* a kind of large vulture.

conducive *adjective* helping to cause or produce something, *Noisy surroundings are not conducive to work.*

conduct[1] (*say* kuhn-**dukt**) *verb* **1** lead or guide. **2** be the conductor of an orchestra or choir. **3** manage or direct something, *conduct an experiment.* **4** allow heat, light, sound, or electricity to pass along or through. **5** behave, *They conducted themselves with dignity.*

conduct[2] (*say* **kon**-dukt) *noun* behaviour. [from *con-*, + Latin *ducere* = to lead]

conduction *noun* the conducting of heat or electricity etc. (see *conduct*[1] 4).

conductor *noun* **1** a person who directs the performance of an orchestra or choir by movements of the arms. **2** a person who collects the fares on a bus etc. **3** something that conducts heat or electricity etc.

conduit (*say* **kon**-joo-uht) *noun* **1** a pipe or channel for liquid. **2** a tube protecting electric wire.

cone *noun* **1** an object that is circular at one end and narrows to a point at the other end. **2** the dry cone-shaped fruit of a pine, fir, or cedar tree.

confection *noun* something made of various things, especially sweet ones, put together.

confectioner *noun* someone who makes or sells sweets. **confectionery** *noun*

confederacy *noun* (*plural* **confederacies**) a union of states; a confederation.

confederate[1] *adjective* allied; joined by an agreement or treaty.

confederate[2] *noun* **1** a member of a confederacy. **2** an ally; an accomplice. [from *con-*, + Latin *foederatum* = allied]

confederation *noun* **1** the process of joining in an alliance. **2** a group of people, organisations, or states joined together by an agreement or treaty.

confer *verb* (**conferred, conferring**) **1** grant; bestow. **2** hold a discussion.

conference *noun* a meeting for holding a discussion.

confess *verb* state openly that you have done something wrong or have a weakness; admit. **confession** *noun*

confessional *noun* an enclosed stall where a priest hears confessions.

confessor *noun* a priest who hears confessions.

confetti *noun* tiny pieces of coloured paper thrown by wedding guests at the bride and bridegroom. [Italian]

confidant *noun* (**confidante** is used of a woman) a person in whom someone confides.

confide *verb* (**confided, confiding**) **1** tell confidentially, *confide a secret to someone* or *confide in someone.* **2** entrust. [from *con-*, + Latin *fidere* = to trust]

confidence *noun* **1** firm trust. **2** a feeling of certainty or boldness; being sure that you can do something. **3** something told confidentially.
in confidence as a secret.
in a person's confidence trusted with a person's secrets.

confidence trick *noun* an act of cheating or tricking someone by gaining their trust and persuading them to believe something that is not true.

confident *adjective* **1** showing or feeling confidence; bold. **2** feeling certain. **confidently** *adverb*

confidential *adjective* **1** that should be kept secret. **2** trusted to keep secrets, *a confidential secretary.* **confidentiality** *noun*, **confidentially** *adverb*

configuration *noun* **1** a method of arrangement (e.g. of parts of a computer system). **2** a shape.

confine *verb* (**confined, confining**) **1** keep within limits; restrict, *Please confine your remarks to the subject being discussed.* **2** keep somebody in a place. [from *con-*, + Latin *finis* = limit, end]

confined *adjective* narrow; restricted, *a confined space.*

confinement *noun* **1** confining. **2** the time of giving birth to a baby.

confines (*say* **kon**-fuynz) *plural noun* the limits or boundaries of an area.

confirm *verb* **1** prove that something is true or correct. **2** make a thing definite, *Please write to confirm your booking.* **3** make a person a full member of the Christian Church. **confirmation** *noun*, **confirmatory** *adjective*

confiscate *verb* (**confiscated, confiscating**) take something away as a punishment. **confiscation** *noun*

conflagration *noun* a great and destructive fire. [same origin as *flagrant*]

conflict[1] (*say* **kon**-flikt) *noun* **1** a fight or struggle. **2** disagreement.

conflict[2] (*say* kuhn-**flikt**) *verb* have a conflict; differ or disagree. [from *con-* = together, + Latin *flictum* = struck]

confluence *noun* the place where two rivers unite. [from *con-*, + Latin *fluens* = flowing]

conform *verb* keep to accepted rules or customs; comply with. **conformist** *noun*, **conformity** *noun* [from Latin *conformare* = shape evenly]

confound *verb* **1** astonish or puzzle someone. **2** confuse.

confront *verb* **1** come or bring face to face, especially in a hostile way. **2** be present and have to be dealt with, *Problems confront us.* **confrontation** *noun*

confuse *verb* (**confused, confusing**) **1** make a person puzzled or muddled. **2** mistake one thing for another. **confusion** *noun*

confute *verb* (**confuted, confuting**) prove a person or statement to be wrong. **confutation** *noun*

congeal (*say* kuhn-**jeel**) *verb* become jelly-like instead of liquid, especially in cooling. [from Latin *congelare* = freeze]

congenial *adjective* pleasant through being similar to yourself or suiting your tastes; agreeable, *a congenial companion.* **congenially** *adverb*

congenital (*say* kuhn-**jen**-uh-tuhl) *adjective* existing in a person from birth. **congenitally** *adverb* [from *con-*, + Latin *genitus* = born]

congested *adjective* crowded; too full of something. **congestion** *noun*

conglomeration *noun* a mass of different things put together. [from *con-*, + Latin *glomus* = mass]

congolli (*Australian*) another name for **tupong**. [from Ngarrindjeri *kunggali*]

congratulate *verb* (**congratulated**, **congratulating**) tell a person that you are pleased about their success or good fortune. **congratulation** *noun*, **congratulatory** *adjective* [from *con-*, + Latin *gratulari* = show joy]

congregate *verb* (**congregated**, **congregating**) assemble; flock together. [from *con-*, + Latin *gregatum* = herded]

congregation *noun* a group who have gathered to take part in worship.

congress *noun* **1** a conference. **2** (**Congress**) the parliament of the USA. [from *con-*, + Latin *-gressus* = going]

congruent *adjective* **1** suitable; consistent; in agreement or harmony. **2** (of geometrical figures) having exactly the same shape and size. **congruence** *noun*

conic *adjective* of a cone.

conical *adjective* cone-shaped. **conically** *adverb*

conifer (*say* **kon**-uh-fuh) *noun* an evergreen tree with cones. **coniferous** *adjective* [from *cone* + Latin *ferens* = bearing]

conjecture *noun* a guess. **conjectural** *adjective*, **conjecture** *verb*

conjoined twins *plural noun* twins who are born with their bodies joined together. Formerly called *Siamese twins*.

conjugal (*say* **kon**-juh-guhl) *adjective* of a husband and wife.

conjugate *verb* (**conjugated**, **conjugating**) give all the different forms of a verb. **conjugation** *noun*

conjunction *noun* **1** a word that joins words or phrases or sentences, e.g. *and, but.* **2** combination, *The four armies acted in conjunction.* [from Latin *conjunctum* = yoked together]

conjure *verb* (**conjured**, **conjuring**) perform puzzling tricks. **conjuror** *noun*
conjure up produce, *Mention of the Arctic conjures up visions of snow and ice.*

con man *noun* a person using confidence tricks.

connect *verb* **1** join together; link. **2** think of as being associated with each other. **connector** *noun* [from *con-*, + Latin *nectere* = bind]

connection *noun* **1** a place where things join together. **2** an association or relationship between things. **3** a train etc. that leaves soon after another arrives, so that passengers can transfer from one to the other. **4** a relative or associate, especially one with influence, *He has connections.*

connective[1] *adjective* connecting.

connective[2] *noun* a word or phrase whose function is to link other linguistic units.

conning tower *noun* a raised structure on a submarine, containing the periscope.

connive (*say* kuh-**nuyv**) *verb* (**connived**, **conniving**) plot or work together secretly to do something that is wrong, *They connived to steal the money.* **connivance** *noun*
connive at take no notice of wrongdoing that ought to be reported or punished. [from Latin *connivere* = shut the eyes]

connoisseur (*say* kon-uh-**ser**) *noun* a person with great experience and appreciation of something, *a connoisseur of wine.* [French, = one who knows]

connotation *noun* a meaning implied in addition to the main meaning.

connote *verb* (**connoted**, **connoting**) **1** (of a word) imply or suggest (an idea or feeling) in addition to the literal or primary meaning. **2** mean; signify.

conquer *verb* defeat; overcome. **conqueror** *noun*

conquest *noun* **1** conquering. **2** conquered territory.

conscience (*say* **kon**-shuhns) *noun* knowing what is right and wrong, especially in your own actions. [from *con-*, + Latin *sciens* = knowing]

conscientious (*say* kon-shee-**en**-shuhs) *adjective* careful and honest, *conscientious workers.* **conscientiously** *adverb*

conscientious objector *noun* a person who refuses to serve in the armed forces because they believe it is wrong.

conscious (*say* **kon**-shuhs) *adjective* **1** awake; aware of what is happening. **2** intentional, *a conscious insult.* **consciously** *adverb*, **consciousness** *noun*

conscript[1] (*say* kuhn-**skript**) *verb* make a person join the armed forces. **conscription** *noun*

conscript[2] (*say* **kon**-skript) *noun* a conscripted person. [from *con-*, + Latin *scriptus* = written in a list, enlisted]

consecrate *verb* (**consecrated**, **consecrating**) make a thing sacred; dedicate to God. **consecration** *noun*

consecutive *adjective* following one after another. **consecutively** *adverb* [from Latin *consecutum* = following]

consensus *noun* (*plural* **consensuses**) general agreement; the opinion of most people. [same origin as *consent*]

consent[1] *noun* agreement to what someone wishes; permission.

consent[2] *verb* say that you are willing to do or allow what someone wishes. [from *con-*, + Latin *sentire* = feel]

consequence *noun* **1** something that happens as the result of an event or action. **2** importance, *It is of no consequence.*

consequent *adjective* happening as a result. **consequently** *adverb* [same origin as *consecutive*]

consequential *adjective* consequent.

conservation *noun* **1** the action of conserving something. **2** preservation, protection, or restoration of the natural environment and of wildlife. **3** preservation and repair of archaeological, historical, and cultural sites and artefacts. **4** prevention of wasteful use of a resource. **conservationist** *noun*

conservative *adjective* **1** liking traditional ways and disliking changes. **2** (of an estimate) moderate; low. **conservatism** *noun*, **conservatively** *adverb*

conservatorium *noun* (*Australian*) a school of music.

conservatory *noun* a greenhouse.

conserve *verb* (**conserved, conserving**) prevent something valuable from being changed, spoilt, or wasted. [from *con-*, + Latin *servare* = keep safe]

consider *verb* **1** think carefully about or give attention to something, especially in order to make a decision. **2** allow for. **3** have an opinion; think to be, *Consider yourself lucky.*

considerable *adjective* fairly great, *a considerable amount.* **considerably** *adverb*

considerate *adjective* taking care not to inconvenience or hurt others. **considerately** *adverb*

consideration *noun* **1** being considerate. **2** careful thought or attention. **3** a fact that must be kept in mind. **4** payment given as a reward.
take into consideration allow for.

considering *preposition* taking something into consideration, *The car runs well considering its age.*

consign *verb* hand something over formally; entrust.

consignment *noun* **1** consigning. **2** a batch of goods sent to someone.

consist *verb* be made up or composed of, *The flat consists of three rooms.*

consistency *noun* (*plural* **consistencies**) **1** being consistent. **2** thickness or stiffness, especially of a liquid.

consistent *adjective* **1** keeping to a regular pattern or style; not changing. **2** not contradictory. **consistently** *adverb*

consolation *noun* **1** consoling. **2** something that consoles someone.

console[1] (*say* kuhn-**sohl**) *verb* (**consoled, consoling**) comfort someone who is unhappy or disappointed. [from *con-*, + Latin *solari* = to comfort]

console[2] (*say* **kon**-sohl) *noun* **1** a panel holding the controls of equipment. **2** a frame containing the keyboard and stops etc. of an organ. **3** a cabinet for a radio or television set. **4** a small machine for playing computerised video games. [French]

consolidate *verb* (**consolidated, consolidating**) **1** make or become secure and strong. **2** combine two or more things into a single more effective or coherent whole. **consolidation** *noun* [from *con-* + *solid*]

consonant *noun* a speech sound in which the breath is at least partly obstructed, and which to form a syllable must be combined with a vowel; a letter or letters representing this, *The word 'cat' has two consonants and one vowel.* (Compare **vowel**.) [from *con-*, + Latin *sonans* = sounding]

consort[1] (*say* **kon**-sawt) *noun* a husband or wife, especially of a monarch.

consort[2] (*say* kuhn-**sawt**) *verb* be in someone's company, *consort with criminals.* [from Latin *consors* = sharer]

consortium *noun* (*plural* **consortia**) a combination of countries, companies, or other groups acting together.

conspicuous *adjective* **1** easily seen; noticeable. **2** remarkable. **conspicuously** *adverb*, **conspicuousness** *noun*

conspiracy *noun* (*plural* **conspiracies**) planning secretly with others to do something bad or illegal; a plot.

conspire *verb* (**conspired, conspiring**) plan secretly with others to do something bad or illegal. **conspirator** *noun*, **conspiratorial** *adjective* [from *con-*, + Latin *spirare* = breathe]

constable *noun* a police officer of the lowest rank. [from Latin, originally = officer in charge of the stable]

constabulary *noun* a police force.

constant[1] *adjective* **1** not changing. **2** happening all the time. **3** faithful; loyal. **constancy** *noun*, **constantly** *adverb*

constant[2] *noun* something that is constant and does not vary. [from *con-*, + Latin *stans* = standing]

constellation *noun* a group of stars. [from *con-*, + Latin *stella* = star]

consternation *noun* anxiety or dismay.

constipated *adjective* unable to empty the bowels easily or regularly. **constipation** *noun*

constituency *noun* (*plural* **constituencies**) an electorate.

constituent *noun* one of the parts that form a whole thing. **constituent** *adjective*

constitute *verb* (**constituted, constituting**) make up or form something, *Twelve months constitute a year.* [from *con-*, + Latin *statuere* = set up]

constitution *noun* **1** the group of laws or principles that state how a country is to be organised and governed. **2** the nature of the body in regard to healthiness, *She has a strong constitution.* **3** constituting. **4** the composition of something. **constitutional** *adjective*

constrain *verb* compel; oblige.

constraint *noun* **1** constraining; compulsion. **2** a restriction. **3** a strained manner caused by holding back feelings.

constrict *verb* squeeze or tighten something by making it narrower. **constriction** *noun* [from *con-*, + Latin *strictum* = bound]

construct *verb* make something by placing parts together; build. **constructor** *noun* [from *con-*, + Latin *structum* = built]

construction *noun* **1** constructing. **2** something constructed; a building. **3** two or more words put together to form a phrase or clause or sentence. **4** an explanation or interpretation, *They put a bad construction on our refusal.*

constructive *adjective* constructing; being helpful, *constructive suggestions.*

construe *verb* (**construed, construing**) interpret; explain.

consul *noun* **1** an official appointed by a state to live in a foreign city and protect the state's citizens and interests there. **2** either of the two chief magistrates in ancient Rome. **consular** *adjective* [Latin]

consulate *noun* the building where a consul works.

consult *verb* seek information or advice from. **consultation** *noun*

consultant *noun* a person who is qualified to give expert advice.

consultative *adjective* for consultation, *a consultative committee.*

consume *verb* (**consumed, consuming**) **1** eat or drink something. **2** use up, *Much time was consumed in waiting.* **3** destroy, *Fire consumed the building.* [from *con-*, + Latin *sumere* = take up]

consumer *noun* **1** a person who buys or uses goods or services. **2** a person or thing that eats or uses something.

consumer price index *noun* a measure of the cost of living based on a standard set of prices.

consummate[1] (*say* **kon**-suh-mayt) *verb* accomplish; make complete. **consummation** *noun*

consummate[2] (*say* kuhn-**sum**-uht) *adjective* perfect; highly skilled, *a consummate artist.* [from *con-*, + Latin *summus* = highest]

consumption *noun* **1** consuming. **2** (*old use*) tuberculosis of the lungs.

contact[1] *noun* **1** touching. **2** being in touch; communication. **3** a person to communicate with when you need information or help.

contact[2] *verb* get in touch with a person. [from *con-*, + Latin *tactum* = touched]

contact lens *noun* a tiny lens worn against the eyeball instead of spectacles.

contactless *adjective* **1** involving minimal or no contact. **2** of or involving technologies that allow a smart card, mobile phone, etc. to connect wirelessly to an electronic reader.

contagion *noun* a contagious disease.

contagious *adjective* spreading by contact with an infected person, *a contagious disease.*

> **Usage** Strictly, a *contagious* disease is one transmitted by physical contact, whereas an *infectious* one is transmitted via microorganisms in the air or water. In practice there is little or no difference in meaning between *contagious* and *infectious* when applied to disease or its spread.

contain *verb* **1** have inside, *The tin contains lollies.* **2** consist of, *A litre contains 1000 millilitres.* **3** restrain; hold back, *Try to contain your laughter.* [from *con-*, + Latin *tenere* = hold]

container *noun* **1** an object for holding or transporting something. **2** a large metal box for transporting goods.

contaminate *verb* (**contaminated, contaminating**) make a thing dirty or impure or diseased; pollute. **contamination** *noun*

contemplate *verb* (**contemplated, contemplating**) **1** look at something thoughtfully. **2** consider or think about something, *We are contemplating a visit to China.* **contemplation** *noun*, **contemplative** *adjective*

contemporary[1] *adjective* **1** belonging to the same period, *Dickens was contemporary with Thackeray.* **2** modern, *contemporary furniture.*

contemporary[2] *noun* (*plural* **contemporaries**) a person who lives at the same time as another or who is about the same age. [from *con-*, + Latin *tempus* = time]

contempt *noun* a feeling of despising a person or thing.

contemptible *adjective* deserving contempt.

contemptuous *adjective* feeling or showing contempt. **contemptuously** *adverb*

contend *verb* **1** strive or fight in competition or against difficulties; compete. **2** assert; declare in an argument etc., *We contend that he is innocent.* **contender** *noun* [from *con-*, + Latin *tendere* = strive]

content[1] (*say* kuhn-**tent**) *adjective* happy with what you have; satisfied. **contentment** *noun*

content[2] *noun* being contented; satisfaction.

content[3] *verb* make a person contented; satisfy. [from Latin *contentum* = restrained]

content[4] (*say* **kon**-tent) *noun* (also **contents**) **1** what something contains. **2** the material dealt with in a speech, literary work, etc. as distinct from its form or style. **3** information made available by a website or other electronic medium. [from Latin *contenta* = things contained]

contented *adjective* happy with what you have; satisfied. **contentedly** *adverb*

contention *noun* **1** contending; arguing. **2** an assertion put forward.

contest[1] (*say* **kon**-test) *noun* a competition; a struggle in which rivals try to obtain something or to do best. **contester** *noun*

contest[2] (*say* kuhn-**test**) *verb* **1** compete for or in, *contest an election.* **2** dispute; argue that something is wrong or not legal. **contestability** *noun*, **contestable** *adjective*

contestant *noun* a person taking part in a contest; a competitor.

context *noun* **1** the circumstances that form the setting for an event, statement, or idea, and in terms of which it can be fully understood, *food shortages were tolerated in the context of war.* **2** the parts of something written or spoken that immediately precede and follow a word or passage and clarify its meaning. [from *con-*, + Latin *textum* = woven]

contiguous *adjective* adjoining.

continent *noun* **1** one of the seven main masses of land in the world, *The continents are Europe, Asia, Africa, North America, South America, Australia, and Antarctica.* **2** (**the Continent**) the mainland of Europe as distinct from the British Isles. **continental** *adjective* [from Latin, = continuous land]

contingency *noun* (*plural* **contingencies**) something that may happen but is not intended.

contingent[1] *adjective* **1** depending, *His future is contingent on success in this exam.* **2** possible but not certain, *other contingent events.*

contingent[2] *noun* a group forming part of a larger group or gathering.

continual *adjective* happening again and again. **continually** *adverb*

> **Usage** *Continual* is often confused with *continuous*. *Continual* is used of something that happens very frequently (e.g. *there were continual interruptions*) while *continuous* is used of something that happens without a pause (e.g. *continuous rain all day*).

continue *verb* (**continued**, **continuing**) **1** do something without stopping. **2** begin again after stopping, *The game will continue after lunch.* **continuation** *noun* [same origin as *contain*]

continuity *noun* **1** being continuous. **2** the uninterrupted succession of things. **3** a state of stability and the absence of disruption.

continuous *adjective* happening without a break. **continuously** *adverb*

> **Usage** See the note at *continual.*

contort *verb* twist or force out of the usual shape. **contorted** *adjective*, **contortion** *noun* [from *con-*, + Latin *tortum* = twisted]

contortionist *noun* a person who can twist their body into unusual postures.

contour *noun* **1** a line (on a map) joining the points that are the same height above sea level. **2** an outline.

contra- *prefix* against. [Latin]

contraband *noun* smuggled goods. [from *contra-*, + Italian *banda* = a ban]

contraception *noun* preventing conception; birth control. [from *contra-* + *conception*]

contraceptive *noun* a substance or device that prevents conception.

contract[1] (*say* **kon**-trakt) *noun* **1** a formal agreement to do something. **2** a document stating the terms of an agreement.

contract[2] (*say* kuhn-**trakt**) *verb* **1** make or become smaller. **2** make a formal agreement to do something. **3** get an illness, *She contracted mumps.* [from *con-*, + Latin *tractum* = pulled]

contraction *noun* **1** contracting. **2** shortening of the muscles of the womb during childbirth. **3** a shortened form of a word or words, *Can't is a contraction of cannot.*

contractor *noun* a person who makes a contract, especially for building.

contradict *verb* **1** say that something said is not true or that someone is wrong. **2** say the opposite of, *These rumours contradict previous ones.* **contradiction** *noun*, **contradictory** *adjective* [from *contra-*, + Latin *dicere* = say]

contralto *noun* (*plural* **contraltos**) a female singer with a low voice. [Italian, from *contra-* + *alto*]

contraption *noun* a strange-looking device or machine.

contrapuntal *adjective* (in music) of or in counterpoint.

contrary[1] *adjective* **1** (*say* **kon**-truh-ree) of the opposite kind or direction; opposed; unfavourable. **2** (*say* kuhn-**trair**-ree) awkward and obstinate.

contrary[2] (*say* **kon**-truh-ree) *noun* the opposite.
on the contrary the opposite is true. [from Latin *contra* = against]

contrast[1] *noun* **1** a difference clearly seen when things are compared. **2** something showing a clear difference.

contrast[2] *verb* **1** compare or oppose two things so as to show that they are clearly different. **2** be clearly different when compared. [from *contra-*, + Latin *stare* = to stand]

contravene *verb* (**contravened**, **contravening**) act against a rule or law. **contravention** *noun* [from *contra-*, + Latin *venire* = come]

contribute *verb* (**contributed**, **contributing**) **1** give jointly with others, especially to a common fund. **2** supply for publication in a newspaper or magazine or book. **3** help to cause something. **contribution** *noun*, **contributor** *noun*, **contributory** *adjective* [from *con-*, + Latin *tribuere* = bestow]

contrite *adjective* very sorry for having done wrong. **contritely** *adverb*, **contrition** *noun*

contrivance *noun* a device.

contrive *verb* (**contrived**, **contriving**) plan cleverly; find a way of doing or making something.

control[1] *verb* (**controlled**, **controlling**) have the power to give orders or to restrain something. **controller** *noun*

control[2] *noun* controlling a person or thing; authority.

controlled burn *noun* the intentional burning of an area, especially of natural bushland, to clear a firebreak or to reduce fuel levels. Also called a *prescribed burn*.

controller *noun* **1** a person or thing that controls. **2** a device used to control a video game.

controversial *adjective* causing controversy.

controversy (*say* **kon**-truh-ver-see or kuhn-**trov**-uh-see) *noun* a long argument or disagreement. [from *contra-*, + Latin *versum* = turned]

> **Usage** The second pronunciation, stressed on the second syllable, is considered incorrect by some people.

contusion *noun* a bruise.

conundrum *noun* a riddle; a hard question.

conurbation *noun* a large urban area where towns have spread into each other. [from *con-*, + Latin *urbs* = city]

convalesce *verb* (**convalesced**, **convalescing**) be recovering from an illness. **convalescence** *noun*, **convalescent** *adjective & noun* [from *con-*, + Latin *valescere* = grow strong]

convection *noun* the passing on of heat within liquid, air, or gas by circulation of the warmed parts. [from *con-*, + Latin *vectum* = carried]

convector *noun* a device that circulates warmed air.

convene *verb* (**convened**, **convening**) come or bring together for a meeting or activity; assemble. **convener** *noun* (also **convenor**) [from *con-*, + Latin *venire* = come]

convenience *noun* **1** being convenient. **2** something that is convenient. **3** a public toilet.
at your convenience whenever you find convenient; as it suits you.

convenient *adjective* **1** easy to use or deal with. **2** easy to reach. **conveniently** *adverb* [from Latin *convenire* = to suit]

convent *noun* a place where nuns live and work. [same origin as *convene*]

convention *noun* **1** an accepted way of doing things. **2** a formal assembly or conference.

conventional *adjective* **1** done or doing things in the accepted way; traditional. **2** (of weapons) not nuclear. **conventionality** *noun*, **conventionally** *adverb*

converge *verb* (**converged**, **converging**) come to or towards the same point from different directions. **convergence** *noun*, **convergent** *adjective* [from *con-*, + Latin *vergere* = turn]

conversant *adjective* familiar with something, *Are you conversant with the rules of this game?* [from *converse*[1]]

conversation *noun* talk between people. **conversational** *adjective*

converse[1] (*say* kuhn-**vers**) *verb* (**conversed**, **conversing**) hold a conversation. [from Latin, = keep company]

converse[2] (*say* **kon**-vers) *adjective* opposite; contrary. **conversely** *adverb*

converse[3] *noun* an opposite idea or statement. [same origin as *convert*[2]]

conversion *noun* converting.

convert[1] (*say* kuhn-**vert**) *verb* **1** change. **2** cause a person to change their beliefs. **3** kick a goal after scoring a try in rugby. **converter** *noun*

convert[2] (*say* **kon**-vert) *noun* someone who has changed their beliefs. [from *con-*, + Latin *vertere* = turn]

convertible *adjective* able to be converted. **convertibility** *noun*

convex *adjective* curved like the outside of a ball or circle. (The opposite is **concave**.) **convexity** *noun*

convey *verb* **1** transport. **2** communicate a message or idea. **conveyor** *noun*

conveyance *noun* **1** conveying. **2** a vehicle for transporting people.

conveyancing *noun* transferring the legal ownership of property from one person to another.

conveyor belt *noun* a continuous moving belt for carrying objects from one place to another.

convict[1] (*say* kuhn-**vikt**) *verb* prove or declare that a certain person is guilty of a crime.

convict[2] (*say* **kon**-vikt) *noun* a convicted person who is in prison or (in former times) transported for a crime. [from *con-*, + Latin *victum* = conquered]

conviction *noun* **1** convicting or being convicted of a crime. **2** being convinced. **3** a firm opinion or belief.

convince *verb* (**convinced, convincing**) make a person feel certain that something is true. [from *con-*, + Latin *vincere* = conquer]

convivial *adjective* sociable and lively. [from Latin *convivium* = feast]

convoke *verb* (**convoked, convoking**) summon people to an assembly or meeting. **convocation** *noun* [from *con-*, + Latin *vocare* = to call]

convoluted *adjective* **1** coiled; twisted. **2** complicated. **convolution** *noun* [from *con-*, + Latin *volutum* = rolled]

convoy *noun* a group of ships or trucks travelling together.

convulse *verb* (**convulse, convulsing**) cause violent movements or convulsions. **convulsive** *adjective* [from *con-*, + Latin *vulsum* = pulled]

convulsion *noun* **1** a violent movement of the body. **2** a violent upheaval.

COO *noun* a senior executive responsible for managing the day-to-day operations of a company or other institution. [from the initials of 'chief operations officer' or 'chief operating officer']

coo *verb* (**cooed, cooing**) make a dove's soft murmuring sound. **coo** *noun*

cooee *interjection* a long loud cry used to attract attention. **cooee** *verb*
within cooee near. [from Sydney language *gawi, guwi* = come here]

cook[1] *verb* make food ready to eat by heating it.
cook up (*informal*) concoct; invent.

cook[2] *noun* a person who cooks.

cooker *noun* a stove for cooking food.

cookery *noun* the action or skill of cooking food.

cookie *noun* **1** a sweet biscuit. **2** a means of identifying a computer user's access to a server.

cool[1] *adjective* **1** fairly cold; not hot or warm. **2** calm. **3** not enthusiastic. **4** (*informal*) excellent; fashionable. **coolly** *adverb*, **coolness** *noun*

cool[2] *verb* make or become cool. **cooler** *noun*

cool[3] *noun* **1** coolness; cool air; a cool place. **2** (*informal*) calmness, composure, *Keep your cool.*

coolamon (*say* **koo**-luh-muhn) *noun* (*Australian*) (in traditional Aboriginal use) a wooden or bark dish used for carrying water. [from Gamilaraay and neighbouring languages *guliman*]

coolibah (*say* **koo**-luh-bah) *noun* an Australian eucalyptus tree that grows along rivers. [from Yuwaaliyaay and neighbouring languages *gulabaa*]

coolie *noun* an unskilled labourer in countries of eastern Asia.

coop[1] *noun* a cage for poultry.

coop[2] *verb* **coop up** confine or shut in.

cooperate *verb* (**cooperated, cooperating**) work helpfully with other people. **cooperation** *noun*

cooperative[1] *adjective* willing to cooperate. **cooperatively** *adverb*

cooperative[2] *noun* a society, business, etc. owned and run jointly by its members with profits shared between them.

co-opt *verb* invite someone to become a member of a group. [from *co-*, + Latin *optare* = choose]

coordinate[1] *verb* (**coordinated, coordinating**) organise people or things to work properly together. **coordination** *noun*, **coordinator** *noun*

coordinate[2] *noun* **1** a coordinated thing. **2** each of a set of quantities used to fix the position of something, e.g. latitude and longitude. [from *co-*, + Latin *ordinare* = arrange]

coordinating conjunction *noun* a conjunction placed between words, phrases, clauses, or sentences of equal rank, e.g. *and, but, or.*

coot *noun* a waterbird with a horny white patch on its forehead.

cop[1] *verb* (**copped**, **copping**) (*informal*) catch; receive, suffer, *He copped a lot of criticism.* **cop it** (*informal*) get into trouble.

cop[2] *noun* (*informal*) a police officer.

cope[1] *verb* (**coped**, **coping**) manage or deal with something successfully.

cope[2] *noun* a long loose cloak worn by clergy in ceremonies.

copha *noun* (*Australian trademark*) solidified coconut oil.

copier *noun* a device for copying things.

copious *adjective* plentiful; in large amounts. **copiously** *adverb*

cop-out *noun* (*informal*) a way of avoiding something one should do.

copper *noun* **1** a reddish-brown metal used to make wire, coins, etc. **2** a reddish-brown colour. **3** a coin made of copper or metal of this colour. **copper** *adjective* [from Latin *cuprum* = Cyprus metal (because the Romans got most of their copper from Cyprus)]

copperplate *noun* neat handwriting.

copra *noun* dried coconut kernels.

copse *noun* a group of small trees.

copulate *verb* (**copulated**, **copulating**) have sexual intercourse with someone. **copulation** *noun*

copy[1] *noun* (*plural* **copies**) **1** a thing made to imitate or be identical to another. **2** something written or typed out again from its original form. **3** a single specimen of a particular book, record, or other publication or issue.

copy[2] *verb* (**copied**, **copying**) **1** make a copy of something. **2** do the same as someone else; imitate. **copyist** *noun*

copycat *noun* (*informal*) someone who copies another person's actions.

copyright *noun* the sole legal right to print, publish, perform, film, or record a literary or artistic or musical work.

coquette (*say* ko-**ket**) *noun* a woman who flirts. **coquettish** *adjective* [French]

cor- *prefix* see **com-**.

coral *noun* **1** a hard red, pink, or white substance formed by the skeletons of tiny sea creatures massed together. **2** a pink colour.

cor anglais *noun* an alto woodwind instrument of the oboe family. [French, = English horn]

corbel *noun* a piece of stone or wood projecting from a roof to support something.

cord *noun* **1** a long thin flexible strip of twisted threads or strands. **2** a piece of flexible insulated wire for carrying electric current. **3** a cord-like structure in the body, *the spinal cord.* **4** corduroy.

cordial[1] *noun* a fruit-flavoured drink.

cordial[2] *adjective* warm and friendly. **cordiality** *noun*, **cordially** *adverb* [from Latin *cordis* = of the heart]

cordon[1] *noun* a line of people, ships, fortifications, etc. placed round an area to guard or enclose it.

cordon[2] *verb* surround with a cordon.

cordon bleu (*say* kaw-don **bler**) *adjective* (of cooks and cookery) first-class. [French, = blue ribbon]

corduroy *noun* cotton cloth with velvety ridges.

core *noun* **1** the hard central part of a piece of fruit, containing the seeds. **2** the central or most important part of something.

corella (*say* kuh-**rel**-uh) *noun* a white Australian cockatoo. [from Wiradjuri, probably *garila*]

corgi *noun* (*plural* **corgis**) a small dog with short legs and upright ears.

cork[1] *noun* **1** the lightweight bark of a kind of oak tree. **2** a stopper for a bottle, made of cork or other material.

cork[2] *verb* **1** close with a cork. **2** (*Australian*) bruise, *He got a corked thigh playing footy.*

corkscrew *noun* **1** a device for removing corks from bottles. **2** a spiral.

corm *noun* a part of a plant rather like a bulb.

cormorant *noun* a large black waterbird.

corn[1] *noun* **1** a cereal plant that has large grains set in rows on a cob; maize. **2** the seed of wheat and similar plants. **3** a plant (such as wheat) grown for its grain.

corn[2] *noun* a small hard lump on the foot.

cornea *noun* the transparent covering over the pupil of the eye. **corneal** *adjective*

corned *adjective* preserved with salt, *corned beef.*

corner[1] *noun* **1** the angle or area where two lines or sides or walls meet or where two streets join. **2** a free hit or kick from the corner of a hockey or football field. **3** a region, *a quiet corner of the world.*

corner[2] *verb* **1** drive someone into a corner or other position from which it is difficult to escape. **2** travel round a corner. **3** obtain possession of all or most of something, *corner the market.*

cornerstone *noun* **1** a stone built into the corner at the base of a building. **2** something that is a vital foundation.

cornet *noun* a musical instrument rather like a trumpet. [from Latin *cornu* = horn, trumpet]

cornflakes *plural noun* toasted flakes of corn eaten for breakfast.

cornflour *noun* flour made from maize or rice, used to thicken sauces.

cornflower *noun* a plant with blue flowers that grows wild in fields of corn.

cornice *noun* a band or ornamental moulding on walls just below a ceiling or at the top of a building.

cornucopia *noun* **1** a symbol of plenty consisting of a horn-shaped container overflowing with fruit and flowers. **2** an abundant supply. [from Latin *cornu* = horn, + *copiae* = of plenty]

corny *adjective* (**cornier**, **corniest**) (*informal*) **1** repeated so often that people are bored, *corny jokes.* **2** sentimental. [from *corn*[1]]

corollary (*say* kuh-**rol**-uh-ree) *noun* (*plural* **corollaries**) a natural consequence or result; something that follows logically after something else is proved.

corona (*say* kuh-**roh**-nuh) *noun* a circle of light round something. [Latin, = crown]

coronary *noun* short for **coronary thrombosis**, blockage of an artery carrying blood to the heart.

coronation *noun* the crowning of a king or queen. [same origin as *corona*]

coronavirus (*say* kuh-**roh**-nuh-vuy-ruhs) *noun* any of a group of RNA viruses that cause a variety of diseases in humans and other animals. [from *corona* + *virus*]

coroner *noun* an official who holds an inquiry into the cause of a death thought to be from unnatural causes. **coronial** *adjective*

coronet *noun* a small crown.

corporal[1] *noun* an officer ranking next below a sergeant.

corporal[2] *adjective* of the body. [from Latin *corpus* = body]

corporal punishment *noun* punishment by being whipped or beaten.

corporate *adjective* shared by members of a group, *corporate responsibility.*

corporate memory *noun* employees' knowledge of the history of an organisation, especially its undocumented procedures.

corporation *noun* a group of people authorised to act as an individual, especially in business.

corps (*say* kaw) *noun* (*plural* **corps**, *say* kawz) **1** a special army unit, *the Medical Corps.* **2** a large group of soldiers. **3** a set of people engaged in the same activity, *the diplomatic corps.*

corpse *noun* a dead body. [from Latin *corpus* = body]

corpulent *adjective* having a bulky body; fat. **corpulence** *noun*

corpuscle *noun* one of the red or white cells in blood. [from Latin, = little body]

corral (*say* ko-**rahl**) *noun* an enclosure for livestock, especially horses and cattle.

correct[1] *adjective* **1** true; accurate; without any mistakes. **2** proper; done or said in an approved way. **correctly** *adverb*, **correctness** *noun*

correct[2] *verb* **1** make a thing correct by altering or adjusting it. **2** mark the mistakes in something. **3** point out or punish a person's faults. **correction** *noun*, **corrective** *adjective* [from *cor-*, + Latin *rectus* = straight]

correlate *verb* (**correlated**, **correlating**) compare or connect things systematically. **correlation** *noun* [from *cor-* + *relate*]

correspond *verb* **1** write letters to each other. **2** agree; match, *Your story corresponds with his.* **3** be similar or equivalent, *Their assembly corresponds to our parliament.* [from *cor-* + *respond*]

correspondence *noun* **1** letters; writing letters. **2** similarity; agreement.

correspondent *noun* **1** a person who writes letters to another. **2** a person employed to gather news and send reports to a newspaper, or radio or television station.

corresponding angles *plural noun* the angles which occupy the same relative position at each intersection where a straight line crosses two others. If the two lines are parallel, the corresponding angles are equal.

corridor *noun* a passage in a building.

corroborate *verb* (**corroborated**, **corroborating**) get or give supporting evidence. **corroboration** *noun*

corroboree (*say* kuh-**rob**-uh-ree) *noun* an Aboriginal dance ceremony with song and rhythmical music. [from Sydney language *garabari*]

corrode *verb* (**corroded**, **corroding**) destroy metal gradually by chemical action. **corrosion** *noun*, **corrosive** *adjective* [from *cor-*, + Latin *rodere* = gnaw]

corrugated *adjective* shaped into alternate ridges and grooves, *corrugated iron.* [from *cor-*, + Latin *ruga* = wrinkle]

corrupt[1] *adjective* **1** dishonest; accepting bribes. **2** wicked. **3** decaying.

corrupt[2] *verb* **1** cause to become dishonest or wicked. **2** spoil; taint. **corruptible** *adjective*, **corruption** *noun* [from *cor-*, + Latin *ruptum* = broken]

corsage (*say* kaw-**sahzh**) *noun* a small bouquet of flowers worn by a woman.

corsair *noun* a pirate ship; a pirate.

corset *noun* a piece of underwear worn to shape or support the body.

cortège (*say* kaw-**tayzh**) *noun* a funeral procession. [French]

cosh *noun* a heavy weapon for hitting people.

cosine *noun* (in a right-angled triangle) the ratio of the length of a side adjacent to one of the acute angles to the length of the hypotenuse. (Compare **sine**.)

cosmetic *noun* a substance (e.g. face powder, lipstick) put on the skin to make it look more attractive.

cosmic *adjective* **1** of the universe. **2** of outer space, *cosmic rays.* [from *cosmos*]

cosmonaut *noun* a Russian astronaut. [from *cosmos* + *astronaut*]

cosmopolitan *adjective* **1** of or from many countries; containing people from many countries. **2** free from national prejudices. [from *cosmos* + Greek *polites* = citizen]

cosmos (*say* **koz**-mos) *noun* the universe. [from Greek, = the world]

cosset *verb* (**cosseted**, **cosseting**) pamper; cherish lovingly.

cossie (*say* **koz**-ee) *noun* (*Australian informal*) a swimming costume.

cost¹ *noun* the price of something.

cost² *verb* (**cost** (in sense 2 **costed**), **costing**) **1** have a certain price. **2** estimate the cost of something.

cost-benefit *adjective* relating to or denoting a process that assesses the relation between the cost of an undertaking and the value of the resulting benefits, *a cost-benefit analysis.*

costly *adjective* (**costlier**, **costliest**) expensive. **costliness** *noun*

costume *noun* clothes, especially for a particular purpose or of a particular place or period.

cosy¹ *adjective* (**cosier**, **cosiest**) warm and comfortable. **cosily** *adverb*, **cosiness** *noun*

cosy² *noun* (*plural* **cosies**) a cover placed over a teapot or boiled egg to keep it hot.

cot *noun* a baby's bed with high sides. [from Hindi *khat* = bedstead]

cot death *noun* (*informal*) the unexplained death of a baby in its sleep. Also called *SIDS*.

coterie (*say* **koh**-tuh-ree) *noun* an exclusive group of people.

cottage *noun* a small house, especially in the country.

cottage cheese *noun* soft white cheese made from curds without pressing.

cotton¹ *noun* **1** a soft white substance covering the seeds of a tropical plant; the plant itself. **2** thread made from this substance. **3** cloth made from cotton thread.

cotton² *verb* **cotton on** (*informal*) begin to understand.

cotton wool *noun* soft fluffy wadding originally made from cotton.

couch¹ *noun* (*plural* **couches**) **1** a long soft seat like a sofa but with only one end raised. **2** a sofa or settee.

couch² *verb* **1** express in words of a certain kind, *The request was couched in polite terms.* **2** lay down.

cougar (*say* **koo**-guh) *noun* (*American*) a puma.

cough¹ (*say* kof) *verb* send out air from the lungs with a sudden sharp sound.

cough² *noun* **1** the act or sound of coughing. **2** an illness that makes you cough.

could *auxiliary verb* **1** past tense of **can³**, *He could have tried harder.* **2** feel inclined to, *I could scream with the pain.* **3** might, *You could be right.*

couldn't could not, *they couldn't find the dog.*

council *noun* a group of people chosen or elected to organise or discuss something, especially those elected to organise the affairs of a town or local government area. [from Latin *concilium* = assembly]

councillor *noun* a member of a council.

counsel¹ *noun* **1** advice, *give counsel.* **2** a barrister or group of barristers representing someone in a lawsuit.
take counsel with consult. [from Latin *consulere* = consult]

counsel² *verb* (**counselled**, **counselling**) give advice to someone; recommend.

counsellor *noun* an adviser.

count¹ *verb* **1** say numbers in their proper order. **2** find the total of something by using numbers. **3** include in a total, *There are six of us, counting the dog.* **4** be important, *It's what you do that counts.* **5** regard; consider, *I should count it an honour to be invited.*
count on rely on.

count² *noun* **1** counting. **2** a number reached by counting a total. **3** any of the points being considered, e.g. in accusing someone of crimes, *guilty on all counts.*

count³ *noun* a European nobleman.

countdown *noun* counting numbers backwards to zero before an event.

countenance¹ *noun* a person's face; the expression on the face.

countenance² *verb* (**countenanced**, **countenancing**) give approval to; allow, *Will they countenance this plan?*

counter[1] *noun* **1** a flat surface over which customers are served or business is transacted. **2** a small disc used for playing or scoring in certain games. **3** a device for counting things.
under the counter sold or obtained in an underhand way.

counter[2] *verb* **1** counteract. **2** counter-attack; return an opponent's blow by hitting back.

counter[3] *adverb* contrary to something, *This is counter to what we really want.*

counter- *prefix* **1** against; opposing; done in return (as in *counter-attack*). **2** corresponding (as in *countersign*). [from Latin *contra* = against]

counteract *verb* act against something and reduce or prevent its effects.
counteraction *noun*

counter-attack *verb* attack to oppose or return an enemy's attack.
counter-attack *noun*

counterbalance *noun* a weight or influence that balances another. **counterbalance** *verb*

counterfeit (*say* **kown**-tuh-fuht) *adjective*, *noun*, & *verb* fake. [from Old French *countrefait* = made in opposition]

counterfoil *noun* a section of a cheque, receipt, ticket, or other document that is detached and kept as a record.

counter-intuitive *adjective* contrary to intuition or to common-sense expectation, *Her ideas sounded counter-intuitive to me at first.*

countermand *verb* cancel a command or instruction that has been given.

counterpane *noun* a bedspread.

counterpart *noun* a person or thing that corresponds to another, *Their president is the counterpart of our prime minister.*

counterpoint *noun* a method of combining melodies in harmony.

counterpoise *noun* & *verb* counterbalance.

countersign[1] *noun* a password or signal that has to be given in response to something.

countersign[2] *verb* add another signature to a document to give it authority.

countertenor *noun* a male singing voice higher than tenor; a singer with this.

counterterrorism *noun* political or military activities designed to prevent terrorism.

counterweight *noun* & *verb* counterbalance.

countess *noun* (*plural* **countesses**) the wife or widow of a count or earl; a female count.

countless *adjective* too many to count.

count noun *noun* (also **countable noun**) a noun that can form a plural or be used with the indefinite article (e.g. *book, cat*). (Compare **mass noun**.)

country *noun* (*plural* **countries**) **1** the land occupied by a nation. **2** all the people of a country. **3** less densely settled districts outside towns and cities. **4** an area of land, *rugged country.* **5** (*Australian*) the traditional territory of an Aboriginal people. **6** (also **country and western**) a type of folk music that originates from the southern US. **country** *adjective*

countryman *noun* (*plural* **countrymen**) **1** a person living in a country area. **2** a person who belongs to the same country as you.
countrywoman *noun* (*plural* **countrywomen**)

countryside *noun* areas outside the towns and cities.

county *noun* (*plural* **counties**) a territorial division in some countries for local government purposes. [originally = the land of a count (*count*[3])]

coup (*say* koo) *noun* a sudden action taken to win power; a clever victory. [French, = a blow]

coup de grâce (*say* koo duh **grahs**) *noun* a stroke or blow that puts an end to something. [French, = mercy-blow]

coup d'état (*say* koo day-**tah**) *noun* the sudden overthrow of a government. [French, = blow of state]

couple[1] *noun* two people or things considered together; a pair.

couple[2] *verb* (**coupled, coupling**) fasten or link together.

couplet *noun* a pair of lines in rhyming verse.

coupon *noun* a piece of paper that gives you the right to receive or do something. [French, = piece cut off]

courage *noun* the ability to face danger or difficulty or pain even when you are afraid; bravery. **courageous** *adjective* [from Latin *cor* = heart]

courgette (*say* kaw-***zh*****et**) another name for **zucchini.**

courier (*say* **kuu**-ree-uh) *noun* **1** a company or employee of a company that transports commercial packages and documents. **2** a messenger. **3** (chiefly *British*) a person employed to guide and help a group of tourists. [from Latin *currere* = to run]

course[1] *noun* **1** an onward movement or progression, *in the ordinary course of events.* **2** the direction in which something goes; a route, *the ship's course.* **3** a series of things one can do to achieve something, *Your best course is to start again.* **4** a series of lessons, exercises, or lectures in a particular subject. **5** part of a meal, *the meat course.* **6** a racecourse. **7** a golf course.
of course without a doubt; as we expected.

course[2] *verb* (**coursed, coursing**) move or flow freely, *Tears coursed down his cheeks.* [from Latin *cursus* = running]

court[1] *noun* **1** a royal household. **2** a lawcourt; the judges in this. **3** an enclosed area for games such as tennis or netball. **4** a courtyard.

court[2] *verb* try to win somebody's love or support. **courtship** *noun*

courteous (*say* **ker**-tee-uhs) *adjective* polite. **courteously** *adverb*, **courtesy** *noun*

courtier *noun* (*old use*) one of a king's or queen's companions at court.

courtly *adjective* dignified and polite.

court martial *noun* (*plural* **courts martial**) **1** a court for trying people who have broken military law. **2** a trial in this court.

court-martial *verb* (**court-martialled, court-martialling**) try a person by a court martial.

courtyard *noun* a space surrounded by walls or buildings.

couscous (*say* **kuus**-kuus) *noun* **1** a type of North African semolina in granules made from crushed wheat. **2** a dish made from this. [French from Arabic]

cousin *noun* a child of your uncle or aunt.

cove[1] *noun* a small bay.

cove[2] *noun* (*informal*) **1** a fellow, a chap. **2** (in early Australia) a manager or overseer.

coven (*say* **kuv**-uhn) *noun* a group of witches.

covenant (*say* **kuv**-uh-nuhnt) *noun* a formal agreement; a contract.

Coventry *noun* **send someone to Coventry** refuse to associate with or speak to someone.

cover[1] *verb* **1** place one thing over or round another; conceal. **2** travel a certain distance, *We covered 15 kilometres a day.* **3** aim a gun at somebody, *I've got you covered.* **4** protect by insurance or a guarantee, *These goods are covered against fire and theft.* **5** be enough money to pay for something, *$5 will cover my fare.* **6** deal with or include, *The book covers many topics.* **7** do someone's job during their absence, *He was able to cover for me.* **coverage** *noun*

cover up conceal (a thing or fact). **cover-up** *noun*

cover[2] *noun* **1** a thing used for covering something else; a lid, wrapper, envelope, etc. **2** the binding of a book. **3** something that hides or shelters or protects you.

coverlet *noun* a bedspread.

covert (*say* **koh**-vert or **kuv**-uht) *adjective* stealthy; done secretly.

covet (*say* **kuv**-uht) *verb* (**coveted, coveting**) wish to have something, especially a thing that belongs to someone else. **covetous** *adjective*

COVID-19 *noun* a contagious respiratory disease caused by a coronavirus. [short for 'coronavirus disease 2019']

cow[1] *noun* the fully grown female of cattle or of certain other large animals (e.g. elephant, whale, seal). (Compare **bull**.)

cow[2] *verb* intimidate; subdue someone by bullying.

coward *noun* a person who shows fear in a shameful way, or who attacks people who cannot defend themselves. **cowardice** *noun*, **cowardly** *adjective*

cowboy *noun* **1** a man in charge of grazing cattle on a ranch in the USA. **2** (*informal*) a person who uses reckless or dishonest methods in business.

cower *verb* crouch or shrink back in fear.

cowl *noun* **1** a monk's hood. **2** a hood-shaped covering, e.g. on a chimney.

cowling *noun* a removable metal cover over an engine.

cowrie *noun* a tropical mollusc with a glossy shell used as money in parts of Africa and Asia. [from Urdu *kauri*]

cowshed *noun* a shed for cattle.

cox *noun* (*plural* **coxes**) a coxswain.

coxswain (*say* **kok**-swayn or **kok**-suhn) *noun* a person who steers a rowing boat.

coy *adjective* pretending to be shy or modest; bashful. **coyly** *adverb*, **coyness** *noun*

coyote (*say* kuy-**oh**-tee) *noun* a North American wolf-like wild dog.

CPI *abbreviation* Consumer Price Index.

CPU *abbreviation* central processing unit.

crab *noun* a shellfish with ten legs.

crab apple *noun* a small sour apple.

crabby *adjective* bad-tempered. **crabbily** *adverb*, **crabbiness** *noun*

crabhole *noun* (*Australian*) a hole or shallow depression in the ground.

crack[1] *noun* **1** a line on the surface of something where it has broken but not come completely apart. **2** a narrow gap. **3** a sudden sharp noise. **4** a knock, *a crack on the head.* **5** (*informal*) a joke; a wisecrack. **6** a drug made from cocaine.

crack[2] *adjective* (*informal*) first-class, *She is a crack shot.*

crack[3] *verb* **1** make or get a crack; split. **2** make a sudden sharp noise. **3** break down, *He cracked under the strain.*

crack a joke tell a joke.

crack down on (*informal*) stop something that is illegal or against rules.

get cracking (*informal*) get busy.

crackdown *noun* (*informal*) action taken to stop something that is illegal or against rules.

cracker *noun* **1** a paper tube that bangs when pulled apart. **2** a firework that explodes with a crack. **3** a thin biscuit.

crackle *verb* (**crackled**, **crackling**) make small cracking sounds. **crackle** *noun*

crackling *noun* crisp skin on roast pork.

-cracy *suffix* forming nouns meaning 'ruling' or 'government' (e.g. *democracy*). [from Greek *-kratia* = rule]

cradle[1] *noun* **1** a small cot for a baby. **2** a supporting framework.

cradle[2] *verb* (**cradled, cradling**) hold gently.

craft *noun* **1** a job that needs skill, especially with the hands. **2** skill. **3** cunning; trickery. **4** (*plural* **craft**) a ship or boat; an aircraft or spacecraft.

craftsman *noun* (*plural* **craftsmen**) a person who is skilled in a craft. **craftsmanship** *noun*

craftswoman *noun* (*plural* **craftswomen**) a woman who is skilled in a craft.

crafty *adjective* (**craftier**, **craftiest**) cunning. **craftily** *adverb*, **craftiness** *noun*

crag *noun* a steep piece of rough rock. **craggy** *adjective*, **cragginess** *noun*

cram *verb* (**crammed**, **cramming**) **1** push many things into a space. **2** fill very full.

cramp[1] *noun* pain caused by a muscle tightening suddenly.

cramp[2] *verb* **1** keep in a very small space. **2** hinder someone's freedom or growth. **cramped** *adjective*

cranberry *noun* (*plural* **cranberries**) a small sour red berry used for making jelly and sauce.

crane[1] *noun* **1** a machine for lifting and moving heavy objects. **2** a large wading bird with long legs and neck.

crane[2] *verb* (**craned**, **craning**) stretch your neck to try and see something.

cranium *noun* the skull. **cranial** *adjective*

crank[1] *noun* **1** an L-shaped part used for changing the direction of movement in machinery. **2** a person with strange or fanatical ideas.

crank[2] *verb* move by means of a crank.

cranky *adjective* **1** bad-tempered. **2** eccentric; strange.

cranny *noun* (*plural* **crannies**) a crevice.

crash[1] *noun* **1** the loud noise of something breaking or colliding. **2** a violent collision or fall. **3** a sudden drop or failure, *a stock market crash; a computer crash.*

crash[2] *verb* **1** make a loud smashing noise. **2** move with a loud noise. **3** collide or cause to collide. **4** drop or fail suddenly.

crash[3] *adjective* intensive, *a crash course.*

crash helmet *noun* a padded helmet worn to protect the head in a crash.

crash-landing *noun* an emergency landing of an aircraft, which usually damages it.

crass *adjective* **1** very obvious or shocking; gross, *crass ignorance.* **2** very stupid. [from Latin *crassus* = thick]

crate *noun* **1** a packing case made of strips of wood. **2** an open container with compartments for carrying bottles.

crater *noun* **1** a bowl-shaped cavity or hollow. **2** the mouth of a volcano.

cravat *noun* a scarf worn inside an open-necked shirt.

crave *verb* (**craved**, **craving**) **1** desire strongly. **2** (*formal*) beg for something.

craven *adjective* cowardly.

craving *noun* a strong desire; a longing.

crawl[1] *verb* **1** move with the body close to the ground or other surface, or on hands and knees. **2** move slowly. **3** be covered with crawling things. **4** (*informal*) flatter someone in the hope of winning favour. **crawler** *noun*

crawl[2] *noun* **1** a crawling movement. **2** a very slow pace. **3** an overarm swimming stroke.

crayfish *noun* (*plural* **crayfish**) **1** a freshwater lobster-like crustacean (e.g. yabby). **2** (*Australian informal*) a marine crustacean (e.g. rock lobster).

crayon *noun* a stick or pencil of coloured wax for drawing.

craze *noun* a temporary enthusiasm.

crazed *adjective* driven insane.

crazy *adjective* (**crazier**, **craziest**) **1** insane. **2** very foolish, *a crazy idea.* **crazily** *adverb*, **craziness** *noun*

creak[1] *noun* a harsh squeak like that of an unoiled hinge. **creaky** *adjective*

creak[2] *verb* make a creak.

cream[1] *noun* **1** the fatty part of milk. **2** a yellowish-white colour. **3** a food containing or looking like cream, *strawberry cream.* **4** a soft substance, *hand cream.* **5** the best part. **creamy** *adjective*

cream[2] *verb* make creamy; beat an ingredient until it is soft like cream.
cream off remove the best part of something.

crease[1] *noun* **1** a line made in something by folding, pressing, or crushing it. **2** a line on a cricket pitch marking a batter's or bowler's position.

crease[2] *verb* (**creased**, **creasing**) make a crease or creases in something.

create *verb* (**created**, **creating**) bring into existence; make or produce, especially something that no one has made before. **creation** *noun*, **creative** *adjective*, **creativity** *noun*

creationism *noun* a theory attributing all matter, biological species, etc. to separate acts of creation by God, rather than to evolution. **creationist** *noun & adjective*

creator *noun* **1** a person who creates something. **2** (**the Creator**) God.

creature *noun* a person or animal.

crèche *noun* a place where babies and young children are minded. [French]

credence *noun* belief, *Don't give it any credence.* [from Latin *credere* = believe]

credentials *plural noun* evidence of a person's achievements or trustworthiness. [same origin as *credit*]

credible *adjective* able to be believed; convincing. **credibility** *noun*, **credibly** *adverb* [same origin as *credit*]

> **Usage** *Credible* is sometimes confused with *credulous*.

credit[1] *noun* **1** honour; acknowledgement. **2** an arrangement trusting a person to pay for something later on. **3** an entry recording a sum received. (Compare **debit**[1] 1.) **4** a payment received. **5** belief; trust, *I put no credit in this rumour.*
on credit with an arrangement to pay later.

credit[2] *verb* (**credited, crediting**) **1** believe. **2** attribute; say that a person has done or achieved something, *Columbus is credited with the discovery of America.* **3** enter something as a credit in an account book. (Compare **debit**[2].) [from Latin *credere* = believe, trust]

creditable *adjective* deserving praise. **creditably** *adverb*

credit card *noun* a card authorising a person to buy on credit.

creditor *noun* a person to whom money is owed.

credits *plural noun* a list of people who have helped to produce a film or television program.

credit union *noun* a financial organisation like a bank, usually for a group of employees.

credulous *adjective* too ready to believe things; gullible.

> **Usage** *Credulous* is sometimes confused with *credible*.

creed *noun* a set or formal statement of beliefs. [from Latin *credi* = I believe]

creek *noun* **1** a small stream, especially an intermittent one. **2** (*British*) a narrow inlet.
up the creek (*informal*) in difficulties.

creep[1] *verb* (**crept, creeping**) **1** move along close to the ground. **2** move quietly or secretly. **3** come gradually. **4** prickle with fear, *It makes my flesh creep.*

creep[2] *noun* **1** a creeping movement. **2** (*informal*) an unpleasant person, especially one who seeks to win favour.
the creeps (*informal*) a nervous feeling caused by fear or dislike.

creeper *noun* a plant that grows along the ground or up a wall.

creepy *adjective* (**creepier, creepiest**) (*informal*) making you feel nervous or frightened.

cremate *verb* (**cremated, cremating**) burn a dead body to ashes. **cremation** *noun*

crematorium *noun* (*plural* **crematoria**) a place where corpses are cremated.

crème de la crème (*say* krem duh lah **krem**) *noun* the very best of something. [French, = cream of the cream]

creosote *noun* an oily brown liquid used to prevent wood from rotting. [from Greek, = flesh-preserver]

crepe (*say* krayp) *noun* (also **crêpe**) **1** cloth, paper, or rubber with a wrinkled surface. **2** a thin pancake.

crept *past tense & past participle* of **creep**[1].

crescendo (*say* kruh-**shen**-doh) *noun* (*plural* **crescendos**) a gradual increase in loudness. [Italian]

crescent *noun* **1** a narrow curved shape (e.g. the new moon) coming to a point at each end. **2** a curved street. [from Latin *crescens* = growing]

cress *noun* a plant with hot-tasting leaves, used in salads and sandwiches.

crest *noun* **1** a tuft of hair, skin, or feathers on an animal's or bird's head. **2** the top of a hill or wave. **3** a design above the shield on a coat of arms, or used on notepaper etc. **crested** *adjective*

crestfallen *adjective* disappointed; dejected.

cretin (*say* **kret**-uhn) *noun* (*informal*) a stupid person.

crevasse (*say* kruh-**vas**) *noun* a deep open crack, especially in a glacier.

crevice *noun* a narrow opening, especially in a rock or wall.

crew[1] *noun* **1** the people working in a ship or aircraft. **2** a group working together, *the camera crew.* **3** (*informal*) a group of people.

crew[2] *past tense* of **crow**[2].

crib[1] *noun* **1** a baby's cot. **2** a framework holding fodder for animals. **3** something copied from another person's work. **4** a translation for use by students. **5** (*Australian*) a worker's packed lunch.

crib[2] *verb* (**cribbed**, **cribbing**) copy someone else's work.

cribbage *noun* a card game.

crick *noun* painful stiffness in the neck or back.

cricket[1] *noun* an outdoor game played with a ball, bats, and two wickets, between two teams of 11 players. **cricketer** *noun*

cricket[2] *noun* an insect like a grasshopper that makes a shrill chirping sound.

cried *past tense & past participle* of **cry**[2].

crime *noun* **1** an action that breaks the law. **2** law-breaking.

criminal *noun* a person who has committed a crime or crimes. **criminal** *adjective*, **criminally** *adverb*

criminology *noun* the study of crime. [from Latin *crimen* offence, + *-logy*]

crimp *verb* press into small ridges.

crimson *adjective & noun* deep red.

cringe *verb* (**cringed**, **cringing**) shrink back in fear or embarrassment; cower.

crinkle *verb* (**crinkled**, **crinkling**) make or become wrinkled. **crinkle** *noun*, **crinkly** *adjective*

crinoline *noun* a long skirt worn over a framework that makes it stand out.

cripple[1] *noun* **1** a person with a severe limitation of a specified kind, *an emotional cripple.* **2** (*offensive*) (in old use) a person who is unable to walk or move normally through disability or because of injury to their back or legs.

cripple[2] *verb* (**crippled**, **crippling**) weaken or damage something seriously.

crisis *noun* (*plural* **crises**) an important and dangerous or difficult situation; a decisive moment.

crisp[1] *adjective* **1** very dry so that it breaks with a snap, *crisp toast.* **2** firm and fresh, *a crisp apple.* **3** cold and dry, *a crisp morning.* **4** brisk and sharp, *a crisp manner.* **crisply** *adverb*, **crispness** *noun*

crisp[2] *noun* a very thin fried slice of potato (usually sold in packets).

criss-cross *adjective & adverb* with crossing lines.

criterion (*say* kruy-**teer**-ree-uhn) *noun* (*plural* **criteria**) a standard by which something is judged. [from Greek, = means of judging]

> **Usage** Note that *criteria* is a plural. It is incorrect to say 'a criteria' or 'this criteria'; correct usage is *this criterion, these criteria.*

critic *noun* **1** a person who gives opinions on books, plays, films, music, etc. **2** a person who criticises. [from Greek *krites* = judge]

critical *adjective* **1** criticising. **2** of critics or criticism. **3** of or at a crisis; very serious. **critically** *adverb*

criticise *verb* (**criticised**, **criticising**) say that a person or thing has faults.

criticism *noun* **1** criticising; pointing out faults. **2** the work of a critic.

croak *noun* a deep hoarse sound like that of a frog. **croak** *verb*, **croaky** *adjective*

crochet (*say* **kroh**-shay) *noun* a kind of needlework done by using a hooked needle to loop a thread into patterns. **crochet** *verb*

crock[1] *noun* an earthenware pot or jar.

crock[2] *noun* (*informal*) a decrepit person or thing.

crockery *noun* cups, saucers, dishes, plates, and other similar items, especially ones made of earthenware or china.

crocodile *noun* **1** a large tropical reptile with a thick skin, long tail, and huge jaws. **2** a long line of schoolchildren walking in pairs. [from Greek = worm of the stones]

crocodile tears *plural noun* sorrow that is not sincere (so called because the crocodile was said to weep while it ate its victim).

crocus *noun* (*plural* **crocuses**) a small plant with yellow, purple, or white flowers.

croissant (*say* **krwah**-song) *noun* a flaky crescent-shaped bread roll. [French, = crescent]

crone *noun* a very old woman.

crony *noun* (*plural* **cronies**) a close friend or companion.

crook[1] *noun* **1** a shepherd's stick with a curved end. **2** something bent or curved. **3** (*informal*) a person who makes a living dishonestly.

crook[2] *verb* bend, *She crooked her finger.*

crook[3] *adjective* (*Australian informal*) **1** bad or unpleasant, *a crook job*; *The weather's crook.* **2** ill, *feeling crook.* **3** angry. **go crook** become angry. [from *crooked*]

crooked *adjective* **1** bent; twisted; not straight. **2** dishonest.

croon *verb* sing softly and gently. **crooner** *noun*

crop[1] *noun* **1** something grown for food, *a good crop of wheat.* **2** a whip with a loop instead of a lash. **3** part of a bird's throat. **4** a very short haircut.

crop[2] *verb* (**cropped**, **cropping**) **1** (of animals) bite off, *Sheep were cropping the grass.* **2** cut very short. **3** produce a crop. **crop up** happen unexpectedly.

cropper *noun* **come a cropper** (*informal*) fall heavily; fall badly.

croquet (*say* **kroh**-kay) *noun* a game played with wooden balls and mallets.

crosier (*say* **kroh**-zee-uh) *noun* a bishop's staff shaped like a shepherd's crook.

cross[1] *noun* **1** a mark or shape made like + or ×. **2** an upright post with another piece of wood across it, used in ancient times for crucifixion. **3** (**the Cross**) that on which Christ was crucified, used as a symbol of Christianity. **4** a mixture of two different things.

cross[2] *verb* **1** go across something. **2** draw a line or lines across something. **3** make the sign or shape of a cross, *Cross your fingers for luck.* **4** produce something from two different kinds.
cross out draw a line across something because it is unwanted or wrong.

cross[3] *adjective* **1** going from one side to another. **2** annoyed; bad-tempered. **crossly** *adverb*, **crossness** *noun*

cross- *prefix* **1** across; crossing something (as in *crossbar*). **2** from two different kinds (as in *cross-breed*).

crossbar *noun* a horizontal bar, especially between two uprights.

crossbow *noun* a powerful bow with a mechanism for pulling and releasing the string.

cross-breed *verb* (**cross-bred**, **cross-breeding**) breed by mating an animal with one of a different kind. **cross-breed** *noun*

cross-country *adjective & adverb* across fields or open country, not following roads.

crosse *noun* a hooked stick with a net across it, used in lacrosse.

cross-examine *verb* question someone closely, especially in a lawcourt, in order to test answers given to previous questions. **cross-examination** *noun*

cross-eyed *adjective* with eyes that look or seem to look towards the nose.

crossfire *noun* lines of gunfire that cross each other.

crossing *noun* a place at which one may cross; a place for pedestrians to cross a road.

cross-legged *adjective & adverb* with ankles crossed and knees spread apart.

cross reference *noun* a reference to another text or part of a text, typically to give further information.

crossroads *noun* a place where two or more roads cross one another.

cross-section *noun* **1** a drawing of something as if it has been cut through. **2** a typical sample.

crosswise *adverb & adjective* with one thing crossing another.

crossword *noun* short for **crossword puzzle**, a puzzle in which words have to be guessed from clues and then written into the blank squares in a diagram.

crotch *noun* the part between the legs where they join the body; a similar angle in a forked part.

crotchet *noun* a note in music, lasting half as long as a minim (written ♩).

crotchety *adjective* peevish.

crouch *verb* lower your body, with your arms and legs bent.

croup (*say* kroop) *noun* a disease causing a hard cough and difficulty in breathing.

crow[1] *noun* a large black bird.
as the crow flies in a straight line.

crow[2] *verb* (**crowed** or **crew**, **crowing**) **1** make a shrill cry as a cock does. **2** boast; be triumphant. **crow** *noun*

crowbar *noun* an iron bar used as a lever.

crowd[1] *noun* a large number of people in one place.

crowd[2] *verb* **1** come together in a crowd. **2** cram; fill uncomfortably full.

crowdfunding *noun* the practice of funding a project or venture by raising money from a large number of people who each contribute a relatively small amount, typically via the Internet. **crowdfund** *verb*

crowdsourcing *noun* the practice of obtaining information or input into a task or project by enlisting the services of a large number of people, typically via the Internet. **crowdsource** *verb*

crowd surf *verb* (especially in a rock concert) ride the body of a crowd as if it were a wave, by being passed over the heads of crowd members.

crown[1] *noun* **1** an ornamental headdress worn by a king or queen. **2** (**the Crown**) the monarch as head of state; the power or authority of the monarch. **3** the highest part, *the crown of the road.* **4** a former coin worth five shillings (50 cents).

crown[2] *verb* **1** place a crown on as a symbol of royal power or victory. **2** form or cover or decorate the top of something. **3** reward; make a successful end to something, *Our efforts were crowned with victory.* **4** (*informal*) hit on the head. [from Latin *corona* = garland or crown]

crown of thorns *noun* a spiny starfish that destroys coral reefs.

crow's nest *noun* a lookout platform high up on a ship's mast.

crucial (*say* **kroo**-shuhl) *adjective* **1** decisive, critical, *The experiment is at a crucial stage.* **2** very important, *This game is crucial to our survival.* **crucially** *adverb* [from Latin *crucis* = of a cross]

crucible *noun* a melting pot for metals.

crucifix *noun* (*plural* **crucifixes**) a model of the Cross or of Jesus Christ on the Cross. [from Latin, = fixed to a cross]

crucify *verb* (**crucified**, **crucifying**) put a person to death by nailing or binding the hands and feet to a cross. **crucifixion** *noun*

crude *adjective* **1** in a natural state; not yet refined, *crude oil.* **2** not well finished; rough, *a crude carving.* **3** vulgar. **crudely** *adverb*, **crudity** *noun* [from Latin *crudus* = raw, rough]

cruel *adjective* (**crueller**, **cruellest**) causing pain or suffering. **cruelly** *adverb*, **cruelty** *noun*

cruet *noun* a small container or set of containers for salt, pepper, oil, or vinegar for use at the table.

cruise[1] *noun* a pleasure trip in a ship.

cruise[2] *verb* (**cruised**, **cruising**) **1** sail or travel at a moderate speed. **2** have a cruise.

cruiser *noun* **1** a fast warship. **2** a large motor boat.

crumb *noun* a small fragment, especially of bread or other food.

crumble *verb* (**crumbled**, **crumbling**) break or fall into small fragments. **crumbly** *adjective*

crumpet *noun* a soft flat cake made with yeast, eaten toasted with butter.

crumple *verb* (**crumpled**, **crumpling**) **1** crush or become crushed into creases. **2** collapse loosely.

crunch[1] *verb* **1** crush something noisily between the teeth. **2** make a sound like crunching. **3** (in computing) process (large quantities of data).

crunch[2] *noun* **1** crunching; a crunching sound. **2** (*informal*) (also **the crunch**) a crucial event. **crunchy** *adjective*

crusade *noun* **1** a military expedition made by Christians in the Middle Ages to recover Palestine from the Muslims who had conquered it. **2** a campaign for a cause. **crusader** *noun*

crush[1] *verb* **1** press something so that it gets broken or harmed. **2** crease or crumple. **3** defeat.

crush[2] *noun* (*plural* **crushes**) **1** a crowd of people pressed together. **2** (*informal*) a strong feeling of love for someone which is usually only temporary.

crust *noun* **1** the hard outer layer of something, especially bread. **2** the rocky outer layer of the earth.

crustacean (*say* krus-**tay**-shuhn) *noun* an animal with a shell, e.g. a crab or yabby.

crusty *adjective* (**crustier**, **crustiest**) **1** having a crisp crust. **2** having a harsh or irritable manner. **crustiness** *noun*

crutch *noun* (*plural* **crutches**) a support like a long walking stick for helping a lame or injured person to walk.

crux *noun* (*plural* **cruces**) the vital part of a problem; the decisive point. [Latin, = a cross]

cry[1] *noun* (*plural* **cries**) **1** a loud wordless sound expressing pain, grief, joy, etc. **2** a shout. **3** crying, *Have a good cry.*

cry[2] *verb* (**cried**, **crying**) **1** shed tears; weep. **2** call out loudly.

crypt *noun* a room under a church, often used as a burial place.

cryptic *adjective* hiding its meaning in a puzzling way. **cryptically** *adverb* [from Greek *kryptos* = hidden]

cryptogram *noun* something written in cipher. [from Greek *kryptos* = hidden, + *-gram*]

crystal *noun* **1** a transparent colourless mineral rather like glass. **2** very clear high-quality glass. **3** a small solid piece of certain substances, *crystals of snow and ice.* **crystalline** *adjective*

crystallise *verb* (**crystallised**, **crystallising**) **1** form into crystals. **2** become definite in form. **crystallisation** *noun*

c-section *noun* Caesarean section.

CS gas *noun* a gas causing tears and choking, used to control riots.

CT scan see **CAT scan**.

cub *noun* **1** the young of certain animals, e.g. lion, tiger, fox, bear. **2** (**Cub** or **Cub Scout**) a member of the junior branch of the Scout Association.

cubby hole *noun* a small compartment.

cubby house *noun* (*Australian*) a child's playhouse.

cube[1] *noun* **1** something that has six equal square sides. **2** the number produced by multiplying something by itself twice, *The cube of 3 is* $3 \times 3 \times 3 = 27$.

cube[2] *verb* (**cubed**, **cubing**) **1** multiply a number by itself twice, *4 cubed is* $4 \times 4 \times 4 = 64$. **2** cut into small cubes.

cube root *noun* the number which produces a particular number if it is multiplied by itself twice, *The cube root of 27 is 3.*

cubic *adjective* three-dimensional.

cubicle *noun* a compartment of a room.

cubic metre *noun* the volume of a cube with sides that are one metre long.

cubism *noun* an early 20th century art movement in which objects are often represented geometrically. **cubist** *noun & adjective*

cuckoo *noun* a bird that makes a sound like 'cuck-oo', and often lays its eggs in the nests of smaller birds.

cucumber *noun* a usually long green-skinned vegetable eaten in salads.

cud *noun* half-digested food that a cow etc. brings back from its first stomach to chew again.

cuddle *verb* (**cuddled**, **cuddling**) put your arms closely round a person or animal that you love. **cuddle** *noun*, **cuddly** *adjective*

cudgel[1] *noun* a short thick stick used as a weapon.

cudgel[2] *verb* (**cudgelled**, **cudgelling**) beat with a cudgel.

cue[1] *noun* something said or done that serves as a signal for something else to be done, e.g. for an actor to speak in a play. [origin unknown]

cue[2] *noun* a long rod for striking the ball in billiards or snooker. [from *queue*]

cuff[1] *noun* **1** the end of a sleeve that fits round the wrist. **2** hitting somebody with your hand; a slap.
off the cuff (*informal*) without preparation.

cuff[2] *verb* hit somebody with your hand.

cuisine (*say* kwuh-**zeen**) *noun* a style of cooking. [French, = kitchen]

cul-de-sac *noun* (*plural* **culs-de-sac**) a street with an opening at one end only; a dead end. [French, = bottom of a sack]

culinary *adjective* of cooking; for cooking.

cull *verb* **1** pick, *culling fruit.* **2** select and use, *culling lines from several poems.* **3** pick out and kill surplus animals from a herd or flock. **cull** *noun*

culminate *verb* (**culminated**, **culminating**) reach its highest or last point. **culmination** *noun* [from Latin *culmen* = summit]

culottes *plural noun* women's shorts designed to look like a skirt.

culpable *adjective* deserving blame. **culpability** *noun* [from Latin *culpare* = to blame]

culprit *noun* the person who has done something wrong.

cult *noun* a religion; devotion to a person or thing.

cultivate *verb* (**cultivated**, **cultivating**) **1** use land to grow crops. **2** grow crops. **3** develop things by looking after them. **cultivation** *noun*, **cultivator** *noun*

cultural burn *noun* (*Australian*) a method of vegetation control by burning, used especially by some Aboriginal communities.

culture *noun* **1** the arts and other manifestations of human intellectual achievement regarded collectively. **2** customs and traditions, *West Indian culture.* **3** improvement by care and training, *physical culture.* **4** cultivating things.
cultural *adjective*

cultured *adjective* educated to appreciate literature, art, music, etc.

cultured pearl *noun* a pearl formed by an oyster when a foreign body is put into its shell.

culvert *noun* a drain that passes under a road or railway.

cumbersome *adjective* clumsy to carry or manage.

cummerbund *noun* a broad sash.

cumquat (*say* **kum**-kwot) *noun* (also **kumquat**) a small orange-like fruit used in jams etc.

cumulative *adjective* accumulating; increasing by continuous additions. [from Latin *cumulus* = heap]

cunjevoi[1] (*say* **kun**-juh-voi) *noun* (also **cunje**) an Australian sea squirt used as fishing bait. [probably from a New South Wales Aboriginal language]

cunjevoi[2] *noun* a rainforest plant of New South Wales and Queensland. [probably from Bundjalung]

cunning[1] *adjective* **1** clever at deceiving people. **2** cleverly designed or planned.

cunning[2] *noun* being cunning.

cup[1] *noun* **1** a small bowl-shaped container for drinking from. **2** anything shaped like a cup. **3** a goblet-shaped ornament given as a prize. **cupful** *noun*

cup[2] *verb* (**cupped**, **cupping**) form into the shape of a cup, *cup your hands.*

cupboard *noun* a recess or piece of furniture with a door, for storing things.

cupcake *noun* a small cake baked in a cup-shaped container.

cupidity (*say* kyoo-**pid**-uh-tee) *noun* greed for gain. [from Latin *cupido* = desire]

cupola (*say* **kyoo**-puh-luh) *noun* a small dome on a roof.

cur *noun* a scruffy or bad-tempered dog.

curable *adjective* able to be cured.

curate *noun* a member of the clergy who helps a vicar. [same origin as *cure*]

curative (*say* **kyoo**-ruh-tiv) *adjective* helping to cure illness.

curator (*say* kyoo-**ray**-tuh) *noun* **1** a person in charge of a museum or other collection. **2** a person who organises an art collection etc. [same origin as *cure*]

curb[1] *verb* restrain, *curb your impatience.*

curb[2] *noun* a restraint, *Put a curb on spending.* [from Latin *curvare* = to curve]

curd *noun* **1** (also **curds**) a thick substance formed when milk turns sour. **2** a substance with a similar consistency, *bean curd.*

curdle *verb* (**curdled, curdling**) form into curds.
make someone's blood curdle fill someone with horror.

cure[1] *verb* (**cured, curing**) **1** get rid of someone's illness. **2** stop something bad. **3** treat something so as to preserve it, *Fish can be cured using smoke.*

cure[2] *noun* **1** something that cures a person or thing; a remedy. **2** curing; being cured, *We cannot promise a cure.* [from Latin *curare* = take care of something]

curfew *noun* **1** a regulation requiring people to remain indoors between specified hours, typically at night. **2** the hour designated as the beginning of a curfew. [from Old French = cover the fire (referring to a time when people had to put out their fires in the evening)]

curio *noun* (*plural* **curios**) a rare or unusual object.

curiosity *noun* (*plural* **curiosities**) **1** being curious. **2** something unusual and interesting.

curious *adjective* **1** wanting to find out about things; inquisitive. **2** strange; unusual. **curiously** *adverb* [from Latin, = careful (compare *cure*)]

curl[1] *noun* a curve or coil, e.g. of hair.

curl[2] *verb* form into curls.
curl up sit or lie with knees drawn up.

curler *noun* a device for curling the hair.

curlew *noun* a wading bird with a long curved bill.

curling *noun* a game played on ice with large flat stones.

curly *adjective* full of curls; curling.

curmudgeon *noun* a bad-tempered person.

currant *noun* **1** a small black dried grape used in cookery. **2** a small round red, black, or white berry.

currawong *noun* an Australian bird like a crow with a loud ringing call. [from Dhanggati *garawang*]

currency *noun* (*plural* **currencies**) **1** the money in use in a country. **2** the general use of something, *Some words have no currency now.* [from *current*]

current[1] *adjective* happening now; used now. **currently** *adverb*

current[2] *noun* **1** water or air moving in one direction. **2** the flow of electricity along a wire or through something. [from Latin *currens* = running]

curricle *noun* an old type of lightweight carriage drawn by two horses.

curriculum *noun* (*plural* **curricula**) a course of study.

curriculum vitae *noun* a brief account of a person's education and previous career.

curry[1] *noun* (*plural* **curries**) food cooked with spices that taste hot. **curried** *adjective* [from Tamil *kari* = sauce]

curry[2] *verb* (**curried, currying**) groom a horse with a rubber or plastic pad (called a *curry comb*).
curry favour seek to win favour by flattering someone.

curse[1] *noun* **1** a call or prayer for a person or thing to be harmed; the evil produced by this. **2** something very unpleasant. **3** an angry word or words.

curse[2] *verb* (**cursed, cursing**) **1** make a curse. **2** use a curse against a person or thing.
be cursed with something suffer from it.

cursive *noun* writing done with joined letters.

cursor *noun* a movable indicator on a display screen. [Latin, = runner (compare *current*)]

cursory *adjective* hasty and not thorough, *a cursory inspection.* **cursorily** *adverb* [from Latin, = of a runner]

curt *adjective* brief and hasty or rude, *a curt reply.* **curtly** *adverb*, **curtness** *noun*

curtail *verb* **1** cut short, *The lesson was curtailed.* **2** reduce, *We must curtail our spending.* **curtailment** *noun*

curtain *noun* **1** a piece of material hung at a window or door. **2** the large cloth screen hung at the front of a stage.

curtsy[1] *noun* (*plural* **curtsies**) a movement of respect made by women and girls, putting one foot behind the other and bending the knees.

curtsy[2] *verb* (**curtsied, curtsying**) make a curtsy. [= *courtesy*]

curvature *noun* curving; a curved shape.

curve[1] *verb* (**curved, curving**) bend smoothly.

curve[2] *noun* a curved line or shape.
curvy *adjective*

cushion[1] *noun* **1** a bag, usually of cloth, filled with soft material so that it is comfortable to sit on or lean against. **2** anything soft or springy that protects or supports something, *The hovercraft travels on a cushion of air.*

cushion[2] *verb* **1** supply with cushions, *cushioned seats.* **2** protect from the effects of a knock or shock, *The bark chips cushioned his fall.*

cushy *adjective* (*informal*) pleasant and easy, *a cushy job.* [from Hindi *khus* = pleasant]

cusp *noun* a pointed end where two curves meet, e.g. a tip of a crescent moon. [from Latin *cuspis* = point]

custard *noun* a dessert made with beaten eggs and milk.

custodian *noun* a person who has custody of something; a keeper.

custody *noun* **1** care and supervision; guardianship. **2** imprisonment.
custodial *adjective*
take into custody arrest. [from Latin *custos* = guardian]

custom *noun* **1** the usual way of behaving or doing something. **2** regular business from customers.

customary *adjective* according to custom; usual. **customarily** *adverb*

customary law *noun* legal practices and rules as prescribed by Aboriginal custom and tradition.

customer *noun* a person who uses a shop, bank, or other business.

custom-made *adjective* made according to a customer's order.

customs *plural noun* **1** taxes charged on goods brought into a country. **2** the place at a port or airport where officials examine your luggage.

cut[1] *verb* (**cut**, **cutting**) **1** divide or wound or separate something by using a knife, axe, scissors, or other sharp object. **2** make a thing shorter or smaller; remove part of something, *They cut their prices.* **3** divide a pack of playing cards. **4** hit a ball with a chopping movement. **5** go through or across something. **6** (*informal*) stay away from something deliberately, *She cut her music lesson.* **7** make a sound recording. **8** switch off electrical power or an engine. **9** delete (part of a text). **10** (in computing) delete part of a text or other display so as to insert a copy of it elsewhere.
cut a corner pass round it very closely.
cut and dried already decided.
cut back reduce.
cut corners fail to do something properly, especially to save time.
cut in interrupt.
cut off 1 interrupt; prevent from continuing. **2** isolate.
cut out 1 omit. **2** shape by cutting. **3** (*informal*) stop doing or using something.

cut[2] *noun* **1** cutting; the result of cutting. **2** a small wound. **3** a reduction. **4** (*informal*) a share.
be a cut above something be superior.

cut and paste *noun* a combination of the functions 'cut' and 'paste', by which text or data is moved from one place in an electronic document or computer system to another.

cutback *noun* a reduction.

cute *adjective* (*informal*) **1** attractive. **2** clever. **cutely** *adverb*, **cuteness** *noun* [from *acute*]

cuticle (*say* **kyoo**-ti-kuhl) *noun* the skin at the base of a nail.

cutlass *noun* (*plural* **cutlasses**) a short sword with a broad curved blade.

cutlery *noun* knives, forks, and spoons.

cutlet *noun* a thick slice of meat for cooking.

cut lunch *noun* (*Australian*) a packed lunch, usually sandwiches.

cut-out *noun* a shape cut out of paper, cardboard, or other material.

cutter *noun* **1** a person or thing that cuts. **2** a small fast sailing ship.

cutting *noun* **1** a steep-sided passage cut through high ground for a road or railway. **2** a piece cut out of a newspaper etc. **3** a piece cut from a plant to form a new plant.

cuttlefish *noun* (*plural* **cuttlefish**) a sea creature that sends out a black liquid when attacked.

CV *abbreviation* curriculum vitae.

cyanide *noun* a very poisonous chemical.

cyber *adjective* relating to or characteristic of the culture of computers, information technology, and virtual reality, *the cyber age.*

cyber- *prefix* forming words relating to electronic communication networks and virtual reality (as in *cyberspace*).

cyberbullying *noun* harassment by email, mobile phone, texting, or on the Internet.

cybercafe *noun* a cafe where customers can sit at computer terminals and log on to the Internet.

cybercrime *noun* crime committed by means of computers or the Internet.

cyberspace *noun* the notional environment in which electronic communication occurs.

cycle[1] *noun* **1** a bicycle or motorcycle. **2** a series of events that are regularly repeated in the same order. **cyclic** *adjective*, **cyclical** *adjective*

cycle[2] *verb* (**cycled**, **cycling**) ride a bicycle. **cyclist** *noun* [from Greek *kyklos* = circle]

cyclone *noun* a wind that rotates round a calm central area. **cyclonic** *adjective*

cygnet (*say* **sig**-nuht) *noun* a young swan.

cylinder *noun* **1** an object with straight sides and circular ends. **2** a machine part shaped like this; the chamber in which a piston moves in an engine. **cylindrical** *adjective* [from Greek *kylindein* = to roll]

cymbal *noun* a percussion instrument consisting of a metal plate that is hit to make a ringing sound.

cynic (*say* **sin**-ik) *noun* a person who believes that people's reasons for doing things are selfish or bad, and shows this by sneering at them. **cynical** *adjective*, **cynically** *adverb*, **cynicism** *noun*

cypress *noun* (*plural* **cypresses**) an evergreen tree with dark leaves.

cyst (*say* sist) *noun* an abnormal swelling containing fluid or soft matter.

czar (*say* zah) *noun* a tsar.

Dd

dab[1] *noun* **1** a quick gentle touch. **2** a small lump, *a dab of butter.*

dab[2] *verb* (**dabbed**, **dabbing**) touch quickly and gently.

dabble *verb* (**dabbled**, **dabbling**) **1** splash something about in water. **2** do something as a hobby, *dabble in chemistry.*

da capo (*say* duh **kah**-poh) *adverb* (in music) repeat from the beginning. [Italian]

dachshund (*say* **daks**-huund) *noun* a small dog with a long body and very short legs. [German, = badger-dog]

dad *noun* (also **daddy**) (*informal*) father, *Her dad likes to cook pasta.*

daddy-long-legs *noun* (*plural* **daddy-long-legs**) a spider with long thin legs.

daffodil *noun* a yellow flower that grows from a bulb.

daft *adjective* (*informal*) silly; crazy.

dag *noun* (*Australian*) **1** a lock of wool clotted with dung on a sheep. **2** (*informal*) an unfashionable or socially awkward person. **3** (*informal*) an eccentric; a character. [from British dialect]

dagger *noun* a pointed knife with two sharp edges, used as a weapon.

daggy *adjective* (*Australian informal*) unfashionable. [from *dag*]

daguerrotype (*say* duh-**gair**-ruh-tuyp) *noun* an early kind of photograph. [named after Louis Daguerre, French inventor]

dahlia (*say* **day**-lee-uh) *noun* a garden plant with brightly coloured flowers. [named after A. Dahl, a Swedish botanist]

daily *adverb & adjective* every day.

dainty *adjective* (**daintier**, **daintiest**) small, delicate, and pretty. **daintily** *adverb*, **daintiness** *noun*

dairy[1] *noun* (*plural* **dairies**) a place where milk and milk products are produced, distributed, or sold.

dairy[2] *adjective* of milk or milk products, *dairy cow.*

dais (*say* **day**-uhs) *noun* a low platform, especially at the end of a room.

daisy *noun* (*plural* **daisies**) a small flower with white petals and a yellow centre. [from *day's eye*]

dak *verb* (**dakked**, **dakking**) (*Australian informal*) pull down a person's trousers or shorts as a joke. [from *daks*]

daks *plural noun* (*Australian trademark*) trousers. [from *Daks* = a British proprietary name for a brand of clothing]

dal (*say* dahl) *noun* (also **daal**, **dahl**, or **dhal**) **1** (in Indian cooking) split pulses, in particular lentils. **2** a dish made with these. [Hindi]

dale *noun* a valley.

dalgyte *noun* (also **dalgite**) a Western Australian name for the bilby. [from Noongar *djalkat*]

dally *verb* (**dallied**, **dallying**) dawdle.

Dalmatian *noun* a large white short-haired dog with dark spots. [named after Dalmatia, a region of Croatia]

dam[1] *noun* **1** a wall built to hold water back. **2** (*Australian*) an artificial pond with earth walls.

dam[2] *verb* (**dammed**, **damming**) hold water back with a dam.

dam[3] *noun* the female parent of an animal, especially a four-footed one. (Compare **sire**.) [from *dame*]

damage[1] *noun* something that reduces the value or usefulness of a thing or spoils its appearance.

damage[2] *verb* (**damaged**, **damaging**) cause damage to something.

damages *plural noun* money paid as compensation for an injury or loss.

Dame *noun* the title of a lady who has been given the equivalent of a knighthood.

damn *verb* curse. [from Latin *damnare* = condemn]

damnation *noun* being damned or condemned to hell.

damp[1] *adjective* slightly wet; not quite dry. **damply** *adverb*, **dampness** *noun*

damp[2] *noun* moisture in the air or on a surface or all through something.

damp[3] *verb* **1** make damp; moisten. **2** reduce the strength of something, *The defeat damped their enthusiasm.*

damp course *noun* a layer of material built into a wall to prevent dampness in the ground from rising.

dampen *verb* damp.

damper *noun* **1** a metal plate that can be moved to increase or decrease the movement of air flowing into a fire or furnace. **2** something that reduces sound or enthusiasm. **3** (*Australian*) a simple kind of bread baked in ashes.

damsel *noun* (*old use*) a young woman.

dan *noun* a grade of proficiency in some martial arts. [Japanese]

dance[1] *verb* (**danced**, **dancing**) move about in time to music.

dance[2] *noun* **1** a set of movements used in dancing. **2** a piece of music for dancing to. **3** a party or gathering where people dance. **dancer** *noun*

dandelion *noun* a yellow wild flower with jagged leaves. [from French *dent-de-lion* = tooth of a lion]

dandruff *noun* tiny white flakes of dead skin in a person's hair.

dandy *noun* (*plural* **dandies**) **1** a man who likes to look very smart. **2** (*Australian*) a small container of ice cream.

danger *noun* something dangerous.

dangerous *adjective* likely to kill or do great harm. **dangerously** *adverb*

dangle *verb* (**dangled**, **dangling**) hang or swing loosely.

dank *adjective* damp and chilly.

dapper *adjective* dressed neatly and smartly.

dappled *adjective* marked with patches of a different colour.

dare[1] *verb* (**dared**, **daring**) **1** be brave or bold enough to do something. **2** challenge a person to do something risky.

dare[2] *noun* a challenge to do something risky.

daredevil *noun* a person who is very bold and reckless.

daring[1] *noun* boldness; courage.

daring[2] *adjective* bold; willing to take risks.

dark[1] *adjective* **1** with little or no light. **2** not light in colour, *a dark suit.* **3** having dark hair. **4** secret, *Keep it dark!* **darkly** *adverb*, **darkness** *noun*

dark[2] *noun* **1** absence of light, *Cats can see in the dark.* **2** the time when darkness has come, *She went out after dark.*

darken *verb* make or become dark.

darkroom *noun* a room kept dark for developing and printing photographs.

darling *noun* someone who is loved very much. [from Old English *dearling* = little dear]

darn[1] *verb* mend a hole by weaving threads across it.

darn[2] *noun* a place that has been darned.

dart[1] *noun* **1** an object with a sharp point thrown at a target. **2** a sudden rapid movement. **3** a tapering tuck stitched in something to make it fit.

dart[2] *verb* run suddenly and quickly.

darts *noun* a game in which darts are thrown at a circular board (**dartboard**).

dash[1] *verb* **1** run quickly; rush. **2** throw a thing violently against something, *The storm dashed the ship against the rocks.*

dash[2] *noun* (*plural* **dashes**) **1** a short quick run; a rush. **2** energy; liveliness. **3** a small amount, *Add a dash of brandy.* **4** a short line (–) used in writing or printing. **5** (*informal*) a dashboard.

dashboard *noun* a panel with dials and controls in front of the driver of a motor vehicle.

dashcam *noun* a video camera mounted on the dashboard or windscreen of a vehicle and used to continuously record the view of the road, traffic, etc.

dashing *adjective* lively and showy.

dastardly *adjective* contemptible and cowardly.

data (*say* **dah**-tuh or **day**-tuh) *plural noun* **1** known facts or things used as a basis for inference or reckoning. **2** quantities or characters operated on by a computer.

> **Usage** Strictly this word is a plural noun (the singular is *datum*). However, it is also widely used nowadays with a singular verb (e.g. *The data has been corrupted*).

database *noun* a structured store of information held in a computer.

data display *noun* a way of presenting data visually, e.g. as a graph or table.

data processing *noun* the carrying out of operations on data, especially by a computer, to retrieve, transform, or classify information.

data set *noun* a collection of related sets of information that is composed of separate elements but can be manipulated as a unit by a computer.

date[1] *noun* **1** the time when something happens or happened or was written, stated as the day, month and year (or any of these). **2** an appointment to meet. **3** (*informal*) a person with whom one has a social engagement.

date[2] *verb* (**dated**, **dating**) **1** give a date to something. **2** have existed from a particular time, *The church dates from 1895.* **3** seem old-fashioned. [from Latin *data* = given (at a certain time)]

date[3] *noun* a small sweet brown fruit that grows on a kind of palm tree.

daub *verb* paint or smear something clumsily. **daub** *noun*

daughter *noun* a girl or woman who is someone's child.

daughter-in-law *noun* (*plural* **daughters-in-law**) a son's wife.

daunt *verb* make somebody afraid or discouraged. **daunting** *adjective*

dauntless *adjective* brave; not to be daunted. **dauntlessly** *adverb*

dawdle *verb* (**dawdled**, **dawdling**) go slowly and lazily. **dawdler** *noun*

dawn[1] *noun* **1** the time when the sun rises. **2** the beginning.

dawn[2] *verb* **1** begin to grow light in the morning. **2** begin to be realised, *The truth dawned on them.*

dawn parade *noun* (also **dawn service**) (*Australian*) a memorial service at dawn on Anzac Day.

day *noun* **1** the 24 hours between midnight and the next midnight, *She spent two days in hospital.* **2** the light part of this time, *The day was cloudy but good for walking.* **3** a particular day, *sports day.* **4** a period of time, *in Queen Victoria's day.*

daybreak *noun* dawn.

daydream[1] *noun* pleasant thoughts of something you would like to happen.

daydream[2] *verb* have daydreams.

daylight *noun* **1** the light of day. **2** dawn.

dazed *adjective* unable to think or see clearly. **daze** *noun*

dazzle *verb* (**dazzled**, **dazzling**) **1** make a person unable to see clearly because of too much bright light. **2** amaze or impress a person by a splendid display.

DC *abbreviation* (also **dc**) direct current.

de- *prefix* **1** removing (as in *defrost*). **2** down, away (as in *descend*). **3** completely (as in *denude*). [from Latin *de* = away from]

deacon *noun* **1** a member of the clergy ranking below bishops and priests. **2** (in some Churches) a church officer who is not a member of the clergy. **deaconess** *noun* [from Greek *diakonos* = servant]

dead *adjective* **1** no longer alive. **2** not lively. **3** not functioning; no longer in use. **4** exact; complete, *a dead loss.*

deaden *verb* deprive of or lose vitality, loudness, or feeling.

dead end *noun* **1** a road or passage with one end closed. **2** a situation where there is no chance of making progress.

dead heat *noun* a race in which two or more competitors finish exactly together.

deadline *noun* a time limit. [originally this meant a line round an American military prison; if a prisoner went beyond it he could be shot]

deadlock *noun* a situation in which no progress can be made.

deadly *adjective* (**deadlier**, **deadliest**) **1** likely to kill, *a deadly weapon.* **2** (*Australian informal*) (especially in Aboriginal English) great, wonderful; terrific, *The school musical was deadly.*

deadpan *adjective* expressionless.

deaf *adjective* **1** unable to hear. **2** unwilling to hear. **deafness** *noun*

deafen *verb* make somebody become deaf, especially by a very loud noise.

deal[1] *verb* (**dealt**, **dealing**) **1** hand something out; give. **2** give out cards for a card game. **3** do business; trade, *He deals in scrap metal.* **dealer** *noun*

deal with 1 be concerned with, *This book deals with words and meanings.* **2** do what is needed, *deal with the problem.*

deal[2] *noun* **1** an agreement or bargain. **2** someone's turn to deal at cards.

a good deal or **a great deal** a large amount.

deal[3] *noun* sawn fir or pine wood.

dean *noun* **1** an important member of the clergy in a cathedral. **2** a college or university official; the head of a university faculty. **deanery** *noun*

dear *adjective* **1** loved very much. **2** a polite greeting in letters, *Dear Sir.* **3** expensive. **dearly** *adverb*, **dearness** *noun*

dearth (*say* derth) *noun* a scarcity.

death *noun* dying; the end of life.

deathly *adjective & adverb* like death.

debacle (*say* day-**bah**-kuhl) *noun* an utter failure or collapse. [from French *débâcler* = unbar]

debar *verb* (**debarred**, **debarring**) forbid; ban, *She was debarred from the contest.*

debase *verb* (**debased**, **debasing**) reduce the quality or value of something. **debasement** *noun*

debatable *adjective* questionable; that can be argued against.

debate[1] *noun* a formal discussion.

debate[2] *verb* (**debated**, **debating**) hold a debate. **debater** *noun*

debilitate *verb* make weak.

debility (*say* duh-**bil**-uh-tee) *noun* weakness.

debit[1] *noun* **1** an entry recording a sum owed. (Compare **credit**[1] 3.) **2** a payment made or owed.

debit² *verb* (**debited**, **debiting**) enter something as a debit in an account book. (Compare **credit**² 3.) [from Latin *debitum* = what is owed]

debonair (*say* deb-uh-**nair**) *adjective* cheerful and confident. [from French *de bon air* = of good disposition]

debris (*say* **deb**-ree or duh-**bree**) *noun* scattered broken pieces of something; rubbish left behind. [from French *débris* = broken down]

debt (*say* det) *noun* something that you owe someone.
in debt owing something. [same origin as *debit*]

debtor (*say* **det**-uh) *noun* a person who owes money to someone.

debut (*say* **day**-byoo) *noun* someone's first public appearance. [from French *débuter* = begin]

debutante (*say* **deb**-yoo-tont) *noun* a young woman making her first appearance in society.

deca- *prefix* ten (as in *decathlon*). [from Greek *deka* = ten]

decade (*say* **dek**-ayd) *noun* a period of ten years.

decadent (*say* **dek**-uh-duhnt) *adjective* **1** characterised by or reflecting a state of moral or cultural decline. **2** luxuriously self-indulgent, *a decadent soak in a scented bath.* **decadence** *noun* [same origin as *decay*]

decamp *verb* **1** pack up and leave a camp. **2** go away suddenly or secretly.

decant (*say* duh-**kant**) *verb* pour liquid gently from one container into another without disturbing the sediment.

decanter (*say* duh-**kan**-tuh) *noun* a glass bottle with a stopper into which wine or spirit is decanted.

decapitate *verb* (**decapitated**, **decapitating**) behead. **decapitation** *noun* [from *de*–, + Latin *caput* = head]

decathlon *noun* an athletic contest in which each competitor takes part in ten events. [from *deca*–, + Greek *athlon* = contest]

decay *verb* **1** go bad; rot. **2** become less good or less strong. **decay** *noun* [from *de*–, + Latin *cadere* = to fall]

decease (*say* duh-**sees**) *noun* death.

deceased *adjective* dead.

deceit (*say* duh-**seet**) *noun* deceiving; a deception. **deceitful** *adjective*, **deceitfully** *adverb*

deceive *verb* (**deceived**, **deceiving**) cause a person to believe something that is not true. **deceiver** *noun*

December *noun* the twelfth month of the year. [from Latin *decem* = ten]

decent *adjective* **1** respectable; conforming to accepted standards of what is proper. **2** (*informal*) kind. **decency** *noun*, **decently** *adverb*

decentre *verb* (**decentred**, **decentring**) **1** displace from the centre or from a central position. **2** remove or displace (the individual human subject, such as the author of a text) from a primary place or central role.

deception *noun* deceiving someone; a trick. **deceptive** *adjective*, **deceptively** *adverb*

deci- (*say* **des**-ee) *prefix* one tenth (as in *decimetre*). [same origin as *decimal*]

decibel (*say* **des**-uh-bel) *noun* a unit for measuring the loudness of sound. [originally one tenth of the unit called a *bel*]

decide *verb* (**decided**, **deciding**) **1** make up your mind; make a choice. **2** settle a contest or argument. **decider** *noun*

decided *adjective* **1** having clear and definite opinions. **2** noticeable, *a decided difference.* **decidedly** *adverb*

deciduous (*say* duh-**sid**-yoo-uhs) *adjective* losing its leaves in autumn, *a deciduous tree.* (Compare **evergreen**.) [from Latin *decidere* = fall off]

decimal¹ *adjective* (of a system of numbers, weights, measures, etc.) based on the number ten, in which the smaller units are related to the principal units as powers of ten (units, tens, hundreds, thousands, etc.).

decimal² *noun* a decimal fraction. [from Latin *decimus* = tenth]

decimal fraction *noun* a fraction with tenths shown as numbers after a dot (3⁄10 is 0.3; 1½ is 1.5).

decimal place *noun* the position of a digit to the right of a decimal point.

decimal point *noun* the dot in a decimal fraction.

decimate (*say* **des**-uh-mayt) *verb* (**decimated**, **decimating**) **1** destroy one tenth of. **2** (loosely) destroy a large part of, *The famine decimated the population.* [from Latin *decimare* = kill every tenth man (this was the ancient Roman punishment for an army guilty of mutiny or other serious crime)]

decipher (*say* duh-**suy**-fuh) *verb* **1** decode. **2** work out the meaning of something written badly. **decipherable** *adjective*

decision *noun* **1** deciding; what you have decided. **2** determination.

decisive (*say* duh-**suy**-siv) *adjective* **1** that settles or ends something, *a decisive battle.* **2** full of determination; resolute. **decisively** *adverb*, **decisiveness** *noun*

deck¹ *noun* **1** a floor on a ship or bus. **2** an outdoor platform attached to a house. **3** a piece of equipment for playing tapes or discs. **4** a pack of cards.

deck[2] *verb* decorate with something.

deckchair *noun* a folding chair with a canvas or plastic seat.

declaim *verb* speak or say impressively or dramatically. **declamation** *noun* [from *de*–, + Latin *clamare* = to shout]

declaration *noun* **1** an official or public statement. **2** the act of declaring an innings of cricket closed.

declarative *adjective* **1** of the nature of or making a declaration, *a declarative statement.* **2** (of a sentence or phrase) taking the form of a simple statement.

declare *verb* (**declared**, **declaring**) **1** say something clearly or firmly. **2** tell customs officials that you have goods on which you ought to pay duty. **3** end a cricket innings before all the batters are out.
declare war announce that you are starting a war against someone. [from *de*–, + Latin *clarare* = make clear]

decline[1] *verb* (**declined**, **declining**) **1** refuse. **2** become weaker or smaller. **3** slope downwards.

decline[2] *noun* a gradual decrease or loss of strength. [from *de*–, + Latin *clinare* = bend]

decode *verb* (**decoded**, **decoding**) **1** find the meaning of something written in code. **2** analyse and interpret (a piece of writing, image, etc.). **decodable** *adjective*, **decoder** *noun*

decompose *verb* (**decomposed**, **decomposing**) decay. **decomposition** *noun*

decompression *noun* reduction of air pressure.

decontamination *noun* getting rid of the harmful effects caused by poisonous chemicals or radioactive material.

décor (*say* **day**-kaw) *noun* the style of furnishings and decorations used in a room. [French (compare *decorate*)]

decorate *verb* (**decorated**, **decorating**) **1** make something look more beautiful or colourful. **2** put fresh paint or paper on walls. **3** give somebody an award. **decoration** *noun*, **decorative** *adjective*, **decorator** *noun* [from Latin *decor* = beauty]

decorous (*say* **dek**-uh-ruhs) *adjective* polite and dignified. **decorously** *adverb*

decorum (*say* duh-**kaw**-ruhm) *noun* polite and dignified behaviour.

decoy[1] (*say* **dee**-koi) *noun* something used to tempt a person or animal into a trap or into danger.

decoy[2] (*say* duh-**koi**) *verb* lure by means of a decoy.

decrease[1] *verb* (**decreased**, **decreasing**) make or become smaller or fewer.

decrease[2] *noun* decreasing; the amount by which something decreased. [from *de*–, + Latin *crescere* = grow]

decree[1] *noun* **1** an official order. **2** a judgement or decision.

decree[2] *verb* (**decreed**, **decreeing**) make a decree.

decrepit (*say* duh-**krep**-uht) *adjective* old and weak; dilapidated. **decrepitude** *noun* [from Latin, = creaking]

decry *verb* (**decried**, **decrying**) speak publicly against something, disparage.

dedicate *verb* (**dedicated**, **dedicating**) **1** devote to a special use, *She dedicated herself to her work.* **2** name a person as a mark of respect, e.g. at the beginning of a book.
dedication *noun*

deduce *verb* (**deduced**, **deducing**) work something out by reasoning. **deducible** *adjective* [from *de*–, + Latin *ducere* = to lead]

deduct *verb* subtract part of something.

deductible *adjective* able to be deducted.

deduction *noun* **1** deducting; something deducted. **2** deducing; something deduced.

deductive *adjective* based on reasoning.

deed *noun* **1** something that someone has done; an act. **2** a legal document.

deem *verb* (*formal*) consider, *I should deem it an honour to be invited.*

deep *adjective* **1** going a long way down or back or in, *a deep well*; *deep cupboards.* **2** measured from top to bottom or front to back, *a hole a metre deep.* **3** intense; strong, *deep colours*; *deep feelings.* **4** low-pitched, not shrill, *a deep voice.* **deeply** *adverb*, **deepness** *noun*

deepen *verb* make or become deeper.

deer *noun* (*plural* **deer**) a fast-running graceful animal, the male of which usually has antlers.

deface *verb* (**defaced**, **defacing**) spoil the surface of something, e.g. by scribbling on it.
defacement *noun*

de facto[1] *adjective* existing in fact (whether by right or not).

de facto[2] *noun* (*Australian*) a person living with another person as if married. [Latin]

defame *verb* (**defamed**, **defaming**) attack a person's good reputation; slander, libel.
defamation (*say* def-uh-**may**-shuhn) *noun*, **defamatory** (*say* duh-**fam**-uh-tuh-ree) *adjective*

default[1] *verb* fail to do what you have agreed to do. **defaulter** *noun*

default[2] *noun* failure to do something.

defeat[1] *verb* **1** win a victory over someone. **2** baffle; be too difficult for someone.

defeat[2] *noun* **1** defeating someone. **2** being defeated; a lost game or battle.

defeatist *noun* a person who expects to be defeated. **defeatism** *noun*

defecate (*say* **def**-uh-kayt) *verb* (**defecated, defecating**) get rid of faeces from your body. **defecation** *noun*

defect[1] (*say* **dee**-fekt or duh-**fekt**) *noun* a flaw.

defect[2] (*say* duh-**fekt**) *verb* desert one's country; abandon one's allegiance to a cause. **defection** *noun*, **defector** *noun*

defective *adjective* having defects; incomplete. **defectiveness** *noun*

defence *noun* **1** defending something. **2** something that defends or protects. **3** a reply put forward by a defendant.

defenceless *adjective* having no defences.

defend *verb* **1** protect, especially against an attack. **2** try to prove that a statement is true or that an accused person is not guilty. **defender** *noun*

defendant *noun* a person accused of something in a lawcourt. (Compare **plaintiff**.)

defensible *adjective* able to be defended. **defensibility** *noun*

defensive *adjective* used or done for defence; protective. **defensively** *adverb*
on the defensive ready to defend yourself.

defer[1] *verb* (**deferred, deferring**) postpone. **deferment** *noun*, **deferral** *noun* [same origin as *differ*]

defer[2] *verb* (**deferred, deferring**) give way to a person's wishes or authority; yield. [from Latin *deferre* = to grant]

deference (*say* **def**-uh-ruhns) *noun* polite respect. **deferential** (*say* def-uh-**ren**-shuhl) *adjective*, **deferentially** *adverb*

defiant *adjective* defying; openly disobedient. **defiance** *noun*, **defiantly** *adverb*

defibrillation *noun* the stopping of fibrillation of the heart by administering a controlled electric shock, to allow restoration of the normal rhythm. **defibrillate** *verb*, **defibrillator** *noun*

deficiency *noun* (*plural* **deficiencies**) **1** a lack; a shortage. **2** a defect. **deficient** *adjective*

deficit (*say* **def**-uh-suht) *noun* **1** the amount by which a total is smaller than what is required. **2** the amount by which spending is greater than income.

defile[1] *verb* (**defiled, defiling**) **1** make a thing dirty or impure. **2** profane. **defilement** *noun* [from an old word *defoul*]

defile[2] *noun* a narrow pass or gorge. [French]

define *verb* (**defined, defining**) **1** explain what a word or phrase means. **2** show clearly what something is; specify. **3** show a thing's outline. **definable** *adjective* [from *de*–, + Latin *finis* = limit]

definite *adjective* **1** clearly stated; exact, *Fix a definite time.* **2** certain; settled, *Is it definite that we are to move?* **definitely** *adverb*

definite article *noun* the word 'the'.

definition *noun* **1** a statement of what a word or phrase means or of what a thing is. **2** being distinct; clearness of outline (e.g. in a photograph).

definitive (*say* duh-**fin**-uh-tiv) *adjective* finally settling something; conclusive, *a definitive victory.*

deflate *verb* (**deflated, deflating**) **1** let out air from a tyre, balloon, or similar object. **2** make someone feel less proud or less confident. **3** reduce or reverse inflation. **deflation** *noun*, **deflationary** *adjective* [from *de-* + *inflate*]

deflect *verb* make something turn aside. **deflection** *noun*, **deflector** *noun* [from *de*–, + Latin *flectere* = to bend]

defoliant *noun* a chemical substance that destroys leaves.

deforest *verb* clear away the trees from an area. **deforestation** *noun*

deform *verb* spoil a thing's shape or appearance. **deformation** *noun*

deformed *adjective* badly or abnormally shaped. **deformity** *noun*

defraud *verb* take something from a person by fraud; cheat, swindle.

defray *verb* (**defrayed, defraying**) provide money to pay costs or expenses. **defrayal** *noun*

defriend *verb* (*informal*) delete someone from a list of friends or contacts associated with a social networking site.

defrost *verb* **1** remove frost or ice from something. **2** thaw out something frozen.

deft *adjective* skilful and quick. **deftly** *adverb*, **deftness** *noun*

defunct *adjective* dead.

defuse *verb* (**defused, defusing**) **1** remove the fuse from a bomb etc. **2** make a situation less dangerous.

defy *verb* (**defied, defying**) **1** resist something openly; refuse to obey, *They defied the law.* **2** challenge a person to do something you believe cannot be done, *I defy you to prove this.* **3** prevent something being done, *The door defied all efforts to open it.*

degenerate[1] *verb* (**degenerated, degenerating**) become worse; lose good qualities. **degeneration** *noun*

degenerate[2] *adjective* having degenerated. **degeneracy** *noun*

degrade *verb* (**degraded**, **degrading**) **1** humiliate; disgrace. **2** decompose. **degradation** *noun*

degree *noun* **1** a unit for measuring temperature. **2** a unit for measuring angles. **3** extent, *to some degree.* **4** a stage in a scale or series. **5** an award to someone at a university or college who has successfully finished a course.

degustation (*say* dee-gus-**tay**-shuhn) *noun* **1** tasting something carefully to appreciate it fully. **2** (of a menu) providing a wide variety of foods in small quantities. [from *de*–, + Latin *gustare* = to taste]

dehydrated *adjective* dried up, with its moisture removed. **dehydration** *noun* [from *de*–, + Greek *hydor* = water]

deify (*say* **dee**-uh-fuy) *verb* (**deified**, **deifying**) treat someone or something as a god. **deification** *noun*

deign (*say* dayn) *verb* condescend, be gracious enough to do something.

deity (*say* **dee**-uh-tee) *noun* (*plural* **deities**) a god or goddess. [from Latin *deux* = god]

déjà vu (*say day-zhah* **voo**) *noun* a feeling that you have already experienced what is happening now. [French, = already seen]

dejected *adjective* sad; gloomy; downcast. **dejectedly** *adverb*, **dejection** *noun* [from *de*–, + Latin *-jectum* = cast]

de jure (*say* day **joor**-ree) *adjective & adverb* rightful; by right. [Latin]

delay[1] *verb* (**delayed**, **delaying**) **1** make someone or something late; hinder. **2** postpone. **3** wait; linger.

delay[2] *noun* delaying; the time for which something is delayed, *a two-hour delay.*

delectable *adjective* delightful. **delectably** *adverb*

delegate[1] (*say* **del**-uh-guht) *noun* a person who represents others and acts on their instructions.

delegate[2] (*say* **del**-uh-gayt) *verb* (**delegated**, **delegating**) **1** appoint as a delegate, *We delegated Jones to represent us.* **2** entrust, *We delegated the work to Jones.* [from Latin *delegare* = entrust]

delegation (*say* del-uh-**gay**-shuhn) *noun* **1** delegating. **2** a group of delegates.

delete (*say* duh-**leet**) *verb* (**deleted**, **deleting**) strike out something written or printed. **deletion** *noun*

deli *noun* (*informal*) a delicatessen.

deliberate[1] (*say* duh-**lib**-uh-ruht) *adjective* **1** done on purpose, intentional. **2** slow and careful. **deliberately** *adverb*

deliberate[2] (*say* duh-**lib**-uh-rayt) *verb* (**deliberated**, **deliberating**) discuss or think carefully. **deliberation** *noun*

delicacy *noun* (*plural* **delicacies**) **1** being delicate. **2** a delicious food.

delicate *adjective* **1** fine; soft; fragile. **2** pleasant and not strong or intense. **3** becoming ill easily. **4** needing great care, *a delicate situation.* **5** taking great care to avoid offence, *The situation requires delicate handling.* **delicately** *adverb*, **delicateness** *noun*

delicatessen *noun* a shop that sells cooked meats, cheeses, salads, and unusual or foreign prepared foods. [from German, = delicacies to eat]

delicious *adjective* tasting or smelling very pleasant. **deliciously** *adverb*

delight[1] *verb* **1** please someone greatly. **2** feel great pleasure.

delight[2] *noun* great pleasure. **delightful** *adjective*, **delightfully** *adverb*

delinquent (*say* duh-**ling**-kwuhnt) *noun* someone who breaks the law or commits an offence. **delinquency** *noun*, **delinquent** *adjective*

delirium (*say* duh-**leer**-ree-uhm) *noun* **1** a state of mental confusion and agitation during a feverish illness. **2** wild excitement. **delirious** *adjective*, **deliriously** *adverb*

deliver *verb* **1** take letters or goods to someone's house or place of work. **2** give a speech or lecture. **3** help with the birth of a baby. **4** aim or strike a blow or an attack. **5** rescue; set free. **deliverance** *noun*, **deliverer** *noun*, **delivery** *noun* [from *de*–, + Latin *liberare* = set free]

dell *noun* a small valley with trees.

delphinium *noun* a garden plant with tall spikes of flowers, usually blue.

delta *noun* a triangular area at the mouth of a river where it spreads into branches. [shaped like the Greek letter delta (= D), written Δ]

delude *verb* (**deluded**, **deluding**) deceive.

deluge[1] *noun* **1** a large flood. **2** a heavy fall of rain. **3** something coming in great numbers, *a deluge of questions.*

deluge[2] *verb* (**deluged**, **deluging**) flood or overwhelm by a deluge.

delusion *noun* a false belief.

deluxe *adjective* of very high quality. [French, = of luxury]

delve *verb* (**delved**, **delving**) search deeply, e.g. for information, *delving into history.* [the original meaning was 'dig']

demagogue (*say* **dem**-uh-gog) *noun* a leader who wins support by making emotional speeches rather than by careful reasoning. [from Greek *demos* = people, + *agogos* = leading]

demand[1] *verb* **1** ask for something firmly or forcefully. **2** need, *It demands skill.*

demand[2] *noun* **1** a firm or forceful request. **2** a desire to have something, *There is a great demand for computers.*
in demand wanted; desired. [from *de*–, + Latin *mandare* = to order]

demarcation (*say* dee-mah-**kay**-shuhn) *noun* marking the boundary of something.

demean *verb* lower a person's dignity, *I wouldn't demean myself to ask for it!*

demeanour (*say* duh-**mee**-nuh) *noun* a person's behaviour or manner.

demented *adjective* driven mad; crazy. [from *de*–, + Latin *mentis* = of the mind]

dementia *noun* a mental disorder marked by memory loss and personality changes.

demerit *noun* a fault; a defect.

demi- *prefix* half (as in *demisemiquaver*).

demigod *noun* a partly divine being.

demise (*say* duh-**muyz**) *noun* (*formal*) death.

demisemiquaver *noun* a note in music, equal to half a semiquaver.

demist *verb* remove misty condensation from a windscreen. **demister** *noun*

demo *noun* (*plural* **demos**) (*informal*) a demonstration.

democracy *noun* (*plural* **democracies**) **1** government of a country by representatives elected by the whole population. **2** a country governed in this way. **3** control of an organisation or group by the majority of its members. **democratic** *adjective*, **democratically** *adverb* [from Greek *demos* = people, + *-cracy*]

democrat *noun* an advocate of democracy.

demographic[1] *adjective* relating to the structure of populations.

demographic[2] *noun* a specific or defined part of the population.

demography *noun* **1** the study of statistics such as births, deaths, diseases, and income levels, which illustrate the changing structure of human populations. **2** the composition of a particular human population. [from Greek *demos* = people, + *-graphy*]

demolish *verb* knock something down and break it up. **demolition** *noun* [from *de*–, + Latin *moliri* = build]

demon *noun* **1** a devil; an evil spirit. **2** a fierce or forceful person. **demonic** (*say* duh-**mon**-ik) *adjective* [from Greek *daimon* = a spirit]

demonstrable (*say* duh-**mon**-struh-buhl) *adjective* able to be shown or proved. **demonstrably** *adverb*

demonstrate *verb* (**demonstrated**, **demonstrating**) **1** show; prove. **2** describe and explain. **3** take part in a demonstration. **demonstrator** *noun*

demonstration *noun* **1** demonstrating; showing how to do or work something. **2** an organised gathering or procession to express the opinion of a group publicly.

demonstrative (*say* duh-**mon**-struh-tiv) *adjective* **1** showing or proving something. **2** showing feelings or affections openly. **3** (in grammar) pointing out the person or thing referred to, *This, that, these, and those are demonstrative adjectives or pronouns.*
demonstratively *adverb*, **demonstrativeness** *noun*

demonstrative pronoun see **pronoun**.

demoralise *verb* (**demoralised**, **demoralising**) dishearten someone; weaken someone's confidence or morale.
demoralisation *noun*

demote *verb* (**demoted**, **demoting**) reduce to a lower position or rank. **demotion** *noun* [from *de-* + *promote*]

demountable *noun* a transportable building, used as temporary accommodation.

demur[1] (*say* duh-**mer**) *verb* (**demurred**, **demurring**) raise objections.

demur[2] *noun* an objection raised.

demure *adjective* quiet and serious. **demurely** *adverb*, **demureness** *noun*

den *noun* **1** a lair. **2** a person's private room. **3** a place where something illegal happens, *a gambling den.*

dendrochronology *noun* a system of dating timber by studying the annual growth rings of trees. [from Greek *dendron* = tree + *chronology*]

dengue (*say* **deng**-gee) *noun* an infectious tropical fever causing acute pain in the joints. [West Indian Spanish from Swahili]

deniable *adjective* able to be denied.

denial *noun* denying or refusing something.

denigrate (*say* **den**-uh-grayt) *verb* (**denigrated**, **denigrating**) blacken someone's reputation. **denigration** *noun*

denim *noun* a kind of strong cotton cloth. [from *serge de Nim* = fabric of Nîmes (a town in southern France)]

denizen (*say* **den**-uh-zuhn) *noun* an inhabitant, *Monkeys are denizens of the jungle.*

denomination *noun* **1** a name or title. **2** a religious group with a special name, *Baptists, Anglicans and other* *denominations.* **3** a unit of weight or of money, *coins of small denomination.*

denominator *noun* the number below the line in a fraction, showing how many parts the whole is divided into, e.g. 4 in ¼. (Compare **numerator.**)

denote *verb* (**denoted**, **denoting**) mean; indicate, *In road signs, P denotes a car park.* **denotation** *noun*

dénouement (*say* day-**noo**-mon) *noun* the final outcome of a plot or story, revealed at the end. [French, = unravelling]

denounce *verb* (**denounced**, **denouncing**) **1** speak strongly against something. **2** accuse, *They denounced him as a spy.* **denunciation** *noun* [from *de*–, + Latin *nuntiare* = announce]

dense *adjective* **1** thick; packed close together. **2** stupid. **densely** *adverb*

density *noun* (*plural* **densities**) **1** thickness. **2** (in physics) the proportion of weight to volume.

dent[1] *noun* a hollow left in a surface where something has pressed or hit it.

dent[2] *verb* make a dent in something.

dental *adjective* of or for the teeth; of dentistry. [from Latin *dentis* = of a tooth]

dentist *noun* a person who is trained to treat diseases and other conditions that affect the teeth and gums. **dentistry** *noun*

denture *noun* a set of false teeth.

denude *verb* (**denuded**, **denuding**) make bare or naked; strip something away. **denudation** *noun*

denunciation *noun* denouncing.

deny *verb* (**denied**, **denying**) **1** say that something is not true. **2** refuse to give or allow something, *deny a request.*

deodorant (*say* dee-**oh**-duh-ruhnt) *noun* a substance that removes smells.

deodorise *verb* (**deodorised**, **deodorising**) remove smells. **deodorisation** *noun* [from *de*–, + Latin *odor* = a smell]

depart *verb* go away; leave.

department *noun* one part of a large organisation. **departmental** *adjective*

department store *noun* a large shop selling various types of goods in different departments.

departure *noun* departing.

depend *verb* **depend on 1** rely on, *We depend on your help.* **2** be controlled by something else, *Whether we can picnic depends on the weather.* [from *de*–, + Latin *pendere* = hang]

dependable *adjective* reliable.

dependant *noun* a person who depends on another, *She has two dependants.*

> **Usage** Note that the spelling ends in *-ant* for this noun but *-ent* for the adjective *dependent.*

dependency *noun* (*plural* **dependencies**) **1** being dependent, *drug dependency.* **2** a country that is controlled by another.

dependent *adjective* **1** depending, *She has two dependent children; they are dependent on her.* **2** unable to do without, *dependent on drugs.* **3** (of a clause, phrase, or word) subordinate to a sentence or word. **4** (of a mathematical variable) having a value determined by that of another variable. **dependence** *noun*

depict *verb* **1** show in the form of a picture. **2** describe. **depiction** *noun* [from *de*–, + Latin *pictum* = painted]

deplete (*say* duh-**pleet**) *verb* (**depleted**, **depleting**) reduce the amount of something by using up large amounts. **depletion** *noun* [from *de*–, + Latin *-pletum* = filled]

deplore *verb* (**deplored**, **deploring**) **1** regret something, *We deplore his death.* **2** find something extremely bad, *She deplores waste.* **deplorable** *adjective*, **deplorably** *adverb* [from *de*–, + Latin *plorare* = weep]

deploy *verb* spread out; bring or come into action systematically, *deploying troops.* **deployment** *noun*

deport *verb* send an unwanted person out of a country. **deportation** *noun*, **deportee** *noun* [from *de*–, + Latin *portare* = carry]

deportment *noun* a person's manner of standing, walking, and behaving.

depose *verb* (**deposed**, **deposing**) **1** remove a person from power. **2** make a sworn statement.

deposit[1] *noun* **1** an amount of money paid into an account. **2** money paid as a first instalment. **3** a layer of matter deposited or accumulated naturally.

deposit[2] *verb* (**deposited**, **depositing**) **1** put down. **2** pay money as a deposit. **depositor** *noun* [from *de*–, + Latin *positum* = placed]

deposition *noun* **1** the action of removing someone from power. **2** a statement made on oath.

depot (*say* **dep**-oh) *noun* **1** a place where things are stored. **2** a headquarters. **3** a place where buses, trams, or trains are kept when not in use. [same origin as *deposit*]

depraved *adjective* behaving wickedly; of bad character. **depravity** *noun*

deprecate (*say* **dep**-ruh-kayt) *verb* (**deprecated**, **deprecating**) say that you disapprove of something. **deprecation** *noun* [from Latin *deprecari* = keep away misfortune by prayer]

depreciate (*say* duh-**pree**-shee-ayt) *verb* (**depreciated**, **depreciating**) make or become lower in value. [from *de*–, + Latin *pretium* = price]

depredation (*say* dep-ruh-**day**-shuhn) *noun* the act of plundering or damaging something.

depress *verb* **1** make somebody sad. **2** lower the value of something, *Threat of war depressed prices.* **3** press down, *Depress the lever.* **depressed** *adjective*, **depressive** *adjective*

depression *noun* **1** a great sadness or feeling of hopelessness. **2** a long period when trade is very slack because people cannot afford to buy things. **3** a shallow hollow in the ground or on a surface. **4** an area of low air pressure which may bring rain. **5** pressing something down.

deprive *verb* (**deprived**, **depriving**) take or keep something away from somebody. **deprival** *noun*, **deprivation** *noun* [from *de*–, + Latin *privare* = rob]

depth *noun* **1** being deep; how deep something is. **2** the deepest or lowest part. **3** sagacity; wisdom. **4** intensity of emotion or colour.
in depth thoroughly.
out of your depth **1** in water that is too deep to stand in. **2** trying to do something that is too hard for you.

deputation *noun* group of people sent as representatives of others.

depute (*say* duh-**pyoot**) *verb* (**deputed**, **deputing**) **1** appoint a person to do something, *We deputed John to take the message.* **2** assign or delegate a task to someone, *We deputed the task to him.*

deputise *verb* (**deputised**, **deputising**) act as someone's deputy.

deputy *noun* (*plural* **deputies**) a person appointed to act as a substitute for another.

deracinate (*say* dee-**ras**-uh-nayt) *verb* **1** to tear up by the roots. **2** to uproot (someone) from their natural environment. [from French *déraciner*]

derail *verb* cause a train to leave the rails. **derailment** *noun*

derange *verb* (**deranged**, **deranging**) **1** throw into confusion; disturb. **2** make a person insane. **derangement** *noun*

derby (*say* **dah**-bee or **der**-bee) *noun* an important sporting contest.

derelict (*say* **de**-ruh-likt) *adjective* abandoned and left to fall into ruin. **dereliction** *noun* [from *de-* = completely, + Latin *relictum* = left behind]

deride *verb* (**derided**, **deriding**) laugh at with contempt or scorn; ridicule. [from *de*–, + Latin *ridere* = to laugh]

de rigueur (*say* **duh** ri-ger) *adjective* proper; required by custom or etiquette. [French, = of strictness]

derision *noun* scorn; ridicule. **derisive** (*say* duh-**ruy**-siv) *adjective*, **derisively** *adverb*, **derisory** *adjective*

derivation *noun* **1** deriving. **2** the origin of a word from another language or from a simple word to which a prefix or suffix is added; etymology.

derivative *adjective* derived from something. **derivative** *noun*

derive *verb* (**derived**, **deriving**) **1** obtain from a source, *She derived great enjoyment from music.* **2** form or originate from something, *Some English words are derived from Latin words.* [from *de*–, + Latin *rivus* = a stream]

dermatology *noun* the study of the skin and its diseases. **dermatologist** *noun* [from Greek *derma* = skin, + *-logy*]

derogatory (*say* duh-**rog**-uh-tuh-ree) *adjective* contemptuous; disparaging.

derrick *noun* **1** a kind of crane for lifting things. **2** a tall framework holding the machinery used in drilling an oil well or bore hole. [this word originally meant 'a gallows', named after Derrick, a London hangman in about 1600]

dervish *noun* (*plural* **dervishes**) a member of a Muslim religious group who vowed to live a life of poverty. [from Persian *darvish* = poor]

desalinate *verb* remove the salt from seawater. **desalination** *noun*

descant *noun* a tune sung or played above the main tune. [from *dis*–, + Latin *cantus* = song]

descend *verb* go down.
be descended from have as an ancestor; come by birth from a certain person or family. [from Latin *descendere* = climb down]

descendant *noun* a person who is descended from another.

descending *adjective* **1** moving or sloping downwards, *We then came to a steep descending track.* **2** moving down a scale of quality, *The movies are ranked in descending order of popularity.*

descent *noun* **1** descending. **2** a downward slope. **3** family origin.

describe *verb* (**described**, **describing**) **1** say what someone or something is like. **2** draw in outline; move in a pattern, *describe a circle.* **description** *noun*, **descriptive** *adjective* [from *de*–, + Latin *scribere* = writer]

desecrate (*say* **des**-uh-krayt) *verb* (**desecrated**, **desecrating**) treat a sacred thing irreverently. **desecration** *noun* [from *de-* + *consecrate*]

desert[1] (*say* **dez**-uht) *noun* a large area of dry often sandy land. **desert** *adjective*

desert[2] (*say* duh-**zert**) *verb* **1** abandon; leave without intending to return. **2** run away from military service. **deserter** *noun*, **desertion** *noun*

desert island *noun* an uninhabited island.

deserts (*say* duh-**zerts**) *plural noun* what a person deserves, *He got his deserts.* [from *deserve*]

deserve *verb* (**deserved**, **deserving**) have a right to something; be worthy of something. **deservedly** *adverb*

desex *verb* make an animal unable to reproduce; castrate or spay.

desiccated *adjective* dried.

design[1] *noun* **1** a drawing that shows how something is to be made. **2** the way something is made or arranged. **3** lines and shapes that form a decoration; a pattern. **4** a mental plan or scheme.
have designs on plan to get hold of.

design[2] *verb* **1** draw a design for something. **2** plan or intend something for a special purpose. **designer** *noun* [from *de*–, + Latin *signare* = mark out]

designate[1] *verb* (**designated**, **designating**) **1** mark or describe as something particular, *They designated the river as the boundary.* **2** appoint someone to a job. **designation** *noun*

designate[2] *adjective* appointed to a job but not yet doing it, *the bishop designate.* [same origin as *design*]

desirable *adjective* **1** causing people to desire it; worth having. **2** worth doing; advisable. **desirability** *noun*

desire[1] *noun* a feeling of wanting something very much. **desirous** *adjective*

desire[2] *verb* (**desired**, **desiring**) have a desire for something.

desist (*say* duh-**zist**) *verb* cease.

desk *noun* **1** a piece of furniture with a flat top and often drawers, used when writing or reading or for other work. **2** a counter at which a cashier or receptionist etc. sits, *an information desk.*

desktop *noun* **1** the working surface of a desk. **2** a computer screen display with icons representing items such as programs and files. **3** a computer suitable for use at an ordinary desk.

desolate *adjective* **1** lonely; sad. **2** uninhabited. **desolation** *noun*

despair[1] *noun* a feeling of hopelessness.

despair[2] *verb* lose all hope. [from *de*–, + Latin *sperare* = to hope]

despatch *noun & verb* dispatch.

desperado (*say* des-puh-**rah**-doh) *noun* (*plural* **desperadoes**) a reckless criminal.

desperate *adjective* **1** extremely serious; hopeless, *a desperate situation.* **2** reckless and ready to do anything. **desperately** *adverb*, **desperation** *noun* [same origin as *despair*]

despicable *adjective* deserving to be despised; contemptible.

despise *verb* (**despised**, **despising**) think someone or something is inferior or worthless. [from *de*–, + Latin *-spicere* = to look]

despite *preposition* in spite of.

despondent *adjective* sad; gloomy. **despondency** *noun*, **despondently** *adverb*

despot (*say* **des**-pot) *noun* a tyrant. **despotic** *adjective*, **despotism** *noun*

dessert (*say* duh-**zert**) *noun* fruit or a sweet food as the last course of a meal. [from French *desservir* = clear the table]

dessertspoon *noun* a medium-sized spoon, often used for eating desserts.

destination *noun* the place to which a person or thing is travelling.

destined *adjective* having as a destiny; intended.

destiny *noun* (*plural* **destinies**) fate.

destitute *adjective* left without anything; living in extreme poverty. **destitution** *noun*

destroy *verb* ruin or put an end to something. **destruction** *noun*, **destructive** *adjective* [from *de*–, + Latin *struere* = build]

destroyer *noun* a fast warship.

desultory (*say* **des**-uhl-tuh-ree) *adjective* casual and disconnected, *desultory talk.*

detach *verb* unfasten; separate. **detachable** *adjective*, **detachment** *noun*

detached *adjective* **1** separated. **2** not prejudiced; not involved in something.

detail *noun* **1** an individual item; a small or subordinate particular. **2** the minor decoration in a building or picture. **3** a small piece of information. **detailed** *adjective*
in detail as regards every feature or aspect; fully.

detain *verb* **1** keep someone waiting. **2** keep someone at a place. [from *de*–, + Latin *tenere* = hold]

detainee *noun* a person who is officially detained or kept in custody.

detect *verb* discover. **detection** *noun*, **detector** *noun* [from *de*–, + Latin *tectum* = covered]

detective *noun* a person who investigates crime.

detention *noun* **1** detaining; being detained. **2** being made to stay late in school as a punishment.

deter *verb* (**deterred**, **deterring**) discourage or prevent a person from doing something. **determent** *noun* [from *de*–, + Latin *terrere* = to frighten]

detergent *noun* a substance used for cleaning or washing things.

deteriorate (*say* duh-**teer**-ree-uh-rayt) *verb* (**deteriorated**, **deteriorating**) become worse. **deterioration** *noun* [from Latin *deterior* = worse]

determination *noun* **1** strong intention; having decided firmly. **2** determining or deciding something.

determine *verb* (**determined**, **determining**) **1** decide, *determine what is to be done.* **2** find out; calculate, *determine the height of the mountain.* [from *de*–, + Latin *terminare* = set a limit]

determined *adjective* full of determination; with your mind firmly made up.

determiner *noun* a word (such as *a, the, many*) that modifies a noun..

deterrent *noun* something that may deter people; a nuclear weapon that deters countries from making war on the one that has it. **deterrence** *noun*

detest *verb* dislike very much; loathe. **detestable** *adjective*, **detestation** *noun*

detonate (*say* **det**-uh-nayt) *verb* (**detonated**, **detonating**) explode; cause something to explode. **detonation** *noun*, **detonator** *noun* [from *de*- = thoroughly, + Latin *tonare* = to thunder]

detour (*say* **dee**-toor) *noun* a roundabout route instead of the normal one. [from French *détourner* = turn away]

detract *verb* lessen the amount or value, *It will not detract from our pleasure.* **detraction** *noun* [from *de*–, + Latin *tractum* = pulled]

detriment (*say* **det**-ruh-muhnt) *noun* harm; damage, *She worked long hours, to the detriment of her health.*

detrimental (*say* det-ruh-**men**-tuhl) *adjective* harmful. **detrimentally** *adverb*

de trop (*say* duh **troh**) *adjective* not wanted; unwelcome. [French, = too much]

deuce *noun* a score in tennis where both sides have 40 points and must gain two consecutive points to win.

devalue *verb* (**devalued**, **devaluing**) reduce a thing's value. **devaluation** *noun*

devastate *verb* (**devastated**, **devastating**) ruin or cause great destruction to something. **devastation** *noun*

devastated *adjective* overwhelmed with shock or grief.

develop *verb* (**developed**, **developing**) **1** make or become bigger or better. **2** come gradually into existence, *Storms developed.* **3** begin to have or use, *They developed bad habits.* **4** convert land to a new purpose by constructing buildings or by making other use of its resources. **5** treat photographic film with chemicals so that the picture becomes visible. **developer** *noun*

development *noun* **1** the process of developing or being developed. **2** a stage of growth or advancement. **3** a new and advanced product or idea. **4** an area of land with new buildings on it.

deviant (*say* **dee**-vee-uhnt) *adjective* deviating from what is accepted as normal. **deviance** *noun*, **deviant** *noun*

deviate (*say* **dee**-vee-ayt) *verb* (**deviated**, **deviating**) turn aside from a course or from what is usual or true. [from *de*–, + Latin *via* = way]

deviation *noun* **1** deviating, digressing; an instance of this. **2** (in statistics) the amount by which a single measurement differs from the mean.

device *noun* **1** something made for a particular purpose, *a device for opening tins.* **2** a design used as a decoration or emblem. **leave them to their own devices** leave them to do as they wish.

devil *noun* **1** an evil spirit. **2** a wicked, cruel, or annoying person. **devilish** *adjective*, **devilry** *noun*

devilment *noun* mischief.

devious (*say* **dee**-vee-uhs) *adjective* **1** roundabout; not direct, *a devious route.* **2** not straightforward; underhand. **deviously** *adverb*, **deviousness** *noun*

devise *verb* (**devised**, **devising**) invent; plan.

devoid *adjective* lacking or without something, *His work is devoid of merit.*

devolution *noun* **1** the delegation or transference of work or power from a central administration to a local or regional one. **2** the descent by natural or due succession from one to another of property or qualities.

devolve *verb* (**devolved**, **devolving**) pass or be passed to a deputy or successor.

devon *noun* (*Australian*) a large bland sausage, eaten cold.

devote *verb* (**devoted**, **devoting**) give completely, *He devoted his time to sport.*

devoted *adjective* very loving or loyal.

devotee (*say* dev-uh-**tee**) *noun* a person who is devoted to something; an enthusiast.

devotion *noun* great love or loyalty; being devoted.

devotions *plural noun* prayers.

devour *verb* eat or swallow something hungrily or greedily. [from *de-*, = completely, + Latin *vorare* = to swallow]

devout *adjective* earnestly religious or sincere. **devoutly** *adverb*, **devoutness** *noun*

dew *noun* tiny drops of water that form during the night on surfaces of things in the open air. **dewdrop** *noun*, **dewy** *adjective*

Dewey system *noun* a decimal system for classifying books in libraries. [named after Melville Dewey, US librarian]

dexterity (*say* dek-**ste**-ruh-tee) *noun* skill in handling things. **dexterous** *adjective* [from Latin *dexter* = on the right-hand side]

dhal alternative spelling of **dal**.

di-[1] *prefix* two; double (as in *dioxide*). [from Greek *dis* = twice]

di-[2] *prefix* see **dis-**.

dia- *prefix* through (as in *diarrhoea*); across (as in *diagonal*). [from Greek *dia* = through]

diabetes (*say* duy-uh-**bee**-teez) *noun* a disease in which there is too much sugar in a person's blood. **diabetic** (*say* duy-uh-**bet**-ik) *adjective & noun*

diabolical *adjective* **1** like a devil; very wicked. **2** very clever or annoying.

diadem (*say* **duy**-uh-dem) *noun* a crown or headband worn by a royal person.

diagnose *verb* (**diagnosed**, **diagnosing**) find out what disease a person has or what is wrong. **diagnosis** *noun*, **diagnostic** *adjective*

diagonal (*say* duy-**ag**-uh-nuhl) *noun* a straight line joining opposite corners. **diagonal** *adjective*, **diagonally** *adverb* [from *dia–*, + Greek *gonia* = angle]

diagram *noun* a kind of drawing or picture that shows the parts of something or how it works. **diagrammatic** *adjective* [from *dia-* + *-gram*]

dial[1] *noun* a circular object with numbers or letters round it.

dial[2] *verb* (**dialled**, **dialling**) telephone a number by turning a telephone dial or pressing numbered buttons.

dialect *noun* a particular form of a language that is peculiar to a specific region or social group.

dialogue *noun* a conversation.

dial-up *adjective* (of a computer system or service) used remotely via a telephone line.

dialysis (*say* duy-**al**-uh-suhs) *noun* a way of removing harmful substances from the blood by letting it flow through a machine. [from *dia–*, + Greek *lysis* = loosening]

diameter (*say* duy-**am**-uh-tuh) *noun* **1** a line drawn straight across a circle or sphere and passing through its centre. **2** the length of this line. [from Greek, = measuring across]

diametrically *adverb* completely, *diametrically opposed.*

diamond *noun* **1** a very hard precious stone that looks like clear glass. **2** a shape with four equal sides and four angles that are not right angles. **3** a playing card with red diamond shapes on it. [from Greek *adamas* = adamant (= a very hard stone)]

diaper *noun* (*American*) a baby's nappy.

diaphanous (*say* duy-**af**-uh-nuhs) *adjective* (of fabric) almost transparent.

diaphragm (*say* **duy**-uh-fram) *noun* **1** the muscular partition inside the body that separates the chest from the abdomen and is used in breathing. **2** a hole that can be altered in size to control the amount of light that passes through a camera lens.

diarrhoea (*say* duy-uh-**ree**-uh) *noun* too frequent and too watery emptying of the bowels. [from *dia–*, + Greek *rhoia* = a flow]

diary *noun* (*plural* **diaries**) a book in which someone writes down what happens each day. **diarist** *noun* [from Latin *dies* = day]

diatribe *noun* a strong verbal attack.

dice[1] *plural noun* **1** small cubes with faces bearing one to six spots, used in games or gambling. **2** (treated as singular) one of those cubes (see *die*[2]).

> **Usage** See the note at *die*[2].

dice[2] *verb* (**diced**, **dicing**) **1** take great risks, *dice with death.* **2** cut into small cubes.

dicey *adjective* (**dicier**, **diciest**) (*informal*) risky.

dictate *verb* (**dictated**, **dictating**) **1** speak or read something aloud for someone else to write down. **2** give orders in an officious way. **dictation** *noun* [from Latin *dictare* = keep saying]

dictates (*say* **dik**-tayts) *plural noun* orders, commands.

dictator *noun* a ruler who has unlimited power. **dictatorial** (*say* dik-tuh-**taw**-ree-uhl) *adjective*, **dictatorship** *noun*

diction *noun* a person's way of speaking words, *clear diction.*

dictionary *noun* (*plural* **dictionaries**) a book that contains words in alphabetical order so that you can find out how to spell them and what they mean. [from Latin *dictio* = word]

did *past tense* of **do**[1].

didactic (*say* duy-**dak**-tik) *adjective* having the manner of someone who is lecturing people. **didactically** *adverb* [from Greek *didaktikos* = teaching]

diddle *verb* (**diddled**, **diddling**) (*informal*) cheat; swindle.

didgeridoo (*say* dij-uh-ree-**doo**) *noun* an Aboriginal musical instrument in the form of a long wooden tube.

didn't did not, *She didn't feel well after eating all that cake.*

die[1] *verb* (**died, dying**) **1** stop living or existing. **2** stop burning or functioning, *The engine died.*
die down become less loud or strong.
die out cease to exist.

die[2] *noun* = **dice**[1] 2.

> **Usage** *Dice*, rather than *die* , is now the standard singular as well as plural form in the games sense (*one dice, two dice*).

die[3] *noun* a device that stamps a design on coins and medals, or that cuts or moulds metal.

diehard *noun* a person who obstinately refuses to give up old ideas or policies.

diesel (*say* **dee**-zuhl) *noun* **1** an engine that works by burning oil in compressed air. **2** fuel for this kind of engine. [named after a German engineer, R. Diesel]

diet[1] *noun* **1** special meals that someone eats in order to be healthy or to become less fat. **2** the sort of foods usually eaten by a person or animal. **dietary** *adjective*

diet[2] *verb* (**dieted, dieting**) keep to a diet. [from Greek *diaita* = way of life]

diet[3] *noun* the parliament of certain countries (e.g. Japan). [from Latin *dieta* = day's business]

dietitian (*say* duy-uh-**tish**-uhn) *noun* an expert in diet and nutrition.

dif- *prefix* see **dis-**.

differ *verb* **1** be different. **2** disagree. [from *dif-* = apart, + Latin *ferre* = carry]

difference *noun* **1** being different; the way in which things differ. **2** the remainder left after one number is subtracted from another, *The difference between 8 and 3 is 5.* **3** a disagreement.

different *adjective* **1** unlike; not the same. **2** separate; distinct. **differently** *adverb*

> **Usage** *Different from* is the preferred phrase; *different to* is acceptable in informal use; *different than* is common in American use.

differential *noun* **1** a difference in wages between one group of workers and another. **2** a differential gear.

differential gear *noun* a system of gears that makes a vehicle's driving wheels revolve at different speeds when going around corners.

differentiate *verb* (**differentiated, differentiating**) **1** make different, *These things differentiate one breed from another.* **2** distinguish; recognise differences, *We do not differentiate between them.*
differentiation *noun*

difficult *adjective* **1** needing much effort or skill. **2** not easy to deal with; troublesome.

difficulty *noun* (*plural* **difficulties**) **1** being difficult. **2** a difficult thing; a problem or hindrance.

diffident (*say* **dif**-uh-duhnt) *adjective* shy and not self-confident; hesitating to put yourself or your ideas forward. **diffidence** *noun*, **diffidently** *adverb* [from *dif-* = not, + Latin *fidere* = to trust]

diffract *verb* cause to undergo diffraction. [from *dif-* = apart, + Latin *fractum* = broken]

diffraction *noun* the process by which a beam of light or other system of waves is spread out as a result of passing through a narrow aperture or across an edge.

diffuse[1] *verb* (**diffused, diffusing**) **1** spread something widely or thinly, *diffused lighting.* **2** mix slowly, *diffusing gases.* **diffusion** *noun*

diffuse[2] *adjective* **1** diffused; spread widely; not concentrated. **2** using many words; not concise. **diffusely** *adverb*, **diffuseness** *noun* [from *dif-* = apart, + Latin *fusum* = poured]

dig[1] *verb* (**dug, digging**) **1** break up soil and move it; make a hole or tunnel by moving soil. **2** poke; push, *Dig a knife into it.* **3** seek or discover by investigating, *We dug up some facts.*

dig[2] *noun* **1** a piece of digging. **2** an archaeological excavation. **3** a poke. **4** a cutting remark.

digest[1] (*say* duy-**jest**) *verb* **1** soften and change food in the stomach and intestines so that the body can absorb it. **2** take information into your mind and think it over. **digestible** *adjective*, **digestion** *noun*

digest[2] (*say* **duy**-jest) *noun* a summary of news or other information.

digestive *adjective* of digestion; digesting, *the digestive system.*

digger *noun* **1** someone who digs. **2** a prospector for gold. **3** (*Australian informal*) an Australian soldier.

digit (*say* **dij**-uht) *noun* **1** any of the numerals from 0 to 9. **2** a finger or toe. [from Latin *digitus* = finger or toe]

digital *adjective* **1** relating to or using signals or information represented by discrete values of a physical quantity such as voltage or magnetic polarisation. (Compare **analog** 1.) **2** involving or relating to the use of computer technology. **3** of or using digits. **digitally** *adverb*

digital camera *noun* a camera that produces digital images that can be stored in a computer and displayed on a screen.

dignified *adjective* having dignity.

dignitary *noun* (*plural* **dignitaries**) an important official.

dignity *noun* **1** a calm and serious manner. **2** a high rank. [from Latin *dignus* = worthy]

digraph *noun* a group of two letters representing one sound, as in *ph* and *ey*. **digraphic** *adjective*

digress *verb* stray from the main subject. **digression** *noun* [from *di-*[2] = away, + Latin *gressum* = gone]

dike alternative spelling of **dyke**.

dilapidated *adjective* falling to pieces. **dilapidation** *noun*

dilate *verb* (**dilated**, **dilating**) make or become wider or larger. **dilation** *noun* [from *di-*[2] = apart, + Latin *latus* = wide]

dilatory (*say* **dil**-uh-tuh-ree) *adjective* slow in doing something; not prompt.

dilemma (*say* duh-**lem**-uh) *noun* **1** a situation where someone has to choose between two possible actions, each of which will bring difficulties. **2** a difficult situation or problem. [from Greek, = double proposal]

> **Usage** The use of *dilemma* in sense 2 is considered incorrect by some people.

diligent (*say* **dil**-uh-juhnt) *adjective* working hard. **diligence** *noun*, **diligently** *adverb* [from Latin *diligens* = conscientious]

dill[1] *noun* a yellow-flowered herb with aromatic seeds.

dill[2] *noun* (*Australian informal*) a fool or simpleton. [from *dilly* = foolish]

dillybag *noun* (also **dilly bag**) (*Australian*) a small bag, originally of plaited grass or fibre. [from Yagara *dili* = coarse grass; a bag woven from this]

dilute[1] *verb* (**diluted**, **diluting**) make a liquid weaker by adding water or other liquid. **dilution** *noun*

dilute[2] *adjective* diluted, *a dilute acid.*

dim[1] *adjective* (**dimmer**, **dimmest**) **1** not bright or clear; only faintly lit. **2** (*informal*) stupid. **dimly** *adverb*, **dimness** *noun*

dim[2] *verb* (**dimmed**, **dimming**) make or become dim. **dimmer** *noun*

dimension *noun* **1** a measurement such as length, width, area, or volume. **2** size; extent. **dimensional** *adjective*

diminish *verb* make or become smaller. **diminution** *noun*

diminutive (*say* duh-**min**-yuh-tiv) *adjective* very small.

dimple *noun* a small hollow or dent, especially in the skin. **dimpled** *adjective*

dim sim *noun* (*Australian*) a Chinese roll of seasoned meat or vegetables wrapped in thin dough and steamed or fried. [from Chinese *tim-sam* = cake, snack]

dim sum *noun* a meal or course of savoury Chinese-style snacks. [from Chinese *dim-sam* = dot of the heart]

din *noun* a loud annoying noise.

dine *verb* (**dined**, **dining**) have dinner.

diner *noun* **1** a person who dines. **2** a railway dining car. **3** (*American*) a small restaurant.

ding[1] *verb* make a ringing sound. **ding** *noun*

ding[2] *noun* (*informal*) **1** a minor collision of motor vehicles. **2** a dent, *a ding in his surfboard.*

ding[3] *verb* (*informal*) dent or damage; smash.

dingbat *noun* (*informal*) a stupid or eccentric person.

ding-dong *noun* the sound of a bell or alternate strokes of two bells.

dinghy (*say* **ding**-gee) *noun* (*plural* **dinghies**) a kind of small boat. [from Hindi, = Indian river boat]

dingo *noun* (*plural* **dingoes**) an Australian wild dog. [from Sydney language *dingu*]

dingy (*say* **din**-jee) *adjective* (**dingier**, **dingiest**) dirty-looking. **dingily** *adverb*, **dinginess** *noun*

dink *verb* (*Australian informal*) give someone a ride on the bar of a bicycle.

dinkum *adjective* (*Australian informal*) genuine, true, *a dinkum Aussie.* [from British dialect = work; a due share of work]

dinner *noun* the main meal of the day, eaten either at midday, or especially in the evening, *On Friday night we eat pizza for dinner.*

dinosaur (*say* **duy**-nuh-saw) *noun* a prehistoric lizard-like animal, often of enormous size. [from Greek *deinos* = terrible, + *sauros* = lizard]

dint *noun* a dent.
by dint of by means of.

diocese (*say* **duy**-uh-suhs) *noun* a district under the care of a bishop. **diocesan** (*say* duy-**os**-uh-suhn) *adjective*

diode (*say* **duy**-ohd) *noun* a rectifier made of semiconducting materials and having two terminals. [from *di-*[1] + *electrode*]

dioxide *noun* an oxide with two atoms of oxygen to one of another element, *carbon dioxide.* [from *di-*[1] + *oxide*]

dip[1] *verb* (**dipped**, **dipping**) **1** put down into a liquid. **2** go down. **3** lower.

dip[2] *noun* **1** dipping. **2** a downward slope or hollow. **3** a quick swim. **4** a substance into which things are dipped.

diphtheria (*say* dif-**theer**-ree-uh) *noun* a serious disease that causes inflammation in the throat. [from Greek, = leather (because a tough skin forms)]

diphthong (*say* **dif**-thong) *noun* a compound vowel sound made up of two sounds, e.g. *oi* in *point* (made up of 'aw' + 'ee') or *ou* in *loud* ('ah' + 'oo'). [from *di*-[1], + Greek *phthongos* = sound]

diploma *noun* a certificate awarded by an educational establishment to show that a person has successfully completed a course of study. [from Greek, = folded paper]

diplomacy *noun* keeping friendly with other nations or other people.

diplomat *noun* **1** an official representing a country abroad. **2** a tactful person.

diplomatic *adjective* **1** of diplomats or diplomacy. **2** tactful. **diplomatically** *adverb*

dire *adjective* dreadful; serious, *dire need.*

direct[1] *adjective* **1** as straight as possible. **2** going straight to the point; frank. **3** exact, *the direct opposite.* **directly** *adverb & conjunction*, **directness** *noun*

direct[2] *verb* **1** tell someone the way. **2** guide or aim in a certain direction. **3** control; manage. **4** order, *He directed his troops to advance.* [from Latin *directum* = kept straight]

direct current *noun* electric current flowing only in one direction.

direct debit *noun* an arrangement for the regular debiting of a bank account at the request of the payee.

direction *noun* **1** directing. **2** the line along which something moves or faces. **directional** *adjective*

directions *plural noun* information on how to use or do something.

directive *noun* a command.

direct object *noun* the word that receives the action of the verb, e.g. *him* in *the dog bit him.*

director *noun* **1** a person who supervises or manages things, especially a member of the board managing a business company on behalf of shareholders. **2** a person who directs a film or play.

directorate *noun* **1** a board of directors. **2** the office of a director.

directory *noun* (*plural* **directories**) **1** a book or website containing a list of people or organisations with details such as telephone numbers and addresses. **2** a computer file listing other files or programs.

dirge *noun* a slow mournful song.

dirt *noun* **1** earth, soil. **2** anything that is not clean.

dirty[1] *adjective* (**dirtier**, **dirtiest**) **1** not clean; soiled. **2** unfair; dishonourable, *a dirty trick.* **3** indecent; obscene. **dirtily** *adverb*, **dirtiness** *noun*

dirty[2] *verb* (**dirtied**, **dirtying**) make or become dirty.

dirty bomb *noun* a bomb dispersed by conventional explosives but containing radioactive material.

dis- *prefix* (changing to **dif-** before words beginning with *f*, and to **di-** before some consonants) **1** not; the reverse of (as in *dishonest*). **2** apart; separated (as in *disarm, disperse*). [from Latin, = not; away]

disability *noun* **1** a physical or mental condition that limits a person's movements, senses, or activities. **2** a disadvantage or handicap.

disabled *adjective* made unable to do something because of illness or injury. **disablement** *noun*

disadvantage *noun* something that hinders or is unhelpful. **disadvantaged** *adjective*, **disadvantageous** *adjective*

disagree *verb* (**disagreed, disagreeing**) **1** have or express a different opinion from someone. **2** have a bad effect, *Rich food disagrees with me.* **disagreement** *noun*

disagreeable *adjective* **1** unpleasant. **2** bad-tempered.

disappear *verb* stop being visible; vanish. **disappearance** *noun*

disappoint *verb* fail to do what someone hopes for. **disappointment** *noun*

disapprobation *noun* disapproval.

disapprove *verb* (**disapproved, disapproving**) have or show an unfavourable opinion; not approve. **disapproval** *noun*

disarm *verb* **1** reduce the size of armed forces. **2** take away someone's weapons. **3** overcome a person's anger or doubt, *Her friendliness disarmed their suspicions.* **disarmament** *noun*

disarray *noun* disorder, confusion.

disaster *noun* **1** a very bad accident or misfortune. **2** a complete failure. **disastrous** *adjective*, **disastrously** *adverb* [literally 'an unlucky star', from *dis*–, + Latin *astrum* = star]

disband *verb* break up a group.

disbelieve *verb* (**disbelieved, disbelieving**) be unable or unwilling to believe something. **disbelief** *noun*

disburse *verb* (**disbursed, disbursing**) pay out money. **disbursement** *noun*

disc *noun* **1** any round flat object. **2** a compact disc. **3** (in computing) a disk. **4** a layer of cartilage between the bones that form the backbone. [from Latin *discus* = disc]

discard *verb* throw away; put something aside as being useless or unwanted.

discern (*say* duh-**sern**) *verb* perceive; see or recognise clearly. **discernible** *adjective*, **discernment** *noun*

discerning *adjective* perceptive; showing good judgement.

discharge[1] *verb* (**discharged, discharging**) **1** release a person. **2** dismiss from employment. **3** send something out, *discharge smoke.* **4** fire a gun or missile. **5** pay or do what was agreed, *discharge the debt.*

discharge[2] *noun* **1** discharging. **2** something that is discharged.

disciple *noun* **1** a follower or pupil of a teacher, leader, or philosopher. **2** any of the original followers of Jesus Christ. [from Latin *discipulus* = learner]

disciplinarian *noun* a person who believes in strict discipline.

discipline[1] *noun* orderly and obedient behaviour. **disciplinary** (*say* **dis**-uh-pluh-nuh-ree) *adjective*

discipline[2] *verb* (**disciplined, disciplining**) **1** train to be orderly and obedient. **2** punish. [from Latin *disciplina* = training]

disc jockey *noun* a person who introduces and plays recorded popular music.

disclaim *verb* disown; say that you are not responsible for something. **disclaimer** *noun*

disclose *verb* (**disclosed, disclosing**) reveal. **disclosure** *noun*

disco *noun* (*plural* **discos**) **1** a discothèque. **2** a type of dance music with a heavy bass rhythm.

discolour *verb* spoil a thing's colour; stain. **discoloration** *noun*

discomfit *verb* (**discomfited, discomfiting**) disconcert; dismay. **discomfiture** *noun*

discomfort *noun* being uncomfortable.

disconcert (*say* dis-kuhn-**sert**) *verb* make a person feel uneasy.

disconnect *verb* break a connection; detach. **disconnection** *noun*

disconnected *adjective* not having a connection between its parts.

disconsolate (*say* dis-**kon**-suh-luht) *adjective* unhappy at the loss of something; disappointed.

discontent *noun* lack of contentment; dissatisfaction. **discontented** *adjective*, **discontentment** *noun*

discontinue *verb* (**discontinued, discontinuing**) put an end to something.

discord *noun* **1** disagreement; quarrelling. **2** musical notes sounded together and producing a harsh or unpleasant sound. **discordant** *adjective* [from *dis-* = not, + Latin *cordis* = of the heart]

discothèque (*say* **dis**-kuh-tek) *noun* a place or party where people dance to recorded music. [French, = record library]

discount[1] *noun* an amount by which a price is reduced.

discount[2] *verb* ignore; disregard, *We cannot discount the possibility.*

discourage *verb* (**discouraged, discouraging**) **1** take away someone's enthusiasm or confidence. **2** try to persuade someone not to do something; dissuade; deter. **discouragement** *noun*

discourse[1] *noun* **1** a formal speech or piece of writing about something. **2** a conversation.

discourse[2] *verb* (**discoursed, discoursing**) speak or write at length about something.

discourteous *adjective* not courteous; rude. **discourteously** *adverb*, **discourtesy** *noun*

discover *verb* **1** find. **2** be the first person to find something. **discoverer** *noun*, **discovery** *noun* [from *dis-* = apart, + *cover*]

discredit[1] *verb* (**discredited, discrediting**) **1** destroy people's confidence in a person or thing; disgrace. **2** distrust.

discredit[2] *noun* **1** disgrace. **2** distrust. **discreditable** *adjective*

discreet *adjective* **1** not giving away secrets. **2** not showy. **discreetly** *adverb*

> **Usage** Do not confuse with *discrete.*

discrepancy (*say* duh-**skrep**-uhn-see) *noun* (*plural* **discrepancies**) difference; lack of agreement, *There are several discrepancies in the two accounts.* **discrepant** *adjective* [from Latin, = discord]

discrete *adjective* separate; distinct from each other.

> **Usage** Do not confuse with *discreet.*

discretion (*say* duh-**skresh**-uhn) *noun* **1** being discreet; keeping secrets. **2** power to take action according to your own judgement, *The treasurer has full discretion.* **discretionary** *adjective*

discriminate *verb* (**discriminated, discriminating**) **1** notice the differences between things; distinguish; prefer one thing to another. **2** treat people differently or unfairly, e.g. because of their race, sex, or religion. **discriminatory** *adjective* [from Latin *discrimen* = separator]

> **Usage** Note that these words have both a 'good' sense and a 'bad' sense. A *discriminating* person can mean someone who judges carefully and well, but it can also mean someone who judges unfairly.

discrimination *noun* **1** the unfavourable or prejudicial treatment of different categories of people, especially on the grounds of race, age, or sex, *discrimination against Chinese nationals.* **2** recognition and understanding of the difference between one thing and another, *discrimination between right and wrong.* **3** the ability to judge what is of high quality; good judgement or taste.

discus *noun* (*plural* **discuses**) a thick heavy disc thrown in athletic contests.

discuss *verb* talk with other people about a subject. **discussion** *noun*

disdain[1] *noun* scorn; contempt. **disdainful** *adjective*, **disdainfully** *adverb*

disdain[2] *verb* **1** regard or treat with disdain. **2** not do something because of disdain, *She disdained to reply.* [from *dis-* = not, + Latin *dignus* = worthy]

disease *noun* an unhealthy condition; an illness. **diseased** *adjective* [from *dis-* = not, + *ease*]

disembark *verb* put or go ashore. **disembarkation** *noun*

disengage *verb* (**disengaged, disengaging**) disconnect; detach.

disentangle *verb* (**disentangled, disentangling**) free from tangles or confusion.

disfavour *noun* disapproval; dislike.

disfigure *verb* (**disfigured, disfiguring**) spoil a person's or thing's appearance. **disfigurement** *noun*

disgrace[1] *noun* **1** shame; loss of approval or respect. **2** something that causes shame. **disgraceful** *adjective*, **disgracefully** *adverb*

disgrace[2] *verb* (**disgraced, disgracing**) bring disgrace upon someone.

disgruntled *adjective* discontented; resentful.

disguise[1] *verb* (**disguised, disguising**) make a person or thing look different so as to deceive people.

disguise[2] *noun* something used for disguising.

disgust[1] *noun* a feeling that something is very unpleasant or disgraceful.

disgust[2] *verb* cause disgust. **disgusted** *adjective*, **disgusting** *adjective* [from *dis-* = not, + Latin *gustare* = to taste]

dish[1] *noun* (*plural* **dishes**) **1** a shallow flat-bottomed container for food. **2** food served on a dish.

dish[2] *verb* **dish up** serve food.

dishearten *verb* cause a person to lose hope or confidence.

dishevelled (*say* di-**shev**-uhld) *adjective* ruffled and untidy. **dishevelment** *noun* [from *dis-* = apart, + Old French *chevel* = hair]

dishonest *adjective* not honest. **dishonestly** *adverb*, **dishonesty** *noun*

dishonour *noun & verb* disgrace. **dishonourable** *adjective*

dishwasher *noun* a machine for washing dishes etc. automatically.

disillusion *verb* get rid of someone's pleasant but wrong beliefs. **disillusionment** *noun*

disincentive *noun* something that discourages an action or effort.

disinclined *adjective* unwilling to do something. **disinclination** *noun*

disinfect *verb* destroy the germs in something. **disinfection** *noun*

disinfectant *noun* a substance used for disinfecting things.

disinherit *verb* deprive a person of the right to inherit something.

disintegrate *verb* (**disintegrated, disintegrating**) break up into small parts or pieces. **disintegration** *noun*

disinterested *adjective* impartial; not biased; not influenced by hope of gaining something yourself, *She gave us some disinterested advice.*

> **Usage** Do not use this word as if it meant 'not interested' or 'bored' (the word for this is *uninterested*).

disjointed *adjective* disconnected.

disk *noun* (in computing) a flat circular device coated with magnetic material on which data can be stored. (See also *floppy disk* and *hard disk*.)

diskette *noun* a floppy disk.

dislike[1] *noun* a feeling of not liking somebody or something.

dislike[2] *verb* (**disliked, disliking**) not to like somebody or something.

dislocate *verb* (**dislocated, dislocating**) **1** dislodge a bone from its proper position in one of the joints. **2** disrupt, *The bus strike dislocated traffic.* **dislocation** *noun*

dislodge *verb* (**dislodged, dislodging**) move or force something from its place.

disloyal *adjective* not loyal. **disloyally** *adverb*, **disloyalty** *noun*

dismal *adjective* gloomy. **dismally** *adverb* [from Latin *dies mali* = unlucky days]

dismantle *verb* (**dismantled, dismantling**) take something to pieces.

dismay[1] *noun* a feeling of surprise and discouragement.

dismay[2] *verb* fill with dismay.

dismiss *verb* **1** send someone away; disband. **2** tell a person that you will no longer employ them. **3** put out of one's thoughts; mention or discuss only briefly. **4** reject without further hearing. **5** (in cricket) get a batter or side out. **dismissal** *noun*, **dismissive** *adjective* [from *dis–*, + Latin *missum* = sent]

dismount *verb* get off a horse or bicycle.

disobedient *adjective* not obedient. **disobedience** *noun*, **disobediently** *adverb*

disobey *verb* (**disobeyed**, **disobeying**) not to obey; disregard orders.

disorder *noun* **1** untidiness. **2** a disturbance. **3** an illness. **disorderly** *adjective*

disorganise *verb* (**disorganised**, **disorganising**) throw into confusion. **disorganisation** *noun*

disown *verb* refuse to acknowledge that a person or thing has any connection with you.

disparage (*say* dis-**pa**-rij) *verb* (**disparaged**, **disparaging**) belittle; declare that something is small or unimportant. **disparagement** *noun*

disparate *adjective* different in kind.

disparity *noun* (*plural* **disparities**) difference; inequality.

dispassionate *adjective* calm and impartial. **dispassionately** *adverb*

dispatch[1] *verb* **1** send off to a destination. **2** kill.

dispatch[2] *noun* **1** dispatching. **2** a report or message sent. **3** promptness; speed.

dispel *verb* (**dispelled**, **dispelling**) drive away; scatter, *Wind dispels fog.* [from *dis-* = apart, + Latin *pellere* = to drive]

dispensary *noun* (*plural* **dispensaries**) a place where medicines are dispensed.

dispense *verb* (**dispensed**, **dispensing**) **1** distribute; deal out. **2** prepare medicine according to prescriptions. **dispensation** *noun*, **dispenser** *noun*
dispense with do without something. [from *dis-* = separately, + Latin *pensum* = weighed]

disperse *verb* (**dispersed**, **dispersing**) scatter. **dispersal** *noun*, **dispersion** *noun* [from Latin *dispersum* = scattered]

displace *verb* (**displaced**, **displacing**) **1** shift from its place. **2** take a person's or thing's place. **displacement** *noun*

display[1] *verb* show; arrange something so that it can be clearly seen.

display[2] *noun* **1** the displaying of something; an exhibition. **2** something displayed. **3** the presentation of signals or data on a visual display unit; a VDU. [from *dis-* = separately, + Latin *plicare* = to fold]

displease *verb* (**displeased**, **displeasing**) annoy or not please someone. **displeasure** *noun*

disposable *adjective* **1** made to be thrown away after it has been used. **2** available for use, *disposable income.*

disposal *noun* getting rid of something.
at your disposal for you to use; ready for you.

dispose *verb* (**disposed**, **disposing**) **1** place in position; arrange, *Dispose your troops in two lines.* **2** make a person ready or willing to do something, *I feel disposed to help him.*
be well disposed be friendly.
dispose of get rid of. [from *dis-* = away, + French *poser* = to place]

disposition *noun* **1** a person's nature or qualities. **2** arrangement.

disproportionate *adjective* out of proportion; too large or too small.

disprove *verb* (**disproved**, **disproving**) show that something is not true.

dispute[1] *verb* (**disputed**, **disputing**) **1** argue; debate. **2** quarrel. **3** raise an objection to, *We dispute their claim.* **disputation** *noun*

dispute[2] *noun* **1** an argument; a debate. **2** a quarrel.
in dispute being argued about. [from *dis-* = apart, + Latin *putare* = consider]

disqualify *verb* (**disqualified**, **disqualifying**) **1** declare a person ineligible for an office, activity or competition because of an offence or infringement. **2** make unsuitable or ineligible, *Weak eyesight disqualifies him from military service.* **disqualification** *noun*

disquiet *noun* anxiety; worry. **disquieting** *adjective*

disregard[1] *verb* ignore.

disregard[2] *noun* the act of ignoring something.

disrepair *noun* bad condition caused by not doing repairs.

disreputable *adjective* not respectable.

disrepute *noun* discredit; bad reputation.

disrespect *noun* lack of respect; rudeness. **disrespectful** *adjective*, **disrespectfully** *adverb*

disrupt *verb* put into disorder; interrupt a continuous flow, *Roadworks disrupted traffic.* **disruption** *noun*, **disruptive** *adjective* [from *dis-* = apart, + Latin *ruptum* = broken]

dissatisfied *adjective* not satisfied. **dissatisfaction** *noun*

dissect (*say* duy-**sekt**) *verb* cut something up so as to examine it. **dissection** *noun* [from *dis-* = apart, + Latin *sectum* = cut]

disseminate *verb* (**disseminated**, **disseminating**) spread something widely, *the news disseminated quickly.* **dissemination** *noun* [from *dis-* = apart, + Latin *seminare* = sow (scatter seeds)]

dissent[1] *noun* disagreement.

dissent[2] *verb* disagree. **dissenter** *noun* [from *dis-* = apart, + Latin *sentire* = feel]

dissertation *noun* a discourse; a long essay or thesis.

disservice *noun* a harmful action done by someone who was intending to help.

dissident *noun* a person who disagrees; someone who opposes the authorities. **dissidence** *noun*, **dissident** *adjective*

dissipate *verb* (**dissipated, dissipating**) **1** dispel; disperse. **2** squander; waste; fritter away. **dissipation** *noun* [from Latin *dissipare* = scatter]

dissociate *verb* (**dissociated, dissociating**) separate something in your thoughts. **dissociation** *noun*

dissolute *adjective* living a frivolous and selfish life.

dissolution *noun* dissolving.

dissolve *verb* (**dissolved, dissolving**) **1** mix something with a liquid so that it becomes part of the liquid. **2** make or become liquid; melt. **3** put an end to a marriage or partnership. **4** dismiss an assembly, *Parliament was dissolved and a general election was held.* [from *dis-* = separate, + Latin *solvere* = loosen]

dissonant *adjective* harsh-toned; unharmonious; discordant. **dissonance** *noun*

dissuade *verb* (**dissuaded, dissuading**) persuade somebody not to do something. **dissuasion** *noun* [from *dis-* = apart, + Latin *suadere* = advise]

distance *noun* the amount of space between two places.
in the distance far away.

distant *adjective* **1** far away. **2** not friendly; not sociable. **distantly** *adverb* [from *dis-* = apart, + Latin *stans* = standing]

distaste *noun* dislike.

distasteful *adjective* unpleasant.

distemper *noun* **1** a disease of dogs and certain other animals. **2** a kind of paint.

distend *verb* make or become swollen because of pressure from inside. **distension** *noun* [from *dis-* = apart, + Latin *tendere* = stretch]

distil *verb* (**distilled, distilling**) purify a liquid by boiling it and condensing the vapour. **distillation** *noun* [from *dis-* = apart, + Latin *stillare* = drip down]

distiller *noun* a person who makes alcoholic liquors by distillation. **distillery** *noun*

distinct *adjective* **1** easily heard or seen; noticeable. **2** clearly separate or different. **distinctly** *adverb*, **distinctness** *noun*

> **Usage** See the note at *distinctive*.

distinction *noun* **1** a difference. **2** distinguishing; making a difference. **3** excellence; honour. **4** an award for excellence; a high mark in an examination.

distinctive *adjective* that distinguishes one thing from another or others, *The school has a distinctive uniform.* **distinctively** *adverb*

> **Usage** Do not confuse this word with *distinct*. A *distinct* mark is a clear mark; a *distinctive* mark is one that is not found anywhere else.

distinguish *verb* **1** make or notice differences between things. **2** see or hear something clearly. **3** bring honour to, *He distinguished himself by his bravery.* **distinguishable** *adjective* [from Latin *distinguere* = to separate]

distinguished *adjective* excellent; famous.

distort *verb* **1** pull or twist out of its normal shape. **2** misrepresent; give a false account of something, *distort the truth.* **distortion** *noun* [from *dis-* = apart, + Latin *tortum* = twisted]

distract *verb* take a person's attention away from something. [from *dis-* = apart, + Latin *tractum* = pulled]

distraction *noun* **1** something that distracts a person's attention. **2** an amusement. **3** great worry or distress.

distraught (*say* dis-**trawt**) *adjective* greatly upset by worry or distress.

distress[1] *noun* great sorrow, pain, or trouble.

distress[2] *verb* cause distress to a person.

distribute *verb* (**distributed, distributing**) **1** deal or share out. **2** spread or scatter. **3** divide into parts; arrange; classify. **distributor** *noun* [from *dis-* = separate, + Latin *tributum* = given]

distribution *noun* **1** the act or an instance of distributing. **2** the dispersal of goods among consumers, brought about by commerce. **3** the extent to which different groups, classes, or individuals share in the total production or wealth of a community. **4** (in statistics) the way in which a characteristic is spread over members of a class.

distributive *adjective* **1** of, concerned with, or produced by distribution. **2** (of a determiner or pronoun) referring to each individual of a class, not to the class collectively, e.g. *each, either.* **3** (in mathematics) (of an operation) fulfilling the condition that, when it is performed on two or more quantities already combined by another operation, the result is the same as when it is performed on each quantity individually and the products then combined.

district *noun* part of a town or country, *an agricultural district.*

distrust[1] *noun* lack of trust; suspicion. **distrustful** *adjective*

distrust[2] *verb* not to trust.

disturb *verb* **1** spoil someone's peace or rest. **2** cause someone to worry. **3** move a thing from its position. **disturbance** *noun* [from *dis-* = thoroughly, + Latin *turbare* = confuse, upset]

disuse *noun* the state of not being used.

disused *adjective* no longer used.

ditch[1] *noun* (*plural* **ditches**) a trench dug to hold water or carry it away, or to serve as a boundary.

ditch[2] *verb* (*informal*) **1** bring an aircraft down in a forced landing on the sea. **2** abandon; discard.

dither *verb* **1** tremble. **2** hesitate nervously.

ditto *noun* (used in lists) the same again.

> **Usage** The word *ditto* is often replaced by ,, under the word or sum to be repeated.

ditty *noun* (*plural* **ditties**) a short song.

ditzy *adjective* (*informal*) silly or scatterbrained. **ditz** *noun*

divan *noun* a bed or couch without a raised back or sides. [Persian, = cushioned bench]

dive *verb* (**dived**, **diving**) **1** go under water, especially head first. **2** move down quickly. **dive** *noun*

> **Usage** In Canada and parts of the United States *dove* is acceptable as the past tense of *dive*. While it is often heard in Australia, it is non-standard.

diver *noun* **1** someone who dives. **2** a person who works under water in a special suit with an air supply. **3** a bird that dives for its food.

diverge *verb* (**diverged**, **diverging**) **1** go aside or in different directions. **2** depart from a set course. **divergence** *noun*, **divergent** *adjective* [from *di-*[2] = apart, + Latin *vergere* = to slope]

divers (*say* **duy**-verz) *adjective* (*old use*) various.

diverse (*say* duy-**vers**) *adjective* varied; of several different kinds. **diversity** *noun*

diversify *verb* (**diversified**, **diversifying**) make or become varied; involve yourself in different kinds of things. **diversification** *noun*

diversion *noun* **1** diverting something from its course; an alternative route for traffic when a road is closed. **2** a recreation; an entertainment. **diversionary** *adjective*

divert *verb* **1** turn something aside from its course. **2** entertain; amuse. [from *di-*[2] = apart, + Latin *vertere* = to turn]

divest *verb* **1** strip of clothes, *He divested himself of his robes.* **2** take away; deprive, *They divested her of power.*

divide *verb* (**divided**, **dividing**) **1** separate from something or into smaller parts; split up. **2** distribute. **3** arrange in separate groups. **4** find how many times one number is contained in another, *Divide six by three* (6 ÷ 3 = 2). **divider** *noun*

dividend *noun* **1** a share of a business's profit. **2** a number that is to be divided by another. (Compare **divisor**.)

dividers *plural noun* a pair of compasses for measuring distances.

divine[1] *adjective* **1** of God; coming from God. **2** like a god. **3** (*informal*) excellent; beautiful. **divinely** *adverb*

divine[2] *verb* (**divined**, **divining**) prophesy or guess what is about to happen. **divination** *noun* [from Latin *divus* = god]

divisible *adjective* **1** capable of being divided, physically or mentally. **2** (of a number) containing another number a number of times without a remainder (*15 is divisible by 3 and 5*). **divisibility** *noun*

division *noun* **1** dividing. **2** a dividing line; a partition. **3** one of the parts into which something is divided. **4** (in parliament) separation of members into two sections for counting votes. **divisional** *adjective*

divisive (*say* duh-**vuy**-siv) *adjective* causing disagreement within a group.

divisor *noun* a number by which another is to be divided. (Compare **dividend** 2.)

divorce[1] *noun* the legal ending of a marriage.

divorce[2] *verb* (**divorced**, **divorcing**) **1** end a marriage by divorce. **2** separate; think of things separately.

divorcee *noun* a divorced person.

divulge *verb* (**divulged**, **divulging**) reveal information. **divulgence** *noun*

Diwali (*say* duh-**wah**-lee) *noun* a Hindu religious festival at which lamps are lit, held in October or November. [from Sanskrit, = row of lamps]

dixie *noun* (*Australian*) a small container of ice cream.

DIY *abbreviation* do-it-yourself.

dizzy *adjective* (**dizzier**, **dizziest**) giddy. **dizzily** *adverb*, **dizziness** *noun*

DJ *noun* **1** disc jockey. **2** a person who uses samples of recorded music to make dance or rap music.

DNA *noun* **1** deoxyribonucleic acid, a substance in chromosomes that stores genetic information. **2** the fundamental and distinctive characteristics or qualities of someone or something, especially when regarded as unchangeable, *Great customer service is part of the company's DNA.*

DNS *abbreviation* **1** domain name server, the system that automatically translates Internet addresses to the numeric machine addresses that computers use. **2** domain name system, the hierarchical method by which Internet addresses are constructed.

do[1] *verb* (**did**, **done**, **doing**) This word has many uses, including **1** perform or carry out a job, duty, etc., **2** produce or make (*do an extra copy*), **3** deal with, attend to (*do your hair; do the dishes*), **4** solve (*do a puzzle*), **5** act or proceed (*do as I say*), **6** fare, get on (*She is doing well at school*), **7** be suitable or enough (*This will do*), **8** be the cause of (*do a lot of harm*), **9** cover a distance in travelling (*do 500 kilometres a day*). The verb is also used with other verbs **1** in questions (*Do you want this?*), **2** in statements with 'not' (*He does not want it*), **3** for emphasis (*I do like nuts*), **4** to avoid repeating a verb that has just been used (*We work as hard as they do*).
do away with get rid of.
do up 1 fasten, *Do your coat up.* **2** repair or redecorate, *Do up the spare room.*
do without manage without, *She can do without the phone today.*

do[2] *noun* (*plural* **dos**) (*informal*) a party; an entertainment.

dob *verb* (**dobbed**, **dobbing**) **dob in** (*Australian informal*) inform on. **dobber** *noun* [probably from British dialect = put down; throw down]

Dobermann *noun* (in full **Dobermann pinscher**) a large dog with a smooth coat. [named after L. Dobermann, German dog breeder, + German *Pinscher* = terrier]

docile (*say* **doh**-suyl) *adjective* willing to obey. **docilely** *adverb*, **docility** *noun* [from Latin *docilis* = easily taught]

dock[1] *noun* **1** a place where ships are loaded, unloaded, or repaired. **2** a device in which a laptop, smartphone, or other mobile device may be placed for charging, providing access to a power supply and to other devices or features.

dock[2] *verb* **1** bring or come into a dock. **2** (of spacecraft) join together in space.

dock[3] *noun* an enclosure for the prisoner on trial in a lawcourt. [from Flemish *dok* = cage]

dock[4] *noun* a weed with broad leaves.

dock[5] *verb* **1** cut short an animal's tail. **2** reduce or take away part of someone's wages or supplies.

docker *noun* a labourer who loads and unloads ships.

docket *noun* **1** a document or label listing the contents of a package. **2** a receipt listing the items purchased.

dockyard *noun* an open area with docks and equipment for building or repairing ships.

doctor *noun* **1** a person who is trained to treat sick or injured people. **2** a person who holds an advanced degree (a **doctorate**) at a university, *Doctor of Music.* [from Latin *doctor* = teacher]

doctrine *noun* a belief held by a religious, political, or other group. **doctrinal** *adjective* [same origin as *doctor*]

document *noun* a piece of written, printed, or electronic matter that provides information or evidence or that serves as an official record. **documentation** *noun*

documentary[1] *adjective* **1** consisting of documents, *documentary evidence.* **2** showing real events or situations.

documentary[2] *noun* (*plural* **documentaries**) a film or television or radio program that provides a factual report on a particular subject.

dodder *verb* totter. **doddery** *adjective*

dodge[1] *verb* (**dodged**, **dodging**) move quickly to avoid someone or something.

dodge[2] *noun* **1** a dodging movement. **2** (*informal*) a trick; a clever way of doing something.

dodgem *noun* a small electrically driven car at a fair or amusement park in which each driver tries to bump some cars and dodge others.

dodgy *adjective* (*informal*) tricky; awkward.

dodo *noun* (*plural* **dodos**) **1** a large heavy bird that used to live on an island in the Indian Ocean but has been extinct for over 200 years. **2** (*informal*) a stupid person. [from Portuguese *doudo* = fool]

doe *noun* a female deer, rabbit, kangaroo, or hare.

doer *noun* a person who does things.

does 3rd person singular present tense of **do**[1].

doesn't does not, *She doesn't like maths.*

doff *verb* take off, *He doffed his hat.* [from *do off*; compare *don*]

dog[1] *noun* a four-legged animal that barks, often kept as a pet, *Greyhounds are very fast dogs.*

dog[2] *verb* (**dogged**, **dogging**) follow closely or persistently, *Reporters dogged his footsteps.*

dog-eared *adjective* (of a book) having the corners of the pages bent from constant use.

dogfish *noun* (*plural* **dogfish**) a kind of small shark.

dogged (*say* **dog**-uhd) *adjective* persistent; obstinate. **doggedly** *adverb*

doggerel *noun* bad verse.

dogma *noun* a belief or principle that a Church or other authority declares is true and must be accepted.

dogman *noun* (*plural* **dogmen**) (*Australian*) a person directing the operation of a crane, often while riding on its load.

dogmatic *adjective* expressing ideas in a very firm authoritative way. **dogmatically** *adverb* [from *dogma*]

dogsbody *noun* (*plural* **dogsbodies**) (*informal*) a person who does the boring or unpleasant jobs for other people; a drudge.

doily *noun* (*plural* **doilies**) a small ornamental lace or paper mat.

do-it-yourself *adjective* suitable for an amateur to make or use.

doldrums *plural noun* **1** the ocean regions near the equator where there is little or no wind. **2** a time of depression or inactivity.

dole[1] *verb* (**doled**, **doling**) distribute.

dole[2] *noun* (*informal*) money paid by the government to unemployed people.

doleful *adjective* mournful. **dolefully** *adverb* [from an old word *dole* = grief]

doll *noun* a toy model of a person.

dollar *noun* a unit of money in Australia, New Zealand, the USA, and various other countries. [from German *thaler* = a silver coin]

dollop *noun* (*informal*) a shapeless lump of something soft.

dolly *noun* (*plural* **dollies**) (*informal*) a doll.

dolour (*say* **dol**-er) *adjective* sorrow, distress. **dolorous** *adjective* [from Latin *dolor* = pain]

dolphin *noun* a sea animal like a small whale with a beak-like snout.

domain (*say* duh-**mayn**) *noun* **1** an area under someone's control; a realm. **2** a field of thought or activity, *the scientific domain.* **3** a distinct subset of the Internet with addresses sharing a common suffix (such as *.au*, *.edu*, *.com*).

domain name *noun* the part of a network address that identifies it as belonging to a particular domain.

dome *noun* a roof shaped like the top half of a ball. **domed** *adjective*

domestic *adjective* **1** of the home or household. **2** (of animals) kept by people, not wild. **domestically** *adverb*, **domesticated** *adjective* [from Latin *domus* = home]

domicile (*say* **dom**-uh-suyl) *noun* a residence; home. **domiciled** *adjective*

dominate *verb* (**dominated**, **dominating**) **1** control by being stronger or more powerful. **2** be conspicuous or prominent, *The mountain dominated the whole landscape.* **dominance** *noun*, **dominant** *adjective*, **domination** *noun* [from Latin *dominus* = master]

domineer *verb* behave in a dominating way. **domineering** *adjective*

dominion *noun* **1** authority to rule others; control. **2** an area over which someone rules; a domain.

domino *noun* (*plural* **dominoes**) a small flat oblong piece of wood or plastic with dots (usually one to six) or a blank space at each end, used in the game of **dominoes**.

don *verb* (**donned**, **donning**) put on, *don a cloak.* [from *do on*; compare *doff*]

donate *verb* (**donated**, **donating**) give money or goods to an organisation or institution like a charity or school. **donation** *noun*

done *past participle* of **do**[1].

donga *noun* **1** a dry watercourse. **2** (*Australian*) a broad shallow depression in dry country. **3** (*Australian*) the bush. **4** (*Australian*) a temporary (usually transportable) building. [from Xhosa and Zulu]

donkey *noun* (*plural* **donkeys**) an animal that looks like a small horse with long ears.

donkey vote *noun* (*Australian*) **1** a vote cast by allocating preferences according to the order in which candidates are listed on the ballot paper. **2** such votes collectively.

donor *noun* someone who gives something, *a blood donor.*

don't do not, *Cats don't bark, and dogs don't meow.*

donut alternative spelling of **doughnut**.

doodle *verb* (**doodled**, **doodling**) scribble or draw absent-mindedly. **doodle** *noun*

doom[1] *noun* a grim fate; death; ruin.

doom[2] *verb* destine to a grim fate.

doomsday *noun* the day of the Last Judgement; the end of the world.

doona *noun* (*Australian trademark*) a thick soft quilt used instead of blankets.

door *noun* a movable barrier on hinges (or one that slides or revolves), used to open or close an entrance, *The door was locked when I came home from school.* **doorknob** *noun*, **doormat** *noun*

doorstep *noun* the step or piece of ground just outside a door.

doorway *noun* the opening into which a door fits.

dope[1] *noun* (*informal*) **1** a drug, especially one taken or given illegally. **2** a stupid person. **dopey** *adjective*

dope[2] *verb* (**doped**, **doping**) (*informal*) give a drug to a person or animal. [from Dutch *doop* = sauce]

doppelgänger (*say* **dop**-uhl-geng-uh) *noun* an apparition or double of a living person. [German, = double-goer]

dork *noun* (*informal*) a stupid or ineffectual person.

dormant *adjective* **1** sleeping. **2** living or existing but not active; not extinct, *a dormant volcano.* **dormancy** *noun* [from French, = sleeping]

dormitory *noun* (*plural* **dormitories**) a room for several people to sleep in, especially in a school or institution. [from Latin *dormire* = to sleep]

dormouse *noun* (*plural* **dormice**) an animal like a large mouse that hibernates in winter.

Dorothy Dix *noun* (also **Dorothy Dixer**) (*Australian informal*) a pre-arranged parliamentary question asked in order to allow a minister to deliver a prepared speech. [named after a US writer of question-and-answer columns]

dorsal *adjective* of or on the back, *Some fish have a dorsal fin.* [from Latin *dorsum* = the back]

dory *noun* (*plural* **dories**) an edible sea fish.

DOS *noun* an operating system for personal computers. [abbreviation of *disk operating system*]

dosage *noun* **1** the giving of medicine in doses. **2** the size of a dose.

dose[1] *noun* an amount of medicine taken at one time.

dose[2] *verb* (**dosed, dosing**) give a dose of medicine to a person or animal.

dossier (*say* **dos**-ee-uh) *noun* a set of documents containing information about a person or event.

dot[1] *noun* a tiny spot.
on the dot (*informal*) exactly on time.

dot[2] *verb* (**dotted, dotting**) mark with dots.

dotage (*say* **doh**-tij) *noun* a condition of weakness of mind caused by old age, *He is in his dotage.*

dotcom *noun* a commercial enterprise operating via the Internet.

dote *verb* (**doted, doting**) **dote on** be very fond of.

dot painting *noun* a style of Aboriginal art from central Australia.

dot plot *noun* (in statistics) a type of graph used for presenting and organising data.

dotty *adjective* (**dottier, dottiest**) (*informal*) crazy; silly. **dottiness** *noun*

double[1] *adjective* **1** twice as much; twice as many. **2** having two things or parts that form a pair, *a double-barrelled gun.* **3** suitable for two people, *a double bed.* **doubly** *adverb*

double[2] *noun* **1** a double quantity or thing. **2** a person or thing that looks exactly like another.

double[3] *verb* (**doubled, doubling**) **1** make or become twice as much or as many. **2** bend or fold in two. **3** turn back sharply, *The fox doubled back on its tracks.* **4** (*Australian*) give someone a ride on the bar of a bicycle.

double bass *noun* a musical instrument with strings, like a large cello.

double-cross *verb* deceive or cheat a trusting friend.

double-decker *noun* a bus or train with two decks.

double entendre (*say* doo-buhl ahn-**tahn**-druh or dub-uhl on-**ton**-druh) *noun* a phrase with two meanings, one of which is usually indecent. [French, = *double understanding*]

doublet *noun* a man's close-fitting jacket worn in the 15th–17th centuries.

doubt[1] *noun* a feeling of not being sure about something.

doubt[2] *verb* feel doubt. **doubter** *noun* [from Latin *dubitore* = hesitate]

doubtful *adjective* **1** feeling doubt. **2** causing doubt. **doubtfully** *adverb*

doubtless *adverb* certainly.

dough *noun* **1** a thick mixture of flour and water used for making bread or pastry. **2** (*informal*) money. **doughy** *adjective*

doughnut *noun* (also **donut**) **1** a round or ring-shaped bun that has been fried and covered in sugar. **2** (*informal*) a tight full-circle turn in a vehicle.

doughty (*say* **dow**-tee) *adjective* valiant.

dour (*rhymes with* tour) *adjective* stern and gloomy-looking. **dourly** *adverb* [from Gaelic *dur* = dull, obstinate]

douse *verb* (**doused, dousing**) put into water; pour water over something, *douse the fire.*

dove *noun* a kind of pigeon.

dovetail[1] *noun* a wedge-shaped joint used to join two pieces of wood.

dovetail[2] *verb* **1** join pieces of wood with a dovetail. **2** fit neatly together, *My plans dovetailed with hers.*

dowager *noun* a woman who holds a title or property after her husband has died, *the dowager duchess.*

dowdy *adjective* (**dowdier, dowdiest**) shabby; unfashionable. **dowdily** *adverb*

dowel *noun* a headless pin or peg for holding together components of a structure.

dowelling *noun* round rods for cutting into dowels.

down[1] *adverb* **1** to or in a lower place or position or level, *It fell down.* **2** to a source or place, *Track them down.* **3** in writing, *Take down these instructions.* **4** as a payment, *We will pay $5 down and the rest later.* **5** out of action, *The computers are down.*
be down on disapprove of, *She is down on smoking.*
down under in or to Australia or New Zealand.

down[2] *preposition* downwards through or along or into, *Pour it down the drain.*

down³ *noun* **have a down on someone** (*Australian informal*) have a prejudice or grudge against someone.

down⁴ *noun* very fine soft feathers or hair. **downy** *adjective*

down⁵ *noun* a grass-covered hill, *Darling Downs.*

downcast *adjective* **1** looking downwards, *downcast eyes.* **2** dejected.

downfall *noun* a fall from power or prosperity.

downhill *adverb & adjective* down a slope.

download¹ *verb* copy data from one computer system to another, typically over the Internet.

download² *noun* **1** an act or process of downloading data. **2** a file or set of files that has been downloaded.

downmarket *adjective & adverb* (*informal*) of or to the cheaper sector of the market.

downpour *noun* a great fall of rain.

downright *adjective* **1** frank; straightforward. **2** thorough; complete, *a downright lie.*

downside *noun* a negative aspect of something.

downsize *verb* (**downsized, downsizing**) reduce in size, *The company was forced to downsize.*

downstairs *adverb & adjective* to or on a lower floor.

downstream *adjective & adverb* in the direction in which a stream flows.

Down syndrome *noun* (also **Down's syndrome**) a condition that some people are born with that results in intellectual impairment, short stature, and a broad facial profile. [named after J.H.L. Down, English physician]

down-to-earth *adjective* sensible and practical.

downturn *noun* a decline in economic or business activity.

downward *adjective & adverb* going towards what is lower. **downwards** *adverb*

dowry *noun* (*plural* **dowries**) property or money brought by a bride to her husband when she marries him.

doze¹ *verb* (**dozed, dozing**) sleep lightly.

doze² *noun* a light sleep. **dozy** *adjective*

dozen *noun* a set of 12, *two dozen eggs.* **dozens of** (*informal*) very many, *dozens of people.*

Dr *abbreviation* Doctor.

drab *adjective* (**drabber, drabbest**) **1** not colourful. **2** dull; uninteresting, *a drab life.* **drably** *adverb*, **drabness** *noun*

draconian (*say* druh-**koh**-nee-uhn) *adjective* very harsh, *draconian laws.* [named after Draco, who established very severe laws in ancient Athens]

draft¹ *noun* **1** a rough sketch or plan. **2** a written order for a bank to pay out money.

draft² *verb* **1** prepare a draft. **2** select for a special duty, *She was drafted to our office in Paris.* **3** (*Australian*) separate sheep or cattle from a flock or herd for some special purpose. **4** conscript.

> **Usage** *Draft* is also the American spelling of *draught.*

drag¹ *verb* (**dragged, dragging**) **1** pull something heavy along. **2** search the bottom of a river, lake, or sea with nets and hooks. **3** continue slowly and dully. **4** move an image or highlighted text across a computer screen using a tool such as a mouse. **drag out** make something last longer than necessary.

drag² *noun* **1** a hindrance; something boring. **2** (*informal*) women's clothes worn by men.

dragon *noun* **1** a mythological monster, usually with wings and able to breathe out fire. **2** a fierce person. [from Greek *drakon* = serpent]

dragonfly *noun* (*plural* **dragonflies**) an insect with a long thin body and two pairs of transparent wings.

dragoon¹ *noun* a member of certain cavalry regiments.

dragoon² *verb* force someone into doing something.

drain¹ *noun* **1** a pipe or channel for taking away water or other liquid. **2** something that takes away strength or resources. **drainpipe** *noun*

drain² *verb* **1** take away water or other liquid through a drain. **2** flow or trickle away. **3** empty liquid out of a container. **4** take away strength or resources gradually; exhaust. **drainage** *noun*

drake *noun* a male duck.

drama *noun* **1** a play. **2** writing or performing plays. **3** a series of exciting events.

drama queen *noun* (*informal*) a person who habitually responds to situations in a melodramatic way.

dramatic *adjective* **1** of drama. **2** exciting; impressive, *a dramatic change.* **dramatically** *adverb*

dramatise *verb* (**dramatised, dramatising**) **1** make a story or incident into a play or film. **2** make something seem exciting. **dramatisation** *noun*

dramatis personae (*say* dram-uh-tuhs per-**soh**-nuy) *plural noun* the characters in a play. [Latin, = persons of the drama]

dramatist *noun* a person who writes plays.

drank *past tense* of **drink**[1].

drape *verb* (**draped, draping**) cover loosely or decorate with cloth or other material.

draper *noun* a shopkeeper who sells cloth or clothes.

drapery *noun* (*plural* **draperies**) **1** a draper's stock. **2** cloth arranged in loose folds.

drastic *adjective* having a strong or violent effect. **drastically** *adverb*

drat *interjection* (*informal*) an expression of annoyance.

draught (*say* drahft) *noun* **1** a current of usually cold air indoors. **2** a haul of fish in a net. **3** the depth of water needed to float a ship. **4** a swallow of liquid.
draughty *adjective*

draughts *noun* a game played with 24 round pieces on a chessboard.

draughtsman *noun* (*plural* **draughtsmen**) **1** a person who makes drawings. **2** a piece used in the game of draughts.

draw[1] *verb* (**drew, drawn, drawing**) **1** produce a picture or outline by making marks on a surface. **2** pull. **3** take out, *draw water.* **4** attract, *The show drew large crowds.* **5** end a game or contest with the same score on both sides. **6** move; come, *The ship drew nearer.* **7** make out by thinking, *draw conclusions.* **8** write out a cheque to be cashed.
draw back move back.
draw out make something last longer.
draw up 1 come to a halt. **2** prepare a document etc.

draw[2] *noun* **1** the drawing of lots (see *lot*). **2** the drawing out of a gun etc., *He was quick on the draw.* **3** an attraction. **4** a drawn game.

drawback *noun* a disadvantage.

drawbridge *noun* a bridge over a moat, hinged at one end so that it can be raised or lowered.

drawer *noun* **1** a sliding box-like compartment in a piece of furniture. **2** a person who draws something. **3** someone who draws (= writes out) a cheque.

drawing *noun* a picture or outline drawn.

drawing pin *noun* a short pin with a flat top to be pressed with your thumb, used for fastening something to a surface.

drawing room *noun* a sitting room.

drawl[1] *verb* speak very slowly or lazily.

drawl[2] *noun* a drawling way of speaking.

dray *noun* a strong low flat cart for carrying heavy loads.

dread[1] *noun* great fear.

dread[2] *verb* fear greatly.

dreadful *adjective* **1** terrible. **2** (*informal*) very bad, *dreadful weather.*
dreadfully *adverb*

dreadlocks *plural noun* hair worn in many ringlets or plaits.

dream[1] *noun* **1** things a person seems to see while sleeping. **2** something imagined; an ambition or ideal. **dreamily** *adverb*, **dreamy** *adjective*

dream[2] *verb* (**dreamt** or **dreamed, dreaming**) **1** have a dream or dreams. **2** have an ambition. **3** think something might happen, *I never dreamt she would leave.* **dreamer** *noun*

dreamtime *noun* (also **dreaming**) (*Australian*) (in traditional Aboriginal belief) events beyond living memory that shaped the physical, spiritual and moral world. [a translation of *alcheringa*]

dreary *adjective* (**drearier, dreariest**) **1** dull; boring. **2** gloomy. **drearily** *adverb*, **dreariness** *noun*

dredge *verb* (**dredged, dredging**) drag something up, especially by scooping at the bottom of a river or the sea. **dredger** *noun*

dregs *plural noun* worthless bits that sink to the bottom of a liquid.

drench *verb* make wet all through.

dress[1] *noun* (*plural* **dresses**) **1** a woman's or girl's garment with a bodice and skirt. **2** clothes; costume, *fancy dress.*

dress[2] *verb* **1** put clothes on. **2** decorate, *dress the shop windows.* **3** prepare food for cooking or eating. **4** put a dressing on a wound. **dresser** *noun*

dressage (*say* **dres**-ah*zh*) *noun* management of a horse to show its obedience and style. [French, = training]

dresser *noun* a sideboard with shelves at the top for dishes and other items.

dressing *noun* **1** a piece of material used to cover and protect a wound. **2** a sauce of oil, vinegar, and other ingredients for a salad. **3** manure or other fertiliser for spreading on the soil.

dressing gown *noun* a loose garment for wearing when you are not fully dressed.

dressmaker *noun* a maker of women's clothes. **dressmaking** *noun*

dress rehearsal *noun* a rehearsal at which the cast wear their costumes.

drew *past tense* of **draw**[1].

dribble *verb* (**dribbled, dribbling**) **1** let saliva trickle out of your mouth. **2** move the ball forward in football or hockey with slight touches of your feet or stick.

dried *past tense & past participle* of **dry**[2].

drier *noun* a machine for drying hair or clothes.

drift[1] *verb* **1** be carried gently along by water or air. **2** move slowly and casually; live casually with no definite objective.
drifter *noun*

drift[2] *noun* **1** a drifting movement. **2** a mass of snow or sand piled up by the wind. **3** the general meaning or tendency of what is said.

driftwood *noun* wood floating on the sea or washed ashore by it.

drill[1] *noun* **1** a tool for making holes; a machine for boring holes or wells. **2** repeated exercises in gymnastics, military training, etc.

drill[2] *verb* **1** make a hole etc. with a drill. **2** do repeated exercises; make people do exercises.

drily *adverb* in a dry way.

drink[1] *verb* (**drank**, **drunk**, **drinking**) **1** swallow liquid. **2** drink a lot of alcoholic drinks.
drinker *noun*

drink[2] *noun* **1** a liquid for drinking. **2** an amount of liquid swallowed. **3** an alcoholic drink.

drip[1] *verb* (**dripped**, **dripping**) fall or let something fall in drops.

drip[2] *noun* **1** liquid falling in drops; the sound it makes. **2** an apparatus for dripping liquid into the veins of a sick person.

drip-dry *adjective* made of material that dries easily and does not need ironing.

dripping *noun* fat melted from roasted meat and allowed to set.

drive[1] *verb* (**drove**, **driven**, **driving**) **1** make something or someone move. **2** operate a motor vehicle or a train. **3** cause; compel, *Hunger drove them to steal.* **4** force someone into a state, *She is driving me crazy.* **5** rush; move rapidly, *Rain drove against the window.* **driver** *noun*

drive[2] *noun* **1** a journey in a vehicle. **2** a hard stroke in cricket or golf. **3** the transmitting of power to machinery, *four-wheel drive.* **4** energy; enthusiasm. **5** an organised effort, *a sales drive.* **6** a track for vehicles through the grounds of a house. **7** (also **disk drive**) a mechanism in a computer that spins a disk so that data can be read from or written to it.

drive-in *adjective* that you can use without getting out of your car.

drivel *noun* silly talk; nonsense.

drizzle *noun* very fine rain. **drizzly** *adjective*

droid *noun* **1** (in science fiction) a robot. **2** (in computing) a program that automatically collects information from remote systems. [from *android*]

droll *adjective* amusing in an odd way.

dromedary *noun* (*plural* **dromedaries**) a camel with one hump, bred for riding on. [from Greek *dromas* = runner]

drone[1] *verb* (**droned**, **droning**) **1** make a deep humming sound. **2** talk in a boring voice.

drone[2] *noun* **1** a droning sound. **2** a male bee. **3** a remote-controlled pilotless aircraft or missile.

drongo *noun* (*plural* **drongos**) **1** a black bird with a long forked tail. **2** (*Australian informal*) a fool or simpleton.

drool *verb* dribble.
drool over be very emotional about liking something.

droop *verb* hang down weakly.

drop[1] *noun* **1** a tiny amount of liquid. **2** a small round sweet. **3** a hanging ornament. **4** a fall; a decrease. **5** a descent.

drop[2] *verb* (**dropped**, **dropping**) **1** fall. **2** let something fall. **3** put down a passenger, *Drop me at the station.* **4** lower; become lower. **5** omit. **6** abandon; give up.
drop in visit someone casually.
drop off fall asleep.
drop out stop taking part in something.
drop-out *noun*

droplet *noun* a small drop.

drought (*say* drowt) *noun* a long period of dry weather.

drove *past tense* of **drive**[1].

drove *noun* a moving herd, flock, or crowd, *People came in droves.*

drover *noun* someone who drives a herd or flock, especially over a long distance.

drown *verb* **1** die or kill by suffocation under water. **2** flood; drench. **3** make so much noise that another sound cannot be heard.

drowsy *adjective* sleepy. **drowsily** *adverb*, **drowsiness** *noun*

drubbing *noun* a beating; a severe defeat.

drudge *noun* a person who does dull work.
drudgery *noun*

drug[1] *noun* **1** a substance used in medicine. **2** a substance that affects your senses or your mind, *a drug addict.*

drug[2] *verb* (**drugged**, **drugging**) give a drug to someone, especially to make them unconscious.

drum[1] *noun* **1** a musical instrument made of a cylinder with a skin or parchment stretched over one or both ends. **2** a cylindrical object or container, *an oil drum.* **3** (*Australian*) a swagman's bundle of possessions. **4** (*Australian informal*) a reliable piece of information.

drum[2] *verb* (**drummed**, **drumming**) **1** play a drum or drums. **2** tap or thump on something. **drummer** *noun*

drumstick *noun* **1** a stick for beating a drum. **2** the lower part of a cooked bird's leg.

drunk[1] *past participle* of **drink**[1].

drunk[2] *adjective* excited or helpless through drinking too much alcohol.

drunk[3] *noun* a person who is drunk.

drunkard *noun* a person who is often drunk.

drunken *adjective* **1** drunk, *a drunken man.* **2** caused by drinking alcohol.

dry[1] *adjective* (**drier, driest**) **1** without water or moisture. **2** thirsty. **3** boring; dull. **4** (of remarks or humour) said in a matter-of-fact or ironical way, *dry wit.* **drily** *adverb*, **dryness** *noun*

dry[2] *verb* (**dried, drying**) make or become dry.

dry-cleaning *noun* a method of cleaning clothes or carpet by a liquid that evaporates quickly.

dry dock *noun* a dock that can be emptied of water so that ships can float in and then be repaired.

dry ice *noun* solid carbon dioxide.

dry season *noun* (also **dry spell**) (*Australian*) a period of low rainfall or drought. (The opposite is **wet season**.)

dual *adjective* composed of two parts; double. [from Latin *duo* = two]

dual carriageway *noun* a road with a dividing strip between lanes of traffic in opposite directions.

dub[1] *verb* (**dubbed, dubbing**) **1** make someone a knight by touching him on the shoulder with a sword. **2** give a person or thing a nickname. [from an old French word, = knight a person]

dub[2] *verb* (**dubbed, dubbing**) **1** change or add new sound to the soundtrack of a film or magnetic tape. **2** copy a recording. [short for *double*]

dubious (*say* **dyoo**-bee-uhs) *adjective* **1** doubtful. **2** questionable, unreliable. **dubiously** *adverb* [from Latin *dubium* = doubt]

ducat (*say* **duk**-uht) *noun* a former gold coin used in Europe.

duchess *noun* (*plural* **duchesses**) a duke's wife or widow.

duchy *noun* (*plural* **duchies**) the territory of a duke.

duck[1] *noun* **1** a swimming bird with a flat beak; the female of this. **2** a batter's score of zero at cricket. **3** a ducking movement.

duck[2] *verb* **1** bend down quickly to avoid something. **2** go or push quickly under water. **3** dodge; avoid doing something.

duckling *noun* a young duck.

duck-shove *verb* (*Australian informal*) evade responsibility. **duck-shover** *noun*

duct *noun* a tube or channel through which liquid, gas, air, or cables can pass. [from Latin *ductum* = conveyed]

ductile *adjective* (of metal) able to be drawn out into fine strands.

dud *noun* (*informal*) something that is useless or a fake or fails to work. **dud** *adjective*

dudgeon (*say* **duj**-uhn) *noun* indignation.

due[1] *adjective* **1** expected; scheduled to do something or to arrive, *The train is due in ten minutes.* **2** owing; needing to be paid. **3** that ought to be given; rightful, *Treat her with due respect.*

due to because of, *His lateness was due to an accident.*

in due course at the appropriate time.

> **Usage** The use of *due to* to mean 'because of' is regarded as unacceptable by some people on the grounds that *due* is an adjective and should not be used as a preposition; *owing to* is often recommended as a better alternative. The prepositional use, however, is well established and is now regarded as standard.

due[2] *adverb* exactly, *We sailed due east.*

due[3] *noun* **1** a person's right; something deserved; proper respect, *Give him his due.* **2** a fee, *harbour dues.*

duel *noun* a fight between two people, especially with pistols or swords. **duelling** *noun*, **duellist** *noun*

> **Usage** Do not confuse this word with *dual.*

duet *noun* a piece of music for two players or singers. [from Latin *duo* = two]

duff *verb* (*Australian*) steal horses or cattle. **duffing** *noun*

duffel coat *noun* a thick overcoat with a hood, fastened with toggles. [named after Duffel, a town in Belgium]

duffer *noun* **1** a person who is stupid or not good at doing something. **2** (*Australian*) a cattle thief or horse thief.

dug *past tense & past participle* of **dig**[1].

dugite (*say* **doo**-guyt) *noun* a highly venomous Australian snake. [from Noongar *dookatj*]

dugong (*say* **doo**-gong) *noun* (*plural* **dugong** or **dugongs**) an Asian sea mammal; a sea cow.

dugout *noun* **1** an underground shelter. **2** a canoe made by hollowing out a tree trunk.

duke *noun* a member of the highest rank of noblemen. **dukedom** *noun* [from Latin *dux* = leader]

dulcet (*say* **dul**-suht) *adjective* sweet-sounding. [from Latin *dulcis* = sweet]

dulcimer *noun* a musical instrument with strings that are struck by two hammers.

dull *adjective* **1** not bright or clear, *dull weather.* **2** stupid. **3** boring, *a dull film.* **4** not sharp, *a dull pain; a dull thud.* **dull** *verb*, **dullness** *noun* **dully** *adverb*

dullard *noun* a stupid person.

duly *adverb* in the due or proper way.

dumb *adjective* **1** (*old use*) unable to speak; silent. **2** (*informal*) stupid. **dumbly** *adverb*, **dumbness** *noun*

> **Usage** Although *dumb* meaning 'unable to speak' is the older sense, it has been overwhelmed by the newer sense (meaning 'stupid') to such an extent that the use of the first sense is now almost certain to cause offence.

dumb down *verb* (*informal*) simplify or reduce the intellectual content of something so as to make it accessible to a larger audience.

dumbfound *verb* greatly astonish or amaze. **dumbfounded** *adjective* [from *dumb* + *confound*]

dummy *noun* (*plural* **dummies**) **1** something made to look like a person or thing. **2** an imitation teat given to a baby to suck. **3** a stupid person. [from *dumb*]

dump[1] *noun* **1** a place where something (especially rubbish) is left or stored. **2** (*informal*) a dull or unattractive place.

dump[2] *verb* **1** get rid of something that is not wanted. **2** put down carelessly.

dumpling *noun* a lump of dough cooked in a stew or baked with fruit inside.

dumps *plural noun* (*informal*) low spirits, *feeling down in the dumps.*

dumpy *adjective* short and fat.

dunce *noun* a person who is slow at learning. [from Duns Scotus, a Scottish philosopher in the Middle Ages, whose followers were said by their opponents to be unable to understand new ideas]

dune *noun* a mound of loose sand shaped by the wind.

dung *noun* solid waste matter excreted by an animal.

dungarees *plural noun* overalls made of thick strong cloth. [from Hindi *dungri*]

dungeon (*say* **dun**-juhn) *noun* an underground cell for prisoners.

dunk *verb* dip something into liquid.

dunnart *noun* a narrow-footed marsupial mouse. [from Noongar *dhanart*]

dunny *noun* (*Australian informal*) a toilet, especially an outside one. [from British dialect *dunnekin*]

duo *noun* (*plural* **duos**) **1** a pair of musicians or singers. **2** a duet.

duodenum (*say* dyoo-uh-**dee**-nuhm) *noun* the part of the small intestine that is just below the stomach. **duodenal** *adjective*

dupe[1] *verb* (**duped**, **duping**) deceive.

dupe[2] *noun* someone who is deceived.

duplicate[1] *noun* **1** something that is exactly the same as something else. **2** an exact copy.

duplicate[2] *verb* (**duplicated**, **duplicating**) make or be a duplicate. **duplication** *noun*, **duplicator** *noun* [from Latin *duplex* = double]

duplicity (*say* dyoo-**plis**-uh-tee) *noun* deceitfulness. [from Latin *duplex* = double]

durable *adjective* strong and likely to last. **durability** *noun* **durably** *adverb* [from Latin *durare* = endure]

duration *noun* the time something lasts.

duress (*say* dyoo-**res**) *noun* the use of force or threats to get what you want.

during *preposition* while something else is going on.

dusk *noun* twilight in the evening.

dusky *adjective* dark; shadowy.

dust[1] *noun* tiny particles of earth or other solid material.

dust[2] *verb* **1** wipe away dust. **2** sprinkle with dust or something powdery.

duster *noun* a cloth for dusting things.

dustpan *noun* a pan into which dust is brushed from a floor.

dust storm *noun* a storm with clouds of dust gathered in the air.

dusty *adjective* (**dustier**, **dustiest**) **1** covered with dust. **2** like dust.

dutiful *adjective* doing your duty; obedient. **dutifully** *adverb* [from *duty* + *full*]

duty *noun* (*plural* **duties**) **1** what you ought to do or must do. **2** a task that must be done. **3** a tax charged on imports and on certain other goods.
on duty actually doing what is your regular work.

duvet (*say* **doo**-vay) *noun* a thick soft quilt used instead of blankets. [French]

dux *noun* the top student in a class or school. [Latin, = leader]

DVD *noun* a type of compact disc that can store both audio and video data. [from the initials of 'digital versatile disc' or 'digital video disc']

DVD-R *noun* a DVD that can be recorded on only once. [from the initials of 'digital versatile disc recordable']

DVD-ROM *noun* a DVD used in a computer for displaying data. [from the initials of 'digital versatile disc read-only memory']

DVD-RW *noun* a DVD on which recordings can be made and erased a number of times. [from the initials of 'digital versatile disc rewritable']

dwarf[1] *noun* (*plural* **dwarfs**) **1** a very small person or thing. **2** a small mythological being.

> **Usage** In sense 1, with regard to people, the term is often considered offensive.

dwarf[2] *verb* make something seem small by contrast.

dwarf planet *noun* a planet-like object that orbits a star, but is not large or solid enough to be designated a planet.

dwell *verb* (**dwelt, dwelling**) live somewhere. **dweller** *noun*
dwell on think or talk about something for a long time.

dwelling *noun* a house, flat, or other place of residence.

dwindle *verb* (**dwindled, dwindling**) get smaller gradually.

dye[1] *verb* (**dyed, dyeing**) colour something by putting it into a liquid. **dyer** *noun*

dye[2] *noun* a substance used to dye things.

dying *present participle* of **die**[1].

dyke *noun* (also **dike**) **1** a long wall or embankment to hold back water and prevent flooding. **2** a ditch for draining water from land.

dynamic *adjective* energetic; active. **dynamically** *adverb* [from Greek *dynamis* = power]

dynamite *noun* **1** a powerful explosive. **2** something likely to make people very excited or angry. [same origin as *dynamic*]

dynamo *noun* (*plural* **dynamos**) a machine that makes electricity.

dynasty (*say* **din**-uh-stee) *noun* (*plural* **dynasties**) a succession of rulers all from the same family. **dynastic** *adjective* [same origin as *dynamic*]

dys- *prefix* bad; difficult. [from Greek]

dysentery (*say* **dis**-uhn-tree) *noun* a disease causing severe diarrhoea. [from *dys-*, + Greek *entera* = bowels]

dyslexia (*say* dis-**lek**-see-uh) *noun* unusually great difficulty in being able to read and spell. **dyslexic** *adjective* [from *dys-*, + Greek *lexis* = speech]

dysmorphia *noun* a deformity or abnormality in the shape or size of a specified part of the body. [Greek = misshapenness, ugliness]

dyspepsia (*say* dis-**pep**-see-uh) *noun* indigestion. **dyspeptic** *adjective* [from *dys-*, + Greek *peptikos* = able to digest]

dystrophy (*say* **dis**-truh-fee) *noun* a disease that weakens the muscles. [from *dys-*, + Greek *-trophia* = nourishment]

Ee

E *abbreviation* east; eastern.

e-[1] *prefix* see **ex-**.

e-[2] *prefix* relating to electronic communication (as in *e-commerce*, *email*).

each *adjective & pronoun* every; every one, *each child*; *each of you*.

eager *adjective* strongly wanting to do something; enthusiastic. **eagerly** *adverb*, **eagerness** *noun*

eagle *noun* a large bird of prey with very strong sight.

ear[1] *noun* **1** the organ of the body that is used for hearing. **2** hearing ability, *She has a good ear for music.*

ear[2] *noun* the spike of seeds at the top of a stalk of wheat or other cereal plant.

earache *noun* pain in the ear.

earbash *verb* (*Australian informal*) talk at great length to someone. **earbashing** *noun*

eardrum *noun* a membrane in the ear that vibrates when sounds reach it.

earl *noun* a British nobleman. **earldom** *noun*

early *adjective & adverb* (**earlier**, **earliest**) **1** before the usual or expected time. **2** near the beginning, *early in the book*. **earliness** *noun*

earmark *verb* put aside for a particular purpose. [from the custom of marking an animal's ear to identify it]

earn *verb* get something by working or in return for what you have done.

earnest *adjective* showing serious feelings or intentions. **earnestly** *adverb*, **earnestness** *noun*

earnings *plural noun* money earned.

earphone *noun* a listening device that fits over the ear.

earring *noun* an ornament worn on the ear.

earshot *noun* the distance within which a sound can be heard.

earth[1] *noun* **1** (also **Earth**) the planet that we live on. **2** its surface; the ground; soil. **3** connection to the ground to complete an electrical circuit.

earth[2] *verb* connect an electrical circuit to the ground.

earthenware *noun* pottery made of coarse baked clay.

earthly *adjective* of this earth or our life on it.

earthquake *noun* a violent movement of part of the earth's surface.

earthworm *noun* a worm that lives in the soil.

earthy *adjective* like earth or soil.

earwig *noun* a crawling insect with pincers at the end of its body.

ease[1] *noun* **1** absence of effort. **2** freedom from trouble or pain.

ease[2] *verb* (**eased**, **easing**) **1** make less painful or less tight or troublesome. **2** move gently or gradually, *ease it in.* **3** become less severe, *The pressure eased.*

easel *noun* a stand for supporting a blackboard or a painting. [from Dutch *ezel* = donkey (which carries a load)]

easily *adverb* **1** without difficulty; with ease. **2** by far, *easily the best.* **3** very likely, *He could easily be lying.*

east[1] *noun* **1** the direction where the sun rises. **2** the eastern part of something. **3** (**the East**) the regions or countries lying to the east of Europe, especially China, Japan, and India.

east[2] *adjective & adverb* towards or in the east; coming from the east. **easterly** *adjective*, **eastern** *adjective*, **easterner** *noun*

Easter *noun* the Sunday (in March or April) when Christians commemorate the resurrection of Christ; the days around it.

eastward *adjective & adverb* towards the east. **eastwards** *adverb*

easy[1] *adjective* (**easier**, **easiest**) **1** able to be done or used or understood without trouble. **2** free from pain, trouble or anxiety. **easiness** *noun*

easy[2] *adverb* in an easy way; with ease; comfortably, *Take it easy!*

easygoing *adjective* relaxed and tolerant.

eat *verb* (**ate**, **eaten**, **eating**) **1** chew and swallow as food. **2** have a meal, *When do we eat?* **3** use up; destroy gradually, *Extra expenses ate up our savings*; *Acid ate into the metal.*

eatable *adjective* fit to be eaten.

eau de Cologne (*say* oh duh kuh-**lohn**) *noun* a perfume first made at Cologne in Germany.

eaves *plural noun* the overhanging edges of a roof.

eavesdrop *verb* (**eavesdropped, eavesdropping**) listen secretly to a private conversation. **eavesdropper** *noun* [as if outside a wall, where water drops from the eaves]

ebb[1] *noun* **1** the movement of the tide when it is going out, away from the land. **2** a low point, *Our courage was at a low ebb.*

ebb[2] *verb* **1** flow away from the land. **2** weaken; become less, *strength ebbed.*

Ebola (*say* uh-**bow**-luh) *noun* a virus that causes uncontrollable internal and external bleeding, often resulting in death. [named after a river in the Democratic Republic of the Congo]

ebony *noun* a hard black wood.

eccentric (*say* uhk-**sen**-trik) *adjective* behaving strangely. **eccentric** *noun*, **eccentrically** *adverb*, **eccentricity** (*say* ek-sen-**tris**-uh-tee) *noun* [from Greek *ekkentros* = away from the centre]

ecclesiastical (*say* uh-klee-zee-**as**-ti-kuhl) *adjective* of the Church or the clergy. [from Greek *ekklesia* = church]

ECG *abbreviation* **1** electrocardiogram. **2** electrocardiograph.

echidna (*say* uh-**kid**-nuh) *noun* a monotreme of Australia and Papua New Guinea, with a covering of spines, a long snout, and long claws.

echo[1] *noun* (*plural* **echoes**) a sound that is heard again as it is reflected off something.

echo[2] *verb* (**echoed, echoing**) **1** make an echo. **2** repeat a sound or saying.

éclair (*say* ay-**klair**) *noun* a finger-shaped cake of pastry with a creamy filling.

eclipse[1] *noun* the blocking of the sun's or moon's light when the moon or the earth is in the way.

eclipse[2] *verb* (**eclipsed, eclipsing**) **1** block the light and cause an eclipse. **2** outshine, seem better or more important, *Her performance eclipsed all the others.*

eco- *prefix* ecology; ecological.

ecological footprint *noun* the amount of land required to sustain a particular person or society.

ecology (*say* ee-**kol**-uh-jee) *noun* the study of living things in relation to each other and to where they live. **ecological** *adjective*, **ecologically** *adverb*, **ecologist** *noun* [from Greek *oikos* = house, + *-logy*]

economic (*say* ee-kuh-**nom**-ik) *adjective* **1** of the economy or economics. **2** profitable.

economical *adjective* using as little as possible. **economically** *adverb*

economic rationalism *noun* (*Australian*) a government's free-market approach to economic management.

economics *noun* the study of how money is used and how goods and services are provided and used. **economist** *noun*

economise *verb* (**economised, economising**) be economical; use or spend less.

economy *noun* (*plural* **economies**) **1** a country's or household's income (e.g. from what it sells or earns) and the way this is spent (e.g. on goods and services). **2** being economical. **3** a saving, *We made economies.* [from Greek *oikos* = house, + *-nomia* = management]

ecosystem *noun* a biological community of interacting organisms and their environment.

ecotourism *noun* a form of tourism that supports conservation efforts in ecologically sensitive areas.

ecstasy (*say* **ek**-stuh-see) *noun* **1** a feeling of great delight. **2** (*informal*) an illegal drug used as a stimulant and hallucinogen. **ecstatic** (*say* ek-**stat**-ik) *adjective*, **ecstatically** *adverb* [from Greek, = standing outside yourself]

ecumenical (*say* ee-kyoo-**men**-uh-kuhl or ek-yoo-**men**-uh-kuhl) *adjective* **1** of the whole Christian world. **2** seeking worldwide Christian unity. [from Greek *oikoumenikos* = of the inhabited world]

eczema (*say* **ek**-suh-muh) *noun* a skin disease causing rough itching patches.

edam (*say* **ee**-dam or **ee**-duhm) *noun* a round cheese with a red rind. [named after the town of Edam in the Netherlands]

eddy[1] *noun* (*plural* **eddies**) a swirling patch of water or air or smoke.

eddy[2] *verb* (**eddied, eddying**) swirl.

edge[1] *noun* **1** the part along the side or end of something. **2** the sharp part of a knife or axe or other cutting instrument.
be on edge be tense and irritable.

edge[2] *verb* (**edged, edging**) **1** be the edge or border of something. **2** put a border on. **3** move gradually, *He edged away.*

edgeways *adverb* with the edge forwards or outwards.

edgy *adjective* tense and irritable. **edginess** *noun*

edible *adjective* suitable for eating, not poisonous, *edible fruits.*

edict (*say* **ee**-dikt) *noun* an official command. [from *e-*[1], + Latin *dictum* = said]

edifice (*say* **ed**-uh-fuhs) *noun* a large building.

edify *verb* (**edified**, **edifying**) be an improving influence on a person's mind. **edification** *noun*

edit *verb* (**edited**, **editing**) **1** make written material ready for publishing. **2** change text on a computer. **3** choose and put the parts of a film or recording into order. **4** be the editor of a newspaper or other publication.

edition *noun* **1** the form in which something is published, *a paperback edition.* **2** the copies of a book, newspaper, or other published material issued at one time, *the first edition.* **3** an instance of a regular broadcast.

editor *noun* **1** the person in charge of a newspaper or a section of it. **2** a person who edits something.

editorial[1] *adjective* of editing or editors.

editorial[2] *noun* a newspaper article giving the editor's comments on something.

educate *verb* (**educated**, **educating**) provide with education. **educative** *adjective*, **educator** *noun* [from Latin *educare* = bring up, train]

education *noun* the process of training people's minds and abilities so that they acquire knowledge and develop skills. **educational** *adjective*, **educationally** *adverb*, **educationist** *noun*

eel *noun* a long fish that looks like a snake.

eerie *adjective* (**eerier**, **eeriest**) strange in a frightening or mysterious way. **eerily** *adverb*, **eeriness** *noun*

ef- *prefix* see **ex-**.

efface *verb* (**effaced**, **effacing**) wipe or rub out. **effacement** *noun*

effect[1] *noun* **1** a change produced by an action or cause; a result. **2** an impression produced, *a cheerful effect.*

effect[2] *verb* cause; produce, *We want to effect a change.* [from *ef-*, + Latin *-fectum* = done]

Usage See the note at *affect*.

effective *adjective* **1** producing an effect. **2** impressive. **effectively** *adverb*, **effectiveness** *noun*

effectual *adjective* producing the result desired. **effectually** *adverb*

effeminate *adjective* (of a man) having qualities that are thought to be feminine. **effeminacy** *noun*

effervesce (*say* ef-uh-**ves**) *verb* (**effervesced**, **effervescing**) give off bubbles of gas; fizz. **effervescence** *noun*, **effervescent** *adjective* [from Latin, = bubble over (compare *fervent*)]

efficacious (*say* ef-uh-**kay**-shuhs) *adjective* able to produce the result desired. **efficacy** (*say* **ef**-uh-kuh-see) *noun*

efficient *adjective* doing work well; effective. **efficiency** *noun*, **efficiently** *adverb* [same origin as *effect*]

effigy *noun* (*plural* **effigies**) a model or sculptured figure.

effort *noun* **1** the use of energy; the energy used. **2** something difficult or tiring. **3** an attempt, *This painting is a good effort.*

effortless *adjective* done with little or no effort. **effortlessly** *adverb*

effusive *adjective* making a great show of affection or enthusiasm. **effusively** *adverb*, **effusiveness** *noun*

EFTPOS *noun* an electronic payment system in which money is transferred from the customer's bank account using a credit or debit card. [from the initials of 'electronic funds transfer (at) point of sale']

e.g. *abbreviation* for example. [short for Latin *exempli gratia* = for the sake of an example]

egalitarian (*say* uh-gal-uh-**tair**-ree-uhn) *adjective* believing that everybody is equal and that nobody should be given special privileges. [from French *égal* = equal]

egg[1] *noun* **1** a more or less round object produced by the female of birds, fishes, reptiles and insects, which may develop into a new individual if fertilised. **2** a hen's or duck's egg used as food.

egg[2] *verb* encourage to do something daring or foolish, *We egged him on.*

eggplant *noun* an egg-shaped fruit with dark purple or white skin, used as a vegetable. Also called an *aubergine.*

ego (*say* **ee**-goh) *noun* (*plural* **egos**) a person's self or self-respect. [Latin, = I]

egotist (*say* **ee**-guh-tist) *noun* a conceited person who is always talking about himself or herself. **egotism** *noun*, **egotistic** *adjective*

egret (*say* **ee**-gruht) *noun* a kind of heron with long feathers.

Eid (*say* eed) *noun* (also **Id**) a Muslim festival, in particular Eid al-Fitr or Eid al-Adha. [Arabic]

eiderdown *noun* a quilt stuffed with soft material. [originally the soft down of the *eider*, a kind of Arctic duck]

eight *noun & adjective* the number 8; one more than seven.

eighteen *noun & adjective* the number 18; one more than seventeen. **eighteenth** *adjective & noun*

eighth *adjective & noun* **1** the next after the seventh. **2** one of eight equal parts of a thing.

eighty *noun & adjective* (*plural* **eighties**) the number 80; eight times ten. **eightieth** *adjective & noun*

eisteddfod (*say* uh-**sted**-fuhd) *noun* **1** an annual gathering of poets and musicians for competitions. **2** any festival for musical etc. competitions. [Welsh]

either[1] (*say* **uy**-*th*uh or **ee**-*th*uh) *adjective & pronoun* **1** one or the other of two, *Either team can win; either of them.* **2** both of two, *There are paths on either side of the river.*

either[2] *adverb* also; similarly, *If you won't go, I won't either.*

either[3] *conjunction* (used with *or*) the first of two possibilities, *He is either ill or drunk; Either come right in or go away.*

ejaculate *verb* (**ejaculated, ejaculating**) **1** eject semen from the penis. **2** say something suddenly. **ejaculation** *noun*

eject *verb* **1** send out forcefully. **2** expel; compel to leave. **ejection** *noun*, **ejector** *noun* [from *e*-[1], + Latin *-jectum* = thrown]

eke (*say* eek) *verb* (**eked, eking**)
eke out make a living with difficulty.

elaborate[1] (*say* uh-**lab**-uh-ruht) *adjective* having many parts or details; complicated. **elaborately** *adverb*, **elaborateness** *noun*

elaborate[2] (*say* uh-**lab**-uh-rayt) *verb* (**elaborated, elaborating**) describe or work out in detail.
elaboration *noun* [from *e*-[1], + Latin *laborare* = to work]

elapse *verb* (**elapsed, elapsing**) (of time) pass or go by. [from *e*-[1], + Latin *lapsum* = slipped]

elastic[1] *noun* cord or material woven with strands of rubber so that it can stretch.

elastic[2] *adjective* able to be stretched or squeezed and then go back to its original length or shape. **elasticity** *noun*

elated *adjective* with raised spirits, feeling very pleased. **elation** *noun* [from *e*-[1], + Latin *latum* = carried]

elbow[1] *noun* the joint in the middle of the arm.

elbow[2] *verb* push with the elbow.

elder[1] *adjective* older, *my elder brother.*

elder[2] *noun* **1** an older person, *Respect your elders!* **2** an official in certain Churches. **3** a person of recognised authority in an Aboriginal community. [an old form of *older*]

elder[3] *noun* a tree with white flowers and black berries. **elderberry** *noun*

elderly *adjective* rather old.

eldest *adjective* oldest. [an old form of *oldest*]

elect *verb* **1** choose by voting. **2** choose to do something; decide. [from *e*-[1], + Latin *lectum* = chosen]

election *noun* electing; the process of electing Members of Parliament.

elective[1] *adjective* **1** having the power to elect. **2** chosen or filled by election, *an elective office.* **3** involving a choice; optional, *elective surgery; elective subjects.*

elective[2] *noun* an elective course of study.

elector *noun* a person who has the right to vote in an election. **electoral** *adjective*

electorate *noun* **1** all the electors. **2** (*Australian*) an area represented by a Member of Parliament elected by the people who live there.

electric *adjective* **1** of or worked by electricity. **2** causing sudden excitement, *The news had an electric effect.* **electrical** *adjective*, **electrically** *adverb* [from Greek *elektron* = amber (which is easily given a charge of static electricity)]

electrician *noun* a person whose job is to deal with electrical equipment.

electricity *noun* a form of energy carried by certain particles of matter (electrons and protons) used for lighting and heating and for making machines work.

electrify *verb* (**electrified, electrifying**) **1** give an electric charge to something. **2** supply with electric power; cause to work with electricity. **3** thrill with sudden excitement. **electrification** *noun*

electro- *prefix* of or using electricity.

electrocardiogram *noun* a record of the heartbeat traced by an electrocardiograph.

electrocardiograph *noun* an instrument recording the electric currents generated by a person's heartbeat. **electrocardiography** *noun*

electrocute *verb* (**electrocuted, electrocuting**) kill by electricity. **electrocution** *noun*

electrode *noun* a conductor through which electricity enters or leaves an object, substance, or region. [from *electro*-, + Greek *hodos* = way]

electrolyte *noun* a substance that conducts electricity when molten or in solution.

electromagnet *noun* a magnet worked by electricity. **electromagnetic** *adjective*

electron *noun* a particle of matter with a negative electric charge. [see *electric*]

electronic *adjective* **1** (of a device) having or operating with components such as microchips and transistors that control and direct electric currents. **2** carried out or accessed by means of a computer or other electronic device, especially over a network. **3** of electrons; of electronics.
electronically *adverb*

electronic mail see **email**.

electronics *noun* the use or study of electronic devices.

elegant *adjective* graceful and dignified. **elegance** *noun*, **elegantly** *adverb*

elegy (*say* **el**-uh-jee) *noun* (*plural* **elegies**) a sorrowful poem or song, especially for the dead.

element *noun* **1** each of the parts that make up a whole thing. **2** each of more than 100 substances composed of atoms that have the same number of protons. **3** a basic or elementary principle, *the elements of algebra.* **4** a wire or coil that gives out heat in an electric heater, oven, or kettle. **5** a suitable or satisfying environment, *in one's element.* **6** (in mathematics) an entity that is a single member of a set.
the elements the forces of weather, such as rain, wind, and cold.

elementary *adjective* dealing with the simplest stages of something; easy.

elephant *noun* a very large animal with a trunk and tusks.
the elephant in the room a major problem or controversial issue that is obviously present but avoided as a subject for discussion because it is more comfortable to do so. [from Greek *elephas* = ivory (the material of its tusks)]

elephantine (*say* el-uh-**fan**-tuyn) *adjective* very large; clumsy.

elevate *verb* (**elevated**, **elevating**) lift up; put high up. **elevation** *noun* [from *e-*[1], + Latin *levare* = to lift]

elevator *noun* **1** something that raises things. **2** a lift.

eleven *adjective & noun* the number 11; one more than ten. **eleventh** *adjective & noun*

elf *noun* (*plural* **elves**) (in fairy tales) a small being with magic powers.

elfin *adjective* (of a person or their face) small and delicate.

elicit (*say* uh-**lis**-uht) *verb* draw out information by reasoning or questioning.

eligible (*say* **el**-uh-juh-buhl) *adjective* qualified or suitable for something. **eligibility** *noun*

eliminate *verb* (**eliminated**, **eliminating**) get rid of; remove. **elimination** *noun* [from Latin *e-* = out, + *limen* = entrance]

elision (*say* uh-**lizh**-uhn) *noun* omitting part of a word in pronouncing it, e.g. in saying *I'm* for *I am.*

elite (*say* ay-**leet**) *noun* a group of people given privileges that are not given to others. [from Old French *élit* = chosen]

elixir (*say* uh-**lik**-suh) *noun* a sweetened and flavoured liquid medicine. [from Arabic *al-iksir* = substance that would cure illness and change metals into gold]

elk *noun* a large kind of deer.

ellipse (*say* uh-**lips**) *noun* an oval shape. **elliptical** *adjective*

ellipsis (*say* uh-**lip**-suhs) *noun* (*plural* **ellipses**) **1** the omission of words needed to complete a meaning or a grammatical construction. **2** a set of dots (...) indicating an ellipsis.

elm *noun* a tall tree with rough leaves.

El Niño (*say* el **nin**-yoh) *noun* an irregular warming of the surface waters of the eastern Pacific Ocean that has far-reaching effects on weather. [from Spanish *El Niño de Navidad* = the Christmas Child]

elocution (*say* el-uh-**kyoo**-shuhn) *noun* speaking clearly. [same origin as *eloquent*]

elongated *adjective* made longer; lengthened. **elongation** *noun*

elope *verb* (**eloped**, **eloping**) run away secretly with a lover. **elopement** *noun*

eloquent *adjective* speaking fluently and expressing ideas vividly. **eloquence** *noun*, **eloquently** *adverb* [from *e-*[1], + Latin *loqui* = speak]

else *adverb* **1** besides; other, *Nobody else knows.* **2** otherwise; if not, *Run or else you'll be late.*

elsewhere *adverb* somewhere else.

elucidate (*say* uh-**loo**-suh-dayt) *verb* (**elucidated**, **elucidating**) make something clear by explaining it. **elucidation** *noun* [compare *lucid*]

elude (*say* uh-**lood**) *verb* (**eluded**, **eluding**) avoid being caught by someone, *The robber eluded the police.* **elusive** *adjective*

em- *prefix* see **en-**.

emaciated (*say* ee-**may**-see-ay-tuhd) *adjective* very thin from illness or starvation. **emaciation** *noun*

email *noun* (also **e-mail**) messages sent from one computer user to another. **email** *verb*, **emailer** *noun* [short for *electronic mail*]

emanate (*say* **em**-uh-nayt) *verb* (**emanated**, **emanating**) come from a source.

emancipate (*say* uh-**man**-suh-payt) *verb* (**emancipated**, **emancipating**) set free from slavery or other restraints. **emancipation** *noun*

embalm *verb* preserve a corpse from decay by using spices or chemicals.

embankment *noun* a long bank of earth or stone to hold back water or support a road or railway.

embargo *noun* (*plural* **embargoes**) a ban. [from Spanish *embargar* = restrain]

embark *verb* put or go on board a ship or aircraft. **embarkation** *noun*
embark on begin, *They embarked on a dangerous exercise.*

embarrass *verb* make someone feel awkward or ashamed. **embarrassment** *noun*

embassy *noun* (*plural* **embassies**) **1** the official residence or offices of an ambassador. **2** the staff working in an embassy.

embed *verb* (**embedded, embedding**) fix firmly in something solid.

embellish *verb* **1** make something more attractive by the addition of decorative details or features. **2** add details to a story or statement to make it more interesting. **embellishment** *noun*

ember *noun* (usually **embers**) a small piece of glowing coal or wood in a dying fire.

ember attack *noun* burning leaves and twigs etc. carried by the wind during a bushfire that can start new fires and threaten property.

embezzle *verb* (**embezzled, embezzling**) take dishonestly money that was left in your care. **embezzlement** *noun*

emblazon *verb* ornament with heraldic or other emblems.

emblem *noun* a symbol; a device representing something, *Wattle is Australia's floral emblem.* **emblematic** *adjective*

embody *verb* (**embodied, embodying**) **1** express principles or ideas in a visible form, *The house embodies our idea of a modern home.* **2** incorporate; include, *Parts of the old treaty are embodied in the new one.* **embodiment** *noun*

embolism *noun* an obstruction of an artery or vein, typically by a clot of blood or an air bubble.

emboss *verb* decorate with a raised design.

embrace[1] *verb* (**embraced, embracing**) hold closely in your arms.

embrace[2] *noun* embracing; a hug. [from *em-*, + Latin *bracchium* = an arm]

embrocation *noun* a lotion for rubbing on parts of the body that ache.

embroider *verb* **1** ornament cloth with needlework. **2** add made-up details to a story to make it more interesting. **embroidery** *noun*

embroil *verb* involve in an argument or quarrel.

embryo (*say* **em**-bree-oh) *noun* (*plural* **embryos**) **1** a baby or young animal as it starts to grow in the womb; a young bird growing in an egg. **2** anything in its earliest stages of development. **embryonic** (*say* em-bree-**on**-ik) *adjective* [from *em-*, + Greek *bryein* = grow]

emcee *noun* **1** a master of ceremonies. **2** an MC at a club or party.

emend *verb* (**emended, emending**) make corrections and revisions to (a text).

> **Usage** See the note at *amend*.

emerald *noun* **1** a bright green precious stone. **2** its colour.

emerge *verb* (**emerged, emerging**) **1** come out; appear. **2** (of facts) become known. **emergence** *noun*, **emergent** *adjective*

emergency *noun* (*plural* **emergencies**) a sudden serious happening needing prompt action.

emery board *noun* a strip of cardboard with a gritty coating like sandpaper, used for filing nails.

emetic (*say* uh-**met**-ik) *noun* a medicine used to make a person vomit.

emigrate *verb* (**emigrated, emigrating**) leave your own country and go and live in another. **emigrant** *noun*, **emigration** *noun* [from *e-*[1] + *migrate*]

> **Usage** People are *emigrants* from the country they leave and *immigrants* in the country where they settle.

eminence *noun* **1** being eminent; distinction. **2** a piece of ground; a hill.
His Eminence a cardinal's title.

eminent *adjective* famous; distinguished; outstanding, *She is one of the world's most eminent mathematicians.* **eminently** *adverb*

emir (*say* e-**meer**) *noun* a Muslim ruler. [from Arabic *amir* = ruler]

emirate (*say* **em**-uh-ruht) *noun* the territory of an emir.

emission *noun* the production and discharge of something, especially gas or radiation, *carbon emmisions.*

emit *verb* (**emitted, emitting**) produce and discharge something, especially gas or radiation. **emitter** *noun* [from *e-*[1], + Latin *mittere* = send]

emoji *noun* (*plural* **emoji** or **emojis**) a small digital image or icon used to express an idea or emotion, *My favourite emoji is the red heart.* [from Japanese *e* = picture, + *moji* = letter, character]

emolument (*say* ee-**mol**-yuh-muhnt) *noun* payment for work; a salary.

emoticon *noun* a representation of a facial expression such as a smile or frown, formed by various combinations of keyboard characters, *When making a joke you can use an emoticon like the smiley face :), to avoid misunderstanding.*

emotion *noun* a strong feeling in the mind, such as love or hate. **emotional** *adjective*, **emotionally** *adverb*

emotive *adjective* causing emotion.

empathise *verb* (**empathised, empathising**) treat someone with empathy.

empathy *noun* the ability to understand and share the feelings of another, *Both authors have the skill to make you feel empathy with their heroines.* [from *em-*, + Greek *pathos* = feeling]

> **Usage** Do not confuse *empathy* with *sympathy*.

emperor *noun* a man who rules an empire.

emphasis (*say* **em**-fuh-suhs) *noun* **1** special importance given to something. **2** the extra force with which you pronounce part of a word or phrase.

emphasise *verb* (**emphasised, emphasising**) put emphasis on something.

emphatic (*say* em-**fat**-ik) *adjective* using emphasis. **emphatically** *adverb*

emphysema (*say* em-fuh-**see**-muh) *noun* a condition in which the air sacs of the lungs enlarge, causing breathlessness. [late Latin, from Greek *emphusema* = puff up]

empire *noun* **1** a group of countries controlled by one person or government. **2** a set of shops or firms under one control.

empirical *adjective* based on observation or experiment, not on theory, *empirical knowledge.* **empirically** *adverb*

employ *verb* **1** pay a person to work for you. **2** make use of, *Our dentist employs the most modern methods.* **employer** *noun*, **employment** *noun*

employee *noun* a person employed by someone (who is the *employer*).

emporium (*say* em-**paw**-ree-uhm) *noun* a large shop.

empower *verb* give someone the power to do something; authorise.

empress *noun* (*plural* **empresses**) **1** a woman who rules an empire. **2** an emperor's wife.

empty[1] *adjective* **1** with nothing in it. **2** with nobody in it. **3** with no meaning or no effect, *empty promises.* **emptily** *adverb*, **emptiness** *noun*

empty[2] *verb* (**emptied, emptying**) make or become empty.

emu *noun* (*plural* **emus**) a large long-legged Australian bird that cannot fly. [from Portuguese]

emulate *verb* (**emulated, emulating**) try to do as well as someone or something, especially by imitating them. **emulation** *noun*

emulsion *noun* **1** a creamy liquid in which particles of one liquid are dispersed in another. **2** a light-sensitive coating on photographic film. **emulsify** *verb*

en- *prefix* (changing to **em-** before words beginning with *b*, *m*, or *p*) in; into; on. [from Latin or Greek, = in]

enable *verb* (**enabled, enabling**) give the means or ability to do something.

enact *verb* **1** make into a law by a formal process, *Parliament enacted new laws against online piracy.* **2** perform, *enact a play.* **enactment** *noun*

enamel[1] *noun* **1** a shiny substance for coating metal. **2** paint that dries hard and shiny. **3** the shiny surface of teeth.

enamel[2] *verb* (**enamelled, enamelling**) coat or decorate with enamel.

enamoured (*say* e-**nam**-uhd) *adjective* in love with someone. [from *en-*, + French *amour* = love]

en bloc (*say* on **blok**) *adverb* all at the same time; in a block. [French]

encamp *verb* settle in a camp.

encampment *noun* a camp.

encase *verb* (**encased, encasing**) enclose in a case.

encephalitis (*say* en-sef-uh-**luy**-tuhs) *noun* inflammation of the brain. [from Greek *enkephalos* = the brain + *-itis*]

enchant *verb* **1** put under a magic spell. **2** fill with intense delight. **enchanter** *noun*, **enchantment** *noun*, **enchantress** *noun*

encircle *verb* (**encircled, encircling**) surround. **encirclement** *noun*

enclave (*say* **en**-klayv) *noun* a small territory belonging to one nation but lying wholly within the boundaries of another.

enclose *verb* (**enclosed, enclosing**) **1** put a wall or fence round; shut in on all sides. **2** put into a box or envelope.

enclosure *noun* **1** enclosing. **2** an enclosed area. **3** something enclosed with a letter or parcel.

encode *verb* (**encoded, encoding**) convert into a coded form.

encompass *verb* **1** surround. **2** contain.

encore (*say* **ong**-kaw) *noun* a repeated or additional performance of an item at the end of a concert, as called for by an audience. [French, = again]

encounter[1] *verb* **1** meet someone unexpectedly. **2** experience, *We encountered some difficulties.*

encounter[2] *noun* **1** an unexpected meeting. **2** a battle.

encourage *verb* (**encouraged, encouraging**) **1** give confidence or hope; hearten. **2** try to persuade; urge. **3** stimulate; help to develop, *Encourage healthy eating.* **encouragement** *noun*

encroach *verb* intrude upon someone's rights; go further than the proper limits, *The extra work would encroach on their free time.* **encroachment** *noun*

encrust *verb* cover with a crust or layer. **encrustation** *noun*

encrypt *verb* (**encrypted, encrypting**) **1** convert (information or data) into a code, especially to prevent unauthorised access. **2** conceal by this means. **encrypted** *adjective*, **encryption** *noun*

encumber *verb* be a burden to; hamper. **encumbrance** *noun*

encyclical (*say* en-**sik**-li-kuhl) *noun* a formal letter from the pope sent to the bishops of the Catholic Church.

encyclopedia *noun* a book or set of books containing all kinds of information. **encyclopedic** *adjective* [from Greek, = general education]

end[1] *noun* **1** the limit of something. **2** an extreme point or part. **3** the part furthest from the front. **4** a remnant. **5** the finish or final part of something. **6** the half of a sports field or court defended or occupied by one team or player. **7** destruction; death. **8** purpose, *She did it to gain her own ends.*

end[2] *verb* bring or come to an end.

endanger *verb* cause danger to.

endangered *adjective* (of a species) seriously at risk of extinction, *The bilby is an endangered animal.*

endear *verb* cause to be loved, *She endeared herself to us all.* **endearing** *adjective*

endeavour[1] (*say* en-**dev**-uh) *verb* attempt.

endeavour[2] *noun* an attempt.

endemic (*say* en-**dem**-ik) *adjective* (of a disease) often found in a certain area or group of people. [from *en-*, + Greek *demos* = people]

ending *noun* the last part.

endless *adjective* **1** never stopping; infinite. **2** continual. **endlessly** *adverb*

endometriosis *noun* a condition resulting from the appearance of endometrial tissue outside the womb and causing pelvic pain.

endometrium *noun* the membrane lining the womb. **endometrial** *adjective*

endorse *verb* (**endorsed, endorsing**) **1** sign your name on the back of a cheque or document. **2** make an official entry on a licence about an offence committed by its holder. **3** confirm or give your approval to something. **endorsement** *noun* [from Latin *in dorsum* = on the back]

endow *verb* **1** provide a source of income to establish something, *She endowed a scholarship.* **2** provide with an ability or quality, *He was endowed with great talent.* **endowment** *noun*

endure *verb* (**endured, enduring**) **1** suffer or put up with pain or hardship; bear patiently. **2** continue to exist; last. **endurable** *adjective*, **endurance** *noun*

enemy *noun* (*plural* **enemies**) **1** one who hates and opposes or seeks to harm another. **2** a hostile nation or its armed forces.

energetic *adjective* full of energy. **energetically** *adverb*

energy *noun* **1** strength to do things; liveliness. **2** the ability of matter or radiation to do work, *electrical energy.* [from *en-*, + Greek *ergon* = work]

enfold *verb* **1** wrap up. **2** clasp.

enforce *verb* (**enforced, enforcing**) compel people to obey a law or rule. **enforceable** *adjective*, **enforcement** *noun*

enfranchise *verb* (**enfranchised, enfranchising**) give the right to vote in elections. **enfranchisement** *noun*

engage *verb* (**engaged, engaging**) **1** arrange to employ or use, *Engage a cleaner.* **2** occupy the attention of, *They engaged her in conversation.* **3** promise. **4** begin a battle with, *We engaged the enemy.*

engaged *adjective* **1** having promised to marry somebody. **2** in use; occupied.

engagement *noun* **1** engaging something. **2** a promise to marry somebody. **3** an arrangement to meet somebody or do something. **4** a battle.

engaging *adjective* attractive; charming.

engender *verb* give rise to.

engine *noun* **1** a machine that provides power. **2** a vehicle that pulls a railway train; a locomotive. [from Latin *ingenium* = clever invention (compare *ingenious*)]

engineer[1] *noun* an expert in engineering.

engineer[2] *verb* plan and construct or cause to happen, *He engineered a meeting between them.*

engineering *noun* the design and building or control of machinery or of structures such as roads and bridges.

engrave *verb* (**engraved, engraving**) carve or cut a design into a hard surface. **engraver** *noun*, **engraving** *noun*

engross *verb* occupy a person's whole attention, *She was engrossed in her book.*

engulf *verb* flow over and cover; swamp.

enhance *verb* (**enhanced, enhancing**) make a thing more attractive; increase its value. **enhancement** *noun*

enigma (*say* uh-**nig**-muh) *noun* something very difficult to understand; a puzzle.

enigmatic (*say* en-ig-**mat**-ik) *adjective* mysterious and puzzling. **enigmatically** *adverb*

enjoy *verb* get pleasure from something. **enjoyable** *adjective*, **enjoyment** *noun*

enlarge *verb* (**enlarged**, **enlarging**) make or become bigger. **enlargement** *noun*

enlighten *verb* give knowledge to a person; inform. **enlightenment** *noun*

enlist *verb* **1** take into or join the armed forces. **2** obtain someone's support or services, *enlist their help.* **enlistment** *noun*

enliven *verb* make more lively. **enlivenment** *noun*

en masse (*say* on **mas**) *adverb* all together. [French, = in a mass]

enmity *noun* being somebody's enemy; hostility.

enoki (*say* uh-**noh**-kee) *noun* an edible Japanese mushroom. [Japanese]

enormity *noun* (*plural* **enormities**) **1** great wickedness, *the enormity of this crime.* **2** great size; hugeness, *the enormity of their task.*

> **Usage** Many people regard the use in sense 2 as incorrect, but it is now standard.

enormous *adjective* very large; huge. **enormously** *adverb*, **enormousness** *noun* [from *e*-[1], + Latin *norma* = standard]

enough *adjective*, *noun*, & *adverb* as much or as many as necessary, *enough food*; *I have had enough*; *Are you warm enough?*

en passant (*say* on pa-**son**) *adverb* by the way. [French, = in passing]

enquire *verb* (**enquired**, **enquiring**) ask, *He enquired if I was well.* **enquirer** *noun*, **enquiry** *noun*

> **Usage** See the note at *inquire.*

enrage *verb* (**enraged**, **enraging**) make very angry.

enrapture *verb* (**enraptured**, **enrapturing**) fill with intense delight.

enrich *verb* make richer. **enrichment** *noun*

enrol *verb* (**enrolled**, **enrolling**) **1** become a member of a society or institution. **2** make into a member. **3** enter one's name on a list. **enrolment** *noun*

en route (*say* on **root**) *adverb* on the way. [French]

ensconce *verb* (**ensconced**, **ensconcing**) settle comfortably, *ensconced in a chair.*

ensemble (*say* on-**som**-buhl) *noun* **1** a group of things that go together. **2** a group of musicians. [French]

enshrine *verb* (**enshrined**, **enshrining**) keep as if in a shrine, *His memory is enshrined in our hearts.*

ensign *noun* a military or naval flag. [the word is related to insignia]

enslave *verb* (**enslaved**, **enslaving**) make a slave of; force into slavery. **enslavement** *noun*

ensue *verb* (**ensued**, **ensuing**) happen afterwards or as a result.

ensuite (*say* **on**-sweet) *noun* (also **en suite**) a bathroom attached to a bedroom. [French]

ensure *verb* (**ensured**, **ensuring**) make certain of; guarantee, *Good food will ensure good health.*

> **Usage** Do not confuse with *insure.*

entail *verb* make necessary; involve, *This plan entails danger.* **entailment** *noun*

entangle *verb* (**entangled**, **entangling**) tangle. **entanglement** *noun*

entente (*say* on-**tont**) *noun* a friendly understanding between nations. [French]

enter *verb* **1** come in; go in. **2** write or key (information) in a book, computer, etc. **3** register as a competitor.

enterprise *noun* **1** being enterprising; adventurous spirit. **2** an undertaking or project. **3** business activity, *private enterprise.*

enterprising *adjective* willing to undertake new or adventurous projects.

entertain *verb* **1** amuse. **2** have people as guests and give them food and drink. **3** consider, *He refused to entertain the idea.*

entertainer *noun* someone who performs before an audience to amuse or interest them.

entertainment *noun* **1** entertaining; being entertained. **2** something performed before an audience to amuse or interest them.

enthral (*say* en-**thrawl**) *verb* (**enthralled**, **enthralling**) hold spellbound; fascinate.

enthusiasm *noun* a strong liking, interest, or excitement. **enthusiast** *noun*

enthusiastic *adjective* full of enthusiasm. **enthusiastically** *adverb*

entice *verb* (**enticed**, **enticing**) attract or persuade by offering something pleasant. **enticement** *noun*

entire *adjective* whole, complete. **entirely** *adverb*

entirety (*say* en-**tuyuh**-ruh-tee) *noun* completeness; the total.
in its entirety in its complete form.

entitle *verb* (**entitled**, **entitling**) give the right to have something, *This coupon entitles you to a ticket.* **entitlement** *noun*

entitled *adjective* having as a title.

entity *noun* (*plural* **entities**) something that exists as a separate thing.

entomb (*say* en-**toom**) *verb* place in a tomb. **entombment** *noun*

entomology (*say* en-tuh-**mol**-uh-jee) *noun* the study of insects. **entomologist** *noun* [from Greek *entomon* = insect, + *-logy*]

entrails *plural noun* the intestines.

entrance[1] (*say* **en**-truhns) *noun* **1** the way into a place. **2** entering, *Her entrance is the signal for applause.* **3** the right to enter. [from *enter*]

entrance[2] (*say* en-**trahns**) *verb* (**entranced**, **entrancing**) fill with intense delight; enchant. [from *en-* + *trance*]

entrant *noun* a person or group that enters or takes part in something.

entreat *verb* request earnestly; beg.

entreaty *noun* an earnest request.

entrée (*say* **on**-tray) *noun* a dish served before the main course of a meal. [French]

entrench *verb* **1** fix or establish firmly, *These ideas are entrenched in his mind.* **2** settle in a well-defended position. **entrenchment** *noun*

entrepreneur (*say* on-truh-pruh-**ner**) *noun* a person who sets up a business or businesses, taking on financial risk in the hope of profit. **entrepreneurial** *adjective*

entrust *verb* place a person or thing in someone's care.

entry *noun* (*plural* **entries**) **1** an entrance. **2** an act of going or coming in. **3** an item written or printed in a list, diary, account book, or reference book.

entwine *verb* (**entwined**, **entwining**) twine round.

enumerate *verb* (**enumerated**, **enumerating**) count; list one by one. [from *e-*[1], + Latin *numerare* = to number]

enunciate *verb* (**enunciated**, **enunciating**) **1** say or pronounce clearly. **2** express (an idea, theory, etc.) in clear or definite terms. **enunciation** *noun*

envelop (*say* en-**vel**-uhp) *verb* (**enveloped**, **enveloping**) wrap thoroughly.

envelope (*say* **en**-vuh-lohp or **on**-vuh-lohp) *noun* a wrapper or covering, especially a folded cover for a letter.

enviable *adjective* likely to be envied.

envious *adjective* feeling envy. **enviously** *adverb*

environment *noun* **1** physical surroundings and conditions, especially those affecting people's lives. **2** (**the environment**) the external conditions affecting the growth, development, and well-being of plants, animals, and humans. **3** the settings or conditions in which a particular activity is carried on. **environmental** *adjective*

environmentalist *noun* a person who wishes to protect or improve the environment.

environs (*say* en-**vuy**-ruhnz) *plural noun* the surrounding districts, *They all lived in the environs of Adelaide.*

envisage (*say* en-**viz**-ij) *verb* (**envisaged**, **envisaging**) picture in the mind; imagine as being possible, *It is difficult to envisage such a change.*

envoy *noun* an official representative, especially one sent by one government to another. [from French *envoyé* = sent]

envy[1] *noun* **1** a feeling of discontent aroused when someone possesses things that others would like to have for themselves. **2** something causing this, *Their car is the envy of all their friends.*

envy[2] *verb* (**envied**, **envying**) feel envy towards someone.

enzyme *noun* a kind of substance that assists chemical processes.

eon alternative spelling of **aeon**.

ephemeral (*say* ee-**fem**-uh-ruhl) *adjective* lasting only a very short time.

epi- *prefix* on; above; in addition. [from Greek *epi* = on]

epic *noun* **1** a long poem or story about heroic deeds or history. **2** a spectacular film.

epicentre *noun* the point where an earthquake reaches the earth's surface.

epidemic *noun* an outbreak of a disease that spreads quickly among the people of an area. [from *epi-*, + Greek *demos* = people]

epidemiology (*say* ep-uh-dee-mee-**ol**-uh-jee) *noun* the study of the incidence, distribution, and possible control of diseases and other factors relating to health. **epidemiologist** *noun* [from Greek *epidēmia* = prevalence of disease, + *-logy*]

epidermis *noun* the outer layer of the skin. [from *epi-*, + Greek *derma* = skin]

epigram *noun* a short witty saying. [from *epi-* + *-gram*]

epilepsy *noun* a disease of the nervous system, causing convulsions. **epileptic** *adjective & noun*

epilogue (*say* **ep**-uh-log) *noun* a short section at the end of a book or play. [from *epi-*, + Greek *logos* = speech]

EpiPen *noun* (*trademark*) a device for administering adrenalin in the treatment of anaphylaxis.

Epiphany (*say* uh-**pif**-uh-nee) *noun* a Christian festival on 6 January, commemorating the showing of the infant Christ to the 'wise men' from the East.

episcopal (*say* uh-**pis**-kuh-puhl) *adjective* **1** of a bishop or bishops. **2** (of a Church) governed by bishops.

episode *noun* **1** one event in a series of happenings. **2** one program in a radio or television serial.

epistle *noun* a letter, especially one forming part of the New Testament.

epitaph *noun* words written on a tomb or describing a person who has died. [from *epi-*, + Greek *taphos* = womb]

epithet *noun* an adjective; words expressing something special about a person or thing, e.g. 'the Great' in *Alfred the Great.*

epitome (*say* uh-**pit**-uh-mee) *noun* a person or thing embodying a quality, *She is the epitome of kindness.* **epitomise** *verb*

epoch (*say* **ee**-pok) *noun* an era.

equable (*say* **ek**-wuh-buhl) *adjective* steady; calm, *She has an equable manner.*

equal[1] *adjective* **1** the same in amount, size, value, or degree. **2** having the necessary strength, courage, or ability to meet a challenge, *He was equal to the task.* **equally** *adverb*

equal[2] *noun* a person or thing that is equal to another, *She has no equal.*

equal[3] *verb* (**equalled**, **equalling**) be the same in amount, size, value, or degree.

equalise *verb* (**equalised**, **equalising**) make things equal. **equalisation** *noun*

equaliser *noun* a goal or point that makes the score equal.

equality *noun* being equal.

equanimity (*say* ek-wuh-**nim**-uh-tee) *noun* calmness of mind or temper. [from *equi-*, + Latin *animus* = mind]

equate *verb* (**equated**, **equating**) say things are equal or equivalent.

equation *noun* a statement that two amounts are equal, e.g. $3 + 4 = 2 + 5$.

equator (*say* ee-**kway**-tuh) *noun* an imaginary line round the earth at an equal distance from the North and South Poles.

equatorial (*say* ek-wuh-**taw**-ree-uhl) *adjective* of or near the equator.

equestrian (*say* uh-**kwes**-tree-uhn) *adjective* of horse riding. [from Latin *equus* = horse]

equi- *prefix* equal; equally. [from Latin *aequus* = equal]

equilateral (*say* ee-kwuh-**lat**-uh-ruhl) *adjective* (of a triangle) having all sides equal. [from *equi-* + *lateral*]

equilibrium (*say* ee-kwuh-**lib**-ree-uhm) *noun* balance; being balanced. [from *equi-*, + Latin *libra* = balance]

equine (*say* **ek**-wuyn) *noun* of or like a horse. [from Latin *equus* = horse]

equinox (*say* **ee**-kwuh-noks) *noun* (*plural* **equinoxes**) the times of year when day and night are equal in length (about 20 March and 22 September). **equinoctial** *adjective* [from *equi-*, + Latin *nox* = night]

equip *verb* (**equipped**, **equipping**) supply with what is needed.

equipment *noun* the things needed for a particular purpose.

equities *plural noun* stocks and shares not bearing fixed interest.

equity (*say* **ek**-wuh-tee) *noun* fairness; justice. **equitable** *adjective*

equivalent *adjective* equal in importance, meaning, value, etc. **equivalence** *noun* [from *equi-*, + Latin *valens* = worth]

equivocal (*say* ee-**kwiv**-uh-kuhl) *adjective* **1** able to be interpreted in two ways; ambiguous. **2** questionable; suspicious, *an equivocal character.* **equivocally** *adverb* [from *equi-*, + Latin *vocare* = to call]

era (*say* **eer**-ruh) *noun* a period of history.

eradicate *verb* (**eradicated**, **eradicating**) get rid of something; remove all traces of it. **eradication** *noun* [from Latin, = root out (*e-* = out, *radix* = a root)]

erase *verb* (**erased**, **erasing**) **1** rub out. **2** remove a recording on magnetic tape. **eraser** *noun* [from *e-*[1], + Latin *rasum* = scraped]

erasure *noun* **1** erasing. **2** the place where something has been erased.

ere (*say* air) *preposition & conjunction* (*old use*) before.

erect[1] *adjective* standing on end; upright.

erect[2] *verb* set up; build. **erection** *noun*, **erector** *noun*

ermine *noun* **1** a kind of weasel with brown fur that turns white in winter; a stoat. **2** this valuable white fur.

erode *verb* (**eroded**, **eroding**) wear away, *Water eroded the rocks.* **erosion** *noun* [from *e-*[1], + Latin *rodere* = gnaw]

erotic *adjective* arousing sexual feelings. **erotically** *adverb*

err (*say* er) *verb* **1** make a mistake. (Compare **error**.) **2** do wrong. [from Latin *errare* = wander]

errand *noun* a short journey undertaken to deliver or collect something.

errant (*say* **e**-ruhnt) *adjective* **1** misbehaving. **2** wandering; travelling in search of adventure, *a knight errant.* [same origin as *err*]

erratic (*say* uh-**rat**-ik) *adjective* not reliable; not regular. **erratically** *adverb*

erroneous (*say* uh-**roh**-nee-uhs) *adjective* incorrect. **erroneously** *adverb*

error *noun* a mistake. [same origin as *err*]

ersatz (*say* **er**-sats) *adjective* used as a substitute. [German, = replacement]

erudite (*say* **e**-roo-duyt) *adjective* having great knowledge or learning. **eruditely** *adverb*, **erudition** *noun*

erupt *verb* **1** burst out. **2** (of a volcano) shoot out lava. **eruption** *noun* [from *e*-¹, + Latin *ruptum* = burst]

escalate *verb* (**escalated**, **escalating**) make or become greater or more serious, *The riots escalated into a war.* **escalation** *noun*

escalator *noun* a staircase with an endless line of steps moving up or down.

escapade (*say* **es**-kuh-payd) *noun* a reckless adventure; a piece of mischief.

escape¹ *verb* (**escaped**, **escaping**) **1** get yourself free; get out or away. **2** avoid something, *He escaped punishment.*

escape² *noun* **1** escaping. **2** a way to escape.

escapee *noun* a person who has escaped.

escapist *noun* a person who seeks distraction and relief from unpleasant realities, especially in the form of entertainment or fantasy. **escapism** *noun*

escarpment *noun* a steep slope at the edge of some high level ground.

escort¹ (*say* **es**-kawt) *noun* **1** a person or group accompanying a person or thing, especially as a protection. **2** a companion for a social event.

escort² (*say* uh-**skawt**) *verb* act as an escort to somebody or something.

Eskimo *noun* (*plural* **Eskimos** or **Eskimo**) a member of a people living in northern Canada, Alaska, Greenland, and eastern Siberia.

> **Usage** In Canada the term *Inuit* is preferred.

esky *noun* (*Australian trademark*) a portable insulated container for keeping food and drink cold.

esoteric (*say* es-uh-**te**-rik) *adjective* intended only for people with special knowledge or interest.

ESP *abbreviation* extrasensory perception.

especial *adjective* special.

especially *adverb* **1** specially. **2** more than anything else.

espionage (*say* **es**-pee-uh-nahzh) *noun* spying. [from French *espion* = spy]

esplanade *noun* a flat open area used as a promenade, especially by the sea.

espresso *noun* (*plural* **espressos**) coffee made by forcing steam through ground coffee beans. [Italian, = pressed out]

esprit de corps (*say* es-pree duh **kaw**) *noun* loyalty to your group. [French, = spirit of the body]

espy *verb* (**espied**, **espying**) catch sight of.

Esq. *abbreviation* (short for **Esquire**) a title written after a man's surname where no title is used before his name. [from Latin *scutarius* = shield-bearer]

essay¹ (*say* **es**-ay) *noun* **1** a short piece of writing in prose. **2** an attempt.

essay² (*say* uh-**say**) *verb* attempt.

essayist *noun* a writer of essays.

essence *noun* **1** the most important quality or element of something. **2** a concentrated liquid. [from Latin *esse* = to be]

essential¹ *adjective* **1** not able to be done without. **2** fundamental. **essentially** *adverb*

essential² *noun* an essential thing.

establish *verb* **1** set up on a firm or permanent basis, *The United Nations was established in 1945.* **2** show to be true; prove, *He established his innocence.*

establishment *noun* **1** establishing something. **2** a business firm or other institution. **3** (**the Establishment**) people who are established in positions of power and influence.

estate *noun* **1** an area of land with a set of houses or factories on it. **2** a large area of land owned by one person. **3** all that a person owns when they die. **4** (*old use*) a condition or status, *the holy estate of matrimony.*

estate agent *noun* a person whose business is selling or letting houses and land.

esteem¹ *verb* think that a person or thing is excellent.

esteem² *noun* respect and admiration. [the word is related to *estimate*]

ester *noun* a kind of chemical compound.

estimable *adjective* worthy of esteem.

estimate¹ (*say* **es**-tuh-muht) *noun* an approximate judgement, especially of cost, value, or size.

estimate² (*say* **es**-tuh-mayt) *verb* (**estimated**, **estimating**) form an estimate or opinion of. **estimation** *noun*

estranged *adjective* unfriendly after having been friendly or loving. **estrangement** *noun*

estrogen *noun* alternative spelling of **oestrogen**.

estuary (*say* **es**-choo-ree) *noun* (*plural* **estuaries**) the mouth of a river where it reaches the sea and the tide flows in and out. **estuarine** *adjective* [from Latin *aestus* = tide]

et al. *abbreviation* and others. [short for Latin *et alii*]

etc. *abbreviation* and other similar things; and so on. [from Latin *et* = and, + *cetera* = the other things]

etch *verb* **1** engrave a picture with acid on a metal plate, especially for printing. **2** cut or impress deeply, *The scene is etched on my memory.* **etcher** *noun*

etching *noun* a picture printed from an etched metal plate.

eternal *adjective* lasting for ever; not ending or changing. **eternally** *adverb*, **eternity** *noun*

ether (*say* **ee**-thuh) *noun* **1** a colourless liquid that evaporates easily into fumes that are used as an anaesthetic. **2** the upper air.

ethereal (*say* ee-**theer**-ree-uhl) *adjective* light and delicate. **ethereally** *adverb*

ethical (*say* **eth**-uh-kuhl) *adjective* **1** of ethics. **2** morally right; honourable. **ethically** *adverb*

ethics (*say* **eth**-iks) *plural noun* standards of right behaviour; moral principles. [from Greek *ethos* = character]

ethnic *adjective* belonging to a particular racial group within a larger set of people. [from Greek *ethnos* = nation]

etiquette (*say* **et**-uh-kuht) *noun* the rules of correct behaviour.

étude (*say* **ay**-tyood) *noun* a short musical composition, especially one designed to develop a player's skill. [French, = a study]

etymology (*say* et-uh-**mol**-uh-jee) *noun* (*plural* **etymologies**) **1** an account of the origin of a word and its meaning. **2** the study of the origins of words. **etymological** *adjective* [from Greek *etymon* = original word, + *-logy*]

EU *abbreviation* European Union.

eu- (*say* yoo) *prefix* well. [from Greek]

eucalypt *noun* a eucalyptus tree.

eucalyptus (*say* yoo-kuh-**lip**-tuhs) *noun* (*plural* **eucalyptuses**) any tree of the *Eucalyptus* genus of evergreen trees, mostly native to Australia.

eucalyptus oil *noun* a strong-smelling oil obtained from eucalyptus leaves.

Eucharist (*say* **yoo**-kuh-ruhst) *noun* the Christian sacrament in which bread and wine are consecrated and swallowed commemorating the Last Supper of Christ and his disciples. [from Greek, = thanksgiving]

eulogy (*say* **yoo**-luh-jee) *noun* a piece of praise for a person or thing. [from *eu-*, + Greek *-logia* = speaking]

euphemism (*say* **yoo**-fuh-miz-uhm) *noun* a mild word or phrase used instead of an offensive or frank one. *'To pass away' is a euphemism for 'to die'.* **euphemistic** *adjective*, **euphemistically** *adverb* [from *eu-*, + Greek *phēme* = speech]

euphonium (*say* yoo-**foh**-nee-uhm) *noun* a large brass wind instrument. [from *eu-*, + Greek *phone* = sound]

euphoria (*say* yoo-**faw**-ree-uh) *noun* a feeling of general happiness. **euphoric** *adjective* [from *eu-*, + Greek *phoros* = bearing]

Eurasian *adjective* having European and Asian parents or ancestors. **Eurasian** *noun* [from *European* + *Asian*]

eureka (*say* yoo-**ree**-kuh) *interjection* I have found it! [Greek]

euro[1] *noun* (*plural* **euros**) a kind of large kangaroo. [from Adnyamathanha *yuru*]

euro[2] *noun* the unit of money in most countries of the European Union.

European *adjective* of Europe or its people. **European** *noun*

euthanase *verb* (also **euthanise**) **1** subject to euthanasia. **2** put an animal to death humanely.

euthanasia (*say* yoo-thuh-**nay**-*zh*ee-uh) *noun* the painless killing of a patient suffering from an incurable and painful disease or in an irreversible coma. [from *eu-*, + Greek *thanatos* = death]

evacuate *verb* (**evacuated**, **evacuating**) **1** move people away from a dangerous place. **2** make a thing empty of air or other contents. **evacuation** *noun* [from *e-*[1], + Latin *vacuus* = empty]

evacuee *noun* a person who has been evacuated.

evade *verb* (**evaded**, **evading**) avoid a person or thing by cleverness or trickery. [from *e-*[1], + Latin *vadere* = go]

evaluate *verb* (**evaluated**, **evaluating**) **1** estimate the value of something; assess. **2** find a numerical expression or equivalent for (an equation, formula, or function). **evaluation** *noun*

evaluative *adjective* based on or relating to an assessment to form an idea of the value of something.

evangelist *noun* **1** any of the writers of the four Gospels (Matthew, Mark, Luke, John). **2** a person who preaches the Christian faith enthusiastically. **evangelical** *adjective*, **evangelism** *noun* [from Greek, = announce good news (*eu-* = well, + *angelos* = messenger)]

evaporate *verb* (**evaporated**, **evaporating**) **1** change from liquid into steam or vapour. **2** cease to exist, *Their enthusiasm had evaporated.* **evaporation** *noun* [from *e-*[1] = out, + Latin *vapor* = steam]

evasion *noun* **1** evading. **2** an evasive answer or excuse.

evasive *adjective* evading something; not frank or straightforward. **evasively** *adverb*, **evasiveness** *noun*

eve *noun* **1** the day or evening before an important day or event, *Christmas Eve.* **2** (*old use*) evening.

even[1] *adjective* **1** level; smooth. **2** not varying. **3** calm; not easily upset, *an even temper.* **4** equal, *Our scores were even.* **5** able to be divided exactly by two, *Six and fourteen are even numbers.* (Compare **odd** 2.) **evenly** *adverb*, **evenness** *noun*

even[2] *verb* make or become even.

even[3] *adverb* (used to emphasise a word or statement) *She ran even faster.*
even so although that is correct.

even[4] *noun* (*old use*) evening.

evening *noun* the time at the end of the day before most people go to bed.

evensong *noun* the service of evening prayer in the Anglican Church.

event *noun* **1** something that happens, especially something important. **2** an item in a sports contest. [from *e-*[1], + Latin *ventum* = come]

eventful *adjective* full of happenings.

event horizon *noun* the gravitational boundary enclosing a black hole, from which no light escapes.

eventual *adjective* happening at last, *his eventual success.* **eventually** *adverb*

eventuality (*say* ee-ven-choo-**al**-uh-tee) *noun* (*plural* **eventualities**) something that may happen.

ever *adverb* **1** at any time, *the best thing I ever did.* **2** always, *ever hopeful.* **3** (*informal*, used for emphasis) *Why ever didn't you tell me?*

evergreen *adjective* having green leaves all the year. (Compare **deciduous.**) **evergreen** *noun*

everlasting *adjective* **1** lasting for ever. **2** lasting for a very long time, *an everlasting problem.*

every *adjective* each without any exceptions, *We enjoyed every minute.*
every one each one, *Every one of them is growing.*
every other day, week, etc. each alternate one; every second one.

everybody *pronoun* every person.

everyday *adjective* ordinary; usual, *everyday clothes.*

everyone *pronoun* everybody.

everything *pronoun* **1** all things; all. **2** the only or most important thing, *Beauty is not everything.*

everywhere *adverb* in every place.

evict *verb* make people move out from where they are living. **eviction** *noun* [from Latin *evictum* = expelled]

evidence *noun* **1** the available body of facts or information indicating whether a belief or proposition is true or valid. **2** statements made or objects produced in a lawcourt to prove something. **3** signs or indications of something.

evident *adjective* obvious; clearly seen. **evidently** *adverb*

evil[1] *adjective* wicked; harmful. **evilly** *adverb*

evil[2] *noun* something evil; a sin.

evoke *verb* (**evoked, evoking**) produce or inspire a memory or feelings, *The photographs evoked happy memories.* **evocation** *noun*, **evocative** *adjective* [from *e-*[1] = out, + Latin *vocare* = call]

evolution (*say* ev-uh-**loo**-shuhn) *noun* **1** evolving; gradual change into something different. **2** the development of animals and plants from earlier or simpler forms. **evolutionary** *adjective*

evolve *verb* (**evolved, evolving**) develop gradually or naturally. [from *e-*[1], + Latin *volvere* = to roll]

ewe (*say* yoo) *noun* a female sheep.

ewer (*say* **yoo**-uh) *noun* a large water jug.

ex- *prefix* (changing to **ef-** before words beginning with *f*; shortened to **e-** before many consonants) **1** out; away (as in *extract*). **2** up; upwards; thoroughly (as in *extol*). **3** formerly (as in *ex-serviceman*). [from Latin *ex* = out of]

exacerbate (*say* ek-**sas**-uh-bayt) *verb* (**exacerbated, exacerbating**) make a pain or disease or other problem worse.

exact[1] *adjective* **1** correct. **2** clearly stated; giving all details, *exact instructions.* **exactly** *adverb*, **exactness** *noun*

exact[2] *verb* insist on something and obtain it, *He exacted obedience from the recruits.* **exaction** *noun* [from *ex-* = out, + Latin *actum* = performed]

exacting *adjective* making great demands, *an exacting task.*

exactitude *noun* exactness.

exaggerate *verb* (**exaggerated, exaggerating**) make something seem greater or more extreme than it really is. **exaggeration** *noun* [from *ex-* = upwards, + Latin *agger* = heap]

exalt (*say* eg-**zawlt**) *verb* **1** raise in rank, power, or dignity. **2** praise highly. **exaltation** *noun* [from *ex-* = up, + Latin *altus* = high]

Usage *Exalt* is often confused with *exult.*

exam *noun* an examination.

examination *noun* **1** a test of a person's knowledge or skill. **2** examining something; an inspection.

examine *verb* (**examined, examining**) **1** test a person's knowledge or skill. **2** inspect; look at something closely. **examiner** *noun*

example *noun* **1** anything that shows what others of the same kind are like or how they work. **2** a person or thing good enough to be worth imitating.

exasperate *verb* (**exasperated, exasperating**) annoy someone greatly. **exasperation** *noun* [from *ex-* = thoroughly, + Latin *asper* = rough]

excavate *verb* (**excavated, excavating**) **1** dig out. **2** uncover by digging. **excavation** *noun*, **excavator** *noun* [from *ex-* = out, + Latin *cavus* = hollow]

exceed *verb* **1** be greater than; surpass. **2** do more than you need or ought to do; go beyond a thing's limits, *She has exceeded her authority.* [from *ex-* = out, beyond, + Latin *cedere* = go]

exceedingly *adverb* very; extremely.

excel *verb* (**excelled, excelling**) be better than others at doing something. [from *ex-*, + Latin *celsus* = lofty]

Excellency *noun* the title of high officials such as ambassadors and governors.

excellent *adjective* extremely good. **excellence** *noun*, **excellently** *adverb*,

except[1] *preposition* excluding; not including, *They all left except me.*

except[2] *verb* exclude; leave out, *I blame you all, no one is excepted.* [from *ex-* = out, + Latin *-ceptum* = taken]

Usage Do not confuse *except* with *accept.*

excepting *preposition* except.

exception *noun* **1** a person or thing that is left out or does not follow the general rule. **2** exclusion; excepting, *All were pardoned with the exception of traitors.*
take exception raise objections to something.

exceptional *adjective* **1** forming an exception; very unusual. **2** outstandingly good. **exceptionally** *adverb*

excerpt (*say* **ek**-serpt) *noun* a short extract from a film, broadcast, or piece of music or writing.

excess *noun* (*plural* **excesses**) **1** too much of something. **2** the amount by which one number or quantity exceeds another. [from *exceed*]

Usage Do not confuse *excess* with *access.*

excessive *adjective* too much; too great. **excessively** *adverb*

exchange[1] *verb* (**exchanged, exchanging**) give something and receive something else for it. **exchangeable** *adjective*

exchange[2] *noun* **1** exchanging. **2** a place where things (especially stocks and shares) are bought and sold, *a stock exchange.* **3** a place where telephone lines are connected to each other when a call is made.

exchequer *noun* a national treasury into which public funds (such as taxes) are paid. [the word refers to the table, covered with a cloth divided into squares (a *chequered* pattern), on which the accounts of the Norman kings were kept by means of counters]

excise[1] (*say* **ek**-suyz) *noun* a tax charged on certain goods and licences. [from a Dutch word meaning 'tax']

excise[2] (*say* ek-**suyz**) *verb* (**excised, excising**) remove something by cutting it away, *The surgeon excised the tumour.* **excision** *noun* [from *ex-* = out, + Latin *caesum* = cut]

excitable *adjective* easily excited.

excite *verb* (**excited, exciting**) **1** rouse a person's feelings; make eager, *The thought of finding gold excited them.* **2** cause a feeling; arouse, *The invention excited great interest.* **excitedly** *adverb* [from *ex-* = out, + Latin *citare* = wake]

excitement *noun* a strong feeling of eagerness or pleasure.

exclaim *verb* shout or cry out in eagerness or surprise. [from *ex-* = out, + Latin *clamare* = cry]

exclamation *noun* **1** exclaiming. **2** a word or words exclaimed expressing joy or pain or surprise.

exclamation mark *noun* the punctuation mark (!) placed after an exclamation.

exclamatory *adjective* (of a cry or remark) expressing surprise, strong emotion, or pain.

exclude *verb* (**excluded, excluding**) **1** keep somebody or something out. **2** leave out, *Do not exclude this possibility.* **exclusion** *noun* [from *ex-* = out, + Latin *claudere* = shut]

exclusive *adjective* **1** allowing only certain people to be members, *an exclusive club.* **2** not shared with others, *This newspaper has an exclusive report.* **exclusively** *adverb*, **exclusiveness** *noun*
exclusive of excluding; not including, *This is the price exclusive of meals.* [same origin as *exclude*]

excommunicate *verb* (**excommunicated, excommunicating**) cut off a person from membership of a Church. **excommunication** *noun* [from Latin, = put out of the community]

excrement (*say* **eks**-kruh-muhnt) *noun* waste matter excreted from the bowels; dung.

excrete *verb* (**excreted, excreting**) expel waste matter from the body. **excretion** *noun*, **excretory** *adjective* [from *ex-* = out, + Latin *cretum* = separated]

excruciating (*say* ek-**skroo**-shee-ay-ting) *adjective* extremely painful; agonising. **excruciatingly** *adverb* [from *ex-* = thoroughly, + Latin *cruciatum* = tortured]

exculpate (*say* **eks**-kul-payt) *verb* (**exculpated, exculpating**) clear a person of blame. **exculpation** *noun* [from *ex-* = away, + Latin *culpa* = blame]

excursion *noun* a short journey made for pleasure. [from *ex-* = out, + Latin *cursus* = course]

excusable *adjective* able to be excused. **excusably** *adverb*

excuse[1] (*say* ek-**skyooz**) *verb* (**excused, excusing**) **1** forgive. **2** allow someone not to do something or to leave a room etc., *Please may I be excused from swimming?*

excuse[2] (*say* ek-**skyoos**) *noun* a reason given to explain why something wrong has been done. [from *ex-* = away, + Latin *causa* = accusation]

execrable (*say* **ek**-suh-kruh-buhl) *adjective* very bad; abominable.

execute *verb* (**executed, executing**) **1** put someone to death as a punishment. **2** perform or produce something, *She executed the somersault perfectly.* **3** (in computing) run (a file or program). **execution** *noun* [from *ex-* = out, + Latin *sequi* = follow]

executioner *noun* an official who executes a condemned person.

executive[1] (*say* eg-**zek**-yuh-tiv) *noun* **1** a senior person with authority in a business or government organisation. **2** (**the executive**) the branch of a government responsible for putting decisions or laws into effect.

executive[2] *adjective* having the authority to carry out plans or laws.

Executive Council *noun* (in Australia) a body presided over by the governor-general or governor and consisting of government ministers, which gives legal form to Cabinet decisions.

executor (*say* eg-**zek**-yuh-tuh) *noun* a person appointed to carry out the instructions in someone's will.

exemplary (*say* eg-**zem**-pluh-ree) *adjective* very good; being an example to others, *His conduct was exemplary.*

exemplify *verb* (**exemplified, exemplifying**) be an example of something.

exempt[1] *adjective* not having to do something that others have to do, *Charities are exempt from paying tax.*

exempt[2] *verb* make someone or something exempt. **exemption** *noun* [from *ex-* = out, + Latin *emptum* = taken]

exercise[1] *noun* **1** using your body to make it strong and healthy. **2** a piece of work done for practice.

exercise[2] *verb* (**exercised, exercising**) **1** use or employ, *exercise patience.* **2** take or cause to take exercise; train by means of exercises. **3** perplex; worry, *He was much exercised by fear for her safety.* [from Latin *exercere* = keep someone working]

exert *verb* use power or influence, *He exerted all his strength.* **exertion** *noun*
exert yourself make an effort.

exeunt (*say* **ek**-see-uunt) *verb* they leave the stage. [Latin, = they go out]

ex gratia (*say* eks **gray**-shuh) *adjective & adverb* given without being legally obliged to be given, *an ex gratia payment.* [Latin, = from favour]

exhale *verb* (**exhaled, exhaling**) breathe out. **exhalation** *noun* [from *ex-*, + Latin *halare* = breathe]

exhaust[1] *verb* **1** make somebody very tired. **2** use up something completely. **exhaustion** *noun*

exhaust[2] *noun* **1** the waste gases or steam from an engine. **2** the pipe or means through which they are sent out. [from *ex-* = out, + Latin *haustum* = drained]

exhaustive *adjective* thorough; trying everything possible, *We made an exhaustive search.* **exhaustively** *adverb*

exhibit[1] *verb* (**exhibited, exhibiting**) show or display something in public. **exhibitor** *noun*

exhibit[2] *noun* something exhibited.

exhibition *noun* a collection of things arranged for people to look at.

exhibitionist *noun* a person who behaves in a way that is meant to attract attention. **exhibitionism** *noun*

exhilarate (*say* eg-**zil**-uh-rayt) *verb* (**exhilarated, exhilarating**) make someone very happy or lively. **exhilaration** *noun* [from *ex-* = thoroughly, + Latin *hilaris* = cheerful]

exhort (*say* eg-**zawt**) *verb* urge someone earnestly. **exhortation** *noun* [from *ex-*, + Latin *hortari* = encourage]

exhume (*say* eks-**hyoom**) *verb* (**exhumed, exhuming**) dig up something that has been buried. **exhumation** *noun* [from *ex-* = out, + Latin *humare* = bury]

exigency *noun* (*plural* **exigencies**) **1** an urgent need or demand. **2** an emergency.

exile[1] *verb* (**exiled, exiling**) banish.

exile[2] *noun* **1** a banished person. **2** having to live away from your own country, *He was in exile for ten years.*

exist *verb* **1** have a place as part of what is real, *Do ghosts exist?* **2** stay alive, *We cannot exist without food.* **existence** *noun*, **existent** *adjective* [from *ex-*, + Latin *sistere* = stand]

exit[1] *verb* go out or leave a place.

exit[2] *noun* **1** the way out of a building. **2** an act of leaving a place, *The singer made her exit.* [Latin, = he or she goes out]

exodus *noun* (*plural* **exoduses**) the departure of many people. [from Greek, = a way out (*ex* = out, *hodos* = way)]

ex officio[1] (*say* eks uh-**fish**-ee-oh) *adverb* as a result of one's status or position, *The director is a member of this committee ex officio.* [Latin, = from office]

ex officio[2] *adjective* holding a position ex officio, *an ex officio member.*

exonerate *verb* (**exonerated**, **exonerating**) declare or prove that a person is not to blame for something. **exoneration** *noun* [from *ex-* = out, + Latin *oneris* = of a burden]

exorbitant *adjective* much too great; excessive, *exorbitant prices.* [from *ex-* = out, + Latin *orbita* = orbit]

exorcise *verb* (**exorcised**, **exorcising**) get rid of an evil spirit. **exorcism** *noun*, **exorcist** *noun*

exotic *adjective* **1** from another part of the world, *exotic plants.* **2** very unusual, *exotic clothes.* **exotically** *adverb* [from Greek *exo* = outside]

expand *verb* **1** make or become larger or fuller. **2** give more details about something, *He expanded on his initial description.* **expansion** *noun*, **expansive** *adjective* [from *ex-* = out, + Latin *pandere* = spread]

expanse *noun* a wide area.

expatriate (*say* eks-**pat**-ree-uht) *noun* a person living away from their own country. [from *ex-* = away, + Latin *patria* = native land]

expect *verb* **1** think or believe that something will happen or that someone will come. **2** think that something ought to happen, *She expects obedience.*
be expecting (*informal*) be pregnant. [from *ex-* = out, + Latin *spectare* = to look]

expectant *adjective* **1** expecting something to happen; hopeful. **2** expecting a baby. **expectancy** *noun*, **expectantly** *adverb*

expectation *noun* **1** expecting something; being hopeful. **2** something you expect to happen or get.

expedient[1] (*say* ek-**spee**-dee-uhnt) *adjective* **1** suitable; convenient. **2** useful and practical though perhaps unfair. **expediency** *noun*, **expediently** *adverb*

expedient[2] *noun* a means of doing something, especially when in difficulty.

expedite (*say* **eks**-puh-duyt) *verb* (**expedited**, **expediting**) make something happen more quickly.

expedition *noun* **1** a journey made in order to do something. **2** speed; promptness. **expeditionary** *adjective*

expeditious (*say* eks-puh-**dish**-uhs) *adjective* quick and efficient. **expeditiously** *adverb*

expel *verb* (**expelled**, **expelling**) **1** send or force something out, *This fan expels stale air.* **2** make a person leave a school, country, or organisation. **expulsion** *noun* [from *ex-* = out, + Latin *pellere* = drive]

expend *verb* spend; use up.

expendable *adjective* **1** able to be expended. **2** able to be sacrificed in order to gain something.

expenditure *noun* **1** expending. **2** the process or an instance of spending or using up.

expense *noun* the cost of doing something.

expensive *adjective* costing a lot. **expensively** *adverb*, **expensiveness** *noun*

experience[1] *noun* **1** what you learn from doing or seeing things. **2** something that has happened to you.

experience[2] *verb* (**experienced**, **experiencing**) have something happen to you. [same origin as *experiment*]

experienced *adjective* having great skill or knowledge from much experience.

experiment[1] *noun* **1** a test made in order to find out what happens or to prove something. **2** a course of action tentatively adopted without being sure of the outcome. **experimental** *adjective*, **experimentally** *adverb*

experiment[2] *verb* carry out an experiment. **experimentation** *noun* [from Latin *experiri* = to test]

expert[1] *noun* a person with great knowledge or skill in something.

expert[2] *adjective* having great knowledge or skill. **expertly** *adverb*, **expertness** *noun*

expertise (*say* ek-sper-**teez**) *noun* expert knowledge or skill.

expiate (*say* **eks**-pee-ayt) *verb* (**expiated**, **expiating**) atone for; make amends for wrongdoing. **expiation** *noun*

expire *verb* (**expired**, **expiring**) **1** come to an end; stop being usable, *Your licence has expired.* **2** die. **3** breathe out air. **expiration** *noun*, **expiry** *noun* [from *ex-*, + Latin *spirare* = breathe]

explain *verb* **1** make something clear to somebody else; show its meaning. **2** account for something, *That explains his absence.* **explanation** *noun* [from *ex-*, + Latin *planare* = make level or plain]

explanatory (*say* ek-**splan**-uh-tuh-ree) *adjective* giving an explanation.

explicit (*say* ek-**splis**-uht) *adjective* stated or stating something openly and exactly. (Compare **implicit** 1.) **explicitly** *adverb* [from Latin, = unfolded]

explode *verb* (**exploded, exploding**) **1** burst or suddenly release energy with a loud noise. **2** cause a bomb to go off. **3** increase suddenly or quickly. [from *ex-* = out, + Latin *plaudere* = clap the hands (originally said of the audience clapping or hissing to drive a player off the stage)]

exploit[1] (*say* **ek**-sploit) *noun* a brave or exciting deed.

exploit[2] (*say* eks-**ploit**) *verb* **1** use or develop resources. **2** use selfishly. **exploitation** *noun*

exploratory (*say* ek-**splo**-ruh-tuh-ree) *adjective* for the purpose of exploring.

explore *verb* (**explored, exploring**) **1** travel through an unfamiliar area in order to learn about it. **2** examine or investigate something, *We explored the possibilities.* **exploration** *noun*, **explorer** *noun* [from Latin, = search out]

explosion *noun* **1** the violent shattering or blowing apart of something, as is caused by a bomb. **2** a sudden great increase.

explosive[1] *adjective* able to explode.

explosive[2] *noun* an explosive substance.

expo *noun* a large public exhibition.

exponent *noun* **1** a person who expounds something. **2** someone who uses a certain technique. **3** the raised number or symbol written to the right of another (e.g. 3 in 2^3) showing how many times the first one is to be multiplied by itself.

exponential (*say* eks-puh-**nen**-shuhl) *adjective* (of an increase) more and more rapid.

export[1] *verb* **1** send goods or services to another country for sale. **2** spread or introduce ideas and beliefs to another country. **exportation** *noun*, **exporter** *noun*

export[2] *noun* **1** exporting things. **2** something exported. [from *ex-* = away, + Latin *portare* = carry]

expose *verb* (**exposed, exposing**) **1** reveal; uncover. **2** allow light to reach a photographic film so as to take a picture. **exposure** *noun* [from *ex-* = out, + Latin *positum* = put]

exposition *noun* **1** expounding; an explanation. **2** a large public exhibition. **3** (in music) the part of a movement in which themes are presented.

expostulate *verb* (**expostulated, expostulating**) make a protest. **expostulation** *noun*

expound *verb* explain in detail.

express[1] *adjective* **1** going or sent quickly. **2** expressed; clearly stated, *This was done against my express orders.*

express[2] *noun* (*plural* **expresses**) a fast train stopping at only a few stations.

express[3] *verb* **1** put ideas etc. into words; make your feelings known. **2** press or squeeze out, *Express the juice.*

expression *noun* **1** the look on a person's face that shows their feelings. **2** a word or phrase. **3** a collection of mathematical symbols expressing a quantity. **4** the conveying of feeling in a work of art or in the performance of a piece of music. **5** expressing, *this expression of opinion.* **expressionless** *adjective*

expressionism *noun* a style of painting, drama, or music seeking to express the artist's or writer's emotional experience rather than to represent the physical world realistically. **expressionist** *noun*

expressive *adjective* full of expression.

expressly *adverb* **1** clearly; plainly, *This was expressly forbidden.* **2** specially, *designed expressly for children.*

expressway *noun* a multi-laned highway for high-speed traffic.

expulsion *noun* expelling; being expelled. **expulsive** *adjective*

expunge *verb* (**expunged, expunging**) erase; wipe out.

expurgate *verb* remove objectionable matter from a text or account. **expurgation** *noun*

exquisite (*say* **eks**-kwuh-zuht) *adjective* very beautiful. **exquisitely** *adverb* [from *ex-* = out, + Latin *quaesitum* = sought]

extant (*say* ek-**stant**) *adjective* still existing, *the last copy extant.*

extemporise *verb* (**extemporised, extemporising**) speak or produce or do something without advance preparation. **extemporisation** *noun* [from Latin *ex tempore* = impromptu (literally 'out of the time')]

extend *verb* **1** stretch out. **2** make something become longer or larger. **3** offer; give, *Extend a warm welcome to our friends.* **extendible** *adjective*, **extensible** *adjective* [from *ex-* = out, + Latin *tendere* = stretch]

extension *noun* **1** extending; being extended. **2** something added on; an addition to a building.

extensive *adjective* covering a large area or range, *extensive gardens*; *extensive knowledge.* **extensively** *adverb*, **extensiveness** *noun*

extent *noun* **1** the area or length over which something extends. **2** the amount, level, or scope of something, *the full extent of his power.*

extenuating *adjective* making a crime seem less great by providing a partial excuse, *There were extenuating circumstances.* **extenuation** *noun*

exterior[1] *adjective* outer.

exterior[2] *noun* the outside of something. [Latin, = further out]

exterminate *verb* (**exterminated**, **exterminating**) destroy or kill all the members or examples. **extermination** *noun*, **exterminator** *noun* [from *ex-* = out, + Latin *terminus* = boundary]

external *adjective* outside. **externally** *adverb*

extinct *adjective* **1** not existing anymore, *The dodo is an extinct bird.* **2** not burning; not active, *an extinct volcano.* [same origin as *extinguish*]

extinction *noun* **1** making or becoming extinct. **2** extinguishing; being extinguished.

extinguish *verb* **1** put out a fire or light. **2** put an end to; nullify; destroy, *Our hopes of victory were extinguished.* [from Latin *extinguere* = quench]

extinguisher *noun* a portable device for sending out water, chemicals, or gases to extinguish a fire.

extol *verb* (**extolled**, **extolling**) praise.

extort *verb* obtain something by force or threats. **extortion** *noun* [from *ex-* = out, + Latin *tortum* = twisted]

extortionate *adjective* charging or demanding far too much.

extra[1] *adjective* additional; more than is usual, *extra strength.*

extra[2] *adverb* more than usually, *extra strong.*

extra[3] *noun* **1** an extra person or thing. **2** a person acting as part of a crowd in a film or play. [Latin, = outside]

extra- *prefix* outside; beyond (as in *extra-terrestrial*). [from Latin, = outside]

extract[1] (*say* ek-**strakt**) *verb* take out, remove. **extractor** *noun*

extract[2] (*say* **ek**-strakt) *noun* **1** a passage taken from a book, speech, film, etc.; an excerpt. **2** a substance separated or obtained from another. [from *ex-* = out, + Latin *tractum* = pulled]

extraction *noun* **1** extracting. **2** descent; ancestry, *He is of Chinese extraction.*

extradite *verb* (**extradited**, **extraditing**) **1** hand over an accused person to the jurisdiction where the crime was committed. **2** obtain such a person for trial or punishment. **extradition** (*say* ek-struh-**dish**-uhn) *noun* [from *ex-*, + Latin *tradere* = hand over]

extraneous (*say* ek-**stray**-nee-uhs) *adjective* **1** added from outside. **2** not belonging to the matter in hand; irrelevant.

extraordinary (*say* ek-**straw**-duh-nuh-ree) *adjective* very unusual or strange. **extraordinarily** *adverb*

extrapolate (*say* ek-**strap**-uh-layt) *verb* make an estimate of something unknown on the basis of available data. **extrapolation** *noun*

extrasensory *adjective* outside the range of the known human senses.

extravagant *adjective* spending or using too much. **extravagance** *noun*, **extravagantly** *adverb* [from *extra-*, + Latin *vagans* = wandering]

extravaganza *noun* a very spectacular show.

extreme[1] *adjective* **1** very great or intense, *extreme cold.* **2** furthest away, *the extreme north.* **3** going to great lengths in actions or opinions; not moderate. **extremely** *adverb*

extreme[2] *noun* **1** something extreme. **2** either end of something. [from Latin, = furthest outside]

extremist *noun* a person who holds extreme (not moderate) opinions in political or other matters.

extremity (*say* ek-**strem**-uh-tee) *noun* (*plural* **extremities**) an extreme point; the very end.

extricate (*say* **eks**-truh-kayt) *verb* (**extricated**, **extricating**) release from a difficult position. **extrication** *noun* [from *ex-*, + Latin *tricae* = entanglements]

extrovert *noun* **1** an outgoing, socially confident person. **2** a person predominantly concerned with external things or objective considerations. (Compare **introvert** 2.) **extroverted** *adjective* [from *extro-* = outside, + Latin *vertere* = to turn]

extrude *verb* (**extruded**, **extruding**) push or squeeze out. **extrusion** *noun* [from *ex-*, + Latin *trudere* = to push]

exuberant (*say* eg-**zyoo**-buh-ruhnt) *adjective* very lively. **exuberance** *noun*, **exuberantly** *adverb*

exude *verb* (**exuded**, **exuding**) **1** send out; emit. **2** ooze out.

exult *verb* rejoice greatly. **exultant** *adjective*, **exultation** *noun*

> **Usage** *Exult* is often confused with *exalt.*

eye[1] *noun* **1** the organ of the body that is used for seeing. **2** the power of seeing, *She has sharp eyes.* **3** the small hole in a needle. **4** a spot or leaf bud that seems like an eye. **5** the centre of a storm.

eye[2] *verb* (**eyed**, **eyeing**) look at; watch.

eyeball *noun* the ball-shaped part of the eye inside the eyelids.

eyebrow *noun* the fringe of hair growing on the face above the eye.

eyelash *noun* (*plural* **eyelashes**) one of the short hairs that grow on an eyelid.

eyelid *noun* either of the two folds of skin that can close over the eyeball.

eyepiece *noun* the lens to which the eye is applied at the end of a telescope or other optical instrument.

eyesight *noun* the ability to see.

eyesore *noun* something that is ugly to look at.

eyewitness *noun* (*plural* **eyewitnesses**) a person who saw an event and can describe it.

eyrie (*say* **eer**-ree) *noun* the nest of an eagle or other bird of prey.

Ff

F *abbreviation* Fahrenheit.

fable *noun* a short story that teaches about behaviour, often with animals as characters. [from Latin *fabula* = story]

fabric *noun* **1** cloth. **2** the framework of a building (walls, floors, and roof).

fabricate *verb* (**fabricated**, **fabricating**) **1** construct; manufacture. **2** invent, *fabricate an excuse.* **fabrication** *noun*

fabulous *adjective* **1** (*informal*) wonderful. **2** incredibly great, *fabulous wealth.* **3** told of in fables. **fabulously** *adverb*

facade (*say* fuh-**sahd**) *noun* (also **façade**) **1** the front of a building. **2** an outward appearance, especially a deceptive one. [French (same origin as *face*)]

face[1] *noun* **1** the front part of the head. **2** the expression on a person's face. **3** the front or upper side of something. **4** a surface, *A cube has six faces.*

face[2] *verb* (**faced**, **facing**) **1** look or have the front towards something, *Our room faced the sea.* **2** meet and have to deal with something; encounter, *Explorers face many dangers.* **3** cover a surface with a layer of different material. [from Latin *facies* = appearance]

Facebook *verb* **1** spend time using the social networking website Facebook. **2** contact someone via Facebook; post information or a piece of data on Facebook. [from *Facebook*, the trademark name of the social networking website]

facelift *noun* **1** cosmetic surgery to remove wrinkles by tightening the skin of the face. **2** an alteration or procedure that improves the appearance of something, *The old building had a facelift.*

facet (*say* **fas**-uht) *noun* **1** one of the many sides of a cut stone or jewel. **2** one aspect of a situation or problem.

facetious (*say* fuh-**see**-shuhs) *adjective* trying to be funny at an unsuitable time, *facetious remarks.* **facetiously** *adverb*

facial (*say* **fay**-shuhl) *adjective* of the face.

facile (*say* **fas**-uyl) *adjective* done or produced easily or with little thought or care. [from Latin *facilis* = easy]

facilitate (*say* fuh-**sil**-uh-tayt) *verb* (**facilitated**, **facilitating**) make easy or easier. **facilitation** *noun*

facility (*say* fuh-**sil**-uh-tee) *noun* (*plural* **facilities**) **1** something that provides you with the means to do things, *sports facilities.* **2** easiness.

facsimile (*say* fak-**sim**-uh-lee) *noun* an exact copy, especially of written or printed material. [from Latin *fac* = make, + *simile* = a likeness]

fact *noun* **1** something that is certainly true. **2** an item of information. [from Latin *factum* = thing done]

faction *noun* a small united group within a larger one, especially in politics.

factor *noun* **1** something that helps to bring about a result, *Hard work was a factor in her success.* **2** a number by which a larger number can be divided exactly, *2 and 3 are factors of 6.*

factorise *verb* (with reference to a number) resolve into factors.

factory *noun* (*plural* **factories**) a large building where machines are used to make things. [from Latin *facere* = make or do]

factual *adjective* based on facts; containing facts. **factually** *adverb*

faculty *noun* (*plural* **faculties**) **1** any of the powers of the body or mind (e.g. sight, speech, understanding). **2** a department teaching a particular subject or group of subjects in a university.

fad *noun* a person's particular like or dislike; a craze. **faddy** *adjective*

fade *verb* (**faded**, **fading**) **1** lose or cause to lose colour or freshness or strength. **2** disappear gradually. **3** make a sound become gradually weaker (*fade it out*) or stronger (*fade it in* or *up*).

faeces (*say* **fee**-seez) *plural noun* solid waste matter expelled from the anus.

fag *noun* **1** tiring work; drudgery. **2** (*informal*) a cigarette.

fagged *adjective* (*informal*) tired out; exhausted.

faggot *noun* a bundle of sticks bound together, especially as firewood.

Fahrenheit *adjective* measuring temperature on a scale where water freezes at 32° and boils at 212°. [named after G.D. Fahrenheit, German scientist]

faience (*say* **fuy**-ahns) *noun* decorated and glazed earthenware and porcelain.

fail[1] *verb* **1** try to do something but be unable to do it. **2** become weak or useless; break down, *The brakes failed.* **3** not to do something, *He failed to warn me.* **4** grade a candidate or be graded as not having passed an examination.

fail[2] *noun* **without fail** for certain; whatever happens.

failing *noun* a weakness; a fault.

failure *noun* **1** not being able to do something. **2** a person or thing that has failed.

fain *adverb* (*old use*) willingly.

faint[1] *adjective* **1** weak; not clear; not distinct. **2** exhausted; nearly unconscious. **faintly** *adverb*, **faintness** *noun*

faint[2] *verb* become unconscious.

fair[1] *adjective* **1** right or just; according to the rules, *a fair fight.* **2** (of hair or skin) light in colour; (of a person) having fair hair. **3** (*old use*) beautiful. **4** fine; favourable, *fair weather.* **5** moderate; quite good, *a fair number of people.* **fairness** *noun* [from Old English *faeger*]

fair[2] *adverb* fairly, *Play fair!*

fair[3] *noun* **1** a group of entertainments such as roundabouts and sideshows. **2** an exhibition. **3** a market. [from Latin *feriae* = holiday]

fair go *noun* (*Australian*) an equal opportunity; a reasonable chance.

fairly *adverb* **1** justly; according to the rules. **2** moderately, *It is fairly hard.*

fairy *noun* (*plural* **fairies**) an imaginary very small creature with magic powers. **fairyland** *noun* [from an old word *fay*, from Latin *fata* = the Fates, three goddesses who were believed to control people's lives]

fairy bread *noun* (*Australian*) bread buttered and sprinkled with hundreds and thousands.

fairy floss *noun* (*Australian*) a fluffy mass of spun sugar.

fairy penguin *noun* a small penguin.

fairy tale *noun* (also **fairy story**) **1** a story about fairies. **2** an unbelievable story; a lie.

fait accompli (*say* fayt ah-**kom**-plee) *noun* a thing that is already done and not reversible. [French, = accomplished fact]

faith *noun* **1** strong belief; trust. **2** a system of religious belief.
in good faith with honest intentions.

faithful *adjective* **1** loyal and trustworthy. **2** sexually loyal to one partner. **faithfully** *adverb*, **faithfulness** *noun*
Yours faithfully see **yours**.

fake[1] *noun* a thing or person that looks genuine but is not; a forgery. **fake** *adjective*

fake[2] *verb* (**faked, faking**) **1** make something that looks genuine, so as to deceive people. **2** pretend, *They faked illness.* **faker** *noun*

falafel (*say* fuh-**laf**-uhl) *noun* (also **felafel**) a Middle Eastern dish of fried balls of mashed chickpeas with spices. [Egyptian Arabic]

falcon *noun* a kind of hawk often used in the sport of hunting other birds or game. **falconry** *noun*

fall[1] *verb* (**fell, fallen, falling**) **1** come or go down freely, e.g. by force of weight, loss of balance, or by becoming detached. **2** decrease; become lower, *Prices fell.* **3** be captured or overthrown, *The city fell.* **4** die in battle. **5** happen, *Darkness fell.* **6** become, *She fell asleep.*
fall back retreat.
fall back on use for support or in an emergency.
fall for (*informal*) **1** be attracted by a person. **2** be taken in by a deception.
fall out quarrel.
fall through fail, *Their plans fell through.*

fall[2] *noun* **1** the action of falling. **2** (*American*) autumn.

fallacy (*say* **fal**-uh-see) *noun* (*plural* **fallacies**) a false idea or belief. **fallacious** (*say* fuh-**lay**-shuhs) *adjective* [from Latin *fallere* = deceive]

fall guy *noun* (*informal*) an easy victim; a scapegoat.

fallible (*say* **fal**-uh-buhl) *adjective* liable to make mistakes, *All people are fallible.* **fallibility** *noun*

fallopian tube (*say* fuh-**loh**-pee-uhn) *noun* either of two tubes carrying egg cells from the ovaries to the womb. [named after G. Fallopio, Italian anatomist]

fallout *noun* particles of radioactive material carried in the air after a nuclear explosion.

fallow *adjective* (of land) ploughed but left without crops in order to restore its fertility.

fallow deer *noun* a kind of light brown deer.

falls *plural noun* a waterfall.

false *adjective* **1** untrue; incorrect. **2** not genuine; sham; faked. **3** treacherous; deceitful. **falsely** *adverb*, **falseness** *noun*, **falsity** *noun* [from Latin *falsum* = deceived]

falsehood *noun* **1** a lie. **2** telling lies.

falsetto *noun* (*plural* **falsettos**) a high-pitched voice above one's natural range, especially when used by male singers.

falsify *verb* (**falsified, falsifying**) alter a thing dishonestly. **falsification** *noun*

falsity *noun* falseness.

falter *verb* **1** stumble; go unsteadily. **2** hesitate when you speak. **3** become weaker; begin to give way, *His courage faltered.*

fame *noun* being famous. **famed** *adjective*

familiar *adjective* **1** well-known; often seen or experienced. **2** knowing something well, *Are you familiar with this book?* **3** very friendly. **4** too informal. **familiarity** *noun*, **familiarly** *adverb* [same origin as *family*]

familiarise *verb* (**familiarised**, **familiarising**) make familiar; accustom. **familiarisation** *noun*

family *noun* (*plural* **families**) **1** parents and their children, sometimes including grandchildren and other relations. **2** a person's children. **3** all the descendants of a common ancestor. **4** a group of things that are alike in some way. [from Latin *familia* = household]

family tree *noun* a diagram showing how people in a family are related.

famine *noun* a very bad shortage of food in an area. [from Latin *fames* = hunger]

famished *adjective* very hungry.

famous *adjective* known to very many people.

famously *adverb* (*informal*) very well, *They get on famously.*

fan[1] *noun* a device for making air move about so as to cool people or things.

fan[2] *verb* (**fanned**, **fanning**) send a current of air on something.

fan[3] *noun* an enthusiast; a great admirer or supporter. [short for *fanatic*]

fanatic *noun* a person who is very enthusiastic or too enthusiastic about something. **fanatical** *adjective*, **fanatically** *adverb*, **fanaticism** *noun*

fanciful *adjective* **1** imagining things. **2** quaint; imaginative, *fanciful designs.*

fancy[1] *noun* (*plural* **fancies**) **1** a liking or desire for something. **2** imagination.

fancy[2] *adjective* decorated; elaborate.

fancy[3] *verb* (**fancied**, **fancying**) **1** believe, *I fancy it's raining.* **2** imagine. **3** have a liking or desire for something. [originally a shortened spelling of *fantasy*]

fanfare *noun* a short piece of loud music played on trumpets.

fang *noun* a long sharp tooth.

fanlight *noun* a window above a door.

fantail *noun* a flycatcher or pigeon with a fan-shaped tail.

fantasia (*say* fan-**tay**-zee-uh) *noun* an imaginative piece of music or writing.

fantasise *verb* (**fantasised**, **fantasising**) imagine in fantasy; daydream.

fantastic *adjective* **1** (*informal*) excellent. **2** designed in a very fanciful way. **fantastically** *adverb*

fantasy *noun* (*plural* **fantasies**) something imaginary or fantastic.

FAQ *abbreviation* frequently asked questions.

far[1] *adverb* **1** at or to a great distance, *We didn't go far.* **2** much; by a great amount, *This is far better.*

far[2] *adjective* distant; remote, *On the far side of the river.*

farce *noun* **1** an exaggerated comedy. **2** events that are ridiculous or a pretence. **farcical** *adjective*

fare[1] *noun* **1** the price charged for a passenger to travel. **2** food and drink, *There was only very plain fare.*

fare[2] *verb* (**fared**, **faring**) get along; progress, *How did they fare?*

farewell[1] *interjection & noun* goodbye.

farewell[2] *verb* (*Australian*) say goodbye to someone leaving a job or district, usually with a formal gathering.

farm[1] *noun* an area of land where someone grows crops or keeps animals for food or other use. **farmhouse** *noun*, **farmyard** *noun*

farm[2] *verb* **1** grow crops or raise livestock. **2** use land for growing crops; cultivate.

farmer *noun* a person who owns or manages a farm.

farrier (*say* **fa**-ree-uh) *noun* a smith who shoes horses. **farriery** *noun* [from Latin *ferrum* = iron, an iron horseshoe]

farrow *noun* a litter of pigs.

farther *adverb & adjective* at or to a greater distance; more distant.

> **Usage** *Farther* and *farthest* are used only in connection with distance (e.g. *She lives farther from the school than I do*), but even in such cases many people prefer to use *further*. Only *further* can be used to mean 'additional', e.g. in *We must make further inquiries*. If you are not sure which is right, use *further*.

farthest *adverb & adjective* at or to the greatest distance; most distant.

farthing *noun* a former coin worth one quarter of a penny. [from Old English *feorthing* = one fourth]

fascinate *verb* (**fascinated**, **fascinating**) be very attractive or interesting to somebody. **fascination** *noun* [from Latin, = cast a spell]

fascism (*say* **fash**-iz-uhm) *noun* an authoritarian and nationalistic right-wing system of government. **fascist** *noun* [from Latin *fasces*, the bundle of rods with an axe through it, carried before a magistrate in ancient Rome as a symbol of his power to punish people]

fashion[1] *noun* **1** the style of clothes or other things that most people like at a particular time. **2** a way of doing something, *Continue in the same fashion.* **fashionable** *adjective*, **fashionably** *adverb*

fashion[2] *verb* make in a particular shape or style.

fast[1] *adjective* **1** moving or done quickly; rapid. **2** allowing fast movement, *a fast road.* **3** showing a time later than the correct time, *Your watch is fast.* **4** firmly fixed or attached. **5** not likely to fade, *fast colours.* **fastness** *noun*

fast[2] *adverb* **1** quickly, *Run fast!* **2** firmly; securely, *They are fast asleep.*

fast[3] *verb* go without food. **fast** *noun*

fasten *verb* fix one thing firmly to another. **fastener** *noun*, **fastening** *noun*

fastidious *adjective* choosing carefully and liking only what is very good. **fastidiously** *adverb*, **fastidiousness** *noun*

fat[1] *noun* **1** the white greasy part of meat. **2** oil or grease used in cooking. **the fat of the land** the best food.

fat[2] *adjective* (**fatter**, **fattest**) **1** having a very thick round body. **2** thick, *a fat book.* **3** full of fat. **fatness** *noun*

fatal *adjective* causing death or disaster, *a fatal accident.* **fatally** *adverb*

fatalist *noun* a person who accepts whatever happens and thinks it could not have been avoided. **fatalism** *noun*, **fatalistic** *adjective*

fatality (*say* fuh-**tal**-uh-tee) *noun* (*plural* **fatalities**) a death caused by an accident, war, or other disaster.

fate *noun* **1** a power that is thought to make things happen. **2** what will happen or has happened to somebody or something; destiny.

fated *adjective* destined by fate; doomed, *the fated lovers, Romeo and Juliet.*

fateful *adjective* bringing events that are important and usually unpleasant. **fatefully** *adverb*

father[1] *noun* **1** a man in relation to his child or children. **2** the title of certain priests. **fatherly** *adjective*

father[2] *verb* be the father of, *He fathered six children.* [from Old English *faeder*]

father-in-law *noun* (*plural* **fathers-in-law**) the father of a married person's husband or wife.

Father's Day *noun* a tribute to fathers, in Australia the first Sunday in September.

fathom[1] *noun* a unit of six feet (about 1.8 metres), used in measuring the depth of water.

fathom[2] *verb* **1** measure the depth of something. **2** get to the bottom of something; work it out. **fathomless** *adjective*

fatigue *noun* **1** tiredness. **2** weakness in metals, caused by stress. **3** (**fatigues**) military clothing. **fatigued** *adjective* [from Latin *fatigare* = tire]

fatten *verb* make or become fat.

fatty *adjective* like fat; containing fat.

fatuous *adjective* silly. **fatuity** *noun*, **fatuously** *adverb*, **fatuousness** *noun*

fault[1] *noun* **1** anything that makes a person or thing imperfect; a flaw or mistake. **2** the responsibility for something wrong, *It wasn't your fault.* **3** a break in a layer of rock.

fault[2] *verb* **1** find faults in something. **2** form a fault. [from Latin *fallere* = deceive]

faultless *adjective* without a fault. **faultlessly** *adverb*, **faultlessness** *noun*

faulty *adjective* having a fault or faults. **faultily** *adverb*, **faultiness** *noun*

faun *noun* (in myths) a god of the woods and fields, with a goat's legs, horns, and tail. [from the name of Faunus, an ancient Roman country-god (see *fauna*)]

fauna *noun* the animals of a certain area or period of time. (Compare **flora**.) [from the name of Fauna, an ancient Roman country-goddess, sister of Faunus (see *faun*)]

faux pas (*say* foh **pah**) *noun* an embarrassing blunder. [French, = false step]

fave *noun & adjective* (*informal*) favourite.

favela *noun* (*say* fah-**vel**-uh) (in Brazil) a shack or shanty town; a slum. [Portuguese]

favour[1] *noun* **1** a kind or helpful act. **2** approval; goodwill. **3** friendly support shown to one person or group but not to another, *without fear or favour.*

favour[2] *verb* **1** be in favour of something. **2** show favour to a person.

favourable *adjective* **1** helpful. **2** approving; pleasing. **favourably** *adverb*

favourite[1] *adjective* liked or preferred above others, *Pizza is my favourite food.*

favourite[2] *noun* **1** a person or thing liked or preferred above others, *Pick your favourite out of the two flavours.* **2** a competitor generally expected to win. **3** a record of the address of a website or other data made to enable quick access; a bookmark.

favourite[3] *verb* record the address of a website or other data to enable quick access in future.

favouritism *noun* unfairly being kinder to one person than to others.

fawn[1] *noun* **1** a young deer. **2** a light brown colour.

fawn[2] *verb* try to win a person's favour or affection by flattery and humility.

fax *noun* **1** a system for transmitting exact copies of documents using telephone networks. **2** a copy produced in this way. **fax** *verb* [from *facsimile*]

faze *verb* (*informal*) disconcert, daunt.

fear[1] *noun* a feeling that something unpleasant may happen.

fear[2] *verb* feel fear; be afraid of somebody or something.

fearful *adjective* **1** feeling fear; afraid. **2** causing fear or horror, *a fearful monster.* **3** (*informal*) very great or bad. **fearfully** *adverb*

fearless *adjective* without fear. **fearlessly** *adverb*, **fearlessness** *noun*

fearsome *adjective* frightening.

feasible *adjective* able to be done; possible. **feasibility** *noun*, **feasibly** *adverb*

feast *noun* **1** a large splendid meal. **2** a religious festival. **feast** *verb* [from Latin *festus* = joyful]

feat *noun* a brave or clever deed.

feather[1] *noun* one of the very light coverings that grow from a bird's skin. **feathery** *adjective*

feather[2] *verb* cover or line with feathers.

featherweight *noun* **1** a person who weighs very little. **2** a boxer weighing between 54 and 57 kilograms.

feature[1] *noun* **1** any part of the face (e.g. mouth, nose, eyes). **2** an important or noticeable part; a characteristic. **3** a long or important film, broadcast program, or newspaper article.

feature[2] *verb* (**featured**, **featuring**) make or be a noticeable part of something.

febrile (*say* **fee**-bruyl) *adjective* feverish. [from Latin *febris* = fever]

February *noun* the second month of the year. [from Latin *februa* = purification feast]

feckless *adjective* feeble and incompetent; irresponsible. [from Scottish *feck* = effect, + *-less* = without]

fed *past tense & past participle* of **feed**[1]. **fed up** (*informal*) discontented.

federal *adjective* **1** of a system in which several states are ruled by a central government but are responsible for their own internal affairs. **2** of the Commonwealth of Australia, as distinct from the states. [from Latin *foederis* = of a treaty]

federation *noun* **1** a federal group of states. **2** (**Federation**) the formation of the Commonwealth of Australia in 1901 by the uniting of the six Australian colonies.

fee *noun* a charge for something.

feeble *adjective* weak; without strength. **feebleness** *noun*, **feebly** *adverb* [from Latin *flebilis* = wept over]

feed[1] *verb* (**fed**, **feeding**) **1** give food to a person or animal. **2** take food. **3** supply; pass a supply of material to, *feed more coins into the parking meter.* **feeder** *noun*

feed[2] *noun* **1** a meal. **2** food for animals. **3** a broadcast distributed from a central source by a satellite or network.

feedback *noun* the return of information about an event or thing; a response.

feel[1] *verb* (**felt**, **feeling**) **1** touch something to find out what it is like. **2** be aware of something. **3** have an opinion. **4** give a certain sensation, *It feels warm.* **feel like** (*informal*) want, be in the mood for.

feel[2] *noun* the sensation caused by feeling something, *I like the feel of silk.*

feeler *noun* **1** a long thin projection on an insect's or crustacean's body, used for feeling; an antenna. **2** a cautious question or suggestion to test people's reactions.

feeling *noun* **1** the ability to feel things; the sense of touch. **2** what a person feels. **3** an idea or opinion.

feet *plural* of **foot**.

feign (*say* fayn) *verb* pretend.

feint[1] (*say* faynt) *noun* a slight attack or movement made to divert attention from the main attack coming elsewhere.

feint[2] *verb* make a feint.

feisty (*say* **fuy**-stee) *adjective* (**feistier**, **feistiest**) (*informal*) spirited; aggressive.

felafel alternative spelling of **falafel**.

felicity *noun* **1** great happiness. **2** a pleasing manner or style, *He expressed himself with great felicity.* **felicitous** *adjective*, **felicitously** *adverb*

feline (*say* **fee**-luyn) *adjective* of cats; cat-like. [from Latin *feles* = cat]

fell[1] *past tense* of **fall**[1].

fell[2] *verb* cause to fall; cut or knock down, *They were felling the trees.*

fell[3] *noun* a piece of wild hilly country, especially in the north of England.

fellow[1] *noun* **1** a friend or companion; one who belongs to the same group. **2** (*informal*) a man or boy. **3** a member of a learned society.

fellow[2] *adjective* of the same group or kind, *Her fellow students supported her.*

fellowship *noun* **1** friendship. **2** a group of friends; a society.

felon (*say* **fel**-uhn) *noun* a criminal. [from Latin *fellonis* = of an evil person]

felony (*say* **fel**-uh-nee) *noun* (*plural* **felonies**) a serious crime.

felt[1] *past tense & past participle* of **feel[1]**.

felt[2] *noun* a thick fabric made of fibres of wool or other material pressed together.

female[1] *adjective* of the sex that can bear offspring or produce eggs or fruit.

female[2] *noun* a female person, animal, or plant.

feminine *adjective* of or like women; suitable for women. **femininity** *noun* [from Latin *femina* = woman]

feminist *noun* a person who believes that women should be given the same rights and status as men. **feminism** *noun*

femur (*say* **fee**-muh) *noun* (*plural* **femurs** or **femora**) the thigh bone.

fen *noun* an area of low-lying marshy or flooded ground.

fence[1] *noun* **1** a barrier, railing, or other upright structure enclosing an area of ground to prevent or control access or escape. **2** a structure for a horse to jump over. **3** (*informal*) a person who buys stolen goods and sells them again.

fence[2] *verb* (**fenced**, **fencing**) **1** put a fence round or along something. **2** fight with long narrow swords (called *foils*) as a sport. **fencer** *noun* [from *defence*]

fend *verb* **fend for** provide things for someone. **fend off** keep a person or thing away from yourself. [from *defend*]

fender *noun* **1** something placed round a fireplace to stop coals from falling into the room. **2** something hung over the side of a boat to protect it from knocks. **3** a car's bumper bar.

feng shui (*say* fung **shway**) *noun* a traditional Chinese system of laws governing the design of buildings and their interiors. [from Chinese *feng* = wind, + *shui* = water]

fennel *noun* a plant with a bulbous stem used as a vegetable, and fragrant seeds used for flavouring.

feral *adjective* **1** wild; untamed, *feral cats in the bush.* **2** (*Australian informal*) (of a person) dirty; wild in behaviour; unconventional.

ferment[1] (*say* fuh-**ment**) *verb* bubble and change chemically by the action of a substance such as yeast. **fermentation** *noun*

ferment[2] (*say* **fer**-ment) *noun* **1** fermenting. **2** an excited or agitated condition.

fermion *noun* any of several subatomic particles. [named after Enrico Fermi, Italian-born US atomic physicist]

fern *noun* a plant with feathery leaves and no flowers.

ferocious *adjective* fierce; savage. **ferociously** *adverb*, **ferocity** *noun* [from Latin *ferox* = bold, fierce]

ferret[1] *noun* a small animal used in catching rabbits and rats.

ferret[2] *verb* (**ferreted**, **ferreting**) **1** hunt with a ferret. **2** search; rummage. [from Latin *fur* = thief]

ferric *adjective* (also **ferrous**) containing iron. [from Latin *ferrum* = iron]

Ferris wheel *noun* a giant revolving vertical wheel with passenger cars on its outer edge. [named after G.W.G. Ferris, US inventor]

ferry[1] *verb* (**ferried**, **ferrying**) transport people or things, especially across water.

ferry[2] *noun* (*plural* **ferries**) a boat or aircraft used in ferrying.

fertile *adjective* **1** producing good crops, *fertile soil.* **2** able to produce offspring. **3** able to produce ideas, *a fertile imagination.* **fertility** *noun*

fertilise *verb* (**fertilised**, **fertilising**) **1** add substances to the soil to make it more fertile. **2** put pollen into a plant or sperm into an egg or female animal so that it develops seed or young. **fertilisation** *noun*, **fertiliser** *noun*

fervent *adjective* (also **fervid**) showing warm or strong feeling. **fervency** *noun*, **fervently** *adverb*, **fervour** *noun* [from Latin *fervens* = boiling]

fester *verb* **1** become septic and filled with pus. **2** cause resentment for a long time.

festival *noun* a time when people arrange special celebrations, performances, or other events. [same origin as *feast*]

festive *adjective* of a festival; suitable for a festival; joyful. **festively** *adverb*

festivity *noun* (*plural* **festivities**) a festive occasion or celebration.

festoon[1] *noun* a chain of flowers, leaves, or ribbons hung as a decoration.

festoon[2] *verb* decorate with ornaments.

festy *adjective* (**festier**, **festiest**) (*informal*) **1** disgusting; revolting. **2** dirty.

feta (*say* **fet**-uh) *noun* a soft white salty cheese originally from Greece.

fetch *verb* **1** go for and bring back, *fetch some milk*; *fetch a doctor.* **2** be sold for a particular price, *The chairs fetched $20.*

fete[1] (*say* fayt) *noun* (also **fête**) an outdoor fundraising event with stalls and sideshows.

fete[2] *verb* (**feted**, **feting**) (also **fête**) honour a person with celebrations. [same origin as *feast*]

fetish *noun* **1** a form of sexual desire in which gratification is linked to an abnormal degree to a particular object, item of clothing, part of the body, etc. **2** an excessive and irrational devotion or commitment to a particular thing. **3** an object supposed to have magical powers. [from Portuguese *feitiço* = a charm]

fetlock *noun* the part of a horse's leg above and behind the hoof.

fetter[1] *noun* a chain or shackle put round a prisoner's ankle.

fetter[2] *verb* put fetters on a prisoner.

fettle *noun* condition, *in fine fettle.*

fettler *noun* a railway maintenance worker.

fetus *noun* alternative spelling of **foetus**.

feud (*say* fyood) *noun* a long-lasting quarrel or enmity.

feudal (*say* **fyoo**-duhl) *adjective* of the system used in the Middle Ages in which people could farm land in exchange for work done for the owner. **feudalism** *noun*

fever *noun* **1** an abnormally high body temperature, usually with an illness. **2** excitement; agitation. **fevered** *adjective*, **feverish** *adjective*, **feverishly** *adverb*

few[1] *adjective* not many. **fewness** *noun*

> **Usage** *Fewer* versus *less*: strictly speaking, the rule is that *fewer*, the comparative form of *few*, is used with words denoting people or countable things ('*fewer students*'; '*fewer books*'). *Less*, on the other hand, is used with mass nouns, denoting things that cannot be counted ('*less butter*'; '*less bother*'). It is regarded as incorrect in standard English to use *less* with count nouns, as in '*less people*' or '*less words*'.

few[2] *noun* a small number of people or things.

fez *noun* (*plural* **fezzes**) a high flat-topped red hat with a tassel, worn by Muslim men in some countries. [named after Fez, a town in Morocco]

fiancé (*say* fee-**on**-say) *noun* a man who is engaged to be married. [French, = betrothed]

fiancée (*say* fee-**on**-say) *noun* a woman who is engaged to be married.

fiasco (*say* fee-**as**-koh) *noun* (*plural* **fiascos**) a complete failure. [from Italian]

fib *noun* a lie about something unimportant. **fib** *verb*, **fibber** *noun*

fibre *noun* **1** a very thin thread. **2** a substance made of thin threads. **3** indigestible material in certain foods that stimulates the action of the intestines. **fibrous** *adjective*

fibreglass *noun* **1** fabric made from glass fibres. **2** plastic containing glass fibres.

fibril *noun* (*say* **fib**-ruhl or **fuy**-bruhl) a small fibre.

fibrillate *verb* **1** (of a muscle, especially in the heart) make a quivering movement due to uncoordinated contraction of the individual fibrils. **2** (of a fibre) split into fibrils. **fibrillation** *noun*

fibro *noun* (*Australian*) (also **fibro-cement**) a building material made from sand, cellulose fibre, and cement.

fibromyalgia (*say* fuy-broh-muy-**al**-jee-uh) *noun* a rheumatic condition with stiffness and tenderness at specific points of the body.

fibula (*say* **fib**-yuh-luh) *noun* (*plural* **fibulae** or **fibulas**) **1** the bone on the outer side of the lower part of the leg. **2** an ancient brooch or clasp. [Latin]

fickle *adjective* often changing; not constant or loyal. **fickleness** *noun*

fiction *noun* **1** writings about events that have not really happened; stories and novels. **2** something imagined or untrue. **fictional** *adjective* [from Latin *fictio* = pretending]

fictitious *adjective* imagined; untrue.

fiddle[1] *noun* **1** a violin. **2** (*informal*) a swindle.

fiddle[2] *verb* (**fiddled**, **fiddling**) **1** play the violin. **2** fidget or tinker with something, using your fingers. **3** (*informal*) swindle; get or change something dishonestly. **fiddler** *noun*

fiddly *adjective* small and awkward to use or do.

fidelity *noun* **1** faithfulness; loyalty. **2** accuracy; the exactness with which sound is reproduced. [from Latin *fidelitas* = faithfulness]

fidget[1] *verb* (**fidgeted**, **fidgeting**) **1** make small restless movements. **2** worry. **fidgety** *adjective*

fidget[2] *noun* a person who fidgets. [from a dialect word *fidge* = twitch]

fief (*say* feef) *noun* (*old use*) an estate held by a noble under feudalism.

field[1] *noun* **1** a piece of land with grass or crops growing on it. **2** a sportsground, *a football field.* **3** an area of activity or study, *recent advances in the field of medicine.* **4** a battlefield. **5** those who are taking part in a race or outdoor game. **6** (in computing) a section of a record, representing a unit of information.

field[2] *verb* **1** stop or catch the ball in cricket or a similar game. **2** be on the side not batting in cricket or a similar game. **3** put a team into a match, *They fielded their best players.* **fielder** *noun*, **fieldsman** *noun*

field day *noun* **1** an exciting or productive time. **2** (*Australian*) a day set aside for the display of agricultural machinery.

field events *plural noun* athletic sports other than races, e.g. long jump.

fieldwork *noun* practical work or research done in various places, not in a library or museum or laboratory.

fiend (*say* feend) *noun* **1** an evil spirit; a devil. **2** a very wicked or cruel person. **3** an enthusiast, *a fresh-air fiend.* **fiendish** *adjective*

fierce *adjective* **1** angry and violent or cruel. **2** intense, *fierce heat.* **fiercely** *adverb*, **fierceness** *noun*

fiery *adjective* **1** full of flames or heat. **2** full of emotion. **3** easily made angry.

fiesta (*say* fee-**es**-tuh) *noun* a holiday or festival.

fife *noun* a small shrill flute.

fifteen *noun & adjective* **1** the number 15; one more than fourteen. **2** a team in rugby union football. **fifteenth** *adjective & noun*

fifth *adjective & noun* next after the fourth. **fifthly** *adverb*

fifty *noun & adjective* (*plural* **fifties**) the number 50; five times ten. **fiftieth** *adjective & noun*

fifty-fifty *adjective & adverb* **1** shared equally between two people or groups. **2** evenly balanced, *a fifty-fifty chance.*

fig *noun* a soft fruit full of small seeds.

fight[1] *noun* **1** a violent confrontation or struggle; a war or battle. **2** an argument or quarrel. **3** an attempt to achieve or overcome something, *the fight against poverty.*

fight[2] *verb* (**fought**, **fighting**) **1** have a fight. **2** attempt to achieve something. **3** attempt to overcome something. **fighter** *noun*

figment *noun* something imagined, *a figment of the imagination.*

figurative *adjective* metaphorical, not literal; using a figure of speech. **figuratively** *adverb*

figure[1] *noun* **1** the symbol of a number. **2** a diagram or illustration. **3** a pattern or shape; the shape of someone's body. **4** a representation of a person or animal in drawing or sculpture. [from Latin *figura* = shape]

figure[2] *verb* (**figured**, **figuring**) **1** imagine. **2** appear or take part in something. **figure out** work something out.

figurehead *noun* **1** a carved figure decorating the prow of a sailing ship. **2** a person who is head of a country or organisation but has no real power.

figure of speech *noun* a word or phrase used for dramatic effect and not intended literally, e.g. '*a flood of emails*'.

filament *noun* a thread or thin wire. [same origin as *file*[4]]

filch *verb* steal something slyly; pilfer.

file[1] *noun* a metal tool with a rough surface that is rubbed on things to shape them or make them smooth.

file[2] *verb* (**filed**, **filing**) shape or smooth with a file.

file[3] *noun* **1** a folder, cover, or box for keeping papers in order. **2** a set of papers kept in this. **3** a set of data stored under one reference in a computer. **4** a line of people one behind the other.

file[4] *verb* (**filed**, **filing**) **1** put into a file. **2** walk in a file, *They filed out.* [from Latin *filum* = thread (because a string of wire was put through papers to hold them in order)]

filial (*say* **fil**-ee-uhl) *adjective* of a son or daughter. [from Latin *filius* = son, *filia* = daughter]

filibuster *verb* try to delay or prevent the passing of a law by making long speeches. **filibuster** *noun*

filigree *noun* ornamental lace-like work of twisted metal wire.

fill[1] *verb* **1** make or become full. **2** block up a hole or cavity. **filler** *noun*

fill[2] *noun* enough to fill a person or thing.

fillet[1] *noun* a piece of fish or meat without bones.

fillet[2] *verb* (**filleted**, **filleting**) remove the bones from fish or meat.

filling *noun* **1** something used to fill a hole or gap, e.g. in a tooth. **2** something put in pastry to make a pie, or between layers of bread to make a sandwich.

filly *noun* (*plural* **fillies**) a young female horse.

film[1] *noun* **1** a story or event recorded by a camera as a set of moving pictures, and shown in a cinema or on television; a copy of this, e.g. on a DVD. **2** a rolled strip or sheet of thin plastic coated with material that is sensitive to light, used for taking photographs or making a motion picture. **3** a very thin layer, *a film of grease.*

film[2] *verb* make a film of a story or event.

filmy *adjective* (**filmier**, **filmiest**) thin and almost transparent. **filminess** *noun*

filter[1] *noun* **1** a device for holding back dirt or other unwanted material from a liquid or gas that passes through it. **2** a piece of software that processes data before passing it to another application, for example to remove unwanted material, *Internet filter.*

filter[2] *verb* **1** pass through a filter. **2** move gradually, *They filtered into the hall.* **filtration** *verb* [from *felt*[2], originally used for making filters]

filth *noun* disgusting dirt.

filthy *adjective* (**filthier**, **filthiest**) **1** disgustingly dirty. **2** obscene. **3** (*informal*) very unpleasant. **4** (*informal*) excellent, *The surf is filthy today.* **filthiness** *noun*

fin *noun* **1** a thin flat part projecting from a fish's body, that helps it to swim. **2** a small projection shaped like a fish's fin, e.g. to improve the stability of an aircraft or surfboard.

final[1] *adjective* **1** coming at the end; last. **2** putting an end to doubt or argument, *You must go, and that's final!* **finality** *noun*, **finally** *adverb*

final[2] *noun* the last in a series of contests. [same origin as *finish*]

finale (*say* fuh-**nah**-lee) *noun* the last part of a piece of music, an entertainment, or a public event.

finalise *verb* (**finalised**, **finalising**) put into its final form. **finalisation** *noun*

finalist *noun* a competitor in the final.

finance[1] *noun* the use or management of money.

finance[2] *verb* (**financed**, **financing**) provide the money for something. **financier** *noun* [from Old French *finer* = to settle a debt]

finances *plural noun* money resources; funds.

financial *adjective* **1** of finance. **2** (*Australian*) having ready money. **financially** *adverb*

finch *noun* (*plural* **finches**) a small bird with a short stubby bill.

find[1] *verb* (**found**, **finding**) **1** get or see something by looking for it or by chance. **2** learn by experience, *She found that digging was hard work.*

find[2] *noun* something found.

fine[1] *adjective* **1** of high quality; excellent. **2** dry and clear; sunny, *fine weather.* **3** very thin; consisting of small particles. **4** in good health; comfortable, *I'm fine.* **finely** *adverb*, **fineness** *noun*

fine[2] *adverb* **1** finely, *chop it fine.* **2** (*informal*) very well, *That will suit me fine.* [same origin as *finish*]

fine[3] *noun* money that has to be paid as a punishment.

fine[4] *verb* (**fined**, **fining**) make somebody pay a fine. [from Latin *finis* = end (in the Middle Ages it referred to the sum paid to settle a lawsuit)]

finery *noun* fine clothes or decorations.

finesse (*say* fuh-**nes**) *noun* clever management; artfulness. [French, = fineness]

finger[1] *noun* **1** one of the separate parts of the hand. **2** a narrow piece of something, *fish fingers.*

finger[2] *verb* touch or feel with your fingers.

fingerprint *noun* a mark made by the tiny ridges on the fingertip, used as a way of identifying someone. **fingerprint** *verb*

fingertip *noun* the tip of a finger.
have something at your fingertips be very familiar with a subject.

finicky *adjective* fussy about details; hard to please.

finish[1] *verb* bring or come to an end.

finish[2] *noun* (*plural* **finishes**) **1** the last stage of something; the end. **2** the surface or coating on woodwork or other manufactured material or object. [from Latin *finis* = end]

finite (*say* **fuy**-nuyt) *adjective* limited; not infinite, *We have only a finite supply of coal.* [from Latin *finitum* = ended]

finite verb *noun* a verb that agrees with its subject in person and number, *'was', 'went', and 'says' are finite verbs; 'going' and 'to say' are not.*

fiord (*say* fee-**awd**) *noun* (also **fjord**) an inlet of the sea between high cliffs, as in Norway. [Norwegian]

fir *noun* an evergreen tree with needle-like leaves, that produces cones.

fire[1] *noun* **1** the process of burning that produces light and heat. **2** destructive burning. **3** a flammable material, such as coal or wood, burning in a grate or furnace to give heat. **4** a device using electricity or gas to heat a room. **5** the shooting of guns, *Hold your fire!*
on fire burning.
set fire to start something burning.

fire[2] *verb* (**fired**, **firing**) **1** set fire to. **2** bake pottery or bricks in a kiln. **3** shoot a gun; send out a bullet or missile. **4** dismiss someone from a job. **5** excite, *fire them with enthusiasm.* **firer** *noun*
fire away (*informal*) begin; go ahead.

firearm *noun* a small gun; a rifle, pistol, or revolver.

firebrand *noun* a person who stirs up trouble.

firebreak *noun* an obstacle to the spread of fire, such as a strip of open space in a forest.

fire engine *noun* a large vehicle fitted with equipment to put out large fires.

fire escape *noun* a special staircase or apparatus by which people may escape from a burning building.

firefighter *noun* a person employed to put out fires.

firefly *noun* (*plural* **fireflies**) a kind of beetle that gives off a glowing light.

fireman *noun* (*plural* **firemen**) a firefighter.

fireplace *noun* an open structure in which a fire may be lit for heating or cooking.

firestick farming *noun* (*Australian*) a method of vegetation control by selective burning, originally carried out by Aboriginal people.

firewall *noun* **1** a fireproof wall that prevents the spread of fire. **2** a part of a computer system that is designed to block unauthorised access.

firewood *noun* wood for use as fuel.

firework *noun* a device containing chemicals that burn attractively or noisily.

firie *noun* (*Australian informal*) a firefighter.

firing squad *noun* a group ordered to shoot a condemned person.

firm[1] *noun* a business organisation.

firm[2] *adjective* **1** not giving way when pressed; hard, solid. **2** steady; not shaking or moving. **3** definite and not likely to change, *a firm belief.* **firmly** *adverb*, **firmness** *noun*

firm[3] *adverb* firmly, *Stand firm!*

firm[4] *verb* make something become firm.

firmament *noun* the sky with its clouds and stars.

first[1] *adjective* coming before all others in time, order, or importance, *She is the first of three daughters.* **firstly** *adverb*

first[2] *adverb* before everything else, *Finish this work first.*

first[3] *noun* a person or thing that is first.

first aid *noun* treatment given to an injured person before a doctor comes.

First Australian *noun* an Aboriginal person.

First Fleet *noun* the 11 ships arriving in Australia in 1788 to begin a penal settlement.

firsthand *adjective & adverb* obtained directly from the original source.

First Nation *noun* an indigenous people, *The First Nations of Australia are the Aboriginal and Torres Strait Islander peoples.*

first person see **person**.

firth *noun* an estuary or inlet of the sea.

fiscal *adjective* of public finances. [from Latin *fiscus* = treasury]

fish[1] *noun* (*plural* **fish** or **fishes**) an animal that always lives and breathes in water, *There are many little fish in the creek near school.*

Usage The normal plural of *fish* is *fish* (e.g. *a shoal of fish; she caught two huge fish*). The older form *fishes* is still used when referring to different kinds of fish (e.g. *freshwater fishes of Tasmania*).

fish[2] *verb* **1** try to catch fish. **2** search for something; try to get something, *He is only fishing for compliments.* **fisher** *noun*

fisher *noun* a person who catches fish for a living or for sport.

fisherman *noun* (*plural* **fishermen**) a fisher.

fishery *noun* (*plural* **fisheries**) **1** a place where fish are caught or reared. **2** the business of fishing.

fishmonger *noun* a shopkeeper who sells fish.

fishy *adjective* (**fishier**, **fishiest**) **1** smelling or tasting of fish. **2** (*informal*) causing doubt or suspicion, *a fishy excuse.* **fishily** *adverb*, **fishiness** *noun*

fissile *adjective* **1** likely to split. **2** capable of undergoing nuclear fission.

fission *noun* splitting something; splitting the nucleus of an atom so as to release energy. **fissionable** *adjective* [from Latin *fissum* = split]

fissure (*say* **fish**-uh) *noun* a narrow opening made where something splits.

fist *noun* a tightly closed hand with the fingers bent into the palm.

fisticuffs *noun* fighting with the fists.

fit[1] *adjective* (**fitter**, **fittest**) **1** suitable; good enough, *a meal fit for a king.* **2** healthy, *Keep fit!* **fitly** *adverb*, **fitness** *noun*

fit[2] *verb* (**fitted**, **fitting**) **1** be the right size and shape for something; be suitable. **2** put into place, *Fit a lock on the door.* **3** alter something to make it the right size and shape. **4** make suitable, *His training fits him for the job.* **fitter** *noun*

fit[3] *noun* the way something fits, *a good fit.*

fit[4] *noun* **1** a sudden illness, especially one that makes you move violently or become unconscious. **2** an outburst, *a fit of rage.*

fitful *adjective* happening in short periods, not steadily. **fitfully** *adverb*

fitment *noun* a piece of fixed furniture.

fitting *adjective* proper; suitable.

fittings *plural noun* the fixtures and fitments of a building.

five *noun & adjective* the number 5; one more than four.

fix[1] *verb* **1** fasten or place firmly. **2** make permanent and unable to change. **3** decide; arrange, *We fixed a date for the party.* **4** repair; put into working condition, *He is*

fixing my bike. **fixer** *noun*
fix up arrange; organise.

fix[2] *noun* (*plural* **fixes**) **1** (*informal*) an awkward situation, *I'm in a fix.* **2** (*informal*) an addict's dose of a drug.

fixation *noun* **1** fixing something. **2** an abnormal emotional attachment to a person or thing. **3** concentration on one idea; an obsession.

fixative *noun* a substance used to keep something in position or make it permanent.

fixedly *adverb* in a fixed way.

fixity *noun* a fixed condition; permanence.

fixture *noun* **1** something fixed in its place. **2** a sports event planned for a particular day.

fizz *verb* make a hissing or spluttering sound; produce a lot of small bubbles. **fizziness** *noun*, **fizzy** *adjective*

fizzer *noun* (*Australian informal*) a failure or fiasco.

fizzle *verb* (**fizzled**, **fizzling**) make a slight fizzing sound.
fizzle out end feebly or unsuccessfully.

fjord *noun* a fiord.

flabbergast *verb* astonish greatly. **flabbergasted** *adjective*

flabby *adjective* fat and soft, not firm. **flabbily** *adverb*, **flabbiness** *noun*

flaccid (*say* **flas**-uhd) *adjective* soft and limp. **flaccidity** *noun*, **flaccidly** *adverb*

flag[1] **1** a piece of cloth with a coloured pattern or shape on it, used as a sign or signal. **2** a small piece of paper or plastic that looks like a flag. **flagpole** *noun*, **flagstaff** *noun*

flag[2] *verb* (**flagged**, **flagging**) **1** become weak; droop. **2** signal with a flag or by waving. [from an old word *flag* = drooping]

flag[3] *noun* a flagstone. [from Old Norse *flaga* = slab of stone]

flagon *noun* a large bottle or container for wine or other drink.

flagrant (*say* **flay**-gruhnt) *adjective* very bad and noticeable, *flagrant disobedience.* **flagrancy** *noun*, **flagrantly** *adverb* [from Latin *flagrans* = blazing]

flagship *noun* a ship that carries an admiral and flies his flag.

flagstone *noun* a flat slab of stone used for paving. [from *flag*³ + *stone*]

flail[1] *noun* an old-fashioned tool for threshing grain.

flail[2] *verb* beat as if with a flail; wave about wildly. [from Latin *flagellum* = a whip]

flair *noun* a natural ability; talent. [French, = power to smell things]

flak *noun* **1** shells fired by anti-aircraft guns. **2** (*informal*) criticism or abuse. [short for German *Fliegerabwehrkanone* = aircraft-defence cannon]

flake[1] *noun* **1** a very light thin piece of something. **2** a small flat piece of falling snow. **3** shark flesh as food. **flaky** *adjective*

flake[2] *verb* (**flaked**, **flaking**) come off in flakes.
flake out (*informal*) collapse or fall asleep from exhaustion.

flak jacket *noun* a heavily padded jacket worn as protection against bullets and shrapnel.

flamboyant *adjective* very showy in appearance or manner. [French, = blazing]

flame[1] *noun* **1** a tongue-shaped portion of fire or burning gas. **2** an abusive email or newsgroup posting.

flame[2] *verb* (**flamed**, **flaming**) **1** produce flames. **2** become bright or glowing. **3** send an abusive email to.

flamenco (*say* fluh-**meng**-koh) *noun* (*plural* **flamencos**) a Spanish gypsy style of song or dance.

flamingo *noun* (*plural* **flamingoes**) a wading bird with long legs, a long neck, and pinkish feathers.

flammable *adjective* able to be set on fire. **flammability** *noun*

> **Usage** See the note at *inflammable*.

flan *noun* a pastry or sponge shell with no cover over the filling.

flange *noun* a projecting rim or edge.

flank[1] *noun* the side of something.

flank[2] *verb* place or be placed at the side of something or somebody.

flannel *noun* **1** a soft cloth for washing yourself. **2** a soft woollen material.

flannelette *noun* cotton fabric made to look and feel like flannel.

flap[1] *verb* (**flapped**, **flapping**) **1** wave about. **2** (*informal*) panic; fuss.

flap[2] *noun* **1** a part that is fixed at one edge on to something else, often to cover an opening. **2** the action or sound of flapping. **3** (*informal*) a panic or fuss, *in a flap.*

flapjack *noun* a kind of pancake.

flare[1] *verb* (**flared**, **flaring**) **1** blaze with a sudden bright flame. **2** become angry suddenly. **3** become gradually wider.

flare[2] *noun* **1** a sudden bright flame or light. **2** a gradual widening.

flash[1] *noun* (*plural* **flashes**) **1** a sudden bright flame or light. **2** a device for making a sudden bright light for taking photographs. **3** a sudden display of something, *a flash of* *inspiration.* **4** a short item of news. **5** an instant.

flash[2] *verb* **1** make a flash. **2** appear suddenly; move quickly, *The train flashed past us.*

flashback *noun* going back in a film or story to something that happened earlier.

flash drive *noun* (in computing) a data storage device containing flash memory.

flash memory *noun* (in computing) memory that retains data in the absence of a power supply.

flashy *adjective* gaudy; showy.

flask *noun* **1** a bottle with a narrow neck. **2** a vacuum flask.

flat[1] *adjective* (**flatter**, **flattest**) **1** with no curves or bumps; smooth and level. **2** spread out; lying at full length, *Lie flat on the ground.* **3** (of a tyre) with no air inside. **4** (of feet) without the normal arch underneath. **5** absolute, *a flat refusal.* **6** dull; not changing. **7** (of a drink) having lost its fizziness. **8** (of a battery) unable to produce anymore electric current. **9** (in music) one semitone lower than the natural note, *E flat.* **flatly** *adverb*, **flatness** *noun*

flat[2] *adverb* **1** so as to be flat, *Press it flat.* **2** (*informal*) exactly, *in ten seconds flat.* **3** (in music) below the correct pitch.
flat out as fast as possible.

flat[3] *noun* **1** a flat thing or area. **2** a set of rooms for living in, usually on one floor of a building. **3** (in music) a note one semitone lower than the natural note; the sign (♭) that indicates this.

flat[4] *verb* (*Australian*) live in a flat.

flathead *noun* an edible sea fish with a flattened head.

flatten *verb* **1** make or become flat. **2** (*informal*) knock down.
flatten the curve take measures designed to reduce the rate at which infection spreads during an epidemic.

flatter *verb* **1** praise somebody more than they deserve. **2** make a person or thing seem better or more attractive than they really are. **flatterer** *noun*, **flattery** *noun* [from Old French *flateri* = smooth down]

flatulent (*say* **flat**-yoo-lent) *adjective* suffering from excess gas in the stomach or intestines. **flatulence** *noun* [from Latin *flatus* = blowing]

flaunt *verb* display something proudly, show it off, *They flaunted the trophy.*

Usage Do not confuse *flaunt* with *flout.*

flautist (*say* **flaw**-tuhst) *noun* a flute player.

flavour[1] *noun* the taste of something.

flavour[2] *verb* give something a flavour, season it. **flavouring** *noun*

flaw *noun* something that makes a person or thing imperfect. **flawed** *adjective*

flawless *adjective* without a flaw; perfect. **flawlessly** *adverb*, **flawlessness** *noun*

flax *noun* a plant that produces fibres from which linen is made and seeds from which linseed oil is obtained.

flaxen *adjective* pale yellow like flax fibres, *flaxen hair.*

flay *verb* strip the skin from an animal.

flea *noun* a small jumping insect that sucks blood.

fleck *noun* **1** a very small patch of colour. **2** a particle; a speck, *flecks of dirt.*
flecked *adjective*

fled *past tense & past participle* of **flee**.

fledged *adjective* (of young birds) having grown feathers and able to fly.
fully fledged fully trained, *a fully fledged engineer.*

fledgling *noun* (also **fledgeling**) a young bird that is just fledged.

flee *verb* (**fled**, **fleeing**) run or hurry away from something.

fleece[1] *noun* the woolly hair of a sheep or similar animal. **fleecy** *adjective*

fleece[2] *verb* (**fleeced**, **fleecing**) **1** shear the fleece from a sheep. **2** swindle a person out of some money.

fleet[1] *noun* a number of ships, aircraft, or vehicles owned by one country or company. [from Old English *fleot* = ships]

fleet[2] *adjective* moving swiftly; nimble.

fleeting *adjective* passing quickly; brief.

Flemish *adjective* of Flanders in Belgium or its people or language. **Flemish** *noun*

flesh *noun* **1** the soft substance of the bodies of people and animals, consisting of muscle and fat. **2** the pulpy part of fruits and vegetables. **fleshly** *adjective*

flew *past tense* of **fly**[2].

flex[1] *verb* bend or stretch something that is flexible, *flex your muscles.*

flex[2] *noun* (*plural* **flexes**) flexible insulated wire for carrying electric current. [from Latin *flexum* = bent]

flexible *adjective* **1** easy to bend or stretch. **2** able to be changed or adapted, *Our plans are flexible.* **flexibility** *noun*

flick[1] *noun* **1** a quick light hit or movement. **2** (*informal*) a cinema film.
get the flick (*Australian informal*) reject; sack, *His boss gave him the flick.*

flick[2] *verb* hit or move with a flick.
flick through turn over pages etc. quickly; glance through a book etc.

flicker[1] *verb* **1** burn or shine unsteadily. **2** move quickly to and fro or up and down.

flicker[2] *noun* a flickering light or movement.

flier *noun* a flyer.

flight[1] *noun* **1** flying. **2** a journey made by air; transport in an aircraft making a particular journey. **3** a series of stairs. **4** the feathers or fins on a dart or arrow.

flight[2] *noun* fleeing; an escape.

flighty *adjective* (**flightier**, **flightiest**) silly and frivolous. **flightiness** *noun*

flimsy *adjective* (**flimsier**, **flimsiest**) **1** light and thin. **2** fragile; not strong. **flimsily** *adverb*, **flimsiness** *noun*

flinch *verb* move or shrink back because you are afraid; wince. **flinch** *noun*

fling[1] *verb* (**flung**, **flinging**) throw something violently or carelessly.

fling[2] *noun* **1** the movement of flinging. **2** a vigorous dance, *the Highland fling.* **3** a short time of enjoyment, *have a fling.*

flint *noun* **1** a very hard kind of stone. **2** a piece of flint or hard metal used to produce sparks. **flinty** *adjective*

flip[1] *verb* (**flipped**, **flipping**) **1** flick. **2** throw something into the air and make it turn over, *flip a coin.* **3** (*informal*) become crazy or very angry. **4** (in mathematics) turn over a shape so it is a mirror image.

flip[2] *noun* a flipping movement.

flippant *adjective* not showing proper seriousness. **flippancy** *noun*, **flippantly** *adverb*

flipper *noun* **1** a limb that water animals use for swimming. **2** a device that you wear on your feet to help you to swim.

flirt[1] *verb* behave lovingly towards somebody to amuse yourself. **flirtation** *noun*

flirt[2] *noun* a person who flirts. **flirtatious** *adjective*, **flirtatiously** *adverb*

flit *verb* (**flitted**, **flitting**) fly or move lightly and quickly. **flit** *noun*

flitter *verb* flit about. **flitter** *noun*

float[1] *verb* **1** stay or move on the surface of a liquid or in air. **2** make something float. **floater** *noun*

float[2] *noun* **1** a device designed to float. **2** a vehicle with a platform used for carrying a display in a parade. **3** a small amount of money kept for paying small bills or giving change.

flock[1] *noun* a group of sheep, goats, or birds.

flock[2] *verb* gather or move in a crowd.

flock[3] *noun* a soft material for stuffing cushions and other soft furnishings.

floe *noun* a sheet of floating ice. [from Norwegian *flo* = layer]

flog *verb* (**flogged**, **flogging**) **1** beat hard with a whip or stick as a punishment. **2** (*informal*) sell. **3** (*informal*) steal.

flood[1] *noun* **1** a large amount of water spreading over a place that is usually dry. **2** a great amount, *a flood of requests.* **3** the movement of the tide when it is coming in towards the land.

flood[2] *verb* **1** cover with a flood. **2** come in great amounts, *Letters flooded in.*

floodlight *noun* a lamp that makes a broad bright beam such as those used to light up a stage. **floodlit** *adjective*

floor[1] *noun* **1** the part of a room that people walk on. **2** a storey of a building; all the rooms at the same level.

floor[2] *verb* **1** put a floor into a building. **2** knock a person down. **3** baffle somebody.

floorboard *noun* one of the boards forming the floor of a room.

flop[1] *verb* (**flopped**, **flopping**) **1** fall or sit down clumsily. **2** hang or sway heavily and loosely. **3** (*informal*) be a failure.

flop[2] *noun* **1** a flopping movement or sound. **2** (*informal*) a failure.

floppy *adjective* hanging loosely; not firm or rigid. **floppiness** *noun*

floppy disk *noun* a flexible computer disk (usually enclosed in a square case) used for storing data.

flora *noun* the plants of a particular area or period. (Compare **fauna**.) [from the name of Flora, the ancient Roman goddess of flowers (Latin *flores* = flowers)]

floral *adjective* of flowers.

florid *adjective* **1** (of the complexion) red or flushed. **2** elaborate and ornate.

florin *noun* a former coin worth two shillings (20 cents).

florist *noun* a shopkeeper who sells flowers.

floss[1] *noun* **1** silky thread or fibres. **2** thread used for cleaning between the teeth. **flossy** *adjective*

floss[2] *verb* clean between the teeth using floss.

flotation *noun* floating something.

flotilla (*say* fluh-**til**-uh) *noun* a fleet of boats or small ships. [Spanish, = little fleet]

flotsam *noun* wreckage or cargo found floating after a shipwreck.

flotsam and jetsam *noun* odds and ends.

flounce[1] *verb* (**flounced**, **flouncing**) go in an impatient or annoyed manner, *She flounced out of the room.* **flounce** *noun*

flounce[2] *noun* a wide frill.

flounder[1] *verb* **1** move clumsily and with difficulty. **2** make mistakes or become confused when trying to do something.

flounder[2] *noun* a small edible flat fish.

flour *noun* a fine powder of wheat or other grain, used in cooking. **floury** *adjective* [old spelling of *flower*]

flourish[1] *verb* **1** grow or develop strongly. **2** be successful; prosper. **3** wave something about dramatically.

flourish[2] *noun* (*plural* **flourishes**) a dramatic sweeping movement, curve, or passage of music. [from Latin *florere* = to flower]

flout *verb* disobey openly and scornfully, *They flouted the rules.*

Usage Do not confuse *flout* with *flaunt.*

flow[1] *verb* **1** move along smoothly or continuously. **2** gush out, *Water flowed from the tap.* **3** hang loosely, *flowing hair.* **4** (of the tide) come in towards the land.

flow[2] *noun* **1** a flowing movement or mass. **2** the movement of the tide when it is coming in towards the land, *the ebb and flow.*

flower[1] *noun* **1** the part of a plant from which seed and fruit develop. **2** a blossom and its stem used for decoration, usually in groups. [compare *flora*]

flower[2] *verb* produce flowers.

flowerpot *noun* a pot in which a plant may be grown.

flowery *adjective* **1** full of flowers. **2** full of ornamental phrases.

flown *past participle* of **fly**[2].

flow-on *noun* (*Australian*) a wage increase granted as a consequence of one already made in a similar or related occupation.

flu *noun* influenza.

fluctuate *verb* (**fluctuated, fluctuating**) rise and fall; vary, *Prices fluctuated.* **fluctuation** *noun* [from Latin *fluctus* = a wave]

flue *noun* a pipe or tube through which smoke or hot gases are drawn off.

fluent (*say* **floo**-uhnt) *adjective* skilful at speaking; using a language easily and well. **fluency** *noun*, **fluently** *adverb* [from Latin *fluens* = flowing]

fluff *noun* a fluffy substance.

fluffy *adjective* having a mass of soft fur or fibres. **fluffiness** *noun*

fluid[1] *noun* a substance that is able to flow freely as liquids and gases do.

fluid[2] *adjective* able to flow freely, not solid or stiff. **fluidity** *noun* [from Latin *fluere* = to flow]

fluke *noun* a piece of good luck that makes you able to do something you thought you could not do.

flummox *verb* (*informal*) baffle.

flung *past tense & past participle* of **fling**[1].

flunk *verb* (*informal*) fail, especially in an examination.

fluorescent (*say* floor-**res**-uhnt) *adjective* creating light from radiation. **fluorescence** *noun*

fluoridation *noun* adding fluoride to drinking water.

fluoride *noun* a chemical substance that is thought to prevent tooth decay.

flurry *noun* (*plural* **flurries**) **1** a sudden whirling gust of wind, rain, or snow. **2** an excited or flustered disturbance.

flush[1] *verb* **1** blush. **2** clean or remove something with a fast flow of water.

flush[2] *noun* **1** a blush. **2** a fast flow of water.

flush[3] *adjective* **1** level; without projections, *The doors are flush with the walls.* **2** having plenty of money.

fluster *verb* make somebody nervous and confused. **fluster** *noun*, **flustered** *adjective*

flute *noun* a musical instrument consisting of a long pipe with holes that are stopped by fingers or keys.

flutter[1] *verb* **1** flap wings quickly. **2** move or flap quickly and irregularly.

flutter[2] *noun* **1** a fluttering movement. **2** a nervously excited condition. **3** (*informal*) a small bet, *Have a flutter.*

flux *noun* continual change or flow.

fly[1] *noun* (*plural* **flies**) **1** a small flying insect with two wings. **2** a real or artificial fly used as bait in fishing.

fly[2] *verb* (**flew, flown, flying**) **1** move through the air by means of wings or in an aircraft. **2** travel through the air or through space. **3** wave in the air, *Flags were flying.* **4** make something fly, *They flew model aircraft.* **5** move or pass quickly, *Time flies.* **6** flee from, *You must fly the country!*

fly[3] *noun* (*plural* **flies**) **1** flying. **2** the front opening of a pair of trousers.

flycatcher *noun* a bird that catches insects in the air, *the restless flycatcher.*

flyer *noun* **1** a person or thing that flies. **2** an information leaflet.

flying doctor *noun* (*Australian*) a doctor who visits outback patients by air.

flying fox *noun* **1** a large fruit-eating bat. **2** (*Australian*) an overhead cable and apparatus for the transport of material over rough terrain; a similar device used for military training or for recreation.

flying saucer *noun* a mysterious saucer-shaped object reported to have been seen in the sky.

flyleaf *noun* (*plural* **flyleaves**) a blank page at the beginning or end of a book.

flyover *noun* a bridge that carries one road or railway over another.

flywheel *noun* a heavy wheel used to regulate machinery.

foal[1] *noun* a young horse.

foal[2] *verb* give birth to a foal.

foam[1] *noun* **1** froth. **2** a spongy kind of rubber or plastic. **foamy** *adjective*

foam[2] *verb* form foam; send out foam.

fob[1] *noun* an ornament hanging from a watch chain; a tab on a key ring.

fob[2] *verb* (**fobbed**, **fobbing**)
fob off get rid of someone by an excuse or a trick.

focal *adjective* of or at a focus.

focus[1] *noun* (*plural* **focuses** or **foci**) **1** the distance from an eye or lens at which an object appears clearest. **2** the point at which rays meet or from which they appear to proceed. **3** the centre of interest or activity.
in focus appearing clearly.
out of focus not appearing clearly.

focus[2] *verb* (**focused**, **focusing**) **1** use or adjust a lens so that objects appear clearly. **2** concentrate, *She focused her attention on it.* [Latin, = hearth (the central point of a household)]

fodder *noun* food for horses and farm animals.

foe *noun* (*old use*) an enemy.

foetus (*say* **fee**-tuhs) *noun* (*plural* **foetuses**) (also **fetus**) a developing embryo, especially an unborn human baby. **foetal** *adjective*

fog *noun* thick mist. **foggy** *adjective*

fogey *noun* (*plural* **fogeys**) (also **fogy**) a person with old-fashioned ideas.

foghorn *noun* a loud horn for warning ships in fog.

FOI *abbreviation* freedom of information.

foible *noun* a slight peculiarity in someone's character or tastes.

foil[1] *noun* **1** a very thin sheet of metal. **2** a person or thing that makes another look better in contrast.

foil[2] *noun* a long narrow sword used in the sport of fencing.

foil[3] *verb* frustrate, prevent from being successful, *We foiled his evil plan.*

foist *verb* make a person accept something inferior or unwelcome, *They foisted the job on me.* [originally = dishonestly substitute a loaded dice]

fold[1] *verb* bend or move so that one part lies on another part.

fold[2] *noun* a line where something is folded.

fold[3] *noun* an enclosure for sheep.

folder *noun* **1** a folding cover for loose papers. **2** (in computing) a directory containing related files or documents.

foliage *noun* the leaves of a tree or plant. [from Latin *folium* = leaf]

folic acid *noun* a vitamin of the B group, deficiency of which causes anaemia.

folk *noun* **1** people. **2** one's relatives.

folklore *noun* old beliefs and legends.

folk song *noun* a song in the traditional style of a country.

follow *verb* **1** go or come after. **2** come next in order or time. **3** take a person or thing as a guide or example. **4** take an interest in the progress of events or a sport or team. **5** understand, *Did you follow what he said?* **6** result from something. **follower** *noun*

following *preposition* after; as a result of, *Following the burglary, we had new locks fitted.*

folly *noun* (*plural* **follies**) foolishness; a foolish action etc. [from French *folie* = madness]

foment (*say* fuh-**ment**) *verb* arouse or stimulate deliberately, *foment trouble.* **fomentation** *noun* [from Latin *fomentum* = poultice]

fond *adjective* **1** loving. **2** foolishly hopeful, *fond hopes.* **fondly** *adverb*, **fondness** *noun* [from *fon* = a fool]

fondle *verb* (**fondled**, **fondling**) touch or stroke lovingly.

font[1] *noun* a basin (often of carved stone) in a church, to hold water for baptism. [from Latin *fontis* = of a fountain]

font[2] *noun* a set of printing type of the same style and size.

food *noun* any substance that a plant or animal can take into its body to help it to grow and be healthy, *I ate too much food at the party.*

food chain *noun* a series of plants and animals each of which serves as food for the one above it in the series.

fool[1] *noun* **1** a stupid person; someone who acts unwisely. **2** a jester or clown, *Stop playing the fool.* **3** a creamy pudding with crushed fruit in it.

fool[2] *verb* **1** behave in a joking way; play about. **2** trick or deceive someone.

foolery *noun* foolish acts or behaviour.

foolhardy *adjective* bold but foolish; reckless. **foolhardiness** *noun*

foolish *adjective* without good sense or judgement; unwise. **foolishly** *adverb*, **foolishness** *noun*

foolproof *adjective* easy to use or do correctly.

fool's paradise *noun* happiness that comes only from being mistaken about something.

foot *noun* (*plural* **feet**) **1** the lower part of the leg below the ankle. **2** any similar part, e.g. one used by certain animals to move or attach themselves to things. **3** the lowest part, *the foot of the hill.* **4** a measure of length, 12 inches (about 30 centimetres). **5** a unit of rhythm in a line of poetry, e.g. each of the four divisions in *Jack /and Jill / went up / the hill.*
on foot walking.

footage *noun* a length of television or cinema film.

foot-and-mouth disease *noun* a contagious disease of cattle and sheep.

football *noun* **1** a game between two teams played with a ball on a field with goals at each end, *What kind of football do you play–Aussie Rules, soccer, or rugby?* **2** the inflated leather or plastic ball used in this game. **footballer** *noun*

foothill *noun* a low hill near the bottom of a mountain or range of mountains.

foothold *noun* **1** a place to put your foot when climbing. **2** a secure position from which further progress may be made.

footing *noun* **1** having your feet placed on something; a foothold, *He lost his footing and slipped.* **2** a status, *We are on a friendly footing with that country.*

footlights *plural noun* a row of lights along the front of the floor of a stage.

footman *noun* (*plural* **footmen**) a male servant whose duties include admitting visitors and waiting at table.

footnote *noun* a note printed at the bottom of the page.

footpath *noun* a path for pedestrians.

footprint *noun* a mark made by a foot or shoe.

footstep *noun* **1** a step taken in walking or running. **2** the sound of this.

footstool *noun* a stool for resting your feet on when you are sitting.

footy *noun* (*Australian informal*) football.

for[1] *preposition* This word is used to show **1** purpose or direction (*This letter is for you; We set out for home*), **2** distance or time (*Walk for six kilometres or two hours*), **3** price or exchange (*We bought it for $2; New lamps for old*), **4** cause (*She was fined for speeding*), **5** defence or support (*He fought for his country; Are you for us or against us?*), **6** reference (*For all her wealth, she is bored*), **7** similarity or correspondence (*We took him for a fool*).
for ever for all time; always.

for[2] *conjunction* because, *They hesitated, for they were afraid.*

for- *prefix* **1** away; off (as in *forgive*). **2** prohibiting (as in *forbid*). **3** abstaining or neglecting (as in *forgo, forsake*).

forage[1] *noun* **1** food for horses and cattle. **2** the action of foraging.

forage[2] *verb* (**foraged, foraging**) go searching for something; rummage.

foray *noun* a raid.

forbear *verb* (**forbore, forborne, forbearing**) **1** refrain from something, *We forbore to mention it.* **2** be patient or tolerant.
forbearance *noun*

forbid *verb* (**forbade, forbidden, forbidding**) **1** order someone not to do something. **2** refuse to allow, *We shall forbid the marriage.*

forbidding *adjective* looking stern or unfriendly.

force[1] *noun* **1** strength; power; intense effort. **2** (in science) an influence, which can be measured, that causes something to move. **3** an organised group of police or soldiers. **4** a person or thing regarded as exerting influence.
in or **into force** in or into effectiveness, *The new law comes into force next week.*
the forces a country's armed forces.

force[2] *verb* (**forced, forcing**) **1** use force in order to get or do something, or to make somebody obey. **2** break something open by force.

forceful *adjective* strong and vigorous.
forcefully *adverb*

forceps *noun* (*plural* **forceps**) surgical pincers or tongs used for gripping things.

forcible *adjective* done by force; forceful.
forcibly *adverb*

ford[1] *noun* a shallow place where you can walk or drive across a river.

ford[2] *verb* cross a river at a ford.

fore[1] *adjective & adverb* at or towards the front, *fore and aft.*

fore[2] *noun* the front part.
to the fore to or at the front; in or to a prominent position.

fore- *prefix* before (as in *forecast*); in front (as in *foreleg*).

forearm[1] *noun* the arm from the elbow to the wrist or fingertips.

forearm[2] *verb* arm or prepare in advance against possible danger.

forebears *plural noun* ancestors.

foreboding *noun* a feeling that trouble is coming.

forecast[1] *noun* a statement that tells in advance what is likely to happen.

forecast[2] *verb* (**forecast, forecasting**) make a forecast. **forecaster** *noun*

forecastle (*say* **fohk**-suhl) *noun* the forward part of certain ships.

forecourt *noun* an enclosed area in front of a building; an outer court.

forefathers *plural noun* ancestors.

forefinger *noun* the finger next to the thumb.

forefoot *noun* (*plural* **forefeet**) an animal's front foot.

forefront *noun* the very front.

foregoing *adjective* preceding; previous.

foregone conclusion *noun* a result that can be foreseen easily and with certainty.

foreground *noun* **1** the front part of a scene or view. **2** the most conspicuous position.

forehand *noun* a stroke made in tennis and other racket sports with the palm of the hand turned forwards.

forehead (*say* **fo**-ruhd or **faw**-hed) *noun* the part of the face above the eyes.

foreign *adjective* **1** of or in another country; of other countries. **2** not belonging; unnatural, *Lying is foreign to her nature.* [from Latin *foris* = outside, abroad]

foreigner *noun* a person from another country.

foreleg *noun* an animal's front leg.

forelimb *noun* either of the front limbs of an animal; a foreleg, wing, flipper, etc.

foreman *noun* (*plural* **foremen**) **1** a worker in charge of a group of other workers. **2** the leader of a jury who speaks on its behalf.

foremost *adjective & adverb* first in position or rank; most important.

forensic (*say* fuh-**ren**-sik) *adjective* of or used in lawcourts.

forensics *plural noun* scientific tests or techniques used in connection with the detection of crime.

forerunner *noun* a person or thing that comes before another; a sign of what is to come.

foresee *verb* (**foresaw, foreseen, foreseeing**) realise what is going to happen.

foreseeable *adjective* able to be foreseen.

foreshadow *verb* be a sign of something that is to come.

foreshore *noun* the shore between high-water mark and low-water mark, or between water and land that is cultivated or built on.

foreshorten *verb* show an object in a drawing with some lines shortened to give an effect of distance or depth.

foresight *noun* the ability to foresee and prepare for future needs.

foreskin *noun* the retractable roll of skin covering the end of the penis.

forest *noun* trees and undergrowth covering a large area, *Tigers can be found in some of the forests of Asia.* **forested** *adjective*

forestall *verb* prevent somebody or something by taking action first. [from Old English *foresteall* = ambush]

forestry *noun* planting forests and looking after them. **forester** *noun*

foretaste *noun* an experience of something that is to come in the future.

foretell *verb* (**foretold, foretelling**) forecast; prophesy.

forethought *noun* careful thought and planning for the future.

forever *adverb* continually; persistently.

forewarn *verb* warn someone beforehand.

foreword *noun* a preface.

forfeit[1] (*say* **faw**-fuht) *verb* pay or give up something as a penalty. **forfeiture** *noun*

forfeit[2] *noun* something forfeited.

forgave *past tense* of **forgive**.

forge[1] *noun* a place where metal is heated and shaped; a blacksmith's workshop.

forge[2] *verb* (**forged, forging**) **1** shape metal by heating and hammering. **2** copy something so as to deceive people. **forger** *noun*, **forgery** *noun*

forge[3] *verb* (**forged, forging**)
forge ahead move forward by a strong effort.

forget *verb* (**forgot, forgotten, forgetting**) **1** fail to remember. **2** stop thinking about, *Forget your troubles.*
forget yourself behave rudely or thoughtlessly.

forgetful *adjective* tending to forget. **forgetfully** *adverb*, **forgetfulness** *noun*

forget-me-not *noun* a plant with small blue flowers.

forgive *verb* (**forgave, forgiven, forgiving**) stop feeling angry with somebody about something. **forgivable** *adjective*, **forgiveness** *noun*

forgo *verb* (**forwent, forgone, forgoing**) give something up; go without.

fork[1] *noun* **1** a small device with prongs for lifting food to your mouth. **2** a large device with prongs used for digging or lifting things. **3** a place where something separates into two or more parts.

fork[2] *verb* **1** lift or dig with a fork. **2** form a fork by separating into two branches. **3** follow one of these branches, *Fork left.*
fork out (*informal*) pay out money.

forklift *noun* (in full **forklift truck**) a vehicle with two metal bars at the front for lifting and moving heavy loads.

forlorn *adjective* left alone and unhappy.

forlorn hope *noun* the only faint hope left.

form[1] *noun* **1** the shape or appearance of something. **2** the way something exists, *Ice is a form of water.* **3** a kind or variety. **4** a class in school. **5** a bench. **6** a piece of paper or digital document with spaces to be filled in. **7** (of a horse or athlete) condition of health and training, *in good form.*

form[2] *verb* **1** shape or construct something; create. **2** come into existence; develop, *Clouds formed.*

formal[1] *adjective* strictly following the accepted rules or customs; ceremonious. **formally** *adverb*

formal[2] *noun* (especially at secondary schools) an official dance or social get-together at which formal dress is often worn.

formaldehyde (*say* for-**mal**-duh-huyd) *noun* a colourless gas used in solution as a preservative and disinfectant.

formalise *verb* (**formalised, formalising**) make something formal or official. **formalisation** *noun*

formality *noun* (*plural* **formalities**) **1** formal behaviour. **2** something done to obey a rule or custom.

format[1] *noun* the shape and size of something; the way it is arranged.

format[2] *verb* (**formatted, formatting**) **1** arrange text in a particular format. **2** (in computing) prepare a disk to receive data.

formation *noun* **1** the act of forming something. **2** a thing formed. **3** a special arrangement or pattern, *flying in formation.* [from Latin *formare* = to mould]

formative *adjective* forming or developing something.

former *adjective* of an earlier period; of past times. **formerly** *adverb*
the former the first of two people or things just mentioned. (Compare **latter**.)

formidable (*say* **faw**-muh-duh-buhl or fuh-**mid**-uh-buhl) *adjective* frightening; difficult to deal with or do, *a formidable task.* **formidably** *adverb* [from Latin *formido* = fear]

formula *noun* (*plural* **formulae**) **1** a set of chemical symbols showing what a substance consists of. **2** a rule or statement expressed in symbols or numbers. **3** a list of substances needed for making something. **4** a fixed series of words, especially one used on social or ceremonial occasions. **5** one of the groups into which racing cars are placed according to the size of their engines. [Latin, = little form]

formulate *verb* (**formulated, formulating**) express clearly and exactly. **formulation** *noun* [from *formula*]

forsake *verb* (**forsook, forsaken, forsaking**) abandon.

fort *noun* a fortified building. [from Latin *fortis* = strong]

forte[1] (*say* **faw**-tay) *noun* a person's strong point. [from French *fort* = strong]

forte[2] *adverb* (in music) loudly.

forth *adverb* **1** out; into view. **2** onwards; forwards, *from this day forth.*
and so forth and so on.

forthcoming *adjective* **1** about to come forth or happen, *forthcoming events.* **2** made available when needed, *Money for the trip was not forthcoming.* **3** (*informal*) willing to give information.

forthright *adjective* frank; outspoken.

forthwith *adverb* immediately.

fortification *noun* **1** fortifying something. **2** a wall or building constructed to make a place strong against attack.

fortify *verb* (**fortified, fortifying**) **1** make a place strong against attack, especially by building fortifications. **2** strengthen. [same origin as *fort*]

fortitude *noun* courage in bearing pain or trouble. [from Latin *fortis* = strong]

fortnight *noun* a period of two weeks. **fortnightly** *adverb & adjective* [from an old word meaning 'fourteen nights']

fortress *noun* (*plural* **fortresses**) a fortified building or town. [same origin as *fort*]

fortuitous (*say* faw-**tyoo**-uh-tuhs) *adjective* happening by chance. **fortuitously** *adverb* [from Latin, = accidental]

fortunate *adjective* **1** lucky. **2** favourable. **fortunately** *adverb*

fortune *noun* **1** luck; chance; fate. **2** a great amount of money. [from Latin *fortuna* = luck]

fortune teller *noun* a person who tells people what will happen to them in the future.

forty *noun & adjective* (*plural* **forties**) the number 40; four times ten. **fortieth** *adjective & noun*
forty winks a short sleep; a nap.

forum *noun* (*plural* **forums** or **fora**) **1** a meeting or medium for an exchange of views. **2** the public square in an ancient Roman city. [Latin]

forward[1] *adjective* **1** going forwards. **2** placed in the front. **3** having made more than the normal progress. **4** too eager or bold. **forwardness** *noun*

forward[2] *adverb* forwards.

forward[3] *noun* an attacking player in football, hockey, and other sports.

forward[4] *verb* **1** send on a letter or email to a new address. **2** help something to improve or make progress.

forwards *adverb* **1** to or towards the front. **2** in the direction you are facing.

forwent *past tense* of **forgo**.

fossick *verb* (*Australian*) search or pick about for gold or other desirable things; rummage. [from British dialect]

fossil *noun* the remains or traces of a prehistoric animal or plant that has been buried in the ground for a very long time and become hardened in rock.

fossil fuel *noun* coal, oil, and natural gas.

fossilise *verb* (**fossilised**, **fossilising**) turn into a fossil. **fossilisation** *noun*

foster *verb* **1** help to grow or develop. **2** bring up a child that is not one's own by birth. **foster child** *noun*, **foster parent** *noun* [from Old English *foster* = food]

fought *past tense & past participle* of **fight**[2].

foul[1] *adjective* **1** disgusting; filthy; tasting or smelling unpleasant. **2** (of weather) rough; stormy. **3** morally offensive; evil. **4** unfair; breaking the rules of a game. **5** colliding or entangled with something. **foully** *adverb*, **foulness** *noun*

foul[2] *noun* an action that breaks the rules of a game.

foul[3] *verb* **1** make or become foul, *Smoke had fouled the air.* **2** commit a foul against a player in a game. **3** entangle or become entangled.

foul play *noun* **1** unfair play. **2** a violent crime, especially murder.

found[1] *past tense & past participle* of **find**[1].

found[2] *verb* **1** establish; provide money for starting, *They founded a hospital.* **2** base, *This novel is founded on fact.* [from Latin *fundus* = bottom]

foundation *noun* **1** the founding of something. **2** a base or basis. **3** the solid base on which a building is built up. **foundation stone** *noun*

founder[1] *noun* a person who founds something, *the founder of the hospital.*

founder[2] *verb* **1** fill with water and sink, *The ship foundered.* **2** stumble; fall. **3** fail completely, *Their plans foundered.* [same origin as *found*[2]]

foundling *noun* a child found abandoned, whose parents are not known.

foundry *noun* (*plural* **foundries**) a factory or workshop where metal or glass is made.

fount *noun* (*poetic*) a fountain.

fountain *noun* a device that makes a jet of water shoot up into the air.

fountain pen *noun* a pen that can be filled with a supply of ink.

four *noun & adjective* the number 4; one more than three.
on all fours on hands and knees.

fourteen *noun & adjective* the number 14; one more than thirteen. **fourteenth** *adjective & noun*

fourth[1] *adjective* next after the third. **fourthly** *adverb*

fourth[2] *noun* **1** the fourth person or thing. **2** one of four equal parts; a quarter.

fowl *noun* a bird, especially one kept for its eggs or meat.

fox[1] *noun* (*plural* **foxes**) a wild animal that looks like a dog with a long furry tail. **foxy** *adjective*

fox[2] *verb* deceive; puzzle.

foxglove *noun* a tall plant with flowers like the fingers of gloves.

foxtrot *noun* a dance with slow and quick steps; the music for this.

foyer *noun* the entrance hall of a theatre, cinema, or hotel. [French, = hearth]

fracking see **hydraulic fracturing**.

fraction *noun* **1** a number that is not a whole number, e.g. ½, 0.5. **2** a tiny part. **fractional** *adjective*, **fractionally** *adverb* [same origin as *fracture*]

fractious (*say* **frak**-shuhs) *adjective* irritable. **fractiously** *adverb*, **fractiousness** *noun*

fracture[1] *noun* the breaking of something, especially of a bone.

fracture[2] *verb* (**fractured**, **fracturing**) break. [from Latin *fractum* = broken]

fragile *adjective* easy to break or damage. **fragilely** *adverb*, **fragility** *noun*

fragment *noun* **1** a small piece broken off. **2** a small part. **fragmentary** *adjective*, **fragmentation** *noun*, **fragmented** *adjective*

fragrant *adjective* having a pleasant smell. **fragrance** *noun*

frail *adjective* **1** (of things) fragile. **2** (of people) not strong; not robust, *a frail old man.* **frailty** *noun*

frame[1] *noun* **1** a holder that fits round the outside of a picture. **2** a rigid structure that supports something. **3** a basic structure that underlies or supports a system, concept, or text. **4** a human or animal body, *He has a small frame.* **5** a single exposure on a cinema film.
frame of mind the way you think or feel for a while.

frame[2] *verb* (**framed**, **framing**) **1** put a frame on or round. **2** construct, *They framed the* *question badly.* **3** formulate (a concept, plan, or system). **4** make an innocent person seem guilty by arranging false evidence.

frame-up *noun* (*informal*) a conspiracy, especially to make an innocent person appear guilty.

framework *noun* **1** a frame supporting something. **2** a basic plan or system.

franchise *noun* **1** the right to vote in elections. **2** a licence to sell a firm's goods or services in a certain area.

frangipani (*say* **fran**-juh-pan-ee) *noun* a small tree with fragrant white and yellow flowers.

frank[1] *adjective* making your thoughts and feelings clear to people; candid. **frankly** *adverb*, **frankness** *noun*

frank[2] *verb* mark a letter or parcel to show that postage has been paid.

frankfurt *noun* (also **frankfurter**) a seasoned smoked sausage. [named after Frankfurt in Germany]

frankincense *noun* a sweet-smelling gum burnt as incense.

frantic *adjective* wildly agitated or excited. **frantically** *adverb* [from Greek *phrenetikos* = mad]

frappé (*say* **frap**-ay) *noun* a drink served with ice or frozen to a slushy consistency. [French]

fraternal (*say* fruh-**ter**-nuhl) *adjective* of a brother or brothers. **fraternally** *adverb* [from Latin *frater* = brother]

fraternise *verb* (**fraternised, fraternising**) associate with other people in a friendly way. **fraternisation** *noun*

fraternity *noun* (*plural* **fraternities**) **1** a brotherly feeling. **2** a group of people who have the same interests or occupation, *the medical fraternity.*

fraud *noun* **1** criminal deception; a dishonest trick. **2** an impostor; a person or thing that is not what it pretends to be. **fraudulence** *noun*, **fraudulent** *adjective*, **fraudulently** *adverb*

fraught *adjective* filled; involving, *The situation is fraught with danger.* [from an old use, = loaded with freight]

fray[1] *noun* a fight; a conflict, *ready for the fray.* [same origin as *affray*]

fray[2] *verb* **1** make or become ragged so that loose threads show. **2** (of tempers or nerves) become strained or upset. **frayed** *adjective*

freak[1] *noun* a very strange or abnormal person, animal, or thing. **freakish** *adjective*

freak[2] *verb* (*informal*) make or become angry or panicky, *He freaked when he saw the damage; Exams freak me out.*

freckle *noun* a small brown spot on the skin. **freckled** *adjective*

free[1] *adjective* (**freer, freest**) **1** able to do what you want to do or go where you want to go. **2** not costing anything. **3** not fixed, *Leave one end free.* **4** not having or affected by something, *free of responsibilities.* **5** available; not being used or occupied. **6** generous, *She is very free with her money.* **freely** *adverb*

free[2] *verb* (**freed, freeing**) **1** set free. **2** clear; disentangle.

freebie *noun* (*informal*) a thing given free of charge.

freedom *noun* **1** being free; independence. **2** liberty of action, *freedom to leave.*

freehand *adjective* (of a drawing) done without the aid of instruments such as rulers.

freehold *noun* possessing land or a house as its absolute owner, not as a tenant renting from a landlord.

freelance *adjective* self-employed and hired to work for different companies on particular assignments, *a freelance journalist.* **freelancer** *noun*

free market *noun* a market governed by unrestricted competition.

Freemason *noun* a member of an international society for men providing mutual support. **Freemasonry** *noun*

freestyle *adjective* (of a swimming race) in which any stroke may be used, in practice usually the crawl.

freeway *noun* a multi-laned highway for high-speed traffic.

freewheel *verb* **1** ride a bicycle without needing to pedal. **2** act without constraint.

freeze[1] *verb* (**froze, frozen, freezing**) **1** turn into ice; become covered with ice. **2** make or be very cold. **3** keep wages or prices at a fixed level. **4** suddenly stand completely still.

freeze[2] *noun* **1** a period of freezing weather. **2** the freezing of wages or prices.

freezer *noun* a refrigerator in which food can be frozen quickly and stored.

freight (*say* frayt) *noun* **1** the transport of goods. **2** goods transported as cargo. **freight** *verb*

freighter (*say* **fray**-tuh) *noun* a ship or aircraft carrying mainly cargo.

French horn *noun* a brass wind instrument with a long tube coiled in a circle.

French knitting *noun* a form of circular knitting in which the yarn is looped over hooks on a hollow reel. Also called *tomboy stitch.*

French window *noun* a long window that serves as a door on an outside wall.

frenzy *noun* wild excitement or agitation. **frenzied** *adjective* [same origin as *frantic*]

frequency *noun* (*plural* **frequencies**) **1** being frequent. **2** how often something happens. **3** the number of oscillations per second of a wave of sound or light etc. **4** (in statistics) the ratio of the number of actual to possible occurrences of an event.

frequency distribution *noun* (in statistics) a measurement of the frequency of occurrence of the values of a variable.

frequent[1] (*say* **free**-kwuhnt) *adjective* happening often. **frequently** *adverb*

frequent[2] (*say* fruh-**kwent**) *verb* be in or go to a place often, *They frequented the club.* [from Latin *frequens* = crowded]

fresco *noun* (*plural* **frescoes**) a picture painted on a wall or ceiling before the plaster is dry. [Italian, = fresh]

fresh *adjective* **1** newly made or produced or arrived; not stale, *fresh bread.* **2** different or new, *a fresh approach.* **3** not tinned; not preserved, *fresh fruit.* **4** cool and clean, *fresh air.* **5** not salty, *fresh water.* **6** alert, not weary. **freshly** *adverb*, **freshness** *noun*

freshen *verb* make or become fresh.

freshwater *adjective* of fresh water not seawater; living in rivers or lakes.

fret[1] *verb* (**fretted**, **fretting**) worry or be upset about something. **fretful** *adjective*, **fretfully** *adverb*

fret[2] *noun* a bar or ridge on the fingerboard of a stringed musical instrument.

fretsaw *noun* a very narrow saw used for cutting decorative patterns in wood.

friable *adjective* easily crumbled.

friar *noun* a man who is a member of certain Roman Catholic religious orders, who has vowed to live a life of poverty. **friary** *noun* [from Latin *frater* = brother]

friction *noun* **1** rubbing. **2** disagreement; quarrelling. **frictional** *adjective* [from Latin *frictum* = rubbed]

Friday *noun* the day of the week following Thursday. [Old English = day of Frigg (the wife of the Norse god Odin)]

fridge *noun* a refrigerator.

friend *noun* **1** a person you like who likes you, *After school I like to play in the park with my friends.* **2** a helpful or kind person.

friendless *adjective* without a friend.

friendly *adjective* behaving like a friend. **friendliness** *noun*

friendly number *noun* (in mathematics) a number that is relatively easy to use in addition and subtraction.

friendship *noun* being friends.

frieze (*say* freez) *noun* a strip of designs or pictures round the top of a wall.

frigate (*say* **frig**-uht) *noun* a small warship.

fright *noun* **1** sudden great fear. **2** a person or thing that looks ridiculous.

frighten *verb* make or become afraid. **be frightened of** be afraid of.

frightful *adjective* awful; very great or bad. **frightfully** *adverb*

frigid *adjective* **1** extremely cold. **2** unfriendly; not affectionate. **frigidity** *noun*, **frigidly** *adverb* [from Latin *frigidus* = cold]

frill *noun* **1** a decorative gathered or pleated trimming on an edge, such as one on a dress or curtain. **2** something extra that is pleasant but unnecessary, *a simple life with no frills.* **frilled** *adjective*, **frilly** *adjective*

fringe *noun* **1** a decorative edging with many threads hanging down loosely. **2** a straight line of short hair hanging down over the forehead. **3** the edge of something. **fringed** *adjective*

fringe benefits *plural noun* benefits provided for an employee or pensioner in addition to income.

frisk *verb* **1** jump or run about playfully. **2** search somebody by running your hands over their clothes.

frisky *adjective* (**friskier**, **friskiest**) lively; playful. **friskily** *adverb*, **friskiness** *noun*

fritter[1] *noun* a slice of meat or fruit or vegetable coated in batter and fried. [from Latin *frictum* = fried]

fritter[2] *verb* waste something gradually; spend money or time on trivial things. [from an old word *fritters* = fragments]

fritz *noun* (*Australian*) a large bland sausage, usually sliced and eaten cold.

frivolous *adjective* seeking pleasure in a light-hearted way; not serious; not sensible. **frivolity** *noun*, **frivolously** *adverb*

frizz *noun* hair curled into a wiry mass. **frizziness** *noun*, **frizzy** *adjective*

frizzle *verb* (**frizzled**, **frizzling**) **1** fry with a spluttering noise. **2** shrivel something by burning it.

fro *adverb* **to and fro** backwards and forwards.

frock *noun* a girl's or woman's dress.

frog *noun* a small jumping animal that can live both in water and on land. **a frog in your throat** hoarseness.

frogman *noun* (*plural* **frogmen**) a swimmer equipped with a rubber suit, flippers, and breathing apparatus for swimming and working underwater.

frogmouth *noun* a nocturnal bird with a large wide beak like a frog's mouth.

frolic[1] *noun* a lively cheerful game or entertainment. **frolicsome** *adjective*

frolic[2] *verb* (**frolicked**, **frolicking**) play about in a lively, cheerful way.

from *preposition* This word is used to show **1** starting point in space or time or order (*We flew from Uluru to Perth; We work from 9 to 5 o'clock; Count from one to ten*), **2** source or origin (*Get water from the tap*), **3** separation or release (*Take the gun from him; She was freed from prison*), **4** difference (*Can you tell margarine from butter?*), **5** cause (*I suffer from headaches*).

frond *noun* a leaf-like part of a fern or other flowerless plant, or of a palm tree. [from Latin *frondis* = of a leaf]

frons *noun* (*plural* **frontes**) the forehead or equivalent part of an animal.

front[1] *noun* **1** the part or side that comes first or is the most important or furthest forward. **2** a road or promenade along the seashore. **3** the place where fighting is happening in a war. **frontal** *adjective* [from Latin *frontis* = of the forehead]

front[2] *adjective* of the front; in front.

front[3] *verb* face; have the front towards, *a house fronting the sea.*
front up (*informal*) show up; appear.

frontage *noun* the front of a building; the land beside this.

frontier *noun* the boundary between two countries or regions.

frontispiece *noun* an illustration opposite the title page of a book.

frost[1] *noun* **1** powdery ice that forms on things in freezing weather. **2** weather with a temperature below freezing point. **frosty** *adjective*

frost[2] *verb* cover with frost or frosting.

frostbite *noun* harm done to the body by very cold weather. **frostbitten** *adjective*

frosted glass *noun* glass made cloudy so that you cannot see through it.

frosting *noun* sugar icing for cakes.

froth *noun* a white mass of tiny bubbles on a liquid. **frothy** *adjective*

frown[1] *verb* wrinkle your forehead because you are angry or worried.

frown[2] *noun* a frowning movement or look.

froze *past tense* of **freeze**[1].

frozen *past participle* of **freeze**[1].

frugal (*say* **froo**-guhl) *adjective* **1** very economical and careful. **2** costing very little money; not plentiful, *a frugal meal.* **frugality** *noun*, **frugally** *adverb*

fruit[1] *noun* (*plural* **fruits** or **fruit**) **1** the seed container that grows on a tree or plant and is often used as food. **2** the result of doing something, *the fruits of his efforts.* **fruity** *adjective*

fruit[2] *verb* produce fruit.

fruitful *adjective* producing good results, *fruitful discussions.* **fruitfully** *adverb*

fruition (*say* froo-**ish**-uhn) *noun* the achievement of what was hoped or worked for, *Our plans never came to fruition.* [from Latin *frui* = enjoy]

fruitless *adjective* producing no results. **fruitlessly** *adverb*

frustrate *verb* (**frustrated, frustrating**) prevent somebody from doing something; prevent from being successful, *frustrate their wicked plans.* **frustration** *noun* [from Latin *frustra* = in vain]

fry[1] *verb* (**fried, frying**) cook something in very hot fat. **fryer** *noun*

fry[2] *plural noun* very young fishes.

frying pan (also **frypan**) *noun* a shallow pan for frying things.

FTA *abbreviation* Free Trade Agreement.

fuchsia (*say* **fyoo**-shuh) *noun* an ornamental plant with flowers that hang down.

fudge *noun* a soft sugary sweet.

fuel[1] *noun* something that is burnt to produce heat or power.

fuel[2] *verb* (**fuelled, fuelling**) supply something with fuel.

fugitive (*say* **fyoo**-juh-tiv) *noun* a person who is running away from something. [from Latin *fugere* = flee]

fugue (*say* fyoog) *noun* a piece of music in which tunes are repeated in a pattern.

fulcrum *noun* the point on which a lever rests.

fulfil *verb* (**fulfilled, fulfilling**) **1** do what is required; satisfy; carry out, *You must fulfil your promises.* **2** make something come true, *It fulfilled an ancient prophecy.* **fulfilment** *noun*

full[1] *adjective* **1** containing as much or as many as possible. **2** having many people or things, *full of ideas.* **3** complete, *the full story.* **4** the greatest possible, *at full speed.* **5** fitting loosely; with many folds, *a full skirt.* **fullness** *noun*

full[2] *adverb* completely; exactly, *It hit him full in the face.*

full-blown *adjective* fully developed.

full moon *noun* the moon when you can see its whole disc.

full stop *noun* the dot used as a punctuation mark at the end of a sentence or an abbreviation.

fully *adverb* completely.

fulsome *adjective* praising something too much or too emotionally.

> **Usage** The original meaning of *fulsome* was 'generous or abundant'; this meaning is now regarded by some people as wrong.

fumble *verb* (**fumbled, fumbling**) hold or handle something clumsily.

fume[1] *noun* (also **fumes**) strong-smelling smoke or gas.

fume[2] *verb* (**fumed, fuming**) **1** give off fumes. **2** be very angry. [from Latin *fumus* = smoke]

fumigate (*say* **fyoo**-muh-gayt) *verb* (**fumigated, fumigating**) disinfect something by fumes. **fumigation** *noun*

fun *noun* amusement; enjoyment, *They had fun riding their bikes.*
make fun of make people laugh at a person or thing.

> **Usage** The use of *fun* as an adjective (e.g. *a fun party*) is common in informal use, but considered incorrect by some people.

function[1] *noun* **1** what somebody or something is there to do, *The function of a knife is to cut things.* **2** an important event or party. **3** a basic operation in a computer. **4** a variable quantity regarded in relation to another or others in terms of which it may be expressed or on which its value depends, *x is a function of y and z.*

function[2] *verb* perform a function; work properly. [from Latin *functum* = performed]

functional *adjective* **1** working properly. **2** practical without being decorative or luxurious. **functionally** *adverb*

fund[1] *noun* **1** money collected or kept for a special purpose. **2** a stock or supply.

fund[2] *verb* supply with money.

fundamental *adjective* basic. **fundamentally** *adverb* [from Latin *fundamentum* = foundation]

fundamentalism *noun* strict maintenance or literal interpretation of traditional religious beliefs. **fundamentalist** *noun & adjective*

fundraise *verb* (**fundraised, fundraising**) seek financial support for a charity, cause, or other enterprise, *We had a sausage sizzle at our school to fundraise for new sporting equipment.* **fundraiser** *noun*

funds *plural noun* money resources.

funeral *noun* the ceremony when a dead person is buried or cremated. [from Latin *funeris* = of a burial]

funereal (*say* fyoo-**neer**-ree-uhl) *adjective* dark; dismal.

fungus *noun* (*plural* **fungi**, *say* **fung**-gee or **fung**-guy) a plant without leaves or flowers that grows on other plants or on decayed material, *Mushrooms are fungi.*

funk *noun* a style of dance music with a strong rhythm that typically accentuates the first beat in the bar.

funky *adjective* (*informal*) **1** (of music) having or using a strong dance rhythm. **2** exciting; excellent.

funnel *noun* **1** a metal chimney on a ship or steam engine. **2** a tube that is wide at the top and narrow at the bottom to help you pour things into a narrow opening. [from Latin *fundere* = pour]

funnel-web *noun* a venomous Australian spider.

funny *adjective* (**funnier, funniest**) **1** that makes you laugh or smile. **2** strange; odd, *a funny smell.* **funnily** *adverb*

fur *noun* **1** the soft hair that covers some animals. **2** animal skin with the fur on it, used for clothing; fabric that looks like animal fur.

furbish *verb* polish or clean; renovate.

furious *adjective* **1** very angry. **2** violent; intense, *furious heat.* **furiously** *adverb*

furl *verb* roll up a sail, flag, or umbrella.

furlong *noun* one eighth of a mile, about 200 metres.

furlough (*say* **fer**-loh) *noun* leave of absence from duty; a holiday.

furnace *noun* a device in which great heat can be produced, e.g. for melting metals or making glass.

furnish *verb* **1** provide a place with furniture. **2** provide; supply.

furnishings *plural noun* furniture, fittings, and other decorative accessories such as curtains and carpets, for a house or room.

furniture *noun* tables, chairs, and other movable things that you need in a room or building.

furore (*say* **fyoo**-raw) *noun* an excited or angry uproar. [from Latin *furor* = madness]

furphy *noun* (*Australian informal*) a rumour; a false report. [named after *Furphy* water carts (centres of gossip during the First World War) made by the firm J. Furphy & Sons]

furrow[1] *noun* **1** a long cut in the ground made by a plough or other implement. **2** a groove. **3** a deep wrinkle in the skin.

furrow[2] *verb* make furrows in something.

furry *adjective* like fur; covered with fur.

further[1] *adverb & adjective* **1** at or to a

greater distance; more distant. **2** more; additional, *We made further enquiries.*

Usage See the note at *farther*.

further[2] *verb* help something to progress, *This success will further your career.* **furtherance** *noun*

further education *noun* education beyond secondary school.

furthermore *adverb* also; moreover.

furthest *adverb & adjective* at or to the greatest distance; most distant.

furtive *adjective* stealthy; trying not to be seen. **furtively** *adverb*, **furtiveness** *noun* [from Latin *furtivus* = stolen]

fury *noun* wild anger; rage. [from Latin *furia* = rage; an avenging spirit]

fuse[1] *noun* a safety device containing a short piece of wire that melts if too much electricity is passed through it.

fuse[2] *verb* (**fused, fusing**) **1** stop working because a fuse has melted. **2** blend together, especially through melting. [from Latin *fusum* = melted]

fuse[3] *noun* a length of material that burns easily, used for setting off an explosive. [from Latin *fusus* = a spindle]

fuselage (*say* **fyoo**-zuh-lah*zh*) *noun* the body of an aircraft.

fusion *noun* **1** the action of blending or uniting things. **2** the uniting of atomic nuclei, usually releasing energy.

fuss[1] *noun* (*plural* **fusses**) **1** unnecessary excitement or bustle. **2** an agitated protest.

fuss[2] *verb* make a fuss about something.

fussy *adjective* (**fussier, fussiest**) **1** fussing; inclined to make a fuss. **2** choosing very carefully; hard to please. **3** full of unnecessary details or decorations. **fussily** *adverb*, **fussiness** *noun*

fusty *adjective* (**fustier, fustiest**) smelling stale or stuffy. **fustiness** *noun*

futile (*say* **fyoo**-tyul) *noun* useless; having no result. **futility** *noun* [from Latin *futilis* = leaking]

future[1] *noun* the time that will come; what is going to happen then.

future[2] *adjective* belonging or referring to the future.

future tense *noun* a form of a verb that shows that something is going to happen in the time that will come, for example *will* in the sentence *I will see you tomorrow*.

fuzz *noun* something fluffy or frizzy.

fuzzy *adjective* **1** fluffy or frizzy. **2** blurred; not clear. **fuzzily** *adverb*, **fuzziness** *noun*

FYI *abbreviation* for your information.

Gg

g *abbreviation* gram(s).

gabardine *noun* a strong fabric woven in a slanting pattern.

gabble *verb* (**gabbled**, **gabbling**) talk so quickly that it is difficult to know what is being said.

gable *noun* the pointed part at the top of an outside wall, between two sloping roofs. **gabled** *adjective*

gad *verb* (**gadded**, **gadding**)
gad about go about in search of pleasure.
gadabout *noun*

gadget *noun* any small useful tool. **gadgetry** *noun*

Gaelic (*say* **gay**-lik) *noun* the Celtic languages of Scotland and Ireland.

gaff *noun* a stick with a metal hook for landing large fish.

gaffe *noun* a blunder. [French]

gag[1] *noun* **1** something put into a person's mouth or tied over it to prevent speaking. **2** a joke.

gag[2] *verb* (**gagged**, **gagging**) **1** put a gag on a person. **2** prevent from making comments, *We cannot gag the press.* **3** retch.

gaggle *noun* a flock of geese.

gaiety *noun* cheerfulness.

gaily *adverb* in a cheerful way.

gain[1] *verb* **1** get something that you did not have before; obtain. **2** (of a clock or watch) become ahead of the correct time. **3** reach; arrive at, *At last we gained the shore.*
gain on come closer to a person or thing in chasing them or in a race.

gain[2] *noun* something gained; a profit or improvement. **gainful** *adjective*

gait *noun* a way of walking or running, *He walked with a shuffling gait.* [from a dialect word *gate* = going]

gaiter *noun* a leather or cloth covering for the lower part of the leg.

gala (*say* **gah**-luh) *noun* a festive occasion.

galah (*say* guh-**lah**) *noun* (*Australian*) **1** a pink-breasted cockatoo with a grey back. **2** (*informal*) a fool or idiot. [from Yuwaalaraay and related languages *gilaa*]

galaxy *noun* (*plural* **galaxies**) a very large group of stars. **galactic** *adjective*

gale *noun* a very strong wind.

gall[1] (*say* gawl) *noun* **1** bile. **2** bitterness of feeling. **3** (*informal*) impudence.

gall[2] (*say* gawl) *noun* a sore spot on an animal's skin.

gall[3] *verb* **1** rub sore. **2** vex or humiliate someone.

gallant (*say* **gal**-uhnt) *adjective* **1** brave; chivalrous. **2** fine; stately, *our gallant ship.* **gallantly** *adverb*, **gallantry** *noun*

gallbladder *noun* an organ beneath the liver that stores bile.

galleon *noun* a large Spanish sailing ship used in the 16th–17th centuries.

gallery *noun* (*plural* **galleries**) **1** a platform jutting out from the wall in a church or hall. **2** the highest balcony in a cinema or theatre. **3** a long room or passage. **4** a room or building for showing works of art.

galley *noun* (*plural* **galleys**) **1** an ancient type of ship driven by oars. **2** the kitchen in a ship or aircraft.

galling (*say* **gaw**-ling) *adjective* vexing; humiliating.

gallivant *verb* go about in search of pleasure.

gallon *noun* a measure of liquid, 8 pints or about 4½ litres.

gallop[1] *noun* **1** the fastest pace a horse can go. **2** a fast ride on a horse.

gallop[2] *verb* (**galloped**, **galloping**) go or ride at a gallop.

gallows *noun* a framework with a noose for hanging criminals.

Gallup poll *noun* (*trademark*) an estimate of public opinion, made by questioning a representative sample of people. [named after G. H. Gallup, the American statistician who devised it]

galore *adverb* in plenty; in great numbers, *bargains galore.*

galoshes *plural noun* a pair of waterproof shoes worn over ordinary shoes.

galvanise *verb* (**galvanised**, **galvanising**) **1** stimulate into sudden activity. **2** coat iron with zinc to protect it from rust.

galvanisation *noun* [named after an Italian scientist, Luigi Galvani]

galvo *noun* (*Australian informal*) galvanised iron.

gambit *noun* **1** a kind of opening move in chess. **2** an action or remark intended to gain an advantage.

gamble[1] *verb* (**gambled**, **gambling**) **1** bet on the result of a game, race, or other event. **2** take great risks in the hope of gaining something. **gambler** *noun*

gamble[2] *noun* **1** gambling. **2** a risky attempt.

gambol *verb* (**gambolled**, **gambolling**) jump or skip about in play.

game[1] *noun* **1** an activity that one engages in for amusement or fun. **2** a form of competitive activity or sport played according to rules. **3** a section of a long game such as tennis. **4** a scheme or plan; a trick. **5** wild animals or birds hunted for sport or food.

game[2] *adjective* **1** able and willing to do something, *She is game for all kinds of tricks.* **2** brave. **gamely** *adverb*

game[3] *verb* **1** manipulate a situation, typically in a way that is unfair or unscrupulous, *The big company gamed the system for its financial advantage.* **2** play a gambling or video game, *Most of her friends like to game and watch movies on the weekend.*

gamepad *noun* an input device for a computer game console or computer that uses buttons to control the motion of an image on the screen.

gamer *noun* a person who plays video games.

gamete (*say* **gam**-eet) *noun* a sexual cell capable of fusing with another in reproduction. [from Greek *gamos* = marriage]

gaming *noun* **1** gambling. **2** playing video or computer games.

gamma *noun* the third letter of the Greek alphabet, = g.

gamma rays *plural noun* very short X-rays.

gammon *noun* a kind of ham.

gamut (*say* **gam**-uht) *noun* the whole range or scope of anything, *the whole gamut of emotion.*

gander *noun* a male goose.

gang[1] *noun* a number of people who do things together.

gang[2] *verb* **gang up on** combine in a group against someone.

gang-gang *noun* a grey cockatoo of south-east Australia. [Wiradjuri, from an imitation of the bird call]

gangling *adjective* tall, thin, and awkward-looking.

gangplank *noun* a plank placed so that people can walk into or out of a boat.

gangrene (*say* **gang**-green) *noun* decay of body tissue in a living person.

gangster *noun* a member of a gang of violent criminals.

gangway *noun* **1** a gap left for people to pass between rows of seats or through a crowd. **2** a movable bridge placed so that people can walk into or out of a ship.

gaol alternative spelling of **jail**[1].

gap *noun* **1** a break or opening in something continuous such as a hedge or fence. **2** an interval. **3** a wide difference in ideas.

gape *verb* (**gaped**, **gaping**) **1** have your mouth open. **2** stare with your mouth open. **3** be open wide; split.

garage (*say* **ga**-rahzh or guh-**rahzh**) *noun* **1** a building in which a motor vehicle or vehicles may be kept. **2** an establishment selling petrol or servicing motor vehicles.

garage sale *noun* a sale of unwanted household goods held in the garage or front garden of someone's house.

garb *noun* special clothing. **garb** *verb*

garbage *noun* rubbish.

garble *verb* (**garbled**, **garbling**) give a confused account of a story or message so that it is misunderstood. **garbled** *adjective*

garbo *noun* (*Australian informal*) a garbage collector.

garden *noun* a piece of ground where flowers, fruit, or vegetables are grown. **gardener** *noun*, **gardening** *noun*

gardenia (*say* gah-**dee**-nee-uh) *noun* a tree or shrub with large fragrant white or yellow flowers. [named after a Scottish naturalist, Dr A. Garden]

garfish *noun* an edible fish with a long spear-like snout.

gargantuan (*say* gah-**gan**-choo-uhn) *adjective* gigantic. [from the name of Gargantua, a giant in a story]

gargle *verb* (**gargled**, **gargling**) hold a liquid at the back of the mouth and breathe air through it to wash the inside of the throat. **gargle** *noun*

gargoyle *noun* an ugly or comical face or figure carved on a building, especially on a water spout.

garish (*say* **gair**-rish) *adjective* too bright or highly coloured; gaudy. **garishly** *adverb*

garland *noun* a wreath of flowers worn or hung as a decoration. **garland** *verb*

garlic *noun* a plant rather like an onion, used for flavouring food.

garment *noun* a piece of clothing.

garner *verb* store up; gather; collect.

garnet *noun* a dark red stone used as a gem.

garnish[1] *verb* decorate.

garnish[2] *noun* something used to decorate food or give it extra flavour.

garret *noun* an attic.

garrison *noun* **1** troops stationed in a town or fort to defend it. **2** the building they occupy. **garrison** *verb*

garrulous (*say* **ga**-ruh-luhs) *adjective* talkative. **garrulousness** *noun*

garter *noun* a band of elastic to hold up a sock or stocking.

gas[1] *noun* (*plural* **gases**) **1** a substance that (like air) can move freely and is not liquid or solid at ordinary temperatures. **2** a flammable gas used for lighting, heating, or cooking.

gas[2] *verb* (**gassed**, **gassing**) **1** kill or injure with gas. **2** (*informal*) talk idly for a long time.

gas[3] *noun* (*American*) gasoline.

gash[1] *noun* along deep cut or wound.

gash[2] *verb* make a gash in something.

gasket *noun* a flat ring or strip of soft material for sealing a joint between metal surfaces.

gasoline *noun* (*American*) petrol.

gasometer (*say* ga-**som**-uh-tuh) *noun* a large round tank in which gas is stored.

gasp *verb* **1** breathe in suddenly when you are shocked or surprised. **2** struggle to breathe with your mouth open when you are tired or ill. **3** speak in a breathless way. **gasp** *noun*

gassy *adjective* of or like gas.

gastric *adjective* of the stomach. [from Greek *gaster* = stomach]

gastroenteritis (*say* gas-troh-en-tuh-**ruy**-tuhs) *noun* inflammation of the stomach and intestines.

gastronomy (*say* gas-**tron**-uh-mee) *noun* the science of good eating. **gastronomic** *adjective* [from Greek *gaster* = stomach, + *nomia* = management]

gastropod *noun* an animal (e.g. a snail) that moves by means of a fleshy 'foot' on its stomach. [from Greek *gaster* = stomach, + *podos* = of the foot]

gate *noun* **1** a movable barrier, usually on hinges, serving as a door in a wall or fence. **2** the opening it covers. **3** a barrier for controlling the flow of water in a dam or lock. **4** the number of people attending a sports game or other event.

gateau (*say* **gat**-oh) *noun* a large rich cream cake. [from French *gâteau* = cake]

gatecrash *verb* go to a private party without being invited. **gatecrasher** *noun*

gateway *noun* **1** an opening containing a gate. **2** a way to reach something, *The gateway to success.*

gather *verb* **1** come or bring together. **2** collect; obtain gradually, *gather information.* **3** collect as harvest; pluck, *gather the grapes.* **4** understand; learn, *We gather you have been on holiday.* **5** pull cloth into folds by running a thread through it. **6** (of a sore) swell up and form pus.

gathering *noun* **1** an assembly of people. **2** a swelling that forms pus.

gaudy *adjective* too showy and bright. **gaudily** *adverb*, **gaudiness** *noun* [from Latin *gaudere* = rejoice]

gauge[1] (*say* gayj) *noun* **1** a standard measurement. **2** the distance between a pair of rails on a railway. **3** a measuring instrument.

gauge[2] *verb* (**gauged**, **gauging**) **1** measure. **2** estimate; form a judgement.

gaunt *adjective* **1** (of a person) lean and haggard. **2** (of a place) grim or desolate-looking. **gauntness** *noun*

gauntlet[1] *noun* a glove with a wide cuff covering the wrist. [from French *gant* = glove]

gauntlet[2] *noun* **run the gauntlet** have to suffer continuous severe criticism or risk. [from a former military and naval punishment in which the victim was made to pass between two rows of men who struck him as he passed; the word is from Swedish *gatlopp* = passage]

gauze *noun* **1** thin transparent woven material. **2** fine wire mesh. **gauzy** *adjective* [from Gaza, a town in Palestine]

gave *past tense* of **give**.

gay[1] *adjective* **1** homosexual. **2** (*old use*) cheerful. **3** (*old use*) brightly coloured. **gayness** *noun*

gay[2] *noun* a homosexual person, especially a male.

gaze[1] *verb* (**gazed**, **gazing**) look at something steadily for a long time.

gaze[2] *noun* a long steady look.

gazebo (*say* guh-**zee**-boh) *noun* (*plural* **gazebos**) a small structure providing shade and seating in a garden or park.

gazelle *noun* a small antelope.

gazette *noun* **1** a newspaper. **2** an official journal.

gazetteer (*say* gaz-uh-**teer**) *noun* a list of place names.

Gb *abbreviation* gigabyte.

g'day *interjection* (*Australian informal*) good-day.

GDP *abbreviation* gross domestic product.

gear[1] *noun* **1** a cogwheel, especially one of a set in a motor vehicle that transmits movement from the engine to the wheels when they are connected. **2** equipment; apparatus, *camping gear.* **3** (*informal*) clothing.

gear[2] *verb* **1** provide with or connect by gears. **2** put in gear.
gear to adjust or adapt, *a factory geared to the export trade.*
gear up get ready, *the resort is gearing up for the tourist season.*

gearbox *noun* a case enclosing gears.

gecko *noun* (*plural* **geckos**) a small tropical lizard. [from Malay]

geek *noun* (*informal*) **1** a dull or socially inept person. **2** a computer fanatic.

geese *plural* of **goose**.

geezer *noun* (*informal*) **1** a person. **2** an old man.

Geiger counter (*say* **guy**-guh) *noun* an instrument that detects and measures radioactivity. [named after the German scientist H. W. Geiger]

gelatine *noun* a clear jelly-like substance made by boiling animal tissue and used to make jellies and other foods and in photographic film. **gelatinous** (*say* juh-**lat**-uh-nuhs) *adjective* [same origin as *jelly*]

gelato (*say* juh-**lah**-toh) *noun* (*plural* **gelati**, *say* juh-**lah**-tee) a kind of ice cream with a soft smooth texture. [Italian]

geld *verb* castrate; spay.

gelding *noun* a castrated horse or other male animal.

gelignite (*say* **jel**-uhg-nuyt) *noun* a kind of explosive. [from *gelatine*, + Latin *ignis* = fire]

gem *noun* **1** a precious stone. **2** an excellent person or thing.

gemfish *noun* (*Australian*) an edible sea fish. Also called *hake.*

Gemini *noun* **1** a constellation and the third sign of the zodiac (the Twins). **2** a person born when the sun is in this sign. [from Latin, = twins]

gen *abbreviation* generation, *the next gen of computers.*

gender *noun* **1** the group in which a noun is classed in the grammar of some languages (e.g. *masculine, feminine, neuter.*) **2** a person's sex. [from Latin *genus* = a kind]

gene (*say* jeen) *noun* a unit of heredity that is transferred from parent to offspring. [from Greek, = born]

genealogy (*say* jee-nee-**al**-uh-jee) *noun* **1** a statement or diagram showing how people are descended from an ancestor; a pedigree. **2** the study of family history and ancestors. **genealogical** (*say* jee-nee-uh-**loj**-i-kuhl) *adjective* [from Greek *genea* = race of people, + *-logy*]

general[1] *adjective* **1** of all or most people or things, *general approval.* **2** usual. **3** not detailed; not exact, *a general account.* **4** chief; head, *the general secretary.*

general[2] *noun* a senior army officer.

general election *noun* a national parliamentary election.

generalise *verb* (**generalised, generalising**) **1** make a statement that is true of most cases. **2** bring into general use.
generalisation *noun*

generality *noun* (*plural* **generalities**) **1** being general. **2** a general statement without exact details.

generally *adverb* **1** usually. **2** in a general sense; without regard to details, *I was speaking generally.*

general practitioner *noun* a doctor who treats cases of all kinds.

generate *verb* (**generated, generating**) produce; create.

generation *noun* **1** generating. **2** a single stage in a family, *Three generations were included: children, parents, and grandparents.* **3** all the people born at about the same time. **4** the average period (regarded as about 30 years) in which children grow up and take the former place of their parents. **5** a single stage in the development of a product, *fourth-generation computers.*

Generation X *noun* the generation born after that of the baby boomers (roughly from the early 1960s to the late 1970s).

Generation Y *noun* the generation born in the 1980s and 1990s.

Generation Z *noun* the generation reaching adulthood in the second decade of the 21st century.

generator *noun* **1** an apparatus for producing gases or steam. **2** a machine for converting mechanical energy into electricity.

generic (*say* juh-**ne**-rik) *adjective* **1** of a whole genus or kind. **2** (of consumer goods) having no brand name. **generically** *adverb*

generous *adjective* **1** willing to give things or share them. **2** given freely; plentiful, *a generous helping.* **3** kindly and not petty in making judgements. **generosity** *noun*, **generously** *adverb*

genesis *noun* a beginning or origin. [Greek, = creation or origin]

genetic (*say* juh-**net**-ik) *adjective* of genes; of characteristics inherited from parents or ancestors. **genetically** *adverb* [from *genesis*]

genetically modified *adjective* (of an organism) containing genetic material that has been artificially altered so as to produce a desired characteristic.

genetic engineering *noun* the manipulation of DNA to modify hereditary features.

genetic screening *noun* the study of a person's DNA to identify susceptibility to particular diseases or abnormalities.

genial (*say* **jee**-nee-uhl) *adjective* kindly and cheerful. **geniality** *noun*, **genially** *adverb*

genie (*say* **jee**-nee) *noun* (in Arabian tales) a spirit with strange powers. [from Arabic *jinni*]

genital (*say* **jen**-uh-tuhl) *adjective* of animal reproduction or reproductive organs.

genitals (*say* **jen**-uh-tuhlz) *plural noun* external sexual organs.

genius *noun* (*plural* **geniuses**) **1** an unusually clever person. **2** a very great natural ability. [Latin, = a spirit]

genocide (*say* **jen**-uh-suyd) *noun* deliberate extermination of a race of people. [from Greek *genos* = a race, + Latin *caedere* = kill]

genome (*say* **jee**-nohm) *noun* the complete set of genetic material of an animal, plant, or other living thing. **genomics** *noun*

genotype *noun* the genetic constitution of an individual.

genre (*say* ***zh*on**-ruh) *noun* a particular kind or style of art, literature, or music, *She reads books in the crime genre.* [French]

gent *noun* (*informal*) a gentleman; a man.

genteel (*say* jen-**teel**) *adjective* trying to seem polite and refined. **genteelly** *adverb*, **gentility** (*say* jen-**til**-uh-tee) *noun*

gentile *noun* a person who is not Jewish.

gentle *adjective* **1** kind and quiet. **2** not rough or severe. **gentleness** *noun*, **gently** *adverb*

gentleman (*plural* **gentlemen**) **1** a well-mannered or honourable man. **2** a man of good social position. **3** (in polite use) a man.

gentry *noun* upper-class people.

genuine *adjective* really what it is said to be, not faked or pretending. **genuinely** *adverb*, **genuineness** *noun*

genus (*say* **jee**-nuhs) *noun* (*plural* **genera**, *say* **jen**-uh-ruh) a group of similar animals or plants, *Lions and tigers belong to the same genus.* [Latin, = family or race]

geo- *prefix* earth. [from Greek *ge* = earth]

geography (*say* jee-**og**-ruh-fee) *noun* the study of the earth's surface and of its climate, peoples, and products. **geographer** *noun*, **geographical** *adjective*, **geographically** *adverb* [from *geo-* + *-graphy*]

geology (*say* jee-**ol**-uh-jee) *noun* the study of the structure of the earth's crust and its layers. **geological** *adjective*, **geologically** *adverb*, **geologist** *noun* [from *geo-* + *-logy*]

geometry (*say* jee-**om**-uh-tree) *noun* the study of lines, angles, surfaces, and solids in mathematics. **geometric** *adjective*, **geometrical** *adjective*, **geometrically** *adverb* [from *geo-*, + Greek *-metria* = measurement]

geomorphic *adjective* relating to the form of the landscape and other natural features of the earth's surface.

geosequestration *noun* the process of capturing and storing carbon dioxide underground. [from *geo-* + *sequestration* = hiding away]

geothermal *adjective* relating to or produced by the internal heat of the earth.

geranium *noun* a garden plant with red, pink, or white flowers.

gerbil (*say* **jer**-buhl) *noun* a small brown animal with long hind legs.

geriatric (*say* je-ree-**at**-rik) *adjective* concerned with the care of old people and their health. [from Greek *geras* = old age, + *iatros* = doctor]

germ *noun* **1** a microorganism, especially one that can cause disease. **2** a tiny living structure from which a plant or animal may develop. **3** part of the seed of a cereal plant.

German measles *noun* rubella.

German shepherd *noun* a large strong dog, often used by the police. Also called *Alsatian.*

germicide *noun* a substance that kills germs. [from *germ*, + Latin *caedere* = kill]

germinate *verb* (**germinated**, **germinating**) begin to grow and develop; put forth shoots. **germination** *noun*

gerrymander *noun* a manipulation of the boundaries of an electorate to gain unfair electoral advantage.

gestation (*say* jes-**tay**-shuhn) *noun* **1** the process or period of carrying a foetus in the womb. **2** the development of something over a period of time.

gesticulate (*say* jes-**tik**-yuh-layt) *verb* (**gesticulated**, **gesticulating**) make expressive movements with hands and arms. **gesticulation** *noun*

gesture (*say* **jes**-chuh) *noun* a movement or action that expresses what a person feels. **gesture** *verb*

get *verb* (**got**, **getting**) **1** obtain or receive, *She got first prize.* **2** become, *Don't get angry!* **3** reach a place, *We got there by midnight.* **4** put or move, *I can't get my shoe on.* **5** prepare, *Will you get the tea?* **6** persuade or order, *Get him to wash up.* **7** catch or suffer from an illness. **8** (*informal*)

understand, *Do you get what I mean?*
get away escape.
get away with 1 escape with something. **2** avoid being punished for what you have done.
get by (*informal*) manage.
get on 1 make progress. **2** be friendly with somebody.
get out of avoid or escape something.
get over 1 overcome a difficulty. **2** recover from an illness or shock.
get up 1 stand up. **2** get out of bed in the morning. **3** prepare or organise.
get your own back (*informal*) have your revenge.
have got to must.

getaway *noun* an escape, especially after committing a crime.

get-together *noun* (*informal*) a social gathering.

get-up *noun* (*informal*) clothing; an outfit.

geyser (*say* **gee**-zuh or **guy**-zuh) *noun* a natural spring that shoots up columns of hot water. [from the name of a hot spring in Iceland (*geysa* = gush)]

ghastly *adjective* **1** very unpleasant or bad. **2** looking pale and ill. **ghastliness** *noun* [related to *aghast* = horrified]

GHB *abbreviation* an illegal drug with anaesthetic properties. [from the scientific name *gamma-hydroxybutyrate*]

gherkin (*say* **ger**-kuhn) *noun* a small pickled cucumber.

ghetto (*say* **get**-oh) *noun* (*plural* **ghettos**) a slum area inhabited by a group of people who are treated unfairly in comparison with others. [from Italian *getto* = foundry (the first ghetto was in Venice, on the site of a foundry)]

ghost *noun* the spirit of a dead person. **ghostly** *adjective*

ghoulish (*say* **gool**-ish) *adjective* enjoying things that are grisly or unpleasant. **ghoulishly** *adverb*, **ghoulishness** *noun* [from *ghoul* = a demon in Muslim stories]

GHz *abbreviation* (also **gHz**) gigahertz.

GI[1] *abbreviation* a private soldier in the US army. [from the initials of *government* (or *general*) *issue*]

GI[2] *abbreviation* glycaemic index.

giant *noun* **1** (in fairy tales) a human-like creature of very great height and size. **2** a human, animal, or plant that is much larger than the usual size.

giantess *noun* (*plural* **giantesses**) a female giant.

giardia (*say* jee-**ah**-dee-uh) *noun* a protozoan that can infect the intestine and cause diarrhoea and other symptoms. [from the name of the French biologist A. Giard]

gibber[1] (*say* **jib**-uh) *verb* make quick meaningless sounds, especially when shocked or terrified.

gibber[2] (*say* **gib**-uh) *noun* (*Australian*) a stone or rock. [from Sydney language *giba*]

gibberish (*say* **jib**-uh-rish) *noun* meaningless speech; nonsense.

gibbet (*say* **jib**-uht) *noun* **1** a gallows. **2** an upright post with an arm from which a criminal's body was hung after execution.

gibbon *noun* an ape with very long arms.

gibe (*say* juyb) *noun & verb* jeer.

giblets (*say* **jib**-luhts) *plural noun* the edible parts of the inside of a bird, taken out before it is cooked.

giddy *adjective* having or causing the feeling that everything is spinning round. **giddily** *adverb*, **giddiness** *noun*

gidgee (*say* **gij**-ee) *noun* a small Australian acacia with a close-grained dark red timber. [from Yuwaalaraay and neighbouring languages *gidji*]

GIF *noun* (in computing) a format for viewing graphics files. [from the initials of 'Graphics Interchange Format']

gift *noun* **1** a present. **2** a talent, *She has a gift for music.*

gifted *adjective* talented.

gig[1] *noun* (*informal*) **1** a show when a musician or band plays music in public. **2** a job, especially one that is temporary or that has an uncertain future.

gig[2] *abbreviation* gigabyte.

giga- *prefix* one thousand million. [from Greek *gigas* = giant]

gigabyte *noun* (in computing) one thousand megabytes.

gigahertz *noun* a measure of frequency equivalent to one thousand million cycles per second.

gigantic *adjective* very large.

gig economy *noun* a labour market characterised by the prevalence of short-term contracts or freelance work as opposed to permanent jobs.

giggle[1] *verb* (**giggled**, **giggling**) laugh in a silly way.

giggle[2] *noun* **1** a silly laugh. **2** (*informal*) something amusing; a joke.

gild *verb* cover with a thin layer of gold or gold paint.

gilgai (*say* **gil**-guy) *noun* (*Australian*) land with hollows and mounds; one of the hollows. [from Wiradjuri and Gamilaraay *gilgaay* = waterhole]

gilgie (*say* **jil**-gee) *noun* a small freshwater crayfish found in Western Australia. [from Noongar *djilgi*]

gills *plural noun* **1** the part of the body through which fishes and certain other water animals breathe while in water. **2** the thin upright parts under the cap of a mushroom.

gilt[1] *noun* a thin gold covering.

gilt[2] *adjective* gilded; gold-coloured.

gimlet *noun* a small tool with a screw-like tip for boring holes.

gimmick *noun* something unusual done or used to attract people's attention. **gimmickry** *noun*, **gimmicky** *adjective*

gin[1] *noun* a colourless alcoholic spirit flavoured with juniper berries. [from the name of Geneva, a city in Switzerland]

gin[2] *noun* **1** a kind of trap for catching animals. **2** a machine for separating the fibres of the cotton plant from its seeds.

gin[3] *verb* (**ginned**, **ginning**) treat cotton in a gin. [from Old French *engin* = engine]

ginger[1] *noun* **1** a flavouring made from the hot-tasting root of a tropical plant. **2** this root. **3** liveliness; energy. **4** reddish-yellow.
ginger *adjective* [from Sanskrit = horn-body (referring to the shape of the root)]

ginger[2] *verb* make more lively, *This will ginger things up!*

gingerbread *noun* a ginger-flavoured cake or biscuit.

gingerly *adverb* cautiously.

gingham (*say* **ging**-uhm) *noun* a cotton fabric usually with a checked pattern.

gipsy alternative spelling of **gypsy**.

giraffe *noun* an African animal with four legs and a very long neck.

gird *verb* **1** fasten with a belt or band, *He girded on his sword.* **2** prepare for an effort, *gird yourself for action.* **3** encircle.

girder *noun* a metal beam supporting part of a building or a bridge.

girdle *noun* a belt or cord worn round the waist.

girl *noun* **1** a female child, *There were mostly girls in her class.* **2** a young woman. **girlhood** *noun*, **girlish** *adjective*

girlfriend *noun* a regular female companion or lover.

girt *adjective* girded.

girth *noun* **1** the distance round a thing. **2** a band passing under a horse's body to hold the saddle in place.

gist (*say* jist) *noun* the essential points or general sense of a speech or text.

give *verb* (**gave**, **given**, **giving**) **1** cause another person to receive something that you have or can provide. **2** make or perform an action or effort, *He gave a laugh.* **3** be flexible or springy; bend or collapse when pressed.
giver *noun*
give away 1 give as a present. **2** (*Australian*) give up; abandon. **3** reveal a secret.
give in acknowledge that you are defeated; yield.
give off send out something.
give up 1 stop doing something. **2** part with; surrender. **3** abandon hope.

giveaway *noun* **1** an unintentional revelation. **2** a thing given as a gift or at a low price.

given *adjective* named or stated in advance, *all the people in a given area.*

gizmo *noun* (*informal*) a gadget.

gizzard *noun* a bird's second stomach, in which food is ground up.

glacé (*say* **glas**-ay) *adjective* iced with sugar; crystallised. [French, = iced]

glacial (*say* **glay**-shuhl) *adjective* icy; of or from ice. **glacially** *adverb* [from Latin *glacies* = ice]

glacier (*say* **glay**-see-uh) *noun* a river of ice that moves very slowly.

glad *adjective* **1** pleased; expressing joy. **2** giving pleasure, *We brought the glad news.*
gladly *adverb*, **gladness** *noun*
glad of grateful for; pleased with.

gladden *verb* make a person glad.

glade *noun* an open space in a forest.

gladiator (*say* **glad**-ee-ay-tuh) *noun* a man trained to fight in public shows in ancient Rome. **gladiatorial** (*say* glad-ee-uh-**taw**-ree-uhl) *adjective* [from Latin *gladius* = sword]

glamorise *verb* (**glamorised**, **glamorising**) make glamorous or romantic.

glamour *noun* attractiveness; romantic charm. **glamorous** *adjective* [from an old use of *grammar* = magic]

glance *verb* (**glanced**, **glancing**) **1** look at something briefly. **2** strike something at an angle and slide off it, *The ball glanced off his bat.* **glance** *noun*

gland *noun* an organ of the body that separates substances from the blood so that they can be used or expelled.
glandular *adjective*

glare *verb* (**glared**, **glaring**) **1** shine with an unpleasant dazzling light. **2** stare angrily or fiercely. **glare** *noun*

glaring *adjective* **1** shining dazzlingly. **2** obvious, *a glaring error.*

glass[1] *noun* (*plural* **glasses**) **1** a hard brittle substance that is usually transparent. **2** a container made of glass for drinking from. **3** a mirror. **4** a lens or telescope.
glassy *adjective*

glass[2] *verb* **1** fit or enclose with glass. **2** (*informal*) hit someone in the face with a beer glass.

glasses *plural noun* **1** spectacles. **2** binoculars.

glaze[1] *verb* (**glazed**, **glazing**) **1** fit or cover with glass. **2** give a shiny surface to something. **3** become glassy.

glaze[2] *noun* a shiny surface or coating, especially on pottery. [from *glass*]

glazier (*say* **glay**-zee-uh) *noun* a person whose job is to fit glass in windows.

gleam[1] *noun* **1** a beam of soft light, especially one that comes and goes. **2** a brief instance of a quality or emotion, *a gleam of hope.*

gleam[2] *verb* send out gleams.

glean *verb* **1** pick up grain left by harvesters. **2** gather bit by bit, *glean some information.* **gleaner** *noun*

glee *noun* lively or triumphant delight. **gleeful** *adjective*, **gleefully** *adverb*

glen *noun* a narrow valley.

glib *adjective* speaking or writing readily but not sincerely or thoughtfully. **glibly** *adverb*, **glibness** *noun* [from an old word *glibbery* = slippery]

glide *verb* (**glided**, **gliding**) **1** fly or move along smoothly. **2** fly without using an engine. **glide** *noun*

glider *noun* **1** an aeroplane that does not use an engine. **2** a tree-dwelling Australian marsupial able to glide through the air, *the sugar glider.*

glimmer[1] *noun* a faint gleam.

glimmer[2] *verb* gleam faintly.

glimpse[1] *noun* a brief view.

glimpse[2] *verb* (**glimpsed**, **glimpsing**) catch a glimpse of.

glint[1] *noun* a very brief flash of light.

glint[2] *verb* send out a glint.

glisten (*say* **glis**-uhn) *verb* shine like something wet or polished.

glitch *noun* (*informal*) a malfunction; a hitch.

glitter *verb & noun* sparkle.

gloaming *noun* the evening twilight.

gloat *verb* be full of greedy or unkind pleasure.

global *adjective* **1** of the whole world; worldwide. **2** of or in the whole system. **globally** *adverb*

globalise *verb* (**globalised**, **globalising**) develop or operate worldwide. **globalisation** *noun*

globe *noun* **1** something shaped like a ball, especially one with a map of the whole world on it. **2** the world, *She has travelled all over the globe.* **3** a hollow round glass object, e.g. a light bulb.

globular (*say* **glob**-yuh-luh) *adjective* shaped like a globe.

globule (*say* **glob**-yool) *noun* a small rounded drop.

glockenspiel (*say* **glok**-uhn-speel) *noun* a musical instrument consisting of steel bars or tubes struck by two hammers. [German, = bell-play]

gloom *noun* **1** darkness. **2** depression.

gloomy *adjective* (**gloomier**, **gloomiest**) **1** almost dark. **2** depressed; depressing; sad. **gloomily** *adverb*, **gloominess** *noun*

glorify *verb* (**glorified**, **glorifying**) **1** give glory or honour. **2** make a thing seem more splendid than it really is. **glorification** *noun*

glorious *adjective* **1** having glory. **2** splendid. **gloriously** *adverb*

glory[1] *noun* **1** fame and honour. **2** praise. **3** beauty; magnificence.

glory[2] *verb* (**gloried**, **glorying**) rejoice; pride yourself, *They gloried in victory.*

gloss[1] *noun* (*plural* **glosses**) the shine on a smooth surface.

gloss[2] *verb* make a thing glossy.
gloss over seek to cover up a mistake or fault, especially by mentioning only briefly.

glossary *noun* (*plural* **glossaries**) a list of difficult words with their meanings explained. [from Greek *glossa* = tongue, language]

glossy *adjective* (**glossier**, **glossiest**) shiny. **glossily** *adverb*, **glossiness** *noun*

glove *noun* a covering for the hand, usually with separate divisions for each finger and thumb. **gloved** *adjective*

glow[1] *noun* **1** brightness and warmth without flames. **2** a warm or cheerful feeling, *We felt a glow of pride.*

glow[2] *verb* produce a glow.

glower (*rhymes with* flower) *verb* stare angrily; scowl.

glow-worm *noun* a kind of beetle whose tail gives out a green light.

glucose *noun* a form of sugar found in fruit juice. [same origin as *glycerine*]

glue[1] *noun* a sticky substance used for joining things. **gluey** *adjective*

glue[2] *verb* (**glued**, **gluing**) **1** stick with glue. **2** attach or hold closely, *His ear was glued to the keyhole.*

glum *adjective* sad and gloomy. **glumly** *adverb*, **glumness** *noun* [from dialect *glum* = to frown]

glut[1] *verb* (**glutted**, **glutting**) **1** supply with much more than is needed. **2** satisfy fully with food.

glut[2] *noun* an excessive supply. [same origin as *glutton*]

gluten (*say* **gloo**-tuhn) *noun* a sticky protein substance in flour. [from Latin, = glue]

glutinous (*say* **gloo**-tuh-nuhs) *adjective* glue-like, sticky. [same origin as *gluten*]

glutton *noun* a person who eats too much. **gluttonous** *adjective*, **gluttony** *noun* [from Latin *gluttire* = to swallow]

glycaemia (*say* gluy-**see**-mee-uh) *noun* (also **glycemia**) the presence of glucose in the bloodstream. **glycaemic** *adjective* [from Greek *glykys* = sweet]

glycaemic index *noun* a measure of how quickly a carbohydrate gets into a person's bloodstream as sugar.

glycerine (*say* **glis**-uh-ruhn) *noun* a thick sweet colourless liquid used in ointments, medicines, and explosives. [from Greek *glykys* = sweet]

GM *abbreviation* genetically modified.

GMT *abbreviation* Greenwich Mean Time.

gnarled (*say* nahld) *adjective* twisted and knobbly, like an old tree.

gnash (*say* nash) *verb* grind teeth together.

gnat (*say* nat) *noun* a tiny fly that bites.

gnaw (*say* naw) *verb* keep on biting something hard.

gnome (*say* nohm) *noun* a kind of dwarf in fairy tales, usually living underground.

GNP *abbreviation* gross national product.

gnu (*say* noo) another name for **wildebeest**.

go[1] *verb* (**went**, **gone**, **going**) **1** move or begin to move, *Where are you going?* **2** leave, *It was time to go.* **3** extend; lead, *The road goes to Darwin.* **4** work or function, *The car doesn't go.* **5** become, *The milk went sour.* **6** belong in some place or position, *Plates go on that shelf.* **7** proceed; turn out, *Things went well.* **8** (of time) pass, *The time went quickly.* **9** be spent or used up, *The money has all gone.* **10** be sold, *The house went very cheaply.* **11** make a particular movement or sound, *The gun went bang.*
go along with agree.
go back on fail to keep a promise.
go off 1 explode. **2** (of food) become bad or stale.
go on continue.
go out stop burning or shining.
go through 1 penetrate. **2** experience; undergo. **3** study; inspect.

go[2] *noun* (*plural* **goes**) **1** a turn or try, *May I have a go?* **2** (*informal*) a success, *They made a go of it.* **3** (*informal*) energy; liveliness, *She is full of go.*
on the go active; always working or moving.

goad[1] *noun* a stick with a pointed end for prodding cattle to move onwards.

goad[2] *verb* stir into action by being annoying, *He goaded me into fighting.*

go-ahead[1] *noun* a signal to proceed.

go-ahead[2] *adjective* energetic; willing to try new methods.

goal *noun* **1** the place where a ball must go to score a point in soccer, hockey, and some other games. **2** a point scored in this way. **3** an objective. [from an old word *gol* = boundary]

goalkeeper *noun* the player whose job is to keep the ball out of the goal.

goalpost *noun* either of the two posts of a goal.
move the goalposts unfairly alter the conditions or rules of a procedure once it has started.

goanna *noun* a large Australian lizard.

goat *noun* a small animal with horns, kept for its milk.

goatee *noun* a short pointed beard.

gobble *verb* (**gobbled**, **gobbling**) eat quickly and greedily.

gobbledegook *noun* (*informal*) pompous language used by officials. [imitation of the sound a turkey-cock makes]

go-between *noun* a person who acts as a messenger or negotiator between others.

goblet *noun* a drinking glass with a stem and a foot.

goblin *noun* a mischievous ugly elf.

go-cart *noun* a billycart.

god *noun* **1** a person or thing that is worshipped, *Mars was a Roman god.* **2** (**God**) the creator and ruler of the universe in some religions.

goddess *noun* (*plural* **goddesses**) a female god.

godly *adjective* (**godlier**, **godliest**) sincerely religious. **godliness** *noun*

godparent *noun* **1** a person who presents a child at baptism and responds on the child's behalf. **2** a person who takes on a similar role at a secular naming ceremony. **godchild** *noun*, **god-daughter** *noun*, **godfather** *noun*, **godmother** *noun*, **godson** *noun*

godsend *noun* a piece of unexpected good luck.

goggle *verb* (**goggled**, **goggling**) stare with wide-open eyes.

goggles *plural noun* large spectacles for protecting the eyes from wind, water, dust, etc.

going[1] *present participle* of **go**[1].
be going to do something be ready or likely to do it.

going[2] *noun* **1** an act of leaving a place; a departure, *comings and goings.* **2** the condition of the ground viewed in terms of suitability for horse racing, riding, or walking, *The soft sand made for slow going on our walk.* **3** conditions for, or progress in, an endeavour, *an opportunity to get out while the going is good.*

going[3] *adjective* **1** existing or available; to be had, *He asked if there were any other jobs going.* **2** current; prevalent, *the going rate.*

goitre (*say* **goy**-tuh) *noun* an enlarged thyroid gland, often showing as a swelling in the neck.

go-kart *noun* (also **go-cart**) a small racing car with a lightweight or skeleton body.

gold *noun* **1** a precious yellow metal. **2** a deep yellow colour. **3** a gold medal, usually given as first prize. **gold** *adjective*

golden *adjective* **1** made of gold. **2** coloured like gold. **3** precious; excellent, *a golden opportunity.*

golden jubilee *noun* a 50th anniversary.

golden staph *noun* a virulent species of (the staphylococcus) bacterium that has developed a resistance to many antibiotics.

goldfield *noun* a place where gold is found and mined.

goldfish *noun* (*plural* **goldfish**) a small red or orange fish, often kept as a pet.

goldsmith *noun* a person who makes things in gold.

golf *noun* an outdoor game played by hitting a small hard ball with a club into a series of holes on a specially prepared ground (a **golf course** or **golf links**). **golfer** *noun*, **golfing** *noun*

golliwog *noun* a black doll with woolly hair.

gondola (*say* **gon**-duh-luh) *noun* a boat with high pointed ends used on the canals in Venice. **gondolier** *noun* [Italian]

gone *past participle* of **go**[1].

gong *noun* a large metal disc that makes an echoing sound when hit.

gonorrhea (*say* gon-uh-**ree**-uh) *noun* a venereal disease causing a thick discharge from the sexual organ. [from Greek *gonos* = semen, + *rhoia* = a flow]

goo *noun* (*informal*) a sticky wet substance.

good[1] *adjective* (**better**, **best**) **1** having the right qualities; of the kind that people like, *a good book.* **2** kind; morally excellent, *It was good of you to help us.* **3** well-behaved, *Be a good boy.* **4** healthy; giving benefit, *Fish is good for you.* **5** competent; skilful. **6** enjoyable, *Have a good time.* **7** thorough, *Give it a good clean.* **8** large; considerable, *It's a good distance from the shops.*

good[2] *noun* **1** something good, *Do good to others.* **2** benefit, *It's for your own good.*
for good for ever.
no good useless.

goodbye *interjection* a word used when you leave somebody or at the end of a phone call. [short for *God be with you*]

Good Friday *noun* the Friday before Easter, commemorating the Crucifixion of Christ.

good-looking *adjective* handsome; physically attractive.

good-natured *adjective* kind; patient; easygoing.

goodness *noun* **1** being good. **2** the good part of something.

goods *plural noun* **1** things that are bought and sold. **2** things that are carried on trains or trucks.

goodwill *noun* a kindly feeling.

goody *noun* (*plural* **goodies**) (*informal*) **1** something good or attractive, especially to eat. **2** a person of good character.

gooey *adjective* (*informal*) soft and sticky.

goog *noun* (also **googie**) (*Australian informal*) an egg. [from British dialect]

google *verb* search for something on the Internet with the use of a search engine. [from the trademark name of a search engine]

goose *noun* (*plural* **geese**) a kind of bird with webbed feet, larger than a duck.

gooseberry *noun* (*plural* **gooseberries**) a small green fruit that grows on a prickly bush.

goosebumps *plural noun* (also **gooseflesh**, **goose pimples**) skin that has turned rough with small bumps on it because a person is cold or afraid.

gore[1] *verb* (**gored**, **goring**) wound by piercing with a horn or tusk.

gore[2] *noun* thickened blood from a cut or wound. [from Old English *gor* = dirt]

gorge[1] *noun* **1** a narrow valley with steep sides. **2** the throat or gullet.

gorge[2] *verb* (**gorged**, **gorging**) eat greedily; stuff with food. [French, = throat]

gorgeous *adjective* magnificent; beautiful. **gorgeously** *adverb*

gorgonzola (*say* gor-guhn-**zoh**-luh) *noun* a rich strong blue-veined cheese, originally from Gorgonzola in north Italy.

gorilla *noun* a large strong African ape.

gorse *noun* a prickly bush with small yellow flowers.

gory *adjective* **1** covered with blood. **2** with much bloodshed, *a gory battle.*

gosh *interjection* an exclamation of surprise.

gosling *noun* a young goose.

gospel *noun* **1** the teachings of Jesus Christ. **2** (**Gospel**) each of the first four books of the New Testament, telling of the life and teachings of Jesus Christ. **3** something you can safely believe. [from Old English *god* = good, + *spel* = news]

gossamer *noun* **1** fine cobwebs made by small spiders. **2** any fine, delicate material.

gossip[1] *verb* (**gossiped**, **gossiping**) talk a lot about other people.

gossip[2] *noun* **1** gossiping talk. **2** a person who enjoys gossiping. **gossipy** *adjective*

got *past tense & past participle* of **get**.
have got possess, *Have you got a car?*
have got to must.

Gothic *adjective* of the style of building common in the 12th–16th centuries, with pointed arches and much carving.

gotten (in the US) *past participle* of **get**.

> **Usage** Except in the adjective *ill-gotten*, the past participle *gotten* is non-standard in Australian English.

gouda (*say* **gow**-duh or **goo**-duh) *noun* a flat round Dutch cheese, originally made in the town of Gouda in the Netherlands.

gouge (*say* gowj) *verb* (**gouged**, **gouging**) scoop or force out by pressing.

goulash (*say* **goo**-lash) *noun* a meat stew seasoned with paprika. [from Hungarian *gulyashus* = herdsman's meat]

gourd (*say* gawd) *noun* the rounded hard-skinned fruit of a climbing plant.

gourmet[1] (*say* **gaw**-may) *noun* a person who understands and appreciates good food and drink. [French, = wine-taster]

gourmet[2] *adjective* of or relating to good food and drink, *a gourmet lunch.*

gout *noun* a disease that causes painful inflammation of the toes, knees, and fingers. **gouty** *adjective*

govern *verb* be in charge of the public affairs of a country or an organisation.

governess *noun* a woman employed to teach children in a private household.

government *noun* **1** the group of people who govern a country. **2** the process of governing. **governmental** *adjective*

governor *noun* **1** a person who governs a state or a colony. **2** the representative of the British Crown in a colony or in a Commonwealth state that regards the monarch as head of state. **3** a member of the governing body of a school or other institution. **4** the person in charge of a prison.

governor-general *noun* (*plural* **governor-generals** or **governors-general**) the British Crown's representative in the Commonwealth of Australia and in any other Commonwealth country that recognises the monarch as head of state.

gown *noun* a loose flowing garment.

GP *abbreviation* general practitioner.

GPO *abbreviation* General Post Office.

GPS *abbreviation* Global Positioning System (a satellite navigational system).

grab *verb* (**grabbed**, **grabbing**) take hold of suddenly or greedily.

grace[1] *noun* **1** beauty of movement or manner or design. **2** goodwill; favour. **3** a short prayer of thanks before or after a meal. **4** the title of a duke, duchess, or archbishop, *His Grace the Duke of York.*

grace[2] *verb* (**graced**, **gracing**) bring honour or dignity to something.

graceful *adjective* full of grace. **gracefully** *adverb*, **gracefulness** *noun*

gracious *adjective* kind and pleasant. **graciously** *adverb*, **graciousness** *noun*

grade[1] *noun* **1** a step in a scale of quality or value or rank; a standard. **2** a mark showing the quality of a student's work. **3** a class in school.

grade[2] *verb* (**graded**, **grading**) **1** arrange in grades. **2** give a mark to a student's work. [from Latin *gradus* = a step]

gradient (*say* **gray**-dee-uhnt) *noun* the amount of slope in a road or railway or of a line or curve on a graph; *the road has a gradient of 1 in 10*, it rises 1 metre in every 10 metres of its length.

gradual *adjective* happening slowly but steadily. **gradually** *adverb*

graduate[1] (*say* **graj**-oo-ayt) *verb* (**graduated**, **graduating**) **1** get an academic degree. **2** divide into graded sections; mark with units of measurement.

graduate[2] (*say* **graj**-oo-uht) *noun* a person who has an academic degree.

graffiti *plural noun* words or drawings scribbled or sprayed on a surface. [Italian, = scratchings]

> **Usage** In Italian the word *graffiti* is a plural noun and its singular form is *graffito*. In English the most common modern use is to treat *graffiti* as if it were a mass noun, similar to a word like *writing*, and not to use *graffito* at all.

graft[1] *noun* **1** a shoot from one plant or tree fixed into another to form a new growth. **2** a piece of living tissue transplanted by a surgeon to replace what is diseased or damaged, *a skin graft.*

graft[2] *verb* insert or transplant as a graft.

graft[3] *noun* (*informal*) **1** hard work. **2** advantage in business or politics obtained by bribery, unfair influence, or other shady means.

graft[4] *verb* (*informal*) work hard.

grain *noun* **1** a small hard seed or similar particle. **2** cereal plants when they are growing or after being harvested. **3** the pattern of lines made by the fibres in a piece of wood. **grainy** *adjective*

gram *noun* a unit of mass or weight in the metric system, *The chocolate bar weighs 80 grams.*

-gram *suffix* forming nouns meaning something written, drawn, or recorded in some way. (e.g. *diagram*). [from Greek *gramma* = thing written]

grammar *noun* **1** the study of words and of the rules for their formation and their relationship to each other in sentences; speech or writing judged as good or bad according to these rules. **2** a book about these rules. [from Greek, = the art of letters]

grammatical *adjective* of grammar; according to its rules. **grammatically** *adverb*

gramophone *noun* a record player. [altered from 'phonogram', from Greek *phone* = a sound, + *-gram*]

grampus *noun* (*plural* **grampuses**) a large dolphin-like sea animal.

Gram stain *noun* a method of differentiating bacteria by staining with a dye, then attempting to remove the dye with solvent, for purposes of identification. [named after H.C.J. Gram, Danish physician]

granary *noun* (*plural* **granaries**) a storehouse for grain.

grand *adjective* **1** splendid; magnificent. **2** including everything; complete, *the grand total.* **grandly** *adverb*, **grandness** *noun*

grandad *noun* (*informal*) grandfather.

grandchild *noun* (*plural* **grandchildren**) the child of a person's son or daughter. **granddaughter** *noun*, **grandson** *noun*

grandeur (*say* **gran**-juh) *noun* grandness; splendour.

grandfather *noun* the father of a person's father or mother.

grandfather clock *noun* a clock in a tall wooden case.

grand final *noun* the concluding match of a competition, *The Tigers played the Giants in the AFL grand final.*

grand finale *noun* the last and most exciting or impressive part of a performance or entertainment, *The concert closed with a grand finale.*

grandiose (*say* **gran**-dee-ohs) *adjective* imposing; trying to seem grand.

grandma *noun* (*informal*) grandmother.

grandmother *noun* the mother of a person's father or mother.

grandpa *noun* (*informal*) grandfather.

grandparent *noun* a grandfather or grandmother.

grand piano *noun* a large piano with the strings fixed horizontally.

Grand Prix (*say* gron **pree**) *noun* any of various international motor or motorcycle racing events. [French, = great or chief prize]

grandstand *noun* a building with a roof and rows of seats for spectators at a racecourse or sportsground.

granite *noun* a very hard kind of rock.

granny *noun* (*plural* **grannies**) (*informal*) grandmother.

granny knot *noun* a reef knot with the strings crossed the wrong way.

Granny Smith *noun* a green-skinned Australian variety of apple. [named after Maria Ann ('Granny') Smith who first cultivated them in Sydney]

grant[1] *verb* **1** give or allow what is asked for, *grant a request.* **2** admit; agree that something is true.
take for granted assume that something is true or will always be available.

grant[2] *noun* something granted, especially a sum of money.

granular *adjective* like grains.

granule *noun* a small grain.

grape *noun* a small green or purple berry that grows in bunches on a vine.

grapefruit *noun* (*plural* **grapefruit**) a large round yellow citrus fruit.

grapevine *noun* **1** a vine on which grapes grow. **2** a way by which news is passed on unofficially.

graph *noun* a diagram consisting of a line or lines showing the relationship between corresponding values of two quantities. [from Greek *graphia* = writing]

-graph *suffix* forming nouns and verbs meaning something written, drawn, or recorded in some way. (e.g. *photograph*). [same origin as *graph*]

grapheme *noun* the smallest meaningful contrastive unit in a writing system.

graphic *adjective* **1** of drawing or painting, *a graphic artist.* **2** giving a lively description. **graphically** *adverb*

graphical user interface *noun* a visual way of interacting with a computer using items such as windows, icons, and menus.

graphics *plural noun* diagrams, lettering, and drawings; computer graphics.

graphite *noun* a soft black form of carbon used for the lead in pencils, as a lubricant, and in nuclear reactors.

-graphy *suffix* forming names of descriptive sciences (e.g. *geography*) or methods of writing or drawing. (e.g. *photography*). [same origin as *graph*]

grapnel *noun* a heavy metal device with claws for hooking things.

grapple *verb* (**grappled**, **grappling**) **1** struggle; wrestle. **2** seize or hold firmly.

grasp *verb* **1** seize and hold firmly. **2** understand. **grasp** *noun*

grasping *adjective* greedy for money or possessions.

grass *noun* (*plural* **grasses**) **1** a plant with green blades and stalks that are eaten by animals. **2** ground covered with grass. **grassy** *adjective*

grasshopper *noun* a jumping insect that makes a shrill noise.

grassland *noun* a wide area covered in grass with few trees.

grass roots *plural noun* the ordinary people in a political party or other group.

grass tree *noun* a small Australian tree with a thick trunk, crown of grass-like leaves, and a tall flowering spike.

grate[1] *noun* **1** a metal framework that keeps fuel in a fireplace. **2** a fireplace.

grate[2] *verb* (**grated**, **grating**) **1** shred into small pieces by rubbing on a rough surface. **2** make an unpleasant noise by rubbing. **3** sound harshly.

grateful *adjective* feeling or showing that you value what was done for you. **gratefully** *adverb* [from Latin *gratus* = thankful, pleasing]

grater *noun* a device with a jagged surface for grating food.

gratify *verb* (**gratified**, **gratifying**) **1** give pleasure. **2** indulge or satisfy, *Please gratify our curiosity.* **gratification** *noun* [from Latin *gratus* = pleasing]

grating[1] *noun* a framework of metal or wooden bars placed across an opening.

grating[2] *adjective* sounding harsh.

gratis (*say* **grah**-tuhs) *adverb & adjective* free of charge, *You can have the leaflet gratis.* [Latin, = out of kindness]

gratitude *noun* being grateful.

gratuitous (*say* gruh-**tyoo**-uh-tuhs) *adjective* given or done without payment or without good reason. **gratuitously** *adverb*

gratuity (*say* gruh-**tyoo**-uh-tee) *noun* (*plural* **gratuities**) money given in gratitude; a tip.

grave[1] *noun* the place where a corpse is buried. [from Old English *graef* = hole dug out]

grave[2] *adjective* **1** serious; solemn. **2** important. **gravely** *adverb* [from Latin *gravis* = heavy]

gravel *noun* small stones mixed with coarse sand. **gravelled** *adjective*, **gravelly** *adjective*

graven (*say* **gray**-vuhn) *adjective* carved.

gravestone *noun* a stone monument over a grave.

graveyard *noun* a burial ground.

gravitas *noun* dignity, seriousness, or solemnity of manner. [from Latin *gravis* = serious]

gravitate *verb* (**gravitated**, **gravitating**) move or be attracted towards something.

gravitation *noun* **1** gravitating. **2** the force of gravity. **gravitational** *adjective*

gravity *noun* **1** the force that pulls everything towards the earth. **2** seriousness. [same origin as *grave*[2]]

gravy *noun* a hot brown sauce served with meat made from the cooking juices.

graze[1] *verb* (**grazed**, **grazing**) **1** feed on growing grass. **2** scrape slightly in passing, *I grazed my elbow on the wall.*

graze[2] *noun* a raw place where skin has been scraped.

grazier *noun* (*Australian*) a large-scale sheep or cattle farmer.

grease[1] *noun* melted fat; any thick oily substance. **greasy** *adjective*

grease[2] *verb* (**greased**, **greasing**) put grease on something.

great *adjective* **1** very large; much above average, *There was a great amount of treasure in the chest.* **2** above average in intensity. **3** very important or talented, *a great composer.* **4** (*informal*) very good or enjoyable, *It's great to see you again.* **5** older or younger by one generation, *great-grandfather.* **greatly** *adverb*, **greatness** *noun*

greatest common divisor *noun* (also **greatest common factor**) (in mathematics) the highest number that can be divided exactly into each of two or more numbers.

grebe (*say* greeb) *noun* a kind of diving bird.

greed *noun* an excessive desire for food, money, or other things.

greedy *adjective* wanting more food, money, or other things than you need. **greedily** *adverb*, **greediness** *noun*

Greek *noun* **1** a person from Greece. **2** the language of Greece or ancient Greece. **Greek** *adjective*

green[1] *noun* **1** the colour of growing grass. **2** an area of grass, *a bowling green.* **3** (**Green**) a member or supporter of a political party or group concerned with protecting the environment.

green[2] *adjective* **1** of the colour green. **2** inexperienced and likely to make mistakes. **3** jealous. **4** concerned with protecting the natural environment. **greenness** *noun*

green belt *noun* an area kept as open land around a city.

greenery *noun* green leaves or plants.

greengrocer *noun* a person who keeps a shop that sells fruit and vegetables. **greengrocery** *noun*

greenhouse *noun* a glass building where plants are protected from cold.

greenhouse effect *noun* the warming up of the earth's surface when radiation from the sun is trapped by the atmosphere.

greenhouse gas *noun* any of the gases, especially carbon dioxide and methane, that contribute to the greenhouse effect.

Green Paper *noun* a preliminary report of government proposals that is published in order to provoke discussion. (Compare **White Paper**.)

green room *noun* a room in a theatre or studio in which performers can relax when they are not performing.

Greenwich Mean Time (*say* **gren**-ich) *noun* time on the line of longitude that passes through Greenwich in London, used as a basis for calculating time throughout the world.

greet *verb* **1** speak to a person who arrives. **2** receive, *They greeted the song with applause.* **3** present itself to, *A strange sight greeted our eyes.*

greeting *noun* **1** words or actions used to greet somebody. **2** good wishes.

gregarious (*say* gruh-**gair**-ree-uhs) *adjective* **1** fond of company. **2** living in flocks or communities. **gregariously** *adverb*, **gregariousness** *noun* [from Latin *gregis* = of a flock]

grenade (*say* gruh-**nayd**) *noun* a small bomb, usually thrown by hand.

grevillea (*say* gruh-**vil**-ee-uh) *noun* an Australian shrub or tree, often with brightly coloured flowers. [from Charles Greville, Scottish botanist]

grew *past tense* of **grow**.

grey[1] *noun* the colour between black and white, like ashes.

grey[2] *adjective* **1** of the colour grey. **2** overcast. **greyness** *noun*

grey area *noun* a situation or topic not clearly defined; a vague area.

greyhound *noun* a slender dog with smooth hair, used in racing.

grey nomad *noun* (*Australian informal*) a retired person who travels extensively.

grid *noun* **1** a framework of bars. **2** a pattern of lines crossing each other.

griddle *noun* a round iron plate for cooking things on.

gridiron *noun* a framework of bars for cooking on.

grid reference *noun* a map reference indicating a location in terms of a series of vertical and horizontal grid lines identified by numbers or letters.

grief *noun* deep sorrow.
come to grief suffer a disaster.

grievance *noun* something that people are discontented about.

grieve *verb* (**grieved, grieving**) **1** cause a person grief. **2** feel grief.

grievous (*say* **gree**-vuhs) *adjective* **1** causing grief. **2** serious. **grievously** *adverb*

griffin *noun* a creature in fables, with an eagle's head and wings on a lion's body.

grill[1] *noun* **1** a device in a cooker for sending heat downwards. **2** food cooked under this. **3** a grille.

grill[2] *verb* **1** cook under a grill. **2** question closely and severely, *The police grilled him for an hour.*

grille *noun* a metal grating covering a window or similar opening.

griller *noun* a device in a cooker for sending heat downwards.

grim *adjective* (**grimmer, grimmest**) **1** stern; severe. **2** without cheerfulness; unattractive, *a grim prospect.* **grimly** *adverb*, **grimness** *noun*

grimace[1] (*say* **grim**-us) *noun* a twisted expression on the face made in pain or disgust.

grimace[2] *verb* (**grimaced, grimacing**) make a grimace.

grime *noun* dirt clinging to a surface or to the skin. **grimy** *adjective*

grin[1] *noun* a broad smile.

grin[2] *verb* (**grinned, grinning**) smile broadly.

grind *verb* (**ground, grinding**) *verb* **1** crush into grains or powder. **2** sharpen or smooth by rubbing on a rough surface. **3** rub harshly together, *He ground his teeth in fury.* **4** move with a harsh grating noise, *The bus ground to a halt.* **grinder** *noun*

grindstone *noun* a thick round rough revolving stone for sharpening or grinding things.

grip[1] *verb* (**gripped, gripping**) **1** hold firmly. **2** hold a person's attention.

grip[2] *noun* **1** a firm hold. **2** understanding. **3** a handle. **4** a suitcase or travel bag.

gripe *verb* (**griped, griping**) (*informal*) grumble. **gripe** *noun*

grisly *adjective* (**grislier, grisliest**) causing horror or disgust; gruesome.

grist *noun* grain for grinding.

gristle *noun* tough rubbery tissue in meat. **gristly** *adjective*

grit[1] *noun* **1** tiny pieces of stone or sand. **2** courage and endurance. **grittiness** *noun*, **gritty** *adjective*

grit[2] *verb* (**gritted**, **gritting**) clench the teeth when in pain or trouble.

grizzle *verb* (**grizzled**, **grizzling**) whimper; whine. **grizzly** *adjective*

grizzled *adjective* streaked with grey hairs.

grizzly *adjective* grey-haired.

grizzly bear *noun* a large fierce bear.

groan *verb* **1** make a long deep sound in pain or distress or disapproval. **2** creak loudly under a heavy load. **groan** *noun*, **groaner** *noun*

grocer *noun* a person who keeps a shop that sells food and household goods.

grocery *noun* (*plural* **groceries**) a grocer's shop or business.
groceries goods sold by a grocer.

grog *noun* **1** a drink of alcoholic spirits, usually rum, mixed with water. **2** (*Australian informal*) any alcoholic drink.

groggy *adjective* (**groggier**, **groggiest**) weak and unsteady, especially after illness. **groggily** *adverb*, **grogginess** *noun*

groin *noun* the groove where the thigh joins the trunk of the body.

grommet *noun* a tube passed through the eardrum in surgery to drain and ventilate the middle ear.

groom[1] *noun* **1** a person whose job is to look after horses. **2** a bridegroom.

groom[2] *verb* **1** clean and brush an animal. **2** make neat and trim. **3** train a person for a certain job or position. **4** (of a paedophile) prepare (a child) for a meeting, especially via the Internet, with the intention of committing a sexual offence.

groomsman *noun* a man attending the bridegroom at a wedding.

groove *noun* a long narrow furrow or channel cut in the surface of something. **grooved** *adjective*

groovy *adjective* (*informal*) excellent; fashionable.

grope *verb* (**groped**, **groping**) feel about for something you cannot see.

groper (*say* **groh**-puh) *noun* a large sea fish with a big head and wide mouth.

gross[1] (*say* grohs) *adjective* **1** fat and ugly. **2** having bad manners; vulgar. **3** very obvious or shocking, *gross stupidity.* **4** total; without anything being deducted, *our gross income.* (Compare **net**[3].) **5** (of weight) including contents, wrappings, or other variable items; overall. **6** (*informal*) disgusting, repulsive. **grossly** *adverb*, **grossness** *noun*

gross[2] *noun* (*plural* **gross**) 12 dozen (144) of something.

gross domestic product *noun* the total value of goods produced and services provided in a country in one year.

gross motor skills *plural noun* the physical skills necessary for movements of the large muscles and joints of the body.

gross national product *noun* the gross domestic product plus the total of net income from abroad.

grotesque (*say* groh-**tesk**) *adjective* very strange; fantastically ugly. **grotesquely** *adverb*, **grotesqueness** *noun*

grotto *noun* (*plural* **grottoes**) a picturesque cave.

grotty *adjective* (*informal*) unpleasant or dirty.

grouch *noun* (*informal*) a discontented person. **grouchy** *adjective*

ground[1] *past tense & past participle* of **grind**.

ground[2] *noun* **1** the solid surface of the earth. **2** soil; earth, *marshy ground.* **3** an area used for a particular purpose, *cricket ground*; *playground.*

ground[3] *verb* **1** run aground. **2** prevent from flying, *All aircraft are grounded because of the fog.* **3** give a good basic training, *Ground them in the rules of spelling.* **4** base, *This theory is grounded on known facts.*

grounding *noun* basic training.

groundless *adjective* without foundation or reasons, *Your fears are groundless.*

grounds *plural noun* **1** an area of enclosed land belonging to a large house or an institution. **2** solid particles that sink to the bottom, *coffee grounds.* **3** reasons, *There are grounds for suspicion.*

groundsheet *noun* a piece of waterproof material for spreading on the ground.

groundsman *noun* (*plural* **groundsmen**) a person whose job is to look after a sportsground or school grounds. **groundsperson** *noun*

groundwork *noun* work that lays the basis for something.

group[1] *noun* a number of people, animals, or things that come together or belong together in some way.

group[2] *verb* **1** put together or come together in a group or groups. **2** classify.

grouse[1] *noun* (*plural* **grouse**) a bird with feathered feet, hunted as game.

grouse[2] *verb* (**groused**, **grousing**) (*informal*) grumble. **grouse** *noun*, **grouser** *noun*

grove *noun* a group of trees; a small wood.

grovel *verb* (**grovelled**, **grovelling**) **1** crawl on the ground, especially in a show of fear or humility. **2** act in an excessively humble way. **groveller** *noun*

grow *verb* (**grew**, **grown**, **growing**) **1** become bigger or greater. **2** develop; put out shoots. **3** cultivate, plant and look after, *She grows roses.* **4** become, *He grew rich.* **grower** *noun*

growl *verb* make a deep angry sound. **growl** *noun*

grown-up *noun* an adult person.

growth *noun* **1** the process of growing; development. **2** something that has grown. **3** a tumour.

groyne *noun* a wall built out into the sea from a beach to prevent sand or pebbles being washed away by the current.

grub[1] *noun* **1** a tiny worm-like creature that will become an insect; a larva. **2** (*informal*) food.

grub[2] *verb* (**grubbed**, **grubbing**) **1** dig up by the roots. **2** rummage.

grubby *adjective* (**grubbier**, **grubbiest**) rather dirty. **grubbiness** *noun*

grudge[1] *noun* a feeling of resentment or ill will.

grudge[2] *verb* (**grudged**, **grudging**) resent having to give or allow something.

gruelling *adjective* exhausting.

gruesome *adjective* causing people to feel horror or disgust.

gruff *adjective* **1** (of a voice) harsh. **2** having a rough unfriendly manner. **gruffly** *adverb*, **gruffness** *noun*

grumble *verb* (**grumbled**, **grumbling**) complain in a bad-tempered way. **grumble** *noun*, **grumbler** *noun*

grumpy *adjective* bad-tempered. **grumpily** *adverb*, **grumpiness** *noun*

grunge *noun* **1** grime; dirt. **2** a kind of rock music with a heavy guitar sound and lo-fi production.

grunt *verb* **1** make a pig's gruff snort. **2** speak or say gruffly. **grunt** *noun*

gruyère (*say* **groo**-yair) *noun* a firm pale cheese with holes, originally made in the district of Gruyère in Switzerland.

GST *abbreviation* goods and services tax, *There is a 10% GST on most things you buy at the supermarket.*

guacamole (*say* gwah-kuh-**moh**-lee) *noun* a dish of mashed avocado mixed with chopped onion, tomatoes, chilli peppers, and seasoning. [from a South American indigenous language = avocado sauce]

guarantee[1] *noun* a formal promise to do something or to repair an object if it breaks or goes wrong.

guarantee[2] *verb* (**guaranteed**, **guaranteeing**) give a guarantee; promise. **guarantor** *noun*

guard[1] *verb* **1** protect; keep safe. **2** watch over and prevent from escaping.

guard[2] *noun* **1** guarding; protection, *Keep the prisoners under close guard.* **2** someone who keeps watch, especially a soldier or other person assigned to protect a person or control a place. **3** a group of soldiers or others acting as a guard. **4** a railway official in charge of a train. **5** a protecting device, *a mouthguard.*

guardian *noun* **1** someone who guards. **2** a person who is legally responsible for the care of someone who is unable to manage their own affairs, especially a child whose parents have died. **guardianship** *noun*

guava (*say* **gwah**-vuh) *noun* the orange-coloured acid fruit of a tropical American tree.

guernsey *noun* (*Australian*) a football jumper.
get a guernsey be selected for a team; win recognition or approval.

guerrilla (*say* guh-**ril**-uh) *noun* a person who fights by making surprise attacks as one of a small group. [Spanish, = little war]

guess[1] *noun* (*plural* **guesses**) an opinion given without making careful calculations or without certain knowledge.

guess[2] *verb* make a guess. **guesser** *noun*

guest *noun* **1** a person who is invited to visit or stay at another's house. **2** a person staying at a hotel. **3** a person who takes part in another's show as a visiting performer.

guestbook *noun* **1** a book at a hotel, museum, or other place where visitors can record their comments. **2** a place on a website where visitors can record their comments.

guffaw *verb* give a noisy laugh. **guffaw** *noun*

GUI *abbreviation* graphical user interface.

guidance *noun* **1** guiding. **2** advising or advice on problems.

guide[1] *noun* **1** a person who shows others the way or points out interesting sights. **2** a book giving information about a place or subject. **3** an adviser. **4** (**Guide**) a member of the Guides Association, an organisation for girls.

guide[2] *verb* (**guided**, **guiding**) act as guide to.

guidebook *noun* a book of information about a place, for travellers or visitors.

guidelines *plural noun* statements that give general advice about something.

guild (*say* gild) *noun* a society of people with similar skills or interests.

guile (*rhymes with* mile) *noun* craftiness.

guillotine[1] (*say* **gil**-uh-teen) *noun* **1** a machine with a heavy blade for beheading criminals. **2** a machine with a long blade for cutting paper or metal. **3** fixing a time for a vote to be taken in parliament in order to cut short a debate.

guillotine[2] *verb* (**guillotined**, **guillotining**) cut with a guillotine. [named after Dr Guillotin, who suggested its use in France in 1789]

guilt *noun* **1** the fact of having committed an offence. **2** a feeling of being to blame for something that has happened.

guilty *adjective* **1** having done wrong. **2** feeling or showing guilt. **guiltily** *adverb*

guinea (*say* **gin**-ee) *noun* (*old use*) **1** the sum of 21 shillings ($2.10), used in stating professional fees, prizes, etc. **2** a British coin worth 21 shillings.

guinea pig *noun* **1** a small furry animal without a tail. **2** a person who is used as the subject of an experiment.

guise (*say* guyz) *noun* an outward disguise or pretence.

guitar *noun* a musical instrument played by plucking its strings. **guitarist** *noun*

gulf *noun* **1** a large area of the sea that is partly surrounded by land. **2** a wide gap; a great difference.

gull *noun* a seagull.

gullet *noun* the tube from the throat to the stomach.

gullible *adjective* easily deceived. [from an old word *gull* = a fool]

gully *noun* (*plural* **gullies**) **1** (*Australian*) a narrow valley. **2** a narrow channel that carries water.

gulp[1] *verb* **1** swallow hastily or greedily. **2** make a loud swallowing noise.

gulp[2] *noun* **1** the act of gulping. **2** a large mouthful of liquid.

gum[1] *noun* the firm flesh in which teeth are rooted. [from Old English *goma*]

gum[2] *noun* **1** a sticky substance produced by some trees and shrubs, used as glue. **2** a sweet made with gum or gelatine, *fruit gums.* **3** chewing gum. **4** a gumtree. **gummy** *adjective.*

gum[3] *verb* (**gummed**, **gumming**) cover or stick with gum. [from Latin *gummi*]

gumboot *noun* a waterproof rubber boot.

gumnut *noun* the woody seed case of a gumtree.

gumtree *noun* (also **gum tree**) a eucalyptus.

gumption *noun* (*informal*) common sense.

gun[1] *noun* **1** a weapon that fires shells or bullets from a tube. **2** a starting pistol. **3** a device that forces a substance out of a tube, *a grease gun; a spray gun.* **gunfire** *noun*, **gunshot** *noun*

gun[2] *verb* (**gunned**, **gunning**) shoot with a gun, *They gunned him down.*

gunboat *noun* a small warship.

gung-ho *adjective* enthusiastic; eager.

gunman *noun* (*plural* **gunmen**) a criminal with a gun.

gunner *noun* a person who operates a gun.

gunnery *noun* the making or use of guns.

gunpowder *noun* a kind of explosive.

gunwale (*say* **gun**-uhl) *noun* the upper edge of a small ship's or boat's side. [from *gun* + *wale* = a ridge (because it was formerly used to support guns)]

gunyah *noun* (*Australian*) (in traditional Aboriginal use) a shelter. [from Sydney language *ganya*= house, hut]

gurdwara (*say* ger-**dwah**-ruh) *noun* (also **gurudwara**) a place where Sikhs meet for worship. [Punjabi from Sanskrit *guru* = teacher + *dvāra* = door]

gurgle *verb* (**gurgled**, **gurgling**) make a low bubbling sound. **gurgle** *noun*

guru (*say* **goo**-roo) *noun* **1** a Hindu spiritual teacher. **2** an influential or revered teacher. [Sanskrit, = teacher]

gush *verb* **1** flow suddenly or quickly. **2** talk effusively. **gush** *noun*

gusset *noun* a piece of cloth inserted in a garment to strengthen or enlarge it.

gust[1] *noun* **1** a sudden rush of wind. **2** a burst of rain, smoke, or sound. **gustily** *adverb*, **gusty** *adjective*

gust[2] *verb* blow in gusts.

gusto *noun* great enjoyment; zest.

gut[1] *noun* the lower part of the digestive system; the intestine.

gut[2] *verb* (**gutted, gutting**) **1** remove the guts from a dead fish or other animal. **2** remove or destroy the inside of something, *The fire gutted the factory.*

guts *plural noun* **1** the digestive system; the inside parts of a person or thing. **2** (*informal*) courage.

gutter[1] *noun* a long narrow channel at the side of a street, or along the edge of a roof, for carrying away rainwater.

gutter[2] *verb* (of a candle) burn unsteadily so that melted wax runs down. [from Latin *gutta* = a drop]

guttering *noun* the gutters of a building.

guttersnipe *noun* a poor child who plays in the streets in a slum.

guttural (*say* **gut**-uh-ruhl) *adjective* throaty; harsh-sounding, *a guttural voice.* [from Latin *guttur* = throat]

guy[1] *noun* (*informal*) **1** a man. **2** (**guys**) people of either sex, *What are you guys doing tomorrow?*

guy[2] *noun* (also **guy rope**) a rope used to hold something in place.

guzzle *verb* (**guzzled**, **guzzling**) eat or drink greedily. **guzzler** *noun*

gym (*say* jim) *noun* (*informal*) **1** a gymnasium. **2** gymnastics.

gymkhana (*say* jim-**kah**-nuh) *noun* a series of horse-riding contests and other sports events.

gymnasium *noun* a place fitted up for gymnastics. [from Greek *gymnos* = naked (because Greek men exercised naked)]

gymnast *noun* an expert in gymnastics.

gymnastics *plural noun* exercises performed to develop the muscles or to show the performer's agility. **gymnastic** *adjective*

gynaecology (*say* guy-nuh-**kol**-uh-jee) *noun* the study of the female reproductive system and its diseases. **gynaecological** *adjective*, **gynaecologist** *noun* [from Greek *gyne* = woman, + *-logy*]

gypsum (*say* **jip**-suhm) *noun* a chalk-like substance from which plaster of Paris is made, also used in the building industry.

gypsy *noun* (*plural* **gypsies**) (also **Gypsy**) a member of a people who live in caravans and wander from place to place. [from *Egyptian*, because Gypsies were originally thought to have come from Egypt]

gyrate (*say* juy-**rayt**) *verb* (**gyrated**, **gyrating**) revolve; move in circles or spirals. **gyration** *noun* [from Greek *gyros* = a ring or circle]

gyroscope (*say* **juy**-ruh-skohp) *noun* a device that keeps steady because of a heavy wheel spinning inside it. [same origin as *gyrate*]

Hh

ha[1] *interjection* an exclamation of triumph, surprise, or suspicion, *Ha! I told you I was right.*

ha[2] *abbreviation* hectare(s).

habeas corpus (*say* hay-bee-uhs **kor**-puhs) *noun* an order requiring a person to be brought before a judge or into court, especially in order to investigate the right of the authorities to keep them imprisoned. [Latin, = you must have the body]

haberdashery *noun* dress accessories and small articles used in sewing, e.g. ribbons, buttons, thread.

habit *noun* **1** something that you do without thinking because you have done it so often; a settled way of behaving. **2** the long dress worn by a monk or nun.

habitat *noun* where an animal or plant lives naturally.

habitation *noun* **1** a dwelling. **2** inhabiting a place.

habitual *adjective* **1** done as a habit; usual. **2** given to a habit, *a habitual liar.*

hack[1] *verb* **1** chop or cut roughly. **2** gain unauthorised access to data in a system or computer. **3** program quickly and roughly. **4** (*informal*) manage; cope, *She can't hack the hot weather.* **hacker** *noun*

hack[2] *noun* **1** a rough cut, blow, or stroke. **2** an act of computer hacking. **3** (*informal*) a piece of computer code providing a quick or rough solution to a particular problem. **4** (*informal*) a strategy or technique for managing your time or activities more efficiently.

hack[3] *noun* a horse for ordinary riding.

hackles *plural noun* **with their hackles up** angry and ready to fight. [*hackles* are the long feathers on some birds' necks]

hackneyed *adjective* used so often that it is no longer interesting.

hacksaw *noun* a saw for cutting metal.

hackwork *noun* dull, routine work.

had *past tense & past participle* of **have**[1], *I had to go to the doctor's yesterday.*

haddock *noun* (*plural* **haddock**) a North Atlantic sea fish like cod but smaller, used as food.

Hadith *noun* (*plural* **Hadith** or **Hadiths**) **1** a collection of traditions containing sayings of the prophet Muhammad. **2** any of the sayings from the Hadith. [Arabic, = tradition]

hadn't had not, *he hadn't seen her for years.*

haemoglobin (*say* hee-muh-**gloh**-buhn) *noun* the red substance that carries oxygen in the blood. [from Greek *haima* = blood]

haemophilia (*say* hee-muh-**fil**-ee-uh) *noun* a disease that causes people to bleed dangerously from even a slight cut. [from Greek *haima* = blood, + *philia* = loving]

haemorrhage (*say* **hem**-uh-rij) *noun* bleeding. [from Greek *haima* = blood, + *rhegnum* = burst]

hag *noun* an ugly old woman.

haggard *adjective* looking ill or very tired.

haggis *noun* (*plural* **haggises**) a Scottish food made from sheep's offal.

haggle *verb* (**haggled**, **haggling**) argue about a price or agreement.

haiku (*say* **huy**-koo) *noun* (*plural* **haiku**) a kind of short poem, usually with three lines. [Japanese]

hail[1] *noun* frozen drops of rain. **hail** *verb*, **hailstone** *noun*, **hailstorm** *noun*

hail[2] *interjection* an exclamation of greeting.

hail[3] *verb* **1** call out to somebody. **2** signal to a taxi to stop. **3** acclaim, *The firefighters were hailed as heroes.*
hail from come from, *He hails from Ireland.*

hair *noun* **1** a soft covering that grows on the heads and bodies of people and animals. **2** one of the threads that make up this covering. **hairbrush** *noun*, **haircut** *noun*

hairdresser *noun* a person whose job is to cut and arrange people's hair.

hairpin *noun* a U-shaped pin for keeping hair in place.

hairpin bend *noun* a sharp bend in a road.

hair-raising *adjective* terrifying.

hair-splitting *adjective & noun* making distinctions of meaning that are too small to be of any real importance; quibbling. **hair-splitter** *noun*

hairy *adjective* **1** with a lot of hair. **2** (*informal*) hair-raising; difficult.

hajj (*say* hahj) *noun* (also **hadj** or **haj**) the annual Muslim pilgrimage to Mecca. [from Arabic (*al-*) *ḥajj* = (the Great) Pilgrimage]

haka (*say* **hah**-kuh) *noun* **1** a Maori ceremonial war dance involving chanting. **2** an imitation of this by a sports team before a match. [Maori]

hake (*plural* **hake**) another name for **gemfish**.

halal (*say* hah-**lahl**) *adjective* **1** denoting or relating to meat prepared as prescribed by Muslim law. **2** religiously acceptable according to Muslim law. **halal** *noun* [Arabic, = according to religious law]

halcyon (*say* **hal**-see-uhn) *noun* happy and peaceful, *halcyon days.*

hale *adjective* strong and healthy, *hale and hearty.*

half[1] *noun* (*plural* **halves**) one of the two equal parts or amounts into which something is or can be divided.

half[2] *adverb* partly; not completely, *This meat is only half cooked.*

half-baked *adjective* (*informal*) not well planned; foolish.

half-brother *noun* a brother to whom you are related by one parent but not by both parents.

half-hearted *adjective* not very enthusiastic. **half-heartedly** *adverb*

halfpenny (*say* **hayp**-nee) *noun* (*plural* **halfpennies** or **halfpence**) a former coin worth half a penny.

half-sister *noun* a sister to whom you are related by one parent but not by both parents.

half-time *noun* the point or interval halfway through a game.

halfway *adjective & adverb* between two others and equally distant from each.

halfwit *noun* a foolish or stupid person.

halibut *noun* (*plural* **halibut**) a large flat fish used as food.

hall *noun* **1** a space or passage into which the front entrance of a house or other building opens. **2** a corridor or passage in a house or other building. **3** a very large room or building used for meetings, concerts, or other events.

hallelujah *interjection & noun* alleluia.

hallmark *noun* an official mark made on gold, silver, and platinum to show its quality.

hallo *interjection* hello.

halloumi *noun* (also **haloumi**) a firm white cheese made from goats' or ewes' milk. [from Egyptian Arabic]

hallow *verb* **1** make a thing holy. **2** honour something as being holy.

Halloween *noun* the night of 31 October, the eve of All Saints' Day, often celebrated by children dressing up in frightening masks and costumes. [from Old English *hallow* = saint, holy person + *even* = evening]

hallucination *noun* something you think you can see or hear that is not really there. **hallucinate** *verb*, **hallucinatory** *adjective*

halo *noun* (*plural* **haloes**) a circle of light around or above something, especially around or above the head of a saint or holy person in paintings.

halt[1] *verb* stop.

halt[2] *noun* **1** a stop, *Work came to a halt.* **2** a small stopping place on a railway.

halter *noun* a rope or strap put round a horse's head so that it can be led or fastened by this.

halve *verb* (**halved**, **halving**) **1** divide into halves. **2** reduce to half its size.

ham *noun* **1** meat from a pig's leg. **2** (*informal*) an actor or performer who is not very good. **3** (*informal*) someone who operates a radio to send and receive messages as a hobby.

hamburger *noun* a flat round cake of minced beef served fried, often in a bread roll. [named after the city Hamburg in Germany]

hamlet *noun* a small village.

hammer[1] *noun* a tool with a heavy metal head used for jobs such as driving in nails and breaking things.
go under the hammer be sold by auction.

hammer[2] *verb* **1** hit with a hammer. **2** strike loudly. **3** (*informal*) defeat.

hammerhead *noun* a shark with a flattened head shaped like a hammer.

hammock *noun* a bed made of a strong net or piece of cloth hung by cords.

hamper[1] *noun* a large box-shaped basket with a lid.

hamper[2] *verb* hinder; prevent from moving or working freely.

hamster *noun* a small furry animal with cheek pouches for carrying grain.

hand[1] *noun* **1** the end part of the arm below the wrist. **2** a pointer on a clock or dial. **3** a worker; a member of a ship's crew, *All hands on deck!* **4** the cards held by one player in a card game. **5** side or direction, *on the other hand.* **6** control; care, *You are in good hands.* **7** influence; help, *Give me a hand with these boxes.* **8** (*informal*) applause, *Give the actors a big hand.*
at hand 1 near. **2** about to happen.
by hand using your hand or hands.
hands down winning easily.
in hand 1 in your possession. **2** being dealt with.

on hand available.
out of hand out of control.

hand² *verb* give or pass something to somebody, *Hand it over.*

handbag *noun* a small bag for holding a purse and personal articles.

handbook *noun* a small book that gives useful facts about something.

handcuff¹ *noun* one of a pair of metal rings linked by a chain, for fastening wrists together.

handcuff² *verb* fasten with handcuffs.

handful *noun* (*plural* **handfuls**) **1** as much as can be carried in one hand. **2** a few people or things. **3** (*informal*) a troublesome person or task.

handicap *noun* **1** a disadvantage. **2** (in some sports) a disadvantage given to a stronger competitor to make the chances more equal. **3** (*offensive*) a condition that significantly restricts a person's ability to function physically, mentally, or socially. **handicap** *verb*, **handicapped** *adjective*

handicraft *noun* artistic work done with the hands, e.g. woodwork, needlework.

handily *adverb* in a handy way.

handiwork *noun* **1** something made by hand. **2** something done, *Is this mess your handiwork?*

handkerchief *noun* a small square of cloth for wiping the nose or face. [from *hand* + *kerchief*]

handle¹ *noun* the part of a thing by which it is carried or controlled.

handle² *verb* (**handled**, **handling**) **1** touch or feel something with your hands. **2** operate something with your hands. **3** deal with; manage, *Will you handle the catering?* **handler** *noun*

handlebar *noun* (also **handlebars**) the bar, with a handle at each end, that steers a bicycle, scooter, or other vehicle.

handout *noun* **1** something given free of charge. **2** a piece of printed information provided free of charge.

handrail *noun* a narrow rail for people to hold as a support.

handset *noun* **1** a telephone mouthpiece and earpiece as one unit. **2** a hand-held control device for a piece of electronic equipment.

handshake *noun* shaking hands with someone as a greeting.

handsome *adjective* **1** good-looking. **2** generous. **handsomely** *adverb*

handstand *noun* balancing on your hands with your feet in the air.

handwriting *noun* writing done by hand. **handwritten** *adjective*

handy *adjective* (**handier**, **handiest**) **1** convenient; useful. **2** ready to hand. **3** good at using the hands. **handily** *adverb*, **handiness** *noun*

handyman *noun* (*plural* **handymen**) a person who does household repairs or odd jobs.

hang¹ *verb* (**hung** (in sense 5 **hanged**), **hanging**) **1** support or be supported from above so that the lower end is free. **2** stick wallpaper to a wall. **3** decorate with drapery or hanging ornaments, *The tree was hung with lights.* **4** droop; lean, *People hung over the gate.* **5** kill someone by tying a rope attached from above around their neck and removing the support from beneath them.
hang about loiter; not go away.
hang back hesitate to go forward or to do something.
hang on 1 hold tightly. **2** (*informal*) wait.
hang up end a telephone conversation by cutting the connection.

hang² *noun* the way something hangs.
get the hang of (*informal*) learn how to do or use something.

hangar *noun* a large shed where aircraft are kept.

hanger *noun* a device on which to hang things, *a coathanger.*

hang-glider *noun* a framework in which a person can glide through the air. **hang-gliding** *noun*

hangman *noun* (*plural* **hangmen**) a man whose job it is to hang people condemned to death.

hangover *noun* an unpleasant feeling after drinking too much alcohol.

hang-up *noun* (*informal*) something that embarrasses or worries you; an inhibition.

hank *noun* a coil or piece of wool, thread, or other material.

hanker *verb* feel a longing for something.

hanky *noun* (*plural* **hankies**) (*informal*) a handkerchief.

Hansard *noun* the official report of the proceedings of parliament. [named after the English printer whose firm originally compiled it]

Hanukkah (*say* **hah**-nuh-kuh) *noun* an eight-day Jewish festival beginning in late November or early December. [Hebrew, = consecration]

haphazard *adjective* done or chosen at random, not by planning. [same origin as *happen*, + *hazard*]

hapless *adjective* having no luck. [same origin as *happen*, + *-less* = without]

happen *verb* **1** take place; occur. **2** do something by chance, *I happened to see him.* [from Old Norse *happ* = luck]

happening *noun* something that happens; an event.

happy *adjective* (**happier**, **happiest**) **1** pleased; contented, *I'm happy when my friend comes over to play.* **2** fortunate. **happily** *adverb*, **happiness** *noun* [same origin as *happen*]

happy-go-lucky *adjective* taking things cheerfully as they happen.

hara-kiri *noun* a form of suicide formerly used by Japanese officers when in disgrace. [from Japanese *hara* = belly, *kiri* = cutting]

harangue (*say* huh-**rang**) *verb* (**harangued**, **haranguing**) make a long speech to somebody. **harangue** *noun*

harass (*say* **ha**-ruhs or huh-**ras**) *verb* trouble or annoy somebody often. **harassment** *noun* [from Old French *harer* = set the dog on someone]

harbour[1] *noun* a place where ships can shelter or unload.

harbour[2] *verb* **1** give shelter to somebody, *harbouring a criminal.* **2** keep in your mind, *harbouring a grudge.*

hard[1] *adjective* **1** firm; solid; not soft. **2** difficult to do, understand, or answer, *hard sums.* **3** severe; stern. **4** causing suffering, *hard luck.* **5** using great effort, *a hard worker.* **6** (of water) containing minerals that prevent soap from making much lather. **hardness** *noun*
hard of hearing slightly deaf.
hard up (*informal*) short of money.

hard[2] *adverb* **1** so as to be hard, *The ground froze hard.* **2** with great effort; intensively, *We worked hard. It is raining hard.* **3** with difficulty, *hard-earned.*

hardboard *noun* stiff board made of compressed wood pulp.

hard case *noun* (*Australian informal*) someone who is amusingly unconventional.

hard copy *noun* material printed on paper from a computer.

hard disk *noun* a rigid disk installed in a computer, capable of storing large quantities of data.

hard drive *noun* a disk drive used to read from and write to a hard disk.

harden *verb* make or become hard or hardy. **hardener** *noun*

hard-hearted *adjective* unsympathetic.

hardly *adverb* only just; only with difficulty, *She can hardly walk.*

hardship *noun* difficult conditions that cause discomfort or suffering.

hardware *noun* **1** metal implements and tools; machinery. **2** the machinery of a computer. (Compare **software**.)

hard-wearing *adjective* able to stand a lot of wear.

hardwood *noun* hard heavy wood from eucalyptus and deciduous trees.

hardy *adjective* (**hardier**, **hardiest**) able to endure cold or difficult conditions. **hardiness** *noun*

hare *noun* an animal like a rabbit but larger.

harem (*say* **hair**-ruhm or hah-**reem**) *noun* the part of a Muslim palace or house where the women live; the women living there. [from Arabic *harim* = forbidden]

hark *verb* listen.
hark back return to an earlier subject.

harlequin *adjective* in mixed colours.

harm[1] *verb* damage; injure.

harm[2] *noun* damage; injury. **harmful** *adjective*, **harmless** *adjective*

harmonic *adjective* of harmony in music.

harmonica *noun* a mouth organ.

harmonise *verb* (**harmonised**, **harmonising**) make harmonious; produce harmony. **harmonisation** *noun*

harmonium *noun* a musical instrument with a keyboard, in which notes are produced by air pumped through brass reeds.

harmony *noun* (*plural* **harmonies**) **1** a pleasant combination, especially of musical notes. **2** being friendly to each other and not quarrelling. **harmonious** *adjective*

harness[1] *noun* (*plural* **harnesses**) the straps put round a horse's head and neck for controlling it.

harness[2] *verb* **1** put a harness on a horse. **2** control and use something, *Could we harness the power of the wind?*

harp[1] *noun* a musical instrument made of strings stretched across a frame and plucked by the fingers. **harpist** *noun*

harp[2] *verb* **harp on** keep on talking about something in a tiresome way, *He is always harping on about manners.*

harpoon *noun* a spear attached to a rope, used especially for catching whales. **harpoon** *verb*

harpsichord *noun* an instrument like a piano but with strings that are plucked (not struck) by a mechanism. [from *harp*, + Latin *chorda* = string]

harrow *noun* a heavy device pulled over the ground to break up the soil.

harrowing *adjective* causing horror and distress.

harry *verb* (**harried**, **harrying**) harass.

harsh *adjective* **1** rough and unpleasant. **2** severe; cruel. **harshly** *adverb*, **harshness** *noun*

hart *noun* a male deer. (Compare **hind**[2].)

harvest[1] *noun* **1** the time when farmers gather in the grain, fruit, or vegetables that they have grown. **2** the crop that is gathered in.

harvest[2] *verb* gather in a crop; reap. **harvester** *noun*

has 3rd person singular present tense of **have**[1], *She has a very cute dog.*

hash[1] *noun* a mixture of small pieces of meat and vegetables, usually fried. **make a hash of** (*informal*) make a mess of something; bungle.

hash[2] *noun* the symbol #.

hashish *noun* a drug made from hemp.

hashtag *noun* the hash symbol (#) preceding a word or phrase on a social media site, used to identify and keep track of a particular subject or topic.

hasn't has not, *She hasn't played piano for ages.*

hassle[1] *noun* (*informal*) trouble.

hassle[2] *verb* (*informal*) annoy; harass.

hassock *noun* a small thick cushion for kneeling on in church.

haste *noun* a hurry. **make haste** act quickly.

hasten *verb* **1** hurry. **2** speed something up.

hasty *adjective* **1** hurried. **2** done too quickly. **hastily** *adverb*, **hastiness** *noun*

hat *noun* a shaped covering for the head.

hatch[1] *noun* (*plural* **hatches**) an opening in a floor, wall, or door, usually with a covering.

hatch[2] *verb* **1** break out of an egg. **2** keep an egg warm until a baby bird comes out. **3** plan, *They hatched a plot.*

hatchback *noun* a car with a sloping back hinged at the top.

hatchet *noun* a small axe.

hate[1] *verb* (**hated**, **hating**) dislike very strongly.

hate[2] *noun* hatred.

hateful *adjective* arousing hatred.

hatred *noun* strong dislike.

hatter *noun* a person who makes hats.

hat trick *noun* getting three goals, wickets, or victories, one after the other.

haughty *adjective* proud of yourself and looking down on other people. **haughtily** *adverb*, **haughtiness** *noun*

haul[1] *verb* pull or drag with great effort. **haulage** *noun*

haul[2] *noun* **1** hauling. **2** the amount obtained by an effort; booty, *The robbers made a good haul.* **3** a distance to be covered, *a long haul.*

haunch *noun* (*plural* **haunches**) the buttock and top part of the thigh.

haunt[1] *verb* **1** (of ghosts) appear often in a place or to a person. **2** visit a place often. **3** stay in your mind, *Memories haunt me.*

haunt[2] *noun* a place often visited by a person.

haute couture (*say* oht koo-**tyoor**) *noun* high fashion; products of the leading fashion houses. [French, = high dressmaking]

haute cuisine (*say* oht kwee-**zeen**) *noun* cookery of a high standard. [French, = high cookery]

have[1] *verb* (**had**, **having**) **1** possess; own, *We have two dogs; She has red hair.* **2** contain, *This tin has lollies in it.* **3** experience, *He had a shock.* **4** give birth to, *She had twins.* **5** be obliged to do something, *We have to go now.* **6** allow, *I won't have him bullied.* **7** receive; accept, *Will you have a lolly?* **8** get something done, *I'm having my tennis racket fixed.* **9** (*informal*) cheat; deceive, *We've been had!* **have somebody on** (*informal*) try to make someone believe something that is untrue, especially as a joke.

have[2] *auxiliary verb* used to form the *past tense* of verbs, for example *she has seen; she had seen; she will have seen.*

haven *noun* a refuge.

haven't have not, *I haven't gone to the movies since last year.*

haversack *noun* a strong bag carried on your back or over your shoulder.

havoc *noun* great destruction or disorder.

hawk[1] *noun* a bird of prey with very strong eyesight.

hawk[2] *verb* carry goods about and try to sell them. **hawker** *noun*

hawthorn *noun* a thorny tree with small red berries (called *haws*).

hay *noun* dried grass for feeding to animals.

hay fever *noun* irritation of the nose, throat, and eyes, caused by pollen or dust.

haystack *noun* (also **hayrick**) a large neat pile of hay packed for storing.

haywire *adjective* (*informal*) badly disorganised; out of control.

hazard *noun* **1** a danger; a risk. **2** an obstacle. **hazardous** *adjective*

hazard reduction *noun* the use of fire, machinery, or other means to reduce the fuel level in areas at risk of bushfire.

haze *noun* thin mist.

hazel *noun* **1** a bush with small nuts. **2** a light brown colour. **hazelnut** *noun*

hazy *adjective* **1** misty. **2** vague; uncertain. **hazily** *adverb*, **haziness** *noun*

HDTV *abbreviation* high-definition television.

he *pronoun* **1** the male person or animal being talked about, *My friends like my father because he lets us play his guitars.* **2** a person (male or female), *He who hesitates is lost.*

> **Usage** Until relatively recently *he* was used to refer to a person of unspecified sex, as in *every child needs to know that he is loved*, but this is now generally regarded as old-fashioned or sexist.

head[1] *noun* **1** the part of the body containing the brains, eyes, and mouth. **2** brains; the mind; intelligence, *Use your head!* **3** a talent or ability, *She has a good head for figures.* **4** the side of a coin on which someone's head is shown. **5** a person, *It costs $2 per head.* **6** the top, *a pinhead*; the leading part of something, *at the head of the procession.* **7** the chief; the person in charge; a headmaster or headmistress. **8** a crisis, *Matters came to a head.*
keep your head stay calm.

head[2] *verb* **1** be at the top or front of something. **2** hit a ball with your head. **3** move in a particular direction, *We headed for the coast.*
head off force someone to turn by getting in front.

headache *noun* **1** a pain in the head. **2** (*informal*) a worrying problem.

headdress *noun* a covering or decoration for the head.

header *noun* **1** heading the ball in soccer. **2** a dive or fall with the head first.

heading *noun* a word or words put at the top of a piece of printing or writing.

headland *noun* a promontory.

headlight *noun* a powerful light at the front of a vehicle.

headline *noun* a heading in a newspaper.
the headlines the main items of news.

headlong *adverb & adjective* **1** head first. **2** in a hasty or thoughtless way.

headmaster *noun* a male principal in charge of a school.

headmistress *noun* a female principal in charge of a school.

head-on *adverb & adjective* with the front parts colliding, *a head-on collision.*

headphones *plural noun* a pair of earphones joined by a band placed over the head, for listening to audio signals such as music or speech.

headquarters *noun & plural noun* the place from which an organisation is controlled.

headset *noun* a set of headphones, typically with a microphone attached.

headstrong *adjective* determined to do as you want.

headway *noun* progress, *make headway.*

heal *verb* **1** make or become healthy again, *The wound healed.* **2** cure, *heal the sick.*

health *noun* **1** the condition of a person's body or mind, *His health is bad.* **2** being healthy, *in sickness and in health.*

healthy *adjective* (**healthier**, **healthiest**) **1** being well; free from illness. **2** producing good health, *healthy activities.* **healthily** *adverb*, **healthiness** *noun*

heap[1] *noun* a pile, especially if untidy.
heaps *plural noun* (*informal*) a great amount; plenty, *There's heaps of time.*

heap[2] *verb* **1** make into a heap. **2** put on large amounts, *She heaped the plate with food.*

hear *verb* (**heard**, **hearing**) **1** take in sounds through the ears. **2** receive news or information. **hearer** *noun*
hear! hear! (in a debate) I agree.

hearing *noun* **1** the ability to hear. **2** a chance to be heard; a trial in a lawcourt.

hearing aid *noun* a device to help a partially deaf person to hear.

hearsay *noun* something heard, e.g. in a rumour or gossip.

hearse *noun* a vehicle for taking the coffin to a funeral.

heart *noun* **1** the organ of the body that makes the blood circulate. **2** a person's feelings or emotions; sympathy. **3** enthusiasm; courage, *Take heart.* **4** the middle or most important part. **5** a curved shape representing a heart; a playing card with red heart shapes on it. **heartbroken** *adjective*
break a person's heart make them very unhappy.
by heart memorised.

heart attack *noun* **1** a sudden blockage of the blood supply to the heart, resulting in death of part of the heart muscle. **2** (*informal*) used in reference to a reaction of shock or great surprise, *I had a heart attack when I saw how much money lunch cost.*

heartburn *noun* a burning sensation in the lower part of the chest resulting from indigestion.

hearten *verb* make a person feel encouraged.

heartfelt *adjective* felt deeply.

hearth *noun* the floor of a fireplace or the area in front of it.

heartland *noun* the central or most important region.

heartless *adjective* without pity or sympathy.

heart-warming *adjective* encouraging; causing people to rejoice.

hearty *adjective* **1** strong; vigorous. **2** enthusiastic; sincere, *hearty congratulations.* **3** (of a meal) large. **heartily** *adverb*, **heartiness** *noun*

heat[1] *noun* **1** hotness or (in scientific use) the form of energy causing this. **2** hot weather. **3** a race or contest to decide who will take part in the final.

heat[2] *verb* make or become hot.

heater *noun* a device for heating something.

heath *noun* **1** flat uncultivated land with low shrubs. **2** a small shrub growing on such land. **3** a small Australian shrub with white, pink, or red flowers.

heathen *noun* a person who does not believe in one of the chief religions. **heathen** *adjective* [from Old English = living in the open (heath) country]

heather *noun* an evergreen plant with small purple, pink, or white flowers.

heatwave *noun* a long period of hot weather.

heave *verb* (**heaved** (in sense 4 **hove**), **heaving**) **1** lift or move something heavy. **2** (*informal*) throw. **3** rise and fall like sea waves; pant; retch. **4** (of ships) come, *heave in sight.*
heave a sigh utter a deep sigh.

heaven *noun* **1** the place where God and angels are thought to live. **2** a very pleasant place or condition.
the heavens the sky.

heavenly *adjective* **1** of heaven. **2** in the sky, *Stars are heavenly bodies.* **3** (*informal*) very pleasing.

heavy *adjective* (**heavier**, **heaviest**) **1** having great weight; difficult to lift or carry. **2** great in amount or force, *heavy rain*; *a heavy penalty.* **3** needing much effort, *heavy work.* **4** full of sadness or worry, *with a heavy heart.* **heavily** *adverb*, **heaviness** *noun*

heavy industry *noun* industry producing metal, machines, and materials in bulk.

heavy metal *noun* **1** metal of a high density. **2** a type of loud rock music with a heavy beat.

heavyweight *noun* **1** a heavy person. **2** a boxer of the heaviest weight.

Hebrew *noun* the language of the Jewish people in ancient Palestine and modern Israel.

heckle *verb* (**heckled**, **heckling**) harass a speaker with interruptions and questions. **heckler** *noun*

hectare (*say* **hek**-tair) *noun* a unit of area equal to 10,000 square metres or nearly 2½ acres.

hectic *adjective* full of activity.

hecto- *prefix* one hundred (as in *hectogram* = 100 grams). [from Greek *hekaton* = a hundred]

hector *verb* frighten by bullying talk.

he'd **1** he had, *he'd seen enough.* **2** he would, *he'd like to see you.*

hedge[1] *noun* a row of bushes forming a barrier or boundary.

hedge[2] *verb* (**hedged**, **hedging**) **1** surround with a hedge or other barrier. **2** make or trim a hedge. **3** avoid giving a definite answer. **hedger** *noun*

hedge fund *noun* an investment fund that engages in speculation using credit or borrowed capital.

hedgehog *noun* a small animal covered with long prickles.

heed[1] *verb* pay attention to.

heed[2] *noun* attention given to something, *take heed.* **heedful** *adjective*, **heedless** *adjective*

hee-haw *noun* a donkey's bray.

heel[1] *noun* **1** the back part of the foot. **2** the part around or under the heel of a sock, shoe, or boot.
take to your heels run away.

heel[2] *verb* lean over to one side; tilt.

heeler *noun* (*Australian*) a cattle dog; a blue heeler.

heft *verb* lift or carry something heavy.

hefty *adjective* (**heftier**, **heftiest**) large and strong. **heftily** *adverb*

Hegira (*say* **hej**-uh-ruh) *noun* the flight of Muhammad from Mecca in AD 622. The Muslim era is reckoned from this date. [from Arabic *hijra* = departure from a country]

heifer (*say* **hef**-uh) *noun* a young cow.

height *noun* **1** how high something is; the distance from the base to the top or from head to foot. **2** a high place. **3** the highest or most intense part, *at the height of her career.*

heighten *verb* make or become higher or more intense.

heinous (*say* **hay**-nuhs or **hee**-nuhs) *adjective* very wicked.

heir (*say* air) *noun* a person who inherits something.

heir apparent *noun* an heir whose right to inherit cannot be cancelled.

heiress (*say* **air**-res) *noun* (*plural* **heiresses**) a female heir, especially to great wealth.

heirloom (*say* **air**-loom) *noun* a valued possession that has been handed down in a family for several generations.

heir presumptive *noun* an heir whose right to inherit will be cancelled if someone with a stronger right is born.

held *past tense & past participle* of **hold**[1].

helicopter *noun* a kind of aircraft with a large horizontal propeller or rotor. [from *helix* + Greek *pteron* = wing]

helium (*say* **hee**-lee-uhm) *noun* a light colourless gas that does not burn. [from Greek *helios* = sun]

helix (*say* **hee**-liks) *noun* (*plural* **helices**, *say* **hee**-luh-seez) a spiral. [Greek, = coil]

hell *noun* **1** a place where wicked people are thought to be punished after they die. **2** a very unpleasant place or condition. **3** (*informal*) an exclamation of anger.

he'll he will.

hello *interjection* a word used to greet somebody or to attract attention.

helm *noun* the handle or wheel used to steer a ship. **helmsman** *noun*

helmet *noun* a strong covering worn to protect the head.

help[1] *verb* **1** do part of another person's work for them. **2** benefit; make something better or easier, *This will help you to sleep.* **3** avoid, *I can't help coughing.* **4** serve food or drink to somebody. **helper** *noun*, **helpful** *adjective*, **helpfully** *adverb*

help[2] *noun* **1** helping somebody. **2** a person or thing that helps.

helping *noun* a portion of food.

helpless *adjective* not able to do things. **helplessly** *adverb*, **helplessness** *noun*

helter-skelter *adverb* in great haste.

hem[1] *noun* the edge of a piece of cloth that is folded over and sewn down.

hem[2] *verb* (**hemmed**, **hemming**) put a hem on something.
hem in surround and restrict.

hemisphere *noun* **1** half a sphere. **2** half the earth. **hemispherical** *adjective* [from Greek *hemi-* = half, + *sphere*]

hemlock *noun* a poisonous plant; poison made from it.

hemp *noun* **1** a plant that produces coarse fibres from which cloth and ropes are made. **2** a drug made from this plant.

hen *noun* **1** a female bird. **2** a female fowl.

hence *adverb* **1** henceforth. **2** therefore. **3** (*old use*) from here.

henceforth *adverb* from now on.

henchman *noun* (*plural* **henchmen**) a trusty supporter.

Hendra virus *noun* a virus carried by fruit bats, and potentially fatal to animals and humans. [named after Hendra, a suburb of Brisbane, where an outbreak of the virus occurred in 1994]

henna *noun* a reddish-brown dye.

hepatitis (*say* hep-uh-**tuy**-tuhs) *noun* inflammation of the liver, often associated with viruses designated A, B, and C, and with varying degrees of severity.

hepato- *prefix* relating to the liver. [from Greek *hepat* = liver]

hepta- *prefix* seven. [from Greek *hepta* = seven]

heptagon *noun* a flat shape with seven sides and seven angles. **heptagonal** *adjective* [from *hepta-*, + Greek *gonia* = angle]

heptathlon (*say* hep-**tath**-luhn) an athletic contest in which competitors take part in seven events.

her[1] *pronoun* the form of *she* used as the object of a verb or after a preposition.

her[2] *adjective* belonging to her, *her book.*

herald[1] *noun* **1** an official in former times who made announcements and carried messages for a king or queen. **2** a person or thing indicating that something is coming.

herald[2] *verb* show that someone or something is coming.

heraldry *noun* the study of coats of arms. **heraldic** (*say* huh-**ral**-dik) *adjective*

herb *noun* a plant used for flavouring or for making medicine. **herbal** *adjective* [from Latin *herba* = grass]

herbaceous (*say* her-**bay**-shuhs) *adjective* **1** of or like herbs. **2** containing many flowering plants, *a herbaceous border.*

herbicide *noun* a substance for killing unwanted plants. [from Latin *herba* = grass, + *caedere* = kill]

herbivorous (*say* her-**biv**-uh-ruhs) *adjective* plant-eating. (Compare **carnivorous.**) **herbivore** *noun* [from Latin *herba* = grass, + *vorare* = devour]

herculean (*say* her-kyuh-**lee**-uhn) *adjective* having or needing great strength or effort, *a herculean task.* [named after Hercules, a hero in ancient Greek legend noted for his great strength]

herd[1] *noun* **1** a group of cattle or other animals that feed together. **2** a mass of people; a mob. **herdsman** *noun*

herd[2] *verb* **1** gather or move or send in a herd, *We were herded into the dining room.* **2** look after a herd of animals.

herd immunity *noun* the resistance to the spread of a contagious disease within a population that results if a sufficiently high proportion of individuals are immune to the disease.

here *adverb* **1** in or to this place, *Bring the book over here so I can see it.* **2** at this point in a process or a series of events.
here and there in various places or directions.

hereafter *adverb* from now on; in future.

hereby *adverb* by this means; as a result of this.

hereditary *adjective* **1** inherited, *a hereditary disease.* **2** inheriting a position, *The Queen is a hereditary monarch.*

heredity (*say* huh-**red**-uh-tee) *noun* inheriting characteristics from parents or ancestors. [from Latin *heredis* = of an heir]

heresy (*say* **he**-ruh-see) *noun* (*plural* **heresies**) an opinion that disagrees with the beliefs accepted by the Christian Church or other authority.

heretic (*say* **he**-ruh-tik) *noun* a person who supports a heresy. **heretical** (*say* huh-**ret**-i-kuhl) *adjective*

heritage *noun* the things that someone has inherited.

hermaphrodite (*say* her-**maf**-ruh-duyt) *noun* an animal or plant that has both male and female sexual organs in one individual.

hermetically *adverb* so as to be airtight, *hermetically sealed.*

hermit *noun* a person who lives alone and keeps away from people. [from Greek *eremites* = of the desert]

hermitage *noun* a hermit's home.

hernia *noun* a condition in which an internal part of the body pushes through another part; a rupture.

hero *noun* (*plural* **heroes**) **1** a man or boy who is admired for doing something very brave or great. **2** the chief male character in a story, play, or poem. **heroic** *adjective*, **heroically** *adverb*, **heroism** *noun*

heroin *noun* a very strong drug.

heroine *noun* **1** a woman or girl who is admired for doing something very brave or great. **2** the chief female character in a story, play, or poem.

heron *noun* a wading bird with long legs and a long neck.

herring *noun* (*plural* **herring** or **herrings**) a sea fish used as food.

herringbone *noun* a zigzag pattern.

hers *possessive pronoun* belonging to her, *This book is hers.*

> **Usage** It is incorrect to write *her's*.

herself *pronoun* she or her and nobody else. The word is used to refer back to the subject of a sentence (e.g. *She cut herself*) or for emphasis (e.g. *She herself has said it*).
by herself alone; on her own.

hertz *noun* (*plural* **hertz**) a unit of frequency of electromagnetic waves, = one cycle per second. [named after the German scientist H.R. Hertz]

he's **1** he is, *he's going to speak.* **2** he has, *he's lost his phone.*

hesitant *adjective* hesitating. **hesitancy** *noun*, **hesitantly** *adverb*

hesitate *verb* (**hesitated**, **hesitating**) **1** show or feel indecision or uncertainty; pause in doubt. **2** be reluctant. **hesitation** *noun* [from Latin *haesitare* = get stuck]

hessian *noun* a strong coarse fabric made from hemp or jute.

hetero- *prefix* other; different. [from Greek *heteros* = other]

heterogeneous (*say* het-uh-roh-**jee**-nee-uhs) *adjective* composed of people or things of different kinds. [from *hetero-*, + Greek *genos* = a kind]

heterosexual *adjective* attracted to people of the opposite sex. **heterosexual** *noun*, **heterosexuality** *noun*

hew *verb* (**hewed**, **hewn**, **hewing**) chop or cut with an axe, sword, or other tool.

hex *noun* a magic spell; a curse.

hexa- *prefix* six. [from Greek *hex* = six]

hexagon *noun* a flat shape with six sides and six angles. **hexagonal** *adjective* [from *hexa-*, + Greek *gonia* = angle]

hey *interjection* an exclamation calling attention or expressing surprise or enquiry.

heyday *noun* the time of a thing's greatest success or prosperity.

hi *interjection* an exclamation calling attention or expressing a greeting.

hiatus (*say* huy-**ay**-tuhs) *noun* (*plural* **hiatuses**) a gap in something that is otherwise continuous. [Latin, = gaping]

hibernate *verb* (**hibernated**, **hibernating**) spend the winter in a state like deep sleep. **hibernation** *noun* [from Latin *hibernus* = of winter]

hibiscus (*say* huy-**bis**-kuhs) *noun* a shrub with brightly coloured flowers.

hiccup *noun* **1** a high gulping sound made when your breath is briefly interrupted. **2** a brief hitch. **hiccup** *verb* (**hiccuped**, **hiccuping**)

hide¹ *verb* (**hid**, **hidden**, **hiding**) **1** keep a person or thing from being seen; conceal. **2** get into a place where you cannot be seen. **3** keep a thing secret.

hide² *noun* an animal's skin.

hide-and-seek *noun* a game in which one person looks for others who are hiding.

hidebound *adjective* narrow-minded.

hideous *adjective* very ugly or unpleasant. **hideously** *adverb*

hideout *noun* a place where somebody hides.

hiding¹ *noun* being hidden, *go into hiding.*

hiding² *noun* a thrashing; a beating.

hierarchy (*say* **huy**-uh-rah-kee) *noun* an organisation that ranks people one above another according to the power or authority that they hold. **hierarchical** *adjective* [from Greek *hieros* = sacred, + *archein* = to rule]

hieroglyphics (*say* huyuh-ruh-**glif**-iks) *plural noun* pictures or symbols used in ancient Egypt to represent words. [from Greek *hieros* = sacred, + *glyphe* = carving]

hi-fi *noun* **1** high fidelity. **2** equipment that gives high fidelity.

higgledy-piggledy *adverb & adjective* completely mixed up; in great disorder.

high[1] *adjective* **1** reaching a long way upwards, *high hills.* **2** far above the ground or above sea level, *high clouds.* **3** measuring from top to bottom, *two metres high.* **4** above average level in importance, quality, or amount, *high rank*; *high prices.* **5** (of a sound or voice) having rapid vibrations; shrill. **6** (of meat) beginning to go bad. **7** (*informal*) affected by a drug.

high[2] *adverb* at or to a high level or position, *They flew high above us.*

highbrow *adjective* intellectual.

High Court *noun* the supreme federal court in Australia.

high definition *noun* a high degree of detail in an image or screen, *The football game was broadcast in high definition on TV.*

higher *adjective & adverb* more high.

higher education *noun* education above the level given in schools, e.g. at university.

highest common factor *noun* the greatest common divisor.

high explosive *noun* a powerful explosive.

high fidelity *adjective* reproducing sound with very little distortion.

highlands *plural noun* mountainous country. **highland** *adjective*, **highlander** *noun*

highlight[1] *noun* **1** a light or bright area in a painting, picture, or design. **2** the most interesting part.

highlight[2] *verb* draw special attention to something.

highlighter *noun* a coloured felt-tipped pen used to mark printed text while leaving it legible.

highly *adverb* **1** extremely, *highly amusing.* **2** very favourably, *We think highly of her.*

Highness *noun* (*plural* **Highnesses**) the title of a prince or princess.

high-rise *adjective* with many storeys.

high school *noun* a secondary school.

high time *noun* fully time, *It's high time we left.*

highway *noun* a main road or route.

highwayman *noun* (*plural* **highwaymen**) a man who robbed travellers on highways in former times.

hijab (*say* hee-**jab**) *noun* a head covering worn in public by some Muslim women.

hijack *verb* seize control of an aircraft or vehicle during a journey. **hijack** *noun*, **hijacker** *noun*

hike *noun* a long walk. **hike** *verb*, **hiker** *noun*

hilarious *adjective* **1** very funny. **2** noisily merry. **hilariously** *adverb*, **hilarity** *noun* [from Greek *hilaros* = cheerful]

hill *noun* a piece of land that is higher than the ground around it. **hillside** *noun*, **hilly** *adjective*

hillock *noun* a small hill; a mound.

hilt *noun* the handle of a weapon or tool, especially a sword, dagger, or knife.
to the hilt completely.

him *pronoun* the form of *he* used as the object of a verb or after a preposition.

himself *pronoun* he or him and nobody else, used to refer back to the subject of a verb, *He has hurt himself.*
by himself on his own; alone, *He did the work all by himself.*

hind[1] *adjective* at the back, *the hind legs.*

hind[2] *noun* a female deer. (Compare **hart**.)

hinder *verb* get in someone's way; make it difficult for a person to do something quickly or for something to happen. **hindrance** *noun*

Hindi *noun* a widely spoken language from northern India.

hindmost *adjective* furthest behind.

hindquarters *plural noun* an animal's hind legs and rear parts.

hindsight *noun* looking back on an event with knowledge or understanding that you did not have at the time.

Hindu *noun* (*plural* **Hindus**) a person whose religion is Hinduism, which is one of the religions of India.

hinge[1] *noun* a joining device on which a lid or door turns when it opens.

hinge[2] *verb* (**hinged, hinging**) **1** fix with a hinge. **2** depend, *Everything hinges on this meeting.*

hint[1] *noun* **1** a slight indication or suggestion, *Give me a hint of what you want.* **2** a useful suggestion, *household hints.*

hint[2] *verb* make a hint.

hinterland *noun* **1** the district behind a coast or port. **2** a remote or fringe area.

hip[1] *noun* the bony part at the side of the body between the waist and the thigh.

hip[2] *interjection* part of a cheer, *Hip, hip, hooray!*

hip hop *noun* a style of music featuring rap with an electronic backing; a dance form associated with this.

hippo *noun* (*plural* **hippos**) (*informal*) a hippopotamus.

hippopotamus *noun* (*plural* **hippopotamuses**) a very large African animal that lives near water. [from Greek *hippos* = horse, + *potamos* = river]

hippy *noun* (also **hippie**) (*informal*) (especially in the 1960s) a person rejecting convention, typically with long hair, beads, etc.

hipster *noun* (*informal*) a person who follows the latest trends and fashions, especially those regarded as being outside the cultural mainstream.

hire[1] *verb* (**hired**, **hiring**) **1** pay to borrow something. **2** lend for payment, *He hires out bicycles.* **3** employ a person. **hirer** *noun*

hire[2] *noun* hiring, *for hire.*

hire purchase *noun* a way of buying something by paying in instalments while having the use of it.

hirsute (*say* **her**-syoot) *adjective* hairy.

his *adjective & possessive pronoun* belonging to him, *That is his book; That book is his.*

hiss *verb* make a sound like an *s, The snakes were hissing.* **hiss** *noun*

histogram *noun* a diagram used in statistics, showing the value of a number of variables by means of columns.

historian *noun* a person who writes or studies history.

historic *adjective* famous or important in history, *a historic town.*

historical *adjective* **1** concerned with history, *a historical society.* **2** belonging to or dealing with history or past events, *a historical novel.* **3** (of the study of a subject) based on an analysis of its development over a period of time. **4** factual, not fictional or legendary. **historically** *adverb*

history *noun* (*plural* **histories**) **1** what happened in the past. **2** study of past events. **3** a description of important events. [from Greek *historia* = finding out, narrative]

hit[1] *verb* (**hit**, **hitting**) **1** come forcefully against a person or thing; knock or strike. **2** have a bad effect on, *Famine has hit the poor countries.* **3** reach, *I can't hit that high note.*

hit back retaliate.

hit on discover something by chance.

hit[2] *noun* **1** hitting; a knock or stroke. **2** a shot that hits the target. **3** a success; something that is successful such as a song, show, or film. **4** (*informal*) a shot or dose of a drug. **5** (in computing) an instance of identifying an item of data that matches the requirements of a search; an instance of a particular website being accessed by a user.

hitch[1] *verb* **1** raise or pull with a slight jerk. **2** fasten or tether. **3** hitchhike.

hitch[2] *noun* **1** a hitching movement. **2** a knot. **3** a difficulty causing delay.

hitchhike *verb* travel by getting free rides in passing vehicles. **hitchhiker** *noun*

hither *adverb* to or towards this place.

hitherto *adverb* until this time.

HIV *abbreviation* human immunodeficiency virus, a virus that can lead to Aids.

hive *noun* **1** a beehive. **2** the bees living in a beehive. **3** a busy place.

hives *plural noun* an itchy rash.

HMAS *abbreviation* Her (or His) Majesty's Australian Ship.

ho *interjection* an exclamation of triumph or scorn, or calling attention.

hoard[1] *noun* a carefully saved store of money, treasure, food, or other items.

hoard[2] *verb* store away. **hoarder** *noun*

hoarding *noun* a tall fence covered with advertisements.

hoar frost *noun* a white frost.

hoarse *adjective* with a rough voice. **hoarsely** *adverb*, **hoarseness** *noun*

hoary *adjective* **1** white or grey from age, *hoary hair.* **2** old, *hoary jokes.*

hoax *verb* deceive somebody as a joke. **hoax** *noun*, **hoaxer** *noun*

hob *noun* a flat surface on a cooker or beside a fireplace, where food can be cooked or kept warm.

hobble *verb* (**hobbled**, **hobbling**) limp.

hobby *noun* (*plural* **hobbies**) something you do for pleasure in your spare time.

hobby horse *noun* **1** a stick with a horse's head, used as a toy. **2** a subject that a person likes to talk about.

hobgoblin *noun* a mischievous or evil spirit.

hobnob *verb* (**hobnobbed**, **hobnobbing**) spend time together in a friendly way, *hobnobbing with pop stars.*

hock *noun* the middle joint of an animal's hind leg.

hockey *noun* a game played by two teams with curved sticks and a hard ball.

hoe[1] *noun* a tool for scraping up weeds.

hoe[2] *verb* (**hoed**, **hoeing**) scrape or dig with a hoe.

hog[1] *noun* **1** a male pig. **2** (*informal*) a greedy person.

go the whole hog (*informal*) do something completely or thoroughly.

hog[2] *verb* (**hogged**, **hogging**) (*informal*) take more than your fair share of something; hoard selfishly.

hoi polloi *noun* the ordinary people; the masses. [Greek, = the many]

hoist[1] *verb* lift; raise something by using ropes and pulleys.

hoist[2] *noun* **1** a device for raising things. **2** (*Australian*) a rotary clothes line of adjustable height.

hokkien (*say* hoh-**keen**) *noun* an egg noodle used widely in Asian cooking.

hold[1] *verb* (**held**, **holding**) **1** have and keep, especially in your hands. **2** possess, *He holds the world record.* **3** keep in a particular position; detain. **4** contain or have room for, *The hall holds 500 people.* **5** support, *This plank won't hold my weight.* **6** stay unbroken; continue, *Will the fine weather hold?* **7** believe; consider, *We shall hold you responsible.* **8** cause to take place, *hold a meeting.* **9** restrain; stop, *Hold everything!*
hold back prevent a person from doing something.
hold forth make a long speech.
hold off delay; not begin.
hold out last; continue.
hold up 1 hinder. **2** stop and rob somebody by threats or force.
hold with approve of, *We don't hold with bullying.*
hold your tongue (*informal*) stop talking.

hold[2] *noun* **1** holding something; a grasp. **2** something to hold on to for support. **3** the part of a ship where cargo is stored, below the deck.
get hold of 1 grasp. **2** obtain. **3** make contact with a person.

holdall *noun* a large portable bag or case.

holder *noun* a person or thing that holds something.

hold-up *noun* **1** a delay. **2** a robbery with threats or force.

hole[1] *noun* **1** a hollow place; a gap or opening. **2** a burrow. **3** (*informal*) an unpleasant place. **4** (*informal*) an awkward situation. **holey** *adjective*

hole[2] *verb* (**holed**, **holing**) **1** make a hole or holes in something. **2** put into a hole.

Holi *noun* a Hindu spring festival celebrated in February or March in honour of Krishna.

holiday *noun* **1** a period of time when people do not go to work or to school. **2** a time when you go away to enjoy yourself. [from *holy* + *day* (because holidays were originally religious festivals)]

holiness *noun* being holy or sacred.
His Holiness the title of the pope.

holistic (*say* hoh-**lis**-tik) *adjective* (of medical treatment) treating the whole person, not just the symptoms. [from Greek *holos* = whole]

hollow[1] *adjective* with an empty space inside; not solid. **hollowly** *adverb*

hollow[2] *noun* **1** a hollow or sunken place. **2** a valley.

hollow[3] *verb* make a thing hollow.

holly *noun* (*plural* **hollies**) an evergreen bush with shiny prickly leaves and red berries.

hollyhock *noun* a plant with large flowers on a very tall stem.

holocaust *noun* **1** an immense destruction, especially by fire, *the nuclear holocaust.* **2** (**the Holocaust**) the mass murder of Jewish people by the Nazis from the 1930s to 1945. [from Greek *holos* = whole, + *kaustos* = burnt]

holster *noun* a leather case in which a pistol or revolver is carried.

holy *adjective* (**holier**, **holiest**) **1** belonging or devoted to God. **2** consecrated, *holy water.* **holiness** *noun*

homage *noun* an act or expression of respect or honour, *We paid homage to his achievements.*

home[1] *noun* **1** the place where you live, *The bushfires forced people to leave their homes.* **2** the place where you were born or where you feel you belong, *She still calls Australia home.* **3** a place where those who need help are looked after, *an old people's home.* **4** the place to be reached in a race or in certain games. **5** a house.

home[2] *adjective* **1** of a person's own home or country, *home produce.* **2** played on a team's own ground, *a home match.*

home[3] *adverb* **1** to or at home, *Is she home yet?* **2** to the point aimed at, *Push the bolt home.*
bring something home to somebody make someone realise the full significance of something.

home[4] *verb* (**homed**, **homing**) move or be aimed towards (a target or destination) with great accuracy, *The missile homed in.*

> **Usage** See the note at *hone*.

home economics *plural noun* the study of household management.

homeless *adjective* having no home.

homely *adverb* simple and ordinary, *a homely meal.* **homeliness** *noun*

home-made *adjective* made at home, not bought from a shop.

homepage *noun* the main page of a document on the World Wide Web.

homesick *adjective* sad because you are away from home. **homesickness** *noun*

homestead *noun* a farmhouse, usually with the land and buildings round it.

home unit *noun* (*Australian*) a residence that is one of several in a building.

homeward *adjective & adverb* going towards home. **homewards** *adverb*

homework *noun* schoolwork that a pupil has to do at home.

homicide *noun* the killing of one person by another. **homicidal** *adjective* [from Latin *homo* = person, + *caedere* = kill]

homily *noun* (*plural* **homilies**) a lecture about behaviour.

homing *adjective* trained to fly home, *a homing pigeon.*

homo- *prefix* same. [from Greek *homos* = same]

homoeopathy (*say* hoh-mee-**op**-uh-thee) *noun* the treatment of a disease with very small doses of natural substances that in a healthy person would produce symptoms like those of the disease itself. **homoeopathic** *adjective* [from Greek *homoios* = alike, + *pathos* = suffering]

homogeneous (*say* hoh-muh-**jee**-nee-uhs) *adjective* composed of people or things of the same kind. [from *homo-*, + Greek *genos* = a kind]

homograph *noun* a word that is spelt like another but has a different meaning or origin, e.g. *bat* (a flying animal) and *bat* (for hitting a ball). [from *homo-* + *-graph*]

homonym (*say* **hom**-uh-nim) *noun* a homograph or homophone. [from *homo-*, + Greek *onyma* = name]

homophone *noun* a word with the same sound as another, e.g. *son* and *sun.* [from *homo-*, + Greek *phone* = sound]

Homo sapiens *noun* the species to which human beings belong. [Latin, = wise man]

homosexual *adjective* attracted to people of the same sex. **homosexual** *noun*, **homosexuality** *noun*

hone (*rhymes with* stone) *verb* **1** sharpen a razor or tool on a fine-grained stone. **2** make sharper or more focused or efficient.

> **Usage** Frequently used in error, as *hone in*, for *home in* (see *home*[4]).

honest *adjective* **1** not stealing or cheating or telling lies. **2** truthful; sincere. **3** fairly earned. **honestly** *adverb*, **honesty** *noun* [from Latin *honestus* = honourable]

honey *noun* a sweet sticky food made by bees.

honeycomb *noun* a wax structure of small six-sided sections made by bees to hold their honey and eggs.

honeydew *noun* a type of melon with pale skin and sweet green flesh.

honeyeater *noun* a bird that feeds on nectar.

honeymoon *noun* **1** a holiday spent together by a newly married couple. **2** an initial period of enthusiasm or goodwill.

honeysuckle *noun* a climbing plant with fragrant yellow or pink flowers.

honk *noun* a loud sound like that made by a goose or a car horn. **honk** *verb*

honorary *adjective* **1** given or received as an honour, *an honorary degree.* **2** unpaid, *the honorary treasurer.*

honorific[1] *adjective* given as a mark of respect.

honorific[2] *noun* a title or word implying or expressing respect.

honour[1] *noun* **1** great respect. **2** a person or thing that brings honour. **3** honesty and loyalty, *a man of honour.* **4** an award for distinction. **5** a title given to certain judges or people of importance, *your Honour.*

honour[2] *verb* **1** feel or show honour for a person. **2** acknowledge and pay a cheque or bill. **3** keep to the terms of an agreement or promise.

honourable *adjective* deserving honour; honest and loyal. **honourably** *adverb*

hood *noun* **1** a covering of soft material for the head and neck. **2** a folding roof or cover. **hooded** *adjective*

hoodwink *verb* deceive.

hoof *noun* (*plural* **hoofs** or **hooves**) the horny part of the foot of a horse and other animals.

hook[1] *noun* a bent or curved piece of metal or other material for hanging things on or for catching hold of something.

hook[2] *verb* **1** catch with a hook. **2** fasten with or on a hook. **3** send a ball in a curving direction.
be hooked on something (*informal*) be addicted to it.

hooked *adjective* hook-shaped.

hookey *noun* **play hookey** (*informal*) stay away from school without permission.

hooligan *noun* a rough lawless young person. **hooliganism** *noun*

hoon[1] *noun* (*Australian informal*) **1** a hooligan. **2** a show-off; an exhibitionist.

hoon[2] *verb* (*Australian informal*) drive dangerously or at reckless speed in order to show off.

hoop *noun* a ring made of metal or wood.

hooray *interjection* **1** a shout of joy or approval; a cheer. **2** (*Australian*) goodbye.

hooroo *interjection* (*Australian*) goodbye.

hoot *noun* **1** the sound made by an owl or a vehicle's horn or a steam whistle. **2** a cry of scorn or disapproval. **3** laughter; a cause of this. **hoot** *verb*, **hooter** *noun*

hop[1] *verb* (**hopped, hopping**) **1** jump on one foot. **2** (of an animal) spring from all feet at once. **3** (*informal*) move quickly, *Here's the car–hop in!*
hop it (*informal*) go away.

hop[2] *noun* a hopping movement.

hop[3] *noun* a climbing plant used to give beer its flavour.

hope[1] *noun* **1** a wish for something to happen. **2** a person or thing that gives hope, *You are our only hope.*

hope[2] *verb* (**hoped, hoping**) feel hope; want and expect something.

hopeful *adjective* feeling or inspiring optimism about a future event, *a hopeful sign.*

hopefully *adverb* **1** in a hopeful manner. **2** it is to be hoped, *Hopefully, we will succeed.*

> **Usage** The use of *hopefully* in sense 2 is extremely common, but it is still considered incorrect by some people.

hopeless *adjective* **1** feeling no hope. **2** admitting no hope, *a hopeless case.* **3** very bad at something. **hopelessly** *adverb*, **hopelessness** *noun*

hopper *noun* **1** one who hops. **2** a V-shaped container with an opening at the bottom.

hopscotch *noun* a game of hopping into squares drawn on the ground.

horde *noun* a large group or crowd.

horizon *noun* the line where the earth and the sky seem to meet. [from Greek *horisein* = form a boundary]

horizontal *adjective* level, so as to be parallel to the horizon; going across from left to right. (The opposite is **vertical**.) **horizontally** *adverb*

hormone *noun* a substance that stimulates an organ of the body or of a plant.

horn *noun* **1** a hard substance that grows into a point on the head of a bull, cow, ram, and certain other animals. **2** a pointed part. **3** a brass instrument played by blowing. **4** a device for making a warning sound. **horned** *adjective*, **horny** *adjective*

hornet *noun* a large kind of wasp.

hornpipe *noun* a sailors' dance.

horoscope *noun* an astrologer's forecast of future events. [from Greek *hora* = hour (of birth), + *skopos* = observer]

horrendous *adjective* horrifying.

horrible *adjective* **1** horrifying. **2** (*informal*) unpleasant. **horribly** *adverb*

horrid *adjective* horrible. **horridly** *adverb*

horrific *adjective* horrifying. **horrifically** *adverb*

horrify *verb* (**horrified, horrifying**) arouse horror in somebody; shock.

horror *noun* **1** great fear and dislike or dismay. **2** a person or thing causing horror.

hors d'oeuvre (*say* aw **derv**) *noun* food served as an appetiser at the start of a meal. [French, = outside the work]

horse *noun* **1** a large four-legged animal, used for riding on or to carry and pull loads. **2** a framework for hanging clothes on to dry. **3** a vaulting horse.
on horseback mounted on a horse.

horseman *noun* (*plural* **horsemen**) a man who rides a horse, especially a skilled rider. **horsemanship** *noun*

horseplay *noun* rough play.

horsepower *noun* a unit for measuring the power of an engine.

horserace *noun* a race between horses with riders. **horseracing** *noun*

horseradish *noun* a plant with a hot-tasting root used to make a sauce.

horseshoe *noun* a U-shaped piece of metal nailed to a horse's hoof.

horsewoman *noun* (*plural* **horsewomen**) a woman who rides a horse, especially a skilled rider.

horticulture *noun* the art of cultivating gardens. **horticultural** *adjective* [from Latin *hortus* = garden, + *culture*]

hose[1] *noun* **1** a flexible tube for taking water to something. **2** (*old use*) breeches, *doublet and hose.*

hose[2] *verb* (**hosed, hosing**) water or spray with a hose.

hosiery *noun* (in shops) socks and stockings.

hospice (*say* **hos**-puhs) *noun* **1** a nursing home for people who are very ill or dying. **2** a lodging house for travellers, especially one kept by a religious institution.

hospitable *adjective* welcoming; liking to give hospitality. **hospitably** *adverb*

hospital *noun* a place providing medical and surgical treatment for people who are ill or injured. [from Latin *hospitium* = hospitality]

hospitality *noun* welcoming people and giving them food and entertainment.

host[1] *noun* **1** a person who has guests and looks after them. **2** the presenter of a television or radio program. **3** an animal or plant on or in which a parasite lives. **4** a computer that stores a website or other data that can be accessed over the Internet. [same origin as *hospital*]

host[2] *noun* a large number of people or things. [same origin as *hostile*]

host[3] *noun* the bread consecrated at Holy Communion. [from Latin *hostia* = sacrifice]

hostage *noun* a person who is held prisoner until the holder gets what they want.

hostel *noun* a lodging house for travellers, students, or other groups.

hostess *noun* **1** a woman who has guests and looks after them. **2** (*informal*) (also **air hostess**) a female steward on an aircraft; a flight attendant.

hostile *adjective* **1** of an enemy. **2** unfriendly, *a hostile glance.* **hostility** *noun* [from Latin *hostis* = an enemy]

hot[1] *adjective* (**hotter**, **hottest**) **1** having great heat or a high temperature. **2** giving a burning sensation when tasted. **3** enthusiastic; excitable, *a hot temper.* **4** (of news) fresh. **5** (*informal*) (of music, an idea, etc.) great; fantastic. **6** (*informal*) (of a person) good-looking; sexy. **hotly** *adverb*, **hotness** *noun*
in hot water (*informal*) in trouble or disgrace.

hot[2] *verb* (**hotted**, **hotting**) **hot up** (*informal*) make or become hot or hotter or more exciting.

hot air *noun* (*informal*) empty or boastful talk.

hot cross bun *noun* a fresh spicy bun marked with a cross, to be eaten on Good Friday.

hot dog *noun* a frankfurt in a soft bread roll.

hotel *noun* **1** a building where people pay to have meals and stay for the night. **2** (*Australian*) a pub.

hotfoot *adverb* in eager haste.

hothead *noun* an impetuous person. **hotheaded** *adjective*

hothouse *noun* a heated greenhouse.

hot key *noun* (in computing) a key or combination of keys providing quick access to a function within a program.

hot link *noun* (in computing) a connection between documents or applications that enables material from one source to be incorporated into another.

hotplate *noun* a heated surface for cooking food or keeping it hot.

hotpot *noun* a stew.

hotspot *noun* **1** a small area with a relatively high temperature in comparison to its surroundings. **2** a place of significant activity, danger, or violence. **3** an area on a computer screen that can be clicked to activate a function. **4** a public place where a wireless signal is made available so that the Internet can be accessed.

houmous alternative spelling of **hummus**.

hound[1] *noun* a dog used in hunting or racing.

hound[2] *verb* chase; harass.

hour *noun* **1** one twenty-fourth part of a day and night; sixty minutes. **2** a time, *Why are you up at this hour?*

hourglass *noun* a glass container with a very narrow part in the middle through which sand runs from the top half to the bottom half, taking one hour.

hourly *adverb & adjective* every hour.

house[1] (*say* hows) *noun* **1** a building made for people to live in. **2** a building or establishment for a special purpose, *the opera house.* **3** a building for a government assembly; the assembly itself, *the House of Representatives.* **4** each of the divisions of a school for games and competitions. **5** a family or dynasty, *the royal house of Tudor.*

house[2] (*say* howz) *verb* (**housed**, **housing**) provide accommodation or room for someone or something.

houseboat *noun* a boat for living in.

household *noun* all the people who live together in the same house.

householder *noun* a person who owns or rents a house.

housekeeper *noun* a person employed to look after a household.

housekeeping *noun* **1** looking after a household. **2** (*informal*) the money for a household's food and other necessities.

House of Representatives *noun* the lower house of the federal parliament of Australia.

house-proud *adjective* very careful to keep a house clean and tidy.

house-trained *adjective* (of an animal) trained to be clean in the house.

house-warming *noun* a party to celebrate moving into a new home.

housewife *noun* (*plural* **housewives**) a woman who does the housekeeping for her family.

housework *noun* the cleaning and cooking done in housekeeping.

housing *noun* **1** accommodation; houses. **2** a stiff cover or guard for a piece of machinery.

housing estate *noun* a set of houses planned and built together in one area.

hove *past tense & past participle* of **heave** (when used of ships).

hovel *noun* a small shabby house.

hover *verb* **1** stay in one place in the air. **2** wait about near someone or something; linger.

hovercraft *noun* (*plural* **hovercraft**) a vehicle that travels just above the surface of land or water, supported by a strong current of air sent downwards from its engines.

how *adverb* **1** in what way; by what means, *How did you do it?* **2** to what extent or amount, *How high can you jump?* **3** in what condition, *How are you?*
how about would you like, *How about a game of football?*
how do you do? a formal greeting.

however *adverb* **1** used to introduce a statement that contrasts with or seems to contradict something that has been said previously, *People tend to put on weight in middle age. However, gaining weight is not inevitable.* **2** in whatever way; regardless of how, *However you look at it, you can't criticise that.* **3** to whatever extent, *She was hesitant to take the risk, however small.*

Usage When *ever* is used for emphasis after *how*, it should be written as a separate word. Thus it is correct to write '*how ever did you manage?*' rather than '*however did you manage?*'.

howl[1] *noun* a long loud sad-sounding cry or sound, such as that made by a dog or wolf.

howl[2] *verb* **1** make a howl. **2** weep loudly.

howler *noun* (*informal*) a foolish mistake.

HQ *abbreviation* headquarters.

HTML *noun* a computer programming language used for World Wide Web applications, involving the linking of text, images, and video clips, and cross-referencing between pages of a website. [from the initials of 'hypertext markup language']

http *noun* a set of instructions made by a computer program that enables a computer to connect to a website. [from the initials of 'hypertext transfer (or transport) protocol']

hub *noun* **1** the central part of a wheel. **2** the effective centre of an activity, region, or network.

hubbub *noun* a loud confused noise of voices.

huddle *verb* (**huddled, huddling**) **1** crowd together into a small space. **2** curl your body closely. **huddle** *noun*

hue[1] *noun* a colour or tint.

hue[2] *noun* **hue and cry** a general outcry of demand, alarm, or protest.

huff[1] *noun* an annoyed or offended mood, *She went away in a huff.* **huffy** *adjective*

huff[2] *verb* blow, *huffing and puffing.*

hug[1] *verb* (**hugged, hugging**) **1** clasp tightly in your arms; embrace. **2** keep close to, *The ship hugged the shore.*

hug[2] *noun* hugging; an embrace.

huge *adjective* extremely large; enormous.
hugely *adverb*, **hugeness** *noun*

hulk *noun* **1** the body or wreck of an old ship. **2** a large clumsy person or thing.
hulking *adjective*

hull *noun* **1** the framework of a ship. **2** the cluster of leaves on a strawberry.

hullabaloo *noun* an uproar.

hullo *interjection* hello.

hum[1] *verb* (**hummed, humming**) **1** sing a tune with your lips closed. **2** make a low continuous sound as some flying insects do.

hum[2] *noun* a humming sound.

hum[3] *verb* (*Australian informal*) cadge. [from *humbug*]

human[1] *adjective* of human beings.

human[2] *noun* a human being.

human being *noun* a man, woman, or child.

humane (*say* hyoo-**mayn**) *adjective* kind-hearted; merciful. **humanely** *adverb*

humanise *verb* (**humanised, humanising**) make human or humane. **humanisation** *noun*

humanist *noun* a humanitarian person.

humanitarian *adjective* concerned with people's welfare and the reduction of suffering. **humanitarian** *noun*

humanities *plural noun* arts subjects such as languages, literature, and history, as opposed to the sciences.

humanity *noun* **1** human beings; people. **2** being human. **3** being humane.

humankind *noun* human beings considered collectively, *This is a discovery for the good of all humankind.*

human right *noun* (usually **human rights**) a right that is believed to belong to every person irrespective of gender, race, status, etc.

humble[1] *adjective* **1** modest; not proud or showy. **2** of low rank or importance.
humbleness *noun*, **humbly** *adverb*

humble[2] *verb* (**humbled, humbling**) make humble. [from Latin *humilis* = lowly]

humbug *noun* **1** deceitful talk or behaviour. **2** a person who tries to win sympathy by deceit. **3** a hard peppermint sweet.

humdrum *adjective* dull and not exciting; commonplace; without variety.

humerus *noun* (*plural* **humeri**) the bone in the upper arm, from shoulder to elbow.
humeral *adjective* [Latin, = shoulder]

humid (*say* **hyoo**-muhd) *adjective* (of air) moist. **humidity** *noun*

humiliate *verb* (**humiliated, humiliating**) make a person feel disgraced. **humiliation** *noun*

humility *noun* being humble.

hummingbird *noun* a small tropical bird that makes a humming sound by moving its wings rapidly.

hummock *noun* a hump in the ground.

hummus (*say* **huum**-uhs) *noun* (also **houmous**) a dip or appetiser made from ground chickpeas, sesame seeds, lemon, and garlic. [Turkish]

humorist *noun* a humorous person.

humorous *adjective* full of humour.

humour[1] *noun* **1** being amusing; what makes people laugh. **2** the ability to enjoy comical things, *a sense of humour.* **3** a mood, *in a good humour.*

humour[2] *verb* keep a person contented by doing what they want.

hump[1] *noun* **1** a rounded projecting part. **2** an abnormal outward curve at the top of a person's back.

hump[2] *verb* **1** form a hump. **2** carry something on your back.

humpback *noun* **1** a hunchback. **2** a whale with a hump on its back. **humpbacked** *adjective*

humpy *noun* (*plural* **humpies**) (*Australian*) (in traditional Aboriginal use) a temporary bush shelter. [from Yagara and neighbouring languages *ngumbi*]

humus (*say* **hyoo**-muhs) *noun* rich earth made by decayed plants.

hunch[1] *noun* (*plural* **hunches**) **1** a hump. **2** a feeling that you can guess what will happen.

hunch[2] *verb* bend into a hump, *He hunched his shoulders.*

hunchback *noun* **1** a back deformed by a sharp forward angle, forming a hump. **2** (*offensive*) a person with a hunchback. **hunchbacked** *adjective*

hundred *noun & adjective* the number 100; ten times ten. **hundredth** *adjective & noun*

hundredfold *adjective & adverb* one hundred times as much or as many.

hundredweight *noun* (*plural* **hundredweight**) a unit of weight equal to 112 pounds (about 50.8 kilograms).

hung *past tense & past participle* of **hang**[1].

hunger *noun* the feeling that you have when you have not eaten for some time; need for food.

hunger strike *noun* refusing to eat, as a way of making a protest.

hungry *adjective* (**hungrier**, **hungriest**) feeling hunger. **hungrily** *adverb*

hunk *noun* **1** a large or roughly cut piece. **2** (*informal*) a muscular good-looking man.

hunt *verb* **1** chase and kill animals for food or as a sport. **2** search for something. **hunt** *noun*, **hunter** *noun*

huntsman *noun* **1** a hunter. **2** a large hairy Australian spider that stalks its prey.

Huon pine *noun* a Tasmanian conifer.

hurdle *noun* **1** an upright frame to be jumped over in hurdling. **2** an obstacle.

hurdling *noun* racing in which the runners jump over hurdles. **hurdler** *noun*

hurdy-gurdy *noun* **1** a musical instrument with a droning sound, played by turning a handle. **2** (*informal*) a barrel organ.

hurl *verb* throw something violently.

hurly-burly *noun* a rough bustle of activity.

hurrah *interjection* (also **hooray** or **hurray**) a shout of joy or approval; a cheer.

hurricane *noun* a storm with violent wind.

hurry[1] *verb* (**hurried**, **hurrying**) **1** move quickly; do something quickly. **2** try to make somebody or something be quick. **hurried** *adjective*, **hurriedly** *adverb*

hurry[2] *noun* hurrying; a need to hurry.

hurt[1] *verb* (**hurt**, **hurting**) **1** cause pain or damage or injury. **2** suffer pain.

hurt[2] *noun* an injury; harm. **hurtful** *adjective*

hurtle *verb* (**hurtled**, **hurtling**) move rapidly, *The train hurtled along.*

husband[1] *noun* a married man considered in relation to his spouse.

husband[2] *verb* manage economically and try to save, *husband your strength.* [from Old English *husbonda* = master of a house (*hus*)]

husbandry *noun* **1** farming. **2** management of resources. [from an old use of *husband* = person who manages things]

hush[1] *verb* make or become silent or quiet.

hush[2] *noun* silence.

husk *noun* the dry outer covering of some seeds and fruits.

husky[1] *adjective* (**huskier**, **huskiest**) **1** hoarse. **2** big and strong; burly. **huskily** *adverb*, **huskiness** *noun*

husky[2] *noun* (*plural* **huskies**) a large dog used in the Arctic and (formerly) in the Antarctic for pulling sledges.

hustle *verb* (**hustled**, **hustling**) hurry; bustle. **hustle** *noun*, **hustler** *noun*

hut *noun* a small roughly made house or shelter.

hutch *noun* (*plural* **hutches**) a box-like cage for rabbits or other small animals.

hyacinth *noun* a fragrant flower that grows from a bulb.

hybrid[1] *noun* **1** a plant or animal produced by combining two different species or varieties. **2** something that combines parts or characteristics of two different things. **hybridisation** *noun*, **hybridise** *verb*, **hybridism** *noun*

hybrid² *adjective* of mixed character; composed of different elements.

hydra *noun* a microscopic freshwater animal with a tubular body.

hydrangea (*say* huy-**drayn**-juh) *noun* a shrub with pink, blue, or white flowers growing in large clusters.

hydrant *noun* a special water-tap in the street to which a hose can be attached for firefighting.

hydraulic *adjective* worked by the force of water or other fluid, *hydraulic brakes.* [from *hydro-*, + *aulos* = pipe]

hydraulic fracturing *noun* the forcing open of fissures in subterranean rocks by introducing liquid at high pressure, especially to extract oil or gas.

hydro- *prefix* **1** water (as in *hydroelectric*). **2** (in chemical names) containing hydrogen (as in *hydrochloric*). [from Greek *hydor* = water]

hydrochloric acid *noun* a colourless acid containing hydrogen and chlorine.

hydroelectric *adjective* using water power to produce electricity. **hydroelectricity** *noun*

hydrofoil *noun* a boat designed to skim over the surface of water.

hydrogen *noun* a lightweight gas that combines with oxygen to form water. [from *hydro-*, + *gen* = producing]

hydrogen bomb *noun* a very powerful bomb using energy created by the fusion of hydrogen nuclei.

hydrophobia *noun* abnormal fear of water, as in someone suffering from rabies. [from *hydro-* + *phobia*]

hyena *noun* a wild animal that looks like a wolf and makes a shrieking howl.

hygiene (*say* **huy**-jeen) *noun* keeping things clean in order to remain healthy and prevent disease. **hygienic** *adjective*, **hygienically** *adverb* [from Greek *hygieine* = of health]

hymn *noun* a religious song, usually of praise to God.

hymnal *noun* a book of hymns.

hype *noun* (*informal*) intensive or extravagant promotion or publicity.

hyper- *prefix* over or above; excessive. [from Greek *hyper* = over]

hyperactive *adjective* (of a person) abnormally active. **hyperactivity** *noun*

hyperbola (*say* huy-**per**-buh-luh) *noun* a kind of curve. [same origin as *hyperbole*]

hyperbole (*say* huy-**per**-buh-lee) *noun* a dramatic exaggeration that is not meant to be taken literally, e.g. '*I've got a stack of work a mile high*'. [from *hyper-*, + Greek *bole* = a throw]

hyperlink *noun* a link from a hypertext document to another location, activated by clicking on a highlighted word or image.

hypertext *noun* a way of joining an image or word to another page of the Internet so that you can move from one to another easily.

hyphen *noun* a short dash used to join words or parts of words together (e.g. in *red-handed*). [from Greek, = together]

hyphenate *verb* (**hyphenated**, **hyphenating**) join with a hyphen. **hyphenation** *noun*

hypnosis (*say* hip-**noh**-suhs) *noun* a condition like a deep sleep in which a person's actions may be controlled by someone else. [from Greek *hypnos* = sleep]

hypnotise *verb* (**hypnotised**, **hypnotising**) produce hypnosis in somebody. **hypnotic** *adjective*, **hypnotism** *noun*, **hypnotist** *noun*

hypo- *prefix* below; under. [from Greek *hypo* = under]

hypochondriac (*say* huy-puh-**kon**-dree-ak) *noun* a person who is abnormally anxious about their health. **hypochondria** *noun*

hypocrite (*say* **hip**-uh-krit) *noun* someone who pretends to be a better person than they really are. **hypocrisy** *noun*, **hypocritical** *adjective* [from Greek, = acting a part]

hypodermic *adjective* injecting something under the skin, *a hypodermic syringe.* [from *hypo-*, + Greek *derma* = skin]

hypotenuse (*say* huy-**pot**-uh-nyooz) *noun* the side opposite the right angle in a right-angled triangle.

hypothermia *noun* being too cold; the condition in which someone's temperature is below normal. [from *hypo-* + Greek *therme* = heat]

hypothesis (*say* huy-**poth**-uh-suhs) *noun* (*plural* **hypotheses**) a supposition or guess put forward to account for certain facts and used as a basis for further investigation by which it may be proved or disproved.

hypothetical (*say* huy-puh-**thet**-i-kuhl) *adjective* **1** of or based on or serving as a hypothesis. **2** supposed but not necessarily real or true.

hysterectomy (*say* his-tuh-**rek**-tuh-mee) *noun* surgical removal of the womb. [from Greek *hystera* = womb, + *-ectomy* = cutting out]

hysteria *noun* wild uncontrollable excitement or emotion. **hysterical** *adjective*, **hysterically** *adverb*, **hysterics** *noun* [from Greek *hystera* = womb (once thought to be the cause of hysterics)]

Ii

I *pronoun* a word used by a person to refer to himself or herself, *I like to go swimming at the beach in summer.*

ibis *noun* (*plural* **ibises**) a wading bird with a long curved bill and long legs.

ice[1] *noun* **1** frozen water; a brittle transparent solid substance. **2** (*informal*) a form of methamphetamine.

ice[2] *verb* (**iced**, **icing**) **1** make or become covered with ice. **2** make very cold. **3** put icing on a cake.

Ice Age *noun* a period when ice covered large areas of the earth.

iceberg *noun* **1** a large mass of ice floating in the sea with most of it under water. **2** (*Australian*) a regular winter swimmer.

iceblock *noun* (*Australian*) a piece of frozen flavoured water usually served on a stick.

ice cream *noun* a sweet creamy frozen food.

icicle *noun* a pointed hanging piece of ice formed when dripping water freezes.

icing *noun* a sugary substance for decorating cakes.

icon (*say* **uy**-kon) *noun* **1** an image or statue, especially a sacred one. **2** a symbol or graphic representation on a screen of a program, option, or window. **3** a famous person or thing that is regarded as a symbol of something or as worthy of veneration, *The Sydney Harbour Bridge is an Australian icon.* **iconic** *adjective* [from Greek *eikon* = image]

ICT *abbreviation* information and communications technology.

ICU *abbreviation* intensive-care unit.

icy *adjective* (**icier**, **iciest**) like ice; very cold. **icily** *adverb*, **iciness** *noun*

ID *abbreviation* identification; identity.

Id alternative spelling of **Eid**.

I'd **1** I had, *I'd decided to go to the movies.* **2** I should, *I thought I'd call and let you know where I am.* **3** I would, *I'd like to go for a swim.*

idea *noun* **1** a plan formed in the mind. **2** an opinion or belief.

ideal[1] *adjective* perfect; completely suitable. **ideally** *adverb*

ideal[2] *noun* a person or thing regarded as perfect or worth trying to achieve.

idealise *verb* (**idealised**, **idealising**) regard or represent a person or thing as perfect. **idealisation** *noun*

idealist *noun* a person who has high ideals and wishes to achieve them. **idealism** *noun*, **idealistic** *adjective*

identical *adjective* exactly the same. **identically** *adverb* [same origin as *identity*]

identify *verb* (**identified**, **identifying**) **1** recognise as being a certain person or thing. **2** treat as being identical, *Don't identify wealth with happiness.* **3** think of yourself as sharing someone's feelings or characteristics, *We can identify with the hero of this play.* **identification** *noun* [from Latin *idem* = same]

identity *noun* (*plural* **identities**) **1** who someone is or who someone thinks they are; the qualities of a person that make them different from others. **2** the typical features of a place that make it different from other places. **3** (*Australian informal*) a well-known person. **4** (in algebra) the equality of two expressions for all values of the quantities expressed by letters; an equation expressing this.

identity theft *noun* the fraudulent practice of using another person's name and personal information in order to obtain credit, loans, etc.

ideology (*say* uy-dee-**ol**-uh-jee) *noun* (*plural* **ideologies**) a set of beliefs and aims, especially in politics, *a socialist ideology.* **ideological** *adjective* [from *idea* + *-logy*]

ides (*say* uydz) *plural noun* the ancient Roman name for the 15th day of March, May, July, and October, and the 13th day of other months.

idiocy *noun* **1** being an idiot. **2** stupid behaviour.

idiom *noun* **1** a phrase that means something different from the meanings of the words in it, e.g. *in hot water* (= in disgrace), *hell for leather* (= at high speed). **2** a special way of using words, e.g. *wash up the dishes* but not e.g. *wash up the baby.* [from Greek *idios* = your own]

idiomatic *adjective* **1** relating to or conforming to idiom. **2** characteristic of a particular language. **idiomatically** *adverb*

idiosyncrasy (*say* id-ee-oh-**sing**-kruh-see) *noun* (*plural* **idiosyncrasies**) one person's own way of behaving or doing something. **idiosyncratic** *adjective* [from Greek *idios* = your own, + *syn* = with, + *krasis* = mixture]

idiot *noun* **1** a person who is mentally deficient. **2** (*informal*) a very stupid person. **idiocy** *noun*, **idiotic** *adjective*, **idiotically** *adverb* [from Greek *idiotes* = private citizen, uneducated person]

idle[1] *adjective* **1** doing no work; lazy. **2** not in use, *The machines were idle.* **3** useless; with no special purpose, *idle gossip.* **idleness** *noun*, **idly** *adverb*

idle[2] *verb* (**idled**, **idling**) **1** be idle. **2** (of an engine) work slowly. **idler** *noun*

idol *noun* **1** a statue or image that is worshipped as a god. **2** a person who is admired intensely. [from Greek *eidolon* = image]

idolatry *noun* worship of idols. **idolatrous** *adjective* [from *idol*, + Greek *latreia* = worship]

idolise *verb* (**idolised**, **idolising**) admire someone intensely. **idolisation** *noun*

idyll (*say* **id**-uhl) *noun* a poem describing a peaceful or romantic scene. **idyllic** (*say* id-**il**-ik) *adjective*

i.e. *abbreviation* that is, *The world's highest mountain (i.e. Mount Everest) is in the Himalayas.* [short for Latin *id est*]

IED *abbreviation* improvised explosive device.

if *conjunction* **1** on condition that; supposing that, *He will do it if you pay him.* **2** even though, *I'll finish this job if it kills me.* **3** whether, *Do you know if dinner is ready?* **if only** I wish, *If only I were rich!*

iffy *adjective* uncertain; doubtful.

igloo *noun* a dome-shaped house built of blocks of hard snow. [from Inuit, = house]

igneous *adjective* formed by the action of a volcano, *igneous rocks.* [from Latin *igneus* = fiery]

ignite *verb* (**ignited**, **igniting**) **1** set fire to something. **2** catch fire. [from Latin *ignis* = fire]

ignition *noun* **1** igniting. **2** the mechanism that starts the fuel burning in an engine.

ignoble *adjective* not noble; shameful.

ignominious *adjective* humiliating; with disgrace. **ignominy** *noun*

ignoramus *noun* (*plural* **ignoramuses**) an ignorant person. [Latin, = we do not know]

ignorant *adjective* **1** not knowing about something or about many things. **2** uneducated. **ignorance** *noun*, **ignorantly** *adverb*

ignore *verb* (**ignored**, **ignoring**) take no notice of a person or thing. [from Latin *ignorare* = not know]

iguana (*say* ig-**wah**-nuh) *noun* a large tree-climbing tropical lizard.

il- *prefix* see **in-**.

ilk *noun* **of that ilk** (*informal*) of that kind.

I'll I shall; I will, *I'll see you tomorrow.*

ill[1] *adjective* **1** unwell; in bad health. **2** bad; harmful, *There were no ill effects.* **ill will** unkind feeling.

ill[2] *adverb* badly, *She was ill-treated.* **ill at ease** uncomfortable; embarrassed.

illegal *adjective* not legal; against the law. **illegality** *noun*, **illegally** *adverb*

illegible *adjective* impossible to read. **illegibility** *noun*, **illegibly** *adverb*

illegitimate *adjective* **1** born of parents not married to each other. **2** contrary to a law or rule. **illegitimacy** *noun*, **illegitimately** *adverb*

illicit *adjective* unlawful; not allowed. **illicitly** *adverb* [from *il-* = not, + Latin *licitus* = allowed]

illiterate *adjective* unable to read or write; uneducated. **illiteracy** *noun*, **illiterately** *adverb*

illness *noun* (*plural* **illnesses**) **1** being ill. **2** a particular form of bad health; a disease.

illogical *adjective* not logical; not reasoning correctly. **illogicality** *noun*, **illogically** *adverb*

illuminate *verb* (**illuminated**, **illuminating**) **1** light something up. **2** decorate streets or buildings with lights. **3** decorate a manuscript with coloured designs. **4** clarify or help to explain something. **illumination** *noun* [from *il-* = in, + Latin *lumen* = light]

illusion *noun* something unreal or imaginary; a false impression, *The train went so fast that we had the illusion that it was flying.* (Compare **delusion.**) **illusive** *adjective*, **illusory** *adjective* [from Latin *illudere* = mock]

illustrate *verb* (**illustrated**, **illustrating**) **1** make clear or explain by examples or pictures. **2** put illustrations in a book or newspaper. **illustrator** *noun*

illustration *noun* **1** a picture in a book or newspaper. **2** illustrating something. **3** an example that helps to explain something.

illustrious *adjective* famous; distinguished.

I'm I am, *I'm going to my cousin's house for the weekend.*

im- *prefix* see **in-**.

image *noun* **1** a picture or statue of a person or thing. **2** the appearance of something as seen in a mirror or through a lens. **3** a person or thing that is very much like another, *He is the image of his father.* **4** reputation.

imagery *noun* **1** a writer's or speaker's use of words to produce effects. **2** images; statues.

imaginable *adjective* able to be imagined.

imaginary *adjective* existing only in the imagination; not real.

imagination *noun* the ability to imagine things, especially in a creative or inventive way. **imaginative** *adjective*

imagine *verb* (**imagined**, **imagining**) form pictures or ideas in your mind.

imam *noun* a Muslim religious leader. [Arabic, = leader]

IMAP *abbreviation* Internet Mail Access Protocol.

imbalance *noun* lack of balance; disproportion.

imbecile (*say* **im**-buh-seel) *noun* (*derogatory*) an idiot. **imbecile** *adjective*, **imbecility** *noun*

imbibe *verb* (**imbibed**, **imbibing**) **1** drink. **2** take ideas into the mind.

imbue *verb* (**imbued**, **imbuing**) **1** fill with feelings, qualities, or opinions. **2** fill with a colour; saturate.

IMF *abbreviation* International Monetary Fund.

imitate *verb* (**imitated**, **imitating**) copy; mimic. **imitative** *adjective*, **imitator** *noun*

imitation *noun* **1** imitating. **2** a copy. **imitation** *adjective*

immaculate *adjective* **1** perfectly clean; spotless. **2** without any fault or blemish. **immaculacy** *noun*, **immaculately** *adverb*

immaterial *adjective* **1** having no physical substance, *as immaterial as a ghost.* **2** unimportant; not mattering, *It is immaterial whether he goes or stays.*

immature *adjective* not mature. **immaturity** *noun*

immediate *adjective* **1** happening or done without any delay. **2** nearest; with nothing or no one between, *our immediate neighbours.* **immediacy** *noun*, **immediately** *adverb*

immemorial *adjective* existing from before what can be remembered or found in histories, *from time immemorial.*

immense *adjective* exceedingly great; huge. **immensely** *adverb*, **immensity** *noun* [from *im-* = not, + Latin *mensum* = measured]

immerse *verb* (**immersed**, **immersing**) **1** put something completely into a liquid. **2** absorb or involve deeply, *She was immersed in her work.* **immersion** *noun* [from *im-* = in, + Latin *mersum* = dipped]

immigrate *verb* (**immigrated**, **immigrating**) come into another country to live there. **immigrant** *noun*, **immigration** *noun* [from *im-* = in, + *migrate*]

> **Usage** See the note at *emigrate.*

imminent *adjective* likely to happen at any moment, *an imminent storm.* **imminence** *noun*

immobile *adjective* not moving; immovable. **immobility** *noun*

immobilise *verb* (**immobilised**, **immobilising**) stop a thing from moving or working. **immobilisation** *noun*

immodest *adjective* **1** without modesty; not decent. **2** conceited.

immoral *adjective* morally wrong; wicked. **immorality** *noun*, **immorally** *adverb*

immortal *adjective* **1** living for ever; not mortal. **2** famous for all time. **immortal** *noun*, **immortalise** *verb*, **immortality** *noun*

immovable *adjective* unable to be moved. **immovably** *adverb*

immune *adjective* safe from or protected against something, *immune from* (or *against* or *to*) *infection.* **immunity** *noun* [from Latin *immunis* = exempt]

immunise *verb* (**immunised**, **immunising**) make a person immune from a disease, e.g. by vaccination. **immunisation** *noun*

immutable (*say* i-**myoo**-tuh-buhl) *adjective* unchangeable. **immutably** *adverb*

imp *noun* **1** a small devil. **2** a mischievous child. **impish** *adjective*

impact *noun* **1** a collision; the force of a collision. **2** an influence or effect, *the impact of mobile phones on our lives.* [from *im-* = in, + Latin *pactum* = driven]

impair *verb* damage; weaken, *Smoking impairs health.* **impairment** *noun* [from *im-* = in, + Latin *pejor* = worse]

impaired *adjective* **1** weakened or damaged. **2** having a disability of a specified kind, *hearing-impaired children.*

impala (*say* im-**pah**-luh) *noun* (*plural* **impala**) a small African antelope. [Zulu]

impale *verb* (**impaled**, **impaling**) pierce or fix something on a sharp pointed object. **impalement** *noun* [from *im-* = in, + Latin *palus* = a stake]

impart *verb* **1** tell, *She imparted the news to her brother.* **2** give, *Lemon imparts a sharp flavour to drinks.*

impartial *adjective* not favouring one side more than the other; not biased; fair. **impartiality** *noun*, **impartially** *adverb*

impassable *adjective* not able to be travelled along or over, *The roads are impassable because of floods.*

impasse (*say* **im**-pahs) *noun* a deadlock. [French, = impassable place]

impassive *adjective* not feeling or not showing emotion. **impassively** *adverb*

impatient *adjective* not patient. **impatience** *noun*, **impatiently** *adverb*

impeach *verb* **1** call into question the integrity or validity of a practice. **2** charge a person with treason or another crime against the state. **3** (*American*) charge the holder of a public office with misconduct. **impeachment** *noun*

impeccable *adjective* faultless. **impeccability** *noun*, **impeccably** *adverb* [from *im-* = not, + Latin *peccare* = to sin]

impede *verb* (**impeded**, **impeding**) hinder. [from Latin *impedire* = to shackle the feet (*im-* = in, + *pedis* = of a foot)]

impediment *noun* **1** a hindrance. **2** a defect, *He has a speech impediment* (= a lisp or stammer). [same origin as *impede*]

impel *verb* (**impelled**, **impelling**) **1** urge or drive someone to do something, *Curiosity impelled her to investigate.* **2** drive forward; propel. [from *im-* = towards, + Latin *pellere* = drive]

impending *adjective* about to happen; imminent. [from *im-* = in, + Latin *pendere* = hang]

impenetrable *adjective* **1** impossible to get through. **2** incomprehensible.

impenitent *adjective* not penitent; not repentant. **impenitence** *noun*

imperative[1] *adjective* **1** expressing a command. **2** essential, *Speed is imperative.*

imperative[2] *noun* a command; the form of a verb used in making commands (e.g. *come* in *Come here!*). [from Latin *imperare* = to command]

imperceptible *adjective* not perceptible; difficult or impossible to see.

imperfect *adjective* not perfect. **imperfection** *noun*, **imperfectly** *adverb*

imperfect tense *noun* a tense of a verb showing an action going on but not completed, e.g. *She was singing.*

imperial *adjective* **1** of an empire or its rulers. **2** (of weights and measures) fixed by British law, *an imperial gallon.* **imperially** *adverb* [from Latin *imperium* = supreme power]

imperialism *noun* the policy of extending a country's empire or its influence; colonialism. **imperialist** *noun*

imperious *adjective* commanding; bossy.

impermanent *adjective* not permanent. **impermanence** *noun*

impersonal *adjective* **1** not affected by personal feelings; showing no emotion. **2** not referring to a particular person. **impersonally** *adverb*

impersonal verb *noun* a verb used only with *it*, e.g. in *It is raining* or *It is hard to find one.*

impersonate *verb* (**impersonated**, **impersonating**) pretend to be another person. **impersonation** *noun*, **impersonator** *noun*

impertinent *adjective* insolent; not showing proper respect. **impertinence** *noun*, **impertinently** *adverb*

imperturbable *adjective* not excitable; calm. **imperturbably** *adverb*

impervious *adjective* **1** not allowing something to pass through, *impervious to water.* **2** not affected or influenced by something, *impervious to criticism.* [from *im-* = not, + Latin *per* = through, *via* = way]

impetuous *adjective* **1** hasty; rash. **2** eager; impulsive.

impetus *noun* force or energy of movement. [Latin, = an attack]

impiety *noun* lack of reverence. **impious** (*say* **im**-pee-uhs) *adjective*

impinge *verb* (**impinged**, **impinging**) **1** make an impact. **2** encroach.

implacable *adjective* not able to be placated; relentless. **implacably** *adverb*

implant *verb* insert; fix something in. **implant** *noun*, **implantation** *noun*

implausible *adjective* not plausible. **implausibility** *noun*, **implausibly** *adverb*

implement[1] *noun* a tool.

implement[2] *verb* put into action, *We shall implement these plans next month.* **implementation** *noun*

implicate *verb* (**implicated**, **implicating**) involve a person in a crime; show that a person is involved, *His evidence implicates his sister.*

implication *noun* **1** implicating. **2** implying; something that is implied.

implicit (*say* im-**plis**-uht) *adjective* **1** implied but not stated openly. (Compare **explicit**.) **2** absolute; unquestioning, *She expects implicit obedience.* **implicitly** *adverb* [from Latin, = folded in]

implore *verb* (**implored**, **imploring**) beg somebody to do something; entreat. [from *im-* = in, + Latin *plorare* = weep]

imply *verb* (**implied**, **implying**) suggest something without actually saying it. **implication** *noun*

> **Usage** See the note at *infer*.

impolite *adjective* not polite.

impolitic *adjective* risky; unwise. **impoliticly** *adverb*

import[1] *verb* bring in from abroad or from an outside source.

import[2] *noun* **1** importing; something imported. **2** meaning; importance, *The message was of great import.* [from *im-* = in, + Latin *portare* = carry]

important *adjective* **1** having or able to have a great effect. **2** having great authority or influence. **importance** *noun*, **importantly** *adverb*

importune *verb* (**importuned, importuning**) bother someone with persistent requests.

impose *verb* (**imposed, imposing**) put; inflict, *It imposes a strain upon us.*
impose on somebody put an unfair burden on them. [from *im-* = on, + Latin *positum* = placed]

imposing *adjective* impressive.

imposition *noun* **1** something imposed; a burden imposed unfairly. **2** imposing something.

impossible *adjective* **1** not possible; unable to be done, exist, or happen. **2** (*informal*) very annoying; unbearable, *He really is impossible!* **impossibility** *noun*, **impossibly** *adverb*

impostor *noun* a person who dishonestly pretends to be someone else.

impotent *adjective* **1** powerless; unable to take action. **2** (of a man) unable to have sexual intercourse. **impotence** *noun*, **impotently** *adverb*

impound *verb* confiscate.

impoverish *verb* **1** make a person poor. **2** make a thing poor in quality, *impoverished soil.* **impoverishment** *noun*

impracticable *adjective* not practicable.

impractical *adjective* not practical; unwise.

imprecise *adjective* not precise.

impregnable *adjective* strong enough to be safe against attack.

impregnate *verb* (**impregnated, impregnating**) **1** fertilise; make pregnant. **2** saturate; fill throughout, *The air was impregnated with the scent.* **impregnation** *noun*

impresario *noun* (*plural* **impresarios**) a person who organises concerts, shows, or other events. [Italian]

impress *verb* **1** affect or influence deeply. **2** cause a person to admire or think something is very good. **3** fix firmly in the mind, *She impressed on them the need for secrecy.* **4** press a mark into something.

impression *noun* **1** an effect produced on the mind. **2** a vague idea. **3** an imitation of a person or a sound. **4** a reprint of a book.

impressionism *noun* a style of painting that gives the general effect of a scene or event but without details. **impressionist** *noun*

impressive *adjective* making a strong impression; seeming very good.

imprint *noun* a mark pressed into or on something. **imprint** *verb*

imprison *verb* put into prison; keep in confinement. **imprisonment** *noun*

improbable *adjective* unlikely. **improbability** *noun*, **improbably** *adverb*

impromptu *adjective & adverb* done without any rehearsal or preparation. [from Latin *in promptu* = in readiness]

improper *adjective* **1** incorrect; wrong. **2** not conforming to accepted standards of behaviour; indecent. **improperly** *adverb*, **impropriety** (*say* im-pruh-**pruy**-uh-tee) *noun*

improper fraction *noun* a fraction that is greater than 1, with the numerator greater than the denominator, e.g. $\frac{5}{4}$.

improve *verb* (**improved, improving**) make or become better. **improvement** *noun*

improvident *adjective* not providing or planning for the future; not thrifty.

improvise *verb* (**improvised, improvising**) **1** compose something impromptu. **2** make something quickly with whatever is available. **improvisation** *noun*

imprudent *adjective* unwise.

impudent *adjective* disrespectful; cheeky. **impudence** *noun*, **impudently** *adverb*

impugn (*say* im-**pyoon**) *verb* call into question, *We do not impugn their motives.*

impulse *noun* **1** a sudden desire to do something. **2** a push; impetus. **3** (in physics) a force acting for a very short time, *electrical impulses.* [same origin as *impel*]

impulsive *adjective* done or doing things on impulse, not after careful thought. **impulsively** *adverb*, **impulsiveness** *noun*

impunity (*say* im-**pyoo**-nuh-tee) *noun* freedom from punishment or injury. [from *im-* = without, + Latin *poena* = penalty]

impure *adjective* not pure. **impurity** *noun*

impute *verb* (**imputed, imputing**) attribute. **imputation** *noun*

in[1] *preposition* This word is used to show position or condition, e.g. **1** at or inside; within the limits of something (*in a box*; *in two hours*), **2** into (*He fell in a puddle*), **3** arranged as; consisting of (*a serial in four parts*), **4** occupied with; a member of (*He is in the army*), **5** by means of (*We paid in cash*).
in all in total number; altogether.

in[2] *adverb* **1** so as to be in something or inside, *Get in.* **2** inwards, *The top caved in.* **3** at home; indoors, *Is anybody in?* **4** in fashion, season, or office. **5** batting, *Which team is in?* **6** having arrived, *The train is in.*
in for likely to get, *You're in for a shock.*
in on (*informal*) aware of or sharing in,

I want to be in on the secret.

in³ *adjective* fashionable.

in- *prefix* (changing to **il-** before *l*, **im-** before *b*, *m*, *p*, **ir-** before *r*) **1** in; into; on; towards (as in *include*, *invade*). **2** not (as in *incorrect*, *indirect*) [Latin].

inability *noun* being unable.

in absentia (*say* in ab-**sen**-tee-ah) *adverb* while not present at the event being referred to, *She graduated in absentia.* [Latin]

inaccessible *adjective* not accessible.

inaccurate *adjective* not accurate.

inactive *adjective* not active. **inaction** *noun*, **inactivity** *noun*

inadequate *adjective* **1** not enough. **2** not capable enough. **inadequacy** *noun*, **inadequately** *adverb*

inadvertent *adjective* unintentional.

inadvisable *adjective* not advisable.

inalienable *adjective* that cannot be taken away, *an inalienable right.*

inane *adjective* silly; without sense. **inanely** *adverb*, **inanity** *noun* [from Latin *inanis* = empty]

inanimate *adjective* **1** not living. **2** not moving.

inappropriate *adjective* not appropriate.

inarticulate *adjective* **1** not able to speak or express yourself clearly, *inarticulate with rage.* **2** not expressed in words, *an inarticulate cry.*

inattentive *adjective* not paying attention. **inattention** *noun*

inaudible *adjective* unable to be heard. **inaudibility** *noun*, **inaudibly** *adverb*

inaugurate *verb* (**inaugurated, inaugurating**) **1** start or introduce something new and important. **2** install a person in office, *inaugurate a new president.* **inaugural** *adjective*, **inauguration** *noun*, **inaugurator** *noun*

inauspicious *adjective* not auspicious.

inborn *adjective* present in a person or animal from birth, *an inborn ability.*

inbox *noun* a folder in which emails received by an individual are held.

inbred *adjective* **1** inborn. **2** produced by inbreeding.

inbreeding *noun* breeding from closely related individuals.

Inc. *abbreviation* Incorporated.

incalculable *adjective* not able to be calculated or predicted.

incandescent *adjective* giving out light when heated; shining. **incandescence** *noun* [from Latin, = becoming white]

incantation *noun* a spoken spell or charm; the chanting of this. [from *in-* = in, + Latin *cantare* = sing]

incapable *adjective* not able to do something, *incapable of working alone.*

incapacitate *verb* (**incapacitated, incapacitating**) make unable to do something; disable.

incapacity *noun* inability; lack of sufficient strength or power.

incarcerate *verb* (**incarcerated, incarcerating**) shut in; imprison. **incarceration** *noun* [from *in-* = in, + Latin *carcer* = prison]

incarnate *adjective* having a body or human form, *a devil incarnate.* **incarnation** *noun* **the Incarnation** the embodiment of God in human form as Jesus Christ. [from *in-* = in, + Latin *carnis* = of flesh]

incautious *adjective* rash.

incendiary *adjective* starting or designed to start a fire, *an incendiary bomb.*

incense¹ (*say* **in**-sens) *noun* a substance producing a spicy smell when burnt.

incense² (*say* in-**sens**) *verb* (**incensed, incensing**) make a person angry.

incentive *noun* something that encourages a person to do something or to work harder.

inception *noun* a beginning.

incessant *adjective* unceasing.

incest *noun* sexual intercourse between close relations. **incestuous** *adjective*

inch *noun* (*plural* **inches**) a measure of length, about 2.5 centimetres.

incidence *noun* the extent or frequency of something, *Study the incidence of the disease.* [from Latin *incidens* = happening]

incident *noun* an event.

incidental *adjective* happening with something else, *incidental expenses.*

incidentally *adverb* by the way.

incinerate *verb* (**incinerated, incinerating**) destroy something by burning. **incineration** *noun* [from *in-* = in, + Latin *cineris* = of ashes]

incinerator *noun* a device in which rubbish is burnt.

incipient (*say* in-**sip**-ee-uhnt) *adjective* just beginning, incipient decay.

incise *verb* (**incised, incising**) cut or engrave something into a surface. [from *in-* = into, + Latin *caesum* = cut]

incision *noun* a cut, especially one made in a surgical operation.

incisive *adjective* clear and sharp, *incisive comments.*

incisor (*say* in-**suy**-zuh) *noun* each of the sharp-edged front teeth in the upper and lower jaws.

incite *verb* (**incited, inciting**) urge a person to do something; stir up, *They incited a riot.* **incitement** *noun* [from *in-* = towards, + Latin *citare* = rouse]

incivility *noun* being uncivil; rudeness.

inclement *adjective* (*formal*) cold, wet, or stormy, *inclement weather.*

inclination *noun* **1** a tendency. **2** a liking or preference. **3** a slope or slant.

incline[1] *verb* (**inclined, inclining**) **1** lean; slope. **2** bend the head or body forward, as in a nod or bow. **3** cause or influence, *Her frank manner inclines me to believe her.*
be inclined have a tendency, *The door is inclined to bang.* [from Latin *inclinare* = to bend]

incline[2] *noun* a slope.

include *verb* (**included, including**) make or consider something as part of a group of things. **inclusion** *noun* [from Latin, = enclose]

inclusive *adjective* including everything.

incognito (*say* in-kog-**nee**-toh) *adjective & adverb* with your name or identity concealed, *The film star was travelling incognito.* [Italian, = unknown]

incoherent *adjective* not speaking or reasoning in an orderly way.

incombustible *adjective* unable to be set on fire.

income *noun* money received regularly for work or through investments.

income tax *noun* tax charged on income.

incoming *adjective* **1** coming in, *the incoming tide.* **2** succeeding another person, *the incoming chairman.*

incomparable *adjective* without an equal; unsurpassed, *incomparable beauty.*

incompatible *adjective* **1** not able to live or exist or be used together. **2** not consistent. **incompatibility** *noun*

incompetent *adjective* not competent.

incomplete *adjective* not complete.

incomprehensible *adjective* not able to be understood. **incomprehension** *noun*

inconceivable *adjective* not able to be imagined; most unlikely.

inconclusive *adjective* not conclusive.

incongruous *adjective* unsuitable; not harmonious; out of place. **incongruity** *noun*, **incongruously** *adverb*

inconsiderable *adjective* of small value.

inconsiderate *adjective* not considerate.

inconsistent *adjective* **1** not consistent; variable. **2** not in keeping. **inconsistency** *noun*, **inconsistently** *adverb*

inconsolable *adjective* not able to be consoled; very sad.

inconspicuous *adjective* not conspicuous. **inconspicuously** *adverb*

incontinent *adjective* not able to control excretion. **incontinence** *noun*

incontrovertible *adjective* unable to be denied.

inconvenient *adjective* causing trouble or difficulty to someone; awkward. **inconvenience** *noun & verb*

incorporate *verb* (**incorporated, incorporating**) include something as a part. **incorporation** *noun*

incorporated *adjective* (of a business firm) formed into a legal corporation.

incorrect *adjective* not correct.

incorrigible *adjective* not able to be reformed, *an incorrigible liar.*

incorruptible *adjective* **1** not liable to decay. **2** not able to be bribed.

increase[1] *verb* (**increased, increasing**) make or become larger or more.

increase[2] *noun* increasing; the amount by which a thing increases. [from *in-* = in, + Latin *crescere* = grow]

incredible *adjective* unbelievable. **incredibility** *noun*, **incredibly** *adverb*

incredulous *adjective* not believing somebody; showing disbelief. **incredulity** *noun*, **incredulously** *adverb*

increment (*say* **in**-kruh-muhnt) *noun* an increase; an added amount. **incremental** *adjective*

incriminate *verb* (**incriminated, incriminating**) show a person to have been involved in a crime. **incrimination** *noun*

incrustation *noun* encrusting; a crust or deposit formed on a surface.

incubate *verb* (**incubated, incubating**) **1** hatch eggs by keeping them warm. **2** cause something to develop, especially in a laboratory. **incubation** *noun*

incubator *noun* **1** a device for incubating something. **2** a device in which a baby born prematurely can be kept warm and supplied with oxygen.

inculcate *verb* implant ideas or habits by persistent urging. **inculcation** *noun*

incumbent[1] *adjective* forming an obligation, *It is incumbent on you to report the matter.*

incumbent[2] *noun* a person who holds a particular office or position. [from *in-* = on, + Latin *-cumbens* = lying]

incur *verb* (**incurred**, **incurring**) bring something on yourself, *incur expense.* [from *in-* = on, + Latin *currere* = to run]

incurable *adjective* not able to be cured. **incurably** *adverb*

incurious *adjective* feeling or showing no curiosity about something.

incursion *noun* a raid or brief invasion. [same origin as *incur*]

indebted *adjective* owing money or gratitude to someone.

indecent *adjective* offending against standards of decency; not appropriate. **indecency** *noun*, **indecently** *adverb*

indecision *noun* being unable to make up your mind; hesitation.

indecisive *adjective* not decisive.

indeed *adverb* **1** really; truly, *I am indeed surprised*; (used to strengthen a meaning), *very nice indeed.* **2** admittedly, *It is, indeed, his first attempt.*

indefatigable *adjective* not becoming tired. **indefatigably** *adverb*

indefensible *adjective* unable to be defended; unable to be justified.

indefinable *adjective* unable to be defined or described clearly.

indefinite *adjective* not clearly stated or fixed; vague.

indefinite article *noun* the word 'a' or 'an'.

indefinitely *adverb* for an unlimited time.

indefinite pronoun see **pronoun**.

indelible *adjective* impossible to rub out or remove. **indelibly** *adverb* [from *in-* = not, + Latin *delere* = destroy]

indelicate *adjective* **1** slightly indecent. **2** tactless. **indelicacy** *noun*

indemnity *noun* **1** protection or insurance against damage or loss. **2** compensation for damage or loss.

indent *verb* **1** make notches or recesses in something. **2** start a line of writing or printing further in from the margin than other lines. **indentation** *noun*

indenture *noun* an agreement binding an apprentice to work for a certain employer. **indentured** *adjective*

independent *adjective* **1** not dependent; not controlled by any other person or thing. **2** (of a country) governing itself. **3** (of a school) non-government. **independence** *noun*, **independently** *adverb*

independent variable *noun* (in mathematics) a variable (often denoted by *x*) whose variation does not depend on that of another.

indescribable *adjective* unable to be described. **indescribably** *adverb*

indestructible *adjective* unable to be destroyed. **indestructibility** *noun*

indeterminate *adjective* not fixed or decided exactly; left vague.

index[1] *noun* **1** (*plural* **indexes**) an alphabetical list of things, especially at the end of a book. **2** a number showing how prices or wages have changed from a previous level. **3** (*plural* **indices**) the exponent of a number.

index[2] *verb* **1** record something in an index; provide an index to. **2** adjust wages or other payments according to changes in the cost of living. **indexation** *noun* [Latin, = pointer]

index finger *noun* the finger next to your thumb.

Indian *adjective* **1** of India or its people. **2** of indigenous North American peoples. **Indian** *noun*

indicate *verb* (**indicated**, **indicating**) **1** point out; make known. **2** be a sign of. **indication** *noun* [from *in-* = towards, + Latin *dicatum* = proclaimed]

indicative[1] *adjective* giving an indication.

indicative[2] *noun* the form of a verb used in making a statement (e.g. 'she said' or 'she is coming'), not in a command or question or wish.

indicator *noun* **1** a thing that indicates or points to something. **2** a flashing light used to signal that a motor vehicle is turning.

indict (*say* in-**duyt**) *verb* charge a person with having committed a crime. **indictment** *noun*

indie *adjective* (*informal*) (of a pop group or record label) independent; not belonging to one of the major companies.

indifferent *adjective* **1** not caring about something; not interested. **2** not very good, *an indifferent footballer.* **indifference** *noun*, **indifferently** *adverb*

indigenous (*say* in-**dij**-uh-nuhs) *adjective* **1** growing or originating in a particular country; native, *The koala is indigenous to Australia.* **2** of or relating to the original inhabitants of a place or country. [from Latin *indigena* = born in a country]

indigent (*say* **in**-di-juhnt) *adjective* needy. **indigence** *noun*

indigestible *adjective* difficult or impossible to digest.

indigestion *noun* pain caused by difficulty in digesting food.

indignant *adjective* angry at something that seems unfair or wicked. **indignantly** *adverb*, **indignation** *noun* [from Latin *indignari* = regard as unworthy]

indignity *noun* (*plural* **indignities**) treatment that makes a person feel undignified or humiliated; an insult.

indigo *noun* a deep blue colour.

indirect *adjective* not direct. **indirectly** *adverb*

indiscreet *adjective* **1** not discreet; revealing secrets. **2** incautious; unwise. **indiscreetly** *adverb*, **indiscretion** *noun*

indiscriminate *adjective* showing no discrimination; not making a careful choice. **indiscriminately** *adverb*

indispensable *adjective* not able to be dispensed with; essential. **indispensability** *noun*

indisposed *adjective* **1** slightly unwell. **2** unwilling, *They seem indisposed to help us.* **indisposition** *noun*

indisputable *adjective* not able to be disputed; undeniable.

indistinct *adjective* not distinct. **indistinctly** *adverb*, **indistinctness** *noun*

indistinguishable *adjective* not distinguishable.

individual[1] *adjective* **1** of or for one person. **2** single; separate, *Count each individual word.* **individually** *adverb*

individual[2] *noun* one person, animal, or plant.

individuality *noun* the things that make one person or thing different from another; distinctive identity.

indivisible *adjective* not able to be divided or separated. **indivisibly** *adverb*

indoctrinate *verb* (**indoctrinated**, **indoctrinating**) teach a person or group to accept a set of beliefs uncritically. **indoctrination** *noun* [from *in-* = in, + *doctrine*]

indolent *adjective* lazy. **indolence** *noun*, **indolently** *adverb*

indomitable *adjective* not able to be overcome or conquered. [from *in-* = not, + Latin *domitare* = to tame]

indoor *adjective* used or placed or done inside a building, *indoor games.*

indoors *adverb* inside a building.

indubitable (*say* in-**dyoo**-buh-tuh-buhl) *adjective* not able to be doubted; certain. **indubitably** *adverb* [from *in-* = not, + Latin *dubium* = doubt]

induce *verb* (**induced**, **inducing**) **1** persuade. **2** produce; cause, *Some substances induce sleep.* **induction** *noun* [from *in-* = in, + Latin *ducere* = to lead]

inducement *noun* an incentive.

induct *verb* install a person formally into office. **induction** *noun* [same origin as *induce*]

indulge *verb* (**indulged**, **indulging**) allow a person to have or do what they wish. **indulgence** *noun*, **indulgent** *adjective*

indulge in allow yourself to have or do something that you like.

industrial *adjective* of industry, working or used in industry. **industrially** *adverb*

industrial action *noun* striking or working to rule.

industrialised *adjective* (of a country or district) having many industries. **industrialisation** *noun*

industrialism *noun* a social or economic system in which manufacturing industries are prevalent.

industrialist *noun* a person who owns or manages an industrial business.

industrious *adjective* hard-working. **industriously** *adverb*

industry *noun* (*plural* **industries**) **1** making or producing goods, especially in factories. **2** a particular branch of this, *the automotive industry.* **3** being industrious. [from Latin *industria* = hard work]

inebriated *adjective* drunk; drunken.

inedible *adjective* not edible.

ineffective *adjective* **1** not producing the desired effect. **2** (of a person) inefficient. **ineffectively** *adverb*

ineffectual *adjective* ineffective; feeble.

inefficient *adjective* **inefficiency** *noun*, **inefficiently** *adverb*

ineligible *adjective* not eligible.

inept *adjective* **1** bungling; unskilful. **2** unsuitable. **ineptitude** *noun*, **ineptly** *adverb* [from *in-* = not, + Latin aptus = *suitable*]

inequality *noun* (*plural* **inequalities**) **1** a lack of equality in any respect. **2** the state of being variable. **3** (in mathematics) a formula affirming that two expressions are not equal.

inequity *noun* (*plural* **inequities**) unfairness. **inequitable** *adjective*

inert *adjective* not moving; not reacting. **inertly** *adverb* [from Latin *iners* = idle]

inertia (*say* in-**er**-shuh) *noun* **1** inactivity; being inert or slow to take action. **2** the tendency for a moving thing to keep moving in a straight line.

inessential *adjective* not essential.

inestimable *adjective* too great or precious to be able to be estimated.

inevitable *adjective* unavoidable; sure to happen. **inevitability** *noun*, **inevitably** *adverb* [from *in-* = not, + Latin *evitare* = avoid]

inexact *adjective* not exact.

inexhaustible *adjective* so great that it cannot be used up completely.

inexorable (*say* in-**ek**-suh-ruh-buhl) *adjective* **1** relentless. **2** not yielding to requests or entreaties. **inexorably** *adverb*

inexpensive *adjective* not expensive; cheap. **inexpensively** *adverb*

inexperience *noun* lack of experience. **inexperienced** *adjective*

inexpert *adjective* unskilful.

inexplicable *adjective* impossible to explain. **inexplicably** *adverb*

in extremis (*say* in ek-**stree**-mis) *adjective* at the point of death; in very great difficulties. [Latin, = in the greatest danger]

infallible *adjective* **1** never wrong. **2** never failing, *an infallible remedy.* **infallibility** *noun*, **infallibly** *adverb*

infamous (*say* **in**-fuh-muhs) *adjective* having a bad reputation; wicked. **infamously** *adverb*, **infamy** *noun*

infancy *noun* **1** early childhood; babyhood. **2** an early stage of development.

infant *noun* a baby or young child. [from Latin, = person unable to speak]

infantile *adjective* **1** of an infant. **2** very childish.

infantry *noun* soldiers who fight on foot. (Compare **cavalry**.) [from Italian *infante* = a youth]

infatuated *adjective* filled with foolish or unreasoning love. **infatuation** *noun* [from *in-* = in, + Latin *fatuus* = foolish]

infect *verb* pass on a disease, bacteria, or virus to a person, animal, or plant. [from Latin *infectum* = tainted]

infection *noun* **1** infecting. **2** an infectious disease or condition.

infectious *adjective* **1** (of a disease or disease-causing organism) able to be spread by air or water etc. **2** quickly spreading to others, *His fear was infectious.*

> **Usage** See the note at *contagious*.

infer *verb* (**inferred, inferring**) form an opinion by reasoning; conclude, *I infer from your look that you disapprove.* **inference** *noun.* [from *in-*, + Latin *ferre* = bring]

> **Usage** There is a distinction in meaning between *infer* and *imply*. In the sentence '*the speaker implied that the general had been a traitor*', *implied* means that the speaker subtly suggested that the general was a traitor (though nothing explicit was actually stated). However, in '*we inferred from his words that the general had been a traitor*', *inferred* means that something in the speaker's words enabled the listeners to deduce that the general was a traitor.

inferior *adjective* less good or less important; low or lower in position, quality, or status. **inferiority** *noun* [Latin, = lower]

infernal *adjective* **1** of or like hell. **2** (*informal*) detestable; tiresome. **infernally** *adverb*

inferno *noun* (*plural* **infernos**) a terrifying fire.

infertile *adjective* not fertile. **infertility** *noun*

infest *verb* (of pests) be numerous and troublesome in a place. **infestation** *noun* [from Latin, = hostile]

infidel (*say* **in**-fuh-del) *noun* a person who does not believe in a religion. [from *in-* = not, + Latin *fidelis* = faithful]

infidelity *noun* unfaithfulness.

infiltrate *verb* (**infiltrated, infiltrating**) get into a place or organisation gradually and without being noticed. **infiltration** *noun*, **infiltrator** *noun*

infinite *adjective* **1** endless; without a limit. **2** too great to be measured. **infinitely** *adverb*

infinitesimal *adjective* extremely small. **infinitesimally** *adverb*

infinitive *noun* a form of a verb that does not indicate a particular tense or number or person, in English used with or without *to*, e.g. *go* in 'Let him go' or 'Allow him to go'. [from *in-* = not, + Latin *finitivus* = definite]

infinity *noun* an infinite number or distance or time.

infirm *adjective* weak, especially from old age or illness. **infirmity** *noun*

infirmary *noun* (*plural* **infirmaries**) **1** a hospital. **2** a place where sick people are cared for in an institution such as a school or prison.

inflame *verb* (**inflamed, inflaming**) **1** arouse strong feelings or anger in people. **2** cause redness, heat, and swelling in a part of the body. **inflammation** *noun*, **inflammatory** *adjective*

inflammable *adjective* able to be set on fire.

> **Usage** This word means the same as *flammable*; its opposite is *non-inflammable*.

inflatable *adjective* able to be inflated.

inflate *verb* (**inflated, inflating**) **1** fill with air or gas and expand. **2** increase too much; raise prices or wages more than is justifiable. [from *in-* = in, + Latin *flatum* = blown]

inflation *noun* **1** inflating. **2** a general rise in prices and fall in the purchasing power of money. **inflationary** *adjective*

inflect *verb* **1** change the ending or form of a word to show its tense or its grammatical relation to other words, e.g. *sing* changes to *sang* or *sung*, *child* changes to *children*. **2** alter the voice in speaking. [from *in-* = in, + Latin *flectere* = to bend]

inflection *noun* **1** a change in the form of a word (typically the ending) to express a grammatical function or attribute such as tense, mood, person, number, case, and gender. **2** the modulation of intonation or pitch in the voice.

inflexible *adjective* **1** not able to be bent. **2** not able to be changed or persuaded. **inflexibility** *noun*, **inflexibly** *adverb*

inflict *verb* make a person suffer something, *She inflicted a severe blow on him.* **infliction** *noun* [from *in-* = on, + Latin *flictum* = struck]

inflow *noun* flowing in; what flows in.

influence[1] *noun* **1** the power to produce an effect. **2** a person or thing with this power.

influence[2] *verb* (**influenced, influencing**) have influence on a person or thing; affect.

influential *adjective* having influence.

influenza *noun* an infectious disease that causes fever, catarrh, and pain.

influx *noun* a flowing in, especially of people or things coming in.

infodemic *noun* a rapid increase in the spread of often unreliable information related to a crisis or event.

infographic *noun* a visual representation of information or data, for example as a chart or diagram.

inform *verb* give information to somebody. **informant** *noun*
inform on give incriminating information about a person to the authorities.

informal *adjective* **1** without ceremony or formality, *an informal chat.* **2** (of language or clothing) everyday; normal; casual. **informality** *noun*, **informally** *adverb*

Usage In this dictionary, words marked *informal* are used in everyday speech but not when you are writing or speaking formally.

informal vote *noun* (*Australian*) a vote that is not valid; a spoiled vote.

information *noun* facts told or heard or discovered, or put into a computer.

information technology *noun* the study or use of electronic systems for storing, retrieving, and sending information.

informative *adjective* giving a lot of useful information.

informed *adjective* knowing about something.

informer *noun* a person who gives information against someone.

infra- *prefix* below. [Latin]

infrared *adjective* below or beyond red in the spectrum.

infrastructure *noun* **1** the basic structural foundations of a society or enterprise. **2** roads, bridges, sewers, etc., regarded as a country's economic foundation.

infrequent *adjective* not frequent.

infringe *verb* (**infringed, infringing**) break a rule or an agreement; violate. **infringement** *noun*

infuriate *verb* (**infuriated, infuriating**) make a person very angry; enrage. **infuriation** *noun*

infuse *verb* (**infused, infusing**) **1** add or inspire with a feeling; instil, *infuse them with courage*; *infuse courage into them.* **2** soak or steep tea or herbs etc. in a liquid to extract the flavour. **infusion** *noun* [from Latin *infusum* = poured in]

ingenious *adjective* clever at inventing things; cleverly made. **ingeniously** *adverb*, **ingenuity** *noun* [from Latin *ingenium* = genius]

ingenuous *adjective* naive; artless. **ingenuously** *adverb*, **ingenuousness** *noun*

ingot *noun* a brick-shaped lump of cast metal, especially gold.

ingrained *adjective* **1** (of dirt) marking a surface deeply. **2** (of feelings, habits, or ideas.) firmly fixed.

ingratiate *verb* (**ingratiated, ingratiating**) **ingratiate yourself** get yourself into favour with someone. **ingratiation** *noun* [from Latin *in gratiam* = into favour]

ingratitude *noun* lack of gratitude.

ingredient *noun* one of the parts of a mixture; one of the things used in a recipe. [from Latin *ingrediens* = going in]

inhabit *verb* (**inhabited, inhabiting**) live in a place. **inhabitant** *noun*

inhale *verb* (**inhaled, inhaling**) breathe in. **inhalation** *noun* [from *in-* = in, + Latin *halare* = breathe]

inherent (*say* in-**he**-ruhnt) *adjective* existing in something as one of its natural or permanent qualities. **inherence** *noun*, **inherently** *adverb* [from *in-* = in, + Latin *haerere* = to stick]

inherit *verb* (**inherited, inheriting**) **1** receive money, property, or a title when its previous owner dies. **2** get certain qualities or characteristics from parents or predecessors. **inheritance** *noun*, **inheritor** *noun* [from *in-* = in, + Latin *heres* = heir]

inhibit *verb* (**inhibited, inhibiting**) restrain; hinder; repress. **inhibition** *noun*

inhospitable *adjective* **1** not welcoming. **2** (of a place) giving no shelter.

inhuman *adjective* cruel; without pity or kindness. **inhumanity** *noun*

inhumane *adjective* not humane.

inimitable *adjective* impossible to imitate.

iniquitous *adjective* very unjust. **iniquity** *noun* [from *in-* = not, + *equity*]

initial[1] *noun* the first letter of a word or name.

initial[2] *verb* (**initialled, initialling**) mark or sign something with the initials of your names.

initial[3] *adjective* of the beginning, *the initial stages.* **initially** *adverb* [from Latin *initium* = the beginning]

initiate *verb* (**initiated, initiating**) **1** start something. **2** admit a person as a member of a society or group, often with special ceremonies. **initiation** *noun*, **initiator** *noun*

initiative (*say* i-**nish**-uh-tiv) *noun* the power or courage to start something; enterprising ability.
take the initiative take action to start something happening.

inject *verb* **1** put a medicine or drug into the body by means of a hollow needle. **2** put liquid into something by means of a syringe or other instrument. **3** add a new quality, *Inject some humour into it.* **injection** *noun* [from *in-* = in, + Latin *-jectum* = thrown]

injunction *noun* a command given with authority, e.g. by a lawcourt.

injure *verb* (**injured, injuring**) harm; damage; hurt. **injurious** *adjective*, **injury** *noun*

injustice *noun* **1** lack of justice. **2** an unjust action or treatment.

ink *noun* a black or coloured liquid used in writing and printing. **inky** *adjective*

inkling *noun* a hint; a slight knowledge or suspicion.

inland *adjective & adverb* in or towards the interior of a country; away from the coast.
the inland the parts of a country away from the coast or frontiers.

in-laws *plural noun* relatives by marriage.

inlay *verb* (**inlaid, inlaying**) set pieces of wood, metal, or other material into a surface to form a design. **inlay** *noun*

inlet *noun* **1** a strip of water reaching into the land from a sea or lake. **2** a passage that lets something in (e.g. to a tank).

in-line skate *noun* a rollerblade.

in loco parentis (*say* in loh-koh puh-**ren**-tis) *adverb* in the place or position of a parent. [Latin]

inmate *noun* one of the occupants of a prison, hospital, or other institution.

in memoriam *preposition* in memory (of). [Latin]

inmost *adjective* most inward.

inn *noun* a small hotel, especially for travellers. **innkeeper** *noun*

innate *adjective* inborn. [from *in-* = in, + Latin *natus* = born]

inner *adjective* inside; internal; nearer to the centre. **innermost** *adjective*

innings *noun* (*plural* **innings**) the time when a cricket team or player is batting.

innocent *adjective* **1** not guilty. **2** not wicked. **3** harmless. **4** naive. **innocence** *noun*, **innocently** *adverb* [from *in-* = not, + Latin *nocens* = doing harm]

innocuous *adjective* harmless.

innovation *noun* **1** introducing new things or new methods. **2** something newly introduced. **innovative** *adjective*, **innovator** *noun* [from *in-* = in, + Latin *novus* = new]

innuendo *noun* (*plural* **innuendoes**) an unpleasant insinuation or hint.

innumerable *adjective* countless.

inoculate *verb* (**inoculated, inoculating**) inject or treat with a vaccine or serum as a protection against a disease.
inoculation *noun*

inoffensive *adjective* harmless.

inoperable *adjective* unable to be cured by a surgical operation.

inopportune *adjective* happening at an unsuitable time. **inopportunely** *adverb*

inordinate *adjective* excessive.
inordinately *adverb*

inorganic *adjective* not of living organisms; of mineral origin.

input *noun* **1** what is put in, taken in, or operated on by any process or system, *There has been little input from other members of the team.* **2** the information put into a computer. **3** a place where, or a device through which, energy or information enters a system. **input** *verb*

inquest *noun* an official inquiry to find out how a person died.

inquire *verb* (**inquired, inquiring**) make an investigation; seek information. **inquirer** *noun*, **inquiry** *noun* [from *in-* = into, + Latin *quaerere* = seek]

Usage *Inquire* and *enquire* may be used interchangeably. However, there is a tendency to use *enquire* as a formal word for 'ask', and *inquire* for 'make an investigation'.

inquisition *noun* **1** a detailed questioning or investigation. **2** (**the Inquisition**) a council of the Roman Catholic Church in the Middle Ages set up to discover and punish heretics. **inquisitor** *noun*

inquisitive *adjective* always asking questions or trying to look at things; prying.
inquisitively *adverb*

inquorate *adjective* not constituting a quorum.

inroads *plural noun* **make inroads on** or **into** use up large quantities of something.

insane *adjective* not sane; mad. **insanely** *adverb*, **insanity** *noun*

insanitary *adjective* unclean and likely to be harmful to health.

insatiable (*say* in-**say**-shuh-buhl) *adjective* impossible to satisfy, *an insatiable appetite.*

inscribe *verb* (**inscribed**, **inscribing**) write or carve words or symbols on something. [from *in-* = on, + Latin *scribere* = write]

inscription *noun* **1** words, names, or symbols inscribed, as on a monument, coin, or stone. **2** inscribing.

inscrutable *adjective* enigmatic; impossible to interpret, *an inscrutable smile.*

insect *noun* a small animal with six legs, no backbone, and a body divided into three parts (head, thorax, abdomen).

insecticide *noun* a substance for killing insects. [from *insect*, + Latin *caedere* = kill]

insectivorous *adjective* feeding on insects and other small invertebrate creatures. **insectivore** *noun* [from *insect*, + Latin *vorare* = devour]

insecure *adjective* not secure; unsafe. **insecurely** *adverb*, **insecurity** *noun*

inseminate *verb* (**inseminated**, **inseminating**) insert semen into the womb. **insemination** *noun*

insensible *adjective* **1** unconscious. **2** unaware.

insensitive *adjective* not sensitive. **insensitively** *adverb*, **insensitivity** *noun*

inseparable *adjective* **1** not able to be separated. **2** liking to be constantly together, *inseparable friends.* **inseparably** *adverb*

insert *verb* put a thing into something else. **insertion** *noun*

inshore *adverb & adjective* near or nearer to the shore.

inside[1] *noun* **1** the inner side or surface of something. **2** the part of a path nearer to a wall or further from a road. **3** the side of a bend where the edge or surface is shorter. **4** the internal appearance of someone or something.
inside out with the inside turned to face outwards.

inside[2] *adjective* **1** situated on or near the interior or internal surface of something, *She put the inside lights on.* **2** (in hockey, soccer, and other sports) denoting positions nearer to the centre of the field. **3** known or done by someone within a group or organisation.

inside[3] *adverb* on or to the inside; indoors, *Come inside*; *It's stuffy inside.*

inside[4] *preposition* **1** in; to or at the interior of, *Leave it inside the door.* **2** internal to, included in, within, *the painting was finished inside an hour.*

insider *noun* a member of a certain group, especially someone with access to private information.

insides *plural noun* (*informal*) the organs in the abdomen; the stomach and bowels.

insidious *adjective* inconspicuous but harmful. **insidiously** *adverb*

insight *noun* being able to perceive the truth about things; understanding.

insignia *plural noun* emblems; a badge.

insignificant *adjective* not important; not influential. **insignificance** *noun*

insincere *adjective* not sincere. **insincerely** *adverb*, **insincerity** *noun*

insinuate *verb* (**insinuated**, **insinuating**) **1** hint indirectly or unpleasantly. **2** introduce gradually or craftily. **insinuation** *noun*

insipid *adjective* **1** lacking flavour. **2** not lively or interesting. **insipidity** *noun*

insist *verb* be very firm in saying or asking for something. **insistence** *noun*, **insistent** *adjective* [from Latin *insistere* = stand firm]

in situ (*say* in **sit**-yoo) *adverb* in its original place. [Latin]

insolent (*say* **in**-suh-luhnt) *adjective* very impudent; insulting. **insolence** *noun*, **insolently** *adverb*

insoluble *adjective* **1** impossible to solve, *an insoluble problem.* **2** impossible to dissolve. **insolubility** *noun*

insolvent *adjective* unable to pay your debts. **insolvency** *noun*

insomnia *noun* being unable to sleep. **insomniac** *noun* [from *in-* = without, + Latin *somnus* = sleep]

inspect *verb* examine carefully and critically. **inspection** *noun* [from *in-* = in, + Latin *specere* = to look]

inspector *noun* **1** a person whose job is to inspect or supervise things. **2** a police officer ranking next above a sergeant.

inspiration *noun* **1** a sudden brilliant idea. **2** inspiring; an inspiring influence.

inspire *verb* (**inspired**, **inspiring**) fill a person with good or useful feelings or ideas, *The applause inspired us with confidence.* [from *in-* = into, + Latin *spirare* = breathe]

instability *noun* lack of stability.

install *verb* **1** put something in position and ready to use, *They installed air conditioning.* **2** put a person into an important position with a ceremony, *He was installed as pope.* **installation** *noun*

instalment *noun* each of the parts in which something is given or paid for gradually, *an instalment of a serial.*

instance *noun* an example, *for instance.*

instant[1] *adjective* **1** happening immediately, *instant success.* **2** (of food) designed to be prepared quickly and easily, *instant coffee.* **instantly** *adverb*

instant[2] *noun* a moment, *not an instant too soon.* [from Latin *instans* = urgent]

instantaneous *adjective* happening immediately. **instantaneously** *adverb*

instant messaging *noun* a service on the Internet that allows you to exchange written messages in real time with someone who is using the service at the same time.

instead *adverb* in place of something else; as a substitute.

instep *noun* the top of the foot between the toes and the ankle.

instigate *verb* (**instigated, instigating**) urge; incite; cause something to be done, *instigate a rebellion.* **instigation** *noun*, **instigator** *noun*

instil *verb* (**instilled, instilling**) put ideas into a person's mind gradually. [from *in-* = in, + Latin *stilla* = a drop]

instinct *noun* a natural tendency or ability, *Birds fly by instinct; He has an instinct for finding a good place.* **instinctive** *adjective*, **instinctively** *adverb*

institute[1] *noun* a society or organisation; the building used by this.

institute[2] *verb* (**instituted, instituting**) establish; found; start an inquiry or custom. [from *in-* = in, + Latin *statuere* = set up]

institution *noun* **1** an institute; a public organisation, e.g. a hospital or university. **2** a habit or custom. **3** instituting something. **institutional** *adjective*

instruct *verb* **1** teach a person a subject or skill. **2** inform. **3** tell a person what they must do. **instructor** *noun* [same origin as *structure*]

instruction *noun* **1** teaching; education. **2** a statement telling a person what they must do; an order. **instructional** *adjective*

instructive *adjective* giving knowledge.

instrument *noun* **1** a device for producing musical sounds. **2** a tool used for delicate or scientific work. **3** a measuring device.

instrumental *adjective* **1** of or using musical instruments. **2** being the means of doing something, *She was instrumental in getting me a job.*

instrumentalist *noun* a person who plays a musical instrument.

instrumentation *noun* **1** the arrangement or composition of music for instruments. **2** the provision or use of mechanical or scientific instruments.

insubordinate *adjective* disobedient; rebellious. **insubordination** *noun*

insufferable *adjective* unbearable.

insufficient *adjective* not sufficient.

insular *adjective* of or like an island.

insulate *verb* (**insulated, insulating**) cover or protect something to prevent heat, cold, or electricity etc. from passing in or out. **insulation** *noun*, **insulator** *noun* [from Latin *insula* = island]

insulin *noun* a substance that controls the amount of sugar in the blood.

insult[1] (*say* in-**sult**) *verb* hurt a person's feelings or pride.

insult[2] (*say* **in**-sult) *noun* an insulting remark or action.

insuperable *adjective* unable to be overcome, *an insuperable difficulty.*

insurance *noun* **1** an agreement to compensate someone for a loss, damage, or injury, in return for a payment (called a *premium*) made in advance. **2** a thing providing protection against a possible eventuality.

insure *verb* (**insured, insuring**) protect with insurance.

> **Usage** Do not confuse with *ensure.*

insurgent *noun* a rebel. **insurgent** *adjective* [from *in-* = against, + Latin *surgere* = to rise]

insurmountable *adjective* unable to be overcome.

insurrection *noun* a rebellion.

intact *adjective* not damaged; complete. [from *in-* = not, + Latin *tactum* = touched]

intake *noun* **1** taking something in. **2** the number of people or things taken in.

intangible *adjective* not tangible.

integer *noun* a whole number (e.g. 0, 3, 19), not a fraction. [Latin, = whole]

integral (*say* **in**-tuh-gruhl) *adjective* **1** (of a part) essential to the whole thing, *An engine is an integral part of a car.* **2** whole; complete.

integrate *verb* (**integrated, integrating**) **1** make parts into a whole; combine. **2** join together harmoniously into a single community. **integration** *noun* [from Latin *integrare* = make whole]

integrity (*say* in-**teg**-ruh-tee) *noun* honesty.

intellect *noun* the ability to think (contrasted with *feeling* and *instinct*).

intellectual[1] *adjective* **1** of or using the intellect. **2** having a good intellect and a liking for knowledge. **intellectually** *adverb*

intellectual[2] *noun* an intellectual person.

intelligence *noun* **1** being intelligent. **2** information, especially of military value; the people who collect and study this information.

intelligent *adjective* able to learn and understand things; having great mental ability. **intelligently** *adverb*

intelligent design *noun* the theory that life, or the universe, cannot have arisen by chance and was designed and created by an intelligent entity.

intelligentsia *noun* intellectual people regarded as a group.

intelligible *adjective* able to be understood. **intelligibility** *noun*, **intelligibly** *adverb*

intend *verb* have something in mind as what you want to do; plan. [from Latin *intendere* = stretch, aim]

intense *adjective* very strong or great. **intensely** *adverb*, **intensity** *noun*

intensify *verb* (**intensified, intensifying**) make or become more intense. **intensification** *noun*

intensive *adjective* concentrated; thorough; using a lot of effort. **intensively** *adverb*

intensive care *noun* special medical treatment in which a patient who is dangerously ill is kept under constant observation.

intent[1] *noun* intention.

intent[2] *adjective* with concentrated attention; very interested. **intently** *adverb* [same origin as *intend*]

intention *noun* what a person intends; a purpose or plan.

intentional *adjective* intended; deliberate; not accidental. **intentionally** *adverb*

inter *verb* (**interred, interring**) bury. [from *in-* = in, + Latin *terra* = earth]

inter- *prefix* between; among. [from Latin]

interact *verb* have an effect upon one another. **interaction** *noun*

interactive *adjective* **1** interacting. **2** (in computers) allowing information to be sent in either direction between a computer system and its user.

inter alia (*say* in-ter **ay**-lee-uh) *adverb* among other things. [Latin]

interbreed *verb* (**interbred, interbreeding**) breed with each other; cross-breed.

intercede *verb* (**interceded, interceding**) intervene on behalf of another person or as a peacemaker. **intercession** *noun* [from *inter-*, + Latin *cedere* = go]

intercept *verb* stop or catch a person or thing that is going from one place to another. **interception** *noun* [from *inter-*, + Latin *captum* = seized]

interchange[1] *verb* (**interchanged, interchanging**) **1** put each of two things into the other's place. **2** exchange. **3** alternate. **interchangeable** *adjective*

interchange[2] *noun* **1** interchanging. **2** a major road or transport junction.

intercom *noun* (*informal*) a system of radio or telephone communication between rooms. [short for *intercommunication*]

intercourse *noun* **1** communication or dealings between people. **2** sexual intercourse.

interdependent *adjective* dependent upon each other. **interdependence** *noun*

interdict *noun* a prohibition. **interdict** *verb* [from *inter-*, + Latin *dictum* = said]

interest[1] *noun* **1** a feeling of wanting to know about or help with something. **2** a thing that interests somebody, *Science fiction is one of his interests.* **3** advantage, *She looks after her own interests.* **4** money paid regularly in return for money lent or deposited.

interest[2] *verb* arouse a person's interest. **interested** *adjective*, **interesting** *adjective* [Latin, = it matters]

interest rate *noun* the proportion of a loan that is charged as interest to the borrower.

interface *noun* **1** a surface forming a common boundary between two regions. **2** a place where two things meet and interact; (in computers) a program or device for connecting two pieces of equipment so that they can be operated jointly, or for enabling a user to access a program.

interfere *verb* (**interfered, interfering**) **1** take part in something that has nothing to do with you. **2** get in the way; obstruct. **interference** *noun*

interim[1] *noun* an interval of time between two events.

interim[2] *adjective* of or in the interim; temporary, *an interim arrangement.* [Latin, = meanwhile]

interior[1] *adjective* inner.

interior[2] *noun* **1** the inside of something. **2** the central or inland part of a country. [Latin, = further in]

interject *verb* break in with a remark while someone is speaking. [from *inter-*, + Latin *jactum* = thrown]

interjection *noun* **1** an exclamation such as *oh!* or *hooray!* **2** interjecting; a remark interjected.

interlock *verb* fit into each other.

interloper *noun* an intruder.

interlude *noun* **1** an interval. **2** something happening in an interval or between other events. [from *inter-*, + Latin *ludus* = game]

intermediary *noun* (*plural* **intermediaries**) a mediator; a go-between.

intermediate *adjective* coming between two things in time, place, or order.

interment *noun* interring; burial.

interminable *adjective* endless; long and boring. **interminably** *adverb*

intermission *noun* an interval or pause.

intermittent *adjective* happening at intervals; not continuous. **intermittently** *adverb* [from *inter-*, + Latin *mittere* = let go]

intern[1] *verb* imprison in a special camp or area, usually in wartime.

intern[2] *noun* **1** a student or trainee who works, sometimes without pay, in order to gain work experience or satisfy requirements for a qualification. **2** a resident junior doctor in a hospital.

internal *adjective* inside. **internally** *adverb*

internal combustion engine *noun* an engine that produces power by burning fuel inside the engine itself.

international *adjective* of or belonging to more than one country; agreed between nations. **internationally** *adverb*

internee *noun* a person who is interned.

Internet *noun* (also **internet**) a global computer network providing a variety of information and communication facilities, consisting of interconnected networks using standardised communication protocols.

Internet relay chat *noun* a tool on the Internet that enables people to take part in a discussion on a particular topic in real time.

internment *noun* being interned.

interpersonal *adjective* between persons.

interplanetary *adjective* between planets.

interplay *noun* interaction.

interpolate *verb* (**interpolated, interpolating**) **1** interject. **2** insert words; put terms into a mathematical series. **interpolation** *noun*

interpose *verb* (**interposed, interposing**) **1** insert; interject. **2** intervene. [from *inter-*, + Latin *positum* = put]

interpret *verb* **1** explain what something means. **2** translate what someone says into another language orally. **interpretation** *noun*, **interpreter** *noun*

interquartile *adjective* (in statistics) situated between the first and third quartiles of a distribution.

interrogate *verb* (**interrogated, interrogating**) question closely or formally. **interrogation** *noun*, **interrogator** *noun* [from *inter-*, + Latin *rogare* = ask]

interrogative *adjective* questioning; expressing a question. **interrogatory** *adjective*

interrogative pronoun see **pronoun**.

interrupt *verb* **1** prevent from continuing. **2** stop a person speaking by saying or doing something. **interruption** *noun* [from *inter-*, + Latin *ruptum* = broken]

intersect *verb* divide a thing by passing or lying across it; (of lines or roads) cross each other. **intersection** *noun* [from *inter-*, + Latin *sectum* = cut]

intersex *adjective* relating to or denoting a person or animal that has both male and female sex organs or other sexual characteristics. **intersex** *noun*

intersperse *verb* (**interspersed, interspersing**) insert things here and there in something. [from *inter-*, + Latin *sparsum* = scattered]

interstate *adjective & adverb* **1** existing or carried on between states. **2** to, in, or from another state, *My friend has gone interstate*; *They were married interstate*; *an interstate visitor.*

intertextuality *noun* the relationship between texts, especially literary ones.

interval *noun* **1** a time between two events or parts of a play or event. **2** a space between two things. **3** (in music) the difference in pitch between two sounds.
at intervals with some time or distance between each one. [from Latin *intervallum* = space between ramparts]

intervene *verb* (**intervened, intervening**) **1** come between two events, *in the intervening years.* **2** interrupt a discussion or fight etc. to try and stop it or change its result. **intervention** *noun* [from *inter-*, + Latin *venire* = come]

interview[1] *noun* a formal meeting with someone to ask them questions or to obtain information.

interview[2] *verb* hold an interview with someone. **interviewer** *noun*

interviewee *noun* a person who is interviewed.

intestine *noun* the long tube along which food passes while being absorbed by the body, between the stomach and the anus. **intestinal** *adjective*

intimate[1] (*say* **in**-tuh-muht) *adjective* **1** very friendly with someone. **2** private and personal, *intimate thoughts.* **3** detailed, *an intimate knowledge of the country.* **intimacy** *noun*, **intimately** *adverb*

intimate[2] (*say* **in**-tuh-mayt) *verb* (**intimated, intimating**) tell or hint. **intimation** *noun*

intimidate *verb* (**intimidated, intimidating**) frighten a person by threats into doing something. **intimidation** *noun* [from *in-* = in, + *timidus* = timid]

into *preposition* used to express **1** movement to the inside (*Go into the house*), **2** change of condition or occupation (*It broke into pieces*; *She went into politics*), **3** division (*4 into 20* = 20 divided by four).

intolerable *adjective* unbearable. **intolerably** *adverb*

intolerant *adjective* not tolerant. **intolerance** *noun*, **intolerantly** *adverb*

intonation *noun* **1** the tone or pitch of the voice in speaking. **2** intoning.

intone *verb* (**intoned**, **intoning**) recite in a chanting voice.

in toto *adverb* completely. [Latin]

intoxicate *verb* (**intoxicated**, **intoxicating**) make a person drunk or very excited. **intoxication** *noun* [from *in-* = in, + Latin *toxicum* = poison]

intra- *prefix* within. [from Latin]

intractable *adjective* unmanageable; difficult to deal with or control. **intractability** *noun*

intransigent *adjective* stubborn. **intransigence** *noun*

intransitive *adjective* (of a verb) used without a direct object after it, e.g. *hear* in *we can hear* (but not in *we can hear you*). (Compare **transitive**.) **intransitively** *adverb*

intravenous (*say* in-truh-**vee**-nuhs) *adjective* into a vein.

intrepid *adjective* fearless; brave. **intrepidity** *noun*, **intrepidly** *adverb* [from *in-* = not, + Latin *trepidus* = alarmed]

intricate *adjective* very complicated. **intricacy** *noun*, **intricately** *adverb* [from Latin *intricatum* = entangled]

intrigue[1] (*say* in-**treeg**) *verb* (**intrigued**, **intriguing**) **1** plot with someone in an underhand way. **2** interest very much, *The subject intrigues me.*

intrigue[2] (*say* **in**-treeg) *noun* **1** plotting; an underhand plot. **2** (*old use*) a secret love affair. [from Latin *intricare* = to tangle]

intrinsic *adjective* belonging naturally in something; inherent. **intrinsically** *adverb*

intro- *prefix* into; inwards. [from Latin]

introduce *verb* (**introduced**, **introducing**) **1** make a person known to other people. **2** announce a broadcast, speaker, etc. **3** bring something into use or for consideration. [from *intro-*, + Latin *ducere* = to lead]

introduction *noun* **1** introducing somebody or something. **2** an explanation put at the beginning of a book or speech etc. **introductory** *adjective*

introspective *adjective* examining your own thoughts and feelings. **introspection** *noun* [from *intro-*, + Latin *specere* = to look]

introvert *noun* **1** a shy, reticent person. **2** a person predominantly concerned with their own thoughts and feelings rather than with external things. (Compare **extrovert** 2.) **introverted** *adjective* [from *intro-*, + Latin *vertere* = to turn]

intrude *verb* (**intruded**, **intruding**) come in or join in without being wanted; interfere. **intrusion** *noun*, **intrusive** *adjective* [from *in-* = in, + Latin *trudere* = to push]

intruder *noun* **1** someone who intrudes. **2** a burglar.

intuition *noun* the power to know or understand things without having to think hard or without being taught. **intuitive** *adjective*, **intuitively** *adverb*

Inuit (*say* **in**-yoo-uht) *noun* **1** a member of a people living in northern Canada, Alaska, and Greenland. **2** the language of the Inuit.

inundate *verb* (**inundated**, **inundating**) flood. **inundation** *noun* [from *in-* = in, + Latin *unda* = a wave]

inure (*say* i-**nyoor**) *verb* (**inured**, **inuring**) accustom, especially to something unpleasant.

in utero (*say* in **yoo**-tuh-roh) *adverb* in the womb; before birth. [Latin]

invade *verb* (**invaded**, **invading**) **1** enter a territory with armed forces in order to attack or occupy it. **2** crowd into a place, *Ants invaded the cat's bowl.* **3** intrude on someone's rights or privacy. **4** penetrate harmfully. **invader** *noun* [from *in-* = into, + Latin *vadere* = go]

invalid[1] (*say* **in**-vuh-lid) *noun* a person who is ill or who is weakened by illness.

invalid[2] (*say* in-**val**-uhd) *adjective* not valid, *This passport is invalid.* **invalidity** *noun*

invalidate *verb* (**invalidated**, **invalidating**) make a thing invalid. **invalidation** *noun*

invaluable *adjective* having a value that is too great to be measured; extremely valuable. [from *in-* = not, + *valuable*]

invariable *adjective* not variable; never changing. **invariably** *adverb*

invasion *noun* invading; being invaded.

invective *noun* abusive words.

inveigle (*say* in-**vay**-guhl) *verb* (**inveigled**, **inveigling**) entice. **inveiglement** *noun*

invent *verb* **1** be the first person to make or think of a particular thing. **2** make up a false story, *invent an excuse.* **invention** *noun*, **inventive** *adjective*, **inventor** *noun*

inventory (*say* **in**-vuhn-tuh-ree) *noun* (*plural* **inventories**) a detailed list of goods or furniture.

inverse *adjective* reversed; opposite. **inversely** *adverb* [same origin as *invert*]

invert *verb* turn something upside down. **inversion** *noun* [from *in-* = in, + Latin *vertere* = to turn]

invertebrate *noun* an animal without a backbone. (The opposite is **vertebrate**.) **invertebrate** *adjective*

inverted commas *plural noun* punctuation marks (" ") or (' ') put round spoken words and quotations.

invest *verb* **1** use money to make a profit, e.g. by lending it in return for interest to be paid, or by buying stocks and shares or property. **2** give somebody a rank, medal, or award in a formal ceremony. **investment** *noun*, **investor** *noun*

investigate *verb* (**investigated**, **investigating**) find out as much as you can about something. **investigative** *adjective*, **investigator** *noun*

investigation *noun* **1** the process or an instance of investigating. **2** a formal examination or study.

investiture *noun* the process of investing someone with an honour.

inveterate *adjective* firmly established; habitual, *an inveterate reader.*

invidious *adjective* causing resentment because of unfairness.

invigilate *verb* (**invigilated**, **invigilating**) supervise candidates at an examination. **invigilation** *noun*, **invigilator** *noun* [from *in-* = on, + Latin *vigilare* = keep watch]

invigorate *verb* (**invigorated**, **invigorating**) give a person strength or courage. [compare *vigour*]

invincible *adjective* not able to be defeated; unconquerable. **invincibility** *noun*, **invincibly** *adverb* [from *in-* = not, + Latin *vincere* = conquer]

invisible *adjective* not visible; not able to be seen. **invisibility** *noun*, **invisibly** *adverb*

invite *verb* (**invited**, **inviting**) **1** ask a person to come or do something. **2** be likely to cause something to happen, *You are inviting disaster.* **invitation** *noun*

inviting *adjective* attractive; tempting. **invitingly** *adverb*

in vitro (*say* in **vee**-troh) *adverb & adjective* (of a biological process) taking place in a test tube or other laboratory equipment, *in vitro fertilisation.* [Latin, = in glass]

invoice *noun* a list of goods sent or work done, with the prices charged. [from French *envoyer* = send]

invoke *verb* (**invoked**, **invoking**) **1** call upon a god in prayer asking for help. **2** appeal to for help or protection, *invoke the law.* **invocation** *noun* [from *in-* = in, + Latin *vocare* = to call]

involuntary *adjective* not deliberate; unintentional. **involuntarily** *adverb*

involve *verb* (**involved**, **involving**) **1** have as a part; make a thing necessary, *The job involves hard work.* **2** make someone share in something, *They involved us in their charity work.* **involvement** *noun* [from *in-* = in, + Latin *volvere* = to roll]

involved *adjective* **1** complicated. **2** concerned; sharing in something.

invulnerable *adjective* not vulnerable.

inward[1] *adjective* **1** on the inside. **2** going or facing inwards.

inward[2] *adverb* inwards.

inwards *adverb* towards the inside.

iodine *noun* a chemical substance used as an antiseptic.

ion *noun* an electrically charged particle.

ionosphere (*say* uy-**on**-uh-sfeer) *noun* a region of the upper atmosphere, containing ions.

IOU *noun* a signed paper acknowledging that you owe somebody a sum of money (= *I owe you*).

IP address *noun* a set of numbers (or words) that identifies each computer linked to the Internet. [from the initials of 'Internet Protocol']

ipso facto (*say* ip-soh **fak**-toh) *adverb* **1** by that very fact or act. **2** thereby. [Latin]

IQ *abbreviation* intelligence quotient, a number showing how a person's intelligence compares with that of an average person.

ir- *prefix* see **in-**.

irascible (*say* i-**ras**-uh-buhl) *adjective* easily becoming angry; irritable.

irate (*say* uy-**rayt**) *adjective* angry.

iridescent *adjective* showing rainbow-like colours. **iridescence** *noun*

iridology *noun* (in alternative medicine) diagnosis by examination of the iris of the eye.

iris *noun* (*plural* **irises**) **1** a plant with long pointed leaves and large flowers. **2** the coloured part of the eyeball. [Greek, = rainbow]

irk *verb* annoy.

irksome *adjective* annoying; tiresome.

iron[1] *noun* **1** a hard grey metal. **2** a device with a flat base that is heated for smoothing clothes or cloth. **3** a tool made of iron. **4** a golf club with an iron or steel head. **iron** *adjective*

iron[2] *verb* smooth clothes or cloth with an iron.

Iron Age *noun* the time when tools and weapons were made of iron.

ironbark *noun* an Australian eucalypt with a thick, solid bark and hard dense timber.

ironic (*say* uy-**ron**-ik) *adjective* using irony; full of irony. **ironical** *adjective*, **ironically** *adverb*

ironmonger *noun* a shopkeeper who sells tools and other metal objects. **ironmongery** *noun*

irony (*say* **uy**-ruh-nee) *noun* (*plural* **ironies**) **1** saying the opposite of what you mean in order to emphasise it, e.g. saying 'What a lovely day' when it is pouring with rain. **2** an oddly contradictory situation, *The irony of it is that I tripped while telling someone else to be careful.*

irradiate *verb* subject something to radiation, especially food in order to preserve it. **irradiation** *noun*

irrational *adjective* **1** not rational; illogical. **2** (of a number, quantity, or expression) not expressible as a ratio of two integers, and having an infinite and non-recurring expansion when expressed as a decimal. **irrationally** *adverb*

irrefutable (*say* i-ruh-**fyoo**-tuh-buhl) *adjective* unable to be refuted.

irregular *adjective* **1** not regular; uneven; not symmetrical. **2** not occurring at regular intervals. **3** against the rules or usual custom. **4** (of troops) not in the regular armed forces. **5** (of a word) not inflected according to the usual rules. **irregularity** *noun*, **irregularly** *adverb*

irrelevant (*say* i-**rel**-uh-vuhnt) *adjective* not relevant. **irrelevance** *noun*, **irrelevantly** *adverb*

irreparable (*say* i-**rep**-uh-ruh-buhl) *adjective* unable to be repaired or replaced. **irreparably** *adverb*

irreplaceable *adjective* unable to be replaced.

irrepressible *adjective* unable to be repressed. **irrepressibly** *adverb*

irreproachable *adjective* blameless; faultless. **irreproachably** *adverb*

irresistible *adjective* unable to be resisted; very attractive. **irresistibly** *adverb*

irresolute *adjective* feeling uncertain; hesitant. **irresolutely** *adverb*

irrespective *adjective* not taking something into account, *Prizes are awarded to winners, irrespective of age.*

irresponsible *adjective* not showing a proper sense of responsibility. **irresponsibility** *noun*, **irresponsibly** *adverb*

irretrievable *adjective* not able to be retrieved. **irretrievably** *adverb*

irreverent *adjective* not reverent; not respectful. **irreverence** *noun*, **irreverently** *adverb*

irrevocable (*say* i-**rev**-uh-kuh-buhl) *adjective* unable to be revoked or altered. **irrevocably** *adverb*

irrigate *verb* (**irrigated**, **irrigating**) supply land with water, especially to enable farming. **irrigation** *noun*

irritable *adjective* easily annoyed; bad-tempered. **irritability** *noun*, **irritably** *adverb*

irritate *verb* (**irritated**, **irritating**) **1** annoy. **2** cause itching. **irritant** *adjective & noun*, **irritation** *noun*

irukandji (*say* i-ruh-**kan**-jee) *noun* a box jellyfish of tropical Australian waters. [from the name of an Aboriginal people near Cairns]

is 3rd person singular present tense of **be**, *Everything is back to normal.*

Islam *noun* the religion of Muslims. **Islamic** *adjective* [Arabic, = submission to God]

island *noun* **1** a piece of land surrounded by water. **2** something resembling an island because it is isolated.

islander *noun* an inhabitant of an island.

isle (*say* uyl) *noun* (*poetic & in names*) an island. [from Latin *insula* = island]

isn't is not, *there isn't any chocolate left.*

iso- *prefix* equal (as in *isobar*). [from Greek *isos* = equal]

isobar (*say* **uy**-suh-bah) *noun* a line (on a map) connecting places that have the same atmospheric pressure.

isolate *verb* (**isolated**, **isolating**) **1** cause a person or place to be or remain alone or apart from others. **2** place a person or animal in quarantine as a precaution against infectious or contagious disease. **3** identify something and examine or deal with it separately. **isolation** *noun* [from Latin *insula* = island]

isosceles (*say* uy-**sos**-uh-leez) *adjective* having two sides equal, *an isosceles triangle.* [from *iso-*, + Greek *skelos* = leg]

isotope *noun* a form of an element that differs from other forms in its nuclear properties but not in its chemical properties.

ISP *abbreviation* Internet service provider.

issue[1] *verb* (**issued**, **issuing**) **1** come out; go out; flow out. **2** supply; give out, *We issued one blanket to each refugee.* **3** put out for sale; publish. **4** send out, *They issued a gale warning.* **5** result.

issue[2] *noun* **1** a subject for discussion or concern, *What are the real issues?* **2** a result, *Await the issue of the trial.* **3** something issued, *The Christmas issue of our magazine.* **4** issuing something, *The issue of passports is held up.*

isthmus (*say* **is**-muhs) *noun* (*plural* **isthmuses**) a narrow strip of land connecting two larger pieces of land.

IT *abbreviation* information technology.

it *pronoun* **1** the thing being talked about, *The ball has a hole in it.* **2** the player who has to catch others in a game. The word is also used **3** in statements about the weather, time, distance, circumstances, etc. (*It is raining*; *It is five o'clock*; *It is nine kilometres to the city*), **4** as an indefinite object (*Run for it!*), **5** to refer to a phrase (*It is unlikely that she will fail*).

italic (*say* i-**tal**-ik) *adjective* printed with sloping letters (called *italics*) *like this.* **italicise** *verb*

itch[1] *verb* **1** have or feel a tickling sensation in the skin that makes you want to scratch it. **2** long to do something.

itch[2] *noun* (*plural* **itches**) **1** an itching feeling. **2** a longing. **itchiness** *noun*, **itchy** *adjective*

item *noun* **1** one thing in a list or group of things. **2** one piece of news in a newspaper or bulletin.

itemise *verb* (**itemised**, **itemising**) list item by item.

itinerant (*say* uy-**tin**-uh-ruhnt) *adjective* travelling from place to place, *an itinerant preacher.*

itinerary (*say* uy-**tin**-uh-ruh-ree) *noun* (*plural* **itineraries**) a list of places to be visited on a journey; a route. [from Latin *itineris* = of a journey]

-itis *suffix* **1** forming names of inflammatory diseases, e.g. *appendicitis; hepatitis.* **2** (*informal*) in extended uses with reference to conditions compared to diseases, e.g. *Mondayitis.*

it'll it will, *It'll be good to get home.*

its *possessive pronoun* belonging to it, *The cat hurt its paw.*

> **Usage** Do not put an apostrophe into *its* unless you mean 'it is'or 'it has' (see the next entry).

it's (*informal*) **1** it is, *It's very hot.* **2** it has, *It's broken all records.*

itself *pronoun* it and nothing else, used to refer back to the subject of a verb, *I think the cat has hurt itself.*
by itself on its own; alone.

IV *abbreviation* intravenous.

I've I have, *I've got an appointment at the doctor's tomorrow.*

IVF *abbreviation* in vitro fertilisation, the fertilisation of a human egg by a sperm in a test tube etc.

ivory *noun* **1** the hard creamy-white substance that forms elephants' tusks. **2** a creamy-white colour.

ivy *noun* (*plural* **ivies**) a climbing evergreen plant with shiny leaves.

Jj

jab[1] *verb* (**jabbed**, **jabbing**) poke roughly; push a thing into something.

jab[2] *noun* **1** a jabbing movement. **2** (*informal*) an injection.

jabber *verb* speak quickly and not clearly; chatter. **jabber** *noun*

jabiru *noun* (*plural* **jabirus**) an Australian stork with greenish-black and white feathers and red legs.

jacaranda *noun* a tropical tree with blue or purple flowers.

jack[1] *noun* **1** a device for lifting something heavy off the ground. **2** a playing card with a picture of a young man. **3** a small white ball aimed at in bowls.

jack[2] *verb* lift with a jack.
jack in (*informal*) give up or abandon an attempt.
jack up (*Australian informal*) refuse to cooperate.

jack[3] *adjective* (*Australian informal*) fed up; tired, *He got jack of the place and cleared out.*

jackal *noun* a wild animal of Africa and Asia, rather like a dog.

jackass *noun* (*plural* **jackasses**) **1** a male donkey. **2** a stupid person. **3** a kookaburra.

jackdaw *noun* a kind of small crow.

jackeroo *noun* (also **jackaroo**) (*Australian*) a trainee on a sheep or cattle station. **jackeroo** *verb* [possibly from an Aboriginal language of the Brisbane area]

jacket *noun* **1** a short coat, usually reaching to the hips. **2** a protective or supportive garment, *life jacket.* **3** a paper etc. wrapper for a book. **4** the skin of a potato that is baked without being peeled.

jackhammer *noun* a pneumatic hammer or drill.

jack-in-the-box *noun* a toy figure that springs out of a box when the lid is lifted.

jackknife *verb* (**jackknifed**, **jackknifing**) fold one part against another, like a folding knife.

jack of all trades *noun* someone who can do many different kinds of work.

jackpot *noun* an amount of prize money that increases until someone wins it.

jade *noun* a green stone that is carved to make ornaments.

jaded *adjective* tired and bored.

jagged (*say* **jag**-uhd) *adjective* having an uneven edge with sharp points.

jaguar *noun* a large fierce South American animal of the cat family rather like a leopard.

jail[1] *noun* (also **gaol**) a prison.

jail[2] *verb* put into prison. **jailer** *noun*

jam[1] *noun* **1** a sweet food made of fruit boiled with sugar until it is thick. **2** a lot of things crowded together so that movement is difficult. **3** (*informal*) a difficult situation, *in a jam.*

jam[2] *verb* (**jammed**, **jamming**) **1** crowd or squeeze into a space. **2** make or become fixed and difficult to move. **3** push something forcibly, *jam the brakes on.* **4** block by crowding or obstructing. **5** block a broadcast by causing interference with the transmission.

jamb (*say* jam) *noun* a side post of a doorway or window frame. [from French *jambe* = leg]

jamboree *noun* **1** a large party or celebration. **2** a large gathering of Scouts.

jam-packed *adjective* (*informal*) packed full and tightly.

jangle *verb* (**jangled**, **jangling**) make a loud harsh ringing sound. **jangle** *noun*

janitor *noun* a caretaker. [from Latin *janua* = door]

January *noun* the first month of the year. [from Latin *Janus* = guardian god of doors]

jar[1] *noun* a container made of glass or pottery. [from Arabic *jarra* = pot]

jar[2] *verb* (**jarred**, **jarring**) **1** cause an unpleasant jolt or shock. **2** sound harshly.

jar[3] *noun* a jarring effect.

jargon *noun* special words used by a group of people, *scientists' jargon.*

jarrah *noun* a Western Australian eucalypt with durable reddish-brown timber. [from Noongar *jarril*]

jasmine *noun* a shrub with yellow or white flowers.

jaundice *noun* a disease in which the skin becomes yellow. [from French *jaune* = yellow]

jaunt *noun* a short trip. **jaunt** *verb*

jaunty *adjective* (**jauntier**, **jauntiest**) lively and cheerful. **jauntily** *adverb*, **jauntiness** *noun*

javelin *noun* a lightweight spear.

jaw *noun* **1** either of the two bones that form the framework of the mouth. **2** the lower part of the face. **3** something shaped like the jaws or used for gripping things. **4** (*informal*) talking.

jay *noun* a noisy chattering bird.

jaywalk *verb* walk across a road carelessly, without paying attention to traffic or signals. **jaywalker** *noun*

jazz *noun* a kind of music with strong rhythm. **jazzy** *adjective*

jealous *adjective* **1** unhappy or resentful because you feel that someone is your rival or is better or luckier than yourself. **2** careful in keeping something, *He is very jealous of his own rights.* **jealously** *adverb*, **jealousy** *noun*

jeans *plural noun* trousers made of strong cotton fabric.

jeer *verb* laugh or shout at somebody rudely or scornfully. **jeer** *noun*

jelly *noun* (*plural* **jellies**) **1** a soft transparent food. **2** any soft slippery substance. **jellied** *adjective* [from Latin *gelare* = freeze]

jellyfish *noun* (*plural* **jellyfish**) a sea animal with a body like jelly.

jemmy *noun* (*plural* **jemmies**) a burglar's crowbar. **jemmy** *verb*

jeopardise (*say* **jep**-uh-duyz) *verb* (**jeopardised**, **jeopardising**) endanger.

jeopardy (*say* **jep**-uh-dee) *noun* danger.

jerk[1] *verb* make a sudden sharp movement; pull suddenly; move unevenly.

jerk[2] *noun* a jerking movement. **jerkily** *adverb*, **jerky** *adjective*

jerkin *noun* a sleeveless jacket.

jerry-built *adjective* built badly and with poor materials.

jersey *noun* (*plural* **jerseys**) **1** a pullover with sleeves. **2** a plain machine-knitted material used for making clothes.

jest[1] *noun* a joke.

jest[2] *verb* make jokes.

jester *noun* a professional entertainer at a royal court in the Middle Ages.

jet[1] *noun* **1** a rapid stream of liquid or gas forced out of a small opening. **2** a narrow opening from which a jet comes. **3** an aircraft driven by engines that send out a high-speed jet of hot gases at the back.

jet[2] *verb* (**jetted**, **jetting**) **1** come or send out in a strong stream. **2** (*informal*) travel in a jet aircraft. [from French *jeter* = to throw]

jet[3] *noun* **1** a hard black mineral substance. **2** a deep glossy black colour.

jetsam *noun* goods thrown overboard and washed ashore from a ship in distress. [from *jettison*]

jettison *verb* throw overboard or away; release or drop something from an aircraft or spacecraft in flight. [same origin as *jet*[2]]

jetty *noun* (*plural* **jetties**) a small landing stage. [same origin as *jet*[2]]

Jew *noun* **1** a member of the people and cultural community who trace their origins through the ancient Hebrew people of Israel to Abraham. **2** a person whose religion is Judaism. **Jewish** *adjective* [from Hebrew, = of the tribe of Judah]

jewel *noun* a precious stone; an ornament containing precious stones. **jewelled** *adjective*

jeweller *noun* a person who sells or makes jewellery.

jewellery *noun* jewels and similar ornaments for wearing.

jib[1] *noun* **1** a triangular sail stretching forward from a ship's front mast. **2** the projecting arm of a crane.

jib[2] *verb* (**jibbed**, **jibbing**) be reluctant or unwilling to do something.

jiffy *noun* (*informal*) a moment.

jig[1] *noun* **1** a lively jumping dance. **2** a device that holds something in place while you work on it with tools.

jig[2] *verb* (**jigged**, **jigging**) move up and down quickly and jerkily.

jiggle *verb* (**jiggled**, **jiggling**) rock or jerk something lightly.

jigsaw *noun* **1** a saw that can cut curved shapes. **2** (in full **jigsaw puzzle**) a picture cut into irregular pieces that are then shuffled and fitted together again for amusement.

jihad *noun* (in Islam) a holy war. [Arabic]

jillaroo *noun* (also **jilleroo**) (*Australian*) a female worker on a sheep or cattle station.

jilt *verb* suddenly reject or abandon a lover.

jingle[1] *verb* (**jingled**, **jingling**) make or cause to make a tinkling sound.

jingle[2] *noun* **1** a jingling sound. **2** a very simple verse or tune.

jinx *noun* (*informal*) a person or thing that is thought to bring bad luck. **jinxed** *adjective*

jitters *plural noun* (*informal*) nervousness. **jittery** *adjective*

jive *noun* a jerky, lively style of dance; music for this.

job *noun* **1** work that someone does regularly to earn a living. **2** a piece of work to be done. **3** (*informal*) a difficult task, *You'll have a job to lift that box.* **4** (*informal*) a thing; a state of affairs, *It's a good job you're here.*

jobless *adjective* without a job.

jockey *noun* (*plural* **jockeys**) a person who rides horses in races.

jockey shorts *plural noun* (also **jocks**) a man's brief underpants or shorts.

jocular *adjective* joking; humorous. **jocularity** *noun*, **jocularly** *adverb*

jodhpurs (*say* **jod**-puhz) *plural noun* trousers for horse riding, fitting closely from the knee to the ankle. [named after Jodhpur in India]

joey *noun* a baby kangaroo or possum.

jog[1] *verb* (**jogged**, **jogging**) **1** run or trot slowly, especially for exercise. **2** give something a slight push. **jogger** *noun*
jog someone's memory help someone to remember something.

jog[2] *noun* **1** a slow run or trot. **2** a slight knock or push.

jogtrot *noun* a slow steady trot.

joie de vivre (*say zh*wah duh **vee**-vruh) *noun* a feeling of great enjoyment of life. [French, = joy of life]

join[1] *verb* **1** put or come together; fasten; unite; connect. **2** do something together with others, *We all joined in the chorus.* **3** become a member of a group or organisation, *Join the navy.*
join up enlist in the armed forces.

join[2] *noun* a place where things join.

joiner *noun* a person whose job is to make furniture and fittings out of wood.
joinery *noun*

joint[1] *noun* **1** a join. **2** the place where two bones fit together. **3** a large piece of meat cut ready for cooking.

joint[2] *adjective* shared or done by two or more people, nations, etc., *a joint project.*
jointly *adverb*

joist *noun* any of the long beams supporting a floor or ceiling.

joke[1] *noun* something said or done to make people laugh.

joke[2] *verb* (**joked**, **joking**) make jokes.

joker *noun* **1** someone who jokes. **2** an extra playing card with a jester on it. **3** (*Australian informal*) a fellow.

jolly[1] *adjective* (**jollier**, **jolliest**) cheerful; merry. **jollity** *noun*

jolly[2] *adverb* (*informal*) very, *jolly good.*

jolly[3] *verb* (**jollied**, **jollying**) (*informal*) keep someone in a good humour.

jolt[1] *verb* **1** shake or dislodge with a sudden sharp movement. **2** move along jerkily, e.g. on a rough road. **3** give someone a shock.

jolt[2] *noun* **1** a jolting movement. **2** a shock.

jostle *verb* (**jostled**, **jostling**) push roughly, especially in a crowd.

jot *verb* (**jotted**, **jotting**) write something quickly, *jot it down.*

joule (*say* jool) *noun* a unit of work or energy. [named after the English scientist J.P. Joule]

journal *noun* **1** a newspaper or magazine. **2** a diary. [from Latin, = by day]

journalist *noun* a person who writes for a newspaper or magazine or prepares news to be broadcast on radio or television.
journalism *noun*, **journalistic** *adjective*

journey[1] *noun* (*plural* **journeys**) **1** going from one place to another. **2** the distance or time taken to travel somewhere, *two days' journey.*

journey[2] *verb* make a journey. [from French, = a day's travel (*jour* = day)]

joust (*say* jowst) *verb* fight on horseback with lances.

jovial *adjective* cheerful and good-humoured.
joviality *noun*, **jovially** *adverb*

jowl *noun* **1** the jaw or cheek. **2** loose skin on the neck.

joy *noun* **1** a feeling of great pleasure; gladness. **2** a thing that causes joy. **joyful** *adjective*, **joyfully** *adverb*, **joyfulness** *noun*, **joyous** *adjective*, **joyously** *adverb*

joyride *noun* a ride taken for pleasure in a stolen car. **joyrider** *noun*, **joyriding** *noun*

joystick *noun* **1** the control lever of an aircraft. **2** a device for moving a cursor or image on a computer screen.

JP *abbreviation* Justice of the Peace.

JPEG *noun* (in computing) a format for compressing images. [from the initials of 'Joint Photographic Experts Group']

jube *noun* a jelly-like sweet.

jubilant *adjective* rejoicing; triumphant.
jubilantly *adverb*, **jubilation** *noun* [from Latin *jubilans* = shouting for joy]

jubilee (*say* **joo**-buh-lee) *noun* a special anniversary, *silver* (25th), *golden* (50th), and *diamond* (60th) *jubilee.*

Judaism (*say* **joo**-day-iz-uhm) *noun* the religion of the Jewish people. [same origin as *Jew*]

judge[1] *noun* **1** a person appointed to hear cases in a lawcourt and decide what should be done. **2** a person deciding who has won a contest or competition. **3** a person who is able to give an authoritative opinion on the value or quality of something.

judge² *verb* (**judged, judging**) **1** act as a judge. **2** form and give an opinion. **3** estimate, *He judged the distance carefully.* [from Latin *judex* = judge]

judgement *noun* (also **judgment**, especially in legal contexts) **1** judging. **2** the decision made by a lawcourt. **3** someone's opinion. **4** the ability to judge wisely. **5** something considered as a punishment from God, *It's a judgement on you!*

judgemental *adjective* (also **judgmental**) **1** involving judgement. **2** condemning; critical. **judgementally** or **judgmentally** *adverb*

judicial *adjective* of lawcourts, judges, or judgements. **judicially** *adverb*

judiciary (*say* joo-**dish**-uh-ree) *noun* all the judges in a country.

judicious (*say* joo-**dish**-uhs) *adjective* having or showing good sense. **judiciously** *adverb*

judo *noun* a Japanese method of self-defence without using weapons. [from Japanese *ju* = gentle, + *do* = way]

jug *noun* a container for holding and pouring liquids, with a handle and a lip.

juggernaut *noun* a huge lorry. [named after a Hindu god whose image was dragged in procession on a huge wheeled vehicle]

juggle *verb* (**juggled, juggling**) **1** toss and keep a number of objects in the air, for entertainment. **2** rearrange or alter things skilfully or in order to deceive people. **juggler** *noun*

jugular *adjective* of or in the throat or neck, *the jugular veins.*

juice *noun* **1** the liquid from fruit, vegetables, or other food. **2** a liquid produced by the body, *the digestive juices.* **juicy** *adjective*

jukebox *noun* a machine that plays a selected recording when you put a coin in.

July *noun* the seventh month of the year. [from Latin *Julius* Caesar]

jumble¹ *verb* (**jumbled, jumbling**) mix things up into a confused mass.

jumble² *noun* a confused mixture of things; a muddle.

jumble sale *noun* a sale of second-hand goods.

jumbo *noun* (*plural* **jumbos**) **1** something very large of its kind. **2** (also **jumbo jet**) a very large jet aircraft.

jumbuck *noun* (*Australian*) a sheep.

jump¹ *verb* **1** move up suddenly from the ground into the air. **2** go over something by jumping, *jump the fence.* **3** omit or skip over part of something and pass on to a further point or stage. **4** move suddenly in surprise. **5** pass quickly to a different place or level; rise or increase.

jump at (*informal*) accept something eagerly.
jump the gun start before you should.
jump the queue not wait your turn.

jump² *noun* **1** a jumping movement. **2** an obstacle to jump over. **3** a sudden rise or change.

jumper *noun* **1** a person or animal that jumps. **2** a knitted garment for the upper part of the body.

jumpy *adjective* (**jumpier, jumpiest**) nervous.

junction *noun* **1** a join. **2** a place where roads or railway lines meet. [from Latin *junctum* = joined]

juncture *noun* **1** a point of time, especially in a crisis. **2** a join.

June *noun* the sixth month of the year. [from Latin *Juno* = name of a goddess]

jungle *noun* a thick tangled forest, especially in the tropics. [from Hindi *jangal* = forest]

junior¹ *adjective* **1** younger. **2** for young children, *a junior school.* **3** lower in rank or importance, *junior officers.*

junior² *noun* a junior person. [from Latin, = younger]

juniper *noun* an evergreen shrub.

junk¹ *noun* rubbish; things of no value.

junk² *noun* a Chinese sailing boat.

junket *noun* **1** a sweet custard-like food made of curdled flavoured milk. **2** a feast; a pleasure outing. **3** an official tour at public expense.

junk food *noun* food that is not nourishing.

junkie *noun* (*informal*) a drug addict.

junk mail *noun* unsolicited advertising material sent by post or email.

Jupiter *noun* the largest planet of the solar system, orbiting between Mars and Saturn. [named after the chief of the Roman gods]

jurisdiction *noun* authority; official power, especially to interpret and apply the law. [from Latin *juris* = of the law, + *dictum* = said]

juror *noun* a member of a jury.

jury *noun* (*plural* **juries**) group of people (usually 12) appointed to give a verdict about a case in a lawcourt. [from Latin *jurare* = take an oath]

just¹ *adjective* **1** based on or behaving according to what is morally right and fair, *She is a just prime minister.* **2** deserved; proper; right in amount, *a just reward.* **justly** *adverb*, **justness** *noun*

just² *adverb* **1** exactly, *It's just what I wanted.* **2** only; simply, *They're just good friends.* **3** barely; by only a small amount, *just below the knee.* **4** at this moment or only a little while ago, *She has just gone.* [from Latin *justus* = rightful]

justice *noun* **1** being just; fair treatment. **2** legal proceedings, *a court of justice.* **3** a judge or magistrate.

Justice of the Peace *noun* a person authorised to witness oaths, written declarations, etc.

justify *verb* (**justified, justifying**) show that something is fair, just, or reasonable. **justifiable** *adjective*, **justification** *noun*

jut *verb* (**jutted, jutting**) stick out. [same origin as *jet*[2]]

jute *noun* fibre from tropical plants, used for making rope, sacks, and matting.

juvenile *adjective* **1** of or for young people. **2** immature. [from Latin *juvenis* = young person]

juvenile delinquent *noun* a young person who has broken the law.

juxtapose *verb* (**juxtaposed, juxtaposing**) place or deal with close together for contrasting effect, *black-and-white photos of slums were starkly juxtaposed with colour images.* **juxtaposition** *noun* [from Latin *juxta* = next, *positum* = put]

Kk

kabbala (*say* kuh-**bah**-luh) *noun* (also **kabbalah**) **1** the Jewish mystical tradition. **2** mystic interpretation; any esoteric doctrine or occult lore. [medieval Latin from Rabbinical Hebrew, = tradition]

kaleidoscope (*say* kuh-**luy**-duh-skohp) *noun* a tube that you look through to see brightly coloured patterns that change as you turn the end of the tube. **kaleidoscopic** *adjective* [from Greek *kalos* = beautiful, + *eidos* = form, + *skopein* = look at]

kangaroo *noun* an Australian marsupial with short front limbs, a large thick tail, and long strong hind legs that enable it to jump along. [from Guugu Yimithirr *gangurru*]

kangaroo bar *noun* a bullbar.

kangaroo paw *noun* an Australian plant with woolly flowers shaped like a kangaroo's paw.

kaput (*say* kuh-**puut**) *adjective* ruined; destroyed; dead; out of order. [from German *kaputt*]

karaoke (*say* ka-ree-**oh**-kee) *noun* a form of entertainment in which people sing along to a backing track. [from Japanese = empty orchestra]

karate (*say* kuh-**rah**-tee) *noun* a Japanese method of self-defence in which the hands and feet are used as weapons. [from Japanese *kara* = empty, *te* = hand]

karma *noun* **1** (in Buddhism and Hinduism) the sum of a person's actions in a previous existence, thought to decide their fate in future existences. **2** (*informal*) the sum of good or bad luck, viewed as resulting from one's actions; destiny. **3** (*informal*) a person's spiritual or emotional state. [Sanskrit, = action, fate]

karri *noun* a tall Western Australian eucalypt yielding hard red wood. [from Noongar]

kayak *noun* a small canoe with a covering that fits round the canoeist's waist. [Inuit]

kebab *noun* small pieces of meat, fish, or vegetables cooked on a skewer.

keel[1] *noun* the long piece of wood or metal along the bottom of a boat.
on an even keel steady.

keel[2] *verb* tilt; overturn, *The ship keeled over.*

keen[1] *adjective* **1** enthusiastic; very interested in or eager to do something, *a keen swimmer.* **2** sharp, *a keen edge.* **3** piercingly cold, *a keen wind.* **keenly** *adverb*, **keenness** *noun*

keen[2] *verb* wail, especially in mourning.

keep[1] *verb* (**kept, keeping**) **1** have something and look after it or not get rid of it. **2** stay or cause to stay in the same condition, position, or state, *keep still; keep it hot.* **3** do something continually, *She keeps laughing.* **4** respect and not break, *keep a promise; keep the law.* **5** celebrate a feast, *keep the sabbath.* **6** make entries in, *keep a diary.* **7** prevent a person from doing something; detain, *What kept you?* **8** guard or protect a person or place, *keep goal.* **9** own and look after animals, *He keeps chickens.* **10** remain in a good condition, *Margarine keeps for a long time.*
keep up 1 make the same progress as others. **2** continue something.

keep[2] *noun* **1** maintenance; the food and resources that you need to live, *She earns her keep.* **2** a strong tower in a castle.
for keeps (*informal*) permanently; to keep, *Is this football mine for keeps?*

keeper *noun* **1** a person who looks after or is in charge of people, an animal, a building, or a thing, *the park keeper.* **2** a goalkeeper or wicketkeeper.

keeping *noun* care; looking after something, *in safe keeping.*
in keeping with conforming to; suiting, *Modern furniture is not in keeping with an old house.*

keepsake *noun* a gift to be kept in memory of the person who gave it.

keffiyeh (*say* ke-**fee**-yay) *noun* a headdress worn by some Arab men. [Arabic]

keg *noun* a small barrel.

keirin (*say* **keer**-ruhn) *noun* a cycling track race in which a motorcyclist sets the pace for the first laps. [Japanese]

kelp *noun* a large seaweed.

kelpie *noun* an Australian breed of short-haired sheepdog.

kennel *noun* a shelter for a dog.

kept *past tense & past participle* of **keep**[1].

keratosis *noun* (*plural* **keratoses**) a horny growth, especially on the skin.

kerb *noun* the edge of a pavement or raised path.

kerchief *noun* a headscarf or neckerchief.

kerfuffle *noun* (*informal*) a fuss; a commotion.

kernel *noun* **1** the softer part inside the shell of a nut or fruit stone. **2** the part of a grain or seed within the husk. **3** the central or most important part of something.

kerosene *noun* a fuel oil distilled from petroleum.

kestrel *noun* a small falcon.

ketchup *noun* a thick sauce made chiefly from tomatoes and vinegar.

kettle *noun* a container with a spout and handle, for boiling water in.

kettledrum *noun* a drum consisting of a large metal bowl with skin or plastic over the top.

key[1] *noun* **1** a piece of metal shaped so that it will open a lock. **2** a similar instrument for grasping and turning something, e.g. for winding a clock or tightening a spring. **3** a small lever or button to be pressed by a finger, e.g. on a piano, typewriter, or computer terminal. **4** a system of notes in music, *the key of C major.* **5** a fact or clue that explains or solves something, *the key to the mystery.* **6** an explanatory list of symbols used in a map, table, etc.

key[2] *verb* **key in** enter or operate on data by means of a computer keyboard or telephone keypad.

key[3] *adjective* very important, *a key point.*

keyboard *noun* **1** the set of keys on a piano, computer, typewriter, or similar device. **2** an electronic musical instrument with keys arranged as on a piano.

keyhole *noun* the hole through which a key is put into a lock.

keynote *noun* **1** the note on which a key in music is based. **2** the main idea in something said, written, or done; a theme.

key signature *noun* (in music) any of several combinations of sharps or flats indicating the key of a composition.

keystone *noun* the central wedge-shaped stone in an arch, locking the others together.

kg *abbreviation* kilogram(s).

khaki *noun* a dull yellowish-brown colour, used for military uniforms. [from Urdu, = dust-coloured]

Khalsa (*say* **kul**-suh) *noun* the body or company of fully initiated Sikhs.

kibbeh (*say* **kib**-ay) *noun* a Middle Eastern dish made with seasoned minced meat. [from Egyptian Arabic *kubba* = ball, lump]

kibble *verb* grind coarsely, *kibbled wheat.*

kibbutz *noun* (*plural* **kibbutzim**) a commune in Israel, especially for farming. [from Hebrew, = gathering]

kick[1] *verb* **1** hit or move a person or thing with your foot. **2** move your legs about vigorously. **3** (of a gun) recoil when fired.
kick out get rid of; dismiss.
kick up (*informal*) make a noise or fuss.

kick[2] *noun* **1** a kicking movement. **2** the recoiling movement of a gun. **3** (*informal*) a thrill. **4** (*informal*) an interest or activity, *She's on a health kick.*

kid[1] *noun* **1** (*informal*) a child. **2** a young goat. **3** fine leather made from a goat's skin.

kid[2] *verb* (**kidded**, **kidding**) (*informal*) deceive in fun; tease.

kidnap *verb* (**kidnapped**, **kidnapping**) abduct, especially in order to obtain a ransom. **kidnapper** *noun*

kidney *noun* (*plural* **kidneys**) either of the two organs in the body that remove waste products from the blood and excrete urine into the bladder.

kill[1] *verb* **1** make a person or thing die. **2** destroy or put an end to something. **killer** *noun*, **killing** *noun*

kill[2] *noun* **1** killing. **2** the animal or animals killed by a hunter.

kiln *noun* an oven for hardening pottery or bricks, for drying hops, or for burning lime. [from Latin *culina* = kitchen]

kilo *noun* (*plural* **kilos**) a kilogram.

kilo- *prefix* one thousand (as in *kilolitre* = 1000 litres, *kilohertz* = 1000 hertz). [from Greek *khilioi* = thousand]

kilobyte *noun* (in computing) 1024 bytes as a measure of memory or data size.

kilogram *noun* a unit of mass or weight equal to 1000 grams, *The baby weighs 3 kilograms.*

kilojoule *noun* 1000 joules, especially used in measuring the energy value of foods.

kilometre (*say* **kil**-uh-mee-tuh or kuh-**lom**-uh-tuh) *noun* a unit of length equal to 1000 metres, *Her school is a two-kilometre walk away.*

kilowatt *noun* a unit of electrical power equal to 1000 watts.

kilt *noun* a kind of pleated skirt worn especially by Scotsmen.

kilter *noun* **out of kilter** not in good working order.

kimono *noun* (*plural* **kimonos**) a long loose Japanese robe.

kin *noun* a person's relatives. **kinsman** *noun*, **kinswoman** *noun*
next of kin a person's closest relative.

kina *noun* the unit of money in Papua New Guinea.

kind[1] *noun* a class of similar things or animals; a sort or type. **payment in kind** payment in goods not in money.

> **Usage** Correct use is *this kind of thing* or *these kinds of things* (not 'these kind of things').

kind[2] *adjective* friendly and helpful; considerate. **kind-hearted** *adjective*, **kindness** *noun*

kinder (*say* **kin**-duh) *noun* (*Australian informal*) kindergarten.

kindergarten *noun* a school or class for very young children. [from German *kinder* = children, + *garten* = garden]

kindle *verb* (**kindled**, **kindling**) **1** start a flame; set light to something. **2** begin burning. **3** stimulate, *kindle interest.*

kindling *noun* small pieces of wood for use in lighting fires.

kindly *adjective* (**kindlier**, **kindliest**) kind, *a kindly smile.* **kindliness** *noun*

kindred[1] *noun* kin.

kindred[2] *adjective* related; similar, *chemistry and kindred subjects.*

kindy *noun* (*Australian informal*) kindergarten.

kinetic *adjective* of or produced by movement, *kinetic energy.* [from Greek *kinetikos* = moving]

king *noun* **1** a man who is the ruler of a country through inheriting the position. **2** a person or thing regarded as supreme, *the lion is the king of beasts.* **3** the most important piece in chess. **4** a playing card with a picture of a king. **kingly** *adjective*

kingdom *noun* **1** a country ruled by a king or queen. **2** the highest category in the classification of living things, *the animal and plant kingdoms.*

kingfisher *noun* a small bird with a long beak that dives to catch fish.

kink *noun* **1** a sharp twist or curve in something that is otherwise straight. **2** a peculiarity. **kinky** *adjective*

kinship *noun* relationship by birth.

kiosk *noun* a small stall or shop where newspapers, refreshments, and snacks are sold. [from Persian, = pavilion]

kip *noun* (*informal*) a sleep.

kipper *noun* a smoked herring.

kipsy *noun* (*plural* **kipsies**) (*Australian informal*) a house or lean-to.

kiss[1] *noun* (*plural* **kisses**) touching somebody with your lips as a sign of affection.

kiss[2] *verb* give somebody a kiss.

kit *noun* **1** equipment or clothes for a particular occupation. **2** a set of parts sold ready to be fitted together.

kitchen *noun* a room in which meals are prepared and cooked.

kite *noun* **1** a light framework covered with cloth, paper, or other material and flown in the wind on the end of a long piece of string. **2** a large hawk. **3** (in geometry) a quadrilateral figure symmetrical about one diagonal.

kith *noun* **kith and kin** friends and relatives.

kitsch *adjective* tasteless, garish, or sentimental. [German]

kitten *noun* a very young cat.

kitty *noun* (*plural* **kitties**) **1** an amount of money that you can win in a card game. **2** a fund for use by several people.

kiwi (*say* **kee**-wee) *noun* (*plural* **kiwis**) **1** a New Zealand bird that cannot fly. **2** (**Kiwi**) a person from New Zealand.

kiwi fruit *noun* a small green-fleshed oval fruit with brown hairy skin.

kleptomania *noun* an uncontrollable tendency to steal things. **kleptomaniac** *noun* [from Greek *kleptes* = thief, + *mania*]

km *abbreviation* kilometre(s).

knack *noun* a special skill.

knapsack *noun* a bag carried on the back, especially by soldiers or hikers.

knave *noun* **1** (*old use*) a dishonest man; a rogue. **2** a jack in playing cards.

knead *verb* press and stretch something soft (especially dough) with your hands.

knee *noun* the joint in the middle of the leg.

kneecap *noun* the small bone covering the front of the knee joint; the patella.

kneel *verb* (**knelt**, **kneeling**) be or get yourself in a position on your knees.

knell *noun* the sound of a bell rung solemnly after death or at a funeral.

knew *past tense* of **know**.

knickerbockers *plural noun* loose-fitting short trousers gathered in at the knees.

knickers *plural noun* a woman's or girl's underpants.

knick-knack *noun* a small ornament.

knife[1] *noun* (*plural* **knives**) a cutting instrument consisting of a sharp blade set in a handle.

knife[2] *verb* (**knifed**, **knifing**) stab with a knife.

knight[1] *noun* **1** a man who has been given the rank that allows him to put 'Sir' before his name. **2** a piece in chess, with a horse's head. **knighthood** *noun*

knight[2] *verb* make someone a knight.

knit *verb* (**knitted** or **knit**, **knitting**) **1** make something by looping together wool or other yarn, using long needles or a machine.

2 (of broken bones) become joined; heal.
knitter *noun*, **knitting needle** *noun*
knit your brow frown.

knob *noun* **1** the round handle of a door or drawer. **2** a round projecting part. **3** a small lump. **knobbly** *adjective*, **knobby** *adjective*

knock[1] *verb* **1** hit a thing hard or so as to make a noise. **2** produce by hitting, *knock a hole in it.* **3** (*informal*) criticise unfavourably, *Stop knocking Britain!*
knock back (*informal*) **1** eat or drink, especially quickly. **2** refuse.
knock down 1 strike to the ground. **2** demolish. **3** lower the price of.
knock off 1 (*informal*) stop working. **2** deduct something from a price. **3** (*informal*) steal.
knock out make a person unconscious, especially by a blow to the head.

knock[2] *noun* the act or sound of knocking.

knocker *noun* a hinged metal device for knocking on a door.

knockout *noun* **1** knocking somebody out. **2** a contest in which the loser in each round has to drop out. **3** (*informal*) an amazing person or thing.

knoll *noun* a small round hill; a mound.

knot[1] *noun* **1** a fastening made by looping a piece of string, rope, or something similar on itself and tightening it. **2** a tangle; a lump. **3** a round spot on a piece of wood where a branch joined it. **4** a cluster of people or things. **5** a unit for measuring the speed of ships and aircraft, 1,852 metres per hour.
knotty *adjective*

knot[2] *verb* (**knotted, knotting**) **1** tie or fasten with a knot. **2** entangle.

knotty *adjective* (**knottier, knottiest**) **1** full of knots. **2** puzzling, *a knotty problem.*

know *verb* (**knew, known, knowing**) **1** have something in your mind that you have learned or discovered, *I know a lot about dinosaurs.* **2** recognise or be familiar with a person or place, *I've known him for years.* **3** understand, *She knows how to please us.*

know-all *noun* a person who behaves as if they know everything.

know-how *noun* skill; ability for a particular job.

knowing *adjective* showing that you know something, *a knowing look.*

knowingly *adverb* **1** in a knowing way. **2** deliberately.

knowledgeable *adjective* (also **knowledgable**) well-informed.
knowledgeably *adverb*

knowledge *noun* **1** knowing. **2** all that a person knows. **3** all that is known.
to my knowledge as far as I know.

knuckle[1] *noun* a joint in the finger.

knuckle[2] *verb* (**knuckled, knuckling**)
knuckle down start working hard.
knuckle under be submissive.

koala (*say* koh-**ah**-luh) *noun* a furry Australian marsupial that lives and feeds in certain eucalypts. [from Sydney language *gula, gulawany*]

kofta (*say* **kof**-tuh) *noun* a savoury ball of minced meat, paneer, or vegetables. [from Urdu and Persian *koftah* = pounded meat]

kookaburra *noun* a large Australian kingfisher with a cry resembling laughter. [from Wiradjuri and nearby languages *gugubarra*, an imitation of the bird call]

Koori *noun* (*Australian*) an Aboriginal person, especially from New South Wales or Victoria. [from Awabakal and other languages *gurri* = man, person]

Koran (*say* kaw-**rahn**) *noun* (also **Quran**) the sacred book of Islam, written in Arabic, believed by Muslims to contain the words of Allah revealed to the prophet Muhammad. [from Arabic *kur'an* = reading]

korma (*say* **kaw**-muh) *noun* a richly spiced Indian dish of meat or fish cooked in yoghurt or curds.

kosher *adjective* keeping to Jewish laws about food, *kosher meat.* [from Hebrew *kasher* = proper]

kowari *noun* a small carnivorous marsupial of inland Australia. [from Dieri *kawiri*]

kowtow *verb* behave with exaggerated respect towards a person. [the *kowtow* was a former Chinese custom of touching the ground with the forehead as a sign of respect or submission]

kransky *noun* (*Australian*) a smoked pork and veal sausage.

kremlin *noun* a citadel in a Russian city. [from Russian *kreml*]

krill *noun* a mass of tiny shrimp-like creatures, the chief food of certain whales. [from Norwegian, = tiny fish]

kudos (*say* **kyoo**-dos) *noun* honour and glory. [from Greek]

kumanjayi (*say* koo-man-**juy**-ee) *noun* (*Australian*) (with many spelling and pronunciation variants) (in traditional Aboriginal society) a substitute name for a person who has recently died. [Western Desert Language]

kung fu *noun* a Chinese method of self-defence, rather like karate.

kurrajong *noun* an Australian evergreen tree with cream and red flowers. [from Sydney language *garrajung* referring to 'fishing line' made from the fibre of this tree]

kylie *noun* (*Australian*) a boomerang. [from Noongar and other languages *garli*]

Grammar and reference guide

Contents

Grammar

Grammar refers to the ways we combine words in phrases, clauses and sentences and organise them in texts. We do this according to conventions that have developed over time that are generally accepted and used. Grammar also refers to the ways we describe how language works as a system.
The language we use to discuss language, its conventions and their use is called metalanguage.

Parts of speech

Each word in a sentence has a job to do and its function is called its part of speech. There are eight parts of speech: nouns, pronouns, adjectives, verbs, adverbs, prepositions, conjunctions, and interjections. Each one is used to *do* different things in a sentence.
We need to see a word in a phrase or clause before we can identify what part of speech it is. The same word can be a different part of speech depending on its relationship to the other words.

water

We need to save **water**. (noun)

We **water** the garden twice a week in summer. (verb)

Nouns

Nouns are words that represent people, creatures, places, things, qualities, feelings, and ideas.

scientist, elephant, lake, monitor, courage, pride, equality

To check if a word in a sentence is a noun, see if it answers the question Who? or What?

Fran plays the **flute**. (Who plays? 'Fran') (Fran plays what? 'the flute')

There are different types of nouns:
Proper nouns usually begin with a capital letter as they specifically name a particular person, place, or thing.

Tom, Mount Everest, Logie

Common nouns do not begin with a capital letter (unless they begin a sentence). They refer to people or things that can be counted

boy, mountain, award

and things that cannot be counted.

air, rice, traffic

Most common nouns are concrete as they name something that we can see, hear, smell, taste or touch.

river, whistle, rose, pineapple, fur

Some common nouns are abstract as they name something we cannot understand with our senses.

love, respect, democracy, talent

Abstract modal nouns can also express judgements about the likelihood of events.

possibility, probability, certainty

Collective nouns name groups of people, animals, or things.

team, flock, bunch

Compound nouns are formed by combining two nouns into one word.

rain/coat, hair/style, foot/ball, house/boat

Noun groups

Noun groups are groups of words that build on a noun and usually consist of an article, one or more adjectives, and a noun.

a simple solution

the economic and social conditions

Nominalisation

To nominalise an adjective or verb is to change it into a noun. A noun can be formed from a verb by adding a suffix such as '-ing', '-ation', '-ance', '-ment' or '-ness'.

argue (verb) argument (noun)
ignore (verb) ignorance (noun)
emit (verb) emission (noun)

A noun can similarly be formed from an adjective.

stagnant (adj) stagnation (noun)
polite (adj) politeness (noun)

Nominalisation can allow complex ideas to be conveyed compactly.

Australia agrees to carbon emission targets

is more concise than

Australia agrees to set targets for how much carbon can be emitted.

Articles

Nouns are often preceded by 'the', 'a' or 'an', known as articles.
'The' is the definite article as it introduces a particular noun.

The car collided with **the** pole.

'A' (or 'an' if the noun begins with a vowel) is an indefinite article as it introduces a general noun.

A car is **an** expensive purchase.

Pronouns

Pronouns help avoid repetition by replacing nouns that have already been mentioned.

The tourists hired a guide. The guide showed the tourists around the town.

The tourists hired a guide. **She** showed **them** around the town.

The tourists hired a guide **who** showed **them** around the town.

Because they replace nouns, pronouns also answer Who?, Whom? or What?

Aunt Mary gave **me** a present. **She** said I would treasure **it**.

(To whom did Aunt Mary give a present? 'me')
(Who said? 'She')
(She said who would treasure it? 'I')
(What would I treasure? 'it')

The noun that the pronoun stands in for is called the antecedent (meaning the word that comes before). It is important that it is clear which noun the pronoun is replacing.

Fran told Gemma **she** had won the competition. (Who has won it?)

Fran boasted to Gemma that **she** had won the competition. (Now it is clear.)

There are several types of pronouns.
Personal pronouns stand in for nouns that name people or things.

I, we, me, us, you, he, she, her, him, it, they, them

He asked **her** if **she** would help **him** move the couch.

She said **she** would be happy to help **him** move **it**.

Possessive pronouns show that someone owns something.

mine, ours, yours, his, hers, its, theirs

The couch was **his**. It was heavier than **hers**.

Reflexive pronouns refer to a noun or pronoun earlier in the sentence.

myself, ourselves, yourself, yourselves, itself, herself, himself, themselves

Sam taught **himself** to play chess.

I see **myself** as a comedian.

With personal, possessive, and reflexive pronouns, we can use the first, second, or third person.

First: **I, me, us, mine, ours, myself, ourselves** (the person or persons speaking)

Second: **you, yours, yourself, yourselves** (the person or persons spoken to)

Third person: **he, she, it, they, them, his, hers, theirs, himself, herself, itself, themselves** (the person or persons spoken about)

I told **you** about **him**.

The cake is **mine**. That biscuit is **yours** and someone has eaten **hers**.

We must save **ourselves** from starvation.

You can help **yourself** to another biscuit.

The kitten gave **itself** a fright.

Relative pronouns relate one part of a sentence to another (a dependent clause to an independent clause).

who, whom, whose, which, what

She was the woman **who** spoke to me.

I addressed the letter to **whom** it may concern.

Whose is this jumper?

He repeated the joke, **which** I didn't think was funny.

The team **that** wins today goes into the final.

Demonstrative pronouns point to someone or something.

this, that, these, those

'This' and 'these' refer to things close in time and/or place. 'That' and 'those' refer to things further away in time and place.

This is my first job.

These are my favourite shoes.

Who gave you **that**?

Those were the days.

Indefinite pronouns do not refer to anyone or anything in particular.

everyone, something, anybody, each, some, many, all, several

Everyone is coming to the party.

Something is wrong with this situation.

Anybody can enter the competition.

Each of you deserves an award.

Some of the money is missing.

Many of my friends play cricket.

All of the cake was eaten.

I had heard **several** of the songs before.

Adjectives

Adjectives modify (give additional information about) nouns.
Usually an adjective precedes the noun that it modifies.

I watched the **happy** children.

She is an **energetic** child.

I bought a pair of **brown** shoelaces.

Sometimes an adjective follows a verb and modifies the subject of the verb.

The children seemed **happy**.

The child is **energetic**.

My shoelaces are **brown**.

Comparison of adjectives

Most adjectives can be used in one of three different forms.
Positive degree (no comparison made):

Sam is a **tall** girl.

Comparative degree (two people or things compared):

Sam is **taller** than her mother.

Superlative (more than two people or things compared):

Sam is the **tallest** person in her family.

If an adjective is a long word, 'more' or 'most', 'less' or 'least' is used.

My sport is **more dangerous** than yours.

My sport is the **most dangerous** of all.

These shoes are **less expensive** than those ones.

This pair is the **least expensive** of all the shoes in the shop.

Some adjectives are irregular and take different forms.

good, better, best

My brother is a **good** athlete.

My sister is a **better** athlete than he is.

I am the **best** athlete in the family.

bad, worse, worst

This medicine tastes **bad**.

My test result was **worse** than yours.

This is the **worst** day of my life.

Compound adjectives

Two or more words can be joined together to form an adjective. Sometimes the words are joined by hyphens.

We booked into a **five-star** hotel.

Our house is a **smoke-free** zone.

The plane was hit by a **surface-to-air** missile.

Sometimes they become one word.

There was **widespread** damage after the cyclone.

Some slang expressions are **overused**.

The steak was **underdone**.

Modal adjectives express judgements about the likelihood of events.

It is **possible** that John will win the competition.

They were **certain** they would finish the job.

Adjective groups

An adjective group is a group of words that are based on an adjective.

disgustingly dirty

frequently outrageously rude

Verbs

A verb is the most important word in a sentence. Each sentence must contain at least one verb. A verb says something about a subject by expressing an action or a state of being.

She **swam** across the pool. (The subject 'she' is performing an action.)

I **understand** grammar now. (The subject 'I' is performing a mental action.)

He **is** a pianist. (The subject 'he' is a pianist.)

My mum **stays** calm in a crisis. (The subject 'my mum' is in a calm state.)

The form of a verb indicates the time an action or a state of being takes place. We call this aspect of a verb its tense.
Simple tenses show whether the action (or state of being) is in the present, past, or future.

I **write** in my diary every day. (simple present tense)

I **wrote** a story last week. (simple past tense)

Auxiliary (or helping) verbs such as am, have, had, has, is, are, was, were and will are used to form some tenses. They add information about when an action happened, whether it has been completed or not, and about whether or not it happened.

I **will write** a poem next week. (future tense, formed by using the auxiliary verb 'will')

I **was writing** a poem. (past tense, formed by using the auxiliary verb 'was')

Modal auxiliary verbs such as can, could, may, might, must, will, would, shall and should are used to express judgements about the likelihood of events.

I **might** go skating tonight.

I **may** visit my Grandma.

Modal verbs are also used to express a degree of obligation.

I **must** visit my Grandma.

Verb groups

Verb groups are groups of words consisting of a verb, often supported by an auxiliary verb or modal verb.

We **were not participating** in the quiz.

We **could have won** the quiz.

Another aspect of a verb is whether it is in the active or passive voice.

Active voice

A verb is described as active if the subject is doing the action of the verb.

The dog **killed** the snake. (The dog is performing the action of killing the snake.)

My brother **kicked** the winning goal.

Passive voice

A verb is described as passive if the subject is receiving the action. Using the passive voice puts the focus on an action, rather than who or what is performing the action.

The snake **was killed** by the dog. (The snake is being killed.)

The winning goal **was kicked** by my brother.

The active voice is more direct and identifies the person performing the action with the action. The passive voice allows us to distance ourselves: 'It was decided that Jake would be dropped from the team' avoids mentioning who decided to drop Jake (The captain decided to drop Jake from the team).

Verb / subject agreement

Another aspect of a verb is agreement with its subject. This means that if a subject is singular, the verb must be singular; if the subject is plural, the verb must be plural.

My brother **plays** football. (singular noun 'brother' takes a singular verb)

His friends **play** football. (plural noun 'friends' takes a plural verb)

A collective noun usually takes a singular verb as it names a group.

His football team **is** at the top of the ladder. (The collective noun 'team' takes the singular verb 'is'.)

The fleet of ships **sails** out of the harbour. (The collective noun 'fleet' takes the singular verb 'sails'.)

When an indefinite pronoun is the subject of a verb, it must agree in number.

Everyone **needs** love. (singular subject 'everyone' takes the singular verb 'needs')

Something **is** out there. (singular subject 'something' takes the singular verb 'is')

Both of my parents **are** Italian. (plural subject 'both' takes the plural verb 'are')

Some of my friends **are** Italian. (plural subject 'some' takes the plural verb 'are')

Adverbs

Adverbs modify (add to the meaning of) verbs. They tell us how, when, where, or how often something happens.

He spoke **clearly**. (How did he speak?)

I started a new job **yesterday**. (When did I start the new job?)

Jim rides his bike **everywhere**. (Where does Jim ride his bike?)

Fran **sometimes** walks to work. (How often does Fran walk to work?)

They can also add to the meaning of adjectives and other adverbs.

That was a **very** boring film. (How boring was the film?)

I eat my food **too** quickly. (How quickly do I eat my food?)

Like adjectives, many adverbs can be used in three different forms.

Positive degree (no comparison):

It is raining **heavily**.

Comparative degree (two people or things compared):

It rained **more heavily** last week.

Superlative (more than two people or things compared):

It rained **most heavily** in June.

Some adverbs are irregular and take different forms.

well, better, best

Sam spoke **well**.

Peter spoke **better** than she did.

Susan spoke the **best** of all.

badly, worse, worst

Sam performed **badly** in the test.

Peter performed **worse** than Sam did.

Susan performed the **worst** of all.

Modal adverbs express judgements about the likelihood of events.

I will **probably** go tomorrow. (probability)

Perhaps it will rain. (possibility)

He will **definitely** be in the school play. (certainty)

Adverb groups

An adverb group is a group of words that are based on an adverb.

It was over **too quickly**. (**too** and **quickly** are adverbs that make up an adverb group.)

Adverbials

An adverbial contributes either additional information to a clause, or information about where or when something takes place, or how. An adverbial can also be used to show how someone feels or acts. An adverb or adverb group can function as an adverbial in a clause.

He made his point **succinctly.**

Personally, I think it was all over **too quickly**.

A prepositional phrase, noun or noun group can also function as an adverbial in a clause.

Jane was misbehaving **in class**. (The prepositional phrase 'in class' adds information about where Jane was misbehaving and functions as an adverbial in this sentence.)

Prepositions

Prepositions indicate the position of something, expressing a relationship between people and things in time or space. Prepositions are usually positioned before a noun or pronoun. ('Pre' means 'before'.) Common prepositions include:

above, across, against, among, at, before, below, beside, beyond, down, during, for, from, in, inside, near, of, off, on, opposite, over, through, towards

Prepositions are sometimes made up of several words, such as:

owing to, next to, because of, in accordance with

Particular prepositions and words are put together according to conventions that have developed over time.

belief **in, in comparison with,** inferior **to**

Conjunctions

Conjunctions join words, clauses or phrases and show how they are related, such as through contrast (although, but), causation (because, since) or addition (and). There are two main types of conjunction.

Coordinating conjunctions

Coordinating conjunctions link words, clauses or phrases of equal status. They include:

and, but, so, yet, or, nor, for, either, neither, then

My cat **and** my dog are great friends. (The conjunction 'and' joins the nouns 'cat' and 'dog'.)

I ran down the stairs **and** out the door. (The conjunction 'and' joins the prepositional phrases 'down the stairs' and 'out the door'.)

I prepared well for the test, **but** I still found it difficult. (The conjunction 'but' joins the independent clauses 'I prepared well for the test' and 'I still found it difficult'.)

Although coordinating conjunctions are usually used to connect clauses, they are sometimes used at the beginning of a sentence for effect.

But what about me?

Subordinating conjunctions

Subordinating conjunctions link dependent clauses to independent clauses. They begin a dependent clause (a clause that is dependent on an independent clause for complete meaning).

I will speak to you **after** you have eaten your dinner. (The subordinating conjunction 'after' begins the dependent clause 'after you have eaten your dinner' and links it to the independent clause 'I will speak to you'.)

Other subordinating conjunctions include:

that, whether, before, when, until, unless, although, where, since, while, because, if, whereas, than

I know **that** I am going.

Eat your dinner **before** it gets cold.

When I was your age, my father made me eat my dinner.

I would have to sit at the table **until** I had eaten all my vegetables.

Interjections

Interjections are words or phrases that express emotions (such as surprise, delight, pain).

What?

Wow!

Ouch!

They can also act as 'fillers' that could easily be taken out of a sentence.

Oh, I don't know about that.

You win, **okay**.

It was, **you know**, just a joke.

Well, I didn't mean it.

Sentences

A sentence is a group of words consisting of one or more clauses that expresses a complete thought. A sentence begins with a capital letter and ends with a full stop, question mark, or exclamation mark. Sentences have several purposes; they can:

Make a statement (ends with a full stop):

The dog barks all night.

Ask a question (ends with a question mark):

Is the dog still barking?

Give a command (ends with a full stop):

Stop the dog from barking.

Voice an exclamation (ends with an exclamation mark):

What a loud bark!

Each sentence consists of two parts: a subject and a predicate. Every word belongs either to the subject or to the predicate.
The subject is the person or thing the sentence is about. It will usually be a noun, noun group or pronoun and go before the verb. To find the subject in a sentence, ask Who? or What? is doing the action stated by the verb.

The dog barks all night. (Who barks all night? The dog.)

The predicate is what is said about the subject. The most important part of the predicate is the verb. (The predicate is 'barks all night'; the verb is 'barks'.)
A subject can consist of more than one noun or pronoun.

My aunt and uncle are coming for a holiday.

A predicate can contain more than one verb.

My relatives **live and work interstate**.

Sometimes the subject is not at the start of a sentence, as in a question or instruction.

Is the dog still barking? (Who is still barking? 'the dog'.)

Another way to find the subject and predicate is to re-order the words as a statement.

The dog is still barking. ('The dog' is the subject, 'is still barking' is the predicate.)

Stop the dog from barking. (The subject is the unstated 'you', as in 'You stop the dog from barking'.)

Types of sentences

Several common structures are used when combining words in sentences.
A simple sentence has a single independent clause that includes a subject and a verb. It expresses a complete thought.

I was late.

A compound sentence has two or more independent clauses usually linked by a coordinating conjunction. Each clause is equally important.

The train was late, **so** I was late for school.

I was late for my first class, **but** the teacher accepted my excuse.

A complex sentence has an independent clause and one or more dependent clauses. The dependent and independent clauses are linked by a subordinating conjunction.

I will get into trouble [independent clause] if [subordinating conjunction] I am late again [dependent clause].

The order of independent and dependent clauses in a sentence can often be changed.

If I am late again, I will get into trouble.

Clauses

A clause is a group of words that contains a subject and a verb. All sentences must have an independent clause. In compound and complex sentences, independent and dependent clauses are combined in different ways.

Independent (or main) clause

An independent clause makes sense on its own, so it can be a sentence.

The school was closed.

If there is more than one independent clause in a sentence, they are joined by a coordinating conjunction.

The school was closed, **so** we went home.

Dependent (or subordinate) clause

A dependent clause adds meaning to an independent clause, but does not make complete sense on its own. A dependent clause must be added to an independent clause, usually by a subordinating conjunction or a relative pronoun.

Because the signals had failed. (This dependent clause beginning with the subordinating conjunction 'because' does not make sense on its own.)

The train was late because the signals had failed. (Now the sentence is complete.)

Who loves chocolate. (This dependent clause beginning with the relative pronoun 'who' does not make sense on its own.)

I am a person who loves chocolate. (Now the sentence is complete.)

A dependent clause can also be introduced by a non-finite verb, such as 'going', 'thinking', 'skating'.

Skating in the park, (The dependent clause beginning with the non-finite verb 'skating' does not make sense on its own)

Skating in the park, I felt both free and afraid. (Now the sentence is complete).

A dependent clause functions as a single part of speech (a noun, an adjective, or an adverb).

A noun clause can be the subject or object of another clause.

I know **that you lied.** (The clause 'that you lied' functions as a **noun**, telling us what I know.)

An adjectival clause adds information about a noun or noun group and often begins with a relative pronoun 'who', 'whom', 'whose', 'which', 'that'.

We took the road **that follows the coast**. (The dependent clause 'that follows the coast' functions as an **adjective**, modifying the noun 'road'.)

An adverbial clause is a dependent clause that provides additional information about time, place, condition, concession, reason, purpose, or result.

We lost the match **because we lacked experience**. (The dependent clause 'because we lacked experience' functions as an **adverb**, modifying the verb 'lost'.)

While most clauses have a verb, verbless clauses are sometimes used for effect.

What a legend! [verbless clause]

An embedded clause is inserted within another clause to add information.

The student, **who came in late,** [embedded clause] was embarrassed.

Phrases

A phrase is a group of words that does not contain a subject and verb. It cannot make sense on its own.

under the bridge
playing the piano
rushing down the stairs

exhausted by the climb

to keep fit

A phrase must be part of a clause.

He hid **under the bridge**.

Playing the piano is his favourite hobby.

Rushing down the stairs, the woman tripped and fell.

Exhausted by the climb, she decided not to go ahead.

I jog **to keep fit**.

As with clauses, phrases function as a single part of speech (nouns, adjectives, adverbs, or prepositions).

I met my friends — **James, Kate and Gino** — and then we had lunch. (The phrase 'James, Kate and Gino' functions as a **noun** because it tells us who the friends are.)

That woman **wearing dark glasses** could be a spy. (The phrase 'wearing dark glasses' functions as an **adjective** because it modifies the noun 'woman'.)

I will meet you **at nine o'clock**. (The phrase 'at nine o'clock' functions as an **adverb** because it modifies the verb 'will meet'.)

She wore a coat **with a hood**. (The phrase 'with a hood' functions as a **preposition** because it tells us the relationship between the coat and the hood.)

Using phrases in a sentence is a useful way to cut down the number of words. A subordinate clause can be reduced to a phrase.

When you make a curry, you need special spices.

To make a curry, you need special spices.

Because I felt sleepy, I went to bed early.

Feeling sleepy, I went to bed early.

I kept the emails that my friend had sent me.

I kept the emails **sent by my friend**.

When you train a dog, you must have patience and skill.

Training dogs requires patience and skill.

Connectives

Connectives are words which signpost how clauses and sentences (and paragraphs) are related to each other. They can sequence ideas or events (firstly, secondly, meanwhile, later), show causes and results (because, consequently, since), add information (also, besides, in addition, furthermore), make comparisons (on the other hand, alternatively, despite this), make conditions or concessions (however, nevertheless, otherwise), and add clarity (for example, in fact).

Firstly, we need more exercise, and **secondly**, we need to eat fewer refined foods.

I am unfit **because** I've stopped training.

The driver was speeding and **also** driving an unregistered car.

The performance could be rescheduled for Monday night. **Alternatively**, it could be held at lunchtime on Tuesday.

Conjunctions function as connectives and are used to join ideas in a sentence.

I don't like eggs, **although** I eat them sometimes.

Using connectives helps give a text cohesion.

Punctuation

We use various punctuation marks to make the meaning of our written communication clear and to assist smooth reading by indicating where a reader should stop, slow down, or speed up.

When we barbecue our neighbour complains about the smoke. (No internal punctuation may make us think the neighbour is being barbecued.)

When we barbecue**,** our neighbour complains about the smoke. (Adding a comma after the dependent clause makes the meaning clear.)

Full stops, question marks, and exclamation marks are used to end sentences.

Full stops (.)

A full stop ends a sentence that is a statement, a command, or an indirect question.

The boat sank. (a statement)

Save the passengers. (a command)

I wonder why the boat sank. (an indirect question)

Question marks (?)

A question mark ends a sentence that is a direct question.

How did the boat sink?

Exclamation marks (!)

An exclamation mark ends a sentence or an interjection that expresses an emotion.

Look out!

Oh, no!

Commas (,)

A comma has many functions.

It precedes a coordinating conjunction joining independent clauses.

I look like my mum, **but** my sister looks more like dad.

It separates additional information included in a phrase, clause, or embedded clause from the rest of the sentence.

The parrot**, which we had only had a week,** fell off its perch.

Freda**, my friend from Sydney,** is coming to stay.

It separates items in a list. Usage varies as to the inclusion of a comma before and in the last item, but its presence often aids clarity.

I love **chocolate, licorice, and cashew nuts.**

The flowers are coloured **red, white, yellow, and blue**.

It separates an introductory word, phrase or dependent clause from the rest of the sentence.

No, you may not buy a puppy.

Laden with parcels, the woman staggered onto the train.

After we had eaten, the dog ate the leftovers.

It separates spoken words from unspoken words in dialogue.

> '**It began with a pain in my leg,**' said the patient, '**and then I developed an itch**.'

It separates the spoken words from the person being addressed.

> '**Doctor,** what should I do about the itch?'

Semicolons (;)

A semicolon usually separates independent clauses that express different ideas or information, but which are also closely connected.

> I was told one half of the story**;** the other half remained a mystery.
>
> The floorboards creaked**;** someone was coming.

Both of the above sentences could be separated by a full stop, but the semicolon strengthens the link between them.
It also separates items in a list if commas are used for other purposes in the sentence.

> Classic science fiction sagas are *Star Trek*, with Mr Spock and his large pointed ears**;** *Battlestar Galactica*, with its cylon raiders**;** and *Star Wars*, with Han Solo, Luke Skywalker, and Darth Vader.

Colons (:)

A colon introduces or announces something. It may be followed by a word, a phrase, or an independent clause.
A colon can introduce a list.

> Choose from the following flavours**: chocolate, mint, strawberry, or toffee.**

A colon is not needed if the list follows on from the previous word.

> I love chocolate, mint, strawberry, and toffee ice cream.

A colon can introduce more information about what precedes it. This may be a single word, a phrase, or an independent clause.

> There is one quality I lack**: modesty.**
>
> I have a new hobby**: collecting spiders.**
>
> The crops failed**: the drought had lasted ten years**.

A colon can introduce a quotation.

> The Prime Minister stated**: 'This country has never been so prosperous. We have eliminated poverty forever.'**

A colon is used after a character's name in a play script.

> TESS: What shall we do now?
>
> JAMES: Let's make a run for it.

A colon may also be used to indicate a subtitle.

> *Social Networking***:** *Youth and community in the 21st century.*

Apostrophes (')

An apostrophe has two purposes: to show ownership or a contraction of two words.
Possessives are used to show that a noun or pronoun owns or possesses something or someone.

> 'This is my **friend's** house.' (instead of 'the house of my friend')

The apostrophe is always placed after the owner's name.
If the noun is singular, add an apostrophe after the owner's name followed by an 's'.

> My **dog's** coat is curly.

If the singular owner's name ends in 's', add an 's'.

The **boss's** instructions are confusing.

Thomas's sister is an actor.

If the noun is plural, add an apostrophe after the 's'.

I was grateful for my **friends'** support.

The **dogs'** barking kept me awake.

If a plural noun does not end in 's', add the apostrophe and then an 's'.

The **children's** party was great fun.

I respect **people's** feelings.

If more than one person owns something, use an apostrophe in the last name only.

We went to **Beth and David's** wedding.

If each owns something separate, use an apostrophe for each owner.

Beth's and **David's** parents sat in the front row.

A possessive pronoun does not require an apostrophe as the word already shows possession.

Is this book yours? (no apostrophe needed)

Contractions are shortened forms of words used in informal texts. Apostrophes signal missing letters.

She's (She is) leaving tomorrow.

There's (There is) a sale on.

I'd (I had) tried my best to win the race.

We **should've** (should have) saved our money. (Note there is no such construction as 'should of'.)

It's (It is) going to be a great weekend. (Do not confuse it's with 'its' as in 'The cat licks its paws'.)

References to decades should not include an apostrophe as they are neither possessive nor contractions.

The band gained in popularity during the **1990s**.

Quotation marks (' ')

Direct (quoted) speech refers to the spoken words of someone.
Quotation marks or inverted commas are used to enclose the spoken words.

The woman said, **'I am knitting a jumper for my grandson.'**

Indirect speech refers to reporting what someone has said. There is no need for quotation marks.

The woman said that she was knitting a jumper for her grandson. (Note that the pronoun changes from 'I' to 'she', and the tense changes from the present 'am knitting' to the past 'was knitting'.)

When using direct speech, there are a few points to remember.
Punctuation that is part of the spoken words is placed inside the quotation marks.

'Mum!' shouted Dylan. **'Where is my skateboard?'**

'Dylan,' said his mother, **'it's where you left it.'**

Punctuation that is part of the sentence as a whole is placed outside the quotation marks.

Did Dylan's mother hear him shout **'Mum'**?

In dialogue, begin a new paragraph every time the speaker changes.

The teacher handed back the tests. 'I expected a better result,' she said. 'Did you study for the test?'

The student looked a little sheepish. 'A bit,' he said.

'It shows,' she said.

If a long speech or quotation covers more than one paragraph, open the quotation marks at the start of each paragraph, closing them only at the end of the last paragraph of the quotation.

If a speech contains other quoted words, use double quotation marks to distinguish them.

'I heard the woman say "Over my dead body" before she got off the tram.'

Use quotation marks to distinguish special words, phrases, or sentences from the writer's own words.

The teacher asked, **'What is the capital city of Thailand?'**

The judge described the building as a **'hovel'**.

My dad always calls me **'petal'**.

Use quotation marks to enclose titles of short works such as poems, short stories, essays, articles, songs, works of art, and radio and television programs.

I wrote a poem called **'View from my Window'**.

My dad loves the song **'Hey, Jude'** by the Beatles.

'Blue Poles' is a famous painting.

Hyphens (-)

Hyphens create words by joining two or more words together.
(Do not confuse hyphens with dashes, which are longer and have a different purpose.)
There is no space between the hyphen and the word or words it joins.

He is a **well-educated** person.

Use hyphens to form compound words (a word formed by joining two or more words). Not all compound words are hyphenated. The dictionary entry will show whether or not hyphens are necessary. Compound words often begin as two separate words. Over time they become hyphenated. Finally they close up.

table cloth

table-cloth

tablecloth

Compound nouns:

My dog Jessie is a **cross-breed**.

The **editor-in-chief** checked the final draft.

Compound adjectives:

I prefer **home-made** soup.

I owned a cat that was **cross-eyed**.

Compound verbs:

The counsel for the defence **cross-examined** the witness.

The shop **gift-wrapped** the parcel.

Use hyphens in numbers and fractions.

My grandmother is **ninety-one**.

Nine-tenths of those surveyed were overweight.

Use hyphens to join a prefix to a word. (Some prefixes do not require a hyphen.)

The patient had a **pre-existing** condition.

The **post-mortem** revealed that the death was suspicious.

My uncle is an **ex-army** officer.

He works for a **non-profit** organisation.

Use a hyphen if the word after the prefix begins with a capital or if figures are used.

The article was **anti-American**.

The **pre-Christian** era is fascinating.

Many migrants arrived in Australia **post-1945**.

Use a hyphen to make the meaning clear.

We had to **re-lay** the carpet after the storm.

Could you relay this message to the director?

He wanted to reform society.

Could we **re-form** the organisation?

There were twenty odd guests at the wedding; everyone else seemed normal.

There were **twenty-odd** guests at the wedding.

Use a hyphen if a vowel is doubled.

We managed to **re-establish** our garden after the drought.

The Historical Society **re-enacted** the battle.

Should we **re-elect** the government?

Note that it is common practice to remove the hyphen from some words.

Will you cooperate or do I have to force you?

I am the coordinator of the program.

Dashes (–)

Dashes have several uses. They are used in pairs unless a full stop, question mark, or exclamation mark ends what follows the dash.

Use dashes instead of a colon in informal texts to introduce a list or an explanation.

Mum says I have too many pets—rabbits, fish, finches, and a ferret.

The man was arrested—he had robbed the bank.

Use dashes to show a change of tone or thought.

The table goes in there—careful!

I bought a new outfit—I just couldn't help myself.

Use dashes instead of brackets or commas to enclose extra information, especially if commas are already present.

The three children—Amy, Tom, and Susan—were found safe and well.

This novel—the latest in the series—is her best.

Use a dash to show that a speaker has been interrupted.

'Come here at once or I'll—'

Round brackets ( ) (or parentheses)

These are always used in pairs. They enclose extra information. The sentence must still make sense without the information in the brackets.

Use brackets to enclose an example, a comment, or an explanation.

I love mystery novels (*The Case of the Missing Leg*, for example).

My grandmother has come to stay (not for too long, I hope), and I have to give up my room.

Your handwriting is illegible (probably through lack of practice), but your typing skills are excellent.

Note that because the information is usually about something mentioned before the first bracket, place any punctuation after the second bracket.

When I was younger (probably about the age of four), I fell off my bike and broke my collar bone.

If the material in brackets is a sentence, punctuate it appropriately.

Now I know about punctuation. (The mystery of the semicolon is solved.)

My mum caught me out. (How did she know I had a ferret in my room?)

It lurches towards me. (I think it's a dinosaur!)

Use brackets to enclose chapter or page numbers.

I particularly enjoyed the part about the crocodile hunt (chapter 7).

Read the second story (page 25).

Square brackets [ ]

Square brackets indicate that someone other than the writer has inserted them.

'He came from Perth [Scotland].' (The reader might not know which Perth the writer is referring to.)

'They [the gymnasts] won the international competition.'
(It may not be clear to the reader who 'they' refers to.)

'The possum fell down the chimley [chimney].' (The correct spelling is given.)

Angle brackets < >

Angle brackets are used to enclose letters, words, or figures. They are used especially to mark off a URL or an email address.

<http://www.anu.edu.au>

<jsmith@anu.edu.au>

Ellipsis points (...)

These are three full stops indicating that words have been left out.
Use them to show that part of a quotation is missing.

'There was movement at the station ... ' (the start of *The Man From Snowy River*)

Use them to show a break in thought or speech (especially in dialogue), or a trailing off at the end of a sentence.

'I don't know what to do ... Should I ask her out or not?'

'Let me tell you about my ...' 'Yes, fascinating I'm sure, but I'm in a hurry.'

The giant cockroach had something else in mind ...

Italics

This slanting typeface is used in printed material for particular purposes.
Use italics for titles of books, plays, musicals, films, newspapers, and magazines.

We are studying *Romeo and Juliet*.
Evita is a musical set in Argentina.
I had a letter published in *The Australian*.

Use italics for the names of ships, aircraft, or trains.

Many people sailed to the UK on the *Fairstar* in the 1960s.
We travelled to Darwin on *The Ghan*.

Use italics for emphasis.

I want to go *today*, not next week.

Use italics for the scientific names of plants and animals.

The red kangaroo, *Macropus rufus*, is native to Australia.

Abbreviations

An abbreviation is a shortened form of a word or words. They are useful in notes and other informal texts.

Abbreviations ending in the same letter as the full word do not need a full stop.

Qld (Queensland), **Cwlth** (Commonwealth), **dept** (department), **Dr** (Doctor), **Rd** (Road)

Abbreviations that do not end in the same letter as the full word need a full stop.

Cres. (Crescent), **Tues.** (Tuesday), **Oct.** (October), **adj.** (adjective)

Abbreviations consisting of the initial letters of each word do not require full stops.

VIP (very important person), **BA** (Bachelor of Arts), **PTO** (please turn over)

Abbreviations that are pronounced as a word are called acronyms.

ANZAC (Australian and New Zealand Army Corps)
EFTPOS (Electronic Funds Transfer at Point of Sale)

Some acronyms are written in lower case.

sonar (sound navigation and ranging)
laser (light amplification by stimulated emission of radiation)

Numbers

Numbers are expressed in figures or words depending on the type of writing and its context.

Use figures in mathematical, scientific, or technical texts.

Print the document and compare it to Figure **5.14** (Chapter **1**).

Use figures for sums of money, dates, addresses, times of day, and percentages.

$4.50, **21** September **2005**, **45** Flinders Street, **6.30** a.m., **99** per cent

Use figures for general texts for numbers over ninety-nine.

I have collected **400** stamps from all over the world.

Use words in general texts for numbers under 100 and for approximations. Always use words if the number begins a sentence.

There were **forty-six** guests at my party.
The snake was approximately **one** metre long.
Twenty-two people were at the auction.

Capital letters

Capital letters (also known as letters in the upper case) have several uses.
Use a capital letter to indicate the start of a sentence (including in direct speech).

Winter is nearly over.

He asked, 'Where are you going for your holidays?'

Use a capital letter to indicate a proper noun. Proper nouns are used to name days of the week, months of the year, holidays and special events, first names and surnames, titles, organisations, historical events, place names, street names, and titles of people, films, books, songs and plays.

My favourite uncle is **U**ncle **J**im, who is a **M**ember of **P**arliament.

In **M**arch we went to **D**reamworld on the **G**old **C**oast.

The worst day of the week is **M**onday, especially in summer.

I have just read a book about the **F**irst **W**orld **W**ar.

My dad recommended I read *The **C**all of the **W**ild*. (Capitalise only the main words of a title.)

Use a capital letter for adjectives formed from proper nouns.

Some people want to change the Australian flag.

Some Shakespearean language is difficult to understand.

Use a capital every time the pronoun 'I' is used.

Whenever I feel afraid, I whistle a happy tune.

Silent letters

Some words contain silent letters which cannot be sounded out. As you meet them, make a list and learn them off by heart.

aghast	honour	qualm
align	hymn	receipt
assign	indict	resign
asthma	irascible	rheumatism
autumn	knave	salmon
ballet	kneel	scintillate
benign	knowledge	scissors
campaign	malign	scythe
catalogue	mnemonic	subtle
condemn	mortgage	succumb
consign	muscle	sword
debt	phlegm	victuals
dialogue	plumber	vogue
epistle	pneumonia	wrangle
gnarled	psalm	wrath
gnaw	psychiatrist	wrench
guardian	psychology	wrinkle
heir	pterodactyl	

Spelling

Some useful rules

Making nouns plural

Normally just add -s:

skirts, socks, ties, pianos, pieces, stars.

But watch out for some words ending in -o, that need -es:

echoes, heroes, potatoes, tomatoes, volcanoes, etc.

To words ending in -ch, -s, -sh, -x, or -z, add -es:

dress — dresses, box — boxes, stitch — stitches.

In some words ending in -f and -fe, change to -ves:

scarf — scarves, life — lives, half — halves.

But watch out for the exceptions:

beliefs, proofs, roofs, etc.

In words ending in a consonant followed by -y, change the y to i and add -es:

copy — copies, cry — cries, party — parties.

Adding -ing and -ed to verbs

Normally just add -ing or -ed:

load — loading — loaded; open — opening — opened;
stay — staying — stayed.

For short words ending in -e, usually leave off the e:

race — raced — racing; blame — blamed — blaming.

For many short words that end with one consonant, double the last consonant:

slam — slamming — slammed; tip — tipping — tipped.

For longer words ending with one consonant and having the stress on the last syllable, double the last consonant:

compel — compelling — compelled; prefer — preferring — preferred.

For words ending in -y after a consonant, change the y to an i before -ed:

try — trying — tried.

For words ending in -ie, change the ie to y before adding -ing:

lie — lying — lied; tie — tying — tied.

Watch out for these exceptions:

lay — laid; pay — paid; say — said.

Adding -er and -est to adjectives

Normally just add -er and -est, unless the word already ends in -e:

cold — colder — coldest; wide — wider — widest.

For many short words that end with one consonant, change to a double consonant:

wet — wetter — wettest; dim — dimmer — dimmest.

If the word has two syllables and ends in -y, change the y to an i:

dirty — dirtier — dirtiest; happy — happier — happiest.

Adding -ly

Adding -ly to an adjective makes it into an adverb:

slowly, badly, awkwardly.

If the word ends in -ll, just add -y:

full — fully.

For words ending in -y and with more than one syllable, leave off the -y and add -ily:

happy — happily; hungry — hungrily.

For words ending in -le, leave off the e:

idle — idly; simple — simply.

For adjectives ending in -ic, you usually add -ally:

basic — basically; drastic — drastically.

But watch out for these special ones:

public — publicly.

Words that are easily confused

When using a spellchecker, remember to select the 'English (Australian)' dictionary option rather than the default 'English (US)' before you begin writing.

Spellcheckers will not pick up every mistake. For example, they will not indicate if you have used the incorrect version of many common homophones (words that sound the same but are spelled differently), such as 'there/they're/their', 'its/it's', or 'desert/dessert'.

These pairs of words can be confused. Check that you know their meaning.

affection/affectation
allowed/aloud
berth/birth
bored/board
bought/brought
brake/break
cell/sell
cereal/serial
check/cheque
coarse/course
complement/compliment
confirm/conform
contemptible/contemptuous
continual/continuous
councillor/counsellor
creak/creek
currant/current
desert/dessert
diseased/deceased
dyeing/dying
emaciated/emancipated
eminent/imminent
except/accept
formally/formerly
gamble/gambol
honourable/honorary
horde/hoard
inedible/indelible
know/no
know/now
lead/led
lightning/lightening
metre/meter
momentary/momentous
moral/morale
officious/official
perpetuate/perpetrate
persecute/prosecute
personal/personnel
piece/peace
plain/plane
political/politic
practise (verb)/practice (noun)
prey/pray
queue/cue
quite/quiet
recent/resent
respective/respectful
sceptic/septic
sealing/ceiling
seam/seem
site/sight
sole/soul
spacious/specious
stationary/stationery
straight/strait
successful/successive
superficial/superfluous
there/their/they're
threw/through
vocation/vacation
waist/waste
wet/whet
wrap/rap

When words sound alike, learn to use them in their correct context as their meaning will make their spelling clear.

The car stopped when I applied the brake. If I drop this glass it will break.
The food was inedible. She labelled her clothes with an indelible pen.

Some commonly misspelt words

accessible
accommodation
adjournment
administrative
admissible
affectation
aghast
alcoholism
align
allotted
ambiguous
annihilate
asthma
benign
bibliography
biographical
brigadier
bureaucracy
capricious
carnivorous
catalogue
chandelier
cheque
chlorinate
colloquial
condemn
confidence
confident
consign
dachshund
definitely
desiccated
dialogue
diesel
discernible
disobedient
drought
effervescent
enthusiasm
entrepreneurial
environmentalist
euthanasia
exception
familiarity
fluorescent
fraudulence
freight
fright
gaiety
genealogy
gnarled
gnawed
gracious
guarantee
guardian
gynaecologist
haemophiliac
haemorrhage
haemorrhoid
hearth
height
heterogeneous
hieroglyphic
hygiene
idiosyncrasy
ignominious
inadequacy
incoherent
indict
irascible
lascivious
liaison
lieutenant
ludicrous
luscious
malign
miscellaneous
mischievous
moratorium
muscle
noxious
numerous
oblique
occasion
oceanic
omitted
onomatopoeia
paradigm
paralleled
perceive
perspicacious
persuadable
pharmaceutical
phlegm
physically
piece
piteous
pneumonia
preferred
psychiatrist
qualm
quarantine
raucous
receive
reconnaissance
rescuing
resign
responsibly

rheumatism
ricochet
salmon
satisfactorily
sceptic
schism
scintillate
scissors
seize
separate
shield
straight
succumb
supersede
synonymous
technologically
thoroughfare
traumatic
ubiquitous
unequalled
vaccination
vaudeville
ventriloquism
vicissitude
vogue
weight
weird
wrangle
wrath
wrench
wrinkle
yacht

List of prefixes and suffixes

Prefixes

Prefixes are meaningful elements added to the beginning of a word. Most prefixes are of classical Greek or Latin origins. Attaching a prefix to a word changes the word's meaning.

a- not: atypical.

Anglo- English: Anglo-Celtic background.

ante- before: antenatal (= before birth).

anti- against: antisocial.

auto- self: autobiography (= the story of the writer's own life).

bi- two: bicycle, bilingual (= using two languages), bimonthly (= twice a month or every two months).

cent-, centi- hundred: centenary (= the hundredth anniversary), centimetre (= one hundredth of a metre).

circum- around: circumnavigate (= sail around).

co- with; together: copilot, coexist, cooperation.

con- (**col-**, **com-**) with; together: context (= the words or sentences that come before and after a particular word or sentence), collide, combine.

contra- against; opposite: contradict (= say the opposite).

counter- against; opposite: counter-revolution, counter-productive (= producing the opposite of the desired effect).

de- taking something away; the opposite: defrost, decentralise.

deci- one tenth: decilitre.

dis- reverse or opposite: displease, disembark, discomfort.

e- electronic: email.

Euro- European: Eurocentric.

ex- former: ex-wife, ex-president.

extra- 1 very; more than usual: extra-thin, extra-special. **2** outside; beyond: extraordinary, extra-terrestrial (= coming from somewhere beyond the earth).

fore- 1 before; in advance: foretell (= say what is going to happen), foreword (= at the beginning of a book). **2** front: foreground (= the front part of a picture), forehead.

in- (il-, im-, ir-) not: incorrect, invalid, illegal, illegible, immoral, impatient, impossible, irregular, irrelevant.

Indo- Indian: Indo-China.

inter- between; from one to another: international, interracial.

kilo- thousand: kilogram, kilowatt.

maxi- most; very large: maximum.

mega- million; very large: megabyte, megastar (= a very famous person).

micro- one millionth; very small: microgram, microorganism.

mid- in the middle of: mid-afternoon, mid-air.

milli- thousandth: milligram, millilitre.

mini- small: miniskirt, minibus.

mis- bad or wrong; not: misunderstand, misbehave, miscalculate.

mono- one; single: monolingual (= using one language), monorail.

multi- many: multinational (= involving many countries).

non- not: nonsense, non-resident, non-smoker.

out- more; to a greater degree: outdo, outrun (= run faster or better than somebody).

over- more than normal; too much: overeat, oversleep (= sleep too long), overestimate (= guess too high).

post- after: postwar.

pre- before: prepaid, preview.

pro- for; in favour of: pro-democracy.

quad- four: quadruple (= multiply by four), quadruplet (= one of four babies born at the same time to the same mother).

re- again: rewrite, rebuild.

semi- half: semicircle, semitrailer.

Sino- Chinese: Sino-Japanese.

sub- 1 below; less than: subzero, subsonic (= less than the speed of sound). **2** under: subway, subtitles (= translation under the pictures of a film).

super- extremely; more than: superhuman (= having greater power than humans normally have), supersonic (= faster than the speed of sound).

tele- far; over a long distance: telecommunications, television, telephoto lens.

trans- across; through: transatlantic, transcontinental.

tri- three: triangle, tricolour (= a flag with three colours).

ultra- extremely; beyond a certain limit: ultra-modern, ultraviolet (= light that is beyond what we can normally see).

un- not; opposite; taking something away: uncertain, uncomfortable, unsure, undo, undress.

uni- one; single: uniform (= having the same form).

Suffixes

Suffixes are meaningful elements added to the end of a word. Attaching a suffix to a word changes the word's meaning.

-able, -ible, -ble to make adjectives; possible to: acceptable, noticeable, convertible, divisible (= possible to divide), irresistible (= that you cannot resist).

-age to make nouns; a process or state: shortage, storage.

-al to make adjectives; connected with: experimental, accidental, environmental.

-ance, -ence (**-ancy, -ency**) to make nouns; an action, process or state: appearance, performance, elegance, importance, existence, intelligence, patience.

-ant, -ent to make nouns; a person who does something: assistant, immigrant, student.

-ation to make nouns; a state or action: examination, imagination, organisation.

-ble look at **-able**.

-ee to make nouns; a person to whom something is done: employee (= one who is employed), trainee (= one who is being trained).

-en to make verbs; to give something a particular quality; to make something more: shorten, widen, blacken, sharpen, loosen.

-ence (**-ency**) look at **-ance**.

-ent look at **-ant**.

-er to make nouns; a person who does something: rider, painter, baker, builder, driver, teacher.

-ese to make adjectives; from a place: Japanese, Chinese, Viennese.

-ess to make nouns; a woman who does something as a job: waitress, actress.

-ful to make adjectives; having a particular quality: helpful, useful, thankful, beautiful.

-hood to make nouns; a state, often during a particular period of time: childhood, motherhood.

-ian to make nouns; a person who does something as a job or hobby: historian, comedian, politician.

-ible look at **-able**.

-ical to make adjectives from nouns ending in -y or -ics; connected with: economical, mathematical, physical.

-ify to make verbs; to produce a state or quality: beautify, simplify, purify.

-ion to make nouns; a state or process: action, connection, exhibition.

-ise, -ize to make verbs; actions producing a particular state: magnetise, standardise, modernise, generalise.

-ish to make adjectives; **1** describing nationality or language: English, Swedish, Polish. **2** similar to something: babyish, foolish. **3** rather, quite: longish (= fairly long, but not very long), youngish, brownish.

-ist to make nouns; **1** a person who has studied something or does something as a job: artist, scientist, typist. **2** a person who believes in something or belongs to a particular group: capitalist, pacifist, feminist.

-ive to make adjectives; able to, having a particular quality: attractive, effective.

-less to make adjectives; not having something: hopeless, friendless.

-like to make adjectives; similar to: childlike.

-ly to make adverbs; in a particular way: badly, beautifully, completely.

-ment to make nouns; a state, action or quality: development, arrangement, excitement, achievement.

-ness to make nouns; a state or quality: kindness, sadness, happiness, weakness.

-ology to make nouns; the study of a subject: biology, psychology, zoology.

-or to make nouns; a person who does something, often as a job: actor, conductor, sailor.

-ous to make adjectives; having a particular quality: dangerous, religious, ambitious.

-ship to make nouns; showing status: friendship, membership, citizenship.

-wards to make adverbs; in a particular direction: backwards, upwards.

-wise to make adverbs; in a particular way: clockwise.

-y to make adjectives; having the quality of the thing mentioned: cloudy, rainy, fatty, thirsty, greeny (= similar to green).

L l

L *abbreviation* learner; a person learning to drive a car.

l *abbreviation* litre(s).

lab *noun* (*informal*) a laboratory.

label[1] *noun* a small piece of paper, cloth, or other material fixed on or beside an object and showing its nature, owner name, destination, or other information about it.

label[2] *verb* (**labelled, labelling**) put a label on something.

Labor *noun* the Australian Labor Party, a political party traditionally representing the interests of workers and, in its ideals, located to the left of the political spectrum.

laboratory *noun* (*plural* **laboratories**) a room or building equipped for scientific experiments. [same origin as *labour*]

laborious *adjective* **1** needing or using much hard work. **2** explaining something at great length and with obvious effort.
laboriously *adverb*

labour[1] *noun* **1** hard work. **2** a task. **3** the contractions of the womb when a baby is being born.

labour[2] *verb* **1** work hard. **2** explain something laboriously, *Don't labour the point.* [from Latin *labor* = toil]

labourer *noun* a person who does hard manual work, especially outdoors.

Labrador *noun* a large black or light brown dog. [named after Labrador, a district of Canada]

labyrinth *noun* a complicated arrangement of paths through which it is difficult to find one's way. **labyrinthine** *adjective*

lace[1] *noun* **1** net-like material with decorative patterns of holes in it. **2** a piece of thin cord or leather threaded through holes or hooks for pulling opposite edges together and securing them, *a shoelace.*

lace[2] *verb* (**laced, lacing**) **1** fasten with a lace. **2** thread a cord or similar material through something; intertwine. **3** add spirits to a drink.

lacerate *verb* (**lacerated, lacerating**) injure flesh by cutting or tearing it; wound.
laceration *noun*

lachrymal (*say* **lak**-ruh-muhl) *adjective* of tears; producing tears, *lachrymal ducts.* [from Latin *lacrima* = a tear]

lack[1] *noun* being without something.

lack[2] *verb* be without, *He lacks courage.*

lackadaisical *adjective* lacking vigour or determination; careless.

lackey *noun* (*plural* **lackeys**) **1** a footman; a servant. **2** a person who is too eager to serve or obey.

lacklustre *adjective* dull; lacking vitality.

laconic *adjective* terse, *a laconic reply.*
laconically *adverb*

lacquer *noun* a hard glossy varnish.
lacquered *adjective*

lacrosse *noun* a game using a stick with a net on it (a *crosse*) to catch and throw a ball. [from French *la crosse* = the crosse]

lactose *noun* a form of sugar found in milk.

lacy *adjective* of or like lace.

lad *noun* a boy; a youth.

ladder[1] *noun* **1** a set of horizontal bars (*rungs*) fixed between two uprights, used for climbing up or down. **2** a vertical strip of unravelled stitching in stockings or tights.

ladder[2] *verb* cause or have a ladder in stockings or tights.

laden *adjective* carrying a heavy load.

ladle[1] *noun* a large deep spoon with a long handle, used for lifting and pouring liquids.

ladle[2] *verb* (**ladled, ladling**) lift and pour with a ladle.

lady *noun* (*plural* **ladies**) **1** a well-mannered woman. **2** a woman of good social position. **3** (in polite use) a woman. **4** (**Lady**) the title of a noblewoman. **ladylike** *adjective*, **ladyship** *noun* [from Old English *hlæfdige* = a person who makes the bread (compare *lord*)]

ladybird *noun* a small flying beetle, usually red with black spots.

lag[1] *verb* (**lagged, lagging**) go too slowly and fail to keep up with others.

lag[2] *noun* lagging; a delay.

lag[3] *verb* (**lagged, lagging**) wrap pipes or boilers etc. in insulating material to keep them warm.

lag[4] *noun* (*Australian old use*) a convict, *an old lag.*

lager (*say* **lah**-guh) *noun* a light beer.

laggard *noun* a person who lags behind.

lagoon *noun* **1** a saltwater lake separated from the sea by sandbanks or reefs. **2** a freshwater lake near a larger lake or river. [from Latin *lacuna* = a pool]

laid *past tense & past participle* of **lay**[1].

laid-back *adjective* (*informal*) relaxed; easygoing.

lain *past participle* of **lie**[3].

lair[1] *noun* a sheltered place where a wild animal lives.

lair[2] *noun* (*Australian informal*) a flashy show-off. **lairy** *adjective*

laissez-faire (*say* la-say-**fair**) *noun* a government's policy of not interfering. [French, = let (them) act]

laity (*say* **lay**-uh-tee) *noun* laypeople, as distinct from the clergy.

lake *noun* a large area of water entirely surrounded by land.

laksa (*say* **luk**-suh) *noun* an Asian dish of rice noodles served in a spicy sauce or curry. [Malay]

lama *noun* a Buddhist priest or monk in Tibet and Mongolia. [from Tibetan *blama* = superior]

Lamarckism *noun* a theory of evolution based on the inheritance of acquired characteristics. [named after Jean Baptiste de Lamarck, French botanist and zoologist]

lamb *noun* **1** a young sheep. **2** meat from a lamb.

lambada *noun* a fast Brazilian dance in which couples dance with their stomachs touching each other. [from Portuguese, = a beating]

lame *adjective* **1** unable to walk normally. **2** weak; not convincing, *a lame excuse.* **lamely** *adverb*, **lameness** *noun*

lament[1] *noun* a statement, song, or poem expressing grief or regret.

lament[2] *verb* express grief or regret about something. **lamentation** *noun* [from Latin *lamentari* = weep]

lamentable (*say* **lam**-uhn-tuh-buhl) *adjective* regrettable; deplorable.

laminated *adjective* **1** made of layers joined together, *laminated glass.* **2** covered with a thin layer of plastic or similar material. [from Latin *lamina* = layer]

lamington *noun* (*Australian*) a block of sponge cake dipped in chocolate and coconut.

lamp *noun* a device for producing light from electricity, gas, or oil. **lamplight** *noun*, **lamppost** *noun*, **lampshade** *noun*

lampoon *noun* a piece of writing that ridicules a person. **lampoon** *verb*

lamprey *noun* (*plural* **lampreys**) a small eel-like water animal.

LAN *abbreviation* local area network.

lance[1] *noun* a long spear.

lance[2] *verb* (**lanced**, **lancing**) cut open with a surgeon's lancet.

lance corporal *noun* a soldier ranking between a private and a corporal.

lancet *noun* a pointed two-edged knife used by surgeons.

land[1] *noun* **1** the part of the earth's surface not covered by sea. **2** the ground or soil. **3** an area of country, *forest land.* **4** the area occupied by a nation; a country.

land[2] *verb* **1** arrive or put on land from a ship or aircraft. **2** reach the ground after jumping or falling. **3** bring a fish out of the water. **4** obtain, *She landed an excellent job.* **5** arrive or cause to arrive at a certain place or position, *They landed up in jail.* **6** present with a problem, *He landed me with this task.*

land council *noun* a group appointed to represent Aboriginal land interests.

landing *noun* **1** bringing or coming to land. **2** a place where people can land. **3** the level area at the top of the stairs.

landing stage *noun* a platform on which people and goods are landed from a boat.

landlady *noun* (*plural* **landladies**) a woman who rents a house or land to someone else, or lets rooms to lodgers.

landline *noun* a conventional telecommunications connection by cable laid across land.

landlocked *adjective* (of a country or region) surrounded by land.

landlord *noun* a person who rents a house or land to someone else, or lets rooms to lodgers.

landlubber *noun* (*informal*) a person unfamiliar with the sea or sailing.

landmark *noun* **1** an object that is easily seen in a landscape. **2** an important event in the history of something.

landowner *noun* a person who owns a large amount of land.

land rights *plural noun* the right of indigenous people to possess land they have traditionally occupied.

landscape *noun* the scenery or a picture of the countryside. (Compare **seascape**.)

landslide *noun* **1** a huge mass of soil and rocks sliding down a slope. **2** an overwhelming victory in an election.

landward *adjective & adverb* towards the land. **landwards** *adverb*

lane *noun* **1** a narrow road. **2** a strip of road for a single line of traffic. **3** a strip of track or water for one competitor in a race.

language *noun* **1** words and their use. **2** the words used in a particular country or by a particular group of people. [from Latin *lingua* = tongue]

languid *adjective* slow because of tiredness, weakness, or laziness. **languidly** *adverb*, **languor** *noun*

languish *verb* **1** become weak or listless and depressed; pine. **2** live in miserable conditions; be neglected.

La Niña (*say* lah **nee**-nyah) *noun* an irregular cooling of the surface waters of the central and eastern Pacific Ocean that has far-reaching effects on the weather. [Spanish = the (girl) child]

lank *adjective* long and limp, *lank hair.*

lanky *adjective* (**lankier**, **lankiest**) awkwardly thin and tall. **lankiness** *noun*

lanolin *noun* a kind of ointment, made of fat from sheep's wool.

lantana *noun* a plant with usually yellow and orange flowers that has become a weed in some parts of Australia.

lantern *noun* a transparent case for holding a light and shielding it from the wind.

lanyard *noun* a short cord for fastening or holding something.

lap[1] *noun* **1** the level place formed by the front of the legs above the knees when a person is sitting down. **2** a single circuit of a racetrack or one length of a swimming pool.

lap[2] *verb* (**lapped**, **lapping**) **1** fold or wrap round. **2** be a lap ahead of someone in a race.

lap[3] *verb* (**lapped**, **lapping**) **1** take up liquid by moving the tongue, as a cat does. **2** make a gentle splash against something, *Waves lapped the shore.*

lapel (*say* luh-**pel**) *noun* a flap folded back at the front edge of a coat or jacket. [from *lap*[1]]

lapidary (*say* **lap**-uh-duh-ree) *adjective* of stones; engraved on stone. [from Latin *lapis* = a stone]

lapis lazuli (*say* lap-uhs **laz**-yoo-lee) *noun* a bright blue semi-precious stone.

lapse[1] *noun* **1** a slight mistake or failure, *a lapse of memory.* **2** an amount of time elapsed, *after a lapse of six months.*

lapse[2] *verb* (**lapsed**, **lapsing**) **1** pass or slip gradually, *He lapsed into unconsciousness.* **2** be no longer valid, through not being renewed, *My insurance policy has lapsed.* [from Latin *lapsum* = slipped]

laptop *noun* a portable computer.

larceny *noun* stealing possessions.

larch *noun* (*plural* **larches**) a tall deciduous tree that bears small cones.

lard *noun* a white greasy substance prepared from pig fat and used in cooking.

larder *noun* a cupboard or small room for storing food.

large *adjective* of more than the ordinary or average size; big. **largeness** *noun*
at large 1 free to roam about; not captured, *The escaped prisoners are still at large.* **2** in general; as a whole, *She is respected by the country at large.*

largely *adverb* to a great extent, *You are largely responsible for the accident.*

largesse (*say* lah-***zh**es*) *noun* money or gifts generously given.

lark[1] *noun* a small sandy-brown bird; the skylark.

lark[2] *noun* (*informal*) something amusing; a bit of fun, *We did it for a lark.*

larrikin *noun* (*Australian*) **1** a person who is unsophisticated but likeable and good-hearted. **2** a person who acts with apparent disregard for social or political conventions. **3** (*old use*) a hooligan. [from British dialect, = mischievous youth]

larva *noun* (*plural* **larvae**) an insect in the first stage of its life, after it comes out of the egg. **larval** *adjective* [from Latin, = ghost, mask]

laryngitis *noun* inflammation of the larynx, causing hoarseness.

larynx (*say* **la**-rinks) *noun* (*plural* **larynxes**) the part of the throat that contains the vocal cords.

lasagne (*say* luh-**sahn**-yuh) *noun* **1** pasta formed into sheets. **2** a baked dish of this pasta layered with meat or vegetable sauce, and cheese. [Italian]

lascivious (*say* luh-**siv**-ee-uhs) *adjective* lustful. **lasciviously** *adverb*, **lasciviousness** *noun*

laser *noun* a device that makes a very strong narrow beam of light or other electromagnetic radiation. [from the initials of 'light amplification (by) stimulated emission (of) radiation']

lash[1] *noun* (*plural* **lashes**) **1** a stroke with a whip or stick. **2** the cord or cord-like part of a whip. **3** an eyelash.

lash[2] *verb* **1** strike with a whip; beat violently. **2** move like a whip. **3** tie with cord or rope, *Lash the sticks together.*
lash out 1 speak or hit out angrily. **2** spend money extravagantly.

lass *noun* (*plural* **lasses**) a girl or young woman.

lassitude *noun* tiredness; listlessness.

lasso[1] (*say* la-**soo**) *noun* (*plural* **lassos** or **lassoes**) a rope with a sliding noose at the end, used especially for catching cattle.

lasso[2] *verb* (**lassoed, lassoing**) catch with a lasso. [from Spanish *lazo* = lace]

last[1] *adjective & adverb* **1** coming after all others; final. **2** latest; most recent, *last night.* **3** least likely, *She is the last person I'd have chosen.*
the last straw a final thing that makes problems unbearable.

last[2] *noun* **1** a person or thing that is last. **2** the end, *He was brave to the last.*
at last or **at long last** finally; after much delay. [originally short for *latest*]

last[3] *verb* **1** continue; go on existing or living or being usable. **2** be enough for, *The food will last us for three days.*

last[4] *noun* a block of wood or metal shaped like a foot, used in making and repairing shoes.

lasting *adjective* able to last for a long time.

lastly *adverb* in the last place; finally.

latch[1] *noun* (*plural* **latches**) a small bar fastening a door or gate, lifted by a lever or spring. **latchkey** *noun*

latch[2] *verb* fasten with a latch.
latch on to (*informal*) **1** attach yourself to someone. **2** understand.

late *adjective & adverb* **1** after the usual or expected time. **2** near the end, *late in the afternoon.* **3** recent, *the latest news.* **4** who has died recently, *the late king.*
of late recently.

latecomer *noun* a person who arrives late.

lately *adverb* recently.

latent (*say* **lay**-tuhnt) *adjective* existing but not yet developed or active or visible, *latent talent.*

lateral *adjective* of, at, or towards the side or sides. **laterally** *adverb* [from Latin *lateris* = of a side]

latex *noun* **1** a milky fluid produced by certain plants, especially the rubber tree. **2** a synthetic product like this, used in paints, glues, and other materials. [Latin, = liquid]

lath *noun* a narrow thin strip of wood.

lathe (*say* lay*th*) *noun* a machine for holding and turning pieces of wood while they are being shaped.

lather[1] *noun* a mass of froth.

lather[2] *verb* **1** cover with lather. **2** form a lather.

Latin *noun* the language of the ancient Romans. [from *Latium*, an ancient district of Italy including Rome]

Latin America *noun* the parts of Central and South America where the main language is Spanish or Portuguese. **Latin American** *adjective & noun* [because these languages developed from Latin]

latitude *noun* **1** the distance of a place from the equator, measured in degrees. **2** freedom from restrictions on what people can do or believe. [from Latin, = breadth]

latrine (*say* luh-**treen**) *noun* a toilet, especially a communal one in a camp or barracks.

latte (*say* **lah**-tay) *noun* a type of coffee made with espresso and hot steamed milk. [from Italian (*caffe*) *latte* = milk (coffee)]

latter *adjective* later, *the latter part of the year.*
the latter the second of two people or things just mentioned. (Compare **former.**)

latterly *adverb* lately; recently.

lattice *noun* a framework of crossed bars or strips of wood with spaces between.

laud *verb* (*formal*) praise. **laudable** *adjective*, **laudably** *adverb* [from Latin *laudare* = to praise]

laugh[1] *verb* **1** make the sounds that show you think something is funny. **2** make fun of someone or something.

laugh[2] *noun* an act or sound of laughing.

laughable *adjective* deserving to be laughed at.

laughing stock *noun* a person or thing that people laugh at or make fun of.

laughter *noun* the act, sound, or manner of laughing.

launch[1] *verb* **1** send a ship from the land into the water. **2** set a thing moving by throwing or pushing it; send a rocket into space. **3** start into action, *launch an attack.*

launch[2] *noun* (*plural* **launches**) the launching of a ship or spacecraft.

launch[3] *noun* (*plural* **launches**) a large motor boat.

launder *verb* **1** wash and iron clothes or linen. **2** (*informal*) transfer funds to conceal their dubious or illegal origin.

laundrette *noun* a laundromat.

laundromat *noun* a place fitted with washing machines and driers that people pay to use.

laundry *noun* (*plural* **laundries**) **1** a room where you wash clothes or linen. **2** clothes or linen that have been or need to be washed. **3** a place where clothes or linen are washed and dried for customers.

laurel *noun* an evergreen shrub with smooth shiny leaves.
rest on your laurels be satisfied with what

you have done and stop striving for further successes. [because a wreath of laurels was worn in ancient times as a sign of victory]

lava *noun* molten rock that flows from a volcano; the solid rock formed when it cools.

lavash (*say* luh-**vahsh**) *noun* a soft thin flat bread originally from the Middle East.

lavatory *noun* (*plural* **lavatories**) a toilet. [from Latin *lavare* = to wash]

lavender *noun* **1** a shrub with sweet-smelling purple flowers. **2** a pale purple colour.

lavish[1] *adjective* **1** generous. **2** plentiful. **lavishly** *adverb*, **lavishness** *noun*

lavish[2] *verb* give generously, *They lavished praise upon him.* [from Old French *lavasse* = downpour of rain]

law *noun* **1** the system of rules that a particular country or community recognises as regulating the actions of its members and that it may enforce by the imposition of penalties; an individual rule as part of a system of law. **2** a scientific statement of something that always happens, *the law of gravity.* **3** (*Australian*) (in Aboriginal culture) the body of religious belief and the social customs arising from it.

law-abiding *adjective* obeying the law.

lawbreaker *noun* a person who breaks the law.

lawcourt *noun* a room or building in which a judge or magistrate hears evidence and decides whether someone has broken the law.

lawful *adjective* allowed or accepted by the law. **lawfully** *adverb*

lawless *adjective* **1** not obeying the law. **2** without proper laws, *a lawless country.* **lawlessly** *adverb*, **lawlessness** *noun*

lawman *noun* (*Australian*) (in Aboriginal culture) a person who is very knowledgeable in the law; a custodian of the law; a leader in ceremony.

lawn[1] *noun* an area of closely cut grass in a garden or park.

lawn[2] *noun* very fine cotton material.

lawnmower *noun* a machine for cutting the grass of lawns.

lawsuit *noun* a dispute or claim brought to a lawcourt for judgement.

law woman *noun* (*Australian*) (in Aboriginal culture) a woman who is very knowledgeable in the law; a custodian of the law; a leader in ceremony.

lawyer *noun* a person who is trained and qualified in matters of law.

lax *adjective* slack; not strict, *discipline was lax.* **laxity** *noun*, **laxly** *adverb* [from Latin *laxus* = loose]

laxative *noun* a medicine that stimulates the bowels to empty.

lay[1] *verb* (**laid, laying**) **1** put something down in a particular place or way. **2** arrange things, especially for a meal, *lay the table.* **3** place, *He laid the blame on his sister.* **4** prepare; arrange, *We laid our plans.* **5** produce an egg.
lay off 1 stop employing somebody for a while. **2** (*informal*) stop doing something.
lay on supply; provide.
lay out 1 arrange or prepare. **2** knock a person unconscious. **3** prepare a corpse for burial. [from Old English *lecgan*]

> **Usage** Do not confuse *lay/laid/laying* = 'put down', with *lie/lay/lain/lying* = 'be in a flat position'. Correct uses are as follows: *Go and lie down; she went and lay down; please lay it on the floor.* 'Go and lay down' is incorrect.

lay[2] *past tense* of **lie**[3].

lay[3] *noun* (*old use*) a poem meant to be sung; a ballad. [from Old French *lai*]

lay[4] *adjective* **1** not belonging to the clergy, *a lay preacher.* **2** not professionally qualified, *lay opinion.* [from Greek *laos* = people]

layabout *noun* a loafer; a person who lazily avoids working for a living.

lay-by *noun* (*plural* **lay-bys**) **1** (*Australian*) a way of reserving something in a shop by paying a deposit and instalments. **2** a place where vehicles can stop beside a main road.

layer *noun* a single thickness or coating.

layman *noun* (also **layperson**) a person who does not have specialised knowledge or training (e.g. as a doctor or lawyer), or who is not ordained as a member of the clergy. [from *lay*[4] + *man*]

layout *noun* **1** the way in which a thing or place is arranged or set out. **2** the way in which text or pictures are arranged on a page.

laze *verb* (**lazed, lazing**) spend time in a lazy way.

lazy *adjective* (**lazier, laziest**) not wanting to work; doing little work. **lazily** *adverb*, **laziness** *noun*

lazybones *noun* (*informal*) a lazy person.

lb *abbreviation* pound(s) (in weight). [from Latin *libra*]

lbw *abbreviation* leg before wicket.

LCD *abbreviation* **1** liquid crystal display. **2** lowest (or least) common denominator.

lea *noun* (*poetic*) a meadow.

leach *verb* remove soluble matter from the soil by the action of a liquid passing through it.

lead[1] (*say* leed) *verb* (**led, leading**) **1** take or guide, especially by going in front. **2** influence a person's actions or opinions. **3** be in charge of something. **4** be winning in a race or contest; be ahead. **5** be a way or route, *This path leads to the beach.* **6** play the first card in a card game. **7** live or experience, *He leads a dull life.*
lead on entice.
lead to have as a result, *Rushing leads to accidents.*

lead[2] (*say* leed) *noun* **1** the action of leading; guidance, *Give us a lead.* **2** a leading place or part or position, *She took the lead.* **3** a strap or cord for leading a dog or other animal. **4** an electrical wire attached to something.

lead[3] (*say* led) *noun* **1** a soft heavy grey metal. **2** the writing substance (graphite) in a pencil. **lead** *adjective*

leaden (*say* **led**-uhn) *adjective* **1** made of lead. **2** heavy and slow. **3** lead-coloured; dark grey, *leaden skies.*

leader *noun* a person or thing that leads; a chief. **leadership** *noun*

leaf *noun* (*plural* **leaves**) **1** a flat usually green part of a plant, growing out from its stem or a branch. **2** the paper forming one page of a book. **3** a very thin sheet of metal, *gold leaf.* **4** a flap that makes a table larger. **leafless** *adjective*, **leafy** *adjective*
turn over a new leaf make a fresh start and improve your behaviour.

leaflet *noun* **1** a piece of paper printed with information. **2** a small leaf.

league[1] *noun* **1** a group of people or nations who agree to work together. **2** a group of teams who compete against each other for a championship.
in league with working or plotting together.

league[2] *noun* an old measure of distance, about five kilometres.

leak[1] *noun* **1** a hole or crack through which liquid or gas can escape. **2** the revealing of secret information. **leaky** *adjective*

leak[2] *verb* **1** get out or let out through a leak. **2** reveal secret information. **leakage** *noun*

lean[1] *adjective* **1** with little or no fat, *lean meat.* **2** thin, *a lean body.*

lean[2] *verb* (**leaned** or **leant, leaning**) **1** bend your body towards or over something. **2** put or be in a sloping position. **3** rest against something.

leaning *noun* a tendency or preference.

lean-to *noun* a building with its roof leaning against the side of a larger building.

leap *verb* (**leaped** or **leapt, leaping**) jump vigorously. **leap** *noun*

leap-frog *noun* a game in which each player jumps with legs apart over another who is bending down.

leap year *noun* a year with an extra day in it (29 February), occurring every four years.

learn *verb* (**learned** or **learnt, learning**) **1** get knowledge or skill. **2** find out about something.

learned (*say* **ler**-nuhd) *adjective* having much knowledge obtained by study.

learner *noun* a person who is learning something, especially to drive a car.

learning *noun* knowledge obtained by study.

lease[1] *noun* an agreement to allow someone to use a building or land etc. for a fixed period in return for payment.
leaseholder *noun*

lease[2] *verb* (**leased, leasing**) allow or obtain the use of something by lease.

leash *noun* (*plural* **leashes**) a dog's lead.

least[1] *adjective & adverb* very small in extent or degree, *the least bit*; *the least expensive bike.*

least[2] *noun* the smallest in amount, extent, or significance.

leather *noun* material made from animal skins. **leathery** *adjective*

leatherjacket *noun* a sea fish with a tough skin.

leatherwood *noun* a Tasmanian tree with highly scented flowers from which bees make a distinctive honey.

leave[1] *verb* (**left, leaving**) **1** go away from a person or place. **2** stop belonging to a group or working for an employer. **3** cause or allow something to stay where it is or as it is, *You left the door open.* **4** go away without taking something, *I left my book at home.* **5** put something to be collected or passed on, *leave a message.* **6** give something to a person when you die.
leave off cease.
leave out omit; not include.

leave[2] *noun* **1** permission. **2** official permission to be away from work; the time for which this permission lasts.

leaven (*say* **lev**-uhn) *noun* a substance (e.g. yeast) used to make dough rise.

lechery *noun* excessive sexual desire.
lecherous *adjective*

lectern *noun* a stand to hold a Bible or other large book or notes for reading. [same origin as *lecture*]

lecture[1] *noun* **1** a talk about a subject to an audience or a class. **2** a long serious warning or rebuke.

lecture[2] *verb* (**lectured, lecturing**) give a lecture. **lecturer** *noun* [from Latin *lectum* = read]

LED *abbreviation* light-emitting diode, a semiconductor diode which glows when a voltage is applied.

led *past tense & past participle* of **lead**[1].

ledge *noun* a narrow shelf or similar projecting part.

ledger *noun* an account book.

lee *noun* the sheltered side or part of something, away from the wind.

leech *noun* (*plural* **leeches**) a small blood-sucking worm.

leek *noun* a long white vegetable of the onion family with broad green leaves.

leer *verb* look at someone in an insulting, sly, or unpleasant way. **leer** *noun*

leeward *adjective* on the lee side.

leeway *noun* **1** a drift to leeward or off course. **2** extra space or time available.

left[1] *adjective & adverb* **1** of or on or towards the side of the body that is on the west when you are facing north; on the same side as the heart is in the body. **2** (of political groups or ideas) left-wing.

left[2] *noun* the left side, part, or direction. [the word originally meant 'weak']

left[3] *past tense & past participle* of **leave**[1].

left field *noun* an unconventional or unusual position or experience, *The proposal came out of left field.*

left-handed *adjective* using the left hand in preference to the right hand.

leftovers *plural noun* food not eaten.

left-wing *adjective* socialist; radical; politically progressive.

leg *noun* **1** each of the projecting parts of a person's or animal's body, on which it stands or moves. **2** the part of a garment covering a leg. **3** each of the projecting supports of a chair or other piece of furniture. **4** one part of a journey. **5** one of a pair of matches between the same teams.

legacy *noun* (*plural* **legacies**) something left to a person in a will.

legal *adjective* **1** lawful. **2** of the law or lawyers. **legality** *noun*, **legally** *adverb* [from Latin *legis* = of a law]

legalise *verb* (**legalised, legalising**) make a thing legal. **legalisation** *noun*

legate *noun* an official representative, especially of the pope.

legato *adverb & adjective* (in music) in a smooth even manner. [Italian]

leg before wicket *adjective & adverb* (of a batter in cricket) out because of stopping the ball, other than with the bat or hand, which would otherwise have hit the wicket.

legend *noun* **1** a traditional story sometimes popularly regarded as historical but not authenticated. **2** an extremely famous or notorious person, especially in a particular field. **3** an inscription, especially on a coin or medal. **4** the wording on a map or diagram explaining the symbols used. **legendary** *adjective* [from Latin *legenda* = things to be read]

leggings *plural noun* **1** close-fitting stretch trousers. **2** protective outer coverings for each leg.

legible *adjective* clear enough to read. **legibility** *noun*, **legibly** *adverb* [from Latin *legere* = to read]

legion *noun* **1** a division of the ancient Roman army. **2** a group of soldiers or former soldiers.

legionnaires' disease *noun* a form of bacterial pneumonia.

legislate *verb* (**legislated, legislating**) make laws. **legislation** *noun*, **legislator** *noun* [from Latin *legis* = of a law, + *latio* = proposing]

legislative *adjective* making laws, *a legislative assembly.*

legislature *noun* a country's legislative assembly.

legitimate *adjective* **1** lawful. **2** born when parents are married to each other. **legitimacy** *noun*, **legitimately** *adverb*

legume (*say* **leg**-yoom) *noun* a plant of the family that bears seeds in pods, e.g. peas and beans. **leguminous** *adjective*

lei (*say* lay) *noun* a garland of flowers worn round the neck.

leisure *noun* time that is free from work, when you can do what you like. **leisured** *adjective*, **leisurely** *adjective*

at leisure having leisure; not hurried.

at your leisure when you have time.

leitmotif (*say* **luyt**-moh-teef) *noun* (also **leitmotiv**) a theme associated with a particular person or idea throughout a musical, literary, or cinematic work. [from German, = leading motive]

lemming *noun* a small mouse-like animal of Arctic regions that migrates in large numbers and is said to run headlong into the sea and drown.

lemon *noun* **1** an oval yellow citrus fruit with a sour taste. **2** a pale yellow colour.

lemonade *noun* a lemon-flavoured drink.

lemur (*say* **lee**-muh) *noun* a monkey-like animal.

lend *verb* (**lent, lending**) **1** allow a person to use something of yours for a short time. **2** provide someone with money that they must repay usually in return for payments (called *interest*). **lender** *noun*

lend a hand help somebody.

length *noun* **1** how long something is. **2** the amount of time that something takes or lasts. **3** a piece of cloth or other material from a larger piece. **4** the amount of thoroughness in an action, *They went to great lengths to make us comfortable.*
at length 1 after a long time. **2** taking a long time; in detail.

lengthen *verb* make or become longer.

lengthways *adverb* (also **lengthwise**) from end to end; along the longest part.

lengthy *adjective* very long; long and boring.
lengthily *adverb*

lenient (*say* **lee**-nee-uhnt) *adjective* merciful; not severe. **lenience** *noun*, **leniently** *adverb* [from Latin *lenis* = gentle]

lens *noun* (*plural* **lenses**) **1** a curved piece of glass or plastic used to focus things. **2** the transparent part of the eye, immediately behind the pupil.

Lent *noun* a time of fasting and penitence observed by Christians for about six weeks before Easter. **Lenten** *adjective*

lent *past tense & past participle* of **lend**.

lentil *noun* a kind of small bean.

Leo *noun* **1** a constellation and the fifth sign of the zodiac (the Lion). **2** a person born when the sun is in this sign. [Latin]

leopard (*say* **lep**-uhd) *noun* a large spotted wild animal of the cat family. Also called a *panther*. **leopardess** *noun*

leotard (*say* **lee**-uh-tahd) *noun* a close-fitting garment worn by acrobats and dancers.

leper *noun* a person who has leprosy.

leprechaun (*say* **lep**-ruh-kawn) *noun* (in Irish folklore) an elf who looks like a little old man. [from Irish, = a small body]

leprosy *noun* an infectious disease that makes parts of the body waste away.
leprous *adjective*

lesbian *noun* a homosexual woman.
lesbian *adjective*

lesion (*say* **lee**-*zh*uhn) *noun* an injury or wound.

less[1] *adjective & adverb* smaller in amount; not so much, *Make less noise; It is less important.*

> **Usage** In standard English *less* should only be used with uncountable things ('*less milk*'; '*less time*'). With countable things it is incorrect to use *less* ('*less people*' and '*less words*'); strictly speaking, the correct use is '*fewer people*' and '*fewer words*'. See also *few* (usage).

less[2] *noun* a smaller amount.

less[3] *preposition* minus; deducting, *She earned $300, less tax.*

lessen *verb* make or become less.

lesser *adjective* not so great as the other, *the lesser evil.*

lesson *noun* **1** an amount of teaching given at one time. **2** something to be learnt by a pupil. **3** an example or experience from which you should learn, *Let this be a lesson to you!* **4** a passage from the Bible read aloud as part of a church service.

lest *conjunction* so that something should not happen, *Remind us, lest we forget.*

let *verb* (**let**, **letting**) **1** allow to do something; not prevent; not forbid, *Let me see it.*
2 cause to, *Let us know what happens.*
3 allow or cause to come or go or pass, *Let me out!* **4** allow someone to use a house or building in return for payment (*rent*).
5 leave, *Let it alone.*
let down 1 deflate. **2** disappoint somebody.
let-down *noun*
let off 1 cause to explode. **2** excuse somebody from a duty or punishment.
let on (*informal*) reveal a secret.
let out 1 allow to go; set free. **2** make clothes looser by adjusting seams.
let up (*informal*) relax. **let-up** *noun*

lethal (*say* **lee**-thuhl) *adjective* deadly; causing death. **lethally** *adverb*

lethargy (*say* **leth**-uh-jee) *noun* extreme lack of energy or vitality; sluggishness. **lethargic** (*say* luh-**thah**-jik) *adjective*

let's let us, *Let's go to the park.*

letter *noun* **1** a symbol representing a sound used in speech. **2** a written message, usually sent by post. [from Latin *littera* = letter of the alphabet]

letter box *noun* a box into which letters are posted or delivered.

lettering *noun* letters drawn or painted.

lettuce *noun* a garden plant with broad crisp leaves eaten as salad.

leucocyte *noun* a white blood cell.

leucoplast *noun* an organelle found in plant cells, used for the storage of starch or oil.

leukaemia (*say* loo-**kee**-mee-uh) *noun* a disease in which there are too many white corpuscles in the blood. [from Greek *leukos* = white, + *haima* = blood]

levee (*say* **lev**-ee) *noun* an embankment built up naturally along a river, or constructed as a protection against floods.

level[1] *adjective* **1** flat; horizontal. **2** at the same height, position, rank, or class as others. **3** steady; uniform.

level[2] *noun* **1** height, depth, position, or value, *Fix the shelves at eye level.* **2** a level surface. **3** a device that shows whether something is level. **4** a floor of a multistorey

building or ship.
on the level (*informal*) honest.

level[3] *verb* (**levelled, levelling**) **1** make or become level. **2** aim a gun or missile. **3** direct an accusation at a person. **4** knock a building down to the ground. [from Latin *libra* = balance]

level crossing *noun* a place where a road crosses a railway at the same level.

lever[1] *noun* **1** a bar that turns on a fixed point (the *fulcrum*) in order to lift something or force something open. **2** a bar used as a handle to operate machinery, *a gear lever.*

lever[2] *verb* lift or move by means of a lever. [from Latin *levare* = raise]

leverage[1] *noun* **1** the action or power of a lever. **2** power, influence.

leverage[2] *verb* **1** use borrowed capital for (an investment), expecting the profits made to be greater than the interest payable. **2** use (something) to maximum advantage.

leveret *noun* a young hare.

levitation *noun* rising into the air and floating there.

levity *noun* being humorous, especially at an unsuitable time; frivolity. [from Latin *levis* = lightweight]

levy[1] *verb* (**levied, levying**) **1** impose or collect a tax or other payment by the use of authority or force. **2** enrol, *levy an army.*

levy[2] *noun* (*plural* **levies**) a fee or tax that must be paid.

lewd *adjective* indecent; obscene. **lewdly** *adverb*, **lewdness** *noun*

lexicography *noun* the process of writing dictionaries. **lexicographer** *noun* [from Greek *lexis* = word, + *-graphy*]

lexicon *noun* **1** a dictionary. **2** the vocabulary of a person, language, group, or branch of knowledge.

LGBTQIA *abbreviation* lesbian, gay, bisexual, transgender, queer (or questioning), intersex, and asexual (or allies).

liability *noun* (*plural* **liabilities**) **1** being liable. **2** a debt or obligation. **3** (*informal*) a disadvantage; a handicap.

liable *adjective* **1** likely to do or get something, *She is liable to colds; The cliff is liable to crumble.* **2** legally responsible for something.

liaise (*say* lee-**ayz**) *verb* (**liaised, liaising**) (*informal*) act as a link or go-between.

liaison (*say* lee-**ay**-zon) *noun* **1** communication and cooperation between people or groups. **2** a person who is a link or go-between. [from French *lier* = bind]

liar *noun* a person who tells lies.

libel[1] (*say* **luy**-buhl) *noun* an untrue written, printed, or broadcast statement that damages a person's reputation. (Compare **slander**[1].) **libellous** *adjective*

libel[2] *verb* (**libelled, libelling**) make a libel against someone. [from Latin *libellus* = little book]

Liberal *noun* a member of the Liberal Party of Australia, a political party traditionally favouring private enterprise and located to the right of the political spectrum.

liberal *adjective* **1** giving generously. **2** given in large amounts. **3** not strict; tolerant. **liberality** *noun*, **liberally** *adverb* [from Latin *liber* = free]

liberalise *verb* (**liberalised, liberalising**) make less strict. **liberalisation** *noun*

liberate *verb* (**liberated, liberating**) set free. **liberation** *noun*, **liberator** *noun* [same origin as *liberty*]

liberty *noun* freedom.
take liberties behave too casually; be presumptuous. [from Latin *liber* = free]

Libra *noun* **1** a constellation and the seventh sign of the zodiac (the Scales). **2** a person born when the sun is in this sign. [Latin = pound weight]

librarian *noun* a person in charge of or assisting in a library. **librarianship** *noun*

library (*say* **luy**-bruh-ree) *noun* (*plural* **libraries**) **1** a place where books and other resources are kept for people to use or borrow. **2** a collection of books, recordings, films, or other items. [from Latin *libri* = books]

libretto *noun* (*plural* **librettos**) the words of an opera or other long musical work. [Italian = little book]

lice *plural* of **louse**.

licence *noun* **1** an official permit to do or use or own something, *a driving licence.* **2** special freedom to avoid the usual rules or customs, *poetic licence.* [from Latin *licere* = be allowed]

license *verb* (**licensed, licensing**) give a licence to a person; authorise, *We are licensed to sell alcohol.*

> **Usage** Note the spelling: *licence* is a noun, *license* is a verb.

licensee *noun* a person who holds a licence, especially to sell alcohol.

licentious (*say* luy-**sen**-shuhs) *adjective* breaking the rules of conduct; immoral. **licentiousness** *noun*

lichen (*say* **luy**-kuhn) *noun* a dry-looking plant that typically grows on rocks, walls, and trees.

lick[1] *verb* **1** pass the tongue over something. **2** (of a wave or flame) move like a tongue; touch lightly. **3** (*informal*) defeat.

lick[2] *noun* **1** the act of licking. **2** (*informal*) a slight application or coating of something, especially paint. **3** (*informal*) a fast pace.

licorice alternative spelling of **liquorice**.

lid *noun* **1** a cover for a container. **2** an eyelid.

lie[1] *noun* a statement that the person who makes it knows to be untrue.

lie[2] *verb* (**lied, lying**) tell a lie or lies; be deceptive.

lie[3] *verb* (**lay, lain, lying**) **1** be or get in a flat or resting position, *He lay on the grass. The cat has lain here all night.* **2** be situated, *The island lies near the coast.* **3** remain, *The machinery lay idle.*
lie low keep yourself hidden.

> **Usage** See the note at *lay*[1].

lie[4] *noun* the way something lies, *the lie of the land.*

liege (*say* leej) *noun* (*old use*) a person entitled to receive feudal service or allegiance (a *liege lord*) or bound to give it (a *liege man*).

lieu (*say* lew) *noun* **in lieu** instead, *He accepted a cheque in lieu of cash.* [French, = place]

lieutenant (*say* lef-**ten**-uhnt or luh-**ten**-uhnt) *noun* **1** an officer in the army or navy. **2** a deputy or chief assistant. [from French *lieu* = place, + *tenant* = holding]

life *noun* (*plural* **lives**) **1** the ability to function and grow; the period between birth and death. **2** living things, *Is there life on Mars?* **3** liveliness, *full of life.* **4** a biography.

lifebelt *noun* a circle of material that will float, used to support someone's body in water.

lifeboat *noun* a boat for rescuing people at sea.

lifebuoy *noun* a device to support someone's body in water.

life jacket *noun* a jacket of material that will float, used to support someone's body in water.

lifeless *adjective* **1** without life. **2** unconscious.
lifelessly *adverb*

lifelike *adjective* looking exactly like a real person or thing.

lifeline *noun* **1** a rope or some other device, used in rescuing people. **2** a sole means of communication or transport or help. **3** a thing that provides a means of escape from a difficult situation.

lifelong *adjective* continuing for the whole of someone's life.

lifesaver *noun* **1** an expert swimmer who supervises beaches, especially to rescue swimmers from drowning. **2** a person or thing that is of great help; a boon.

lifetime *noun* the time for which someone is alive.

lift[1] *verb* **1** raise; pick up. **2** rise; go upwards. **3** (*informal*) steal. **4** remove; abolish, *The ban has been lifted.*

lift[2] *noun* **1** the act of lifting. **2** a device for taking people or goods from one floor or level to another in a building. **3** a free ride in somebody else's vehicle.

lift-off *noun* the vertical take-off of a rocket or spacecraft.

ligament *noun* a piece of the tough flexible tissue that holds bones together or keeps organs in place in the body. [from Latin *ligare* = bind]

ligature *noun* **1** a thing used in tying something, especially in surgical operations. **2** (in music) a tie or slur. [from Latin *ligare* = bind]

light[1] *noun* **1** radiation that stimulates the sense of sight and makes things visible. **2** something that provides light, especially an electric lamp. **3** a flame.
bring or **come to light** make or become known.

light[2] *adjective* **1** full of light; not dark. **2** pale, *light blue.*

light[3] *verb* (**lit** or **lighted, lighting**) **1** start a thing burning; kindle. **2** provide the light.
light up 1 put lights on, especially at dusk. **2** make or become light or bright.

> **Usage** Say *He lit the lamps*; *The lamps were lit* (not 'lighted'), but *She carried a lighted torch* (not 'a lit torch').

light[4] *adjective* **1** having little weight; not heavy. **2** small in amount or force, *light rain*; *a light punishment.* **3** needing little effort, *light work.* **4** cheerful; not sad, *with a light heart.* **5** not serious or profound, *light music.*
lightly *adverb*, **lightness** *noun*

light[5] *adverb* lightly; with only a small load, *We were travelling light.*

lighten[1] *verb* **1** make or become lighter or brighter. **2** producing lighting.

lighten[2] *verb* make or become lighter or less heavy.

lighter *noun* a device that produces a small flame, used to light cigarettes.

light-headed *adjective* feeling slightly faint or giddy.

light-hearted *adjective* cheerful; free from worry; not serious.

lighthouse *noun* a tower with a bright light at the top to guide or warn ships.

light industry *noun* industry producing small or light articles.

lighting *noun* lamps, or the light they provide.

lightning *noun* a flash of bright light produced by natural electricity during a thunderstorm.
like lightning with very great speed.

lightning conductor *noun* a metal rod or wire fixed on a building to divert lightning into the earth.

lightweight *noun* **1** a person who is not heavy. **2** a boxer weighing between 57 and 60 kilograms. **lightweight** *adjective*

light year *noun* the distance that light travels in one year (about 9.5 million million kilometres).

like[1] *verb* (**liked, liking**) **1** think a person or thing is pleasant or satisfactory, *I like swimming when it's hot.* **2** wish, *I should like to come.* **3** (in the context of social media) indicate your approval of or support for someone or something by means of a particular icon or link.

like[2] *noun* **1** the things one likes or prefers. **2** (in the context of social media) an indication of approval of or support for someone or something, expressed by means of a particular icon or link.

like[3] *adjective* similar; having some or all of the qualities of another person or thing, *the grouping of children of like ability together.*

like[4] *noun* a similar person or thing, *We shall not see his like again.*

like[5] *preposition* **1** similar to; in the manner of, *He swims like a fish.* **2** in a suitable state for, *It looks like rain.*

likeable *adjective* easy to like; pleasant.

likelihood *noun* being likely; probability.

likely *adjective* (**likelier, likeliest**) **1** probable; expected to happen or be true, *Rain is likely.* **2** expected to be successful, *a likely lad.*

liken *verb* compare, *He likened the human heart to a pump.*

likeness *noun* (*plural* **likenesses**) **1** being like; a resemblance. **2** a portrait.

likewise *adverb* similarly.

liking *noun* a feeling that you like something, *She has a liking for cherries.*

lilac *noun* **1** a bush with fragrant purple or white flowers. **2** pale purple.

lilly-pilly *noun* a small eastern Australian tree or its edible purplish to white berries.

lilt *noun* a light pleasant rhythm.
lilting *adjective*

lily *noun* (*plural* **lilies**) a garden plant with trumpet-shaped flowers, growing from a bulb.

lily-livered *adjective* cowardly.

limb *noun* **1** a leg, arm, or wing. **2** a projecting part, e.g. a bough of a tree.
out on a limb isolated; stranded.

limber *verb* **limber up** exercise in preparation for an athletic activity.

limbo[1] *noun* **1** intermediate state where nothing is happening, *Lack of money has left our plans in limbo.* **2** a condition of being neglected and forgotten. [from the name of a region formerly thought to exist on the border of hell]

limbo[2] *noun* a kind of dance in which the dancer bends back to pass under a horizontal bar which is progressively lowered.

lime[1] *noun* a white substance (calcium oxide) used in making cement and as a fertiliser.

lime[2] *noun* a round green citrus fruit like a small lemon.

limelight *noun* great publicity. [from *lime*[1] which gives a bright light when heated, formerly used to light up the stage of a theatre]

limerick *noun* a type of comical poem with five lines. [named after Limerick, a town in Ireland]

limestone *noun* a kind of rock from which lime (calcium oxide) is obtained.

limit[1] *noun* **1** a line, point, or level where something ends. **2** the greatest amount allowed, *the speed limit.*

limit[2] *verb* **1** keep within certain limits. **2** be a limit to something. **limitation** *noun*, **limited** *adjective* [from Latin *limes* = boundary]

limited company *noun* (also **limited liability company**) a company whose members would have to pay only some of its debts.

limousine (*say* lim-uh-**zeen**) *noun* a luxurious car.

limp[1] *verb* walk lamely.

limp[2] *noun* a limping walk.

limp[3] *adjective* **1** not stiff or firm. **2** without strength or energy. **limply** *adverb*, **limpness** *noun*

limpet *noun* a small shellfish that attaches itself firmly to rocks.

limpid *adjective* (of liquids) clear; transparent. **limpidity** *noun*

linchpin *noun* a pin passed through the end of an axle to keep a wheel in position.

line[1] *noun* **1** a long thin mark. **2** a crease or wrinkle in the skin. **3** a limit or boundary. **4** a row or series of people or things; a row of words. **5** a length of rope, string, or wire used for a particular purpose, *a fishing line.* **6** a railway; a line of railway track. **7** a company that provides ships, aircraft, or buses on particular routes on a regular basis. **8** a way of doing things or behaving. **9** a type of business or activity.
in line 1 forming a straight line. **2** conforming.

line[2] *verb* (**lined**, **lining**) **1** mark with lines, *Use lined paper.* **2** form into a line or lines, *Line them up.* [from Latin *linea* = linen thread]

line[3] *verb* (**lined**, **lining**) cover the inside of something. [from *linen* (used for linings)]

lineage (*say* **lin**-ee-ij) *noun* ancestry; a line of descendants from an ancestor.

lineal (*say* **lin**-ee-uhl) *adjective* of or in a line, especially as a descendant.

linear (*say* **lin**-ee-uh) *adjective* **1** of a line; of length. **2** arranged in a line.

linear equation *noun* an equation between two variables that gives a straight line when plotted on a graph.

line-ball *noun* **1** a ball striking the boundary line in tennis. **2** (*Australian*) an indecisive event; a borderline case.

linen *noun* **1** cloth made from flax. **2** shirts, sheets, and tablecloths etc. (which were formerly made of linen). [from Latin *linum* = flax]

liner[1] *noun* a large ship or aircraft on a regular route, usually carrying passengers.

liner[2] *noun* a removable lining, *bin liners.*

linesman *noun* (*plural* **linesmen**) **1** an official in football, tennis and certain other games who decides whether the ball has crossed a line. **2** a person who maintains railway, electrical, or telephone lines.

ling *noun* (*plural* **ling**) a long slender sea fish.

linger *verb* stay for a long time, as if unwilling to leave; be slow to leave.

lingerie (*say* **lon**-*zh*uh-ray) *noun* women's underwear. [from French *linge* = linen]

lingo *noun* (*plural* **lingos** or **lingoes**) (*informal*) **1** a foreign language. **2** the vocabulary of a special subject or group.

lingua franca (*say* ling-gwuh **frang**-kuh) *noun* a common language used by people whose native languages are different. [from Italian, = Frankish tongue]

linguist *noun* an expert in languages. [from Latin *lingua* = language]

linguistics *noun* the study of languages. **linguistic** *adjective*

liniment *noun* a liquid for rubbing on the skin to relieve soreness.

lining *noun* a layer that covers the inside of something. (Compare **line**[3].)

link[1] *noun* **1** one ring or loop of a chain. **2** a connection. **3** a hyperlink.

link[2] *verb* join things together; connect. **linkage** *noun*

lino *noun* linoleum.

linocut *noun* a print made from a design cut into a block of thick linoleum.

linoleum *noun* a stiff shiny floor covering. [from Latin *linum* = flax, + *oleum* = oil]

linseed *noun* the seed of flax, from which oil is obtained. [from Latin *linum* = flax, + *seed*]

lint *noun* **1** a soft material for covering wounds. **2** fluff.

lintel *noun* a horizontal piece of wood, stone, or other material above a door or other opening.

lion *noun* a large strong flesh-eating animal of the cat family, found in Africa and India. **lioness** *noun*

lip *noun* **1** either of the two fleshy edges of the mouth. **2** the edge of something hollow, such as a cup or crater. **3** a projecting part of such an edge shaped for pouring.

lipid *noun* any of a group of fat-like compounds including fatty acids, oils, waxes, and steroids.

lipo- *prefix* relating to fat or other lipids. [from Greek *lipos* = fat]

lipoma *noun* (*plural* **lipomas** or **lipomata**) a benign tumour of fatty tissue.

lip-read *verb* understand what a person says by watching the movements of their lips.

lip-service *noun* **pay lip-service to something** say that you approve of it but do nothing to support it.

lipstick *noun* a stick of a waxy substance for colouring the lips.

liquefy *verb* (**liquefied**, **liquefying**) make or become liquid. **liquefaction** *noun*

liqueur (*say* luh-**kyoor**) *noun* a strong sweet alcoholic drink. [French, = liquor]

liquid[1] *noun* a substance (such as water or oil) that flows freely but is not a gas.

liquid[2] *adjective* **1** in the form of a liquid; flowing freely. **2** easily converted into cash, *the firm's liquid assets.* [from Latin *liquidus* = flowing]

liquidate *verb* (**liquidated**, **liquidating**) **1** pay off or settle a debt. **2** close down a business and divide its value between its creditors. **3** get rid of, especially by killing. **liquidation** *noun*, **liquidator** *noun*

liquid crystal display *noun* a form of visual display used in electronic devices, in which a layer of liquid crystal is sandwiched between two transparent electrodes.

liquidise *verb* (**liquidised**, **liquidising**) cause to become liquid; crush into a liquid pulp. **liquidiser** *noun*

liquidity *noun* **1** being liquid. **2** the availability of cash (or assets that can be easily converted to cash) to a market or company; such cash or assets.

liquor *noun* **1** alcoholic drink. **2** juice produced in cooking; liquid in which food has been cooked.

liquorice *noun* **1** a black substance used in medicine and as a sweet. **2** the plant from whose root this substance is obtained. [from Greek *glykys* = sweet, + *rhiza* = root]

lisp *noun* a fault in speech in which *s* and *z* are pronounced like *th*. **lisp** *verb*

list[1] *noun* a number of names, items, figures, or other pieces of information written or printed one after another.

list[2] *verb* make a list of people or things. [from Old English *liste* = border]

list[3] *verb* (of a ship) lean over to one side; tilt. **list** *noun*

listen *verb* pay attention in order to hear something. **listener** *noun*
listen in listen to a private conversation, especially secretly.

listless *adjective* too tired to be active or enthusiastic. **listlessly** *adverb*, **listlessness** *noun* [from an old word *list* = desire, + *-less*]

lit *past tense & past participle* of **light**[3].

litany *noun* (*plural* **litanies**) a formal prayer with fixed responses.

literacy *noun* being literate; the ability to read and write.

literal *adjective* **1** using or taking words in their most basic sense; not metaphorical or exaggerated. **2** precise; word for word, *a literal translation.* [same origin as *letter*]

literally *adverb* **1** in a literal manner or sense; exactly. **2** (*informal*) used for emphasis while not being actually true.

> **Usage** *Literally* and *literal* are sometimes used in contexts where they are not meant to be literal at all, and serve primarily as intensifiers: *he literally exploded, a literal avalanche of complaints*. This can lead to unintentional humorous effects, and such usages should be avoided in formal contexts.

literary (*say* **lit**-uh-ruh-ree) *adjective* of literature; interested in literature.

literate *adjective* able to read and write. [same origin as *letter*]

literature *noun* **1** books and other writings, especially those considered to have been written well. **2** printed material, leaflets, etc. about a subject. [same origin as *letter*]

lithe *adjective* flexible; supple; agile.

lithosphere (*say* **lith**-uh-sfeer) *noun* the earth's crust and upper mantle.

litigant *noun* a person who is involved in a lawsuit. [from Latin *litigare* = start a lawsuit]

litigation *noun* a lawsuit; the process of carrying on a lawsuit.

litigious *adjective* fond of going to law.

litmus *noun* a blue substance that is turned red by acids and can be turned back to blue by alkalis.

litmus paper *noun* paper stained with litmus.

litre *noun* a measure of liquid, 1000 millilitres, equivalent to four standard cups, *We bought two litres of milk from the shop.*

litter[1] *noun* **1** rubbish or untidy things left lying about. **2** straw or other plant matter put down as bedding for animals. **3** the young animals born to one mother at one time. **4** a kind of stretcher. **5** granulated material for use by pets as an indoor toilet, *cat litter.*

litter[2] *verb* make a place untidy with litter.

litterbug *noun* a person who carelessly drops rubbish in public places.

little[1] *adjective* (**littler**, **littlest**; **less**, **least**) **1** small in amount or size or intensity; not great or big or much, *She has a little dog*; *We have very little time.* **2** trivial; unimportant, *I can't remember every little detail.*
little by little gradually; by a small amount at a time.

little[2] *adverb* not much, *I eat very little.*

little[3] *pronoun* a small amount of; a short time or distance, *You only see a little of what she can do*; *After a little, the rain stopped.*

liturgy *noun* (*plural* **liturgies**) a fixed form of public worship used in churches.
liturgical *adjective*

live[1] (*rhymes with* give) *verb* (**lived**, **living**) **1** have life; be alive; stay alive, *Her cat lived to a very old age.* **2** have your home, *She lives in Albury.* **3** pass your life in a certain way, *He lived as a hermit.*
live on 1 use something as food. **2** depend on for your living.

live[2] (*rhymes with* hive) *adjective* **1** alive. **2** burning, *live coals.* **3** carrying electricity. **4** broadcast while it is actually happening, not from a recording.

livelihood *noun* a way of earning money or providing enough food to support yourself.

lively *adjective* (**livelier**, **liveliest**) full of life or action; vigorous and cheerful. **liveliness** *noun*

liven *verb* make or become lively, *liven things up.*

liver *noun* **1** a large organ of the body, found in the abdomen, that processes digested food and produces bile. **2** an animal's liver used as food.

livery *noun* (*plural* **liveries**) **1** a distinctive uniform worn by servants or certain officials. **2** the distinctive colours and design used on the vehicles, aircraft, or products of a particular company.
livery stables a place where horses are kept for their owner or for hire.

lives *plural* of **life**.

livestock *noun* farm animals.

livestream[1] *noun* (also **live stream**) a live transmission of an event over the Internet.

livestream[2] *verb* (also **live stream**) transmit or receive live video and audio coverage of (an event) over the Internet.

live wire *noun* **1** a wire carrying electricity. **2** a forceful energetic person.

livid *adjective* **1** bluish-grey, *a livid bruise.* **2** (*informal*) furiously angry.

living[1] *adjective* alive.

living[2] *noun* **1** being alive. **2** the way that a person lives, *a high standard of living.* **3** a way of earning money or providing enough food to support yourself.

living room *noun* a room for general use during the day.

lizard *noun* a reptile with a rough or scaly skin, four legs, and a long tail.

llama (*say* **lah**-muh) *noun* a South American animal with woolly fur, like a camel but with no hump. [from Quechua, an indigenous South American language]

lo *interjection* (*old use*) see; behold.

load[1] *noun* **1** something carried; a burden. **2** the quantity that can be carried. **3** the total amount of electric current supplied. **4** (*informal*) a large amount, *a load of nonsense*; *loads of time.*

load[2] *verb* **1** put a load in or on something. **2** fill heavily. **3** weight with something heavy, *loaded dice.* **4** put a bullet or shell into a gun; put a film into a camera. **5** transfer a program or data into memory, or into the central processor from storage.

loading *noun* (*Australian*) payment in addition to wages for skill, productivity, or as a holiday bonus.

loaf[1] *noun* (*plural* **loaves**) **1** a shaped mass of bread baked in one piece. **2** minced or chopped meat moulded into an oblong shape. **3** (*informal*) the head, *Use your loaf.* [from Old English *hlaf*]

loaf[2] *verb* spend time idly; loiter or stand about. **loafer** *noun*

loam *noun* rich soil containing clay, sand, and decayed vegetable matter. **loamy** *adjective*

loan *noun* **1** something lent, especially money. **2** lending; being lent, *These books are on loan from the library.* **loan** *verb*

loath (*rhymes with* both) *adjective* unwilling, *I was loath to go.*

loathe (*rhymes with* clothe) *verb* (**loathed**, **loathing**) feel great hatred and disgust for something; detest. **loathing** *noun*

loathsome *adjective* arousing a feeling of loathing; detestable.

loaves *plural* of **loaf**[1].

lob *verb* (**lobbed**, **lobbing**) send a ball in a high curve into the air. **lob** *noun*

lobby[1] *noun* (*plural* **lobbies**) **1** an entrance hall. **2** a group of people seeking to influence legislators on a particular issue.

lobby[2] *verb* (**lobbied**, **lobbying**) try to influence a legislator in favour of a special interest.

lobe *noun* a rounded fairly flat part of a leaf or an organ of the body; the rounded soft part at the bottom of an ear. **lobar** *adjective*, **lobed** *adjective*

lobster *noun* a large crustacean with eight legs and two long claws.

local[1] *adjective* **1** belonging to a particular place or a small area. **2** of or affecting a particular part. **locally** *adverb*

local[2] *noun* (*informal*) someone who lives in a particular district. [from Latin *locus* = place]

local anaesthetic *noun* an anaesthetic affecting only the part of the body where it is applied.

local area network *noun* a communication network linking a number of computers in close proximity.

local government *noun* the system of administration of a city, town, municipality, or shire by people elected by those who live there.

localise *verb* (**localised**, **localising**) keep something within a particular area. **localisation** *noun*

locality *noun* (*plural* **localities**) a district; a location.

locate *verb* (**located**, **locating**) **1** discover where something is, *locate the electrical fault.* **2** situate something in a particular place, *The cinema is located in Pitt Street.*

location *noun* **1** the place where something is situated. **2** discovering where something is; locating.
on location filmed in natural surroundings, not in a studio.

loch *noun* a lake in Scotland.

lock[1] *noun* **1** a fastening that is opened with a key or other device. **2** a section of a canal or river fitted with gates and sluices so that boats can be raised or lowered to the level beyond each gate. **3** a wrestling hold that keeps an opponent's arm or leg from moving. **4** the distance that a vehicle's front wheels can be turned by the steering wheel.

lock[2] *verb* **1** fasten or secure by means of a lock. **2** store away securely. **3** become fixed in one place; jam.
lock up imprison.

lock[3] *noun* a clump of hair.

lockdown *noun* a state of isolation or restricted access instituted as a security or safety measure.

locker *noun* a small cupboard or compartment where things can be stowed safely.

locket *noun* a small ornamental case for holding a portrait or lock of hair, worn on a chain around the neck.

locks *plural noun* the hair of the head.

locksmith *noun* a person whose job is to make and mend locks.

lock, stock, and barrel *adverb* completely.

locomotive[1] *noun* a railway engine.

locomotive[2] *adjective* of movement or the ability to move, *locomotive power.* **locomotion** *noun* [from Latin *locus* = place, + *motivus* = moving]

locum *noun* a doctor or member of the clergy who takes the place of another who is temporarily away. [short for Latin *locum tenens* = person holding the place]

locus (*say* **loh**-kuhs) *noun* (*plural* **loci**, *say* **loh**-kee) **1** the exact place of something. **2** (in geometry) the path traced by a moving point, or made by points placed in a certain way. [Latin, = place]

locust *noun* a kind of grasshopper that travels in large swarms that eat all the plants in an area.

locution *noun* a word or phrase. [from Latin *locutum* = spoken]

lodestone *noun* a kind of stone that can be used as a magnet.

lodge[1] *noun* **1** a cabin or hut; a holiday house, *a ski lodge.* **2** a small house, especially at the gates of a park. **3** (**the Lodge**) the official residence of the Australian prime minister in Canberra.

lodge[2] *verb* (**lodged, lodging**) **1** stay somewhere as a lodger. **2** provide a person with somewhere to live temporarily. **3** deposit; be or become fixed, *The ball lodged in the tree.* **4** present formally for attention, *lodge a complaint.*

lodger *noun* a person who pays to live in another person's house.

lodgings *plural noun* a room or rooms (not in a hotel) rented for living in.

lo-fi *adjective* of or employing sound reproduction of a lower quality than hi-fi.

loft *noun* a room or storage space under the roof of a house, barn, or other building.

lofty *adjective* **1** tall. **2** noble. **3** haughty. **loftily** *adverb*, **loftiness** *noun*

log[1] *noun* **1** a large piece of a tree that has fallen or been cut down; a piece cut off this. **2** a detailed record of a ship's voyage or aircraft's flight; any similar record.

log[2] *verb* (**logged, logging**) enter facts in a logbook.
log in or **on** enter a user name and password in order to gain access to a computer system.
log out or **off** go through the procedures to finish using a computer system.

log[3] *noun* a logarithm, *log tables.*

loganberry *noun* (*plural* **loganberries**) a dark red fruit like a blackberry.

logarithm *noun* **1** one of a series of numbers set out in tables that make it possible to do sums by adding and subtracting instead of multiplying and dividing. **2** the power to which a fixed number or base must be raised to produce a given number. [from Greek *logos* = reckoning, + *arithmos* = number]

logbook *noun* a book containing a detailed record or log.

loggerheads *plural noun* **at loggerheads** arguing; quarrelling.

logging *noun* cutting down trees for timber. **logger** *noun*

logic *noun* **1** reasoning; a system of reasoning. **2** the principles used in designing a computer; the circuits involved in this. [from Greek *logos* = word, reason]

logical *adjective* using logic; reasoning or reasoned correctly. **logicality** *noun*, **logically** *adverb*

Logie *noun* an Australian award for excellence in television acting or directing. [named after John Logie Baird, Scottish inventor of television]

logistics *plural noun* the detailed organisation and implementation of a plan or operation. **logistic** *adjective*, **logistical** *adjective*, **logistically** *adverb*

logjam *noun* **1** a crowded mass of logs in a river. **2** a deadlock. **3** a backlog.

logo (*say* **loh**-goh) *noun* (*plural* **logos**) a symbol used by an organisation as its emblem.

-logy *suffix* forming nouns meaning a subject of study (e.g. *biology*). [from Greek *-logia* = study]

loin *noun* the side and back of the body between the ribs and the hip bone.

loincloth *noun* a piece of cloth worn round the hips as a garment.

loiter *verb* linger or stand about idly. **loiterer** *noun*

LOL *abbreviation* (especially in electronic communication) laughing out loud.

loll *verb* lean lazily against something.

lollipop *noun* a large round hard sweet on a stick.

lollipop lady *noun* (also **lollipop woman**) (*informal*) a woman who is employed to help children cross the road safely near a school by holding up a sign to stop the traffic.

lollipop man *noun* (*informal*) a man who is employed to help children cross the road safely near a school by holding up a sign to stop the traffic.

lolly *noun* (*plural* **lollies**) **1** (*Australian*) a sweet, *I like chewy lollies more than hard ones.* **2** (*informal*) money.

lone *adjective* solitary. [from *alone*]

lonely *adjective* (**lonelier**, **loneliest**) **1** sad because you are on your own. **2** solitary. **3** far from inhabited places; not often visited or used, *a lonely road.* **loneliness** *noun* [from *lone*]

lonesome *adjective* lonely.

long[1] *adjective* **1** measuring a lot or a certain amount from one end to the other. **2** taking a lot of time, *a long speech.* **3** having a certain length, *The line is five centimetres long.* **4** lasting, *a long friendship.*

long[2] *adverb* **1** for a long time, *Have you been waiting long?* **2** at a long time before or after, *They left long ago.* **3** throughout a time, *all night long.*
as long as or **so long as** provided that; on condition that.

long[3] *verb* feel a strong desire.

long division *noun* dividing one number by another and writing down all the calculations.

longevity (*say* lon-**jev**-uh-tee) *noun* long life. [from Latin *longus* = long, + *aevum* = age]

longhand *noun* ordinary writing, contrasted with shorthand, typing, or printing.

longing *noun* a strong desire.

longitude *noun* the distance east or west, measured in degrees, from the Greenwich meridian.

longitudinal *adjective* **1** of longitude. **2** of length; measured lengthwise.

long paddock *noun* (*Australian*) the grassy sides of a public road, used to graze stock during a drought.

long-sighted *adjective* able to see clearly only what is at a distance.

long-suffering *adjective* putting up with things patiently.

long-winded *adjective* talking or writing at great length.

loo *noun* (*informal*) a toilet.

loofah *noun* a rough sponge made from a dried gourd. [from Arabic *lufa*]

look[1] *verb* **1** use your eyes; turn your eyes in a particular direction, *She looked everywhere for her friend but couldn't find her.* **2** face in a particular direction. **3** have a certain appearance; seem, *You look sad.*
look after 1 protect. **2** attend to somebody's needs. **3** be in charge of something.
look down on despise.
look forward to be waiting eagerly for something you expect.
look in make a short visit.
look into investigate.
look out be careful.
look up 1 search for information about something. **2** improve in prospects, *Things are looking up.*
look up to admire or respect.

look[2] *noun* **1** the act of looking; a gaze or glance. **2** appearance, *I don't like the look of this place.*

looker-on *noun* (*plural* **lookers-on**) a spectator; someone who sees what happens but takes no part in it.

looking glass *noun* a glass mirror.

lookout *noun* **1** looking out or watching for something. **2** a place from which you can keep watch. **3** a person whose job is to keep watch. **4** a place from which you can admire a view. **5** a future prospect, *It's a poor lookout for us.* **6** (*informal*) a person's own concern, *If he wastes his money, that's his lookout.*

loom[1] *noun* an apparatus for weaving cloth.

loom[2] *verb* appear suddenly; seem large or close and threatening, *An iceberg loomed up through the fog.*

loop[1] *noun* the shape made by a curve crossing itself; a piece of string, ribbon, or similar material made into this shape.

loop[2] *verb* **1** make into a loop. **2** enclose in a loop.

loophole *noun* **1** an ambiguity or inadequacy in the law or a set of rules. **2** a narrow opening in the wall of a fort.

loose[1] *adjective* **1** not tight; slack; not firmly fixed, *a loose tooth.* **2** not tied up or shut in, *There's a lion loose!* **3** not packed in a box, packet, or other container. **4** not exact, *a loose translation.* **loosely** *adverb*, **looseness** *noun*
at a loose end with nothing to do.

loose[2] *verb* (**loosed**, **loosing**) **1** loosen. **2** untie; release.

loose-leaf *adjective* with each leaf or page removable, *a loose-leaf notebook.*

loosen *verb* make or become loose or looser.

loot[1] *noun* stolen things; goods taken from an enemy.

loot[2] *verb* **1** rob a place or an enemy, especially in a time of war or disorder. **2** take as loot. **looter** *noun*

lop *verb* (**lopped**, **lopping**) cut away branches or twigs; cut off.

lope *verb* (**loped**, **loping**) run with a long jumping stride. **lope** *noun*

lopsided *adjective* with one side lower than the other; uneven.

loquacious (*say* luh-**kway**-shuhs) *adjective* talkative. **loquacity** (*say* luh-**kwas**-uh-tee) *noun* [from Latin *loqui* = speak]

lord[1] *noun* **1** a nobleman, especially one who is allowed to use the title 'Lord' in front of his name. **2** a master or ruler. **3** (**the Lord**) God; Jesus Christ. **lordly** *adjective*, **lordship** *noun*

lord[2] *verb* domineer; behave in a masterful way, *lording it over the whole club.* [from Old English *hlaford* = person who keeps the bread (compare *lady*)]

Lord Mayor *noun* the mayor of a large city.

lore *noun* a set of traditional facts or beliefs, *gypsy lore.* [from *learn*]

lorikeet *noun* a small brightly coloured Australian parrot.

lorry *noun* (*plural* **lorries**) a truck.

lose *verb* (**lost, losing**) **1** be without something that you once had, especially because you cannot find it. **2** be deprived of something; fail to keep or obtain, *We lost control.* **3** be defeated in a contest or argument. **4** cause the loss of, *That fall lost us the game.* **5** (of a clock or watch) become behind the correct time. **loser** *noun*

lose out (*informal*) **1** be unsuccessful. **2** be at a disadvantage.

lose your life be killed.

lose your way not know where you are or which is the right path.

loss *noun* (*plural* **losses**) **1** losing something. **2** a person or thing lost.

be at a loss be puzzled; not know what to do or say.

lost[1] *past tense & past participle* of **lose**.

lost[2] *adjective* not knowing where you are; unable to find your way.

lost cause *noun* **1** a hopeless effort or undertaking. **2** a person one can no longer help or influence.

lot *noun* **1** a number of people or things. **2** one of a set of objects used in choosing or deciding something by chance, *We drew lots to see who should go first.* **3** a person's share. **4** a person's fate. **5** something for sale at an auction. **6** a piece of land.

a lot or **lots** (*informal*) a large amount; plenty.

the lot or **the whole lot** everything; all. [from Old English *hlot* = share]

> **Usage** *A lot of* and *lots of* are very common in speech and writing but are not considered acceptable for formal English, where alternatives such as *many* or *a large number* are used instead.

LOTE (*say* **loht**) *noun* languages other than English.

lotion *noun* a liquid for putting on the skin.

lottery *noun* (*plural* **lotteries**) a way of raising money by selling numbered tickets and giving prizes to people who hold winning numbers, which are chosen by a method depending on chance. (Compare **lot** 2.)

lotto *noun* **1** a game like bingo. **2** a lottery.

lotus *noun* (*plural* **lotuses**) a kind of tropical water lily.

loud *adjective* **1** easily heard; producing much noise. **2** unpleasantly bright; gaudy, *loud colours.* **loudly** *adverb*, **loudness** *noun*

loudspeaker *noun* a device that changes electrical impulses into sound.

lounge[1] *noun* **1** a sitting room. **2** a long soft seat with back and arms; a sofa.

lounge[2] *verb* (**lounged, lounging**) sit or stand lazily; loll.

louring (*rhymes with* flowering) *adjective* looking dark and threatening, *a louring sky.*

louse *noun* (*plural* **lice**) a small insect that lives as a parasite on animals or plants.

lousy *adjective* (**lousier, lousiest**) **1** full of lice. **2** (*informal*) very bad.

lout *noun* a rough or bad-mannered man. **loutish** *adjective*

louvre (*say* **loo**-vuh) *noun* one of a set of overlapping slats arranged to let in air but exclude light or rain. [from Old French *lovier* = skylight]

lovable *adjective* easy to love.

love[1] *noun* **1** great liking or affection, *I love my dad*; *Her mother has a great love for classical music.* **2** sexual affection or passion. **3** a person or thing that you love, *His greatest loves are football and swimming.* **4** (in games) no score; nil, *The score was love 15.*

in love feeling strong love.

make love have sexual intercourse.

love[2] *verb* (**loved, loving**) **1** feel love for a person or thing. **2** like very much. **lover** *noun*, **loving** *adjective*, **lovingly** *adverb*

loveless *adjective* without love.

lovelorn *adjective* pining with love, especially when abandoned by a lover.

lovely *adjective* (**lovelier, loveliest**) **1** beautiful. **2** (*informal*) very pleasant or enjoyable. **loveliness** *noun*

lovesick *adjective* languishing with love.

low[1] *adjective* **1** not high or tall. **2** not far above the ground or above sea level. **3** below average level in importance, quality, or status, *low rank.* **4** of less than normal amount, extent, or intensity, *low prices.* **5** (of a sound) not shrill or loud. **6** depressed, *in low spirits.* **7** mean; vulgar. **lowness** *noun*

low[2] *adverb* at or to a low level or position etc., *The plane was flying low.*

low³ *verb* make the deep sound of a cow; moo.

lower¹ *adjective & adverb* less high.

lower² *verb* **1** make or become lower. **2** bring something down, *lower the flag.*

lower case *noun* letters that are not capitals.

lowest common denominator *noun* the lowest common multiple of the denominators of several fractions.

lowest common multiple *noun* the lowest quantity that is a multiple of two or more given numbers.

low-key *adjective* restrained; not ostentatious.

lowlands *plural noun* low-lying country.

lowly *adjective* (**lowlier**, **lowliest**) humble. **lowliness** *noun*

loyal *adjective* always firmly supporting a person, country, or institution. **loyally** *adverb*, **loyalty** *noun*

loyalist *noun* a person who is loyal to the government during a revolt.

lozenge *noun* **1** a small flavoured tablet, especially as medicine. **2** a diamond shape.

LPG *abbreviation* liquefied petroleum gas.

Ltd *abbreviation* limited. (See **limited company**.)

lubricant *noun* a lubricating substance.

lubricate *verb* (**lubricated**, **lubricating**) oil or grease something so that it moves smoothly. **lubrication** *noun* [from Latin *lubricus* = slippery]

lucerne (*say* **loo**-suhn) *noun* a clover-like plant used for fodder.

lucid *adjective* **1** clear and easy to understand. **2** sane. **lucidity** *noun*, **lucidly** *adverb* [from Latin *lucidus* = bright]

luck *noun* **1** the way things happen without being planned; chance. **2** good fortune, *It will bring you luck.*

luckless *adjective* unlucky.

lucky *adjective* (**luckier**, **luckiest**) **1** having good luck. **2** bringing good luck. **3** resulting from good luck. **luckily** *adverb*

lucrative (*say* **loo**-kruh-tiv) *adjective* profitable; producing much money. [from Latin *lucrari* = to gain]

Luddite (*say* **lud**-uyt) *noun* a person who opposes the introduction of new technology or new working methods. [Probably named after Ned Lud, a person who destroyed machinery in England c. 1779]

ludicrous *adjective* ridiculous. **ludicrously** *adverb*

lug¹ *verb* (**lugged**, **lugging**) drag or carry something heavy.

lug² *noun* an ear-like part on an object, by which it may be carried or fixed.

luggage *noun* suitcases and bags holding things for taking on a journey.

lugubrious (*say* luh-**goo**-bree-uhs) *adjective* dismal. **lugubriously** *adverb* [from Latin *lugubris* = mourning]

lukewarm *adjective* **1** only slightly warm. **2** not very enthusiastic. [from *luke* = tepid, + *warm*]

lull¹ *verb* soothe or calm; send to sleep.

lull² *noun* a short period of quiet or inactivity.

lullaby *noun* (*plural* **lullabies**) a song that is sung to send a baby to sleep.

lumbar *adjective* of the loins. [from Latin *lumbus* = loin]

lumber¹ *noun* **1** unwanted furniture; junk. **2** partly prepared timber.

lumber² *verb* **1** leave someone with something unwanted or unpleasant. **2** fill up space with junk. **3** move in a heavy clumsy way.

lumberjack *noun* (*American*) a person whose job is to cut or carry timber.

luminescent *adjective* giving out light. **luminescence** *noun* [from Latin *lumen* = light]

luminous *adjective* glowing in the dark. **luminosity** *noun* [from Latin *lumen* = light]

lump¹ *noun* **1** a solid piece of something. **2** a swelling. **lumpy** *adjective*

lump² *verb* put things together as being similar; deal with things together.

lump³ *verb* **lump it** (*informal*) put up with something you dislike.

lump sum *noun* a single payment, especially one covering a number of items.

lunacy *noun* (*plural* **lunacies**) **1** insanity. **2** great folly, madness. [from *lunatic*]

lunar *adjective* of the moon. [from Latin *luna* = moon]

lunatic *noun* an insane person. **lunatic** *adjective* [from Latin *luna* = moon (because formerly people were thought to be affected by changes of the moon)]

lunch *noun* (*plural* **lunches**) a meal eaten in the middle of the day. **lunch** *verb*

luncheon *noun* (*formal*) lunch.

lung *noun* either of the two parts of the body, in the chest, used in breathing.

lunge *verb* (**lunged**, **lunging**) thrust the body forward suddenly. **lunge** *noun*

lurch¹ *verb* stagger; lean suddenly to one side.

lurch² *noun* an unsteady swaying movement to one side.
leave somebody in the lurch leave somebody in difficulties.

lure *verb* (**lured**, **luring**) tempt a person or animal into a trap; entice. **lure** *noun*

lurid (*say* **loo**-ruhd) *adjective* **1** in very bright colours; gaudy. **2** sensational and shocking, *the lurid details of the murder.* **luridly** *adverb*, **luridness** *noun*

lurk[1] *verb* wait where you cannot be seen.

lurk[2] *noun* (*Australian informal*) a dodge or stratagem.

luscious (*say* **lush**-uhs) *adjective* delicious. **lusciously** *adverb*, **lusciousness** *noun*

lush *adjective* **1** growing thickly and strongly, *lush grass.* **2** luxurious. **lushly** *adverb*, **lushness** *noun*

lust *noun* powerful desire, especially sexual desire. **lustful** *adjective*

lustre *noun* brightness; brilliance. **lustrous** *adjective* [from Latin *lustrare* = illuminate]

lusty *adjective* (**lustier, lustiest**) strong and vigorous. **lustily** *adverb*, **lustiness** *noun*

lute *noun* a musical instrument rather like a guitar.

Lutheran *noun* a member of a Christian denomination based on the doctrines of Martin Luther (1483–1546). **Lutheran** *adjective*

luxuriant *adjective* growing abundantly.

luxuriate *verb* (**luxuriated, luxuriating**) enjoy something as a luxury, *luxuriating in the warm sunshine.*

luxury *noun* (*plural* **luxuries**) **1** something expensive that you enjoy but do not really need. **2** expensive and comfortable surroundings or possessions. **luxurious** *adjective*, **luxuriously** *adverb* [from Latin *luxus* = plenty]

lychee *noun* a small fruit with sweet white flesh in a thin rough shell.

Lycra *noun* (*trademark*) a stretch fabric used especially for sports clothing.

lying *present participle* of **lie**[2] and **lie**[3].

lymph (*say* limf) *noun* a colourless fluid from the flesh or organs of the body, containing white blood cells. **lymphatic** *adjective* [from Latin *lympha* = water]

lynch *verb* join together to execute or punish someone violently without a proper trial. [named after William Lynch, an American judge who allowed this kind of punishment in about 1780]

lynx *noun* (*plural* **lynxes**) a wild animal of the cat family with thick spotted fur and very sharp sight.

lyre *noun* an ancient musical instrument like a small harp.

lyrebird *noun* an Australian bird, the male with a lyre-shaped tail display.

lyric (*say* **li**-rik) *noun* **1** a short poem that expresses thoughts and feelings. **2** the words of a song. **lyrical** *adjective*, **lyrically** *adverb* [from *lyre*]

Mm

m *abbreviation* **1** metre(s). **2** mile(s). **3** million(s).

m- *prefix* denoting commercial activity conducted via mobile phones (as in *m-commerce*).

macabre (*say* muh-**kah**-buh) *adjective* gruesome.

macadam *noun* layers of broken stone rolled flat to make a firm road surface. **macadamised** *adjective* [named after a Scottish engineer, J. McAdam]

macadamia *noun* an edible nut with a hard round shell from an Australian evergreen tree. [named after an Australian chemist, J. Macadam]

macaque (*say* muh-**kak**) *noun* a monkey of India and south-east Asia.

macaroni *noun* pasta formed into tubes.

macaroon *noun* a small sweet cake or biscuit made with egg whites and ground almonds.

macaw *noun* a brightly coloured parrot.

macchiato (*say* mak-ee-**ah**-toh) *noun* (*plural* **macchiatos**) a strong coffee in a small cup with a small amount of milk or cream. [Italian]

mace *noun* an ornamental staff carried or placed in front of an official.

mach (*say* mahk) *noun* **mach number** the ratio of the speed of a moving object to the speed of sound, *mach one is the speed of sound.* [named after the Austrian scientist Ernst Mach]

machete (*say* muh-**shet**-ee) *noun* a broad heavy knife used as a tool or weapon.

machiavellian (*say* mak-ee-uh-**vel**-ee-uhn) *adjective* very cunning or deceitful. [named after an Italian political writer, Niccolo dei Machiavelli (1469–1527)]

machine[1] *noun* something with parts that work together to do a job.

machine[2] *verb* (**machined**, **machining**) make something with a machine. [from Greek *mechane* = device]

machine gun *noun* a gun that can keep firing bullets quickly one after another.

machinery *noun* **1** machines. **2** mechanism. **3** an organised system for doing something.

macho (*say* **mach**-oh) *adjective* showing off masculine strength. [Spanish, = male]

mackerel *noun* (*plural* **mackerel**) a sea fish used as food.

mackintosh *noun* (*plural* **mackintoshes**) a raincoat. [named after the Scottish inventor of a waterproof material, C. Macintosh]

macro *noun* (in computing) a set of instructions grouped together as a single instruction.

macro- *prefix* large; large-scale; long. [from Greek *makros* = long, large]

macrobiotic *adjective* relating to or following a diet intended to prolong life, comprising pure vegetable foods, brown rice, etc.

macrocosm (*say* **mak**-roh-koz-uhm) *noun* **1** the universe. **2** any great whole. [from *macro-* + *cosmos*]

macropod (*say* **mak**-ruh-pod) *noun* any of many plant-eating marsupials such as the kangaroo and wallaby. [from *macro-* + Greek *podos* = foot]

mad *adjective* (**madder**, **maddest**) **1** mentally ill; not sane. **2** extremely foolish. **3** (*informal*) very keen, *He is mad about football.* **4** (*informal*) very excited or annoyed. **madly** *adverb*, **madman** *noun*, **madness** *noun*, **madwoman** *noun*
like mad (*informal*) with great speed, energy, or enthusiasm.

madam *noun* a word used when speaking politely to a woman, *Can I help you, madam?* [from French *ma dame* = my lady]

madcap *adjective* wildly impulsive.

madden *verb* make a person mad or angry.

made *past tense & past participle* of **make**[1].

madison *noun* (in cycling) a long-distance track race for teams of riders. [from Madison Square Garden]

madonna *noun* a picture or statue of the Virgin Mary. [from Old Italian *ma donna* = my lady]

madras *noun* **1** a strong cotton fabric with colourful stripes or checks. **2** a dish of meat, fish, or vegetables in a hot curry sauce. [named after Madras, the former name of the Indian city Chennai]

madrasa *noun* (also **madrasah or medrese**) a college for Islamic instruction. [from Arabic *darasa* = to study]

madrigal *noun* a song for several voices singing different parts together.

maelstrom (*say* **mayl**-struhm) *noun* a great whirlpool. [from Dutch *malen* = whirl, + *stroom* = stream]

maestro (*say* **muy**-stroh) *noun* (*plural* **maestros**) a master, especially a musician. [Italian, = master]

mafia *noun* **1** (**the Mafia**) an organised group of criminals originating in Sicily. **2** a network of people regarded as exerting a hidden sinister influence. [Italian]

magazine *noun* **1** a publication that comes out regularly, with articles or stories by a number of writers. **2** the part of a gun that holds the cartridges. **3** a store for weapons and ammunition or for explosives. **4** a device that holds film for a camera or slides for a projector. [from Arabic *makhazin* = storehouses]

magenta (*say* muh-**jen**-tuh) *noun* a colour between bright red and purple. [named after Magenta, a town in north Italy]

maggot *noun* the larva of some kinds of fly. **maggoty** *adjective*

Magi (*say* **may**-juy) *plural noun* the 'wise men' from the East who brought offerings to the infant Jesus at Bethlehem.

magic *noun* the art or pretended art of making things happen by secret or unusual powers. **magic** *adjective*, **magical** *adjective*, **magically** *adverb*

magician *noun* a person who is skilled in magic; a wizard.

magic square *noun* a square divided into smaller squares each containing a number such that the sums of all vertical, horizontal, or diagonal rows are equal.

magisterial *adjective* **1** of a magistrate. **2** masterful; full of authority; imperious. [same origin as *magistrate*]

magistrate *noun* an official who hears and judges minor cases and holds preliminary hearings. **magistracy** *noun* [from Latin *magister* = master]

magma *noun* a molten substance beneath the earth's crust.

magnanimous (*say* mag-**nan**-uh-muhs) *adjective* generous and forgiving; not petty-minded. **magnanimity** *noun*, **magnanimously** *adverb* [from Latin *magnus* = great, + *animus* = mind]

magnate *noun* a wealthy influential person, especially in business. [from Latin *magnus* = great]

magnesium *noun* a silvery-white metal that burns with a very bright flame.

magnet *noun* a piece of iron or steel that can attract iron and that points north and south when it is hung up. **magnetism** *noun*

magnetic *adjective* **1** having the powers of a magnet. **2** very attractive, *a magnetic personality.* **magnetically** *adverb*

magnetic tape *noun* a plastic strip coated with a magnetic substance for recording sound.

magnetise *verb* (**magnetised, magnetising**) **1** make into a magnet. **2** attract like a magnet. **magnetisation** *noun*

magneto (*say* mag-**nee**-toh) *noun* (*plural* **magnetos**) a small electric generator using magnets. [from *magnet*]

magnificent *adjective* **1** extremely beautiful, elaborate, or impressive. **2** excellent. **magnificence** *noun*, **magnificently** *adverb* [same origin as *magnify*]

magnify *verb* (**magnified, magnifying**) **1** make something look or seem bigger than it really is. **2** (*old use*) praise, *My soul doth magnify the Lord.* **magnification** *noun*, **magnifier** *noun* [from Latin *magnus* = great, + *facere* = make]

magnifying glass *noun* a lens that magnifies things.

magnitude *noun* **1** largeness; size. **2** importance. [from Latin *magnus* = great]

magnolia *noun* a tree with large white or pale pink flowers.

magnum *noun* a large bottle containing about 1.5 litres of wine or spirits. [Latin, = large thing]

magnum opus *noun* **1** a great work of art, literature, or music. **2** the greatest work of an artist, writer, or composer. [Latin, = great work]

magpie *noun* **1** a black and white Australian bird with a melodious song. **2** (in the northern hemisphere) a noisy black and white crow.

magpie lark *noun* a black and white Australian bird with a loud piping call.

maharajah *noun* the title of certain Indian princes. [Hindi, = great rajah]

mah-jong *noun* a Chinese game for four people, played with pieces called *tiles.*

mahogany *noun* a hard brown wood.

maid *noun* **1** a female servant. **2** (*old use*) a girl. **maidservant** *noun*

maiden[1] *noun* (*old use*) a girl. **maidenhood** *noun*

maiden[2] *adjective* **1** not married, *a maiden aunt.* **2** first, *a maiden voyage.*

maiden name *noun* a woman's family name before she married.

maiden over *noun* a cricket over in which no runs are scored.

mail[1] *noun* **1** letters or parcels sent by post. **2** email.

mail[2] *verb* **1** send by post. **2** send an email.

mail[3] *noun* armour made of metal rings joined together, *a suit of chain mail.*

mailbox *noun* **1** a box into which letters are posted or delivered. **2** a computer file in which email messages are stored.

mail order *noun* the purchase of goods by post.

maim *verb* wound or injure a person or animal so that part of the body is permanently damaged.

main[1] *adjective* principal; most important; largest.

main[2] *noun* **1** (also **mains**) the main pipe or cable in a public system carrying water, gas, or electricity to a building. **2** (*old use*) the seas, *Drake sailed the Spanish main.*

mainframe *noun* the central processing unit of a large computer; a large computer system.

mainland *noun* the main part of a country or continent, not the islands round it.

mainly *adverb* chiefly; almost completely.

mainstay *noun* the chief support.

mainstream *noun* the dominant trend in opinion, fashion etc.

maintain *verb* **1** cause something to continue; keep in existence. **2** keep a thing in good condition. **3** provide money for a person to live on. **4** state that something is true.

maintenance *noun* **1** the process of maintaining or being maintained. **2** money payable to a spouse after separation or divorce.

maisonette *noun* **1** a semi-detached house. **2** a flat.

maize another name for **corn**[1] 1.

majestic *adjective* stately and dignified; imposing. **majestically** *adverb*

majesty *noun* (*plural* **majesties**) **1** the title of a king or queen, *Her Majesty the Queen.* **2** being majestic.

major[1] *adjective* **1** greater; very important, *major roads.* **2** of the musical scale that has a semitone after the third and seventh notes. (Compare **minor**[1] 2.) [Latin, = larger, greater]

major[2] *noun* an army officer ranking next above a captain.

majority *noun* (*plural* **majorities**) **1** the greatest part of a group of people or things. (Compare **minority** 1.) **2** the difference between numbers of votes, *She had a majority of 25 over her opponent.* **3** the age at which a person becomes an adult according to the law, *He attained his majority.*

makarrata (*say* mak-uh-**rah**-tuh) *noun* (*Australian*) an Aboriginal ceremonial ritual symbolising peace after a dispute; an agreement. [from Yolngu *makarrartha*]

make[1] *verb* (**made, making**) **1** bring something into existence, especially by putting things together. **2** gain or earn, *She makes $30,000 a year.* **3** cause or compel, *Make him repeat it.* **4** achieve, *The swimmer just made the shore.* **5** reckon, *What do you make the time?* **6** perform an action, *make an effort.* **7** arrange for use, *make the beds.* **8** cause to be successful or happy, *Her visit made my day.* **9** compose; draw up, *make a list*; *make a will.* **10** amount to, *3 and 3 make 6.* **11** decide on, *They made a time for the next meeting.*

make do manage with something that is not what you really want.

make for go towards.

make off go away quickly.

make out 1 manage to see, hear, or understand something. **2** pretend.

make up 1 build or put together. **2** invent a story. **3** compensate for something. **4** be reconciled. **5** put on make-up.

make up your mind decide.

make[2] *noun* **1** making; how something is made. **2** a brand of goods; something made by a particular firm.

make-believe *noun* pretending; imagining things.

makeover *noun* a transformation or remodelling, *a bedroom makeover.*

maker *noun* the person or firm that has made something.

makeshift *adjective* improvised or used because you have nothing better, *We used a box as a makeshift table.*

make-up *noun* **1** cosmetics. **2** the way something is made up. **3** a person's character.

mal- *prefix* bad; badly (as in *malnourished*). [from Latin *male* = badly]

maladjusted *adjective* failing to cope with the demands of a normal social environment.

maladministration *noun* bad administration, especially of business affairs.

malady *noun* (*plural* **maladies**) an illness or disease. [from French *malade* = ill]

malapropism *noun* a comical confusion of words, e.g. using *hooligan* instead of *hurricane.* [named after Mrs Malaprop in Sheridan's play *The Rivals*, who made mistakes of this kind]

malaria *noun* a feverish disease spread by mosquitoes. **malarial** *adjective* [from Italian *mala aria* = bad air, which was once thought to cause the disease]

Malay *noun* **1** a member of a people from Malaysia and Indonesia. **2** the language of the Malays.

malcontent *noun* a discontented person.

male[1] *adjective* **1** of the sex that reproduces by fertilising egg cells produced by the female. **2** of men, *a male voice choir.*

male[2] *noun* a male person, animal, or plant.

malediction (*say* mal-uh-**dik**-shuhn) *noun* a curse. [from Latin *male* = evilly, + *diction*]

malefactor (*say* **mal**-uh-fak-tuh) *noun* a wrongdoer. [from Latin *male* = evilly, + *factor* = doer]

malevolent (*say* muh-**lev**-uh-luhnt) *adjective* wishing to harm people. **malevolence** *noun*, **malevolently** *adverb* [from Latin *male* = evilly, + *volens* = wishing]

malformed *adjective* faultily formed.

malfunction *noun* faulty functioning. **malfunction** *verb*

malice *noun* a desire to harm others or to tease. **malicious** *adjective*, **maliciously** *adverb* [from Latin *malus* = evil]

malign[1] (*say* muh-**luyn**) *adjective* **1** harmful, *a malign influence.* **2** showing malice. **malignity** (*say* muh-**lig**-nuh-tee) *noun*

malign[2] *verb* say unpleasant and untrue things about somebody. [same origin as *malice*]

malignant *adjective* **1** (of a tumour) growing uncontrollably. **2** full of ill will. **malignancy** *noun*, **malignantly** *adverb*

malinger *verb* pretend to be ill in order to avoid work. **malingerer** *noun*

mall (*say* mawl or mal) *noun* **1** an area without traffic where people can walk and shop. **2** a shopping centre.

malleable *adjective* **1** able to be pressed or hammered into shape. **2** easy to influence; adaptable. **malleability** *noun* [from Latin *malleare* = to hammer]

mallee *noun* (*Australian*) **1** a eucalypt flourishing in dry areas, with several trunks or stems growing from a common base. **2** (also **mallee scrub**) scrub formed by these trees. [from Woiwurrung *mali*]

mallet *noun* **1** a large hammer, usually made of wood. **2** an implement with a long handle, used in croquet or polo for striking the ball. [from Latin *malleus* = a hammer]

malnutrition *noun* not having enough food to eat. **malnourished** *adjective*

malpractice *noun* wrongdoing.

malt *noun* dried barley used in brewing, distilling, and making vinegar. **malted** *adjective*

maltreat *verb* ill-treat. **maltreatment** *noun*

mama *noun* (*old use*) mother.

mammal *noun* any animal of which the female can feed her babies with her own milk. **mammalian** (*say* ma-**may**-lee-uhn) *adjective* [from Latin *mamma* = breast]

mammary *adjective* of the breasts.

mammoth[1] *noun* an extinct elephant with a hairy skin and curved tusks.

mammoth[2] *adjective* huge. [from Russian]

man[1] *noun* (*plural* **men**) **1** a grown-up male human being. **2** an individual person. **3** mankind. **4** a piece used in chess and other board games. [from Old English *mann*]

> **Usage** Traditionally the word *man* has been used to refer not only to adult males but also to human beings in general, regardless of sex. This use is now generally regarded as sexist or old-fashioned.

man[2] *verb* (**manned, manning**) supply with people to work something, *Man the pumps.*

manacle[1] *noun* a fetter or handcuff.

manacle[2] *verb* (**manacled, manacling**) fasten with manacles. [from Latin *manus* = hand]

manage *verb* (**managed, managing**) **1** be able to do something difficult. **2** control. **3** be in charge of an organisation or group of staff. **4** meet your needs with limited resources; cope. **manageable** *adjective* [from Latin *manus* = hand]

management *noun* **1** managing. **2** managers; the people in charge.

manager *noun* a person who manages something. **manageress** *noun*, **managerial** (*say* man-uh-**jeer**-ree-uhl) *adjective*

manchester *noun* (*Australian*) household linen. [named after the city Manchester in England]

mandarin *noun* **1** an important official. **2** a kind of small orange.

mandate *noun* authority given to someone to carry out a certain task or policy, *An elected government has a mandate to govern the country.* [from Latin *mandatum* = commanded]

mandatory *adjective* obligatory; compulsory.

mandible *noun* **1** a jaw, especially the lower one. **2** either part of a bird's beak or the similar part in insects etc. (Compare **maxilla.**)

mandir (*say* **man**-deer) *noun* a Hindu temple. [from Hindi and Sanskrit *mandira* = dwelling place, temple]

mandolin *noun* a musical instrument rather like a guitar.

mandrake *noun* a poisonous plant with white or purple flowers and large yellow fruit.

mane *noun* the long hair on a horse's or lion's neck.

manful *adjective* brave. **manfully** *adverb*

manga *noun* Japanese cartoons, comic books, and animated films, often intended for a mature audience. [from Japanese *man* = indiscriminate, + *ga* = picture]

manganese *noun* a hard brittle metal.

mange *noun* a skin disease affecting hairy animals such as dogs.

manger *noun* a long trough for horses or cattle to feed from.

mangle[1] *noun* a wringer. **mangle** *verb*

mangle[2] *verb* (**mangled, mangling**) damage something by crushing or cutting it roughly.

mango *noun* (*plural* **mangoes**) a tropical fruit with yellow pulp.

mangrove *noun* a tropical tree growing in mud and swamps, with many tangled roots above the ground.

mangy *adjective* **1** having mange. **2** squalid; shabby.

manhandle *verb* (**manhandled, manhandling**) treat or push roughly.

manhole *noun* a space or opening, usually with a cover, by which a person can get into a sewer or roof to inspect or repair it.

manhood *noun* **1** the condition of being a man. **2** manly qualities.

mania *noun* **1** mental illness marked by periods of great excitement and violence. **2** great enthusiasm, *football mania.* [Greek, = madness]

maniac *noun* a person with mania.

manic *adjective* of or affected with mania.

manic depression *noun* bipolar disorder. **manic-depressive** *adjective*

manicure *noun* care and treatment of the hands and nails. **manicure** *verb*, **manicurist** *noun* [from Latin *manus* = hand, + *cura* = care]

manifest[1] *adjective* clear and obvious. **manifestly** *adverb*

manifest[2] *verb* show a thing clearly. **manifestation** *noun*

manifesto *noun* (*plural* **manifestos**) a public statement of a group's or person's policy or principles.

manifold *adjective* of many kinds; very varied. [from *many* + *-fold*]

manikin *noun* **1** a little man; a dwarf. **2** an anatomical model of the human body.

manila *noun* a kind of brown paper used for wrapping and for envelopes.

manioc *noun* cassava; the flour made from this.

manipulate *verb* (**manipulated, manipulating**) **1** handle something skilfully. **2** handle or arrange something cleverly or cunningly. **manipulation** *noun*, **manipulator** *noun* [from Latin *manus* = hand]

mankind *noun* human beings in general.

> **Usage** The word *mankind* is often considered sexist or old-fashioned now. *Humankind* or the *human race* can be used instead.

manly *adjective* **1** suitable for a man. **2** strong; brave. **manliness** *noun*

man-made *adjective* made or caused by human beings.

> **Usage** See the note at *man*[1].

manna *noun* **1** (in the Bible) a substance miraculously supplied as food to the Israelites while they were in the wilderness. **2** an edible white sweet substance exuded by many eucalypts.

mannequin (*say* **man**-uh-kuhn or **man**-uh-kwuhn) *noun* **1** a person who models clothes. **2** a dressmaker's or window dummy.

manner *noun* **1** the way something happens or is done. **2** a person's way of behaving. **3** sort, *all manner of things.*

mannerism *noun* **1** a person's habit or way of doing something. **2** a style of European art in the 16th century, involving contorted figures.

manners *plural noun* **1** how a person behaves with other people. **2** politeness.

mannish *adjective* like a man.

manoeuvre[1] (*say* muh-**noo**-vuh) *noun* a difficult or skilful or cunning action.

manoeuvre[2] *verb* (**manoeuvred, manoeuvring**) make a difficult or skilful or cunning action. **manoeuvrable** *adjective* [from Latin, = work by hand (*manus* = hand, *operari* = to work)]

man-of-war *noun* (*plural* **men-of-war**) a warship.

manor *noun* (*British*) a large country house; the land belonging to it. **manorial** *adjective*

manpower *noun* the number of people who are working or needed or available for work on something.

manse *noun* a church minister's house.

mansion *noun* a large stately house.

manslaughter *noun* killing a person unlawfully but without meaning to.

mantelpiece *noun* a shelf above a fireplace.

mantle *noun* a cloak.

manual[1] *adjective* of or done with the hands, *manual work*; *a manual gear change.* **manually** *adverb*

manual[2] *noun* **1** a handbook. **2** an organ keyboard played with the hands. **3** a vehicle with gears that are changed by hand. [from Latin *manus* = hand]

manufacture *verb* (**manufactured, manufacturing**) make things. **manufacture** *noun*, **manufacturer** *noun* [from Latin *manu* = by hand, + *facere* = make]

manure *noun* fertiliser, especially dung.

manuscript *noun* **1** something written by hand. **2** an author's work as written or typed, submitted for publication. [from Latin *manu* = by hand, + *scriptum* = written]

many[1] *adjective* (**more, most**) great in number; numerous, *many people.*
how many what number of.

many[2] *pronoun* a large number of people or things, *the solution to many of our problems.*

many[3] *plural noun* (**the many**) the majority of people, *music for the many.*

Maori (*say* **mow**-ree) *noun* (*plural* **Maoris**) **1** a member of the indigenous people of New Zealand. **2** their language.

map[1] *noun* a diagram of part or all of the earth's surface or of the sky.

map[2] *verb* (**mapped, mapping**) make a map of an area.
map out plan the details of something.

maple *noun* a tree with broad leaves.

mar *verb* (**marred, marring**) spoil.

marathon *noun* a long-distance running race, usually of about 42 kilometres. [named after Marathon in Greece, from which a messenger ran to Athens in 490 BC to announce that the Greeks had defeated the Persian army]

marauding *adjective* going about in search of plunder or prey. **marauder** *noun* [from French *maraud* = rogue]

marble *noun* **1** a small glass ball used in games. **2** a kind of limestone polished and used in sculpture or building.

marbled *adjective* having a veined or mottled appearance.

March *noun* the third month of the year. [from Latin *Martius* = of the god Mars]

march[1] *verb* **1** walk with regular steps. **2** make somebody walk somewhere, *He marched them up the hill.* **marcher** *noun*

march[2] *noun* (*plural* **marches**) **1** marching. **2** music suitable for marching to. **3** a procession as demonstration. [from Latin *marcus* = hammer]

marchioness *noun* (*plural* **marchionesses**) the wife or widow of a marquis.

mare *noun* a female horse or donkey.

margarine (*say* mah-juh-**reen**) *noun* a substance used like butter, made from animal or vegetable fats.

margin *noun* **1** an edge or border. **2** the blank space between the edge of a page and the writing or pictures on it. **3** the difference between two scores or prices, *She won by a narrow margin.*

marginal *adjective* **1** of or in a margin, *marginal notes.* **2** very slight, *a marginal difference.* **marginally** *adverb*

marginalise *verb* (**marginalised, marginalising**) treat as insignificant or less important.

marginal seat *noun* a seat where a Member of Parliament was elected with only a small majority and may be defeated in the next election.

marigold *noun* a yellow or orange garden flower.

marijuana (*say* ma-ruh-**wah**-nuh) *noun* a drug made from hemp.

marina (*say* muh-**ree**-nuh) *noun* a harbour for yachts and pleasure boats.

marinade *noun* a flavoured liquid in which meat or fish is soaked before being cooked. **marinade** *verb*

marine[1] (*say* muh-**reen**) *adjective* **1** of or concerned with the sea. **2** of shipping.

marine[2] *noun* a soldier trained to serve on land and at sea. [from Latin *mare* = sea]

mariner (*say* **ma**-ruh-nuh) *noun* a sailor.

marionette *noun* a puppet worked by strings or wires.

marital *adjective* of marriage. [from Latin *maritus* = husband]

maritime *adjective* **1** of the sea or ships. **2** found near the sea. [same origin as *marine*]

mark[1] *noun* **1** a line or area that differs in appearance from the rest of a surface, especially one that spoils it. **2** a number or letter put on a piece of work to show its quality. **3** a distinguishing feature. **4** a symbol. **5** a target. **6** the position from which you start a race, *On your marks!* **7** (in Australian Rules football) a catch of the ball after it has been kicked at least 15 metres.

mark[2] *verb* **1** put a mark on something. **2** give a mark to a piece of work; correct. **3** pay attention to something, *Mark my words!* **4** keep close to an opposing player in sport. **5** (in Australian Rules football) catch the ball after it has been kicked at least 15 metres. **marker** *noun*
mark down reduce the price of.
mark time 1 march on one spot without moving forward. **2** occupy your time without making progress.
mark up 1 increase the price of. **2** mark or correct text.

markdown *noun* a reduction in price.

marked *adjective* noticeable, *a marked improvement.* **markedly** *adverb*

market[1] *noun* **1** a place where things are bought and sold, usually from stalls in the open air. **2** demand for things; trade, *There is hardly any market for typewriters now.*

market[2] *verb* (**marketed, marketing**) **1** offer things for sale. **2** advertise or promote something. **marketable** *adjective* [from Latin *merx* = merchandise]

marketplace *noun* **1** an open space for a market. **2** the commercial world.

marksman *noun* (*plural* **marksmen**) an expert in shooting at a target. **marksmanship** *noun*, **markswoman** *noun*

markup *noun* **1** the amount added to the cost price of goods to cover overheads and profit, *a markup of 50%.* **2** the process or result of correcting text in preparation for printing.

marlin *noun* a long-nosed sea fish.

marloo *noun* a Western Australian name for the red kangaroo. [Western Desert Language]

marmalade *noun* jam made from oranges, lemons, or other citrus fruit.

marmoset *noun* a kind of small monkey.

marmot *noun* a small burrowing animal of the squirrel family.

maroon[1] (*say* muh-**roon**) *verb* abandon or isolate somebody in a deserted place; strand.

maroon[2] (*say* muh-**rohn** or muh-**roon**) *noun* dark brownish-red.

marquee (*say* mah-**kee**) *noun* a large tent used for social or commercial functions.

marquis *noun* (*plural* **marquises**) a nobleman ranking next above an earl.

marriage *noun* **1** the formal union of two people, typically as recognised by law. **2** a wedding. **3** a close union; a combination.

marron *noun* (*plural* **marron**) a large freshwater crayfish found in Western Australia. [from Noongar *marran*]

marrow *noun* **1** a large gourd eaten as a vegetable. **2** the soft substance inside bones.

marry *verb* (**married, marrying**) **1** become a person's husband or wife. **2** unite or give or take in marriage. **3** unite; combine. [from Latin *maritus* = husband]

Mars *noun* one of the planets, with a characteristic red colour. **Martian** *adjective & noun* [named after the Roman god of war]

marsh *noun* (*plural* **marshes**) an area of very wet ground. **marshy** *adjective*

marshal[1] *noun* **1** an official who supervises a contest or ceremony. **2** an officer of very high rank, *a field marshal.*

marshal[2] *verb* (**marshalled, marshalling**) **1** arrange neatly. **2** usher; escort.

marshmallow *noun* a soft spongy sweet.

marsupial (*say* mah-**soo**-pee-uhl) *noun* an animal such as a kangaroo or koala, the female of which has a pouch in which its babies are carried. [from Greek *marsypion* = pouch]

mart *noun* a market or shop.

martial *adjective* **1** of war. **2** warlike. [from Latin, = of Mars, the Roman god of war]

martial arts *plural noun* fighting sports, such as judo and karate.

martial law *noun* government of a country by the armed forces during a crisis.

martinet *noun* a very strict person.

martyr[1] *noun* a person who is killed or suffers because of their beliefs. **martyrdom** *noun*

martyr[2] *verb* kill or torment someone as a martyr. [from Greek, = witness]

marvel[1] *noun* a wonderful thing.

marvel[2] *verb* (**marvelled, marvelling**) be filled with wonder.

marvellous *adjective* wonderful.

Marxism *noun* the Communist theories of the German writer Karl Marx (1818–83). **Marxist** *noun & adjective*

marzipan *noun* a soft sweet food made of ground almonds and sugar.

mascara *noun* a cosmetic for darkening the eyelashes. [from Italian, = mask]

mascarpone (*say* mas-kuh-**poh**-nee) *noun* a soft creamy Italian cheese. [Italian]

mascot *noun* a person, animal, or thing that is believed to bring good luck.

masculine *adjective* of or like men; suitable for men. **masculinity** *noun*

mash *verb* crush into a soft mass.

mask[1] *noun* a covering worn over the face to disguise or protect it.

mask[2] *verb* **1** cover with a mask. **2** disguise; screen; conceal.

masochist (*say* **mas**-uh-kist) *noun* a person who enjoys things that seem painful or tiresome. **masochism** *noun*, **masochistic** *adjective*

mason *noun* **1** a person who builds or works with stone. **2** (**Mason**) a Freemason.

masonry *noun* **1** the stone parts of a building; stonework. **2** a mason's work.

masquerade[1] *noun* a pretence.

masquerade[2] *verb* (**masqueraded, masquerading**) pretend to be something, *He masqueraded as a policeman.* [from Spanish *mascara* = mask]

Mass *noun* (*plural* **Masses**) the Communion service in a Roman Catholic church.

mass[1] *noun* (*plural* **masses**) **1** a large number or amount. **2** a heap, lump, or other collection of matter. **3** (in scientific use) the quantity of matter that a thing contains. In non-scientific use this is called *weight.*
the masses ordinary people.

mass[2] *verb* collect into a mass.

massacre *noun* the killing of a large number of people. **massacre** *verb*

massage (*say* **mas**-ah*zh*) *verb* (**massaged, massaging**) rub and press the body to make it less stiff or less painful. **massage** *noun*, **masseur** *noun*, **masseuse** *noun*

massive *adjective* large and heavy; huge.

mass noun *noun* a noun that is not normally countable and not used with the indefinite article, e.g. *rice.* (Compare **count noun.**)

mass production *noun* manufacturing goods in large quantities. **mass-produced** *adjective*

mast *noun* a tall pole that holds up a ship's sail or a flag or an aerial.

master[1] *noun* **1** a person who is in charge of something. **2** a person who is very good at something; a great artist or musician. **3** something from which copies are made. **4** (**Master**) a title put before a boy's name. **5** (usually in titles) a person who holds a second or further degree, *a master's degree*; *a Master of Arts.* **6** a male teacher.

master[2] *verb* **1** learn a subject or a skill thoroughly. **2** overcome; bring under control. [from Latin *magister* = master]

masterful *adjective* **1** domineering. **2** very skilful. **masterfully** *adverb*

masterly *adjective* very skilful.

mastermind[1] *noun* **1** a very clever person. **2** the person who is planning and organising a scheme etc.

mastermind[2] *verb* plan and organise a scheme etc.

masterpiece *noun* **1** an excellent piece of work. **2** a person's best piece of work.

mastery *noun* **1** complete control. **2** thorough knowledge or skill in something.

masticate *verb* (**masticated, masticating**) chew food. **mastication** *noun* [from Greek *mastichan* = gnash the teeth]

mastiff *noun* a large kind of dog.

masturbate *verb* (**masturbated, masturbating**) excite sexually by stimulating the genitals. **masturbation** *noun*

mat *noun* **1** a small carpet; a doormat. **2** a small piece of material put on a table to protect the surface.

matador *noun* a bullfighter who fights on foot. [from Spanish *matar* = kill]

match[1] *noun* (*plural* **matches**) a small thin stick with a head made of a substance that gives a flame when rubbed on something rough. **matchbox** *noun*, **matchstick** *noun*

match[2] *noun* (*plural* **matches**) **1** a game or contest between two teams or players. **2** one person or thing that matches another. **3** a marriage.

match[3] *verb* **1** be equal or similar to another person or thing. **2** put teams or players to compete against each other. **3** find something that is similar or corresponding.

mate[1] *noun* **1** a companion or friend. **2** one of a mated pair. **3** an officer on a merchant ship.

mate[2] *verb* (**mated, mating**) **1** come or put together so as to have offspring. **2** put together as a pair or as corresponding.

mate[3] *noun & verb* (in chess) checkmate.

material *noun* **1** anything used for making or doing something. **2** cloth; fabric. [from Latin *materia* = matter]

materialise *verb* (**materialised, materialising**) **1** become visible; appear, *The ghost didn't materialise.* **2** become a fact; happen, *The trip did not materialise.* **materialisation** *noun*

materialism *noun* regarding possessions as very important. **materialist** *noun*, **materialistic** *adjective*

maternal *adjective* **1** of a mother. **2** motherly. **maternally** *adverb* [from Latin *mater* = mother]

maternity[1] *noun* motherhood.

maternity[2] *adjective* to do with having a baby, *maternity hospital.* [same origin as *maternal*]

mateship *noun* the bond between partners; comradeship as an ideal.

matey *adjective* friendly; sociable.

mathematics *noun* the study of numbers, measurements, and shapes. **mathematical** *adjective*, **mathematically** *adverb*, **mathematician** *noun*

maths *noun* mathematics.

matilda *noun* (*Australian*) a swag.
waltzing matilda carrying a swag.

matinée *noun* (also **matinee**) an afternoon performance at a theatre or cinema.

matins *noun* the church service of morning prayer. [from Latin *matutinus* = of morning]

matriarch (*say* **may**-tree-ahk) *noun* a woman who is the head of a family or community. (Compare **patriarch** 1.) **matriarchal** *adjective*, **matriarchy** *noun* [from Latin *mater* = mother, + Greek *archein* = to rule]

matriculate *verb* admit or be admitted to a university. **matriculation** *noun*

matrimony *noun* marriage. **matrimonial** *adjective*

matrix (*say* **may**-triks) *noun* (*plural* **matrices**) **1** the cultural, social, or political environment in which something develops. **2** (in mathematics) a set of numbers or quantities arranged in rows and columns. **3** a mould in which something is shaped.

matron *noun* **1** an older married woman, especially one who is staid or dignified. **2** a woman nurse and housekeeper at a boarding school or institution. **3** (*old use*) the person in charge of the nursing staff in a hospital. **matronly** *adjective*

matron of honour *noun* a woman, usually married, as the chief attendant of the bride at a wedding.

matt *adjective* not shiny, *matt paint.*

matted *adjective* tangled into a mass.

matter[1] *noun* **1** something you can touch or see, not spirit or mind or qualities. **2** that which has mass and occupies space. **3** things of a certain kind, *printed matter.* **4** something to be thought about or done, *It's a serious matter.* **5** a quantity, *in a matter of minutes.*
what is the matter? what is wrong? [same origin as *material*]

matter[2] *verb* be important.

matter-of-fact *adjective* keeping to facts; not imaginative or emotional.

matting *noun* rough material for covering floors.

mattress *noun* (*plural* **mattresses**) soft or springy material in a fabric covering, used on or as a bed.

mature[1] *adjective* **1** fully grown or developed; grown-up. **2** ripe. **maturely** *adverb*, **maturity** *noun*

mature[2] *verb* (**matured, maturing**) make or become mature. [from Latin *maturus* = ripe]

maudlin *adjective* sentimental in a silly or tearful way.

maul *verb* injure by handling or clawing, *He was mauled by a lion.*

maulana (*say* mow-**lah**-nuh) *noun* a Muslim man revered for his religious learning or piety. [Arabic]

mausoleum (*say* maw-suh-**lee**-uhm) *noun* a magnificent tomb. [named after the tomb of Mausolus, a king in the 4th century BC in what is now Turkey]

mauve *noun* pale purple.

maverick *noun* a person who belongs to a group but often disagrees with its beliefs.

maw *noun* the jaws, mouth, or stomach of a hungry or fierce animal.

maxilla *noun* (*plural* **maxillae**) the upper jaw; a similar part in a bird or insect etc. (Compare **mandible**.)

maxim *noun* a short saying giving a general truth or rule of behaviour, e.g. 'Waste not, want not'.

maximise *verb* (**maximised, maximising**) **1** make as large or great as possible. **2** make the best use of. **maximisation** *noun*

maximum *noun* (*plural* **maxima**) the greatest possible number or amount. (The opposite is **minimum.**) **maximum** *adjective* [Latin, = greatest thing]

May *noun* the fifth month of the year. [from Latin *Maius* = of the goddess Maia]

may *auxiliary verb* (*past tense* **might**) used to express **1** permission (*You may go now*), **2** possibility (*It may be true*), **3** wish (*Long may she reign*), **4** uncertainty (*whoever it may be*).

maybe *adverb* perhaps; possibly.

mayday *noun* an international radio signal calling for help. [from French *m'aidez* = help me]

mayhem *noun* violent confusion or damage.

mayonnaise *noun* a creamy sauce made from eggs, oil, and vinegar.

mayor *noun* the person in charge of the council in a town or city. **mayoral** *adjective*, **mayoress** *noun*

maze *noun* a network of paths, especially one designed as a puzzle in which to try and find your way.

Mbps *abbreviation* megabits per second.

MC[1] *abbreviation* Master of Ceremonies.

MC[2] *noun* a rapper.

me *pronoun* the form of *I* used as the object of a verb or after a preposition.

mea culpa *noun & interjection* an acknowledgement of guilt or error. [Latin, = by my fault]

mead *noun* an alcoholic drink made from honey and water.

meadow *noun* a field of grass.

meagre *adjective* scanty in amount.

meal[1] *noun* food served and eaten at one sitting. **mealtime** *noun*

meal[2] *noun* coarsely ground grain. **mealy** *adjective*

mean[1] *verb* (**meant, meaning**) **1** have as an equivalent, *'Maybe' means 'perhaps'.* **2** have as a purpose; intend, *I mean to win.* **3** indicate, *Dark clouds mean rain.*

mean[2] *adjective* **1** not generous; miserly. **2** unkind; spiteful, *a mean trick.* **3** poor in quality or appearance, *a mean little house.* **meanly** *adverb*, **meanness** *noun*

mean[3] *noun* **1** the value obtained by dividing the sum of several quantities by their number; an average. **2** a middle point or condition.

mean[4] *adjective* **1** (of a quantity) calculated as a mean; average, *Participants in the study had a mean age of 35 years.* **2** equally far from two extremes.

meander (*say* mee-**an**-duh) *verb* **1** take a winding course. **2** wander. **meander** *noun* [named after the Meander, a river in Turkey]

meaning *noun* what something means. **meaningful** *adjective*, **meaningless** *adjective*

means[1] *noun* a way of achieving something or producing a result, *We transport our goods by means of trucks.*
by all means certainly.
by no means not at all.

means[2] *plural noun* money or other wealth. [from *mean*[3]]

means test *noun* an official investigation into a person's financial circumstances to determine their eligibility for state assistance.

meant *past tense & past participle* of **mean**[1].

meantime *noun* the time between two events or while something else is happening, *in the meantime.* [from *mean*[3] + *time*]

meanwhile *adverb* **1** in the time between two events. **2** while something else is happening. [from *mean*[3] + *while*]

measles *noun* an infectious disease that causes small red spots on the skin.

measly *adjective* (*informal*) very small.

measure[1] *verb* (**measured**, **measuring**) **1** find how big or heavy something is by comparing it with a unit of standard size or weight. **2** be a certain size. **measurable** *adjective*, **measurement** *noun*

measure[2] *noun* **1** a unit used for measuring, *A kilometre is a measure of length.* **2** a device used in measuring. **3** the size or quantity of something. **4** the rhythm of poetry; time in music. **5** something done for a particular purpose; a law, *We took measures to stop vandalism.*

meat *noun* animal flesh used as food. **meaty** *adjective*

mechanic *noun* a person who uses or repairs machinery.

mechanical *adjective* **1** of machines; produced or worked by machines. **2** automatic; done or doing things without thought. **mechanically** *adverb* [from Greek *mechane* = machine]

mechanics *noun* **1** the study of movement and force. **2** the study or use of machines.

mechanised *adjective* operated by or equipped with machines. **mechanisation** *noun*

mechanism *noun* **1** the moving parts of a machine. **2** the way a machine works.

medal *noun* a piece of metal shaped like a coin, star, or cross, given to a person for bravery or for achieving something.

medallion *noun* a large medal.

medallist *noun* a winner of a medal.

meddle *verb* (**meddled**, **meddling**) **1** interfere. **2** tinker, *Don't meddle with it.* **meddler** *noun*, **meddlesome** *adjective*

media *noun* **1** *plural* of **medium**[2]. **2** (**the media**) newspapers, radio, television, and the Internet, which convey information and ideas to the public.

> **Usage** Although *media* is a Latin plural form, in sense 2 it is commonly used as a collective noun, and can take either a plural or singular verb: *the media are to blame for these false reports*; *the media is to blame for these false reports.*

medial *adjective* in the middle; average. [from Latin *medius* = middle]

median[1] *adjective* in the middle.

median[2] *noun* **1** a point, line, artery, etc. situated in the middle. **2** the middle value of a series of values arranged in order or size. **3** (in geometry) a straight line drawn from any vertex of a triangle to the middle of the opposite side.

median strip *noun* a usually raised strip in the middle of a road, separating opposing lanes of traffic.

mediate *verb* (**mediated**, **mediating**) negotiate between the opposing sides in a dispute. **mediation** *noun*, **mediator** *noun* [from Latin *medius* = middle]

medical *adjective* connected with the treatment of disease and injury. **medically** *adverb* [from Latin *medicus* = doctor]

medicament *noun* a medicine or ointment.

medicated *adjective* treated with a medicinal substance. **medication** *noun*

medicine *noun* **1** a drug or other preparation for the treatment or prevention of disease. **2** the study and treatment of disease and injury. **medicinal** (*say* muh-**dis**-uh-nuhl) *adjective*, **medicinally** *adverb*

medieval (*say* med-ee-**ee**-vuhl) *adjective* of the Middle Ages. [from Latin *medius* = middle, + *aevum* = age]

mediocre (*say* mee-dee-**oh**-kuh) *adjective* not very good; of only medium quality; middling. **mediocrity** *noun*

meditate *verb* (**meditated**, **meditating**) **1** think deeply and quietly. **2** focus one's mind for a period of time, in silence or with the aid of chanting, for spiritual purposes or as a method of relaxation. **meditation** *noun*, **meditative** *adjective*

Mediterranean *adjective* of the Mediterranean Sea (which lies between Europe and Africa) or the countries round it. [from Latin, = sea in the middle of the earth (*media* = middle, + *terra* = land)]

medium[1] *adjective* of middle size or degree or quality; moderate; average.

medium[2] *noun* (*plural* **media**) **1** a middle size or degree or quality. **2** a thing in which something exists, moves, or is expressed, *Air is the medium in which sound travels; Television is used as a medium for advertising.* (See **media**.) **3** (*plural* **mediums**) a person who claims to be able to communicate with the dead. [Latin, = middle thing]

medley *noun* (*plural* **medleys**) an assortment or mixture of things.

meek *adjective* quiet and obedient. **meekly** *adverb*, **meekness** *noun*

meet[1] *verb* (**met**, **meeting**) **1** come together from different places; come face to face. **2** make the acquaintance of. **3** come into contact; touch. **4** go to receive an arrival, *We will meet your train.* **5** pay a bill or the cost of something. **6** deal with a problem, demand, etc.

meet[2] *noun* a meeting of athletes for a competition.

meet[3] *adjective* (*old use*) suitable; proper.

meeting *noun* **1** coming together. **2** a number of people who have come together for a discussion or contest.

meg *noun* one megabyte of computer memory or storage.

mega- *prefix* **1** large; great (as in *megaphone*). **2** one million (as in *megahertz* = one million hertz). [from Greek *megas* = great]

megabit *noun* (in computing) a unit of data size or network speed, equal to one million or (strictly) 1,048,576 bits (per second).

megabyte *noun* (in computing) a measure of how much data a disk or memory can hold, = 1,048,576 bytes.

megafauna *noun* the large animals of a particular region, habitat, or geological period. [from *mega-* + *fauna*]

megahertz *noun* a unit of frequency of electromagnetic waves, = one million cycles per second.

megalomania *noun* an exaggerated idea of your own importance. **megalomaniac** *noun* [from *mega-* + *mania*]

megaphone *noun* a funnel-shaped device for amplifying a person's voice. [from *mega-*, + Greek *phone* = voice]

meiosis (*say* muy-**oh**-suhs) *noun* the process of division of the nuclei of cells in which gametes are formed, each containing half the normal number of chromosomes. [modern Latin from Greek, = lessening]

melamine *noun* a strong kind of plastic.

melancholy[1] *adjective* sad; gloomy.

melancholy[2] *noun* sadness; gloom. [from Greek *melas* = black, + *chole* = bile]

melanoma *noun* a malignant skin tumour.

mêlée (*say* **mel**-ay) *noun* **1** a confused fight. **2** a muddle. [French, = medley]

mellow[1] *adjective* **1** not harsh; soft and rich in flavour, colour, or sound. **2** kindly and genial. **mellowness** *noun*

mellow[2] *verb* make or become mellow.

melodeon *noun* (also **melodion**) a small organ or harmonium.

melodic *adjective* of melody.

melodious *adjective* full of melody.

melodrama *noun* a play full of dramatic excitement and emotion. **melodramatic** *adjective* [from Greek *melos* = music, + *drama*]

melody *noun* (*plural* **melodies**) a tune, especially a pleasing tune. [from Greek *melos* = music, + *oide* = song]

melon *noun* a large sweet fleshy fruit with a thick skin, e.g. watermelon, rockmelon.

melt *verb* **1** make or become liquid by heating. **2** disappear slowly. **3** soften.

meltdown *noun* **1** a disastrous collapse or breakdown. **2** (*informal*) an uncontrolled emotional outburst or a mental collapse. **3** an accident in a nuclear reactor in which the fuel overheats and melts the reactor core or shielding.

member *noun* **1** a person or thing that belongs to a particular society or group. **2** a part of something. **membership** *noun* [from Latin *membrum* = limb]

membrane *noun* a thin skin or similar covering. **membranous** *adjective*

meme *noun* **1** an image, video, piece of text, etc., typically humorous in nature, that is copied and spread rapidly by Internet users, often with slight variations. **2** an element of a culture or system of behaviour that may be considered to be passed from one individual to another by non-genetic means, especially imitation. **memetic** *adjective*

memento *noun* (*plural* **mementoes**) a souvenir. [Latin, = remember]

memo (*say* **mem**-oh) *noun* (*plural* **memos**) (*informal*) a memorandum.

memoir (*say* **mem**-wah) *noun* a historical account or biography written from personal knowledge.

memoirs *plural noun* an autobiography.

memorable *adjective* worth remembering; easy to remember. **memorably** *adverb*

memorandum *noun* (*plural* **memoranda**) a written note, especially to remind yourself of something. [from Latin, = thing to be remembered]

memorial *noun* something to remind people of a person or event, *a war memorial.* **memorial** *adjective*

memorise *verb* (**memorised**, **memorising**) get something into your memory.

memory *noun* (*plural* **memories**) **1** the ability to remember things. **2** something that you remember. **3** the part of a computer where information is stored. [from Latin *memor* = remembering]

memory card *noun* a removable data storage device used in digital cameras, video game consoles, and certain other electronic devices.

memory stick *noun* (*trademark*) a USB flash drive.

men *plural* of **man**[1].

menace[1] *noun* **1** a threat or danger. **2** a troublesome person or thing.

menace[2] *verb* (**menaced**, **menacing**) threaten with harm or danger.

menagerie *noun* a small zoo.

mend[1] *verb* **1** repair. **2** make or become better; improve. **mender** *noun*

mend[2] *noun* a repair.

mendacious (*say* men-**day**-shuhs) *adjective* untruthful; telling lies. **mendaciously** *adverb*, **mendacity** *noun* [from Latin *mendax* = lying]

mendicant *noun* a beggar. [from Latin *mendicans* = begging]

menial (*say* **mee**-nee-uhl) *adjective* lowly; needing little or no skill, *menial tasks.* **menially** *adverb*

meningitis *noun* a disease causing inflammation of the membranes (*meninges*) around the brain and spinal cord.

meningococcus (*say* muh-nin-joh-**kok**-uhs) *noun* (*plural* **meningococci**) a bacterium involved in some forms of meningitis.

menopause *noun* the time of life when a woman finally ceases to menstruate. [from Greek *menos* = of a month, + *pause*]

menorah *noun* a seven-branched Jewish candelabrum.

menstruate *verb* (**menstruated**, **menstruating**) bleed from the womb about once a month, as normally happens to girls and women from their teens until middle age. **menstrual** *adjective*, **menstruation** *noun* [from Latin *menstruus* = monthly]

mental *adjective* **1** of or in the mind. **2** (*informal*) mad. **mentally** *adverb* [from Latin *mentis* = of the mind]

mentality *noun* (*plural* **mentalities**) a person's mental ability or attitude.

menthol *noun* a solid white peppermint-flavoured substance. [from Latin *mentha* = mint]

mention[1] *verb* speak or write about a person or thing briefly; refer to.

mention[2] *noun* mentioning something.

mentor *noun* a trusted adviser; a counsellor. [from Mentor in Greek legend, who advised Odysseus' son]

menu (*say* **men**-yoo) *noun* **1** a list of the food available in a restaurant or served at a meal. **2** a list of things, shown on a screen, from which you decide what you want a computer to do.

meow *verb & noun* mew.

mercantile *adjective* trading; of trade.

mercenary[1] *adjective* working only for money or some other reward.

mercenary[2] *noun* (*plural* **mercenaries**) a soldier hired to serve in a foreign army.

merchandise *noun* goods for sale.

merchant *noun* a person involved in trade.

merciful *adjective* showing mercy. **mercifully** *adverb*

merciless *adjective* showing no mercy; cruel. **mercilessly** *adverb*

mercurial *adjective* **1** of mercury. **2** having sudden changes of mood.

Mercury *noun* the innermost planet of the solar system. [named after a Roman god, the messenger of the gods]

mercury *noun* a heavy silvery metal that is usually liquid, used in thermometers. Also called *quicksilver*. **mercuric** *adjective* [from the name of the planet Mercury]

mercy *noun* (*plural* **mercies**) **1** kindness or pity shown in not punishing or harming a wrongdoer or enemy. **2** something to be thankful for.

mere[1] *adjective* not more than, *He's a mere child.*

mere[2] *noun* (*poetic*) a lake.

merely *adverb* only; simply.

merest *adjective* very small, *the merest trace of colour.*

merge *verb* (**merged**, **merging**) combine; blend. [from Latin *mergere* = dip]

merger *noun* the combining of two things into one, especially companies.

meridian *noun* a line on a map or globe from the North Pole to the South Pole. The meridian that passes through Greenwich is shown on maps as 0° longitude.

meringue (*say* muh-**rang**) *noun* a crisp cake made from egg white and sugar.

merino *noun* (*plural* **merinos**) a kind of sheep with fine soft wool.

merit[1] *noun* **1** a quality that deserves praise; excellence. **2** a quality or good point. **meritorious** *adjective*

merit[2] *verb* (**merited, meriting**) deserve. [from Latin *meritum* = deserved]

mermaid *noun* a mythical sea creature with a woman's body but with a fish's tail instead of legs. **merman** *noun* [from *mere*[2] + *maid*]

merry *adjective* (**merrier, merriest**) cheerful and lively. **merrily** *adverb*, **merriment** *noun*

merry-go-round *noun* a machine with a revolving platform fitted with horses, cars, etc. for riding on.

mesclun *noun* a salad of edible leaves and flowers. [Provençal]

mesh[1] *noun* **1** the open spaces in a net, sieve, or other criss-cross structure. **2** material made like a net; network.

mesh[2] *verb* (of gears) engage.

mesmerise *verb* hypnotise; fascinate or hold a person's attention completely. **mesmerism** *noun*

mess[1] *noun* (*plural* **messes**) **1** a dirty or untidy condition or thing. **2** a difficult or confused situation; trouble. **3** (in the armed forces) a dining room.
make a mess of bungle.

mess[2] *verb* **1** make a thing dirty or untidy. **2** bungle; spoil by muddling, *They messed up our plans.*
mess about 1 behave stupidly. **2** potter.
mess with interfere or tinker with.

message[1] *noun* **1** a piece of information sent from one person to another. **2** the central theme of a book etc.

message[2] *verb* send a message to someone, especially by mobile phone or email.

messenger *noun* a person who carries a message.

Messiah (*say* muh-**suy**-uh) *noun* **1** the promised deliverer of the Jewish nation prophesied in the Hebrew Bible. **2** Jesus regarded by Christians as the Messiah of the Hebrew prophecies and the saviour of humankind. **Messianic** *adjective* [from Hebrew, = the anointed one]

messmate *noun* a rough-barked eucalypt.

messy *adjective* **1** dirty; untidy. **2** difficult to deal with; awkward. **messily** *adverb*, **messiness** *noun*

met *past tense & past participle* of **meet**[1].

metabolism (*say* muh-**tab**-uh-liz-uhm) *noun* the process by which food is built up into living material in a plant or animal, or used to supply it with energy. **metabolic** *adjective*, **metabolise** *verb* [from Greek *metabole* = change]

metacarpus *noun* (*plural* **metacarpi**) the part of the hand between the wrist and the fingers; the set of bones in this. **metacarpal** *adjective*

metadata *noun* a set of data that describes and gives information about other data.

metafiction *noun* a kind of fiction that self-consciously comments on its own fictional status.

meta key *noun* (in computing) a key on some keyboards that activates a particular function when held down simultaneously with another key.

metal *noun* a hard mineral substance (e.g. gold, silver, copper, iron) that melts when it is heated. **metallic** *adjective*

metalanguage *noun* **1** a form of language used to discuss a language. **2** a system of propositions about propositions.

metallurgy (*say* **met**-uh-ler-jee) *noun* the study of metals; the craft of making and using metals. **metallurgical** *adjective*, **metallurgist** *noun* [from *metal*, + Greek *-ourgia* = working]

metamorphic *adjective* (of rock) formed or changed by heat or pressure, *Marble is a metamorphic rock.* [from Greek *meta-* = change, + *morphe* = form]

metamorphosis (*say* met-uh-**maw**-fuh-suhs) *noun* (*plural* **metamorphoses**) a change of form or character. **metamorphose** *verb* [same origin as *metamorphic*]

metaphor *noun* the transfer of a word or phrase to something that it does not apply to literally, e.g. *a burning ambition*; *Her heart was on fire.* (Compare **simile**.) **metaphorical** *adjective*, **metaphorically** *adverb* [from Greek *metapherein* = transfer]

metatarsus *noun* (*plural* **metatarsi**) the part of the foot between the ankle and the toes; the set of bones in this. **metatarsal** *adjective*

mete *verb* (**meted, meting**) (usually as **mete out**) deal out; allot, *mete out punishment.*

meteor (*say* **mee**-tee-aw) *noun* a piece of rock or metal that moves through space and burns up when it enters the earth's atmosphere. [from Greek *meteoros* = high in the air]

meteoric (*say* mee-tee-**o**-rik) *adjective* **1** of meteors. **2** like a meteor in brilliance or sudden appearance, *a meteoric career.*

meteorite *noun* a meteor that has landed on the earth.

meteorology *noun* the study of the conditions of the atmosphere, especially in order to forecast the weather. **meteorological** *adjective*, **meteorologist** *noun* [from Greek *meteoros* = high in the air, + *-logy*]

meter *noun* a device for measuring something, e.g. the amount supplied, *a gas meter.* **meter** *verb* [from *mete*]

methadone *noun* a strong narcotic drug used to relieve pain, and as a substitute for heroin or morphine.

methamphetamine (*say* meth-am-**fet**-uh-meen) *noun* a synthetic drug used illegally as a stimulant.

methane (*say* **mee**-thayn) *noun* a flammable gas found in marshy areas and in coalmines.

method *noun* **1** a procedure or way of doing something. **2** methodical behaviour; orderliness. [from Greek *methodos* = pursuit of knowledge]

methodical *adjective* doing things in an orderly or systematic way.
methodically *adverb*

methylated spirits *plural noun* (also **methylated spirit**) a liquid fuel made from alcohol.

meticulous *adjective* very careful and exact.
meticulously *adverb*

métier (*say* **met**-ee-ay) *noun* one's trade, profession, or field of activity; what one does best. [French]

metonymy (*say* muh-**ton**-uh-mee) *noun* using a word denoting an attribute or part of a thing in place of the thing itself, e.g. *crown* for *king*, thus *They swore allegiance to the crown.* [from Latin]

metre *noun* **1** a unit of length in the metric system equal to 100 centimetres, *The tree is seven metres high.* **2** rhythm in poetry. [from Greek *metron* = measure]

metric *adjective* **1** of the metric system. **2** of metre in poetry. **metrically** *adverb*

metrical *adjective* of or in rhythmic metre, not prose, *metrical psalms.*

metric system *noun* a measuring system based on decimal units (the metre, litre, and gram).

metronome *noun* a device that makes a regular clicking noise to help a person keep in time when practising music. [from Greek *metron* = measure, + *nomos* = law]

metropolis *noun* the chief city of a country or region. **metropolitan** *adjective* [from Greek *meter* = mother, + *polis* = city]

mettle *noun* courage; strength of character.
mettlesome *adjective*
be on your mettle be determined to show your courage or ability.

mew *verb* make a cat's cry. **mew** *noun*

mezzanine (*say* **mez**-uh-neen) *noun* an extra storey between two others, often in the form of a wide balcony. [from Italian *mezzano* = middle]

mezzo[1] *adverb* (in music) half; moderately.

mezzo[2] *noun* (also **mezzo-soprano**) a voice between soprano and contralto; a singer with this voice.

mia-mia (*say* **muy**-uh-muy-uh) *noun* (in traditional Aboriginal use) a hut. [from Wathaurong and Woiwurrung *miam miam*]

miaow *verb & noun* mew.

miasma (*say* mee-**az**-muh) *noun* unpleasant or unhealthy air. [Greek, = pollution]

mica *noun* a mineral substance used to make electrical insulators.

mice *plural* of **mouse**.

mickey *noun* **take the mickey out of** (*informal*) tease or ridicule someone.

micro- *prefix* very small (as in *microfilm*). [from Greek *mikros* = small]

microbe *noun* a microorganism. [from *micro-*, + Greek *bios* = life]

microchip *noun* a very small piece of silicon or other material made to work like a complex wired electric circuit.

microcomputer *noun* a very small computer.

microcosm *noun* a world in miniature; something regarded as resembling something else on a very small scale. [from Greek *mikros kosmos* = little world]

microfilm *noun* a length of film on which written or printed material is photographed in greatly reduced size.

micron *noun* one millionth of a metre.

microorganism *noun* a microscopic creature, e.g. a bacterium or virus.

microphone *noun* an electrical device that picks up sound waves for recording, amplifying, or broadcasting. [from *micro-*, + Greek *phone* = sound]

microprocessor *noun* a miniature computer (or a unit of this) consisting of one or more microchips.

microscope *noun* an instrument with lenses that magnify tiny objects or details. [from *micro-*, + Greek *skopein* = look at]

microscopic *adjective* **1** extremely small; too small to be seen without the aid of a microscope. **2** of a microscope.

microsurgery *noun* intricate surgery using a microscope and special small instruments.

microwave *noun* **1** a very short electromagnetic wave. **2** (in full **microwave oven**) an oven that uses microwaves to heat food very quickly.

mid *adjective* in the middle of; middle.

midday *noun* the middle of the day; noon.

midden *noun* **1** a dung heap; a rubbish heap. **2** a rubbish heap that marks an ancient settlement, chiefly containing bones, shells, and stone implements.

middle[1] *noun* **1** the place or part of something that is at the same distance from all its sides or edges or from both its ends. **2** someone's waist.

middle² *adjective* **1** placed or happening in the middle. **2** moderate in size or rank etc.

Middle Ages *noun* the period in history from about AD 1000 to 1400.

middle class *noun* the class of people between the upper class and the working class, including business and professional people.

Middle East *noun* an extensive area of south-western Asia and northern Africa, stretching from the Mediterranean to Pakistan and including the Arabian peninsula. **Middle Eastern** *adjective*

Middle English *noun* the English language from about 1150 to 1500.

middleman *noun* (*plural* **middlemen**) **1** a trader who buys from a producer and sells to a consumer. **2** an intermediary.

middling¹ *adjective* moderately good.

middling² *adverb* fairly or moderately.

midge *noun* a small insect like a gnat.

midget *noun* an extremely small person or thing. **midget** *adjective*

midnight *noun* twelve o'clock at night.

midpoint *noun* **1** the exact middle point, *the midpoint of a line.* **2** a point somewhere in the middle, *at the midpoint of her career.*

midriff *noun* the front part of the body just above the waist.

midshipman *noun* (*plural* **midshipmen**) a sailor ranking next above a cadet.

midst *noun* the middle of something. **in the midst of** among; in the middle of.

midway *adverb* halfway.

midwife *noun* (*plural* **midwives**) a person trained to look after a woman who is giving birth to a baby. **midwifery** *noun*

mien (*say* meen) *noun* a person's manner.

miffed *adjective* (*informal*) offended; put out.

might¹ *noun* great strength or power.

might² *auxiliary verb* used **1** as the *past tense* of *may* (*We told her she might go*), **2** to express possibility (*It might be true*).

mighty *adjective* very strong or powerful. **mightily** *adverb*, **mightiness** *noun*

mignonette (*say* min-yuh-**net**) *noun* **1** a plant with fragrant leaves. **2** a kind of lettuce.

migraine (*say* **muy**-grayn) *noun* a severe kind of headache.

migrant *noun* a person or animal that migrates or has migrated.

migrate *verb* (**migrated**, **migrating**) **1** leave one place or country and settle in another. **2** (of birds or animals) move periodically from one area to another. **migration** *noun*, **migratory** *adjective* [from Latin *migrare* = migrate]

mike *noun* (*informal*) a microphone.

mild *adjective* **1** gentle; not harsh or severe. **2** (of weather) moderately warm. **3** not strongly flavoured. **mildly** *adverb*, **mildness** *noun*

mildew *noun* a tiny fungus that forms a white coating on things kept in damp conditions. **mildewed** *adjective*

mile *noun* a measure of distance, about 1.6 kilometres. [from Latin *mille* = thousand (paces)]

mileage *noun* the number of miles or kilometres travelled.

milestone *noun* **1** a stone of a kind that used to be fixed beside a road to mark the distance between towns. **2** an important event in life or history.

milieu (*say* mee-**lyer**) *noun* environment; surroundings. [French, from *mi* = mid + *lieu* = place]

militant *adjective* eager to fight or be aggressive. **militancy** *noun*, **militant** *noun*

militarism *noun* belief in the use of military strength and methods. **militarist** *noun*, **militaristic** *adjective*

military *adjective* of soldiers or the armed forces. [from Latin *miles* = soldier]

militate *verb* (**militated**, **militating**) have a strong effect or influence, *The weather militated against the success of our plans.*

militia (*say* muh-**lish**-uh) *noun* a military force, especially one raised from civilians. [same origin as *military*]

milk¹ *noun* **1** a white liquid that female mammals produce in their bodies to feed their babies. **2** the milk of cows, used as food by human beings. **3** a milky liquid, e.g. that in a coconut.

milk² *verb* get the milk from a cow or other animal.

milkman *noun* (*plural* **milkmen**) a person who delivers milk to customers' houses.

milk tooth *noun* a first (temporary) tooth in young mammals.

milky *adjective* like milk; white.

Milky Way *noun* the broad bright band of stars formed by our galaxy.

mill¹ *noun* **1** machinery for grinding corn to make flour; a building containing this machinery. **2** a grinding machine, *a pepper mill.* **3** a factory for processing certain materials, *a paper mill.*

mill² *verb* **1** grind or crush in a mill. **2** cut markings round the edge of a coin. **3** move in a confused crowd, *The animals were milling around.* **miller** *noun*

millennial¹ *adjective* **1** of or relating to a period of 1000 years. **2** denoting people reaching young adulthood in the early 21st century.

millennial² *noun* a person reaching young adulthood in the early 21st century.

millennium *noun* (*plural* **millennia** or **millenniums**) a period of 1000 years. [from Latin *mille* = thousand, + *annus* = year]

millet *noun* a kind of cereal with tiny seeds.

milli- *prefix* **1** one thousand (as in *millipede*). **2** one thousandth (as in *milligram*). [from Latin *mille* = thousand]

milligram *noun* one thousandth of a gram, *The tablet weighs ten milligrams.*

millilitre *noun* one thousandth of a litre, *The spoon holds five millilitres of medicine.*

millimetre *noun* one thousandth of a metre, *The ant is nine millimetres long.*

milliner *noun* a person who makes or sells women's hats. **millinery** *noun*

million *noun & adjective* one thousand thousand (1,000,000). **millionth** *adjective & noun*

millionaire *noun* a person whose assets are worth one million dollars or more.

millipede *noun* (also **millepede**) a small crawling creature like a centipede, with many legs. [from Latin *mille* = thousand, + *pedes* = feet]

millstone *noun* **1** either of a pair of large circular stones between which corn is ground. **2** a heavy responsibility.

milt *noun* a male fish's sperm.

mime *noun* acting with movements of the body, not using words. **mime** *verb*

mimic¹ *verb* (**mimicked**, **mimicking**) imitate. **mimicry** *noun*

mimic² *noun* a person who mimics others, especially to amuse people.

mimosa *noun* a tropical tree or shrub with small ball-shaped flowers.

minaret *noun* the tall tower of a mosque. [from Arabic *manara* = lighthouse]

mince¹ *verb* (**minced**, **mincing**) **1** cut into very small pieces in a machine. **2** walk in an affected way. **mincer** *noun*
not to mince matters speak bluntly.

mince² *noun* minced meat.

mincemeat *noun* a sweet mixture of currants, raisins, apple, or other fruits used in pies.

mince pie *noun* a pie containing mincemeat.

mind¹ *noun* **1** the ability to think, feel, understand, and remember, originating in the brain. **2** a person's thoughts and feelings or opinion, *I changed my mind.*

mind² *verb* **1** look after, *He was minding the baby.* **2** be careful about, *Mind the step.* **3** be sad or upset about something; object to, *We don't mind waiting.* **minder** *noun*

mind-boggling *adjective* (*informal*) amazing; unbelievable.

mindful *adjective* taking thought or care, *She was mindful of her reputation.*

mindless *adjective* **1** without intelligence. **2** not requiring thought or skill, *a mindless job.*

mindset *noun* a mental attitude.

mine¹ *possessive pronoun* belonging to me.

mine² *noun* **1** a place where coal or other minerals are dug out of the ground. **2** an explosive placed in or on the ground or in the sea to destroy people or things that come close to it.

mine³ *verb* (**mined**, **mining**) **1** dig from a mine. **2** lay explosive mines in a place.

minefield *noun* an area where explosive mines have been laid.

miner¹ *noun* a person who works in a mine.

miner² *noun* an Australian bird of the honeyeater family, *noisy miner*; *bell miner.*

mineral *noun* a hard inorganic substance found in the ground. [from Latin *minera* = ore]

mineralogy (*say* min-uh-**ral**-uh-jee) *noun* the study of minerals. **mineralogist** *noun* [from *mineral* + *-logy*]

minestrone (*say* min-uh-**stroh**-nee) *noun* an Italian soup containing vegetables and pasta.

mingle *verb* (**mingled**, **mingling**) **1** mix. **2** move about among people.

mingy *adjective* (*informal*) mean; stingy.

mini- *prefix* miniature; very small. [short for *miniature*]

miniature¹ *adjective* very small; copying something on a very small scale.

miniature² *noun* **1** a very small portrait. **2** a small-scale model.

minibus *noun* (*plural* **minibuses**) a small bus.

minim *noun* a note in music, lasting half as long as a semibreve (written 𝅗𝅥).

minimal *adjective* very small; the least possible. **minimally** *adverb*

minimalism *noun* **1** the use of simple or basic forms in design and art. **2** including only the minimum. **minimalist** *adjective & noun*

minimise *verb* (**minimised**, **minimising**) reduce something to a minimum.

minimum *noun* (*plural* **minima**) the lowest possible number or amount. (The opposite is **maximum**.) [Latin, = least thing]

minion *noun* (*derogatory*) a very obedient assistant or servant.

minister[1] *noun* **1** a person in charge of a government department. **2** a member of the clergy. **ministerial** *adjective*

minister[2] *verb* attend to people's needs. [Latin, = servant]

ministry *noun* (*plural* **ministries**) **1** the body of ministers of a government. **2** the work of the clergy.

mink *noun* **1** a small animal of the weasel family. **2** this animal's valuable brown fur.

minke *noun* a small whale with a pointed snout.

minkey *noun* (*Australian*) a form of hockey for younger players.

minnow *noun* a tiny freshwater fish.

minor[1] *adjective* **1** less important; not very important. **2** of the musical scale that has a semitone after the second note. (Compare **major**[1] 2.) [Latin, = smaller, lesser]

minor[2] *noun* a person under the full legal age.

minority *noun* (*plural* **minorities**) **1** the smallest part of a group of people or things. **2** a small group that is different from others. (Compare **majority** 1.)

minster *noun* a large or important church.

minstrel *noun* a travelling singer and musician in the Middle Ages.

mint[1] *noun* **1** a plant with fragrant leaves that are used for flavouring things. **2** peppermint; a sweet flavoured with this. [from Latin *mentha* = mint]

mint[2] *noun* the place where a country's coins are made.

mint[3] *adjective* clean and new or unused.

mint[4] *verb* make coins. [from Latin *moneta* = money]

minuet *noun* a slow stately dance.

minus[1] *preposition* with the next number or thing subtracted, *Ten minus four equals six* (10 – 4 = 6).

minus[2] *adjective* less than zero, *temperatures of minus ten degrees* (–10°).

minus[3] *noun* a disadvantage. [Latin, = less]

minuscule (*say* **min**-uh-skyool) *adjective* extremely small.

minute[1] (*say* **min**-uht) *noun* **1** one sixtieth of an hour. **2** a very short time; a moment. **3** a particular time, *Come here this minute!* **4** one sixtieth of a degree (used in measuring angles).

minute[2] (*say* muy-**nyoot**) *adjective* **1** very small, *a minute insect.* **2** very detailed, *a minute examination.* **minutely** *adverb* [from Latin *minutus* = little]

minutes *plural noun* a written summary of what was said at a meeting.

minx *noun* (*plural* **minxes**) a cheeky or mischievous girl.

miracle *noun* something wonderful and good that happens, especially something believed to have a supernatural or divine cause. **miraculous** *adjective*, **miraculously** *adverb* [from Latin *mirari* = to wonder]

mirage (*say* muh-**rahzh**) *noun* an illusion; something that seems to be there but is not, especially when a lake seems to appear in a desert. [from French *se mirer* = be reflected]

mire *noun* swampy ground; mud.

mirror[1] *noun* a device or surface of reflecting material, usually glass.

mirror[2] *verb* reflect in or like a mirror. [from Latin *mirare* = look at]

mirror image *noun* **1** an image or object that is identical in form to another, but with the structure reversed, as in a mirror. **2** a person or thing that closely resembles another.

mirror site *noun* (in computing) a site on a network that stores some or all of the contents from another site.

mirth *noun* merriment; laughter. **mirthful** *adjective*, **mirthless** *adjective*

mis- *prefix* badly; wrongly.

misadventure *noun* a piece of bad luck.

misanthropy *noun* dislike of people. **misanthropic** *adjective*, **misanthropist** *noun* [from Greek *misos* = hatred, + *anthropos* = human being]

misapprehend *verb* misunderstand. **misapprehension** *noun*

misappropriate *verb* take something dishonestly. **misappropriation** *noun*

misbehave *verb* behave badly. **misbehaviour** *noun*

miscalculate *verb* calculate incorrectly. **miscalculation** *noun*

miscarriage *noun* **1** the birth of a baby before it has developed enough to live. **2** failure to achieve the right result, *a miscarriage of justice.*

miscellaneous (*say* mis-uh-**lay**-nee-uhs) *adjective* of various kinds; mixed. **miscellany** (*say* muh-**sel**-uh-nee) *noun* [from Latin *miscellus* = mixed]

mischance *noun* misfortune.

mischief *noun* **1** naughty or troublesome behaviour. **2** trouble caused by this. **mischievous** *adjective*, **mischievously** *adverb*

misconception *noun* a mistaken idea.

misconduct *noun* **1** bad behaviour. **2** improper or unprofessional behaviour.

misconstrue *verb* (**misconstrued**, **misconstruing**) misinterpret. **misconstruction** *noun*

miscreant (*say* **mis**-kree-uhnt) *noun* a wrongdoer; a villain.

misdeed *noun* a wrong or improper action.

misdemeanour *noun* a misdeed; an unlawful act.

mis en scène (*say* meez on **sen**) *noun* **1** the scenery and properties for a play. **2** the surroundings of an event. [French, = putting on stage]

miser *noun* a person who hoards money and spends as little as possible. **miserliness** *noun*, **miserly** *adjective* [same origin as *misery*]

miserable *adjective* **1** full of misery; very unhappy, poor, or uncomfortable. **2** disagreeable; unpleasant, *miserable weather.* **miserably** *adverb*

misery *noun* (*plural* **miseries**) **1** great unhappiness or discomfort or suffering. **2** something causing this. **3** (*informal*) a discontented or disagreeable person. [from Latin *miser* = wretched]

misfire *verb* (**misfired, misfiring**) fail to fire; fail to function correctly or to have the required effect, *The joke misfired.*

misfit *noun* **1** a person whose behaviour or attitude sets them apart from others in an uncomfortably conspicuous way. **2** a garment that does not fit.

misfortune *noun* **1** bad luck. **2** an unlucky event or accident.

misgiving *noun* a feeling of doubt or slight fear or mistrust.

misguided *adjective* mistaken.

mishap (*say* **mis**-hap) *noun* an unlucky accident.

misinform *verb* give wrong information to someone; mislead. **misinformation** *noun*

misinterpret *verb* interpret incorrectly. **misinterpretation** *noun*

misjudge *verb* (**misjudged, misjudging**) judge wrongly; form a wrong opinion or estimate. **misjudgement** or **misjudgment** *noun*

mislay *verb* (**mislaid, mislaying**) lose something for a short time.

mislead *verb* (**misled, misleading**) give somebody a wrong idea; deceive.

mismanage *verb* manage something badly. **mismanagement** *verb*

misnomer (*say* mis-**noh**-muh) *noun* an unsuitable name for something. [from *mis-*, + Latin *nomen* = name]

miso (*say* **mee**-soh) *noun* a paste made from fermented soy beans and barley or rice malt, used in Japanese cookery. [Japanese]

misogyny (*say* muh-**soj**-uh-nee) *noun* **1** hatred or dislike of women. **2** prejudice against women. **misogynist** *noun* [from Greek *misos* = hatred, + *gyne* = woman]

misplace *verb* (**misplaced, misplacing**) put something in the wrong place. **misplacement** *noun*

misprint *noun* a mistake in printing.

mispronounce *verb* pronounce incorrectly. **mispronunciation** *noun*

misquote *verb* (**misquoted, misquoting**) quote incorrectly. **misquotation** *noun*

misread *verb* read or interpret incorrectly.

misrepresent *verb* represent in a false or misleading way. **misrepresentation** *noun*

Miss *noun* (*plural* **Misses**) a title put before a girl's or unmarried woman's name. [short for *mistress*]

miss[1] *verb* **1** fail to hit, reach, catch, see, hear, or find something. **2** fail to attend an event or appointment. **3** fail to seize an opportunity. **4** be sad because someone or something is not with you. **5** notice that something has gone. **6** avoid. [from Old English *missan*]

miss[2] *noun* (*plural* **misses**) missing something, *Was that shot a hit or a miss?*

misshapen *adjective* badly shaped.

missile *noun* a weapon or other object for firing or throwing at a target. [from Latin *missum* = sent]

missing *adjective* **1** lost; not in the proper place. **2** absent.

mission *noun* **1** an important job that somebody is sent to do or feels they must do. **2** a place or building where missionaries work. [from Latin *missio* = a sending]

missionary *noun* (*plural* **missionaries**) a person who is sent to another country to spread a religious faith.

mist *noun* **1** damp cloudy air near the ground. **2** condensed water vapour on a surface such as a window or mirror.

mistake[1] *noun* something done wrongly; an incorrect opinion.

mistake[2] *verb* (**mistook, mistaken, mistaking**) **1** misunderstand, *Don't mistake my meaning.* **2** choose or identify wrongly, *We mistook her for her sister.*

mistaken *adjective* incorrect; wrong.

mistime *verb* (**mistimed, mistiming**) do or say something at a wrong time.

mistletoe *noun* a plant with white berries that grows as a parasite on trees.

mistook *past tense* of **mistake**[2].

mistreat *verb* treat badly. **mistreatment** *noun*

mistress *noun* (*plural* **mistresses**) **1** a woman who is in charge of something. **2** a female teacher. **3** a woman who is a man's lover but not his wife.

mistrust *verb* feel no trust in somebody or something. **mistrust** *noun*

misty *adjective* full of mist; not clear. **mistily** *adverb*, **mistiness** *noun*

misunderstand *verb* (**misunderstood**, **misunderstanding**) get a wrong idea or impression of something.

misuse *verb* (**misused**, **misusing**) **1** use incorrectly. **2** treat badly. **misuse** *noun*

mite *noun* **1** a tiny spider-like creature, often found on plants and animals as a parasite. **2** a very small amount. **3** a small child.

mitigate *verb* (**mitigated**, **mitigating**) make a thing less intense or less severe. **mitigation** *noun* [from Latin *mitigare* = make mild]

mitigating circumstances *plural noun* facts that may partially excuse wrongdoing.

mitochondrion (*say* muy-toh-**kon**-dree-uhn) *noun* (*plural* **mitochondria**) an organelle present in most living cells, containing enzymes. [from Greek *mitos* = thread, + *khondrion* = granule]

mitosis (*say* muy-**toh**-suhs) *noun* the process of division of a cell or its nucleus, in which each chromosome splits lengthways into two identical sets, one for each of the two new cells. [from Greek *mitos* = thread]

mitre[1] *noun* **1** the tall tapering hat worn by a bishop. **2** a mitred join.

mitre[2] *verb* (**mitred**, **mitring**) join two tapered pieces of wood, cloth, or other material so that they form a right angle.

mitt *noun* **1** a mitten. **2** a fielder's glove in baseball or softball. **3** (*informal*) a hand or fist.

mitten *noun* a kind of glove without separate parts for the fingers.

mix[1] *verb* **1** put different things together so that they form one substance; blend; combine. **2** (of a person) get together with others. **mixer** *noun*
mix up 1 mix thoroughly. **2** confuse.

mix[2] *noun* (*plural* **mixes**) a mixture.

mixed *adjective* containing two or more kinds of things or people.

mixed number *noun* a number that includes a whole number and a fraction.

mixture *noun* **1** something made of different things mixed together. **2** the process of mixing.

mizzenmast *noun* the mast that is next aft of the mainmast on a ship.

ml *abbreviation* millilitre(s).

MLA *abbreviation* Member of the Legislative Assembly.

MLC *abbreviation* Member of the Legislative Council.

mm *abbreviation* millimetre(s).

MMOG *abbreviation* massively multiplayer online game, a type of computer game in which numerous people can play simultaneously over the Internet.

MMR *abbreviation* measles, mumps, and rubella (a vaccination given to children).

MMS *abbreviation* Multimedia Messaging Service, a system that enables mobile phones to send and receive colour pictures and sound clips as well as text messages.

mnemonic (*say* nuh-**mon**-ik) *noun* a verse or saying that helps you to remember something. [from Greek *mnemonikos* = for the memory]

moan *verb* **1** make a long low sound of pain or suffering. **2** grumble. **moan** *noun*

moat *noun* a deep wide ditch round a castle, usually filled with water. **moated** *adjective*

mob[1] *noun* **1** a large disorderly crowd; a rabble. **2** a gang. **3** (*Australian*) a flock or herd, *a mob of kangaroos.* **4** (*Australian*) an Aboriginal extended family or community.

mob[2] *verb* (**mobbed**, **mobbing**) crowd round somebody. [from Latin *mobile vulgus* = excitable crowd]

mobile[1] *adjective* moving easily. **mobility** *noun*

mobile[2] *noun* **1** a decoration for hanging up so that its parts move in currents of air. **2** a mobile phone. [from Latin *movere* = move]

mobile home *noun* a large caravan usually permanently parked and used for living in.

mobile phone *noun* a portable telephone without physical connection to a network.

mobilise *verb* (**mobilised**, **mobilising**) assemble people or things for a particular purpose, especially for war. **mobilisation** *noun*

moccasin *noun* a soft leather shoe.

mocha *noun* a kind of coffee; flavouring made with this.

mock[1] *verb* **1** make fun of a person or thing. **2** imitate; mimic.

mock[2] *adjective* sham; imitation, not real, *a mock battle.*

mockery *noun* **1** ridicule. **2** a ridiculous representation.

mock-up *noun* a model of something, made in order to test or study it.

modal *adjective* **1** of or relating to mode or form as opposed to substance. **2** of or denoting the mood of a verb. **3** of or relating to nouns, adjectives, and adverbs that express possibility or likelihood.

modality *noun* **1** the state of being modal. **2** a particular method or procedure.

modal verb *noun* an auxiliary verb that expresses necessity or possibility, e.g. *must, shall, will, should, would, can, could, may,* and *might.*

mode *noun* **1** the way a thing is done. **2** what is fashionable. **3** (in music) each of a number of traditional scale systems. **4** (in statistics) the value that occurs most frequently in a given set of data.

model[1] *noun* **1** a copy of an object, usually on a smaller scale. **2** a particular design. **3** a simplified (often mathematical) description of a system etc., to assist calculations and predictions. **4** a person who poses for an artist or displays clothes by wearing them. **5** a person or thing that is worth copying.

model[2] *adjective* **1** miniature. **2** excellent; being an example to others, *a model pupil.*

model[3] *verb* (**modelled, modelling**) **1** make a model of something. **2** make according to a model. **3** work as an artist's model or a fashion model.

modem *noun* a device linking a computer and communication line (such as a telephone line) so that data can be transmitted and received. [short for *mo*dulator-*dem*odulator]

moderate[1] (*say* **mod**-uh-ruht) *adjective* medium; not extremely small or great or hot, *a moderate climate.* **moderately** *adverb*

moderate[2] (*say* **mod**-uh-rayt) *verb* (**moderated, moderating**) make or become moderate. **moderation** *noun*
in moderation in moderate amounts.

modern *adjective* **1** of the present or recent times; in fashion now. **2** using the most up-to-date techniques, ideas, or equipment. **modernity** *noun*

modernise *verb* (**modernised, modernising**) make a thing more modern. **modernisation** *noun*

modernism *noun* modern views or methods, especially the rejection of realism and traditionalism in the art and literature of the first half of the 20th century.

modest *adjective* **1** not vain; not boasting. **2** moderate, *a modest income.* **3** not showy or splendid. **4** rather shy; decorous. **modestly** *adverb*, **modesty** *noun* [from Latin, = keeping the proper measure]

modicum *noun* a small amount.

modify *verb* (**modified, modifying**) **1** change something slightly. **2** qualify a word by describing it, *Adjectives modify nouns.* **modification** *noun*

modulate *verb* (**modulated, modulating**) **1** adjust; regulate. **2** vary in pitch or tone. **modulation** *noun*

module *noun* **1** an independent or separate part of a spacecraft, building, or other structure. **2** a section of a course of study. **3** a unit used in measuring. **modular** *adjective*

modus operandi (*say* moh-duhs op-uh-**ran**-duy) *noun* **1** a person's way of working. **2** the way a thing works. [Latin, = way of working]

modus vivendi (*say* moh-duhs viv-**en**-duy) *noun* **1** a way of living or coping. **2** an arrangement whereby those in dispute can carry on pending a settlement. [Latin, = way of living]

mogul (*say* **moh**-guhl) *noun* (*informal*) an important or influential person. [the Moguls were the ruling dynasty in India in the 16th–19th centuries]

mohair *noun* fine silky wool from an angora goat. [from Arabic, = special]

mohawk *noun* a hairstyle in which the head is shaved except for a strip of hair running centrally from the middle of the forehead to the back of the neck. [from the name of an indigenous North American people]

moist *adjective* slightly wet; damp. **moistly** *adverb*, **moistness** *noun*

moisten *verb* make or become moist.

moisture *noun* water or other liquid diffused in a small quantity as vapour, within a solid, or condensed on a surface.

moisturiser *noun* a cosmetic preparation used to prevent dryness in the skin.

molar *noun* any of the wide teeth at the back of the jaw, used in chewing. [from Latin *mola* = millstone]

molasses *noun* syrup from raw sugar.

mole[1] *noun* **1** a small furry animal that burrows under the ground. **2** a person who secretly gives confidential information to an enemy or rival.

mole[2] *noun* a small dark spot on the skin.

mole[3] *noun* a stone wall built out into the sea as a breakwater or causeway.

molecule *noun* the smallest part into which a substance can be divided without changing its chemical nature; a group of atoms. **molecular** *adjective* [from Latin, = little mass]

molehill *noun* a small pile of earth thrown up by a burrowing mole.
make a mountain out of a molehill treat a small difficulty as if it were a great one.

moleskin *noun* a strong cotton fabric, the surface of which is shaved before dyeing.

molest *verb* **1** assault or abuse a person sexually. **2** (*old use*) pester. **molestation** *noun*, **molester** *noun* [from Latin *molestus* = troublesome]

mollify *verb* (**mollified, mollifying**) make someone less angry. **mollification** *noun* [from Latin, = soften]

mollusc *noun* an invertebrate animal with a soft body and hard shell (e.g. snails, oysters, mussels) or no shell (e.g. slugs, octopuses).

mollycoddle *verb* (**mollycoddled**, **mollycoddling**) coddle excessively; pamper.

Molotov cocktail *noun* a kind of incendiary bomb thrown by hand. [named after V.M. Molotov, a Russian statesman]

molten *adjective* melted; made liquid by great heat.

moment *noun* **1** a very short time. **2** a particular time, *Call me the moment she arrives.* **3** importance, *These are matters of great moment.*

momentary *adjective* lasting for only a moment. **momentarily** *adverb*

momentous (*say* muh-**men**-tuhs) *adjective* very important.

momentum *noun* amount or force of movement, *The stone gathered momentum as it rolled downhill.* [Latin, = movement]

monarch *noun* **1** a king, queen, emperor, or empress ruling a country. **2** a large orange and black butterfly. **monarchic** *adjective* [from Greek *monos* = alone, + *archein* = to rule]

monarchy *noun* (*plural* **monarchies**) a country ruled by a monarch. (Compare **republic.**) **monarchist** *noun*

monastery *noun* (*plural* **monasteries**) a building where monks live and work. (Compare **nunnery.**) **monastic** *adjective* [from Greek *monazein* = live alone]

Monday *noun* the day of the week following Sunday. [Old English, = day of the moon]

monetary *adjective* of money.

money *noun* **1** coins and banknotes. **2** wealth. [same origin as *mint*[4]]

mongoose *noun* (*plural* **mongooses**) a small carnivorous mammal that can kill snakes.

mongrel (*say* **mung**-gruhl) *noun* a dog of mixed breeds. [from *mingle*]

monic *adjective* (of a polynomial) having the coefficient of the term of highest degree equal to one.

monitor[1] *noun* **1** a device for watching or testing how something is working. **2** a visual display unit, a computer screen. **3** a pupil who is given a special responsibility in a school. **4** a large lizard of Australia, Asia, and Africa.

monitor[2] *verb* watch or test how something is working. [from Latin *monere* = warn]

monk *noun* a member of a community of men who live according to the rules of a religious organisation. (Compare **nun.**) [same origin as *mono-*]

monkey *noun* (*plural* **monkeys**) **1** an animal with long arms, hands with thumbs, and often a tail. **2** a mischievous person.

mono *adjective* (of sound reproduction) using only one transmission channel. [short for *monophonic* (from *mono-*, + Greek *phone* = sound)]

mono- *prefix* one; single. [from Greek *monos* = alone]

monochrome *adjective* done in one colour or in black and white. [from *mono-*, + Greek *chroma* = colour]

monocle *noun* an eyeglass for one eye. [from *mono-*, + Latin *oculus* = eye]

monogamy *noun* the practice of marrying or state of being married to one person at a time. (Compare **polygamy.**) **monogamous** *adjective* [from *mono-*, + Greek *gamos* = marriage]

monogram *noun* a design made up of a letter or letters, especially a person's initials. **monogrammed** *adjective* [from *mono-* + *-gram*]

monograph *noun* a scholarly book or article on one particular subject. [from *mono-* + *-graph*]

monolith *noun* a large single upright block of stone. [from *mono-*, + Greek *lithos* = stone]

monolithic *adjective* **1** consisting of monoliths. **2** single and huge.

monologue *noun* a speech by one person. [from *mono-*, + Greek *logos* = word]

monoplane *noun* a type of aeroplane with only one set of wings.

monopolise *verb* (**monopolised**, **monopolising**) take the whole of something for yourself, *One girl monopolised my attention.* **monopolisation** *noun*

monopoly *noun* (*plural* **monopolies**) complete possession or control of something by one group, *The company had a monopoly in supplying electricity.* [from *mono-*, + Greek *polein* = sell]

monorail *noun* a railway that uses a single rail, not a pair of rails.

monosyllable *noun* a word with only one syllable. **monosyllabic** *adjective*

monotheism (*say* **mon**-oh-thee-iz-uhm) *noun* belief that there is only one god. **monotheist** *noun* [from *mono-*, + Greek *theos* = god]

monotone *noun* a level, unchanging tone of voice in speaking or singing.

monotonous *adjective* boring because it does not change. **monotonously** *adverb*, **monotony** *noun*

monotreme *noun* an egg-laying mammal, e.g. the platypus and the echidna.

monoxide *noun* an oxide with one atom of oxygen.

monsoon *noun* **1** a strong wind in and near the Indian Ocean, bringing heavy rain in summer. **2** the rainy season brought by this wind. [from Arabic *mausim* = fixed season]

monster[1] *noun* **1** a large frightening creature. **2** a huge thing.

monster[2] *adjective* huge. [from Latin *monstrum* = marvel]

monstrosity *noun* (*plural* **monstrosities**) a monstrous thing.

monstrous *adjective* **1** like a monster. **2** huge. **3** very shocking; outrageous.

montage (*say* mon-**tah*zh***) *noun* something produced by putting together pieces from other pictures or compositions.

month *noun* each of the 12 parts into which a year is divided. [related to *moon* (because time was measured by the changes in the moon's appearance)]

monthly *adjective & adverb* happening or done once a month.

monument *noun* anything (especially a structure) designed or serving to celebrate a person or event.

monumental *adjective* **1** of or as a monument. **2** extremely great; huge. **3** (of a literary or artistic work) of lasting value.

moo *verb* make the low deep sound of a cow. **moo** *noun*

mooch *verb* (*informal*) wander around aimlessly.

mood *noun* the way someone feels, *She is in a cheerful mood.*

moody *adjective* **1** gloomy or sullen. **2** likely to become bad-tempered suddenly. **moodily** *adverb*, **moodiness** *noun*

moon *noun* **1** the natural satellite of the earth that can be seen in the sky at night. **2** a satellite of any planet. **moonbeam** *noun*, **moonlight** *noun*, **moonlit** *adjective*

Moor *noun* a member of a Muslim people of north-west Africa. **Moorish** *adjective*

moor[1] *noun* (*British*) an area of open uncultivated land with bushes but no trees.

moor[2] *verb* fasten a boat or other floating thing to a fixed object by means of a cable.

moorhen *noun* a small waterbird.

moorings *plural noun* **1** cables, ropes, or anchors by which something is moored. **2** a place where a boat is moored.

moose *noun* (*plural* **moose**) a North American elk.

moot[1] *adjective* debatable; undecided, *That's a moot point.*

moot[2] *verb* put forward an idea for discussion.

mop[1] *noun* **1** a bunch or pad of soft material fastened on the end of a stick, used for cleaning floors. **2** a thick mass of hair.

mop[2] *verb* (**mopped**, **mopping**) clean or wipe with a mop; wipe away.

mope *verb* (**moped**, **moping**) be sad and listless. **mopy** *adjective*

mopoke (*say* **moh**-pohk) *noun* (*Australian*) a boobook.

moraine *noun* a mass of stones and earth carried down by a glacier.

moral[1] *adjective* **1** connected with what is right and wrong in behaviour. **2** virtuous. **morality** *noun*, **morally** *adverb*

moral[2] *noun* a lesson in right behaviour taught by a story or event. [from Latin *mores* = customs]

morale (*say* muh-**rahl**) *noun* confidence; the state of someone's spirits, *Morale was high after the victory.*

moral hazard *noun* lack of incentive to guard against risk where one is protected from its consequences, e.g. by insurance.

moralise *verb* (**moralised**, **moralising**) talk or write about right and wrong behaviour. **moralist** *noun*

morals *plural noun* standards of behaviour; virtuousness.

moral support *noun* encouragement.

morass *noun* (*plural* **morasses**) **1** a marsh or bog. **2** a confused mass.

moratorium *noun* a temporary ban. [from Latin *morari* = to delay]

morbid *adjective* **1** thinking about gloomy or unpleasant things. **2** unhealthy. **morbidity** *noun*, **morbidly** *adverb* [from Latin *morbus* = disease]

morbillivirus *noun* any of a group of viruses causing diseases such as measles.

more[1] *adjective* (comparative of **much**[1] and **many**[1]) greater in quantity or intensity etc., *I had more energy after lunch.*

more[2] *noun* a greater quantity or number.

more[3] *adverb* **1** to a greater extent, *more beautiful.* **2** again, *once more.* **more or less** about; approximately.

moreover *adverb* besides; in addition to what has been said.

morgue *noun* a mortuary.

moribund *adjective* in a dying state.

Mormon *noun* a member of a religious group (the Church of Jesus Christ of Latter-Day Saints) founded in the USA.

morn *noun* (*poetic*) morning.

morning *noun* the early part of the day, before noon or before lunchtime.

moron *noun* (*informal*) a very stupid person. [from Greek *moros* = foolish]

morose *adjective* sullen and gloomy. **morosely** *adverb*, **moroseness** *noun*

morph[1] *noun* a variant form of something. [Greek, = form]

morph² *verb* **1** change smoothly and gradually from one image to another using computer animation techniques. **2** change shape or form.

morpheme *noun* a meaningful unit of language that cannot be further divided, e.g. *in*, *come*, *-ing* are morphemes forming *incoming*.

morphine (*say* **maw**-feen) *noun* (also **morphia**) a drug made from opium, used to lessen pain. [named after Morpheus, the Roman god of dreams]

morris dance *noun* a traditional English folk dance, usually performed by people in a costume with ribbons and bells.

morrow *noun* (*poetic*) the following day.

Morse code *noun* a signalling code using short and long sounds or flashes of light (dots and dashes) to represent letters. [named after its American inventor, S. F. B. Morse]

morsel *noun* a small piece of food; a small amount. [from Latin *morsus* = bite]

mortadella *noun* (*plural* **mortadelle**) a large spiced pork sausage.

mortal¹ *adjective* **1** that can die, *All of us are mortal.* **2** causing death; fatal, *a mortal wound.* **3** deadly, *mortal enemies.* **mortality** *noun*, **mortally** *adverb*

mortal² *noun* a human being. [from Latin *mortis* = of death]

mortar *noun* **1** a mixture of sand, cement, and water used in building to stick bricks together. **2** a hard bowl in which substances are pounded with a pestle. **3** a short cannon.

mortarboard *noun* an academic headdress with a stiff square top.

mortgage¹ (*say* **maw**-gij) *noun* an arrangement to borrow money to buy a house or other property, with the house or property as security for the loan.

mortgage² *verb* (**mortgaged, mortgaging**) give someone a claim on a house or other property as security for payment of a debt or loan.

mortify *verb* (**mortified, mortifying**) humiliate a person greatly. **mortification** *noun* [same origin as *mortal*]

mortuary *noun* a place where dead bodies are kept before being buried. [from Latin *mortuus* = dead]

morwong (*say* **maw**-wong) *noun* an edible sea fish of southern Australia and New Zealand. [probably from a New South Wales Aboriginal language]

mosaic (*say* moh-**zay**-ik) *noun* a picture or design made from small coloured pieces of stone or glass.

mosque (*say* mosk) *noun* a place where Muslims meet for worship. [from Arabic *masjid*]

mosquito *noun* (*plural* **mosquitoes**) a kind of gnat that sucks blood. [Spanish, = little fly]

moss *noun* (*plural* **mosses**) a plant that grows in damp places and has no flowers. **mossy** *adjective*

mossie alternative spelling of **mozzie**.

most¹ *adjective* (superlative of **much¹** and **many¹**) greatest in quantity or intensity etc., *Most people come by bus.*

most² *noun* the greatest quantity or number; the majority, *Most of the food was eaten.*

most³ *adverb* **1** to the greatest extent; more than any other, *most beautiful.* **2** very; extremely, *most impressive.*

mostly *adverb* mainly.

motel *noun* a hotel providing accommodation for motorists and parking for their cars. [from *motor* + *hotel*]

moth *noun* an insect rather like a butterfly, that usually flies at night.

mothball¹ *noun* a small ball of naphthalene for keeping moths away from clothes.

mothball² *verb* **1** store clothes with mothballs. **2** leave unused. **3** cancel or postpone work on a plan or project.

mother¹ *noun* a woman in relation to her child or children. **motherhood** *noun*

mother² *verb* look after someone in a motherly way. [from Old English *modor*]

motherboard *noun* a printed circuit board containing the principal components of a computer or other electronic device, to which other boards may be connected.

mother-in-law *noun* (*plural* **mothers-in-law**) the mother of a person's husband or wife.

motherly *adjective* kind and gentle like a mother. **motherliness** *noun*

mother-of-pearl *noun* a pearly substance lining the shells of some molluscs, especially oysters and abalones.

Mother's Day *noun* a day in honour of mothers, in Australia the second Sunday in May.

motif *noun* a repeated design or theme.

motion¹ *noun* **1** moving; movement. **2** a formal statement to be discussed and voted on at a meeting.

motion² *verb* signal by a gesture, *She motioned him to sit beside her.* [from Latin *motio* = movement]

motionless *adjective* not moving.

motivate *verb* (**motivated, motivating**) give a person a motive or incentive to do something. **motivation** *noun*

motive[1] *noun* what makes a person do something, *a motive for murder.*

motive[2] *adjective* providing movement, *The engine provides motive power.* [from Latin *motivus* = moving]

motley *adjective* **1** multicoloured. **2** made up of various sorts of things.

motor[1] *noun* a machine providing power to drive machinery; an engine.

motor[2] *verb* go or take someone in a car. [from Latin *motor* = mover]

motorbike *noun* a motorcycle.

motorcade *noun* a procession of cars. [from *motor* + *cavalcade*]

motor car *noun* a car.

motorcycle *noun* a two-wheeled motor vehicle. **motorcyclist** *noun*

motorised *adjective* **1** equipped with a motor. **2** equipped with motor vehicles.

motorist *noun* a person who drives a car.

motor neuron *noun* a nerve cell forming part of a pathway along which impulses pass from the brain or spinal cord to a muscle or gland.

motor vehicle *noun* a road vehicle powered by an internal combustion engine.

motorway *noun* a multi-laned highway for high-speed traffic.

mottled *adjective* marked with spots or patches of colour. [from *motley*]

motto *noun* (*plural* **mottoes**) a short saying used as a guide for behaviour, *Their motto is 'Who dares, wins'.* [Italian, = word]

motza *noun* (also **motser** or **motzer**) (*Australian informal*) **1** a large sum of money, *The car was worth a motza.* **2** a certainty, *She's a motza to win the race.* [probably from Yiddish *matse* = bread (in the sense 'money')]

mould[1] *noun* a hollow container of a particular shape, in which a liquid or soft substance is put to set into this shape.

mould[2] *verb* make something have a particular shape or character.

mould[3] *noun* a fine furry growth of very small fungi. **mouldy** *adjective*

moulder *verb* rot away; decay into dust.

moult *verb* shed feathers, hair, or skin while a new growth forms.

mound *noun* **1** a pile of earth or stones; a heap or pile. **2** a small hill.

mount[1] *verb* **1** climb or go up; ascend. **2** get on a horse or bicycle to ride it. **3** increase in amount, *Our costs mounted.* **4** place or fix in position for use or display, *Mount your photos in an album.*

mount[2] *noun* **1** a mountain, *Mount Everest.* **2** something on which an object is mounted. **3** a horse for riding. [from Latin *mons* = mountain]

mountain *noun* **1** a very high hill. **2** a large heap or pile or quantity.
mountainous *adjective*

mountaineer *noun* a person who climbs mountains. **mountaineering** *noun*

mounted *adjective* serving on horseback, *mounted police.*

mourn *verb* be sad, especially because someone has died. **mourner** *noun*

mournful *adjective* sad; sorrowful.
mournfully *adverb*

mouse *noun* (*plural* **mice**) a small animal with a long thin tail and a pointed nose.
mousetrap *noun*, **mousy** *adjective*

mousse (*say* moos) *noun* **1** a creamy dessert flavoured with fruit or chocolate. **2** a frothy creamy substance, *hair mousse.* [French, = froth]

moustache (*say* muh-**stahsh**) *noun* hair left to grow on a man's upper lip.

mouth[1] *noun* **1** the opening through which food is taken into the body. **2** the place where a river enters the sea. **3** an opening or outlet. **mouthful** *noun*

mouth[2] *verb* form words carefully with your lips, especially without saying them aloud.

mouth organ *noun* a small musical instrument that you play by blowing and sucking while passing it along your lips.

mouthpiece *noun* the part of a musical or other instrument that you put to your mouth.

movable *adjective* able to be moved.

move[1] *verb* (**moved**, **moving**) **1** take or go from one place to another; change a person's or thing's position. **2** make progress. **3** affect a person's feelings, *Their sad story moved us deeply.* **4** put forward a formal statement (a *motion*) to be discussed and voted on at a meeting. **mover** *noun*

move[2] *noun* **1** moving; a movement. **2** a moving of a piece in a board game; a player's turn to do this. **3** an action taken to achieve a purpose.
get a move on (*informal*) hurry up.
on the move moving; making progress. [from Latin *movere* = to move]

movement *noun* **1** the action of moving or being moved. **2** a group of people working together to achieve something. **3** one of the main divisions of a symphony or other long musical work. **4** progress; a trend.

movie *noun* a film for viewing in a cinema or on television, video, DVD, etc. [short for *moving picture*]

mow *verb* (**mowed, mown, mowing**) cut down grass. **mower** *noun*
mow down knock down and kill.

mozzarella (*say* mot-suh-**rel**-uh) *noun* a soft Italian curd cheese.

mozzie (*say* **moz**-ee) *noun* (also **mossie**) (*Australian informal*) a mosquito.

MP *abbreviation* Member of Parliament.

MPEG *noun* an international standard for encoding and compressing video images; a file so compressed. [from the initials of 'Motion Pictures Experts Group']

MP3 *noun* a means of compressing a sound sequence into a very small file, used as a way of downloading audio files from the Internet; a file so compressed. [as *MPEG*]

MP3 player *noun* a device for playing MP3 files, *I listen to music on my MP3 player.*

Mr (*say* **mis**-tuh) *noun* (*plural* **Messrs**) a title put before a man's name. [short for *mister*]

Mrs (*say* **mis**-uhz) *noun* (*plural* **Mrs**) a title put before a married woman's name. [short for *mistress*]

Ms (*say* muhz) *noun* a title put before a woman's name. [from *Mrs* and *Miss*]

Mt *abbreviation* mount or mountain.

much[1] *adjective* (**more, most**) existing in a large amount, *much noise.*

much[2] *noun* a large amount of something.

much[3] *adverb* **1** greatly; considerably, *much to my surprise.* **2** approximately, *It is much the same.*

muck[1] *noun* **1** farmyard manure. **2** (*informal*) dirt; filth. **3** (*informal*) a mess.
mucky *adjective*

muck[2] *verb* make dirty; mess.
muck about (*informal*) fool about.
muck up (*informal*) **1** mess up; spoil. **2** (*Australian*) misbehave.

mucous (*say* **myoo**-kuhs) *adjective* like mucus; covered with mucus, *a mucous membrane.*

mucus (*say* **myoo**-kuhs) *noun* the moist sticky substance on the inner surface of the throat etc.

mud *noun* wet soft earth. **muddiness** *noun*, **muddy** *adjective*

muddle[1] *verb* (**muddled, muddling**) **1** mix things up. **2** bewilder; confuse. **muddler** *noun*

muddle[2] *noun* a muddled condition or thing; confusion; disorder.

mudflat *noun* a stretch of muddy land uncovered at low tide.

mudguard *noun* a curved cover over the top part of the wheel of a vehicle (especially a bicycle or motorbike) to protect the rider and vehicle from the mud and water thrown up by the wheel.

muesli (*say* **myoo**-zlee) *noun* a food made of mixed cereals, dried fruit, and nuts.

muff[1] *noun* a short tube-shaped piece of warm material into which the hands are pushed from opposite ends.

muff[2] *verb* (*informal*) bungle.

muffin *noun* **1** a large cupcake. **2** a kind of spongy cake eaten toasted and buttered.

muffle *verb* (**muffled, muffling**) **1** cover or wrap something to protect it or keep it warm. **2** deaden the sound of something, *a muffled scream.* [from *muff*[1]]

muffler *noun* **1** something used to muffle sound, especially a device fitted to a vehicle's exhaust system. **2** a warm scarf.

mufti[1] *noun* ordinary clothes worn by someone who usually wears a uniform.

mufti[2] *noun* a Muslim legal expert empowered to give rulings on religious matters.

mug[1] *noun* **1** a kind of large cup, usually used without a saucer. **2** (*informal*) a fool; a person who is easily deceived. **3** (*informal*) a person's face.

mug[2] *verb* (**mugged, mugging**) attack and rob somebody in the street. **mugger** *noun*

muggy *adjective* unpleasantly warm and damp, *muggy weather.* **mugginess** *noun*

mulberry *noun* (*plural* **mulberries**) a purple or white fruit rather like a blackberry.

mulch *noun* a mixture of wet straw, grass clippings, leaves, etc., spread on the ground to protect plants or retain moisture.
mulch *verb*

mule *noun* an animal that is the offspring of a donkey and a mare, known for being stubborn. **mulish** *adjective*

mulga *noun* **1** a scrubby acacia of inland Australia. **2** (**the Mulga**) the outback. [from Gamilaraay, Yuwaalaraay, and other languages *malga*]

mulgara (*say* **mul**-guh-ruh) *noun* a small carnivorous marsupial of inland Australia. [from Arabana *mardagura*]

mull[1] *verb* heat wine or beer with sugar and spices, as a drink, *mulled ale.*

mull[2] *verb* think about something carefully; ponder, *mull it over.*

mullet *noun* **1** an edible sea fish. **2** a type of haircut with the hair short at the top and front and long at the back.

mulloway *noun* a large edible Australian sea and estuarine fish. [from Ngarrindjeri *malowe*]

multi- *prefix* many (as in *multicoloured* = with many colours). [from Latin *multus* = many]

multicultural *adjective* made up of various cultural and ethnic groups, *a multicultural society.* **multiculturalism** *noun*

multifarious (*say* mul-tuh-**fair**-ree-uhs) *adjective* of many kinds; very varied.

multilateral *adjective* (of an agreement or treaty) made between three or more parties.

multimedia *adjective* **1** (of art, education, etc.) using more than one medium of expression or communication. **2** (of a computer application) combining text, sound, and video.

multimillionaire *noun* a person with a fortune of several million dollars.

multinational *adjective* (of a business company) operating in several countries.

multiple[1] *adjective* having many parts.

multiple[2] *noun* a number that contains another number (a *factor*) an exact amount of times without remainder, *8 and 12 are multiples of 4.*

multiplicity *noun* a great variety.

multiply *verb* (**multiplied, multiplying**) **1** take a number a given quantity of times, *Five multiplied by four equals twenty* ($5 \times 4 = 20$). **2** make or become many; increase. **multiplication** *noun*, **multiplier** *noun*

multiracial *adjective* consisting of people of many different races.

multiskilling *noun* the training of employees to perform tasks requiring a number of skills.

multitude *noun* a great number of people or things. **multitudinous** *adjective*

mum[1] *noun* (*informal*) mother.

mum[2] *adjective* (*informal*) silent, *keep mum.*

mum[3] *verb* (**mummed, mumming**) act in a mime. **mummer** *noun*

mumble *verb* (**mumbled, mumbling**) speak indistinctly and not be easy to hear. **mumble** *noun*, **mumbler** *noun*

mumbo-jumbo *noun* talk or ceremony that has no real meaning.

mummy[1] *noun* (*plural* **mummies**) (*informal*) mother.

mummy[2] *noun* (*plural* **mummies**) a corpse treated with preservatives before being buried, as was the custom in ancient Egypt. **mummify** *verb*

mumps *noun* an infectious disease that causes the neck to swell painfully.

munch *verb* chew vigorously.

mundane *adjective* **1** ordinary, not exciting. **2** concerned with practical matters, not ideals. [from Latin *mundus* = world]

municipal (*say* myoo-**nis**-uh-puhl) *adjective* of a town or city.

municipality *noun* (*plural* **municipalities**) a town or district with its own local government.

munificent *adjective* extremely generous. **munificence** *noun*, **munificently** *adverb* [from Latin *munus* = gift]

munitions *plural noun* military weapons, ammunition, equipment, and stores. [from Latin *munitum* = fortified]

mural[1] *adjective* of or on a wall.

mural[2] *noun* a wall painting. [from Latin *murus* = wall]

murder[1] *verb* kill a person unlawfully and deliberately. **murderer** *noun*, **murderess** *noun*

murder[2] *noun* the murdering of somebody. **murderous** *adjective*

murky *adjective* **1** dark and gloomy. **2** (of liquid) dirty or cloudy. **murk** *noun*, **murkiness** *noun*

murmur *verb* **1** make a low continuous sound. **2** speak in a soft voice. **murmur** *noun*

Murray cod *noun* a large edible Australian river fish. [named after the River Murray]

muscle *noun* **1** a band or bundle of fibrous tissue that can contract and relax and so produce movement in parts of the body. **2** the power of muscles; strength.

muscular *adjective* **1** of or affecting the muscles. **2** having well-developed muscles. **muscularity** *noun*

muscular dystrophy *noun* a hereditary condition causing progressive wasting of the muscles.

musculoskeletal *adjective* to do with the workings of the muscles, tendons, bones, and joints of the body.

muse *verb* (**mused, musing**) think deeply about something; ponder; meditate.

museum *noun* a place where objects of historical, scientific, or cultural interest are displayed for people to see. [from Greek, = place of the Muses (goddesses of the arts and sciences)]

mush *noun* soft pulp. **mushy** *adjective*

mushroom[1] *noun* an edible fungus with a stem and a dome-shaped top.

mushroom[2] *verb* grow or appear suddenly in large numbers, *Blocks of flats mushroomed in the city.*

music *noun* **1** pleasant or interesting sounds made by instruments or by the voice. **2** printed or written instructions for making music. [from Greek, = of the Muses (see *museum*)]

musical[1] *adjective* **1** of or with music; producing music. **2** melodious; harmonious. **3** good at music; interested in music. **musically** *adverb*

musical[2] *noun* a play or film containing a lot of songs.

musician *noun* someone who plays a musical instrument.

musk *noun* a strong-smelling substance used in perfumes. **musky** *adjective*

musket *noun* a kind of gun with a long barrel, formerly used by soldiers.

musketeer *noun* a soldier armed with a musket.

Muslim *noun* a person who follows the religious teachings of Muhammad (who lived in about 570–632), set out in the Koran.

muslin *noun* very thin cotton cloth.

mussel *noun* a black shellfish.

must[1] *auxiliary verb* used to express **1** necessity or obligation (*You must go*), **2** certainty (*You must be joking!*).

must[2] *noun* (*informal*) a thing that should not be missed.

mustang *noun* a wild horse of Mexico and California.

mustard *noun* a yellow paste or powder used to give food a hot taste.

muster[1] *verb* **1** assemble; gather together. **2** (*Australian*) round up livestock.

muster[2] *noun* an assembly of people or things.
pass muster be up to the required standard.

mustn't (*informal*) must not.

musty *adjective* smelling or tasting mouldy or stale. **mustiness** *noun*

mutable (*say* **myoo**-tuh-buhl) *adjective* able or likely to change. **mutability** *noun* [from Latin *mutare* = to change]

mutation *noun* a change or alteration in the form of something. **mutate** *verb*

mute[1] *adjective* **1** silent; not speaking. **2** (*old use*) not able to speak. **3** not pronounced, *The k in 'knight' is mute.* **mutely** *adverb*, **muteness** *noun*

mute[2] *noun* **1** a device on a television, telephone, or other appliance that temporarily turns off the sound. **2** a device fitted to a musical instrument to deaden its sound. **3** (*old use*) a person who cannot speak.

mute[3] *verb* (**muted**, **muting**) make a thing quieter or less intense.

mutilate *verb* (**mutilated**, **mutilating**) damage something by breaking or cutting off part of it. **mutilation** *noun*

mutineer *noun* a person who mutinies.

mutiny[1] *noun* (*plural* **mutinies**) rebellion against authority; refusal by members of the armed forces to obey orders. **mutinous** *adjective*, **mutinously** *adverb*

mutiny[2] *verb* (**mutinied**, **mutinying**) take part in a mutiny.

mutter *verb* **1** speak in a low voice. **2** grumble. **mutter** *noun*

mutton *noun* meat from a sheep.

muttonbird *noun* a kind of sea bird, breeding especially on Bass Strait islands.

mutual (*say* **myoo**-choo-uhl) *adjective* given to each other; felt by each for the other, *mutual affection.* **mutually** *adverb*

muzzle[1] *noun* **1** an animal's nose and mouth. **2** a cover put over an animal's nose and mouth so that it cannot bite. **3** the open end of a gun.

muzzle[2] *verb* (**muzzled**, **muzzling**) **1** put a muzzle on an animal. **2** silence; prevent a person from expressing opinions.

my *adjective* belonging to me.

myall[1] *noun* an Australian acacia with silvery foliage. [probably from Gamilaraay *maayaal*]

myall[2] *noun* (*Australian*) an Aboriginal person living in a traditional manner. [from Sydney language *mayal*, *myal* = a stranger; a person from another tribe]

myna *noun* a noisy bird of the starling family, introduced into Australia from Asia.

myopia (*say* muy-**oh**-pee-uh) *noun* short-sightedness. **myopic** *adjective*

myriad (*say* **mi**-ree-uhd) *adjective* innumerable.

myriads *plural noun* a very great number, *myriads of ants.* [from Greek *myrioi* = 10,000]

myrrh (*say* mer) *noun* a substance used in perfumes and incense and medicine.

myrtle *noun* **1** an evergreen European shrub with dark leaves and white flowers. **2** a tall Australian tree with dark green leaves and valuable timber.

myself *pronoun* I or me and nobody else, used to refer back to the person who is speaking, *I have hurt myself.*
by myself on my own; alone, *I did the work all by myself.*

mysterious *adjective* full of mystery; puzzling. **mysteriously** *adverb*

mystery *noun* (*plural* **mysteries**) something that cannot be explained or understood; something puzzling.

mystic[1] *adjective* **1** having a spiritual meaning. **2** mysterious and filling people with wonder. **mystical** *adjective*, **mystically** *adverb*, **mysticism** *noun*

mystic[2] *noun* a person who seeks to obtain spiritual contact with God by deep religious meditation.

mystify *verb* (**mystified, mystifying**) puzzle; bewilder. **mystification** *noun*

mystique (*say* mis-**teek**) *noun* an air of mystery or mystical power.

myth (*say* mith) *noun* **1** a traditional story, especially one concerning the early history of a people or explaining a natural or social phenomenon, and typically involving supernatural beings or events. **2** an untrue story or belief. [from Greek *mythos* = story]

mythical *adjective* **1** imaginary. **2** found in myths, *a mythical animal.*

mythology *noun* myths; the study of myths. **mythological** *adjective* [from *myth* + *-logy*]

myxomatosis (*say* mik-suh-muh-**toh**-suhs) *noun* a disease that kills rabbits.

Nn

N *abbreviation* north; northern.

naan (*say* nahn) *noun* (also **nan**) an Indian flat bread. [Persian from Urdu]

nab *verb* (**nabbed**, **nabbing**) (*informal*) catch or arrest; grab.

nabarlek *noun* a small wallaby of northern Australia. [from Gunwinygu]

nadir (*say* **nay**-deer) *noun* the lowest point. [from Arabic *nazir* = opposite (i.e. to the zenith)]

nag[1] *verb* (**nagged**, **nagging**) **1** pester a person by keeping on criticising, complaining, or asking for things. **2** keep on hurting, *a nagging pain.*

nag[2] *noun* (*informal*) a horse.

nail[1] *noun* **1** the hard covering over the end of a finger or toe. **2** a small sharp piece of metal driven in with a hammer to hold things together.

nail[2] *verb* **1** fasten with a nail or nails. **2** (*informal*) catch; arrest.

naive (*say* nuy-**eev**) *adjective* (also **naïve**) showing a lack of experience or good judgement; innocent and unsophisticated. **naively** *adverb*, **naivety** *noun*

naked *adjective* without any clothes or coverings on. **nakedly** *adverb*, **nakedness** *noun*
the naked eye the eye when it is not helped by an optical device such as a telescope or microscope.

naltrexone *noun* a synthetic drug that blocks opiate receptors in the nervous system.

name[1] *noun* **1** the word or words by which a person, animal, place, or thing is known. **2** a reputation.

name[2] *verb* (**named**, **naming**) **1** give a name to. **2** state the name or names of.

nameless *adjective* without a name.

namely *adverb* that is to say, *I chose my favourite dessert, namely apple pie.*

namesake *noun* a person or thing with the same name as another.

nan *noun* (*informal*) grandmother

nanna *noun* (*informal*) grandmother.

nanny *noun* (*plural* **nannies**) **1** a person employed to look after young children. **2** grandmother.

nannygai (*say* **nan**-ee-guy) (*Australian*) another name for **redfish**. [possibly from Sydney language]

nanny goat *noun* a female goat. (Compare **billy goat**.)

nanny state *noun* the government regarded as overprotective or as too interfering.

nano- *prefix* **1** one thousand-millionth part (as in *nanosecond*). **2** extremely small. [from Greek *nanos* = dwarf]

nanosecond *noun* **1** one thousand-millionth of a second. **2** (*informal*) a very short time, *She tidied her room in a nanosecond.*

nanotechnology *noun* technology on a molecular or atomic scale.

nap[1] *noun* a short sleep.
catch a person napping catch a person unprepared for something or not alert.

nap[2] *noun* short raised fibres on the surface of cloth or leather.

napalm (*say* **nay**-pahm) *noun* a substance made of petrol, used in some incendiary bombs.

naphthalene (*say* **naf**-thuh-leen) *noun* a strong-smelling white substance obtained from coal tar, used in dyes and as a moth repellent.

napkin *noun* **1** a piece of cloth or paper used to keep your clothes clean or to wipe your lips or fingers; a serviette, *a table napkin.* **2** a nappy.

nappy *noun* (*plural* **nappies**) a piece of cloth or other absorbent material put round a baby's bottom.

narcissism (*say* **nah**-suh-siz-uhm) *noun* abnormal self-love or self-admiration. **narcissistic** *adjective* [from Narcissus, the name of a youth in Greek mythology who fell in love with his own reflection in water]

narcissus *noun* (*plural* **narcissi**) a garden flower like a daffodil.

narcosis *noun* a state of sleep or drowsiness, especially one produced by drugs.

narcotic *noun* a drug that makes a person sleepy or unconscious. **narcotic** *adjective*

nardoo *noun* an Australian clover-like fern whose seeds may be ground into flour and used as food. [from various Aboriginal languages of south-eastern Australia]

nark[1] *noun* (*Australian informal*) an annoying person or thing.

nark[2] *verb* (*informal*) annoy someone.

narky *adjective* (**narkier**, **narkiest**) (*informal*) bad-tempered, irritable.

narrate *verb* (**narrated**, **narrating**) tell a story; give an account of something. **narration** *noun*

narrative *noun* a spoken or written account of something; a story.

narrator *noun* **1** a person who delivers a commentary in a film, broadcast, etc. **2** a person who narrates.

narrow[1] *adjective* **1** not wide; not broad. **2** uncomfortably close; with only a small margin of safety, *a narrow escape.* **narrowly** *adverb*

narrow[2] *verb* make or become narrower.

narrow-minded *adjective* not tolerant of other people's beliefs and ways.

nasal *adjective* **1** of the nose. **2** sounding as if the breath comes out through the nose, *a nasal voice.* **nasally** *adverb* [from Latin *nasus* = nose]

nashi *noun* an apple-like pear. [Japanese]

nasturtium (*say* nuh-**ster**-shuhm) *noun* a garden plant with round leaves and red, yellow, or orange flowers.

nasty *adjective* **1** unpleasant. **2** unkind. **nastily** *adverb*, **nastiness** *noun*

natal (*say* **nay**-tuhl) *adjective* of birth; from birth. [from Latin *natus* = born]

nation *noun* a large community of people most of whom have the same ancestors, language, history, and customs, and who usually live in the same part of the world under one government. **national** *adjective & noun*, **nationally** *adverb* [from Latin *natio* = birth; race]

nationalise *verb* (**nationalised**, **nationalising**) put an industry or commercial enterprise under public ownership. **nationalisation** *noun*

nationalism *noun* **1** patriotic feeling, principles, or ideas; an extreme form of this; chauvinism. **2** a policy of national independence.

nationalist *noun* **1** a person who is very patriotic. **2** a person who wants their country to be independent and not to form part of another country. **nationalistic** *adjective*

nationality *noun* (*plural* **nationalities**) the condition of belonging to a particular nation, *What is his nationality?*

national park *noun* an area of natural beauty protected by the federal, state, or territory government for the use of the public.

National Party *noun* an Australian political party formed to represent rural interests.

native[1] *noun* **1** a person born in a particular place, *He is a native of Sweden.* **2** an indigenous plant or animal.

native[2] *adjective* **1** belonging to a person because of the place of their birth, *my native country.* **2** born in a place, *a native inhabitant.* **3** natural; belonging to a person by nature, *native ability.* [from Latin *nativus* = born]

native title *noun* the right of indigenous people to own their traditional land.

nativity *noun* **1** a person's birth. **2** (**the Nativity**) the birth of Jesus Christ.

natter *verb* (*informal*) chat. **natter** *noun*

natty *adjective* (**nattier**, **nattiest**) neat and trim; dapper. **nattily** *adverb*

natural[1] *adjective* **1** produced or done by nature, not by people or machines. **2** normal; not surprising. **3** inborn. **4** without pretence. **5** (of a note in music) neither sharp nor flat. **naturally** *adverb*, **naturalness** *noun*

natural[2] *noun* **1** a person who is naturally good at something. **2** a natural note in music; a sign (♮) that shows this.

natural gas *noun* gas found under the ground or sea, not manufactured.

natural history *noun* the study of plants and animals.

naturalise *verb* (**naturalised**, **naturalising**) **1** admit a foreigner to the citizenship of a country. **2** cause a plant or animal to grow or live naturally in a country that is not its own. **naturalisation** *noun*

naturalist *noun* a person who studies plants and animals.

natural numbers *plural noun* the positive integers (whole numbers) 1, 2, 3, etc., and sometimes zero as well.

nature *noun* **1** everything in the world that was not made by people. **2** the qualities and characteristics of a person or thing, *She has a loving nature.* **3** a kind or sort of thing, *He likes things of that nature.* [from Latin *natus* = born]

nature strip *noun* (*Australian*) **1** a piece of publicly owned land (usually lawn) between the front boundary of a property and the street. **2** a median strip between two lanes of traffic, usually grassed or planted with shrubs etc.

naturopathy *noun* the treatment of illness without drugs, usually involving diet, exercise, and massage. **naturopath** *noun*, **naturopathic** *adjective*

naught *noun* (*old use*) nothing.

naughty *adjective* behaving badly; disobedient. **naughtily** *adverb*, **naughtiness** *noun* [from *naught*]

nausea (*say* **naw**-zee-uh) *noun* a feeling of sickness or disgust. **nauseating** *adjective*, **nauseous** *adjective* [originally 'seasickness', from Greek *naus* = ship]

nautical *adjective* of ships or sailors. [from Greek *nautes* = sailor]

nautical mile *noun* a measure of distance used in navigating, 2,025 yards (1.852 kilometres).

naval *adjective* of a navy.

nave *noun* the main central part of a church (the other parts are the chancel, aisles, and transepts).

navel *noun* the small hollow in the centre of the abdomen, where the umbilical cord was attached.

navigable *adjective* **1** suitable for ships to sail in, *a navigable river.* **2** able to be steered. **navigability** *noun*

navigate *verb* (**navigated, navigating**) **1** sail in or through a river or sea etc., *The ship navigated the Suez Canal.* **2** make sure that a ship, aircraft, or vehicle is going in the right direction. **3** move around a website or the Internet. **navigation** *noun*, **navigator** *noun* [from Latin *navis* = ship, + *agere* = to drive]

navy *noun* (*plural* **navies**) **1** the part of the armed forces of a country that conducts military operations at sea. **2** (also **navy blue**) very dark blue, the colour of naval uniforms. [from Latin *navis* = ship]

nay *adverb* (*old use*) no.

Nazi (*say* **naht**-see) *noun* (*plural* **Nazis**) **1** a member of the National Socialist Party in Germany in Hitler's time, with Fascist beliefs. **2** (*derogatory*) a person with extreme racist or authoritarian views. **3** (*derogatory*) a person who seeks to impose their views on others in a very autocratic or inflexible way. **Nazism** *noun*

NB *abbreviation* note well. [short for Latin *nota bene*]

NBN *abbreviation* National Broadband Network.

NE *abbreviation* north-east; north-eastern.

near[1] *adverb & adjective* not far away in space or time.

near[2] *preposition* not far away from, *near the shops.*

near[3] *verb* come near to, *The ship neared the harbour.*

nearby *adjective & adverb* near, *a nearby house; He lives nearby.*

nearly *adjective* **1** almost, *We have nearly finished.* **2** closely, *They are nearly related.*

neat *adjective* **1** simple and clean and tidy. **2** skilful. **3** undiluted, *neat whisky.* **neatly** *adverb*, **neatness** *noun*

neaten *verb* make or become neat.

nebula *noun* (*plural* **nebulae**) a bright or dark patch in the sky, caused by a distant galaxy or a cloud of dust or gas. [Latin, = mist]

nebulous *adjective* indistinct; vague, *nebulous ideas.* [from *nebula*]

necessary *adjective* **1** not able to be done without; essential. **2** unavoidable. **necessarily** *adverb*

necessitate *verb* (**necessitated, necessitating**) make a thing necessary.

necessitous *adjective* very poor; needy.

necessity *noun* (*plural* **necessities**) **1** need. **2** something necessary.

neck *noun* **1** the part of the body that joins the head to the shoulders. **2** the part of a garment round the neck. **3** a narrow part of something, especially of a bottle.
neck and neck level in a race or other competition.
stick your neck out say or do something that you know could get you into trouble.

neckerchief *noun* a square of cloth worn round the neck.

necklace *noun* an ornament worn round the neck.

nectar *noun* **1** a sweet liquid collected by bees from flowers. **2** a delicious drink.

nectarine *noun* a kind of peach with a smooth skin and firm flesh.

née (*say* nay) *adjective* born (used in giving a married woman's maiden name), *Mrs Smith, née Jones.* [French]

need[1] *verb* **1** be without something you should have; require, *We need two more chairs.* **2** have to do something, *You need not answer.*

need[2] *noun* **1** something needed; a necessary thing. **2** a situation where something is necessary, *There is no need to cry.* **3** great poverty or hardship. **needful** *adjective*, **needless** *adjective*

needle[1] *noun* **1** a very thin pointed piece of steel that can be threaded and used in sewing. **2** something long and thin and sharp, *a knitting needle.* **3** the pointer of a meter or compass.

needle[2] *verb* (*informal*) annoy or provoke someone.

needlework *noun* sewing or embroidery.

needy *adjective* very poor; lacking things necessary for life. **neediness** *noun*

ne'er *adverb* (*poetic*) never.

nefarious (*say* nuh-**fair**-ree-uhs) *adjective* wicked. [from Latin *nefas* = wrong]

negate *verb* (**negated**, **negating**) **1** make a thing ineffective. **2** disprove. **negation** *noun* [from Latin *negare* = deny]

negative[1] *adjective* **1** that says 'no', *a negative answer.* (Compare **affirmative**.) **2** not definite; not positive. **3** less than zero; minus. **4** of the kind of electric charge carried by electrons.
negatively *adverb*

> **Usage** The opposite of sense 1 is *affirmative*, and of senses 2, 3, 4 *positive*.

negative[2] *noun* **1** something negative. **2** a photograph on film with the dark parts light and the light parts dark, from which a positive print (with the dark and light or colours correct) can be made. (Compare **positive**[2].) [from Latin *negare* = deny]

neglect[1] *verb* **1** not look after or attend to a person or thing. **2** not do something; forget, *She neglected to lock the door.*

neglect[2] *noun* neglecting; being neglected. **neglectful** *adjective*

negligence *noun* lack of proper care or attention; carelessness. **negligent** *adjective*, **negligently** *adverb*

negligible *adjective* not big enough or important enough to be worth bothering about.

negotiable *adjective* **1** able to be changed after being discussed, *The salary is negotiable.* **2** (of a cheque) able to be changed for cash or transferred to another person.

negotiate *verb* (**negotiated**, **negotiating**) **1** bargain or discuss with others in order to reach an agreement. **2** arrange after discussion, *They negotiated a treaty.* **3** get over an obstacle or difficulty. **negotiation** *noun*, **negotiator** *noun* [from Latin *negotium* = business]

Negro *noun* (*plural* **Negroes**) (*old use*) a member of a dark-skinned people originally from Africa. **Negress** *noun* [from Latin *niger* = black]

> **Usage** The terms *Negro and Negress are now considered offensive, and Black is usually preferred.*

neigh *verb* make the high-pitched cry of a horse. **neigh** *noun*

neighbour *noun* a person who lives next door or near to another. **neighbouring** *adjective*, **neighbourly** *adjective* [from Old English *neahgebur* = near dweller]

neighbourhood *noun* the surrounding district or area.

neither[1] (*say* **nuy**-*th*uh or **nee**-*th*uh) *adjective & pronoun* not either.

> **Usage** Correct use is *Neither of them likes it. Neither he nor his children like it.* Use a singular verb (e.g. *likes*) unless one of its subjects is plural (e.g. *children*).

neither[2] *adverb & conjunction* **neither ... nor** not one thing and not the other, *She neither knew nor cared.*

nemesis (*say* **nem**-uh-suhs) *noun* retribution; justifiable punishment that comes upon somebody who hoped to escape it. [named after Nemesis, goddess of retribution in Greek mythology]

neo- *prefix* new. [from Greek *neos* = new]

neolithic (*say* nee-o-**lith**-ik) *adjective* of the later part of the Stone Age. [from *neo-*, + Greek *lithos* = stone]

neologism (*say* nee-**ol**-uh-jiz-uhm) *noun* a new word or expression.

neon *noun* a gas that glows when electricity passes through it, used in glass tubes to make illuminated signs.

nephew *noun* the son of a person's brother or sister. [from Latin *nepos*]

nepotism (*say* **nep**-uh-tiz-uhm) *noun* showing favouritism to relatives in appointing them to jobs. [from Latin *nepos* = nephew]

Neptune *noun* the third-largest of the planets. [named after the Roman god of the sea]

nerd *noun* (*informal*) a person who is socially inept or boringly studious. **nerdy** *adjective*

nerve[1] *noun* **1** any of the fibres in the body that carry messages to and from the brain, so that parts of the body can feel and move. **2** courage; calmness in a dangerous situation, *Don't lose your nerve.* **3** (*informal*) impudence, *She had the nerve to ask for more.*

nerve[2] *verb* (**nerved**, **nerving**) give strength or courage to someone. [from Latin *nervus* = sinew]

nerve-racking *adjective* causing anxiety.

nerves *plural noun* nervousness.

nervous *adjective* **1** easily upset or agitated; excitable. **2** slightly afraid; timid. **3** of the nerves, *a nervous illness.* **nervously** *adverb*, **nervousness** *noun*

nervy *adjective* nervous.

nest[1] *noun* **1** a structure or place in which a bird lays its eggs and feeds its young. **2** a place where some small creatures (e.g. mice, wasps) live. **3** a set of similar things that fit inside each other, *a nest of tables.*

nest[2] *verb* **1** have or make a nest. **2** fit inside something.

nest egg *noun* a sum of money saved up for future use.

nestle *verb* (**nestled**, **nestling**) curl up comfortably.

nestling *noun* a bird that is too young to leave the nest.

net[1] *noun* **1** material made of pieces of thread, cord, or something similar joined together in a criss-cross pattern with holes between. **2** something made of this. **3** (**the Net**) the Internet. **4** (in mathematics) a flat shape that can be folded to form a polyhedron.

net[2] *verb* (**netted**, **netting**) cover or catch with a net.

net[3] *adjective* remaining when nothing more is to be deducted, *The net weight, without the box, is 100 grams.* (Compare **gross**[1] 4.)

net[4] *verb* (**netted**, **netting**) obtain or produce as net profit.

netball *noun* a game between two teams of seven players in which goals are scored by throwing a ball through a net hanging from a ring on a high post.

nether *adjective* lower, *the nether regions.*

netting *noun* a piece of net.

nettle[1] *noun* a wild plant with leaves that sting when they are touched.

nettle[2] *verb* (**nettled**, **nettling**) annoy or provoke someone.

network *noun* **1** a net-like arrangement of connected lines or parts. **2** a group or system of interconnected people or things; a set of computers or broadcasting stations that are connected to each other.

neurology *noun* the study of nerves and their diseases. **neurological** *adjective*, **neurologist** *noun* [from *neuron* + *-logy*]

neuron *noun* (also **neurone**) a nerve cell. [Greek, = nerve]

neurotic (*say* nyoo-**rot**-ik) *adjective* always very worried about something.

neuter[1] *adjective* neither masculine nor feminine. [Latin, = neither]

neuter[2] *verb* make an animal unable to reproduce; castrate or spay.

neutral *adjective* **1** not supporting either side in a war or quarrel. **2** not very distinctive, *a neutral colour such as grey.* **neutrality** *noun*, **neutrally** *adverb* [from Latin *neuter* = neither]

neutral gear *noun* a gear that is not connected to the driving parts of an engine.

neutralise *verb* (**neutralised**, **neutralising**) make a thing neutral or ineffective. **neutralisation** *noun*

neutron *noun* a particle with no electric charge. [from *neutral*]

never *adverb* at no time; not ever; not at all. [from *ne* = not, + *ever*]

never-never *noun* **1** (*informal*) hire purchase. **2** (*Australian*) the remote outback.

nevertheless *adverb & conjunction* in spite of this; although this is a fact.

new[1] *adjective* **1** not existing before; just made, invented, discovered, received, or experienced, *We built a new house.* **2** different or unfamiliar, *We have a new teacher this year.* **3** additional. **4** changed or renewed. **newly** *adverb*, **newness** *noun*

new[2] *adverb* newly, *newborn; new-laid.*

new chum *noun* (*Australian*) a newcomer; a novice.

newcomer *noun* **1** a person who has arrived recently. **2** a beginner.

newel *noun* the upright post to which the handrail of a stair is fixed, or that forms the centre pillar of a winding stair.

newfangled *adjective* needlessly new in method or style. [from *new*, + *fang* = seize]

newly *adverb* **1** recently. **2** in a new way.

new moon *noun* the moon when it is seen as a crescent.

news *noun* **1** information about recent events; a broadcast report of this. **2** a piece of new information.

newsagent *noun* a shopkeeper who sells newspapers. **newsagency** *noun*

newsgroup *noun* a group of Internet users who exchange email on a topic of mutual interest.

newsletter *noun* a printed report giving news of a club, society, or other organisation.

newspaper *noun* **1** a daily or weekly publication on large sheets of paper, containing news reports, articles, advertisements, and correspondence. **2** the sheets of paper forming a newspaper, *Wrap it in newspaper.*

newsy *adjective* (*informal*) full of news.

newt *noun* a small animal rather like a lizard, that lives near or in water.

newton *noun* a unit of force. [named after Sir Isaac Newton]

New Year's Day *noun* 1 January.

next[1] *adjective* **1** nearest. **2** coming immediately after, *on the next day.* **next door** in the next house or room.

next[2] *adverb* **1** in the next place. **2** on the next occasion, *What happens next?*

nexus *noun* (*plural* **nexus** or **nexuses**) an important connection between parts of a system or group of things.

NGO *abbreviation* non-governmental organisation.

niacin *noun* a vitamin of the B group.

nib *noun* the pointed metal part of a pen.

nibble *verb* (**nibbled, nibbling**) take small quick or gentle bites. **nibble** *noun*

nibblies *plural noun* (*Australian informal*) small snacks, *We had cheese and crackers for nibblies.*

nice *adjective* **1** pleasant; satisfactory. **2** kind; good-natured. **3** precise; careful, *a nice distinction.* **nicely** *adverb*, **niceness** *noun* [the word originally meant 'stupid', from Latin *nescius* = ignorant]

nicety (*say* **nuy**-suh-tee) *noun* (*plural* **niceties**) **1** precision. **2** a small detail or difference pointed out.

niche (*say* neesh) *noun* **1** a small recess, especially in a wall. **2** a suitable place or position, *She found her niche in the drama club.* [from Latin *nidus* = nest]

nick[1] *noun* **1** a small cut or notch. **2** (*informal*) a police station or prison. **3** (*informal*) condition, *in good nick.* **in the nick of time** only just in time.

nick[2] *verb* **1** make a nick in something. **2** (*informal*) steal. **3** (*informal*) catch; arrest. **nick off** (*Australian informal*) depart quickly.

nickel *noun* **1** a silvery-white metal. **2** (*American*) a five-cent coin.

nickname *noun* a name given to a person instead of their real name. [originally *a nekename*, from *an eke-name* (*eke* = addition, + *name*)]

nicotine *noun* a poisonous substance found in tobacco. [from the name of J. Nicot, who introduced tobacco into France in 1560]

niece *noun* the daughter of a person's brother or sister.

nifty *adjective* (**niftier, niftiest**) clever or smart, *a nifty invention.*

niggardly *adjective* mean; stingy. **niggardliness** *noun*

niggle *verb* (**niggled, niggling**) fuss over details or very small faults.

nigh *adverb & preposition* (*old use*) near.

night *noun* **1** the dark hours between sunset and sunrise. **2** a particular night or evening, *the first night of the play.*

nightclub *noun* a place that is open late into the night where people can go to drink and dance.

nightdress *noun* a loose garment for wearing in bed.

nightfall *noun* the coming of darkness at the end of the day.

nightie *noun* (*informal*) a nightdress.

nightingale *noun* a small brown bird that sings sweetly.

nightly *adjective & adverb* happening every night.

nightmare *noun* a frightening dream. **nightmarish** *adjective*

nil *noun* nothing; nought. [from Latin *nihil* = nothing]

nimble *adjective* able to move quickly; agile. **nimbly** *adverb*

nine *noun & adjective* the number 9; one more than eight. **ninth** *adjective & noun*

ninepins *noun* the game of skittles played with nine objects.

nineteen *noun & adjective* the number 19; one more than eighteen. **nineteenth** *adjective & noun*

ninety *noun & adjective* (*plural* **nineties**) the number 90; nine times ten. **ninetieth** *adjective & noun*

ninja (*say* **nin**-juh) *noun* **1** a person skilled in the Japanese art of ninjutsu. **2** (*informal*) a person who excels in a particular skill or activity. [Japanese, = spy]

ninjutsu (*say* nin-**juut**-soo) *noun* the traditional Japanese art of stealth, camouflage, and sabotage, developed in feudal times for espionage and now practised as a martial art. [from Japanese *nin* = stealth, + *jutsu* = art, science]

nip[1] *verb* (**nipped, nipping**) **1** pinch or bite quickly. **2** (*informal*) go quickly.

nip[2] *noun* **1** a quick pinch or bite. **2** sharp coldness, *There's a nip in the air.*

nipper *noun* (*informal*) a young child.

nipple *noun* a small projecting part, especially at the front of a person's breast.

nippy *adjective* (**nippier, nippiest**) (*informal*) **1** quick; nimble. **2** cold.

niqab (*say* ni-**kahb**) *noun* a veil worn by some Muslim women, covering all the face and having two holes for the eyes. [Arabic]

nirvana *noun* **1** (in Buddhist and Hindu teaching) the state of perfect bliss attained when the soul is freed from all suffering and absorbed into the supreme spirit. **2** a state of perfect happiness. [Sanskrit]

nit *noun* a parasitic insect; its egg.

nit-picking *noun* pointing out very small faults.

nitrate *noun* a chemical compound containing nitrogen.

nitric acid (*say* **nuy**-trik) *noun* a very strong colourless acid containing nitrogen.

nitrogen (*say* **nuy**-truh-juhn) *noun* a gas that makes up about four fifths of the air.

nitty-gritty *noun* (*informal*) the basic facts or practical details of a matter.

nitwit *noun* (*informal*) a stupid person.

no[1] *adjective* not any, *We have no money.*

no[2] *adverb* **1** used to deny or refuse something, *Will you come? No.* **2** not at all, *She is no better.*

no. *abbreviation* (*plural* **nos.**) number. [from Latin *numero* = by number]

noble[1] *adjective* **1** of high social rank; aristocratic. **2** having a very good character or qualities. **3** stately; impressive, *a noble building.* **nobility** *noun*, **nobly** *adverb*

noble[2] *noun* a person of high social rank. **nobleman** *noun*, **noblewoman** *noun*

nobody[1] *pronoun* no person; no one.

nobody[2] *noun* a person of no importance.

nocturnal *adjective* of or in the night; active at night, *nocturnal animals.* [from Latin *noctis* = of night]

nocturne *noun* a piece of music with the quiet dreamy feeling of night.

nod *verb* (**nodded, nodding**) **1** move the head up and down, especially as a way of agreeing with somebody or as a greeting. **2** be drowsy. **nod** *noun*

node *noun* a swelling like a small knob.

nodule *noun* a small node.

noise *noun* a sound, especially one that is loud or unpleasant. **noiseless** *adjective*, **noisily** *adverb*, **noisy** *adjective*

nomad *noun* **1** a member of a people that moves from place to place looking for pasture for their animals. **2** a person who does not stay long in the same place. **nomadic** *adjective*

no man's land *noun* an area that does not belong to anybody.

nom de plume *noun* a writer's pseudonym. [French, = pen-name (this phrase is not used in France)]

nomenclature (*say* nuh-**men**-kluh-chuh) *noun* a system of names, e.g. those used in a particular science.

nominal *adjective* **1** in name only, not real or actual, *He is the nominal ruler, but the real power is held by the generals.* **2** small, *We charged them only a nominal fee.* **3** of, like, or as a noun. **nominally** *adverb* [from Latin *nomen* = name]

nominalise *verb* form a noun from a verb or adjective, e.g. *output, truth*, from *put out, true.* **nominalisation** *noun*

nominate *verb* (**nominated, nominating**) name a person or thing to be appointed or chosen. **nomination** *noun*, **nominator** *noun* [from Latin *nominare* = to name]

nominee *noun* a person who is nominated.

non- *prefix* not. [from Latin *non* = not]

nonagenarian *noun* a person aged between 90 and 99. [from Latin *nonageni* = ninety each]

non-believer *noun* a person who does not believe or who has no faith.

nonchalant (*say* **non**-shuh-luhnt) *adjective* calm and casual; showing no anxiety or excitement. **nonchalance** *noun*, **nonchalantly** *adverb* [from French *non* = not, + *chaloir* = be concerned]

non-commissioned *adjective* not holding a commission, *Non-commissioned officers include corporals and sergeants.*

non-committal *adjective* not committing yourself; not showing what you think.

nonconformist *noun* a person who does not conform to established principles.

nondescript *adjective* having no special or distinctive qualities and therefore difficult to describe.

none[1] *pronoun* **1** not any. **2** no one, *None can tell.*

> **Usage** In sense 1 it is better to use a singular verb (e.g. *None of them is here*), but the plural is not incorrect (e.g. *None of them are here*).

none[2] *adverb* not at all, *He is none too bright.* [from *not one*]

nonentity (*say* non-**en**-tuh-tee) *noun* (*plural* **nonentities**) an unimportant person. [from *non-* + *entity*]

non-event *noun* an event that was expected to be important but proves to be disappointing.

non-existent *adjective* not existing; unreal.

non-fiction *noun* writings that are not fiction; books about real people and things and true events.

nong *noun* (*Australian informal*) a simpleton.

nonplus *verb* (**nonplussed, nonplussing**) puzzle someone completely. [from Latin *non plus* = not further]

nonplussed *adjective* **1** confused; puzzled. **2** (*informal*) not disconcerted; not worried.

non-profit *adjective* not making or conducted primarily to make a profit, *charities and other non-profit organisations.*

nonsense *noun* **1** words put together in a way that does not mean anything. **2** stupid ideas or behaviour. **nonsensical** (*say* non-**sen**-si-kuhl) *adjective* [from *non-* + *sense*]

non sequitur (*say* non **sek**-wi-tuh) *noun* a conclusion that does not follow from the evidence given. [Latin, = it does not follow]

non-stick *adjective* having a special coating to which food etc. will not stick, *non-stick frying pan.*

non-stop *adjective* **1** not stopping, *non-stop chatter.* **2** not stopping between two main stations, *a non-stop train.*

noodles *plural noun* pasta made in narrow strips.

nook *noun* a sheltered corner; a recess.

noon *noun* twelve o'clock at midday.

no one *pronoun* no person; nobody.

noose *noun* a loop in a rope that gets smaller when the rope is pulled.

nor *conjunction* and not, *She cannot do it; nor can I.*

norm *noun* a standard or average type, amount, level, etc.

normal *adjective* **1** usual or ordinary. **2** natural and healthy; without a physical or mental illness. **normality** *noun*, **normally** *adverb*

north[1] *noun* **1** the direction to the left of a person who faces east. **2** the northern part of something.

north[2] *adjective & adverb* towards or in the north. **northerly** *adjective*, **northern** *adjective*, **northerner** *noun*, **northernmost** *adjective*

north-east *noun*, *adjective*, *& adverb* midway between north and east. **north-easterly** *adjective*, **north-eastern** *adjective*

north pole see **pole**[2].

northward *adjective & adverb* towards the north. **northwards** *adverb*

north-west *noun*, *adjective*, *& adverb* midway between north and west. **north-westerly** *adjective*, **north-western** *adjective*

nos. *plural* of **no.**

nose[1] *noun* **1** the part of the face that is used for breathing and for smelling things. **2** the front end or part.
on the nose (*Australian informal*) **1** offensively smelly. **2** unacceptable.

nose[2] *verb* (**nosed, nosing**) **1** push the nose into or near something. **2** pry or search, *nosing around.* **3** go forward cautiously, *The car nosed past the roadworks.*

nosedive *noun* a steep downward dive, especially of an aircraft. **nosedive** *verb*

nosegay *noun* a small bunch of flowers. [from *nose* + *gay*[1] = ornament]

nostalgia (*say* nos-**tal**-juh) *noun* sentimental remembering or longing for the past. **nostalgic** *adjective*, **nostalgically** *adverb* [from Greek *nostos* = return home, + *algos* = pain (= homesickness)]

nostril *noun* either of the two openings in the nose.

nosy *adjective* (**nosier, nosiest**) unduly inquisitive. **nosily** *adverb*, **nosiness** *noun*

not *adverb* used to change the meaning of something to its opposite or absence, *We are not playing soccer this weekend.*

nota bene (*say* noh-tuh **ben**-ay) *verb* (usually shortened to **NB**) note carefully. [Latin, = note well]

notable *adjective* **1** worth noticing; remarkable. **2** famous. **notability** *noun*, **notably** *adverb*

notation *noun* a system of symbols representing numbers, quantities, or elements in something such as music.

notch[1] *noun* (*plural* **notches**) a small V-shape cut into a surface.

notch[2] *verb* cut a notch or notches in.
notch up score.

note[1] *noun* **1** something written down as a reminder or as a comment or explanation. **2** a short letter. **3** a banknote, *a $10 note.* **4** a single sound in music. **5** any of the black or white keys on a piano or similar instrument (see **key**[1] 3). **6** a sound or quality that indicates something, *a note of warning.* **7** notice.

note[2] *verb* (**noted, noting**) **1** make a note about something; write down. **2** notice; pay attention to, *Note what we say.* [from Latin *nota* = a mark]

notebook *noun* **1** a book with blank pages on which to write notes. **2** a laptop computer.

noted *adjective* famous; well-known.

notepad *noun* a set of sheets of writing paper fastened together at one edge.

notepaper *noun* paper for writing letters.

nothing[1] *noun* **1** no thing; not anything. **2** no amount; nought. **nothingness** *noun*
for nothing 1 without payment; free. **2** without a result.

nothing[2] *adverb* not at all; in no way, *It's nothing like as good.*

notice[1] *noun* **1** something written or printed and displayed for people to see. **2** attention, *It escaped my notice.* **3** information that something is going to happen; warning that you are about to end an agreement or a person's employment, *We gave him a month's notice.*

notice[2] *verb* (**noticed, noticing**) see; become aware of something. [from Latin *notus* = known]

noticeable *adjective* easily seen or noticed. **noticeably** *adverb*

noticeboard *noun* a board on which notices may be displayed.

notifiable *adjective* that must be reported.

notify *verb* (**notified, notifying**) **1** inform, *Notify the police.* **2** report; make something known. **notification** *noun*

notion *noun* an idea, especially one that is vague or incorrect.

notional *adjective* guessed and not definite. **notionally** *adverb*

notorious *adjective* well known for something bad. **notoriety** (*say* noh-tuh-**ruy**-uh-tee) *noun*, **notoriously** *adverb* [from Latin *notus* = known]

notwithstanding *preposition* in spite of.

nougat (*say* **noo**-gah) *noun* a chewy sweet made from nuts, sugar or honey, and egg white. [French]

nought (*say* nawt) *noun* **1** the figure 0. **2** nothing.

noun *noun* a word that is the name of a person, place, thing, or idea. **Common nouns** are words such as *boy, dog, river, sport, table*, that are used of a whole kind of people or things; **proper nouns** are words such as *George, Uluru*, and *Sydney*, that name a particular person or thing. [from Latin *nomen* = name]

nourish *verb* keep a person, animal, or plant alive and well by means of food. **nourishment** *noun* [from Latin *nutrio* = to feed]

nous (*rhymes with* house) *noun* (*informal*) common sense. [Greek, = the mind]

nouveau riche (*say* noo-voh **reesh**) *noun* a person who has only recently become rich. [French, = new rich]

novel[1] *noun* a story that fills a whole book.

novel[2] *adjective* of a new and unusual kind, *a novel experience.* [from Latin *novus* = new]

novelist *noun* a person who writes novels.

novella *noun* (*plural* **novellas**) a short novel or narrative story. [Italian]

novelty *noun* **1** the quality of being new and unusual. **2** something new and unusual. **3** a small toy or trinket. [same origin as *novel*]

November *noun* the eleventh month of the year. [from Latin *novem* = nine (originally the ninth month of the Roman year)]

novice *noun* a beginner.

now[1] *adverb* **1** at this time. **2** by this time. **3** immediately, *You must go now.* **4** I insist or I wonder, *Now behave yourself; Now why didn't I think of that?*
now and again or **now and then** sometimes; occasionally.

now[2] *conjunction* as a result of or at the same time as something, *Now that you have come, we'll start.*

now[3] *noun* this moment, *They will be at home by now.*

nowadays *adverb* at the present time, as contrasted with years ago.

nowhere[1] *adverb* not anywhere.

nowhere[2] *noun* no place, *Nowhere is as beautiful as New Zealand.*

noxious *adjective* unpleasant and harmful. [from Latin *noxius* = harmful]

nozzle *noun* the spout of a hose, pipe, or tube used to control a jet of gas or liquid. [= little nose]

nuance (*say* **nyoo**-ons) *noun* a slight difference or shade of meaning.

nub *noun* **1** a small knob or lump. **2** the central point of a problem.

nuclear *adjective* **1** of a nucleus. **2** using the energy that is created by reactions in the nuclei of atoms.

nucleic acid *noun* an acid of either of the two types (DNA and RNA) present in all living cells.

nucleus *noun* (*plural* **nuclei**) **1** the part in the centre of something, round which other things are grouped. **2** the central part of an atom or of a seed or a biological cell. [Latin, = kernel]

nude *adjective* not wearing any clothes; naked. **nudism** *noun*, **nudist** *noun*, **nudity** *noun*

nudge *verb* (**nudged, nudging**) **1** poke a person gently with your elbow. **2** push slightly or gradually. **nudge** *noun*

nugget *noun* **1** a rough lump of gold or other precious metal found in the earth. **2** a small chunk or lump of another substance.

nuggety *adjective* (*Australian*) thickset; stocky, *a nuggety man.*

nuisance *noun* an annoying person or thing.

null *adjective* not valid, *null and void.* [from Latin *nullus* = none]

nulla-nulla *noun* a wooden club, used traditionally by Aboriginal people in fighting and hunting. [from Sydney language *ngala ngala*]

nullify *verb* (**nullified, nullifying**) make a thing null. **nullification** *noun*

numb[1] *adjective* unable to feel or move. **numbly** *adverb*, **numbness** *noun*

numb[2] *verb* make numb.

numbat *noun* a small reddish-brown Australian marsupial that feeds on termites. [from Noongar *nhumbad*]

number[1] *noun* **1** a symbol or word indicating how many; a numeral or figure. **2** a numeral given to a thing to identify it, *a telephone number.* **3** a quantity of people or things, *the number of people present.* **4** one issue of a magazine or newspaper. **5** a song or piece of music.

number[2] *verb* **1** mark with numbers. **2** count. **3** amount to, *The crowd numbered 10,000.*

numberless *adjective* too many to count.

number line *noun* (in mathematics) a line on which numbers are marked at intervals, used to illustrate simple numerical operations.

number plate *noun* a plate on a motor vehicle showing its registration number.

number sentence *noun* a record of calculations using numbers and symbols, such as 2 + 5 = 7.

numeral *noun* a symbol that represents a certain number; a figure, *The numeral for the number two is 2.* [from Latin *numerus* = number]

numerate *adjective* having a good basic knowledge of mathematics. **numeracy** *noun* [same origin as *numeral*]

numeration *noun* numbering.

numerator *noun* the number above the line in a fraction, showing how many parts are to be taken, e.g. 2 in ⅔. (Compare **denominator**.)

numerical (*say* nyoo-**me**-ri-kuhl) *adjective* of a number or series of numbers, *in numerical order.* **numerically** *adverb*

numerous *adjective* many. [from Latin *numerus* = number]

numismatics (*say* new-muhz-**mat**-iks) *noun* the study of coins. **numismatist** *noun* [from Greek *nomisma* = coin]

nun *noun* a member of a community of women who live according to the rules of a religious organisation. (Compare **monk**.) [from Latin *nonna* = nun]

nunnery *noun* (*plural* **nunneries**) a convent for nuns. (Compare **monastery**.)

nuptial *adjective* of marriage; of a wedding.

nurse[1] *noun* a person trained to look after people who are ill or injured.

nurse[2] *verb* (**nursed**, **nursing**) **1** look after someone who is ill or injured. **2** hold carefully. **3** feed a baby. [same origin as *nourish*]

nursery *noun* (*plural* **nurseries**) **1** a place where young children are looked after or play. **2** a place where young plants are grown and usually for sale.

nursery rhyme *noun* a simple rhyme or song of the kind that young children like.

nursing home *noun* a small hospital or home for invalids or elderly people.

nurture[1] *verb* (**nurtured**, **nurturing**) **1** nourish. **2** train and educate; bring up.

nurture[2] *noun* nurturing; nourishment.

nut *noun* **1** a fruit with a hard shell. **2** a kernel. **3** a small piece of metal with a hole in the middle, for screwing on to a bolt. **4** (informal) the head. **5** (informal) a mad or eccentric person. **nutty** *adjective*

nutcracker *noun* an implement for cracking the shells of nuts.

nutmeg *noun* the hard seed of a tropical tree, grated and used in cooking.

nutrient (*say* **nyoo**-tree-uhnt) *noun* a nourishing substance. [from Latin *nutrire* = nourish]

nutriment (*say* **nyoo**-truh-muhnt) *noun* nourishing food.

nutrition (*say* nyoo-**trish**-uhn) *noun* nourishment; the study of what nourishes people. **nutritional** *adjective*, **nutritionally** *adverb*

nutritious (*say* new-**trish**-uhs) *adjective* nourishing; giving good nourishment. **nutritiousness** *noun*

nutritive (*say* **nyoo**-truh-tiv) *adjective* nourishing.

nutshell *noun* the shell of a nut. **in a nutshell** stated very briefly.

nuzzle *verb* (**nuzzled**, **nuzzling**) rub gently with the nose.

NW *abbreviation* north-west; north-western.

nylon *noun* a synthetic lightweight very strong cloth or fibre.

nymph (*say* nimf) *noun* (in myths) a young goddess living especially in the sea or woods.

NZ *abbreviation* New Zealand.

Oo

O *interjection* oh.

oaf *noun* (*plural* **oafs**) a stupid lout.

oak *noun* a large deciduous tree with seeds called *acorns.* **oaken** *adjective*

oar *noun* a pole with a flat blade at one end, used for rowing a boat. **oarsman** *noun*

oasis (*say* oh-**ay**-suhs) *noun* (*plural* **oases**) **1** a fertile place in a desert, with a spring or well of water. **2** a pleasant or peaceful area or period in the midst of a difficult or hectic place or situation.

oath *noun* **1** a solemn promise to do something or that something is true, often appealing to God or a holy person as witness. **2** use of the name of God in anger or to emphasise something.

oatmeal *noun* ground oats.

oats *plural noun* a cereal used to make food for people and animals.

ob- *prefix* (changing to **oc-** before *c*, **of-** before *f*, **op-** before *p*) **1** to; towards (as in *observe*). **2** against (as in *opponent*). **3** in the way; blocking (as in *obstruct*). [from Latin *ob* = towards, against]

obedient *adjective* doing what you are told; willing to obey. **obedience** *noun*, **obediently** *adverb*

obeisance (*say* oh-**bay**-suhns) *noun* a deep bow or curtsy.

obelisk *noun* a tall pillar set up as a monument. [from Greek, = little rod]

obese (*say* oh-**bees**) *adjective* very fat or overweight. **obesity** *noun* [from Latin *obesus* = having overeaten]

obey *verb* do what you are told to do by a person, law, or rule.

obituary *noun* (*plural* **obituaries**) a notice of a death, typically including a brief biography of the deceased person.

object[1] (*say* **ob**-jekt) *noun* **1** something that can be seen or touched. **2** a purpose or intention. **3** (in grammar) the word or words naming who or what is acted upon by a verb or by a preposition, e.g. *him* in *the dog bit him* and *against him.*

object[2] (*say* uhb-**jekt**) *verb* say that you are not in favour of something or do not agree; protest. **objector** *noun* [from *ob* = in the way, + Latin *-jectum* = thrown]

objection *noun* **1** objecting to something. **2** a reason for objecting.

objectionable *adjective* unpleasant; not liked. **objectionably** *adverb*

objective[1] *noun* what you are trying to reach or do; an aim.

objective[2] *adjective* **1** real; actual, *Dreams have no objective existence.* **2** not influenced by personal feelings or opinions, *an objective account of the quarrel.* (Compare **subjective.**) **objectively** *adverb*, **objectivity** *noun*

objet d'art (*say* ob-*zh*ay **dah**) *noun* a small artistic object. [French, = object of art]

obligation *noun* **1** being obliged to do something. **2** what you are obliged to do; a duty.
under an obligation owing gratitude to someone who has helped you.

obligatory (*say* uh-**blig**-uh-tuh-ree) *adjective* compulsory; not optional.

oblige *verb* (**obliged, obliging**) **1** compel. **2** help and please someone, *The bank will oblige you with a loan.*
be obliged to someone feel gratitude to a person who has helped you. [from *ob-* = to, + Latin *ligare* = bind]

obliging *adjective* polite and helpful.

oblique (*say* uh-**bleek**) *adjective* **1** slanting. **2** not saying something straightforwardly, *an oblique reply.* **obliquely** *adverb*

obliterate *verb* (**obliterated, obliterating**) blot out; destroy and remove all traces of something. **obliteration** *noun* [from Latin, = erase (*ob* = over, *littera* = letter)]

oblivion *noun* **1** being forgotten. **2** being oblivious.

oblivious *adjective* not aware of or concerned about what is happening around you, *They were enjoying the game so much that they were oblivious to the storm outside.*

oblong *adjective* rectangular in shape and longer than it is wide (like a page of this book). **oblong** *noun*

obnoxious *adjective* very unpleasant; objectionable.

oboe *noun* a high-pitched woodwind instrument. **oboist** *noun* [from French *haut* = high, + *bois* = wood]

obscene (*say* uhb-**seen**) *adjective* indecent in a very offensive way. **obscenely** *adverb*, **obscenity** *noun*

obscure[1] *adjective* **1** dark; indistinct. **2** difficult to understand; not clear. **3** not famous. **obscurely** *adverb*, **obscurity** *noun*

obscure[2] *verb* (**obscured**, **obscuring**) make a thing obscure; darken or conceal, *Clouds obscured the sun.*

obsequious (*say* uhb-**see**-kwee-uhs) *adjective* respectful in an excessive or sickening way. **obsequiously** *adverb*, **obsequiousness** *noun*

observable *adjective* able to be noticed or perceived; discernible. **observability** *noun*, **observably** *adverb*

observance *noun* obeying or keeping a law, custom, religious festival, or rule.

observant *adjective* quick at observing or noticing things. **observantly** *adverb*

observation *noun* **1** observing; watching. **2** a comment or remark.

observatory *noun* (*plural* **observatories**) a building with telescopes and other equipment for observation of the stars or weather.

observe *verb* (**observed**, **observing**) **1** see and notice; watch carefully. **2** obey a law. **3** keep or celebrate a custom or religious festival. **4** make a remark. **observer** *noun* [from *ob-* = towards, + Latin *servare* = to watch]

obsess *verb* occupy a person's thoughts continually. **obsession** *noun*, **obsessive** *adjective*

obsolescent *adjective* becoming obsolete; going out of use or fashion. **obsolescence** *noun*

obsolete *adjective* not used anymore; out of date. [from Latin *obsoletus* = worn out]

obstacle *noun* something that stands in the way or obstructs progress. [from *ob* = in the way, + Latin *stare* = to stand]

obstetrics *noun* the branch of medicine and surgery that deals with the birth of babies. **obstetrician** *noun* [from Latin, = of a midwife]

obstinate *adjective* keeping firmly to your own ideas or ways, even though they may be wrong. **obstinacy** *noun*, **obstinately** *adverb*

obstreperous (*say* uhb-**strep**-uh-ruhs) *adjective* noisy and unruly.

obstruct *verb* **1** stop a person or thing from getting past. **2** hinder. **obstruction** *noun*, **obstructive** *adjective*

obtain *verb* get; come into possession of something by buying, taking, or being given it. **obtainable** *adjective* [from *ob-* = to, + Latin *tenere* = hold]

obtrude *verb* (**obtruded**, **obtruding**) force yourself or your ideas on someone; be unpleasantly noticeable. **obtrusion** *noun* [from *ob-*, + Latin *trudere* = push]

obtrusive *adjective* **1** obtruding. **2** unpleasantly noticeable. **obtrusiveness** *noun*

obtuse *adjective* stupid; slow to understand. **obtusely** *adverb*, **obtuseness** *noun* [from *ob-* = towards, + Latin *tusum* = blunted]

obtuse angle *noun* an angle of more than 90° but less than 180°. (Compare **acute angle**.)

obverse *noun* the side of a coin or medal showing the head or chief design (the other side is the *reverse*). [from *ob-* = towards, + Latin *versum* = turned]

obviate *verb* get round or do away with a need or inconvenience.

obvious *adjective* easy to see or understand. **obviously** *adverb* [from Latin *ob viam* = in the way]

oc- *prefix* see **ob-**.

ocarina *noun* a small egg-shaped ceramic or metal wind instrument.

occasion[1] *noun* **1** the time when something happens. **2** a special event. **3** a suitable time; an opportunity.

occasion[2] *verb* cause.

occasional *adjective* **1** happening at intervals. **2** for special occasions, *occasional music.* **occasionally** *adverb*

Occident (*say* **ok**-suh-duhnt) *noun* the countries of the West, especially Europe and America. (Compare **Orient**.) **occidental** *adjective* [from Latin, = sunset]

occipital bone (*say* ok-**sip**-uh-tuhl) *noun* the bone that forms the back and base of the skull and encircles the spinal cord.

occult *adjective* **1** mysterious; magical; supernatural, *occult powers.* **2** secret except when people have special knowledge. [from Latin *occultum* = hidden]

occupant *noun* someone who occupies a place. **occupancy** *noun*

occupation *noun* **1** an activity that keeps a person busy; a job. **2** occupying.

occupational *adjective* of or caused by an occupation, *an occupational hazard.* **occupational therapy** mental or physical activity designed to help people to recover from certain illnesses.

occupy *verb* (**occupied**, **occupying**) **1** live in a place; inhabit. **2** fill a space or position. **3** capture enemy territory and place troops there. **4** keep somebody busy; fill with activity. **occupier** *noun*

occur *verb* (**occurred**, **occurring**) **1** happen; come into existence as an event or process. **2** be found to exist. **3** come into a person's mind, *An idea occurred to me.*

occurrence *noun* **1** occurring. **2** an incident or event; a happening.

ocean *noun* the seas that surround the continents of the earth, especially one of the large named areas of this, *the Pacific Ocean.* **oceanic** *adjective* [from Oceanus, the river that the ancient Greeks thought surrounded the world]

ocelot (*say* **os**-uh-lot) *noun* a leopard-like cat of Central and South America.

ochre (*say* **oh**-kuh) *noun* **1** a mineral used as a pigment. **2** pale brownish-yellow.

ocker *noun* (*Australian informal*) a rough and uncultivated male (especially as a stereotype). **ocker** *adjective*

o'clock *adverb* by the clock, *Lunch is at one o'clock.* [short for *of the clock*]

octa- *prefix* (also **octo-**) eight. [from Greek *okto* = eight]

octagon *noun* a flat shape with eight sides and eight angles. **octagonal** *adjective* [from *octa-*, + Greek *gonia* = angle]

octahedron *noun* a solid shape with eight faces. [from *octa-*, + Greek *hedra* = base]

octave *noun* the interval of eight steps between one musical note and the next note of the same name above or below it. [from Latin *octavus* = eighth]

octet *noun* **1** a group of eight musicians. **2** a piece of music for eight musicians. [from *octo-*]

octo- *prefix* see **octa-**.

October *noun* the tenth month of the year. [from Latin *octo* = eight (originally the eighth month of the Roman year)]

octogenarian *noun* a person aged between 80 and 89. [from Latin *octogeni* = 80 each]

octopus *noun* (*plural* **octopuses**) a sea animal with eight long tentacles. [from *octo-*, + Greek *pous* = foot]

ocular *adjective* of or for the eyes; visual. [from Latin *oculus* = eye]

odd *adjective* **1** strange; unusual. **2** not an even number; not able to be divided exactly by two. (Compare **even**[1] 5.) **3** left over from a pair or set, *I've got one odd sock.* **4** of various kinds; not regular, *odd jobs.* **oddity** *noun*, **oddly** *adverb*, **oddness** *noun*

oddments *plural noun* small things of various kinds.

odds *plural noun* the chances that a certain thing will happen; a measure of this, *When the odds are 10 to 1, you will win $10 if you bet $1.*

odds and ends *plural noun* oddments.

ode *noun* a poem addressed to a person or thing. [from Greek *oide* = song]

odious (*say* **oh**-dee-uhs) *adjective* hateful. **odiously** *adverb*, **odiousness** *noun*

odium (*say* **oh**-dee-uhm) *noun* general hatred or disgust felt towards a person or actions. [Latin, = hatred]

odometer (*say* oh-**dom**-uh-tuh) *noun* a device in a vehicle for measuring the distance travelled. [from Greek *hodos* = way, + *meter*]

odour *noun* a smell. **odorous** *adjective*, **odourless** *adjective* [Latin *odor* = smell]

odyssey (*say* **od**-uh-see) *noun* (*plural* **odysseys**) a long adventurous journey. [named after the *Odyssey*, a Greek poem telling of the wanderings of Odysseus]

OECD *adjective* Organisation for Economic Cooperation and Development.

o'er *preposition & adverb* (*poetic*) over.

oesophagus (*say* uh-**sof**-uh-guhs) *noun* (*plural* **oesophagi**) the gullet.

oestrogen (*say* **ees**-truh-juhn) *noun* (also **estrogen**) a sex hormone developing and maintaining female characteristics of the body.

of *preposition* **1** belonging to, *the mother of the child.* **2** concerning; about, *news of the disaster.* **3** made from, *built of stone.* **4** from, *north of the town.*

> **Usage** *Of* should not be used instead of *have* in constructions such as *You should have asked*; *She couldn't have known*, although in rapid speech they sound the same.

of- *prefix* see **ob-**.

off[1] *preposition* **1** not on; away or down from, *He fell off the ladder.* **2** not taking or wanting, *She is off her food.* **3** deducted from, *$5 off the price.*
off colour slightly unwell.

> **Usage** *Off of* is often used in place of the preposition *off* in contexts such as '*she picked it up off of the floor*' (compared with '*she picked it up off the floor*'). Although *off of* is recorded from the 16th century, it is regarded as incorrect in standard modern English.

off[2] *adverb* **1** away or down from something, *His hat blew off.* **2** not working; not happening, *The heating is off.* **3** to the end; completely, *Finish it off.* **4** as regards money or supplies, *How are you off for cash?* **5** behind or at the side of a stage, *There were noises off.* **6** (of food) beginning to go bad.

offal *noun* the organs of an animal (e.g. liver, kidneys) that can be used as food.

offbeat *adjective* unconventional; eccentric.

offcut *noun* a piece of timber or other material remaining after cutting.

offence *noun* **1** an illegal action. **2** a feeling of annoyance or resentment.

offend *verb* **1** cause offence to someone; hurt a person's pride. **2** do wrong, *offend against the law.* **offender** *noun*

offensive[1] *adjective* **1** causing offence; insulting. **2** disgusting, *an offensive smell.* **3** used in attacking, *offensive weapons.* **offensively** *adverb*, **offensiveness** *noun*

offensive[2] *noun* an attack.
take the offensive be the first to attack.

offer[1] *verb* (**offered**, **offering**) **1** present something so that people can accept it if they want to. **2** say that you are willing to do or give something or to pay a certain amount. [from *of-* = to, + Latin *ferre* = bring]

offer[2] *noun* **1** offering something. **2** an amount offered.

offering *noun* what is offered.

offhand *adjective* **1** without preparation. **2** casual; curt. **offhanded** *adjective*

office *noun* **1** a room or building used for business, especially for clerical work or for a special department; the people who work there. **2** a government department, *the Tax Office.* **3** an important job or position.

officer *noun* **1** a person who is in charge of others, especially in the armed forces. **2** an official. **3** a member of the police.

official[1] *adjective* **1** done or said by someone with authority. **2** of officials, *her official duties.* **officially** *adverb*

official[2] *noun* a person who holds a position of authority.

officiate *verb* (**officiated**, **officiating**) act in an official capacity; be in charge.

officious *adjective* too ready to give orders; bossy. **officiously** *adverb*

offing *noun* **in the offing** not far away; likely to happen.

offline[1] *adjective* not controlled by or directly connected to a computer or the Internet.

offline[2] *adverb* while not directly controlled by or connected to a computer or the Internet, *The website remained offline while the technical issues were fixed.*

offload *verb* get rid of something that you do not want by giving it to someone else.

off-peak *adjective* in or used at a time that is less popular or less busy, *off-peak travel.*

off-putting *adjective* repellent.

offset *verb* (**offset**, **offsetting**) counterbalance or make up for something, *Defeats are offset by successes.*

offshoot *noun* **1** a sideshoot on a plant. **2** a by-product.

offshore *adjective* **1** from the land towards the sea, *an offshore breeze.* **2** in the sea some distance from the shore, *an offshore island.* **3** overseas, *an offshore investment.*

offside *adjective & adverb* **1** (of a player, especially in soccer, rugby, or hockey) in a position where they may not legally play the ball. **2** opposed; hostile.

offsider *noun* (*Australian*) an assistant.

offspring *noun* (*plural* **offspring**) **1** a person's child or children. **2** the young of an animal.

off-white *adjective* white with a grey or yellowish tinge.

oft *adverb* (*old use*) often.

often *adverb* many times; in many cases.

ogle *verb* (**ogled**, **ogling**) stare at someone whom you find attractive.

ogre *noun* **1** a cruel giant in fairy tales. **2** a terrifying person.

oh *interjection* an exclamation of pain, surprise, delight, etc., or used for emphasis, *Oh yes I will!*

ohm *noun* a unit of electrical resistance. [named after a German scientist, G. S. Ohm]

oil[1] *noun* **1** a thick slippery liquid that will not dissolve in water. **2** a kind of petroleum used as fuel.

oil[2] *verb* put oil on something, especially to make it work smoothly. [from Latin *oleum* = olive oil]

oilfield *noun* an area where oil is found.

oil paint *noun* paint made by mixing powdered pigment in oil.

oilskin *noun* cloth made waterproof by treatment with oil.

oil well *noun* a deep hole drilled in the ground or under the sea from which oil is drawn.

oily *adjective* **1** of or like oil; covered or soaked with oil. **2** unpleasantly smooth in manner. **oiliness** *noun*

ointment *noun* a cream or slippery paste for putting on sore skin and cuts.

OK *adverb & adjective* (also **okay**) (*informal*) all right. [perhaps from the initials of *oll* (or *orl*) *korrect*, a humorous spelling of *all correct*, first used in the USA in 1839]

old *adjective* **1** not new; born or made or existing from a long time ago, *We live in a very old house.* **2** of a particular age, *I'm ten years old.* **3** shabby from age or wear. **4** former; original, *I liked my old school better than the one I go to now.* **5** (*informal*) used casually or for emphasis, *good old mum!* **oldness** *noun*

olden *adjective* (*old use*) of former times.

Old English *noun* the English language from about 700 to 1150.

old-fashioned *adjective* in or according to a fashion or tastes no longer current; antiquated.

old hand *noun* (*Australian*) an experienced person.

old wives' tale *noun* a foolish or unscientific tradition or belief.

oleander *noun* a poisonous evergreen shrub with white, pink, red, or yellow flowers.

olfactory *adjective* of the sense of smell.

oligarchy *noun* (*plural* **oligarchies**) a country ruled by a small group of people. **oligarch** *noun*, **oligarchic** *adjective* [from Greek *oligoi* = few, + *archein* = to rule]

olive *noun* **1** an evergreen tree with a small bitter fruit. **2** this fruit, from which an oil (*olive oil*) is made. **3** a shade of green like an unripe olive.

olive branch *noun* something done or offered that shows you want to make peace.

Olympic Games *plural noun* (also **Olympics**) a series of international sports contests held every fourth year in a different part of the world. **Olympian** *noun*, **Olympic** *adjective* [from the name of Olympia, a city in Greece where they were held in ancient times]

ombudsman *noun* (*plural* **ombudsmen**) an official whose job is to investigate complaints against government organisations. [from Swedish, = legal representative]

omega (*say* **oh**-muh-guh) *noun* the last letter of the Greek alphabet, a long *o*. [from Greek *o mega* = big O]

omelette *noun* eggs beaten together and cooked in a pan, often with a filling.

omen *noun* an event regarded as a sign of what is going to happen.

ominous *adjective* seeming as if trouble is coming. **ominously** *adverb* [from *omen*]

omission *noun* **1** omitting. **2** something that has been omitted or not done.

omit *verb* (**omitted**, **omitting**) **1** miss something out. **2** fail to do something.

omni- *prefix* all. [from Latin *omnis* = all]

omnibus *noun* (*plural* **omnibuses**) **1** a book containing several stories or books that were previously published separately. **2** (*formal*) a bus. [Latin, = for everybody]

omnipotent *adjective* having unlimited power or very great power. **omnipotence** *noun* [from *omni-* + *potent*]

omniscient (*say* om-**nis**-ee-uhnt) *adjective* knowing everything. **omniscience** *noun* [from *omni-*, + Latin *sciens* = knowing]

omnivorous (*say* om-**niv**-uh-ruhs) *adjective* feeding on all kinds of food. (Compare **carnivorous**, **herbivorous**.) **omnivore** *noun* [from *omni-*, + Latin *vorare* = devour]

on[1] *preposition* **1** supported by; covering; added or attached to, *the sign on the door.* **2** close to; towards, *The army advanced on Paris.* **3** during; at the time of, *on my birthday.* **4** by reason of, *Arrest him on suspicion.* **5** concerning, *a book on butterflies.* **6** in a state of; using or showing, *The house was on fire.*

on[2] *adverb* **1** so as to be on something, *Put your gloves on.* **2** further forward, *Move on.* **3** working; in action, *Is the heater on?*
on and off not continually.

once[1] *adverb* **1** for one time or on one occasion only, *They came only once.* **2** formerly, *They once lived here.*

once[2] *noun* one time, *Once is enough.*

once[3] *conjunction* as soon as, *You can go once I have taken your names.*

oncology *noun* the study of tumours. [from Greek *ogkos* = mass]

oncoming *adjective* approaching; coming towards you, *oncoming traffic.*

oncost *noun* an overhead expense.

one[1] *adjective* single; individual; united.

one[2] *noun* **1** the smallest whole number; 1. **2** a person or thing alone.
one another each other.

one[3] *pronoun* a person; any person, *One likes to help.* **oneself** *pronoun*

one-eyed *adjective* strongly biased towards someone or something.

onerous (*say* **oh**-nuh-ruhs) *adjective* burdensome. [from Latin *onus* = burden]

one-sided *adjective* **1** unfairly giving or dealing with only one side of a contentious issue; biased, *He gave you a very one-sided story of what happened.* **2** (of a contest or conflict) having a marked inequality of strength or ability between the participants, *It will be a very one-sided game.*

onesie *noun* a loose-fitting one-piece garment combining trousers and a top. [from a trademark name for a garment of this type]

one-way *adjective* where traffic is allowed to travel in one direction only.

ongoing *adjective* continuing to exist or progress.

onion *noun* a round vegetable with a strong flavour. **oniony** *adjective*

online[1] *adjective* **1** controlled by or connected to a computer. **2** (of an activity or service) available on or performed using the Internet or other computer network, *online shopping.*

online[2] *adverb* **1** while connected to a computer or under computer control. **2** by means of the Internet or other computer network, *Some people would rather go to the shops than buy online.* **3** in or into operation or existence, *The new power plant will go online this month.*

onlooker *noun* a spectator.

only[1] *adjective* being the one person or thing of a kind; sole, *my only wish.*
only child a child who has no brothers or sisters.

only[2] *adverb* no more than; and that is all, *There are only three cakes left.*

only[3] *conjunction* but then; however, *She makes promises, only she never keeps them.*

onomatopoeia (*say* on-uh-mat-uh-**pee**-uh) *noun* the formation of words that imitate what they stand for, e.g. *cuckoo, plop.* **onomatopoeic** *adjective* [from Greek *onoma* = name, + *poiein* = make]

onset *noun* **1** a beginning, *the onset of winter.* **2** an attack.

onset and rime *noun* (as used in language teaching) the 'onset' is the first sound in a syllable (as 'b' in *bark*, 'm' in *mark*, and 'p' in *park*) and the 'rime' is the sound in the rest of the syllable (the sound 'ark' in *bark*, *mark*, and *park*).

onshore *adjective* **1** from the sea towards the land, *an onshore breeze.* **2** on land.

onside *adjective & adverb* not offside.

onslaught *noun* a fierce attack.

onto *preposition* to a position on.

> **Usage** The form *onto* is still not fully accepted in the way that *into* is, although it is in wide use. It is however useful in distinguishing sense as between *we drove on to the beach* (i.e. in that direction) and *we drove onto the beach* (i.e. in contact with it).

onus (*say* **oh**-nuhs) *noun* the duty or responsibility of doing something. [Latin, = burden]

onward *adverb & adjective* going forward; further on. **onwards** *adverb*

onyx *noun* a stone rather like marble, with different colours in layers.

oodles *plural noun* (*informal*) a great quantity.

ooze[1] *verb* (**oozed**, **oozing**) **1** flow out slowly; trickle. **2** allow something to flow out slowly, *The wound oozed blood.*

ooze[2] *noun* mud at the bottom of a river or sea.

op- *prefix* see **ob-**.

opal *noun* a kind of stone with a rainbow sheen. **opalescent** *adjective*

opaque (*say* oh-**payk**) *adjective* not transparent; not translucent.

open[1] *adjective* **1** allowing people or things to go in and out; not closed or covered; not blocked up. **2** spread out; unfolded. **3** not limited; not restricted, *an open contest.* **4** letting in visitors or customers. **5** with wide spaces between solid parts. **6** honest; frank; not secret or secretive, *Be open about the danger.* **7** undisguised, *open hostility.* **8** not decided, *an open mind.* **openness** *noun*
in the open air not inside a house or building. **open-air** *adjective*

open[2] *verb* **1** make or become open or more open. **2** begin. **opener** *noun*

open-cut *adjective* (of a mine) worked by removing layers of earth from the surface, not underground.

opening *noun* **1** a space or gap; a place where something opens. **2** the beginning of something. **3** an opportunity.

openly *adverb* without secrecy.

open-minded *adjective* ready to consider new ideas; unprejudiced.

open-source *adjective* (in computing) denoting software for which the original source code is made freely available.

opera[1] *noun* a play in which all or most of the words are sung. **operatic** *adjective*

opera[2] *plural* of **opus**.

operate *verb* (**operated**, **operating**) **1** make something work. **2** be in action; work. **3** perform a surgical operation on somebody. **operable** *adjective* [from Latin *operari* = to work]

operating system *noun* software that is used to control a computer and to allow applications or programs to be run.

operation *noun* **1** operating; working. **2** a piece of work. **3** something done to the body to take away or repair a part of it. **4** a planned military activity. **5** (in mathematics) the subjection of a number or quantity or function to a process affecting its value or form, e.g. multiplication, differentiation. **operational** *adjective*

operative[1] *adjective* working; functioning.

operative[2] *noun* **1** a worker, especially a skilled one. **2** a secret agent, private detective, or similar covert worker.

operator *noun* a person who works something, especially a telephone switchboard or exchange.

operetta *noun* a short light opera.

ophthalmic (*say* of-**thal**-mik) *adjective* of or for the eyes. [from Greek *ophthalmos* = eye]

ophthalmology (*say* of-thal-**mol**-uh-jee) *noun* the study of the eye and its diseases.

ophthalmologist *noun* [from Greek *ophthalmos* = eye]

opinion *noun* what you think of something; a belief or judgement. [from Latin *opinari* = believe]

opinionated *adjective* having strong opinions and holding them obstinately.

opinion poll *noun* an estimate of what people think, made by questioning a sample of them.

opium *noun* a drug made from the juice of certain poppies, used in medicine.

opponent *noun* a person or group opposing another in a contest or war. [from Latin *opponere* = set against]

opportune *adjective* **1** (of time) suitable for a purpose. **2** done or happening at a suitable time. **opportunely** *adverb* [from *op-*, + Latin *portus* = harbour (originally used of wind blowing a ship towards a harbour)]

opportunist *noun* a person who is quick to seize opportunities.

opportunistic *adjective* exploiting immediate opportunities, especially in an unplanned or selfish way.

opportunity *noun* (*plural* **opportunities**) a time or set of circumstances that are suitable for doing a particular thing. [same origin as *opportune*]

opportunity shop *noun* (*Australian*) a shop run by a charity to sell donated secondhand clothes and other pre-owned items.

oppose *verb* (**opposed**, **opposing**) **1** argue or fight against; resist. **2** contrast, *'Soft' is opposed to 'hard'.*

opposite[1] *adjective* **1** placed on the other or further side; facing, *on the opposite side of the road.* **2** moving away from or towards each other, *The trains were travelling in opposite directions.* **3** completely different, *opposite characters.*

opposite[2] *noun* an opposite person or thing.

opposite[3] *adverb* in an opposite position or direction, *I'll sit opposite.*

opposite[4] *preposition* facing, *They live opposite the school.* [from Latin *oppositum* = placed against]

opposition *noun* **1** opposing something; resistance. **2** the people who oppose something. **3** (the Opposition) the chief political party opposing the one that is in power.

oppress *verb* **1** govern or treat somebody cruelly or unjustly. **2** weigh down with care. **oppression** *noun*, **oppressor** *noun* [from *op-* = against, + *press*]

oppressive *adjective* **1** oppressing; harsh or cruel. **2** (of weather) sultry.

opprobrium (*say* uh-**proh**-bree-uhm) *noun* disgrace brought by shameful conduct.

op shop *noun* an opportunity shop.

opt *verb* choose.
opt out decide not to join in. [from Latin *optare* = wish for]

optic *adjective* of the eye or sight. [from Greek *optos* = seen]

optical *adjective* of sight; aiding sight, *optical instruments.* **optically** *adverb* [from *optic*]

optical illusion *noun* a deceptive appearance that makes you see something wrongly.

optician *noun* a person who makes or sells spectacles.

optimist *noun* a person who expects that things will turn out well. (Compare **pessimist**.) **optimism** *noun*, **optimistic** *adjective*, **optimistically** *adverb* [from Latin *optimus* = best]

optimum *adjective* best; most favourable. **optimal** *adjective*, **optimum** *noun* [Latin, = best thing]

option *noun* **1** the right or power to choose something. **2** something chosen or that may be chosen. [same origin as *opt*]

optional *adjective* that you can choose, not compulsory. **optionally** *adverb*

optometrist *noun* a person who tests eyesight and supplies lenses to correct defects of vision. **optometry** *noun*

opulent *adjective* **1** wealthy; rich. **2** luxurious. **3** plentiful. **opulence** *noun*, **opulently** *adverb* [from Latin *opes* = wealth]

opus (*say* **oh**-puhs) *noun* (*plural* **opera**) a numbered musical composition, *Beethoven opus 15.* [Latin, = work]

or *conjunction* used to show that there is a choice or an alternative, *Do or die.*

oracle *noun* **1** a shrine where the ancient Greeks consulted one of their gods for advice or a prophecy. **2** a wise adviser. **oracular** *adjective* [from Latin *orare* = speak]

oral *adjective* **1** spoken, not written. **2** of or using the mouth. **orally** *adverb* [from Latin *oris* = of the mouth]

orange *noun* **1** a round juicy citrus fruit with reddish-yellow peel. **2** a reddish-yellow colour. **orange** *adjective* [from Persian *narang*]

orang-utan *noun* a large ape of Borneo and Sumatra. [from Malay, = wild man]

oration *noun* a long formal speech. [from Latin *orare* = speak]

orator *noun* a person who makes speeches. **oratorical** *adjective*, **oratory** *noun*

oratorio *noun* (*plural* **oratorios**) a piece of music for voices and an orchestra, usually on a religious subject.

orb *noun* a sphere or globe.

orbit[1] *noun* **1** the curved path taken by something moving around a planet or star. **2** the range of someone's influence or control. **orbital** *adjective*

orbit[2] *verb* (**orbited**, **orbiting**) move in an orbit round something, *The spacecraft orbited the earth.* [from Latin *orbis* = circle]

orchard *noun* a piece of ground planted with fruit trees. [from Latin *hortus* = garden, + *yard*]

orchestra *noun* a large group of people playing various musical instruments together. **orchestral** *adjective* [Greek, = space where the chorus danced during a play]

orchestrate *verb* (**orchestrated**, **orchestrating**) **1** compose or arrange music for an orchestra. **2** coordinate things deliberately, *They orchestrated their campaigns.*
orchestration *noun*

orchid (*say* **aw**-kuhd) *noun* a plant with beautiful long-lasting flowers, often with unevenly shaped petals.

ordain *verb* **1** appoint a person ceremonially to perform spiritual duties in the Christian Church. **2** destine. **3** declare authoritatively; decree.

ordeal *noun* something very hard to endure.

order[1] *noun* **1** a command. **2** a request for something to be supplied. **3** the way things are arranged, *in alphabetical order.* **4** a condition in which everything is in its right place; tidiness. **5** the condition or state of something, *in working order.* **6** obedience to rules or laws, *law and order.* **7** a kind or sort, *She showed courage of the highest order.* **8** a special group; a religious organisation, *an order of monks.*
in order that or **in order to** so that; for the purpose of.

order[2] *verb* **1** command. **2** ask for something to be supplied. **3** put into order; arrange neatly.
order about keep giving somebody commands.

orderly[1] *adjective* **1** arranged neatly or well; methodical. **2** well-behaved; obedient.
orderliness *noun*

orderly[2] *noun* (*plural* **orderlies**) **1** a soldier whose job is to assist an officer. **2** an assistant in a hospital.

ordinal number *noun* a number showing a thing's position in a series, e.g. *first, fifth, twentieth.* (Compare **cardinal number**.) [same origin as *ordinary*]

ordinance *noun* a command; a decree.

ordinary *adjective* normal; usual; not special. **ordinarily** *adverb* [from Latin *ordinis* = of a row or an order]

ordination *noun* ordaining or being ordained as a member of the clergy.

ordnance *noun* military equipment.

ore *noun* rock with metal or other useful substances in it, *iron ore.*

oregano (*say* o-ruh-**gah**-noh) *noun* a kind of herb used for flavouring food.

organ *noun* **1** a musical instrument from which sounds are produced by air forced through pipes, played by keys and pedals. **2** a part of the body with a particular function, *the digestive organs.* [from Greek *organon* = tool]

organelle *noun* any of various organised or specialised structures within a living cell.

organic *adjective* **1** of organs of the body, *organic diseases.* **2** of or formed from living things, *organic matter.* **3** produced without the use of artificial fertilisers or pesticides, *organic vegetables.* **organically** *adverb*

organisation *noun* **1** an organised group of people. **2** the organising of something. **3** the way something is organised.
organisational *adjective*

organise *verb* (**organised**, **organising**) **1** plan and prepare something, *We organised a picnic.* **2** form people into a group to work together. **3** put things in order. **organiser** *noun* [same origin as *organ*]

organism *noun* a living thing; an individual animal or plant.

organist *noun* a person who plays the organ.

orgasm *noun* the climax of sexual excitement.

orgy *noun* (*plural* **orgies**) **1** a wild party. **2** an extravagant activity, *an orgy of spending.*

Orient *noun* the countries of the East, especially East Asia. (Compare **Occident**.) [from Latin, = sunrise]

orient *verb* (also **orientate**) place something or face in a certain direction.
orient yourself 1 get your bearings. **2** become accustomed to a new situation.

> **Usage** Many people object to *orientate* as an unnecessary duplication of *orient*, but the variant form has been in existence since the 19th century.

oriental *adjective* of the Orient, of the eastern or Asian world or its civilisation.

orientation *noun* **1** orienting; being oriented. **2** the position of something relative to its surroundings. **3** an introduction to a subject or situation.

orienteering *noun* the sport of finding your way across rough country with a map and compass.

orifice (*say* **o**-ruh-fuhs) *noun* an opening. [from Latin *oris* = of the mouth]

origami (*say* o-ruh-**gah**-mee) *noun* folding paper into decorative shapes. [from Japanese *ori* = fold, + *kami* = paper]

origin *noun* **1** the start of something; the point or cause from which something began, *a book about the origins of life on earth.* **2** a person's ancestry. **3** (in mathematics) a fixed point from which coordinates are measured. [from Latin *origo* = source]

original *adjective* **1** existing from the start; earliest, *the original inhabitants.* **2** new in design or character; not a copy. **3** producing new ideas; inventive. **original** *noun*, **originality** *noun*, **originally** *adverb*

originate *verb* (**originated**, **originating**) **1** cause to begin; create. **2** have its origin, *The quarrel originated in rivalry.* **origination** *noun*, **originator** *noun*

ornament[1] *noun* a decoration. **ornamental** *adjective*

ornament[2] *verb* decorate with things. **ornamentation** *noun* [from Latin *ornare* = adorn]

ornate *adjective* elaborately ornamented. **ornately** *adverb* [from Latin *ornatum* = adorned]

ornithology *noun* the study of birds. , **ornithological** *adjective*, **ornithologist** *noun* [from Greek *ornithos* = of a bird, + *-logy*]

orphan *noun* a child whose parents are dead. **orphaned** *adjective*

orphanage *noun* a home for orphans.

ortho- *prefix* right; straight; correct. [from Greek *orthos* = straight]

orthodontics *plural noun* the correction of irregularities in the teeth and jaws. **orthodontist** *noun*

orthodox *adjective* holding beliefs that are correct. **orthodoxy** *noun* [from *ortho-*, + Greek *doxa* = opinion]

Orthodox Church *noun* the Christian Churches of eastern Europe.

orthography *noun* **1** the conventional spelling system of a language. **2** the study of spelling and how letters combine to represent sounds and form words. **orthographic** *adjective*

orthopaedics (*say* aw-thuh-**pee**-diks) *plural noun* the treatment of deformities and injuries to bones and muscles. **orthopaedic** *adjective* [from *ortho-*, + Greek *paideia* = rearing of children (because the treatment was originally of children)]

orthotics *plural noun* the branch of medicine concerned with the provision and use of artificial supports or braces.

OS *abbreviation* operating system.

Oscar *noun* a statuette awarded by the American Academy of Motion Picture Arts and Sciences for excellence in the film industry.

oscillate *verb* (**oscillated**, **oscillating**) **1** move or swing back and forth like a pendulum; vibrate. **2** waver; vary. **oscillation** *noun*, **oscillator** *noun*

osmosis *noun* the passing of fluid through a porous partition into another more concentrated fluid. **osmotic** *adjective* [from Greek *osmos* = push]

osprey *noun* (*plural* **ospreys**) a large bird that preys on fish.

ostensible *adjective* pretended; used to conceal the true reason, *Their ostensible reason for travelling was to visit friends.* **ostensibly** *adverb* [from Latin *ostendere = to show*]

ostentatious *adjective* making a showy display of something to impress people. **ostentation** *noun*, **ostentatiously** *adverb*

osteopath *noun* a person who treats medical disorders by manipulating a patient's bones and muscles. **osteopathic** *adjective*, **osteopathy** *noun* [from Greek *osteon* = bone, + *-patheia* = suffering]

osteoporosis *noun* a condition in which the bones become brittle, often caused by hormonal changes or calcium deficiency. [from Greek *osteon* = bone, + *poros* = passage, pore]

ostracise *verb* (**ostracised**, **ostracising**) exclude; ignore someone completely. **ostracism** *noun* [from Greek *ostrakon* = piece of pottery (because people voted that a person should be banished by writing his name on this)]

ostrich *noun* (*plural* **ostriches**) a large long-legged African bird that can run very fast but cannot fly.

other[1] *adjective* **1** different, *some other time.* **2** remaining, *Try the other shoe.* **3** additional, *my other friends.* **4** just recent or past, *I saw him the other day.*

other[2] *noun & pronoun* the other person or thing, *Where are the others?*

otherwise *adverb* **1** if things happen differently; if you do not, *Write it down, otherwise you'll forget.* **2** in other ways, *It rained, but otherwise the holiday was good.* **3** differently, *We could not do otherwise.*

otter *noun* a fish-eating animal with webbed feet, a flat tail, and thick brown fur, living near water.

ottoman *noun* **1** a long padded seat. **2** a storage box with a padded top.

ought *auxiliary verb* expressing duty (*We ought to feed them*), rightness or advisability (*You ought to take more exercise*), or probability (*At this speed, we ought to be there by noon*).

oughtn't (*informal*) ought not.

ounce *noun* a unit of weight equal to one-sixteenth of a pound (about 28 grams).

our *adjective* belonging to us.

ours *possessive pronoun* belonging to us, *These seats are ours.*

> **Usage** It is incorrect to write *our's*.

ourselves *pronoun* we or us and nobody else, used to refer back to the subject of a verb, *We have hurt ourselves.*
by ourselves on our own; alone, *We did the work all by ourselves.*

oust *verb* drive out; expel; eject from a position or place.

out *adverb* **1** away from or not in a particular place or position or state etc.; not at home, *They lived a long way out of town.* **2** into the open; into existence or sight, *The sun came out.* **3** not in action or use; (of a batter in cricket) having had the innings ended; (of a fire) not burning. **4** to or at an end; completely, *sold out; tired out.* **5** without restraint; boldly; loudly, *Speak out!*
be out to be seeking or wanting, *They are out to make trouble.*
out of date 1 old-fashioned. **2** not valid anymore.
out of doors in the open air.
out of the way 1 remote. **2** unusual.

> **Usage** The use of *out* as a preposition, e.g. *he walked out the room*, is non-standard: *out of* should be used.

out- *prefix* **1** out of; away from (as in *outcast*). **2** external; separate (as in *outpost*). **3** more than; so as to defeat or exceed (as in *outdo*).

out-and-out *adjective* thorough; complete, *an out-and-out villain.*

outback *noun* the remote inland districts of Australia.

outboard motor *noun* a motor fitted to the outside of a boat's stern.

outbox *noun* a folder in which emails written by an individual are held before being sent.

outbreak *noun* a sudden breaking out of something, especially something unpleasant like a war or disease.

outbuilding *noun* a small building (e.g. a shed or barn) that belongs to a house but is separate from it.

outburst *noun* the bursting out of something, especially of strong or violent emotion.

outcast *noun* a person who has been rejected by family, friends, or society.

outcome *noun* the result of what happens or has happened.

outcrop *noun* a piece of rock from a lower level that sticks out on the surface of the ground.

outcry *noun* (*plural* **outcries**) **1** a loud cry. **2** a strong protest.

outdated *adjective* out of date.

outdistance *verb* (**outdistanced**, **outdistancing**) get far ahead of someone in a race or other endeavour.

outdo *verb* (**outdid**, **outdone**, **outdoing**) be superior to in action or performance; surpass.

outdoor *adjective* done or used outdoors.

outdoors *adverb* in the open air.

outer *adjective* outside; external; nearer to the outside. **outermost** *adjective*

outfit *noun* **1** a set of clothes worn together. **2** a set of equipment. **3** (*informal*) an organisation.

outflow *noun* **1** flowing out; what flows out. **2** a pipe for liquid flowing out.

outgoing *adjective* **1** going out, *the outgoing president.* **2** sociable and friendly.

outgoings *plural noun* expenditure.

outgrow *verb* (**outgrew**, **outgrown**, **outgrowing**) **1** grow out of clothes or habits etc. **2** grow faster or larger than another person or thing.

outgrowth *noun* **1** something that grows out of another thing, *Feathers are outgrowths on a bird's skin.* **2** a natural development.

outhouse *noun* **1** an outbuilding. **2** an outdoor toilet.

outing *noun* a journey for pleasure.

outlandish *adjective* looking or sounding strange or foreign.

outlast *verb* last longer than something else.

outlaw[1] *noun* a person who is punished by being excluded from legal rights and the protection of the law.

outlaw[2] *verb* **1** make a person an outlaw. **2** declare something to be illegal; forbid.

outlay *noun* what is spent on something.

outlet *noun* **1** a way for something to get out. **2** a market for goods.

outlier *noun* **1** an outlying part or member. **2** (in statistics) a result differing greatly from others in the same sample. **3** (in geology) a younger rock formation isolated in older rocks.

outline[1] *noun* **1** a line round the outside of something, showing its boundary or shape. **2** a summary.

outline[2] *verb* (**outlined**, **outlining**) **1** make an outline of something. **2** summarise.

outlive *verb* (**outlived**, **outliving**) live longer than.

outlook *noun* **1** a view on which people look out. **2** a person's mental attitude to something. **3** future prospects.

outlying *adjective* far from a centre; remote, *the outlying districts.*

outmoded *adjective* out of date.

outnumber *verb* be more numerous than another group.

outpatient *noun* a person who visits a hospital for treatment but does not stay there.

outpoll *verb* receive more votes than.

outpost *noun* a distant settlement.

output *noun* **1** the amount of something produced by a person, machine, or industry. **2** the action or process of producing something. **3** the power, energy, or other results supplied by a device or system. **4** a place where power or information leaves a system. **output** *verb*

outrage[1] *noun* **1** something that shocks people by being very wicked or cruel. **2** great anger. **outrageous** *adjective*, **outrageously** *adverb*

outrage[2] *verb* (**outraged**, **outraging**) shock and anger people greatly.

outrider *noun* a person riding on horseback or on a motorcycle as an escort.

outrigger *noun* a projecting framework attached to a boat, e.g. to prevent a canoe from capsizing.

outright[1] *adverb* **1** completely; entirely. **2** not gradually. **3** frankly, *We told him this outright.*

outright[2] *adjective* thorough; complete, *an outright fraud.*

outrun *verb* (**outran**, **outrun**, **outrunning**) **1** run faster or further than another. **2** go on for longer than it should.

outset *noun* the beginning, *from the outset of her career.*

outside[1] *noun* **1** the external side or surface of something. **2** the part of a path nearer to a road or further from a wall. **3** the side of a bend or curve where the edge or surface is longer in extent. **4** the external appearance of someone or something.

outside[2] *adjective* **1** situated on or near the exterior or external surface of something, *She put the outside lights on.* **2** (in hockey, soccer, and other sports) denoting positions nearer to the sides of the field. **3** not belonging to or coming from within a particular group, *the use of outside contractors will speed up the process.* **4** beyond one's own immediate personal concerns, *I was able to face the outside world again.* **5** remote; unlikely, *an outside chance.*

outside[3] *adverb* on or to the outside; outdoors, *Leave it outside; It's cold outside.*

outside[4] *preposition* **1** not in; to or at the exterior of, *Leave it outside the door.* **2** external to; not included in; beyond the limits of, *one of her interests outside work.*

outsider *noun* **1** a person who does not belong to a certain group. **2** a horse or person thought to have little chance of winning a race or competition.

outsize *adjective* much larger than average.

outskirts *plural noun* the outer parts or districts, especially of a town.

outsource *verb* contract out part of the work of an industry or office.

outspoken *adjective* speaking or spoken very frankly.

outspread *adjective* spread out.

outstanding *adjective* **1** extremely good or distinguished. **2** conspicuous. **3** not yet paid or dealt with.

outstation *noun* (*Australian*) an outlying sheep or cattle station or Aboriginal settlement.

outstretched *adjective* stretched out.

outstrip *verb* (**outstripped**, **outstripping**) **1** outrun. **2** surpass.

outvote *verb* (**outvoted**, **outvoting**) defeat by a majority of votes.

outward *adjective* **1** going towards the outside. **2** on the outside. **outwardly** *adverb*, **outwards** *adverb*

outweigh *verb* be greater in weight or importance than something else.

outwit *verb* (**outwitted**, **outwitting**) deceive somebody by being crafty.

ova *plural* of **ovum**.

oval[1] *adjective* shaped like an O, rounded and longer than it is broad. [from Latin *ovum* = egg]

oval[2] *noun* **1** an oval shape. **2** (*Australian*) a sportsground.

ovary *noun* (*plural* **ovaries**) **1** either of the two organs in which ova or egg cells are produced in a woman's or female animal's body. **2** part of the pistil in a plant, from which fruit is formed. [from Latin *ovum* = egg]

ovation *noun* enthusiastic applause. [from Latin *ovare* = rejoice]

oven *noun* a closed space in which things are cooked or heated.

over[1] *preposition* **1** above. **2** more than, *It's over an hour ago.* **3** concerning, *They quarrelled over money.* **4** across the top of; on or to the other side of, *a bridge over the river.* **5** during, *We can talk over dinner.* **6** in superiority or preference to, *their victory over Carlton.*

over² *adverb* **1** out and down from the top or edge; from an upright position, *He fell over.* **2** so that a different side shows, *Turn it over.* **3** at or to a place; across, *Walk over to our house.* **4** remaining, *There is nothing left over.* **5** all through; thoroughly, *Think it over.* **6** at an end, *The lesson is over.* **over and over** many times; repeatedly.

over³ *noun* a series of six balls bowled in cricket.

over- *prefix* **1** over (as in *overturn*). **2** too much; too (as in *over-anxious*).

overact *verb* act in an exaggerated manner.

overall *adjective* including everything; total, *the overall cost.*

overalls *plural noun* a garment worn over other clothes to protect them.

overarm *adjective & adverb* with the arm lifted above shoulder level and coming down in front of the body.

overawe *verb* (**overawed**, **overawing**) overcome a person with awe.

overbalance *verb* (**overbalanced**, **overbalancing**) lose balance and fall over; cause to lose balance.

overbearing *adjective* domineering.

overboard *adverb* from in or on a ship into the water, *She jumped overboard.*

overcast *adjective* covered with cloud.

overcoat *noun* a warm outdoor coat.

overcome *verb* (**overcame**, **overcome**, **overcoming**) **1** win a victory over somebody; defeat. **2** make a person helpless, *He was overcome by the fumes.* **3** find a way of dealing with a problem or obstacle.

overcrowd *verb* crowd too many people into a place.

overdo *verb* (**overdid**, **overdone**, **overdoing**) **1** do something too much; exaggerate. **2** cook food for too long.

overdose *noun* too large a dose of a drug. **overdose** *verb*

overdraft *noun* the amount by which a bank account is overdrawn.

overdraw *verb* (**overdrew**, **overdrawn**, **overdrawing**) draw more money from a bank account than the amount you have in it.

overdue *adjective* late; past the expected time for payment, arrival, or return.

overestimate *verb* (**overestimated**, **overestimating**) estimate too highly.

overflow *verb* flow over the edge or limits of something. **overflow** *noun*

overgrown *adjective* covered with weeds or unwanted plants.

overhang *verb* (**overhung**, **overhanging**) jut out over something. **overhang** *noun*

overhaul *verb* **1** examine something thoroughly and repair it if necessary. **2** overtake. **overhaul** *noun*

overhead¹ *adjective & adverb* **1** above the level of your head. **2** in the sky.

overhead² *noun* an expense arising from the cost of running a business.

overhear *verb* (**overheard**, **overhearing**) hear something accidentally or without the speaker intending you to hear it.

overjoyed *adjective* filled with great joy.

overland¹ *adjective & adverb* travelling over the land, not by sea or air.

overland² *verb* (*Australian*) drive stock a long distance over land. **overlander** *noun*

overlap *verb* (**overlapped**, **overlapping**) **1** lie across part of something. **2** happen partly at the same time. **overlap** *noun*

overlay¹ *verb* (**overlaid**, **overlaying**) cover with a layer; lie on top of something.

overlay² *noun* a thing laid over another.

overleaf *adverb* on the other side of the page.

overlie *verb* (**overlay**, **overlain**, **overlying**) be or lie over something.

overload *verb* load too heavily. **overload** *noun*

overlook *verb* **1** not notice or consider something. **2** not punish an offence. **3** have a view over something.

overly *adverb* excessively.

overnight *adjective & adverb* of or during a night, *an overnight stop in Bangkok.*

overpower *verb* overcome.

overpowering *adjective* very strong.

overrate *verb* (**overrated**, **overrating**) have too high an opinion of something.

overreach *verb* **overreach yourself** fail through being too ambitious.

override *verb* (**overrode**, **overridden**, **overriding**) **1** overrule. **2** be more important than, *Safety overrides all other considerations.*

overripe *adjective* too ripe.

overrule *verb* (**overruled**, **overruling**) reject or disallow by exercising one's superior authority, *We voted for having a party but the principal overruled the idea.*

overrun *verb* (**overran**, **overrun**, **overrunning**) **1** spread over and occupy or harm something, *Mice overran the place.* **2** go on for longer than it should, *The broadcast overran its time.*

overseas *adverb & adjective* across or beyond the sea; abroad.

oversee *verb* (**oversaw, overseen, overseeing**) supervise. **overseer** *noun*

overshadow *verb* **1** cast a shadow over something. **2** make a person or thing seem unimportant in comparison.

overshoot *verb* (**overshot, overshooting**) go beyond a target or limit, *The plane overshot the runway.*

oversight *noun* **1** a mistake made by not noticing something. **2** supervision.

oversleep *verb* (**overslept, oversleeping**) sleep for longer than intended.

overstate *verb* exaggerate. **overstatement** *noun*

overstep *verb* (**overstepped, overstepping**) go beyond a limit.

overt *adjective* done or shown openly, *overt hostility.* **overtly** *adverb*

overtake *verb* (**overtook, overtaken, overtaking**) **1** pass a moving vehicle or person. **2** catch up with someone.

overtax *verb* **1** tax too heavily. **2** put too heavy a burden or strain on someone.

overthrow[1] *verb* (**overthrew, overthrown, overthrowing**) cause the downfall of, *They overthrew the government.*

overthrow[2] *noun* **1** overthrowing; downfall. **2** throwing a ball too far.

overtime *noun* time spent working outside the normal hours; payment for this.

overtone *noun* an extra quality, *There were overtones of envy in his speech.*

overture *noun* **1** a piece of music written as an introduction to an opera, ballet, etc. **2** a friendly attempt to start a discussion, *They made overtures of peace.*

overturn *verb* **1** turn over or upside down. **2** overthrow.

overview *noun* a general review or summary of a subject.

overweight *adjective* above a weight considered normal or desirable.

overwhelm *verb* **1** bury or drown beneath a huge mass. **2** overcome completely.

overwork *verb* **1** work or cause to work too hard. **2** use too often, *'Nice' is an overworked word.* **overwork** *noun*

overwrought *adjective* very upset and nervous or worried.

ovine *adjective* of or like sheep. [from Latin *ovis* = sheep]

ovulate *verb* (**ovulated, ovulating**) produce an ovum from an ovary. [from Latin *ovum* = egg]

ovum (*say* **oh**-vuhm) *noun* (*plural* **ova**) a female cell that can develop into a new individual when fertilised. [Latin, = egg]

owe *verb* (**owed, owing**) **1** have a duty to pay or give something to someone, especially money. **2** have something because of the action of another person or thing, *They owed their lives to the pilot's skill.*
owing to because of; caused by, *The bus was late owing to smoke on the road.*

owl *noun* a bird of prey with large eyes, usually flying at night.

own[1] *adjective* belonging to yourself or itself.
get your own back get revenge.
on your own alone.

own[2] *verb* **1** possess; have something as your property. **2** acknowledge; admit, *I own that I made a mistake.*
own up (*informal*) confess; admit guilt.

owner *noun* the person who owns something. **ownership** *noun*

ox *noun* (*plural* **oxen**) a large animal kept for its meat and for pulling carts.

oxidant *noun* an oxidising agent.

oxide *noun* a compound of oxygen and one other element.

oxidise *verb* (**oxidised, oxidising**) **1** combine or cause to combine with oxygen. **2** coat with an oxide. **oxidation** *noun*

oxygen *noun* a colourless, odourless, tasteless gas that exists in the air and is essential for living things.

oyster *noun* a kind of shellfish whose shell sometimes contains a pearl.

Oz *noun* (*informal*) Australia.

oz *abbreviation* ounce(s).

ozone *noun* a form of oxygen with a sharp smell. [from Greek *ozein* = to smell]

ozone layer *noun* a layer of ozone high in the atmosphere, protecting the earth from harmful amounts of the sun's rays.

Ozzie alternative spelling of **Aussie**[1].

Pp

P *abbreviation* (of a driver's licence) provisional, *P-plates.*

p *abbreviation* penny; pence.

p. *abbreviation* (*plural* **pp.**) page.

P2P *abbreviation* peer-to-peer.

pa *noun* (*informal*) father. [short for *papa*]

pace[1] *noun* **1** one step in walking, marching, or running. **2** speed.

pace[2] *verb* (**paced, pacing**) **1** walk with slow or regular steps. **2** measure a distance in paces, *pace it out.*

pacemaker *noun* **1** a person who sets the pace for another in a race. **2** an electrical device to keep the heart beating.

pacific (*say* puh-**sif**-ik) *adjective* peaceful; making or loving peace. **pacifically** *adverb* [from Latin *pacis* = of peace]

pacifist (*say* **pas**-uh-fuhst) *noun* a person who believes that war is always wrong. **pacifism** *noun*

pacify *verb* (**pacified, pacifying**) make peaceful or calm. **pacification** *noun* [from Latin *pacis* = of peace]

pack[1] *noun* **1** a bundle; a collection of things wrapped or tied together. **2** a backpack. **3** a set of playing cards (usually 52). **4** a group of wild animals, especially wolves. **5** a group of people; a group of Brownies or Cubs. **6** a large amount, *a pack of lies.*
go to the pack (*Australian informal*) deteriorate.

pack[2] *verb* **1** put things into a suitcase, bag, box, or other container in order to move or store them. **2** crowd together; fill tightly. **packer** *noun*
pack off send a person away.
send a person packing dismiss them.

package *noun* **1** a parcel or packet. **2** a number of things offered or accepted together. **packaging** *noun*

packet *noun* a small parcel.

pact *noun* an agreement; a treaty.

pad[1] *noun* **1** a soft thick mass of material, used e.g. to protect or stuff something. **2** a device worn to protect the leg in cricket and other games. **3** a set of sheets of paper fastened together at one edge. **4** the soft fleshy part under an animal's foot or the end of a finger or toe. **5** a flat surface from which spacecraft are launched or where helicopters take off and land. **6** (*Australian*) a path made by animals.

pad[2] *verb* (**padded, padding**) put a pad on or in something.
pad out make a speech or piece of writing longer with unnecessary material.

pad[3] *verb* (**padded, padding**) walk softly.

padding *noun* material used to pad things.

paddle[1] *verb* (**paddled, paddling**) walk about in shallow water. **paddle** *noun*

paddle[2] *noun* a short oar with a broad blade; something shaped like this.

paddle[3] *verb* (**paddled, paddling**) move a boat along with a paddle or paddles; row gently.

paddock *noun* **1** (*Australian*) an enclosed piece of land, usually part of a rural property. **2** (*British*) a small field where horses are kept.

paddy[1] *noun* (*plural* **paddies**) (also **paddy field**) a field where rice is grown.

paddy[2] *noun* (*plural* **paddies**) (*informal*) a temper; a rage.

pademelon *noun* (also **paddymelon**) a small wallaby of eastern Australia. [probably from Sydney language *badimaliyan*]

padlock *noun* a detachable lock with a U-shaped bar.

padre (*say* **pah**-dray) *noun* a chaplain in the armed forces. [Italian, = father]

paean (*say* **pee**-uhn) *noun* a song of praise or triumph. [from Greek, = hymn]

paediatrics (*say* pee-dee-**at**-riks) *noun* the study of children's diseases. **paediatric** *adjective*, **paediatrician** *noun* [from Greek *paidos* = of a child, + *iatros* = doctor]

paedophile (*say* **ped**-uh-fuyl or **pee**-duh-fuyl) *noun* (also **pedophile**) an adult displaying paedophilia.

paedophilia (*say* ped-uh-**fil**-ee-uh or pee-duh-**fil**-ee-uh) *noun* (also **pedophilia**) sexual attraction felt by an adult towards a child. [from Greek *paid* = child, + *philos* = loving]

pagan (*say* **pay**-guhn) *adjective & noun* heathen. [same origin as *peasant*]

page[1] *noun* **1** a piece of paper that is part of a book, newspaper, or other collection of bound sheets; one side of this. **2** (in computing) a section of stored data, especially that which can be displayed on a screen at one time. **3** (on the World Wide Web) a file referenced by one URL; a webpage. [from Latin *pagina* = page]

page[2] *noun* a boy or man employed to go on errands or be an attendant. [from Greek *paidion* = small boy]

pageant *noun* **1** a play or entertainment about historical events and people. **2** a procession of people in costume as an entertainment. **pageantry** *noun*

pagoda (*say* puh-**goh**-duh) *noun* a Buddhist tower, or a Hindu temple shaped like a pyramid, in India and East Asia.

paid *past tense & past participle* of **pay**[1].
put paid to (*informal*) destroy the hopes, chances, or activities of.

pail *noun* a bucket.

pain[1] *noun* **1** an unpleasant feeling caused by injury or disease. **2** suffering in the mind. **3** (**pains**) careful effort; trouble taken, *got nothing for my pains.* **painful** *adjective*, **painfully** *adverb*, **painless** *adjective*

pain[2] *verb* cause pain to someone. [from Latin *poena* = punishment]

painstaking *adjective* careful; thorough.

paint[1] *noun* a liquid substance put on something to colour it. **paintbox** *noun*, **paintbrush** *noun*

paint[2] *verb* **1** put paint on something. **2** make a picture with paints.

painter[1] *noun* a person who paints.

painter[2] *noun* a rope used to tie up a boat. [from Old French *penteur* = rope]

painting *noun* a painted picture.

pair[1] *noun* **1** a set of two things or people; a couple. **2** something made of two joined parts, *a pair of scissors.*

pair[2] *verb* put together as a pair. [from Latin *paria* = equal things]

pal *noun* (*informal*) a friend. [from a gypsy word *pal* = brother]

palace *noun* a mansion where a king, queen, or other important person lives. [from Palatium, the name of a hill on which the house of the emperor Augustus stood in ancient Rome]

palaeolithic (*say* pal-ee-oh-**lith**-ik) *adjective* of the early part of the Stone Age. [from Greek *palaios* = old, + *lithos* = stone]

palatable *adjective* **1** tasting pleasant. **2** acceptable or satisfactory.

palate *noun* **1** the roof of the mouth. **2** a person's sense of taste.

palatial (*say* puh-**lay**-shuhl) *adjective* like a palace; large and splendid.

palaver (*say* puh-**lah**-vuh) *noun* fuss and bother. [from Portuguese *palavra* = word]

pale[1] *adjective* **1** almost white, *a pale face.* **2** not bright in colour or light, *pale green*; *the pale moonlight.* **palely** *adverb*, **paleness** *noun* [from Latin *pallidus* = pallid]

pale[2] *verb* **1** turn pale. **2** become less important, *pale into insignificance.*

pale[3] *noun* a boundary.
beyond the pale beyond the limits of good taste or behaviour. [from Latin *palus* = pointed stick set in the ground]

palette *noun* a board on which an artist mixes colours ready for use.

palindrome *noun* a word or phrase that reads the same backwards as forwards, e.g. *Glenelg.* [from Greek *palindromos* = running back again]

paling *noun* a fence made of wooden posts or railings; one of its posts.

palisade *noun* a fence of pointed sticks or boards. [same origin as *pale*[3]]

pall[1] (*say* pawl) *noun* **1** a cloth spread over a coffin. **2** a dark covering, *A pall of smoke lay over the town.* [from Latin *pallium* = cloak]

pall[2] (*say* pawl) *verb* become uninteresting or boring to someone. [from *appal*]

pallbearer *noun* a person helping to carry the coffin at a funeral.

pallet *noun* **1** a mattress stuffed with straw. **2** a hard narrow bed. **3** a portable wooden platform for transporting and storing loads.

palliate *verb* (**palliated**, **palliating**) make a thing less serious or less severe. **palliation** *noun*, **palliative** *adjective & noun* [same origin as *pall*[1]]

palliative care *noun* the care of the terminally ill and their families, usually by a hospice.

pallid *adjective* pale, especially because of illness. **pallor** *noun*

pally *adjective* (*informal*) friendly.

palm[1] *noun* **1** the inner part of the hand, between the fingers and the wrist. **2** a palm tree.

palm[2] *verb* **palm off** deceive a person into accepting something.

palmistry *noun* fortune-telling by looking at the creases in the palm of a person's hand. **palmist** *noun*

Palm Sunday *noun* the Sunday before Easter, commemorating Jesus Christ's entry into Jerusalem when people spread palm leaves in his path.

palmtop *noun* a computer small and light enough to be held in one hand.

palm tree *noun* a tropical tree with large leaves and no branches.

palpable *adjective* **1** able to be touched or felt. **2** obvious, *a palpable lie.* **palpably** *adverb* [from Latin *palpare* = touch]

palpitate *verb* (**palpitated**, **palpitating**) **1** (of the heart) beat hard and quickly. **2** (of a person) quiver with fear or excitement. **palpitation** *noun*

palsy (*say* **pawl**-zee) *noun* paralysis.

paltry (*say* **pawl**-tree) *adjective* very small and almost worthless, *a paltry amount.*

pampas *noun* wide grassy plains in South America.

pampas grass *noun* a tall ornamental grass with feathery flowers.

pamper *verb* treat very kindly and indulgently; coddle.

pamphlet *noun* a leaflet or booklet giving information on a subject.

pan[1] *noun* **1** a wide container with a flat base, used for cooking. **2** something shaped like this. **3** the bowl of a toilet.

pan[2] *verb* (**panned**, **panning**) **1** wash gravel in a pan in search of gold. **2** (*informal*) criticise severely.
pan out (*informal*) turn out in a particular way.

pan- *prefix* **1** all (as in *panorama*). **2** of the whole of a continent or group etc. (as in *pan-African*). [from Greek *pan* = all]

panacea (*say* pan-uh-**see**-uh) *noun* a cure for all kinds of diseases or troubles. [from *pan-*, + Greek *akos* = remedy]

panama *noun* a hat made of a fine straw-like material. [from Panama in Central America]

pancake *noun* a thin round cake of batter fried on both sides. [from *pan* + *cake*]

pancreas (*say* **pang**-kree-uhs) *noun* a gland near the stomach, producing insulin and digestive juices. [from *pan-*, + Greek *kreas* = flesh]

panda *noun* a large bear-like black and white animal found in China.

pandemic *adjective* (of a disease) occurring over a whole country or the whole world. [from *pan-*, + Greek *demos* = people]

pandemonium *noun* uproar. [from *pan-* + *demon*]

pander *verb* **pander to** indulge someone by providing things, *Don't pander to his taste for sweet things!*

pane *noun* a sheet of glass in a window.

paneer *noun* a type of milk curd cheese.

panegyric (*say* pan-uh-**ji**-rik) *noun* a piece of praise; a eulogy.

panel *noun* **1** a strip of board or other material forming a separate section of a wall, door, or cabinet; a section of the metal bodywork of a vehicle; a distinct section of a surface. **2** a group of people appointed to discuss or decide something. **panelled** *adjective*, **panelling** *noun*

panel van *noun* (*Australian*) a vehicle like a station wagon but with a single row of seats.

pang *noun* a sudden sharp pain.

panic[1] *noun* sudden uncontrollable fear. **panicky** *adjective*, **panic-stricken** *adjective*

panic[2] *verb* (**panicked**, **panicking**) fill or be filled with panic. [from the name of Pan, an ancient Greek god thought to be able to cause sudden fear]

panna cotta *noun* an Italian dessert consisting of a rich solidified custard, often served with caramel syrup. [Italian, = cooked cream]

pannier *noun* a large bag, basket, or box, especially one of a pair carried on either side of a bicycle, motorcycle, or pack animal. [from Latin *panarium* = bread basket]

pannikin *noun* a small metal cup.

panoply *noun* (*plural* **panoplies**) a splendid array. [from *pan-*, + Greek *hopla* = weapons]

panorama *noun* a view or picture of a wide area. **panoramic** *adjective* [from *pan-*, + Greek *horama* = view]

pan pipes *plural noun* a musical instrument made of a series of short pipes graduated in length. [named after Pan, a Greek god]

pansy *noun* (*plural* **pansies**) a small brightly coloured garden flower with velvety petals. [from French *pensée* = thought]

pant *verb* take short quick breaths, usually after running or working hard.

pantaloons *plural noun* baggy trousers.

panther *noun* a leopard.

panties *plural noun* (*informal*) underpants for women and girls.

pantihose *noun* women's tights. [from *panties* + *hose* = hosiery]

pantomime *noun* **1** a theatrical entertainment based on a fairy tale. **2** mime. [from *pan-* + *mime* (because in its most ancient form an actor mimed the different parts)]

pantry *noun* (*plural* **pantries**) a cupboard or room where food is stored. [from Latin *panis* = bread]

pants *plural noun* **1** trousers. **2** underpants. [short for *pantaloons*]

pap *noun* soft food suitable for babies.

papa *noun* (*old use*) father.

papacy (*say* **pay**-puh-see) *noun* the position of pope. [from Latin *papa* = pope]

papadum *noun* (also **papadam**, **pappadum**, **poppadum**, etc.) a thin, crisp, fried lentil wafer. [Tamil]

papal (*say* **pay**-puhl) *adjective* of the pope.

paparazzi (*say* pap-uh-**raht**-see) *plural noun* photographers who pursue celebrities to photograph them. [Italian]

paper[1] *noun* **1** a substance made in thin sheets from the pulp of wood or other fibrous substances and used for writing, printing, or drawing on or for wrapping things. **2** a newspaper. **3** wallpaper. **4** a document.

paper[2] *verb* cover with wallpaper. [from *papyrus*]

paperback *noun* a book with a thin flexible cover.

paperbark *noun* an Australian tree with papery bark.

paper clip *noun* a piece of bent wire used for holding sheets of paper together.

papier mâché (*say* pay-puh **mash**-ay) *noun* paper made into pulp and moulded to make boxes and ornaments. [French, = chewed paper]

papilloma (*say* pap-uh-**loh**-muh) *noun* (*plural* **papillomas** or **papillomata**) a wartlike usually benign tumour.

papillomavirus *noun* any of a group of DNA viruses that cause the formation of papillomas or warts.

paprika (*say* puh-**pree**-kuh) *noun* red pepper. [Hungarian]

pap smear *noun* (also **pap test**) a smear taken from the cervix or vagina and used to test for cancer.

papyrus (*say* puh-**puy**-ruhs) *noun* (*plural* **papyri**) **1** a kind of paper made from the stems of a plant like a reed, used in ancient Egypt. **2** a document written on this paper.

par *noun* **1** an average or normal amount or condition. **2** (in golf) the number of strokes that a first-class player should normally require for a hole or course. [from Latin *par* = equal]

para-[1] *prefix* **1** beside (as in *parallel*). **2** beyond (as in *paradox*). [from Greek *para* = beside or past]

para-[2] *prefix* protecting (as in *parasol*). [from Italian *para* = defend]

parable *noun* a story told to teach people something, especially one of those told by Jesus Christ. [from Greek *parabole* = comparison (same origin as *parabola*)]

parabola (*say* puh-**rab**-uh-luh) *noun* an open plane curve formed by the intersection of a cone with a plane parallel to its side, resembling the path of an object thrown into the air and falling down again. **parabolic** *adjective* [from *para-*[1] = beside, + Greek *bole* = a throw]

parachute *noun* an expanding device on which people or things can float slowly to the ground from an aircraft. **parachute** *verb*, **parachutist** *noun* [from *para-*[2] + *chute*]

parade[1] *noun* **1** a procession that displays people or things. **2** an assembly of troops for inspection or display; a ground for this. **3** a public square, promenade, or street.

parade[2] *verb* (**paraded**, **parading**) **1** move in a parade. **2** assemble for a parade.

paradigm (*say* **pa**-ruh-duym) *noun* a typical example of something; a model or pattern. [from *para-*[1], + Greek *deiknunai* = show]

paradise *noun* **1** heaven; a heavenly place. **2** the Garden of Eden. [from ancient Persian, = a park or garden]

paradox *noun* (*plural* **paradoxes**) a statement that seems to contradict itself but which contains a truth, e.g. 'More haste, less speed'. **paradoxical** *adjective*, **paradoxically** *adverb* [from *para-*[1], + *doxa* = opinion]

paraffin *noun* a kind of oil used as fuel.

paragon *noun* a person or thing that seems to be perfect.

paragraph *noun* one or more sentences on a single subject, forming a section of a piece of writing and beginning on a new line. [from *para-*[1] + *-graph*]

parakeet *noun* a kind of small parrot.

parallax *noun* what seems to be a change in the position of something when you look at it from a different place.

parallel[1] *adjective* **1** (of lines, planes, or surfaces) always at the same distance from each other, like the rails on which a train runs. **2** similar; corresponding, *When petrol prices rise there is a parallel rise in bus fares.* **parallelism** *noun*

parallel[2] *noun* **1** a line etc. that is parallel to another. **2** a line of latitude. **3** something similar or corresponding. **4** a comparison.

parallel[3] *verb* (**paralleled**, **paralleling**) find or be a parallel to something. [from *para-*[1], + Greek *allelos* = each other]

parallel imports *plural noun* goods imported by unlicensed distributors for sale at less than the manufacturer's official retail price.

parallelogram *noun* a quadrilateral with its opposite sides equal and parallel. [from *parallel* + *-gram*]

Paralympics *plural noun* an international athletic competition, modelled on the Olympic Games, for disabled athletes.

paralyse *verb* (**paralysed**, **paralysing**) **1** affect with paralysis; make unable to move or act normally. **2** bring to a standstill.

paralysis *noun* being unable to move, especially because of a disease or an injury to the nerves. **paralytic** *adjective* [from Greek *para* = on one side, + *lysis* = loosening]

paramedical *adjective* supplementing and supporting medical work. **paramedic** *noun*

parameter (*say* puh-**ram**-uh-tuh) *noun* **1** (in mathematics) a quantity that is constant in the case considered but varies in different cases. **2** a variable quantity or quality that restricts or gives a particular form to the thing it characterises. **3** a limit or boundary, especially of a subject or discussion. [from *para-*[1] = beside, + Greek *metron* = measure]

paramilitary *adjective* organised like a military force but not part of the armed services. [from *para-*[1] = beside, + *military*]

paramount *adjective* more important than anything else, *Secrecy is paramount.*

paranoia *noun* an abnormal mental condition in which a person has delusions or suspects and distrusts people. **paranoid** *adjective* [Greek, = distraction]

parapet *noun* a low wall along the edge of a balcony, bridge, or roof.

paraphernalia *noun* a mixed assortment of articles or pieces of equipment. [from Greek, = personal articles that a woman could keep after her marriage, as opposed to her dowry which went to her husband (Greek *para* = beside, *pherne* = dowry)]

paraphrase *verb* (**paraphrased**, **paraphrasing**) give the meaning of something by using different words. **paraphrase** *noun* [from *para-*[1] + *phrase*]

paraplegia *noun* paralysis of the legs and part or all of the trunk. **paraplegic** *adjective & noun* [from *para-*[1], + Greek *plexis* = a stroke]

parasite *noun* an animal or plant that lives in or on another, from which it gets its food. **parasitic** *adjective* [from Greek *parasitos* = guest at a meal]

parasol *noun* a lightweight umbrella used to shade yourself from the sun. [from *para-*[2], + Italian *sole* = sun]

paratroops *plural noun* troops trained to come down from aircraft by parachute. **paratrooper** *noun* [from *parachute* + *troops*]

parboil *verb* boil food until it is partly cooked.

parcel[1] *noun* **1** something wrapped up to be sent by post or carried. **2** a quantity of something considered as a unit. **3** a piece of land.

parcel[2] *verb* (**parcelled**, **parcelling**) **1** wrap up as a parcel. **2** divide into portions, *parcel out the work.* [same origin as *particle*]

parched *adjective* very dry or thirsty.

parchment *noun* a kind of heavy paper, originally made from animal skins. [from the city of Pergamum, now in Turkey, where parchment was made in ancient times]

pardon[1] *noun* forgiveness.

pardon[2] *verb* **1** forgive. **2** excuse somebody for a minor fault. **pardonable** *adjective*, **pardonably** *adverb*

pare (*say* pair) (**pared**, **paring**) **1** trim by cutting away the edges; peel. **2** reduce gradually, *We had to pare down our expenses.* [from Latin *parare* = prepare]

parent *noun* **1** a father or mother; a living thing that has produced others of its kind. **2** a source from which others are derived, *the parent company.* **parental** (*say* puh-**ren**-tuhl) *adjective*, **parenthood** *noun*, **parenting**, *noun* [from Latin *parens* = producing offspring]

parentage *noun* descent from parents; lineage; ancestry.

parenthesis (*say* puh-**ren**-thuh-suhs) *noun* (*plural* **parentheses**) **1** something extra that is inserted in a sentence, usually between brackets or dashes. **2** either of the pair of brackets (like these) used to mark off words from the rest of a sentence. **parenthetical** *adjective* [Greek, = putting in besides]

par excellence (*say* pah **ek**-suh-luhns) *adverb* more than all the others; to the greatest degree. [French, = because of special excellence]

pariah (*say* puh-**ruy**-uh) *noun* an outcast.

parietal bone (*say* puh-**ruy**-uh-tuhl) *noun* either of a pair of bones forming part of the sides and top of the skull.

parish *noun* (*plural* **parishes**) a district with its own church. **parishioner** *noun* [from Greek, = neighbourhood (Greek *para* = beside, *oikein* = dwell)]

parity *noun* equality. [from *par*]

park[1] *noun* **1** a large garden or recreation ground for public use. **2** a large area of land kept in its natural state, *a national park.* **car park** an area where cars may be parked.

park[2] *verb* leave a vehicle somewhere for a time.

parka *noun* a warm jacket with a hood attached.

Parkinson's disease *noun* a disease of the nervous system causing tremor and weakness of the muscles. [named after J. Parkinson, English surgeon]

parley *verb* (**parleyed**, **parleying**) hold a discussion with someone. **parley** *noun* [from French *parler* = speak]

parliament *noun* the assembly that makes a country's laws. **parliamentarian** *noun*, **parliamentary** *adjective* [same origin as *parley*]

parlour *noun* **1** (*old use*) a sitting room. **2** a shop providing particular goods or services, *a beauty parlour.* [from French *parler* = speak]

parmesan *noun* a kind of hard cheese made originally at Parma in Italy, usually grated before use.

parochial (*say* puh-**roh**-kee-uhl) *adjective* **1** of a parish. **2** local; interested only in your own area, *a narrow parochial attitude.*

parody[1] *noun* (*plural* **parodies**) an imitation that makes fun of a person or thing.

parody[2] *verb* (**parodied**, **parodying**) make or be a parody of a person or thing. [from *para-*[1] = beside, + Greek *oide* = song]

parole *noun* the release of a prisoner before the end of their sentence on condition of good behaviour, *He was on parole.* [French, = word of honour]

paroxysm (*say* **pa**-ruhk-siz-uhm) *noun* a spasm; a sudden outburst of a particular emotion or activity, *a paroxysm of laughter.*

parquet (*say* **pah**-kay) *noun* wooden blocks arranged in a pattern to make a floor.

parrot[1] *noun* a brightly coloured tropical bird.

parrot[2] *verb* repeat someone's words mechanically.

parry *verb* (**parried**, **parrying**) **1** turn aside an opponent's weapon or blow by using your own to block it. **2** avoid an awkward question skilfully.

parse *verb* (**parsed**, **parsing**) state what is the grammatical form and function of a word or words in a sentence. [from Latin *pars* = part (of speech)]

parsimonious *adjective* stingy; very sparing in the use of something. **parsimony** *noun*

parsley *noun* a plant with crinkled green leaves used to flavour and decorate food.

parsnip *noun* a plant with a pointed pale yellow root used as a vegetable.

parson *noun* a member of the clergy.

parsonage *noun* a parson's house.

part[1] *noun* **1** some but not all of a thing or number of things; anything that belongs to something bigger. **2** a region. **3** the character played by an actor or actress. **4** the words spoken by a character in a play. **5** one side in an agreement or in a dispute or quarrel.
take in good part not be offended at something.
take part join in an activity.

part[2] *verb* separate; divide.
part up (*Australian*) pay out money.
part with give away or get rid of something.

partake *verb* (**partook**, **partaken**, **partaking**) **1** participate. **2** eat or drink something, *We all partook of the food.*

Parthian shot *noun* a sharp remark made by a person who is just leaving. [named after the horsemen of Parthia (an ancient kingdom in what is now Iran), who were famous for shooting arrows at the enemy while retreating]

partial *adjective* **1** of a part; not complete; not total, *a partial eclipse.* **2** biased; unfair. **partiality** *noun*, **partially** *adverb*
be partial to be fond of something.

participate *verb* (**participated**, **participating**) take part or have a share in something. **participant** *noun*, **participation** *noun* [from Latin *pars* = part, + *capere* = take]

participle *noun* a word formed from a verb (e.g. *gone, going*; *guided, guiding*) and used with an auxiliary verb to form certain tenses (e.g. *It has gone; It is going*) or the passive (e.g. *We were guided to our seats*), or as an adjective (e.g. *a guided missile*; *a guiding light*). The **past participle** (e.g. *gone, guided*) describes a completed action or past condition. The **present participle** (which ends in *-ing*) describes a continuing action or condition.

particle *noun* a very small portion or amount. [from Latin, = little part]

particoloured *adjective* partly of one colour and partly of another; variegated.

particular[1] *adjective* **1** of this one and no other; individual, *This particular stamp is very rare.* **2** special, *Take particular care of it.* **3** giving something close attention; choosing carefully, *He is very particular about his clothes.* **particularity** *noun*, **particularly** *adverb*

particular[2] *noun* a single fact; a detail.
in particular 1 especially, *We liked this one in particular.* **2** special, *We did nothing in particular.* [same origin as *particle*]

parting *noun* **1** leaving; separation. **2** a line where hair is combed away in different directions.

partisan *noun* **1** a strong supporter of a party, cause, or person. **2** a member of an organisation resisting the authorities in a conquered country.

partition[1] *noun* **1** a thin wall that divides a room or space. **2** dividing something into parts.

partition[2] *verb* **1** divide into parts. **2** divide a room or space by means of a partition.

partly *adverb* to some extent but not completely.

partner[1] *noun* **1** one of a pair of people who do something together, e.g. in business or dancing or playing a game. **2** either member of a married or unmarried couple.
partnership *noun*

partner[2] *verb* be a person's partner; put together as partners.

part of speech *noun* any of the groups into which words are divided in grammar (noun, pronoun, adjective, verb, adverb, preposition, conjunction, interjection).

partook *past tense* of **partake**.

partridge *noun* a game bird with brown feathers.

part-time *adjective & adverb* working for only some of the normal hours.
part-timer *noun*

party[1] *noun* (*plural* **parties**) **1** a gathering of people to enjoy themselves, *a birthday party.* **2** a group working or travelling together. **3** an organised group of people with similar political beliefs, *the Labor Party.* **4** a person who is involved in an action or lawsuit, *the guilty party.* [from *part*]

party[2] *verb* attend a party; celebrate.

pash *noun* (*Australian informal*) a passionate kiss. **pash** *verb*

pashmina *noun* a shawl made from fine quality goat's wool. [Persian]

pass[1] *verb* (**passed, passing**) **1** go past something. **2** go onwards. **3** cause to move, *Pass the cord through the ring.* **4** give or transfer to another person, *Pass the butter to your father.* **5** be successful in a test or examination. **6** approve or accept, *They passed a law.* **7** occupy time. **8** happen, *We heard what passed when they met.* **9** (of time) go by. **10** disappear. **11** utter, *She passed a remark.* **12** let your turn go by at cards or in a competition, *Pass!*
pass away die.
pass out (*informal*) faint.

pass[2] *noun* (*plural* **passes**) **1** passing something. **2** a permit to go in or out of a place. **3** a route through a gap in a range of mountains. **4** a critical state of affairs, *Things have come to a pretty pass!* [from Latin *passus* = pace]

passable *adjective* **1** able to be passed. **2** satisfactory but not especially good.
passably *adverb*

passage *noun* **1** a way through something; a corridor. **2** a journey by sea or air. **3** a section of a piece of writing or music. **4** passing, *the passage of time.*
passageway *noun*

passbook *noun* a special notebook in which a bank or building society records how much a customer has paid in or drawn out.

passenger *noun* a person who is driven or carried in a vehicle, ship, or aircraft.

passer-by *noun* (*plural* **passers-by**) a person who happens to be going past something.

passim (*say* **pas**-im) *adverb* (of allusions or references in a published work) to be found at various places throughout the text. [Latin, = everywhere]

passing *adjective* not lasting long; casual.

passion *noun* **1** strong emotion. **2** great enthusiasm. **3** (**the Passion**) the sufferings of Jesus Christ at the Crucifixion. [from Latin *passia* = suffering]

passionate *adjective* full of passion.
passionately *adverb*

passionfruit *noun* a small purple-skinned fruit with edible seeds and pulp.

passive *adjective* **1** acted upon and not active; not resisting or fighting against something. **2** (of a form of a verb) used when the subject of the sentence receives the action, e.g. *was hit* in 'She was hit on the head'. (Compare **active.**) **passively** *adverb*, **passiveness** *noun*, **passivity** *noun*

Passover *noun* a Jewish religious festival commemorating the freeing of the Jews from slavery in Egypt. [from *pass over*, because God spared the Jews from the fate that affected the Egyptians]

passport *noun* an official document that entitles the person holding it to travel abroad. [from *pass* + *port*[1]]

password *noun* **1** a string of characters that allows access to a computer system or service. **2** a secret word or phrase that must be used to gain admission to a place.

past[1] *adjective* of the time before now, *during the past week.*

past[2] *noun* past times or events.

past[3] *preposition* **1** beyond, *Walk past the school.* **2** after, *It is past midnight.*
past it (*informal*) too old to be able to do something.

pasta *noun* a type of dough made into various shapes (e.g. macaroni and spaghetti) and cooked in boiling water. [Italian, = paste]

paste[1] *noun* **1** a soft and moist or gluey substance. **2** a hard glassy substance used to make imitation gems.

paste[2] *verb* (**pasted, pasting**) **1** stick by using paste. **2** coat something with paste. **3** (*informal*) beat or thrash. **4** (in computing) insert a piece of text or other data copied from elsewhere.

pasteboard *noun* a kind of thin board made of layers of paper or wood fibres pasted together.

pastel *noun* **1** a crayon that is like chalk. **2** a light delicate colour. **pastel** *adjective*

pasteurise *verb* (**pasteurised**, **pasteurising**) purify milk by heating and then cooling it. [named after a French scientist, Louis Pasteur]

pastille *noun* a small flavoured sweet for sucking.

pastime *noun* something done to make time pass pleasantly; a recreation.

pastor *noun* a member of the clergy who is in charge of a church or congregation. [Latin, = shepherd]

pastoral *adjective* **1** of country life, *a pastoral scene.* **2** of a pastor or a pastor's duties. **3** of or used for raising stock, *pastoral districts.*

pastoralist *noun* (*Australian*) a large-scale sheep or cattle farmer; a grazier.

past participle see **participle**.

pastry *noun* (*plural* **pastries**) **1** dough made with flour, fat, and water, rolled flat and baked. **2** something made of pastry. [from *paste*]

past tense *noun* a form of a verb used to describe an action that happened at a time before now, for example *took* is the past tense of *take.*

pasture[1] *noun* land covered with grass that cattle, sheep, or horses can eat.

pasture[2] *verb* (**pastured**, **pasturing**) put animals to graze in a pasture. [same origin as *pastor*]

pasty[1] (*say* **pas**-tee or **pahs**-stee) *noun* (*plural* **pasties**) pastry with a filling of meat, vegetables, or other ingredients, baked without a dish.

pasty[2] (*say* **pays**-tee) *adjective* **1** like paste. **2** looking pale and unhealthy.

pat[1] *verb* (**patted**, **patting**) tap gently with the open hand or with something flat.

pat[2] *noun* **1** a patting movement or sound. **2** a small piece of butter or other soft substance. **a pat on the back** praise.

pat[3] *adverb & adjective* known and ready for any occasion, *She had her answer pat.*

patch[1] *noun* (*plural* **patches**) **1** a piece of cloth or other material put over a hole or damaged place. **2** a pad or dressing put over a wound. **3** an area that is different from its surroundings. **4** a piece of ground, *the cabbage patch.* **5** a small area or piece of something, *There are patches of fog.* **6** (in computing) a small piece of code inserted to correct or enhance a program.
not a patch on (*informal*) not nearly as good as.

patch[2] *verb* **1** put a patch on something. **2** piece things together.
patch up 1 repair something roughly. **2** settle a quarrel.

patchwork *noun* needlework in which small pieces of different cloth are sewn edge to edge.

patchy *adjective* occurring in patches; uneven. **patchily** *adverb*, **patchiness** *noun*

pâté (*say* **pat**-ay) *noun* paste made of meat or fish. [French]

pâté de foie gras (*say* duh fwah **grah**) *noun* a paste of fatted goose liver. [French, = paste of fat liver]

patella (*say* puh-**tel**-uh) *noun* the kneecap.

patent[1] (*say* **pay**-tuhnt) *noun* the official right given to an inventor to make or sell their invention and to prevent other people from copying it.

patent[2] *adjective* **1** protected by a patent, *patent medicines.* **2** obvious. **patently** *adverb*

patent[3] *verb* get a patent for something.

patentee *noun* a person who holds a patent.

patent leather *noun* glossy leather.

paternal *adjective* **1** of a father. **2** fatherly. **paternally** *adverb* [from Latin *pater* = father]

paternalistic *adjective* treating people in a paternal way, providing for their needs but giving them no responsibility.
paternalism *noun*

paternity *noun* **1** fatherhood. **2** being the father of a particular baby. [from Latin *pater* = father]

path *noun* **1** a narrow way along which people or animals can walk. **2** a line along which a person or thing moves.
pathway *noun*

pathetic *adjective* **1** arousing pity or sadness. **2** miserably inadequate or useless, *a pathetic attempt.* **pathetically** *adverb* [same origin as *pathos*]

pathogen *noun* a bacterium, virus, or other microorganism that can cause disease.

pathology *noun* the study of diseases of the body. **pathological** *adjective*, **pathologist** *noun* [from Greek *pathos* = suffering, + *-logy*]

pathos (*say* **pay**-thos) *noun* a quality that arouses pity or sadness. [Greek, = feeling or suffering]

patience *noun* **1** the ability to wait or put up with annoyances without becoming angry. **2** perseverance. **3** a card game for one person.

patient[1] *adjective* **1** able to wait or put up with annoyances without becoming angry. **2** able to persevere. **patiently** *adverb*

patient[2] *noun* a person receiving or seeking medical or surgical treatment. [from Latin *patiens* = suffering]

patio (*say* **pat**-ee-oh) *noun* (*plural* **patios**) a paved area beside a house. [Spanish]

patka *noun* a small piece of cloth wrapped around the head and tied in a topknot, worn especially by young Sikhs.

patriarch (*say* **pay**-tree-ahk) *noun* **1** a man who is the head of a family or community. (Compare **matriarch**.) **2** a bishop of high rank in certain Churches. **patriarchal** *adjective* [from Greek *patria* = family, + *archein* = to rule]

patrician *noun* an ancient Roman noble. (Compare **plebeian**.) **patrician** *adjective* [from Latin, = having a noble father]

patriot (*say* **pay**-tree-uht or **pat**-ree-uht) *noun* a person who loves their country and supports it loyally. **patriotic** *adjective*, **patriotically** *adverb*, **patriotism** *noun* [from Greek *patris* = fatherland]

patrol[1] *verb* (**patrolled**, **patrolling**) walk or travel regularly over an area so as to guard it and see that all is well.

patrol[2] *noun* **1** a patrolling group of people, ships, aircraft, etc. **2** a group of Scouts or Guides.
on patrol patrolling. [from French *patouiller* = paddle in mud]

patron (*say* **pay**-truhn) *noun* **1** someone who supports a person or cause with money or encouragement. **2** a regular customer. **patronage** (*say* **pat**-ruh-nij) *noun* [from Latin *patronus* = protector]

patronise (*say* **pat**-ruh-nuyz) *verb* (**patronised**, **patronising**) **1** be a patron or supporter of something. **2** treat someone in a condescending way.

patron saint *noun* a saint who is thought to protect a particular place or activity.

patter[1] *noun* **1** a series of light tapping sounds. **2** rapid and often glib or deceptive speech, e.g. that used by a conjuror or salesman.

patter[2] *verb* make light tapping sounds.

pattern *noun* **1** an arrangement of lines, shapes, or colours. **2** a thing to be copied in order to make something, *a dress pattern.* **3** an excellent example; a model. **4** a regular form, order, or arrangement of parts.

patty *noun* (*plural* **patties**) **1** a small pie or pasty. **2** a small cake of minced food, especially meat.

paucity *noun* scarcity; shortage. [from Latin *pauci* = few]

paunch *noun* a large belly.

pauper *noun* a person who is very poor. [Latin, = poor]

pause[1] *noun* a temporary stop in speaking or doing something.

pause[2] *verb* (**paused**, **pausing**) make a pause. [from Greek *pauein* = to stop]

pave *verb* (**paved**, **paving**) cover a piece of ground with stones, bricks, or other hard material. **paving** *noun*
pave the way prepare for something. [from Latin *pavire* = ram down]

pavement *noun* a paved path along the side of a street.

pavilion *noun* **1** a building for use by players and spectators. **2** an ornamental building or shelter used for dances, concerts, exhibitions, and other social occasions.

pavlova *noun* (*Australian*) an open meringue tart filled with cream and fruit. [named after the Russian ballerina Anna Pavlova]

paw[1] *noun* the foot of an animal that has claws.

paw[2] *verb* touch with a hand or foot.

pawl *noun* a bar with a catch that fits into the notches of a ratchet.

pawn[1] *noun* **1** any of the least valuable pieces in chess. **2** a person whose actions are controlled by somebody else. [from Latin *pedo* = foot-soldier]

pawn[2] *verb* leave something with a pawnbroker as security for a loan. [from Old French *pan* = pledge]

pawnbroker *noun* a shopkeeper who lends money to people in return for objects that they leave as security. **pawnshop** *noun*

pawpaw *noun* a large oval-shaped tropical fruit with orange-coloured flesh.

pay[1] *verb* (**paid**, **paying**) **1** give money in return for goods or services. **2** give what is owed, *pay your debts*; *pay the rent.* **3** be profitable or worthwhile, *It pays to advertise.* **4** give or express, *pay attention*; *pay them a visit*; *pay compliments.* **5** suffer a penalty. **6** let out a rope by loosening it gradually. **payer** *noun*
pay back 1 give back money you owe. **2** take revenge on someone.
pay off 1 pay in full what is owed. **2** be worthwhile or give good results, *The hard work paid off.*
pay up 1 pay fully. **2** pay what is asked.

pay[2] *noun* payment; wages. [from Latin *pacare* = appease]

payable *adjective* that must be paid.

payee *noun* a person to whom money is paid or is to be paid.

payment *noun* **1** paying. **2** money paid.

payroll *noun* a list of a company's employees receiving regular pay.

pay television *noun* television broadcasting in which viewers pay by subscription to watch a particular channel.

paywall *noun* (on a website) an arrangement whereby access is restricted to users who have paid to subscribe to the site.

PC *abbreviation* personal computer.

PCI *abbreviation* a standard for connecting computers and their peripherals. [from the initials of 'Peripheral Component Interconnect']

PDA *abbreviation* personal digital assistant, a basic palmtop computer.

PDF *noun* a file format for capturing and sending electronic documents in exactly the intended format; a file in this format. [from the initials of 'Portable Document Format']

PE *abbreviation* physical education.

pea *noun* the small round green seed of a climbing plant, growing inside a pod and used as a vegetable.

peace *noun* **1** a condition in which there is no war, violence, or disorder. **2** quietness; calm. **peaceful** *adjective*, **peacefully** *adverb*, **peacefulness** *noun*, **peacemaker** *noun* [from Latin *pax* = peace]

peaceable *adjective* peaceful; not quarrelsome. **peaceably** *adverb*

peach *noun* (*plural* **peaches**) a round soft juicy fruit with a pinkish or yellowish downy skin and a large stone.

peacharine *noun* a kind of peach with a smooth skin.

peacock *noun* a male bird with a long brightly coloured tail that it can spread out like a fan. **peahen** *noun*

peak[1] *noun* **1** a pointed top, especially of a mountain. **2** the highest or most intense part of something, *Traffic reaches its peak at 5 p.m.* **3** the part of a cap that sticks out in front. **peaked** *adjective*

peak[2] *verb* reach its highest point.

peak hour *noun* the time when traffic is busiest.

peaky *adjective* looking pale and ill.

peal[1] *noun* **1** the loud ringing of a bell or set of bells. **2** a loud burst of thunder or laughter.

peal[2] *verb* sound in a peal.

peanut *noun* a small round nut that grows in a pod in the ground.

peanut butter *noun* (also **peanut paste**) roasted peanuts crushed into a paste.

peanuts *plural noun* (*informal*) a very small amount of money.

pear *noun* a juicy fruit that gets narrower near the stalk.

pearl *noun* **1** a small shiny white ball found in the shells of some oysters and used as a jewel. **2** something shaped like this. **pearly** *adjective*

pear-shaped *adjective* having hips and thighs disproportionately wide in relation to the upper part of the body.
go pear-shaped (*informal*) go wrong; become disordered, *the plan went pear-shaped.*

peasant *noun* (in some countries) a person who works on a farm. **peasantry** *noun* [from French *paisant* = country dweller]

peat *noun* rotted plant material that can be dug out of the ground and used as fuel or in gardening. **peaty** *adjective*

pebble *noun* a small round stone. **pebbly** *adjective*

pec *noun* (*informal*) a pectoral muscle.

pecan (*say* **pee**-kahn) *noun* a pinkish-brown nut with an edible kernel.

peccadillo *noun* (*plural* **peccadilloes**) an unimportant offence. [Spanish, = little sin]

peck[1] *verb* **1** bite or eat something with the beak. **2** kiss lightly.

peck[2] *noun* a pecking movement.

peckish *adjective* (*informal*) hungry.

pecorino (*say* pek-uh-**ree**-noh) *noun* an Italian cheese made from ewes' milk. [Italian from *pecorino* = of ewes]

pectin *noun* a substance found in ripe fruits, causing jam to set firmly.

pectoral *adjective* of the chest or breast, *pectoral muscles.* [from Latin *pectoris* = of the breast]

peculiar *adjective* **1** strange; unusual. **2** particular; special, *This point is of peculiar interest.* **3** restricted, *This dialect is peculiar to this part of the country.* **peculiarity** *noun*, **peculiarly** *adverb* [from Latin *peculium* = private property]

pecuniary *adjective* of money, *pecuniary aid.* [from Latin *pecunia* = money (from *pecu* = cattle, because in early times wealth consisted in cattle and sheep)]

pedagogue (*say* **ped**-uh-gog) *noun* a teacher who teaches in a pedantic way. [from Greek, = slave who led a boy to school]

pedagogy *noun* the method and practice of teaching

pedal[1] *noun* a lever pressed by the foot to operate a bicycle, vehicle, machine, or in certain musical instruments.

pedal[2] *verb* (**pedalled**, **pedalling**) use a pedal; move or work something by means of pedals. [from Latin *pedis* = of a foot]

pedant *noun* a pedantic person. **pedantry** *noun*

pedantic *adjective* being very careful and strict about exact meanings and facts in learning. **pedantically** *adverb* [same origin as *pedagogue*]

peddle *verb* (**peddled**, **peddling**) **1** sell goods as a pedlar. **2** sell drugs illegally. [from *pedlar*]

pedestal *noun* the raised base on which a statue or pillar stands.
put someone on a pedestal give someone uncritical respect or admiration; treat someone as an ideal rather than a real person. [from Italian *piede* = foot, + *stall*]

pedestrian *noun* a person who is walking. [from Latin *pedis* = of a foot]

pedigree *noun* a list of a person's or animal's ancestors, especially to show how well an animal has been bred.

pediment *noun* a wide triangular part decorating the top of a building.

pedlar *noun* a person who goes from house to house selling small things.

pedophile alternative spelling of **paedophile**.

pedophilia alternative spelling of **paedophilia**.

peek *verb & noun* peep.

peel[1] *noun* the skin of certain fruits and vegetables.

peel[2] *verb* **1** remove the peel or covering from something. **2** come off in strips or layers. **3** lose a covering or skin.

peep *verb* **1** look quickly or secretly. **2** look through a narrow opening. **3** show slightly or briefly, *The moon peeped out from behind the clouds.* **peep** *noun*, **peephole** *noun*

peer[1] *verb* look at something closely or with difficulty. [from *appear*]

peer[2] *noun* **1** someone who is equal to another in age, rank, merit, or ability. **2** a noble. **peerage** *noun*, **peeress** *noun* [from Latin *par* = equal]

peering *noun* (in computing) the exchange of data directly between Internet service providers, rather than via the Internet.

peerless *adjective* without an equal; superb.

peer-to-peer *adjective* denoting a network in which each computer can act as a server for the others.

peeve *verb* (*informal*) annoy.

peevish *adjective* irritable.

peewit *noun* (also **peewee**) a magpie lark.

peg[1] *noun* a piece of wood or metal or plastic for fastening things together or for hanging things on.

peg[2] *verb* (**pegged**, **pegging**) **1** fix with pegs. **2** keep wages or prices at a fixed level.
peg away work diligently; persevere.
peg out (*informal*) die.

pejorative (*say* puh-**jo**-ruh-tiv) *adjective* disparaging; derogatory; insulting. **pejoratively** *adverb* [from Latin *pejor* = worse]

Pekingese *noun* (*plural* **Pekingese**) a small kind of dog with short legs, a flat face, and long silky hair. [from Peking, now Beijing, the capital of China]

pelican *noun* a large bird with a pouch in its long beak.

pellagra *noun* a disease characterised by cracking of the skin, diarrhoea, and mental disturbance, caused by deficiencies in diet.

pellet *noun* a tiny ball of metal, food, paper, or other material.

pelmet *noun* an ornamental strip of wood or other material above a window, especially to conceal a curtain rail.

pelt[1] *verb* **1** throw a lot of things at someone. **2** run fast. **3** rain very hard.

pelt[2] *noun* an animal skin, especially with the fur still on it.

pelvis *noun* (*plural* **pelvises**) the round framework of bones at the lower end of the spine. **pelvic** *adjective*

pen[1] *noun* a device with a point for writing with ink. [from Latin *penna* = feather (because a pen was originally a sharpened quill)]

pen[2] *noun* an enclosure for cattle, sheep, hens, or other animals.

pen[3] *verb* (**penned**, **penning**) shut into a pen or other enclosed space.

pen[4] *noun* a female swan. (The male is a *cob*.)

penal (*say* **pee**-nuhl) *adjective* of punishment; used for punishment. [from Latin *poena* = punishment]

penal colony *noun* a colony to which convicts were transported, *New South Wales was formerly a British penal colony.*

penalise *verb* (**penalised**, **penalising**) punish; put a penalty on someone. **penalisation** *noun*

penalty *noun* (*plural* **penalties**) **1** a punishment. **2** a point or advantage given to one side in a game when a member of the other side has broken a rule.

penalty rates *plural noun* (*Australian*) rates of pay for employees working overtime or on public holidays.

penance *noun* something done to show penitence.

pence *plural noun* see **penny**.

penchant (*say* **pon**-shon or **pen**-shuhnt) *noun* a liking or inclination, *a penchant for music.* [French]

pencil[1] *noun* a device for drawing or writing, usually a thin stick of graphite enclosed in a cylinder of wood.

pencil[2] *verb* (**pencilled**, **pencilling**) **1** write, draw, or mark with a pencil. **2** arrange provisionally, *Let's pencil in the 29th.*

pendant *noun* an ornament worn hanging on a cord or chain round the neck. [from Latin *pendens* = hanging]

pendent *adjective* hanging.

pending[1] *preposition* **1** until, *Please take charge, pending his return.* **2** during, *pending these discussions.*

pending[2] *adjective* waiting to be decided or settled. [same origin as *pendant*]

pendulous *adjective* hanging down.

pendulum *noun* a weight hung so that it can swing to and fro, especially in the works of a clock.

penetrable *adjective* able to be penetrated.

penetrate *verb* (**penetrated**, **penetrating**) **1** make or find a way through or into something; pierce. **2** permeate. **penetration** *noun*, **penetrative** *adjective* [from Latin *penitus* = inside]

penfriend *noun* a friend to whom you write without meeting.

penguin *noun* an Antarctic sea bird that cannot fly but uses its wings as flippers for swimming.

penicillin *noun* an antibiotic obtained from mould. [from the Latin name of the mould used]

peninsula *noun* a piece of land that is almost surrounded by water. **peninsular** *adjective* [from Latin *paene* = almost, + *insula* = island]

penis (*say* **pee**-nuhs) *noun* (*plural* **penises**) the part of the body with which a male urinates and has sexual intercourse. [Latin, = tail]

penitence *noun* regret for having done wrong. **penitent** *adjective*, **penitently** *adverb*

penitentiary *noun* (*American*) a prison.

penknife *noun* (also **pocketknife**) (*plural* **penknives** or **pocketknives**) a small folding knife. [originally used for sharpening quill pens]

pen name *noun* an author's pseudonym.

pennant *noun* a long pointed flag.

penniless *adjective* having no money; very poor.

penny *noun* (*plural* **pennies** or **pence**) **1** a British coin worth one hundredth of a pound. **2** a former Australian coin worth less than one cent.

pension[1] *noun* an income consisting of regular payments made by a government or firm to someone who is retired, widowed, or disabled.

pension[2] *verb* pay a pension to someone. [from Latin *pensio* = payment]

pensioner *noun* a person who receives a pension.

pensive *adjective* thinking deeply; thoughtful. **pensively** *adverb* [from Latin *pensare* = consider]

penta- *prefix* five. [from Greek *pente* = five]

pentagon *noun* **1** a flat shape with five sides and five angles. **2** (**the Pentagon**) a five-sided building in Washington, headquarters of the American armed forces. **pentagonal** *adjective* [from *penta-*, + Greek *gonia* = angle]

pentameter *noun* a line of verse with five rhythmic beats. [from *penta-*, + Greek *metron* = measure]

pentathlon *noun* an athletic contest consisting of five events. [from *penta-*, + Greek *athlon* = contest]

pentatonic *adjective* (in music) consisting of five notes.

Pentecost *noun* **1** the Jewish harvest festival, 50 days after Passover. **2** the seventh Sunday after Easter, commemorating the coming of the Holy Spirit. Also called *Whit Sunday.* [from Greek, = fiftieth day]

penthouse *noun* a flat at the top of a tall building.

pent-up *adjective* shut in, *pent-up anger.* [from *pen*[3]]

penultimate *adjective* last but one. [from Latin *paene* = almost, + *ultimate*]

penumbra *noun* an area that is partly but not fully shaded, e.g. during an eclipse. [from Latin *paene* = almost, + *umbra* = shade]

penurious (*say* puh-**nyoo**-ree-uhs) *adjective* **1** in great poverty. **2** mean; stingy. **penury** (*say* **pen**-yuh-ree) *noun* [from Latin *penuria* = poverty]

peony *noun* (*plural* **peonies**) a plant with large round red, pink, or white flowers.

people[1] *plural noun* **1** human beings; men, women, and children, *People think I'm funny.* **2** persons, especially those belonging to a particular country, area, or group.

people[2] *noun* a community or nation, *a warlike people*; *the English-speaking peoples.*

people[3] *verb* fill a place with people; populate. [from Latin *populus* = people]

pep *noun* (*informal*) vigour; energy. [from *pepper*]

pepper[1] *noun* **1** a hot-tasting powder used to flavour food. **2** a bright green, red, or yellow vegetable; a capsicum. **peppery** *adjective*

pepper[2] *verb* **1** sprinkle with pepper. **2** pelt with small objects.

peppercorn *noun* the dried black berry from which pepper is made.

peppermint *noun* **1** a kind of mint used for flavouring. **2** a sweet flavoured with this mint.

per *preposition* for each, *The charge is $10 per person.* [from Latin, = through]

per- *prefix* **1** through (as in *perforate*). **2** thoroughly (as in *perturb*). **3** away entirely; towards badness (as in *pervert*). [from Latin *per* = through]

perambulate *verb* (**perambulated, perambulating**) walk through or round an area. **perambulation** *noun* [from *per-* + Latin *ambulare* = to walk]

perambulator *noun* (*old use*) a baby's pram.

per annum *adverb* for each year; yearly. [Latin]

per capita (*say* puh **kap**-uh-tuh) *adjective & adverb* for each person. [Latin, = for heads]

perceive *verb* (**perceived, perceiving**) **1** see; notice. **2** understand. [from Latin *percipere* = seize, understand]

per cent[1] *adverb* (also **percent**) for or in every hundred, *three per cent (3%).*

per cent[2] *noun* (also **percent**) **1** percentage. **2** one part in every hundred, *half a per cent.*

percentage *noun* the amount per cent; a proportion or part.

perceptible *adjective* able to be perceived. **perceptibility** *noun*, **perceptibly** *adverb*

perception *noun* perceiving.

perceptive *adjective* quick to notice things.

perch[1] *noun* (*plural* **perches**) **1** a place where a bird sits or rests. **2** a seat high up.

perch[2] *verb* rest or place on a perch. [from Latin *pertica* = pole]

perch[3] *noun* (*plural* **perch**) an edible freshwater or sea fish.

percolate *verb* (**percolated, percolating**) flow through small holes or spaces. **percolation** *noun* [from *per-*, + Latin *colum* = strainer]

percolator *noun* a pot for making coffee, in which boiling water percolates through coffee grounds.

percussion *noun* the striking of one thing against another. **percussive** *adjective* [from Latin *percussum* = hit]

percussion instrument *noun* a musical instrument (e.g. drum, cymbals) played by being struck or shaken.

perdition *noun* eternal damnation. [from Latin *perditum* = destroyed]

peregrination *noun* travelling about; a journey. [from Latin *per* = through, + *ager* = field]

peregrine *noun* a kind of falcon.

peremptory *adjective* giving commands; imperious.

perennial[1] *adjective* lasting for many years; keeping on recurring. **perennially** *adverb*

perennial[2] *noun* a plant that lives for many years. [from *per-*, + Latin *annus* = year]

perentie *noun* the largest Australian lizard, a giant monitor lizard of desert country. [from Dieri and neighbouring languages *pirrinthi*]

perfect[1] (*say* **per**-fuhkt) *adjective* **1** so good that it cannot be made any better. **2** exact; precise. **3** complete, *a perfect stranger.* **perfectly** *adverb*

perfect[2] (*say* puh-**fekt**) *verb* make a thing perfect. **perfection** *noun*
to perfection perfectly. [from Latin *perfectum* = completed]

perfectionist *noun* a person who likes everything to be done perfectly.

perfect tense *noun* a tense of a verb showing a completed action, e.g. *He has arrived.*

perfidious *adjective* treacherous; disloyal. **perfidiously** *adverb*, **perfidy** *noun* [from *per-* = becoming bad, + Latin *fides* = faith]

perforate *verb* (**perforated, perforating**) **1** make tiny holes in something, especially so that it can be torn off easily. **2** pierce. **perforation** *noun* [from *per-*, + Latin *forare* = bore through]

perforce *adverb* by necessity; unavoidably.

perform *verb* **1** do something in front of an audience, *perform a play*; *perform in a show.* **2** do something, *perform an operation.* **3** function, *The car performed well.* **performance** *noun*, **performer** *noun*

perfume *noun* **1** a pleasant smell. **2** a liquid for giving something a pleasant smell; scent. **perfume** *verb*, **perfumery** *noun* [from *per-* + *fume* (originally used of smoke from a burning substance)]

perfunctory *adjective* done without much care or interest, *a perfunctory glance.* **perfunctorily** *adverb*

pergola (*say* puh-**goh**-luh or **per**-guh-luh) *noun* a framework over which climbing plants are grown.

perhaps *adverb* it may be; possibly.

peri- *prefix* around (as in *perimeter*). [from Greek *peri* = around]

peril *noun* danger. **perilous** *adjective*, **perilously** *adverb* [from Latin *periculum* = danger]

perimeter *noun* **1** the outer edge or boundary of something. **2** the distance round the edge. [from *peri-*, + Greek *metron* = measure]

period[1] *noun* **1** a length of time. **2** the time allocated for a lesson in school. **3** the time when a woman or girl menstruates. **4** (in punctuation) a full stop.

period[2] *adjective* to do with a past historical time, especially in style or design, *period furniture.*

periodic *adjective* occurring at regular intervals.

periodical[1] *adjective* periodic; at set times. **periodically** *adverb*

periodical[2] *noun* a magazine published at regular intervals (e.g. monthly).

periodic table *noun* a list of the symbols of chemical elements, arranged in rows and columns according to similarities in chemical behaviour.

periodontics (*say* pe-ree-oh-**don**-tiks) *noun* the branch of dentistry concerned with the structures surrounding and supporting the teeth. [from *peri-*, + Greek *odous* = tooth]

periodontitis *noun* inflammation of the tissue around the teeth.

peripatetic *adjective* going from place to place. [from *peri-*, + Greek *patein* = to walk]

peripheral[1] *adjective* **1** of minor importance; marginal. **2** of the periphery; on the fringe.

peripheral[2] *noun* any input, output, or storage device that can be controlled by a computer's central processing unit, e.g. a keyboard or printer.

periphery (*say* puh-**rif**-uh-ree) *noun* the part at the edge or boundary. [from Greek, = circumference]

periphrasis (*say* puh-**rif**-ruh-suhs) *noun* (*plural* **periphrases**) a roundabout way of saying something; a circumlocution. [from *peri-*, + Greek *phrasis* = speech]

periscope *noun* a device with a tube and mirrors by which a person in a trench or submarine can see things that are otherwise out of sight. [from *peri-*, + Greek *skopein* = look at]

perish *verb* **1** die; be destroyed. **2** rot, *The rubber ring has perished.* **3** (*informal*) suffer from cold, hunger, thirst, or heat. **perishable** *adjective*

periwinkle[1] *noun* a trailing plant with blue or white flowers.

periwinkle[2] *noun* a winkle.

perjure *verb* (**perjured**, **perjuring**) **perjure yourself** commit perjury.

perjury *noun* telling a lie while you are on oath to speak the truth. [from Latin *perjurare* = break an oath]

perk[1] *verb* raise the head quickly or cheerfully.
perk up make or become more cheerful. [from *perch*[2]]

perk[2] *noun* (*informal*) something extra given to a worker, *A company car is one of the perks of this job.* [short for *perquisite*]

perky *adjective* lively and cheerful. **perkily** *adverb*

perm *noun* a method of setting the hair in waves or curls and then treating it with chemicals so that the style lasts for several months. **perm** *verb*

permanent *adjective* lasting for always or for a very long time. **permanence** *noun*, **permanency** *noun*, **permanently** *adverb* [from *per-*, + Latin *manens* = remaining]

permeable *adjective* (of a material or membrane) allowing liquids or gases to pass through it. **permeability** *noun*

permeate (*say* **per**-mee-ayt) *verb* (**permeated**, **permeating**) spread into every part of something; pervade, *Smoke had permeated the hall.* **permeation** *noun* [from *per-*, + Latin *meare* = to pass]

permissible *adjective* allowable.

permission *noun* the right to do something, given by someone in authority; authorisation.

permissive *adjective* permitting things; allowing much freedom to do things.

permit[1] (*say* puh-**mit**) *verb* (**permitted**, **permitting**) give permission or consent or a chance to do something; allow.

permit[2] (*say* **per**-muht) *noun* written or printed permission to do something or go somewhere. [from *per-*, + Latin *mittere* = send]

permutation *noun* **1** the order of a set of things. **2** a changed order, *3, 1, 2, is a permutation of 1, 2, 3.* [from *per-*, + Latin *mutare* = to change]

pernicious *adjective* very harmful.

perpendicular *adjective* upright; at a right angle (90°) to a line or surface. [from Latin, = plumb-line]

perpetrate *verb* (**perpetrated**, **perpetrating**) commit or be guilty of, *perpetrate a crime or an error.* **perpetration** *noun*, **perpetrator** *noun*

perpetual *adjective* **1** lasting for a long time. **2** continual. **perpetually** *adverb* [from Latin, = uninterrupted]

perpetuate *verb* (**perpetuated**, **perpetuating**) make a thing perpetual; cause to be remembered for a long time, *The statue will perpetuate his memory.* **perpetuation** *noun*

perpetuity *noun* being perpetual.
in perpetuity for ever.

perplex *verb* bewilder or puzzle somebody. **perplexity** *noun* [from *per-*, + Latin *plexus* = twisted together]

per se (*say* per **say**) *adverb* by or in itself; intrinsically. [Latin]

persecute *verb* (**persecuted**, **persecuting**) be continually cruel to somebody, especially because you disagree with their beliefs; harass. **persecution** *noun*, **persecutor** *noun* [from Latin *persecutum* = pursued]

persevere *verb* (**persevered**, **persevering**) go on doing something even though it is difficult. **perseverance** *noun* [from *per-*, + Latin *severus* = strict]

Persian *noun* **1** a person from ancient or modern Persia (now Iran). **2** the language of the Persians.

persimmon (*say* per-**sim**-uhn) *noun* an orange-coloured fruit that looks rather like a tomato.

persist *verb* **1** continue firmly or obstinately, *She persists in breaking the rules.* **2** continue to exist, *The custom persists in some countries.* **persistence** *noun*, **persistent** *adjective*, **persistently** *adverb* [from *per-*, + Latin *sistere* = to stand]

person *noun* (*plural* **persons** or **people**) **1** a human being; a man, woman, or child. **2** (in grammar) any of the three groups of personal pronouns and forms taken by verbs. The **first person** (= *I*, *me*, *we*, *us*) refers to the person(s) speaking; the **second person** (= *thou*, *thee*, *you*) refers to the person(s) spoken to; the **third person** (= *he*, *him*, *she*, *her*, *it*, *they*, *them*) refers to the person(s) spoken about.
in person being actually present oneself, *She was there in person.* [from Latin *persona* = mask used by an actor]

persona *noun* (*plural* **personas** or **personae**) **1** the personality that a person presents to other people. **2** a role or character adopted by an author or an actor.

personable *adjective* good-looking.

personage *noun* a person; someone important.

persona grata (*say* puh-soh-nuh **grah**-tuh) *noun* a person who is acceptable to someone. (The opposite is **persona non grata.**) [Latin, = pleasing person]

personal *adjective* **1** belonging to, done by, or concerning a particular person. **2** private, *a personal diary.* **3** criticising a person, *making personal remarks.* **personally** *adverb*

personalise *verb* (**personalised**, **personalising**) make something personal; design something for a particular person, *personalised number plates.*

personality *noun* (*plural* **personalities**) **1** a person's character, *She has a cheerful personality.* **2** a well-known person.

personal pronoun see **pronoun**.

personify *verb* (**personified**, **personifying**) **1** represent an idea in human form or a thing as having human characteristics, *Justice is personified as a blindfolded woman holding a pair of scales.* **2** embody in one's life or behaviour, *he was meanness personified.* **personification** *noun*

personnel *noun* the body of people employed in any work; staff. [French, = personal]

perspective *noun* **1** the impression of depth and space in a picture or scene. **2** a view of a scene or of facts or events. **3** a mental view of the relative importance of things.
in perspective giving a well-balanced view of things. [from Latin *perspectum* = looked through]

perspex *noun* (*trademark*) a tough transparent plastic material.

perspicacious *adjective* perceptive. **perspicacity** *noun*

perspire *verb* (**perspired**, **perspiring**) sweat. **perspiration** *noun* [from *per-*, + Latin *spirare* = breathe]

persuade *verb* (**persuaded**, **persuading**) cause a person to believe or agree to do something. **persuasion** *noun*, **persuasive** *adjective* [from *per-*, + Latin *suadere* = induce]

pert *adjective* cheeky. **pertly** *adverb*, **pertness** *noun*

pertain *verb* be relevant to something, *evidence pertaining to the crime.* [from Latin *pertinere* = belong]

pertinacious *adjective* persistent and determined. **pertinaciously** *adverb*, **pertinacity** *noun* [from *per-* + *tenacious*]

pertinent *adjective* pertaining; relevant. **pertinence** *noun*, **pertinently** *adverb*

perturb *verb* worry someone. **perturbation** *noun* [from *per-*, + Latin *turbare* = disturb]

pertussis medical term for **whooping cough.**

peruse (*say* puh-**rooz**) *verb* (**perused**, **perusing**) read something carefully. **perusal** *noun* [from *per-* + *use*]

pervade *verb* (**pervaded**, **pervading**) spread all through something; permeate. **pervasion** *noun*, **pervasive** *adjective* [from *per-*, + Latin *vadere* = go]

perverse *adjective* obstinately doing something different from what is reasonable or required. **perversely** *adverb*, **perversity** *noun* [same origin as *pervert*]

pervert[1] (*say* puh-**vert**) *verb* **1** turn something from the right course of action, *By false evidence they perverted the course of justice.* **2** cause a person to behave wickedly or abnormally. **perversion** *noun*

pervert[2] (*say* **per**-vert) *noun* a person who behaves wickedly or abnormally. [from *per-*, + Latin *vertere* = to turn]

pessimist *noun* a person who expects that things will turn out badly. (Compare **optimist.**) **pessimism** *noun*, **pessimistic** *adjective*, **pessimistically** *adverb* [from Latin *pessimus* = worst]

pest *noun* **1** a destructive insect or animal, such as a locust or a mouse. **2** a nuisance. [from Latin *pestis* = plague]

pester *verb* keep annoying someone by frequent questions or requests.

pesticide *noun* a substance for killing harmful insects. [from *pest*, + Latin *caedere* = kill]

pestilence *noun* a deadly epidemic. [same origin as *pest*]

pestle *noun* a tool with a heavy rounded end for pounding substances in a mortar.

pesto *noun* an Italian sauce of crushed basil leaves, pine nuts, garlic, parmesan cheese, and olive oil. [from Italian *pestare* = pound, crush]

pet[1] *noun* **1** a tame animal kept for companionship and amusement. **2** a person treated as a favourite, *teacher's pet.*

pet[2] *adjective* **1** kept as a pet, *a pet wallaby.* **2** favourite, *a pet subject.*

pet[3] *verb* (**petted**, **petting**) treat or fondle affectionately.

petal *noun* any of the separate coloured outer parts of a flower.

peter *verb* **peter out** become gradually less and cease to exist.

petition[1] *noun* a formal request for something, especially a written one signed by many people.

petition[2] *verb* request by a petition. **petitioner** *noun* [from Latin *petere* = seek]

petrel *noun* a kind of sea bird.

Petri dish *noun* a shallow covered dish used in laboratories for growing microorganisms such as bacteria. [named after Julius Petri, a German bacteriologist]

petrify *verb* (**petrified**, **petrifying**) **1** paralyse someone with terror, surprise, etc. **2** change into a stony mass. **petrifaction** *noun* [from Greek *petra* = rock]

petrol *noun* a liquid made from petroleum, used as fuel for engines.

petroleum *noun* an oil found underground that can be used to make fuels. [from Greek *petra* = rock, + *oleum* = oil]

petticoat *noun* a woman's or girl's dress-length undergarment. [from *petty* = little, + *coat*]

pettifogging *adjective & noun* paying too much attention to unimportant details.

petting *noun* affectionate treatment or fondling.

petty *adjective* (**pettier**, **pettiest**) unimportant; trivial, *petty regulations.* **pettily** *adverb*, **pettiness** *noun* [from French *petit* = small]

petty cash *noun* cash kept by an office for small payments.

petty officer *noun* a non-commissioned officer in the navy.

petulant *adjective* peevish; irritable. **petulance** *noun*, **petulantly** *adverb*

petunia *noun* a garden plant with funnel-shaped flowers.

pew *noun* a long wooden seat, usually fixed in rows, in a church.

pewter *noun* a grey alloy of tin and lead.

phalanger *noun* an Australian marsupial, such as a possum, that lives in trees.

phalanx *noun* (*plural* **phalanxes** or **phalanges**) **1** a number of people or soldiers in a close formation. **2** a bone of the finger or toe. [Greek]

phantasm *noun* a phantom.

phantom *noun* a ghost; something that is not real. [from Greek, = made visible]

pharaoh (*say* **fair**-roh) *noun* the title of the king of ancient Egypt. [from ancient Egyptian *pr- 'o* = great house]

pharisee (*say* **fa**-ruh-see) *noun* a hypocritical self-righteous person. **pharisaical** *adjective* [named after the Pharisees, an ancient Jewish sect distinguished by strict observance of the traditional and written law]

pharmaceutical (*say* fah-muh-**syoo**-ti-kuhl) *adjective* of pharmacy; of medicines.

pharmacist *noun* a person who is trained in pharmacy; a pharmaceutical chemist.

pharmacology *noun* the study of medicinal drugs. **pharmacological** *adjective*, **pharmacologist** *noun* [from Greek *pharmakon* = drug, + *-logy*]

pharmacy *noun* (*plural* **pharmacies**) **1** a shop selling medicines; a dispensary. **2** the process of preparing medicines. [from Greek *pharmakon* = drug]

pharynx (*say* **fa**-ringks) *noun* (*plural* **pharynges**) **1** the cavity at the back of the mouth and nose. **2** the part of the alimentary canal immediately behind the mouth in invertebrates.

phase[1] *noun* a stage in the progress or development of something.

phase[2] *verb* (**phased**, **phasing**) do something in stages, *a phased withdrawal.*

pheasant (*say* **fez**-uhnt) *noun* a game bird with a long tail.

phenome (*say* **fee**-nohm) *noun* **1** the phenotypic counterpart or expression of a genome. **2** the complete set of phenotypic characteristics of an organism. **phenomic** *adjective*

phenomenal *adjective* amazing; remarkable. **phenomenally** *adverb*

phenomenon *noun* (*plural* **phenomena**) an event or fact, especially one that is remarkable. [from Greek, = thing appearing]

> **Usage** Note that *phenomena* is a plural; it is incorrect to say 'this phenomena' or 'these phenomenas'.

phenotype (*say* **fee**-noh-tuyp) *noun* the observable characteristics of an individual resulting from the interaction of its genotype with the environment. **phenotypic** *adjective*

pheromone (*say* **fe**-ruh-mohn) *noun* a substance, secreted by an animal, that is detected by others of the same species and produces a response in them.

phial *noun* a small glass bottle.

phil- *prefix* see **philo-**.

philander *verb* flirt. **philanderer** *noun*

philanthropy *noun* love of mankind, especially as shown by kind and generous acts that benefit large numbers of people. **philanthropic** *adjective*, **philanthropist** *noun* [from *phil-*, + Greek *anthropos* = human being]

philately (*say* fuh-**lat**-uh-lee) *noun* stamp-collecting. **philatelist** *noun* [from *phil-*, + Greek *ateleia* = not needing to pay (because postage has been paid for by buying a stamp)]

philharmonic *adjective* (in names of orchestras and music societies) devoted to music.

philistine (*say* **fil**-uh-stuyn) *noun* a person who is hostile or indifferent to culture, or one whose interests or tastes are commonplace or material. **philistine** *adjective* [named after the Philistines, who were enemies of the Israelites in the Old Testament]

philo- *prefix* (becoming **phil-** before vowels and *h*) fond of; lover of (as in *philosophy*). [from Greek *philein* = to love]

philology *noun* the study of languages. **philologist** *noun*, **philological** *adjective* [from *philo-*, + Greek *logos* = word]

philosopher *noun* an expert in philosophy.

philosophical *adjective* **1** of philosophy. **2** calm and not upset, *Be philosophical about losing.* **philosophically** *adverb*

philosophy *noun* (*plural* **philosophies**) **1** the use of reason and argument in seeking truth and knowledge of reality, especially of the causes and nature of things and of the principles governing existence, the material universe, perception of physical phenomena, and human behaviour. **2** a set of ideas or principles or beliefs. [from *philo-*, + Greek *sophia* = wisdom]

philtre (*say* **fil**-tuh) *noun* a magic drink; a love potion.

phishing (*say* **fish**-ing) *noun* the process of sending an email that directs the receiver to a bogus website where bank account or credit card numbers are requested.

phlegm (*say* flem) *noun* thick mucus that forms in the throat and lungs when someone has a bad cold.

phlegmatic (*say* fleg-**mat**-ik) *adjective* not easily excited or worried; sluggish. **phlegmatically** *adverb*

phobia (*say* **foh**-bee-uh) *noun* great or abnormal fear of something. [from Greek *phobos* = fear]

phoenix (*say* **fee**-niks) *noun* (*plural* **phoenixes**) a mythical bird that was said to burn itself to death in a fire and be born again from the ashes.

phone[1] *noun* a telephone.

phone[2] *verb* (**phoned**, **phoning**) telephone. [short for *telephone*]

phone-in *noun* a broadcast in which people phone the studio and take part.

phoneme (*say* **foh**-neem) *noun* a unit of sound in a specified language that distinguishes one word from another, for example *p*, *b*, *d*, and *t* in the English words *pad*, *pat*, *bad*, and *bat*. **phonemic** *adjective*

phonetic (*say* fuh-**net**-ik) *adjective* of speech sounds. **phonetically** *adverb* [from Greek *phonein* = speak]

phoney *adjective* (*informal*) sham; not genuine.

phonic *adjective* of sound; acoustic; of vocal sounds. [from Greek *phone* = voice]

phonics *noun* **1** a method of teaching reading based on sounds. **2** the branch of science that deals with spoken sounds.

phonology *noun* the study of sounds in a language. **phonological** *adjective*

phosphate *noun* a substance containing phosphorus.

phosphorescent (*say* fos-fuh-**res**-uhnt) *adjective* luminous. **phosphorescence** *noun*

phosphorus *noun* a chemical substance that glows in the dark. **phosphoric** *adjective*, **phosphorous** *adjective* [from Greek *phos* = light, + *-phoros* = bringing]

photo *noun* (*plural* **photos**) a photograph.

photo- *prefix* light (as in *photograph*). [from Greek *photos* = of light]

photocopy *noun* (*plural* **photocopies**) a copy of a document made by photographing the original. **photocopier** *noun*, **photocopy** *verb*

photoelectric *adjective* using the electrical effects of light.

photogenic *adjective* looking attractive in photographs.

photograph[1] *noun* **1** a picture made by the effect of light or other radiation on film or special paper. **2** a picture made with a digital camera.

photograph[2] *verb* take a photograph of a person or thing. **photographer** *noun* [from *photo-* + *-graph*]

photography *noun* taking photographs. **photographic** *adjective*

photon *noun* an indivisible unit of electromagnetic radiation.

photoshop *verb* (**photoshopped**, **photoshopping**) edit or alter (an image) digitally using computer software. [from *Adobe Photoshop*, the proprietary name of such a software package]

photosynthesis *noun* the process by which green plants use sunlight to turn carbon dioxide and water into complex substances, giving off oxygen. [from *photo-* + *synthesis*]

phrase[1] *noun* **1** a group of words that form a unit in a sentence or clause, e.g. *on the mat* in 'The cat sat on the mat'. **2** a short section of a tune.

phrase[2] *verb* (**phrased**, **phrasing**) **1** put something into words. **2** divide music into phrases. [from Greek *phrazein* = declare]

phraseology (*say* fray-zee-**ol**-uh-jee) *noun* wording; the way something is worded. [from *phrase* + *-logy*]

phylum (*say* **fuy**-luhm) *noun* (*plural* **phyla**) a major division of the plant or animal kingdom. [from Greek *phylon* = race]

physical *adjective* **1** of the body. **2** of things that you can touch or see. **3** of physics. **physically** *adverb* [same origin as *physics*]

physical education *noun* instruction in physical exercise and games, especially in schools.

physician *noun* a doctor, especially one who is not a surgeon.

physicist (*say* **fiz**-uh-sist) *noun* an expert in physics.

physics (*say* **fiz**-iks) *noun* the study of the properties of matter and energy (e.g. heat, light, sound, movement). [from Greek *physikos* = natural]

physiognomy (*say* fiz-ee-**on**-uh-mee) *noun* the features of a person's face. [from Greek *physis* = nature, + *gnomon* = indicator]

physiology (*say* fiz-ee-**ol**-uh-jee) *noun* the study of the body and its parts and how they function. **physiological** *adjective*, **physiologist** *noun* [from Greek *physis* = nature, + *-logy*]

physiotherapy (*say* fiz-ee-oh-**the**-ruh-pee) *noun* the treatment of a disease or weakness by physical methods such as massage and exercises rather than by drugs and surgery. **physiotherapist** *noun* [from Greek *physis* = nature, + *therapy*]

physique (*say* fuh-**zeek**) *noun* a person's build. [French]

phytochemistry (*say* **fuy**-toh-) *noun* a branch of chemistry dealing with plants and plant products. [from Greek *phuton* = plant]

pi (*rhymes with* my) *noun* a letter of the Greek alphabet (= p) used as a symbol for the ratio of the circumference of a circle to its diameter (approximately 3.14).

pianist *noun* a person who plays the piano.

piano[1] (*say* pee-**an**-oh) *noun* (*plural* **pianos**) a large musical instrument with a keyboard. [short for *pianoforte*, from Italian *piano* = soft, + *forte* = loud (because it can produce soft notes and loud notes)]

piano[2] (*say* **pyah**-noh) *adverb & adjective* (in music) softly.

piccolo *noun* (*plural* **piccolos**) a small high-pitched flute. [Italian, = small]

pick[1] *verb* **1** separate a flower or fruit from its plant, *We picked apples.* **2** choose; select carefully. **3** pull bits off or out of something. **4** open a lock by using something pointed, not with a key.
pick holes in find fault with.
pick on keep criticising or harassing a particular person.
pick someone's pocket steal from it.
pick up **1** lift; take up. **2** collect. **3** take someone into a vehicle. **4** manage to hear something. **5** get better; recover.

pick[2] *noun* **1** choice. **2** the best of a group.

pick[3] *noun* **1** a pickaxe. **2** a plectrum.

pickaxe *noun* a heavy pointed tool with a long handle, used for breaking up hard ground and stones.

picket[1] *noun* **1** a striker or group of strikers who try to persuade other people not to go into a place during a strike. **2** a group of sentries. **3** a pointed post as part of a fence.

picket[2] *verb* (**picketed**, **picketing**) act as a picket; place people as pickets. [from French *piquet* = pointed post]

pickle[1] *noun* **1** a strong-tasting food made of pickled vegetables. **2** (*informal*) a mess.

pickle[2] *verb* (**pickled**, **pickling**) preserve in vinegar or salt water.

pickpocket *noun* a thief who steals from people's pockets.

pickup *noun* **1** the part of a record player that holds the stylus. **2** an open truck for carrying small loads. **3** a device on an electric guitar that converts string vibrations into electrical signals.

picky *adjective* (**pickier**, **pickiest**) (*informal*) choosy; fussy.

picnic[1] *noun* **1** a meal eaten in the open air away from home. **2** (*informal*) an easy task.

3 (*Australian informal*) an awkward situation.

picnic[2] *verb* (**picnicked**, **picnicking**) have a picnic. **picnicker** *noun*

pictorial *adjective* with or using pictures. **pictorially** *adverb*

picture[1] *noun* **1** a representation of a person or thing made by painting, drawing, or photography. **2** a film at the cinema. **3** how something seems; an impression.

picture[2] *verb* (**pictured**, **picturing**) **1** show in a picture. **2** imagine. [from Latin *pictum* = painted]

picturesque *adjective* **1** forming an attractive scene, *a picturesque village.* **2** vividly described; expressive, *picturesque language.* **picturesquely** *adverb*

pide (*say* **pee**-day) *noun* a flat Turkish bread. [Turkish]

pidgin *noun* a simplified form of English or another language used between people who speak different languages. [from the Chinese pronunciation of *business* (because it was used by traders)]

pie *noun* a baked dish of meat, fish, or fruit covered with pastry.

piebald *adjective* with patches of black and white, *a piebald donkey.* [from *pie* = magpie, + *bald*]

piece[1] *noun* **1** a part or portion of something; a fragment. **2** a separate thing or example, *a fine piece of work.* **3** something written, composed, or painted, *a piece of music.* **4** any of the objects used to play a game on a board, *a chess piece.* **5** a coin, *a ten-cent piece.*

piece[2] *verb* (**pieced**, **piecing**) put pieces together to make something.

pièce de résistance (*say* pyes duh ray-**zis**-tons) *noun* the most important item. [French]

piecemeal *adjective & adverb* done or made one piece at a time.

pie chart *noun* a diagram representing quantities as sectors of a circle.

pier *noun* **1** a long structure built out into the sea for people to walk on. **2** a pillar supporting a bridge or arch.

pierce *verb* (**pierced**, **piercing**) make a hole through something; penetrate.

piercing[1] *adjective* **1** very loud. **2** penetrating; very strong, *a piercing wind.*

piercing[2] *noun* a small hole in a part of the body for inserting a ring, stud, or other piece of jewellery.

piety *noun* piousness. [from Latin *pietas* = dutiful behaviour]

piffle *noun* (*informal*) nonsense.

pig *noun* **1** a fat animal with short legs and a blunt snout, kept for its meat. **2** (*informal*) someone greedy, dirty, or unpleasant. **piggy** *adjective & noun*

pigeon *noun* a bird with a fat body and a small head. [from Old French *pijon* = young bird]

pigeonhole[1] *noun* one of a set of small compartments in a desk or on a wall, used for holding letters or papers.

pigeonhole[2] *verb* decide that someone belongs in a particular category.

piggery *noun* (*plural* **piggeries**) a place where pigs are bred or kept.

piggyback *adverb* carried on somebody else's back or shoulders. **piggyback** *noun* [from *pick-a-back*]

piggy bank *noun* a money-box made in the shape of a hollow pig.

pigheaded *adjective* obstinate.

pig iron *noun* iron that has been processed in a smelting furnace.

piglet *noun* a young pig.

pigment *noun* a substance that colours something. **pigmentation** *noun*, **pigmented** *adjective* [from Latin *pingere* = to paint]

pigsty *noun* (*plural* **pigsties**) a partly covered pen for pigs.

pigtail *noun* a plait or bunch of hair worn singly at the back or on each side of the head.

pike[1] *noun* **1** a heavy spear. **2** (*plural* **pike**) a large northern-hemisphere freshwater fish with a long narrow snout; any of several similar Australian sea fishes.

pike[2] *verb* **pike out** (*Australian informal*) go back on your word, an arrangement, etc. **piker** *noun*

pikelet *noun* a small thick pancake.

Pilates *noun* a system of exercises using special apparatus, designed to improve physical strength, flexibility, and posture, and enhance mental awareness. [named after Joseph Pilates, German physical fitness specialist]

pilchard *noun* a small sea fish.

pile[1] *noun* **1** a number of things on top of one another. **2** (*informal*) a large quantity; a lot of money. **3** a tall building.

pile[2] *verb* (**piled**, **piling**) put things into a pile; make a pile. [from Latin *pila* = pillar]

pile[3] *noun* a heavy beam made of metal, concrete, or timber driven into the ground to support something. [from Latin *pilum* = spear]

pile[4] *noun* a raised surface on fabric, made of upright threads, *a carpet with a thick pile.* [from Latin *pilus* = hair]

pilfer *verb* steal small things. **pilferer** *noun*

pilgrim *noun* a person who travels to a holy place for religious reasons. **pilgrimage** *noun*

pill *noun* **1** a small solid piece of medicinal substance for swallowing. **2** (**the pill**) a contraceptive pill. [from Latin *pila* = ball]

pillage *verb* (**pillaged**, **pillaging**) plunder. **pillage** *noun*

pillar *noun* a tall stone or wooden post. [from Latin *pila* = pillar]

pillion *noun* a seat behind the driver on a motorcycle.

pillory[1] *noun* (*plural* **pillories**) a wooden framework with holes for a person's head and hands, in which offenders were formerly made to stand and be ridiculed and scorned by the public as punishment.

pillory[2] *verb* (**pilloried**, **pillorying**) **1** put into a pillory. **2** expose a person to public ridicule and scorn, *He was pilloried in the newspapers for what he had done.*

pillow[1] *noun* a cushion for a person's head to rest on, especially in bed.

pillow[2] *verb* rest or prop up on or as if on a pillow.

pillowcase *noun* (also **pillowslip**) a cloth cover for a pillow.

pilot[1] *noun* **1** a person who works the controls for flying an aircraft. **2** a person qualified to steer a ship in and out of a port or through a difficult stretch of water. **3** a guide.

pilot[2] *verb* (**piloted**, **piloting**) **1** be pilot of an aircraft or ship. **2** guide; steer.

pilot[3] *adjective* testing on a small scale how something will work, *a pilot scheme.*

pilot light *noun* **1** a small jet of gas kept alight to light a larger burner when this is turned on. **2** an electric indicator light.

pimp *noun* **1** a man who lives off the earnings of prostitutes. **2** (*Australian informal*) an informer; a telltale. **pimp** *verb*

pimple *noun* a small round raised spot on the skin. **pimply** *adjective*

PIN *abbreviation* personal identification number, a secret number used with a plastic card for certain banking transactions.

pin[1] *noun* **1** a short thin piece of metal with a sharp point and a rounded head, used to fasten pieces of fabric or paper together. **2** a pointed device for fixing or marking something. **3** a bottle-shaped wooden object that players try to knock down in tenpin bowling or skittles.

pin[2] *verb* (**pinned**, **pinning**) **1** fasten with a pin or pins. **2** make a person or thing unable to move, *He was pinned under the wreckage.* **3** fix, *They pinned the blame on her.*

pinafore *noun* **1** an apron. **2** (also **pinafore dress**) a sleeveless dress worn over a blouse or jumper. [from *pin* + *afore* = before]

piñata (*say* peen-**yah**-tuh) *noun* a decorated object containing toys and sweets that is suspended from a height and broken open by blindfolded children as part of a celebration. [Spanish, = pot]

pincers *plural noun* **1** the front claws of a shellfish such as a lobster. **2** a tool with two parts that are pressed together for gripping and holding things.

pinch[1] *verb* **1** squeeze tightly or painfully between two things, especially between the finger and thumb. **2** (*informal*) steal.

pinch[2] *noun* (*plural* **pinches**) **1** a pinching movement. **2** difficulty; stress or pressure of circumstances, *They began to feel the pinch.* **3** the amount that can be held between the tips of the thumb and forefinger, *a pinch of salt.*

at a pinch if necessary.

pincushion *noun* a small pad into which pins are stuck to keep them ready for use.

pine[1] *noun* an evergreen tree with needle-shaped leaves.

pine[2] *verb* (**pined**, **pining**) **1** feel an intense longing. **2** become weak through longing for somebody or something.

pineapple *noun* a large tropical fruit with a tough prickly skin and yellow flesh.

ping[1] *noun* a short sharp ringing sound.

ping[2] *verb* **1** make or cause to make a ping. **2** send an email or other electronic message to (someone).

ping pong *noun* table tennis.

pinion[1] *noun* a bird's wing, especially the outer end.

pinion[2] *verb* **1** clip a bird's wings to prevent it from flying. **2** hold or fasten a person's arms or legs so as to prevent movement.

pinion[3] *noun* a small cogwheel that engages with another or with a rod (called a *rack*).

pink[1] *adjective* pale red. **pinkness** *noun*

pink[2] *noun* **1** pink colour. **2** a garden plant with fragrant flowers, often pink or white. **in the pink** (*informal*) in very good health.

pink[3] *verb* **1** pierce slightly. **2** cut a zigzag edge on cloth.

pinkie *noun* (also **pinky**) the little finger.

pinnacle *noun* **1** a pointed ornament on a roof. **2** a peak. **3** the highest point, *the pinnacle of her career.*

pinpoint[1] *adjective* exact; precise, *with pinpoint accuracy.*

pinpoint[2] *verb* find or identify something precisely.

pinprick *noun* a small annoyance.

pins and needles *plural noun* a prickling feeling.

pinstripe *noun* a very narrow stripe.
pinstriped *adjective*

pint *noun* a measure for liquids, one eighth of a gallon (about 0.57 litres).

pin-up *noun* (*informal*) a picture of an attractive or famous person for pinning on a wall.

pioneer *noun* one of the first people to go to a place or do or investigate something.
pioneer *verb* [from French *pionnier* = foot-soldier]

pious *adjective* very religious; devout. **piously** *adverb*, **piousness** *noun* [from Latin *pius* = dutiful]

pip[1] *noun* **1** a small hard seed in a fruit. **2** one of the spots on playing cards, dice, or dominoes. **3** a short high-pitched sound, *She heard the six pips of the time signal on the radio.*

pip[2] *verb* (**pipped**, **pipping**) (*informal*) defeat.

pipe[1] *noun* **1** a tube through which liquid or gas can flow from one place to another. **2** a short narrow tube with a bowl at one end in which tobacco can burn for smoking. **3** a tube forming a musical instrument or part of one.
the pipes bagpipes.

pipe[2] *verb* (**piped**, **piping**) **1** send something along pipes. **2** transmit music or other sound by wire or cable. **3** play music on a pipe or the bagpipes. **4** trim or ornament with piping.
pipe down (*informal*) be quiet.

pipe dream *noun* an impossible wish.

pipeline *noun* a pipe for carrying liquid or gas a long distance.
in the pipeline in the process of being made or organised.

piper *noun* a person who plays a pipe or bagpipes.

pipette *noun* a small glass tube used in a laboratory, usually filled by suction.

pipi *noun* an edible shellfish. [Maori]

piping[1] *noun* **1** pipes; a length of pipe. **2** a long narrow pipe-like fold or line decorating something.

piping[2] *adjective* shrill, *a piping voice.*
piping hot very hot.

piping shrike another name for **magpie** 1.

piquant (*say* **pee**-kuhnt) *adjective* pleasantly sharp and appetising or stimulating, *a piquant smell.* **piquancy** *noun* [same origin as *pique*]

pique (*say* peek) *noun* a feeling of hurt pride.
pique *verb* [from French *piquer* = to prick]

piracy *noun* **1** the practice of attacking and robbing ships at sea. **2** the unauthorised use or reproduction of another's work, *software piracy.*

piranha (*say* puh-**rah**-nuh) *noun* a fierce South American freshwater fish. [Portuguese]

pirate *noun* **1** a person on a ship who robs other ships at sea or makes a plundering raid on the shore. **2** someone who produces or publishes or broadcasts without authorisation, *a pirate radio station.* **piratical** *adjective* [from Greek *peiraein* = to attack]

pirouette (*say* pi-roo-**et**) *noun* a spinning movement of the body made while balanced on the point of the toe or on one foot.
pirouette *verb* [French, = spinning-top]

Pisces *noun* **1** a constellation and the twelfth sign of the zodiac (the Fish or Fishes). **2** a person born when the sun is in this sign. [from Latin *piscis* = fish]

pistachio *noun* (*plural* **pistachios**) a nut with an edible green kernel.

pistil *noun* the part of a flower that produces the seed, consisting of the ovary, style, and stigma.

pistol *noun* a small handgun.

piston *noun* a disc or cylinder that fits inside a tube in which it moves up and down as part of an engine or pump.

pit[1] *noun* **1** a deep hole or depression. **2** a coalmine. **3** the part of a racecourse where racing cars are refuelled and repaired during a race.

pit[2] *verb* (**pitted**, **pitting**) **1** make pits or depressions in something, *The ground was pitted with holes.* **2** put somebody in competition with somebody else, *She was pitted against the champion.* [from Latin *puteus* = a well]

pit[3] *noun* the stone of a fruit.

pit[4] *verb* remove stones from fruit.

pitch[1] *noun* (*plural* **pitches**) **1** a piece of ground marked out for games. **2** the highness or lowness of a voice or a musical note. **3** intensity; strength, *Excitement was at fever pitch.* **4** the steepness of a slope, *the pitch of the roof.*

pitch[2] *verb* **1** throw; fling. **2** erect and fix a tent or camp. **3** fall heavily. **4** move up and down on a rough sea. **5** set something at a particular level, *They pitched their hopes high.* **6** (of a bowled ball in cricket) strike the ground.
pitch in (*informal*) **1** start working or eating vigorously. **2** contribute money.

pitch[3] *noun* a black sticky substance rather like tar.

pitch-black *adjective* (also **pitch black**) very black or very dark.

pitchblende *noun* a mineral ore (uranium oxide) from which radium is obtained.

pitched battle *noun* a battle between troops in prepared positions.

pitcher[1] *noun* a large jug.

pitcher[2] *noun* the person who throws the ball to the batter in baseball or softball.

pitchfork[1] *noun* a large fork with two prongs, used for lifting hay.

pitchfork[2] *verb* **1** lift with a pitchfork. **2** put a person somewhere suddenly.

piteous *adjective* causing pity. **piteously** *adverb*

pitfall *noun* an unsuspected danger or difficulty.

pith *noun* the spongy substance in the stems of certain plants or lining the rind of oranges and other citrus fruits.

pithy *adjective* **1** like pith; containing much pith. **2** short and full of meaning, *pithy comments.*

pitiable *adjective* pitiful.

pitiful *adjective* **1** arousing pity. **2** miserably inadequate. **pitifully** *adverb*

pitiless *adjective* showing no pity. **pitilessly** *adverb*

pittance *noun* a very small allowance of money. [same origin as *pity* and *piety* (the word *pittance* originally meant 'pious gift')]

pity[1] *noun* **1** the feeling of being sorry because someone is in pain or trouble. **2** a cause for regret, *It's a pity that you can't come.*
take pity on feel sorry for and help someone.

pity[2] *verb* (**pitied**, **pitying**) feel pity for someone. [same origin as *piety*]

pivot[1] *noun* a point or part on which something turns or swings. **pivotal** *adjective*

pivot[2] *verb* (**pivoted**, **pivoting**) turn or place something to turn on a pivot.

pixel *noun* any of the minute illuminated areas making up an image displayed on a screen. **pixelate** *verb* [from 'picture element']

pixie *noun* a small fairy; an elf.

pizza (*say* **peet**-suh) *noun* an Italian food consisting of a layer of dough baked with a savoury topping. [Italian, = pie]

pizzicato (*say* pit-see-**kah**-toh) *adjective & adverb* plucking the strings of a musical instrument. [Italian]

placard *noun* a poster; a notice.

placate *verb* (**placated**, **placating**) pacify; conciliate. **placatory** *adjective*

place[1] *noun* **1** a particular part of space, especially where something belongs; an area; a position. **2** a particular town, district, or location. **3** a seat, *Save me a place.* **4** a job; employment. **5** a building; a home, *Come round to our place.* **6** a duty or function, *It's not my place to interfere.* **7** a point in a series of things, *In the first place, the date is wrong.*
out of place 1 in the wrong position. **2** unsuitable.

place[2] *verb* (**placed**, **placing**) put something in a particular place. **placement** *noun* [from Greek *plateia* = broad way]

placebo (*say* pluh-**see**-boh) *noun* (*plural* **placebos**) a harmless substance given as if it were medicine, to humour a patient or as a dummy pill etc. in a controlled experiment. [Latin, = I shall please]

placenta *noun* a piece of body tissue that forms in the womb during pregnancy and supplies the foetus with nourishment.

place value *noun* the numerical value that a digit has by virtue of its position in a number.

placid *adjective* calm and peaceful; not easily made anxious or upset. **placidity** *noun*, **placidly** *adverb* [from Latin *placidus* = gentle]

placket *noun* an opening in a garment to make it easy to put on and take off.

plagiarise (*say* **play**-juh-ruyz) *verb* (**plagiarised**, **plagiarising**) copy and use someone else's writings or ideas as if they were your own. **plagiarism** *noun*, **plagiarist** *noun* [from Latin *plagiarius* = kidnapper]

plague[1] *noun* **1** a dangerous illness that spreads very quickly. **2** a large number of pests, *a plague of locusts.*

plague[2] *verb* (**plagued**, **plaguing**) pester; annoy.

plaice *noun* (*plural* **plaice**) a flat edible sea fish.

plaid (*say* plad) *noun* cloth with a tartan or similar pattern.

plain[1] *adjective* **1** not decorated; not elaborate; not flavoured. **2** not beautiful. **3** easy to see or hear or understand. **4** frank; straightforward. **plainly** *adverb*, **plainness** *noun*

plain[2] *noun* a large area of flat country. [from Latin *planus* = flat]

plain clothes *plural noun* civilian clothes worn instead of a uniform, e.g. by police.

plaintiff *noun* the person who brings a complaint against somebody else to a lawcourt. (Compare **defendant**.) [same origin as *complain*]

plaintive *adjective* sounding sad. [same origin as *complain*]

plait[1] (*say* plat) *verb* weave three or more strands to form one length.

plait[2] *noun* something plaited. [from Latin *plicatum* = folded]

plan[1] *noun* **1** a way of doing something thought out in advance. **2** a drawing showing the arrangement of parts of something. **3** a map of a town or district.

plan[2] *verb* (**planned, planning**) **1** make a plan for something. **2** intend. **planner** *noun*

plane[1] *noun* **1** an aeroplane. **2** a tool for making wood smooth by scraping its surface. **3** a flat or level surface; an imaginary surface of this kind. **4** a level of attainment, thought, knowledge, or existence.

plane[2] *verb* (**planed, planing**) smooth wood with a plane.

plane[3] *adjective* flat; level, *a plane surface.* [same origin as *plain*]

plane[4] *noun* a tall tree with broad leaves.

planet *noun* any of the heavenly bodies that move in an orbit around a star, *The planets in our solar system are Mercury, Venus, Earth, Mars, Jupiter, Saturn, Uranus, Neptune, and the dwarf planet Pluto.* **planetary** *adjective* [from Greek *planetes* = wanderer (because it was not a 'fixed star')]

plank *noun* a long flat piece of wood.

plankton *noun* microscopic plants and animals that float in the sea or fresh water. [from Greek, = wandering]

plant[1] *noun* **1** a living thing that cannot move and that makes its food from chemical substances, *Flowers, trees, and shrubs are plants.* **2** a small plant, as opposed to a tree or shrub. **3** a factory or its equipment. **4** (*informal*) something planted to deceive people (see *plant*[2] 3).

plant[2] *verb* **1** put something in soil for growing. **2** fix firmly in place. **3** place something where it will be found, usually to mislead people or cause trouble. **planter** *noun* [from Latin *planta* = a shoot]

plantation *noun* **1** a large area of land where crops such as cotton, tobacco, or tea are planted. **2** a group of planted trees.

plaque (*say* plahk) *noun* **1** a flat piece of metal or porcelain fixed on a wall as an ornament or memorial. **2** a filmy substance that forms on teeth and gums, where bacteria can live.

plasma *noun* **1** the colourless liquid part of blood, carrying the corpuscles. **2** a gas of positive ions and free electrons.

plasma screen *noun* a flat television screen filled with a special gas that makes the picture very clear.

plaster[1] *noun* **1** a mixture of lime, sand, and water etc. for covering walls and ceilings. **2** plaster of Paris. **3** a strip of adhesive material for covering cuts.

plaster[2] *verb* **1** cover with plaster. **2** cover thickly; daub.

plaster of Paris *noun* a white paste used for making moulds or for casts around a broken limb.

plastic[1] *noun* a strong light synthetic substance that can be moulded into a permanent shape.

plastic[2] *adjective* **1** made of plastic. **2** soft and easy to mould, *Clay is a plastic substance.* **plasticity** *noun*

plasticine *noun* (*trademark*) a plastic substance used for modelling things.

plastic surgery *noun* surgery to repair deformed or injured parts of the body.

plate[1] *noun* **1** an almost flat usually circular object from which food is eaten or served. **2** a thin flat sheet of metal, glass, or other hard material. **3** an illustration on special paper in a book. **plateful** *noun*

plate[2] *verb* (**plated, plating**) **1** coat metal with a thin layer of gold, silver, or tin. **2** cover with sheets of metal.

plateau (*say* **plat**-oh) *noun* (*plural* **plateaux**, *say* **plat**-ohz) a flat area of high land. [from French *plat* = flat]

platform *noun* **1** a flat surface that is above the level of the ground or the rest of the floor, e.g. in a hall or beside a railway line at a station. **2** the policy that a political party puts forward when there is an election.

platinum *noun* a valuable silver-coloured metal that does not tarnish. [from Spanish *plata* = silver]

platitude *noun* a very ordinary remark. **platitudinous** *adjective*

platonic *adjective* (of a relationship) friendly but not sexual.

platoon *noun* a small group of soldiers.

platter *noun* a flat dish or plate.

platypus *noun* (*plural* **platypuses**) an Australian animal with a beak like that of a duck, that lays eggs like a bird but is a mammal and suckles its young. [from Greek *platys* = broad, + *pous* = foot]

plaudits *plural noun* applause; expressions of approval. [same origin as *applaud*]

plausible *adjective* seeming to be honest or worth believing but perhaps deceptive, *a plausible excuse.* **plausibility** *noun*, **plausibly** *adverb*

play[1] *verb* **1** take part in a game or other amusement, *They played tennis on Friday.* **2** make music or sound with a musical instrument, *She plays the guitar.* **3** perform a part in a play or film, *He plays Voldemort in the Harry Potter movies.* **4** make a disc, music player, or other device produce sounds or recorded images.

play down give people the impression that something is not important.

play for time seek to gain time by delaying.

play up (*informal*) be mischievous or annoying.

play[2] *noun* **1** a story acted on a stage or on radio or television. **2** playing.

playback *noun* playing back something that has been recorded.

player *noun* **1** a person who plays a game or a musical instrument, *a football player*; *a piano player.* **2** a device for playing recorded music or video.

playful *adjective* **1** wanting to play. **2** full of fun; not serious. **playfully** *adverb*, **playfulness** *noun*

playground *noun* a piece of ground for children to play on.

playgroup *noun* a group of very young children who play together regularly, supervised by adults.

playing card *noun* see **card**[1] 2.

playlist *noun* **1** a list of recorded music to be broadcast on a radio station. **2** a list of digital files to be played on a portable media player, computer, etc.

playlunch *noun* (*Australian*) a snack eaten at playtime.

playmate *noun* a person you play games with.

plaything *noun* a toy.

playtime *noun* the time when young schoolchildren may go out to play.

playwright *noun* a dramatist. [from *play*, + *wright* = maker]

plaza (*say* **plah**-zuh) *noun* **1** an open square in a city or town. **2** (used in names) a set of shops. [Spanish, = place]

plea *noun* **1** a request; an appeal, *a plea for mercy.* **2** an excuse, *He stayed at home on the plea of a headache.* **3** a formal statement of 'guilty' or 'not guilty' made in a lawcourt by someone accused of a crime. [same origin as *please*]

plead *verb* make a plea.

pleasant *adjective* **1** pleasing; giving pleasure. **2** friendly. **pleasantly** *adverb*, **pleasantness** *noun*

pleasantry *noun* (*plural* **pleasantries**) being humorous; a humorous remark.

please *verb* (**pleased**, **pleasing**) **1** make a person feel satisfied or glad. **2** (used to make a request or an order polite), *Please ring the bell.* **3** like; think suitable, *Do as you please.* [from Latin *placere* = satisfy]

pleasurable *adjective* causing pleasure.

pleasure *noun* **1** a feeling of satisfaction or gladness; enjoyment. **2** something that pleases you.

pleat *noun* a flat fold made by doubling cloth upon itself. **pleated** *adjective* [from *plait*]

plebeian (*say* pluh-**bee**-uhn) *noun* a member of the common people in ancient Rome. (Compare **patrician.**) **plebeian** *adjective* [from Latin *plebs* = the common people]

plebiscite (*say* **pleb**-uh-suyt) *noun* a referendum. [from Latin *plebs* = the common people, + *scitum* = decree]

plectrum *noun* (*plural* **plectrums** or **plectra**) a small piece of plastic or other material for plucking or strumming the strings of a musical instrument.

pledge[1] *noun* **1** a solemn promise. **2** a thing handed over as security for a loan or contract.

pledge[2] *verb* (**pledged**, **pledging**) **1** promise solemnly. **2** hand something over as security.

plenary (*say* **plee**-nuh-ree) *adjective* attended by all members, *a plenary session of the council.* [from Latin *plenus* = full]

plenipotentiary (*say* plen-uh-puh-**ten**-shuh-ree) *adjective* having full authority to make decisions on behalf of a government, *Our ambassador has plenipotentiary power.* **plenipotentiary** *noun* [from Latin *plenus* = full, + *potentia* = power]

plentiful *adjective* quite enough in amount; abundant. **plentifully** *adverb*

plenty[1] *noun* quite enough; as much as is needed or wanted.

plenty[2] *adverb* (*informal*) quite; fully, *It's plenty big enough.* [from Latin *plenus* = full]

pleurisy (*say* **ploo**-ruh-see) *noun* inflammation of the membrane round the lungs. [from Greek *pleura* = ribs]

pliable *adjective* **1** easy to bend; flexible. **2** easy to influence. **pliability** *noun* [from French *plier* = to bend]

pliant *adjective* pliable.

pliers *plural noun* pincers that have jaws with flat surfaces for gripping things.

plight[1] *noun* a difficult situation.

plight[2] *verb* (*old use*) pledge.

Plimsoll line *noun* a mark on a ship's side showing how deeply it may legally go down in the water when loaded. [named after an English politician, S. Plimsoll, who in the 1870s protested about ships being overloaded]

plinth *noun* a block or slab forming the base of a column or a support for a statue or vase.

plod *verb* (**plodded**, **plodding**) **1** walk slowly and heavily. **2** work slowly but steadily. **plodder** *noun*

plonk[1] *verb* set down heavily.

plonk[2] *noun* (*Australian informal*) cheap or inferior wine.

plop *noun* the sound of something dropping into water. **plop** *verb*

plot[1] *noun* **1** a secret plan. **2** the story in a play, novel, or film. **3** a small piece of land.

plot[2] *verb* (**plotted, plotting**) **1** make a secret plan. **2** make a chart or graph of something, *We plotted the ship's route on our map.*

plough[1] *noun* a farming implement for turning the soil over.

plough[2] *verb* **1** turn over soil with a plough. **2** go through something with great effort or difficulty, *She ploughed through the book.* **plough back** reinvest profits in the business that produced them.

ploughshare *noun* the cutting blade of a plough.

plover (*say* **pluv**-uh) *noun* a kind of wading bird. [from Latin *pluvia* = rain]

ploy *noun* a cunning manoeuvre to gain an advantage; a ruse.

pluck[1] *verb* **1** pick a flower or fruit. **2** pull the feathers off a bird. **3** pull something up or out. **4** pull a string (e.g. on a guitar) and let it go again. **5** pull at something. **pluck up courage** summon up courage and overcome fear.

pluck[2] *noun* **1** courage; bravery. **2** plucking; a pull.

plucky *adjective* (**pluckier, pluckiest**) brave; spirited. **pluckily** *adverb*

plug[1] *noun* **1** something used to stop up a hole. **2** a device that fits into a socket to connect wires to a supply of electricity. **3** (*informal*) a piece of publicity for something.

plug[2] *verb* (**plugged, plugging**) **1** stop up a hole. **2** (*informal*) publicise something. **plug in** put a plug into an electrical socket.

plum *noun* **1** a soft juicy fruit with a pointed stone in the middle. **2** (*old use*) a dried grape or raisin used in cooking, *plum pudding.* **3** reddish-purple colour. **4** (*informal*) something good, *a plum job.*

plumage (*say* **ploo**-mij) *noun* a bird's feathers. [same origin as *plume*]

plumb[1] *verb* **1** measure how deep something is. **2** get to the bottom of a matter, *We could not plumb the mystery.* **3** fit with a plumbing system.

plumb[2] *adjective* exactly upright; vertical, *The wall was plumb.*

plumb[3] *adverb* (*informal*) exactly, *It fell plumb in the middle.* [from Latin *plumbum* = *lead*[3] (the metal)]

plumber *noun* a person who fits and mends plumbing.

plumbing *noun* **1** the water pipes, water tanks, and drainage pipes in a building. **2** the work of a plumber.

plumb line *noun* a cord with a weight on the end, used to find how deep something is or whether an upright surface is vertical.

plume[1] *noun* **1** a large feather. **2** something shaped like a feather, *a plume of smoke.*

plume[2] *verb* (**plumed, pluming**) preen, *The bird plumed itself.* [from Latin *pluma* = feather]

plummet[1] *noun* a plumb line or the weight on its end.

plummet[2] *verb* (**plummeted, plummeting**) drop downwards quickly.

plump[1] *adjective* slightly fat; rounded. **plumpness** *noun*

plump[2] *verb* make or become plump, *She plumped up the pillows.*

plump[3] *verb* drop or fall quickly. **plump for** (*informal*) choose.

plunder[1] *verb* rob a person or place forcibly or systematically; loot. **plunderer** *noun*

plunder[2] *noun* **1** plundering. **2** goods that have been plundered; loot.

plunge[1] *verb* (**plunged, plunging**) **1** go or push forcefully into something; dive. **2** fall or go downwards suddenly. **3** go or force into action, *They plunged the world into war.* **4** immerse something completely. **plunger** *noun*

plunge[2] *noun* plunging; a dive. **take the plunge** start a bold course of action.

plural *noun* the form of a noun or verb used when it stands for more than one person or thing, *The plural of 'child' is 'children'.* (Compare **singular**[1].) **plural** *adjective*, **plurality** *noun* [from Latin *pluris* = of more]

pluralism *noun* a form of society with many minority groups and cultures; multiculturalism. **pluralist** *noun*, **pluralistic** *adjective*

plus[1] *preposition* with the next number or thing added, *Two plus two equals four* (2 + 2 = 4).

plus[2] *noun* an advantage. [Latin, = more]

plush *noun* a thick velvety cloth used in furnishings. **plushy** *adjective* [from Latin *pilus* = hair]

Pluto *noun* the ninth planet of the solar system (technically now regarded as a dwarf planet). [named after the Roman god of the Underworld]

plutocrat *noun* a person who is powerful because of wealth. **plutocracy** *noun*, **plutocratic** *adjective* [from Greek *ploutos* = wealth, + *-kratia* = power]

plutonium *noun* a radioactive substance used in nuclear weapons and reactors. [named after the planet Pluto]

ply[1] *noun* **1** a thickness or layer of certain materials, especially wood or cloth. **2** a strand in yarn, *four-ply wool.* [same origin as *pliable*]

ply[2] *verb* (**plied**, **plying**) **1** use or wield a tool or weapon. **2** work at, *Tailors plied their trade.* **3** keep offering, *They plied her with food* or *with questions.* **4** go regularly, *The boat plies between the two harbours.* **5** drive or wait about looking for custom, *Taxis are allowed to ply for hire.* [from *apply*]

plywood *noun* strong thin board made of layers of wood glued together.

PM *abbreviation* prime minister.

p.m. *abbreviation* post meridiem. [Latin, = after noon]

pneumatic (*say* nyoo-**mat**-ik) *adjective* filled with or worked by compressed air, *a pneumatic drill.* **pneumatically** *adverb* [from Greek *pneuma* = wind]

pneumonia (*say* nyoo-**moh**-nee-uh) *noun* inflammation of one or both lungs. [from Greek *pneumon* = lung]

PNG *abbreviation* Papua New Guinea.

poach *verb* **1** cook an egg (removed from its shell) in simmering water. **2** cook by simmering in a small amount of liquid. **3** steal game or fish from someone else's land or water. **4** take unfairly, *One club was poaching members from another.* **poacher** *noun* [same origin as *pouch*]

pocket[1] *noun* **1** a small bag-shaped part, especially in a garment. **2** a person's supply of money, *The expense is beyond my pocket.* **3** an isolated part or area, *small pockets of rain.* **pocketful** *noun*
be out of pocket have spent more money than you have gained.

pocket[2] *adjective* small enough to fit in a pocket, *a pocket calculator.*

pocket[3] *verb* (**pocketed**, **pocketing**) put something into a pocket. [from Old French *pochet* = little pouch]

pocketknife another name for **penknife**.

pocket money *noun* a small amount of money given to a child by their parents, typically on a regular basis.

pod[1] *noun* a long seed case of the kind found on a pea or bean plant.

pod[2] *noun* a small herd of marine animals, especially whales.

podcast *noun* a digital audio file made available on the Internet for downloading to a computer or mobile device, typically available as a series. **podcast** *verb* [from *iPod*, trademark name for a digital audio player]

poddy *noun* (*plural* **poddies**) (*Australian*) a hand-fed calf.

podgy *adjective* (**podgier**, **podgiest**) short and fat.

podiatry *noun* the treatment of ailments of the feet. **podiatrist** *noun* [from Greek *podos* = foot, + *iatreia* = healing]

podium (*say* **poh**-dee-uhm) *noun* (*plural* **podia**) a platform or pedestal. [from Greek *podion* = little foot]

poem *noun* a composition in verse. [from Greek *poiema* = thing made]

poet *noun* a person who writes poems.

poetic *adjective* **1** of or like poetry or poets; written in verse. **2** elevated or sublime in expression. **poetical** *adjective*, **poetically** *adverb*

poetic justice *noun* suitable and well-deserved punishment or reward.

poetry *noun* poems.

pogrom *noun* an organised massacre. [Russian, = destruction]

poignant (*say* **poi**-nyuhnt) *adjective* very distressing; affecting the feelings, *poignant memories.* **poignancy** *noun* [from French, = pricking]

point[1] *noun* **1** the narrow or sharp end of something. **2** a dot, *the decimal point.* **3** a particular place, *a meeting point.* **4** a particular time, *At this point she was winning.* **5** a detail; a characteristic, *He has his good points.* **6** the important or essential idea, *Keep to the point!* **7** purpose; value, *There is no point in hurrying.* **8** an electrical socket. **9** a device for changing a train from one track to another.
to the point relevant.

point[2] *verb* **1** aim; direct, *She pointed a gun at me.* **2** show where something is, especially by holding out a finger towards it. **3** fill in the parts between bricks with mortar or cement.
point out draw attention to something. [from Latin *punctum* = pricked]

point-blank[1] *adjective* **1** aimed or fired from close to the target. **2** direct; straightforward, *a point-blank refusal.*

point-blank[2] *adverb* in a point-blank manner, *He refused point-blank.*

point duty *noun* traffic control by a police officer at a road junction.

pointed *adjective* **1** with a point at the end. **2** clearly directed at a person, *a pointed remark.* **pointedly** *adverb*

pointer *noun* **1** a thing that points or is used to point to something; an indicator on a dial or scale. **2** a dog that points with its muzzle towards birds that it scents. **3** an indication or hint.

pointless *adjective* without a point; with no purpose. **pointlessly** *adverb*

point of view *noun* a way of looking at or thinking of something.

poise[1] *verb* (**poised**, **poising**) balance.

poise[2] *noun* **1** balance; the way something is poised. **2** a dignified self-confident manner.

poison[1] *noun* a substance that can harm or kill a living thing. **poisonous** *adjective*

poison[2] *verb* **1** give poison to; kill with poison. **2** put poison in something. **3** corrupt; fill with prejudice, *She poisoned their minds.* **poisoner** *noun* [same origin as *potion*]

poke *verb* (**poked**, **poking**) **1** prod; jab. **2** push out or forward; stick out. **3** search, *I was poking about in the cupboard.* **poke** *noun*
poke fun at ridicule.

poker[1] *noun* a stiff metal rod for poking a fire.

poker[2] *noun* a card game in which players bet on who has the best cards.

poker face *noun* a face that does not reveal thoughts or feelings.

poker machine *noun* (*Australian*) a coin-operated gambling machine.

pokie *noun* (*Australian informal*) a poker machine.

poky *adjective* (**pokier**, **pokiest**) small and cramped, *poky little rooms.* [from *poke*]

polar *adjective* **1** of or near the North Pole or South Pole. **2** of either pole of a magnet. **polarity** *noun*

polar bear *noun* a white bear living in Arctic regions.

polarise *verb* (**polarised**, **polarising**) **1** keep vibrations of light-waves etc. to a single direction. **2** set at opposite extremes of feeling, *Opinions had polarised.* **polarisation** *noun*

pole[1] *noun* a long slender rounded piece of wood or metal. [same origin as *pale*[2]]

pole[2] *noun* **1** a point on the earth's surface that is as far north (**North Pole**) or as far south (**South Pole**) as possible. **2** either of the ends of a magnet. **3** either terminal of an electric cell or battery. [from Greek *polos* = axis]

polecat *noun* an animal of the weasel family with an unpleasant smell.

polemic (*say* puh-**lem**-ik) *noun* an attack in words against someone's opinion or actions. **polemical** *adjective* [from Greek *polemos* = war]

polenta *noun* cornmeal; a food made by boiling this in water to a thick paste.

pole-vault *noun* a jump over a high bar done with the help of a long pole held in the hands.

police[1] *noun* the people whose job is to catch criminals and make sure that the law is kept. **policeman** *noun*, **policewoman** *noun*

police[2] *verb* (**policed**, **policing**) keep order in a place by means of police.

police force *noun* an organised body of police officers responsible for a country, district, or town.

police officer *noun* a member of the police force.

policy[1] *noun* (*plural* **policies**) the aims or plan of action of a person or group. [same origin as *political*]

policy[2] *noun* (*plural* **policies**) a document stating the terms of a contract of insurance. [from Greek, = evidence]

polio *noun* poliomyelitis.

poliomyelitis (*say* poh-lee-oh-muy-uh-**luy**-tuhs) *noun* an infectious disease caused by a virus, producing temporary or permanent paralysis.

polish[1] *verb* **1** make a thing smooth and shiny by rubbing. **2** make a thing better by making corrections and alterations. **polisher** *noun*
polish off finish off.

polish[2] *noun* (*plural* **polishes**) **1** a substance used in polishing. **2** a shine. **3** elegance of manner.

polite *adjective* having good manners. **politely** *adverb*, **politeness** *noun* [from Latin *politus* = polished]

politic (*say* **pol**-uh-tik) *adjective* showing good judgement; prudent.

political *adjective* **1** of or engaged in politics. **2** of the way a country is governed. **3** concerned with power, policy, or status rather than with principle. **politically** *adverb* [from Greek *politeia* = government]

politician *noun* a person who is involved in politics.

politics *noun* the science and art of government; political matters.

polka *noun* a lively dance for couples. [from Czech = half step]

polka dot *noun* a round dot as one of many forming a pattern on fabric or other surface.

poll[1] *noun* **1** voting or votes at an election. **2** an opinion poll (see **opinion**). **3** (*old use*) the head.

poll[2] *verb* **1** vote at an election. **2** receive a stated number of votes. **polling booth** *noun*, **polling station** *noun*

pollarded *adjective* (of trees) with the tops trimmed so that young shoots start to grow thickly there. [from *poll*[1] 3]

polled *adjective* (of cattle) with the horns trimmed. [from *poll*[1] 3]

pollen *noun* powder produced by the anthers of flowers, containing male cells for fertilising other flowers. [Latin, = fine flour]

pollinate *verb* (**pollinated**, **pollinating**) fertilise with pollen. **pollination** *noun*

pollster *noun* a person who conducts an opinion poll.

pollute *verb* (**polluted, polluting**) make a place or thing dirty or impure. **pollutant** *noun*, **pollution** *noun*

Pollyanna *noun* an excessively cheerful or optimistic person. [from the name of a heroine created by American writer Eleanor Porter]

polo *noun* a game rather like hockey, with players on horseback.

polo neck *noun* a high round turned-over collar.

poltergeist *noun* a ghost or spirit that throws things about noisily. [from German *poltern* = make a disturbance, + *geist* = ghost]

poly- *prefix* many (as in *polyhedron*). [from Greek *polys* = much]

polychromatic *adjective* (also **polychrome**) having many colours. [from *poly-*, + Greek *chroma* = colour]

polyester *noun* a kind of synthetic substance.

polygamy (*say* puh-**lig**-uh-mee) *noun* the practice or custom of having more than one wife or husband at the same time. (Compare **monogamy**.) **polygamist** *noun*, **polygamous** *adjective* [from *poly-*, + Greek *gamos* = marriage]

polyglot *adjective* knowing or using several languages. [from *poly-*, + Greek *glotta* = language]

polygon *noun* a shape with many sides, e.g. a hexagon or octagon. **polygonal** *adjective* [from *poly-*, + Greek *gonia* = corner]

polygraph *noun* a machine for reading physiological characteristics (e.g. pulse rate), used as a lie detector.

polyhedron *noun* a solid shape with many sides. [from *poly-*, + Greek *hedra* = base]

polymath *noun* a person of great or varied learning.

polymer *noun* a substance whose molecule is formed from a large number of simple molecules combined. [from *poly-*, + Greek *meros* = part]

polynomial[1] *noun* an expression of more than two algebraic terms, especially the sum of several terms that contain different powers of the same variable(s).

polynomial[2] *adjective* of or being a polynomial.

polyp *noun* **1** a tiny creature with a tube-shaped body. **2** a small abnormal growth.

polyphony *noun* contrapuntal music.

polystyrene *noun* a polymer used to make hard plastic or expanded with gas to produce a lightweight white material for packaging etc.

polytheism (*say* **pol**-ee-thee-iz-uhm) *noun* belief in more than one god. **polytheist** *noun* [from *poly-*, + Greek *theos* = god]

polythene *noun* a tough light plastic.

pom *noun* (*Australian informal*) (often offensive) a British (especially English) person. **pommy** *noun & adjective* [from an abbreviation of rhyming slang *pomegranate* = immigrant]

pomegranate *noun* a hard red fruit with many seeds. [from Latin *pomum* = apple, + *granatum* = having many seeds]

pommel *noun* **1** a knob on the handle of a sword. **2** the raised part at the front of a saddle. [from Latin *pomum* = apple]

pomp *noun* stately and splendid ceremonial. [from Greek, = procession]

pompom *noun* a ball of coloured threads used as a decoration.

pompous *adjective* full of great dignity and self-importance. **pomposity** *noun*, **pompously** *adverb* [from *pomp*]

poncho *noun* (*plural* **ponchos**) a blanket-like piece of material with a slit in the centre for the head, worn as a cloak. [South American Spanish]

pond *noun* a small lake.

ponder *verb* think deeply and seriously; muse. [from Latin *ponderare* = weight]

ponderous *adjective* **1** heavy and awkward. **2** laborious, *He writes in a ponderous style.* **ponderously** *adverb* [from Latin *ponderis* = of weight]

pong *noun* (*informal*) a stink. **pong** *verb*, **pongy** *adjective*

pontiff *noun* the pope. **pontifical** *adjective* [from Latin *pontifex* = chief priest]

pontificate *verb* (**pontificated, pontificating**) speak or write pompously. **pontification** *noun*

pontoon[1] *noun* a boat or float used to support a bridge (a **pontoon bridge**) over a river. [from Latin *pontis* = of a bridge]

pontoon[2] *noun* **1** a card game in which players try to get cards whose value totals 21. **2** a score of 21 from two cards in this game. [from French *vingt-et-un* = 21]

pony *noun* (*plural* **ponies**) a small horse.

ponytail *noun* a bunch of long hair tied at the back of the head.

Ponzi scheme *noun* a form of fraud in which belief in the success of a non-existent enterprise is fostered by the payment of quick returns to the first investors from money invested by later investors. [named after Charles Ponzi, who carried out such a scheme]

poodle *noun* a dog with thick curly hair.

pooh *interjection* an exclamation of contempt.

pooh-pooh *verb* dismiss an idea or suggestion scornfully.

pool[1] *noun* **1** a pond. **2** a puddle. **3** a swimming pool.

pool[2] *noun* **1** the fund of money staked in a gambling game. **2** a group of things shared by several people.

pool[3] *verb* put money or things together for sharing.

poop *noun* the stern of a ship.

poor *adjective* **1** having very little money or other resources. **2** not good; inadequate, *a poor piece of work.* **3** unfortunate; deserving pity, *Poor fellow!* **poorness** *noun*

poorly *adverb* **1** in a poor way, *She was poorly dressed.* **2** rather ill.

POP *abbreviation* **1** point of presence, denoting equipment that acts as access to the Internet. **2** Post Office Protocol, a standard protocol for accessing email.

pop[1] *noun* **1** a small explosive sound. **2** a fizzy drink.

pop[2] *verb* (**popped, popping**) **1** make a pop. **2** (*informal*) put or go quickly, *Pop down to the shop*; *Pop in any time.*

pop[3] *noun* (also **pop music**) modern popular music. [short for *popular*]

pop art *noun* art that uses themes drawn from popular culture.

popcorn *noun* corn kernels heated to burst and form fluffy balls.

pope *noun* the bishop of Rome, leader of the Roman Catholic Church. [from Greek *papas* = father]

pop-eyed *adjective* with bulging eyes.

popgun *noun* a toy that shoots a cork or pellet with a popping sound.

poplar *noun* a tall slender tree.

poplin *noun* a plain woven cotton material.

poppadom alternative spelling of **papadum**.

poppy *noun* (*plural* **poppies**) a plant with showy flowers, often red.

populace *noun* the general public.

popular *adjective* **1** liked or enjoyed by many people. **2** of or for the general public. **popularity** *noun*, **popularly** *adverb* [from Latin *populus* = people]

popularise *verb* (**popularised, popularising**) make a thing generally liked or known. **popularisation** *noun*

populate *verb* (**populated, populating**) **1** supply with a population; inhabit. **2** (in computing) fill in (data).

population *noun* the people who live in a district or country; inhabitants; the total number of these or of any group of living things.

pop-up *adjective* **1** with parts that come upwards automatically, *a pop-up book.* **2** (in computing) (of a menu or other utility) able to be superimposed on the screen being worked on and suppressed rapidly. **3** of a shop or other business that opens quickly in a temporary location and is intended to operate for only a short period of time.

porcelain *noun* the finest kind of china.

porch *noun* (*plural* **porches**) a shelter outside the entrance to a building. [from Latin *porticus* (compare *portico*)]

porcupine *noun* a small animal covered with long prickles. [from Latin *porcus* = pig, + *spine*]

pore[1] *noun* a tiny opening on the skin through which moisture can pass in or out. [from Greek *poros* = passage]

pore[2] *verb* (**pored, poring**)
pore over study with close attention, *She was poring over her books.* [related to *peer*[1]]

pork *noun* meat from a pig. [from Latin *porcus* = pig]

pork barrel *noun* government funds allocated so as to derive political benefit. **pork barrelling** *noun*

pornography (*say* paw-**nog**-ruh-fee) *noun* printed or visual material containing the explicit description or display of sexual organs or activity. **pornographic** *adjective* [from Greek *porne* = prostitute, + *-graphy*]

porous *adjective* allowing liquid or air to pass through. **porosity** *noun* [same origin as *pore*[1]]

porphyry (*say* **paw**-fuh-ree) *noun* a kind of rock containing crystals of minerals. [from Latin, = purple stone]

porpoise (*say* **paw**-puhs) *noun* a sea animal rather like a small whale. [from Latin *porcus* = pig, + *piscis* = fish]

porridge *noun* a food made by boiling oatmeal to a thick paste.

port[1] *noun* **1** a harbour. **2** a place where goods pass in and out of a country by ship or aircraft. **3** the left-hand side of a ship or aircraft when you are facing forward. (Compare **starboard**.) [from Latin *portus* = harbour]

port[2] *noun* a sweet strong red wine. [from the city of Oporto in Portugal]

port[3] *noun* (*Australian*) a suitcase, schoolbag, or travelling bag. [from *portmanteau*]

portable *adjective* able to be carried. [from Latin *portare* = carry]

portable media player *noun* a portable device that can play audio and video files downloaded from the Internet etc.

portal *noun* **1** a doorway or gateway. **2** an Internet site providing a directory of links to other sites. [from Latin *porta* = gate]

portcullis *noun* (*plural* **portcullises**) a strong heavy vertical grating that can be lowered in grooves to block the gateway to a castle. [from French, = sliding door (*porte* = door)]

portend *verb* foreshadow; be a sign that something will happen, *Dark clouds portend a storm.* [from Latin *pro-* = forwards, + *tendere* = stretch]

portent *noun* an omen; a sign that something will happen. **portentous** *adjective*

porter[1] *noun* a person whose job is to carry luggage or other goods. [from Latin *portare* = carry]

porter[2] *noun* a person whose job is to look after the entrance to a large building. [from Latin *porta* = gate]

portfolio *noun* (*plural* **portfolios**) **1** a case for holding documents or drawings. **2** a government minister's special responsibility. **3** a set of investments held by one investor. [from Italian *portare* = carry, + *foglio* = sheet of paper]

porthole *noun* a small window in the side of a ship or aircraft (formerly a hole for pointing a ship's cannon through).

portico *noun* (*plural* **porticoes**) a roof supported on columns, usually forming a porch to a building. [from Latin *porticus* = porch]

portion[1] *noun* a part or share given to somebody.

portion[2] *verb* divide into portions, *Portion it out.*

portly *adjective* (**portlier**, **portliest**) stout and dignified. **portliness** *noun*

portmanteau (*say* pawt-**man**-toh) *noun* a trunk that opens into two equal parts for holding clothes etc. [from French *porter* = carry, + *manteau* = coat]

portmanteau word *noun* a word made from the sounds and meanings of two others, e.g. *motel* (from *motor* + *hotel*).

portrait *noun* a picture of a person or animal.

portray *verb* **1** make a picture of. **2** describe or show, *The play portrays the king as a fool.* **portrayal** *noun*

pose[1] *noun* **1** a position or posture of the body, e.g. for a portrait or photograph. **2** a pretence; unnatural behaviour to impress people.

pose[2] *verb* (**posed**, **posing**) **1** take up a pose. **2** put someone into a pose. **3** pretend. **4** put forward, *pose a question.*

poser *noun* **1** a puzzling question or problem. **2** a person who behaves affectedly.

posh *adjective* (*informal*) very smart; high-class; luxurious.

position[1] *noun* **1** the place where something is or should be. **2** the way a person or thing is placed or arranged, *in a sitting position.* **3** a situation or condition, *I am in no position to help you.* **4** paid employment; a job. **5** a point of view. **positional** *adjective*

position[2] *verb* place a person or thing in a certain position. [from Latin *positum* = placed]

positive[1] *adjective* **1** definite; certain, *We have positive proof that he is guilty.* **2** holding an opinion confidently. **3** agreeing; saying 'yes', *We received a positive reply.* **4** greater than zero. **5** constructive and helpful, *some positive suggestions.* **6** of the kind of electric charge that lacks electrons. **7** (of an adjective or adverb) in the simple form, not comparative or superlative, *The positive form is 'big', the comparative is 'bigger', the superlative is 'biggest'.* **positively** *adverb*

positive[2] *noun* **1** something positive. **2** a photograph with the light and dark parts or colours as in the thing photographed. (Compare **negative**[2].)

positron *noun* a particle of matter with a positive electric charge. [from *positive*]

posse (*say* **pos**-ee) *noun* a strong group, especially one that helps a sheriff. [same origin as *possible*]

possess *verb* **1** have or own something. **2** control someone's thoughts or behaviour, *I don't know what possessed you to do such a thing!* **possessor** *noun*

possessed *adjective* seeming to be controlled by strong emotion or an evil spirit, *He fought like a man possessed.*

possession *noun* **1** something you possess or own. **2** possessing. **3** control of something, *She got possession of the ball and scored a goal.*

possessive *adjective* **1** wanting to possess and keep things for yourself. **2** showing that somebody owns something, *a possessive pronoun.*

possessive pronoun see **pronoun**.

possibility *noun* (*plural* **possibilities**) **1** being possible. **2** something that may exist or happen.

possible *adjective* able to exist, happen, be done, or be used. [from Latin *posse* = be able]

possibly *adverb* **1** in any way, *I can't possibly do it.* **2** perhaps.

possie (*say* **poz**-ee) *noun* (*Australian informal*) a position.

possum *noun* a furry long-tailed marsupial that lives in trees.

post[1] *noun* **1** an upright piece of wood, concrete, or other material set in the ground. **2** a piece of writing, image, or other item of content published online. **3** the starting point or finishing point of a race, *He was left at the post.*

post[2] *verb* **1** put up a notice or poster to announce something. **2** publish a piece of writing, image, or other item of content online. [from Latin *postis* = post]

post[3] *noun* **1** the collecting and delivering of letters and parcels. **2** these letters and parcels.

post[4] *verb* put a letter or parcel into a postbox or post office for collection.
keep someone posted keep them informed. [same origin as *position*]

post[5] *noun* **1** a position of paid employment; a job. **2** the place where someone is on duty, *a sentry post.* **3** a place occupied by soldiers, traders, etc.
last post a military bugle-call sounded at sunset and at military funerals or ceremonies.

post[6] *verb* place someone on duty, *We posted sentries.*

post- *prefix* after (as in *post-war*). [from Latin *post* = after]

postage *noun* the charge for sending something by post.

postage stamp *noun* a stamp for sticking on things to be posted, showing the amount paid.

postal *adjective* of or by the post.

postbox *noun* a box into which letters and parcels are put for collection.

postcard *noun* a card for sending messages by post without an envelope.

postcode *noun* a group of numbers or letters and numbers included in an address to help in sorting the post.

poster *noun* a large sheet of paper announcing or advertising something, for display in a public place. [from *post*[2]]

posterior[1] *adjective* situated at the back of something. (The opposite is **anterior**.)

posterior[2] *noun* the buttocks. [Latin, = further back]

posterity *noun* future generations of people.

postgraduate *adjective* (of studies) carried on after taking a first degree.
postgraduate *noun*

post-haste *adverb* with great speed or haste. [from *post*[3] + *haste*]

posthumous (*say* **pos**-chuh-muhs) *adjective* happening after a person's death.
posthumously *adverb* [from Latin *postumus* = last]

postie *noun* (*informal*) a postman or postwoman.

postilion (*say* pos-**til**-yuhn) *noun* a person riding one of the horses pulling a carriage.

postman *noun* (*plural* **postmen**) a person who delivers or collects letters and parcels.

postmark *noun* an official mark put on something sent by post to show where and when it was posted.

postmodern *adjective* (in the arts etc.) of the movement reacting against modernism, especially by drawing attention to former conventions. **postmodernism** *noun*, **postmodernist** *noun & adjective*

post-mortem *noun* an examination of a dead body to discover the cause of death. [Latin, = after death]

post office *noun* a building or room where postal business is carried on.

postpone *verb* (**postponed**, **postponing**) fix a later time for something, *They postponed the meeting for a fortnight.* **postponement** *noun* [from *post-*, + Latin *ponere* = to place]

postscript *noun* something extra added at the end of a letter (after the writer's signature) or at the end of a book. [from *post-*, + Latin *scriptum* = written]

postulant *noun* a person who applies to be admitted to an order of monks or nuns.

postulate[1] *verb* (**postulated**, **postulating**) assume that something is true and use it in reasoning. **postulation** *noun*

postulate[2] *noun* something postulated. [from Latin *postulare* = to claim]

posture[1] *noun* the way a person stands, sits or walks; a pose.

posture[2] *verb* (**postured**, **posturing**) pose, especially to impress people. [same origin as *position*]

postwoman *noun* (*plural* **postwomen**) a woman who delivers or collects letters and parcels.

posy *noun* (*plural* **posies**) a small bunch of flowers.

pot[1] *noun* **1** a deep usually round container. **2** (*informal*) a lot of something, *pots of money.*
go to pot (*informal*) lose quality; be ruined.
take pot luck (*informal*) take whatever is available.

pot[2] *verb* (**potted**, **potting**) **1** put into a pot. **2** (*informal*) abridge, *a potted version of the story.*

pot[3] *noun* (*informal*) marijuana. [short for Spanish *potiguaya* = drink of grief]

potash *noun* potassium carbonate. [from *pot*[1] + *ash*[1] (because it was first obtained from vegetable ashes washed in a pot)]

potassium *noun* a soft silver-white metal substance that is essential for living things. [from *potash*]

potato *noun* (*plural* **potatoes**) a starchy white tuber growing underground, used as a vegetable. [from South American *batata* (potatoes were first brought to Europe from South America)]

potent (*say* **poh**-tuhnt) *adjective* powerful. **potency** *noun* [from Latin *potens* = able]

potentate (*say* **poh**-tuhn-tayt) *noun* a powerful monarch or ruler. [from *potent*]

potential[1] (*say* puh-**ten**-shuhl) *adjective* capable of happening or being used or developed, *a potential winner.* **potentiality** *noun*, **potentially** *adverb*

potential[2] *noun* an ability or capacity for development or use. [from Latin *potentia* = power]

pothole *noun* **1** a deep natural hole in the ground. **2** a hole in a road.

potholing *noun* exploring underground potholes. **potholer** *noun*

potion *noun* a liquid medicine, poison, or drug. [from Latin *potus* = having drunk something]

potoroo *noun* a small long-nosed Australian marsupial. Also called a *rat-kangaroo.* [probably from Sydney language *badaru*]

pot-pourri (*say* poh-**poor**-ee) *noun* a scented mixture of dried petals and spices. [French, = rotten pot]

potter[1] *noun* a person who makes pottery.

potter[2] *verb* work or move about in a leisurely way.

pottery *noun* (*plural* **potteries**) **1** vessels and other objects made of baked clay. **2** a place where a potter works.

potty[1] *adjective* (**pottier**, **pottiest**) (*informal*) mad.

potty[2] *noun* (*plural* **potties**) (*informal*) a child's chamber pot.

pouch *noun* (*plural* **pouches**) **1** a small bag. **2** something shaped like a bag. **3** a pocket-like part of the body in which marsupials carry their undeveloped young. [from French *poche* = bag or pocket]

pouffe (*say* poof) *noun* a padded stool or footrest. [French]

poultice (*say* **pohl**-tuhs) *noun* a soft hot dressing put on a sore or inflamed place.

poultry (*say* **pohl**-tree) *noun* birds (e.g. chickens, geese, turkeys) kept for their eggs and meat.

pounce *verb* (**pounced**, **pouncing**) jump or swoop down quickly on something. **pounce** *noun*

pound[1] *noun* **1** a unit of money in Britain and certain other countries and formerly in Australia. **2** a unit of weight equal to 16 ounces or about 454 grams.

pound[2] *noun* **1** a place where stray animals are taken. **2** a public enclosure for vehicles officially removed.

pound[3] *verb* **1** hit something often, especially so as to crush it. **2** run or go heavily, *pounding along.* **3** thump, *My heart was pounding.*

pour *verb* **1** flow; cause to flow. **2** rain heavily, *It poured all day.* **3** come or go in large amounts, *Letters poured in.* **pourer** *noun*

pout *verb* push out your lips when you are annoyed or sulking. **pout** *noun*

poverty *noun* being poor.

powder[1] *noun* **1** a mass of fine dry particles of something. **2** a medicine or cosmetic made as a powder. **3** gunpowder. **powdery** *adjective*

powder[2] *verb* **1** put powder on something. **2** make into powder. [from Latin *pulveris* = of dust]

power *noun* **1** strength; energy; vigour. **2** the ability to do something. **3** authority. **4** a powerful country, person, or organisation. **5** mechanical or electrical energy; the electricity supply, *There was a power failure after the storm.* **6** (in mathematics) the product of a number multiplied by itself a given number of times, *The third power of 2 = 2 × 2 × 2 = 8.* **powered** *adjective*, **powerless** *adjective*

powerful *adjective* **1** having great power or strength. **2** influential. **powerfully** *adverb*

powerhouse *noun* a power station.

power station *noun* a building where electricity is produced.

powwow *noun* a meeting for discussion.

pp. *abbreviation* pages.

PPE *abbreviation* personal protective (or protection) equipment.

P-plate *noun* (*Australian*) a sign bearing the letter P, denoting a provisional licence. **P-plater** *noun*

PPP *abbreviation* point to point protocol, a protocol that allows a computer to use a telephone line and a modem.

practicable *adjective* able to be done.

practical *adjective* **1** able to do useful things, *a practical person.* **2** likely to be useful, *a very practical invention.* **3** actually doing something, *She has had practical experience.* **practicality** *noun* [from Greek *praktikos* from *prattein* = do]

practical joke *noun* a trick played on somebody.

practically *adverb* **1** in a practical way. **2** almost, *I've practically finished.*

practice *noun* **1** practising, *Have you done your piano practice?* **2** actually doing something; action, not theory, *It works well in practice.* **3** the professional business of a doctor, dentist, or lawyer. **4** a habit or custom, *It is his practice to work until midnight.*
out of practice no longer skilful because you have not practised recently.

practise *verb* (**practised, practising**) **1** do something repeatedly in order to become better at it. **2** do something actively or habitually, *Practise what you preach.* **3** work as a doctor, dentist, or lawyer. [same origin as *practical*]

> **Usage** Note the spelling: *practice* is a noun, *practise* is a verb.

practised *adjective* experienced; expert.

practitioner *noun* a professional worker, especially a doctor.

pragmatic *adjective* treating things in a practical way, *Take a pragmatic approach to the problem.* **pragmatically** *adverb*, **pragmatism** *noun*, **pragmatist** *noun* [from Greek, = businesslike]

prairie *noun* a large area of flat grass-covered land in North America. [from Latin *pratum* = meadow]

praise[1] *verb* (**praised, praising**) **1** say that somebody or something is very good. **2** honour God in words.

praise[2] *noun* words that praise somebody or something. **praiseworthy** *adjective* [from Latin *pretium* = value]

pram *noun* a four-wheeled carriage for a baby, pushed by a person walking. [short for *perambulator*]

prance *verb* (**pranced, prancing**) move about in a lively or happy way.

prang *noun* (*informal*) a car crash. **prang** *verb*

prank *noun* a piece of mischief; a practical joke. **prankster** *noun*

prat *noun* (*informal*) a silly or foolish person.

prattle *verb* (**prattled, prattling**) chatter like a young child. **prattle** *noun*

prawn *noun* an edible shellfish like a large shrimp.
come the raw prawn (*Australian informal*) try to trick someone.

pray *verb* **1** talk to God. **2** ask earnestly for something; entreat. **3** (*formal*) please, *Pray be seated.*

prayer *noun* praying; words used in praying.

praying mantis *noun* an insect rather like a grasshopper.

pre- *prefix* before (as in *prehistoric*). [from Latin *prae* = before]

preach *verb* give a religious or moral talk. **preacher** *noun*

preamble *noun* the introduction to a speech or book or document. [from *pre-*, + Latin *ambulare* = go]

prearranged *adjective* arranged beforehand. **prearrangement** *noun*

precarious (*say* pruh-**kair**-ree-uhs) *adjective* not safe or secure. **precariously** *adverb* [from Latin *precarious* = uncertain]

precaution *noun* something done to prevent future trouble or danger. **precautionary** *adjective* [from *pre-* + *caution*]

precede *verb* (**preceded, preceding**) come or go in front of or before a person or thing. [from *pre-*, + Latin *cedere* = go]

precedence (*say* **pres**-uh-duhns or pree-**see**-duhns) *noun* priority; a first or earlier place.

precedent (*say* **pree**-suh-duhnt or **pres**-uh-duhnt) *noun* a previous case that is taken as an example to be followed.

precept (*say* **pree**-sept) *noun* a rule for action or conduct; an instruction.

precinct (*say* **pree**-singkt) *noun* an enclosed or specially defined area, *a shopping precinct.* [from *pre-*, + Latin *cinctum* = surrounded]

precincts *plural noun* the area surrounding a place.

precious[1] *adjective* **1** very valuable. **2** greatly loved. **preciousness** *noun*

precious[2] *adverb* (*informal*) very, *We have precious little time.* [from Latin *pretium* = value]

precipice *noun* a very steep place, such as the face of a cliff. [from Latin *praeceps* = headlong]

precipitate[1] *verb* (**precipitated, precipitating**) **1** make something happen suddenly or soon, *The insult precipitated a quarrel.* **2** throw or send down; cause to fall, *The push precipitated him through the window.* **3** cause a solid substance to separate chemically from a solution.

precipitate[2] *noun* a substance precipitated from a solution.

precipitate[3] *adjective* hurried; hasty, *a precipitate departure.* [from Latin *praeceps* = headlong]

precipitation *noun* **1** rain, dew or snow; the amount of this. **2** precipitating or being precipitated.

precipitous *adjective* like a precipice; steep. **precipitously** *adverb*

precis (*say* **pray**-see) *noun* (*plural* **precis**, *say* **pray**-seez) (also **précis**) a summary. [French, = precise]

precise *adjective* **1** exact; clearly stated. **2** taking care to be exact. **precisely** *adverb*, **precision** *noun* [from Latin *praecisum* = cut short]

preclude *verb* (**precluded**, **precluding**) prevent. [from *pre-*, + Latin *claudere* = shut]

precocious (*say* pruh-**koh**-shuhs) *adjective* developed or having abilities earlier than is usual, *a precocious child.* **precociously** *adverb*, **precocity** *noun* [from Latin *praecox* = ripe very early]

preconceived *adjective* (of an idea) formed in advance, before full information is available. **preconception** *noun*

precursor *noun* a forerunner.

predator (*say* **pred**-uh-tuh) *noun* an animal that hunts or preys upon others. **predatory** *adjective* [from Latin, = plunderer]

predecessor (*say* **pree**-duh-ses-uh) *noun* an earlier person or thing, e.g. an ancestor or the former holder of a job. [from *pre-*, + Latin *decessor* = person departed]

predestine *verb* (**predestined**, **predestining**) destine beforehand. **predestination** *noun*

predicament (*say* pruh-**dik**-uh-muhnt) *noun* a difficult or unpleasant situation.

predicate *noun* the part of a sentence that says something about the subject, e.g. 'is short' in *Life is short.* [from Latin *praedicare* = proclaim]

predicative (*say* pruh-**dik**-uh-tiv) *adjective* forming part of the predicate, e.g. 'old' in *The dog is old.* (Compare **attributive.**) **predicatively** *adverb*

predict *verb* forecast; prophesy. **predictable** *adjective*, **prediction** *noun*, **predictor** *noun* [from *pre-*, + Latin *dicere* = to say]

predispose *verb* (**predisposed**, **predisposing**) cause a tendency; influence in advance, *Lack of exercise may predispose an individual to high blood pressure.* **predisposition** *noun*

predominate *verb* (**predominated**, **predominating**) be the largest or most important or most powerful. **predominance** *noun*, **predominant** *adjective*

pre-eminent *adjective* excelling others; outstanding. **pre-eminence** *noun*, **pre-eminently** *adverb*

pre-empt *verb* **1** obtain something before anyone else can do so. **2** prevent something from happening by taking action first; do or say something before someone else does. **pre-emption** *noun*, **pre-emptive** *adjective*

preen *verb* (of a bird) smooth its feathers with its beak.
preen yourself 1 smarten yourself. **2** congratulate yourself.

prefab *noun* (*informal*) a prefabricated building.

prefabricated *adjective* made in sections ready to be assembled on a site. **prefabrication** *noun*

preface (*say* **pref**-uhs) *noun* an introduction to a book or speech. **preface** *verb*

prefect *noun* **1** a school pupil given authority to help to keep order. **2** a district official in France, Japan, and other countries. [from Latin *praefectus* = overseer]

prefer *verb* (**preferred**, **preferring**) **1** like one person or thing more than another. **2** put forward, *They preferred charges of forgery against her.* [from Latin *prae* = before, + *ferre* = carry]

preferable (*say* **pref**-uh-ruh-buhl) *adjective* liked better; more desirable. **preferably** *adverb*

preference *noun* **1** preferring. **2** something preferred.

preferential (*say* pref-uh-**ren**-shuhl) *adjective* being favoured above others, *preferential treatment.*

preferment *noun* promotion.

prefix *noun* (*plural* **prefixes**) a word or syllable joined to the front of a word to change or add to its meaning, as in *dis*order, *out*stretched, *un*happy.

pregnant *adjective* having a baby developing in the womb. **pregnancy** *noun* [from *pre-*, + Latin *gnasci* = be born]

prehensile *adjective* (chiefly of an animal's limb or tail) able to grasp things. [from Latin *prehendere* = seize]

prehistoric *adjective* belonging to very ancient times, before written records of events were made. **prehistory** *noun*

prejudice *noun* a fixed opinion formed without examining the facts fairly. **prejudiced** *adjective* [from Latin *prae* = before, + *judicium* = judgement]

preliminary *adjective* coming before an important action or event and preparing for it. [from *pre-*, + Latin *limen* = threshold]

prelude *noun* **1** a thing that introduces or leads up to something else. **2** a short piece of music. [from *pre-*, + Latin *ludere* = to play]

premature *adjective* too early; coming before the usual or proper time. **prematurely** *adverb*

premeditated *adjective* planned beforehand, *a premeditated crime.*

premier[1] (*say* **prem**-ee-uh or **prem**-yuh) *adjective* first in importance, order, or time.

premier[2] *noun* (in Australia) the leader of a state government; (in some countries) a prime minister. [French, = first]

premiere (*say* **prem**-ee-air) *noun* (also **première**) the first public performance of a play or film. [French, = first]

premiers *plural noun* the sporting team that wins a premiership.

premiership *noun* an organised competition amongst sporting clubs.

premise (*say* **prem**-uhs) *noun* (also **premiss**) a statement used as the basis for a piece of reasoning.

premises *plural noun* a building and its grounds.

premium[1] *noun* **1** an amount or instalment paid to an insurance company. **2** an extra payment; a bonus.
at a premium above the normal price; highly valued.

premium[2] *adjective* of the best quality and therefore more expensive, *premium mince.* [from Latin *praemium* = reward]

premonition *noun* a feeling that something is about to happen. [from *pre-*, + Latin *monere* = warn]

preoccupied *adjective* having your thoughts completely busy with something.
preoccupation *noun*

prep *noun* homework. [short for *preparation*]

preparation *noun* **1** preparing. **2** something prepared.

preparatory *adjective* preparing for something.

prepare *verb* (**prepared**, **preparing**) make ready; get ready.
be prepared to be ready and willing to do something. [from *pre-*, + Latin *parare* = make ready]

preparedness *noun* readiness.

preponderate *verb* (**preponderated**, **preponderating**) be more than others or more powerful. **preponderance** *noun*, **preponderant** *adjective* [from Latin *praeponderare* = outweigh]

preposition *noun* a word used with a noun or pronoun to show place, position, time, or means, e.g. *at* home, *in* the hall, *on* Sunday, *by* train. [from *pre-*, + Latin *positum* = placed]

prepossessing *adjective* attractive, *Its appearance is not very prepossessing.*

preposterous *adjective* very absurd; outrageous. [from Latin, = back to front (from *prae* = before, + *posterus* = behind)]

prerequisite *noun* something required as a condition or in preparation for something else, *The ability to swim is a prerequisite for learning to sail.* **prerequisite** *adjective*

prerogative *noun* a right or privilege that belongs to one person or group. [from Latin, = people voting first]

Presbyterian (*say* prez-buh-**teer**-ree-uhn) *noun* a member of a Protestant church that is governed by elders who are chosen by the congregation. [from Greek *presbyteros* = elder]

preschool[1] *adjective* of the time before a child is old enough to attend school.

preschool[2] *noun* a kindergarten or child care centre.

prescribe *verb* (**prescribed**, **prescribing**) **1** advise a person to use a particular medicine or treatment. **2** say what should be done or what rule should be followed. [from *pre-*, + Latin *scribere* = write]

> **Usage** Do not confuse *prescribe* with *proscribe.*

prescribed burn another name for **controlled burn**.

prescription *noun* **1** a doctor's written order for a medicine. **2** the medicine prescribed. **3** prescribing.

preselection *noun* the choice of a candidate for a forthcoming election by (local) members of a political party.

presence *noun* being present in a place, *Your presence is required.*

presence of mind *noun* the ability to act quickly and sensibly in an emergency.

present[1] *adjective* **1** in a particular place, *No one else was present.* **2** belonging or referring to what is happening now; existing now, *the present prime minister.*

present[2] *noun* present times or events. [from Latin *praesens* = being at hand]

present[3] *noun* something given or received without payment; a gift.

present[4] (*say* pruh-**zent**) *verb* **1** give, especially with a ceremony, *Who is to present the prizes?* **2** introduce someone to another person or to an audience. **3** put on a play or other entertainment. **4** show. **5** cause, *Writing a dictionary presents many problems.* **presenter** *noun*

presentable *adjective* fit to be presented to someone; looking good.

presentation *noun* **1** a formal talk showing or demonstrating something. **2** a ceremony in which someone is given a gift or prize. **3** the way something looks when it is shown to other people, *The presentation of the food is designed to make you hungry.*

presentiment *noun* a feeling that something is about to happen; a foreboding.

presently *adverb* **1** soon, *I shall be with you presently.* **2** now, *the person who is presently in charge.*

present participle see **participle**.

present tense *noun* a form of a verb used to describe something that is happening now, for example *likes* in the sentence *He likes swimming.*

preserve[1] *verb* (**preserved, preserving**) **1** keep something safe or in good condition. **2** treat food so that it can be kept for future use. **preservation** *noun*, **preservative** *adjective & noun*, **preserver** *noun*

preserve[2] *noun* **1** preserved fruit; jam. **2** an activity that belongs to a particular person or group. [from *pre-*, + Latin *servare* = keep]

preside *verb* (**presided, presiding**) be president or chairperson; be in authority or control. [from Latin *prae* = in front, + *-sidere* = sit]

president *noun* **1** the person in charge of a club, society, or council. **2** the head of a republic. **3** the presiding officer in a legislative council or senate. **presidency** *noun*, **presidential** *adjective* [from *preside*]

press[1] *verb* **1** put weight or force steadily on something; squeeze. **2** make something by pressing. **3** flatten; smooth; iron. **4** urge, *They pressed him to come.* **5** make demands, *They pressed for an increase in wages.*

press[2] *noun* (*plural* **presses**) **1** the action of pressing something. **2** a device for pressing things. **3** a device for printing things. **4** a printing or publishing company, *Oxford University Press.* **5** (**the press**) newspapers; journalists. [from Latin *pressum* = squeezed]

press conference *noun* an interview with a group of journalists.

pressure[1] *noun* **1** continuous pressing. **2** the force with which something presses. **3** an influence that persuades or compels you to do something, *under pressure to resign*; *financial pressures.*

pressure[2] *verb* try to compel a person to do something.

pressurise *verb* (**pressurised, pressurising**) **1** keep a compartment at the same air pressure all the time. **2** try to compel a person to do something. **pressurisation** *noun*

prestige (*say* pres-**teezh**) *noun* good reputation. **prestigious** (*say* pres-**tij**-uhs) *adjective* [from Latin, = an illusion]

presto *adverb & adjective* (especially in music) very quickly.
hey presto! a conjuror, words used at a moment of sudden change. [Italian]

presumably *adverb* according to what you may presume.

presume *verb* (**presumed, presuming**) **1** suppose; assume something to be true. **2** take the liberty of doing something; venture, *May we presume to advise you?* **presumption** *noun*

presumptive *adjective* presuming something. **heir presumptive** see **heir**.

presumptuous *adjective* too bold or confident. **presumptuously** *adverb*

presuppose *verb* (**presupposed, presupposing**) suppose or assume something beforehand. **presupposition** *noun*

pretence *noun* **1** pretending. **2** a pretext.
false pretences pretending to be something that you are not, in order to deceive people.

pretend *verb* **1** behave as if something is true or real when you know that it is not, either in play or so as to deceive people. **2** put forward a claim (to a right or title). **pretender** *noun* [from Latin *prae* = in front, + *tendere* = offer]

pretension *noun* **1** pretentious or showy behaviour. **2** a doubtful claim.

pretentious *adjective* **1** showy; ostentatious. **2** claiming to have great merit or importance. **pretentiously** *adverb*, **pretentiousness** *noun*

pretext *noun* a reason put forward to conceal the true reason. [from Latin *praetextus* = an outward display]

pretty[1] *adjective* (**prettier, prettiest**) attractive in a delicate way. **prettily** *adverb*, **prettiness** *noun*

pretty[2] *adverb* quite, *It's pretty cold.*

prevail *verb* **1** be the most frequent or general, *The prevailing wind is from the north.* **2** be victorious. [from *pre-*, + Latin *valere* = have power]

prevalent (*say* **prev**-uh-luhnt) *adjective* most frequent or common; widespread. **prevalence** *noun* [same origin as *prevail*]

prevaricate *verb* (**prevaricated, prevaricating**) say something that is not actually a lie but is evasive or misleading. **prevarication** *noun* [from Latin, = walk crookedly]

prevent *verb* **1** stop something from happening. **2** stop a person from doing something. **preventable** *adjective*, **prevention** *noun*, **preventive** or **preventative** *adjective & noun* [from *pre-* + Latin *ventum* = come]

preview *noun* **1** an opportunity to view something before it is acquired or becomes generally available. **2** the showing of a film, play, or exhibition before it is seen by the general public.

previous *adjective* coming before this; preceding. **previously** *adverb* [from *pre-*, + Latin *via* = way]

prey[1] (*say* pray) *noun* an animal that is hunted or killed by another for food; a victim.
bird or **beast of prey** one that kills and eats other birds or four-footed animals.

prey[2] *verb* **prey on 1** hunt or take as prey. **2** cause to worry, *The problem preyed on his mind.* [from Latin *praeda* = booty]

price[1] *noun* **1** the amount of money for which something is bought or sold. **2** what must be given or done in order to achieve something.

price[2] *verb* (**priced, pricing**) decide the price of something.

price fixing *noun* the maintaining of prices at a certain level by agreement between competing sellers.

priceless *adjective* **1** very valuable. **2** (*informal*) very amusing.

pricey *adjective* (*informal*) expensive.

prick *verb* **1** pierce slightly; make a tiny hole in. **2** worry; make one feel guilty. **prick** *noun* **prick up your ears** start listening suddenly.

prickle[1] *noun* **1** a small thorn. **2** a sharp-pointed projection on an echidna or cactus etc. **3** a feeling that something is pricking you.

prickle[2] *verb* (**prickled, prickling**) feel or cause a pricking feeling.

prickly *adjective* **1** having prickles. **2** (of a person) easily offended.

prickly pear *noun* a cactus bearing prickly pear-shaped fruits.

pride[1] *noun* **1** pleasure or satisfaction with yourself or someone else who has done well. **2** something that makes you feel proud. **3** self-respect. **4** an unduly high opinion of your own merits or importance. **5** a group of lions.

pride[2] *verb* (**prided, priding**) **pride yourself on** be proud of.

pride of place *noun* the most important or most honoured position.

priest *noun* **1** a member of the clergy. **2** a person who conducts religious ceremonies. **priestess** *noun*, **priesthood** *noun*, **priestly** *adjective*

prig *noun* a self-righteous person. **priggish** *adjective*

prim *adjective* (**primmer, primmest**) formal and correct in manner; disliking anything rough or rude. **primly** *adverb*, **primness** *noun*

primacy (*say* **pruy**-muh-see) *noun* being the first or most important.

prima donna (*say* pree-muh **don**-uh) *noun* **1** the chief female singer in an opera. **2** a temperamental person with an inflated view of their own importance. [Italian, = first lady]

prima facie (*say* pruy-muh **fay**-see) *adverb* at first sight; judging by the first impression. [Latin, = on first appearance]

primary *adjective* **1** first. **2** most important. (Compare **secondary**.) **primarily** *adverb* [same origin as *prime*]

primary colours *plural noun* the colours from which all others can be made by mixing (red, yellow, and blue for paint; red, green, and violet for light).

primary industry *noun* agriculture, forestry, fishing, etc., as distinct from manufacturing industry.

primary school *noun* a school for the first stage of a child's education.

primary source *noun* a document, firsthand account, or other source that constitutes direct evidence of an object of study. (Compare **secondary source**.)

primate (*say* **pruy**-mayt) *noun* **1** an animal of the group that includes human beings, apes, and monkeys. **2** an archbishop.

prime[1] *adjective* **1** chief; most important, *the prime cause.* **2** excellent; first-rate, *prime beef.* **3** (of a number) divisible only by itself and one.

prime[2] *noun* the best time or stage of something, *in the prime of life.*

prime[3] *verb* (**primed, priming**) **1** prepare something for use or action. **2** put a coat of liquid on something to prepare it for painting. **3** equip a person with information. [from Latin *primus* = first]

prime minister *noun* the leader of a government, in Australia of the Federal Government.

prime number *noun* a number (e.g. 2, 3, 5, 7, 11) that can be divided exactly only by itself and one.

primer *noun* **1** a liquid for priming a surface. **2** an elementary textbook.

primeval (*say* pruy-**mee**-vuhl) *adjective* of the earliest times of the world. [from Latin *primus* = first, + *aevum* = age]

primitive *adjective* of or at an early stage of development or civilisation; not complicated or sophisticated.

primordial *adjective* primeval.

primrose *noun* a pale yellow flower that blooms in spring. [from Latin *prima rosa* = first rose]

prince *noun* **1** the son of a king or queen. **2** a man or boy in a royal family. **princely** *adjective* [from Latin *princeps* = chieftain]

princess *noun* (*plural* **princesses**) **1** the daughter of a king or queen. **2** a woman or girl in a royal family. **3** the wife of a prince.

principal[1] *adjective* chief; most important. **principally** *adverb*

principal[2] *noun* **1** the head of a college or school. **2** a sum of money that is invested or lent, *Interest is paid on the principal.* [same origin as *prince*]

> **Usage** Do not confuse *principal* with *principle*.

principality *noun* a country ruled by a prince.

principle *noun* **1** a general truth, belief, or rule, *She taught me the principles of*

geometry. **2** a code of conduct, *Cheating is against his principles*; *a man of principle.*
in principle in general, not in details.
on principle because of your principles of behaviour. [from Latin *principium* = source]

Usage Do not confuse *principle* with *principal.*

print[1] *verb* **1** put words or pictures on paper by using a machine. **2** write with letters that are not joined together. **3** press a mark or design on a surface. **4** make a picture from the negative of a photograph. **printer** *noun*

print[2] *noun* **1** printed lettering or words. **2** a mark made by something pressing on a surface. **3** a printed picture, photograph, or design.

printed circuit *noun* an electric circuit made by pressing thin metal strips on to a surface.

printout *noun* material produced in printed form by a computer.

prior[1] *adjective* earlier or more important than something else.

prior[2] *noun* a monk who is the head of a religious house or order. **prioress** *noun* [Latin, = former, more important]

prioritise *verb* (**prioritised, prioritising**) give priority to.

priority *noun* (*plural* **priorities**) **1** being earlier or more important than something else; precedence. **2** something considered more important than other things, *Safety is a priority.* [from *prior*]

priory *noun* (*plural* **priories**) a religious house governed by a prior or prioress.

prise *verb* (**prised, prising**) lever something out or open, *Prise the lid off the crate.*

prism (*say* **priz**-uhm) *noun* **1** a solid shape with ends that are triangles or polygons that are equal and parallel. **2** a glass prism that breaks up light into the colours of the rainbow. **prismatic** *adjective*

prison *noun* a place where criminals are kept as a punishment.

prisoner *noun* **1** a person kept in prison. **2** a captive.

prissy *adjective* (**prissier, prissiest**) prim, prudish. **prissily** *adverb*, **prissiness** *noun*

pristine *adjective* ancient and unspoilt; original, *in its pristine form.* [from Latin *pristinus* = former]

private[1] *adjective* **1** belonging to a particular person or group, *private property.* **2** confidential. **3** secluded. **4** not holding public office, *a private citizen.* **5** independent; not organised by a government, *private enterprise.* **privacy** *noun*, **privately** *adverb*
in private where only particular people can see or hear; not in public.

private[2] *noun* a soldier of the lowest rank.

private school *noun* a non-government school funded mainly by pupils' fees. Also called an *independent school.*

privation *noun* loss or lack of something; lack of necessities. [from Latin *privatus* = deprived]

privatise *verb* (**privatised, privatising**) transfer a business, industry, or service from public to private ownership and control. **privatisation** *noun*

privet *noun* an evergreen shrub with small leaves, used to make hedges.

privilege *noun* a special right or advantage given to one person or group. **privileged** *adjective* [from Latin *privus* = of an individual, + *legis* = of law]

privy *adjective* (*old use*) hidden; secret.
privy to sharing in the knowledge of something secret or private. [from Latin, = private]

prize[1] *noun* **1** an award given to the winner of a game or competition. **2** something striven for or worth striving for.

prize[2] *verb* (**prized, prizing**) value something greatly. [from *price*]

pro[1] *noun* (*plural* **pros**) (*informal*) a professional.

pro[2] *preposition* in favour of.

pro[3] *noun* a reason for or in favour of something.
pros and cons reasons for and against something. [from Latin *pro* = for, + *contra* = against]

pro- *prefix* **1** favouring or supporting (as in *pro-life*). **2** deputising or substituted for (as in *pronoun*). **3** onwards; forwards (as in *proceed*). [from Latin *pro* = for; in front of]

proactive *adjective* taking the initiative.

probability *noun* **1** the state or condition of being probable. **2** the likelihood of something happening. **3** (in mathematics) the extent to which an event is likely to occur, measured by the ratio of the favourable cases to the whole number of cases possible.

probable *adjective* likely to happen or be true. **probably** *adverb* [same origin as *prove*]

probate *noun* the official process of proving that a person's will is valid. [from Latin *probatum* = tested, proved]

probation *noun* **1** the testing of a person's character and abilities, especially at the start of a new job. **2** the supervision of an offender by an official (a **probation officer**) as an alternative to imprisonment.

probationary *adjective*, **probationer** *noun* [same origin as *prove*]

probe[1] *noun* **1** an instrument for exploring something. **2** an investigation.

probe[2] *verb* (**probed**, **probing**) **1** explore with a probe. **2** investigate. [from Latin *probare* = to test]

probity (*say* **proh**-buh-tee) *noun* honesty. [from Latin *probus* = good]

problem *noun* **1** something difficult to deal with or understand. **2** something that has to be done or answered. **problematic** or **problematical** *adjective* [from Greek, = an exercise]

proboscis (*say* pruh-**bos**-kuhs) *noun* (*plural* **proboscises**) **1** a long flexible snout. **2** an insect's long mouth-part. [from Greek *pro* = in front, + *boskein* = feed]

procedure *noun* an orderly way of doing something. **procedural** *adjective*

proceed *verb* **1** go forward or onward. **2** continue; go on with an action, *She proceeded to explain the plan.* [from *pro-* + Latin *cedere* = go]

proceedings *plural noun* **1** things that happen; activities. **2** a lawsuit.

proceeds *plural noun* the money made from a sale or show; profit.

process[1] (*say* **proh**-ses) *noun* (*plural* **processes**) **1** a series of actions for making or doing something. **2** an outgrowth.

process[2] *verb* put something through a manufacturing or other process, *processed cheese.* [same origin as *proceed*]

process[3] (*say* pruh-**ses**) *verb* go in procession. [from *procession*]

procession *noun* a number of people or vehicles moving steadily forward following each other.

processor *noun* a machine that processes things.

proclaim *verb* announce officially or publicly. **proclamation** *noun*

procrastinate *verb* (**procrastinated**, **procrastinating**) put off doing something. **procrastination** *noun*, **procrastinator** *noun* [from *pro-*, + Latin *crastinus* = of tomorrow]

procreate *verb* (**procreated**, **procreating**) produce offspring by the natural process of reproduction. **procreation** *noun*

procure *verb* (**procured**, **procuring**) obtain; acquire. **procurement** *noun* [from *pro-*, + Latin *curare* = look after]

prod *verb* (**prodded**, **prodding**) **1** poke. **2** stimulate into action. **prod** *noun*

prodigal *adjective* wasteful; extravagant. **prodigality** *noun*, **prodigally** *adverb* [from Latin *prodigus* = generous]

prodigious *adjective* **1** wonderful. **2** enormous. **prodigiously** *adverb*

prodigy *noun* (*plural* **prodigies**) **1** a person with wonderful abilities. **2** a wonderful thing. [from Latin *prodigium* = good omen]

produce[1] (*say* pruh-**dyoos**) *verb* (**produced**, **producing**) **1** make or create something; bring into existence. **2** bring out so that it can be seen. **3** organise the performance of a play, making of a film, etc. **4** extend a line further, *Produce the base of the triangle.*

produce[2] (*say* **prod**-yoos) *noun* things produced, especially by farmers. [from *pro-*, + Latin *ducere* = to lead]

producer *noun* **1** a person, company, or country that makes, grows, or supplies goods or commodities for sale. **2** a person or thing that makes or causes something. **3** a person who produces a play or film or other entertainment.

product *noun* **1** something produced. **2** the result of multiplying two numbers. (Compare **quotient**.)

production *noun* **1** producing. **2** the thing or amount produced.

productive *adjective* **1** producing a lot of things. **2** profitable; useful. **productivity** *noun*

profane[1] *adjective* irreverent; blasphemous. **profanely** *adverb*, **profanity** *noun*

profane[2] *verb* (**profaned**, **profaning**) treat irreverently. [from Latin *profanus* = outside the temple]

profess *verb* **1** declare. **2** claim; pretend, *She professed interest in our work.* **professedly** *adverb*

profession *noun* **1** an occupation that needs special education and training, *The professions include being a doctor, nurse, or lawyer.* **2** a declaration, *They made professions of loyalty.*

professional *adjective* **1** of a profession. **2** doing a certain kind of work as a full-time job for payment, not as an amateur, *a professional footballer.* **professional** *noun*, **professionally** *adverb*

professor *noun* a university lecturer of the highest rank. **professorship** *noun*

proffer *verb & noun* offer. [from *pro-* + *offer*]

proficient *adjective* doing something properly because of training or practice; skilled. **proficiency** *noun* [from Latin *proficiens* = making progress]

profile *noun* **1** a side view of a person's face. **2** a short description of a person's character or career.
keep a low profile not make yourself noticeable.

profiling *noun* psychological and other assessments of a person to determine their likelihood of doing something.

profit[1] *noun* **1** the extra money obtained by selling something for more than it cost to buy or make. **2** an advantage gained by doing something. **profitable** *adjective*, **profitably** *noun*

profit[2] *verb* (**profited, profiting**) get a profit.

profiteer *noun* a person who makes a great profit unfairly. **profiteering** *noun*

profiterole *noun* a small ball of soft, sweet pastry filled with cream and covered with chocolate sauce. [French]

profligate *adjective* wasteful; unrestrained. **profligacy** *noun*

profound *adjective* **1** very deep or intense, *We take a profound interest in it.* **2** showing or needing great study. **profoundly** *adverb*, **profundity** *noun* [from Latin *profundus* = deep]

profuse *adjective* lavish; plentiful. **profusely** *adverb*, **profuseness** *noun*, **profusion** *noun* [from *pro-*, + Latin *fusum* = poured]

progenitor *noun* an ancestor.

progeny (*say* **proj**-uh-nee) *noun* offspring; descendants.

prognosis (*say* prog-**noh**-suhs) *noun* (*plural* **prognoses**) a forecast or prediction, especially about a disease. **prognostication** *noun* [from Greek *pro-* = before, + *gnosis* = knowing]

program[1] *noun* (also **programme**) **1** a list of planned events; a leaflet giving details of a play, concert, or other event. **2** a radio or television broadcast. **3** (always **program**) a series of coded instructions for a computer to carry out. **programmer** *noun* [from Greek *programma* = public notice]

program[2] *verb* (**programmed, programming**) prepare a computer by means of a program.

progress[1] (*say* **proh**-gres) *noun* **1** forward movement; an advance. **2** a development or improvement.

progress[2] (*say* pruh-**gres**) *verb* make progress. **progression** *noun* [from *pro-*, + Latin *gressus* = going]

progressive *adjective* **1** moving forward. **2** proceeding step by step. **3** favouring rapid progress or reform.

prohibit *verb* (**prohibited, prohibiting**) forbid; ban, *Smoking is prohibited.* **prohibition** *noun* [from Latin, = keep off]

prohibitive *adjective* **1** prohibiting. **2** (of prices) so high that people will not buy things.

project[1] (*say* **proj**-ekt or **proh**-jekt) *noun* **1** a plan or scheme. **2** the task of finding out as much as you can about something and writing about it.

project[2] (*say* pruh-**jekt**) *verb* **1** stick out. **2** throw outwards. **3** show a picture on a screen. **4** forecast. **projection** *noun* [from *pro-*, + Latin *-jectum* = thrown]

projectile *noun* a missile.

projectionist *noun* a person who works a projector.

projector *noun* a machine for showing films or photographs on a screen.

proletariat (*say* proh-luh-**tair**-ree-uht) *noun* working people. **proletarian** *adjective & noun*

proliferate *verb* (**proliferated, proliferating**) increase rapidly in numbers. **proliferation** *noun* [from Latin *proles* = offspring, + *ferre* = to bear]

prolific *adjective* producing much fruit or many flowers or other things. **prolifically** *adverb*

prologue (*say* **proh**-log) *noun* an introduction to a poem, play, or book; an act or event serving as an introduction. [from Greek *pro-* = before, + *logos* = speech]

prolong *verb* make a thing longer or make it last for a long time. **prolongation** *noun*

prom *noun* (*informal*) **1** a promenade concert. **2** (*American*) a formal dance, especially one held at the end of high school or college.

promenade (*say* prom-uh-**nahd**) *noun* **1** a place suitable for walking, especially beside the seashore. **2** a leisurely walk. **promenade** *verb* [from French *se promener* = to walk]

promenade concert *noun* a concert where part of the audience may stand or walk about.

prominent *adjective* **1** sticking out; projecting. **2** conspicuous. **3** important. **prominence** *noun*, **prominently** *adverb*

promiscuous *adjective* **1** indiscriminate. **2** having many casual sexual relationships. **promiscuity** *noun*, **promiscuously** *adverb*

promise[1] *noun* **1** a statement that you will definitely do or not do something. **2** an indication of future success or good results, *His work shows promise.*

promise[2] *verb* (**promised, promising**) make a promise.

promising *adjective* likely to be good or successful, *a promising pianist.*

promo (*say* **proh**-moh) *noun* (*plural* **promos**) (*informal*) an advertisement; publicity. [short for *promotion*]

promontory *noun* (*plural* **promontories**) a piece of high land that sticks out into a sea or lake.

promote *verb* (**promoted, promoting**) **1** move a person to a higher rank or position. **2** help the progress of something. **3** publicise a product. **promoter** *noun*, **promotion** *noun* [from *pro-*, + Latin *motum* = moved]

prompt[1] *adjective* **1** without delay, *a prompt reply.* **2** punctual. **promptitude** *noun*, **promptly** *adverb*, **promptness** *noun*

prompt[2] *verb* **1** cause or encourage a person to do something. **2** remind an actor or speaker of words when they have forgotten them. **prompter** *noun* [from Latin *promptum* = produced]

promulgate *verb* (**promulgated**, **promulgating**) make known to the public; proclaim. **promulgation** *noun*

prone *adjective* lying face downwards. (The opposite is **supine** 1.)
be prone to be likely to do or suffer something, *He is prone to headaches.*

prong *noun* a spike of a fork. **pronged** *adjective*

pronoun *noun* a word used instead of a noun. **demonstrative pronouns** are *this*, *that*, *these*, *those*; **indefinite pronouns** are *anything*, *something*, *anyone*, *everyone*, etc.; **interrogative pronouns** are *who? what? which?*, etc.; **personal pronouns** are *I*, *me*, *we*, *us*, *thou*, *thee*, *you*, *ye*, *he*, *him*, *she*, *her*, *it*, *they*, *them*; **possessive pronouns** are *my*, *mine*, *your*, *yours*, *their*, *theirs*, etc.; **reflexive pronouns** are *myself*, *yourself*, etc.; **relative pronouns** are *who*, *what*, *which*, *that*.

pronounce *verb* (**pronounced**, **pronouncing**) **1** say a sound or word in a particular way, *'Two' is pronounced like 'too'*. **2** declare formally, *I now pronounce you man and wife.* [from *pro-*, + Latin *nuntiare* = announce]

pronounced *adjective* noticeable, *She walks with a pronounced limp.*

pronouncement *noun* a declaration.

pronunciation (*say* pruh-nun-see-**ay**-shuhn) *noun* **1** the way a word is pronounced. **2** the way a person pronounces words.

proof[1] *noun* **1** a fact or thing that shows something is true. **2** a trial impression of printed matter, produced so that corrections can be made.

proof[2] *adjective* able to resist something or not be penetrated, *a bulletproof vest.*

proofread *verb* read and correct printed proofs or a draft document. **proofreader** *noun*

prop[1] *noun* a support, especially one made of a long piece of wood or metal.

prop[2] *verb* (**propped**, **propping**) support something by leaning it against something else.

prop[3] *noun* (*Australian*) a sudden stop by a horse when galloping. **prop** *verb*

prop[4] *noun* a movable object used on a theatre stage or in a film. [from *property*]

propaganda *noun* publicity intended to make people believe something.

propagate *verb* (**propagated**, **propagating**) **1** breed; reproduce. **2** spread news or ideas. **3** transmit. **propagation** *noun*, **propagator** *noun*

propel *verb* (**propelled**, **propelling**) push something forward. [from *pro-*, + Latin *pellere* = to drive]

propellant *noun* a substance that propels things, *Liquid fuel is the propellant used in these rockets.*

propeller *noun* a device with blades that spin round to drive an aircraft or ship.

propensity *noun* (*plural* **propensities**) a tendency.

proper *adjective* **1** suitable; right, *the proper way to hold a bat.* **2** respectable, *prim and proper.* **3** (*informal*) complete; great, *You're a proper nuisance!* **properly** *adverb* [from Latin *proprius* = your own]

proper fraction *noun* a fraction that is less than 1, with the numerator less than the denominator, e.g. ⅔.

proper noun see **noun**.

property *noun* (*plural* **properties**) **1** a thing or things that belong to somebody. **2** a building or someone's land. **3** a quality or characteristic. **4** a movable object (other than furniture or scenery) used on stage during a performance of a play. [same origin as *proper*]

prophecy (*say* **prof**-uh-see) *noun* (*plural* **prophecies**) **1** a statement that prophesies something. **2** the action of prophesying.

prophesy (*say* **prof**-uh-suy) *verb* (**prophesied**, **prophesying**) forecast; foretell. [from Greek *pro* = before, + *phanai* = speak]

prophet *noun* **1** a person who makes prophecies. **2** a religious teacher who is believed to be inspired by God. **3** (**the Prophet**) Muhammad, who founded the Muslim faith. **prophetess** *noun*, **prophetic** *adjective*

propinquity *noun* nearness.

propitiate (*say* pruh-**pish**-ee-ayt) *verb* (**propitiated**, **propitiating**) win a person's favour or forgiveness. **propitiation** *noun*, **propitiatory** *adjective*

propitious (*say* pruh-**pish**-uhs) *adjective* favourable.

proponent (*say* pruh-**poh**-nuhnt) *noun* the person who puts forward a proposal. [from *pro-*, + Latin *ponere* = to place]

proportion *noun* **1** a part or share of a whole thing. **2** a ratio. **3** the correct relationship in size, amount, or importance between two things. **proportional** *adjective*, **proportionally** *adverb*, **proportionate** *adjective* [from *pro-* + *portion*]

proportional representation *noun* a system in which each political party has a number of Members of Parliament in proportion to the number of votes for all its candidates.

proportions *plural noun* size, *a ship of large proportions.*

propose *verb* (**proposed, proposing**) **1** put forward for consideration. **2** have and declare as one's intention, *we propose to wait.* **3** ask a person to marry you. **proposal** *noun* [from *pro-*, + Latin *positum* = put]

proposition *noun* **1** a suggestion. **2** a statement. **3** (*informal*) an undertaking; a matter, *a difficult proposition.*

propound *verb* put forward an idea for consideration. [same origin as *propose*]

proprietary (*say* pruh-**pruy**-uh-tuh-ree) *adjective* **1** made or sold by one firm; branded, *proprietary medicines.* **2** of an owner or ownership. [same origin as *property*]

proprietary company *noun* (*Australian*) a private company with a restricted membership and no public share issue.

proprietary name *noun* the name of a product or service registered by its owner as a trademark and not able to be used by others without permission.

proprietor *noun* the owner of a shop or business. **proprietress** *noun*

propriety (*say* pruh-**pruy**-uh-tee) *noun* (*plural* **proprieties**) **1** being proper. **2** correct behaviour.

propulsion *noun* propelling something.

pro rata (*say* proh **rah**-ta) *adjective & adverb* proportional; proportionally, *if costs increase, there will be a pro rata increase in prices; prices will increase pro rata.* [Latin, = according to the rate]

prorogue *verb* (**prorogued, proroguing**) stop the meetings of parliament temporarily without dissolving it. **prorogation** *noun* [from Latin *prorogare* = prolong]

prosaic *adjective* plain or dull and ordinary. **prosaically** *adverb* [from *prose*]

proscenium (*say* pruh-**see**-nee-uhm) *noun* the part of a theatre stage in front of the curtain, with its enclosing arch. [from Greek *pro* = before, + *skene* = stage]

prosciutto (*say* pruh-**shoo**-toh) *noun* Italian cured ham. [Italian]

proscribe *verb* (**proscribed, proscribing**) forbid by law. [from Latin *proscribere* = to outlaw]

> **Usage** Do not confuse *proscribe* with *prescribe.*

prose *noun* writing or speech that is not in verse.

prosecute *verb* (**prosecuted, prosecuting**) **1** make someone go to a lawcourt to be tried for a crime. **2** perform; carry on, *prosecuting their trade.* **prosecution** *noun*, **prosecutor** *noun* [from Latin *prosecutus* = pursued]

proselyte *noun* a person converted, especially recently, from one opinion, religion, or party to another.

prosody (*say* **pros**-uh-dee) *noun* **1** the patterns of rhythm and sound used in poetry. **2** the patterns of stress and intonation in a language. **3** the theory or study of prosody.

prospect[1] (*say* **pros**-pekt) *noun* **1** a possibility, *There is no prospect of success.* **2** a wide view.

prospect[2] (*say* pruh-**spekt**) *verb* explore in search of something, *prospecting for gold.* **prospector** *noun* [from Latin *pro* = forward, + *spectere* = to look]

prospective *adjective* expected to be or to happen; possible, *prospective customers.*

prospectus *noun* (*plural* **prospectuses**) a booklet describing and advertising something, especially an educational institution or business company.

prosper *verb* be successful.

prosperous *adjective* successful; rich. **prosperity** *noun*

prostate *noun* a gland surrounding the neck of the bladder in male mammals and releasing a fluid forming part of the semen.

prostitute *noun* a person who takes part in sexual acts for payment. **prostitution** *noun* [from Latin, = for sale]

prostrate[1] *adjective* lying face downwards.

prostrate[2] *verb* (**prostrated, prostrating**) cause to be prostrate. **prostration** *noun* [from Latin *prostratum* = laid flat]

protagonist *noun* **1** the leading character or one of the major characters in a play, film, novel, etc. **2** the main figure or one of the most prominent figures in a situation. [from *proto-*, + Greek *agonistes* = actor]

protect *verb* keep safe from harm or injury. **protection** *noun*, **protective** *adjective*, **protector** *noun* [from *pro-*, + Latin *tectum* = covered]

protectorate *noun* a country that is under the official protection of a stronger country.

protégé (*say* **prot**-uh-*zh*ay or **proh**-tuh-*zh*ay) *noun* a person who is given helpful protection or encouragement by another. [French, = protected]

protein *noun* a substance that is found in all living things and is an essential part of the food of animals.

protest[1] (*say* **proh**-test) *noun* **1** a statement or action showing that you disapprove of something. **2** an organised public demonstration expressing strong objection to something, *There was a large protest on the weekend against the new coalmine.*

protest² (*say* pruh-**test**) *verb* **1** make a protest. **2** declare firmly, *They protested their innocence.* **protestation** *noun*, **protester** *noun* [from *pro-*, + Latin *testari* = say on oath]

Protestant *noun* a member of any of the western Christian Churches separated from the Roman Catholic Church. [because in the 16th century many people protested (= declared firmly) their opposition to the Catholic Church]

proto- *prefix* first. [from Greek *protos* = first or earliest]

protocol *noun* **1** etiquette connected with people's rank. **2** a formal international agreement. **3** (in computing) the set of rules governing the exchange or transmission of data electronically between devices.

proton *noun* a particle of matter with a positive electric charge.

prototype *noun* the first model of something, from which others are copied or developed. [from *proto-* + *type*]

protract *verb* prolong in time; lengthen. **protraction** *noun* [from *pro-*, + Latin *tractum* = drawn out]

protractor *noun* a device for measuring angles, usually a semicircle marked off in degrees.

protrude *verb* (**protruded**, **protruding**) project; stick out. **protrusion** *noun* [from *pro-*, + Latin *trudere* = push]

protuberance *noun* a protuberant part.

protuberant *adjective* sticking out from a surface. [from *pro-*, + Latin *tuber* = a swelling]

proud *adjective* **1** very pleased with yourself or with someone else who has done well. **2** causing pride, *This is a proud moment for us.* **3** full of self-respect and independence, *They were too proud to ask for help.* **4** having an unduly high opinion of your own merits or importance. **proudly** *adverb* [from Old French *prud* = brave]

prove *verb* (**proved** or **proven**, **proving**) **1** show that something is true. **2** turn out, *The forecast proved to be correct.* **provable** *adjective* [from Latin *probare* = to test]

proven *adjective* **1** demonstrated by evidence or argument to be true or existing, *a proven ability to work hard.* **2** (of a new method, system, or treatment) tried and tested, *a system based on proven technologies.*

provender *noun* fodder; food.

proverb *noun* a short well-known saying that states a truth, e.g. 'Many hands make light work'. [from *pro-*, + Latin *verbum* = word]

proverbial *adjective* **1** of or in a proverb. **2** well-known.

provide *verb* (**provided**, **providing**) **1** make something available; supply. **2** prepare for something, *Try to provide against emergencies.* **provider** *noun* [from Latin *providere* = foresee]

provided *conjunction* on condition, *You can stay provided that you help.*

providence *noun* **1** being provident. **2** God's or nature's care and protection.

provident *adjective* wisely providing for the future; thrifty. [same origin as *provide*]

providential *adjective* happening very luckily. **providentially** *adverb*

providing *conjunction* provided.

province *noun* **1** a section of a country. **2** the area of a person's special knowledge or responsibility, *Teaching you to swim is not my province.* **provincial** *adjective*
the provinces the parts of a country outside its capital city.

provision *noun* **1** providing something. **2** a statement in a document, *the provisions of the treaty.*

provisional *adjective* arranged or agreed upon temporarily but possibly to be altered later. **provisionally** *adverb*

provisional licence *noun* (*Australian*) an initial driver's licence that imposes certain restrictions.

provisions *plural noun* supplies of food and drink.

proviso (*say* pruh-**vuy**-zoh) *noun* (*plural* **provisos**) a requirement before agreeing to something.

provoke *verb* (**provoked**, **provoking**) **1** make a person angry. **2** arouse; stimulate, *The joke provoked laughter.* **provocation** *noun*, **provocative** *adjective* [from *pro-*, + Latin *vocare* = summon]

provost *noun* **1** the head of certain colleges or schools. **2** the head of a chapter etc. of certain religious foundations. **3** (**provost marshal**) the head of military police in camp or on active service.

prow *noun* the front end of a ship.

prowess *noun* **1** great ability. **2** daring.

prowl *verb* move about quietly or cautiously. **prowl** *noun*, **prowler** *noun*

proximity *noun* **1** nearness. **2** the part near something, *in the proximity of the station.* [from Latin *proximus* = nearest]

proxy *noun* (*plural* **proxies**) a person authorised to represent or act for another person.

prude *noun* a person who is easily shocked by sexual matters. **prudery** *noun*, **prudish** *adjective*

prudent *adjective* careful, not rash or reckless. **prudence** *noun*, **prudently** *adverb* [same origin as *provide*]

prune[1] *noun* a dried plum.

prune[2] *verb* (**pruned, pruning**) **1** cut off unwanted parts of a tree or bush. **2** shorten or reduce and improve something by removing unnecessary parts.

pry *verb* (**pried, prying**) look or ask inquisitively.

PS *abbreviation* postscript.

psalm (*say* sahm) *noun* a religious song, especially one from the Book of Psalms in the Bible. **psalmist** *noun* [from Greek, = song sung to the harp]

pseudo- (*say* **syoo**-doh) *prefix* false; pretended. [Greek, = false]

pseudonym *noun* a fictitious name used by an author. [from *pseudo-*, + Greek *onyma* = name]

psoriasis (*say* suh-**ruy**-uh-suhs) *noun* a skin disease causing red scaly patches. [from Greek *psora* = itch]

psych (*say* suyk) *verb* **psych yourself up** (*informal*) prepare yourself psychologically for something.

psyche (*say* **suy**-kee) *noun* the human soul, spirit, or mind. [Greek]

psychiatrist (*say* suy-**kuy**-uh-truhst) *noun* a doctor who treats mental illnesses. **psychiatric** *adjective*, **psychiatry** *noun* [from *psycho-*, + Greek *iatreia* = healing]

psychic (*say* **suy**-kik) *adjective* **1** of powers or events that seem to be supernatural. **2** of the mind or soul. **psychical** *adjective* [same origin as *psycho-*]

psycho- *prefix* of the mind. [from Greek *psyche* = life or soul]

psychoanalysis *noun* investigation of a person's mental processes, especially in psychotherapy.

psychology *noun* the study of the mind and how it works. **psychological** *adjective*, **psychologist** *noun* [from *psycho-* + *-logy*]

psychopath *noun* a person suffering from a severe mental disorder, especially with aggressive antisocial behaviour. **psychopathic** *adjective*

psychotherapy *noun* treatment of mental illness by psychological methods.

pterodactyl (*say* te-ruh-**dak**-tuhl) *noun* an extinct reptile with wings. [from Greek *pteron* = wing, + *daktylos* = finger]

PTO *abbreviation* please turn over.

Pty *abbreviation* proprietary.

pub *noun* (*informal*) a place licensed to serve alcoholic drinks to the public.

puberty (*say* **pyoo**-buh-tee) *noun* the time when a young person is developing physically into an adult.

pubic (*say* **pyoo**-bik) *adjective* of the lower front part of the abdomen.

public[1] *adjective* belonging to or known by everyone, not private. **publicly** *adverb*

public[2] *noun* all the people. **in public** openly, not in private. [from Latin *publicus* = of the people]

publican *noun* the person in charge of a pub; a hotel-keeper.

publication *noun* **1** publishing. **2** something published, e.g. a book or a newspaper.

publicise *verb* (**publicised, publicising**) bring something to people's attention; advertise.

publicity *noun* **1** public attention. **2** doing things (e.g. advertising) to draw people's attention to something.

public school *noun* a school funded and run by the state or territory. Also called a *government school*.

public servant *noun* (*Australian*) an employee of the public service.

public service *noun* (*Australian*) people employed by the government in various departments other than the armed forces.

publish *verb* **1** prepare and issue a book, journal, piece of music, etc. for public sale, distribution, or readership. **2** make content available online. **3** announce something in public. **publisher** *noun* [from *public*]

puce *noun* brownish-purple colour. [French, = flea-colour]

puck *noun* a hard rubber disc used in ice hockey.

pucker *verb* wrinkle. **pucker** *noun*

pudding *noun* a sweet or savoury cooked food, especially one containing flour, milk, and eggs, *sticky date pudding*; *Yorkshire pudding*.

puddle *noun* a shallow patch of liquid, especially of rainwater on a road.

pudgy *adjective* podgy.

puerile (*say* **pyoor**-ruyl) *adjective* silly and childish. **puerility** *noun* [from Latin *puer* = boy]

puff[1] *noun* **1** a short blowing of breath, wind, or smoke. **2** a soft pad for putting powder on the skin. **3** a cake of very light pastry filled with cream.

puff[2] *verb* **1** blow out puffs of smoke etc. **2** breathe with difficulty; pant. **3** inflate or swell something, *He puffed out his chest.*

puffin *noun* a sea bird with a large striped beak.

puffy *adjective* puffed out; swollen. **puffiness** *noun*

pug *noun* a small dog with a flat face like a bulldog.

pugilist (*say* **pyoo**-juh-luhst) *noun* a boxer.

pugnacious *adjective* wanting to fight; aggressive. **pugnaciously** *adverb*, **pugnacity** *noun* [from Latin *pugnare* = to fight]

puke *verb* (**puked**, **puking**) (*informal*) vomit.

pull *verb* **1** make a thing come towards or after you by using force on it. **2** move by a driving force, *The car pulled out into the road.* **3** damage a muscle by abnormal strain. **pull** *noun*
pull a face make a strange face.
pull off achieve something.
pull somebody's leg deceive them playfully.
pull through recover from an illness.
pull up stop.
pull yourself together become calm or sensible.

pullet *noun* a young hen.

pulley *noun* (*plural* **pulleys**) a wheel with a rope, chain, or belt over it, used for lifting or moving heavy things.

pullover *noun* a knitted garment (with no fastenings) for the top half of the body.

pulmonary (*say* **pul**-muh-nuh-ree) *adjective* of the lungs. [from Latin *pulmo* = lung]

pulp *noun* **1** the soft moist part of fruit. **2** any soft moist mass. **pulpy** *adjective*

pulpit *noun* a small enclosed platform for the preacher in a church or chapel. [from Latin *pulpitum* = platform]

pulsate *verb* (**pulsated**, **pulsating**) expand and contract rhythmically; vibrate. **pulsation** *noun*

pulse[1] *noun* **1** the rhythmical movement of the arteries as blood is pumped through them by the beating of the heart, *The pulse can be felt in a person's wrists.* **2** a throb.

pulse[2] *verb* (**pulsed**, **pulsing**) throb. [from Latin *pulsum* = driven, beaten]

pulse[3] *noun* the edible seed of peas, beans, lentils, and other legumes.

pulverise *verb* (**pulverised**, **pulverising**) crush into powder. **pulverisation** *noun* [from Latin *pulveris* = of dust]

puma (*say* **pyoo**-muh) *noun* a large wild American animal of the cat family. Also called a *cougar* or *mountain lion.*

pumice *noun* a kind of porous volcanic rock used for rubbing stains from the skin or as powder for polishing things.

pummel *verb* (**pummelled**, **pummelling**) keep on hitting something.

pump[1] *noun* a device that pushes air or liquid into or out of something, or along pipes.

pump[2] *verb* **1** move air or liquid with a pump. **2** fill something such as a tyre or balloon with liquid or gas using a pump; inflate. **3** move vigorously up and down. **4** (*informal*) question a person to obtain information.
pump up inflate.

pumpkin *noun* a large round fruit with a hard skin and orange-coloured flesh, cooked as a vegetable.

pun[1] *noun* the humorous use of a word to suggest different meanings, or of words of the same sound and different meanings, e.g. 'Deciding where to bury him was a *grave* decision'.

pun[2] *verb* (**punned**, **punning**) make a pun or puns.

punch[1] *verb* **1** hit with a fist. **2** make a hole in something.

punch[2] *noun* (*plural* **punches**) **1** a hit with a fist. **2** a device for making holes in paper, metal, or leather. **3** vigour. [same origin as *puncture*]

punch[3] *noun* a drink made by mixing wine or spirits and fruit juice in a bowl.

punchline *noun* words that give the climax of a joke or story.

punch-up *noun* (*informal*) a fight.

punctilious *adjective* very careful about details; conscientious. **punctiliously** *adverb*, **punctiliousness** *noun* [from Latin *punctillum* = little point]

punctual *adjective* doing things exactly at the time arranged; not late. **punctuality** *noun*, **punctually** *adverb*

punctuate *verb* (**punctuated**, **punctuating**) **1** put punctuation marks into something. **2** put in at intervals, *Her speech was punctuated with cheers.* [from Latin *punctum* = a point]

punctuation *noun* **1** marks such as commas, full stops, and brackets put into a piece of writing to make it easier to read. **2** the action of punctuating.

puncture[1] *noun* a small hole made by something sharp, especially in a tyre.

puncture[2] *verb* (**punctured**, **puncturing**) make a puncture in something. [from Latin *punctum* = pricked]

pundit *noun* a person who is an authority on something. [from Hindi *pandit* = learned (person)]

pungent (*say* **pun**-juhnt) *adjective* **1** having a strong taste or smell. **2** (of remarks) sharp. **pungency** *noun*, **pungently** *adverb* [from Latin *pungens* = pricking]

punish *verb* make a person suffer because they have done something wrong. **punishable** *adjective*, **punishment** *noun* [from Latin *poena* = penalty]

punitive (*say* **pyoo**-nuh-tiv) *adjective* inflicting punishment.

Punjabi *noun* **1** a person from the Punjab region of north-western India and Pakistan. **2** a language spoken in this region.

punk *noun* **1** (in full **punk rock**) a loud, fast-moving, and aggressive form of rock music. **2** a follower or performer of punk. **3** a young hooligan or thug.

punnet *noun* a small container for soft fruit such as strawberries.

punt[1] *noun* a flat-bottomed boat, usually moved by pushing a pole against the bottom of a river while standing in the punt.

punt[2] *verb* move a punt with a pole.

punt[3] *verb* kick a football after dropping it from your hands and before it touches the ground.

punt[4] *verb* gamble; bet on a horserace. **punt** *noun*, **punter** *noun*

puny (*say* **pyoo**-nee) *adjective* (**punier, puniest**) small or undersized; feeble.

pup *noun* **1** a puppy. **2** a young seal.

pupa (*say* **pyoo**-puh) *noun* (*plural* **pupae**) a chrysalis.

pupate (*say* pyoo-**payt**) *verb* (**pupated, pupating**) become a pupa. **pupation** *noun*

pupil *noun* **1** someone who is being taught by another person. **2** the opening in the centre of the eye. [from Latin *pupilla* = little girl or doll (the use of sense 2 refers to the tiny images of people and things that can be seen in the eye)]

puppet *noun* **1** a kind of doll that can be made to move by fitting it over your hand or working it by strings or wires. **2** a person whose actions are controlled by someone else. **puppetry** *noun*

puppy *noun* (*plural* **puppies**) a young dog.

purchase[1] *verb* (**purchased, purchasing**) buy. **purchaser** *noun*

purchase[2] *noun* **1** something bought. **2** buying. **3** a firm hold to pull or raise something.

purdah *noun* the Muslim or Hindu custom of keeping women from the sight of men or strangers. [Urdu, = veil]

pure *adjective* **1** not mixed with anything else; clean. **2** free from evil or sin. **3** mere; nothing but, *pure nonsense.* **purely** *adverb*, **pureness** *noun*

purée (*say* **pyoo**-ray) *noun* fruit or vegetables made into pulp. [French, = squeezed]

purgative *noun* a strong laxative.

purgatory *noun* (in Roman Catholic belief) a place or condition in which souls are purified by punishment. [same origin as *purge*]

purge[1] *verb* (**purged, purging**) get rid of unwanted people or things.

purge[2] *noun* **1** purging. **2** a purgative. [from Latin *purgare* = make pure]

purify *verb* (**purified, purifying**) make a thing pure. **purification** *noun*, **purifier** *noun*

purist *noun* a person who likes things to be exactly right, especially in people's use of words.

puritan *noun* **1** (**Puritan**) a Protestant in the 16th and 17th centuries who wanted simpler religious ceremonies and strictly moral behaviour. **2** a person with very strict morals. **puritanical** *adjective* [from Latin *puritas* = purity]

purity *noun* pureness.

purl *noun* a knitting stitch that makes a ridge towards the knitter. **purl** *verb* [from Scottish *pirl* = twist]

purloin *verb* take something without permission.

purple *noun* deep reddish-blue colour. **purple** *adjective*

purport[1] (*say* per-**pawt**) *verb* claim, *The letter purports to be from the council.* **purportedly** *adverb*

purport[2] (*say* **per**-pawt) *noun* meaning.

purpose *noun* **1** what you intend to do; a plan or aim. **2** determination. **purposeful** *adjective*, **purposefully** *adverb*, **purposeless** *adjective*
on purpose by intention, not by accident. [same origin as *propose*]

purposely *adverb* on purpose.

purr *verb* make the low murmuring sound that a cat does when it is pleased. **purr** *noun*

purse[1] *noun* a small pouch for carrying money.

purse[2] *verb* (**pursed, pursing**) draw into folds, *She pursed her lips.* [from Latin *bursa* = a bag]

purser *noun* a ship's officer in charge of accounts. [from *purse*]

pursue *verb* (**pursued, pursuing**) **1** chase in order to catch or kill. **2** continue with something; work at, *We are pursuing our enquiries.* **pursuer** *noun*

pursuit *noun* **1** the action of pursuing. **2** a regular activity.

purvey *verb* (**purveyed, purveying**) supply food, drink, or other goods as a trade. **purveyor** *noun* [same origin as *provide*]

pus *noun* a thick yellowish substance produced in inflamed or infected tissue, e.g. in an abscess or boil.

push[1] *verb* **1** make a thing go away from you by using force on it. **2** move yourself by using force, *He pushed in front of me.* **3** try to force someone to do or use something; urge.
push off (*informal*) go away.

push² *noun* (*plural* **pushes**) **1** a pushing movement or effort. **2** (*Australian*) a gang.
at a push if necessary but only with difficulty.

pushchair *noun* a folding chair on wheels, in which a child can be pushed along.

pusher *noun* **1** a seller of illegal drugs. **2** (*Australian*) a pushchair; a stroller.

pushover *noun* (*informal*) **1** something that is easily done. **2** a person who is easily convinced or defeated.

pushy *adjective* unpleasantly self-confident and eager to do things.

pusillanimous (*say* pyoo-suh-**lan**-uh-muhs) *adjective* timid; cowardly. [from Latin *pusillus* = small, + *animus* = mind]

puss *noun* (*informal*) a cat.

pussy *noun* (*plural* **pussies**) (*informal*) a cat.

pussyfoot *verb* (*informal*) act cautiously; avoid committing yourself.

pustule *noun* a pimple containing pus.

put *verb* (**put**, **putting**) **1** move a person or thing to a place or position, *Put the lamp on the table.* **2** cause a person or thing to do or experience something or be in a certain condition, *Put the light on*; *Put her in a good mood.* **3** express in words, *She put it tactfully.* **4** estimate, *He put the cost at $500.*
be hard put have difficulty in doing something.
put by save for future use.
put down 1 suppress, *put down a rebellion.* **2** humiliate; snub. **3** kill an old or sick animal.
put forward suggest; propose.
put off 1 postpone. **2** dissuade. **3** stop someone wanting something, *The smell puts me off.*
put on 1 clothe yourself with. **2** pretend to have something, *She put on a posh voice.* **3** increase, *He has put on weight.* **4** stage a play or other event.
put out 1 stop a fire from burning or a light from shining. **2** annoy or inconvenience, *Our lateness has put her out.*
put up 1 build. **2** raise. **3** give someone a place to sleep. **4** provide, *Who will put up the money?*
put up with endure; tolerate.

putrefy (*say* **pyoo**-truh-fuy) *verb* (**putrefied**, **putrefying**) decay; rot. **putrefaction** *noun* [from Latin *puter* = rotten]

putrid (*say* **pyoo**-truhd) *adjective* **1** decomposed; rotting. **2** smelling bad.

putt *verb* hit a golf ball gently towards the hole. **putt** *noun*, **putter** *noun*

putty *noun* a soft paste that sets hard, used for fitting the glass into a window frame.

puzzle¹ *noun* **1** a difficult question; a problem. **2** a game or toy that sets a problem or difficult task. **3** a jigsaw puzzle.

puzzle² *verb* (**puzzled**, **puzzling**) **1** give someone a problem so that they have to think hard. **2** think patiently about how to solve something. **puzzlement** *noun*

pygmy (*say* **pig**-mee) *noun* (*plural* **pygmies**) **1** a member of certain peoples of very short stature in equatorial Africa and parts of south-east Asia. **2** (*derogatory*) a very small person or thing. **pygmy** *adjective*

pyjamas *plural noun* a loose jacket and trousers worn in bed. [from Urdu *pay jama* = leg-clothes]

pylon *noun* **1** a tall framework made of steel, supporting electricity cables. **2** a monumental gate-tower. [from Greek *pyle* = gate]

pyramid *noun* **1** a structure with a square base and with sloping sides that meet in a point at the top. **2** an ancient Egyptian tomb shaped like this. **pyramidal** (*say* puh-**ram**-uh-duhl) *adjective*

pyre *noun* a pile of wood or other combustible material for burning a dead body as part of a funeral ceremony. [from Greek *pyr* = fire]

pyrrhic victory (*say* **pi**-rik) *noun* a victory gained at too great a cost, like that of Pyrrhus (king of Epirus) over the Romans in 279 BC.

Pythagoras' theorem *noun* the mathematical theorem that the square on the hypotenuse of a right-angled triangle is equal to the sum of the squares on the other two sides. [named after Pythagoras, a Greek philosopher and mathematician]

python *noun* a large snake that squeezes its prey so as to suffocate it.

Qq

QC *abbreviation* Queen's Counsel.

QED *abbreviation* which was to be proved. [Latin, *quod erat demonstrandum*]

quack[1] *verb* make the harsh cry of a duck. **quack** *noun* [imitation of the sound]

quack[2] *noun* **1** a person who falsely claims to have medical skill or have remedies to cure diseases. **2** (*informal*) a doctor. [from Dutch *quacken* = to boast]

quad (*say* kwod) *noun* **1** a quadrangle. **2** a quadruplet.

quadrangle *noun* a rectangular courtyard with large buildings round it. [from *quadri-* + *angle*]

quadrant *noun* **1** a quarter of a circle. **2** each of four parts of a plane, sphere, space, or body divided by two lines or planes at right angles. **3** (*old use*) an instrument for measuring angles, especially altitudes.

quadratic *noun* (also **quadratic equation**) (in mathematics) an equation involving the square (and no higher power) of one or more of the unknown quantities or variables.

quadri- *prefix* four. [from Latin *quattuor* = four]

quadrilateral *noun* a flat geometric shape with four sides. [from *quadri-* + *lateral*]

quadriplegia *noun* paralysis of both arms and both legs. **quadriplegic** *adjective & noun* [from *quadri-* + Greek *plexis* = a stroke]

quadruped *noun* an animal with four feet. [from *quadri-*, + Latin *pedis* = of a foot]

quadruple[1] *adjective* **1** four times as much or as many. **2** having four parts.

quadruple[2] *verb* (**quadrupled, quadrupling**) make or become four times as much or as many. [from *quadri-*]

quadruplet *noun* each of four children born to the same mother at one time.

quaff (*say* kwof) *verb* drink.

quagmire *noun* a bog or marsh.

quail[1] *noun* (*plural* **quail** or **quails**) a small game bird related to the partridge.

quail[2] *verb* flinch; feel or show fear.

quaint *adjective* attractive through being unusual or old-fashioned. **quaintly** *adverb*, **quaintness** *noun*

quake[1] *verb* (**quaked, quaking**) tremble; shake with fear.

quake[2] *noun* (*informal*) an earthquake.

Quaker *noun* a member of a religious group called the Society of Friends, founded by George Fox in the 17th century.

qualify *verb* (**qualified, qualifying**) **1** make or become able to do something through having certain qualities or training, or by passing a test. **2** make a statement less extreme, limit its meaning. **3** (of an adjective) add meaning to a noun. **qualification** *noun*

qualitative *adjective* of quality as opposed to quantity, *a qualitative study.*

quality *noun* (*plural* **qualities**) **1** how good or bad something is. **2** excellence. **3** a characteristic; something that is special in a person or thing. [from Latin *qualis* = of what kind]

qualm (*say* kwahm) *noun* a misgiving; a scruple.

quandary *noun* (*plural* **quandaries**) a difficult situation where you are uncertain what to do.

quandong *noun* an Australian tree, especially one with red fruit containing an edible kernel. [from Wiradjuri *guwandhaang*]

quantify *verb* (**quantifies, quantified**) **1** determine the quantity of. **2** express as a quantity.

quantitative *adjective* of quantity as opposed to quality.

quantity *noun* (*plural* **quantities**) **1** how much there is of something; how many things there are of one sort. **2** a large amount. [from Latin *quantus* = how much]

quantum *noun* (*plural* **quanta**) a quantity or amount.

quantum mechanics *plural noun* a scientific theory assuming that energy exists in discrete units.

quarantine[1] *noun* a state, period, or place of isolation in which people or animals that have arrived from elsewhere or been exposed to infectious or contagious disease are placed. [from Italian *quaranta* = forty (the original period of isolation was 40 days)]

quarantine[2] *verb* (**quarantined, quarantining**) put a person or animal in quarantine.

quark (*say* kwahk) *noun* a hypothetical component of elementary particles.

quarrel[1] *noun* an angry disagreement.

quarrel[2] *verb* (**quarrelled, quarrelling**) have a quarrel. **quarrelsome** *adjective* [from Latin *querela* = complaint]

quarry[1] *noun* (*plural* **quarries**) an open place where stone or slate is dug or cut out of the ground.

quarry[2] *verb* (**quarried, quarrying**) dig or cut from a quarry.

quarry[3] *noun* (*plural* **quarries**) an animal being hunted or pursued; something that is being sought or pursued.

quart *noun* a liquid measure equal to a quarter of a gallon (about 1.14 litres).

quarter[1] *noun* **1** each of four equal parts into which a thing is or can be divided. **2** three months; one fourth of a year. **3** a district or region, *People came from every quarter.* **4** mercy towards an enemy, *They gave no quarter.*
at close quarters very close together.

quarter[2] *verb* **1** divide something into quarters. **2** put soldiers etc. into lodgings. [from Latin *quartus* = fourth]

quarterdeck *noun* the part of a ship's upper deck nearest the stern, usually reserved for the officers.

quarterly[1] *adjective & adverb* happening or produced once in every three months.

quarterly[2] *noun* (*plural* **quarterlies**) a quarterly magazine or other publication.

quarters *plural noun* lodgings.

quartet *noun* **1** a group of four musicians. **2** a piece of music for four musicians. **3** a set of four people or things.

quartile *noun* any of three points at which a range of statistical data is divided to make four groups of equal size; any of these groups.

quartz *noun* a hard mineral.

quasar (*say* **kway**-zah) *noun* a star-like object that is the source of intense electromagnetic radiation. [from *quasi-* + *stellar*]

quash *verb* cancel or annul something, *The judges quashed his conviction.*

quasi- (*say* **kway**-zuy or **kwah**-zee) *prefix* seeming to be something but not really so, *a quasi-scientific explanation.* [from Latin *quasi* = as if]

quatrain *noun* a stanza with four lines. [from French *quatre* = four]

quaver[1] *verb* tremble; quiver.

quaver[2] *noun* **1** a quavering sound. **2** a note in music (♪) lasting half as long as a crotchet.

quay (*say* kee) *noun* a landing place where ships can be tied up for loading and unloading; a wharf. **quayside** *noun*

queasy *adjective* feeling slightly sick. **queasily** *adverb*, **queasiness** *noun*

queen *noun* **1** a woman who is the ruler of a country through inheriting the position. **2** the wife of a king. **3** a female bee or ant that produces eggs. **4** an important piece in chess. **5** a playing card with a picture of a queen on it. **queenly** *adjective*

Queen's Counsel *noun* a senior barrister.

queer[1] *adjective* **1** strange; eccentric. **2** slightly ill or faint. **3** (*informal*) (sometimes offensive) homosexual. **queerly** *adverb*, **queerness** *noun*

queer[2] *verb*
queer someone's pitch spoil someone's plans or chances of doing something.

quell *verb* suppress; subdue.

quench *verb* **1** satisfy your thirst by drinking. **2** put out a fire or flame.

querulous (*say* **kwe**-ruh-luhs) *adjective* complaining peevishly. **querulously** *adverb* [same origin as *quarrel*]

query[1] (*say* **kweer**-ree) *noun* (*plural* **queries**) **1** a question. **2** a question mark.

query[2] *verb* (**queried, querying**) ask a question or express doubt about something. [from Latin *quaere* = ask]

quesadilla (*say* kay-suh-**dee**-yuh) *noun* a tortilla filled with cheese and heated. [Spanish]

quest *noun* a search, *the quest for gold.*

question[1] *noun* **1** a sentence asking something. **2** a matter to be discussed, *Parliament debated the question of immigration.* **3** a problem to be solved. **4** doubt, *Whether we shall win is open to question.*
in question being discussed or disputed, *Her honesty is not in question.*
out of the question impossible.

question[2] *verb* **1** ask someone questions. **2** express doubt about something. **questioner** *noun* [from Latin *quaesitum* = sought for]

questionable *adjective* causing doubt; not certainly true or honest or advisable.

question mark *noun* the punctuation mark (?) placed after a question.

questionnaire *noun* a list of questions.

question time *noun* a period in parliament when MPs may question ministers.

queue[1] (*say* kyoo) *noun* a line of people or vehicles waiting for something.

queue[2] *verb* (**queued, queuing**) wait in a queue. [from Latin *cauda* = tail]

quibble[1] *noun* a petty objection.

quibble[2] *verb* (**quibbled, quibbling**) make petty objections.

quiche (*say* keesh) *noun* an open tart with a savoury filling. [French]

quick[1] *adjective* **1** taking only a short time to do something. **2** done in a short time. **3** able to notice or learn or think quickly. **4** nimble; agile. **5** (*old use*) alive, *the quick and the dead.* **quickly** *adverb*, **quickness** *noun*

quick[2] *noun* the sensitive flesh below the nails.

quicken *verb* **1** make or become quicker. **2** stimulate; make or become livelier.

quicksand *noun* an area of loose wet sand which is so deep that heavy objects sink into it.

quicksilver *noun* mercury.

quid *noun* (*plural* **quid**) (*informal*) (in Britain and formerly in Australia) one pound.

quid pro quo (*say* kwid proh **kwoh**) *noun* something given or done in return for something. [Latin, = something for something]

quiescent (*say* kwee-**es**-uhnt) *adjective* inactive; quiet. **quiescence** *noun* [from Latin *quiescens* = becoming quiet]

quiet[1] *adjective* **1** silent, *Be quiet!* **2** with little sound; not loud or noisy. **3** calm; without disturbance; peaceful, *a quiet life.* **4** shy; reserved. **5** (of colours) not bright. **quietly** *adverb*, **quietness** *noun*

quiet[2] *noun* quietness. [from Latin *quietus* = calm]

quieten *verb* make or become quiet.

quiff *noun* an upright tuft of hair.

quill *noun* **1** a large feather. **2** a pen made from a large feather. **3** one of the spines on an echidna or porcupine.

quilt[1] *noun* a padded bed-cover.

quilt[2] *verb* line material with padding and fix it with lines of stitching.

quilt[3] *verb* (*Australian informal*) beat soundly; thrash.

quin *noun* a quintuplet.

quince *noun* a hard yellow pear-shaped fruit that has to be cooked before it can be eaten.

quinine (*say* kwin-**een**) *noun* a bitter-tasting medicine used to cure malaria.

quinoa (*say* **keen**-wah) *noun* the seed of a South American plant used as food. [from a Spanish spelling of an indigenous South American word *kinua, kinoa*]

quintessence *noun* **1** the essence of something. **2** a perfect example of a quality.

quintet *noun* **1** a group of five musicians. **2** a piece of music for five musicians. [from Latin *quintus* = fifth]

quintuplet *noun* each of five children born to the same mother at one time. [from Latin *quintus* = fifth]

quip *noun* a witty remark.

quirk *noun* **1** a peculiarity of a person's behaviour. **2** a trick of fate.

quit *verb* (**quitted** or **quit, quitting**) **1** leave. **2** abandon. **3** (*informal*) stop doing something. **quitter** *noun*

quite *adverb* **1** completely; entirely, *I am quite all right.* **2** somewhat; rather, *She is quite a good swimmer.* **3** really, *It's quite a change.*

quits *adjective* even or equal after retaliating or paying someone.

quiver[1] *noun* a container for arrows.

quiver[2] *verb* tremble. **quiver** *noun*

quixotic (*say* kwik-**sot**-ik) *adjective* very chivalrous and unselfish, often to an impractical extent. **quixotically** *adverb* [named after Don Quixote, hero of a Spanish story]

quiz[1] *noun* (*plural* **quizzes**) a series of questions, especially as an entertainment or competition.

quiz[2] *verb* (**quizzed, quizzing**) question someone closely.

quizzical *adjective* **1** in a questioning way. **2** gently amused. **quizzically** *adverb* [from *quiz*]

quoit (*say* koit) *noun* a ring thrown at a peg in the game of **quoits**.

quokka *noun* a small greyish-brown short-tailed wallaby found in Western Australia. [from Noongar *kwoka*]

quoll *noun* a small predatory Australian marsupial. Also called a *native cat.* [from Guugu Yimithirr *dhigul*]

quorum *noun* the smallest number of people that must be present at a meeting before its proceedings are valid. [Latin, = of which people]

quota *noun* **1** a fixed share that must be given or received or done. **2** a limited amount. [from Latin *quot* = how many]

quotation *noun* **1** quoting. **2** something quoted. **3** a statement of the price.

quotation marks *plural noun* punctuation marks (“ ”) or (‘ ’) put around quotations and spoken words. Also called *inverted commas.*

quote[1] *verb* (**quoted, quoting**) **1** repeat words that were first written or spoken by someone else. **2** mention something as proof. **3** state the price of goods or services that you can supply.

quote² *noun* (*informal*) **1** a passage quoted. **2** a price quoted.

quoth *verb* (*old use*) said.

quotient (*say* **kwoh**-shuhnt) *noun* the result of dividing one number by another. (Compare **product** 2.) [from Latin, = how many times]

Quran alternative spelling of **Koran**.

Rr

rabbi (*say* **rab**-uy) *noun* (*plural* **rabbis**) a Jewish religious leader. **rabbinical** *adjective* [Hebrew, = my master]

rabbit *noun* a furry animal with long ears that digs burrows.

rabble *noun* a disorderly crowd; a mob.

rabid (*say* **rab**-uhd) *adjective* **1** fanatical, *a rabid tennis fan.* **2** suffering from rabies. [from Latin *rabidus* = raving]

rabies (*say* **ray**-beez) *noun* a fatal disease that affects dogs and similar animals, transmitted to humans by the bite of an infected animal and causing madness.

raccoon *noun* (also **racoon**) an American animal with a bushy tail.

race[1] *noun* **1** a competition to be the first to reach a particular place or to do something. **2** a strong fast current of water, *the tidal race.* **3** (*Australian*) a fenced passageway for drafting sheep or cattle.

race[2] *verb* (**raced**, **racing**) **1** compete in a race. **2** move very fast. **racer** *noun*

race[3] *noun* a very large group of people thought to have the same ancestors and with physical characteristics (e.g. colour of skin and hair, shape of eyes and nose) that differ from those of other groups. **racial** *adjective*

racecourse *noun* a place where horseraces are run.

racetrack *noun* **1** a racecourse. **2** a track for motor racing.

racialism (*say* **ray**-shuh-liz-uhm) *noun* racism. **racialist** *noun*

racism (*say* **ray**-siz-uhm) *noun* **1** belief that a particular race of people is better than others. **2** hostility towards people of other races. **racist** *noun*

rack[1] *noun* **1** a framework used as a shelf or container. **2** a cogged or toothed bar or rail engaging with a wheel or pinion, or using pegs to adjust the position of something. **3** an ancient device for torturing people by stretching them.

rack[2] *verb* torment, *He was racked with pain.* **rack your brains** think hard in trying to solve a problem.

rack[3] *noun* destruction, *The place has gone to rack and ruin.*

racket[1] *noun* (also **racquet**) a bat with strings stretched across a frame used in tennis and similar games. [from Arabic *rahat* = palm of the hand]

racket[2] *noun* **1** a loud noise; a din. **2** dishonest business; a swindle.

racketeer *noun* a person involved in a dishonest business. **racketeering** *noun*

racoon *noun* see **raccoon**.

racquet alternative spelling of **racket**[1].

racy *adjective* lively in style, *She gave a racy account of her travels.*

radar *noun* a system or apparatus that uses radio waves to reveal the position of objects that cannot be seen because of darkness, fog, distance, or other obstacles. [from the initials of 'radio detection and ranging']

radial *adjective* **1** of rays or radii. **2** having spokes or lines that radiate from a central point. **radially** *adverb*

radiant *adjective* **1** giving out rays of light or heat. **2** radiated, *radiant heat.* **3** looking very bright and happy. **radiance** *noun*, **radiantly** *adverb*

radiate *verb* (**radiated**, **radiating**) **1** send out light, heat, or other energy in rays. **2** spread out from a central point like the spokes of a wheel. [from Latin *radius* = ray]

radiation *noun* **1** the process of radiating. **2** light, heat, or other energy radiated. **3** radioactivity.

radiator *noun* **1** a device that gives out heat, especially a metal case that is heated electrically or through which steam or hot water flows. **2** a device that cools the engine of a motor vehicle.

radical[1] *adjective* **1** basic; thorough, *radical changes.* **2** wanting to make great reforms, *a radical politician.* **radically** *adverb*

radical[2] *noun* a person who wants to make great reforms. [from Latin *radicis* = of a root]

radicle *noun* a root that forms in the seed of a plant. [from Latin, = little root]

radio *noun* (*plural* **radios**) **1** the process of sending and receiving sound or pictures by means of electromagnetic waves without a connecting wire. **2** an apparatus for receiving sound (a *receiver*) or sending it out (a *transmitter*) in this way. **3** sound broadcasting. [from Latin *radius* = ray]

radio- *prefix* **1** of rays or radiation. **2** of radio.

radioactive *adjective* having atoms that break up and send out radiation which produces electrical and chemical effects and penetrates things. **radioactivity** *noun*

radiography *noun* the production of X-ray photographs. **radiographer** *noun* [from *radio-* + *-graphy*]

radiology *noun* the study of X-rays and similar radiation. **radiologist** *noun* [from *radio-* + *-logy*]

radish *noun* (*plural* **radishes**) a plant with a crisp hot-tasting root, eaten raw. [from Latin *radix* = root]

radium *noun* a radioactive substance found in pitchblende. [from Latin *radius* = ray]

radius *noun* (*plural* **radii** or **radiuses**) **1** a straight line from the centre of a circle or sphere to the circumference; the length of this line. **2** a range or distance from a central point, *The school takes pupils living within a radius of ten kilometres.* **3** the thicker and shorter of the two bones in the human forearm. [from Latin *radius* = a spoke or ray]

Rafferty's rules *plural noun* (*Australian informal*) no rules at all.

raffia *noun* soft fibre from the leaves of a kind of palm tree.

raffish *adjective* looking disreputable.

raffle[1] *noun* a kind of lottery, usually to raise money for a charity.

raffle[2] *verb* (**raffled**, **raffling**) offer something as a prize in a raffle.

raft *noun* a flat floating structure, used as a boat.

rafter *noun* any of the long sloping pieces of wood that hold up a roof.

rag[1] *noun* **1** an old or torn piece of cloth. **2** a piece of ragtime music. **3** (*informal*) a newspaper, *the local rag.*

rag[2] *verb* (**ragged**, **ragging**) (*informal*) tease.

ragamuffin *noun* a person in ragged dirty clothes.

rage[1] *noun* **1** great or violent anger. **2** a craze, *Skateboarding was all the rage.* **3** (*Australian informal*) a lively party.

rage[2] *verb* (**raged**, **raging**) **1** be very angry. **2** be violent or noisy, *A storm was raging.* **3** (*Australian informal*) enjoy oneself thoroughly.

ragged *adjective* **1** torn or frayed. **2** wearing torn clothes. **3** jagged. **4** irregular; uneven, *a ragged performance.*

raglan *noun* a sleeve joined to a garment by sloping seams. [named after Lord Raglan, British military commander (died 1855)]

ragtime *noun* a kind of jazz music.

raid[1] *noun* **1** a sudden attack. **2** a surprise visit by police to arrest people or seize illegal goods.

raid[2] *verb* **1** make a raid on a place. **2** plunder. **raider** *noun*

rail[1] *noun* **1** a level or sloping bar for hanging things on or forming part of a fence or barrier. **2** a long metal bar forming part of a railway track.
by rail on a train.

rail[2] *verb* protest angrily.

railings *plural noun* a fence made of metal bars.

railway *noun* **1** the parallel metal bars that trains travel on. **2** a system of transport using rails.

raiment *noun* (*old use*) clothing.

rain[1] *noun* drops of water that fall from the sky. **rainy** *adjective*

rain[2] *verb* **1** fall as rain or like rain. **2** send down like rain, *They rained blows on him.*

rainbow *noun* a curved band of colours seen in the sky when the sun shines through rain.

rainbow serpent *noun* (*Australian*) (in traditional Aboriginal belief) the widely venerated spirit of sacred lore, especially associated with the fashioning of the earth in the dreamtime.

rain check *noun* a voucher issued to a shopper promising that an out-of-stock item advertised in a sale will be made available later at the sale price.

raincoat *noun* a waterproof coat.

raindrop *noun* a single drop of rain.

rainfall *noun* the amount of rain that falls in a particular place or time.

rainforest *noun* thick forest in tropical areas where there is heavy rainfall.

raise[1] *verb* (**raised**, **raising**) **1** move something to a higher place or an upright position. **2** increase the amount or level of something. **3** collect; manage to obtain, *They raised $500 for charity.* **4** bring up young children or animals, *raise a family.* **5** rouse; cause, *She raised a laugh with her joke.* **6** put forward, *We raised objections.* **7** end a siege.

raise[2] *noun* an increase in a wage or salary.

raisin *noun* a dried grape.

raison d'être (*say* ray-zon **det**-ruh) *noun* the purpose of a thing's existence. [French, = reason for being]

raj (*say* rahj) *noun* the period of Indian history when the country was ruled by Britain. [Hindi, = reign]

rajah *noun* an Indian king or prince. [Hindi]

rake[1] *noun* a gardening tool with a row of short spikes fixed to a long handle.

rake² *verb* (**raked, raking**) **1** gather or smooth with a rake. **2** search. **3** gather; collect, *raking it in.*
rake up 1 collect; find. **2** reveal; expose, *Don't rake that up.*

rake³ *noun* a man who lives an irresponsible and immoral life. **rakish** *adjective*

rally¹ *noun* (*plural* **rallies**) **1** a large meeting to support something or share an interest. **2** a competition to test skill in driving. **3** a series of strokes in tennis before a point is scored. **4** a recovery.

rally² *verb* (**rallied, rallying**) **1** bring or come together for a united effort, *They rallied support; People rallied round.* **2** revive; recover strength.

RAM *abbreviation* random-access memory, a type of computer memory with parts that can be located directly.

ram¹ *noun* **1** a male sheep. **2** a device for ramming things.

ram² *verb* (**rammed, ramming**) **1** push one thing hard against another. **2** crash into something.

Ramadan *noun* the ninth month of the Muslim year, when Muslims fast between sunrise and sunset. [Arabic]

ramble¹ *noun* a long walk in the country.

ramble² *verb* (**rambled, rambling**) **1** go for a ramble; wander. **2** talk or write a lot without keeping to the subject. **rambler** *noun*

ramen (*say* **rah**-muhn) *noun* (in Asian cuisine) quick-cooking noodles. [Japanese from Chinese]

ramifications *plural noun* **1** the branches of a structure. **2** the many effects of a plan or action. [from Latin *ramus* = branch]

ramp¹ *noun* a slope or grid joining two different levels.

rampage *verb* (**rampaged, rampaging**) rush about wildly or destructively. **rampage** *noun*

rampant *adjective* **1** growing or increasing unrestrained, *Disease was rampant in the poorer districts.* **2** (of an animal on coats of arms) standing upright on a hind leg, *a lion rampant.* [from *ramp*]

rampart *noun* a wide bank of earth built as a fortification; a wall on top of this.

ram raid *noun* a robbery in which a shop window is rammed with a vehicle and looted.

ramrod *noun* a straight rod formerly used for ramming an explosive into a gun.

ramshackle *adjective* badly made and rickety, *a ramshackle hut.*

ran *past tense* of **run¹**.

ranch *noun* (*plural* **ranches**) a large farm in America where cattle or other animals are bred.

rancid *adjective* smelling or tasting unpleasant like stale fat.

rancour (*say* **rang**-kuh) *noun* bitter resentment or ill will. **rancorous** *adjective*

r & b *abbreviation* **1** rhythm and blues. **2** a style of pop music with elements of soul.

r & d *abbreviation* research and development.

random¹ *noun* **at random** using no particular order or method, *In bingo, numbers are chosen at random.*

random² *adjective* done or taken at random, *a random sample.*

rang *past tense* of **ring³**.

range¹ *noun* **1** a line or series of things, *a range of mountains.* **2** the limits between which things exist or are available; an extent, *a wide range of goods.* **3** the distance that a gun can shoot, an aircraft can travel, a sound can be heard, etc. **4** a place with targets for shooting practice. **5** a large open area of grazing land or hunting ground. **6** a kitchen fireplace with ovens; an electric or gas stove.

range² *verb* (**ranged, ranging**) **1** exist between two limits; extend, *Prices ranged from $10 to $50.* **2** arrange. **3** move over a wide area; wander.

ranger *noun* **1** someone who looks after or patrols a park, forest, or wilderness area. **2** (**Ranger**) a senior Guide.

rank¹ *noun* **1** a line of people or things. **2** a place where taxis stand to await customers. **3** a position in a series of different levels, *He holds the rank of sergeant.*
the rank and file ordinary people.

rank² *verb* **1** arrange in a rank or ranks. **2** have a certain rank or place, *She ranks among the greatest novelists.*

rank³ *adjective* **1** growing too thickly and coarsely. **2** smelling very unpleasant. **3** complete; unmistakably bad, *rank injustice.* **rankly** *adverb*, **rankness** *noun*

rankle *verb* (**rankled, rankling**) cause lasting annoyance or resentment.

ransack *verb* **1** search thoroughly or roughly. **2** rob or pillage a place.

ransom¹ *noun* money that has to be paid for a prisoner to be set free.
hold to ransom hold someone captive or in your power and demand ransom.

ransom² *verb* **1** free someone by paying a ransom. **2** get a ransom for someone. [same origin as *redeem*]

ransomware *noun* a type of harmful software designed to block access to a computer system until a sum of money is paid.

rant *verb* speak loudly and violently.

rap[1] *verb* (**rapped, rapping**) **1** knock loudly. **2** (*informal*) reprimand. **3** perform rap music. **4** (*Australian informal*) praise extravagantly.

rap[2] *noun* **1** a rapping movement or sound. **2** (*informal*) blame; punishment, *take the rap.* **3** a form of music of US black origin in which words are recited rapidly and rhythmically over an instrumental backing. **4** (*Australian informal*) extravagant praise. **rapper** *noun*

rapacious (*say* ruh-**pay**-shuhs) *adjective* greedy; plundering. **rapaciously** *adverb*, **rapacity** *noun* [from Latin *rapax* = grasping]

rape[1] *noun* the crime of forcing another person to have sexual intercourse against their will.

rape[2] *verb* (**raped, raping**) commit rape on a person. **rapist** *noun* [from Latin *rapere* = seize]

rape[3] *noun* a plant grown as food for sheep and for its seed from which oil is obtained.

rapid *adjective* quick; swift. **rapidity** *noun*, **rapidly** *adverb*

rapids *plural noun* part of a river where the water flows very quickly.

rapier *noun* a thin lightweight sword.

rapport (*say* ra-**paw**) *noun* a harmonious and understanding relationship between people.

rapt *adjective* **1** very intent and absorbed; enraptured. **2** (*informal*) overjoyed; delighted. **raptly** *adverb* [from Latin *raptum* = seized]

rapture *noun* very great delight. **rapturous** *adjective*, **rapturously** *adverb*

rare[1] *adjective* **1** unusual; not often found or happening. **2** (of air) thin; below normal pressure. **rarely** *adverb*, **rareness** *noun*, **rarity** *noun*

rare[2] *adjective* (of meat) cooked so that the inside is still red.

rarefied *adjective* **1** (of air) thin, like that on high mountains. **2** very subtle; highly intellectual; select.

raring *adjective* (*informal*) eager, *raring to go.*

rascal *noun* **1** a dishonest person; a rogue. **2** a mischievous person. **rascally** *adjective*

rash[1] *adjective* doing something or done without thinking of the possible risks or effects. **rashly** *adverb*, **rashness** *noun*

rash[2] *noun* (*plural* **rashes**) an outbreak of spots or patches on the skin.

rasher *noun* a slice of bacon.

rasp[1] *noun* **1** a file with sharp points on its surface. **2** a rough grating sound.

rasp[2] *verb* **1** scrape roughly. **2** make a rough grating sound or effect.

raspberry *noun* (*plural* **raspberries**) a small soft red fruit.

rat *noun* **1** an animal like a large mouse. **2** an unpleasant or treacherous person.

ratbag *noun* (*Australian informal*) someone who is unpleasant or eccentric.

ratchet *noun* a row of notches on a bar or wheel in which a device (a *pawl*) catches to prevent it running backwards.

rate[1] *noun* **1** speed, *The train travelled at a great rate.* **2** a measure of cost or value or charge, *Postage rates went up.* **3** quality; standard, *first-rate.*
at any rate anyway.

rate[2] *verb* (**rated, rating**) **1** put a value on something. **2** regard as, *He rated me among his friends.* [from Latin *ratum* = reckoned]

rates *plural noun* a local government tax assessed on the value of land and buildings.

rather *adverb* **1** slightly; somewhat, *It's rather dark.* **2** more willingly; preferably, *I would rather not go.* **3** more exactly, *He is lazy rather than stupid.* **4** (*informal*) definitely; yes, *'Do you like it?' 'Rather!'*

ratify *verb* (**ratified, ratifying**) confirm or agree to something officially, *They ratified the treaty.* **ratification** *noun*

rating *noun* **1** the way something is rated. **2** a sailor who is not an officer.

ratio (*say* **ray**-shee-oh) *noun* (*plural* **ratios**) **1** the relationship between two numbers, given by the quotient, *The ratio of 2 to 10 = 2:10 =* $\frac{2}{10} = \frac{1}{5}$. **2** proportion, *Mix flour and butter in the ratio of two to one* (= two measures of flour to one measure of butter). [from Latin, = reckoning]

ration[1] *noun* an amount allowed to one person.

ration[2] *verb* share something out in fixed amounts. [same origin as *ratio*]

rational *adjective* **1** reasonable; sane. **2** able to reason, *Plants are not rational.* **3** (of a quantity or ratio) expressible as a ratio of whole numbers. **rationality** *noun*, **rationally** *adverb*

rationalise *verb* (**rationalised, rationalising**) **1** make a thing logical and consistent, *Attempts to rationalise English spelling have failed.* **2** invent a reasonable explanation of something, *She rationalised her meanness by calling it economy.* **3** make an industry or process more efficient by reorganising it. **rationalisation** *noun*

rat-kangaroo another name for **bettong** and **potoroo**.

rat race *noun* a fiercely competitive struggle to maintain one's position in work or life.

rattle[1] *verb* (**rattled, rattling**) **1** make a series of short sharp hard sounds. **2** say something quickly, *She rattled off the poem.* **3** (*informal*) make a person nervous or flustered.

rattle² *noun* **1** a rattling sound. **2** a device or baby's toy that rattles.

rattlesnake *noun* a poisonous American snake with a tail that rattles.

rattling *adjective* **1** that rattles. **2** vigorous; brisk, *a rattling pace.*

ratty *adjective* (*informal*) irritable.

raucous (*say* **raw**-kuhs) *adjective* loud and harsh, *a raucous voice.*

ravage *verb* (**ravaged**, **ravaging**) do great damage to something; devastate. **ravages** *plural noun*

rave¹ *verb* (**raved**, **raving**) **1** talk wildly or angrily or madly. **2** talk rapturously about something. **3** (*informal*) attend a rave party.

rave² *noun* **1** (*informal*) a very enthusiastic review of a book, play, or other artistic work. **2** (*informal*) an all-night dance party with loud electronic music.

ravel *verb* (**ravelled**, **ravelling**) tangle.

raven *noun* a large black bird.

ravenous *adjective* very hungry. **ravenously** *adverb*

ravine (*say* ruh-**veen**) *noun* a deep narrow gorge or valley.

ravish *verb* **1** rape. **2** enrapture.

ravishing *adjective* very beautiful.

raw *adjective* **1** not cooked. **2** in the natural state; not yet processed, *raw materials.* **3** without experience, *raw recruits.* **4** with the skin removed, *a raw wound.* **5** cold and damp, *a raw morning.* **rawness** *noun*

raw deal *noun* (*informal*) unfair treatment.

ray¹ *noun* **1** a thin line of light, heat, or other radiation. **2** (in mathematics) any of a set of straight lines passing through one point. **3** a thing that is arranged radially. [from Latin *radius* = ray]

ray² *noun* a large sea fish with a flat body.

rayon *noun* a synthetic fibre or cloth made from cellulose.

raze *verb* (**razed**, **razing**) destroy a building or town completely, *raze it to the ground.* [from Latin *rasum* = scraped]

razoo (*say* rah-**zoo**) *noun* (*Australian*) an imaginary very small coin, *I haven't got a brass razoo.*

razor *noun* a device with a very sharp blade, especially one used for shaving. [from *raze*]

razzamatazz *noun* (*informal*) showy publicity.

RDI *abbreviation* recommended daily (or dietary) intake of nutrients necessary to maintain good health.

re- *prefix* **1** again (as in *rebuild*). **2** back again, to an earlier condition (as in *reopen*). **3** in return; to each other (as in *react*). **4** against (as in *rebel*). **5** away or down (as in *recede*). [Latin]

reach¹ *verb* **1** go as far as; arrive at a place or thing. **2** stretch out your hand to get or touch something. **reachable** *adjective*

reach² *noun* (*plural* **reaches**) **1** the distance a person or thing can reach. **2** a distance you can easily travel, *We live within reach of the sea.* **3** a straight stretch of a river.

react *verb* have a reaction.

reaction *noun* **1** something done, felt, or thought in response to a situation or event. **2** a person's ability to respond physically and mentally to external stimuli, *she's got quick reactions.* **3** a chemical change caused when substances act upon each other.

reactionary *adjective* wanting to undo progress or reform.

reactor *noun* an apparatus for producing nuclear power in a controlled way.

read *verb* (**read** (*say* red), **reading**) **1** look at something written or printed and understand it or say it aloud. **2** (of a computer) copy or transfer data. **3** indicate; register, *The thermometer reads 20°* Celsius. **readable** *adjective*

reader *noun* **1** a person who reads. **2** a book that helps you learn to read. **3** a device or piece of software used for reading or obtaining data stored on tape, cards, or other media.

readily (*say* **red**-uh-lee) *adverb* **1** willingly. **2** easily; without any difficulty.

ready¹ *adjective* (**readier**, **readiest**) **1** able to do something or be used immediately; prepared. **2** willing. **3** quick; prompt, *a ready answer.* **readiness** *noun*
at the ready ready for use or action.

ready² *adverb* beforehand, *This meat is ready cooked.* **ready-made** *adjective*

real *adjective* **1** existing; true; not imaginary. **2** genuine; not an imitation, *real pearls.*

real estate *noun* property in the form of land or buildings.

realise *verb* (**realised**, **realising**) **1** be fully aware of something; accept something as true. **2** make a hope or plan happen, *She realised her ambition to become a racing driver.* **3** convert into money; be sold for; produce as profit. **realisation** *noun*

realism *noun* seeing or showing things as they really are or appear to be. **realist** *noun*

realistic *adjective* **1** showing things as they really are, *a realistic painting.* **2** facing facts; based on facts rather than ideals, *a realistic proposal.* **realistically** *adverb*

reality *noun* (*plural* **realities**) what is real; something real.

reality television *noun* television programs that show real people, not actors, living in real-life situations, often as part of a competition.

really *adverb* **1** in actual fact, as opposed to what is said or imagined to be true or possible, *So what really happened?* **2** used to emphasise a statement or opinion, *I really want to go home.* **3** very, *It's a really cold day.* **4** seriously, *Do you really expect me to believe that?*

realm (*say* relm) *noun* **1** a kingdom. **2** a field of activity or interest, *in the realms of science.*

real time *noun* the actual time during which something occurs.

ream *noun* 500 (originally 480) sheets of paper.

reams *plural noun* a large quantity of writing.

reap *verb* **1** cut down and gather a grain crop when it is ripe. **2** obtain as the result of something done, *They reaped great benefit from their training.* **reaper** *noun*

reappear *verb* appear again.

rear[1] *noun* the back part.

rear[2] *adjective* placed at the rear.

rear[3] *verb* **1** bring up young children or animals. **2** rise up; raise itself on hind legs, *The horse reared in fright.* **3** build or set up something.

rearguard *noun* troops protecting the rear of an army.

rearrange *verb* (**rearranged, rearranging**) arrange in a different way or order. **rearrangement** *noun*

reason[1] *noun* **1** a cause or explanation of something. **2** reasoning; common sense, *Listen to reason.*

> **Usage** Do not use the phrase *the reason is* with the word *because* (which means the same thing). Correct usage is *We cannot come. The reason is that we both have flu* (not 'The reason is because ...').

reason[2] *verb* **1** use your ability to think and draw conclusions. **2** try to persuade someone by giving reasons, *We reasoned with the rebels.*

reasonable *adjective* **1** ready to use or listen to reason; sensible; logical. **2** fair; moderate; not expensive, *reasonable prices.* **reasonably** *adverb*

reassure *verb* (**reassured, reassuring**) restore someone's confidence by removing doubts and fears. **reassurance** *noun*

rebate *noun* a reduction in the amount to be paid; a partial refund. [from *re-* + *abate*]

rebel[1] (*say* ruh-**bel**) *verb* (**rebelled, rebelling**) refuse to obey someone in authority, especially the government; fight against the rulers of your own country.

rebel[2] (*say* **reb**-uhl) *noun* someone who rebels. **rebellion** *noun*, **rebellious** *adjective* [from *re-*, + Latin *bellare* = fight]

rebirth *noun* a return to life or activity; a revival of something.

reboot[1] *verb* **1** (with reference to a computer system) boot or be booted again. **2** restart or revive something; give fresh impetus to, *The prime minister pledged to reboot the economy if elected.*

reboot[2] *noun* **1** an act of booting a computer system again. **2** something that has been restarted or revived.

rebound *verb* bounce back after hitting something. **rebound** *noun*

rebuff *noun* an unkind refusal; a snub. **rebuff** *verb*

rebuild *verb* (**rebuilt, rebuilding**) build something again after it has been destroyed.

rebuke *verb* (**rebuked, rebuking**) speak severely to a person who has done wrong. **rebuke** *noun*

rebut *verb* (**rebutted, rebutting**) refute; disprove. **rebuttal** *noun* [from *re-* + *butt*]

recalcitrant *adjective* disobedient. **recalcitrance** *noun* [from Latin, = kicking back]

recall[1] *verb* **1** ask a person to come back. **2** bring back into the mind; remember.

recall[2] *noun* recalling.

recant *verb* withdraw something you have said. **recantation** *noun* [from *re-*, + Latin *cantare* = sing]

recap *verb* (**recapped, recapping**) (*informal*) recapitulate. **recap** *noun*

recapitulate *verb* (**recapitulated, recapitulating**) state again the main points of what has been said. **recapitulation** *noun* [from *re-*, + Latin *capitulum* = chapter]

recapture *verb* (**recaptured, recapturing**) capture again; recover. **recapture** *noun*

recede *verb* (**receded, receding**) go back from a certain point, *The floods receded.* [from *re-*, + Latin *cedere* = go]

receipt (*say* ruh-**seet**) *noun* **1** a written statement that money has been paid or something has been received. **2** receiving something.

receive *verb* (**received, receiving**) **1** take or get something that is given or sent. **2** greet a guest. [from *re-* = back again, + Latin *capere* = take]

receiver *noun* **1** a person or thing that receives something. **2** an official who takes charge of a bankrupt person's property. **3** a radio or television set that receives broadcasts. **4** the part of a telephone that receives the sound and is held to a person's ear.

recent *adjective* not long past; happening or made a short time ago. **recently** *adverb*

receptacle *noun* something for holding or containing what is put into it.

reception *noun* **1** the way a person or thing is received. **2** a formal party to receive guests, *a wedding reception.* **3** a place in a hotel or office where visitors are received and registered. **4** a first class at school.

receptionist *noun* a person whose job is to receive and direct visitors, patients, or callers.

receptive *adjective* quick or willing to receive ideas, knowledge, or suggestions.

recess (*say* ree-**ses**) *noun* (*plural* **recesses**) **1** an alcove. **2** a time when work or business is stopped for a while. **3** the mid-morning break between classes at school; a snack eaten during this break. [same origin as *recede*]

recession *noun* **1** receding from a point. **2** a reduction in trade or prosperity.

recharge *verb* (**recharged**, **recharging**) **1** charge again. **2** restore electrical energy in a battery or a battery-operated device by connecting it to a power supply. **3** (of a person) return to a normal state of mind or strength after a period of exertion. **rechargeable** *adjective*

recipe (*say* **res**-uh-pee) *noun* instructions for preparing or cooking food. [Latin, = take]

recipient *noun* a person who receives something.

reciprocal[1] (*say* ruh-**sip**-ruh-kuhl) *adjective* given and received; mutual, *reciprocal help.* **reciprocally** *adverb*, **reciprocity** *noun*

reciprocal[2] *noun* a reversed fraction, *3/2 is the reciprocal of 2/3.* [from Latin, = moving backwards and forwards]

reciprocate *verb* (**reciprocated**, **reciprocating**) give and receive; do the same thing in return, *She did not reciprocate his love.* **reciprocation** *noun*

recital *noun* **1** reciting something. **2** a musical entertainment given by one performer or group.

recitative (*say* res-uh-tuh-**teev**) *noun* a speech sung to music in an oratorio or opera.

recite *verb* (**recited**, **reciting**) repeat a passage aloud from memory, especially before an audience. **recitation** *noun* [from Latin, = read aloud]

reckless *adjective* rash; heedless. **recklessly** *adverb*, **recklessness** *noun* [from *reck* = heed, + *-less* = without]

reckon *verb* **1** calculate; count up. **2** have as an opinion; feel confident, *I reckon we shall win.*

reclaim *verb* **1** claim or get something back. **2** make a thing usable again, *reclaimed land.* **reclamation** *noun*

recline *verb* (**reclined**, **reclining**) lean or lie back. [from *re-*, + Latin *-clinare* = to lean]

recluse *noun* a person who lives alone and avoids mixing with people. [from *re-* = away, + Latin *clausum* = shut]

recognise *verb* (**recognised**, **recognising**) **1** know who someone is or what something is because you have seen that person or thing before. **2** realise, *We recognise the truth of what you said.* **3** accept something as genuine, welcome, or lawful, *Nine countries recognised the island's new government.* **recognisable** *adjective*, **recognition** *noun* [from *re-*, + Latin *cognoscere* = know]

recoil *verb* **1** spring back suddenly. **2** draw back in fear or disgust.

recollect *verb* remember. **recollection** *noun*

recommend *verb* **1** say that a person or thing would be a good one to do a job or achieve something. **2** advise doing something. **recommendation** *noun*

recompense *verb* (**recompensed**, **recompensing**) repay or reward someone; compensate. **recompense** *noun*

reconcile *verb* (**reconciled**, **reconciling**) **1** make people who have quarrelled become friendly again. **2** persuade a person to put up with something, *New frames reconciled him to wearing glasses.* **3** make things agree, *I cannot reconcile what you say with what you do.* **reconciliation** *noun* [from *re-* + *conciliate*]

recondition *verb* overhaul and repair.

reconnaissance (*say* ruh-**kon**-uh-suhns) *noun* an exploration of an area, especially in order to gather information about it for military purposes. [French, = recognition]

reconnoitre *verb* (**reconnoitred**, **reconnoitring**) make a reconnaissance of an area.

reconsider *verb* consider something again and perhaps change an earlier decision. **reconsideration** *noun*

reconstitute *verb* (**reconstituted**, **reconstituting**) put together again; reconstruct; reorganise.

reconstruct *verb* **1** construct or build something again. **2** create or act past events again, *Police reconstructed the robbery.* **reconstruction** *noun*

record[1] (*say* **rek**-awd) *noun* **1** information kept in a permanent form, e.g. written or printed. **2** a disc on which sound has been recorded. **3** facts known about a person's past life or career, *She has a good school* *record.* **4** the best performance (especially in sport), or the most remarkable event of its kind, *He holds the record for the high jump.*

record[2] (*say* ruh-**kawd**) *verb* **1** put something down in writing or other permanent form. **2** store sounds or scenes (e.g. television pictures) on a disc or magnetic tape etc. so that you can play or show them later.

recorder *noun* **1** a kind of flute held downwards from the player's mouth. **2** a person or thing that records something.

recording *noun* **1** the process of storing sound or pictures on a disc or tape etc. for later reproduction. **2** the disc or tape etc. produced. **3** the recorded material.

record player *noun* an apparatus for reproducing sound from discs on which it is recorded.

recount *verb* give an account of, *We recounted our adventures.* [from Old French *reconter* = tell]

re-count *verb* count something again.

recoup (*say* ruh-**koop**) *verb* recover what one has lost or its equivalent.

recourse *noun* a source of help.
have recourse to go to a person or thing for help.

recover *verb* **1** get something back again after losing it; regain. **2** get well again after being ill or weak. **recovery** *noun*

recreation *noun* **1** the process or means of entertaining oneself or relaxing. **2** a pleasurable activity. **recreational** *adjective* [from *re-* + *creation*]

recrimination *noun* an angry retort or accusation made against a person who has criticised or blamed you. [from *re-*, + Latin *criminare* = accuse]

recruit[1] *noun* **1** a person who has just joined the armed forces. **2** a new member of an organisation or group.

recruit[2] *verb* enlist recruits. **recruitment** *noun*

rectal *adjective* of the rectum.

rectangle *noun* a shape with four sides and four right angles. **rectangular** *adjective* [from Latin *rectus* = straight or right, + *angle*]

rectangular hyperbola *noun* a hyperbola with rectangular asymptotes.

rectifier *noun* a device that converts alternating current to direct current.

rectify *verb* (**rectified, rectifying**) correct or put something right. **rectification** *noun* [from Latin *rectus* = right]

rectilinear *adjective* with straight lines, *Squares and triangles are rectilinear figures.* [from Latin *rectus* = straight, + *linear*]

rectitude *noun* moral goodness; rightness of behaviour or procedure. [from Latin *rectus* = right]

rector *noun* a member of the clergy in charge of a parish. [Latin, = ruler]

rectory *noun* (*plural* **rectories**) the house of a rector.

rectum *noun* the last part of the large intestine, ending at the anus. [Latin, = straight (intestine)]

recumbent *adjective* lying down. [from *re-*, + Latin *cumbens* = lying]

recuperate *verb* (**recuperated, recuperating**) get better after an illness. **recuperation** *noun*

recur *verb* (**recurred, recurring**) happen again; keep on happening. **recurrence** *noun*, **recurrent** *adjective* [from *re-*, + Latin *currere* = to run]

recurring decimal *noun* a decimal fraction in which the same figures are repeated indefinitely.

recycle *verb* (**recycled, recycling**) convert waste material into a form in which it can be reused.

recycling *noun* **1** the action or process of converting waste into reusable material. **2** waste material set aside to be recycled.

red[1] *adjective* (**redder, reddest**) **1** of the colour of blood or a colour rather like this. **2** (*informal*) Communist; favouring Communism. **redness** *noun*

red[2] *noun* **1** red colour. **2** (*informal*) a Communist.
in the red in debt (debts were entered in red in account books).

redback *noun* a small venomous Australian spider with a distinctive red or orange-red stripe on the female.

red-blooded *adjective* full of vigour; virile.

redden *verb* make or become red.

redeem *verb* **1** buy something back; pay off a debt. **2** save a person from damnation, *Christians believe that Christ redeemed us all.* **3** make up for faults, *His one redeeming feature is his kindness.* **redeemer** *noun*, **redemption** *noun* [from *re-*, + Latin *emere* = buy]

redeploy *verb* send troops or workers to a new place or task. **redeployment** *noun*

redevelop *verb* (**redeveloped, redeveloping**) replan or rebuild an urban area. **redevelopment** *noun*

redfin *noun* a fish, the European perch, introduced to Australia.

redfish *noun* a native Australian sea fish. Also called *nannygai.*

red-handed *adjective* while actually committing a crime, *He was caught red-handed.*

redhead *noun* a person with reddish hair.

red herring *noun* something that draws attention away from the main subject; a misleading clue.

redneck *noun* a person with extremely conservative views.

redolent (*say* **red**-uh-luhnt) *adjective* **1** having a strong smell, *redolent of onions.* **2** full of memories, *a castle redolent of romance.* [from *re-*, + Latin *olens* = smelling]

redoubtable *adjective* formidable. [from French *redouter* = to fear]

redound *verb* come back as an advantage or disadvantage, *This will redound to our credit.* [from Latin *redundare* = overflow]

redress[1] (*say* ruh-**dres**) *verb* set right; rectify, *redress the balance.*

redress[2] *noun* redressing; compensation, *You should seek redress for this damage.*

red tape *noun* the use of too many rules and forms in official business.

reduce *verb* (**reduced**, **reducing**) **1** make or become smaller or less. **2** force someone into a condition or situation, *She was reduced to borrowing the money.* **reduction** *noun* [from *re-*, + Latin *ducere* = bring]

redundant *adjective* not needed, especially for a particular job. **redundancy** *noun* [same origin as *redound*]

redwood *noun* a very tall Californian conifer.

re-echo *verb* (**re-echoed**, **re-echoing**) echo; go on echoing.

reed *noun* **1** a tall plant that grows in water or marshy ground. **2** a thin strip that vibrates to make the sound in a clarinet, saxophone, and certain other wind instruments.

reedy *adjective* **1** full of reeds. **2** (of a voice) having a thin high tone like a reed instrument. **reediness** *noun*

reef[1] *noun* a ridge of rock, coral, or sand, especially one near the surface of the sea.

reef[2] *verb* shorten a sail by drawing in a strip (called a *reef*) at the top or bottom to reduce the area exposed to the wind.

reef-knot *noun* a symmetrical double knot that is very secure.

reek *verb* smell strongly or unpleasantly. **reek** *noun*

reel[1] *noun* **1** a spool. **2** a lively Scottish dance.

reel[2] *verb* **1** wind something on to or off a reel. **2** stagger.
reel off say something quickly.

re-elect *verb* elect again. **re-election** *noun*

re-enact *verb* act out a past event. **re-enactment** *noun*

re-enter *verb* enter again. **re-entry** *noun*

re-examine *verb* examine again.

ref *noun* (*informal*) a referee.

refectory *noun* (*plural* **refectories**) the dining room in an educational or religious institution. [from Latin *refectum* = refreshed]

refer *verb* (**referred**, **referring**) **1** make an allusion; direct people's attention by words. **2** send on or direct a person to some authority, specialist, or source of information. **referral** *noun*
refer to 1 mention; speak about, *I wasn't referring to you.* **2** look in a book etc. for information, *We referred to our dictionary.* [from *re-* = back, + Latin *ferre* = bring]

referee[1] *noun* **1** someone appointed to see that people keep to the rules of a game. **2** a person whose opinion or judgement is sought in some connection, or who is referred to for a decision in a dispute. **3** a person willing to testify to the character of an applicant for employment.

referee[2] *verb* (**refereed**, **refereeing**) act as a referee; umpire.

reference *noun* **1** referring to something, *There was no reference to recent events.* **2** a direction to a book or page or file etc. where information can be found. **3** a letter describing someone's abilities, character, etc.
in or **with reference to** concerning; about.

reference book *noun* a book (such as a dictionary or encyclopedia) that gives information systematically.

referendum *noun* (*plural* **referendums** or **referenda**) voting by all the people of a country (not by parliament) to decide whether something shall be done. Also called a *plebiscite.* [Latin, = referring]

refill *verb* fill again. **refill** *noun*

refine *verb* (**refined**, **refining**) **1** purify. **2** improve something, especially by making small changes.

refined *adjective* **1** purified. **2** cultured; with good manners.

refinement *noun* **1** the action of refining. **2** being refined. **3** something added to improve a thing.

refinery *noun* (*plural* **refineries**) a factory for refining something, *an oil refinery.*

reflect *verb* **1** send back light, heat, or sound from a surface. **2** form an image of something as a mirror does. **3** think something over; consider. **4** show; be influenced by something, *Prices reflect the cost of producing things.* **5** (in mathematics) turn a shape over so it is a mirror image. **reflection** *noun*, **reflective** *adjective*, **reflector** *noun* [from *re-*, + Latin *flectere* = to bend]

reflex *noun* (*plural* **reflexes**) a movement or action done without any conscious thought. [from *reflect*]

reflex angle *noun* an angle of more than 180°.

reflexive *adjective* **1** referring back. **2** (of a word or form) referring back to the subject of a sentence (for example *myself*). **3** (of a verb) having a reflexive pronoun as its object (as in *wash oneself*).

reflexive pronoun see **pronoun**.

reflexive verb *noun* a verb where the subject and the object are the same person or thing, as in *The child behaved himself.*

reflexology *noun* massaging points on the feet, hands, and head to relieve tension and treat illness. **reflexologist** *noun*

reflux *noun* a backward flow.

reform[1] *verb* make or become better by removing faults. **reformative** *adjective*, **reformatory** *adjective & noun*, **reformer** *noun*

reform[2] *noun* **1** reforming. **2** a change made in order to improve something.

reformation *noun* **1** reforming. **2** (**the Reformation**) a religious movement in Europe in the 16th century to reform certain teachings and practices of the Church, which resulted in the establishment of the Reformed or Protestant Churches.

refract *verb* bend a ray of light at the point where it enters water, glass, or air at an angle. **refraction** *noun*, **refractive** *adjective*, **refractor** *noun* [from *re-*, + Latin *fractum* = broken]

refractory *adjective* **1** difficult to control; stubborn. **2** (of substances) resistant to heat.

refrain[1] *verb* stop yourself from doing something, *Refrain from talking.*

refrain[2] *noun* **1** the lines of a song that are repeated at the end of each verse. **2** the main part of a song, after the verse.

refresh *verb* **1** give new strength or energy to. **2** stimulate the memory by reminding. **3** (in computing) update the display on a screen.

refreshment *noun* refreshing.

refreshments *plural noun* drinks and snacks.

refrigerate *verb* (**refrigerated, refrigerating**) make a thing extremely cold, especially in order to preserve it and keep it fresh. **refrigeration** *noun* [from *re-*, + Latin *frigus* = cold]

refrigerator *noun* a cabinet or room in which food is stored at a very low temperature.

refuel *verb* (**refuelled, refuelling**) supply with more fuel, especially a ship or aircraft.

refuge *noun* **1** shelter from pursuit or danger. **2** a place where a person is safe from pursuit or danger. [from *re-*, + Latin *fugere* = flee]

refugee *noun* a person who has had to leave home and seek refuge somewhere, e.g. because of war or persecution or famine.

refund[1] *verb* pay money back.

refund[2] *noun* money paid back.

refurbish *verb* freshen something up; redecorate.

refuse[1] (*say* ruh-**fyooz**) *verb* (**refused, refusing**) say that you are unwilling to do or give or accept something. **refusal** *noun*

refuse[2] (*say* **ref**-yoos) *noun* waste material, *Trucks collected the refuse.*

refute *verb* (**refuted, refuting**) prove that a person or statement is wrong. **refutation** *noun*

regain *verb* **1** get something back after losing it. **2** reach a place again.

regal (*say* **ree**-guhl) *adjective* of or by a monarch; fit for a king or queen. [from Latin *regis* = of a king]

regale (*say* ruh-**gayl**) *verb* (**regaled, regaling**) feed or entertain well, *They regaled us with stories.*

regalia *plural noun* the emblems of royalty or rank.

regard[1] *verb* **1** look or gaze at. **2** think of in a certain way; consider to be, *We regard the matter as serious.*

regard[2] *noun* **1** a gaze. **2** consideration; heed, *You acted without regard to people's safety.* **3** respect, *We have a great regard for her.* **with regard to** concerning.

regarding *preposition* concerning, *There are laws regarding drugs.*

regardless *adverb* without considering something, *Do it, regardless of the cost.*

regards *plural noun* kind wishes sent in a message, *Give him my regards.*

regatta *noun* a meeting for boat or yacht races. [from Italian]

regency *noun* being a regent.

regenerate *verb* (**regenerated, regenerating**) give new life or strength to something. **regeneration** *noun*

regent *noun* a person appointed to rule a country while the monarch is too young or unable to rule. [from Latin *regens* = ruling]

reggae (*say* **reg**-ay) *noun* a West Indian style of music with a strong beat.

regime (*say* ray-***zheem***) *noun* a system of government or organisation, *a Communist regime.*

regiment *noun* an army unit, usually divided into battalions or companies. **regimental** *adjective*

region *noun* an area; a part of a country or of the world, *in tropical regions.* **regional** *adjective*, **regionally** *adverb*
in the region of near, *The cost will be in the region of $100.*

register[1] *noun* **1** an official list of things or names. **2** a book in which items are recorded for reference. **3** a device that records the amount of something automatically, *a cash register.* **4** the range of a voice or musical instrument. **5** a variety of language (informal, literary, etc.) used in particular circumstances, *The Queen used a very formal register in her speech.*

register² *verb* **1** list something in a register. **2** indicate; show, *The thermometer registered 100°.* **3** make an impression on someone's mind. **4** pay extra for a letter or parcel to be sent with special care.

registrar *noun* **1** an official whose job is to keep written records or registers. **2** a doctor undergoing hospital training to be a specialist.

registration *noun* **1** the action or process of registering or of being registered. **2** a certificate that attests to the registering of a person, car, etc. **3** an annual fee payable by the owner of a motor vehicle.

registry *noun* (*plural* **registries**) a place where registers are kept.

registry office *noun* an office where marriages are performed and records of births, marriages, and deaths are kept.

rego *noun* (*Australian informal*) motor vehicle registration.

regress *verb* return to an earlier or less advanced state. **regression** *noun*, **regressive** *adjective* [from *re-*, + Latin *gressus* = gone]

regret¹ *noun* a feeling of sorrow or disappointment about something that has happened or been done. **regretful** *adjective*, **regretfully** *adverb*

regret² *verb* (**regretted, regretting**) feel regret about something. **regrettable** *adjective*, **regrettably** *adverb*

regular *adjective* **1** always happening or doing something at certain times. **2** even; symmetrical, *regular teeth.* **3** normal; standard; correct, *the regular procedure.* **4** of a country's permanent armed forces, *a regular soldier.* **5** (of a word) following the normal pattern of inflection. **6** (in geometry) (of a figure) having all sides and all angles equal. **regularity** *noun*, **regularly** *adverb* [from Latin *regula* = a rule]

regulate *verb* (**regulated, regulating**) **1** adjust. **2** control. **regulator** *noun*

regulation *noun* **1** regulating. **2** a rule or law. [same origin as *regular*]

regurgitate *verb* (**regurgitated, regurgitating**) bring swallowed food up again into the mouth. **regurgitation** *noun*

rehabilitation *noun* restoring a person to a normal life or a building to a good condition. **rehabilitate** *verb*

rehash *verb* (*informal*) repeat something without changing it very much.

rehearse *verb* (**rehearsed, rehearsing**) practise something before performing to an audience. **rehearsal** *noun*

reign¹ *verb* **1** rule a country as king or queen. **2** be supreme; be the strongest influence, *Silence reigned.*

reign² *noun* the time when someone reigns. [from Latin *regnum* = royal authority]

reimburse *verb* (**reimbursed, reimbursing**) repay. **reimbursement** *noun*

rein¹ *noun* a strap used to guide a horse.

rein² *verb* control with reins.
rein in restrain or control, *rein in spending.* [same origin as *retain*]

reincarnation *noun* being born again into a new body.

reindeer *noun* (*plural* **reindeer**) a kind of deer that lives in Arctic regions.

reinforce *verb* (**reinforced, reinforcing**) strengthen or support by additional persons or material or an added quantity.

reinforcement *noun* **1** reinforcing. **2** something that reinforces.

reinforcements *plural noun* extra troops sent to strengthen a force.

reinstate *verb* (**reinstated, reinstating**) put a person or thing back into a former position. **reinstatement** *noun*

reiterate *verb* (**reiterated, reiterating**) say something again and again. **reiteration** *noun* [from *re-*, + Latin *iterum* = again]

reject¹ *verb* **1** refuse to accept a person or thing. **2** throw away; discard. **rejection** *noun*

reject² *noun* a person or thing that is rejected. [from *re-* = away, + Latin *-jectum* = thrown]

rejoice *verb* (**rejoiced, rejoicing**) feel or show great joy.

rejoin *verb* **1** join again. **2** answer; retort.

rejoinder *noun* a reply or retort.

rejuvenate *verb* (**rejuvenated, rejuvenating**) make a person seem young again. **rejuvenation** *noun* [from *re-*, + Latin *juvenis* = young]

relapse *verb* (**relapsed, relapsing**) return to a previous condition; become worse after improving. **relapse** *noun* [from *re-*, + Latin *lapsum* = slipped]

relate *verb* (**related, relating**) **1** narrate. **2** connect or compare one thing with another. **3** behave happily towards people or animals, *Some people cannot relate to animals.*

related *adjective* **1** belonging to the same family. **2** connected.

relation *noun* **1** a relative. **2** the way one thing is related to another.

relationship *noun* **1** how people or things are related. **2** how people get on with each other.

relative[1] *noun* a person who is related to another.

relative[2] *adjective* **1** connected or compared with something; compared with the average, *They live in relative comfort.* **2** (in grammar) referring to an earlier noun, clause, or sentence, *'Who' in 'the girl who lives there' is a relative pronoun.* **relatively** *adverb*

relative pronoun see **pronoun**.

relax *verb* **1** make or become less tight or stiff. **2** make or become less strict, *relax the rules.* **3** stop working; rest. **relaxation** *noun* [from *re-* = back, + Latin *laxus* = loose]

relay[1] *verb* pass on a message or broadcast.

relay[2] *noun* **1** a fresh group taking the place of another, *The firefighters worked in relays.* **2** a relay race. **3** a device for relaying a broadcast.

relay race *noun* a race between teams in which each person covers part of the distance.

release[1] *verb* (**released, releasing**) **1** set free; unfasten. **2** let a thing fall or fly or go out. **3** make information or a film or recording etc. available to the public.

release[2] *noun* **1** being released. **2** something released. **3** a device that unfastens something.

relegate *verb* (**relegated, relegating**) **1** put into a less important place. **2** put a sports team into a lower division of a league. **relegation** *noun* [from *re-* = back, + Latin *legatum* = sent]

relent *verb* become less severe or more merciful. [from *re-* = back, + Latin *lentus* = flexible]

relentless *adjective* **1** not relenting; pitiless. **2** unceasing. **relentlessly** *adverb*

relevant *adjective* connected with what is being discussed or dealt with. (The opposite is **irrelevant**.) **relevance** *noun*

reliable *adjective* able to be relied on; trustworthy. **reliability** *noun*, **reliably** *adverb*

reliance *noun* relying; trust. **reliant** *adjective*

relic *noun* something that has survived from an earlier time. [same origin as *relinquish*]

relief *noun* **1** ease given by reduction or removal of pain, anxiety, or a burden. **2** something that gives relief or help. **3** a person who takes over a turn of duty when another finishes. **4** a method of making a design that stands out from a surface. [from *re-*, + Latin *levis* = lightweight]

relief map *noun* a map that shows hills and valleys by shading or moulding.

relieve *verb* (**relieved, relieving**) **1** end or lessen a person's pain, anxiety, or burden. **2** release a person from a duty by acting as or providing a replacement.

religion *noun* **1** the belief in and worship of a superhuman controlling power, especially a personal God or gods. **2** a particular system of faith and worship. **3** a pursuit or interest followed with great devotion, *Football is her religion.* [from Latin *religio* = reverence]

religious *adjective* **1** of religion. **2** believing firmly in a religion and taking part in its customs. **religiously** *adverb*

relinquish *verb* give up; let go. **relinquishment** *noun* [from *re-* = behind, + Latin *linquere* = leave]

relish[1] *noun* **1** great enjoyment. **2** something tasty that adds flavour to plainer food.

relish[2] *verb* enjoy greatly.

rellie *noun* (*Australian informal*) a relative.

reluctant *adjective* unwilling; not keen. **reluctance** *noun*, **reluctantly** *adverb* [from Latin, = struggling against something]

rely *verb* (**relied, relying**) **rely on** trust a person or thing to help or support you.

remain *verb* **1** be there after other parts have gone or been dealt with; be left over. **2** continue to be in the same place or condition; stay. [from *re-* = behind, + Latin *manere* = stay]

remainder *noun* **1** the remaining part of people or things. **2** the number left after subtraction or division.

remains *plural noun* **1** all that is left over after other parts have been removed or destroyed. **2** ancient ruins or objects; relics. **3** a dead body.

remand *verb* send back a prisoner into custody while further evidence is sought. **remand** *noun* [from *re-*, + Latin *mandare* = entrust]

remark[1] *noun* something said; a comment.

remark[2] *verb* **1** make a remark; say. **2** notice.

remarkable *adjective* unusual; extraordinary. **remarkably** *adverb*

remedial *adjective* helping to cure an illness or deficiency.

remedy[1] *noun* (*plural* **remedies**) **1** something that cures or relieves a disease or illness. **2** something that puts a matter right.

remedy[2] *verb* (**remedied, remedying**) be a remedy for something; put right. [from *re-*, + Latin *mederi* = heal]

remember *verb* **1** keep something in your mind. **2** bring something back into your mind. **remembrance** *noun* [from *re-*, + Latin *memor* = mindful]

remind *verb* help or cause a person to remember something. **reminder** *noun*

reminisce (*say* rem-uh-**nis**) *verb* (**reminisced, reminiscing**) think or talk about things that you remember. **reminiscence** *noun*

reminiscent *adjective* **1** tending to remind you of something. **2** suggesting something by resemblance.

remiss *adjective* negligent; careless about doing what you ought to do.

remit *verb* (**remitted, remitting**) **1** send, especially money. **2** forgive; reduce or cancel a punishment. **3** make or become less intense; slacken, *We must not remit our efforts.* **remission** *noun* [from *re-* = back, + Latin *mittere* = send]

remittance *noun* **1** sending money. **2** the money sent.

remnant *noun* a part or piece left over from something. [compare *remain*]

remonstrate *verb* (**remonstrated, remonstrating**) make a protest, *We remonstrated with him about his behaviour.* [from *re-* = against, + Latin *monstrare* = to show]

remorse *noun* deep regret for having done wrong. **remorseful** *adjective*, **remorsefully** *adverb* [from *re-* = back, + Latin *morsum* = bitten]

remorseless *adjective* relentless.

remote *adjective* **1** far away. **2** some but very little; unlikely, *a remote chance.* **remotely** *adverb*, **remoteness** *noun* [from Latin *remotum* = removed]

remote control *noun* controlling something from a distance, usually by radio or electronic signals; a device used for this.

removable *adjective* able to be removed.

removal *noun* removing or moving something.

removalist *noun* (*Australian*) a person or firm that moves household or office furniture.

remove *verb* (**removed, removing**) **1** take something away or off. **2** move or take to another place. **3** dismiss a person from a job. **4** get rid of, *remove graffiti.*

remunerate *verb* (**remunerated, remunerating**) pay or reward someone. **remuneration** *noun*, **remunerative** *adjective* [from *re-*, + Latin *muneris* = of a gift]

Renaissance (*say* ruh-**nay**-suhns) *noun* the revival of classical styles of art and literature in Europe in the 14th–16th centuries. [French, = rebirth]

renal (*say* **ree**-nuhl) *adjective* of the kidneys.

rend *verb* (**rent, rending**) rip; tear.

render *verb* **1** give or perform something, *render help to the victims.* **2** cause to become, *The shock rendered us speechless.* **3** cover (stone or brick) with a coat of plaster or other material. **4** (in computing) process an image in order to make it appear solid and three-dimensional. [from Latin *reddere* = give back]

rendezvous (*say* **ron**-day-voo) *noun* (*plural* **rendezvous**, *say* **ron**-day-vooz) a meeting with somebody; a place arranged for this. [from French *rendezvous* = present yourselves]

renegade (*say* **ren**-uh-gayd) *noun* a person who deserts a group, cause, or faith. [from *re-* = back, + Latin *negare* = deny]

renege (*say* ree-**neg**) *verb* **1** fail to keep a promise; go back on one's word. **2** (in card games) fail to follow suit when able to do so.

renew *verb* **1** restore something to its original condition or replace it with something new. **2** begin or make or give again, *We renewed our request.* **renewal** *noun*

renewable *adjective* **1** (of a contract, agreement, etc.) capable of being renewed. **2** (of a natural resource or source of energy) not depleted when used, *a shift away from fossil fuels to renewable energy.*

renewables *plural noun* a natural resource or source of energy that is not depleted by use, such as water, wind, or solar power.

rennet *noun* a substance used to curdle milk in making cheese or junket.

renounce *verb* (**renounced, renouncing**) give up; reject. **renunciation** *noun* [from *re-* = back, + Latin *nuntiare* = announce]

renovate *verb* (**renovated, renovating**) repair a thing and make it look new. **renovation** *noun* [from *re-*, + Latin *novus* = new]

renown *noun* fame. **renowned** *adjective*

rent[1] *noun* a regular payment for the use of something especially a house that belongs to another person.

rent[2] *verb* have or allow the use of something in return for rent.

rent[3] *past tense & past participle* of **rend**.

rent[4] *noun* a torn place; a split.

rental *noun* **1** an amount paid or received as rent. **2** renting.

renunciation *noun* renouncing something.

reorganise *verb* organise again or in a new way. **reorganisation** *noun*

repair[1] *verb* **1** restore to good condition after damage or the effects of wear and tear. **2** put right; make amends for. **repairable** *adjective*

repair[2] *noun* repairing; being repaired. [from *re-*, + Latin *parare* = make ready]

repair[3] *verb* (*formal*) go, *The guests repaired to the dining room.* [same origin as *repatriate*]

reparation *noun* compensation; amends.

repartee *noun* quick retorts.

repast *noun* (*formal*) a meal.

repatriate *verb* (**repatriated, repatriating**) send a person back to their own country. **repatriation** *noun* [from *re-*, + Latin *patria* = native country]

repay *verb* (**repaid, repaying**) **1** pay back, especially money. **2** give in return, *repay their kindness.* **repayable** *adjective*, **repayment** *noun*

repeal *verb* cancel a law officially. **repeal** *noun*

repeat[1] *verb* say or do the same thing again. **repeatedly** *adverb*

repeat[2] *noun* **1** the action of repeating. **2** something that is repeated. [from *re-*, + Latin *petere* = seek]

repel *verb* (**repelled, repelling**) **1** drive away; repulse, *repel the attack.* **2** disgust somebody. **repellent** *adjective & noun* [from *re-*, + Latin *pellere* = to drive]

repent *verb* be sorry for what you have done. **repentant** *adjective*, **repentance** *noun* [from *re-* + *penitent*]

repercussion *noun* a result or reaction produced indirectly by something.

repertoire (*say* **rep**-uh-twah) *noun* **1** a stock of plays, dances, or items that a company or a performer knows or is prepared to perform. **2** a stock of skills or types of behaviour that a person often uses.

repertory *noun* a repertoire.

repertory company *noun* (also **repertory theatre**) a company or theatre giving performances of various plays for short periods.

repetition *noun* repeating; something repeated. **repetitious** *adjective*

repetitive *adjective* full of repetitions. **repetitively** *adverb*

replace *verb* (**replaced, replacing**) **1** put a thing back in its place. **2** take the place of another person or thing. **3** put a new or different thing in place of something. **replacement** *noun*

replay *verb* play a sports match or a recording again. **replay** *noun*

replenish *verb* fill again; add a new supply of something. **replenishment** *noun* [from *re-*, + Latin *plenus* = full]

replete *adjective* **1** well supplied. **2** feeling full after eating. [from *re-*, + Latin *-pletum* = filled]

replica *noun* an exact copy.

reply[1] *noun* (*plural* **replies**) something said or written to deal with a question, letter, etc.; an answer.

reply[2] *verb* (**replied, replying**) give a reply to; answer.

report[1] *verb* **1** describe something that has happened or that you have done or studied. **2** make a complaint or accusation against somebody. **3** go and tell somebody that you have arrived or are ready for work.

report[2] *noun* **1** a description or account of something. **2** a regular statement of how someone has worked or behaved, e.g. at school. **3** an explosive sound. [from *re-* = back, + Latin *portare* = carry]

reporter *noun* a person whose job is to report news for publication or broadcasting.

repose[1] *noun* rest; sleep.

repose[2] *verb* (**reposing, reposing**) rest or lie somewhere.

repository *noun* (*plural* **repositories**) a place where things are stored.

reprehensible *adjective* deserving blame or rebuke.

represent *verb* **1** show a person or thing in a work of art. **2** symbolise; stand for, *In Roman numerals, V represents 5.* **3** be an example or equivalent of something. **4** help someone by speaking or doing something on their behalf. **representation** *noun*

representative[1] *noun* a person or thing that represents another or others.

representative[2] *adjective* **1** representing others. **2** typical of a group.

repress *verb* keep down; restrain; suppress. **repression** *noun*, **repressive** *adjective*

reprieve[1] *noun* postponement or cancellation of a punishment, especially the death penalty.

reprieve[2] *verb* (**reprieved, reprieving**) give a reprieve to.

reprimand[1] *noun* a rebuke, especially a formal or official one.

reprimand[2] *verb* give someone a reprimand.

reprisal *noun* an act of revenge.

reproach *verb* rebuke. **reproach** *noun*, **reproachful** *adjective*, **reproachfully** *adverb*

reproduce *verb* (**reproduced, reproducing**) **1** cause to be seen or heard or happen again. **2** make a copy of something. **3** produce offspring. **reproduction** *noun*, **reproductive** *adjective*

reproof *noun* an expression of condemnation for a fault or offence.

reprove *verb* (**reproved, reproving**) rebuke; reproach.

reptile *noun* a cold-blooded animal that has a backbone and very short legs or no legs at all, e.g. a snake, lizard, crocodile, or tortoise. **reptilian** *adjective* [from Latin *reptilis* = crawling]

republic *noun* a country that has a president, especially one who is elected. (Compare

monarchy.) **republican** *adjective* [from Latin *res publica* = public affairs]

repudiate *verb* (**repudiated, repudiating**) reject; deny. **repudiation** *noun*

repugnant *adjective* distasteful; objectionable. **repugnance** *noun* [from *re-* = against, + Latin *pugnans* = fighting]

repulse *verb* (**repulsed, repulsing**) **1** drive away; repel. **2** reject an offer or suggestion; rebuff. [same origin as *repel*]

repulsion *noun* **1** repelling; repulsing. **2** a feeling of disgust.

repulsive *adjective* **1** disgusting. **2** repelling things. **repulsively** *adverb*, **repulsiveness** *noun*

reputable (*say* **rep**-yuh-tuh-buhl) *adjective* having a good reputation; respected. **reputably** *adverb*

reputation *noun* what people say about a person or things. [from Latin *reputare* = consider]

repute *noun* reputation.

reputed *adjective* said or thought to be something, *This is reputed to be the best hotel.* **reputedly** *adverb*

request[1] *verb* **1** ask for a thing. **2** ask a person to do something.

request[2] *noun* **1** asking for something. **2** a thing asked for. [same origin as *require*]

requiem (*say* **rek**-wee-uhm) *noun* a special Mass for someone who has died; music for the words of this. [Latin, = rest]

require *verb* (**required, requiring**) **1** need. **2** make somebody do something; oblige, *Drivers are required to pass a test.* [from *re-*, + Latin *quaerere* = seek]

requirement *noun* what is required; a need.

requisite[1] (*say* **rek**-wuh-zit) *adjective* required; needed.

requisite[2] *noun* a thing needed for something. [same origin as *require*]

requisition *verb* take something over for official use.

rescind (*say* ruh-**sind**) *verb* repeal or cancel a law or agreement. **rescission** *noun* [from *re-*, + Latin *scindere* = to cut]

rescue[1] *verb* (**rescued, rescuing**) save from danger, harm, etc.; bring away from captivity. **rescuer** *noun*

rescue[2] *noun* the action of rescuing.

research[1] (*say* ruh-**serch** or **ree**-serch) *noun* careful study or investigation to discover facts or information.

research[2] *verb* do research into something.

resemblance *noun* likeness.

resemble *verb* (**resembled, resembling**) be like another person or thing. [from *re-*, + Latin *similis* = like]

resent *verb* feel indignant about or insulted by something. **resentful** *adjective*, **resentfully** *adverb*, **resentment** *noun* [from *re-* = against, + Latin *sentire* = feel]

reservation *noun* **1** reserving. **2** something reserved. **3** an area of land kept for a special purpose. **4** a limit on how far you agree with something, *I believe most of his story, but I have some reservations.*

reserve[1] *verb* (**reserved, reserving**) **1** keep something for a particular person or a special use. **2** order a place in a theatre, hotel, etc. in advance. **3** postpone, *reserve judgement.*

reserve[2] *noun* **1** something kept ready to be used if necessary. **2** an extra player chosen as a substitute in a team. **3** an area of land kept for a special purpose, *a nature reserve.* **4** shyness; keeping your thoughts and feelings private. [from *re-* = back, + Latin *servare* = keep]

reserve bank *noun* a country's central bank, responsible for the administration of the monetary policy of that country.

reserved *adjective* (of a person) showing reserve of manner (see **reserve**[2] 4).

reservoir (*say* **rez**-uh-vwah) *noun* a place where water is stored, especially an artificial lake.

reshuffle *noun* a rearrangement, especially an exchange of jobs between members of a group, *a Cabinet reshuffle.* **reshuffle** *verb*

reside *verb* (**resided, residing**) live in a particular place; dwell. [from *re-*, + Latin *-sidere* = sit]

residence *noun* **1** a place where a person lives. **2** residing.

resident *noun* **1** a person living or residing in a particular place. **2** a guest staying in a hotel. **resident** *adjective* [from *re-*, + Latin *-sidens* = sitting]

residential *adjective* containing people's homes, *a residential area.*

residue *noun* what is left over. **residual** *adjective*

resign *verb* give up your job or position. **resignation** *noun*

be resigned or **resign yourself to something** accept that you must put up with it. [from Latin *resignare* = unseal]

resilient *adjective* **1** springy. **2** recovering quickly from illness or trouble. **resilience** *noun* [from *re-* = back, + Latin *-siliens* = jumping]

resin *noun* a sticky substance that comes from plants or is manufactured, used in varnish, plastics, etc. **resinous** *adjective*

resist *verb* oppose; fight or act against something. **resistance** *noun*, **resistant**

adjective [from *re-* = against, + Latin *sistere* = stand firmly]

resistor *noun* a device that increases the resistance to an electric current.

resolute *adjective* showing great determination. **resolutely** *adverb* [same origin as *resolve*]

resolution *noun* **1** being resolute. **2** something you have resolved to do, *New Year resolutions.* **3** a formal decision made by a committee or legislative body. **4** the solving of a problem. **5** the degree of detail visible in a photographic or screen image, *high-resolution monitor.* **6** the smallest interval measurable by a telescope or other scientific instrument.

resolve[1] *verb* (**resolved**, **resolving**) **1** decide firmly or formally. **2** solve a problem etc. **3** overcome doubts or disagreements. **4** separate into constituent parts.

resolve[2] *noun* **1** something you have decided to do; a resolution. **2** great determination. [from *re-*, + Latin *solvere* = loosen]

resonant *adjective* resounding; echoing. **resonance** *adjective* [from *re-*, + Latin *sonans* = sounding]

resort[1] *verb* turn to or make use of something, *They resorted to violence.*

resort[2] *noun* **1** a place where people go for relaxation or holidays. **2** resorting, *without resort to cheating.*
the last resort something to be tried when everything else has failed.

resound *verb* fill a place with sound; echo.

resounding *adjective* very great; outstanding, *a resounding victory.*

resource *noun* **1** something that can be used; an asset, *The country's natural resources include coal and oil.* **2** an ability; ingenuity.

resourceful *adjective* clever at finding ways of doing things. **resourcefully** *adverb*, **resourcefulness** *noun*

respect[1] *noun* **1** admiration for a person's or thing's good qualities. **2** politeness; consideration, *Have respect for people's feelings.* **3** a detail or aspect, *In this respect he is like his sister.* **4** reference, *The rules with respect to bullying are quite clear.*

respect[2] *verb* have respect for a person or thing. [from *re-* = back, + Latin *specere* = to look]

respectable *adjective* **1** having good manners and character; proper in appearance or behaviour. **2** fairly good, *a respectable score.* **respectability** *noun*, **respectably** *adverb*

respectful *adjective* showing respect. **respectfully** *adverb*

respecting *preposition* concerning.

respective *adjective* of or for each individual, *We went to our respective rooms.* **respectively** *adverb*

respiration *noun* breathing. **respiratory** *adjective*

respirator *noun* **1** a device that fits over a person's nose and mouth to purify air before it is breathed. **2** an apparatus for giving artificial respiration.

respire *verb* (**respired**, **respiring**) breathe. [from *re-*, + Latin *spirare* = breathe]

respite *noun* an interval of rest, relief, or delay.

resplendent *adjective* brilliant with colour or decorations. [from *re-*, + Latin *splendens* = glittering]

respond *verb* **1** reply. **2** react. [from *re-*, + Latin *spondere* = promise]

respondent *noun* the person answering.

response *noun* **1** a reply. **2** a reaction.

responsibility *noun* (*plural* **responsibilities**) **1** being responsible. **2** something for which a person is responsible.

responsible *adjective* **1** looking after a person or thing and having to take the blame if something goes wrong. **2** reliable; trustworthy. **3** with important duties, *a responsible job.* **4** causing something, *His carelessness was responsible for their deaths.* **responsibly** *adverb*

responsive *adjective* responding readily.

rest[1] *noun* **1** a time of sleep or freedom from work as a way of regaining strength. **2** a support, *a headrest.* **3** an interval of silence between notes in music.
at rest not moving.

rest[2] *verb* **1** have a rest; be still. **2** allow to rest, *Sit down and rest your feet.* **3** be supported. **4** be left without further investigation or discussion, *And there the matter rests.* [from Old English *raest* = bed]

rest[3] *noun* **the rest** the remaining part; the others.

rest[4] *verb* remain, *Rest assured, it will be a success.*
rest with be left to someone to deal with, *It rests with you to suggest a date.* [from Latin *restare* = stay behind]

restart[1] *verb* start again, *I tried to restart the computer when it stopped working.*

restart[2] *noun* a new start or beginning, *They scored a goal ten seconds after the restart.*

restaurant *noun* a place where you can buy a meal and eat it.

restaurateur *noun* a restaurant keeper.

restful *adjective* giving rest or a feeling of rest.

restitution *noun* **1** restoring something. **2** compensation. [from *re-*, + Latin *statutum* = established]

restive *adjective* restless or impatient because of delay, boredom, etc.

restless *adjective* unable to rest or keep still. **restlessly** *adverb*

restore *verb* (**restored, restoring**) **1** bring something back to its original condition. **2** put something back in its original place. **restoration** *noun*, **restorative** *adjective*

restrain *verb* hold a person or thing back; keep under control. **restraint** *noun*

restrict *verb* limit. **restriction** *noun*, **restrictive** *adjective*

result[1] *noun* **1** something produced by an action or condition; an effect or consequence. **2** the score or situation at the end of a game, competition, or race. **3** the answer to a sum or calculation.

result[2] *verb* **1** happen as a result. **2** have a particular result. **resultant** *adjective*

resume *verb* (**resumed, resuming**) **1** begin again after stopping for a while. **2** take or occupy again, *After the interval we resumed our seats.* **resumption** *noun* [from *re-*, + Latin *sumere* = take up]

resumé (*say* **rez**-yuh-may) *noun* (also **résumé** or **resume**) **1** a summary. **2** a curriculum vitae. [French, = summed up]

resurgence *noun* a rise or revival of something, *a resurgence of interest in grammar.* [from *re-*, + Latin *surgens* = rising]

resurrect *verb* bring back into use or existence, *resurrect an old custom.*

resurrection *noun* **1** coming back to life after being dead. **2** the revival of something. [same origin as *resurgence*]

resuscitate *verb* (**resuscitated, resuscitating**) **1** revive a person from unconsciousness. **2** revive a custom, idea, or institution. **resuscitation** *noun*

retail[1] *verb* **1** sell goods to the general public. **2** tell what happened; recount; relate. **retailer** *noun*

retail[2] *noun* selling to the general public. (Compare **wholesale**[1].)

retain *verb* **1** continue to have something; keep in your possession. **2** keep in your memory. **3** hold something in place. [from *re-*, + Latin *tenere* = to hold]

retainer *noun* **1** a fee paid to secure someone's services. **2** (*old use*) an attendant of a person of high rank.

retaliate *verb* (**retaliated, retaliating**) repay an injury or insult etc. with a similar one; counter-attack. **retaliation** *noun* [from *re-*, + Latin *talis* = the same kind]

retard *verb* slow down or delay the progress or development of something. **retardation** *noun*, **retarded** *adjective* [from *re-*, + Latin *tardus* = slow]

retch *verb* strain your throat as if being sick.

retention *noun* retaining; keeping. **retentive** *adjective*

reticent (*say* **ret**-uh-suhnt) *adjective* not telling people what you feel or think; discreet. **reticence** *noun*

retina *noun* a layer of membrane at the back of the eyeball, sensitive to light.

retinol *noun* either of two forms of vitamin A.

retinue *noun* a group of people accompanying an important person.

retire *verb* (**retired, retiring**) **1** give up your regular work because you are getting old. **2** retreat. **3** go to bed or to your private room. **retirement** *noun* [from French *retirer* = draw back]

retiree *noun* a retired person.

retiring *adjective* shy; avoiding company.

retort[1] *noun* **1** a quick or witty or angry reply. **2** a glass bottle with a long downward-bent neck, used in distilling liquids. **3** a receptacle used in making steel or gas.

retort[2] *verb* make a quick, witty, or angry reply. [from *re-*, + Latin *tortum* = twisted]

retrace *verb* (**retraced, retracing**) go back over something, *We retraced our steps and returned to the ferry.*

retract *verb* **1** pull back or in, *The snail retracts its horns.* **2** withdraw, *She refused to retract her comments.* **retractable** *adjective*, **retractile** *adjective*, **retraction** *noun* [from *re-*, + Latin *tractum* = pulled]

retreat[1] *verb* go back after being defeated or to avoid danger or difficulty; withdraw.

retreat[2] *noun* **1** retreating. **2** a quiet place to which someone can withdraw. [same origin as *retract*]

retrench *verb* **1** reduce the amount of something; economise. **2** dismiss staff in order to reduce costs. **retrenchment** *noun*

retribution *noun* a deserved punishment. [from *re-*, + Latin *tributum* = assigned]

retrieve *verb* (**retrieved, retrieving**) get something back; rescue. **retrievable** *adjective*, **retrieval** *noun* [from Old French *retrover* = find again]

retriever *noun* a kind of dog that is often trained to retrieve game.

retro- *prefix* back; backward (as in *retrograde*). [from Latin *retro* = backwards]

retrograde *adjective* **1** going backwards. **2** becoming less good.

retrogress *verb* **1** move backwards. **2** deteriorate. **retrogression** *noun*, **retrogressive** *adjective* [from *retro-* + *progress*]

retrospect *noun* a survey of past events. **in retrospect** when you look back at what has happened. [from *retro-* + *prospect*]

retrospective *adjective* **1** looking back on the past. **2** applying to the past as well as the future, *The law could not be made retrospective.* **retrospection** *noun*

retrovirus *noun* any of a group of RNA viruses, including HIV.

return[1] *verb* **1** come back or go back. **2** bring, give, put, or send back.

return[2] *noun* **1** returning. **2** something returned. **3** profit, *He gets a good return on his savings.* **4** a return ticket. **5** a formal report, *a tax return.*

returned soldier *noun* a soldier who has returned from war.

return match *noun* a second match played between the same teams.

return ticket *noun* a ticket for a journey to a place and back again.

reunion *noun* **1** reuniting. **2** a meeting of people who have not met for some time.

reunite *verb* (**reunited, reuniting**) unite again after being separated.

reuse[1] *verb* (**reused, reusing**) use again. **reusable** *adjective*

reuse[2] *noun* using again.

rev[1] *verb* (**revved, revving**) (*informal*) make an engine run quickly, especially when starting.

rev[2] *noun* (*informal*) a revolution of an engine. [short for *revolution*]

Rev. *abbreviation* Reverend.

revamp *verb* renovate or revise.

reveal *verb* **1** let something be seen. **2** make known. [from Latin *revelare* = unveil]

reveille (*say* ruh-**val**-ee) *noun* a military waking-signal sounded on a bugle or drums. [from French *réveillez* = wake up!]

revel *verb* (**revelled, revelling**) **1** take great delight in something. **2** celebrate in a lively or noisy way. **reveller** *noun*
revels *plural noun* noisy festivities.

revelation *noun* **1** revealing. **2** something revealed, especially something surprising.

revelry *noun* revelling; revels.

revenge[1] *noun* harming somebody in return for harm that they have caused.

revenge[2] *verb* (**revenged, revenging**) avenge; take vengeance.

revenue *noun* **1** income, especially of a large amount, from any source. **2** a country's income from taxes etc., used for paying public expenses. [French, = returned]

reverberate *verb* (**reverberated, reverberating**) resound; re-echo. **reverberation** *noun* [from *re-*, + Latin *verberare* = to lash]

revere (*say* ruh-**veer**) *verb* (**revered, revering**) respect deeply or with reverence.

reverence *noun* a feeling of awe and deep or religious respect.

Reverend *noun* the title of a member of the clergy, *the Reverend John Smith.* [from Latin, = person to be revered]

reverent *adjective* feeling or showing reverence. **reverently** *adverb* [from Latin, = revering]

reverie (*say* **rev**-uh-ree) *noun* a daydream.

reversal *noun* reversing.

reverse[1] *adjective* facing or moving in the opposite direction; opposite in character or order; upside down.

reverse[2] *noun* **1** the reverse side. **2** the opposite or contrary. **3** a piece of misfortune, *They suffered several reverses.* **in reverse** the opposite way round.

reverse[3] *verb* (**reversed, reversing**) **1** turn in the opposite direction or order; turn something inside out or upside down. **2** move backwards. **3** cancel a decision or decree. **reversible** *adjective* [same origin as *revert*]

reverse gear *noun* a gear that allows a vehicle to be driven backwards.

revert *verb* return to a former condition, habit, or type. **reversion** *noun* [from *re-* = back, + Latin *vertere* = to turn]

review[1] *noun* **1** an inspection or survey. **2** a published description and opinion of a book, film, play, etc.

review[2] *verb* **1** make a review of something. **2** write a review of a book, film, play, etc. **reviewer** *noun*

revile *verb* (**reviled, reviling**) criticise angrily. **revilement** *noun*

revise *verb* (**revised, revising**) **1** go over work that you have already done, especially in preparing for an examination. **2** alter or correct something. **revision** *noun* [from *re-*, + Latin *visere* = examine]

revive *verb* (**revived, reviving**) **1** come or bring back to life, strength, or consciousness. **2** come or bring back into use, activity, or fashion. **revival** *noun* [from *re-*, + Latin *vivere* = to live]

revoke *verb* (**revoked, revoking**) withdraw or cancel a decree or licence etc. [from *re-*, + Latin *vocare* = to call]

revolt[1] *verb* **1** rebel. **2** disgust somebody.

revolt[2] *noun* **1** a rebellion. **2** a feeling of disgust. [same origin as *revolve*]

revolting *adjective* disgusting.

revolution *noun* **1** a rebellion that overthrows the government. **2** a complete change. **3** revolving; rotation; one complete turn of a wheel, engine, etc. [same origin as *revolve*]

revolutionary *adjective* **1** involving a great change. **2** of a political revolution.

revolutionise *verb* (**revolutionised, revolutionising**) make a great change in something.

revolve *verb* (**revolved, revolving**) turn or keep on turning round. [from *re-*, + Latin *volvere* = to roll]

revolver *noun* a pistol with a revolving mechanism that makes it possible to fire it a number of times without reloading.

revue *noun* an entertainment consisting of a number of items. [French]

revulsion *noun* **1** strong disgust. **2** a sudden violent change of feeling.

reward[1] *noun* something given in return for a useful action or merit.

reward[2] *verb* give a reward to someone.

rewrite *verb* (**rewrote, rewritten, rewriting**) write something again or differently.

rhapsody (*say* **rap**-suh-dee) *noun* (*plural* **rhapsodies**) **1** a statement of great delight about something. **2** a romantic piece of music. **rhapsodise** *verb* [from Greek *rhapsoidos* = one who stitches songs together]

rhetoric (*say* **ret**-uh-rik) *noun* **1** the art of using words impressively, especially in public speaking. **2** affected or exaggerated expressions used because they sound impressive. **rhetorical** *adjective*, **rhetorically** *adverb* [from Greek *rhetor* = orator]

rhetorical question *noun* something put as a question so that it sounds dramatic, not to get an answer, e.g. *Who cares?* (= nobody cares).

rheumatism *noun* a disease that causes pain and stiffness in joints and muscles. **rheumatic** *adjective*, **rheumatoid** *adjective*

rhinoceros *noun* (*plural* **rhinoceroses**) a large heavy animal with a horn or two horns on its nose. [from Greek *rhinos* = of the nose, + *keras* = horn]

rhododendron *noun* an evergreen shrub with large trumpet-shaped flowers. [from Greek *rhodon* = rose, + *dendron* = tree]

rhombus *noun* (*plural* **rhombuses**) a quadrilateral with equal sides but no right angles, like the diamond on playing cards.

rhubarb *noun* a plant with thick reddish stalks that are used as fruit.

rhyme[1] *noun* **1** a similar sound in the endings of words, e.g. *bat/fat/mat, batter/fatter/matter.* **2** a poem with rhymes. **3** a word that rhymes with another.

rhyme[2] *verb* (**rhymed, rhyming**) form a rhyme; have rhymes.

rhythm *noun* a regular pattern of beats, sounds, or movements. **rhythmic** *adjective*, **rhythmical** *adjective*, **rhythmically** *adverb*

rib *noun* **1** each of the curved bones round the chest. **2** a curved part that looks like a rib or supports something, *the ribs of an umbrella.* **ribbed** *adjective*

ribald (*say* **ruy**-bawld or **rib**-awld) *adjective* funny in a vulgar or disrespectful way. **ribaldry** *noun*

riband *noun* a ribbon.

ribbon *noun* a narrow strip of material used for decoration or for tying something.

rice *noun* the white seeds of a plant that is grown in marshes in hot countries, used as food.

rich *adjective* **1** having a lot of money or property or resources; wealthy. **2** having a large amount of something, *rich in minerals.* **3** costly; luxurious. **4** (of colours, sounds, or smells) deep; strong. **richly** *adverb*, **richness** *noun*

riches *plural noun* wealth.

Richter scale (*say* **rik**-tuh) *noun* a scale for measuring the strength of earthquakes. [named after the American seismologist C. F. Richter]

rick[1] *noun* a large neat stack of hay or straw.

rick[2] *verb* sprain; wrench.

rickets *noun* a disease caused by lack of vitamin D, causing deformed bones.

rickety *adjective* unsteady.

rickshaw *noun* a two-wheeled carriage pulled by one or more people, used in Asian countries. [from Japanese *jin-riki-sha* = person-power-vehicle]

ricochet (*say* **rik**-uh-shay) *verb* (**ricocheted, ricocheting**) bounce off something; rebound, *The bullets ricocheted off the wall.* **ricochet** *noun*

ricotta *noun* a soft Italian cheese.

rid *verb* (**rid, ridding**) make a person or place free from something unwanted, *He rid the town of rats.* **riddance** *noun*
get rid of cause to go away.

ridden *past participle* of **ride**[1].

riddle[1] *noun* a puzzling question, especially as a joke.

riddle[2] *noun* a coarse sieve.

riddle[3] *verb* (**riddled, riddling**) **1** pass material through a riddle. **2** pierce with many holes, *They riddled the target with bullets.*

ride[1] *verb* (**rode**, **ridden**, **riding**) **1** sit on a horse, bicycle, etc. and be carried along on it. **2** travel in a car, bus, train, or other vehicle. **3** float or be supported on something, *The ship rode the waves.*

ride[2] *noun* riding; a journey on a horse, bicycle, etc. or in a vehicle.

rider *noun* **1** someone who rides. **2** an extra comment or statement.

ridge *noun* a long narrow part higher than the rest of something. **ridged** *adjective*

ridicule *verb* (**ridiculed**, **ridiculing**) make fun of a person or thing. **ridicule** *noun* [from Latin *ridere* = to laugh]

ridiculous *adjective* so silly that it makes people laugh or despise it. **ridiculously** *adverb*

riesling (*say* **reez**-ling) *noun* a kind of grape; a dry white wine made from this. [German]

rife *adjective* widespread; happening frequently, *Crime was rife in the town.*

riff[1] *noun* **1** a short repeated phrase in popular music and jazz. **2** a monologue or spoken improvisation.

riff[2] *verb* **1** play riffs. **2** perform a monologue or spoken improvisation

riff-raff *noun* the rabble; disreputable people.

rifle[1] *noun* a long gun with spiral grooves (called *rifling*) inside the barrel that make the bullet spin and so travel more accurately.

rifle[2] *verb* (**rifled**, **rifling**) search and rob, *They rifled his desk.*

rift *noun* **1** a crack or split. **2** a disagreement that separates friends.

rift valley *noun* a steep-sided valley formed where the land has sunk.

rig[1] *verb* (**rigged**, **rigging**) **1** provide a ship with ropes, spars, sails, etc. **2** set something up quickly or out of makeshift materials. **rig out** provide with clothes or equipment.

rig[2] *noun* **1** a framework supporting the machinery for drilling an oil well. **2** the way a ship's masts and sails etc. are arranged. **3** (*informal*) an outfit of clothes. **4** a large truck; a semitrailer.

rig[3] *verb* (**rigged**, **rigging**) arrange or control fraudulently, *The election was rigged.*

rigging *noun* the ropes etc. that support a ship's mast and sails.

right[1] *adjective* **1** of or on or towards the side of the body that is on the east when you are facing north. **2** correct; true, *the right answer.* **3** morally good; fair; just, *Is it right to cheat?* **4** most suitable, *the right person for the job.* **5** (of political groups) right-wing. **rightly** *adverb*, **rightness** *noun*
she'll be right (*Australian informal*) all will be well.

right[2] *adverb* **1** on or towards the right-hand side, *Turn right.* **2** straight, *Go right on.* **3** completely, *Go right round it.* **4** exactly, *right in the middle.* **5** rightly, *You did right to tell me.*
right away immediately.

right[3] *noun* **1** the right-hand side or part or region. **2** what is morally good or fair or just. **3** something that people are allowed to do or have, *the right to vote.*

right[4] *verb* make a thing right or upright, *They righted the boat.*

right angle *noun* an angle of 90°.

righteous *adjective* doing what is right; virtuous. **righteously** *adverb*, **righteousness** *noun*

rightful *adjective* deserved; proper, *in her rightful place.* **rightfully** *adverb*

right-hand *adjective* of or on the right of something.

right-handed *adjective* using the right hand in preference to the left hand.

right-hand man *noun* an indispensable assistant.

right-wing *adjective* conservative or reactionary.

rigid *adjective* **1** stiff; firm; not bending, *a rigid support.* **2** strict, *rigid rules.* **rigidity** *noun*, **rigidly** *adverb*

rigmarole *noun* **1** a long rambling statement. **2** a complicated procedure.

rigor mortis (*say* rig-uh **maw**-tuhs) *noun* stiffening of the body after death. [Latin, = stiffness of death]

rigorous *adjective* strict; severe. **rigorously** *adverb*

rigour *noun* **1** strictness; severity. **2** harshness of weather or conditions, *the rigours of winter.*

rile *verb* (**riled**, **riling**) (*informal*) annoy.

rill *noun* a very small stream.

rim *noun* the outer edge of a cup, wheel, or other round object.

rime see **onset and rime**.

rimmed *adjective* edged.

rind *noun* the tough skin on bacon, cheese, or fruit.

ring[1] *noun* **1** a circle. **2** a thin circular piece of metal worn on a finger. **3** the space where a circus performs. **4** a square area in which a boxing match or wrestling match takes place.

ring[2] *verb* (**ringed**, **ringing**) put a ring round something; encircle.

ring[3] *verb* (**rang**, **rung**, **ringing**) **1** cause a bell to sound. **2** make a loud clear sound like that of a bell. **3** be filled with sound, *The hall rang with cheers.* **4** telephone, *Please ring me tomorrow.*

ring[4] *noun* **1** the act or sound of ringing. **2** a telephone call.

ringbark *verb* (*Australian*) kill a tree by cutting a ring of bark from around the trunk.

ringbinder *noun* a loose-leaf binder with ring-shaped clasps.

ringer *noun* (*Australian*) **1** the fastest shearer in a shed. **2** someone or something that is very good.

ring-in *noun* (*Australian*) a replacement, especially a dishonest one.

ringleader *noun* a person who leads others in wrongdoing or in opposition to authority.

ringlet *noun* a tube-shaped curl.

ringmaster *noun* the person in charge of a performance in a circus ring.

ringtail *noun* (in full **ringtail possum**) an Australian possum with a long tail that curls at the end.

ringtone *noun* a sound made by a mobile phone when an incoming call is received.

ringworm *noun* a skin disease producing round scaly patches, caused by a fungus.

rink *noun* a place made for skating.

rinse *verb* (**rinsed**, **rinsing**) **1** wash something lightly. **2** wash in clean water to remove soap. **rinse** *noun*

riot[1] *noun* wild or violent behaviour by a crowd of people.

riot[2] *verb* (**rioted**, **rioting**) take part in a riot.

riotous *adjective* **1** disorderly; unruly. **2** boisterous, *riotous laughter.*

RIP *abbreviation* rest in peace (used on graves). [short for Latin *requiescat* (or *requiescant*) *in pace*]

rip[1] *verb* (**ripped**, **ripping**) **1** tear roughly. **2** rush. **3** use a program to copy data on to a computer's hard drive.
rip off (*informal*) swindle. **rip-off** *noun*

rip[2] *noun* **1** a torn place. **2** rough water with strong currents.

ripe *adjective* **1** ready to be harvested or eaten. **2** ready and suitable, *The time is ripe for revolution.* **3** mature; advanced, *She lived to a ripe old age.* **ripeness** *noun*

ripen *verb* make or become ripe.

riposte (*say* ruh-**post**) *noun* **1** a quick counterstroke in fencing. **2** a quick retort.

ripper *noun* (*Australian informal*) an excellent person or thing, *a ripper of a day.*

ripple[1] *noun* a small wave or series of waves.

ripple[2] *verb* (**rippled**, **rippling**) form ripples.

rise[1] *verb* (**rose**, **risen**, **rising**) **1** go upwards. **2** get up from lying, sitting, or kneeling; get out of bed. **3** come to life again after death, *Christ is risen.* **4** rebel, *They rose in revolt against the tyrant.* **5** (of a river) begin its course. **6** (of the wind) begin to blow more strongly. **7** increase in number, size, or intensity.

rise[2] *noun* **1** the action of rising; an upward movement. **2** an increase in amount, number, intensity, or wages. **3** an upward slope.
give rise to cause.

rising *noun* a revolt.

risk[1] *noun* a chance of danger or loss.

risk[2] *verb* take the chance of damaging or losing something.

risky *adjective* (**riskier**, **riskiest**) full of risk.

rissole *noun* a fried cake of minced meat or fish.

Ritalin *noun* (*trademark*) a drug that stimulates the nervous system, used to treat ADD.

rite *noun* a religious ceremony; a solemn ritual.

ritual *noun* the series of actions used in a religious or other ceremony. **ritual** *adjective*, **ritually** *adverb*

rival[1] *noun* a person or thing that competes with another or tries to do the same thing. **rivalry** *noun*

rival[2] *verb* (**rivalled**, **rivalling**) be a rival of a person or thing. [from Latin *rivalis* = person using the same stream (*rivus* = stream)]

riven *adjective* split; torn apart.

river *noun* a large stream of water flowing in a natural channel. [from Latin *ripa* = bank]

rivet[1] *noun* a strong nail or bolt for holding pieces of metal together. The end opposite the head is flattened to form another head when it is in place.

rivet[2] *verb* (**riveted**, **riveting**) **1** fasten with rivets. **2** hold firmly, *She stood riveted to the spot.* **3** fascinate, *The concert was riveting.*

rivulet *noun* a small stream.

RNA *noun* ribonucleic acid, a substance in living cells that carries instructions from DNA, involved in protein synthesis.

road *noun* **1** a level way with a hard surface made for traffic to travel on. **2** a way or course, *the road to success.* **roadside** *noun*, **roadway** *noun*

roadhouse *noun* a petrol station with restaurant on a main road in a country area.

roadkill *noun* animals killed on the road by vehicles.

road map *noun* **1** a map showing the roads of an area. **2** a plan or strategy intended to achieve a particular goal, *a road map for peace.*

road rage *noun* anger provoked by another driver's actions.

road train *noun* (*Australian*) a truck pulling two or three long trailers.

roadworthy *adjective* safe to be used on roads.

roam *verb* wander. **roam** *noun*

roaming *noun* the use or ability to use a mobile phone on another operator's network, typically while overseas.

roan *adjective* (of a horse) brown or black with many white hairs.

roar¹ *noun* **1** a loud deep sound like that made by a lion. **2** a loud laugh.

roar² *verb* make a roar.
a roaring trade brisk selling of something.

roast¹ *verb* **1** cook meat or other food in an oven or by exposing it to heat. **2** make or be very hot.

roast² *adjective* roasted, *roast beef.*

roast³ *noun* meat for roasting; roast meat.

rob *verb* (**robbed**, **robbing**) take or steal from somebody, *He robbed me of my watch.* **robber** *noun*, **robbery** *noun* [from Old French *robe* = booty]

robe¹ *noun* a long loose garment.

robe² *verb* (**robed**, **robing**) dress in a robe.

robin *noun* **1** a small European bird with a red breast. **2** any of several Australian birds, some with a brightly coloured breast.

robot *noun* **1** a machine that looks and acts like a person. **2** a machine capable of carrying out a complex series of actions automatically, especially one programmable by a computer. **robotic** *adjective* [from Czech *robota* = compulsory labour]

robust *adjective* strong; vigorous. **robustly** *adverb*, **robustness** *noun* [from Latin *robur* = strength]

rock¹ *noun* **1** a large stone or boulder. **2** the hard part of the earth's crust, under the soil.

rock² *verb* **1** move gently backwards and forwards while supported on something. **2** shake violently, *The earthquake rocked the city.*

rock³ *noun* **1** a rocking movement. **2** (also **rock music**) popular music with a heavy beat.

rock bottom *noun* the very lowest level.

rocker *noun* **1** a thing that rocks something or is rocked. **2** a rocking chair.
off your rocker (*informal*) mad.

rockery *noun* (*plural* **rockeries**) a mound or bank in a garden, where plants are made to grow between large rocks.

rocket¹ *noun* **1** a firework that shoots high into the air. **2** a structure that flies by expelling burning gases, used to send up a missile or a spacecraft. **rocketry** *noun*

rocket² *verb* (**rocketed**, **rocketing**) move quickly upwards or away.

rocket³ *noun* a plant whose leaves are used in salads.

rocking chair *noun* a chair that can be rocked by a person sitting in it.

rocking horse *noun* a model of a horse that can be rocked by a child sitting on it.

rock lobster *noun* (*Australian*) a marine crustacean.

rockmelon *noun* a small round orange-coloured melon; a cantaloupe.

rocky¹ *adjective* (**rockier**, **rockiest**) like rock; full of rocks.

rocky² *adjective* (**rockier**, **rockiest**) unsteady. **rockiness** *noun*

rococo¹ *noun* an ornate style of decoration common in Europe in the 18th century.

rococo² *adjective* of or in the form of rococo.

rod *noun* **1** a long thin stick or bar. **2** a stick with a line attached for fishing.

rode *past tense* of **ride**¹.

rodent *noun* an animal that has large front teeth for gnawing things, e.g. a rat, mouse, or squirrel. [from Latin *rodens* = gnawing]

rodeo (*say* roh-**day**-oh or **roh**-dee-oh) *noun* (*plural* **rodeos**) an exhibition of cowboy-like skills in handling animals.

roe¹ *noun* a mass of eggs or reproductive cells in a fish's body.

roe² *noun* (*plural* **roes** or **roe**) a kind of small deer. The male is called a **roebuck.**

rogaine *noun* (*Australian*) a marathon orienteering event usually taking 24 hours to complete. **rogainer** *noun*, **rogaining** *noun*

rogan josh *noun* (also **roghan josh**) a dish of curried meat cooked in a rich sauce. [Urdu from Persian]

rogue *noun* **1** a dishonest person. **2** a mischievous person. **roguish** *adjective*

Rohypnol (*say* roh-**hip**-nol) *noun* (*trademark*) a powerful sedative drug.

role *noun* **1** a performer's part in a play or film etc. **2** a person's or thing's function.

roll¹ *verb* **1** move along by turning over and over, like a ball or wheel. **2** form something into the shape of a cylinder or ball. **3** flatten something by rolling a rounded object over it. **4** rock from side to side. **5** pass steadily, *The years rolled on.* **6** make a long vibrating sound, *The thunder rolled.*
roll up (*Australian*) arrive.

roll² *noun* **1** a cylinder made by rolling something up. **2** a small individual portion of bread baked in a rounded shape. **3** an official list of names. **4** a long vibrating

sound, *a drum roll.*
on a roll (*informal*) experiencing a prolonged spell of success or good luck. [from Latin *rotula* = little wheel]

roll-call *noun* the calling of a list of names to check that everyone is present.

roller *noun* **1** a cylinder for rolling over things, or on which something is wound. **2** a long swelling wave.

rollerblade *noun* (*trademark*) a roller skate with the four wheels one behind the other.
rollerblader *noun*

roller coaster *noun* a railway at a showground or amusement park with a series of steep slopes up and down alternately.

roller derby *noun* a contact sport where two teams compete on roller skates.

roller skate *noun* a framework with wheels, fitted under a shoe so that the wearer can roll smoothly over the ground.
roller skating *noun*

rollicking *adjective* boisterous and full of fun. [from *romp* + *frolic*]

rolling pin *noun* a heavy cylinder for rolling over pastry to flatten it.

rolling stock *noun* railway engines and carriages and wagons etc.

roll-up *noun* (*Australian*) the number of people attending a meeting etc.

ROM *abbreviation* read-only memory, a type of computer memory with information that can be accessed but not changed by the user.

Roman *adjective* of ancient or modern Rome or its people. **Roman** *noun*

roman *noun* plain upright type (not italic).

Roman Catholic see **catholic** 2.

romance (*say* roh-**mans**) *noun* **1** tender feelings, experiences, and qualities connected with love. **2** a love story. **3** a love affair. **4** an imaginative story about the adventures of heroes, *a romance of King Arthur's court.* **romantic** *adjective*, **romantically** *adverb*

Roman numerals *plural noun* letters that represent numbers (I = 1, V = 5, X = 10, etc.), used by the ancient Romans.

romanticism *noun* a movement in the arts and literature that originated in the late 18th century, emphasising inspiration, subjectivity, and the primacy of the individual.

Romany *noun* (*plural* **Romanies**) **1** a Gypsy. **2** the language of Gypsies. [from a Romany word *rom* = man]

romp *verb* play in a lively way. **romp** *noun*

rondo *noun* (*plural* **rondos**) a piece of music whose first part recurs several times.

roo *noun* (*Australian informal*) a kangaroo.

roo bar *noun* (*Australian*) a bullbar.

rood *noun* a crucifix in a church.

roof *noun* (*plural* **roofs**) **1** the part that covers the top of a building, shelter, or vehicle. **2** the upper part of the mouth.

rook[1] *noun* a black crow that nests in large groups. [from Old English *hroc*]

rook[2] *verb* (*informal*) swindle; charge people an unnecessarily high price.

rook[3] *noun* a chess piece shaped like a castle. [from Arabic *rukk*]

rookery *noun* (*plural* **rookeries**) a place where many rooks nest.

rookie *noun* (*informal*) a new recruit.

room *noun* **1** a part of a building with its own walls and ceiling. **2** enough space, *Is there room for me?* **roomful** *noun*

roomy *adjective* (**roomier**, **roomiest**) containing plenty of room; spacious.

roost[1] *noun* a place where birds perch or settle for sleep.

roost[2] *verb* perch; settle for sleep.

rooster *noun* a male domestic fowl.

root[1] *noun* **1** that part of a plant that grows under the ground and absorbs water and nourishment from the soil. **2** a source or basis, *The love of money is the root of all evil.* **3** a number in relation to the number it produces when multiplied by itself, *9 is the square root of 81 (9 × 9 = 81).*
take root 1 grow roots. **2** become established.

root[2] *verb* **1** take root; cause something to take root. **2** fix firmly, *Fear rooted us to the spot.*
root out get rid of something.

root[3] *verb* rummage; (of an animal) turn up ground in search of food.

rope[1] *noun* a strong thick cord made of twisted strands of fibre.
show someone the ropes show them how to do something.

rope[2] *verb* (**roped**, **roping**) fasten with a rope.
rope in persuade a person to take part in something.

ropeable *adjective* (*Australian informal*) angry.

rort[1] *noun* (*Australian informal*) **1** an act of fraud or sharp practice. **2** a wild party.

rort[2] *verb* (*Australian informal*) engage in sharp practice; manipulate or rig a ballot.

rosary *noun* (*plural* **rosaries**) a string of beads for keeping count of a set of prayers as they are said.

rose[1] *noun* **1** a shrub that has showy flowers often with thorny stems. **2** deep pink colour.

rose[2] *past tense* of **rise**[1].

roseate *adjective* deep pink; rosy.

rosella[1] *noun* a brightly coloured Australian parakeet. [from an alteration of the name *Rose Hill*, the original name of Parramatta, west of Sydney]

rosella[2] *noun* an Australian shrub with fruit used for jam.

rosemary *noun* an evergreen shrub with fragrant leaves.

rosette *noun* a large circular badge or ornament. [French, = little rose]

rosin *noun* a kind of resin.

roster[1] *noun* a list showing people's turns to be on duty etc.

roster[2] *verb* place on a roster.

rostrum *noun* (*plural* **rostra** or **rostrums**) a platform for one person.

rosy *adjective* (**rosier**, **rosiest**) **1** deep pink. **2** hopeful; cheerful, *a rosy future.* **rosiness** *noun*

rot[1] *verb* (**rotted**, **rotting**) go soft or bad and become useless; decay.

rot[2] *noun* **1** rotting; decay. **2** (*informal*) nonsense.

rotate *verb* (**rotated**, **rotating**) **1** move or cause to move in a circle round an axis or centre; revolve, *the wheel continued to rotate.* **2** arrange or happen in a series; take turns at doing something. **rotation** *noun*, **rotary** *adjective*, **rotatory** *adjective* [from Latin *rota* = wheel]

rote *noun* **by rote** from memory or by routine, without full understanding of the meaning, *We used to learn French songs by rote.*

rotor *noun* a rotating part of a machine or helicopter.

rotten *adjective* **1** rotted, *rotten apples.* **2** (*informal*) worthless; unpleasant; ill. **rottenness** *noun*

rotter *noun* (*informal*) a dishonourable person.

Rottweiler (*say* **rot**-wuy-luh) *noun* a tall black and tan dog, often used as a guard dog.

rotund *adjective* rounded; plump. **rotundity** *noun* [from Latin, = round]

rotunda *noun* a circular domed building.

rouge (*say* roozh) *noun* a reddish cosmetic for colouring the cheeks. [French, = red]

rough[1] *adjective* **1** not smooth; uneven. **2** not gentle or careful; violent, *a rough push.* **3** made or done quickly; lacking finish, *a rough job.* **4** not exact, *a rough guess.* **5** unpleasant or unfortunate; difficult, *He's had a rough trot.* **roughly** *adverb*, **roughness** *noun*

rough[2] *verb* make rough.
rough it do without ordinary comforts.
rough out draw or plan something roughly.
rough up (*informal*) treat a person violently.

roughage *noun* fibre in food that helps digestion.

roughen *verb* make or become rough.

roughy *noun* **1** tommy rough. **2** a small reef-dwelling Australian fish.

roulette (*say* roo-**let**) *noun* a gambling game where players bet on where the ball in a rotating disc will come to rest. [French, = little wheel]

round[1] *adjective* **1** shaped like a circle or ball or cylinder; curved. **2** full; complete, *a round dozen.* **3** returning to the start, *a round trip.* **roundness** *noun*
in round figures approximately, without giving exact units.

round[2] *adverb* **1** in a circle or curve; round something, *Go round to the back of the house.* **2** in every direction, *Hand the cakes round.* **3** in a new direction, *Turn your chair round.* **4** to someone's house or office etc., *Go round after dinner.* **5** into being conscious again, *Has she come round from the anaesthetic yet?*
round about 1 near by. **2** approximately.

round[3] *preposition* **1** on all sides of, *Put a fence round the pool.* **2** in a curve or circle at an even distance from, *The earth moves round the sun.* **3** to all parts of, *Show them round the house.* **4** on the further side of, *The shop is round the corner.*

round[4] *noun* **1** a round object. **2** a series of visits made by a doctor, chaplain, etc. **3** one section or stage in a competition, *Winners go on to the next round.* **4** a shot or volley of shots from a gun; ammunition for this. **5** a song in which people sing the same words but start at different times.

round[5] *verb* **1** make or become round, *A lathe was used to round the chair legs.* **2** travel round, *The car rounded the corner.* **3** express a number approximately, *round up* or *round down.*
round off finish something.
round up gather people or animals together. **round-up** *noun*

roundabout[1] *noun* **1** a road junction where traffic has to pass round a circular structure in the road. **2** a merry-go-round.

roundabout[2] *adjective* indirect; not using the shortest way of going or of saying or doing something, *I heard the news in a roundabout way.*

rounders *noun* a game in which players try to hit a ball and run round a circuit.

roundly *adverb* **1** thoroughly; severely, *We were roundly told off for being late.* **2** in a rounded shape.

round robin *noun* a contest in which each competitor plays every other.

rouse[1] (*rhymes with* cows) *verb* (**roused, rousing**) **1** make or become awake. **2** cause to become active or excited.

rouse[2] (*rhymes with* house) *verb* (**roused, rousing**) (*Australian*) scold, *He roused on me for scratching the car.*

rouseabout *noun* (*Australian*) a general hand on a rural property or in a shearing shed. [from British dialect = a person who roams about]

rousing *adjective* exciting; stirring, *a rousing speech.*

rout *verb* defeat and chase away an enemy. **rout** *noun*

route (*say* root) *noun* the way taken to get to a place.

router[1] *noun* a type of plane used for cutting groves etc. into wood; a similar power tool.

router[2] *noun* a device forwarding computer messages to the correct part of a network.

routine (*say* roo-**teen**) *noun* a regular way of doing things. **routine** *adjective*, **routinely** *adverb*

rove *verb* (**roved, roving**) roam. **rover** *noun*

row[1] (*rhymes with* go) *noun* a line of people or things.

row[2] (*rhymes with* go) *verb* make a boat move by using oars. **rower** *noun*, **rowing boat** *noun*

row[3] (*rhymes with* cow) *noun* (*informal*) **1** a loud noise. **2** a quarrel. **3** a scolding.

rowdy *adjective* (**rowdier, rowdiest**) noisy and disorderly. **rowdiness** *noun*

rowlock (*say* **rol**-uhk) *noun* a device on the side of a boat, keeping an oar in place.

royal *adjective* of or connected with a king or queen. **royally** *adverb* [from Latin *regalis* = regal]

royal blue *noun* a deep vivid blue.

royalty *noun* (*plural* **royalties**) **1** being royal. **2** a royal person or persons, *in the presence of royalty.* **3** the most successful, famous, or highly regarded members of a particular group. **4** a sum paid to a patentee for the use of a patent or to an author or composer for each copy of a book sold or for each public performance of a work. **5** payment by a mining or oil company to the owner of the land used.

RPG *abbreviation* **1** report program generator, a high-level commercial programming language. **2** rocket-propelled grenade. **3** role-playing game.

RSVP *abbreviation* répondez s'il vous plaît. [French, = please reply]

rub *verb* (**rubbed, rubbing**) **1** move something backwards and forwards while pressing it on something else. **2** apply polish, ointment, etc. by rubbing. **3** polish or clean by rubbing. **4** make sore or bare by rubbing. **rub** *noun* **rub out** remove something by rubbing.

rubber *noun* **1** a strong elastic substance used for making tyres, balls, hoses, etc. **2** a piece of rubber for rubbing out pencil or ink marks. **rubbery** *adjective*

rubbish[1] *noun* **1** things that are worthless or not wanted; refuse or litter. **2** nonsense.

rubbish[2] *verb* (*Australian*) belittle; disparage.

rubble *noun* broken pieces of brick or stone.

rubella (*say* roo-**bel**-uh) *noun* a contagious disease like mild measles.

rubicund *adjective* ruddy; red-faced. [same origin as *ruby*]

rubric (*say* **roo**-brik) *noun* **1** a heading on a document. **2** a category. **3** a set of instructions or rules. **4** a statement of purpose or function.

ruby *noun* (*plural* **rubies**) a red jewel. [from Latin *rubeus* = red]

ruck *noun* a dense crowd.

rucksack *noun* a bag on straps for carrying on the back. [from German *Rücken* = back, + *sack*]

ruckus *noun* (*informal*) a row; a commotion.

ructions *plural noun* (*informal*) protests and noisy argument.

rudder *noun* a hinged upright piece at the back of a ship or aircraft, used for steering.

ruddy *adjective* red and healthy-looking, *a ruddy complexion.*

rude *adjective* **1** impolite. **2** indecent; improper. **3** roughly made; crude, *a rude shelter.* **4** vigorous; hearty, *in rude health.* **rudely** *adverb*, **rudeness** *noun* [from Latin *rudis* = raw, wild]

rudimentary *adjective* **1** of rudiments; elementary. **2** not fully developed, *Penguins have rudimentary wings.*

rudiments (*say* **roo**-duh-muhnts) *plural noun* the elementary principles of a subject, *Learn the rudiments of chemistry.*

rue *verb* (**rued, ruing**) regret, *I rue the day I started this!*

rueful *adjective* regretful. **ruefully** *adverb*

ruff *noun* **1** a starched pleated frill worn round the neck in the 16th century. **2** a collar-like ring of feathers or fur round a bird's or animal's neck.

ruffian *noun* a violent lawless person. **ruffianly** *adjective*

ruffle[1] *verb* (**ruffled, ruffling**) **1** disturb the smoothness of a thing. **2** upset or annoy someone.

ruffle[2] *noun* a gathered ornamental frill.

rug *noun* **1** a thick mat for the floor. **2** a piece of thick fabric used as a blanket.

rugby *noun* (also **rugby football**) a kind of football game using an oval ball that players may carry or kick. [named after Rugby School in England, where it was first played]

rugby league *noun* a form of rugby played by teams of 13.

rugby union *noun* a form of rugby played by teams of 15.

rugged *adjective* **1** having an uneven surface or outline; craggy. **2** sturdy.

ruin[1] *noun* **1** severe damage or destruction to something. **2** a building that has fallen down.

ruin[2] *verb* damage a thing so severely that it is useless; destroy. **ruination** *noun* [from Latin *ruere* = to fall]

ruinous *adjective* **1** causing ruin. **2** in ruins; ruined.

rule[1] *noun* **1** something that people have to obey. **2** the customary or normal state of things. **3** ruling; governing, *under French rule.* **4** a carpenter's ruler.
as a rule usually; more often than not.

rule[2] *verb* (**ruled**, **ruling**) **1** govern; reign. **2** make a decision, *The referee ruled that it was a foul.* **3** draw a straight line with a ruler or other straight edge.
rule out exclude. [from Latin *regula* = rule]

rule of law *noun* the restriction of the arbitrary exercise of power by subordinating it to well-defined and established laws.

ruler *noun* **1** a person who governs. **2** a strip of wood, metal, or plastic with straight edges, used for measuring and drawing straight lines.

ruling *noun* a judgement.

rum *noun* a strong alcoholic drink made from sugar or molasses.

rumba (*say* **rum**-buh) *noun* a rhythmic dance with Spanish and African elements, originating in Cuba; music for this.

rumble *verb* (**rumbled**, **rumbling**) make a deep heavy continuous sound like thunder. **rumble** *noun*

ruminant[1] *adjective* ruminating.

ruminant[2] *noun* an animal that chews the cud (see **cud**).

ruminate *verb* (**ruminated**, **ruminating**) **1** chew the cud. **2** meditate; ponder. **rumination** *noun*, **ruminative** *adjective*

rummage *verb* (**rummaged**, **rummaging**) turn things over or move them about while looking for something. **rummage** *noun*

rummy *noun* a card game in which players try to form sets or sequences of cards.

rumour[1] *noun* information that spreads to a lot of people but may not be true.

rumour[2] *verb* **be rumoured** be spread as a rumour. [from Latin *rumor* = noise]

rump *noun* the hind part of an animal.

rumple *verb* (**rumpled**, **rumpling**) crumple; make a thing untidy.

rumpus *noun* (*plural* **rumpuses**) (*informal*) an uproar; an angry protest.

run[1] *verb* (**ran**, **run**, **running**) **1** move with quick steps so that both or all feet leave the ground at each stride. **2** go or travel; flow, *Tears ran down his cheeks.* **3** produce a flow of liquid, *Run some water into it.* **4** work or function, *The engine was running smoothly.* **5** manage; organise, *She runs a deli.* **6** compete in a contest, *He ran for President.* **7** extend, *A fence runs round the property.* **8** go or take in a vehicle, *I'll run you to the station.*
run after pursue.
run away leave a place secretly or quickly.
run down 1 knock down with a moving vehicle. **2** stop gradually. **3** criticise; disparage.
run into 1 collide with. **2** happen to meet.
run out 1 have used up your stock of something. **2** (in cricket) knock over the wicket of a running batter.
run over 1 overflow. **2** knock down or crush with a moving vehicle.
run through study or repeat quickly.

run[2] *noun* **1** the action of running; a time spent running, *Go for a run.* **2** a short trip or journey. **3** a point scored in cricket or baseball. **4** a continuous stretch, sequence, or spell, *She had a run of good luck.* **5** an enclosure for animals, *a chicken run.* **6** (*Australian*) a sheep or cattle station. **7** a track, *a ski run.* **8** a ladder in stockings etc.
on the run running away from pursuit or capture.

runaway[1] *noun* someone who has run away.

runaway[2] *adjective* **1** having run away or out of control. **2** won easily, *a runaway victory.*

run-down *noun* a summary or analysis.

rung[1] *noun* a crosspiece in a ladder.

rung[2] *past participle* of **ring**[3].

run-in *noun* (*informal*) a quarrel.

runner *noun* **1** a person or animal that runs, especially in a race. **2** a stem that grows away from a plant and roots itself. **3** a groove, rod, or roller for a thing to move on; each of the long strips under a sledge. **4** a long narrow strip of carpet or covering.

runner bean *noun* a kind of climbing bean.

runners *plural noun* (*Australian*) running shoes.

runner-up *noun* (*plural* **runners-up**) someone who comes second in a competition.

running[1] *noun* **in the running** competing and with a chance of winning.

running[2] *adjective* continuous; consecutive; without an interval, *It rained for four days running.*

runny *adjective* flowing like liquid; producing a flow of liquid.

runt *noun* the smallest animal in a litter.

runway *noun* a long hard surface on which aircraft take off and land.

rupiah (*say* roo-**pee**-uh) *noun* the unit of money in Indonesia.

rupture *verb* (**ruptured**, **rupturing**) break; burst. **rupture** *noun* [from Latin *ruptum* = broken]

rural *adjective* of or like the countryside. [from Latin *ruris* = of the country]

ruse *noun* a deception or trick.

rush[1] *verb* **1** hurry. **2** move or flow quickly. **3** attack or capture by rushing.

rush[2] *noun* (*plural* **rushes**) **1** a hurry. **2** a sudden movement towards something. **3** a sudden great demand for something.

rush[3] *noun* (*plural* **rushes**) a plant with a thin stem that grows in marshy places.

rusk *noun* a kind of biscuit, especially for feeding babies.

russet *noun* reddish-brown colour. [from Latin *russus* = red]

rust[1] *noun* **1** a red or brown substance that forms on iron or steel exposed to damp and corrodes it. **2** reddish-brown colour.

rust[2] *verb* make or become rusty.

rustic *adjective* **1** rural. **2** made of rough timber or branches, *a rustic bridge.*

rustle *verb* (**rustled**, **rustling**) **1** make a sound like paper being crumpled. **2** steal horses or cattle, *cattle rustling.* **rustle** *noun*, **rustler** *noun*
rustle up (*informal*) produce quickly, *rustle up a meal.*

rusty *adjective* (**rustier**, **rustiest**) **1** coated with rust. **2** weakened by lack of use or practice, *My French is a bit rusty.* **rustiness** *noun*

rut *noun* **1** a deep track made by wheels in soft ground. **2** a settled and usually dull way of life, *We are getting into a rut.*
rutted *adjective*

ruthless *adjective* pitiless; merciless; cruel. **ruthlessly** *adverb*, **ruthlessness** *noun* [from *ruth* = pity]

rye *noun* a cereal used for making flour or as a food for cattle.

Ss

S *abbreviation* south; southern.

sabbath *noun* (often **the Sabbath**) a day of religious observance and abstinence from work, kept by Jews from Friday evening to Saturday evening, and by most Christians on Sunday. [from Hebrew, = rest]

sable *noun* **1** a kind of dark fur. **2** (*poetic*) black.

sabotage *noun* deliberate damage or disruption to hinder an enemy, employer, etc. **sabotage** *verb*, **saboteur** *noun*

sabre *noun* **1** a heavy sword with a curved blade. **2** a light fencing sword.

sac *noun* a bag-shaped part in an animal or plant.

saccharin (*say* **sak**-uh-ruhn) *noun* a very sweet substance used as a substitute for sugar. [from Greek *saccharon* = sugar]

saccharine (*say* **sak**-uh-reen) *adjective* unpleasantly sweet, *a saccharine smile.*

sachet (*say* **sash**-ay) *noun* a small sealed bag or packet holding a scented substance or a single portion of something. [French, = little sack]

sack[1] *noun* a large bag made of strong material. **sacking** *noun*
get the sack (*informal*) be dismissed from a job.

sack[2] *verb* (*informal*) dismiss someone from a job.

sack[3] *verb* plunder a captured town in a violent destructive way. **sack** *noun*

sackbut *noun* an early form of trombone.

sacrament *noun* an important Christian religious ceremony such as baptism or Holy Communion. [same origin as *sacred*]

sacred *adjective* to do with God or a god, or religion; holy. [from Latin *sacer* = holy]

sacred site *noun* a place of spiritual significance, especially to Aboriginal people.

sacrifice[1] *noun* **1** giving something that you think will please a god. **2** giving up a thing you value, so that something good may happen. **3** a thing sacrificed.
sacrificial *adjective*

sacrifice[2] *verb* (**sacrificed**, **sacrificing**) give something as a sacrifice. [from Latin, = make a thing sacred]

sacrilege (*say* **sak**-ruh-lij) *noun* disrespect or damage to something people regard as sacred. **sacrilegious** *adjective* [from Latin *sacer* = sacred, + *legere* = take away]

sacrosanct *adjective* sacred or respected and therefore not to be harmed. [from Latin *sacro* = by a sacred rite, + *sanctus* = holy]

sacrum (*say* **say**-kruhm) *noun* (*plural* **sacra** or **sacrums**) the triangular bone that forms the back of the pelvis.

sad *adjective* (**sadder**, **saddest**) **1** unhappy; showing sorrow. **2** causing sorrow. **sadly** *adverb*, **sadness** *noun*

sadden *verb* make a person sad.

saddle[1] *noun* **1** a seat for putting on the back of a horse or other animal. **2** the seat of a bicycle. **3** a ridge of high land between two peaks.

saddle[2] *verb* (**saddled**, **saddling**) **1** put a saddle on a horse or other animal. **2** burden someone with a task or responsibility.

sadist (*say* **say**-duhst) *noun* a person who enjoys hurting other people. **sadism** *noun*, **sadistic** *adjective* [named after a French novelist, the Marquis de Sade, noted for his crimes]

safari *noun* (*plural* **safaris**) an expedition to see or hunt wild animals. [from Arabic *safara* = travel]

safe[1] *adjective* **1** free from risk or danger; not dangerous. **2** providing protection, *a safe place.* **3** reliable; certain, *a safe method.* **4** unharmed. **safely** *adverb*, **safeness** *noun*, **safety** *noun*

safe[2] *noun* a strong cupboard or box in which valuables can be locked safely. [from Latin *salvus* = uninjured]

safeguard[1] *noun* a protection.

safeguard[2] *verb* protect.

safety net *noun* **1** a net placed to catch an acrobat etc. in case of a fall. **2** a safeguard against possible hardship or adversity; welfare measures etc. that protect the disadvantaged.

safety pin *noun* a U-shaped pin with a clip fastening over the point.

safflower *noun* a thistle-like plant yielding a red dye and a cooking oil.

saffron *noun* the orange-coloured stigmas of a kind of crocus, used to colour or flavour food. [Arabic]

sag *verb* (**sagged**, **sagging**) go down in the middle because something heavy is pressing on it; droop. **sag** *noun*

saga (*say* **sah**-guh) *noun* a long story with many episodes.

sagacious (*say* suh-**gay**-shuhs) *adjective* shrewd and wise. **sagaciously** *adverb*, **sagacity** *noun* [from Latin *sagax* = wise]

sage[1] *noun* a kind of herb.

sage[2] *adjective* wise. **sagely** *adverb*

sage[3] *noun* a wise and respected person.

Sagittarius *noun* **1** a constellation and the ninth sign of the zodiac (the Archer). **2** a person born when the sun is in this sign. [Latin = archer]

sago *noun* a starchy white food used to make puddings.

said (*say* sed) *past tense & past participle* of **say**[1], *I can't remember what she said.*

sail[1] *noun* **1** a large piece of strong cloth attached to a mast etc. to catch the wind and make a ship or boat move. **2** a short voyage. **3** an arm of a windmill.

sail[2] *verb* **1** travel in a ship or boat. **2** start a voyage, *We sail at noon.* **3** control a ship or boat. **4** move quickly and smoothly. **sailing ship** *noun*

sailor *noun* a person who sails; a member of a ship's crew or of a navy.

saint *noun* a holy or very good person. **saintliness** *noun*, **saintly** *adverb* [from Latin *sanctus* = holy]

sake *noun* **for the sake of** so as to help or please a person, get a thing, etc.

salaam *noun* a low bow with the right hand on the forehead. [from Arabic *salam* = peace]

salad *noun* a mixture of vegetables eaten raw or cold.

salamander *noun* a lizard-like animal formerly thought to live in fire.

salami *noun* a spiced sausage.

salary *noun* (*plural* **salaries**) a fixed regular payment, typically paid on a monthly basis but often expressed as an annual sum, made by an employer to an employee. **salaried** *adjective* [from Latin *salarium* = salt-money, money given to Roman soldiers to buy salt]

salary sacrifice *noun* (*Australian*) a financial scheme whereby part of an employee's pre-tax salary is paid into a superannuation fund or used for a non-cash benefit such as a computer or car.

sale *noun* **1** selling. **2** a time when things are sold at reduced prices.

salesman *noun* (*plural* **salesmen**) a man employed to sell goods.

salesperson *noun* (*plural* **salespersons** or **salespeople**) a person employed to sell goods.

saleswoman *noun* (*plural* **saleswomen**) a woman employed to sell goods.

salience *noun* (also **saliency**) the quality of being particularly noticeable or important; prominence.

salient (*say* **say**-lee-uhnt) *adjective* **1** projecting; prominent; conspicuous; most noticeable. **2** main; most pertinent, *the salient points of his argument.* **saliently** *adverb* [from Latin *saliens* = leaping]

saline *adjective* containing salt.

saliva *noun* the natural liquid in a person's or animal's mouth. **salivary** *adjective*

salivate (*say* **sal**-uh-vayt) *verb* (**salivated**, **salivating**) form saliva. **salivation** *noun*

sallow *adjective* slightly yellow, *a sallow complexion.* **sallowness** *noun*

sally[1] *noun* (*plural* **sallies**) **1** a sudden rush forward. **2** an excursion. **3** a lively or witty remark.

sally[2] *verb* (**sallied, sallying**) make a sudden attack or an excursion. [same origin as *salient*]

sally[3] *noun* a eucalypt or wattle resembling a willow.

salmon (*say* **sam**-uhn) *noun* (*plural* **salmon**) a large edible fish with pink flesh.

salmonella (*say* sal-muh-**nel**-uh) *noun* a bacterium that can cause food poisoning and various diseases.

salon *noun* **1** a large elegant room. **2** a room or shop where a hairdresser etc. receives customers.

saloon *noun* **1** a car with a hard roof. **2** a room where people can sit, drink, etc.

salsa *noun* **1** a kind of dance music of Cuban origin, with jazz and rock elements; a dance associated with this. **2** (especially in Latin American cooking) a spicy sauce served with meat or as a dip. [Spanish, = sauce]

salt[1] *noun* **1** sodium chloride, the white substance that gives seawater its taste and is used for flavouring food. **2** a chemical compound formed by a metal and an acid. **salty** *adjective*

salt[2] *verb* flavour or preserve food with salt.

saltbush *noun* an Australian plant growing in saline areas especially in desert country.

salt cellar *noun* a small dish or perforated pot holding salt for use at meals.

saltie *noun* (*Australian informal*) a saltwater crocodile.

saltwater *adjective* of or living in seawater, *a saltwater crocodile.*

salubrious *adjective* good for people's health. **salubrity** *noun* [from Latin *salus* = health]

salutary *adjective* beneficial; having a good effect, *She gave us some salutary advice.* [from Latin *salus* = health]

salutation *noun* a greeting.

salute[1] *verb* (**saluted**, **saluting**) **1** raise your right hand to your forehead as a sign of respect. **2** greet. **3** say that you respect or admire something, *We salute this achievement.*

salute[2] *noun* **1** the act of saluting. **2** the firing of guns as a sign of greeting or respect. [from Latin *salus* = health]

salvage *verb* (**salvaged**, **salvaging**) save or rescue something so that it can be used again. **salvage** *noun* [from Latin *salvare* = save]

salvation *noun* **1** preservation from loss or calamity; a person or thing that preserves from these. **2** saving of the soul from sin; the state of being saved.

Salvation Army *noun* a worldwide evangelical Christian organisation doing charitable work.

salve[1] *noun* **1** a soothing ointment. **2** something that soothes.

salve[2] *verb* (**salved**, **salving**) soothe a person's conscience or wounded pride.

salver *noun* a small tray, usually of metal.

Salvo *noun* (*plural* **Salvos**) (*informal*) a member of the Salvation Army.

salvo *noun* (*plural* **salvoes** or **salvos**) a volley of shots or of applause.

samba *noun* a dance of Brazilian origin; music for this. [Portuguese]

sambal (*say* **sam**-bahl) *noun* a spicy condiment used in Malaysian and Indonesian cooking. [Malay]

same *adjective* **1** of one kind; exactly alike or equal; not different. **2** not changing. **sameness** *noun*

samosa *noun* a small case of crisp pastry filled with a mixture of spicy meat or vegetables. [Persian from Urdu]

samovar *noun* a Russian tea-urn. [Russian, = self-boiler]

sampan *noun* a small flat-bottomed boat used in China. [from Chinese *sanpan* (*san* = three, *pan* = boards)]

sample[1] *noun* a small amount that shows what something is like; a specimen.

sample[2] *verb* (**sampled**, **sampling**) **1** take a sample of something. **2** record or extract a small piece of music or sound for reuse as part of a composition or song.

sampler *noun* a piece of embroidery worked in various stitches to show skill in needlework.

sanatorium *noun* a hospital for treating chronic diseases (e.g. tuberculosis) or convalescents. [from Latin *sanara* = heal]

sanctify *verb* (**sanctified**, **sanctifying**) make holy or sacred. **sanctification** *noun* [from Latin *sanctus* = holy]

sanctimonious *adjective* making a show of being virtuous or pious.

sanction[1] *noun* **1** permission; authorisation. **2** action taken against a nation that is considered to have broken an international law or agreement, *Sanctions against that country include refusing to trade with it.*

sanction[2] *verb* permit; authorise. [from Latin *sancire* = make holy]

sanctity *noun* being sacred; holiness.

sanctuary *noun* (*plural* **sanctuaries**) **1** a safe place; a refuge. **2** a sacred place; the part of a church where the altar stands. **3** a place where wildlife is protected. [from Latin *sanctus* = holy]

sanctum *noun* a person's private room. [Latin, = holy thing]

sand[1] *noun* the tiny particles that cover the ground in deserts, on seashores, etc.

sand[2] *verb* smooth or polish with sandpaper or some other rough material. **sander** *noun*

sandal *noun* a lightweight shoe with straps over the foot. **sandalled** *adjective*

sandalwood *noun* a scented wood from a tropical tree.

sandbag *noun* a bag filled with sand, used to build defences.

sandbank *noun* a bank of sand under water.

sandpaper *noun* strong paper coated with sand or a similar substance, rubbed on rough surfaces to make them smooth.

sands *plural noun* a sandy area.

sandshoe *noun* a canvas shoe with a rubber sole, worn especially for sport.

sandstone *noun* rock made of compressed sand.

sandstorm *noun* a desert storm of wind with clouds of sand.

sandwich[1] *noun* (*plural* **sandwiches**) two or more slices of bread with food between them. [named after the Earl of Sandwich (1718–92), who is said to have eaten this form of food so as not to have to leave the gambling table]

sandwich[2] *verb* put a thing between two other things.

sandy *adjective* **1** like sand; covered with sand. **2** yellowish-red, *sandy hair.* **sandiness** *noun*

sane *adjective* **1** having a healthy mind; not mad. **2** sensible. **sanely** *adverb*, **sanity** *noun* [from Latin *sanus* = healthy]

sang *past tense* of **sing**.

sanger *noun* (*Australian informal*) a sandwich.

sangfroid (*say* sahng-**frwah**) *noun* calmness in danger or difficulty. [French, = cold blood]

sanguinary *adjective* bloodthirsty. [from Latin *sanguis* = blood]

sanguine (*say* **sang**-gwuhn) *adjective* hopeful; optimistic.

sanitary *adjective* **1** free from germs and dirt; hygienic. **2** of sanitation. [from Latin *sanus* = healthy]

sanitary pad *noun* an absorbent pad worn during menstruation.

sanitation *noun* arrangements for drainage and the disposal of sewage.

sanitise *verb* (**sanitised**, **sanitising**) **1** make clean and hygienic; disinfect. **2** (*informal*) make something more acceptable by removing elements that are likely to be unacceptable or controversial.

sanitiser *noun* a substance used to make something clean and hygienic, *hand sanitiser.*

sanity *noun* being sane.

sank *past tense* of **sink**[1].

Sanskrit *noun* the ancient language of the Hindus in India.

sans serif *noun* (also **sanserif**) a form of typeface without serifs (like the headwords in this dictionary).

sap[1] *noun* the liquid inside a plant, carrying food to all its parts.

sap[2] *verb* (**sapped**, **sapping**) take away a person's strength gradually.

sapling *noun* a young tree. [from *sap*]

sapphire *noun* a bright blue jewel.

saprophyte *noun* a fungus or similar plant living on dead organic matter. [from Greek *sapros* = putrid, + *phuton* = plant]

sarcastic *adjective* saying amusing or contemptuous things that hurt someone's feelings; using irony. **sarcasm** *noun*, **sarcastically** *adverb* [from Greek *sarkazein* = tear the flesh]

sarcophagus *noun* (*plural* **sarcophagi**) a stone coffin, often decorated with carvings. [from Greek *sarkos* = of flesh, + *phagos* = eating]

sardine *noun* a small sea fish, often sold in tins, packed tightly in oil.

sardonic *adjective* funny in a grim or sarcastic way. **sardonically** *adverb*

sari *noun* (*plural* **saris**) a length of cloth worn wrapped round the body as a garment, especially by Indian women and girls. [Hindi]

sarod (*say* suh-**rohd**) *noun* an Indian musical instrument that is like a sitar. [Urdu from Persian *surod* = song, melody]

sarong *noun* a skirt-like garment consisting of a strip of cloth wrapped round the body and tucked at the waist or under the armpits. [Malay]

SARS (*say* sahz) *noun* severe acute respiratory syndrome, a contagious viral disease.

sartorial *adjective* of clothes. [from Latin *sartor* = tailor]

SAS *abbreviation* Special Air Service, an armed regiment trained in commando techniques.

sash *noun* (*plural* **sashes**) a strip of cloth worn round the waist or over one shoulder. [from Arabic *shash* = turban]

sashimi (*say* sa-**shee**-mee) *noun* a Japanese dish of slices of raw fish served with grated horseradish and soy sauce.

sash window *noun* a window that slides up and down. [from French *châssis* = frame]

sat *past tense & past participle* of **sit**.

satanic (*say* suh-**tan**-ik) *adjective* of or like Satan. [from *Satan*, the Devil in Jewish and Christian teaching]

satay (*say* sah-**tay**) *noun* **1** Indonesian and Malaysian dish consisting of small pieces of meat grilled on a skewer and usually served with a spiced sauce. **2** a spicy sauce containing peanuts, chilli, etc. [Malay and Indonesian]

satchel *noun* a bag worn on the shoulder or over the back, especially for carrying books to and from school. [from Latin *saccellus* = little sack]

sate *verb* (**sated**, **sating**) satiate.

satellite *noun* **1** a heavenly body or spacecraft etc. that moves in an orbit round a planet, *The moon is a satellite of the earth.* **2** a country that is under the influence of a more powerful country. [from Latin *satelles* = guard]

satiate (*say* **say**-shee-ayt) *verb* (**satiated**, **satiating**) satisfy an appetite or desire etc. fully; glut. [from Latin *satis* = enough]

satiety (*say* suh-**tuy**-uh-tee) *noun* being or feeling satiated.

satin *noun* a silky material that is shiny on one side. **satin** *adjective*, **satiny** *adjective*

satire *noun* **1** using humour or exaggeration to make fun of a person or thing. **2** a play or poem etc. that does this. **satirical** *adjective*, **satirically** *adverb*, **satirise** *verb*, **satirist** *noun*

satisfaction *noun* **1** satisfying. **2** being satisfied and pleased because of this. **3** something that satisfies a desire or gratifies a feeling. [from Latin *satis* = enough, + *facere* = make]

satisfactory *adjective* good enough; sufficient. **satisfactorily** *adverb*

satisfy *verb* (**satisfied**, **satisfying**) **1** give a person etc. what is needed or wanted. **2** make someone feel certain; convince, *The firemen were satisfied that the fire was out.* [same origin as *satisfaction*]

saturate *verb* (**saturated**, **saturating**) **1** make a thing very wet. **2** make something take in as much as possible of a substance or goods etc. **saturation** *noun*

Saturday *noun* the day of the week following Friday. [Old English = day of Saturn (a Roman god)]

Saturn *noun* a large planet of the solar system, with 'rings' composed of small icy particles. [named after a Roman god of agriculture]

saturnine *adjective* looking gloomy and forbidding, *a saturnine face.*

satyr (*say* **sat**-uh) *noun* (in Greek myths) a woodland god with a man's body and a goat's ears, tail, and legs.

sauce *noun* **1** a thick liquid served with food to add flavour. **2** (*informal*) being cheeky; impudence.

saucepan *noun* a cooking pan with a handle at the side.

saucer *noun* a small shallow dish on which a cup is placed.

saucy *adjective* (**saucier**, **sauciest**) cheeky; impudent. **saucily** *adverb*, **sauciness** *noun*

sauna *noun* a room or compartment filled with steam, used as a kind of bath (originally in Finland). [Finnish]

saunter *verb* walk slowly and casually. **saunter** *noun*

sausage *noun* a tube of skin or plastic stuffed with minced meat and other filling.

sausage sizzle *noun* (*Australian*) **1** a fundraising or social event at which barbecued sausages served on a slice of bread are sold or provided. **2** a barbecued sausage in a slice of bread sold or provided at such an event.

sauté (*say* **soh**-tay) *adjective* fried quickly in a small amount of fat. **sauté** *verb* (**sautéd** or **sautéed**, **sautéing**) [from French *sauter* = to jump]

sauvignon (*say* **soh**-vin-yon) *noun* a variety of white grape; the white wine made from this. [French]

savage[1] *adjective* **1** wild; primitive. **2** fierce; cruel. **savage** *noun*, **savagely** *adverb*, **savageness** *noun*, **savagery** *noun*

savage[2] *verb* attack viciously; maul, *She was savaged by the dog.* [from Latin *silvaticus* = of the woods, wild]

savannah *noun* a grassy plain in a hot country, with few or no trees.

save[1] *verb* (**saved**, **saving**) **1** keep safe; free a person or thing from danger or harm. **2** keep something, especially money, so that it can be used later. **3** avoid wasting something, *This will save time.* **4** (in computing) keep data by moving a copy to a storage location. **5** (in sports) prevent an opponent from scoring. **save** *noun*, **saver** *noun*

save[2] *preposition* except, *All the trains save one were late.* [from Latin *salvus* = safe]

saveloy (*say* **sav**-uh-loi) *noun* a kind of pork sausage.

savings *plural noun* money saved.

saviour *noun* **1** a person who saves someone. **2** (**the** or **our Saviour**) Jesus Christ as the saviour of mankind.

savour[1] *noun* the taste or smell of something.

savour[2] *verb* **1** taste or smell. **2** enjoy; relish. [from Latin *sapor* = flavour]

savoury[1] *adjective* **1** tasty but not sweet. **2** having an appetising taste or smell.

savoury[2] *noun* (*plural* **savouries**) a savoury dish.

savvy *adjective* (*informal*) knowing; wise.

saw[1] *noun* a tool with a zigzag edge for cutting wood, metal, etc.

saw[2] *verb* (**sawed**, **sawn**, **sawing**) **1** cut with a saw. **2** move to and fro as a saw does.

saw[3] *past tense* of **see**, *I saw a kangaroo yesterday.*

sawdust *noun* powder that comes from wood cut by a saw.

sawmill *noun* a mill where timber is cut into planks etc. by machinery.

sawyer *noun* a person whose job is to saw timber.

saxophone *noun* a brass wind instrument with a reed in the mouthpiece. **saxophonist** *noun* [from the name of A. Sax, its Belgian inventor]

say[1] *verb* (**said**, **saying**) **1** speak or express something in words, *Mum says I'm not allowed to leave the house today.* **2** give an opinion. **3** convey information.

say[2] *noun* the power to decide something, *I have no say in the matter.*

saying *noun* a well-known phrase or proverb or other statement.

SC *abbreviation* Senior Counsel.

scab[1] *noun* **1** a hard crust that forms over a cut or graze while it is healing. **2** (*informal*) a person who works while fellow workers are on strike. **scabby** *adjective*

scab[2] *verb* (**scabbed**, **scabbing**) **1** form a scab. **2** (*informal*) work while fellow workers are on strike. **3** (*Australian informal*) cadge or borrow something.

scabbard *noun* the sheath of a sword or dagger.

scabies (*say* **skay**-beez) *noun* a contagious skin disease that causes itching.

scaffold *noun* **1** a platform on which criminals are executed. **2** scaffolding.

scaffolding *noun* a structure of poles or tubes and planks making platforms for workers to stand on while building or repairing a house or other structure.

scald *verb* **1** burn yourself with very hot liquid or steam. **2** heat milk until it is nearly boiling. **3** clean pans etc. with boiling water. **scald** *noun*

scale[1] *noun* **1** a series of units, degrees, or qualities etc. for measuring something. **2** a series of musical notes going up or down in a fixed pattern. **3** proportion; ratio, *The scale of this map is one centimetre to the kilometre.* **4** the relative size or importance of something, *They entertain friends on a large scale.*

scale[2] *verb* (**scaled**, **scaling**) **1** climb, *She scaled the ladder.* **2** alter or arrange something in proportion to something else, *Scale your spending according to your income!* [from Latin *scala* = ladder]

scale[3] *noun* **1** each of the thin overlapping parts on the outside of fish, snakes, etc.; a thin flake or part like this. **2** a hard substance formed in a kettle or boiler by hard water, or on teeth. **scaly** *adjective*

scale[4] *verb* (**scaled**, **scaling**) remove scales or scale from something. [from Old French *escale* = flake, from an old Germanic word *skalo*]

scale[5] *noun* an instrument for weighing. [from Old Norse *skal* = bowl, from *skalo* (see *scale*[4])]

scalene (*say* **skay**-leen) *adjective* (of a triangle) having unequal sides. [from Greek *skalenos* = unequal]

scallop *noun* **1** a shellfish with two hinged fan-shaped shells. **2** each curve in an ornamental wavy border. **3** (*Australian*) a slice of potato battered and deep fried. **scalloped** *adjective*

scallywag *noun* a rascal.

scalp[1] *noun* the skin on the top of the head.

scalp[2] *verb* cut or tear the scalp from.

scalpel *noun* a small straight knife used by a surgeon or artist.

scam *noun* (*informal*) a trick or swindle; a racket.

scamp *noun* a rascal.

scamper *verb* run hurriedly. **scamper** *noun*

scampi *plural noun* large prawns. [Italian]

scan *verb* (**scanned**, **scanning**) **1** look at every part of something. **2** glance at something. **3** sweep a radar or electronic beam over an area in search of something. **4** examine internal areas of the body using X-rays, ultrasound, or other devices. **5** convert a document or picture into digital form for storage or processing on a computer. **6** count the beats of a line of poetry; be correct in rhythm, *This line doesn't scan.* **scan** *noun*, **scanner** *noun*

scandal *noun* **1** something shameful or disgraceful. **2** gossip about people's faults and wrongdoing. **scandalous** *adjective* [from Greek, = stumbling block]

scandalise *verb* (**scandalised**, **scandalising**) shock a person by something considered shameful or disgraceful.

scandalmonger *noun* a person who invents or gossips about scandal.

Scandinavian *adjective* of Scandinavia (= Norway, Sweden, and Denmark; sometimes also Finland and Iceland). **Scandinavian** *noun*

scansion *noun* the scanning of verse.

scant *adjective* scanty.

scanty *adjective* (**scantier**, **scantiest**) small in amount or extent; meagre, *a scanty harvest.* **scantily** *adverb*, **scantiness** *noun*

scapegoat *noun* a person who is made to bear the blame or punishment for what others have done. [named after the goat which the ancient Jews allowed to escape into the desert after the priest had symbolically laid the people's sins upon it]

scapula (*say* **scap**-yuh-luh) *noun* (*plural* **scapulae** or **scapulas**) the shoulder blade. [Latin]

scar[1] *noun* a mark left where a wound or sore has healed.

scar[2] *verb* (**scarred**, **scarring**) make a scar or scars on skin etc.

scarab *noun* an ancient Egyptian ornament or symbol carved in the shape of a beetle.

scarce *adjective* not enough to supply people; rare. **scarcity** *noun*
make yourself scarce (*informal*) go away; keep out of the way.

scarcely *adverb* only just; only with difficulty, *She could scarcely walk.*

scare[1] *verb* (**scared**, **scaring**) frighten.

scare[2] *noun* a fright; alarm. **scary** *adjective*

scarecrow *noun* a figure of a person dressed in old clothes, set up to frighten birds away from crops.

scarf *noun* (*plural* **scarves**) a strip of material worn round the neck or head.

scarlet *adjective & noun* bright red.

scarlet fever *noun* an infectious fever producing a scarlet rash.

scarp *noun* a steep slope on a hill.

scarper *verb* (*informal*) run away.

scathing (*say* **skay**-*thing*) *adjective* severely criticising a person or thing.

scatter *verb* throw or send or move in various directions.

scatterbrain *noun* a careless forgetful person. **scatterbrained** *adjective*

scavenge *verb* (**scavenged**, **scavenging**) **1** search for useful things amongst rubbish. **2** (of a bird or animal) search for decaying flesh as food. **scavenger** *noun*

scenario *noun* (*plural* **scenarios**) **1** a summary of the plot of a play, film, or novel. **2** a postulated sequence or development of events, *A possible scenario is that she became lost after school.* [Italian]

scene *noun* **1** the place where something happens, *the scene of the crime.* **2** a part of a play or film. **3** a view as seen by a spectator. **4** an angry or noisy outburst, *He made a scene about the money.* **5** stage scenery. [from Greek *skene* = stage]

scenery *noun* **1** the natural features of a landscape. **2** things put on a stage to make it look like a place.

scenic *adjective* having fine natural scenery, *a scenic road along the coast.*

scent[1] *noun* **1** a pleasant smell. **2** a liquid perfume. **3** an animal's smell that other animals can detect.

scent[2] *verb* **1** discover something by its scent; detect. **2** put scent on something; make fragrant. **scented** *adjective* [from Latin *sentire* = perceive]

sceptic (*say* **skep**-tik) *noun* a sceptical person.

sceptical (*say* **skep**-tuh-kuhl) *adjective* inclined to disbelieve things; doubting or questioning the truth or claims of statements etc. **sceptically** *adverb*, **scepticism** *noun* [from Greek *skeptikos* = thoughtful]

sceptre *noun* a rod carried by a king or queen as a symbol of sovereignty.

schadenfreude *noun* the enjoyment of another's misfortune. [German]

schedule[1] (**shed**-yool or **sked**-jool) *noun* a program or timetable of planned events or work.

schedule[2] *verb* (**scheduled, scheduling**) put into a schedule; plan. [from Latin *scedula* = little piece of paper]

schematic (*say* skuh-**mat**-ik) *adjective* in the form of a diagram or chart.

scheme[1] *noun* **1** a plan of action. **2** a secret plan. **3** an orderly pattern or arrangement, *a colour scheme.*

scheme[2] *verb* (**schemed**, **scheming**) make plans; plot. **schemer** *noun* [from Greek *schema* = form]

scherzo (*say* **skairt**-soh) *noun* (*plural* **scherzos**) a lively piece of music. [Italian, = joke]

schism (*say* **siz**-uhm or **skiz**-uhm) *noun* the splitting of a group into two opposing sections because they disagree about something important. [from Greek *schisma* = split]

schizophrenia (*say* skit-suh-**free**-nee-uh) *noun* a kind of mental illness. **schizophrenic** *adjective & noun* [from Greek *schizein* = to split, + *phren* = mind]

schmick *adjective* (also **smick**) (*Australian informal*) stylish; excellent.

schnitzel (*say* **shnit**-suhl) *noun* a thin slice of veal or other meat, crumbed and fried. [German, = slice]

scholar *noun* **1** a person who has studied a subject thoroughly. **2** a person who has been awarded a scholarship. **scholarly** *adjective* [same origin as *school*[1]]

scholarship *noun* **1** a grant of money given to someone to help to pay for their education. **2** academic study or achievement; learning at a high level.

scholastic *adjective* of schools or education; academic.

school[1] *noun* **1** a place where teaching is done, especially of pupils aged 5–18, *He likes the teachers at his new school.* **2** the pupils and staff of a school, *The whole school had a holiday.* **3** the time when teaching takes place in a school, *School begins at 9 a.m.* **4** a group of people who have the same beliefs or style of work etc. **schoolboy** *noun*, **schoolchild** *noun*, **schoolgirl** *noun*, **schoolteacher** *noun* [from Greek *schole* = leisure, lecture-place]

school[2] *verb* train, *She was schooling her horse for the competition.*

school[3] *noun* a group of fish or sea mammals, *a school of dolphins.* [from an old word *scolu* = troop]

schoolie *noun* (*Australian informal*) a secondary school student, especially one who has just completed year 12.

schooling *noun* training; education, especially in a school.

School of the Air *noun* (*Australian*) education for outback children, originally by two-way radio, now also using computers and satellite communications technology.

schooner (*say* **skoo**-nuh) *noun* **1** a sailing ship with two or more masts and with sails rigged along its length, not crosswise. **2** a large beer glass; the beer contained in it.

sciatica (*say* suy-**at**-i-kuh) *noun* pain in the sciatic nerve (a large nerve in the hip and thigh).

science *noun* the systematic study of the physical or natural world through observation and experiment, *We learnt about biology and chemistry in science today.* [from Latin *scientia* = knowledge]

science fiction *noun* stories about imaginary scientific discoveries or space travel and life on other planets.

scientific *adjective* **1** of science or scientists. **2** studying things systematically and testing ideas carefully. **scientifically** *adverb*

scientist *noun* an expert in science; someone who studies science.

scimitar (*say* **sim**-uh-tuh) *noun* a curved sword, used originally in Eastern countries.

scintillate *verb* (**scintillated**, **scintillating**) **1** sparkle. **2** be brilliant, *a scintillating discussion.* **scintillation** *noun* [from Latin *scintilla* = spark]

scion (*say* **suy**-uhn) *noun* a descendant, especially of a noble family. [from Old French *cion* = a twig]

scissors *plural noun* a cutting instrument used with one hand, with two blades pivoted so that they can close against each other. [from Latin *scissum* = cut]

scoff[1] *verb* jeer; speak contemptuously. **scoffer** *noun*

scoff[2] *verb* (*informal*) eat greedily.

scold *verb* rebuke; find fault with someone angrily. **scolding** *noun*

scone (*say* skon) *noun* a small soft cake, eaten with butter, jam, or cream.

scoop[1] *noun* **1** a kind of deep spoon for serving ice cream etc. **2** a deep shovel for lifting grain, sugar, etc. **3** a scooping movement. **4** an important piece of news published by only one newspaper.

scoop[2] *verb* lift or hollow something out with a scoop.

scoot *verb* run or go away quickly.

scooter *noun* **1** a board for riding on, with wheels and a long handle. **2** a kind of lightweight motorcycle.

scope *noun* **1** opportunity to work, *This job gives scope for your musical abilities.* **2** the range or extent of a subject. [from Greek *skopos* = target]

scorch *verb* make something go brown by burning it slightly.

scorching *adjective* (*informal*) very hot.

score[1] *noun* **1** the number of points or goals made in a game; a result. **2** twenty, *three score years and ten* (= 70 years). **3** written or printed music. **4** a reason, *You needn't worry on that score.*

score[2] *verb* (**scored**, **scoring**) **1** get a point or goal in a game. **2** keep a count of the score. **3** mark with lines or cuts. **4** write out a musical score; arrange music for instruments. **scorer** *noun*

scorn[1] *noun* contempt. **scornful** *adjective*, **scornfully** *adverb*

scorn[2] *verb* treat or refuse scornfully.

Scorpio *noun* **1** a constellation and the eighth sign of the zodiac (the Scorpion). **2** a person born when the sun is in this sign. [from Greek *skorpios* = scorpion]

scorpion *noun* an animal that looks like a tiny lobster, with a poisonous sting.

scotch *verb* put an end to, *scotched the rumour.*

scot-free *adjective* **1** without harm or punishment. **2** free of charge. [from *scot* = tax, + *free*]

Scottish *adjective* of Scotland or its people or their form of the English language.

scoundrel *noun* a dishonest person.

scour[1] *verb* **1** rub something until it is clean and bright. **2** clear a channel or pipe by the force of water flowing through it. **scourer** *noun*

scour[2] *verb* search thoroughly.

scourge[1] (*say* skerj) *noun* **1** a whip for flogging people. **2** something that inflicts suffering or punishment.

scourge[2] *verb* (**scourged**, **scourging**) **1** flog with a whip. **2** cause suffering or punishment.

scout[1] *noun* **1** someone sent out to collect information. **2** (**Scout**) a member of the Scout Association, an international youth organisation.

scout[2] *verb* act as a scout; search an area thoroughly.

scowl[1] *noun* a bad-tempered frown.

scowl[2] *verb* make a scowl.

scrabble *verb* (**scrabbled**, **scrabbling**) **1** scratch or claw at something with the hands or feet. **2** grope or struggle to get something.

scraggy *adjective* thin and bony.

scram *verb* (*informal*) go away. [from *scramble*]

scramble[1] *verb* (**scrambled**, **scrambling**) **1** move quickly and awkwardly. **2** struggle to do or get something. **3** (of aircraft or their crew) hurry and take off quickly. **4** cook eggs by mixing them up and heating them in a pan. **5** mix things together. **6** alter a telephone signal so that it cannot be used without a special receiver. **scrambler** *noun*

scramble[2] *noun* **1** a climb or walk over rough ground. **2** a struggle to do or get something. **3** a motorcycle race over rough ground.

scrap[1] *noun* **1** a small piece. **2** rubbish; waste material, especially metal that is suitable for reprocessing.

scrap[2] *verb* (**scrapped**, **scrapping**) get rid of something that is useless or unwanted.

scrap[3] *noun* (*informal*) a fight.

scrap[4] *verb* (**scrapped**, **scrapping**) (*informal*) fight.

scrapbook *noun* a book with blank pages for drawing and sticking cuttings in.

scrape[1] *verb* (**scraped**, **scraping**) **1** clean or smooth something by passing something hard over it. **2** damage by scraping. **3** remove by scraping, *Scrape the mud off your shoes.* **4** pass with difficulty, *We scraped through.* **5** get something by great effort or care, *They scraped together enough money for a holiday.* **scraper** *noun*

scrape[2] *noun* **1** a scraping movement or sound. **2** a scraped mark or injury. **3** an awkward situation caused by mischief or foolishness.

scrappy *adjective* made of scraps or bits or disconnected things. **scrappiness** *noun*

scratch[1] *verb* **1** mark or cut the surface of a thing with something sharp. **2** rub the skin with fingernails or claws because it itches. **3** withdraw from a race or competition.

scratch[2] *noun* (*plural* **scratches**) **1** a mark made by scratching. **2** the action of scratching. **scratchy** *adjective*
start from scratch start from the beginning or with nothing prepared.
up to scratch up to the proper standard.

scrawl[1] *noun* untidy handwriting.

scrawl[2] *verb* write in a scrawl.

scrawny *adjective* thin and bony.

scream[1] *noun* **1** a loud piercing cry of pain, fear, anger, or excitement. **2** (*informal*) a very amusing person or thing.

scream[2] *verb* make a scream.

scree *noun* a mass of loose stones on the side of a mountain.

screech *noun* a harsh high-pitched scream or sound. **screech** *verb*

screed *noun* a very long piece of writing.

screen[1] *noun* **1** a thing that protects, hides, or divides something. **2** a flat panel or area on an electronic device such as a television, computer, or smartphone, on which images and data are displayed. **3** a windscreen.

screen[2] *verb* **1** protect, hide, or divide with a screen. **2** show a film or television pictures on a screen. **3** examine carefully, e.g. to check whether a person is suitable for a job or whether a substance is present in something. **4** sift gravel etc.

screen door *noun* (*Australian*) a door fitted with fine mesh to keep flies out.

screenplay *noun* the script of a film.

screw[1] *noun* **1** a metal pin with a spiral ridge (the *thread*) round it, holding things together by being twisted in. **2** a twisting movement. **3** something twisted. **4** a propeller, especially for a ship or motor boat.

screw[2] *verb* **1** fasten with a screw or screws. **2** twist.

screwdriver *noun* a tool for turning screws.

scribble *verb* (**scribbled**, **scribbling**) **1** write quickly or untidily or carelessly. **2** make meaningless marks. **scribble** *noun* [same origin as *scribe*]

scribe *noun* **1** a person who made copies of writings before printing was invented. **2** (in biblical times) a professional religious scholar. [from Latin *scribere* = write]

scrimmage *noun* a confused struggle.

scrimp *verb* skimp, *scrimp and save.*

script *noun* **1** handwriting. **2** a manuscript. **3** the text of a play, film, broadcast talk, etc. **4** (in computing) an automated series of instructions carried out in a specific order. [from Latin *scriptum* = written]

scripture *noun* sacred writings, especially the Bible. [same origin as *script*]

scroggin *noun* (*Australian*) a mixture of dried fruit and nuts eaten as a snack, especially by bushwalkers.

scroll *noun* **1** a roll of paper or parchment used for writing on. **2** a spiral design.

scrotum (*say* **skroh**-tuhm) *noun* the pouch of skin behind the penis, containing the testicles.

scrounge *verb* (**scrounged**, **scrounging**) cadge. **scrounger** *noun*

scrub[1] *verb* (**scrubbed**, **scrubbing**) **1** rub with a hard brush, especially to clean something. **2** (*informal*) cancel. **scrub** *noun*

scrub[2] *noun* low trees and bushes; land covered with these. **scrubby** *adjective*

scruff *noun* the back of the neck.

scruffy *adjective* (**scruffier**, **scruffiest**) shabby and untidy. **scruffily** *adverb*, **scruffiness** *noun*

scrum *noun* (also **scrummage**) a group of players from each side in rugby who push against each other and try to heel out the ball which is thrown between them.

scrumptious *adjective* (*informal*) delicious.

scrunch *verb & noun* crunch.

scruple[1] *noun* a feeling of doubt or hesitation when your conscience tells you that an action would be wrong.

scruple[2] *verb* (**scrupled**, **scrupling**) have scruples, *He would not scruple to betray us.*

scrupulous *adjective* **1** very careful and conscientious. **2** strictly honest or honourable. **scrupulously** *adverb*

scrutinise *verb* (**scrutinised**, **scrutinising**) examine or look at something carefully. **scrutiny** *noun*

scuba diving *noun* swimming underwater breathing air from a supply carried on your back. [from the initials of 'self-contained underwater breathing apparatus']

scud *verb* (**scudded**, **scudding**) move fast, *Clouds scudded across the sky.*

scuff *verb* **1** drag your feet while walking. **2** scrape with your foot; mark or damage something by doing this.

scuffle[1] *noun* a confused fight or struggle.

scuffle[2] *verb* (**scuffled**, **scuffling**) take part in a scuffle.

scull[1] *noun* a small or lightweight oar.

scull[2] *verb* row with sculls.

scullery *noun* (*plural* **sculleries**) a room where dishes etc. are washed up.

sculptor *noun* a person who makes sculptures.

sculpture *noun* making shapes by carving wood or stone or casting metal; a shape made in this way. **sculpture** *verb* [from Latin *sculptere* = carve]

scum *noun* **1** froth or dirt on top of a liquid. **2** worthless people.

scungy *adjective* (*Australian informal*) disagreeable, sordid.

scupper[1] *noun* an opening in a ship's side to let water drain away.

scupper[2] *verb* **1** sink a ship deliberately. **2** (*informal*) wreck, *It scuppered our plans.*

scurf *noun* flakes of dry skin. **scurfy** *adjective*

scurrilous *adjective* **1** very insulting. **2** vulgar. **scurrilously** *adverb*

scurry *verb* (**scurried**, **scurrying**) run with short steps; hurry.

scurvy *noun* a disease caused by lack of vitamin C in food.

scutter *verb* scurry.

scuttle[1] *noun* a bucket or container for coal in a house. [from Latin *scutella* = dish]

scuttle[2] *verb* (**scuttled**, **scuttling**) scurry; hurry away. [from *scud*]

scuttle[3] *noun* a small opening with a lid in a ship's deck or side.

scuttle[4] *verb* (**scuttled**, **scuttling**) sink a ship deliberately by letting water into it. [from Spanish *escotar* = cut out]

scythe *noun* a tool with a long curved blade for cutting grass or corn.

SDTV *abbreviation* standard-definition television.

SE *abbreviation* south-east; south-eastern.

se- *prefix* **1** apart; aside (as in *secluded*). **2** without (as in *secure*). [Latin]

sea *noun* **1** the salt water that covers most of the earth's surface; a part of this. **2** a large lake, *the Sea of Galilee.* **3** a large area of something, *a sea of faces.*
at sea 1 on the sea. **2** not knowing what to do.

sea anemone *noun* a sea creature with short tentacles round its mouth.

seaboard *noun* the coast.

sea change *noun* a dramatic change.

seadragon *noun* a fish like a seahorse found in Australian waters.

seafaring *adjective & noun* working or travelling on the sea. **seafarer** *noun*

seafood *noun* fish or shellfish from the sea eaten as food.

seagull *noun* a sea bird with long wings and webbed feet.

seahorse *noun* a small fish that swims upright, with a head rather like a horse's head.

seal[1] *noun* a sea mammal with thick fur or bristles that eats fish.

seal[2] *noun* **1** a piece of metal with an engraved design for pressing on a soft substance to leave an impression. **2** this impression. **3** something designed to close an opening and prevent air or liquid etc. from getting in or out. **4** a small decorative sticker.

seal[3] *verb* **1** close something by sticking two parts together. **2** close securely; stop up. **3** press a seal on something. **4** coat a surface with a protective substance; coat a road with tar, bitumen, or concrete. **5** settle or decide something, *Her fate was sealed.*
seal off prevent people getting to an area.

sea level *noun* the level of the sea halfway between high and low tide.

sealing wax *noun* a substance that is soft when heated but hardens when cooled, used for sealing documents or for marking with a seal.

sea lion *noun* a kind of large seal.

seam *noun* **1** the line where two edges of cloth, wood, or other material join. **2** a layer of coal in the ground.

seaman *noun* (*plural* **seamen**) a sailor.

seamanship *noun* skill in seafaring.

seamy *adjective* the less attractive side or part, *Police see a lot of the seamy side of life.*

seance (*say* **say**-ons) *noun* a spiritualist meeting. [French, = a sitting]

seaplane *noun* an aeroplane that can land on and take off from water.

seaport *noun* a port on the coast.

sear *verb* scorch or burn the surface of something.

search *verb* look very carefully in a place etc. in order to find something. **search** *noun*, **searcher** *noun*

search engine *noun* (in computing) a program used to find information on a database or the Internet, *If you type 'UFO' into your search engine you'll find some interesting websites.*

searchlight *noun* a light with a strong beam that can be turned in any direction.

search warrant *noun* a legal document allowing the police to enter and search a house or other premises.

seascape *noun* a picture or view of the sea. (Compare **landscape**.)

seashore *noun* the land next to the sea.

seasick *adjective* sick because of the movement of a ship. **seasickness** *noun*

season[1] *noun* **1** each of the four main parts of the year (spring, summer, autumn, winter). **2** the time of year when something happens, *the football season.* **3** a set or sequence of related television programs; a series. **in season** available and ready for eating, *Apples are in season in the autumn.*

season[2] *verb* **1** give extra flavour to food by adding salt, pepper, or other strong-tasting substances. **2** dry and treat timber etc. to make it ready for use.

seasonable *adjective* suitable for the season, *Hot weather is seasonable in summer.* **seasonably** *adverb*

seasonal *adjective* of or for a season; happening in a particular season, *Fruit picking is seasonal work.* **seasonally** *adverb*

seasoning *noun* a substance used to season food.

season ticket *noun* a ticket that can be used as often as you like throughout a period of time.

sea squirt *noun* a marine invertebrate that has a body with orifices through which water flows into and out of a central pharynx.

seat[1] *noun* **1** a thing made or used for sitting on. **2** the right to be a member of a council, committee, parliament, etc., *She won the seat ten years ago.* **3** the buttocks; the part of a skirt or trousers covering these. **4** the place where something is based or located, *Canberra is the seat of our government.*

seat[2] *verb* **1** place in or on a seat. **2** have seats for, *The theatre seats 3,000 people.*

seatbelt *noun* a strap to hold a person securely in a seat.

sea urchin *noun* a sea animal with a shell covered in sharp spikes.

seaward *adjective & adverb* towards the sea. **seawards** *adverb*

seaweed *noun* a plant or plants that grow in the sea.

seaworthy *adjective* (of a ship) fit for a sea voyage. **seaworthiness** *noun*

secateurs *plural noun* clippers held in the hand for pruning plants. [from Latin *secare* = to cut]

secede (*say* suh-**seed**) *verb* (**seceded**, **seceding**) withdraw from being a member of an organisation. **secession** *noun* [from *se-* = aside, + Latin *cedere* = go]

secluded *adjective* screened or sheltered from view. **seclusion** *noun* [from *se-* = aside, + Latin *claudere* = shut]

second[1] *adjective* **1** next after the first. **2** another, *a second chance.* **3** less good, *second quality.* **secondly** *adverb*

second[2] *noun* **1** a person or thing that is second. **2** an attendant of a fighter in a boxing match or duel. **3** a thing that is of second (not the best) quality. **4** one sixtieth of a minute (of time or of a degree used in measuring angles). **5** a very short time.

second[3] *verb* **1** assist someone. **2** state formally that one supports a motion that has been put forward by another person as a means of bringing it to be voted on. **seconder** *noun* [from Latin *secundus* = next]

second[4] (*say* suh-**kond**) *verb* transfer a person temporarily to another job or department etc. **secondment** *noun*

secondary *adjective* **1** coming after or from something. **2** less important. (Compare **primary**.)

secondary colours *plural noun* colours made by mixing two primary colours.

secondary school *noun* a school providing education after primary school and before employment or further study at university or college etc.

secondary source *noun* a book, article, or other source that provides information about an object of study but does not constitute direct, firsthand evidence. (Compare **primary source**.)

second-degree burn *noun* a burn causing blistering but not scars.

secondhand *adjective* (also **second-hand**) **1** bought or used after someone else has owned it. **2** selling used goods, *a secondhand shop.*

second nature *noun* behaviour that has become automatic or a habit, *Lying is second nature to him.*

second person see **person**.

second sight *noun* the ability to foresee the future.

secret[1] *adjective* **1** that must not be told or shown to other people. **2** not known by everybody. **3** working secretly, *a secret agent.* **secrecy** *noun*, **secretly** *adverb*

secret[2] *noun* **1** something secret. **2** a mystery. **3** a method for achieving something, *the secret of her success.* [from Latin *secretum* = set apart]

secretariat *noun* an administrative department of a large organisation such as the United Nations.

secretary (*say* **sek**-ruh-tuh-ree) *noun* (*plural* **secretaries**) **1** a person whose job is to help with letters, answer the telephone, and make business arrangements for a person or organisation. **2** the head of a public service department. **secretarial** *adjective*

secrete (*say* suh-**kreet**) *verb* (**secreted**, **secreting**) **1** hide something. **2** produce a substance in the body, *Saliva is secreted in the mouth.* **secretion** *noun* [from *secret*]

secretive (*say* **see**-kruh-tiv) *adjective* liking or trying to keep things secret. **secretively** *adverb*, **secretiveness** *noun*

sect *noun* a group whose beliefs differ from those of others in the same religion; a faction.

sectarian (*say* sek-**tair**-ree-uhn) *adjective* belonging to or supporting a sect.

section *noun* **1** a part of something. **2** a cross-section. **sectional** *adjective* [from Latin *sectum* = cut]

sector *noun* **1** one part of an area. **2** a part of something, *the private sector of industry.*

secular *adjective* of worldly affairs, not of spiritual or religious matters.

secure[1] *adjective* **1** safe, especially against attack. **2** certain not to slip or fail. **3** reliable. **securely** *adverb*

secure[2] *verb* (**secured**, **securing**) **1** make a thing secure. **2** obtain, *We secured two tickets for the show.* [from Latin, = free from worry (*se-* = apart, *cura* = care)]

security *noun* (*plural* **securities**) **1** being secure; safety. **2** precautions against theft or spying etc. **3** something given as a guarantee that a promise will be kept or a debt repaid. **4** investments such as stocks and shares.

sedan *noun* an enclosed car seating four or more people.

sedate *adjective* calm and dignified. **sedately** *adverb*, **sedateness** *noun* [from Latin *sedatum* = made calm]

sedative (*say* **sed**-uh-tiv) *noun* a medicine that makes a person calm. **sedation** *noun*

sedentary (*say* **sed**-uhn-tuh-ree) *adjective* done sitting down, *sedentary work.* [from Latin *sedens* = sitting]

sedge *noun* a grass-like plant growing in marshes or near water.

sediment *noun* fine particles of solid matter that float in liquid or sink to the bottom of it. [from Latin *sedere* = sit]

sedimentary *adjective* formed from particles that have settled on a surface, *sedimentary rocks.*

sedition *noun* inciting people to rebel against the authority of the state. **seditious** *adjective*

seduce *verb* (**seduced**, **seducing**) **1** persuade a person to have sexual intercourse. **2** attract or lead astray by offering temptations. **seducer** *noun*, **seduction** *noun*, **seductive** *adjective* [from *se-* = aside, + Latin *ducere* = to lead]

sedulous *adjective* diligent and persevering. **sedulously** *adverb*

see *verb* (**saw**, **seen**, **seeing**) **1** perceive with the eyes. **2** meet or visit somebody, *See a doctor about your cough.* **3** understand, *She saw what I meant.* **4** imagine, *Can you see yourself as a teacher?* **5** consider, *I will see what can be done.* **6** make sure, *See that the windows are shut.* **7** discover, *See who is at the door.* **8** escort, *See her to the door.* **see through** not be deceived by something. **see to** attend to.

seed[1] *noun* (*plural* **seeds** or **seed**) **1** a fertilised part of a plant, capable of growing into a new plant. **2** (*old use*) descendants. **3** a seeded player.

seed[2] *verb* **1** plant or sprinkle seeds in something. **2** name the best players and arrange for them not to play against each other in the early rounds of a tournament.

seedling *noun* a very young plant growing from a seed.

seedy *adjective* (**seedier**, **seediest**) **1** full of seeds. **2** shabby and disreputable. **3** (*informal*) unwell. **seediness** *noun*

seeing *conjunction* considering, *Seeing that we have all finished, let's go.*

seek *verb* (**sought**, **seeking**) search for; try to find or obtain.

seem *verb* give the impression of being something, *She seems worried about her work.* **seemingly** *adverb*

seemly *adjective* proper; suitable; in accordance with accepted standards of good taste. **seemliness** *noun*

seep *verb* ooze slowly out or through something. **seepage** *noun*

seer *noun* a prophet. [from *see*]

seersucker *noun* fabric woven with a puckered surface. [from Persian, = milk and sugar, or a striped garment]

see-saw *noun* a plank balanced in the middle so that two people can sit, one on each end, and make it go up and down.

seethe *verb* (**seethed**, **seething**) **1** bubble and surge like water boiling. **2** be very angry or excited.

see-through *adjective* able to be seen through; transparent.

segment *noun* a part that is cut off or separates naturally from other parts, *the segments of an orange.* **segmented** *adjective*

segregate *verb* (**segregated**, **segregating**) **1** separate people of different religions, races, etc. **2** isolate a person or thing. **segregation** *noun* [from *se-* = apart, + Latin *-gregatum* = herded]

segue (*say* **seg**-way) *verb* move smoothly from one topic or situation to another. **segue** *noun* [Italian, = follows]

seismic (*say* **suyz**-mik) *adjective* of earthquakes or other vibrations of the earth.

seismograph *noun* an instrument for measuring the strength of earthquakes. [from Greek *seismos* = earthquake, + *-graph*]

seize *verb* (**seized**, **seizing**) **1** take hold of a person or thing suddenly or forcibly. **2** arrest a person. **3** take possession of goods etc. **4** take eagerly, *Seize your chance!* **5** have a sudden effect on, *Panic seized us.*
seize up become jammed, especially because of friction or overheating.

seizure *noun* **1** seizing. **2** a sudden fit, as in epilepsy or a heart attack.

seldom *adverb* rarely; not often.

select[1] *verb* choose a person or thing. **selection** *noun*, **selector** *noun*

select[2] *adjective* **1** carefully chosen, *a select group of students.* **2** (of a club or other organisation) choosing its members carefully; exclusive. [from *se-* = apart, + Latin *legere* = pick]

selective *adjective* choosing or chosen carefully. **selectively** *adverb*, **selectivity** *noun*

self *noun* (*plural* **selves**) **1** a person as an individual. **2** a person's particular nature, *She has recovered and is her old self again.* **3** a person's own advantage, *He always puts self first.*

self- *prefix* **1** of or to or done by yourself or itself. **2** automatic (as in *self-loading*).

self-addressed *adjective* addressed to yourself.

self-assured *adjective* self-confident. **self-assurance** *noun*

self-centred *adjective* selfish.

self-confident *adjective* confident of your own abilities. **self-confidence** *noun*

self-conscious *adjective* embarrassed or unnatural because you know that people are watching you. **self-consciousness** *noun*

self-contained *adjective* **1** complete in itself; (of accommodation) having all the necessary facilities. **2** (of a person) able to do without the company of others.

self-control *noun* the ability to control your own behaviour. **self-controlled** *adjective*

self-defence *noun* defending yourself.

self-denial *noun* deliberately going without things you would like to have.

self-employed *adjective* working independently, not for an employer.

self-esteem *noun* a good opinion of yourself.

self-evident *adjective* obvious and not needing proof or explanation.

selfie *noun* (*informal*) a photograph that one has taken of oneself.

self-important *adjective* having a high opinion of your own importance. **self-importance** *noun*

self-interest *noun* concern for your own personal advantage.

selfish *adjective* doing what you want and not thinking of other people; keeping things for yourself. **selfishly** *adverb*, **selfishness** *noun*

self-isolate *verb* (**self-isolated, self-isolating**) isolate oneself, especially to avoid catching or transmitting a contagious disease.

selfless *adjective* unselfish.

self-pity *noun* feeling sorry for yourself.

self-possessed *adjective* calm and dignified.

self-quarantine *verb* (**self-quarantined**, **self-quarantining**) quarantine oneself, especially to avoid catching or transmitting a contagious disease.

self-raising *adjective* (of flour) containing a substance that makes cakes rise.

self-respect *noun* your own proper respect for yourself.

self-righteous *adjective* smugly sure that you are behaving virtuously.

selfsame *adjective* the very same.

self-satisfied *adjective* very pleased with yourself. **self-satisfaction** *noun*

self-seeking *adjective* selfishly trying to benefit yourself.

self-service *adjective* where customers help themselves to things and pay a cashier for what they have taken.

self-sufficient *adjective* able to provide what you need without help from others.

self-willed *adjective* obstinately doing what you want; stubborn.

sell *verb* (**sold, selling**) **1** exchange something for money. **2** offer goods for people to buy, *Do you sell hats?* **3** persuade someone to accept something. **seller** *noun*
sell out 1 sell all your stock of something. **2** (*informal*) betray someone. **sell-out** *noun*

selvedge *noun* (also **selvage**) an edge of cloth woven so that it does not unravel. [from *self* + *edge*]

selves *plural* of **self**.

semantic *adjective* relating to the meaning of words. **semantically** *adverb*

semantics *noun* the study of meaning in language. [from Greek *sema* = sign]

semaphore *noun* a system of signalling by holding the arms in positions that indicate letters of the alphabet. [from Greek *sema* = sign, + *phoros* = carrying]

semblance *noun* an outward appearance.

semen (*say* **see**-muhn) *noun* a white liquid produced by males and containing sperm. [Latin, = seed]

semester *noun* a half-year term in a university or college. [from Latin *semestris* = six-monthly]

semi *noun* (*informal*) **1** (*Australian*) a semitrailer. **2** a semifinal. **3** a semi-detached house.

semi- *prefix* half; partly. [Latin, = half]

semibreve *noun* the longest musical note normally used (𝅝), equal to two minims in length.

semicircle *noun* half a circle.
semicircular *adjective*

semicolon *noun* a punctuation mark (;) used to mark a break that is more pronounced than that marked by a comma.

semiconductor *noun* a substance that can conduct electricity but not as well as most metals do.

semi-detached *adjective* (of a house) joined to another house on one side only.

semifinal *noun* a match or round whose winner will take part in the final.

seminar *noun* a meeting for advanced discussion and research on a subject.

seminary *noun* (*plural* **seminaries**) a training college for priests or rabbis.

semiquaver *noun* a note in music (𝅘𝅥𝅯), equal to half a quaver in length.

Semitic (*say* suh-**mit**-ik) *adjective* of the Semites, the group of people that includes the Jews and Arabs.
Semite (*say* **see**-muyt) *noun*

semitone *noun* half a tone in music.

semitrailer *noun* an articulated vehicle consisting of a driver's cabin and a detachable trailer.

semolina *noun* hard round grains of wheat used to make milk puddings and pasta. [from Italian *semola* = bran]

senate *noun* **1** the upper house of the parliament of Australia, France, the United States, and certain other countries. **2** the governing council in ancient Rome. **senator** *noun* [from Latin *senatus* = council of elders]

send *verb* (**sent, sending**) **1** make a person or thing go somewhere. **2** cause a message or computer file to be transmitted electronically. **3** cause to become, *It sent him mad.* **sender** *noun*
send for order a person or thing to come or be brought to you.
send up (*informal*) make fun of something by imitating it. **send-up** *noun*

senile (*say* **see**-nuyl or **sen**-uyl) *adjective* suffering from weakness of the body or mind because of old age. **senility** *noun* [from Latin *senilis* = old]

senior[1] *adjective* **1** older in age. **2** higher in rank. **3** for older children, *a senior school.* **seniority** *noun*

senior[2] *noun* **1** a person who is older or higher in rank than you are, *She is my senior.* **2** a member of a senior school. [Latin, = older]

Senior Counsel *noun* a senior barrister.

sensation *noun* **1** a feeling, *a sensation of warmth.* **2** a very excited condition; something causing this, *The news caused a great sensation.* **sensational** *adjective*, **sensationally** *adverb* [same origin as *sense*]

sensationalism *noun* deliberate use of dramatic words or style etc. to arouse excitement. **sensationalist** *noun & adjective*

sense[1] *noun* **1** the ability to see, hear, smell, touch, or taste things. **2** the ability to feel or appreciate something; awareness, *a sense of humour.* **3** the power to think or make wise decisions, *He hasn't got the sense to come in out of the rain.* **4** meaning, *The word 'run' has many senses.*
make sense 1 have a meaning. **2** be a sensible idea.

sense[2] *verb* (**sensed, sensing**) **1** feel; get an impression, *I sensed that she did not like me.* **2** detect something, *This device senses radioactivity.* **sensor** *noun*

senseless *adjective* **1** stupid; not showing good sense. **2** unconscious.

senses *plural noun* sanity, *come to your senses.*

sensibility *noun* (*plural* **sensibilities**) sensitiveness; feeling, *The criticism hurt the artist's sensibilities.*

sensible *adjective* **1** wise; having or showing good sense. **2** (of an object) practical and functional rather than decorative, *Do you have sensible shoes for the bushwalk?* **3** aware, *We are sensible of the honour you have done us.* **sensibly** *adverb*

sensitise *verb* (**sensitised, sensitising**) make a thing sensitive to something.

sensitive *adjective* **1** receiving impressions quickly and easily, *sensitive fingers.* **2** easily hurt or offended, *She is very sensitive about her height.* **3** affected by something, *Photographic paper is sensitive to light.* **4** considerate of other people's feelings. **sensitively** *adverb*, **sensitivity** *noun*

sensory *adjective* of the senses; receiving sensations, *sensory nerves.*

sensual *adjective* of the senses; pleasing the body, *sensual pleasures.*

sensuous *adjective* giving pleasure to the senses, especially by being beautiful or delicate.

sentence[1] *noun* **1** a group of words that express a complete thought and form a statement, question, exclamation, or command. **2** the punishment announced to a convicted person in a lawcourt.

sentence[2] *verb* (**sentenced, sentencing**) give someone a sentence in a lawcourt, *The judge sentenced him to a year in prison.* [from Latin *sententia* = opinion]

sententious *adjective* giving moral advice in a pompous way.

sentient *adjective* capable of feeling and perceiving things, *sentient beings.* [from Latin *sentiens* = feeling]

sentiment *noun* **1** an opinion. **2** sentimentality. [from Latin *sentire* = feel]

sentimental *adjective* showing or arousing tenderness or romantic feelings or foolish emotion. **sentimentality** *noun*, **sentimentally** *adverb*

sentinel *noun* **1** a soldier or guard whose job is to stand and keep watch. **2** an indicator of the presence of disease.

sentry *noun* (*plural* **sentries**) a soldier stationed to keep guard or to control access to a place.

sepal *noun* each of the leaves forming the calyx of a bud.

separable *adjective* able to be separated.

separate[1] *adjective* not joined to anything; on its own; not shared. **separately** *adverb*

separate[2] *verb* (**separated, separating**) **1** make or keep separate; divide. **2** become separate. **3** stop living together as a couple. **separation** *noun*, **separator** *noun* [from *se-* = apart, + Latin *parare* = make ready]

separation of powers *noun* the vesting of the legislative, executive, and judiciary powers of government in separate bodies, thus ensuring their independence.

sepia *noun* reddish-brown. [from Greek, = cuttlefish (from which the dye was originally obtained)]

sepsis *noun* a septic condition.

September *noun* the ninth month of the year. [from Latin *septem* = seven (originally the seventh month of the Roman year)]

septet *noun* **1** a group of seven musicians. **2** a piece of music for seven musicians. [from Latin *septem* = seven]

septic *adjective* infected with harmful bacteria that cause pus to form. [from Greek *septikos* = made rotten]

septicaemia (*say* sep-**tuh**-see-mee-uh) *noun* blood poisoning. [from *septic*, + Greek *haima* = blood]

septic tank *noun* a tank in which sewage is broken down through bacterial activity.

sepulchral (*say* suh-**pul**-kruhl) *adjective* **1** of a sepulchre. **2** (of a voice) sounding deep and hollow.

sepulchre (*say* **sep**-uhl-kuh) *noun* a tomb. [from Latin *sepultum* = buried]

sequel *noun* **1** a book or film that continues the story of an earlier one. **2** something that follows or results from an earlier event.

sequence *noun* **1** the following of one thing after another; the order in which things happen. **2** a series of things. **sequential** *adjective* [from Latin *sequens* = following]

sequin *noun* a tiny bright disc sewn on clothes to decorate them. **sequinned** *adjective*

seraph *noun* (*plural* **seraphim** or **seraphs**) a kind of angel. **seraphic** *adjective*

serenade[1] *noun* music played for a lover, or suitable for this.

serenade[2] *verb* (**serenaded, serenading**) sing or play a serenade to someone.

serendipity *noun* the making of pleasant discoveries by accident; the knack of doing this. **serendipitous** *adjective*

serene *adjective* calm and cheerful. **serenely** *adverb*, **serenity** *noun*

serf *noun* a farm labourer who worked for a landowner in the Middle Ages. **serfdom** *noun* [same origin as *servant*]

serge *noun* a kind of strong woven fabric.

sergeant (*say* **sah**-juhnt) *noun* a soldier or police officer who is in charge of others.

sergeant major *noun* a soldier who is one rank higher than a sergeant.

serial[1] *noun* a story that is presented in separate parts.

serial[2] *adjective* **1** of or forming a series. **2** repeatedly committing the same offence and typically following a characteristic, predictable behaviour pattern, *a serial killer.* **serial number** a number identifying one item in a series of things.

serialise *verb* (**serialised**, **serialising**) produce a story as a serial. **serialisation** *noun*

series *noun* (*plural* **series**) a number of things following or connected with each other. [Latin, = row or chain]

serif *noun* a slight projection finishing off the stroke of a printed letter (as in T contrasted with sans serif T).

serious *adjective* **1** solemn and thoughtful; not smiling. **2** sincere; not casual; not light-hearted, *a serious attempt.* **3** causing anxiety; not trivial, *a serious accident.* **4** important, *a serious decision.* **seriously** *adverb*, **seriousness** *noun*

sermon *noun* a talk given by a preacher, especially as part of a religious service.

serpent *noun* a snake. [from Latin *serpens* = creeping]

serpentine *adjective* twisting and curving like a snake, *a serpentine road.*

serrated *adjective* having a notched edge. [from Latin *serratum* = sawn]

serried *adjective* arranged in rows close together, *serried ranks of troops.*

serum (*say* **seer**-ruhm) *noun* the thin yellowish liquid that remains from blood when the rest has clotted; this fluid used medically. [Latin, = whey]

servant *noun* a person whose job is to work or serve in someone else's house. [from Latin *servus* = slave]

serve[1] *verb* (**served**, **serving**) **1** work for a person or organisation or country. **2** sell things to people in a shop. **3** give out food to people at a meal. **4** spend time in something; undergo, *He served a prison sentence.* **5** be suitable for something, *This box will serve as a table.* **6** start play in tennis etc. by hitting the ball.
it serves you right you deserve it.

serve[2] *noun* **1** a service in tennis etc. **2** a helping of food. **3** (*Australian informal*) a severe reprimand.

server *noun* **1** a person or thing that serves. **2** a computer or program that manages access to a centralised resource or service in a network.

service[1] *noun* **1** working for a person or organisation or country. **2** use; assistance, *be of service.* **3** something that helps people or supplies what they want, *a bus service.* **4** the army, navy, or air force, *the armed services.* **5** a religious ceremony. **6** providing people with goods, food, etc., *quick service.* **7** a set of dishes and plates etc. for a meal, *a dinner service.* **8** the servicing of a vehicle or machine. **9** the action of serving in tennis etc.

service[2] *verb* (**serviced**, **servicing**) **1** repair or keep a vehicle or machine in working order. **2** supply with services.

serviceable *adjective* **1** usable. **2** suitable for ordinary use or wear.

serviceman *noun* (*plural* **servicemen**) a man who is a member of the armed services.

service station *noun* an establishment selling petrol or servicing motor vehicles.

servicewoman *noun* (*plural* **servicewomen**) a woman who is a member of the armed services.

serviette *noun* a piece of cloth or paper used to keep your clothes or hands clean at a meal.

servile *adjective* **1** having or showing an excessive willingness to serve or please others. **2** of or like a slave. **servility** *noun* [same origin as *servant*]

servitude *noun* the condition of being obliged to work for someone else and having no independence; slavery.

servo *noun* (*Australian informal*) a service station.

sesame (*say* **ses**-uh-mee) *noun* a small oval-shaped seed used in cooking or crushed to make oil.

session *noun* **1** a meeting or series of meetings, *The governor will open the next session of parliament.* **2** a time spent doing one thing, *a recording session.* [from Latin *sessio* = sitting]

set[1] *verb* (**set**, **setting**) **1** put or place, *Set the vase on the table.* **2** fix in position, *Set the post in concrete.* **3** adjust the hands of a clock to show the right time. **4** prepare or arrange, *Set the table for dinner.* **5** fix or appoint, *Set a date for the wedding.* **6** make or become firm or hard, *Leave the jelly to set.* **7** give someone a task, *The teacher sets us homework.* **8** put into a condition, *Set them free.* **9** go down below the horizon, *The sun was setting.*
set about 1 start doing something. **2** (*informal*) attack somebody.
set back stop or slow the progress of something.
set off 1 begin a journey. **2** start something happening. **3** cause to explode.
set out 1 begin a journey. **2** display or make known.
set sail begin a voyage.
set to 1 begin doing something vigorously. **2** begin fighting or arguing.
set up 1 place in position. **2** organise; establish, *set up house.* **3** cause or start, *set up a din.*

set[2] *noun* **1** a group of people or things that belong together. **2** the way something is placed, *the set of his jaw.* **3** the scenery or stage for a play or film. **4** a group of games in a tennis match. **5** a radio or television receiver. **6** (*Australian informal*) a grudge, *The authorities had a set on the local youth.*

setback *noun* something that stops progress or slows it down.

set square *noun* a device shaped like a right-angled triangle, used in drawing lines parallel to each other etc.

settee *noun* a long soft seat with a back and arms.

setter *noun* a dog of a long-haired breed that can be trained to stand rigid when it scents game.

setting *noun* **1** the way or place in which something is set. **2** music for the words of a song etc.

settle[1] *verb* (**settled**, **settling**) **1** arrange; decide or solve something, *That settles the problem.* **2** make or become calm or comfortable or orderly; stop being restless, *Stop chattering and settle down!* **3** go and live somewhere, *They settled in Canada.* **4** sink; come to rest on something, *Dust had settled on his books.* **5** pay a bill or debt. **settler** *noun*

settle[2] *noun* a long wooden seat with a high back and arms.

settlement *noun* **1** settling something. **2** the way something is settled. **3** a small number of people or houses established in a new area.

set-top box *noun* a device that converts a digital television signal to analogue for viewing on a conventional set.

set-up *noun* (*informal*) the way something is organised or arranged.

seven *noun & adjective* the number 7; one more than six. **seventh** *adjective & noun*

seventeen *noun & adjective* the number 17; one more than sixteen. **seventeenth** *adjective & noun*

seventy *noun & adjective* (*plural* **seventies**) the number 70; seven times ten. **seventieth** *adjective & noun*

sever *verb* (**severed**, **severing**) cut or break off. **severance** *noun*

several *adjective & noun* more than two but not many.

severally *adverb* separately.

severe *adjective* **1** strict; not gentle or kind. **2** intense; forceful, *severe gales.* **3** very plain, *a severe style of dress.* **severely** *adverb*, **severity** *noun*

sew *verb* (**sewed**, **sewn** or **sewed**, **sewing**) **1** join things together by using a needle and thread. **2** work with a needle and thread or with a sewing machine.

sewage (*say* **soo**-ij) *noun* liquid waste matter carried away in drains.

sewer (*say* **soo**-uh) *noun* a drain for carrying away sewage.

sewing machine *noun* a machine for sewing things.

sex *noun* (*plural* **sexes**) **1** each of the two groups (*male* and *female*) into which living things are placed according to their functions in the process of reproduction. **2** the instinct that causes members of the two sexes to be attracted to one another. **3** sexual intercourse. [from Latin *secus* = division]

sexism *noun* discrimination against people of a particular sex, especially women. **sexist** *adjective & noun*

sextant *noun* an instrument for measuring the angle of the sun and stars, used for finding your position when navigating. [from Latin *sextus* = sixth (because early sextants contained 60°, one sixth of a circle)]

sextet *noun* **1** a group of six musicians. **2** a piece of music for six musicians. [from Latin *sextus* = sixth]

sexting *noun* (*informal*) the sending of sexually explicit material by mobile phone.

sextuplet *noun* each of six children born to the same mother at one time. [from Latin *sextus* = sixth]

sexual *adjective* **1** of sex or the sexes. **2** (of reproduction) happening by the fusion of male and female cells. **sexuality** *noun*, **sexually** *adverb*

sexual intercourse *noun* sexual contact between two individuals involving penetration, especially by the man putting his penis into the woman's vagina.

sexy *adjective* (**sexier**, **sexiest**) **1** sexually attractive. **2** concerned with sex. **3** (*informal*) very exciting or appealing.

SGML *noun* standard generalised markup language, a form of generic coding used for producing printed material in electronic form.

shabby *adjective* (**shabbier**, **shabbiest**) **1** in a poor or worn-out condition; dilapidated. **2** poorly dressed. **3** unfair; dishonourable, *a shabby trick.* **shabbily** *adverb*, **shabbiness** *noun*

shack *noun* a roughly built hut; a small holiday house.

shackle[1] *noun* an iron ring for fastening a prisoner's wrist or ankle to something.

shackle[2] *verb* (**shackled**, **shackling**) put shackles on a prisoner.

shade[1] *noun* **1** slight darkness produced where something blocks the sun's light. **2** a device that reduces or shuts out bright light. **3** a colour; how light or dark a colour is. **4** a slight difference, *The word had several shades of meaning.* **5** a ghost.

shade[2] *verb* (**shaded**, **shading**) **1** shelter something from bright light. **2** make part of a drawing darker than the rest.

shadow[1] *noun* **1** the dark shape that falls on a surface when something is between the surface and a light. **2** an area of shade. **shadowy** *adjective*

shadow[2] *verb* **1** cast a shadow on something. **2** follow a person secretly.

Shadow Cabinet *noun* members of the Opposition in parliament who comment on important matters.

shady *adjective* (**shadier**, **shadiest**) **1** giving shade, *a shady tree.* **2** in the shade, *a shady place.* **3** not completely honest; disreputable, *a shady deal.*

shaft *noun* **1** a long slender rod or straight part, *the shaft of an arrow.* **2** a ray of light. **3** a deep narrow hole, *a mine shaft.*

shag *noun* a kind of cormorant.

shaggy *adjective* (**shaggier**, **shaggiest**) **1** having long rough hair or fibre. **2** rough, thick, and untidy, *shaggy hair.*

shah *noun* the former ruler of Iran. [Persian, = king]

shake[1] *verb* (**shook**, **shaken**, **shaking**) **1** move quickly up and down or from side to side. **2** disturb; shock; upset, *The news shook us.* **3** tremble; be unsteady, *His voice was shaking.* **shaker** *noun*
shake hands clasp a person's right hand with yours in greeting or parting or as a sign of agreement.

shake[2] *noun* **1** shaking; a shaking movement. **2** (*informal*) a moment, *I'll be there in two shakes.* **shakily** *adverb*, **shaky** *adjective*

shale *noun* a kind of stone that splits easily into layers. [same origin as *scale*[4]]

shall *auxiliary verb* **1** used with *I* and *we* to express the ordinary future tense, e.g. *I shall arrive tomorrow*, and in questions, e.g. *Shall I shut the door?* (but *will* is used with other words, e.g. *they will arrive*; *will you shut the door?*). **2** used with words other than *I* and *we* in promises, e.g. *Cinderella, you shall go to the ball!* (but *I will go* = I promise or intend to go).

> **Usage** If you want to be strictly correct, keep to the rules given here, but nowadays many people use *will* after *I* and *we* and it is not usually regarded as wrong.

shallot *noun* a kind of small onion.

shallow *adjective* **1** not deep, *shallow water.* **2** not showing deep thought; not capable of deep feelings. **shallowness** *noun*

shallows *plural noun* a shallow part of a stretch of water.

sham[1] *noun* something that is not genuine; a pretence. **sham** *adjective*

sham[2] *verb* (**shammed**, **shamming**) pretend.

shamble *verb* (**shambled**, **shambling**) walk or run in a lazy or awkward way.

shambles *noun* a scene of great disorder or bloodshed. [the word originally meant 'slaughterhouse']

shame[1] *noun* **1** a feeling of great sorrow or guilt because you have done wrong. **2** something you regret, *It's a shame that it rained.* **shameful** *adjective*, **shamefully** *adverb*

shame[2] *verb* (**shamed**, **shaming**) make a person feel ashamed.

shamefaced *adjective* looking ashamed.

shameless *adjective* not feeling or looking ashamed. **shamelessly** *adverb*

shampoo[1] *noun* **1** a liquid substance for washing the hair. **2** a substance for cleaning a carpet or washing a car.

shampoo[2] *verb* wash or clean with a shampoo. [from Hindi *champo* = press]

shamrock *noun* a plant rather like clover.

shandy *noun* (*plural* **shandies**) a mixture of beer and lemonade or some other soft drink.

shanghai *noun* (*Australian*) a catapult.

shank *noun* **1** the leg, especially the part from knee to ankle. **2** a long narrow part, *the shank of a pin.*

shan't shall not, *we shan't be gone long.*

shanty[1] *noun* (*plural* **shanties**) a roughly built hut.

shanty[2] *noun* (*plural* **shanties**) a sailors' song with a chorus. [from French *chantez* = sing]

shanty town *noun* a settlement consisting of shanties.

shape[1] *noun* **1** a thing's outline; the appearance an outline produces. **2** proper form or condition, *Get it into shape.*

shape[2] *verb* (**shaped**, **shaping**) **1** make into a particular shape. **2** develop, *It's shaping up nicely.* **3** adapt.

shapeless *adjective* having no definite shape.

shapely *adjective* (**shapelier**, **shapeliest**) having an attractive shape.

shard *noun* a broken piece of pottery or glass.

share[1] *noun* **1** a part given to one person or thing out of something that is being divided. **2** each of the equal parts forming a business company's capital, giving the person who holds it the right to receive a portion (a *dividend*) of the company's profits. **3** an instance of posting or reposting something on a social media website or application.

share[2] *verb* (**shared**, **sharing**) **1** give portions of something to two or more people. **2** have or use or experience something that others have too, *share a room*; *share the responsibility.* **3** post or repost something on a social media website or application.

shareholder *noun* an owner of shares in a company.

sharemarket *noun* (*Australian*) a place for selling and buying stocks and shares; a stock exchange.

shareware *noun* (in computing) software that is available free of charge.

sharia (*say* **shah**-ree-uh) *noun* (also **shariah**) the sacred law of Islam, prescribing religious and other duties.

shark *noun* a large sea fish with sharp teeth.

sharp[1] *adjective* **1** with an edge or point that can cut or make holes. **2** quick at noticing or learning things, *sharp eyes.* **3** steep or pointed; not gradual, *a sharp bend.* **4** intense; severe, *sharp pain.* **5** distinct, *a sharp image.* **6** loud and shrill, *a sharp cry.* **7** slightly sour. **8** (in music) one semitone higher than the natural note, *C sharp.* **9** (of words) harsh. **sharply** *adverb*, **sharpness** *noun*

sharp[2] *adverb* **1** sharply, *turn sharp right.* **2** punctually, *at six o'clock sharp.* **3** (in music) above the correct pitch, *You were singing sharp.*

sharp[3] *noun* (in music) a note one semitone higher than the natural note; the sign (♯) that indicates this.

sharpen *verb* make or become sharp. **sharpener** *noun*

sharp practice *noun* dishonest or barely honest dealings in business.

sharpshooter *noun* a skilled marksman.

shatter *verb* **1** break violently into small pieces. **2** destroy, *It shattered our hopes.* **3** upset greatly, *We were shattered by the news.*

shave[1] *verb* (**shaved**, **shaving**) **1** scrape growing hair off the skin. **2** cut or scrape a thin slice off something. **shaver** *noun*

shave[2] *noun* the act of shaving the face. **close shave** (*informal*) a narrow escape.

shavings *plural noun* thin strips shaved off a piece of wood or metal.

shawl *noun* a large piece of material worn round the shoulders or head or wrapped round a baby.

she *pronoun* **1** the female person or animal being talked about, *Mum said she would be home late tonight.* **2** (*Australian informal*) a thing, material or not, *she's a hot day; she'll be right.*

sheaf *noun* (*plural* **sheaves**) **1** a bundle of stalks of wheat etc. tied together. **2** a bundle of arrows, papers, etc. held together.

shear *verb* (**sheared**, **shorn** or **sheared**, **shearing**) cut or trim; cut the wool off a sheep. **shearer** *noun*

shears *plural noun* a shearing, clipping or cutting tool shaped like a very large pair of scissors.

shearwater *noun* a sea bird with long wings.

sheath *noun* a close-fitting cover; a cover for the blade of a knife or sword.

sheathe *verb* (**sheathed**, **sheathing**) **1** put into a sheath, *He sheathed his sword.* **2** put a close covering on something.

shed[1] *noun* a building used for storing things or sheltering animals, or as a workshop.

shed[2] *verb* (**shed**, **shedding**) **1** let something fall or flow, *The tree shed its leaves. We shed tears. The snake shed its skin.* **2** give off, *A heater sheds warmth.* **3** get rid of, *The company has shed 100 workers.*

she'd **1** she had, *she'd seen enough.* **2** she would, *she'd like to see you.*

sheen *noun* a shine; a gloss.

sheep *noun* (*plural* **sheep**) an animal that eats grass and has a thick fleecy coat, kept in flocks for its wool and its meat.

sheepdog *noun* a dog trained to guard and herd sheep.

sheepish *adjective* bashful; embarrassed. **sheepishly** *adverb*, **sheepishness** *noun*

sheepshank *noun* a knot used to shorten a rope.

sheer[1] *adjective* **1** complete; thorough, *sheer stupidity.* **2** vertical, with almost no slope, *a sheer drop.* **3** (of material) very thin; transparent.

sheer[2] *verb* swerve; move sharply away.

sheet[1] *noun* **1** a large piece of lightweight material used on a bed in pairs for a person to sleep between. **2** a whole flat piece of paper, glass, or metal. **3** a wide area of water, ice, flame, or other material. **4** a layer or covering.

sheet[2] *noun* a rope or chain fastening a sail.

sheikh (*say* shayk) *noun* the leader of an Arab community, family, or village. [Arabic, = old man]

sheila *noun* (*Australian informal*) a girl or woman.

shelf *noun* (*plural* **shelves**) **1** a flat piece of wood, metal, or glass etc. fixed to a wall or in a piece of furniture so that things can be placed on it. **2** a flat level surface that sticks out; a ledge.

shelf life *noun* the length of time for which an item remains usable or fit for consumption.

shell[1] *noun* **1** the hard outer covering of a nut, egg, snail, tortoise, etc. **2** the walls or framework of a building, ship, or other structure. **3** a metal case filled with explosive, fired from a large gun. [from Old English *sciell*, which has the same origin as *scale*[4]]

shell[2] *verb* **1** take something out of its shell. **2** fire explosive shells at something. **shell out** (*informal*) pay out money.

she'll she will.

shellfish *noun* (*plural* **shellfish**) an aquatic animal that has a shell.

shell shock *noun* a nervous breakdown resulting from exposure to battle conditions.

shelter[1] *noun* **1** something that protects people from rain, wind, danger, etc. **2** protection, *Seek shelter from the rain.*

shelter[2] *verb* **1** provide with shelter. **2** protect. **3** find a shelter, *They sheltered under the trees.*

shelve *verb* (**shelved**, **shelving**) **1** put things on a shelf or shelves. **2** fit a wall or cupboard with shelves. **3** put aside for later consideration; postpone. **4** slope, *The bed of the river shelves steeply.*

she-oak *noun* a casuarina.

shepherd[1] *noun* a person whose job is to look after sheep. **shepherdess** *noun*

shepherd[2] *verb* **1** guide or direct people. **2** (in sport) guard a teammate in possession of the ball by blocking opponents. [from *sheep* + *herd*]

sherbet *noun* a fizzy sweet powder or drink. [from Arabic *sharab* = a drink]

sheriff *noun* **1** (*Australian*) an administrative officer of the Supreme Court. **2** (*American*) the chief law-enforcing officer of a county. [from *shire* + *reeve* = officer]

sherry *noun* (*plural* **sherries**) a kind of strong wine. [named after Jerez in Spain]

she's **1** she is, *she's going to speak.* **2** she has, *she's lost her phone.*

Shia (*say* **shee**-uh) *noun* (also **Shi'a**, **Shiah**) (*plural* **Shia** or **Shias**) **1** one of the two main branches of Islam that rejects the first three Sunni caliphs and regards Ali, the fourth caliph, as Muhammad's first true successor. **2** a Muslim who adheres to the Shia branch of Islam. [Arabic, = party (of Ali)]

shickered *adjective* (*Australian informal*) drunk.

shield[1] *noun* **1** a large piece of metal, wood, etc. carried to protect the body. **2** a model of a triangular shield used as a trophy. **3** a protection.

shield[2] *verb* protect from harm or from being discovered.

shift[1] *verb* **1** move; change. **2** move house. **3** manage, *Learn to shift for yourself.*

shift[2] *noun* **1** a change of position or condition etc. **2** a group of workers who start work as another group finishes; the time when they work, *the night shift.* **3** a straight dress.

shifty *adjective* evasive, not straightforward; untrustworthy. **shiftily** *adverb*, **shiftiness** *noun*

Shiite (*say* **shee**-uyt) *noun* (also **Shi'ite**) an adherent of the Shia branch of Islam. **Shiite** *adjective*

shilling *noun* a former coin worth two pence.

shilly-shally *verb* (**shilly-shallied**, **shilly-shallying**) be unable to make up your mind. [from *shall I? shall I?*]

shimmer *verb* shine with a quivering light. **shimmer** *noun*

shin[1] *noun* the front of the leg between the knee and the ankle.

shin[2] *verb* (**shinned**, **shinning**) climb by using the arms and legs, not on a ladder.

shindig *noun* (*informal*) **1** a lively party. **2** a shindy.

shindy *noun* (*plural* **shindies**) (*informal*) a din; a brawl.

shine[1] *verb* (**shone** (in sense 4 **shined**), **shining**) **1** give out or reflect light; be bright. **2** be excellent, *He shines in maths.* **3** aim a light, *Shine a torch on it.* **4** polish, *Shine your shoes.*

shine[2] *noun* **1** brightness. **2** a polish.

shingle *noun* **1** pebbles on a beach. **2** a wooden tile used on roofs.

shingles *plural noun* a painful disease caused by a virus, with a rash and blisters.

shiny *adjective* (**shinier**, **shiniest**) shining; glossy.

ship[1] *noun* a large boat, especially one that goes to sea.

ship[2] *verb* (**shipped**, **shipping**) send goods by ship; transport.

shipment *noun* **1** the process of shipping goods. **2** the amount shipped.

shipping *noun* **1** ships. **2** transporting goods by ship.

shipshape *adjective* in good order; tidy.

shipwreck *noun* the wrecking of a ship. **shipwrecked** *adjective*

shipyard *noun* a place where ships are built or repaired.

shiralee *noun* (*Australian*) a swag.

shiraz (*say* shuh-**raz**) (also **Shiraz**) a variety of black grape; the red wine made from this. [named after Shiraz, a city in Iran]

shire *noun* a rural municipality.

shirk *verb* avoid a duty or work etc. selfishly or unfairly. **shirker** *noun*

shirr *verb* gather cloth into folds by rows of threads run through it.

shirt *noun* a loose-fitting garment for the top half of the body.

shirty *adjective* (*informal*) annoyed.

shish kebab *noun* pieces of meat and vegetables grilled on skewers. [Turkish, = skewer roast meat]

shiver[1] *verb* tremble with cold or fear. **shiver** *noun*, **shivery** *adjective*

shiver[2] *verb* shatter into pieces.

shivoo *noun* (*Australian informal*) a celebration; a boisterous party.

shoal[1] *noun* a large number of fish swimming together.

shoal[2] *noun* a shallow place; an underwater sandbank.

shock[1] *noun* **1** a sudden unpleasant surprise. **2** great weakness caused by pain or injury etc. **3** the effect of a violent shake or knock. **4** an effect caused by electric current passing through the body.

shock[2] *verb* **1** give someone a shock; surprise or upset a person greatly. **2** seem very improper or scandalous to a person.

shock[3] *noun* a bushy mass of hair.

shod *past tense & past participle* of **shoe**[2].

shoddy *adjective* (**shoddier**, **shoddiest**) of poor quality; badly made or done, *shoddy work.* **shoddily** *adverb*, **shoddiness** *noun*

shoe[1] *noun* **1** a strong covering for the foot. **2** a horseshoe. **3** something shaped or used like a shoe. **shoelace** *noun*
be in somebody's shoes be in their situation or predicament.
on a shoestring with only a small amount of money.

shoe[2] *verb* (**shod**, **shoeing**) fit with a shoe or shoes.

shoehorn *noun* a curved piece of stiff material for easing your heel into the back of a shoe.

shone *past tense & past participle* of **shine**[1].

shonky *adjective* (*Australian informal*) unreliable; dishonest.

shoo *interjection* a word used to frighten animals away. **shoo** *verb*

shook *past tense* of **shake**[1].

shoot[1] *verb* (**shot**, **shooting**) **1** fire a gun or missile. **2** hurt or kill by shooting. **3** move or send very quickly, *The car shot past us.* **4** kick or hit a ball at a goal. **5** (of a plant) put out buds or shoots. **6** slide the bolt of a door into or out of its fastening. **7** film or photograph something, *They shot the film in Africa.*
shoot through (*Australian informal*) depart, especially suddenly.

shoot[2] *noun* **1** a young branch or new growth of a plant. **2** an expedition for shooting animals.

shooting star *noun* a meteor.

shop[1] *noun* **1** a building or room where goods or services are on sale to the public, *A new bike shop opened up near our apartment.* **2** a workshop. **3** talk that is about your own work or job, *She is always talking shop.*

shop[2] *verb* (**shopped**, **shopping**) **1** visit one or more shops or websites to buy goods, *Many people shop online now for clothes.* **2** (**shop around**) look for the best available price or rate for something. **shopper** *noun*

shopkeeper *noun* a person who owns or manages a shop.

shoplifter *noun* a person who steals goods from a shop after entering as a customer. **shoplifting** *noun*

shopping *noun* **1** buying goods in shops. **2** the goods bought.

shop steward *noun* a person elected by workers, for example in a factory, to represent them in dealings with management.

shore[1] *noun* the land along the edge of a sea or of a lake.

shore[2] *verb* (**shored**, **shoring**) prop something up with a piece of wood; support or hold something up.

shorn *past participle* of **shear**.

short[1] *adjective* **1** not long; occupying a small distance or time, *a short walk.* **2** not tall, *a short person.* **3** not enough; not having enough of something, *We are short of water.* **4** concise. **5** curt. **6** (of pastry) rich and crumbly because it contains a lot of fat. **shortness** *noun*
for short as an abbreviation, *Joanna is called Jo for short.*
short for an abbreviation of, *'Jo' is short for 'Joanna'.*

short[2] *adverb* suddenly, *She stopped short.*

shortage *noun* lack or scarcity of something; insufficiency.

shortbread *noun* a rich sweet biscuit.

short circuit *noun* a fault in an electrical circuit in which current flows along a shorter route than the normal one. **short-circuit** *verb*

shortcoming *noun* a fault or failure to reach a good standard.

short cut *noun* a route or method that is quicker than the usual one.

short division *noun* dividing one number by another without writing down the calculations.

shorten *verb* make or become shorter.

shorthand *noun* a set of special signs for writing words down quickly.

short-handed *adjective* not having enough staff.

shortly *adverb* **1** in a short time; soon, *They will arrive shortly.* **2** in a few words. **3** curtly.

shorts *plural noun* trousers reaching to the knees or higher.

short-sighted *adjective* **1** unable to see distant things clearly. **2** lacking imagination or foresight.

short-tempered *adjective* easily becoming angry.

shot[1] *past tense & past participle* of **shoot**[1].

shot[2] *noun* **1** the firing of a gun or missile; the sound of this. **2** something fired from a gun; lead pellets for firing from small guns. **3** a person judged by skill in shooting, *She's a good shot.* **4** a heavy metal ball thrown as a sport. **5** a stroke in tennis, cricket, billiards, etc. **6** a photograph; a filmed scene. **7** an attempt, *Have a shot at the crossword.* **8** an injection.

shot[3] *adjective* (of fabric) woven so that different colours show at different angles, *shot silk.*

shotgun *noun* a gun for firing small shot at close range.

shot put *noun* a sporting event based on throwing a heavy ball.

should *auxiliary verb* used to express **1** obligation or duty, = ought to (*You should have told me*), **2** something expected (*They should be here by ten o'clock*), **3** a possible event (*if you should happen to see him*), **4** with *I* and *we* to make a polite statement (*I should like to come*) or in a conditional clause (*If they had supported us we should have won*).

> **Usage** In sense 4, although *should* is strictly correct, many people nowadays use *would* and this is not regarded as wrong.

shoulder[1] *noun* **1** the part of the body between the neck and the arm, foreleg, or wing. **2** a side that juts out, *the shoulder of the bottle.*

shoulder[2] *verb* **1** take something on your shoulder or shoulders. **2** push with your shoulder. **3** accept responsibility or blame.

shoulder blade *noun* either of the two large flat bones at the top of your back; the scapula.

shouldn't (*informal*) should not.

shout[1] *noun* **1** a loud cry or call. **2** (*Australian informal*) a person's turn to buy a round of drinks; any treat.

shout[2] *verb* **1** give a shout; call loudly. **2** (*Australian informal*) buy a round of drinks; pay for someone else's drink or meal etc.

shove *verb* (**shoved**, **shoving**) push roughly.
shove *noun*
shove off (*informal*) go away.

shovel[1] *noun* a tool like a spade with the sides turned up, used for lifting earth, sand, etc.

shovel[2] *verb* (**shovelled**, **shovelling**) **1** move or clear with a shovel. **2** scoop or push roughly, *He was shovelling food into his mouth.*

show[1] *verb* (**showed**, **shown**, **showing**) **1** allow or cause something to be seen, *Show me your new bike.* **2** indicate your feelings etc. **3** make a person understand; demonstrate, *Show me how to use it.* **4** guide, *Show him in.* **5** treat in a certain way, *She showed us much kindness.* **6** be visible, *That scratch won't show.* **7** prove your ability to someone, *We'll show them!*
show off 1 show something proudly. **2** try to impress people. **show-off** *noun*
show up 1 make or be clearly visible. **2** reveal a fault. **3** (*informal*) arrive.

show[2] *noun* **1** a display or exhibition, *a flower show*; *an agricultural show.* **2** an entertainment. **3** (*informal*) something that happens or is done, *She runs the whole show.*

showdown *noun* a final test or confrontation.

shower[1] *noun* **1** a brief fall of rain or snow. **2** a lot of small things coming or falling like rain, *a shower of stones.* **3** a device or cabinet for spraying water to wash a person's body; a wash in this. **4** a party for giving gifts, especially to a prospective bride, *bridal shower.*

shower[2] *verb* **1** fall or send things in a shower. **2** wash under a shower.

showery *adjective* (of weather) with many showers.

showjumping *noun* a competition in which riders make their horses jump over fences and other obstacles. **showjumper** *noun*

showman *noun* (*plural* **showmen**) **1** a person who presents entertainments. **2** someone who is good at attracting attention.
showmanship *noun*

showroom *noun* a room where goods are displayed for people to look at.

showy *adjective* (**showier**, **showiest**) likely to attract attention; brightly or highly decorated. **showily** *adverb*, **showiness** *noun*

shrank *past tense* of **shrink**.

shrapnel *noun* **1** pieces of metal scattered from an exploding shell. **2** (*Australian informal*) small change. [named after H. Shrapnel, the British officer who invented it in about 1806]

shred[1] *noun* **1** a tiny piece torn or cut off something. **2** a small amount, *There is not a shred of evidence.*

shred[2] *verb* (**shredded**, **shredding**) cut into shreds. **shredder** *noun*

shrew *noun* **1** a small mouse-like animal. **2** a bad-tempered woman who is constantly scolding people. **shrewish** *adjective*

shrewd *adjective* having common sense and good judgement; clever. **shrewdly** *adverb*, **shrewdness** *noun*

shriek[1] *noun* a shrill cry or scream.

shriek[2] *verb* give a shriek.

shrift *noun* **short shrift** curt treatment.

shrill *adjective* sounding very high and piercing. **shrillness** *noun*, **shrilly** *adverb*

shrimp *noun* **1** a small shellfish, pink when boiled. **2** (*informal*) a small person.

shrine *noun* an altar, chapel, or other sacred place.

shrink *verb* (**shrank**, **shrunk**, **shrinking**) **1** make or become smaller. **2** move back to avoid something. **3** avoid doing something because of fear, conscience, embarrassment, etc. **shrinkage** *noun*

shrivel *verb* (**shrivelled**, **shrivelling**) make or become dry and wrinkled.

shroud[1] *noun* **1** a cloth in which a dead body is wrapped. **2** each of a set of ropes supporting a ship's mast.

shroud[2] *verb* **1** wrap in a shroud. **2** cover or conceal, *The town was shrouded in mist.*

Shrove Tuesday *noun* the day before Ash Wednesday.

shrub *noun* a woody plant smaller than a tree; a bush. **shrubby** *adjective*

shrubbery *noun* (*plural* **shrubberies**) an area planted with shrubs.

shrug *verb* (**shrugged**, **shrugging**) raise your shoulders as a sign that you do not care, do not know, etc. **shrug** *noun*
shrug off dismiss something as unimportant.

shrunk *past participle* of **shrink**.

shrunken *adjective* having shrunk.

shudder *verb* **1** shiver violently with horror, fear, or cold. **2** make a strong shaking movement. **shudder** *noun*

shuffle *verb* (**shuffled**, **shuffling**) **1** walk without lifting the feet from the ground. **2** slide playing cards over each other to get them into random order. **3** shift; rearrange. **4** play or arrange tracks on a music player in a random order. **shuffle** *noun*

shun *verb* (**shunned**, **shunning**) avoid.

shunt *verb* move a train or wagons on to another track; divert. **shunt** *noun*, **shunter** *noun*

shut *verb* (**shut**, **shutting**) **1** move a door, lid, or cover so that it blocks an opening; make or become closed. **2** bring or fold parts together, *Shut the book.*
shut down 1 stop work. **2** stop business. **3** turn off a computer or computer system.
shut out exclude something from a place.
shut up 1 shut securely. **2** imprison. **3** (*informal*) stop talking or making a noise.

shutdown *noun* **1** the closure of a factory or system. **2** the ending or suspension of an activity, operation, etc. **3** a turning off of a computer or computer system.

shutter *noun* **1** a panel or screen that can be closed over a window. **2** the device in a camera that opens and closes to let light fall on the film. **shuttered** *adjective* [from *shut*]

shuttle[1] *noun* **1** a holder carrying the weft-thread across a loom in weaving. **2** a train, bus, or aircraft that makes frequent short journeys between two points. **3** a space shuttle (see *space*[1]).

shuttle[2] *verb* (**shuttled**, **shuttling**) move, travel, or send backwards and forwards.

shuttlecock *noun* a small rounded piece of cork or plastic with a crown of feathers, struck to and fro by players in badminton.

shy[1] *adjective* (**shyer**, **shyest**) afraid to meet or talk to other people; timid. **shyly** *adverb*, **shyness** *noun*

shy[2] *verb* (**shied**, **shying**) move suddenly in alarm, *The horse shied at the sound.*

shy[3] *verb* (**shied**, **shying**) fling or throw something at a target.

shy[4] *noun* (*plural* **shies**) a fling or throw.

SI *abbreviation* Système International d'Unités. [French, = International System of Units]

Siamese twins (*old use*) another name for **conjoined twins**. [named after two famous twins born in Siam (now called Thailand), who were joined near the waist]

sibilant[1] *adjective* having a hissing sound, *a sibilant whisper.*

sibilant[2] *noun* a speech sound that sounds like hissing, e.g. *s*, *sh*. [from Latin *sibilans* = hissing]

sibling *noun* a brother or sister.

sibyl *noun* a prophetess in ancient Greece or Rome.

sic *adverb* used in brackets after a copied or quoted word that appears odd or erroneous to show that the word is quoted exactly as it stands in the original, as in *she likes to eat aples* (*sic*) *after lunch.* [Latin, = so, thus]

sick *adjective* **1** ill; physically or mentally unwell. **2** vomiting or likely to vomit, *I feel sick.* **3** distressed; disgusted.
sick of tired of.

sickbay *noun* the place you go to when you are feeling ill at school.

sicken *verb* **1** begin to be ill. **2** make or become distressed or disgusted, *Vandalism sickens us all.* **sickening** *adjective*

sickie *noun* (*Australian informal*) a day's sick leave, especially if without medical evidence.

sickle *noun* **1** a tool with a narrow curved blade, used for cutting plants etc. **2** something shaped like this blade, e.g. the crescent moon.

sickly *adjective* **1** often ill; unhealthy. **2** making people feel sick, *a sickly smell.* **3** weak, *a sickly smile.*

sickness *noun* **1** illness. **2** a disease. **3** vomiting.

side¹ *noun* **1** a surface, especially one joining the top and bottom of something. **2** a line that forms part of the boundary of a triangle, square, or other plane figure. **3** either of the two halves into which something can be divided by a line down its centre. **4** the part near the edge and away from the centre. **5** the place or region next to a person or things, *She stood at my side.* **6** one aspect or view of something, *Study all sides of the problem.* **7** one of two groups or teams etc. who oppose each other.
on the side as a sideline.
side by side next to each other.

side² *adjective* at or on a side, *the side door.*

side³ *verb* (**sided**, **siding**) take a person's side in an argument, *He sided with his son.*

sideboard *noun* a long piece of furniture with drawers and cupboards, used for storing crockery, glasses, and table linen.

sidecar *noun* a small compartment for a passenger, fixed to the side of a motorcycle.

sideline *noun* **1** something done in addition to the main work or activity. **2** a line at the side of a football field etc.; the area just outside this.

sidelong *adjective* towards one side; sideways, *a sidelong glance.*

sidereal (*say* suy-**deer**-ree-uhl) *adjective* of or measured by the stars. [from Latin *sideris* = of a star]

sideshow *noun* **1** a small show or stall forming part of a fair, exhibition, or circus. **2** a minor incident or issue.

sidestep *verb* avoid by stepping sideways; evade a problem etc.

sidetrack *verb* divert from the main course or issue.

sidewalk *noun* (*American*) a pavement.

sideways *adverb & adjective* **1** to or from one side, *Move it sideways.* **2** with one side facing forwards, *We sat sideways in the bus.*

siding *noun* a short railway line by the side of a main line.

sidle *verb* (**sidled**, **sidling**) walk in a shy or nervous manner. [from *sidelong*]

SIDS *noun* sudden infant death syndrome, a technical term for **cot death**.

siege *noun* the besieging of a place.
lay siege to begin besieging.

sienna *noun* a kind of clay used in making brownish paints. [from Siena, a town in Italy]

sierra *noun* a range of mountains with sharp peaks, in Spain or parts of America. [from Latin *serra* = a saw]

siesta (*say* see-**es**-tuh) *noun* an afternoon rest. [Spanish, from Latin *sexta* = sixth (hour)]

sieve¹ (*say* siv) *noun* a device made of mesh or perforated metal or plastic, used to separate the smaller or soft parts of something from the larger or hard parts.

sieve² *verb* (**sieved**, **sieving**) put something through a sieve.

sift *verb* **1** sieve. **2** examine and analyse facts or evidence carefully. **sifter** *noun*

sigh¹ *noun* a sound made by breathing out heavily when you are sad, tired, relieved, etc.

sigh² *verb* make a sigh.

sight¹ *noun* **1** the ability to see. **2** a thing that can be seen or is worth seeing, *Our roses are a wonderful sight.* **3** an unsightly thing, *You do look a sight in those clothes!* **4** a device looked through to help aim a gun or optical instrument.
at sight or **on sight** as soon as a person or thing has been seen.
in sight **1** visible. **2** clearly near, *Victory was in sight.*

sight² *verb* **1** see or observe something. **2** aim a gun or telescope etc.

sightless *adjective* blind.

sight-reading *noun* playing or singing music at sight, without preparation.

sightseeing *noun* visiting places of interest. **sightseer** *noun*

sign¹ *noun* **1** something that shows that a thing exists, *There are signs of decay.* **2** a symbol, *a dollar sign.* **3** a board etc. displaying information. **4** an action or movement giving information or a command etc. **5** any of the 12 divisions of the zodiac, represented by a symbol.

sign² *verb* **1** make a sign or signal. **2** write your signature on something; accept a

contract etc. by doing this. **3** communicate in sign language.
sign up 1 enlist in the armed forces. **2** enrol. [from Latin *signum* = a mark]

signal[1] *noun* **1** a device, gesture, or sound etc. that gives information or a command; a message made up of such things. **2** a sequence of electrical impulses or radio waves.

signal[2] *verb* (**signalled, signalling**) make a signal to somebody. **signaller** *noun*

signal[3] *adjective* remarkable, *a signal success.* **signally** *adverb* [same origin as sign]

signal box *noun* a building from which railway signals are controlled.

signalman *noun* (*plural* **signalmen**) a person who controls railway signals.

signatory *noun* (*plural* **signatories**) a person who signs a treaty or other agreement.

signature *noun* a person's name written by himself or herself. [same origin as *sign*]

signature tune *noun* a special tune always used to announce a particular program, performer, etc.

signet *noun* a seal with an engraved design, especially one set in a person's ring (a **signet ring**). [same origin as *sign*]

significant *adjective* **1** having a meaning; full of meaning. **2** important, *a significant event.* **significance** *noun*, **significantly** *adverb*

signification *noun* meaning.

signify *verb* (**signified, signifying**) **1** be a sign or symbol of; mean. **2** indicate, *She signified her approval.* **3** be important; matter. [from Latin *signum* = sign]

sign language *noun* (also **signing**) a system of communication using visual gestures and signs, as used by deaf people.

signpost *noun* a sign at a road junction etc. showing the names and distances of places down each road.

Sikh (*say* seek) *noun* a follower of a religion founded in India and believing in one God. **Sikhism** *noun* [Hindi, = disciple]

silage *noun* fodder made from green crops stored in a silo.

silence[1] *noun* absence of sound or talk.

silence[2] *verb* (**silenced, silencing**) make a person or thing silent. [from Latin *silere* = to be silent]

silencer *noun* a device for reducing the sound made by a gun or a vehicle's exhaust system.

silent *adjective* **1** without any sound. **2** not speaking. **silently** *adverb*

silhouette (*say* sil-oo-**et**) *noun* a dark shadow seen against a light background. **silhouette** *verb* [named after E. de Silhouette, French author]

silica *noun* a hard white mineral that is a compound of silicon. [from Latin *silicis* = of flint]

silicon *noun* a substance found in many rocks, used in making transistors, microchips, etc.

silicone *noun* a compound of silicon used in paints, varnish, and lubricants.

silk *noun* a fine soft thread or cloth made from the fibre produced by silkworms for making their cocoons. **silken** *adjective*, **silky** *adjective*

silkworm *noun* the caterpillar of a kind of moth that feeds on mulberry leaves and spins itself a cocoon of silk.

sill *noun* a strip of stone, wood, or metal underneath a window or door.

silly *adjective* (**sillier, silliest**) foolish; unwise. **silliness** *noun* [the word originally meant 'feeble' (from an older word *seely* = happy or fortunate)]

silo (*say* **suy**-loh) *noun* (*plural* **silos**) **1** a pit or tower for storing green crops (see **silage**) or grain or cement etc. **2** an underground place for storing a missile ready for firing.

silt[1] *noun* sand or mud laid down by a river or sea etc.

silt[2] *verb* block or clog or become blocked with silt, *The harbour had silted up.*

silvan alternative spelling of **sylvan**.

silver[1] *noun* **1** a shiny white precious metal. **2** the colour of silver. **3** coins or objects made of silver or silver-coloured metal. **4** a silver medal, usually given as second prize. **silvery** *adjective*

silver[2] *adjective* **1** made of silver. **2** coloured like silver.

silver[3] *verb* make or become silvery.

silverbeet *noun* a plant with large green leaves and white stalks, used as a vegetable.

silver bullet *noun* a simple and seemingly magical solution to a complex problem.

silver jubilee *noun* a 25th anniversary.

SIM *noun* (also **SIM card**) a small plastic chip in a mobile phone that contains personal information, and that allows use of the phone. [from the initials of 'Subscriber Identification Module']

sim *noun* (*informal*) a video game that simulates an activity such as flying an aircraft or playing a sport. [short for *simulation*]

simian *adjective* like a monkey. [from Latin *simia* = monkey]

similar *adjective* nearly the same as another person or thing; of the same kind. **similarity** *noun*, **similarly** *adverb* [from Latin *similis* = like]

simile (*say* **sim**-uh-lee) *noun* a comparison of one thing with another, e.g. *He is as strong as a horse; We ran like the wind.* [from Latin *similis* = like]

similitude *noun* similarity.

simmer *verb* boil very gently.
simmer down calm down.

simper *verb* smile in a silly affected way.
simper *noun*

simple *adjective* **1** easy, *a simple question.* **2** not complicated or elaborate, *a simple plan.* **3** plain, not showy, *a simple dress.* **4** without much sense or intelligence. **5** not of high rank; ordinary. **simplicity** *noun*

simple interest *noun* interest payable on a capital sum only. (Compare **compound interest.**)

simpleton *noun* a foolish person.

simplify *verb* (**simplified**, **simplifying**) make a thing simple or easy to understand.
simplification *noun*

simplistic *adjective* treating complex issues and problems as if they were much simpler than they really are. **simplistically** *adverb*

simply *adverb* **1** in a simple way, *Explain it simply.* **2** without doubt; completely, *It's simply marvellous.* **3** only; merely, *It's simply a question of time.*

simulate *verb* (**simulated**, **simulating**) **1** reproduce the appearance or conditions of something; imitate, *This device simulates a space flight.* **2** pretend, *They simulated fear.* **simulation** *noun*, **simulator** *noun* [from Latin *similis* = like]

simultaneous (*say* sim-uhl-**tay**-nee-uhs) *adjective* happening at the same time.
simultaneously *adverb*

sin[1] *noun* **1** the breaking of a religious or moral law. **2** a very bad action.

sin[2] *verb* (**sinned**, **sinning**) commit a sin.
sinner *noun*

since[1] *conjunction* **1** from the time when, *Where have you been since I last saw you?* **2** because, *Since we have missed the bus we must walk home.*

since[2] *preposition* from a certain time, *She has been here since Christmas.*

since[3] *adverb* between then and now, *He ran away and hasn't been seen since.*

sincere *adjective* without pretence; truly felt or meant, *my sincere thanks.* **sincerely** *adverb*, **sincerity** *noun*
Yours sincerely see **yours.** [from Latin *sincerus* = pure]

sine *noun* (in a right-angled triangle) the ratio of the length of a side opposite one of the acute angles to the length of the hypotenuse. (Compare **cosine.**)

sinecure (*say* **sin**-uh-kyoor) *noun* a paid job that requires no work. [from Latin *sine cura* = without care]

sine qua non (*say* see-nay kwah **nohn**) *noun* an indispensable condition or qualification. [Latin, = without which not]

sinew *noun* **1** a tendon. **2** strength; muscular power. **sinewy** *adjective*

sinful *adjective* guilty of sin; wicked. **sinfully** *adverb*, **sinfulness** *noun*

sing *verb* (**sang**, **sung**, **singing**) **1** make musical sounds with the voice. **2** perform a song. **3** make a humming or whistling sound.
singer *noun*

singe (*say* sinj) *verb* (**singed**, **singeing**) burn something slightly.

single[1] *adjective* **1** one only; not double or multiple. **2** suitable for one person, *single beds.* **3** separate, *We sold every single thing.* **4** not married. **5** for the journey to a place but not back again, *a single ticket.*
singly *adverb*

single[2] *noun* **1** a single person or thing. **2** a single ticket.

single[3] *verb* (**singled**, **singling**) **single out** pick out or distinguish from other people or things.

single file *noun* a line of people one behind the other.

single-handed *adjective* without help.

single-minded *adjective* with your mind set on one purpose only.

singlet *noun* a garment worn under or instead of a shirt; a vest.

singsong *adjective* having a monotonous tone or rhythm, *a singsong voice.*

singular[1] *noun* the form of a noun or verb used when it stands for only one person or thing, *The singular is 'man', the plural is 'men'.* (Compare **plural.**)

singular[2] *adjective* **1** of the singular. **2** uncommon; extraordinary, *a woman of singular courage.* **singularity** *noun*, **singularly** *adverb*

Sinhalese *noun* **1** a member of a people from Sri Lanka. **2** the language of the Sinhalese.

sinister *adjective* **1** looking evil or harmful. **2** wicked. [from Latin, = on the left (which was thought to be unlucky)]

sink[1] *verb* (**sank**, **sunk**, **sinking**) **1** go or cause to go under the surface or to the bottom of the sea etc., *The ship sank; They sank the ship.* **2** go or fall slowly downwards, *He sank to his knees.* **3** dig or drill, *They sank a well.* **4** invest money in something.
sink in become understood.

sink[2] *noun* a fixed basin with a drainpipe and usually a tap or taps to supply water.

sinuous *adjective* with many bends or curves. [same origin as *sinus*]

sinus (*say* **suy**-nuhs) *noun* (*plural* **sinuses**) a hollow part in the bones of the skull, connected with the nose. [Latin, = curve]

sip *verb* (**sipped**, **sipping**) drink in small mouthfuls. **sip** *noun*

siphon[1] *noun* **1** a pipe or tube in the form of an upside-down U, arranged so that liquid is forced up it and down to a lower level. **2** a bottle containing soda water that is released through a tube.

siphon[2] *verb* flow or draw out through a siphon. [Greek, = pipe]

sir *noun* **1** a word used when speaking politely to a man, *Please sir, may I go?* **2** (**Sir**) the title given to a knight or baronet, *Sir Henry Parkes.* [from *sire*]

sire *noun* **1** the male parent of an animal, especially a horse or dog. (Compare **dam**[3].) **2** a word formerly used when speaking to a king. [same origin as *senior*]

siren *noun* **1** a device that makes a long loud sound as a signal. **2** a dangerously attractive woman. [named after the Sirens in Greek legend, women who by their sweet singing lured seafarers to shipwreck on the rocks]

sirloin *noun* beef from the upper part of the loin. [from *sur-* = over, + *loin*]

sirocco (*say* suh-**rok**-oh) *noun* a hot wind that blows from northern Africa to southern Europe.

sisal (*say* **suy**-suhl) *noun* fibre from a tropical plant, used for making ropes.

sissy *noun* (*plural* **sissies**) a timid or cowardly person. [from *sis* = sister]

sister *noun* **1** a daughter of the same parents as another person, *My sister plays the drums.* **2** a woman who is a fellow member of an association etc. **3** a nun. **4** (*old use*) a nurse. **sisterhood** *noun*, **sisterly** *adjective*

sister-in-law *noun* (*plural* **sisters-in-law**) the sister of a married person's spouse; the wife of a person's sibling.

sit *verb* (**sat**, **sitting**) **1** rest with the body supported on the buttocks; occupy a seat, *We were sitting in the front row.* **2** seat; cause someone to sit. **3** (of birds) perch; stay on the nest to hatch eggs. **4** be a candidate for an examination. **5** be situated; stay. **6** (of a parliament, committee, court of law, etc.) be engaged in its business. **sitter** *noun*

sitar *noun* an Indian musical instrument that is like a guitar. [Hindi, = three-stringed]

site[1] *noun* **1** the place where something happens or happened or is built etc., *a camping site*; *a building site.* **2** a website.

site[2] *verb* (**sited**, **siting**) provide with a site; locate. [from Latin *situs* = position]

sitemap *noun* (also **site map**) (on a website) a list or diagram of pages and other information that shows the organisation of the content.

sitting room *noun* a room with comfortable chairs for sitting in.

situated *adjective* in a particular place or situation.

situation *noun* **1** a position, with its surroundings. **2** a state of affairs at a certain time, *The police faced a difficult situation.* **3** a job. [same origin as *site*]

six *noun & adjective* (*plural* **sixes**) the number 6; one more than five. **sixth** *adjective & noun*
at sixes and sevens in disorder.

sixteen *noun & adjective* the number 16; one more than fifteen. **sixteenth** *adjective & noun*

sixty *noun & adjective* (*plural* **sixties**) the number 60; six times ten. **sixtieth** *adjective & noun*

size[1] *noun* **1** the measurements or extent of something. **2** any of the series of standard measurements in which certain things are made, *a size eight shoe.*

size[2] *verb* (**sized**, **sizing**) arrange things according to their size.
size up 1 estimate the size of something. **2** (*informal*) form an opinion or judgement about a person or thing.

size[3] *noun* a gluey substance used to glaze paper or stiffen cloth etc.

size[4] *verb* (**sized**, **sizing**) treat with size.

sizeable *adjective* large; fairly large.

sizzle *verb* (**sizzled**, **sizzling**) make a crackling or hissing sound.

skate[1] *noun* **1** a boot with a steel blade attached to the sole, used for sliding smoothly over ice. **2** a roller skate.

skate[2] *verb* (**skated**, **skating**) move on skates. **skater** *noun*

skate[3] *noun* (*plural* **skate**) a large flat edible sea fish.

skateboard *noun* a small board with wheels, used for riding on (as a sport) while standing. **skateboarding** *noun*

skedaddle *verb* (*informal*) run away; depart quickly.

skein *noun* a coil of yarn or thread.

skeleton *noun* **1** the framework of bones of the body. **2** the shell or other hard part covering or supporting an invertebrate animal such as crab. **3** a framework, e.g. of a building. **skeletal** *adjective* [from Greek *skeletos* = dried-up]

skerrick *noun* (*Australian informal*) slightest amount, *not a skerrick left.* [from British dialect]

sketch[1] *noun* (*plural* **sketches**) **1** a rough or unfinished drawing or painting, often made to assist in making a more finished picture. **2** a rough or unfinished version of any creative work. **3** a short amusing play or performance.

sketch[2] *verb* make a sketch. [from Greek *schedios* = impromptu]

sketchy *adjective* rough and not detailed or careful.

skew[1] *adjective* askew; slanting.

skew[2] *verb* make a thing askew.

skewer *noun* a long pin pushed through meat to hold it together while it is being cooked. **skewer** *verb*

ski[1] (*say* skee) *noun* (*plural* **skis**) each of a pair of long narrow strips of wood, metal, or plastic fixed under the feet for moving quickly over snow.

ski[2] *verb* (**ski'd** or **skied**, **skiing**) travel on skis. **skier** *noun* [Norwegian]

skid[1] *verb* (**skidded**, **skidding**) slide accidentally.

skid[2] *noun* **1** a skidding movement. **2** a runner on a helicopter, for use in landing.

skilful *adjective* having or showing great skill. **skilfully** *adverb*

skill *noun* the ability to do something well. **skilled** *adjective*

skillion *noun* (*Australian*) a lean-to attached to a house.

skim *verb* (**skimmed**, **skimming**) **1** remove something from the surface of a liquid; take the cream off milk. **2** move quickly over a surface or through the air. **3** read something quickly. **4** steal or embezzle money in small amounts over a period of time.

skimp *verb* supply or use less than is needed, *Don't skimp on the food.*

skimpy *adjective* (**skimpier**, **skimpiest**) scanty; too small.

skin[1] *noun* **1** the flexible outer covering of a person's or animal's body. **2** an outer layer or covering, e.g. of a fruit. **3** a skin-like film formed on the surface of a liquid.

skin[2] *verb* (**skinned**, **skinning**) take the skin off something.

skin diving *noun* swimming under water with flippers and breathing apparatus but without a diving suit. **skin diver** *noun*

skinflint *noun* a miserly person.

skinhead *noun* a youth with very closely cropped hair.

skink *noun* a small lizard.

skinny *adjective* (**skinnier**, **skinniest**) very thin.

skip[1] (**skipped**, **skipping**) **1** move along lightly, especially by hopping on each foot in turn. **2** jump with a skipping rope. **3** go quickly from one subject to another. **4** miss something out, *You can skip chapter six.* **5** (*informal*) not attend something, *He skipped his maths lesson.*

skip[2] *noun* a skipping movement.

skip[3] *noun* a large metal container for taking away builders' rubbish etc.

skip counting *noun* (in mathematics) counting forwards or backwards by the same number each time.

skipper *noun* a captain.

skipping rope *noun* a rope, usually with a handle at each end, that is swung over your head and under your feet as you jump.

skirmish *noun* (*plural* **skirmishes**) a small fight or conflict. **skirmish** *verb*

skirt[1] *noun* a piece of clothing that hangs down from the waist and does not have legs, usually worn by women and girls.

skirt[2] *verb* **1** go round the edge of something. **2** avoid dealing with an issue.

skirting *noun* (also **skirting board**) a narrow board round the wall of a room, close to the floor.

skit *noun* a parody, *She wrote a skit on 'Hamlet'.*

skite[1] *verb* (*Australian informal*) boast.

skite[2] *noun* (*Australian informal*) **1** a boaster. **2** boasting.

skittish *adjective* frisky.

skittle *noun* one of a set of wooden pins that people try to knock down by bowling a ball in the game of **skittles**.

skive *verb* (**skived**, **skiving**) (*informal*) dodge work or a duty. **skiver** *noun*

skivvy *noun* a thin high-necked long-sleeved garment.

skulk *verb* loiter stealthily.

skull *noun* the framework of bones of the head.

skunk *noun* a black furry American animal that can spray a bad-smelling fluid.

sky *noun* (*plural* **skies**) the space above the earth, appearing blue in daylight on fine days.

skylark[1] *noun* a lark that sings while it hovers high in the air.

skylark[2] *verb* play about light-heartedly.

skylight *noun* a window in a roof.

skyline *noun* **1** the horizon, where earth and sky appear to meet. **2** the outline of buildings etc. against the sky.

sky marshal *noun* a plain-clothes armed guard on an aeroplane.

skyscraper *noun* a very tall building.

slab *noun* a thick flat piece.

slack[1] *adjective* **1** not pulled tight. **2** not busy. **3** not working hard; careless. **slackly** *adverb*, **slackness** *noun*

slack[2] *verb* avoid work. **slacker** *noun*

slacken *verb* make or become slack.

slacks *plural noun* trousers for informal occasions.

slag *noun* waste material separated from metal in smelting.

slain *past tense & past participle* of **slay**.

slake *verb* (**slaked**, **slaking**) quench, *slake your thirst.*

slalom (*say* **slay**-luhm or **slah**-luhm) *noun* **1** a ski race down a zigzag course. **2** an obstacle race in canoes or on skateboards. [Norwegian]

slam *verb* (**slammed**, **slamming**) **1** shut loudly. **2** hit violently. **slam** *noun*

slander[1] *noun* a spoken statement that damages a person's reputation and is untrue. (Compare **libel**[1].) **slanderous** *adjective*

slander[2] *verb* make a slander against someone. **slanderer** *noun*

slang *noun* words that are used very informally to add vividness or humour to what is said. **slangy** *adjective*

slant *verb* **1** slope. **2** present news or information etc. from a particular point of view. **slant** *noun*

slant height *noun* (in mathematics) the height of a cone from the vertex to the periphery of the base.

slap *verb* (**slapped**, **slapping**) **1** hit with the palm of the hand or with something flat. **2** put forcefully or carelessly, *We slapped paint on the walls.* **slap** *noun*

slapdash *adjective* hasty and careless.

slapstick *noun* comedy with people hitting each other, falling over, etc.

slash[1] *verb* **1** make large cuts in something; cut or strike with a long sweeping movement. **2** reduce greatly, *Prices were slashed.*

slash[2] *noun* (*plural* **slashes**) **1** a slashing cut. **2** an oblique stroke.

slat *noun* each of the thin strips of wood or metal or plastic arranged so that they overlap and form a screen, e.g. in a venetian blind.

slate[1] *noun* **1** a kind of grey rock that is easily split into flat plates. **2** a piece of this rock used in covering a roof or (formerly) for writing on. **slaty** *adjective*

slate[2] *verb* (**slated**, **slating**) **1** cover a roof with slates. **2** (*informal*) criticise severely; reprimand.

slater *noun* a small crustacean that lives in decaying wood and damp soil.

slather *noun* **open slather** (*Australian informal*) freedom to operate without restraint.

slattern *noun* a slovenly woman. **slatternly** *adjective*

slaughter *verb* **1** kill an animal for food. **2** kill people or animals ruthlessly or in great numbers. **slaughter** *noun*

slaughterhouse *noun* a place where animals are killed for food.

slave[1] *noun* a person who is owned by another and obliged to work for them without being paid. **slavery** *noun*

slave[2] *verb* (**slaved**, **slaving**) work very hard.

slave-driver *noun* a person who makes others work very hard.

slaver (*say* **slav**-uh) *verb* have saliva flowing from the mouth, *a slavering dog.*

slavish *adjective* **1** like a slave. **2** showing no independence or originality.

slay *verb* (**slew**, **slain**, **slaying**) kill.

sleazy *adjective* (**sleazier**, **sleaziest**) (*informal*) **1** dirty and slovenly. **2** corrupt and immoral. **3** promiscuous. **sleaziness** *noun*

sled *noun* a sledge.

sledge[1] *noun* a vehicle for travelling over snow, with strips of metal or wood instead of wheels. **sledging** *noun*

sledge[2] *verb* (**sledged**, **sledging**) (*Australian informal*) **1** (in cricket) make taunting or teasing remarks to an opposing player in order to disturb their concentration. **2** criticise or insult in a mocking way. **sledge** *noun*, **sledging** *noun*

sledgehammer *noun* a very large heavy hammer.

sleek *adjective* smooth and shiny.

sleep[1] *noun* the condition or time of rest in which the eyes are closed, the body relaxed, and the mind unconscious. **sleepily** *adverb*, **sleepiness** *noun*, **sleepy** *adjective*

sleep[2] *verb* (**slept**, **sleeping**) have a sleep.

sleeper *noun* **1** someone who is asleep. **2** each of the wooden or concrete beams on which the rails of a railway rest. **3** a railway carriage with beds or berths for passengers to sleep in; a place in this.

sleepless *adjective* unable to sleep.

sleepout *noun* (*Australian*) part of a verandah closed off as a bedroom.

sleepover *noun* a night spent by children or young people at a friend's house.

sleepwalker *noun* a person who walks about while asleep. **sleepwalking** *noun*

sleet *noun* a mixture of rain and snow or hail.

sleeve *noun* **1** the part of a garment that covers the arm. **2** the cover of a record. **up your sleeve** hidden but ready for use.

sleeveless *adjective* without sleeves.

sleigh (*say* slay) *noun* a sledge, especially a large one pulled by horses.

sleight (*rhymes with* bite) *noun* **sleight of hand** skill in using the hands to do conjuring tricks etc. [from Norse *slægth* = slyness]

slender *adjective* **1** slim. **2** small, *a slender hope.* **slenderness** *noun*

sleuth (*say* slooth) *noun* a detective.

slew *past tense* of **slay**.

slice[1] *noun* **1** a thin piece cut off something. **2** a portion.

slice[2] *verb* (**sliced**, **slicing**) **1** cut into slices. **2** cut from a larger piece, *Slice the top off the egg.* **3** cut cleanly, *The knife sliced through the apple.*

slick[1] *adjective* **1** quick and clever or cunning. **2** slippery.

slick[2] *noun* **1** a large patch of oil floating on water. **2** a slippery place.

slide[1] *verb* (**slid**, **sliding**) **1** move or cause to move smoothly on a surface. **2** move quietly or secretly, *The thief slid behind the door.* **3** (in mathematics) move a shape to a new position without flipping or turning it.

slide[2] *noun* **1** a sliding movement. **2** a smooth surface or structure on which people or things can slide. **3** a photograph that can be projected on a screen. **4** a small glass plate on which things are placed to be examined under a microscope. **5** a fastener to keep hair tidy.

slight[1] *adjective* very small; not serious or important. **slightly** *adverb*, **slightness** *noun*

slight[2] *verb* insult a person by treating them without respect.

slim[1] *adjective* (**slimmer**, **slimmest**) **1** thin and graceful. **2** small, *a slim chance.* **slimness** *noun*

slim[2] *verb* (**slimmed**, **slimming**) make yourself thinner. **slimmer** *noun*

slime *noun* unpleasant wet slippery stuff. **sliminess** *noun*, **slimy** *adjective*

sling[1] *noun* **1** a loop or band placed round something to support or lift it. **2** a looped strap used to throw a stone or other missile.

sling[2] *verb* (**slung**, **slinging**) **1** support or lift with a sling. **2** (*informal*) throw. **sling off at** (*Australian informal*) mock; ridicule.

slink *verb* (**slunk**, **slinking**) move in a stealthy or guilty way.

slinky *adjective* (**slinkier**, **slinkiest**) **1** stealthy. **2** (of a garment) close-fitting; sinuous.

slip[1] *verb* (**slipped**, **slipping**) **1** slide accidentally; lose your balance by sliding. **2** move or put quickly and quietly, *Slip it in your pocket; We slipped away from the party.* **3** escape from, *The dog slipped its leash; It slipped my memory.* **slip up** make a mistake. **slip-up** *noun*

slip[2] *noun* **1** an accidental slide or fall. **2** a mistake. **3** a small piece of paper. **4** a petticoat. **5** a pillowcase. **give someone the slip** escape or avoid them skilfully.

slipper *noun* a soft comfortable shoe to wear indoors.

slippery *adjective* smooth or wet so that it is difficult to stand on or hold. **slipperiness** *noun*

sliprail *noun* (*Australian*) a movable rail in a fence making a gateway.

slipshod *adjective* careless; not systematic.

slit[1] *noun* a narrow straight cut or opening.

slit[2] *verb* (**slitted**, **slitting**) make a slit or slits in something.

slither *verb* slip or slide unsteadily.

sliver (*say* **sliv**-uh) *noun* a thin strip of wood or glass etc.

slob *noun* (*informal*) a lazy and untidy person.

slobber *verb* slaver; dribble.

slog *verb* (**slogged**, **slogging**) **1** hit hard. **2** work hard and steadily. **3** walk with effort. **slog** *noun*, **slogger** *noun*

slogan *noun* a phrase used to advertise something or to sum up the aims of a campaign etc.

sloop *noun* a small sailing ship with one mast.

slop *verb* (**slopped**, **slopping**) spill liquid over the edge of its container.

slope[1] *verb* (**sloped**, **sloping**) lie or turn at an angle; slant. **slope off** (*informal*) go away.

slope[2] *noun* **1** a sloping surface. **2** the amount by which something slopes.

sloppy *adjective* (**sloppier**, **sloppiest**) **1** liquid and splashing easily. **2** careless; slipshod, *sloppy work.* **3** weakly sentimental, *a sloppy story.* **sloppily** *adverb*, **sloppiness** *noun*

slops *plural noun* dirty waste water or other waste liquids.

slosh *verb* (*informal*) **1** splash; slop; pour liquid carelessly. **2** hit.

slot *noun* a narrow opening to put things in. **slotted** *adjective*

sloth (*rhymes with* both) *noun* **1** laziness. **2** a South American animal that lives in trees and moves very slowly. **slothful** *adjective*

slouch *verb* stand, sit, or move in a lazy awkward way, not with an upright posture. **slouch** *noun*

slouch hat *noun* a hat with a wide flexible brim, especially with the left brim turned up, associated with the Australian army.

slough[1] (*rhymes with* plough) *noun* a swamp or marshy place.

slough[2] (*say* sluf) *verb* shed, *A snake sloughs its skin periodically.*

slovenly (*say* **sluv**-uhn-lee) *adjective* careless; untidy. **slovenliness** *noun*

slow[1] *adjective* **1** not quick; taking more time than is usual. **2** showing a time earlier than the correct time, *Your watch is slow.* **3** not quick to learn or understand. **slowly** *adverb*, **slowness** *noun*

slow[2] *adverb* slowly.

> **Usage** The use of *slow* as an adverb is chiefly confined to compounds such as *slow-acting*, *slow-burning*, *slow-moving*. It is also established in the expression *go slow* and the noun *go-slow*. In sentences such as *he drives too slow* and *go as slow as you can*, *slowly* is preferable in formal contexts. Compare *fast* which is fully acceptable as an adverb in standard English

slow[3] *verb* go more slowly; cause to go more slowly, *The storm slowed us down.*

slowcoach *noun* (*informal*) a slow person.

sludge *noun* thick mud.

slug[1] *noun* **1** a small slimy animal like a snail without a shell. **2** a pellet for firing from a gun.

slug[2] *verb* (**slugged**, **slugging**) **1** hit hard. **2** (*Australian informal*) charge an excessive price.

sluggish *adjective* slow-moving; not alert or lively.

sluice[1] (*say* sloos) *noun* **1** a sliding barrier for controlling a flow of water. **2** a channel carrying off water.

sluice[2] *verb* (**sluiced**, **sluicing**) **1** wash with a flow of water. **2** let out water.

slum *noun* an area of dirty overcrowded houses.

slumber *noun & verb* sleep. **slumberer** *noun*

slump[1] *verb* fall heavily or suddenly.

slump[2] *noun* a sudden great fall in prices or trade.

slung *past tense & past participle* of **sling**[1].

slunk *past tense & past participle* of **slink**.

slur[1] *verb* (**slurred**, **slurring**) **1** pronounce words indistinctly by running the sounds together. **2** mark with a slur in music.

slur[2] *noun* **1** a slurred sound. **2** discredit, *It casts a slur on her reputation.* **3** a curved line placed over notes in music to show that they are to be sung or played smoothly without a break.

slush *noun* partly melted snow on the ground; watery mud. **slushy** *adjective*

sly *adjective* (**slyer**, **slyest**) **1** unpleasantly cunning or secret. **2** mischievous, *a sly smile.* **slyly** *adverb*, **slyness** *noun*

smack[1] *noun* a slap; a hard hit.

smack[2] *verb* slap; hit hard.
smack your lips close and then part them noisily in enjoyment.

smack[3] *adverb* (*informal*) with a smack; directly, *The ball went smack through the window.*

smack[4] *noun* a slight flavour of something; a trace.

smack[5] *verb* have a slight flavour or trace, *His manner smacks of conceit.*

smack[6] *noun* a small sailing boat used for fishing.

small *adjective* **1** not large; less than the usual size. **2** insignificant. **smallness** *noun*
the small of the back the smallest part of the back (at the waist).

smallgoods *plural noun* (*Australian*) cooked meats and meat products.

small-minded *adjective* selfish; petty.

smallpox *noun* a contagious disease with spots that leave bad scars on the skin.

smart[1] *adjective* **1** neat and elegant; dressed well. **2** clever. **3** forceful; brisk, *She ran at a smart pace.* **smartly** *adverb*, **smartness** *noun*

smart[2] *verb* feel a stinging pain. **smart** *noun*

smart card *noun* a plastic card with a built-in microprocessor, used for electronic processes such as financial transactions and personal identification.

smarten *verb* (also **smarten up**) make or become smarter, *Smarten up your bedroom!*

smartphone *noun* a mobile phone that performs many of the functions of a computer.

smash[1] *verb* **1** break noisily into pieces. **2** hit hard; collide. **3** move with great force. **4** destroy or defeat completely.

smash[2] *noun* (*plural* **smashes**) **1** the action or sound of smashing. **2** a collision.

smash hit *noun* (*informal*) something very successful.

smashing *adjective* (*informal*) excellent; beautiful.

smattering *noun* a slight knowledge of a subject or a foreign language.

smear *verb* **1** rub something greasy or sticky or dirty on a surface. **2** try to damage someone's reputation. **smear** *noun*, **smeary** *adjective*

smell[1] *verb* (**smelt**, **smelling**) **1** be aware of something by means of the sense organs of the nose, *I can smell smoke.* **2** give out a smell, *The food smells delicious.*

smell[2] *noun* **1** something you can smell; a quality in something that makes people able to smell it. **2** an unpleasant quality of this kind. **3** the ability to smell things. **smelly** *adjective*

smelt *verb* melt ore to get the metal it contains.

smile[1] *noun* an expression on the face that shows pleasure or amusement with the lips stretched and turning upwards at the ends.

smile[2] *verb* (**smiled**, **smiling**) give a smile.

smirch *verb* **1** soil. **2** disgrace or dishonour a reputation. **smirch** *noun*

smirk *noun* a self-satisfied smile. **smirk** *verb*

smite *verb* (**smote**, **smitten**, **smiting**) hit hard. **be smitten with** be affected by a disease or desire or fascination etc.

smith *noun* a person who makes things out of metal; a blacksmith.

smithereens *plural noun* (*informal*) small fragments.

smithy *noun* a blacksmith's workshop.

smitten *past participle* of **smite**.

smock[1] *noun* an overall shaped like a very long shirt.

smock[2] *verb* stitch into close gathers with embroidery. **smocking** *noun*

smog *noun* a mixture of smoke and fog. [from *smoke* + *fog*]

smoke[1] *noun* **1** the mixture of gas and solid particles given off by a burning substance. **2** an act or spell of smoking tobacco. **3** a cigarette or cigar. **smoky** *adjective*

smoke[2] *verb* (**smoked**, **smoking**) **1** give out smoke. **2** have a lighted cigarette, cigar, or pipe between your lips and draw its smoke into your mouth; do this as a habit. **3** preserve meat or fish by treating it with smoke, *smoked salmon.* **smoker** *noun*

smokescreen *noun* **1** a mass of smoke used to hide the movement of troops. **2** something that conceals what is happening.

smoking ceremony *noun* (*Australian*) (in traditional Aboriginal culture) a ceremony in which smoke is used for ritual purposes, especially after death.

smoko *noun* (*Australian informal*) a break from work (originally time to have a cigarette etc.).

smoodge *verb* (*Australian informal*) **1** kiss and caress. **2** behave ingratiatingly; toady.

smooth[1] *adjective* **1** having a surface without any lumps, wrinkles, roughness, etc. **2** moving without bumps or jolts etc. **3** not harsh, *a smooth flavour.* **4** pleasantly polite but perhaps insincere. **smoothly** *adverb*, **smoothness** *noun*

smooth[2] *verb* make a thing smooth.

smorgasbord *noun* **1** a buffet meal with a variety of meals to choose from. **2** (*informal*) a medley; a wide variety or choice. [Swedish]

smote *past tense* of **smite**.

smother *verb* **1** suffocate. **2** put out a fire by covering it. **3** cover thickly, *The buns were smothered in sugar.* **4** restrain; conceal, *She smothered a smile.*

smoulder *verb* **1** burn slowly without a flame. **2** continue to exist inwardly, *Their anger smouldered.*

SMS[1] *noun* Short Message (or Messaging) Service, a system that allows mobile phone users to send and receive text messages; a message sent in this way.

SMS[2] *verb* (**SMSs**, **SMSing**, **SMSed**) send someone a text message using SMS.

SMTP *abbreviation* Simple Mail Transfer (or Transport) Protocol, a standard for the transmission of electronic mail on a computer network.

smudge[1] *noun* a dirty mark made by rubbing something. **smudgy** *adjective*

smudge[2] *verb* (**smudged**, **smudging**) make a smudge on something; become smudged.

smug *adjective* self-satisfied. **smugly** *adverb*, **smugness** *noun*

smuggle *verb* (**smuggled**, **smuggling**) bring something into a country etc. secretly or illegally. **smuggler** *noun*, **smuggling** *noun*

smut *noun* **1** a small piece of soot or dirt. **2** indecent talk or images. **smutty** *adjective*

snack *noun* **1** a small meal; food eaten between meals. **2** (*Australian informal*) an easy task.

snaffle *verb* (*informal*) steal; seize, *snaffle up a bargain.*

snag[1] *noun* **1** a difficulty. **2** a sharp projection. **3** a tear in material that has been caught on something sharp.

snag[2] *verb* (**snagged**, **snagging**) catch or tear or be caught on a snag.

snag[3] *noun* (*Australian informal*) a sausage. [from British dialect = a small morsel]

snail *noun* a small animal with a soft body and a shell.

snail's pace *noun* a very slow pace.

snake *noun* a reptile with a long narrow body and no legs.

snaky *adjective* (*Australian informal*) irritable; angry.

snap[1] *verb* (**snapped**, **snapping**) **1** break suddenly or with a sharp sound. **2** bite suddenly or quickly. **3** say something quickly and angrily. **4** take something or move quickly. **5** take a snapshot of something.

snap[2] *noun* **1** the action or sound of snapping. **2** a snapshot. **3** a card game in which players shout 'Snap!' when they see two similar cards.

snap[3] *adjective* sudden, *a snap decision.*

snapdragon *noun* a plant with flowers that have a mouth-like opening.

snapper *noun* an edible pink sea fish.

snappy *adjective* **1** snapping at people. **2** quick; lively. **snappily** *adverb*

snapshot *noun* **1** an informal photograph. **2** a brief look or summary.

snare[1] *noun* **1** a trap for catching birds or animals. **2** something liable to entangle a person or expose them to danger or failure. **3** twisted strings of gut, hide, or wire stretched across the lower head of a side drum to produce a rattling sound.

snare[2] *verb* (**snared**, **snaring**) catch in a snare.

snare drum *noun* a drum with snares.

snarl[1] *verb* **1** growl angrily. **2** speak in a bad-tempered way. **snarl** *noun*

snarl[2] *verb* make or become tangled or jammed, *Traffic was snarled up.* **snarl** *noun*

snatch *verb* seize; take quickly.

sneak[1] *verb* (**sneaked**, **sneaking**) **1** move quietly and secretly. **2** (*informal*) take secretly, *He sneaked a biscuit from the tin.* **3** (*informal*) tell tales.

> **Usage** The traditional standard past form of *sneak* is *sneaked* (*she sneaked round the corner*). An alternative past form, *snuck* (*she snuck past me*), arose in the US in the 19th century. While this form often appears in Australian English, it should be avoided in formal contexts.

sneak[2] *noun* (*informal*) a telltale.
sneakily *adverb*, **sneaky** *adjective*

sneakers *plural noun* soft-soled shoes made of canvas, leather, etc.

sneer *verb* speak or behave in a scornful way. **sneer** *noun*

sneeze *verb* (**sneezed**, **sneezing**) send out air suddenly and uncontrollably through the nose and mouth in order to get rid of something irritating the nostrils.
sneeze *noun*
not to be sneezed at (*informal*) not to be despised; worth having.

sniff *verb* **1** make a sound by drawing in air through the nose. **2** smell something. **sniff** *noun*, **sniffer** *noun*

sniffle *verb* (**sniffled**, **sniffling**) sniff slightly; keep on sniffing. **sniffle** *noun*

snigger *verb* giggle slyly. **snigger** *noun*

snip *verb* (**snipped**, **snipping**) cut with scissors or shears in small quick cuts. **snip** *noun*

snipe *verb* (**sniped**, **sniping**) **1** shoot at people from a hiding place. **2** make a sly critical attack. **sniper** *noun*

snippet *noun* a small piece of news, information, etc. [from *snip*]

snivel *verb* (**snivelled**, **snivelling**) cry or complain in a whining way. **snivel** *noun*

snob *noun* a person who despises those who have not got wealth, power, or particular tastes or interests. **snobbery** *noun*, **snobbish** *adjective*

snooker *noun* a game played with cues and coloured balls on a special cloth-covered table.

snoop *verb* (*informal*) pry. **snooper** *noun*

snooze *noun* a nap. **snooze** *verb*

snore *verb* (**snored**, **snoring**) breathe very noisily while sleeping. **snore** *noun*

snorkel *noun* a tube through which a person swimming under water can take in air. **snorkelling** *noun* [from German]

snort *verb* make a rough sound by breathing forcefully through the nose. **snort** *noun*

snout *noun* an animal's projecting nose, or nose and jaws.

snow[1] *noun* frozen drops of water that fall from the sky in small white flakes.
snowy *adjective*

snow[2] *verb* send down snow.
be snowed under be overwhelmed with a mass of work.

snowdrop *noun* a small white flower that blooms in early spring.

snowman *noun* (*plural* **snowmen**) a figure made of snow.

snow-white *adjective* pure white.

snub *verb* treat someone in a scornful or unfriendly way. **snub** *noun*

snub-nosed *adjective* having a short thick nose.

snuck see the note at **sneak**[1].

snuff[1] *noun* powdered tobacco for taking into the nose by sniffing.

snuff[2] *verb* put out a candle by covering or pinching the flame. **snuffer** *noun*

snuffle *verb* (**snuffled**, **snuffling**) sniff in a noisy way. **snuffle** *noun*

snug *adjective* (**snugger**, **snuggest**) **1** cosy. **2** close-fitting. **snugly** *adverb*, **snugness** *noun*

snuggle *verb* (**snuggled**, **snuggling**) press closely and comfortably; nestle.

so[1] *adverb* **1** in this way; to such an extent, *Why are you so cross?* **2** very, *Cricket is so boring.* **3** also, *I was wrong but so were you.*
or so or about that number.
so far up to now.
so-so (*informal*) only moderately good or well.
so what? (*informal*) that is not important.

so[2] *conjunction* for that reason, *They threw me out, so I came here.*

soak[1] *verb* make a person or thing very wet.
soak up take in a liquid in the way that a sponge does.

soak[2] *noun* **1** the process of soaking. **2** (*Australian*) a hollow in the ground where water collects.

so-and-so *noun* (*plural* **so-and-so's**) a person or thing that need not be named.

soap[1] *noun* **1** a substance used with water for washing and cleaning things. **2** (*informal*) a soap opera. **soapy** *adjective*

soap[2] *verb* put soap on something.

soap opera *noun* a broadcast serial with a domestic setting (so called because originally sponsored in the US by soap manufacturers).

soar *verb* **1** rise high in the air. **2** rise very high, *Prices were soaring.*

sob *verb* (**sobbed**, **sobbing**) make a gasping sound when crying. **sob** *noun*

soba (*say* **soh**-buh) *noun* a type of noodle used in Asian cuisine. [Japanese]

sober[1] *adjective* **1** not intoxicated. **2** serious and calm. **3** (of colours) not bright. **soberly** *adverb*, **sobriety** (*say* suh-**bruy**-uh-tee) *noun*

sober[2] *verb* make or become sober.

so-called *adjective* named in what may be the wrong way, *This so-called gentleman slammed the door.*

soccer *noun* a kind of football game played by sides of 11 with a round ball.

sociable *adjective* liking to be with other people; friendly. **sociability** *noun*, **sociably** *adverb*

social[1] *adjective* **1** living in a community, not alone, *Bees are social insects.* **2** of life in a community, *social science.* **3** concerned with people's welfare, *social worker.* **4** helping people to meet each other, *a social club.* **5** sociable. **socially** *adverb*

social[2] *noun* a social gathering, *the school social.* [from Latin *socius* = companion]

social distancing *noun* the action of keeping a specified distance from other people, or of restricting contact between people.

socialism *noun* a political system where wealth is shared equally between people, and the main industries and trade are controlled by the government. (Compare **capitalism.**) **socialist** *noun*

social media *noun* websites and applications that enable users to create and share content or to participate in social networking.

social networking *noun* the use of particular websites and applications to interact with other users, or to find people with similar interests to one's own.

social security *noun* money provided by the government for those in need through being unemployed, ill, disabled, or poor.

society *noun* (*plural* **societies**) **1** a community; people living together in a group or nation. **2** a group of people organised for a particular purpose, *the school dramatic society.* **3** company; companionship, *We enjoy the society of our friends.* [same origin as *social*]

socio-economic *adjective* relating to the difference between groups of people based on their financial situation.

sociology (*say* soh-see-**ol**-uh-jee) *noun* the study of human society and social behaviour. **sociological** *adjective*, **sociologist** *noun* [from *socio-* = of society, + *-logy*]

sock[1] *noun* a garment covering the foot.

sock[2] *verb* (*informal*) hit hard; punch, *He socked me on the jaw.* **sock** *noun*

socket *noun* **1** a hollow into which something fits, *a tooth socket.* **2** a device into which an electric plug or bulb is put to make a connection.

sod *noun* a piece of turf.

soda *noun* **1** a compound of sodium used in washing, cooking, etc. **2** soda water.

soda water *noun* water made fizzy with carbon dioxide, used in drinks.

sodden *adjective* made very wet.

sodium *noun* a soft white metal.

sofa *noun* a long soft seat with a back and arms. [from Arabic *suffa*]

soft *adjective* **1** not hard or firm; easily pressed. **2** smooth, not rough or stiff. **3** gentle; not loud. **4** (of colours) not harsh or bright. **5** lenient; sympathetic. **6** (*informal*) easy, *a soft job.* **softly** *adverb*, **softness** *noun*

softball *noun* a modified form of baseball.

soft drink *noun* a drink that is not alcoholic.

soften *verb* make or become soft or softer. **softener** *noun*

soft-hearted *adjective* compassionate; tender.

software *noun* computer programs. (Compare **hardware** 2.)

softwood *noun* wood from coniferous trees, which is easily sawn.

soggy *adjective* (**soggier**, **soggiest**) very wet and heavy, *soggy ground.*

soil[1] *noun* **1** the loose earth in which plants grow. **2** territory, *on Australian soil.*

soil[2] *verb* make a thing dirty.

sojourn[1] (*say* **so**-jern) *verb* stay at a place temporarily.

sojourn[2] *noun* a temporary stay.

solace (*say* **sol**-uhs) *noun* comfort in sadness or disappointment. **solace** *verb* [from Latin *solari* = console]

solar *adjective* of or from the sun. [from Latin *sol* = sun]

solar system *noun* the sun and the planets that revolve around it.

sold *past tense & past participle* of **sell**.

solder *noun* a soft alloy that is melted to join pieces of metal together. **solder** *verb* [from Latin *solidare* = make firm or solid]

soldier *noun* a member of an army.

sole[1] *noun* **1** the bottom surface of a foot or shoe. **2** an edible flatfish.

sole[2] *verb* (**soled**, **soling**) put a sole on a shoe.

sole[3] *adjective* single; only, *She was the sole survivor.* **solely** *adverb*

solemn *adjective* **1** not smiling; not cheerful. **2** dignified; formal. **solemnity** *noun*, **solemnly** *adverb*

solemnise *verb* (**solemnised**, **solemnising**) celebrate a festival; perform a marriage ceremony. **solemnisation** *noun*

solenoid *noun* a coil of wire that becomes magnetic when an electric current is passed through it.

sol-fa *noun* a system of syllables (*doh, ray, me, fah, soh, la, te*) used to represent the notes of the musical scale.

solicit *verb* (**solicited**, **soliciting**) ask for; try to obtain, *solicit votes* or *solicit for votes.* **solicitation** *noun*

solicitor *noun* a lawyer who advises clients, prepares legal documents, and instructs barristers who argue the case in court.

solicitous *adjective* anxious and concerned about a person's comfort or welfare. **solicitously** *adverb*, **solicitude** *noun* [from Latin *sollicitus* = worrying]

solid[1] *adjective* **1** not hollow; with no space inside. **2** keeping its shape; not liquid or gas. **3** continuous, *for two solid hours.* **4** firm or strongly made; not flimsy, *a solid foundation.* **5** showing solidarity; unanimous. **solidity** *noun*, **solidly** *adverb*

solid[2] *noun* **1** a solid thing; solid food. **2** a shape that has three dimensions (length, width, and height or depth).

solidarity *noun* unity and support for each other because of shared interests, feelings, or sympathies.

solidify *verb* (**solidified**, **solidifying**) make or become solid.

soliloquy (*say* suh-**lil**-uh-kwee) *noun* (*plural* **soliloquies**) a speech in which a person speaks their thoughts aloud without addressing anyone. **soliloquise** *verb* [from Latin *solus* = alone, + *loqui* = speak]

solipsism *noun* (in philosophy) the view that the self is all that exists or can be known. **solipsist** *noun*

solitaire *noun* **1** a game for one person. **2** a diamond or other precious stone set by itself.

solitary *adjective* **1** alone; without companions. **2** single, *a solitary example.* **3** lonely, *a solitary valley.* [from Latin *solus* = alone]

solitude *noun* being solitary.

solo *noun* (*plural* **solos**) something sung, played, danced, or done by one person. **solo** *adjective & adverb*, **soloist** *noun* [Italian, = alone]

solstice (*say* **sol**-stuhs) *noun* either of the two times in each year when the sun is at its furthest point north or south of the equator (about 21 June and 22 December). [from Latin *sol* = sun, + *sistere* = stand still]

soluble *adjective* **1** able to be dissolved. **2** able to be solved. **solubility** *noun* [same origin as *solve*]

solution *noun* **1** a liquid in which something is dissolved. **2** the answer to a problem or puzzle. [same origin as *solve*]

solve *verb* (**solved**, **solving**) find the answer to a problem or puzzle. [from Latin *solvere* = unfasten]

solvent[1] *adjective* **1** having enough money to pay all your debts. **2** able to dissolve another substance. **solvency** *noun*

solvent[2] *noun* a liquid used for dissolving something.

sombre *adjective* dark and gloomy. [from Latin *sub* = under, + *umbra* = shade]

sombrero (*say* som-**brair**-roh) *noun* (*plural* **sombreros**) a hat with a very wide brim. [from Spanish *sombra* = shade (same origin as *sombre*)]

some[1] *adjective* **1** a few; a little, *some apples*; *some sugar.* **2** an unknown person or thing, *Some animal got into our picnic basket.* **3** about, *We waited some 20 minutes.*

some[2] *pronoun* a certain number or amount that is less than the whole, *Some of them were late.*

somebody[1] *pronoun* some person.

somebody[2] *noun* an important person.

somehow *adverb* in some way.

somen *noun* a type of very thin noodle that is popular in Japan.

someone *pronoun* somebody.

somersault *noun* a movement in which you turn head over heels before landing on your feet. **somersault** *verb* [from Latin *supra* = above, + *saltus* = a leap]

something *pronoun* a thing that is unspecified or unknown, *I knew something terrible had happened.*
something like rather like, *It's something like a rabbit*; approximately, *It cost something like $10.*

sometime *adjective* former, *her sometime friend.*

sometimes *adverb* at some times but not always, *We sometimes walk to school.*

somewhat *adverb* to some extent, *She was somewhat annoyed.*

somewhere *adverb* in or to some place.

somnambulist *noun* a sleepwalker. **somnambulism** *noun* [from Latin *somnus* = sleep, + *ambulare* = to walk]

somnolent *adjective* sleeping; sleepy. **somnolence** *noun* [from Latin *somnus* = sleep]

son *noun* a boy or man who is someone's child.

sonar *noun* a device for finding objects under water by the reflection of sound waves. [from *so*und *na*vigation and *r*anging]

sonata *noun* a musical composition for one instrument or two, in several movements. [from Italian *sonare* = to sound]

song *noun* **1** a tune for singing. **2** singing, *He burst into song.*
a song and dance (*informal*) a great fuss.
for a song bought or sold very cheaply.

songbird *noun* a bird that sings sweetly.

songline *noun* (*Australian*) (in traditional Aboriginal culture) a route taken by an ancestral being or beings on a journey through a particular landscape and recorded in song.

songman *noun* (*plural* **songmen**) (*Australian*) (in Aboriginal culture) a man who memorises and performs the traditional songs of a community.

songwoman *noun* (*plural* **songwomen**) (*Australian*) (in Aboriginal culture) a woman who memorises and performs the traditional songs of a community.

sonic *adjective* of sound or sound waves. [from Latin *sonus* = sound]

son-in-law *noun* (*plural* **sons-in-law**) a daughter's husband.

sonnet *noun* a kind of poem with 14 lines.

sonorous (*say* **son**-uh-ruhs) *adjective* giving a loud deep sound; resonant. [from Latin *sonor* = sound]

sook (*rhymes with* book) *noun* (*Australian informal*) a timid or cowardly person. **sooky** *adjective* [from Scottish *souk* = suck (in reference to a child feeding from the breast)]

sool (*rhymes with* tool) *verb* (*Australian informal*) urge a dog to attack. **sooler** *noun*

soon *adverb* **1** in a short time from now. **2** not long after something.
as soon as willingly, *I'd just as soon stay here.*
as soon as at the moment that.
sooner or later at some time in the future.

soot *noun* the black powder left by smoke in a chimney or on a building etc.
sooty *adjective*

soothe *verb* (**soothed**, **soothing**) calm; ease pain or distress. **soothingly** *adverb*

soothsayer *noun* a prophet. [from an old word *sooth* = truth, + *say*]

sop *noun* **1** a piece of bread dipped in liquid before being eaten or cooked. **2** something given to pacify or bribe a troublesome person.

sophisticated *adjective* **1** of or accustomed to fashionable life and its ways. **2** complicated, *a sophisticated machine.* **sophistication** *noun*

sophistry (*say* **sof**-uhs-tree) *noun* (*plural* **sophistries**) a piece of reasoning that is clever but false or misleading. [from Greek *sophos* = wise]

soporific *adjective* causing sleep. [from Latin *sopor* = sleep, + *facere* = make]

sopping *adjective* very wet; drenched.

soppy *adjective* (*informal*) very sentimental.

soprano *noun* (*plural* **sopranos**) **1** a woman, girl, or boy with a high singing voice. **2** an instrument with a high or the highest pitch in its family. [from Italian *sopra* = above]

sorbet (*say* **saw**-bay) *noun* a frozen dessert made with fruit or liqueur, syrup, egg whites, etc. [same origin as *sherbet*]

sorcerer *noun* a wizard. **sorceress** *noun*, **sorcery** *noun*

sordid *adjective* **1** dirty; squalid. **2** dishonourable; selfish and mercenary, *sordid motives.* **sordidly** *adverb*, **sordidness** *noun*

sore[1] *adjective* **1** painful; smarting. **2** (*informal*) annoyed; offended. **3** serious; distressing, *in sore need.* **soreness** *noun*

sore[2] *noun* a sore place.

sorely *adverb* seriously; very, *I was sorely tempted to run away.*

sorrel[1] *noun* a herb with sharp-tasting leaves.

sorrel[2] *noun* a reddish-brown colour; a horse of this colour.

sorrow[1] *noun* unhappiness or regret caused by loss or disappointment. **sorrowful** *adjective*, **sorrowfully** *adverb*

sorrow[2] *verb* feel sorrow; grieve.

sorry *adjective* (**sorrier**, **sorriest**) **1** feeling regret. **2** feeling pity or sympathy. **3** wretched, *His clothes were in a sorry state.* **4** (*Australian*) (in Aboriginal English) of or relating to death and mourning, *sorry business.*

sort[1] *noun* **1** a group of things or people that are similar; a kind or variety. **2** (*informal*) a person, *He's a decent sort.*
out of sorts slightly unwell or depressed.
sort of (*informal*) rather; to some extent, *I sort of expected it.*

sort[2] *verb* arrange things in groups according to their size, kind, etc. **sorter** *noun*
sort out 1 disentangle; put into order. **2** select. **3** resolve a problem or disagreement. **4** (*informal*) deal with and punish someone.

sortie *noun* **1** an attack by troops coming out of a besieged place. **2** an attacking expedition by a military aircraft. [from French *sortir* = go out]

SOS *noun* (*plural* **SOSs**) an urgent appeal for help. [the international Morse code signal of extreme distress]

sotto voce (*say* sot-oh **voh**-chay) *adverb* in a very quiet voice. [Italian, = under the voice]

sought *past tense & past participle* of **seek**.

soul *noun* **1** the invisible part of a person that is believed to go on living after the body has died. **2** a person's mind and emotions. **3** a person, *There isn't a soul about.* **4** emotional or intellectual energy or intensity, *She put a lot of soul into her performance.* **5** a kind of music incorporating elements of rhythm and blues and gospel music.

soulful *adjective* having or showing deep feeling. **soulfully** *adverb*

sound[1] *noun* **1** vibrations that travel through the air and can be detected by the ear; the sensation they produce. **2** sound reproduced in a film etc. **3** a mental impression, *We don't like the sound of his plans.*

sound[2] *verb* **1** produce or cause to produce a sound. **2** give an impression when heard, *She sounds angry.* **3** test by noting the sounds heard, *A doctor sounds a patient's lungs with a stethoscope.* [from Latin *sonus* = a sound]

sound[3] *verb* test the depth of water beneath a ship.
sound out try to find out what a person thinks or feels about something. [from Latin *sub* = under, + *unda* = wave]

sound[4] *adjective* **1** in good condition; not damaged. **2** healthy; not diseased. **3** reasonable; correct, *His ideas are sound.* **4** reliable; secure, *a sound investment.* **5** thorough; deep, *a sound sleep.* **soundly** *adverb*, **soundness** *noun* [from Old English *gesund* = healthy]

sound[5] *noun* a strait; an inlet, *Milford Sound.* [from Old English *sund* = swimming or sea]

sound barrier *noun* the resistance of the air to objects moving at nearly supersonic speed.

soundtrack *noun* the sound that goes with a cinema film.

soup *noun* liquid food made from stewed bones, meat, fish, vegetables, etc.
in the soup (*informal*) in trouble.

sour[1] *adjective* **1** tasting sharp like unripe fruit. **2** stale and unpleasant; not fresh, *sour milk.* **3** bad-tempered. **sourly** *adverb*, **sourness** *noun*

sour[2] *verb* make or become sour.

source *noun* **1** the place from which something comes. **2** something providing information. **3** writing, artefacts, etc. that can be used as evidence for the study of history or for research.

source code *noun* a text listing of commands to be compiled into an executable computer program.

sourdough *noun* fermenting dough, usually left over from a previous baking, used as leaven; bread made from this.

soursob *noun* (*Australian*) a garden weed with yellow flowers.

souse *verb* (**soused**, **sousing**) **1** soak; drench. **2** soak fish in pickle.

south[1] *noun* **1** the direction to the right of a person who faces east. **2** the southern part of something.

south[2] *adjective & adverb* towards or in the south. **southerly** (*say* **suth**-uh-lee) *adjective*, **southern** *adjective*, **southerner** *noun*, **southernmost** *adjective*

south-east *noun*, *adjective*, *& adverb* midway between south and east. **south-easterly** *adjective*, **south-eastern** *adjective*

south pole see **pole**[2].

southward *adjective & adverb* towards the south. **southwards** *adverb*

south-west *noun*, *adjective*, *& adverb* midway between south and west. **south-westerly** *adjective*, **south-western** *adjective*

souvenir (*say* soo-vuh-**neer**) *noun* something that you keep to remind you of a person, place, or event. [from French *se souvenir* = remember]

sou'wester *noun* a waterproof hat.

sovereign[1] *noun* **1** a king or queen who is the ruler of a country; a monarch. **2** an old British gold coin. **sovereignty** *noun*

sovereign[2] *adjective* **1** supreme, *sovereign power.* **2** having sovereign power; independent, *sovereign states.* **3** very effective, *a sovereign remedy.* [from Latin *super* = over]

sow[1] (*rhymes with* go) *verb* (**sowed, sown** or **sowed, sowing**) put seeds into the ground so that they will grow into plants. **sower** *noun*

sow[2] (*rhymes with* cow) *noun* a female pig.

soy *noun* (also **soya**) **1** soybean. **2** soy milk; soy sauce.

soybean *noun* (also **soy bean** or **soya bean**) **1** a leguminous plant yielding edible oil and flour. **2** the seed of this plant.

soy milk *noun* a drink made from soy beans, often used as a substitute for milk.

soy sauce *noun* (also **soya sauce**) a salty black sauce made from soy beans and used traditionally in Asian cooking.

spa *noun* **1** a health resort where there is a spring of water containing mineral salts. **2** a bath or pool with underwater jets of water that massage the body. [from Spa, a town in Belgium with a mineral spring]

space[1] *noun* **1** the whole area outside the earth, where the stars and planets are. **2** an area or volume, *This table takes up too much space.* **3** an empty area; a gap. **4** an interval of time, *within the space of an hour.*

space[2] *verb* (**spaced, spacing**) arrange things with spaces between, *Space them out.* [from Latin *spatium* = a space]

spacecraft *noun* (*plural* **spacecraft**) a vehicle for travelling in outer space.

spaceship *noun* a spacecraft.

space shuttle *noun* a spacecraft for repeated use to and from outer space.

spacious *adjective* providing a lot of space; roomy. **spaciousness** *noun*

spade[1] *noun* a tool with a long handle and a wide blade for digging. [from Old English *spadu*]

spade[2] *noun* a playing card with black shapes like upside-down hearts on it, each with a short stem. [from Italian *spada* = sword]

spadework *noun* hard work done in preparation for something.

spaghetti *noun* pasta made in long thin sticks. [from Italian, = little strings]

spam[1] *noun* **1** unwanted messages or email sent over the Internet, typically for the purposes of advertising or swindling. **2** (*trademark*) a tinned meat product made mainly from ham.

spam[2] *verb* (**spammed, spamming**) send the same message indiscriminately to a large number of Internet users.

span[1] *noun* **1** the length from end to end or across something. **2** the distance from the tip of the thumb to the tip of the little finger when the hand is spread out. **3** the part between two uprights of an arch or bridge. **4** the length of a period of time.

span[2] *verb* (**spanned, spanning**) reach across, *A bridge spans the river.*

spangle *noun* a small piece of glittering material. **spangled** *adjective*

spaniel *noun* a kind of dog with long ears and silky fur. [from French, = Spanish dog]

spank *verb* smack a person on the bottom as a punishment.

spanner *noun* a tool for gripping and turning the nut on a bolt etc.

spar[1] *noun* a strong pole used for a mast or boom etc. on a ship.

spar[2] *verb* (**sparred, sparring**) **1** practise boxing. **2** quarrel or argue.

spare[1] *verb* (**spared, sparing**) **1** afford to give something, *Can you spare a moment?* **2** be merciful towards someone; not hurt or harm a person or thing. **3** use or treat economically, *No expense will be spared; Spare the rod and spoil the child!*

spare[2] *adjective* **1** not used but kept ready in case it is needed; extra, *a spare wheel; spare time.* **2** thin; lean. **sparely** *adverb*, **spareness** *noun*

sparing (*say* **spair**-ring) *adjective* economical; grudging. **sparingly** *adverb*

spark[1] *noun* **1** a tiny glowing particle. **2** a flash produced electrically.

spark[2] *verb* give off a spark or sparks. **spark off** start something happening.

sparkle *verb* (**sparkled, sparkling**) **1** shine with tiny flashes of light. **2** show brilliant wit or liveliness.

sparkler *noun* a sparkling firework.

sparkling *adjective* (of a liquid) giving off bubbles of gas; fizzy.

spark plug *noun* a device that makes a spark to ignite the fuel in an engine.

sparrow *noun* a small brown bird.

sparse *adjective* thinly scattered; not numerous, *a sparse population.* **sparsely** *adverb*, **sparseness** *noun* [from Latin *sparsum* = scattered]

spartan *adjective* simple and without comfort or luxuries. [named after the people of Sparta in ancient Greece, famous for their hardiness]

spasm *noun* **1** a sudden involuntary movement of a muscle. **2** a sudden brief spell of activity.

spasmodic *adjective* in spasms; happening or done at irregular intervals. **spasmodically** *adverb*

spastic *adjective* **1** of or affected by muscle spasm. **2** of a form of muscular weakness (spastic paralysis) typical of cerebral palsy.

> **Usage** The use of the word *spastic* in the medical sense may be considered offensive as a result of its use as an offensive slang term.

spat[1] *past tense & past participle* of **spit**[1].

spat[2] *noun* a short gaiter.

spat[3] *noun* a petty quarrel.

spate *noun* a sudden flood or rush.

spathe (*rhymes with* bathe) *noun* a large petal-like part of a flower, round a central spike.

spatial *adjective* of or in space. [same origin as *space*]

spatter *verb* scatter in small drops; splash. **spatter** *noun*

spatula *noun* **1** an implement with a broad, flat, blunt blade, used for mixing and spreading things. **2** a kitchen utensil with a broad flat blade for lifting and turning food.

spawn[1] *noun* **1** the eggs of fish, frogs, toads, or shellfish. **2** the thread-like matter from which fungi grow.

spawn[2] *verb* **1** put out spawn; produce from spawn. **2** produce something in great quantities.

spay *verb* sterilise a female animal by removing the ovaries.

speak *verb* (**spoke**, **spoken**, **speaking**) **1** say something; talk. **2** hold a conversation. **3** give a speech. **4** talk or be able to talk in a foreign language, *Do you speak French?* **speak up 1** speak more loudly. **2** give your opinion.

speaker *noun* **1** a person who is speaking; someone who makes a speech. **2** a loudspeaker. **3** (**the Speaker**) the presiding officer in a legislative assembly, for example the House of Representatives.

spear[1] *noun* a weapon for throwing or stabbing, with a long shaft and a pointed tip.

spear[2] *verb* pierce with a spear or with something pointed.

spearhead *noun* the person or group that leads an attack etc. **spearhead** *verb*

spearmint *noun* mint used in cookery and for flavouring chewing gum.

special *adjective* **1** of a particular kind; for some purpose, not general, *special training.* **2** exceptional, *Take special care of it.*

specialise *verb* (**specialised**, **specialising**) give particular attention or study to one subject or thing, *She specialised in biology.* **specialisation** *noun*

specialist *noun* an expert in one subject, *a skin specialist.*

speciality *noun* (*plural* **specialities**) a special quality or product; something in which a person specialises.

specially *adverb* in a special way; for a special purpose.

specialty *noun* (*plural* **specialties**) a speciality.

species (*say* **spee**-sheez or **spee**-seez) *noun* (*plural* **species**) **1** a group of animals or plants that are very similar. **2** a kind or sort, *a species of sledge.* [Latin, = appearance]

specific *adjective* **1** definite; precise. **2** of or for a particular thing, *The money was given for a specific purpose.* **specifically** *adverb*

specific gravity *noun* the weight of something as compared with the same volume of water or air.

specify *verb* (**specified**, **specifying**) name or list things precisely, *The recipe specified cream, not milk.* **specification** *noun*

specimen *noun* **1** a sample. **2** an example, *a fine specimen of a waratah.*

specious (*say* **spee**-shuhs) *adjective* seeming good but lacking real merit, *specious reasoning.* [from Latin *speciosus* = attractive]

speck *noun* a small spot or particle.

speckle *noun* a small spot or mark. **speckled** *adjective*

spectacle *noun* **1** an impressive sight or display. **2** a public show. **3** a ridiculous sight. [from Latin *spectare* = look at]

spectacles *plural noun* a pair of lenses set in a frame, worn in front of the eyes to help the wearer to see clearly. **spectacled** *adjective*

spectacular *adjective* impressive.

spectator *noun* a person who watches a game, show, incident, or other event.

spectre *noun* a ghost. **spectral** *adjective* [same origin as *spectrum*]

spectrum *noun* (*plural* **spectra**) **1** the bands of colours seen in a rainbow. **2** a wide range of things, ideas, etc. [Latin, = image]

speculate *verb* (**speculated**, **speculating**) **1** form opinions without having any definite evidence. **2** make investments in the hope of making a profit but risking a loss. **speculation** *noun*, **speculative** *adjective*, **speculator** *noun* [from Latin *speculari* = spy out]

speculative fiction *noun* a genre of fiction including fantasy, horror, and science fiction.

sped *past tense & past participle* of **speed**[2].

speech *noun* (*plural* **speeches**) **1** the action or power of speaking. **2** words spoken; a talk to an audience.

speechless *adjective* unable to speak because of great emotion.

speed[1] *noun* **1** a measure of the time in which something moves or happens. **2** quickness; swiftness.
at speed quickly.

speed[2] *verb* (**sped** (in senses 3 and 4 **speeded**), **speeding**) **1** go quickly, *The train sped by.* **2** send quickly, *to speed you on your way.* **3** travel too fast. **4** make or become quicker, *This will speed things up.*

speedboat *noun* a fast motor boat.

speedo *noun* (*informal*) a speedometer.

speedometer *noun* a device in a vehicle, showing its speed. [from *speed* + *meter*]

speedway *noun* a track for motorcycle racing.

speedy *adjective* (**speedier**, **speediest**) quick; swift. **speedily** *adverb*

speleology (*say* spee-lee-**ol**-uh-jee) *noun* the exploration and study of caves. [from Greek *spelaion* = cave, + *-logy*]

spell[1] *noun* a saying or action supposed to have magical power.

spell[2] *noun* **1** a period of time. **2** a period of a certain work or activity. **3** (*Australian*) a period of rest from work.

spell[3] *verb* (**spelt**, **spelling**) rest; allow a person or animal to rest.

spell[4] *verb* (**spelt**, **spelling**) **1** put letters in the right order to make a word or words. **2** have as a result, *Drought spells ruin for crops.*
speller *noun*
spell out explain in detail.

spellbound *adjective* entranced as if by a magic spell.

spencer *noun* a woman's undergarment like a thin jumper, worn for warmth.

spend *verb* (**spent**, **spending**) **1** use money to pay for things. **2** use up, *Don't spend too much time on it.* **3** pass time, *We spent a holiday in Bali.*

spendthrift *noun* a person who spends money extravagantly and wastefully.

sperm *noun* (*plural* **sperms** or **sperm**) the male cell that fuses with an ovum. [from Greek *sperma* = seed]

spew *verb* **1** vomit. **2** cast out in a stream, *The volcano spewed out lava.*

sphere *noun* **1** a perfectly round solid shape; the shape of a ball. **2** a field of action or interest etc., *a sphere of influence.* **spherical** *adjective* [from Greek *sphaira* = ball]

spheroid *noun* a sphere-like but not perfectly spherical solid.

sphinx *noun* (*plural* **sphinxes**) a stone statue with the body of a lion and a human head, especially the huge one (almost 5,000 years old) in Egypt.

spice *noun* a substance used to flavour food, often made from dried parts of plants.
spicy *adjective*

spick and span *adjective* neat and clean.

spider *noun* **1** a small animal with eight legs that spins webs to catch insects on which it feeds. **2** (*Australian*) a soft drink with a scoop of ice cream in it. **spidery** *adjective*

spiel (*say* speel or shpeel) *noun* (*informal*) a glib or lengthy speech, usually intended to persuade. [German, = game]

spike[1] *noun* **1** a pointed piece of metal; a sharp point. **2** a long narrow projecting part. **spiky** *adjective*

spike[2] *verb* (**spiked**, **spiking**) **1** put spikes on something. **2** pierce with a spike. **3** (*informal*) add alcohol to a drink.

spill[1] *verb* (**spilt** or **spilled**, **spilling**) **1** let something fall out of a container. **2** become spilt, *The coins came spilling out.*
spillage *noun*

spill[2] *noun* **1** spilling. **2** a fall.

spill[3] *noun* a thin strip of wood or rolled paper used to carry a flame, e.g. to light a pipe.

spin[1] *verb* (**spun**, **spinning**) **1** turn round and round quickly. **2** make raw wool or cotton into threads by pulling and twisting its fibres. **3** (of a spider or silkworm) make a web or cocoon out of threads from its body. **4** tell a story, *spin a yarn.*
spin out cause to last a long time.

spin[2] *noun* **1** a spinning movement. **2** a short excursion in a vehicle. **3** (*Australian informal*) a run of luck, *He's had a rough spin.* **4** a favourable bias or slant to a news story.

spinach *noun* a vegetable with dark green leaves.

spinal *adjective* of the spine.

spindle *noun* **1** a thin rod on which thread is wound. **2** a pin or bar that turns round or on which something turns.

spindly *adjective* thin and long or tall.

spin doctor *noun* a person whose job is to promote a positive impression of events to the media.

spindrift *noun* spray blown along the surface of the sea.

spine *noun* **1** the line of bones down the middle of the back. **2** a thorn or prickle. **3** the part of a book where the pages are joined together.

spine-chilling *adjective* frightening.

spineless *adjective* **1** without a backbone. **2** lacking in determination or strength of character.

spinet *noun* a small harpsichord.

spinifex *noun* a coarse grass with spiny leaves found in inland Australia.

spinnaker (*say* **spin**-uh-kuh) *noun* a large triangular extra sail on a racing yacht.

spinney *noun* (*plural* **spinneys**) a small wood; a thicket.

spinning wheel *noun* a household device for spinning fibre into thread.

spin-off *noun* (*plural* **spin-offs**) a by-product; an extra benefit from a process.

spinster *noun* a woman who has not married. [the original meaning was 'one who spins']

spiny *adjective* full of spines; prickly.

spiral[1] *adjective* going round and round a central point and becoming gradually closer to it or further from it; twisting continually round a central line or cylinder etc.
spirally *adverb*

spiral[2] *noun* a spiral line or course.

spiral[3] *verb* (**spiralled**, **spiralling**) move in a spiral.

spire *noun* a tall pointed part on top of a church tower.

spirit[1] *noun* **1** the soul. **2** a person's mood or mind and feelings, *He was in good spirits.* **3** a ghost; a supernatural being. **4** courage; liveliness, *She answered with spirit.* **5** a kind of quality in something, *the romantic spirit of the book.* **6** a person's nature. **7** a strong distilled alcoholic drink.

spirit[2] *verb* carry off quickly and secretly, *They spirited her away.* [from Latin *spiritus* = breath]

spirited *adjective* brave; lively.

spiritual[1] *adjective* **1** to do with the human soul and with a person's deepest thoughts and feelings; not physical. **2** of religion or religious belief. **spirituality** *noun*, **spiritually** *adverb*

spiritual[2] *noun* a religious folk song, especially of Black people in America.

spiritualism *noun* the belief that the spirits of dead people communicate with living people. **spiritualist** *noun*

spirituous *adjective* containing a lot of alcohol; distilled, *spirituous liquors.*

spit[1] *verb* (**spat** or **spit**, **spitting**) **1** send out drops of liquid forcibly from the mouth, *He spat at me.* **2** fall lightly, *It's spitting with rain.* **3** perform rap music.
spit the dummy (*Australian informal*) **1** be very angry. **2** give up (contesting, participating, etc.) prematurely.

spit[2] *noun* saliva; spittle.

spit[3] *noun* **1** a long thin metal spike put through meat to hold it while it is being roasted. **2** a narrow strip of land sticking out into the sea.

spite *noun* a desire to hurt or annoy somebody. **spite** *verb*, **spiteful** *adjective*, **spitefully** *adverb*, **spitefulness** *noun*
in spite of not being prevented by, *We went out in spite of the rain.*

spitfire *noun* a fiery-tempered person.

spitting image *noun* an exact likeness.

spittle *noun* saliva, especially that spat out.

splash[1] *verb* **1** make liquid fly about in drops. **2** (of liquid) fly about in drops. **3** wet by scattering drops of liquid, *The bus splashed us.*

splash[2] *noun* (*plural* **splashes**) **1** the action or sound of splashing. **2** a mark made by splashing. **3** a striking display or effect.

splatter *verb* splash noisily.

splay *verb* spread or slope apart.

spleen *noun* **1** an organ of the body, close to the stomach, that helps to keep the blood in good condition. **2** bad temper; spite, *He vented his spleen on us.*

splendid *adjective* **1** magnificent; full of splendour. **2** excellent. **splendidly** *adverb* [from Latin *splendidus* = shining]

splendour *noun* a brilliant display or appearance.

splice *verb* (**spliced**, **splicing**) **1** join pieces of rope etc. by twisting their strands together. **2** join pieces of film or wood etc. by overlapping the ends.

splint[1] *noun* a straight piece of wood or metal etc. tied to a broken arm or leg to hold it firm.

splint[2] *verb* hold with a splint.

splinter[1] *noun* a thin sharp piece of wood, glass, stone, etc. broken off a larger piece.

splinter[2] *verb* break into splinters.

split[1] *verb* (**split**, **splitting**) **1** break into parts. **2** divide. **3** (*informal*) reveal a secret.
split hairs make small and unnecessary distinctions.
split up (of a couple) separate.

split[2] *noun* **1** the splitting or dividing of something. **2** a place where something has split.
the splits an acrobatic position in which the legs are stretched widely in opposite directions.

splurge[1] *noun* a sudden extravagance; a spending spree.

splurge[2] *verb* (**splurged**, **splurging**) spend money freely.

splutter *verb* **1** make a quick series of spitting sounds. **2** speak quickly but not clearly.
splutter *noun*

spoil[1] *verb* (**spoilt** or **spoiled**, **spoiling**) **1** damage something and make it useless or unsatisfactory. **2** make someone selfish by always letting them have what they want. **3** (of food) go bad.

spoil[2] *noun* (also **spoils**) plunder or other things gained by a victor, *the spoils of war.* [from Latin *spolium* = plunder]

spoilsport *noun* a person who spoils other people's enjoyment of things.

spoke[1] *noun* each of the bars or rods that go from the centre of a wheel to its rim.

spoke[2] *past tense* of **speak**.

spoken *past participle* of **speak**.

spokesman *noun* (*plural* **spokesmen**) a man who speaks on behalf of a group.

spokesperson *noun* (*plural* **spokespersons** or **spokespeople**) a person who speaks on behalf of a group.

spokeswoman *noun* (*plural* **spokeswomen**) a woman who speaks on behalf of a group.

spoliation *noun* pillaging.

sponge[1] *noun* **1** a sea creature with a soft porous body. **2** the skeleton of this creature, or a piece of a similar substance, used for washing or padding things. **3** a soft lightweight cake or pudding.
spongy *adjective*

sponge[2] *verb* (**sponged**, **sponging**) **1** wipe or wash something with a sponge. **2** (*informal*) live off the generosity of other people, *She sponged on her friends.* **sponger** *noun*

sponsor[1] *noun* someone who provides money or help for a person or thing, or who gives money to a charity in return for something achieved by another person.
sponsorship *noun*

sponsor[2] *verb* be a sponsor for a person or thing. [from Latin *sponsum* = promised]

spontaneous (*say* spon-**tay**-nee-uhs) *adjective* happening or done naturally; not forced or suggested by someone else.
spontaneity *noun*, **spontaneously** *adverb* [from Latin *sponte* = of your own accord]

spoof *noun* (*informal*) a hoax; a parody.

spook *noun* (*informal*) a ghost.
spookiness *noun*, **spooky** *adjective*

spool *noun* a rod or cylinder on which something is wound.

spoon[1] *noun* a small device with a rounded bowl on a handle, used for lifting things to the mouth or for stirring or measuring things. **spoonful** *noun* (*plural* **spoonfuls**)

spoon[2] *verb* take or lift something with a spoon.

spoonbill *noun* a wading bird with a very broad flat tip to its bill.

spoonerism *noun* an accidental exchange of the initial letters of two words, e.g. by saying *a boiled sprat* instead of *a spoiled brat.* [named after Canon Spooner (1844–1930), said to have made mistakes of this kind]

spoor *noun* the track left by an animal.

sporadic *adjective* happening or found at irregular intervals; scattered. **sporadically** *adverb* [from Greek *sporas* = scattered]

spore *noun* a tiny reproductive cell of a plant such as a fungus or fern. [from Greek *spora* = seed]

sporran *noun* a pouch worn in front of a kilt.

sport[1] *noun* **1** an athletic activity; a game or pastime, especially outdoors. **2** games of this kind, *Are you keen on sport?* **3** (*informal*) a person who behaves fairly and generously, *Come on, be a sport!*

sport[2] *verb* **1** play; amuse yourself. **2** wear, *He sported a gold watch.*

sporting *adjective* **1** connected with sport; interested in sport. **2** behaving fairly and generously.
a sporting chance a reasonable chance of success.

sportive *adjective* playful.

sports car *noun* an open low-built fast car.

sports coat *noun* (also **sports jacket**) a man's jacket for informal wear (not part of a suit).

sportsground *noun* a piece of land for sports.

sportsman *noun* (*plural* **sportsmen**) **1** a man who takes part in sport, especially as a professional. **2** a person who behaves fairly and generously.

sportsmanship *noun* being generous in victory or defeat in sports.

sportsperson *noun* (*plural* **sportspeople** or **sportspersons**) a person who takes part in sport, especially as a professional.

sportswoman *noun* (*plural* **sportswomen**) **1** a woman who takes part in sport, especially as a professional. **2** a woman who behaves fairly and generously.

spot[1] *noun* **1** a small round mark. **2** a pimple; a blemish. **3** a small amount, *We had a spot of trouble.* **4** a place. **5** a drop, *a few spots of rain.*
on the spot 1 without delay or change of place. **2** under pressure to take action, *This really puts him on the spot!*

spot[2] *verb* (**spotted**, **spotting**) **1** mark with spots. **2** (*informal*) notice, *We spotted her in the crowd.* **3** watch for and take note of, *trainspotting.* **4** (of a bushfire) break out in patches ahead of the main fire. **spotter** *noun*

spotless *adjective* perfectly clean.

spotlight *noun* a strong light that can shine on one small area.

spotty *adjective* marked with spots.

spouse *noun* a person's husband or wife. [from Latin *sponsus* = betrothed]

spout[1] *noun* **1** a pipe or similar opening from which liquid can pour. **2** a jet of liquid.

spout[2] *verb* **1** come or send out as a jet of liquid. **2** (*informal*) speak for a long time.

sprain *verb* injure a joint by twisting it. **sprain** *noun*

sprang *past tense* of **spring**[1].

sprat *noun* a small edible fish.

sprawl *verb* **1** sit or lie with the arms and legs spread out loosely. **2** spread out loosely or untidily. **sprawl** *noun*

spray[1] *verb* scatter tiny drops of liquid over something.

spray[2] *noun* **1** tiny drops of liquid sprayed. **2** a device for spraying liquid.

spray[3] *noun* **1** a single shoot with its leaves and flowers. **2** a small bunch of flowers.

spread[1] *verb* (**spread**, **spreading**) **1** open or stretch something out to its full size, *The bird spread its wings.* **2** make something cover a surface, *We spread jam on the bread.* **3** become longer or wider, *The stain was spreading.* **4** make or become more widely known or felt or distributed, *We spread the news; Panic spread.*

spread[2] *noun* **1** the action or result of spreading. **2** a thing's breadth or extent. **3** a paste for spreading on bread. **4** (*informal*) a huge meal.

spread-eagle *verb* (**spread-eagled**, **spread-eagling**) spread out a person's body with arms and legs stretched out.

spree *noun* (*informal*) a lively outing or bout of activity.

sprig *noun* a small branch; a shoot.

sprightly *adjective* (**sprightlier**, **sprightliest**) lively; full of energy.

spring[1] *verb* (**sprang**, **sprung**, **springing**) **1** jump; move quickly or suddenly, *He sprang to his feet.* **2** originate; arise, *The trouble has sprung from carelessness.* **3** present or produce suddenly, *He sprang a test on us.* **4** appear suddenly.

spring[2] *noun* **1** a springy coil or bent piece of metal. **2** a springing movement. **3** a place where water comes up naturally from the ground. **4** the season when most plants begin to grow.

springboard *noun* a springy board from which people jump in diving and gymnastics.

springbok *noun* a South African gazelle.

spring-clean *verb* clean a house thoroughly, especially in spring.

springy *adjective* (**springier**, **springiest**) able to spring back easily after being bent or squeezed. **springiness** *noun*

sprinkle *verb* (**sprinkled**, **sprinkling**) make tiny drops or pieces fall on something. **sprinkler** *noun*

sprinkling *noun* a few here and there.

sprint *verb* run very fast for a short distance. **sprint** *noun*, **sprinter** *noun*

sprite *noun* an elf, fairy, or goblin.

sprocket *noun* each of the row of teeth round a wheel, fitting into links on a chain.

sprout[1] *verb* start to grow; put out shoots.

sprout[2] *noun* a shoot of a plant.

sprouts *plural noun* the young shoots of plants, such as alfalfa and mung beans, eaten as a vegetable.

spruce[1] *noun* a kind of fir tree.

spruce[2] *adjective* neat and trim; smart.

spruce[3] *verb* (**spruced**, **sprucing**) smarten, *Spruce yourself up.*

spruik (*say* sprook) *verb* (*Australian*) hold forth in public, especially to advertise a show etc. **spruiker** *noun*

sprung *past participle* of **spring**[1].

spry *adjective* (**spryer**, **spryest**) active; nimble; lively.

spud *noun* (*informal*) a potato.

spume *noun* froth; foam.

spun *past tense & past participle* of **spin**[1].

spunk *noun* (*informal*) **1** courage. **2** (*Australian*) an attractive person. **spunky** *adjective*

spur[1] *noun* **1** a sharp device worn on the heel of a rider's boot to urge a horse to go faster. **2** a stimulus or incentive. **3** a projecting part. **on the spur of the moment** on an impulse; without planning.

spur[2] *verb* (**spurred**, **spurring**) urge on; encourage.

spurious *adjective* not genuine.

spurn *verb* reject scornfully.

spurt[1] *verb* **1** gush out. **2** increase your speed suddenly.

spurt[2] *noun* **1** a sudden gush. **2** a sudden increase in speed or effort.

sputter *verb* splutter. **sputter** *noun*

spy[1] *noun* (*plural* **spies**) someone who works secretly to find out things about another country, person, etc.

spy[2] *verb* (**spied**, **spying**) **1** be a spy; keep watch secretly. **2** see; notice, *She spied a house.* **3** pry.

spyware *noun* software that enables a user to secretly obtain information from another computer's hard drive.

squabble *verb* (**squabbled**, **squabbling**) quarrel; bicker. **squabble** *noun*

squad *noun* a small group of people working or being trained together.

squadron *noun* part of an army, navy, or air force.

squalid *adjective* dirty and unpleasant. **squalidly** *adverb*, **squalor** *noun* [from Latin *squalidus* = rough, dirty]

squall[1] *noun* **1** a sudden storm or gust of wind. **2** a baby's loud cry.

squall[2] *verb* (of a baby) cry loudly.

squander *verb* waste something in a reckless and foolish manner.

square[1] *noun* **1** a flat shape with four equal sides and four right angles. **2** an area surrounded by buildings, *Victoria Square.* **3** the number produced by multiplying something by itself, *nine is the square of three ($9 = 3 \times 3$).* **4** (*informal*) an old-fashioned or conventional person.

square[2] *adjective* **1** having the shape of a square. **2** forming a right angle, *The desk has square corners.* **3** equal; even, *The teams are all square with six points each.* **4** honest; fair, *a square deal.* **5** (*informal*) old-fashioned. **squarely** *adverb*, **squareness** *noun*

square[3] *verb* (**squared**, **squaring**) **1** make a thing square. **2** multiply a number by itself, *5 squared is 25.* **3** match; make or be consistent, *His story doesn't square with yours.* **4** settle an account. **5** (*informal*) bribe. [from Latin *quadra* = square]

square meal *noun* a satisfying meal.

square metre *noun* the area of a surface with sides that are one metre long.

square-rigged *adjective* with the sails set across the ship, not lengthways.

square root *noun* the number that gives a particular number if it is multiplied by itself, *three is the square root of nine ($3 \times 3 = 9$).*

squash[1] *verb* **1** press something so that it loses its shape; crush. **2** pack tightly. **3** suppress; quash.

squash[2] *noun* (*plural* **squashes**) **1** a crowded condition. **2** a fruit-flavoured soft drink. **3** a game played with rackets and a soft ball in a special indoor court.

squash[3] *noun* (*plural* **squashes**) a kind of gourd used as a vegetable.

squat[1] *verb* (**squatted**, **squatting**) **1** sit on your heels; crouch. **2** use an unoccupied house for living in without permission. **squat** *noun*

squat[2] *adjective* short and fat.

squatter *noun* **1** someone who squats. **2** (*Australian*) a grazier.

squaw *noun* (*offensive*) a North American indigenous woman or wife.

squawk *verb* make a loud harsh cry. **squawk** *noun*

squeak *verb* make a short high-pitched cry or sound. **squeak** *noun*, **squeakily** *adverb*, **squeaky** *adjective*

squeal *verb* make a long shrill cry or sound. **squeal** *noun*

squeamish *adjective* easily disgusted or shocked. **squeamishness** *noun*

squeeze[1] *verb* (**squeezed**, **squeezing**) **1** press from opposite sides; press something so as to get liquid out of it. **2** force into or through a place, *We squeezed through a gap in the fence.* **squeezer** *noun*

squeeze[2] *noun* **1** the action of squeezing. **2** a drop of liquid squeezed out, *Add a squeeze of lemon.* **3** a time when money is difficult to get or borrow. **4** a clasp or hug.

squelch *verb* make a sound like someone treading in thick mud. **squelch** *noun*

squib *noun* a small firework that hisses and then explodes.

squid *noun* a sea animal with eight short tentacles and two long ones.

squiggle *noun* a short curly line. **squiggly** *adjective*

squint *verb* **1** be cross-eyed. **2** peer; look with half-shut eyes at something. **squint** *noun*

squire *noun* (*British*) a country gentleman, especially the chief landowner in a district.

squirm *verb* wriggle.

squirrel *noun* a small animal with a bushy tail and red or grey fur, living in trees.

squirt *verb* send or come out in a jet of liquid.

squizz *noun* (*Australian informal*) a look.

St *abbreviation* **1** Saint. **2** Street.

stab[1] *verb* (**stabbed**, **stabbing**) pierce or wound with something sharp.

stab[2] *noun* **1** the action of stabbing. **2** a sudden sharp pain, *She felt a stab of fear.* **3** (*informal*) an attempt, *I'll have a stab at it.*

stabilise *verb* (**stabilised**, **stabilising**) make or become stable. **stabilisation** *noun*, **stabiliser** *noun*

stability *noun* being stable.

stable[1] *adjective* steady; firmly fixed. **stably** *adverb* [from Latin *stabilis* = standing firm]

stable[2] *noun* a building where horses are kept.

stable[3] *verb* (**stabled**, **stabling**) put or keep in a stable.

staccato *adverb & adjective* (in music) played with each note short and separate. [Italian, = detached]

stack[1] *noun* **1** a neat pile. **2** a haystack. **3** (*informal*) a large amount, *a stack of work.* **4** a chimney.

stack[2] *verb* pile things up.

stadium *noun* a sportsground surrounded by seats for spectators. [from Greek *stadion*]

staff[1] *noun* **1** the people employed in a particular business or organisation. **2** the teachers in a school or college. **3** a stick or pole used as a weapon or support or as a symbol of authority. **4** (*plural* **staves**) a set of five horizontal lines on which music is written.

staff[2] *verb* provide with a staff of people.

stag *noun* a male deer.

stage[1] *noun* **1** a platform for performances in a theatre or hall. **2** a point or part of a process, journey, etc., *the final stage.*

stage[2] *verb* (**staged**, **staging**) **1** present a performance on a stage. **2** organise, *We decided to stage a protest.*

stagecoach *noun* a horse-drawn coach that formerly ran regularly from one point to another along the same route.

stagflation *noun* a state of inflation without a corresponding increase in demand and employment.

stagger *verb* **1** walk unsteadily. **2** shock deeply; amaze, *We were staggered at the price.* **3** arrange things so that they do not coincide, *Please stagger your holidays so that there is always someone here.* **stagger** *noun*

stagnant *adjective* not flowing or not changing, *a pool of stagnant water.*

stagnate *verb* (**stagnated**, **stagnating**) **1** be stagnant. **2** be dull through lack of activity or variety. **stagnation** *noun* [from Latin *stagnum* = a pool]

staid *adjective* steady and serious in manner; sedate.

stain[1] *noun* **1** a dirty mark on something. **2** a blemish on someone's character or past record. **3** a liquid used for staining things.

stain[2] *verb* **1** make a stain on something. **2** colour with a liquid that sinks into the surface.

stainless *adjective* without a stain.

stainless steel *noun* steel that does not rust easily.

stair *noun* a fixed step in a series that leads from one level or floor to another in a building.

staircase *noun* a flight of stairs.

stairway *noun* a staircase.

stairwell *noun* a shaft in which a staircase is built.

stake[1] *noun* **1** a thick pointed stick to be driven into the ground. **2** the post to which people used to be tied for execution by being burnt alive. **3** an amount of money bet on something. **4** an investment that gives a person a share or interest in an enterprise.
at stake being risked.

stake[2] *verb* (**staked**, **staking**) **1** fasten, support, or mark out with stakes. **2** bet or risk money etc. on an event.
stake a claim claim or obtain a right to something.

stalactite *noun* a stony spike hanging like an icicle from the roof of a cave. [from Greek *stalaktos* = dripping]

stalagmite *noun* a stony spike standing like a pillar on the floor of a cave. [from Greek *stalagma* = a drop]

stale *adjective* not fresh. **staleness** *noun*

stalemate *noun* **1** a situation in which further action or progress by opposing or competing parties seems impossible. **2** a drawn position in chess when a player cannot make a move without putting their king in check.

stalk[1] *noun* a stem of a plant etc.

stalk[2] *verb* **1** track or hunt stealthily. **2** walk in a stiff or dignified way. **3** harass or persecute a person with unwanted and obsessive attention.

stall[1] *noun* **1** a table or counter from which things are sold. **2** a place for one animal in a stable or shed.
the stalls the seats in the lowest part of a theatre.

stall[2] *verb* **1** stop suddenly, *The car engine stalled.* **2** put an animal into a stall.

stall[3] *verb* delay things deliberately so as to avoid having to take action. [from *stall* = pickpocket's helper]

stallion *noun* a male horse.

stalwart *adjective* sturdy; strong and faithful, *my stalwart supporters.*

stamen *noun* the part of a flower bearing pollen.

stamina *noun* strength and ability to endure things for a long time.

stammer *verb* keep repeating the same syllables when you speak. **stammer** *noun*

stamp[1] *noun* **1** a postage stamp; a small piece of gummed paper with a special design on it. **2** a small device for pressing words or marks on something; the words or marks made by this. **3** a distinctive characteristic, *His story bears the stamp of truth.*

stamp[2] *verb* **1** bang a foot heavily on the ground; crush or flatten in this way. **2** walk with loud heavy steps. **3** stick a stamp on something. **4** press a mark or design on something.
stamp out 1 put out a fire by stamping. **2** stop something, *stamp out cruelty.*

stampede *noun* a sudden rush by animals or people. **stampede** *verb*

stance *noun* **1** the way a person or animal stands. **2** an attitude.

stanchion *noun* an upright bar or post forming a support.

stand[1] *verb* (**stood**, **standing**) **1** be on your feet without moving, *We were standing at the back of the hall.* **2** set or be upright; place, *We stood the vase on the table.* **3** stay the same, *My offer still stands.* **4** be a candidate for election, *She stood for parliament.* **5** tolerate; endure, *I can't stand that noise.* **6** provide and pay for, *I'll stand you a drink.*
it stands to reason it is reasonable or obvious.
stand by be ready for action. **standby** *noun*
stand down 1 withdraw from a position or candidacy. **2** suspend an employee.
stand for 1 represent. **2** tolerate.
stand in for act in place of another.
stand-in *noun*
stand out stick out; be noticeable.
stand up for support; defend.
stand up to 1 resist bravely. **2** stay in good condition in hard use.

stand[2] *noun* **1** something made for putting things on, *a music stand.* **2** a stall where things are sold or displayed. **3** a grandstand. **4** a stationary condition or position, *He took his stand near the door.* **5** resistance to attack, *We made a stand.*

standard[1] *noun* **1** how good something is, *a high standard of work.* **2** a thing used to measure or judge something else. **3** a special flag, *the royal standard.* **4** an upright support.

standard[2] *adjective* **1** of the usual or average quality or kind. **2** regarded as the best and widely used, *the standard book on spiders.*

standard deviation *noun* (in statistics) a quantity calculated to indicate the extent of deviation for a group as a whole.

standardise *verb* (**standardised**, **standardising**) make things be of a standard size, quality, etc. **standardisation** *noun*

standard lamp *noun* a lamp on an upright pole that stands on the floor.

standard of living *noun* the degree of wealth and material comfort available to a person or community.

standoffish *adjective* aloof in manner.

standover *adjective* (*Australian*) threatening; intimidating, *standover tactics.*

standpoint *noun* a point of view.

standstill *noun* a stop; an end to movement or activity.

stank *past tense* of **stink**[1].

stanza *noun* a verse of poetry.

staphylococcus *noun* (*plural* **staphylococci**) a bacterium that can sometimes cause pus formations in the skin and mucous membranes. **staphylococcal** *adjective*

staple[1] *noun* **1** a small piece of metal pushed through papers and clenched to fasten them together. **2** a U-shaped nail. **staple** *verb*, **stapler** *noun*

staple[2] *adjective* main; usual, *Rice is their staple food.* **staple** *noun*

star[1] *noun* **1** a heavenly body that is seen as a speck of light in the sky at night. **2** a shape with rays from it; an asterisk; a mark of this shape showing that something is good, *a five-star hotel.* **3** a famous performer; one of the chief performers in a play or show etc.

star[2] *verb* (**starred**, **starring**) **1** perform or present as a star in a show etc. **2** mark with an asterisk or star symbol.

starboard *noun* the right-hand side of a ship or aircraft when you are facing forward. (Compare **port**[1] 3.)

starch[1] *noun* (*plural* **starches**) **1** a white carbohydrate in bread, potatoes, and certain other foods. **2** this or a similar substance used to stiffen clothes. **starchy** *adjective*

starch[2] *verb* stiffen with starch.

stardom *noun* being a star performer.

stare *verb* (**stared**, **staring**) look at something fixedly. **stare** *noun*

starfish *noun* (*plural* **starfish** or **starfishes**) a sea animal shaped like a star with five or more points.

stark[1] *adjective* **1** complete; unmistakable, *stark nonsense.* **2** desolate; without cheerfulness, *the stark lunar landscape.* **starkly** *adverb*, **starkness** *noun*

stark[2] *adverb* completely, *stark naked.*

starlight *noun* light from the stars.

starling *noun* a noisy black bird with speckled feathers.

starry *adjective* full of stars.

start[1] *verb* **1** begin or cause to begin. **2** establish or found, *start a company.* **3** begin a journey. **4** make a sudden movement of pain or surprise. **starter** *noun*

start[2] *noun* **1** the beginning; the place where a race starts. **2** an advantage that someone starts with, *We gave the younger ones ten minutes' start.* **3** a sudden movement.

startle *verb* (**startled**, **startling**) surprise or alarm someone.

start-up *noun* **1** the action or process of setting something in motion. **2** a newly established business.

starve *verb* (**starved**, **starving**) suffer or die from lack of food; cause to do this. **starvation** *noun*

stash *verb* (*informal*) hoard; put something in a safe place. **stash** *noun*

state[1] *noun* **1** the quality of a person's or thing's characteristics or circumstances; condition. **2** a grand style, *She arrived in state.* **3** (also **State**) an organised community under one government (*the state of Israel*) or forming part of a federation (*the 50 states of the USA*). **4** (also **State**) a country's government, *Help for the bushfire victims was provided by the state.* **5** (*informal*) an excited or upset condition, *Don't get into a state about the robbery.*

state[2] *verb* (**stated**, **stating**) express something in spoken or written words. [same origin as *status*]

stately *adjective* (**statelier**, **stateliest**) dignified; imposing; grand. **stateliness** *noun*

statement *noun* **1** words stating something. **2** a formal account of facts, *The witness made a statement to the police.* **3** a written report of a financial account, *a bank statement.*

state school *noun* a public school.

statesman *noun* (*plural* **statesmen**) an experienced and respected political leader. **statesmanship** *noun*

stateswoman *noun* (*plural* **stateswomen**) a woman who is an experienced and respected political leader.

static *adjective* not moving; not changing. [from Greek *statikos* = standing]

static electricity *noun* electricity that is present in something, not flowing as a current.

station[1] *noun* **1** a place where a person or thing stands or is stationed; a position. **2** a stopping place on a railway with buildings for passengers and goods. **3** a building equipped for people who serve the public or for certain activities, *the police station.* **4** a broadcasting establishment with its own frequency. **5** (*Australian*) a large sheep or cattle farm.

station[2] *verb* put someone in a certain place for a purpose, *He was stationed at the door to take the tickets.* [from Latin *statio* = a standing]

stationary *adjective* not moving, *The car was stationary when the van hit it.*

Usage Do not confuse with *stationery*.

stationer *noun* a shopkeeper who sells stationery.

stationery *noun* paper, envelopes, pens, and other articles used in writing etc.

station wagon *noun* a car with a rear door, having luggage space behind the back seat (which can be folded down to create more space).

statistic *noun* a piece of information expressed as a number, *These statistics show that the population has doubled.* **statistical** *adjective*, **statistically** *adverb*

statistician (*say* stat-uh-**stish**-uhn) *noun* an expert in statistics.

statistics *plural noun* the practice or science of collecting and analysing numerical data in large quantities.

statuary *noun* statues.

statue *noun* a sculptured, cast, or moulded figure of a person or animal.

statuesque (*say* sta-choo-**esk**) *adjective* like a statue in stillness or dignity.

statuette *noun* a small statue.

stature *noun* **1** the natural height of the body. **2** importance or reputation gained by ability or achievement, *an artist of international stature.*

status (*say* **stay**-tuhs or **stat**-uhs) *noun* (*plural* **statuses**) **1** a person's or thing's position or rank in relation to others. **2** high rank or prestige. **3** a posting on a social networking website that indicates a user's current situation, state of mind, or opinion about something. [from Latin *status* = a standing]

status quo (*say* stay-tuhs **kwoh**) *noun* the existing state of affairs. [Latin, = the state in which]

statute *noun* a law passed by a parliament. **statutory** *adjective* [from Latin *statutum* = set up]

staunch *adjective* firm and loyal, *our staunch supporters.* **staunchly** *adverb*

stave[1] *noun* **1** each of the curved strips of wood forming the side of a cask or tub. **2** a staff in music (see *staff*[1] 4).

stave[2] *verb* (**staved** or **stove**, **staving**) dent or break a hole in something, *The collision stove in the front of the ship.*
stave off keep something away, *We staved off the disaster.*

stay[1] *verb* **1** continue to be in the same place or condition; remain. **2** spend time in a place as a visitor. **3** satisfy temporarily, *We stayed our hunger with a sandwich.* **4** pause. **5** show endurance in a race or task.
stay put (*informal*) remain in place.

stay[2] *noun* **1** a time spent somewhere, *We had a short stay in Rome.* **2** a postponement, *a stay of execution.*

stay[3] *noun* a support, especially a rope or wire holding up a mast.

STD *abbreviation* sexually transmitted disease.

stead *noun* the place or role that someone or something should have or fill (used in referring to a substitute), *He can stay home and you can go in his stead.*
stand a person in good stead be advantageous or useful to a person in the future, *Her years of training stood her in good stead.*

steadfast *adjective* firm and not changing, *a steadfast refusal.*

steady[1] *adjective* (**steadier**, **steadiest**) **1** not shaking or moving; firm. **2** regular; continuing the same, *a steady pace.* **steadily** *adverb*, **steadiness** *noun*

steady[2] *verb* make or become steady.

steak *noun* a thick slice of meat or fish.

steal *verb* (**stole**, **stolen**, **stealing**) **1** take and keep something that does not belong to you; take secretly or dishonestly. **2** move secretly or without being noticed, *He stole out of the room.*

stealthy (*say* **stel**-thee) *adjective* (**stealthier**, **stealthiest**) quiet and secret, so as not to be noticed. **stealth** *noun*, **stealthily** *adverb*, **stealthiness** *noun*

steam[1] *noun* **1** the gas or vapour that comes from boiling water; this used to drive machinery. **2** energy, *She ran out of steam.* **steamy** *adjective*

steam[2] *verb* **1** give out steam. **2** cook or treat by steam, *a steamed pudding.* **3** move by the power of steam, *The ship steamed down the river.*

steam engine *noun* an engine driven by steam.

steamer *noun* **1** a steamship. **2** a container in which things are steamed.

steamroller *noun* a heavy vehicle with a large roller used to flatten surfaces when making roads.

steamship *noun* a ship driven by steam.

steed *noun* (*poetic*) a horse.

steel *noun* **1** a strong metal made from iron and carbon. **2** a steel rod for sharpening knives. **steely** *adjective*

steep[1] *adjective* **1** sloping very sharply, not gradually. **2** (*informal*) unreasonably high, *a steep price.* **steeply** *adverb*, **steepness** *noun*

steep[2] *verb* soak thoroughly; saturate.

steepen *verb* make or become steeper.

steeple *noun* a church tower with a spire on top.

steeplechase *noun* a race across country or over hedges or fences. [so called because the race originally had a distant church steeple in view as its goal]

steer[1] *verb* make a car, ship, or bicycle etc. go in the direction you want; guide. **steersman** *noun*

steer[2] *noun* a young bull kept for its beef.

steering wheel *noun* a wheel for steering a car, boat, etc.

stellar *adjective* of a star or stars. [from Latin *stella* = star]

stem[1] *noun* **1** the main central part of a tree, shrub, or plant. **2** a thin part on which a leaf, flower, or fruit is supported. **3** a thin upright part; the thin part of a wineglass between the bowl and the foot. **4** the main part of a verb or other word, to which endings are attached. **5** the front part of a ship, *from stem to stern.*

stem[2] *verb* (**stemmed**, **stemming**)
stem from arise from; have as its source.

stem[3] *verb* (**stemmed**, **stemming**) stop the flow of something.

stem cell *noun* a cell, especially one taken from a person or animal in a very early stage of development, that can develop into any other type of cell.

stench *noun* (*plural* **stenches**) a very unpleasant smell.

stencil[1] *noun* a piece of card, metal, or plastic with pieces cut out of it, used to produce a picture or design.

stencil[2] *verb* (**stencilled**, **stencilling**) produce or decorate with a stencil.

stentorian *adjective* very loud, *a stentorian voice.* [from the name of Stentor, a herald in ancient Greek legend]

step[1] *noun* **1** a movement made by lifting the foot and setting it down. **2** the sound or rhythm of stepping. **3** a level surface for placing the foot on in climbing up or down. **4** each of a series of things done in some process or action, *The first step is to find somewhere to practise.*
in step 1 stepping in time with others in marching or dancing. **2** in agreement.
watch your step be careful.

step[2] *verb* (**stepped**, **stepping**) tread; walk.
step in intervene.
step on it (*informal*) hurry.
step up increase something.

step- *prefix* related through remarriage of one parent.

stepchild *noun* (*plural* **stepchildren**) a child that a person's husband or wife has from an earlier marriage. **stepbrother**, **stepdaughter**, **stepsister**, **stepson** *nouns*

stepfather *noun* the husband of your parent by a later marriage.

stepladder *noun* a folding ladder with flat treads.

stepmother *noun* the wife of your parent by a later marriage.

steppe *noun* a grassy plain with few trees, in south-east Europe or Asia.

stepping stone *noun* **1** each of a line of stones put into a shallow stream so that people can walk across. **2** a way of achieving something, or a stage in achieving it.

stereo[1] *adjective* stereophonic.

stereo[2] *noun* (*plural* **stereos**) **1** sound that is directed through two or more speakers so that it seems to surround the listener and to come from more than one source. **2** a music player that has two or more speakers and produces stereo sound.

stereophonic *adjective* using sound that comes from two different directions so as to give a natural effect. [from Greek *stereos* = solid, + *phone* = sound]

stereotype *noun* an image or idea of a particular person or thing that has become fixed through being widely held, *The stereotype of a hero is one who is tall, strong, brave, and good-looking.* **stereotypical** *adjective* [from Greek *stereos* = solid, + *type* (= fixed type formerly used in printing)]

sterile *adjective* **1** not fertile; barren. **2** free from germs. **sterility** *noun*

sterilise *verb* (**sterilised**, **sterilising**) **1** make a thing free from germs, e.g. by heating it. **2** make a person or animal unable to reproduce. **sterilisation** *noun*, **steriliser** *noun*

sterling[1] *noun* British money. [from *steorling* = Norman coin with a star on it]

sterling[2] *adjective* **1** genuine, *sterling silver.* **2** excellent; of great worth, *her sterling qualities.*

stern[1] *adjective* strict and severe, not lenient or kindly. **sternly** *adverb*, **sternness** *noun*

stern[2] *noun* the back part of a ship.

sternum *noun* (*plural* **sternums** or **sterna**) the breastbone.

steroid *noun* a substance of a kind that includes certain hormones and other natural secretions.

stethoscope *noun* a device used for listening to sounds in a person's body, e.g. heartbeats and breathing. [from Greek *stethos* = breast, + *skopein* = look at]

stevedore *noun* a person employed in loading and unloading ships.

stew[1] *verb* cook slowly in liquid.

stew[2] *noun* a dish of stewed food, especially meat and vegetables.

steward *noun* **1** a person whose job is to look after the passengers on a ship, aircraft, or train. **2** an official who looks after something. **3** a person employed to manage another's property. **4** a person whose responsibility is to take care of something. **stewardess** *noun*, **stewardship** *noun*

stick[1] *noun* **1** a long thin piece of wood. **2** a walking stick. **3** the implement used to hit the ball in hockey, polo, etc. **4** a long thin piece of something, *a stick of liquorice.*
the sticks (*informal*) a remote rural area.

stick[2] *verb* (**stuck**, **sticking**) **1** push a thing into something, *Stick a pin in it.* **2** fix or be fixed by glue or as if by this, *Stick stamps on the parcel.* **3** become fixed and unable to move, *The boat stuck on a sandbank.* **4** (*informal*) stay, *We must stick together.* **5** (*informal*) endure; tolerate, *I can't stick that noise!* **6** (*informal*) impose a task on someone, *We were stuck with the clearing up.*
stick at (*informal*) persevere.
stick out 1 come or push out from a surface; stand out from the surrounding area. **2** be very noticeable.
stick to 1 remain faithful to a friend or promise. **2** keep to and not alter, *He stuck to his story.*
stick up for (*informal*) stand up for.

sticker *noun* an adhesive label or sign for sticking to something.

stickleback *noun* a small fish with sharp spines on its back.

stickler *noun* a person who insists on something, *a stickler for punctuality.*

sticky *adjective* (**stickier**, **stickiest**) **1** able or likely to stick to things. **2** (of weather) hot and humid, causing perspiration. **3** (*informal*) difficult; awkward, *a sticky problem.* **stickily** *adverb*, **stickiness** *noun*

stickybeak *noun* (*Australian informal*) **1** an inquisitive person. **2** an inquisitive look. **stickybeak** *verb*

sticky note *noun* **1** a small piece of paper with a sticky strip along one edge of the reverse side, enabling it to be stuck to a surface, and to be easily removed when necessary. **2** (in computing) a note or comment attached to selected content in an electronic document.

stiff *adjective* **1** not bending or moving or changing its shape easily. **2** not fluid; hard to stir, *a stiff dough.* **3** difficult, *a stiff examination.* **4** formal in manner; not friendly. **5** strong, *a stiff breeze.* **6** severe, *a stiff sentence.* **stiffly** *adverb*, **stiffness** *noun*

stiffen *verb* make or become stiff. **stiffener** *noun*

stifle *verb* (**stifled**, **stifling**) **1** suffocate. **2** suppress, *She stifled a yawn.*

stigma *noun* **1** a mark of disgrace; a stain on a reputation. **2** the part of a pistil that receives the pollen in pollination. [Greek, = a mark]

stigmatise *verb* (**stigmatised**, **stigmatising**) brand as something disgraceful, *He was stigmatised as a coward.*

stile *noun* an arrangement of steps or bars for people to climb over a fence.

stiletto *noun* (*plural* **stilettos**) a dagger with a narrow blade.
stiletto heel a high pointed heel on a shoe. [Italian, = little dagger]

still[1] *adjective* **1** not moving, *still water.* **2** silent. **3** not fizzy. **stillness** *noun*

still[2] *adverb* **1** without moving, *Stand still.* **2** up to this or that time, *He was still there.* **3** in a greater amount or degree, *You can do still better.* **4** nevertheless, *They've lost. Still,*

they tried, and that was good.
still life a painting of lifeless things such as ornaments and fruit.

still³ *verb* make or become still; quieten.

still⁴ *noun* an apparatus for distilling alcohol or other liquid. [from *distil*]

stillborn *adjective* born dead.

stilted *adjective* stiffly formal.

stilts *plural noun* **1** a pair of poles with supports for the feet so that the user can walk high above the ground. **2** posts for supporting a house etc. above marshy or flood-prone ground.

stimulant *noun* something that stimulates.

stimulate *verb* (**stimulated**, **stimulating**) make more lively or active; excite or interest.
stimulation *noun*

stimulus *noun* (*plural* **stimuli**) something that stimulates or produces a reaction. [Latin, = goad]

sting¹ *noun* **1** a sharp-pointed part of an animal or plant that can cause a wound. **2** a painful wound caused by this part.

sting² *verb* (**stung**, **stinging**) **1** wound or hurt with a sting. **2** feel a sharp pain. **3** stimulate sharply, *I was stung into answering rudely.* **4** (*informal*) cheat a person by overcharging; extort money from someone.

stingray *noun* a large sea fish with a flat body and a long poisonous spine.

stingy (*say* **stin**-jee) *adjective* (**stingier**, **stingiest**) mean, not generous; giving or given in small amounts. **stingily** *adverb*, **stinginess** *noun*

stink¹ *noun* **1** an unpleasant smell. **2** (*informal*) an unpleasant fuss or protest.

stink² *verb* (**stank** or **stunk**, **stinking**) have an unpleasant smell.

stint¹ *noun* **1** a fixed amount of work to be done. **2** limitation of a supply or effort, *They gave help without stint.*

stint² *verb* limit; be niggardly, *Don't stint them of food.*

stipend (*say* **stuy**-pend) *noun* a salary.
stipendiary *adjective* [from Latin *stips* = wages, + *pendere* = to pay]

stipple *verb* (**stippled**, **stippling**) paint, draw, or engrave in small dots.

stipulate *verb* (**stipulated**, **stipulating**) insist on something as part of an agreement.
stipulation *noun*

stir¹ *verb* (**stirred**, **stirring**) **1** mix a liquid or soft mixture by moving a spoon etc. round and round in it. **2** move slightly; start to move. **3** excite; stimulate, *They stirred up trouble.* **4** (*Australian informal*) provoke someone to exasperation; cause trouble.
stirrer *noun*

stir² *noun* **1** the action of stirring. **2** a disturbance; excitement, *The news caused a stir.*

stirrup *noun* a metal part that hangs from each side of a horse's saddle, for a rider to put their foot in.

stitch¹ *noun* (*plural* **stitches**) **1** a loop of thread made in sewing or knitting. **2** a method of arranging the threads, *cross stitch.* **3** a sudden sharp pain in the side of the body, caused by running.

stitch² *verb* sew or fasten with stitches.

stoat *noun* a kind of weasel. Also called an *ermine.*

stobie pole *noun* (in South Australia) a pole of steel and concrete carrying electricity lines. [named after an Australian engineer, J. C. Stobie]

stock¹ *noun* **1** a number of things kept ready to be sold or used. **2** livestock. **3** a line of ancestors, *a man of Irish stock.* **4** liquid made by stewing meat, fish, or vegetables, used for making soup etc. **5** a garden flower with a sweet smell. **6** shares in a business company's capital (see *share*¹ 2). **7** the main stem of a tree or plant. **8** the base, holder, or handle of an implement etc. **9** a kind of cravat.

stock² *verb* **1** keep goods in stock. **2** provide a place with a stock of something.

stockade *noun* a fence made of stakes.

stockbroker *noun* a broker who deals in stocks and shares.

stock exchange *noun* a place where stocks and shares are bought and sold; a sharemarket.

stocking *noun* a garment covering the foot and part or all of the leg.

stockman *noun* (*plural* **stockmen**) a person employed to look after livestock.

stockpile *noun* a large stock of things kept in reserve. **stockpile** *verb*

stocks *plural noun* a wooden framework with holes for people's legs and arms, in which criminals were formerly locked as a punishment.

stock-still *adjective* quite still.

stocktaking *noun* making a list of the stock in a shop etc.

stockwoman *noun* (*plural* **stockwomen**) a woman employed to look after livestock.

stocky *adjective* (**stockier**, **stockiest**) short and solidly built, *a stocky man.*

stodge *noun* stodgy food.

stodgy *adjective* (**stodgier**, **stodgiest**) **1** (of food) heavy and filling. **2** dull and boring, *a stodgy book.* **stodginess** *noun*

stoical (*say* **stoh**-uh-kuhl) *adjective* bearing pain or difficulties calmly without complaining. **stoically** *adverb*, **stoicism** *noun* [named after ancient Greek philosophers called Stoics]

stoke *verb* (**stoked**, **stoking**) put fuel in a furnace or on a fire. **stoker** *noun*

stole[1] *noun* a wide piece of material worn round the shoulders.

stole[2] *past tense* of **steal**.

stolen *past participle* of **steal**.

stolid *adjective* not excitable; not feeling or showing emotion. **stolidity** *noun*, **stolidly** *adverb*

stomach[1] *noun* **1** the part of the body where food starts to be digested. **2** the abdomen.

stomach[2] *verb* endure; tolerate.

stone[1] *noun* **1** a piece of rock. **2** stones or rock as material, e.g. for building. **3** a jewel. **4** the hard case round the kernel of plums, cherries, and certain other fruits. **5** a unit of weight equal to 6.35 kilograms.

stone[2] *verb* (**stoned**, **stoning**) **1** throw stones at somebody. **2** remove the stones from fruit.

stone- *prefix* completely, *stone-cold.*

Stone Age *noun* the time when tools and weapons were made of stone.

stoned *adjective* (*informal*) very drunk or drugged.

stonewall *verb* obstruct a discussion etc. by giving evasive replies.

stonkered *adjective* (*Australian informal*) exhausted; defeated, thwarted.

stony *adjective* **1** full of stones. **2** like stone; hard. **3** cold; unfeeling, *a stony silence.*

stony-broke *adjective* (*informal*) having spent all your money.

stood *past tense & past participle* of **stand**[1].

stooge *noun* (*informal*) **1** a comedian's assistant, used as a target for jokes. **2** an assistant who does dull or routine work.

stool *noun* a movable seat without arms or a back; a footstool.

stoop *verb* **1** bend your body forwards and down. **2** lower yourself, *She would not stoop to cheating.* **stoop** *noun*

stop[1] *verb* (**stopped**, **stopping**) **1** bring or come to an end; not continue working or moving. **2** stay. **3** prevent or obstruct something. **4** fill a hole, especially in a tooth. **stoppage** *noun*

stop[2] *noun* **1** stopping; a pause or end. **2** a place where a bus or train etc. regularly stops. **3** a punctuation mark, especially a full stop. **4** a lever or knob that controls pitch in a wind instrument or allows organ pipes to sound.

stopcock *noun* a valve controlling the flow of liquid or gas in a pipe.

stopgap *noun* a temporary substitute.

stopper *noun* a plug for closing a bottle.

stop press *noun* late news put into a newspaper after printing has started.

stopwatch *noun* a watch that can be started and stopped when you wish, used for timing races etc.

storage *noun* the storing of things.

store[1] *noun* **1** a stock of things kept for future use. **2** a place where these are kept. **3** a shop, especially a large one.
in store 1 being stored. **2** going to happen, *There's a surprise in store for you.*
set store by something value it greatly.

store[2] *verb* (**stored**, **storing**) keep things until they are needed.

storey *noun* (*plural* **storeys**) one whole floor of a building.

stork *noun* a large bird with long legs and a long beak.

storm[1] *noun* **1** a very strong wind usually with thunder, rain, dust, etc. **2** a violent attack or outburst, *a storm of protest.* **stormy** *adjective*

storm[2] *verb* **1** move or behave violently or angrily, *He stormed out of the room.* **2** attack or capture by a sudden assault, *They stormed the building.*

storm in a teacup *noun* a great fuss over something unimportant.

story *noun* (*plural* **stories**) **1** an account of a real or imaginary event. **2** the plot of a play or novel etc. **3** (*informal*) a lie, *Don't tell stories!* [same origin as *history*]

storyboard *noun* a sequence of drawings representing the shots planned for a film or television production.

stoush[1] *verb* (*Australian informal*) thrash; punch.

stoush[2] *noun* (*Australian informal*) a fight; fighting.

stout[1] *adjective* **1** rather fat. **2** thick and strong. **3** brave. **stoutly** *adverb*, **stoutness** *noun*

stout[2] *noun* a kind of dark beer.

stove[1] *noun* **1** a device containing an oven or ovens. **2** a device for heating a room.

stove[2] *past tense* of **stave**[2].

stow *verb* pack or store something away. **stowage** *noun*
stow away hide on a ship or aircraft so as to travel without paying. **stowaway** *noun* [from *bestow*]

straddle *verb* (**straddled**, **straddling**) be astride; sit or stand across something, *A long bridge straddles the river.*

straggle *verb* (**straggled**, **straggling**) **1** grow or spread in an untidy way. **2** lag behind;

wander on your own. **straggler** *noun*, **straggly** *adjective*

straight[1] *adjective* **1** going continuously in one direction; not curving or bending. **2** tidy; in proper order. **3** honest; frank, *a straight answer.* **straightness** *noun*

straight[2] *adverb* **1** in a straight line or manner. **2** directly; without delay, *Go straight home.*
straight away immediately.

straight angle *noun* an angle of 180 degrees.

straighten *verb* make or become straight.

straightforward *adjective* **1** easy, not complicated. **2** honest; frank.

strain[1] *verb* **1** stretch tightly. **2** injure or weaken something by stretching or working it too hard. **3** make a great effort. **4** put something through a sieve or filter to separate liquid from solid matter.

strain[2] *noun* **1** straining; the force of straining. **2** an injury caused by straining. **3** something that uses up strength, patience, resources, etc. **4** exhaustion. **5** a part of a tune.

strain[3] *noun* **1** a breed or variety of animals, plants, etc.; a line of descent. **2** an inherited characteristic, *There's an artistic strain in the family.*

strainer *noun* a device for straining liquids, *a tea strainer.*

strait *noun* a narrow stretch of water connecting two seas, *Bass Strait.*
in dire straits in difficulty or distress.

straitened *adjective* restricted; made narrow.
in straitened circumstances short of money.

straitjacket *noun* (also **straightjacket**) **1** a strong garment with long sleeves which can be tied together to confine the arms of a violent prisoner or mental patient. **2** a severe restriction on freedom of action, development, or expression.

strait-laced *adjective* (also **straight-laced**) having or showing very strict moral attitudes.

strand[1] *noun* **1** each of the threads or wires twisted together to form a rope, yarn, or cable. **2** a single thread. **3** a lock of hair.

strand[2] *noun* a shore.

strand[3] *verb* **1** run or cause to run on to sand or rocks in shallow water. **2** leave in a difficult or helpless position, *We were stranded when our car broke down.*

strange *adjective* **1** unusual. **2** not known or seen or experienced before. **strangely** *adverb*, **strangeness** *noun*

stranger *noun* **1** a person you do not know. **2** a person who does not know, or is not known in, a particular place or community.

strangle *verb* (**strangled**, **strangling**) kill by squeezing the throat to prevent breathing. **strangler** *noun* [from Greek *strangale* = a halter]

strangulate *verb* (**strangulated**, **strangulating**) strangle; squeeze so that nothing can pass through. **strangulation** *noun*

strap[1] *noun* a flat strip of leather or cloth etc. for fastening things or holding them in place.

strap[2] *verb* (**strapped**, **strapping**) fasten with a strap or straps; bind.

strapping *adjective* tall and healthy-looking, *a strapping lad.*

strata *plural* of **stratum**.

stratagem *noun* a cunning method of achieving something; a trick.

strategic *adjective* **1** of strategy. **2** giving an advantage. **strategical** *adjective*, **strategically** *adverb*

strategist *noun* an expert in strategy.

strategy *noun* (*plural* **strategies**) **1** a plan or policy to achieve something, *our economic strategy.* **2** the planning of a war or campaign. (Compare **tactics**.) [from Greek *strategos* = a general]

stratified *adjective* arrange in strata. **stratification** *noun*

stratosphere *noun* a layer of the atmosphere between about 10 and 60 kilometres above the earth's surface. [from *stratum* + *sphere*]

stratum (*say* **strah**-tuhm) *noun* (*plural* **strata**) **1** a layer, especially of rock. **2** a social level or class. [Latin, = thing spread]

> **Usage** The word *strata* is a plural. It is incorrect to say 'a strata' or 'this strata'; correct use is *this stratum* or *these strata.*

straw *noun* **1** dry cut stalks of grain. **2** a narrow tube for drinking through.

strawberry *noun* (*plural* **strawberries**) a small red juicy fruit.

stray[1] *verb* leave a group or proper place and wander; get lost.

stray[2] *adjective* that has strayed, *a stray cat.* **stray** *noun*

streak[1] *noun* **1** a long thin line or mark. **2** a trace, *a streak of cruelty.* **streaky** *adjective*

streak[2] *verb* **1** mark with streaks. **2** move very quickly.

stream[1] *noun* **1** water flowing in a channel; a creek or river. **2** a flow of liquid or of things or people. **3** (in computing) a continuous flow of data or instructions; a continuous flow of video and audio material transmitted or received over the Internet. **4** a group in which children of similar ability are placed in a school.

stream^2 *verb* **1** move in or like a stream. **2** produce a stream of liquid. **3** (in computing) transmit or receive data, especially video and audio material, over the Internet as a steady, continuous flow. **4** arrange schoolchildren in streams according to their ability.

streamer *noun* a long narrow ribbon or strip of paper etc.

streaming *noun* a method of transmitting or receiving data, especially video and audio material, over a computer network as a steady continuous stream.

streamline *verb* (**streamlined**, **streamlining**) **1** give something a smooth shape that helps it to move easily through air or water. **2** organise something so that it works more efficiently. **streamlined** *adjective*

street *noun* a road with houses beside it in a city or town. [from Latin *strata via* = paved way]

strength *noun* **1** how strong a person or thing is; being strong. **2** a good quality of a person or thing.

strengthen *verb* make or become stronger.

strenuous *adjective* **1** needing or using great effort. **2** energetic. **strenuously** *adverb*

strep throat *noun* (*informal*) an acute sore throat and fever caused by streptococcal infection.

streptococcus *noun* (*plural* **streptococci**) any of a group of bacteria that cause serious infections. **streptococcal** *adjective*

stress^1 *noun* (*plural* **stresses**) **1** a force that acts on something, e.g. by pressing, pulling, or twisting it; strain. **2** emphasis, especially the extra force with which you pronounce part of a word or phrase. **3** mental or physical distress caused by difficult circumstances. **stressful** *adjective*

stress^2 *verb* lay stress on something; emphasise. [from *distress*]

stretch^1 *verb* **1** pull something or be pulled so that it becomes longer or wider or larger. **2** be continuous, *The wall stretches right round the prison.* **3** push out your arms and legs.

stretch^2 *noun* (*plural* **stretches**) **1** the action of stretching. **2** the ability to be stretched, *The elastic has lost its stretch.* **3** a continuous period of time or area of land or water.

stretcher *noun* **1** a framework for carrying a sick or injured person. **2** (*Australian*) a collapsible single bed.

strew *verb* (**strewed**, **strewn** or **strewed**, **strewing**) scatter things over a surface.

striated (*say* struy-**ay**-tuhd) *adjective* marked with lines or ridges. **striation** *noun*

stricken *adjective* overcome or strongly affected by an illness, grief, fear, etc.

strict *adjective* **1** demanding obedience and good behaviour, *a strict teacher.* **2** complete; exact, *the strict truth*; *a strict translation.* **strictly** *adverb*, **strictness** *noun*

stricture *noun* **1** criticism. **2** constriction.

stride^1 *verb* (**strode**, **stridden**, **striding**) **1** walk with long steps. **2** stand astride something.

stride^2 *noun* **1** a long step when walking or running. **2** progress.
get into your stride settle into a fast and steady pace of working.

strident (*say* **struy**-duhnt) *adjective* loud and harsh. **stridency** *noun*, **stridently** *adverb* [from Latin *stridens* = creaking]

strife *noun* **1** a conflict; fighting or quarrelling. **2** (*Australian informal*) trouble of any kind, *You'll be in strife if you don't get your homework finished.*

strike^1 *verb* (**struck**, **striking**) **1** hit. **2** attack suddenly. **3** produce by pressing or stamping something, *They are striking some special coins.* **4** light a match by rubbing it against a rough surface. **5** sound, *The clock struck ten.* **6** make an impression on someone's mind, *She strikes me as truthful.* **7** find gold or oil etc. by digging or drilling. **8** stop work until the people in charge agree to improve wages or conditions etc. **9** go in a certain direction, *We struck north through the forest.*
strike off or **out** cross out.
strike up 1 begin playing or singing. **2** start a friendship etc.

strike^2 *noun* **1** a hit. **2** an attack. **3** a stoppage of work, as a way of making a protest (see sense 8 of the verb). **4** a sudden discovery of gold or oil etc.
on strike (of workers) striking.

striker *noun* **1** a person or thing that strikes something. **2** a worker who is on strike. **3** a hockey or soccer player whose function is to try to score goals.

striking *adjective* **1** that strikes. **2** noticeable. **strikingly** *adverb*

Strine *noun* a jocular imitation of Australian speech. [= *Australian* in Strine]

string^1 *noun* **1** cord used to fasten or tie things; a piece of this or similar material. **2** a piece of wire or cord stretched and vibrated to produce sounds in a musical instrument. **3** a line or series of things, *a string of buses.*

string^2 *verb* (**strung**, **stringing**) **1** fit or fasten with string. **2** thread on a string. **3** remove the tough fibre from beans.
string out 1 spread out in a line. **2** cause something to last a long time.

stringed *adjective* (of musical instruments) having strings.

stringent (*say* **strin**-jent) *adjective* strict, *There are stringent rules.* **stringency** *noun*, **stringently** *adverb*

strings *plural noun* stringed instruments.

stringy *adjective* **1** like string. **2** containing tough fibres.

stringybark *noun* an Australian eucalypt with tough fibrous bark.

strip[1] *verb* (**stripped**, **stripping**) **1** take a covering or layer off something. **2** undress. **3** deprive a person of something. **stripper** *noun*

strip[2] *noun* a long narrow piece or area.

stripe *noun* **1** a long narrow band of colour. **2** a strip of cloth worn on the sleeve of a uniform to show the wearer's rank. **striped** *adjective*, **stripy** *adjective*

stripling *noun* a youth.

striptease *noun* an entertainment in which a person slowly undresses.

strive *verb* (**strove**, **striven**, **striving**) **1** try hard to do something. **2** carry on a conflict.

strobe *noun* (in full **stroboscope**) a light that flashes on and off continuously. [from Greek *strobos* = whirling]

strode *past tense* of **stride**[1].

stroke[1] *noun* **1** a hit; a movement or action. **2** the sound made by a clock striking. **3** a sudden interruption in the flow of blood to the brain that often causes paralysis.

stroke[2] *verb* (**stroked**, **stroking**) move your hand gently along something. **stroke** *noun*

stroll *verb* walk in a leisurely way. **stroll** *noun*

stroller *noun* **1** a person who strolls. **2** a folding chair on wheels, in which a child can be pushed along.

strong[1] *adjective* **1** having great power, energy, effect, etc. **2** not easy to break, damage, or defeat. **3** firmly held; deeply felt, *a strong faith.* **4** having a lot of flavour, smell, colour, etc. **5** having a certain number of members, *an army 5,000 strong.* **strongly** *adverb*

strong[2] *adverb* strongly, *going strong.*

stronghold *noun* a fortified place.

strontium *noun* a soft silvery metal.

strop[1] *noun* a strip of leather or canvas on which a razor is sharpened.

strop[2] *verb* (**stropped**, **stropping**) sharpen on a strop.

stroppy *adjective* (*informal*) bad-tempered; awkward to deal with.

strove *past tense* of **strive**.

struck *past tense & past participle* of **strike**[1].

structure *noun* **1** something that has been constructed or built. **2** the way something is constructed or organised. **structural** *adjective*, **structurally** *adverb*, **structure** *verb* [from Latin *structura* = thing built]

struggle[1] *verb* (**struggled**, **struggling**) **1** move your arms, legs, etc. in trying to get free. **2** make strong efforts to do something. **3** try to overcome an opponent or a problem.

struggle[2] *noun* **1** the action of struggling. **2** a determined effort under difficulties. **3** a hard or confused contest.

strum *verb* (**strummed**, **strumming**) **1** sound a guitar by running your fingers across its strings. **2** play badly or casually on a musical instrument.

strung *past tense & past participle* of **string**[2].

strut[1] *verb* (**strutted**, **strutting**) walk proudly or stiffly.

strut[2] *noun* **1** a bar of wood or metal strengthening a framework. **2** a strutting walk.

strychnine (*say* **strik**-neen) *noun* a bitter poisonous substance.

stub[1] *noun* **1** a short stump left when the rest has been used or worn down. **2** a counterfoil.

stub[2] *verb* (**stubbed**, **stubbing**) bump your toe painfully. **stub out** put out a cigarette by pressing it against something hard.

stubble *noun* **1** the short stalks of a cereal plant left in the ground after the harvest is cut. **2** short hairs growing after shaving.

stubborn *adjective* obstinate. **stubbornly** *adverb*, **stubbornness** *noun*

stubby *adjective* short and thick.

stucco *noun* plaster or cement used for coating walls and ceilings, often moulded into decorations. **stuccoed** *adjective* [from Italian]

stuck *past tense & past participle* of **stick**[2].

stuck-up *adjective* (*informal*) conceited; snobbish.

stud[1] *noun* **1** a small curved lump or knob. **2** a short nail with a large head. **3** a piece of jewellery for wearing in pierced ears etc.

stud[2] *verb* (**studded**, **studding**) set or decorate with studs etc., *The necklace was studded with jewels.*

stud[3] *noun* a place where horses are kept for breeding.

student *noun* a person who studies a subject, especially at a college or university. [from Latin *studens* = studying]

studio *noun* (*plural* **studios**) **1** the room where a painter or photographer etc. works. **2** a place where cinema films are made. **3** a room from which radio or television broadcasts are made or recorded. [same origin as *study*]

studious *adjective* **1** keen on studying. **2** deliberate, *with studious politeness.* **studiously** *adverb*, **studiousness** *noun*

study[1] *verb* (**studied**, **studying**) **1** spend time learning about something. **2** look at something carefully.

study[2] *noun* (*plural* **studies**) **1** the process of studying. **2** a subject studied; a piece of research. **3** a room where someone studies. **4** a piece of music for playing as an exercise. [from Latin *studium* = zeal]

stuff[1] *noun* **1** a substance or material. **2** things, *Leave your stuff outside.* **3** (*informal*) valueless matter, *stuff and nonsense!*

stuff[2] *verb* **1** fill tightly. **2** fill with stuffing. **3** push a thing into something, *He stuffed the catapult into his pocket.* **4** (*informal*) eat greedily.

stuffing *noun* **1** material used to fill the inside of something; padding. **2** a savoury mixture put into meat or poultry etc. before cooking.

stuffy *adjective* (**stuffier**, **stuffiest**) **1** badly ventilated; without fresh air. **2** with blocked breathing passages, *a stuffy nose.* **3** formal; boring. **stuffily** *adverb*, **stuffiness** *noun*

stultify *verb* (**stultified**, **stultifying**) prevent from being effective, *Their stubbornness stultified the discussions.* **stultification** *noun* [from Latin *stultus* = foolish]

stumble *verb* (**stumbled**, **stumbling**) **1** trip and lose your balance. **2** speak or do something hesitantly or uncertainly. **stumble** *noun* **stumble across** or **on** find accidentally.

stumbling block *noun* an obstacle; something that causes difficulty.

stump[1] *noun* **1** the bottom of a tree trunk left in the ground when the rest has fallen or been cut down. **2** something left when the main part is cut off or worn down. **3** each of the three upright sticks of a wicket in cricket.

stump[2] *verb* **1** walk stiffly or noisily. **2** (of a wicketkeeper in cricket) dismiss a batter by dislodging the bails with the ball while the batter is out of the crease but not running. **3** (*informal*) be too difficult for somebody, *The question stumped her.*

stumpy *adjective* short and thick. **stumpiness** *noun*

stun *verb* (**stunned**, **stunning**) **1** knock a person unconscious. **2** daze or shock, *She was stunned by the news.*

stung *past tense & past participle* of **sting**[2].

stunk *past tense & past participle* of **stink**[2].

stunt[1] *verb* prevent a thing from growing or developing normally, *a stunted tree.*

stunt[2] *noun* something unusual or difficult done as a performance or to attract attention.

stupa (*say* **stoo**-puh) *noun* a Buddhist shrine in the shape of a dome. [Sanskrit]

stupefy *verb* (**stupefied**, **stupefying**) make a person dazed. **stupefaction** *noun* [from Latin *stupere* = be amazed]

stupendous *adjective* amazing; tremendous. **stupendously** *adverb*

stupid *adjective* not clever or thoughtful; without reason or common sense. **stupidity** *noun*, **stupidly** *adverb* [from Latin *stupidus* = dazed]

stupor (*say* **styoo**-puh) *noun* a dazed condition. [same origin as *stupefy*]

sturdy *adjective* (**sturdier**, **sturdiest**) **1** strong and vigorous. **2** solid; strongly built. **sturdily** *adverb*, **sturdiness** *noun*

sturgeon *noun* (*plural* **sturgeon**) a large edible fish.

stutter *verb & noun* stammer.

sty[1] *noun* (*plural* **sties**) a pigsty.

sty[2] *noun* (also **stye**) (*plural* **sties** or **styes**) a sore swelling on an eyelid.

style[1] *noun* **1** the way something is done, made, said, or written etc. **2** a shape or design. **3** elegance. **4** the part of a pistil that supports the stigma in a plant.

style[2] *verb* (**styled**, **styling**) design or arrange something, especially in a fashionable style. **stylist** *noun* [same origin as *stylus*]

styling *noun* **1** the way in which something is made, designed, or performed. **2** the arranging of hair in a particular way.

stylish *adjective* in a fashionable style.

stylistic *adjective* of literary or artistic style. **stylistically** *adverb*

stylus *noun* (*plural* **styluses**) **1** the device like a needle that travels in the grooves of a record to produce the sound. **2** a pointed writing tool. **3** a pen-like device used to input instructions, handwritten text, or drawings directly into a computer etc. [from Latin *stilus* = pointed writing-instrument]

suave (*say* swahv) *adjective* smoothly polite. **suavely** *adverb*, **suavity** *noun* [from Latin *suavis* = agreeable]

sub *noun* (*informal*) **1** a submarine. **2** a subscription. **3** a substitute.

sub- *prefix* (often changing to **suc-**, **suf-**, **sum-**, **sup-**, **sur-**, **sus-** before certain consonants) **1** under (as in *submarine*). **2** subordinate, secondary (as in *subsection*). [from Latin *sub* = under]

subaltern *noun* an army officer ranking below a captain.

subconscious *adjective* of our own mental activities of which we are not fully aware. **subconscious** *noun*

subcontinent *noun* a large mass of land not large enough to be called a continent, *the Indian subcontinent.*

subdivide *verb* (**subdivided**, **subdividing**) divide again or into smaller parts. **subdivision** *noun*

subdue *verb* (**subdued**, **subduing**) **1** overcome; bring under control. **2** make quieter or gentler.

subitising *noun* recognising the number of objects etc. in a small group without consciously counting them.

subject[1] *noun* **1** the person or thing being talked about or written about etc. **2** something that is studied. **3** (in grammar) the word or words naming who or what does the action of a verb, e.g. '*the cat*' in *the cat caught a mouse.* **4** someone who is ruled by a particular king, government, etc.

subject[2] *adjective* ruled by a king or government etc.; not independent. **subject to 1** having to obey. **2** liable to, *The land is subject to frequent flooding.* **3** depending upon, *Our decision is subject to your approval.*

subject[3] (*say* suhb-**jekt**) *verb* **1** make a person or thing undergo something, *They subjected him to torture.* **2** bring a country under your control. **subjection** *noun* [from *sub-*, + Latin *-jectum* = thrown]

subjective *adjective* **1** existing in a person's mind and not produced by things outside it. **2** depending on a person's own taste or opinions. (Compare **objective**[2].)

sub judice (*say* sub **joo**-duh-see) *adjective* under judicial consideration and therefore prohibited from public discussion elsewhere. [Latin, = under a judge]

subjugate *verb* (**subjugated**, **subjugating**) bring under your control; conquer. **subjugation** *noun* [from Latin *sub* = under, + *jugum* = a yoke]

subjunctive *noun* the form of a verb used to indicate what is imagined or wished or possible. There are only a few cases where it is commonly used in English, e.g. '*were*' in *if I were you* and '*save*' in *God save the Queen.* [from *sub-*, + Latin *junctum* = joined]

sublet *verb* (**sublet**, **subletting**) let to another person a house etc. that is let to you by a landlord.

sublime *adjective* **1** noble; impressive. **2** extreme; not caring about the consequences, *with sublime indifference.*

submarine[1] *adjective* under the sea, *We laid a submarine cable.*

submarine[2] *noun* a ship that can travel under water.

submerge *verb* (**submerged**, **submerging**) go under or put under water or other liquid. **submergence** *noun*, **submersion** *noun* [from *sub-*, + Latin *mergere* = dip]

submissive *adjective* willing to obey.

submit *verb* (**submitted**, **submitting**) **1** let someone have authority over you; surrender. **2** put forward for consideration, testing, etc., *Submit your plans to the committee.* **submission** *noun* [from *sub-* + Latin *mittere* = send]

subnormal *adjective* below normal.

subordinate[1] *adjective* **1** less important. **2** lower in rank.

subordinate[2] *verb* (**subordinated**, **subordinating**) treat as being less important than another person or thing. **subordination** *noun* [from *sub-*, + Latin *ordinare* = arrange]

subordinate clause *noun* a clause that is not the main clause in a sentence.

subplot *noun* a secondary plot in a play etc.

subpoena[1] (*say* suh-**pee**-nuh) *noun* an official document ordering a person to appear in a lawcourt.

subpoena[2] *verb* (**subpoenaed**, **subpoenaing**) summon by a subpoena. [from Latin *sub poena* = under a penalty (because there is a punishment for not obeying)]

subscribe *verb* (**subscribed**, **subscribing**) **1** contribute money; pay regularly so as to be a member of a society, get a periodical, have the use of a telephone, etc. **2** sign, *subscribe your name.* **3** say that you agree, *We cannot subscribe to this theory.* **subscriber** *noun*, **subscription** *noun* [from *sub-*, + Latin *scribere* = write]

subsequent *adjective* coming after in time or order; later. **subsequently** *adverb* [from *sub-*, + Latin *sequens* = following]

subservient *adjective* under someone's power; submissive. **subservience** *noun* [from *sub-*, + Latin *serviens* = serving]

subset *noun* a group that is part of a larger group.

subside *verb* (**subsided**, **subsiding**) **1** sink. **2** become less intense, *Her fear subsided.* **subsidence** *noun* [from *sub-*, + Latin *sidere* = settle]

subsidiary *adjective* **1** less important; secondary. **2** (of a business) controlled by another, *a subsidiary company.* [same origin as *subsidy*]

subsidise *verb* (**subsidised**, **subsidising**) pay a subsidy to a person or firm etc.

subsidy *noun* (*plural* **subsidies**) money paid to an industry etc. that needs help, or to keep down the price at which its goods etc. are sold to the public. [from Latin *subsidium* = assistance]

subsist *verb* exist; keep yourself alive, *We subsisted on nuts.* **subsistence** *noun* [from Latin *subsistere* = stand firm]

subsoil *noun* soil lying just below the surface layer.

subsonic *adjective* not as fast as the speed of sound. (Compare **supersonic.**)

substance *noun* **1** matter of a particular kind. **2** the main or essential part of something, *We agree with the substance of your report but not with all its details.* [from Latin *substantia* = essence]

substantial *adjective* **1** of great size, value, or importance, *a substantial fee.* **2** solidly built, *substantial houses.* **3** actually existing. **substantially** *adverb*

substantiate *verb* (**substantiated**, **substantiating**) produce evidence to prove something. **substantiation** *noun*

substation *noun* a subsidiary station for distributing electric current.

substitute[1] *noun* a person or thing that acts or is used instead of another.

substitute[2] *verb* (**substituted**, **substituting**) put or use a person or thing as a substitute. **substitution** *noun* [from *sub-*, + Latin *statuere* = to set up]

subsume *verb* (**subsumed**, **subsuming**) include something under a particular rule or classification etc. [from *sub-*, + Latin *sumere* = take up]

subterfuge *noun* a deception.

subterranean *adjective* underground. [from *sub-*, + Latin *terra* = ground]

subtitle *noun* **1** a subordinate title. **2** words shown on the screen during a film, e.g. to translate a foreign language.

subtle (*say* **sut**-uhl) *adjective* **1** slight, *a subtle difference.* **2** delicate, *a subtle perfume.* **3** ingenious; not immediately obvious, *a subtle joke.* **subtlety** *noun*, **subtly** *adverb*

subtotal *noun* the total of part of a group of figures.

subtract *verb* deduct; take away a part, quantity, or number from a greater one. **subtraction** *noun* [from *sub-*, + Latin *tractum* = pulled]

subtropical *adjective* of regions that border on the tropics.

suburb *noun* a district with houses that is outside the central part of a city. **suburban** *adjective*, **suburbia** *noun* [from *sub-*, + Latin *urbs* = city]

subvert *verb* get people to be disloyal to their government, religion, standards of behaviour, etc.; overthrow a government etc. in this way. **subversion** *noun*, **subversive** *adjective* [from *sub-*, + Latin *vertere* = to turn]

subway *noun* an underground passage, e.g. for pedestrians to cross below a road or for a railway.

subwoofer *noun* a loudspeaker component designed to reproduce very low bass frequencies.

suc- *prefix* see **sub-**.

succeed *verb* **1** be successful. **2** come after another person or thing; become the next king or queen, *She succeeded to the throne; Edward VII succeeded Queen Victoria.* [from *suc-*, + Latin *cedere* = go]

success *noun* (*plural* **successes**) **1** doing or getting what you wanted or intended. **2** a person or thing that does well, *The show was a great success.*

successful *adjective* having success; being a success. **successfully** *adverb*

succession *noun* **1** a series of people or things. **2** the process of following in order. **3** succeeding to the throne; the right of doing this.

successive *adjective* following one after another, *on five successive days.* **successively** *adverb*

successor *noun* a person or thing that succeeds another.

succinct (*say* suhk-**singkt**) *adjective* concise. **succinctly** *adverb* [from Latin *succinctum* = tucked up]

succour (*say* **suk**-uh) *noun & verb* help. [from Latin *succurrere* = run to a person's aid]

succulent *adjective* juicy.

succumb (*say* suh-**kum**) *verb* give way to something overpowering. [from *suc-*, + Latin *cumbere* = to lie]

such *adjective* **1** of the same kind; similar, *Cakes, biscuits and all such foods are fattening.* **2** of the kind described, *There's no such person.* **3** so great or intense, *It gave me such a fright!*

such-and-such *adjective* particular but not now named, *She promises to come at such-and-such a time but is always late.*

suchlike *adjective* (*informal*) of that kind.

suck *verb* **1** take in liquid or air through almost-closed lips. **2** squeeze something in your mouth by using your tongue, *sucking a toffee.* **3** draw in, *The canoe was sucked into the whirlpool.* **suck** *noun*
suck in (*informal*) **1** involve someone in something. **2** deceive someone.
suck up to (*informal*) flatter someone in the hope of winning favour.

sucker *noun* **1** a thing that sucks something. **2** something that can stick to a surface by suction. **3** a shoot coming up from a root or underground stem. **4** (*informal*) a person who is easily deceived.

suckle *verb* (**suckled**, **suckling**) feed on milk at the mother's breast or udder.

suckling *noun* a child or animal that has not yet been weaned.

suction *noun* **1** sucking. **2** producing a vacuum so that things are sucked into the empty space, *Vacuum cleaners work by suction.*

sudden *adjective* happening or done quickly or without warning. **suddenly** *adverb*, **suddenness** *noun*

sudoku (*say* soo-**doh**-koo) *noun* a Japanese number puzzle. [from Japanese *su* = number, + *doku* = place]

suds *plural noun* froth on soapy water.

sue *verb* (**sued**, **suing**) start a lawsuit to claim money from somebody.

suede (*say* swayd) *noun* leather with one side rubbed to make it velvety. [from *Suède*, the French name for Sweden, where it was first made]

suet *noun* hard fat from cattle and sheep, used in cooking.

suf- *prefix* see **sub-**.

suffer *verb* **1** feel pain or sadness. **2** experience something bad, *suffer damage.* **3** (*old use*) allow; tolerate. **sufferer** *noun*, **suffering** *noun* [from *suf-*, + Latin *ferre* = to bear]

sufferance *noun* **on sufferance** allowed but only reluctantly.

suffice *verb* (**sufficed**, **sufficing**) be enough for someone's needs.

sufficient *adjective* enough. **sufficiency** *noun*, **sufficiently** *adverb*

suffix *noun* (*plural* **suffixes**) a letter or set of letters joined to the end of a word to make another word (e.g. in forget*ful*, lion*ess*, rust*y*) or a form of a verb (e.g. sing*ing*, wait*ed*). [from *suf-* + *fix*]

suffocate *verb* (**suffocated**, **suffocating**) **1** make it difficult or impossible for someone to breathe. **2** suffer or die because breathing is prevented. **suffocation** *noun* [from *suf-*, + Latin *fauces* = throat]

suffrage *noun* the right to vote in political elections. [from Latin, = vote]

suffragette *noun* a woman who campaigned in the early 20th century for women to have the right to vote.

suffuse *verb* (**suffused**, **suffusing**) spread through or over something, *A blush suffused her cheeks.* [from *suf-*, + Latin *fusum* = poured]

sugar *noun* a sweet food obtained from the juices of various plants (e.g. sugar cane, sugar beet). **sugar** *verb*, **sugary** *adjective* [from Arabic *sukkar*]

suggest *verb* **1** give somebody an idea that you think is useful. **2** cause an idea or possibility to come into the mind. **suggestion** *noun*, **suggestive** *adjective*

suggestible *adjective* easily influenced by people's suggestions.

suicide *noun* **1** killing yourself deliberately, *commit suicide.* **2** a person who deliberately kills himself or herself. **suicidal** *adjective* [from Latin *sui* = of yourself, + *caedere* = kill]

suit[1] *noun* **1** a matching jacket and trousers, or a jacket and skirt, that are meant to be worn together. **2** clothing for a particular activity, *a diving suit.* **3** any of the four sets of cards (clubs, hearts, diamonds, spades) in a pack of playing cards. **4** a lawsuit.

suit[2] *verb* **1** be suitable or convenient for a person or thing. **2** make a person look attractive.

suitable *adjective* satisfactory or right for a particular person, purpose, or occasion. **suitability** *noun*, **suitably** *adverb*

suitcase *noun* a rectangular container for carrying clothes, usually with a hinged lid and a handle.

suite (*say* sweet) *noun* **1** a set of furniture, rooms, etc. **2** a set of short pieces of music.

suitor *noun* a man who is courting a woman. [from Latin *secutor* = follower]

sulfur see **sulphur**.

sulk *verb* be silent and bad-tempered because you are not pleased. **sulkily** *adverb*, **sulkiness** *noun*, **sulks** *plural noun*, **sulky** *adjective*

sullen *adjective* sulking and gloomy. **sullenly** *adverb*, **sullenness** *noun*

sully *verb* (**sullied**, **sullying**) soil or stain something; blemish, *The scandal sullied his reputation.*

sulphur *noun* (also **sulfur**) **1** a yellow chemical used in industry and in medicine. **2** a pale greenish-yellow colour. **sulphurous** *adjective*

> **Usage** The traditional spelling is *sulphur* and the US spelling is *sulfur*. In chemistry and other technical uses, however, *sulfur* is now the standard form.

sulphuric acid *noun* a strong colourless acid containing sulphur.

sultan *noun* the ruler of certain Muslim countries. [from Arabic, = ruler]

sultana *noun* **1** a seedless raisin. **2** a sultan's wife, mother, or daughter.

sultry *adjective* hot and humid, *sultry weather.* **sultriness** *noun*

sum[1] *noun* **1** a total. **2** a problem in arithmetic. **3** an amount of money.

sum[2] *verb* (**summed**, **summing**) **sum up 1** summarise, especially at the end of a talk etc. **2** form an opinion of a person, *sum him up.* [from Latin *summa* = main thing]

sum- *prefix* see **sub-**.

summarise *verb* (**summarised, summarising**) make or give a summary of something.

summary[1] *noun* (*plural* **summaries**) a statement of the main points of something said or written.

summary[2] *adjective* **1** brief. **2** done or given hastily, without delay, *summary punishment.* **summarily** *adverb* [same origin as *sum*]

summer *noun* the warm season between spring and autumn. **summery** *adjective*

summit *noun* **1** the top of a mountain or hill. **2** a meeting between the leaders of powerful countries, *a summit conference.* [from Latin *summus* = highest]

summon *verb* **1** order someone to come or appear. **2** request firmly, *He summoned the rebels to surrender.*
summon up gather or prepare, *Can you summon up the energy to get out of bed?* [from *sum-*, + Latin *monere* = warn]

summons *noun* (*plural* **summonses**) a command to appear in a lawcourt.

sump *noun* a metal case that holds oil round an engine.

sumptuous *adjective* splendid and expensive-looking. **sumptuously** *adverb* [from Latin *sumptus* = cost]

sun[1] *noun* **1** the large ball of fire round which the earth travels. **2** light and warmth from the sun, *Go and sit in the sun.*

sun[2] *verb* (**sunned, sunning**) warm something in the sun, *sunning ourselves on the beach.*

sunbake *verb* (**sunbaked, sunbaking**) (*Australian*) sunbathe.

sunbathe *verb* (**sunbathed, sunbathing**) expose your body to the sun.

sunbeam *noun* a ray of sun.

sunblock *noun* sunscreen.

sunburn *noun* redness of the skin caused by the sun. **sunburnt** *adjective*

sundae (*say* **sun**-day) *noun* a mixture of ice cream and fruit, nuts, cream, etc.

Sunday *noun* the first day of the week, *I sometimes go fishing on Sundays.* [Old English = day of the sun]

sunder *verb* (*poetic*) break apart; sever.

sundial *noun* a device that shows the time by a shadow on a dial.

sundown *noun* sunset.

sundowner *noun* (*Australian*) a swagman arriving at sundown, too late to work for his meal.

sundries *plural noun* various small things.

sundry *adjective* various; several.
all and sundry everyone.

sunflower *noun* a very tall flower with golden petals round a dark centre.

sung *past participle* of **sing**.

sunglasses *plural noun* dark glasses to protect your eyes from strong sunlight.

sunk *past participle* of **sink**[1].

sunken *adjective* sunk deeply into a surface, *Their cheeks were pale and sunken.*

sunlight *noun* light from the sun.
sunlit *adjective*

Sunna *noun* the traditional portion of Muslim law based on Muhammad's words or acts. [Arabic, = form, way, course, rule]

Sunni (*say* **suu**-nee or **sun**-ee) *noun* (*plural* **Sunni** or **Sunnis**) **1** one of the two main branches of Islam, commonly described as orthodox, and differing from Shia in its understanding of the Sunna and in its acceptance of the first three caliphs. **2** a Muslim who adheres to the Sunni branch of Islam. [Arabic, = custom, normative rule]

sunnies *plural noun* (*Australian informal*) sunglasses.

sunny *adjective* (**sunnier, sunniest**) **1** full of sunshine. **2** cheerful, *She was in a sunny mood.* **sunnily** *adverb*

sunrise *noun* the rising of the sun; dawn.

sunscreen *noun* (also **sunblock**) a lotion used to protect the skin from the sun's harmful ultraviolet rays.

sunset *noun* the setting of the sun.

sunshade *noun* a parasol or other device to protect people from the sun.

sunshine *noun* sunlight with no cloud between the sun and the earth.

sunspot *noun* **1** a dark place on the sun's surface. **2** an area of skin damage caused by too much exposure to the sun.

sunstroke *noun* illness caused by being in the sun too long.

suntan *noun* brownish skin colour caused by exposure to the sun. **suntanned** *adjective*

sup *verb* (**supped, supping**) **1** drink liquid in sips or spoonfuls. **2** eat supper.

sup- *prefix* see **sub-**.

super[1] *adjective* (*informal*) excellent; superb.

super[2] *noun* (*informal*) **1** superannuation. **2** superphosphate.

super- *prefix* **1** over; on top (as in *superstructure*). **2** of greater size or quality etc. (as in *supermarket*). **3** extremely (as in *superabundant*). **4** beyond (as in *supernatural*). [from Latin *super* = over]

superannuation *noun* a pension paid to a retired worker; regular payments made by the employee or employer towards this. **superannuant** *noun* (*Australian*) [from *super-*, + Latin *annus* = a year]

superb *adjective* magnificent; excellent. **superbly** *adverb* [from Latin *superbus* = proud]

supercilious *adjective* haughty and scornful. **superciliously** *adverb* [from Latin *supercilium* = eyebrow]

superficial *adjective* **1** on the surface; not deep. **2** hasty; not thorough. **superficiality** *noun*, **superficially** *adverb* [from *super*-, + Latin *facies* = face]

superfluous *adjective* more than is needed. **superfluity** *noun* [from *super*-, + Latin *fluere* = flow]

superhuman *adjective* **1** beyond ordinary human ability, *superhuman strength.* **2** higher than human; divine.

superimpose *verb* (**superimposed, superimposing**) place a thing on top of something else. **superimposition** *noun*

superintend *verb* supervise. **superintendent** *noun*

superior[1] *adjective* **1** higher in position or rank, *She is your superior officer.* **2** better than another person or thing. **3** conceited. **superiority** *noun*

superior[2] *noun* a person or thing that is superior to another. [Latin, = higher]

superlative[1] *adjective* of the highest degree or quality, *superlative skill.* **superlatively** *adverb*

superlative[2] *noun* the form of an adjective or adverb that expresses 'most', *The superlative of 'great' is 'greatest'.* (Compare **positive**[1] 7, **comparative.**) [from Latin *superlatum* = carried above]

superman *noun* (*plural* **supermen**) a man with superhuman powers.

supermarket *noun* a large self-service shop that sells food and other goods.

supernatural *adjective* not belonging to the natural world, *supernatural beings such as ghosts.*

superphosphate *noun* a fertiliser made from phosphate rock.

superpower *noun* **1** a very powerful and influential nation. **2** (in fiction) an exceptional or extraordinary power or ability, *Her superpowers allow her to fly.*

supersede *verb* (**superseded, superseding**) take the place of something, *Cars superseded horse-drawn carriages.* [from *super*-, + Latin *sedere* = sit]

supersonic *adjective* faster than the speed of sound. (Compare **subsonic.**)

superstition *noun* a belief or action that is not based on reason or evidence, e.g. the belief that it is unlucky to walk under a ladder. **superstitious** *adjective*

superstructure *noun* a structure that rests on something else; a building as distinct from its foundations.

supertanker *noun* a very large tanker.

supervene *verb* (**supervened, supervening**) happen and interrupt or change something, *The country was prosperous until an earthquake supervened.* [from *super*-, + Latin *venire* = come]

supervise *verb* (**supervised, supervising**) be in charge of a person or thing and inspect what is done. **supervision** *noun*, **supervisor** *noun*, **supervisory** *adjective* [from *super*-, + Latin *visum* = seen]

supine (*say* **soo**-puyn) *adjective* **1** lying face upwards. (The opposite is **prone.**) **2** not taking action.

supper *noun* a meal eaten in the evening.

supplant *verb* take the place of a person or thing that has been ousted.

supple *adjective* bending easily; flexible. **supplely** *adverb*, **suppleness** *noun*

supplejack *noun* a climbing or twining shrub.

supplement[1] *noun* **1** something added as an extra. **2** an extra section added to a book or newspaper, *the colour supplement.* **supplementary** *adjective*

supplement[2] *verb* add to something, *She supplements her pocket money by working on Saturdays.* [same origin as *supply*]

supplementary angle *noun* either of two angles whose sum is 180°.

suppliant (*say* **sup**-lee-uhnt) *noun* a person who asks humbly for something.

supplicate *verb* (**supplicated, supplicating**) beg humbly; beseech. **supplication** *noun* [from Latin, = kneel]

supply[1] *verb* (**supplied, supplying**) give or sell or provide what is needed or wanted. **supplier** *noun*

supply[2] *noun* (*plural* **supplies**) **1** an amount of something that is available for use when needed. **2** the action of supplying something; the thing supplied. [from *sup*-, + Latin *-plere* = fill]

support[1] *verb* **1** keep a person or thing from falling or sinking. **2** give strength, help, or encouragement to someone, *Support your local team.* **3** provide with the necessities of life, *She has two children to support.* **4** help to confirm a statement etc. **supporter** *noun*, **supportive** *adjective*

support[2] *noun* **1** the action of supporting. **2** a person or thing that supports. [from *sup*-, + Latin *portare* = carry]

suppose *verb* (**supposed, supposing**) think that something is likely to happen or be true. **supposedly** *adverb*, **supposition** *noun*
be supposed to be expected to do something; have as a duty.

suppress *verb* **1** put an end to something forcibly or by authority, *Troops suppressed the rebellion.* **2** keep something from being known or seen, *They suppressed the truth.* **suppression** *noun*, **suppressor** *noun*

supreme *adjective* **1** highest in rank; most important. **2** greatest, *supreme courage.* **supremacy** *noun*, **supremely** *adverb* [from Latin *supremus* = highest]

sur-[1] *prefix* see **sub-**.

sur-[2] *prefix* = super- (as in *surcharge*, *surface*).

surcharge *noun* an extra charge.

surd *noun* a mathematical quantity (especially a root) that cannot be expressed in finite terms of whole numbers or quantities; an irrational number.

sure[1] *adjective* **1** convinced; feeling no doubt. **2** certain to happen or do something, *team is sure to win.* **3** reliable. **4** undoubtedly true. **sureness** *noun*
for sure definitely.
make sure 1 find out exactly. **2** make something happen or be true, *Make sure the door is locked.* [from Latin *securus* = secure]

sure[2] *adverb* (*informal*) surely.
sure enough certainly; in fact.

surely *adverb* **1** in a sure way; certainly; securely. **2** it must be true; I feel sure, *Surely we met last year?*

surety *noun* (*plural* **sureties**) **1** a guarantee. **2** a person who promises to pay a debt or fulfil a contract etc. if another person fails to do so.

surf[1] *noun* the white foam of waves breaking on a rock or shore.

surf[2] *verb* **1** ride waves on a board or by streamlining your body and letting it be carried by the waves. **2** move from site to site on the Internet. **surfer** *noun*, **surfie** *noun* (*informal*), **surfing** *noun*

surface[1] *noun* **1** the outside of something. **2** any of the sides of an object, especially the top part. **3** an outward appearance, *On the surface he was a kindly man.*

surface[2] *verb* (**surfaced**, **surfacing**) **1** put a surface on something (especially a road). **2** come up to the surface from under water.

surfboard *noun* a board used in surfing.

surfeit (*say* **ser**-fuht) *noun* too much of something. **surfeited** *adjective*

surge *verb* (**surged**, **surging**) move forwards or upwards like waves. **surge** *noun* [from Latin *surgere* = rise]

surgeon *noun* a doctor who treats disease or injury by cutting or repairing the affected parts of the body.

surgery *noun* (*plural* **surgeries**) **1** the place where a doctor or dentist regularly gives advice and treatment to patients. **2** the time when patients can visit the doctor etc. **3** the work of a surgeon. **surgical** *adjective*, **surgically** *adverb* [from Greek, = handiwork]

surly *adjective* (**surlier**, **surliest**) bad-tempered and unfriendly. **surliness** *noun*

surmise *noun* a guess. **surmise** *verb*

surmount *verb* **1** overcome a difficulty. **2** get over an obstacle. **3** be on top of something.

surname *noun* the name held by all members of a family.

surpass *verb* do or be better than all others; excel.

surplice *noun* a loose white garment worn over a cassock by clergy and the choir at a religious service.

surplus *noun* (*plural* **surpluses**) an amount left over after spending or using all that was needed.

surprise[1] *noun* **1** something unexpected. **2** the feeling caused by something that was not expected.

surprise[2] *verb* (**surprised**, **surprising**) **1** be a surprise to somebody. **2** come upon or attack somebody unexpectedly. **surprisingly** *adverb*

surreal *adjective* bizarre; unreal; dreamlike.

surrealism *noun* a style of painting that shows strange shapes like those seen in dreams and fantasies. **surrealist** *noun*, **surrealistic** *adjective* [from *sur-*[2] +*real*]

surrender *verb* **1** give yourself up to an enemy. **2** hand something over to another person, especially when compelled to do so. **surrender** *noun* [from *sur-*[2] + *render*]

surreptitious (*say* su-ruhp-**tish**-uhs) *adjective* stealthy. **surreptitiously** *adverb* [from Latin, = seized secretly]

surrogate (*say* **su**-ruh-guht) *noun* a deputy; a substitute. **surrogacy** *noun*

surround *verb* come or be all round a person or thing; encircle.

surroundings *plural noun* the things or conditions round a person or thing.

surveil *verb* (**surveilled**, **surveilling**) (also **surveille**) keep a person or place under surveillance.

surveillance (*say* ser-**vay**-luhns) *noun* a close watch kept on a person or thing, *Police kept him under surveillance.*

survey[1] (*say* **ser**-vay) *noun* **1** a general look at something. **2** an inspection of an area or building. **3** an investigation of the opinions or experience of a group of people, based on a series of questions.

survey[2] (*say* suh-**vay**) *verb* **1** make a survey of something; inspect. **2** measure and map out an area. **surveyor** *noun* [from *sur-*², + Latin *videre* = see]

survive *verb* (**survived**, **surviving**) **1** stay alive. **2** go on living or existing after someone has died or after a disaster. **survival** *noun*, **survivor** *noun* [from *sur-*², + Latin *vivere* = to live]

sus- *prefix* see **sub-**.

susceptible (*say* suh-**sep**-tuh-buhl) *adjective* likely to be affected by something, *She is susceptible to colds.* **susceptibility** *noun* [from Latin *susceptum* = caught up]

sushi (*say* **soo**-shee or **suu**-shee) *noun* a Japanese dish consisting of small balls or rolls of rice served with a garnish of vegetables, egg, or raw seafood. [Japanese]

suspect¹ (*say* suh-**spekt**) *verb* **1** think that a person is not to be trusted or has committed a crime; distrust. **2** have a feeling that something is likely or possible.

suspect² (*say* **sus**-pekt) *noun* a person thought to be guilty of a crime or offence. **suspect** *adjective*

suspend *verb* **1** hang something up. **2** postpone; stop something temporarily. **3** deprive a person of a job or position etc. for a time. [from *sus-*, + Latin *pendere* = hang]

suspender *noun* a fastener to hold up a stocking by its top.

suspense *noun* an anxious or uncertain feeling while waiting for something to happen or become known.

suspension *noun* suspending.

suspension bridge *noun* a bridge supported by cables.

suspicion *noun* **1** suspecting a person or thing; being suspected; distrust. **2** a slight belief. **3** a slight trace.

suspicious *adjective* **1** feeling suspicion. **2** causing suspicion. **suspiciously** *adverb*

suss¹ *adjective* (*informal*) suspect; suspicious.

suss² *verb* (**sussed**, **sussing**)
suss out (*informal*) investigate; inspect; work out.

sustain *verb* **1** support. **2** keep someone alive. **3** keep something happening. **4** undergo; suffer, *We sustained a defeat.* [from *sus-*, + Latin *tenere* = hold]

sustainable *adjective* **1** able to be sustained or upheld. **2** (of economic development or the utilisation of natural resources) able to be maintained at a particular level without causing damage to the environment or depletion of the resource.

sustenance *noun* food; nourishment.

suture (*say* **soo**-chuh) *noun* surgical stitching of a cut. [from Latin *sutura* = sewing]

suzerainty (*say* **soo**-zuh-ruhn-tee) *noun* **1** the partial control of a weaker country by a stronger one. **2** the power of an overlord in feudal times.

svelte *adjective* slim and graceful.

SW *abbreviation* south-west; south-western.

swab¹ (*say* swob) *noun* a mop or pad for cleaning or wiping something.

swab² *verb* (**swabbed**, **swabbing**) clean or wipe with a swab.

swaddle *verb* (**swaddled**, **swaddling**) wrap in warm clothes or blankets.

swag *noun* **1** (*Australian*) a collection of possessions, food, etc. carried by a person travelling, usually on foot, in the outback. **2** (*Australian*) portable bedding rolled into a bundle. **3** (*Australian*) a large quantity, *a swag of letters to answer.* **4** loot.

swagger *verb* walk or behave in a conceited way; strut. **swagger** *noun*

swagman *noun* (*plural* **swagmen**) (*Australian*) a tramp.

swain *noun* (*old use*) **1** a country lad. **2** a suitor.

swallow¹ *verb* **1** make something go down your throat. **2** believe something that ought not to be believed. **swallow** *noun*
swallow up take in and cover; engulf, *She was swallowed up in the crowd.*

swallow² *noun* a small bird with a forked tail and pointed wings.

swam *past tense* of **swim**¹.

swamp¹ *noun* a marsh. **swampy** *adjective*

swamp² *verb* **1** flood. **2** overwhelm with a great mass or number of things.

swan *noun* a large black or white swimming bird with a long neck.

swank¹ *verb* (*informal*) boast; swagger.

swank² *noun* (*informal*) swanking; boasting.

swansong *noun* a person's last performance or work. [from the old belief that a swan sang sweetly when about to die]

swap *verb* (**swapped**, **swapping**) (*informal*) exchange. **swap** *noun*

sward *noun* (*literary*) an expanse of short grass.

swarm¹ *noun* a large number of insects, birds, small animals, or people moving about together.

swarm² *verb* **1** gather or move in a swarm. **2** (of a place) be crowded or overrun, *swarming with tourists.*

swarthy *adjective* having a dark complexion. **swarthiness** *noun*

swashbuckling *adjective* swaggering aggressively; showing flamboyant daring. **swashbuckler** *noun*

swastika *noun* an ancient symbol formed by a cross with its ends bent at right angles, adopted by the Nazis as their sign.

swat *verb* (**swatted, swatting**) hit or crush a fly etc. **swatter** *noun*

swathe *verb* (**swathed, swathing**) wrap in layers of bandages, paper, or clothes etc.

sway *verb* **1** swing gently; move from side to side. **2** influence, *His speech swayed the crowd.* **sway** *noun*

swear *verb* (**swore, sworn, swearing**) **1** make a solemn promise, *She swore to tell the truth.* **2** make a person take an oath, *We swore him to secrecy.* **3** use curses or coarse words in anger or surprise etc. **swear word** *noun*
swear by have great confidence in something.
swear in admit someone to office by making them take an oath.

sweat[1] (*say* swet) *noun* moisture given off by the body through the pores of the skin; perspiration. **sweaty** *adjective*

sweat[2] *verb* give off sweat; perspire.

sweated *adjective* (of goods, workers, or labour) produced by or subjected to long hours under poor conditions.

sweater *noun* a jumper or pullover.

sweatshirt *noun* a cotton sweater with a fleecy lining.

sweatshop *noun* a workshop or factory where sweated labour is used.

swede *noun* a large yellow kind of turnip.

sweep[1] *verb* (**swept, sweeping**) **1** clean or clear with a broom or brush. **2** move or remove quickly, *The floods swept away the bridge.* **3** go smoothly, quickly, or proudly, *She swept out of the room.* **sweeper** *noun*

sweep[2] *noun* **1** the process of sweeping, *Give the path a sweep.* **2** a chimney sweep. **3** a sweepstake.

sweeping *adjective* general; wide-ranging, *He made sweeping changes.*

sweepstake *noun* a kind of lottery used in gambling on the result of a horserace etc.

sweet[1] *adjective* **1** tasting as if it contains sugar; not bitter. **2** very pleasant, *a sweet smell.* **3** melodious. **4** (*informal*) charming. **sweetly** *adverb*, **sweetness** *noun*

sweet[2] *noun* **1** a small shaped piece of sweet food made with sugar, chocolate, etc. **2** the sweet course in a meal. **3** a beloved person.

sweetbread *noun* an animal's pancreas or thymus used as food.

sweetcorn *noun* the seeds of maize.

sweeten *verb* make or become sweet. **sweetener** *noun*

sweetheart *noun* a person you love very much.

sweet pea *noun* a climbing plant with fragrant flowers.

swell[1] *verb* (**swelled, swollen** or **swelled, swelling**) make or become larger in size or amount or force.
swelled head (*informal*) conceit.

swell[2] *noun* **1** the process of swelling. **2** the rise and fall of the sea's surface.

swell[3] *adjective* (*informal*) excellent.

swelling *noun* a swollen place.

swelter *verb* feel uncomfortably hot. **sweltering** *adjective*

swerve *verb* (**swerved, swerving**) turn to one side suddenly. **swerve** *noun*

swift[1] *adjective* quick; rapid. **swiftly** *adverb*, **swiftness** *noun*

swift[2] *noun* a small bird rather like a swallow.

swiftie *noun* (*Australian informal*) a trick or piece of deception, *He pulled a swiftie.*

swig *verb* (**swigged, swigging**) (*informal*) drink; swallow. **swig** *noun*

swill[1] *verb* pour water over or through something; wash or rinse.

swill[2] *noun* **1** the process of swilling, *Give it a swill.* **2** a sloppy mixture of waste food given to pigs.

swim[1] *verb* (**swam, swum, swimming**) **1** move the body through the water; be in the water for pleasure. **2** cross by swimming, *She swam the English Channel.* **3** float. **4** be covered with or full of liquid, *Our eyes were swimming in tears.* **5** feel dizzy, *His head swam.* **swimmer** *noun*

swim[2] *noun* the action of swimming, *We went for a swim.*

swimmers *plural noun* (*Australian*) a swimming costume.

swimming costume *noun* a garment worn for swimming.

swimming pool *noun* an artificial pool for swimming in.

swimsuit *noun* a swimming costume.

swindle *verb* (**swindled, swindling**) cheat a person; obtain by fraud. **swindle** *noun*, **swindler** *noun*

swine *noun* (*plural* **swine**) **1** a pig. **2** a very unpleasant person or thing.

swing[1] *verb* (**swung, swinging**) **1** move to and fro while hanging; move or turn in a curve, *The door swung open.* **2** change from one opinion or mood etc. to another.

swing[2] *noun* **1** a swinging movement. **2** a seat hung on chains or ropes so that it can be moved backwards and forwards. **3** the amount by which votes or opinions etc.

change from one side to another. **4** a kind of jazz music.
in full swing full of activity; working fully.

swingeing (*say* **swin**-jing) *adjective* **1** (of a blow) very powerful. **2** huge in amount, *a swingeing increase in taxes.*

swinging voter *noun* a person who does not support any political party permanently.

swipe *verb* (**swiped**, **swiping**) (*informal*) **1** hit hard. **2** steal something. **3** slide a credit card etc. through an electronic device that reads it. **swipe** *noun*

swirl *verb* move round quickly in circles; whirl. **swirl** *noun*

swish[1] *verb* move with a hissing sound. **swish** *noun*

swish[2] *adjective* (*informal*) smart; fashionable.

switch[1] *noun* (*plural* **switches**) **1** a device that is pressed or turned to start or stop something working, especially by electricity. **2** a change of opinion, policy, or methods. **3** mechanism for moving the points on a railway track. **4** a flexible rod or whip.

switch[2] *verb* **1** turn something on or off by means of a switch. **2** change or transfer or divert something.

switchback *noun* a road or railway with steep slopes up and down alternately; a roller coaster.

switchboard *noun* a panel with switches for making telephone connections or operating electric circuits.

swivel *verb* (**swivelled**, **swivelling**) turn round.

swollen *past participle* of **swell**[1].

swoon *verb* faint. **swoon** *noun*

swoop *verb* **1** come down with a rushing movement. **2** make a sudden attack. **swoop** *noun*

swop *verb* (**swopped**, **swopping**) swap.

sword (*say* sawd) *noun* a weapon with a long pointed blade fixed in a handle or hilt. **swordsman** *noun*

swordfish *noun* a sea fish with a long upper jaw like a sword.

swore *past tense* of **swear**.

sworn *past participle* of **swear**.

swot *verb* (**swotted**, **swotting**) (*informal*) study hard. **swot** *noun* [a dialect word for *sweat*]

swum *past participle* of **swim**[1].

swung *past tense & past participle* of **swing**[1].

sycamore *noun* a kind of maple tree.

sycophant (*say* **sik**-uh-fuhnt) *noun* a person who tries to win people's favour by flattering them. **sycophancy** *noun*, **sycophantic** *adjective*, **sycophantically** *adverb*

syl- *prefix* see **syn-**.

syllabification *noun* division into or articulation by syllables. **syllabify** *verb*

syllable *noun* a word or part of a word that has one sound when you say it, *'Cat' has one syllable, 'el-e-phant' has three syllables.* **syllabic** *adjective* [from *syl-*, + Greek *lambenein* = take]

syllabus *noun* (*plural* **syllabuses**) a summary of the things to be studied by a class or for an examination.

sylph *noun* a slender and graceful girl or woman.

sylvan *adjective* of the woods; wooded; rural. [from Latin *silva* = a wood]

sym- *prefix* see **syn-**.

symbol *noun* **1** a thing that suggests something, *The cross is a symbol of Christianity.* **2** a mark or sign with a special meaning (e.g. +, –, and ÷ in mathematics). **symbolic** *adjective*, **symbolical** *adjective*, **symbolically** *adverb* [from Greek *symbolon* = token]

symbolise *verb* (**symbolised**, **symbolising**) make or be a symbol of something.

symbolism *noun* the use of symbols to represent things.

symmetrical *adjective* able to be divided into two halves that are exactly the same but the opposite way round, *Butterflies are symmetrical.* **symmetrically** *adverb* [from *sym-* + *metrical*]

symmetry *noun* **1** being symmetrical. **2** pleasing proportion between parts of a whole.

sympathise *verb* (**sympathised**, **sympathising**) **1** show or feel sympathy. **2** agree. **sympathiser** *noun*

sympathy *noun* (*plural* **sympathies**) **1** feelings of pity and sorrow for someone else's misfortune, *We have great sympathy for the bushfire victims.* **2** understanding between people; common feeling. **sympathetic** *adjective*, **sympathetically** *adverb* [from *sym-*, + Greek *pathos* = feeling]

Usage Do not confuse *sympathy* with *empathy*.

symphony *noun* (*plural* **symphonies**) a long piece of music for an orchestra. **symphonic** *adjective* [from *sym-*, + Greek *phone* = sound]

symptom *noun* a sign that a disease or condition exists, *Red spots are a symptom of measles.* **symptomatic** *adjective*

syn- *prefix* (changing to **syl-** or **sym-** before certain consonants) **1** with; together (as in *synchronise*). **2** alike (as in *synonym*). [from Greek *syn* = with]

synagogue (*say* **sin**-uh-gog) *noun* a place where Jews meet for worship. [from Greek, = assembly]

synchronise (*say* **sing**-kruh-nuyz) *verb* (**synchronised, synchronising**) **1** make things happen at the same time. **2** make watches or clocks show the same time. **3** happen at the same time. **synchronisation** *noun* [from *syn-*, + Greek *chronos* = time]

syncopate (*say* **sing**-kuh-payt) *verb* (**syncopated, syncopating**) change the strength of beats in a piece of music. **syncopation** *noun*

syndicate *noun* a group of people or firms who work together in business.

syndrome *noun* a group of concurrent symptoms of a disease.

synod (*say* **sin**-uhd) *noun* a council attended by clergy and (in some Churches) laypeople. [from Greek, = meeting]

synonym (*say* **sin**-uh-nim) *noun* a word that means the same or almost the same as another word, *'Large' and 'great' are synonyms of 'big'.* **synonymous** (*say* suh-**non**-uh-muhs) *adjective* [from *syn-*, + Greek *onyma* = name]

synopsis (*say* suh-**nop**-suhs) *noun* (*plural* **synopses**) a summary. [from *syn-*, + Greek *opsis* = seeing]

syntax (*say* **sin**-taks) *noun* the way words are arranged to make phrases or sentences. **syntactic** *adjective*, **syntactically** *adverb* [from *syn-*, + Greek *taxis* = arrangement]

synthesis (*say* **sin**-thuh-suhs) *noun* (*plural* **syntheses**) combining different things to make something. **synthesise** *verb* [from *syn-*, + Greek *thesis* = placing]

synthesiser *noun* an electronic musical instrument that can make a large variety of sounds.

synthetic *adjective* artificially made; not natural. **synthetically** *adverb*

syphilis (*say* **sif**-uh-luhs) *noun* a contagious venereal disease. **syphilitic** *adjective*

syringe *noun* a device for sucking in a liquid and squirting it out.

syrup *noun* a thick sweet liquid. **syrupy** *adjective* [from Arabic *sharab* = a drink]

system *noun* **1** a set of parts, things, or ideas that form a whole or work together. **2** a way of doing something, *a new system of training drivers.* **3** a set of rules, principles, or practices forming a particular philosophy or form of government etc. **4** orderliness; being systematic. **5** a method of classification, notation, or measurement, *the metric system.* [from Greek, = setting up]

systematic *adjective* methodical; carefully planned. **systematically** *adverb*

Tt

tab[1] *noun* **1** a small flap or strip that sticks out. **2** (in computing) a second or further document or page that can be opened on a spreadsheet or browser.
keep tabs on (*informal*) keep account of; keep under observation.

tab[2] *noun* a tabulator.

tabard *noun* a kind of tunic decorated with a coat of arms.

tabbouleh (*say* tuh-**boo**-lee) *noun* (also **tabouli**) a Middle Eastern salad made with bulgur, parsley, onion, mint, lemon juice, oil, and spices. [Arabic]

tabby *noun* (*plural* **tabbies**) a grey or brown cat with dark stripes.

tabernacle *noun* (in the Bible) the portable shrine used by the ancient Jews during their wanderings in the desert.

tablature *noun* (in music) a form of notation in which lines, figures, and letters are used, e.g. to indicate fingering for the guitar.

table[1] *noun* **1** a piece of furniture with a flat top supported on legs. **2** a list of facts or figures arranged in order; a list of the results of multiplying a number by other numbers, *multiplication tables.* [from Latin *tabula* = plank]

table[2] *verb* (**tabled**, **tabling**) present formally for discussion or consideration.

tableau (*say* **tab**-loh) *noun* (*plural* **tableaux**, *say* **tab**-lohz) a dramatic or picturesque scene, especially one posed on a stage by a group of people who do not speak or move. [French, = little table]

tablecloth *noun* a cloth for covering a table, especially at meals.

table d'hôte (*say* **tah**-buhl doht) *noun* a restaurant meal served at a fixed inclusive price. (Compare **à la carte.**) [French, = host's table]

tableland *noun* an extensive high area of flat land.

tablespoon *noun* a large spoon for serving food. **tablespoonful** *noun*

tablet *noun* **1** a small amount of medicine in solid form; a pill. **2** a solid piece of soap. **3** a flat piece of stone or wood etc. with words carved or written on it. **4** a portable computer that can be used without a keyboard and mouse.

table tennis *noun* a game played with bats and a light hollow ball on a table with a net across it.

tabloid *noun* a newspaper with pages that are half the size of larger newspapers.

taboo *adjective* not to be touched or done or used. **taboo** *noun*

tabor (*say* **tay**-buh) *noun* a small drum.

tabular *adjective* arranged in a table or in columns.

tabulate *verb* (**tabulated**, **tabulating**) arrange information or figures in a table or list. **tabulation** *noun*

tabulator *noun* a device on a typewriter or computer keyboard that automatically sets the positions for columns.

tachograph (*say* **tak**-uh-grahf) *noun* a device that automatically records the speed and travelling time of a motor vehicle in which it is fitted. [from Greek *tachos* = speed, + *-graph*]

tacit (*say* **tas**-uht) *adjective* implied or understood without being put into words; silent, *tacit approval.* **tacitly** *adverb* [from Latin *tacitus* = not speaking]

taciturn (*say* **tas**-uh-tern) *adjective* saying very little. **taciturnity** *noun*

tack[1] *noun* **1** a short nail with a flat top. **2** a tacking stitch. **3** (in sailing) direction taken when tacking. **4** a course of action.

tack[2] *verb* **1** nail down with tacks. **2** fasten material together with long stitches. **3** sail a zigzag course so as to use what wind there is.
tack on (*informal*) add an extra thing.

tack[3] *noun* harness, saddles, etc. [from *tackle* = equipment]

tackle[1] *verb* (**tackled**, **tackling**) **1** try to do something that needs doing. **2** (in some sports) intercept or stop a player running with the ball.

tackle[2] *noun* **1** equipment, especially for fishing. **2** a set of ropes and pulleys. **3** the action of tackling someone.

tacky *adjective* **1** sticky, not quite dry, *The paint is still tacky.* **2** (*informal*) cheap and of poor quality. **tackiness** *noun*

tact *noun* skill in not offending people. **tactful** *adjective*, **tactfully** *adverb*, **tactless** *adjective*, **tactlessly** *adverb* [from Latin *tactus* = sense of touch]

tactics *noun* the method of arranging troops etc. skilfully for a battle, or of doing things to achieve something. (Compare **strategy**.) **tactic** *noun*, **tactical** *adjective*, **tactically** *adverb*, **tactician** *noun* [from Greek *taktika* = things arranged]

> **Usage** *Strategy* is a general plan for a whole campaign, *tactics* is for one part of this.

tactile *adjective* of or using the sense of touch. [from Latin *tactum* = touched]

tad *noun* (*informal*) a small amount.

tadpole *noun* a young frog or toad that has developed from the egg and lives entirely in water. [from old words *tad* = toad, + *poll* = head]

taekwondo (*say* tuy-kwon-**doh**) *noun* a modern Korean martial art.

TAFE *abbreviation* Technical and Further Education, a system of mainly vocational education and training; an institution providing this.

taffeta *noun* a stiff silky material.

tag¹ *noun* **1** a label tied on or stuck into something. **2** a metal or plastic point at the end of a shoelace. **3** (in computing) a character or set of characters appended to an item of data in order to identify it.

tag² *verb* (**tagged, tagging**) **1** label something with a tag. **2** add as an extra thing, *A postscript was tagged on to her letter.* **3** (*informal*) go with other people, *Her sister tagged along.*

tag³ *noun* a game in which one person chases the others.

tahini *noun* (also **tahina**) a Middle Eastern paste or sauce made from sesame seeds.

t'ai chi (*say* tuy **chee**) *noun* a Chinese martial art and system of exercises with slow controlled movements.

tail¹ *noun* **1** the part that sticks out from the rear end of the body of a bird, fish, or animal. **2** the part at the end or rear of something. **3** the side of a coin opposite the head.

tail² *verb* **1** remove stalks etc. from fruit or vegetables, *top and tail beans.* **2** follow a person or thing. **3** (*Australian*) follow, herd, and tend livestock.
tail off become fewer, smaller, or slighter; cease gradually.

tailless *adjective* without a tail.

tailor¹ *noun* **1** a person who makes men's clothes. **2** a sea fish of Australian waters.

tailor² *verb* **1** make or fit clothes. **2** adapt or make something for a special purpose.

taint¹ *noun* a small amount of decay, pollution, or a bad quality that spoils something.

taint² *verb* give something a taint. [same origin as *tint*]

taipan (*say* **tuy**-pan) *noun* a large venomous Australian snake. [from Wik-Mungkan *thaypan*]

take *verb* (**took, taken, taking**) **1** get something into your hands, *He took the cup.* **2** get possession of something; win, receive, *She took all the prizes.* **3** capture, *They took many prisoners.* **4** make use of; indulge in, *He takes the bus; Let's take a holiday.* **5** carry or convey, *Take this parcel to the post office*; *Take the man to the station.* **6** remove; steal, *Who took my watch?* **7** perform or deal with, *When do you take your music exam?* **8** study or teach a subject, *Who takes you for maths?* **9** make an effort, *take trouble.* **10** experience a feeling, *Don't take offence.* **11** accept; endure, *I'll take a risk.* **12** require, *It takes a strong man to lift this.* **13** write down, *take notes.* **14** make a photograph. **15** subtract, *take 4 from 10.* **16** assume, *I take it that you agree.* **taker** *noun*
take after be like a parent etc.
take away 1 remove something. **2** subtract.
take back withdraw something you have said.
take in 1 understand. **2** deceive somebody.
take leave of say goodbye to.
take off 1 remove clothes. **2** (of an aircraft) leave the ground and become airborne. **3** mimic satirically. **take-off** *noun*
take on 1 begin to employ someone. **2** play or fight against someone. **3** agree to do something.
take out 1 remove something. **2** escort someone on an outing.
take over take control. **takeover** *noun*
take place happen; occur.
take up 1 start something **2** occupy space or time etc. **3** accept an offer.

takeaway *noun* a place that sells cooked meals for customers to take away; a meal from this.

takings *plural noun* money received.

talcum powder *noun* a scented powder put on the skin to make it feel smooth and dry.

tale *noun* a story.

talent *noun* a special or very great ability. **talented** *adjective* [from Greek *talanton* = sum of money]

talisman *noun* (*plural* **talismans**) an object supposed to bring good luck. [from Greek *telesma* = consecrated object]

talk[1] *verb* speak; have a conversation.
talker *noun*
talk down to speak to someone in a way that shows that you feel superior.
talk into persuade by talking.
talk out of dissuade by talking.

talk[2] *noun* **1** talking; a conversation. **2** an informal lecture. **3** rumour or gossip.

talkative *adjective* talking a lot.

tall *adjective* **1** higher than the average, *a tall tree.* **2** measured from the bottom to the top, *It is ten metres tall.* **tallness** *noun*

tallboy *noun* a tall chest of drawers.

tall order *noun* (*informal*) a difficult task.

tallow *noun* animal fat used to make candles, soap, lubricants, etc.

tall poppy *noun* (*Australian informal*) a person who is conspicuously successful and whose distinction frequently attracts envious notice or hostility.

tall story *noun* (*informal*) a story that is hard to believe.

tally[1] *noun* (*plural* **tallies**) the total amount of a debt or score.

tally[2] *verb* (**tallied**, **tallying**) correspond or agree with something else, *Does your list tally with mine?*

Talmud *noun* a collection of writings on Jewish religious law. [from Hebrew = instruction]

talon *noun* a strong claw.

talus *noun* (*plural* **tali**) the ankle bone supporting the tibia (the shin bone).

tamarillo *noun* an egg-shaped acidic red fruit. Also called a *tree tomato.*

tambourine *noun* a circular musical instrument with metal discs round it, tapped or shaken to make it jingle.

tame[1] *adjective* **1** (of animals) gentle and not afraid of people; not wild or dangerous. **2** not exciting; dull. **tamely** *noun*, **tameness** *noun*

tame[2] *verb* (**tamed**, **taming**) make an animal become tame. **tamer** *noun*

Tamil *noun* **1** a member of a people from southern India and Sri Lanka. **2** the language of the Tamils.

tammar *noun* a small greyish-brown wallaby of southern and south-western Australia. [from Noongar *damar*]

tamp *verb* pack or ram down tightly.

tamper *verb* meddle or interfere with something.

tampon *noun* a plug of absorbent material especially to absorb menstrual blood.

tan[1] *noun* **1** a light brown colour. **2** brown colour in skin that has been exposed to sun.

tan[2] *adjective* light brown.

tan[3] *verb* (**tanned**, **tanning**) **1** make or become brown by exposing skin to the sun. **2** make an animal's skin into leather by treating it with chemicals.

tandem *noun* a bicycle for two riders, one behind the other. [Latin, = at length]

tandoori (*say* tan-**door**-ree) *adjective* of a style of Indian cooking based on the use of a clay oven called a tandoor, *tandoori chicken.* **tandoori** *noun* [Urdu from Persian]

tang *noun* a strong flavour or smell.
tangy *adjective*

tangelo *noun* a cross between a tangerine and a grapefruit.

tangent *noun* **1** a straight line that touches the outside of a curve or circle. **2** the ratio of the sides opposite and adjacent to an angle in a right-angled triangle.
at a tangent diverging from a previous course of action or thought, *go off at a tangent.* [from Latin *tangens* = touching]

tangerine *noun* a kind of small orange. [named after Tangier in Morocco]

tangible *adjective* able to be touched; real.
tangibility *noun*, **tangibly** *noun* [from Latin *tangere* = touch]

tangle *verb* (**tangled**, **tangling**) make or become twisted into a confused mass. **tangle** *noun*, **tangled** *adjective*

tango *noun* (*plural* **tangos**) a ballroom dance with gliding steps.

tank *noun* **1** a large container for a liquid or gas. **2** a heavy armoured vehicle used in war. **3** (*Australian*) a reservoir formed by excavation and a dam.

tankard *noun* a large mug for drinking from, usually made of silver or pewter.

tanker *noun* **1** a large ship for carrying oil. **2** a large truck for carrying a liquid.

tanner *noun* a person who tans animal skins into leather. **tannery** *noun*

tannin *noun* a substance obtained from the bark or fruit of various trees (also found in tea), used in tanning and dyeing things.

tantalise *verb* (**tantalised**, **tantalising**) tease or torment a person by showing them something good but keeping it out of reach. [from the name of Tantalus in Greek mythology, who was punished by being made to stand near water and fruit which moved away when he tried to reach them]

tantamount *adjective* equivalent, *The Queen's request was tantamount to a command.* [from Italian *tanto montare* = amount to so much]

tantrum *noun* an outburst of bad temper.

tap[1] *noun* a device for letting out liquid or gas in a controlled flow.

tap[2] *verb* (**tapped**, **tapping**) **1** take liquid out of something, especially through a tap. **2** obtain supplies or information from a source. **3** fix a device to a telephone line so that you can overhear conversations on it.

tap[3] *noun* **1** a quick light hit; the sound of this. **2** tap-dancing.

tap[4] *verb* (**tapped**, **tapping**) hit a person or thing quickly and lightly.

tap and go *noun* a contactless payment system for making payments with a bank card, mobile phone etc. by tapping it on or hovering over a reader at the point of sale.

tap dance *noun* a dance in which rhythms are tapped with the feet, wearing shoes with metal pieces on the toes and heels. **tap-dance** *verb*

tape[1] *noun* **1** a narrow strip of cloth, paper, plastic, etc. **2** a narrow plastic strip coated with a magnetic substance and used for making recordings. **3** a tape recording. **4** a tape measure.

tape[2] *verb* (**taped**, **taping**) **1** fix, cover, or surround something with tape. **2** record something on magnetic tape.

tape measure *noun* a long strip of tape or flexible metal marked in centimetres or inches for measuring things.

taper[1] *verb* make or become narrower gradually.

taper[2] *noun* a very thin candle.

tape recorder *noun* a device for recording sounds or computer data on magnetic tape and reproducing them. **tape recording** *noun*

tapestry *noun* (*plural* **tapestries**) a piece of strong cloth with pictures or patterns woven or embroidered on it. [from French *tapis* = carpet]

tapeworm *noun* a long flat worm that can live as a parasite in the intestines of people and animals.

tapioca *noun* a starchy substance in hard white grains obtained from cassava, used for making puddings.

tapir (*say* **tay**-puh) *noun* a pig-like animal with a long flexible snout.

tar[1] *noun* a thick black liquid made from coal or wood etc. and used in making roads.

tar[2] *verb* (**tarred**, **tarring**) coat something with tar.

tarantula *noun* **1** (*Australian*) a huntsman spider. **2** a large kind of spider found in southern Europe and in tropical countries.

tardy *adjective* (**tardier**, **tardiest**) slow; late. **tardily** *adverb*, **tardiness** *noun* [from Latin *tardus* = slow]

target[1] *noun* **1** something aimed at; a thing that someone tries to hit or reach. **2** a person or thing that people criticise, ridicule, etc.

target[2] *verb* (**targeted**, **targeting**) aim at or have as a target.

tariff *noun* a list of prices or charges.

tarmac *noun* an area surfaced with tarmacadam, especially on an airfield. [*Tarmac* is a trademark]

tarmacadam *noun* (*trademark*) a mixture of tar and broken stone, used for making a hard surface on roads, paths, etc.

tarnish *verb* **1** make or become less shiny, *The silver had tarnished.* **2** spoil; blemish, *The scandal tarnished his reputation.* **tarnish** *noun*

tarpaulin *noun* a large sheet of waterproof canvas. [from *tar* + *pall*[1]]

tarragon *noun* a plant with leaves that are used as a flavouring.

tarry[1] (*say* **tah**-ree) *adjective* of or like tar.

tarry[2] (*say* **ta**-ree) *verb* (**tarried**, **tarrying**) (*old use*) linger.

tarsal[1] *adjective* of the tarsus.

tarsal[2] *noun* one of the tarsal bones.

tarsus *noun* (*plural* **tarsi**) the seven small bones that make up the ankle. [Greek]

tart[1] *noun* a pastry case containing fruit, jam, etc.

tart[2] *adjective* **1** sour. **2** sharp in manner, *a tart reply.* **tartly** *adverb*, **tartness** *noun*

tartan *noun* a pattern with coloured stripes crossing each other, especially one associated with a Scottish clan.

tartar[1] *noun* a person who is fierce or difficult to deal with. [named after the Tartars, warriors from central Asia in the 13th century]

tartar[2] *noun* a hard chalky deposit that forms on teeth. [medieval Latin from Greek]

tartlet *noun* a small pastry tart.

taser *noun* (*trademark*) a weapon firing barbs that cause temporary paralysis.

task *noun* a piece of work to be done. **take a person to task** reprimand or criticise a person severely for a fault or mistake.

taskbar *noun* a bar at the edge of the display of a computer screen that allows quick access to current or favourite applications.

task force *noun* a group specially organised for a particular task.

taskmaster *noun* a person imposing tasks on others, *a hard taskmaster.*

Tasmanian devil *noun* a small black carnivorous marsupial found in Tasmania.

Tasmanian tiger *noun* an extinct carnivorous marsupial with brown-striped sandy fur; a thylacine.

tassel *noun* a bundle of threads tied together at the top and used to decorate something. **tasselled** *adjective*

taste[1] *verb* (**tasted**, **tasting**) **1** take a small amount of food or drink to try its flavour. **2** be able to perceive flavours. **3** have a certain flavour.

taste[2] *noun* **1** the feeling caused in the tongue by something placed on it. **2** the ability to taste things. **3** the ability to enjoy beautiful things or to choose what is suitable, *Her choice of clothes shows her good taste.* **4** a liking, *He always had a taste for camping.* **5** a very small amount of food or drink.

tasteful *adjective* showing good taste. **tastefully** *adverb*, **tastefulness** *noun*

tasteless *adjective* **1** having no flavour. **2** showing poor taste. **tastelessly** *adverb*, **tastelessness** *noun*

tasty *adjective* (**tastier**, **tastiest**) having a strong pleasant taste.

tattered *adjective* badly torn; ragged.

tatters *plural noun* rags; badly torn pieces, *My coat was in tatters.*

tatting *noun* a kind of handmade lace.

tattle *verb* (**tattled**, **tattling**) gossip. **tattle** *noun*

tattoo[1] *verb* mark a person's skin with a picture or pattern by using a needle and some dye.

tattoo[2] *noun* a tattooed mark.

tattoo[3] *noun* **1** a drumming or tapping sound. **2** an entertainment consisting of military music and marching.

tatty *adjective* **1** ragged; shabby and untidy. **2** cheap and gaudy. **tattily** *adverb*, **tattiness** *noun*

taught *past tense & past participle* of **teach**.

taunt *verb* jeer at or insult someone. **taunt** *noun* [from French *tant pour tant* = tit for tat]

taupe (*say* tawp or tohp) *noun & adjective* brownish-grey.

Taurus *noun* **1** a constellation and the second sign of the zodiac (the Bull). **2** a person born when the sun is in this sign. [Latin = bull]

taut *adjective* stretched tightly. **tautly** *adverb*, **tautness** *noun*

tauten *verb* make or become taut.

tautology *noun* (*plural* **tautologies**) saying the same thing again in different words, e.g. *You can get the book free for nothing* (where *free* and *for nothing* mean the same). [from Greek *tauto* = the same, + *logos* = word]

tavern *noun* (*old use*) an inn or public house. [from Latin *taberna* = hut]

tawdry *adjective* cheap and gaudy. **tawdriness** *noun* [from *St Audrey's lace* (cheap finery formerly sold at St Audrey's fair at Ely, England)]

tawny *adjective* brownish-yellow.

tax[1] *noun* (*plural* **taxes**) **1** money that people or business firms have to pay to the government, to be used for public purposes. **2** a strain or burden, *The long walk was a tax on his strength.*

tax[2] *verb* **1** put a tax on something. **2** charge someone a tax. **3** put a strain or burden on a person or thing, *Will it tax your strength?* **4** accuse, *I taxed him with leaving the door open.* **taxable** *adjective*, **taxation** *noun*, **taxing** *adjective* [from Latin *taxare* = calculate]

taxi[1] *noun* (*plural* **taxis**) a car that carries passengers for payment, usually with a meter to record the fare payable. **taxicab** *noun* [short for *taximeter cab*]

taxi[2] *verb* (**taxied**, **taxiing**) (of an aircraft) move along the ground or water, especially before or after flying.

taxidermist *noun* a person who prepares and stuffs the skins of animals in a lifelike form. **taxidermy** *noun* [from Greek *taxis* = arrangement, + *derma* = skin]

taxpayer *noun* a person who pays tax.

TB *abbreviation* tuberculosis.

TBA *abbreviation* (also **tba**) to be announced.

T-bone *noun* a T-shaped bone, especially in a steak.

tbsp *abbreviation* tablespoonful.

TCP/IP *abbreviation* (*trademark*) transmission control protocol/Internet protocol, used to govern the connection of computer systems to the Internet.

tea *noun* **1** a drink made by pouring hot water on the dried leaves of an evergreen shrub (the *tea plant*). **2** these dried leaves. **3** a meal in the afternoon or evening at which tea is served (often the main evening meal). [from Chinese *t'e*]

tea bag *noun* a small bag holding about a teaspoonful of tea.

teach *verb* (**taught**, **teaching**) **1** give a person knowledge or skill; train. **2** give lessons, especially in a particular subject. **3** show someone what to do or avoid, *That will teach you not to meddle.*

teachable *adjective* able to be taught.

teacher *noun* a person who teaches others, especially in a school.

teaching *noun* **1** the profession of a teacher. **2** what is taught, *the Church's teachings.*

teacup *noun* a cup for drinking tea.

teak *noun* the hard strong wood of an evergreen Asian tree.

teal *noun* (*plural* **teal**) a kind of duck.

team[1] *noun* **1** a set of players forming one side in certain games and sports. **2** a set of people working together. **3** two or more animals harnessed to pull a vehicle or a plough etc. **teamwork** *noun*

team[2] *verb* put together in a team; combine.

teammate *noun* (also **team-mate**) a fellow member of a team or group.

teapot *noun* a pot with a lid and a handle, for making and pouring tea.

tear[1] (*say* teer) *noun* a drop of the water that comes from the eyes when a person cries. **teardrop** *noun*
in tears crying.

tear[2] (*say* tair) *verb* (**tore**, **torn**, **tearing**) **1** pull something apart or into pieces. **2** become torn, *Newspaper tears easily.* **3** run or travel hurriedly. **4** pull something away.

tear[3] *noun* a split made by tearing.

tearful *adjective* in tears; crying easily. **tearfully** *adverb*

tear gas *noun* a gas that makes people's eyes water painfully.

tease[1] *verb* (**teased**, **teasing**) **1** amuse yourself by deliberately annoying or making fun of someone. **2** pick threads apart into separate strands.

tease[2] *noun* a person who often teases others.

teasel *noun* a plant with bristly heads formerly used to brush up the surface of cloth. [from *tease*[1] 2]

teaser *noun* a difficult problem.

teaspoon *noun* a small spoon for stirring tea etc. **teaspoonful** *noun*

teat *noun* **1** a nipple through which a baby sucks milk. **2** the cap of a baby's feeding-bottle.

tea towel *noun* a cloth for drying washed dishes, cutlery, etc.

tea-tree *noun* any of various Australian shrubs with aromatic leaves. [so called because the leaves of some species were used as a substitute for tea]

technical *adjective* **1** concerned with technology. **2** of a particular subject and its methods, *the technical terms of chemistry.* **technically** *adverb* [from Greek *technikos* = skilful]

technicality *noun* (*plural* **technicalities**) **1** being technical. **2** a technical word or phrase; a special detail.

technician *noun* **1** an expert in the techniques of a particular subject or craft. **2** a skilled mechanic.

technique *noun* the method of doing something skilfully.

techno *noun* a style of music making extensive use of electronic instruments and synthesised sound.

techno- *prefix* relating to technology or its use (as in *technology*). [from Greek *techne* = skill]

technology *noun* (*plural* **technologies**) **1** the application of scientific knowledge for practical purposes, especially in industry. **2** machinery and equipment developed from such scientific knowledge. **technological** *adverb*, **technologist** *noun* [from Greek *techne*, + *-logy*]

teddy bear *noun* a soft furry toy bear. [named after US president Theodore ('Teddy') Roosevelt in about 1906]

tedious *adjective* annoyingly slow or long; boring. **tediously** *adverb*, **tediousness** *noun*, **tedium** *noun* [from Latin *taedium* = tiredness]

tee[1] *noun* **1** the flat area from which golfers strike the ball at the start of play for each hole. **2** a small piece of wood or plastic on which the ball is placed for being struck.

tee[2] *verb* (**teed**, **teeing**) place a ball on a tee in golf.
tee off play the ball from the tee.
tee up (*informal*) arrange.

teem *verb* **1** be full of something, *The river was teeming with fish.* **2** rain very hard; pour.

teen *noun* **1** (also **teens**) the time of life from 13 to 19 years of age. **2** (*informal*) a teenager.

teenage *adjective* of teenagers.

teenaged *adjective* in your teens.

teenager *noun* a person aged between 13 and 19 years.

teeny *adjective* (**teenier**, **teeniest**) (*informal*) tiny.

teeter *verb* stand or move unsteadily.

teeth *plural* of **tooth**.

teething *noun* (of a baby) having its first teeth beginning to grow through the gums.

teetotal *adjective* never drinking alcohol. **teetotaller** *noun*

teflon *noun* (*trademark*) a non-stick coating for kitchen utensils.

telco *noun* (*plural* **telcos**) a telecommunications company.

tele- *prefix* far; at a distance (as in *telescope*). [from Greek *tele* = far off]

telecast[1] *noun* a television broadcast.

telecast[2] *verb* transmit by television.

telecommunication *noun* communication over a distance by cable, the Internet, telephone, or broadcasting.

telegram *noun* a message sent by telegraph. [from *tele-* + *-gram*]

telegraph *noun* a way of sending messages from a distance, especially by using electric current along wires. **telegraphic** *adverb*, **telegraphy** *noun* [from *tele-* + *-graph*]

telehealth *noun* the provision of healthcare remotely by means of telecommunications technology. [from *tele-*+ *health*]

telemarketing *noun* attempting to sell goods or services by telephone. **telemarketer** *noun*

telepathy (*say* tuh-**lep**-uh-thee) *noun* communication of thoughts from one person's mind to another without speaking, writing, or gestures. **telepathic** *adjective* [from *tele-*, + Greek *pathos* = feeling]

telephone[1] *noun* a device or system using electric wires or radio etc. to enable one person to speak to another who is some distance away.

telephone[2] *verb* (**telephoned**, **telephoning**) speak to a person on the telephone. [from *tele-*, + Greek *phone* = voice]

telephonist (*say* tuh-**lef**-uh-nuhst) *noun* a person who operates a telephone switchboard.

telephoto lens *noun* a lens producing a large image of a distant object that is photographed.

telescope[1] *noun* an instrument using lenses to magnify distant objects. **telescopic** *adjective* [from *tele-*, + Greek *skopein* = look at]

telescope[2] *verb* (**telescoped**, **telescoping**) **1** make or become shorter by sliding overlapping sections into each other. **2** compress or condense so as to take less space or time.

televise *verb* (**televised**, **televising**) broadcast something by television.

television *noun* **1** a system for transmitting visual images with sound and reproducing them on a screen. **2** an apparatus for receiving these pictures. **3** televised programs. [from *tele-* + *vision*]

telex *noun* **1** a system for sending printed messages by telegraphy. **2** a message sent or received by telex. **telex** *verb*

tell *verb* (**told**, **telling**) **1** make a thing known to someone, especially by words. **2** speak, *Tell the truth.* **3** order, *Tell them to wait.* **4** reveal a secret, *Promise you won't tell*; *We won't tell on you.* **5** decide; distinguish, *Can you tell the difference between butter and margarine?* **6** produce an effect, *The strain began to tell on him.* **7** count, *There are ten of them, all told.*
tell off (*informal*) reprimand.

teller *noun* a bank cashier.

telling *adjective* having a strong effect, *a very telling reply.*

telltale[1] *noun* a person who tells tales.

telltale[2] *adjective* revealing or indicating something, *There was a telltale spot of jam on her chin.*

telly *noun* (*plural* **tellies**) (*informal*) **1** television. **2** a television set.

temerity (*say* tuh-**me**-ruh-tee) *noun* rashness; boldness.

temper[1] *noun* **1** a person's mood, *He is in a good temper.* **2** an angry mood, *She was in a temper.*
lose your temper lose your calmness and become angry.

temper[2] *verb* **1** harden or strengthen metal by heating and cooling it. **2** moderate or soften the effects of something, *tempering justice with mercy.* [from Latin *temperare* = mix]

temperament *noun* a person's or animal's nature as shown in the way they usually behave, *a nervous temperament.*

temperamental *adjective* **1** of a person's temperament. **2** likely to become excitable or moody suddenly. **temperamentally** *adverb*

temperance *noun* **1** moderation; self-restraint. **2** drinking little or no alcohol.

temperate *adjective* neither extremely hot nor extremely cold, *Tasmania has a temperate climate.*

temperature *noun* **1** how hot or cold a person or thing is. **2** an abnormally high temperature of the body.

tempest *noun* a violent storm. [from Latin *tempestas* = weather]

tempestuous *adjective* stormy; full of commotion.

template *noun* **1** a piece of rigid material used as a pattern or guide for cutting metal, wood, fabric, etc. **2** something serving as a model or base for producing other similar things.

temple[1] *noun* a building where a god is worshipped. [from Latin *templum* = consecrated place]

temple[2] *noun* the part of the head between the forehead and the ear. [from Latin *tempora* = sides of the head]

tempo *noun* (*plural* **tempos** or **tempi**) the speed or rhythm of something, especially of a piece of music. [Italian, from Latin *tempus* = time]

temporal *adjective* **1** secular; of worldly affairs as opposed to spiritual. **2** of or denoting time. **3** of the temples of the head.

temporary *adjective* lasting for a limited time only; not permanent. **temporarily** *adverb* [from Latin *temporis* = of a time]

temporise *verb* (**temporised**, **temporising**) avoid giving a definite answer, in order to postpone something.

tempt *verb* try to persuade or attract someone, especially into doing something wrong or unwise. **temptation** *adverb*, **tempter** *noun*, **tempting** *adjective*, **temptress** *noun* [from Latin *temptare* = test]

tempura (*say* tem-**poo**-ruh) *noun* a Japanese dish of fish, shellfish, etc., fried in batter.

ten *noun & adjective* the number 10; one more than nine.

tenable *adjective* able to be held, *a tenable theory; the job is tenable for one year only.* [from Latin *tenere* = to hold]

tenacious (*say* tuh-**nay**-shuhs) *adjective* **1** holding or clinging firmly to something. **2** persistent; determined. **tenaciously** *adverb*, **tenacity** *noun*

tenant *noun* a person who rents a house, building, or land etc. from a landlord. **tenancy** *noun* [from Latin *tenens* = holding]

tend[1] *verb* have a certain tendency, *Prices tend to rise.* [from Latin *tendere* = stretch]

tend[2] *verb* look after, *Shepherds were tending their sheep.* [from *attend*]

tendency *noun* (*plural* **tendencies**) the way a person or thing is likely to behave, *She has a tendency to be lazy.*

tender[1] *adjective* **1** easy to chew; not tough or hard. **2** easily hurt or damaged; sensitive; delicate, *tender plants.* **3** gentle and loving, *a tender smile.* **tenderly** *adverb*, **tenderness** *noun* [from Latin *tener* = soft]

tender[2] *verb* offer something formally, *He tendered his resignation.*

tender[3] *noun* a formal offer to supply goods or carry out work at a stated price, *The council asked for tenders to build a library.* **legal tender** kinds of money that are legal for making payments, *Are two-cent coins still legal tender?* [same origin as *tend*[1]]

tender[4] *noun* **1** a truck attached to a steam locomotive to carry its coal and water. **2** a small boat carrying stores or passengers to and from a larger one. [from *tend*[2]]

tender-hearted *adjective* compassionate.

tendon *noun* a strong strip of tissue that joins muscle to bone.

tendril *noun* **1** a threadlike part by which a climbing plant clings to a support. **2** a thin curl of hair etc.

tenement *noun* a large house or building divided into flats or rooms that are let to separate tenants.

tenet (*say* **ten**-uht) *noun* a firm belief held by a person or group. [Latin, = he or she holds]

tennis *noun* a game played with rackets and a ball on a court with a net across the middle. [from French *tenez!* = receive (called by the person serving)]

tenor *noun* **1** the general routine or course of something, *disrupting the even tenor of her life.* **2** the general meaning or drift, *the tenor of his speech.* **3** a male singer with a high voice. **4** a musical instrument with approximately the range of a tenor voice.

tenpin bowling *noun* a game in which players try to knock down a set of ten pins by rolling a ball towards them.

tense[1] *noun* the form of a verb that shows when something happens, e.g. *she came* (**past tense**), *she comes* or *is coming* (**present tense**), *she will come* (**future tense**). [from Latin *tempus* = time]

tense[2] *adjective* **1** tightly stretched. **2** with muscles tight because you are nervous or excited; unable to relax. **3** causing tenseness, *a tense situation.* **tensely** *adverb*, **tenseness** *noun*

tense[3] *verb* (**tensed**, **tensing**) make or become tense. [from Latin *tensum* = stretched]

tensile *adjective* **1** of tension. **2** able to be stretched.

tension *noun* **1** pulling so as to stretch something; being stretched. **2** tenseness; the condition when feelings are tense. **3** voltage, *high-tension cables.*

tent *noun* a shelter made of canvas or other material. [same origin as *tense*[3]]

tentacle *noun* a long flexible part of the body of certain animals (e.g. octopuses), used for feeling or grasping things or for moving.

tentative *adjective* cautious; trying something out, *a tentative suggestion.* **tentatively** *adverb* [same origin as *tempt*]

tenterhooks *plural noun* **on tenterhooks** tense and anxious. [from *tenter* = a machine with hooks for stretching cloth to dry]

tenth *adjective & noun* next after the ninth.

tenuous *adjective* very slight or thin, *tenuous threads; a tenuous connection.* [from Latin *tenuis* = thin]

tenure (*say* **ten**-yuh) *noun* the holding of office or of land, accommodation, etc.

tepee (*say* **tee**-pee) *noun* a conical tent, traditionally used by some indigenous North Americans.

tepid *adjective* only slightly warm; lukewarm, *tepid water.*

terabyte *noun* (in computing) one thousand gigabytes.

teriyaki (*say* te-ree-**yah**-kee) *noun* a Japanese dish of grilled marinated meat or fish.

term[1] *noun* **1** the period of weeks when a school or college is open. **2** a definite period, *a term of imprisonment.* **3** a word or expression, *technical terms.* **4** each of the quantities in a ratio, series, or mathematical expression.

term[2] *verb* name; call by a certain term, *This music is termed jazz.* [from Latin *terminus* = boundary]

termagant *noun* a shrewish bullying woman.

terminable *adjective* able to be terminated.

terminal[1] *noun* **1** the place where something ends; a terminus. **2** a building where air passengers arrive or depart. **3** a place where a wire is connected in an electric circuit or battery. **4** a device for sending information to a computer, or for receiving it.

terminal[2] *adjective* **1** of or at the end or boundary of something. **2** of or in the last stage of a fatal disease, *terminal cancer.* **terminally** *adverb*

terminate *verb* (**terminated**, **terminating**) end; stop finally. **termination** *noun* [same origin as *terminus*]

terminology *noun* the technical terms of a subject. **terminological** *adjective* [from *term* + *-logy*]

terminus *noun* (*plural* **termini**) the end of something; the last station on a railway or bus route. [Latin, = the end]

termite *noun* a small insect that is very destructive to timber.

terms *plural noun* **1** a relationship between people, *They are on friendly terms.* **2** conditions offered or accepted, *peace terms.*

tern *noun* a sea bird with long wings.

terrace *noun* **1** a level area on a slope or hillside. **2** a paved area beside a house. **3** a row of houses joined together. **terraced** *adjective* [from Latin *terra* = earth]

terracotta *noun* **1** a kind of pottery. **2** the brownish-red colour of flowerpots. [Italian, = baked earth]

terra firma *noun* dry land; the ground. [Latin, = firm land]

terrain *noun* a stretch of land, *hilly terrain.* [from Latin *terra* = earth]

terra nullius *noun* land belonging to no one. [Latin]

terrapin *noun* an edible freshwater turtle of North America.

terrestrial *adjective* **1** of the earth. **2** of land; living on land. [from Latin *terra* = earth]

terrible *adjective* very bad; distressing. **terribly** *adverb* [from Latin *terrere* = frighten]

terrier *noun* a kind of small lively dog.

terrific *adjective* (*informal*) **1** very great, *a terrific storm.* **2** excellent. **terrifically** *adverb*

terrify *verb* (**terrified**, **terrifying**) fill someone with terror.

territory *noun* (*plural* **territories**) **1** an area of land, especially one that belongs to a country or person. **2** an organised division of a country, especially one not yet admitted to the full rights of a state, *the Australian Capital Territory.* **3** (**the Territory**) the Northern Territory. **territorial** *adjective* [from Latin *terra* = earth]

terror *noun* **1** very great fear. **2** a terrifying person or thing. [from Latin *terrere* = frighten]

terrorise *verb* (**terrorised**, **terrorising**) fill someone with terror; control or compel someone by frightening them. **terrorisation** *noun*

terrorism *noun* the use of violence and intimidation, especially for political purposes.

terrorist *noun* a person who uses or favours violent and intimidating methods of coercing a government or community.

terse *adjective* concise; curt. **tersely** *adverb*, **terseness** *noun* [from Latin *tersum* = polished]

tertiary (*say* **ter**-shuh-ree) *adjective* of the third stage of something; coming after secondary. [from Latin *tertius* = third]

tessellate *verb* (**tessellated**, **tessellating**) fit shapes into a pattern without overlapping. **tessellation** *noun*

test[1] *noun* **1** a short examination; a way of discovering the qualities or abilities etc. of a person or thing. **2** (also **test match**) an international cricket match.

test[2] *verb* make a test of a person or thing. **tester** *noun*

testament *noun* **1** a written statement. **2** either of the two main parts of the Bible, the Old Testament or the New Testament. [from Latin *testis* = witness]

testator *noun* a person who has made a will.

testicle *noun* either of the two glands in the scrotum where semen is produced.

testify *verb* (**testified**, **testifying**) give evidence; swear that something is true. [from Latin *testis* = witness]

testimonial *noun* **1** a letter describing someone's abilities, character, or qualifications. **2** a gift presented to someone as a mark of respect.

testimony *noun* (*plural* **testimonies**) **1** what someone testifies. **2** evidence in support of something.

testosterone *noun* a male sex hormone formed in the testicles.

test tube *noun* a tube of thin glass with one end closed, used for scientific experiments.

testy *adjective* easily annoyed; irritable.

tetanus *noun* a disease that makes the muscles become stiff, caused by bacteria. [from Greek *tetanos* = a spasm]

tête-à-tête (*say* tay-tah-**tayt**) *noun* a private conversation, especially between two people. [French, = head to head]

tether[1] *verb* **1** tie an animal so that it cannot move far. **2** use a smartphone in order to connect a computer or other device to the Internet.

tether[2] *noun* a rope for tethering an animal. **at the end of your tether** unable to endure something anymore.

tetra- *prefix* four. [Greek, = four]

tetrahedron *noun* a solid with four sides (e.g. a pyramid with a triangular base). [from *tetra-*, + Greek *hedra* = base]

text[1] *noun* **1** the words of something written or printed. **2** a book or play etc. prescribed for study. **3** a sentence from the Bible used as the subject of a sermon etc. **4** (in computing) data in the form of words or alphabetic characters. **5** a text message. **textual** *adjective* [from Latin *textus* = literary style]

text[2] *verb* send someone a text message.

texta *noun* (*Australian trademark*) a pen with a felt or fibre tip.

textbook *noun* a book that teaches you about a subject.

textiles *plural noun* kinds of cloth; fabrics. [from Latin *textum* = woven]

text message *noun* an electronic communication sent and received by mobile phone.

texture *noun* the way that the surface of something feels.

thalidomide *noun* a medicinal drug that was found to have caused malformation of the limbs of babies whose mothers took it during pregnancy.

than *conjunction* compared with another person or thing, *His brother is taller than he is* or *taller than him.*

> **Usage** Do not confuse *than* with *then.*

thank *verb* express gratitude to someone, especially by saying 'thank you'. **thank you** a polite expression used when acknowledging a gift, service, or compliment, or accepting or refusing an offer.

thankful *adjective* grateful. **thankfully** *adverb*

thankless *adjective* not likely to win thanks from people, *a thankless task.*

thanks *plural noun* **1** statements of gratitude. **2** (*informal*) thank you. **thanks to** as a result of; because of, *Thanks to your help, we succeeded.*

thanksgiving *noun* an expression of gratitude, especially to God.

that[1] *adjective & pronoun* (*plural* **those**) the one there, *That book is mine*; *Whose is that?*

that[2] *adverb* to such an extent, *I'll come that far but no further.*

that[3] *relative pronoun* which, who, or whom, *This is the book that I wanted*; *We liked the people that we met on holiday.*

> **Usage** See the note at *which.*

that[4] *conjunction* used to introduce a wish, reason, result, etc., *I hope that you are well; The puzzle was so hard that no one could solve it.*

thatch *noun* straw or reeds used to make a roof. **thatch** *verb*

thaw *verb* melt; stop being frozen. **thaw** *noun*

the *adjective* (called the *definite article*) a particular one; that or those, *The dog next door came into our yard*; *How did the game go?*

theatre *noun* **1** a building where plays etc. are performed to an audience. **2** a special room where surgical operations are done, *the operating theatre.* [from Greek *theatron* = place for seeing things]

theatrical *adjective* of plays or acting. **theatrically** *adverb*, **theatricals** *plural noun*

thee *pronoun* (*old use*) the form of *thou* used as the object of a verb or after a preposition.

theft *noun* stealing.

their *adjective* **1** belonging to or associated with the people or things previously mentioned or easily identified, *Their jumpers are in the washing machine.* **2** belonging to or associated with a person of unspecified sex, *Somebody has left their jumper on the bus.*

> **Usage** See the note at *they.*

theirs *possessive pronoun* belonging to them, *These coats are theirs.*

> **Usage** It is incorrect to write *their's.*

them *pronoun* **1** the form of *they* used as the object of a verb or after a preposition, *We saw them.* **2** referring to a person of unspecified sex, *How well do you have to know someone before you call them a friend?*

> **Usage** See the note at *they.*

theme *noun* **1** the subject about which a person speaks, writes, or thinks. **2** a melody. **thematic** *adjective*, **thematically** *adverb*

themselves *pronoun* **1** they or them and nobody else, used to refer back to the

subject of a verb, *They have hurt themselves.* **2** used instead of 'himself' or 'herself' to refer to a person of unspecified sex, *This is a movie for anyone who considers themselves a fan of thrillers.*
by themselves on their own; alone, *They did the work all by themselves.*

> **Usage** See the note at *they*.

then *adverb* **1** at that time, *We were younger then.* **2** after that; next, *Make the tea, then pour it out.* **3** in that case, *If this is yours, then this must be mine.*

thence *adverb* from that place.

theology *noun* the study of religion. **theologian** *noun*, **theological** *adjective* [from Greek *theos* = a god, + *-logy*]

theorem *noun* a mathematical statement that can be proved by reasoning. [from Greek *theorema* = theory]

theoretical *adjective* based on theory not on experience. **theoretically** *adverb*

theorise *verb* (**theorised**, **theorising**) form a theory or theories.

theory *noun* (*plural* **theories**) **1** an idea or set of ideas formulated (by reasoning from known facts) to explain something, *the theory of evolution.* **2** an opinion or supposition. **3** ideas (contrasted with *practice*). **4** the principles of a subject.

therapeutic (*say* the-ruh-**pyoo**-tik) *adjective* **1** treating or curing a disease; administered or applied for reasons of health. **2** soothing; conducive to well-being.

therapy *noun* the treatment of physical or mental disorders, other than by surgery. **therapist** *noun* [from Greek *therapeia* = healing]

there *adverb* **1** in or to that place etc., *They went to Brisbane and stayed there for a week.* **2** used to call attention to something (*There's a good boy!*) or to introduce a sentence where the verb comes before its subject (*There was plenty to eat*).

thereabouts *adverb* near there.

thereafter *adverb* from then or there onwards.

thereby *adverb* by that means; because of that.

therefore *adverb* for that reason.

therm *noun* a unit for measuring heat, especially from gas. [from Greek *therme* = heat]

thermal *adjective* **1** of heat; worked by heat. **2** hot, *thermal springs.*

thermo- *prefix* heat.

thermodynamics *noun* the science dealing with the relation between heat and other forms of energy.

thermometer *noun* a device for measuring temperature. [from *thermo-* + *meter*]

thermos *noun* (*trademark*) a kind of vacuum flask.

thermostat *noun* a device that automatically keeps the temperature of a room or device steady. **thermostatic** *adjective*, **thermostatically** *adverb* [from *thermo-*, + Greek *statos* = standing]

thesaurus (*say* thuh-**saw**-ruhs) *noun* (*plural* **thesauruses** or **thesauri**) a kind of dictionary in which words with similar meanings are listed in groups together, instead of one long list in alphabetical order. [from Greek, = treasury]

these *plural* of **this**[1].

thesis *noun* (*plural* **theses**) a theory put forward, especially a long essay written by a candidate for a university degree. [from Greek, = placing]

thews *plural noun* (*literary*) muscles; muscular strength.

they *pronoun* **1** the people or things being talked about. **2** people in general, *They say the show is a great success.* **3** used to refer to a person of unspecified gender, *ask a friend if they could help.*

> **Usage** The use of *they* (and its counterparts *them*, *their*, and *themselves*) as a singular pronoun (see sense 3) is now well established. It is particularly useful when the sex of the person is unspecified or unknown.

they'd **1** they had, *they'd lost their way.* **2** they would, *they'd arrive tomorrow.*

they'll they will, *they'll be here soon.*

they're they are, *they're happy.*

they've they have, *they've run out of money.*

thiamine *noun* a vitamin of the B group, important in energy production and for healthy muscles and nerves, found in unrefined cereals, beans, and liver.

thick *adjective* **1** measuring a lot or a certain amount between opposite surfaces. **2** (of a line) broad, not fine. **3** crowded with things; dense, *a thick forest*; *thick fog.* **4** fairly stiff, *thick cream.* **5** (*informal*) stupid. **thickly** *adverb*, **thickness** *noun*

thicken *verb* make or become thicker.

thicket *noun* a number of shrubs and small trees growing close together.

thickset *adjective* **1** with parts placed or growing close together. **2** having a stocky or burly body.

thief *noun* (*plural* **thieves**) a person who steals things. **thievery** *noun*, **thieving** *noun*, **thievish** *adjective*

thigh *noun* the part of the leg between the hip and the knee.

thimble *noun* a small metal or plastic cap worn on the end of the finger to push the needle in sewing.

thin[1] *adjective* (**thinner, thinnest**) **1** not thick; not fat. **2** made of thin material, *thin curtains.* **3** lean; not plump. **4** not dense or plentiful, *thin hair.* **5** runny, *thin soup.* **6** feeble, *a thin excuse.* **thinly** *adverb*, **thinness** *noun*

thin[2] *verb* (**thinned, thinning**) make or become less thick. **thinner** *noun*

thine *adjective & possessive pronoun* (*old use*) belonging to thee.

thing *noun* **1** an object; that which can be seen, touched, thought about, etc. **2** an act, fact, idea, event, etc., *a funny thing to happen; things to discuss.*
things *plural noun* **1** personal belongings. **2** circumstances or conditions.

think *verb* (**thought, thinking**) **1** use your mind; form connected ideas. **2** have as an idea or opinion, *We think we shall win.* **thinker** *noun*
think up (*informal*) devise, *Can you think up a plan to get us out of here?*

think tank *noun* a group providing ideas and advice on national or commercial problems.

third[1] *adjective* next after the second. **thirdly** *adverb*

third[2] *noun* **1** the third person or thing. **2** one of three equal parts of something.

third-degree burn *noun* a burn of the most severe kind.

third-party insurance *noun* insurance covering damage or injury suffered by a person other than the insured.

third party *noun* a person or group besides the two primarily involved in a situation.

third person see **person**.

Third World *noun* the developing countries of Asia, Africa, and Latin America.

thirst *noun* **1** a feeling of dryness in the mouth and throat, causing a desire to drink. **2** a strong desire, *a thirst for adventure.* **thirstily** *adverb*, **thirsty** *adjective*

thirteen *noun & adjective* the number 13; one more than twelve. **thirteenth** *adjective & noun*

thirty *noun & adjective* (*plural* **thirties**) the number 30; three times ten. **thirtieth** *adjective & noun*

this[1] *adjective & pronoun* (*plural* **these**) the one here, *This house is ours; Whose is this?*

this[2] *adverb* to such an extent, *I'm surprised he got this far.*

thistle *noun* a prickly wild plant with purple, white, or yellow flowers.

thistledown *noun* the very light fluff on thistle seeds.

thither *adverb* (*old use*) to that place.

thong *noun* **1** a narrow strip of leather etc. used for fastening things. **2** (*Australian*) a light backless sandal with a thong between the big toe and the other toes.

thorax *noun* (*plural* **thoraxes**) the part of the body between the head or neck and the abdomen. **thoracic** *adjective* [Greek, = breastplate]

thorn *noun* a small pointed growth on the stem of a plant.

thorny *adjective* (**thornier, thorniest**) **1** having many thorns. **2** like a thorn. **3** difficult, *a thorny problem.*

thorough *adjective* **1** done or doing things carefully and in detail. **2** complete in every way, *a thorough mess.* **thoroughly** *adverb*, **thoroughness** *noun*

thoroughbred *adjective* bred of pure or pedigree stock. **thoroughbred** *noun*

thoroughfare *noun* a public road or path that is open at both ends.

those *plural* of **that**[1].

thou *pronoun* (*old use*, in speaking to one person) you.

though[1] *conjunction* in spite of the fact that; even if, *We must look for it, though we probably shan't find it.*

though[2] *adverb* however, *She's right, though.*

thought[1] *noun* **1** something that you think; an idea or opinion. **2** the process of thinking, *She was deep in thought.*

thought[2] *past tense & past participle* of **think**.

thoughtful *adjective* **1** thinking a lot. **2** showing thought for other people's needs; considerate. **thoughtfully** *adverb*, **thoughtfulness** *noun*

thoughtless *adjective* **1** careless; not thinking of what may happen. **2** inconsiderate. **thoughtlessly** *adverb*, **thoughtlessness** *noun*

thousand *noun & adjective* the number 1000; ten hundred. **thousandth** *adjective & noun*

thrall *noun* slavery; servitude, *in thrall.*

thrash *verb* **1** beat with a stick or whip; keep hitting very hard. **2** defeat someone thoroughly. **3** move violently, *The crocodile thrashed its tail.*
thrash out discuss something thoroughly.

thread[1] *noun* **1** a thin length of any substance. **2** a length of spun cotton, wool, etc. used for making cloth or in sewing or knitting. **3** the spiral ridge round a screw. **4** a theme or characteristic running throughout a situation or piece of writing, *Bravery is the common thread in her latest book.* **5** (in online communication) a sequence of linked posts or messages.

thread[2] *verb* **1** put a thread through the eye of a needle. **2** pass a strip of film etc. through or round something. **3** put beads on a thread.

threadbare *adjective* (of cloth) with the surface worn away so that the threads show.

threat *noun* **1** a warning that you will punish, hurt, or harm a person or thing. **2** a sign of something undesirable. **3** a person or thing causing danger.

threaten *verb* **1** make threats against someone. **2** be a threat or danger to a person or thing.

three *noun & adjective* the number 3; one more than two.

three-dimensional *adjective* (also **3D**) having three dimensions (length, width, and height or depth).

thresh *verb* beat wheat etc. so as to separate the grain from the husks.

threshold *noun* **1** a slab of stone or board etc. forming the bottom of a doorway; the entrance. **2** the beginning, *We are on the threshold of a great discovery.*

threw *past tense* of **throw**.

thrice *adverb* (*old use*) three times.

thrift *noun* **1** being economical with money or resources. **2** a plant with pink flowers. **thriftily** *adverb*, **thrifty** *adjective* [same origin as *thrive*]

thrill[1] *noun* a feeling of excitement.

thrill[2] *verb* feel or cause someone to feel a thrill. **thrilling** *adjective*

thriller *noun* **1** an exciting story, play, or film, usually about crime. **2** a very exciting contest or experience.

thrive *verb* (**thrived** or **throve**, **thrived** or **thriven**, **thriving**) grow strongly; prosper or be successful. [from Old Norse *thrifask* = prosper]

throat *noun* **1** the tube in the neck that takes food and drink down into the body. **2** the front of the neck.

throaty *adjective* **1** produced deep in the throat, *a throaty chuckle.* **2** hoarse. **throatily** *adverb*

throb *verb* (**throbbed**, **throbbing**) beat or vibrate with a strong rhythm, *My heart throbbed.* **throb** *noun*

throes *plural noun* severe pangs of pain.
in the throes of (*informal*) struggling with, *We are in the throes of exams.*

thrombosis *noun* the formation of a clot of blood in the body. [from Greek *thrombos* = lump]

throne *noun* a special chair for a king, queen, or bishop at ceremonies. [from Greek *thronos* = high seat]

throng[1] *noun* a crowd of people.

throng[2] *verb* crowd, *People thronged the streets.*

throttle[1] *noun* a device controlling the flow of fuel to an engine; an accelerator.

throttle[2] *verb* (**throttled**, **throttling**) strangle.

through[1] *preposition* **1** from one end or side to the other end or side of, *Climb through the window.* **2** by means of; because of, *We lost it through carelessness.* **3** at the end of; having finished successfully, *He is through his exam.*

through[2] *adverb* **1** through something, *We squeezed through.* **2** with a telephone connection made, *I'll put you through to the manager.* **3** finished, *Wait till I'm through with these papers.*

through[3] *adjective* **1** going through something, *No through road.* **2** going all the way to a destination without a change of line or vehicle, *a through train.*

throughout *preposition & adverb* all the way through.

throve *past tense* of **thrive**.

throw *verb* (**threw**, **thrown**, **throwing**) **1** send a person or thing through the air. **2** put carelessly or hastily. **3** move part of your body quickly, *He threw his head back.* **4** cause to be in a certain condition etc., *It threw us into confusion.* **5** move a switch or lever so as to operate it. **6** shape a pot on a potter's wheel. **throw** *noun*, **thrower** *noun*
throw away 1 put something out as being useless or unwanted. **2** waste, *You threw away an opportunity.*
throw up (*informal*) vomit.

throwback *noun* an animal etc. showing characteristics of an ancestor earlier than its parents.

thrum *verb* (**thrummed**, **thrumming**) sound monotonously; strum. **thrum** *noun*

thrush[1] *noun* (*plural* **thrushes**) any of several songbirds, especially one with a speckled breast.

thrush[2] *noun* a disease causing tiny white patches in the mouth and throat.

thrust *verb* (**thrust**, **thrusting**) **1** push hard. **2** pierce; stab; lunge suddenly. **thrust** *noun*

thud *verb* (**thudded**, **thudding**) make the dull sound of a heavy knock or fall. **thud** *noun*

thug *noun* a violent ruffian. **thuggery** *noun* [the Thugs were robbers in India in the 17th–19th centuries]

thumb[1] *noun* the short thick finger set apart from the other four.
be under someone's thumb be completely under someone's influence or control.

thumb[2] *verb* turn the pages of a book etc. quickly with your thumb.
thumb a lift hitchhike.

thumb drive *noun* a USB flash drive.

thumbnail *noun* **1** the nail of a thumb. **2** (in computing) a miniature picture to be clicked on if the full-sized picture is required.

thump *verb* **1** hit or knock something heavily. **2** punch. **3** thud. **thump** *noun*

thunder[1] *noun* **1** the loud noise that goes with lightning. **2** a similar noise, *thunder of applause.* **thunderous** *adverb*, **thunderstorm** *noun*, **thundery** *adjective*

thunder[2] *verb* **1** sound with thunder. **2** make a noise like thunder; speak loudly.

thunderbolt *noun* **1** a lightning flash with a crash of thunder. **2** a very startling event or statement.

thunderstruck *adjective* amazed.

Thursday *noun* the day of the week following Wednesday. [Old English = day of Thor (Norse god of Thunder)]

thus *adverb* **1** in this way, *Hold the wheel thus.* **2** therefore.

thwart *verb* stop something from happening or someone from doing something.

thy *adjective* (*old use*) belonging to thee.

thylacine (*say* **thuy**-luh-seen) another name for **Tasmanian tiger**.

thyme (*say* time) *noun* a herb with fragrant leaves. [from Greek *thymon*]

thymus *noun* a gland near the base of the neck.

thyroid gland *noun* a large gland at the front of the neck. [from Greek *thyreos* = shield]

thyself *pronoun* (*old use*) thou or thee and nobody else.

tiara (*say* tee-**ah**-ruh) *noun* a woman's jewelled crescent-shaped ornament worn like a crown.

tibia *noun* (*plural* **tibiae** or **tibias**) the inner of the two bones extending from the knee to the ankle; the shin bone. **tibial** *adjective* [Latin]

tic *noun* an unintentional twitch of a muscle, especially of the face. [French]

tick[1] *noun* **1** a small mark (usually ✓) put by something to show that it is correct or has been checked. **2** a regular clicking sound, especially that made by a clock or watch. **3** (*informal*) a moment.

tick[2] *verb* **1** put a tick by something. **2** make the sound of a tick.
tick off (*informal*) reprimand someone.

tick[3] *noun* a blood-sucking insect.

ticket *noun* **1** a printed piece of paper or card that entitles the holder to a certain right (e.g. to travel by train or bus or to a seat in a cinema). **2** a label showing a thing's price.

tickle *verb* (**tickled**, **tickling**) **1** touch a person's skin lightly so as to cause a slight tingling feeling. **2** (of a part of the body) have a slight tingling or itching feeling. **3** amuse or please somebody.

ticklish *adjective* **1** likely to laugh or wriggle when tickled. **2** awkward; difficult, *a ticklish situation.*

tidal *adjective* of or affected by tides.

tidal wave *noun* a huge ocean wave.

tiddler *noun* (*informal*) a very small fish.

tiddlywinks *plural noun* a game in which small counters are flicked into a cup.

tide[1] *noun* **1** the regular rise and fall in the level of the sea that usually happens twice a day. **2** (*old use*) a time or season, *Yuletide.*

tide[2] *verb* (**tided**, **tiding**) **tide a person over** help a person through a difficult period, especially with financial assistance.

tidings *plural noun* news.

tidy[1] *adjective* (**tidier**, **tidiest**) **1** with everything in its right place; orderly. **2** (*informal*) fairly large, *It costs a tidy amount.* **tidily** *adverb*, **tidiness** *noun*

tidy[2] *verb* (**tidied**, **tidying**) make a thing tidy.

tie[1] *verb* (**tied**, **tying**) **1** fasten with string, ribbon, or something similar. **2** arrange something into a knot or bow. **3** make the same score as another competitor.

tie[2] *noun* **1** a strip of material worn passing under the collar of a shirt and knotted in front. **2** a result when two or more competitors have equal scores. **3** a curved line (in a musical score) over two notes of the same pitch, indicating that the second is not sounded separately.

tiebreak *noun* (also **tiebreaker**) a means of deciding the winner when competitors have tied.

tier (*say* teer) *noun* each of a series of rows, ranks, or units placed one above the other. **tiered** *adjective*

tiff *noun* a slight quarrel.

tiger *noun* a large wild animal of the cat family, with yellow and black stripes.

tiger snake *noun* a very venomous Australian snake.

tight *adjective* **1** fitting very closely. **2** firmly fastened. **3** fully stretched; tense. **4** in short supply, *Money is tight at the moment.* **5** stingy, *She is very tight with her money.* **6** (*informal*) drunk. **tightly** *adverb*, **tightness** *noun*

tighten *verb* make or become tighter.

tightrope *noun* a tightly stretched rope high above the ground, on which acrobats perform.

tights *plural noun* a garment that fits tightly over the feet, legs, and lower part of the body.

tigress *noun* a female tiger.

tikka *noun* an Indian dish of small pieces of meat or vegetables marinated in a spice mixture. [Punjabi]

tile *noun* a thin piece of baked clay or other hard material, used in rows for covering roofs, walls, or floors. **tiled** *adjective*

till[1] *preposition & conjunction* until. [from Old English *til* = to]

> **Usage** It is better to use *until* rather than *till* when the word stands first in a sentence (e.g. *Until last year we had never been overseas*) or when you are speaking or writing formally.

till[2] *noun* a drawer or box for money in a shop; a cash register. [origin unknown]

till[3] *verb* cultivate land. [from Old English *tilian* = try]

tiller *noun* a handle used to turn a boat's rudder.

tilt[1] *verb* move into a sloping position.

tilt[2] *noun* a sloping position.
at full tilt at full speed or force.

timber *noun* **1** wood for building or making things. **2** a wooden beam.

timbre (*say* **tam**-buh) *noun* the quality of a voice or musical sound. [French]

time[1] *noun* **1** all the years of the past, present, and future; the continuous existence of the universe. **2** a particular portion of time; a period in the past. **3** a particular point of time. **4** an occasion, *the first time I saw him.* **5** a period suitable or available for something, *Is there time for a cup of tea?* **6** a system of measuring time, *Greenwich Mean Time.* **7** (in music) rhythm depending on the number and accentuation of beats in the bar. **8** (**times**) multiplied by, *Five times three is fifteen* ($5 \times 3 = 15$).
in time 1 not late. **2** eventually.
on time punctual.

time[2] *verb* (**timed**, **timing**) **1** measure how long something takes. **2** arrange when something is to happen. **timer** *noun*

timeless *adjective* not affected by the passage of time; eternal.

time limit *noun* a fixed amount of time within which something must be done.

timeline *noun* a visual representation of a period of time, on which important events are marked.

timely *adjective* happening at a suitable or useful time, *a timely warning.*

time signature *noun* an indication of the speed and rhythm of a piece of music following the clef.

timetable *noun* a list showing the times when things will happen, e.g. when buses or trains will arrive and depart, or when school lessons will take place.

timid *adjective* easily frightened. **timidity** *noun*, **timidly** *adverb* [from Latin *timidus* = nervous]

timing *noun* the way something is timed.

timorous *adjective* timid. [from Latin *timor* = fear]

timpani *plural noun* kettledrums. [Italian]

tin[1] *noun* **1** a silvery-white metal. **2** a metal container for food.

tin[2] *verb* (**tinned**, **tinning**) seal food in a tin to preserve it.

tincture *noun* **1** a solution of medicine in alcohol. **2** a slight trace of something. [same origin as *tint*]

tinder *noun* any dry substance that catches fire easily.

tine *noun* a point or prong of a fork, harrow, or antler.

tinge *verb* (**tinged**, **tingeing**) colour something slightly; tint. **tinge** *noun* [same origin as *tint*]

tingle *verb* (**tingled**, **tingling**) have a slight pricking or stinging feeling. **tingle** *noun*

tinker[1] *noun* (*old use*) a person travelling about to mend pots and pans.

tinker[2] *verb* work at something casually, trying to improve or mend it.

tinkle *verb* (**tinkled**, **tinkling**) make a gentle ringing sound. **tinkle** *noun*

tinnitus *noun* a condition causing repeated ringing or other sounds in the ears.

tinny *adjective* of tin; like tin.

tinsel *noun* strips of glittering material used for decoration.

tint[1] *noun* a shade of colour, especially a pale one.

tint[2] *verb* colour something slightly. [from Latin *tinctum* = stained]

tiny *adjective* (**tinier**, **tiniest**) very small.

tip[1] *noun* the part right at the top or end of something.

tip[2] *verb* (**tipped**, **tipping**) put a tip on something.

tip[3] *noun* **1** a small present of money given to someone who has helped you. **2** a small but useful piece of advice; a hint.

tip[4] *verb* (**tipped**, **tipping**) **1** give a person a tip. **2** name as a likely winner, *Which team would you tip to win the championship?*
tipper *noun*
tip off give someone secret information, or a warning, etc. **tip-off** *noun*

tip[5] *verb* (**tipped**, **tipping**) **1** tilt; topple. **2** empty rubbish somewhere.

tip[6] *noun* **1** a slight tilt or push. **2** a place where rubbish etc. is tipped.

tipsy *adjective* drunk. [from *tip*[5]]

tiptoe *verb* (**tiptoed**, **tiptoeing**) walk on your toes very quietly or carefully.
on tiptoe walking or standing on your toes.

tiptop *adjective* (*informal*) excellent; very best, *in tiptop condition.* [from *tip*[1]]

tirade (*say* tuy-**rayd**) *noun* a long angry or violent speech.

tiramisu (*say* ti-ruh-muh-**soo**) *noun* an Italian dessert consisting of layers of mascarpone cheese, chocolate, and sponge cake soaked in coffee and brandy. [from Italian *tira mi sù* = pick me up]

tire *verb* (**tired**, **tiring**) make or become tired.

tired *adjective* feeling that you need to sleep or rest. **tiredness** *noun*
tired of having had enough of something and impatient or bored with it.

tireless *adjective* not tiring easily; energetic.

tiresome *adjective* annoying.

tiro *noun* (*plural* **tiros**) a beginner. [Latin, = recruit]

tissue *noun* **1** tissue paper. **2** a paper handkerchief. **3** the substance forming any part of the body of an animal or plant, *bone tissue.*

tissue paper *noun* very thin soft paper used for wrapping and packing things.

tit[1] *noun* a kind of small bird.

tit[2] *noun* **tit for tat** something equal given in return; retaliation.

titanic (*say* tuy-**tan**-ik) *adjective* huge. [from the Titans, gods and goddesses in Greek mythology]

titbit *noun* a nice little piece of something, e.g. of food, gossip, or information.

tithe *noun* **1** one tenth of a year's produce or earnings, formerly paid as tax to support the clergy and church. **2** (in certain religious denominations) a tenth of an individual's income pledged to the church. [from Old English *teotha* = tenth]

titillate *verb* (**titillated**, **titillating**) stimulate something pleasantly. **titillation** *noun*

titivate *verb* (**titivated**, **titivating**) put the finishing touches to something; smarten up. **titivation** *noun*

title *noun* **1** the name of a book, film, song, etc. **2** a word used to show a person's rank or position, e.g. *Dr, Lord, Mrs.* **3** a championship in sport, *the world heavyweight title.* **4** a legal right to something. [from Latin *titulus* = title]

titled *adjective* having a title as a noble.

titter *verb & noun* giggle.

tizzy[1] *noun* (*informal*) a state of nervous agitation or confusion, *He gets into a tizzy when things go wrong.*

tizzy[2] *verb* (**tizzied**, **tizzying**) (*Australian*) titivate; adorn, *She tizzied herself up for the party.*

TNT *abbreviation* trinitrotoluene, a powerful explosive.

to[1] *preposition* This word is used to show **1** direction or arrival at a position (*We walked to school; He rose to power*), **2** limit (*from noon to two o'clock*), **3** comparison (*We won by six goals to three*), **4** receiving or being affected by something (*Give it to me; Be kind to animals*).

to[2] Used before a verb to form an infinitive (*I want to see him*) or to show purpose etc. (*She does that to annoy us*), or alone when the verb is understood (*We meant to go but forgot to*).

to[3] *adverb* **1** to or in the proper or closed position or condition, *Push the door to.* **2** into a state of activity, *We set to and cleaned the kitchen.*
to and fro backwards and forwards.

toad *noun* a frog-like animal that lives chiefly on land.

toadfish *noun* a poisonous sea and estuarine fish that inflates its body.

toadstool *noun* a fungus (usually poisonous) with a round top on a stalk.

toady *verb* (**toadied**, **toadying**) flatter someone so as to make them want to like or help you. **toady** *noun*

toast[1] *verb* **1** heat bread etc., to make it brown and crisp. **2** warm something in front of a fire etc. **3** drink in honour of someone.

toast[2] *noun* **1** toasted bread. **2** the call to drink in honour of someone; the person honoured in this way. [from Latin *tostum* = dried up]

toaster *noun* an electrical device for toasting bread.

tobacco *noun* the dried leaves of certain plants prepared for smoking or making snuff.

tobacconist *noun* a shopkeeper who sells tobacco products.

toboggan *noun* a small sledge used for sliding downhill. **tobogganing** *noun*

tocsin *noun* a bell rung as an alarm signal.

today[1] *noun* this present day, *Today is Monday.*

today[2] *adverb* on this day, *Have you seen him today?*

toddler *noun* a young child who has only recently learnt to walk. **toddle** *verb*

toddy *noun* a sweetened drink made with spirits and hot water.

to-do *noun* a fuss; a commotion.

toe *noun* **1** any of the separate parts (five in humans) at the end of each foot. **2** the part of a shoe or sock that covers the toes.

toehold *noun* **1** a small foothold. **2** a small beginning or advantage.

toey *adjective* (*Australian informal*) restless; touchy.

toffee *noun* a sticky sweet made from heated butter and sugar.

tofu (*say* **toh**-foo) *noun* a soft white curd made from soy beans.

toga (*say* **toh**-guh) *noun* a long loose garment worn by men in ancient Rome.

together *adverb* **1** with another person or thing; with each other, *They went to the party together.* **2** at the same time. [from *to* + *gather*]

toggle *noun* a short piece of wood or metal etc. used like a button.

togs *plural noun* (*informal*) **1** (*Australian*) a swimming costume. **2** clothes.

toil[1] *verb* **1** work hard. **2** move slowly and with difficulty. **toiler** *noun*

toil[2] *noun* hard work.

toilet *noun* **1** a large bowl-like fitment, usually flushed by running water, used for getting rid of urine and faeces. **2** a room containing a toilet. **3** the process of washing, dressing, and tidying yourself.

toilet paper *noun* paper for use in a toilet.

toiletries *plural noun* articles such as soap, toothpaste, etc. used in washing and grooming yourself.

token *noun* **1** a piece of metal or plastic bought for use instead of money, *parking tokens.* **2** a voucher or coupon that can be exchanged for goods. **3** a sign or signal of something, *a token of our friendship.*

told *past tense & past participle* of **tell**.

tolerable *adjective* **1** able to be tolerated. **2** fairly good. **tolerably** *adverb*

tolerant *adjective* tolerating things, especially other people's behaviour or beliefs. **tolerance** *noun*, **tolerantly** *adverb*

tolerate *verb* (**tolerated**, **tolerating**) allow something without protesting or interfering. **toleration** *noun* [from Latin *tolerare* = endure]

toll[1] *noun* **1** a charge made for using a road, bridge, etc. **2** loss or damage caused, *The death toll in the earthquake is rising.* [from Greek *telos* = tax]

toll[2] *verb* ring a bell slowly. **toll** *noun*

tollgate *noun* a gate across a road to prevent anyone passing until the toll has been paid.

tollway *noun* a road for which users pay a fee.

tom *noun* (also **tomcat**) a male cat. [short for *Thomas*]

tomahawk *noun* **1** a small axe traditionally used by indigenous North Americans. **2** (*Australian*) a hatchet. [from an indigenous North American word, = he cuts]

tomato *noun* (*plural* **tomatoes**) a soft round red or yellow fruit eaten as a vegetable.

tomb (*say* toom) *noun* a place where someone is buried; a monument built over this.

tombola *noun* a kind of lottery.

tomboy *noun* an energetic girl who enjoys activities traditionally or stereotypically associated with boys.

tomboy stitch *noun* French knitting.

tombstone *noun* a memorial stone set up over a grave.

tome *noun* a large heavy book.

tommy rough *noun* (also **tommy ruff**) a small sea fish of southern Australian waters.

tomography *noun* a method of radiography displaying details in a selected plane within the body.

tomorrow *noun & adverb* the day after today.

tom-tom *noun* **1** a medium-sized drum, of which one to three may be used in a drum kit. **2** a type of drum that you beat with the palms of your hands.

ton (*say* tun) *noun* **1** a unit of weight equal to about 1,016 kilograms. **2** a large amount, *There's tons of room.* **3** (*informal*) a speed of 100 kilometres per hour. **4** (*informal*) a score of 100 in cricket.
metric ton a tonne; 1000 kilograms.

tone[1] *noun* **1** a sound in music or of the voice. **2** each of the five larger intervals between notes in a musical scale (the smaller intervals are *semitones*). **3** a shade of a colour. **4** the quality or character of something, *a cheerful tone.* **tonal** *adjective*, **tonally** *adverb*

tone[2] *verb* (**toned**, **toning**) **1** give a particular tone or quality to something. **2** be harmonious in colour.
tone down make a thing quieter or less bright or less harsh.
tone up make a thing brighter or stronger.
[from Greek *tonos* = tension]

toner *noun* a powdered substance like ink used in photocopiers and laser printers.

tongs *plural noun* a tool with two arms joined at one end, used to pick up or hold things.

tongue *noun* **1** the long soft muscular part that moves about inside the mouth. **2** a language. **3** a projecting strip or flap. **4** a pointed flame.

tongue-tied *adjective* too shy to speak.

tongue-twister *noun* something that is difficult to say quickly and correctly, e.g. '*She sells sea shells*'.

tonic *noun* **1** a medicine etc. that makes a person healthier or stronger. **2** a keynote in music. **tonic** *adjective* [same origin as *tone*]

tonic sol-fa *noun* a system of representing notes of a musical scale by syllables *doh, ray, me,* etc.

tonight *noun & adverb* this evening or night.

tonnage *noun* the amount a ship or ships can carry, expressed in tons.

tonne (*say* ton or tun) *noun* a metric unit of weight equal to 1000 kilograms.

tonsil *noun* either of two small masses of soft tissue at the sides of the throat.

tonsillitis *noun* inflammation of the tonsils.

too *adverb* **1** also, *Take the others too.* **2** more than is wanted or allowed etc., *That's too much sugar for me; She is too generous.*

took *past tense* of **take**.

tool *noun* **1** a device or implement, especially one held in the hand, used to carry out a particular function, *gardening tools.* **2** a thing used to help perform a job, *A computer is an essential tool for many jobs.* **3** a person used or exploited by another. **4** (in computing) a piece of software that carries out a particular function.

toolbar *noun* (in computing) a strip of icons used to perform certain functions.

toot[1] (*rhymes with* boot) *noun* a short sound produced by a horn. **toot** *verb*

toot[2] (*rhymes with* foot) (*Australian informal*) *noun* a toilet.

tooth *noun* (*plural* **teeth**) **1** any of the hard white bony parts that are rooted in the gums, used for biting and chewing things. **2** each of a row of sharp parts or projections, *the teeth of a saw.* **toothache** *noun*, **toothbrush** *noun*, **toothed** *adjective*
fight tooth and nail fight very fiercely.

toothpaste *noun* a paste for cleaning your teeth.

toothpick *noun* a small pointed piece of wood etc. for removing bits of food from between your teeth.

toothy *adjective* having many or large teeth.

top[1] *noun* **1** the highest part of something. **2** the upper surface. **3** the covering or stopper of a bottle, jar, etc. **4** a garment for the upper part of the body.
on top of in addition to something.

top[2] *adjective* highest in position, degree, or importance, *at top speed; the top designer.*

top[3] *verb* (**topped**, **topping**) **1** put a top on something. **2** be at the top of something, *She tops the list.* **3** remove the top of something.
top up fill up something that is half empty.

top[4] *noun* a toy that can be made to spin on its point.

topaz *noun* a kind of gem, often yellow.

Top End *noun* (*Australian*) the northern part of the Northern Territory. **Top Ender** *noun*

top hat *noun* a man's tall stiff hat worn with formal clothes.

top-heavy *adjective* too heavy at the top and likely to overbalance.

topiary (*say* **toh**-pee-uh-ree) *noun* the art of clipping shrubs or trees into ornamental shapes.

topic *noun* a subject to write, learn, or talk about. [from Greek *topos* = place]

topical *adjective* connected with things that are happening now, *a topical film.* **topicality** *noun*, **topically** *adverb*

topless *adjective* not wearing any clothes on the top half of the body.

topmost *adjective* highest.

topography (*say* tuh-**pog**-ruh-fee) *noun* the position of the rivers, mountains, roads, buildings, etc. in a place. **topographical** *adjective* [from Greek *topos* = place, + *-graphy*]

topple *verb* (**toppled**, **toppling**) **1** fall over; totter and fall. **2** cause to fall; overthrow. [from *top*[1]]

topsy-turvy *adverb & adjective* upside-down; muddled.

torch *noun* (*plural* **torches**) **1** a small electric lamp for carrying in the hand. **2** a stick with burning material on the end, used as a light.

tore *past tense* of **tear**[2].

toreador (*say* **to**-ree-uh-daw) *noun* a bullfighter. [from Spanish *toro* = bull]

torment[1] *verb* **1** cause a person to suffer greatly. **2** tease; keep annoying someone. **tormentor** *noun*

torment[2] *noun* great suffering. [from Latin *tortum* = twisted]

torn *past participle* of **tear**[2].

tornado (*say* taw-**nay**-doh) *noun* (*plural* **tornadoes**) a violent storm or whirlwind. [from Spanish, = thunderstorm]

torpedo[1] *noun* (*plural* **torpedoes**) a long tubular missile that can be sent under water to destroy ships. [Latin, = large sea fish that can give an electric shock that causes numbness]

torpedo[2] *verb* (**torpedoed**, **torpedoing**) attack or destroy with a torpedo.

torpid *adjective* slow-moving; not lively. **torpidity** *noun*, **torpidly** *adverb*, **torpor** *noun* [from Latin *torpidus* = numb]

torrent *noun* **1** a rushing stream; a great flow. **2** a great downpour. **torrential** *adjective*

torrid *adjective* very hot and dry. [from Latin *torridus* = parched]

torsion *noun* twisting, especially of one end of a thing while the other is held in a fixed position. [same origin as *torture*]

torso *noun* (*plural* **torsos**) the trunk of the human body. [Italian, = stump]

tortilla (*say* taw-**tee**-yuh) *noun* (in Mexican cooking) a thin, flat pancake made from corn flour. [Spanish]

tortoise (*say* **taw**-tuhs) *noun* a slow-moving animal with a shell over its body.

tortoiseshell *noun* **1** the mottled brown and yellow shell of certain turtles, used for making combs etc. **2** a cat or butterfly with mottled brown colouring.

tortuous *adjective* full of twists and turns. **tortuosity** *noun* [from Latin *tortum* = twisted]

torture *verb* (**tortured**, **torturing**) make a person feel great pain or worry. **torture** *noun*, **torturer** *noun* [from Latin *tortum* = twisted]

toss *verb* **1** throw, especially up into the air. **2** spin a coin to decide something according to which side of it is upwards after it falls. **3** move restlessly or unevenly from side to side. **toss** *noun*

toss-up *noun* **1** the tossing of a coin. **2** an even chance.

tot[1] *noun* **1** a small child. **2** (*informal*) a small amount of spirits, *a tot of rum.*

tot[2] *verb* (**totted**, **totting**)
tot up (*informal*) add up. [short for *total*]

total[1] *adjective* **1** including everything, *the total amount.* **2** complete, *total darkness.* **totally** *adverb*

total[2] *noun* the amount you get by adding everything together.

total[3] *verb* (**totalled**, **totalling**) **1** reckon up the total. **2** amount to something. [from Latin *totum* = the whole]

totalitarian *adjective* using a form of government where people are not allowed to form rival political parties.

totality *noun* **1** being total. **2** a total.

totem (*say* **toh**-tuhm) *noun* a natural object or animal that is believed by a particular society to have spiritual significance and that is adopted by it as an emblem. [from an indigenous North American language]

totem pole *noun* a pole on which totems are hung or on which the images of totems are carved.

totter *verb* walk unsteadily; wobble. **tottery** *adjective*

toucan (*say* **too**-kan) *noun* a tropical American bird with a huge beak.

touch[1] *verb* **1** put your hand or fingers etc. on something lightly. **2** be or come together so that there is no space between. **3** hit gently. **4** move or meddle with something. **5** reach, *The thermometer touched 40°*. **6** arouse sympathy etc. in someone, *The sad story touched our hearts.* **7** (*informal*) persuade someone to give or lend money.
touch down 1 (of an aircraft) land. **2** (in rugby) touch the ball on the ground behind the goal line.
touch up improve something by making small additions or changes.

touch[2] *noun* (*plural* **touches**) **1** the action of touching. **2** the ability to feel things by touching them. **3** a small amount; a small thing done, *the finishing touches.* **4** a special skill or style of workmanship, *She hasn't lost her touch.* **5** communication with someone, *We lost touch with him.* **6** the part of a football field outside the playing area.

touchable *adjective* able to be touched.

touch-and-go *adjective* uncertain; risky.

touchdown *noun* the action of touching down.

touching *adjective* arousing kindly feelings such as pity or sympathy.

touchpad *noun* a computer input device in the form of a small panel containing different touch-sensitive areas.

touchscreen *noun* a display device that allows the user to interact with a computer by touching areas on the screen.

touchstone *noun* a test by which the quality of something is judged. [formerly, a kind of stone against which gold and silver were rubbed to test their purity]

touchy *adjective* (**touchier**, **touchiest**) easily offended. **touchily** *adverb*, **touchiness** *noun*

tough *adjective* **1** strong; difficult to break or damage. **2** difficult to chew. **3** (of a person) strong; hardy. **4** firm; stubborn; rough or violent, *tough criminals.* **5** difficult, *a tough job.* **toughly** *adverb*, **toughness** *noun*

toughen *verb* make or become tough.

tour[1] *noun* a journey visiting several places.

tour[2] *verb* make a tour. [same origin as *turn*]

tour de force (*say* toor duh **faws**) *noun* (*plural* **tours de force**) an outstandingly skilful performance or achievement. [French]

tourist *noun* a person who makes a tour or visits a place for pleasure. **tourism** *noun*

tournament *noun* a series of contests.

tourniquet (*say* **taw**-nuh-kay) *noun* a strip of material pulled tightly round an arm or leg to stop bleeding from an artery.

tousle (*say* **tow**-zuhl) *verb* (**tousled**, **tousling**) ruffle someone's hair.

tout[1] (*rhymes with* scout) *verb* try to obtain orders for goods or services.

tout[2] *noun* a person who touts things, *ticket touts.*

tow[1] (*rhymes with* go) *verb* pull something along behind you. **tow** *noun*

tow[2] (*rhymes with* go) *noun* short light-coloured fibres of flax or hemp.

toward *preposition* towards.

towards *preposition* **1** in the direction of, *She walked towards the sea.* **2** in relation to; regarding, *He behaved kindly towards his children.* **3** as a contribution to, *Put the money towards a new bicycle.* **4** near, *towards four o'clock.*

towel *noun* a piece of absorbent cloth for drying things. **towelling** *noun*

tower[1] *noun* a tall narrow building.

tower[2] *verb* be very high; be taller than others, *Skyscrapers towered over the city.* [from Latin *turris* = tower]

town *noun* a place with many houses, shops, offices, and other buildings. [from Old English *tun* = enclosure]

town hall *noun* a building with offices for the local council and usually a hall for public events.

townhouse *noun* a terrace house or a house in a planned group in a town.

townie *noun* (*derogatory*) a town dweller, especially as opposed to a country dweller.

township *noun* (*Australian*) a small town.

toxic *adjective* **1** poisonous; caused by poison. **2** very bad, unpleasant, or harmful. **toxicity** *noun* [from Greek, = poison for arrows (*toxa* = arrows)]

toxicology *noun* the study of poisons. **toxicologist** *noun* [from *toxic* + *-logy*]

toxin *noun* a poisonous substance, especially one formed in the body by germs. [from *toxic*]

toy[1] *noun* a thing to play with.

toy[2] *adjective* **1** made as a toy. **2** (of a dog) of a very small breed kept as a pet, *a toy poodle.*

toy[3] *verb* **toy with** handle a thing or consider an idea casually.

toyshop *noun* a shop that sells toys.

trace[1] *noun* **1** a mark left by a person or thing; a sign, *There was no trace of the thief.* **2** a very small amount.

trace[2] *verb* (**traced**, **tracing**) **1** copy a picture or map etc. by drawing over it on transparent paper. **2** follow the traces of a person or thing; find. **tracer** *noun*

trace[3] *noun* each of the two straps or ropes by which a horse pulls a cart.
kick over the traces (of a person) become disobedient or reckless.

traceable *adjective* able to be traced.

tracery *noun* a decorative pattern of holes in stone, e.g. in a church window. [from *trace*[1]]

trachea (*say* truh-**kee**-uh) *noun* (*plural* **tracheae** or **tracheas**) the windpipe.

trachoma (*say* truh-**koh**-muh) *noun* a contagious disease of the eye causing grainy inflammation of the inner surface of the eyelids and leading eventually to blindness.

track[1] *noun* **1** a mark or marks left by a moving person or thing. **2** a rough path made by being used. **3** a road or area of ground specially prepared for something (e.g. racing). **4** a set of rails for trains or trams etc. **5** a recording of one song or piece of music. **6** a continuous band round the wheels of a tank or tractor etc.
keep track of keep yourself informed about where something is or what someone is doing.

track[2] *verb* **1** follow the tracks left by a person or animal. **2** follow or observe something as it moves. **tracker** *noun*
track down find by searching.

track pants *plural noun* warm loose trousers worn for exercising etc.

tracksuit *noun* a warm loose set of trousers and top worn when exercising or for casual wear.

tract[1] *noun* **1** an area of land. **2** a series of connected parts along which something passes, *the digestive tract.*

tract[2] *noun* a pamphlet containing a short essay, especially about religion.

traction *noun* **1** pulling a load. **2** the grip of a tyre on the road. **3** the extent to which an idea or product gains popularity or acceptance. [from Latin *tractum* = pulled]

tractor *noun* a motor vehicle for pulling farm machinery or other heavy loads. [same origin as *traction*]

trade[1] *noun* **1** buying, selling, or exchanging goods. **2** business of a particular kind; the people working in this. **3** an occupation, especially a skilled craft.

trade[2] *verb* (**traded**, **trading**) buy, sell, or exchange things. **trader** *noun*
trade in give a thing as part of the payment for something new, *He traded in his motorcycle for a car.* **trade-in** *noun*

trademark *noun* a symbol, word, or words legally registered or established by use as representing a company or product.

tradesman *noun* a male tradesperson.

tradesperson *noun* a person engaged in or skilled in a trade.

tradeswoman *noun* a female tradesperson.

trade union *noun* a group of workers organised to help and protect workers in their own trade.

tradie *noun* (*Australian informal*) a tradesperson.

tradition *noun* **1** the passing down of beliefs or customs etc. from one generation to another. **2** something passed on in this way. **traditional** *adjective*, **traditionally** *adverb* [from Latin *traditum* = handed on]

traditional owner *noun* (*Australian*) an Aboriginal person who is a member of a local descent group having certain rights over a tract of land.

traffic[1] *noun* **1** vehicles, ships, or aircraft moving along a route. **2** trading, especially when it is illegal or wrong, *drug traffic.*

traffic[2] *verb* (**trafficked**, **trafficking**) trade. **trafficker** *noun*

traffic lights *plural noun* coloured lights used as a signal to traffic at road junctions etc.

tragedian (*say* truh-**jee**-dee-uhn) *noun* **1** a person who writes tragedies. **2** an actor in tragedies.

tragedy *noun* (*plural* **tragedies**) **1** a play with unhappy events or a sad ending. **2** a very sad event. [from Greek *tragos* = goat, + *oide* = song]

tragic[1] *adjective* **1** very sad; causing sadness; calamitous. **2** of tragedies, *a great tragic actor.* **tragically** *adverb*

tragic[2] *noun* a person devoted to a specified activity or interest, *a cricket tragic.*

trail[1] *noun* **1** a track, scent, or other sign left where something has passed. **2** a path or track made through a wild region.

trail[2] *verb* **1** follow the trail of something; track. **2** drag or be dragged along behind. **3** lag behind. **4** hang down or float loosely. [from Latin *tragula* = net for dragging a river]

trailer *noun* **1** a vehicle designed to be pulled along by another vehicle. **2** a short piece from a film or television program, shown in advance to advertise it.

train[1] *noun* **1** a railway engine pulling a line of carriages or trucks that are linked together. **2** a number of people or animals moving in a line, *a camel train.* **3** a series of things, *a train of events.* **4** part of a long dress or robe that trails on the ground at the back.

train[2] *verb* **1** give a person instruction or practice so that they become skilled. **2** practise, *She was training for the race.* **3** make something grow in a particular direction. **4** aim a gun etc., *Train that gun on the bridge.* [same origin as *traction*]

trainee *noun* a person being trained.

trainer *noun* **1** a person who trains people or animals. **2** a rubber-soled running shoe.

traipse *verb* (**traipsed**, **traipsing**) trudge.

trait (*say* trayt or tray) *noun* a distinguishing quality or characteristic, typically one belonging to a person. [French]

traitor *noun* a person who betrays someone or something, such as a friend, cause, or principle. **traitorous** *adjective* [same origin as *tradition*]

trajectory *noun* (*plural* **trajectories**) the path taken by a moving object such as a bullet or rocket. [from *trans*-, + Latin *-jectum* = thrown]

tram *noun* a public passenger vehicle running on rails in the road.

tramlines *plural noun* **1** rails for a tram. **2** the pair of parallel lines at the side of a tennis court.

tramp[1] *noun* **1** a person without a home or job who walks from place to place. **2** a long walk. **3** the sound of heavy footsteps.

tramp[2] *verb* **1** walk with heavy footsteps. **2** walk for a long distance.

trample *verb* (**trampled**, **trampling**) tread heavily on something; crush something by treading on it.

trampoline *noun* a large piece of canvas joined to a frame by springs, used for jumping on in acrobatics. [from Italian *trampoli* = stilts]

trance *noun* a dreamy or unconscious condition rather like sleep. [same origin as *transit*]

tranquil *adjective* calm and quiet. **tranquillity** *noun*, **tranquilly** *adverb*

tranquilliser *noun* a medicine used to make a person feel calm.

trans- *prefix* **1** across; through. **2** beyond. [from Latin *trans* = across]

transact *verb* carry out business. **transaction** *noun*

transatlantic *adjective* across or on the other side of the Atlantic Ocean.

transcend *verb* **1** go or be beyond the range of human experience, belief, or powers of description etc. **2** surpass. **transcendence** *noun*, **transcendent** *adjective* [from *trans*-, + Latin *scandere* = climb]

transcribe *verb* (**transcribed**, **transcribing**) copy or write something out. **transcription** *noun* [from *trans*-, + Latin *scribere* = write]

transcript *noun* a written copy.

transept *noun* the part that is at right angles to the nave in a cross-shaped church. [from *trans-*, + Latin *septum* = partition]

trans-fatty acid *noun* (also **trans-fat**) an unsaturated fatty acid that occurs especially in margarines and cooking oils.

transfer[1] *verb* (**transferred, transferring**) **1** move a person or thing to another place. **2** hand over. **transferable** *adjective*, **transference** *noun*

transfer[2] *noun* **1** the transferring of a person or thing. **2** a picture or design that can be transferred on to another surface. [from *trans-*, + Latin *ferre* = carry]

transfigure *verb* (**transfigured, transfiguring**) change the appearance of something greatly. **transfiguration** *noun*

transfix *verb* **1** pierce and fix with something pointed. **2** make a person or animal unable to move because of fear or surprise etc.

transform *verb* change the form or appearance or character of a person or thing. **transformation** *noun*

transformer *noun* a device used to change the voltage of an electric current.

transfusion *noun* putting blood taken from one person into another person's body. **transfuse** *verb* [from *trans-*, + Latin *fusum* = poured]

transgender *adjective* (also **transgendered**) of a person whose sense of personal identity and gender does not correspond with their birth sex.

transgenic *adjective* containing genetic material into which DNA from a different organism has been artificially introduced.

transgress *verb* **1** break a rule or law. **2** sin. **transgression** *noun* [from *trans-*, + Latin *gressus* = gone]

transient *adjective* passing away quickly; not lasting. **transience** *noun* [from *trans-*, + Latin *iens* = going]

transistor *noun* a semiconductor device, usually with three electrodes, capable of amplification. **transistorised** *adjective* [from *trans*fer + res*istor*]

transit *noun* the process of travelling across or through. [from *trans-*, + Latin *itum* = gone]

transition *noun* the process of changing from one condition or style etc. to another. **transitional** *adjective*

transitive *adjective* (of a verb) used with a direct object after it, e.g. *change* in *change your shoes* (but not in *change into dry shoes*). (Compare **intransitive**.) **transitively** *adverb*

transitory *adjective* existing for a time but not lasting.

translate *verb* (**translated, translating**) **1** express in another language or in simpler words, or in code for use in a computer. **2** interpret, *we translated his silence as disapproval.* **3** move or change, especially from one person, place, or condition to another. **4** (in mathematics) move a shape to a new position without flipping or turning it. **translatable** *adjective*, **translation** *noun*, **translator** *noun* [from *trans-*, + Latin *latum* = carried]

transliterate *verb* (**transliterated, transliterating**) put letters or words into letters of a different alphabet. **transliteration** *noun* [from *trans-*, + Latin *littera* = letter]

translucent (*say* tranz-**loo**-suhnt) *adjective* allowing light to shine through but not transparent. **translucence** *noun* [from *trans-*, + Latin *lucens* = shining]

transmission *noun* **1** transmitting something. **2** a broadcast. **3** the gears by which power is transmitted from the engine to the wheels of a vehicle.

transmit *verb* (**transmitted, transmitting**) **1** send or pass on from one person or place to another. **2** send out a signal or broadcast etc. **transmitter** *noun* [from *trans-*, + Latin *mittere* = send]

transmute *verb* change something from one form or substance into another. **transmutation** *noun*

transom *noun* **1** a horizontal bar of wood or stone dividing a window or separating a door from a window above it. **2** a small window above a door.

transparency *noun* (*plural* **transparencies**) **1** being transparent. **2** a transparent photograph that can be projected on to a screen.

transparent *adjective* able to be seen through. [from *trans-*, + Latin *parens* = appearing]

transpire *verb* (**transpired, transpiring**) **1** (of information) become known; leak out. **2** (of plants) give off watery vapour from leaves. **transpiration** *noun* [from *trans-*, + Latin *spirare* = breathe]

transplant[1] *verb* **1** remove a plant and put it to grow somewhere else. **2** transfer a part of the body to another person or animal. **transplantation** *noun*

transplant[2] *noun* **1** the process of transplanting. **2** something transplanted.

transport[1] *verb* **1** take a person, animal, or thing from one place to another. **2** (*old use*) send a convicted person to a penal settlement. **transportable** *adjective*, **transportation** *noun*, **transporter** *noun*

transport[2] *noun* **1** the action of transporting people, animals, or things. **2** the means of transporting people, animals, or things. [from *trans*-, + Latin *portare* = carry]

transpose *verb* (**transposed**, **transposing**) **1** change the position or order of something. **2** put a piece of music into a different key. **transposition** *noun* [from *trans*-, + Latin *positum* = placed]

transsexual *noun* a person who feels they should have been born the opposite sex, and therefore behaves and dresses like a member of that sex; a person who has had a medical operation to change their sex.

trans-Tasman *adjective* **1** across the Tasman Sea. **2** between Australia and New Zealand.

transversal *noun* a line that intersects a set of two or more lines on a flat surface.

transverse *adjective* lying across something. **transversely** *adverb* [from *trans*-, + Latin *versum* = turned]

transvestite *noun* a person who wears particular clothes in order to assume the image of the opposite sex.

trap[1] *noun* **1** a device for catching and holding animals. **2** an arrangement for capturing, detecting, or cheating someone. **3** a device for collecting water etc. or preventing it from passing. **4** a two-wheeled carriage pulled by a horse.

trap[2] *verb* (**trapped**, **trapping**) **1** catch or hold in a trap. **2** catch or catch out a person by means of a trick, etc. **trapper** *noun*

trapdoor *noun* a door in a floor, ceiling, or roof.

trapdoor spider *noun* a large spider that digs a burrow, covering it with a hinged flap like a trapdoor.

trapeze *noun* a bar hanging from two ropes as a swing for acrobats.

trapezium *noun* a quadrilateral in which two opposite sides are parallel and the other two are not. [from Greek *trapeza* = table]

trapezoid *noun* a quadrilateral in which no sides are parallel.

trappings *plural noun* **1** ornamental accessories or equipment etc., e.g. for officials. **2** ornamental harness for a horse.

trash *noun* rubbish; nonsense. **trashy** *adjective*

trauma (*say* **traw**-muh) *noun* a shock that produces a lasting effect on a person's mind. **traumatic** *adjective*, **traumatise** *verb* [Greek, = a wound]

travail *noun* (*old use*) hard or laborious work. **travail** *verb*

travel *verb* (**travelled**, **travelling**) move from place to place. **travel** *noun*, **traveller** *noun* [the original meaning was 'travail']

traverse *verb* (**traversed**, **traversing**) go across something. **traversal** *noun* [same origin as *transverse*]

travesty *noun* (*plural* **travesties**) a bad or ridiculous form of something, *Her story is a travesty of the truth.* [from French *travesti* = having changed clothes]

trawl *verb* fish by dragging a large net along the seabed.

trawler *noun* a boat used in trawling.

tray *noun* **1** a flat piece of wood, metal, or plastic, usually with raised edges, for carrying cups, plates, food, etc. **2** an open container for holding letters or documents in an office. **3** (*Australian*) the flat open part of a truck on which goods are carried.

treacherous *adjective* **1** betraying someone; disloyal. **2** not to be trusted, *treacherous roads.* **treacherously** *adverb*, **treachery** *noun*

treacle *noun* a thick sticky liquid produced when sugar is purified. **treacly** *adjective*

tread[1] *verb* (**trod**, **trodden**, **treading**) walk or put your foot on something.

tread[2] *noun* **1** a sound or way of walking. **2** the top surface of a stair; the part you put your foot on. **3** the part of a tyre that touches the ground.

treadle *noun* a lever that you press with your foot to turn a wheel that works a machine.

treadmill *noun* a wide mill-wheel turned by the weight of people or animals treading on steps fixed round its edge.

treason *noun* the action of betraying your country. **treasonable** *adjective*, **treasonous** *adjective* [same origin as *tradition*]

treasure[1] *noun* **1** a store of precious metals or jewels. **2** a precious thing or person.

treasure[2] *verb* (**treasured**, **treasuring**) value greatly something that you have. [from Greek *thesauros* = treasury]

treasure hunt *noun* a game in which people try to find a hidden object.

treasurer *noun* **1** a person in charge of the money of a club, society, or other organisation. **2** (**Treasurer**) the minister responsible for Treasury.

treasure trove *noun* treasure found hidden and with no known owner.

treasury *noun* (*plural* **treasuries**) **1** a place where money and valuables are kept. **2** (**Treasury**) the government department in charge of a country's income.

treat[1] *verb* **1** behave in a certain way towards a person or thing. **2** deal with a subject etc. **3** give medical care in order to cure a person or animal. **4** put something through a chemical or other process, *The fabric has been treated to make it waterproof.* **5** pay for someone else's food, drink, or entertainment, *I'll treat you to an ice cream.*

treat[2] *noun* **1** something special that gives pleasure. **2** the process of treating someone to food, drink, or entertainment. [from Latin *tractare* = to handle]

treatise *noun* a book or long essay on a subject. [same origin as *treat*]

treatment *noun* the process or manner of dealing with a person, animal, or thing.

treaty *noun* (*plural* **treaties**) a formal agreement between two or more countries. [same origin as *treat*]

treble[1] *adjective* **1** three times as much or as many. **2** (of a voice etc.) high-pitched or soprano.

treble[2] *noun* **1** a treble amount. **2** a person with a high-pitched or soprano voice.

treble[3] *verb* (**trebled**, **trebling**) make or become three times as much or as many. [same origin as *triple*]

tree *noun* a tall plant with a single very thick hard stem or trunk that is usually without branches for some distance above the ground.

tree diagram *noun* a diagram with a structure of branching connecting lines.

trefoil *noun* a plant with three small leaves (e.g. clover). [from Latin *tres* = three, + *folium* = leaf]

trek[1] *noun* a long walk or ride.

trek[2] *verb* (**trekked**, **trekking**) make a trek. [from Dutch *trekken* = pull]

trellis *noun* (*plural* **trellises**) a framework with crossing bars of wood or metal etc. to support climbing plants.

tremble *verb* (**trembled**, **trembling**) shake gently, especially with fear. **tremble** *noun*

tremendous *adjective* **1** very large; huge. **2** (*informal*) excellent. **tremendously** *adverb* [from Latin, = causing people to tremble]

tremolo *noun* **1** a wavering effect in a musical tone. **2** a device in an organ or on an electric guitar used to produce tremolo.

tremor *noun* a shaking or trembling movement.

tremulous *adjective* trembling from nervousness or weakness. **tremulously** *adverb* [from Latin *tremulus* = trembling]

trench *noun* (*plural* **trenches**) a long narrow hole cut in the ground.

trenchant *adjective* strong and effective, *trenchant criticism.*

trend[1] *noun* **1** a general direction in which something is developing or changing. **2** a fashion. **3** a topic that is the subject of many posts on a social media website within a short period of time.

trend[2] *verb* **1** change or develop in a general direction. **2** (of a topic) be the subject of many posts on a social media website or application within a short period of time.

trendy *adjective* (*informal*) fashionable; following the latest trends. **trendily** *adverb*, **trendiness** *noun*

trepidation *noun* fear and anxiety; nervousness. [from Latin *trepidare* = be afraid]

trespass[1] *verb* **1** go on someone's land or property unlawfully. **2** (*old use*) do wrong; sin. **trespasser** *noun*

trespass[2] *noun* (*plural* **trespasses**) (*old use*) wrongdoing; sin. [from Old French *trespasser* = pass over (same origin as *trans-* + *pass*)]

tress *noun* (*plural* **tresses**) a lock of hair.

trestle *noun* each of a set of supports on which a board is rested to form a table. **trestle table** *noun*

trevally *noun* (*plural* **trevally** or **trevallies**) any of several Australian sea fish.

tri- *prefix* three (as in *triangle*). [from Latin *tres* or Greek *treis* = three]

triad *noun* a group of three connected persons or things, especially notes in a chord.

trial[1] *noun* **1** testing a thing to see how good it is. **2** a test of qualities or ability. **3** the trying of a person in a lawcourt. **4** an annoying person or thing; a hardship. **trial** *adjective*
on trial being tried. [from *try*]

trial[2] *verb* test something, especially a new product, to assess its suitability or performance.

triangle *noun* **1** a flat shape with three sides and three angles. **2** a percussion instrument made from a metal rod bent into a triangle. **triangular** *adjective* [from *tri-* + *angle*]

triantelope (*say* truy-**an**-tuh-lohp) *noun* (*Australian*) a huntsman spider. [from *tarantula*]

triathlon *noun* an athletic contest in which competitors take part in three events (usually swimming, cycling, and running).

tribe *noun* **1** a group of families or communities, linked by social, religious, or blood ties, and usually having a common culture and a recognised leader. **2** (*informal*) a set of people. **tribal** *adjective*, **tribally** *adverb*

tribesman *noun* (*plural* **tribesmen**) a man belonging to a tribe in a traditional society or group.

tribeswoman *noun* (*plural* **tribeswomen**) a woman belonging to a tribe in a traditional society or group.

tribulation *noun* great troubles.

tribunal (*say* truy-**byoo**-nuhl) *noun* a committee appointed to hear evidence and give judgements when there is a dispute.

tribune *noun* an official chosen by the people in ancient Rome.

tributary *noun* (*plural* **tributaries**) a river or stream that flows into a larger one or into a lake.

tribute *noun* **1** something said, done, or given to show respect or admiration. **2** payment that one country or ruler was formerly obliged to pay to a more powerful one. [from Latin *tributum* = assigned]

trice *noun* **in a trice** in a moment.

triceps *noun* the large muscle at the back of the upper arm that straightens the elbow.

trick[1] *noun* **1** a crafty or deceitful action. **2** a practical joke. **3** a special technique for doing things. **4** a skilful action, especially one done for entertainment. **5** one round of a card game such as bridge.

trick[2] *verb* **1** deceive or cheat someone by a trick. **2** decorate, *The building was tricked out with little flags.*

trickery *noun* the use of tricks.

trickle *verb* flow or move slowly. **trickle** *noun*

trickster *noun* a person who tricks or cheats people.

tricky *adjective* (**trickier**, **trickiest**) **1** difficult; needing skill, *a tricky job.* **2** cunning; deceitful. **trickiness** *noun*

tricolour (*say* **truy**-kul-uh) *noun* a flag with three coloured stripes, e.g. the national flag of France or Ireland. [from *tri-* + *colour*]

tricycle *noun* a vehicle like a bicycle but with three wheels.

trident *noun* a three-pronged spear. [from *tri-*, + Latin *dens* = tooth]

tried *past tense & past participle* of **try**[1].

triennial (*say* truy-**en**-ee-uhl) *adjective* happening every third year. [from *tri-*, + Latin *annus* = year]

trier *noun* a person who tries hard.

trifecta *noun* **1** a form of betting in which the first three places in a race must be predicted in the correct order. **2** (*informal*) a run of three 'wins' or good fortune etc.

trifle[1] *noun* **1** a dessert made of sponge cake covered in custard, fruit, cream, etc. **2** a very small amount. **3** something that has very little importance or value.

trifle[2] *verb* (**trifled**, **trifling**) behave frivolously; toy with something.

trifling *adjective* trivial.

trigger[1] *noun* a lever that is pulled to fire a gun.

trigger[2] *verb* **trigger off** start something happening.

trigonometry (*say* trig-uh-**nom**-uh-tree) *noun* the calculation of distances and angles by using triangles. [from Greek *trigonon* = triangle, + *metria* = measurement]

trike *noun* (*informal*) a tricycle.

trilateral *adjective* having three sides. [from *tri-* + *lateral*]

trilby *noun* (*plural* **trilbies**) a man's soft felt hat.

trill *verb* make a quivering musical sound. **trill** *noun*

trillion *noun* **1** a million million. **2** (*old use*) a million million million. **trillionth** *adjective & noun* [from *tri-* + *million*]

trilogy *noun* (*plural* **trilogies**) a group of three stories, poems, plays or films about the same people or things. [from *tri-*, + Greek *-logia* = writings]

trim[1] *adjective* neat and orderly. **trimly** *adverb*, **trimness** *noun*

trim[2] *verb* (**trimmed**, **trimming**) **1** cut the edges or unwanted parts off something. **2** ornament a piece of clothing etc. **3** arrange sails to suit the wind. **4** balance a boat or aircraft evenly by arranging the people or cargo in it.

trim[3] *noun* **1** condition, *in good trim.* **2** cutting or trimming, *Your beard needs a trim.* **3** ornamentation. **4** the balance of a boat or aircraft.

Trinity *noun* God regarded as three persons (Father, Son, and Holy Spirit).

trinket *noun* a small ornament or piece of jewellery.

trio *noun* (*plural* **trios**) **1** a group of three people or things. **2** a group of three musicians or singers. **3** a piece of music for three musicians. [from Latin *tres* = three]

trip[1] *verb* (**tripped**, **tripping**) **1** catch your foot on something and fall; cause a person to do this. **2** move with quick light steps. **3** operate a switch.
trip up 1 stumble; cause a person to stumble. **2** make a slip or blunder; cause a person to do this.

trip[2] *noun* **1** a journey or excursion. **2** the action of tripping; a stumble.

tripartite *adjective* having three parts; involving three groups, *tripartite talks.*

tripe *noun* **1** part of an ox's stomach used as food. **2** (*informal*) nonsense.

triple[1] *adjective* **1** consisting of three parts. **2** involving three people or groups, *a triple alliance.* **3** three times as much or as many. **triply** *adverb*

triple[2] *verb* (**tripled**, **tripling**) treble. [from Latin *triplus* = three times as much]

triplet *noun* each of three children or animals born to the same mother at one time. [from *triple*]

triplicate *noun* **in triplicate** as three identical copies. [from Latin *triplex* = triple]

tripod (*say* **truy**-pod) *noun* a stand with three legs, e.g. to support a camera. [from *tri*-, + Greek *podos* = of a foot]

tripper *noun* a person who is making a pleasure trip.

trireme (*say* **truy**-reem) *noun* an ancient warship with three banks of oars. [from *tri*-, + Latin *remus* = oar]

trisect *verb* divide into three equal parts. **trisection** *noun* [from *tri*-, + Latin *sectum* = cut]

trite (*rhymes with* kite) *adjective* commonplace; hackneyed, *a few trite remarks.* [from Latin *tritum* = worn by use]

triumph[1] *noun* **1** a great success or victory; a feeling of joy at this. **2** a celebration of a victory. **triumphal** *adjective*, **triumphant** *adjective*, **triumphantly** *adverb*

triumph[2] *verb* **1** be successful or victorious. **2** rejoice in success or victory.

triumvirate *noun* a ruling group of three people. [from Latin *trium virorum* = of three men]

trivet *noun* an iron stand for a pot or kettle etc., placed over a fire. [from Latin, = three-footed (compare *tripod*)]

trivia *plural noun* unimportant things.

trivial *adjective* of only small value or importance. **triviality** *noun*, **trivially** *adverb* [from Latin, = commonplace]

trod *past tense* of **tread**[1].

trodden *past participle* of **tread**[1].

troglodyte *noun* **1** a person who lives in a cave, especially in ancient times. **2** a hermit. **3** (*informal*) an ignorant or old-fashioned person. [from Greek *trogle* = hole]

troll[1] (*rhymes with* hole) *noun* **1** (in folklore) an ugly creature depicted as either a giant or a dwarf. **2** a person who makes a deliberately offensive or provocative online post. **3** a deliberately offensive or provocative online post.

troll *verb* **1** make a deliberately offensive or provocative online post with the aim of upsetting someone or eliciting an angry response from them. **2** carefully and systematically search an area for something.

trolley *noun* (*plural* **trolleys**) **1** a basket, stand, or table on wheels or castors. **2** a low truck running on rails.

trombone *noun* **1** a large brass musical instrument with a sliding tube. **2** a large variety of pumpkin. [from Italian *tromba* = trumpet]

tromp l'oeil (*say* trom **ler**-ee) *noun* a painting on a wall or other surface designed to give an illusion of reality. [French, = deceives the eye]

troop[1] *noun* **1** an organised group of soldiers, Scouts, etc. **2** a number of people moving along together.

troop[2] *verb* move along as a group or in large numbers, *They all trooped in.*

trooper *noun* a soldier in the cavalry or in an armoured unit.

troops *plural noun* armed forces.

trophy *noun* (*plural* **trophies**) a prize or souvenir for a victory or other success.

tropic *noun* a line of latitude about 23½° north of the equator (**tropic of Cancer**) or 23½° south of the equator (**tropic of Capricorn**). **tropical** *adjective*
the tropics the region between these two latitudes. [from Greek *trope* = turning (because the sun seems to turn back when it reaches these points)]

troposphere *noun* the layer of the atmosphere extending about six to ten kilometres upwards from the earth's surface. [from Greek *tropos* = turning, + *sphere*]

troppo *adjective* (*Australian informal*) mad; crazy, *gone troppo.*

trot[1] *verb* (**trotted**, **trotting**) (of a horse) run, going faster than when walking but more slowly than when cantering.
trot out (*informal*) produce, *He trotted out the usual excuses.*

trot[2] *noun* **1** a trotting run. **2** (*Australian informal*) a continuous sequence; a run of luck, *having a bad trot.*
on the trot (*informal*) one after the other without a break, *She worked for ten days on the trot.*

troth (*rhymes with* both) *noun* (*old use*) loyalty; a solemn promise. [from *truth*]

trotter *noun* an animal's foot as food, *pigs' trotters.*

troubadour (*say* **troo**-buh-daw) *noun* a poet and singer in southern France in the 11th–13th centuries.

trouble[1] *noun* **1** difficulty, inconvenience, or distress. **2** a cause of any of these. **3** conflict; public disturbance.
take trouble take great care in doing something.

trouble[2] *verb* (**troubled**, **troubling**) **1** cause trouble to someone. **2** give yourself trouble or inconvenience etc., *Don't trouble to reply.* [same origin as *turbid*]

troublemaker *noun* a person who habitually causes trouble.

troubleshoot *verb* **1** analyse and solve serious problems for a company or other organisation. **2** trace and correct faults in a mechanical or electronic system. **troubleshooter** *noun*

troublesome *adjective* causing trouble or annoyance.

trough (*say* trof) *noun* **1** a long narrow open container, especially one holding water or food for animals. **2** a channel for liquid. **3** the low part between two waves or ridges. **4** a long region of low air pressure.

trounce *verb* (**trounced**, **trouncing**) **1** thrash. **2** defeat someone heavily.

troupe (*say* troop) *noun* a company of actors or other performers.

trousers *plural noun* a garment worn over the lower half of the body, with a separate part for each leg.

trousseau (*say* **troo**-soh) *noun* a bride's collection of clothing etc. to begin married life. [from French, = bundle]

trout *noun* (*plural* **trout**) a freshwater fish that is caught as a sport and for food.

trowel *noun* **1** a small garden tool with a curved blade for lifting plants or scooping things. **2** a small tool with a flat blade for spreading mortar etc. [from Latin *trulla* = scoop]

troy weight *noun* a system of weights used for precious metals and gems, in which 1 pound = 12 ounces. [said to be from a weight used at Troyes in France]

truant *noun* a child who stays away from school without permission. **truancy** *noun* **play truant** be a truant. [the word originally meant 'idle rogue', from a Celtic word related to Welsh *truan* = miserable]

truce *noun* an agreement to stop fighting for a while.

truck[1] *noun* **1** a large powerful motor vehicle for transporting goods etc.; a lorry. **2** an open railway wagon for freight.

truck[2] *noun* **have no truck with** have no dealings with.

truckie *noun* (*Australian informal*) a truck driver.

truculent (*say* **truk**-yuh-luhnt) *adjective* defiant and aggressive. **truculence** *noun*, **truculently** *adverb*

trudge *verb* (**trudged**, **trudging**) walk slowly and heavily.

true *adjective* (**truer**, **truest**) **1** representing what has happened or exists, *a true story*. **2** genuine; not false, *He was the true heir.* **3** accurate. **4** loyal; faithful, *Be true to your friends.*
true-blue 1 extremely loyal. **2** (*Australian*) genuine, *a true-blue Aussie battler.*

truffle *noun* **1** a soft sweet made with chocolate. **2** a fungus that grows underground and is valued as food because of its rich flavour.

truism *noun* a statement that is obviously true, especially one that is hackneyed, e.g. 'Nothing lasts for ever'.

truly *adverb* **1** truthfully. **2** sincerely; genuinely, *We are truly grateful.* **3** accurately. **4** loyally; faithfully.
Yours truly see **yours**.

trump[1] *noun* a playing card of a suit that ranks above the others for one game.

trump[2] *verb* defeat a card by playing a trump.
trump up invent an excuse or an accusation etc. [from *triumph*]

trump[3] *noun* (*old use*) the sound of a trumpet.

trumpery *adjective* showy but worthless, *trumpery ornaments.* [from French *tromper* = deceive]

trumpet[1] *noun* **1** a metal wind instrument with a narrow tube that widens near the end. **2** something shaped like this.

trumpet[2] *verb* (**trumpeted**, **trumpeting**) **1** blow a trumpet. **2** (of an elephant) make a loud sound with its trunk. **3** shout or announce something loudly.

trumpeter *noun* **1** a person who plays a trumpet. **2** an edible Australian sea fish.

truncate *verb* (**truncated**, **truncating**) shorten something by cutting off its top or end. **truncation** *noun*

truncheon *noun* a short thick stick carried as a weapon, especially by police. [from Latin *truncus* = tree trunk]

trundle *verb* (**trundled**, **trundling**) roll along heavily, *She was trundling a wheelbarrow; A bus trundled up.*

trundle bed *noun* a low bed on wheels that can be pushed under another.

trunk *noun* **1** the main stem of a tree. **2** an elephant's long flexible nose. **3** a large box with a hinged lid for transporting or storing clothes and other items. **4** the human body except for the head, arms, and legs.

trunks *plural noun* shorts worn by men and boys for swimming, boxing, etc.

truss[1] *noun* (*plural* **trusses**) **1** a framework of beams or bars supporting a roof or bridge etc. **2** a bundle of hay etc.

truss[2] *verb* **1** tie up a person or thing securely. **2** support a roof or bridge etc. with trusses.

trust[1] *verb* **1** believe that a person or thing is good, truthful, or strong. **2** entrust. **3** hope, *I trust that you are well.*
trust to rely on, *trusting to luck.*

trust[2] *noun* **1** the belief that a person or thing can be trusted. **2** responsibility; being trusted, *Being a prefect is a position of trust.* **3** money legally entrusted to a person with instructions about how to use it. **trustful** *adjective*, **trustfully** *adverb*, **trustworthy** *adjective* [from Norse *traustr* = strong]

trustee *noun* a person who looks after money entrusted to them.

trusting *adjective* having trust.

trusty *adjective* (*old use*) trustworthy; reliable, *my trusty sword.*

truth *noun* **1** something that is true. **2** the quality of being true.

truthful *adjective* **1** telling the truth, *a truthful boy.* **2** true, *a truthful account of what happened.* **truthfully** *adverb*, **truthfulness** *noun*

try[1] *verb* (**tried**, **trying**) **1** attempt. **2** test something by using or doing it, *Try sleeping on your back.* **3** examine the accusations against someone in a lawcourt. **4** be a strain on, *Very small print tries your eyes.*
try on put on clothes etc. to see if they fit.

> **Usage** The use of *try* followed by *and* + infinitive (*try and be early*; *don't try and get the better of me*) is common in informal speech, but is considered incorrect by some people, and should be avoided in formal writing. Say instead *try to be early*, etc.

try[2] *noun* (*plural* **tries**) **1** an attempt. **2** (in rugby) putting the ball down behind the opponents' goal line so as to score points. [the original meaning was 'to separate or distinguish things']

trying *adjective* putting a strain on someone's patience; annoying.

tsar (*say* zah) *noun* the title of the former ruler of Russia. [Russian, from Latin *Caesar*]

tsetse fly (*say* **tset**-see) *noun* a tropical African fly that can transmit sleeping sickness to people whom it bites.

T-shirt *noun* a short-sleeved shirt shaped like a T.

tsp *abbreviation* teaspoonful.

tsunami (*say* tsoo-**nah**-mee) *noun* a long high sea wave caused by underwater earth movement. [Japanese]

tuan (*say* **tyoo**-uhn) *noun* a largely tree-dwelling brush-tailed carnivorous Australian marsupial. [from Wathawarung *duwan*]

tub *noun* a round open container holding liquid, ice cream, soil for plants, etc.

tuba (*say* **tyoo**-buh) *noun* a large brass wind instrument with a deep tone. [Latin, = trumpet]

tubby *adjective* (**tubbier**, **tubbiest**) short and fat. **tubbiness** *noun* [from *tub*]

tube *noun* **1** a long hollow piece of metal, plastic, rubber, glass, etc., especially for liquids or air to pass along. **2** a container made of flexible material with a screw cap, *a tube of toothpaste.*

tuber *noun* a short thick rounded root (e.g. of a dahlia) or underground stem (e.g. of a potato) that produces buds from which new plants will grow. [Latin, = a swelling]

tuberculosis *noun* a disease of people and animals, producing small swellings in the parts affected by it, especially in the lungs. **tubercular** *adjective* [from Latin *tuberculum* = little swelling]

tubing *noun* tubes; a length of tube.

tubular *adjective* shaped like a tube.

tuck[1] *verb* **1** push a loose edge into something so that it is hidden or held in place. **2** put something away in a small space, *Tuck this in your pocket.*
tuck in (*informal*) eat heartily.

tuck[2] *noun* a flat fold stitched in a garment.

tucker *noun* (*Australian informal*) food. [from British dialect]

tuckshop *noun* a school shop selling lunches, snacks, and drinks; a canteen.

Tuesday *noun* the day of the week following Monday. [Old English = day of Tiw (Norse god of war)]

tuft *noun* a bunch of threads, grass, hair, or feathers etc. growing close together. **tufted** *adjective*

tug[1] *verb* (**tugged**, **tugging**) **1** pull hard or suddenly. **2** tow.

tug[2] *noun* **1** a hard or sudden pull. **2** a small powerful boat used for towing others.

tug of war *noun* a contest between two teams pulling a rope from opposite ends.

tuition *noun* teaching. [from Latin *tuitio* = looking after something]

tulip *noun* a large cup-shaped flower on a tall stem growing from a bulb. [from old Turkish *tuliband* = turban (because the flowers are this shape)]

tulle (*say* tyool) *noun* a very fine silky net material used for veils, wedding dresses, etc.

tumble *verb* (**tumbled**, **tumbling**) **1** fall. **2** cause to fall. **3** move or push quickly and carelessly. **tumble** *noun*
tumble to (*informal*) realise what something means.

tumbledown *adjective* falling into ruins.

tumbler *noun* **1** a drinking glass with no stem or handle. **2** a part of a lock that is lifted when a key is turned to open it.

tumbrel *noun* (*old use*) an open cart of the kind used to carry condemned people to the guillotine during the French Revolution.

tummy *noun* (*plural* **tummies**) (*informal*) the stomach.

tumour (*say* **tyoo**-muh) *noun* an abnormal lump growing on or in the body.

tumult (*say* **tyoo**-mult) *noun* an uproar; a state of confusion and agitation.

tumultuous (*say* tyoo-**mul**-choo-uhs) *adjective* making a tumult; noisy.

tun *noun* a large cask or barrel.

tuna (*say* **tyoo**-nuh) *noun* (*plural* **tuna**) a large edible sea fish with pink flesh.

tundra *noun* the vast level Arctic regions of Europe, Asia, and America where there are no trees and the subsoil is always frozen.

tune[1] *noun* a short piece of music; a pleasant series of musical notes. **tuneful** *adjective*, **tunefully** *adverb*
in tune at the correct musical pitch.

tune[2] *verb* (**tuned**, **tuning**) **1** put a musical instrument in tune. **2** adjust a radio or television set to receive a certain channel. **3** adjust an engine so that it runs smoothly. **tuner** *noun*

tungsten *noun* a grey metal used to make a kind of steel. [from Swedish *tung* = heavy, + *sten* = stone]

tunic *noun* **1** a jacket worn as part of a uniform. **2** a sleeveless dress worn over a shirt etc., especially as part of a school uniform.

tunnel[1] *noun* an underground passage.

tunnel[2] *verb* (**tunnelled**, **tunnelling**) make a tunnel.

tupong (*say* **too**-pong) *noun* a small, chiefly sea fish, of south-eastern Australia. Also called *congolli*. [from Gunditjmara *dubong*]

turban *noun* a covering for the head made by wrapping a strip of cloth round a cap. [from old Turkish *tuliband* (compare *tulip*)]

turbid *adjective* (of liquids) muddy; not clear. **turbidity** *noun*, **turbidly** *adverb* [from Latin *turba* = crowd, disturbance]

turbine *noun* a machine or motor driven by a flow of water, steam, or gas. [from Latin *turbinis* = of a whirlwind]

turbojet *noun* a jet engine or aircraft with turbines.

turbot *noun* (*plural* **turbot**) a large flat edible sea fish.

turbulent *adjective* **1** moving violently and unevenly, *turbulent seas.* **2** unruly. **turbulence** *noun*, **turbulently** *adverb* [same origin as *turbid*]

tureen *noun* a deep dish with a lid, from which soup is served at the table.

turf[1] *noun* short grass and the earth round its roots.

turf[2] *verb* cover ground with turf.
turf out (*informal*) throw out.

turgid (*say* **ter**-juhd) *adjective* **1** swollen and not flexible. **2** (of language) pompous.

turkey *noun* (*plural* **turkeys**) a large bird kept for its meat. [the name was originally used of a kind of fowl imported through Turkey in the 16th century]

turmoil *noun* a disturbance; confusion.

turn[1] *verb* **1** move round; move to a new direction. **2** change in position so that a different side becomes uppermost or outermost. **3** change in appearance etc.; become, *He turned pale.* **4** make something change, *You can turn milk into butter.* **5** move a switch or tap to control something, *Turn that radio off.* **6** pass a certain time, *It has turned midnight.* **7** shape something on a lathe.
turn down 1 fold down. **2** reduce the flow or sound of something. **3** reject, *We offered her a job but she turned it down.*
turn out 1 send out; expel. **2** empty something, especially to search or clean it. **3** happen. **4** prove to be, *The visitor turned out to be my uncle.*
turn up 1 appear or arrive. **2** increase the flow or sound of something.

turn[2] *noun* **1** the action of turning; a turning movement. **2** a change. **3** the point where something turns. **4** an opportunity or duty etc. that comes to each person etc. in succession, *It's your turn to wash up.* **5** a short performance in an entertainment. **6** (*informal*) an attack of illness; a nervous shock, *It gave me a nasty turn.*
good turn a helpful action.
in turn in succession; one after another.
[from Greek *tornos* = lathe]

turncoat *noun* a person who deserts one party or cause in order to join an opposing one.

turner *noun* a person who makes things on a lathe. **turnery** *noun*

turning *noun* a place where one road meets another, forming a corner.

turning point *noun* a point where an important change takes place.

turnip *noun* a plant with a large round white root used as a vegetable.

turnout *noun* the number of people who attend a meeting etc.

turnover *noun* **1** a small pie made by folding pastry over fruit, jam, etc. **2** the amount of money received by a firm selling things. **3** the rate at which goods are sold or workers leave and are replaced.

turnpike *noun* **1** (*old use*) a tollgate; a road with tollgates. **2** (*American*) a motorway on which a toll is charged.

turnstile *noun* a revolving gate that admits one person at a time.

turntable *noun* a circular revolving platform or support, e.g. for the record in a record player.

turpentine *noun* a kind of oil used for thinning paint, cleaning paintbrushes, etc.

turpitude *noun* wickedness. [from Latin *turpis* = shameful]

turps *noun* (*informal*) turpentine.

turquoise *noun* **1** a sky-blue or greenish-blue colour. **2** a blue jewel. [French, = Turkish stone]

turret *noun* **1** a small tower on a castle or other building. **2** a revolving structure containing a gun. **turreted** *adjective* [from French *tour* = tower]

turtle *noun* a sea animal that looks like a tortoise.
turn turtle capsize.

tusk *noun* a long pointed tooth projecting outside the mouth of an elephant, walrus, and certain other animals.

tussle[1] *noun* a struggle; a conflict.

tussle[2] *verb* (**tussled**, **tussling**) take part in a tussle.

tussock *noun* a tuft or clump of grass.

tutor *noun* **1** a private teacher. **2** a teacher directing the studies of a small group of students, especially in a university. **tutor** *verb* [Latin, = guardian]

tutorial *noun* a period of tuition and discussion led by a tutor.

tutu (*say* **too**-too) *noun* a ballet dancer's short stiff frilled skirt. [French]

tuxedo *noun* (*plural* **tuxedos** or **tuxedoes**) a dinner jacket; a suit including this.

TV *abbreviation* television.

twaddle *noun* nonsense.

twain *noun & adjective* (*old use*) two.

twang *verb* **1** play a guitar or other stringed instrument by plucking its string. **2** make a sharp sound like that of a wire when plucked. **twang** *noun*

tweak *verb* pinch and twist or pull something sharply. **tweak** *noun*

tweed *noun* thick woollen twill, often woven of mixed colours. [originally a mistake; the Scottish word *tweel* (= twill) was wrongly read as *tweed* by being confused with the River Tweed]

tweet *noun* **1** the chirping sound made by a small bird. **2** a posting on the Twitter social networking site. **tweet** *verb*

tweezers *plural noun* small pincers for picking up or pulling very small things.

twelve *noun & adjective* the number 12; one more than eleven. **twelfth** *adjective & noun*

twenty *noun & adjective* (*plural* **twenties**) the number 20; two times ten. **twentieth** *adjective & noun*

24-7 *adverb* (also **24/7**) (*informal*) twenty-four hours a day, seven days a week; all the time.

twice *adverb* **1** two times; on two occasions. **2** double the amount.

twiddle *verb* (**twiddled**, **twiddling**) twirl or finger something in an idle way; twist something quickly to and fro. **twiddle** *noun*, **twiddly** *adjective* [from *twirl* and *fiddle*]

twig[1] *noun* a small shoot or branch on a tree or shrub.

twig[2] *verb* (**twigged**, **twigging**) (*informal*) realise what something means.

twilight *noun* dim light from the sky just after sunset or just before sunrise.

twill *noun* material woven so that there is a pattern of diagonal lines.

twin[1] *noun* **1** either of two children or animals born to the same mother at one time. **2** either of two things that are exactly alike.

twin[2] *verb* (**twinned**, **twinning**) put things together as a pair. [from Old English *twinn* = double]

twine[1] *noun* strong thin string.

twine[2] *verb* (**twined**, **twining**) twist or wind together or round something.

twinge *noun* a sudden pain; a pang.

twinkle *verb* (**twinkled**, **twinkling**) sparkle. **twinkle** *noun*

twirl *verb* twist quickly. **twirl** *noun*

twist[1] *verb* **1** pass threads or strands round something or round each other. **2** turn the ends of something in opposite directions. **3** turn round or from side to side, *The road twisted through the hills.* **4** bend something out of its proper shape. **5** (*informal*) swindle somebody. **twister** *noun*

twist[2] *noun* a twisting movement or action. **twisty** *adjective*

twit *noun* (*informal*) a silly person.

twitch *verb* pull or move with a slight jerk. **twitch** *noun*

twitter[1] *verb* make quick chirping sounds.

twitter[2] *noun* an act of twittering.

two *noun & adjective* (*plural* **twos**) the number 2; one more than one.
be in two minds be undecided about something.

two-dimensional *adjective* (also **2D**) having two dimensions (length and width); flat.

two-faced *adjective* insincere; deceitful.

tycoon *noun* a rich and influential business person. [from Japanese *taikun* = great prince]

tying *present participle* of **tie**[1].

type[1] *noun* **1** a kind or sort. **2** letters, figures, or symbols designed for use in printing.

type[2] *verb* (**typed, typing**) write something by using a keyboard, typewriter, etc. [from Greek *typos* = impression]

typecast *verb* (**typecast, typecasting**) cast an actor repeatedly in the same kind of part.

typeface *noun* a set of printing types in one design.

typewriter *noun* a machine with keys that are pressed to print letters, figures, or symbols on a piece of paper. **typewritten** *adjective*

typhoid fever *noun* a serious infectious disease with fever, caused by harmful bacteria in food or water etc. [from *typhus*]

typhoon *noun* a violent hurricane in the western Pacific or East Asian seas. [from Chinese *tai fung* = great wind]

typhus *noun* an infectious disease causing fever, weakness, and a rash. [from Greek *typhos* = vapour]

typical *adjective* **1** having the qualities of a particular type of person or thing, *a typical school playground.* **2** usual in a particular person or thing, *She worked with typical carefulness.* **typically** *adverb* [same origin as *type*]

typify (*say* **tip**-uh-fuy) *verb* (**typified, typifying**) be a typical example of something.

typist *noun* a person who types.

typography (*say* tuy-**pog**-ruh-fee) *noun* the style or appearance of the letters, figures, and symbols in printed material. [from *type + -graphy*]

tyrannise (*say* **ti**-ruh-nuyz) *verb* (**tyrannised, tyrannising**) rule or behave like a tyrant.

tyranny (*say* **ti**-ruh-nee) *noun* (*plural* **tyrannies**) **1** government by a tyrant. **2** the way a tyrant behaves towards people. **tyrannical** *adjective*, **tyrannous** *adjective*

tyrant (*say* **tuy**-ruhnt) *noun* a person who rules cruelly and unjustly; someone who insists on being obeyed. [from Greek *tyrannos* = ruler with full power]

tyre *noun* a covering of rubber fitted round a wheel to make it grip the road and run more smoothly.

Uu

uber- (*say* **oo**-buh) *prefix* denoting an outstanding or an extreme example of a particular person or thing. [from German *über* = over]

ubiquitous (*say* yoo-**bik**-wuh-tuhs) *adjective* found everywhere, *The ubiquitous television aerials spoil the view.* **ubiquity** *noun* [from Latin *ubique* = everywhere]

udder *noun* the bag-like part of a cow, ewe, female goat, etc. from which milk is taken.

udon *noun* (in Japanese cookery) wheat pasta made in thick strips. [Japanese]

uey (*say* **yoo**-ee) *noun* (*Australian informal*) a U-turn.

UFO *abbreviation* unidentified flying object.

ugg boot *noun* (also **ugh boot**) (*Australian trademark*) a boot made of sheepskin with the wool on the inside.

ugly *adjective* (**uglier**, **ugliest**) **1** unpleasant to look at; not beautiful. **2** hostile and threatening, *The crowd was in an ugly mood.* **ugliness** *noun* [from Old Norse *uggligr* = frightening]

ugly duckling *noun* someone without early promise but blossoming later.

UHF *abbreviation* ultra-high frequency (between 300 and 3,000 megahertz).

UK *abbreviation* United Kingdom.

ukulele (*say* yoo-kuh-**lay**-lee) *noun* a small guitar with four strings.

ulcer *noun* an open sore. **ulcerated** *adjective*, **ulceration** *noun*

ulna *noun* (*plural* **ulnae** or **ulnas**) the thinner and longer of the two bones in the human forearm. [Latin]

ulterior *adjective* beyond what is obvious or stated, *an ulterior motive.* [Latin, = further (compare *ultra-*)]

ultimate *adjective* **1** furthest in a series of things; final, *Our ultimate destination is London.* **2** basic; fundamental, *the ultimate cause.* **ultimately** *adverb* [from Latin *ultimus* = last]

ultimatum (*say* ul-tuh-**may**-tuhm) *noun* a final demand; a statement that unless something is done by a certain time action will be taken or war will be declared. [same origin as *ultimate*]

ultra- *prefix* **1** beyond (as in *ultraviolet*). **2** extremely; excessively (as in *ultra-modern*). [from Latin *ultra* = beyond]

ultralight *noun* a small lightweight usually one-seater aircraft.

ultramarine *noun* deep bright blue.

ultrasonic *adjective* (of sound) beyond the range of human hearing.

ultrasound *noun* ultrasonic waves; the use of such waves as a diagnostic medical procedure.

ultraviolet *adjective* (of light rays) beyond the violet end of the spectrum.

ultraviolet protection factor *noun* (of sunscreen etc.) the degree of protection against the harmful ultraviolet rays of the sun.

umber *noun* a kind of brown pigment.

umbilical (*say* um-**bil**-uh-kuhl) *adjective* of the navel.

umbilical cord *noun* the tube through which a baby receives nourishment before it is born, connecting its body with the mother's womb.

umbrage *noun* **take umbrage** take offence. [from Latin *umbra* = shadow]

umbrella *noun* **1** a circular piece of material stretched over a folding frame with a central stick used as a handle, or a central pole, opened to protect the user from rain or sun. **2** a general protection. [from Italian *ombrella* = a little shade]

umpire[1] *noun* a referee in cricket, tennis, and some other games.

umpire[2] *verb* (**umpired**, **umpiring**) act as an umpire.

umpteen *adjective* (*informal*) very many. **umpteenth** *adjective*

UN *abbreviation* United Nations.

un- *prefix* **1** not (as in *uncertain*). **2** (before a verb) reversing the action (as in *unlock* = release from being locked).

> **Usage** The number of words with this prefix is almost unlimited, and many of those whose meaning is obvious are not listed here.

unable *adjective* not able to do something.

unacceptable *adjective* not satisfactory or allowable.

unaccountable *adjective* **1** unable to be explained. **2** not accountable for what you do. **unaccountably** *adverb*

unadulterated *adjective* pure; not mixed with things that are less good.

unafraid *adjective* feeling no fear or anxiety.

unaided *adjective* without help.

unalienated *adjective* (of land) not transferred in respect to ownership.

unanimous (*say* yoo-**nan**-uh-muhs) *adjective* with everyone agreeing, *a unanimous decision.* **unanimity** (*say* yoo-nuh-**nim**-uh-tee) *noun*, **unanimously** *adverb* [from Latin *unus* = one, + *animus* = mind]

unassuming *adjective* modest; not arrogant or pretentious.

unattractive *adjective* not pleasing or appealing to look at.

unauthorised *adjective* not having official permission or approval.

unavoidable *adjective* not able to be avoided.

unaware *adjective* not aware.

unawares *adverb* unexpectedly; without noticing.

unbalanced *adjective* **1** not balanced; uneven. **2** biased. **3** emotionally unstable.

unbearable *adjective* not able to be endured. **unbearably** *adverb*

unbeatable *adjective* unable to be defeated or surpassed.

unbeaten *adjective* not defeated; not surpassed.

unbecoming *adjective* **1** not making a person look attractive. **2** not suitable; improper.

unbeknown *adjective* without someone knowing about it, *Unbeknown to us, they were working for our enemies.*

unbelievable *adjective* not able to be believed; incredible. **unbelievably** *adverb*

unbend *verb* (**unbent**, **unbending**) **1** change or become changed from a bent position. **2** relax and become friendly.

unbiased *adjective* not biased.

unbidden *adjective* not commanded; not invited, *He arrived unbidden.*

unblock *verb* remove an obstruction from something.

unborn *adjective* not yet born.

unbreakable *adjective* not liable to break or able to be broken easily.

unbridled *adjective* unrestrained.

unbroken *adjective* not broken; not interrupted.

unburden *verb* remove a burden from the person etc. carrying it.
unburden yourself tell someone what you know.

uncalled-for *adjective* not justified; impertinent.

uncanny *adjective* (**uncannier**, **uncanniest**) **1** strange and rather frightening. **2** extraordinary, *They forecast the exam results with uncanny accuracy.* **uncannily** *adverb*, **uncanniness** *noun*

uncaring *adjective* not displaying sympathy or concern for others.

unceremonious *adjective* without proper formality or dignity.

uncertain *adjective* **1** not certain. **2** not reliable, *Her aim is rather uncertain.* **uncertainly** *adverb*, **uncertainty** *noun*
in no uncertain terms clearly and forcefully.

unchangeable *adjective* not liable to variation or able to be altered.

uncharitable *adjective* making unkind judgements of people or actions. **uncharitably** *adverb*

uncivilised *adjective* **1** not civilised. **2** rough, uncultured.

uncle *noun* the brother of your father or mother; your aunt's husband. [from Latin *avunculus* = uncle]

uncomfortable *adjective* not comfortable. **uncomfortably** *adverb*

uncommon *adjective* not common; unusual.

uncommunicative *adjective* unwilling to talk or impart information.

uncompressed *adjective* (especially of computer data) not compressed.

uncompromising (*say* un-**kom**-pruh-muy-zing) *adjective* not allowing a compromise; inflexible.

unconcerned *adjective* not caring about something; not worried.

unconditional *adjective* without any conditions; absolute, *unconditional surrender.* **unconditionally** *adverb*

unconscious *adjective* **1** not conscious. **2** not aware of things. **3** not intentional. **unconsciously** *adverb*, **unconsciousness** *noun*

uncontrollable *adjective* unable to be controlled or stopped. **uncontrollably** *adverb*

unconventional *adjective* not based on or conforming to what is generally done or believed.

unconvincing *adjective* failing to make someone believe that something is true or valid.

uncooperative *adjective* not cooperative.

uncouple *verb* (**uncoupled**, **uncoupling**) disconnect.

uncouth (*say* un-**kooth**) *adjective* rude and awkward in manner; boorish. [from *un-* + Old English *cuth* = known]

uncover *verb* **1** remove the covering from something. **2** reveal; expose, *They uncovered a plot to kill the president.*

unction *noun* **1** anointing with oil, especially in a religious ceremony. **2** unctuousness. [from Latin *unctum* = oiled]

unctuous (*say* **ungk**-choo-uhs) *adjective* unpleasantly smooth in manner; polite in an exaggerated way. **unctuously** *adverb*, **unctuousness** *noun*

uncultivated *adjective* **1** (of land) not used for growing crops. **2** (of a person) not highly educated.

undecided *adjective* **1** not yet settled, not certain. **2** not having made up your mind yet.

undeniable *adjective* impossible to deny; undoubtedly true. **undeniably** *adverb*

under[1] *preposition* **1** below; beneath, *Hide it under the desk.* **2** less than, *under five years old.* **3** inferior to; of lower rank than. **4** governed or controlled by, *The country prospered under his rule.* **5** in the process of; undergoing, *The road is under repair.* **6** using, *She writes under a pseudonym.* **7** according to the rules of, *This is permitted under our agreement.*
under way in motion; in progress.

under[2] *adverb* in or to a lower place or level or condition, *Slowly the diver went under.*

under[3] *adjective* lower, *the under layers.*

under- *prefix* **1** below; beneath (as in *underwear*). **2** lower; subordinate (as in *under-manager*). **3** not enough; incompletely (as in *undercooked*).

underarm *adjective & adverb* **1** moving the hand and arm forward and upwards. **2** in or for the armpit.

undercarriage *noun* an aircraft's landing wheels and their supports.

underclothes *plural noun* underwear. **underclothing** *noun*

undercover *adjective* done or doing things secretly, *an undercover agent.*

undercurrent *noun* **1** a current that is below the surface or below another current. **2** an underlying feeling or influence, *an undercurrent of fear.*

undercut *verb* (**undercut**, **undercutting**) **1** cut away the part below something. **2** sell something for a lower price than someone else sells it.

underdog *noun* a person or team that is expected to lose a contest or struggle.

underdone *adjective* not thoroughly done; undercooked.

underestimate *verb* (**underestimated**, **underestimating**) make too low an estimate of a person or thing.

underfoot *adverb* on the ground; under your feet.

undergarment *noun* a piece of underwear.

undergo *verb* (**underwent**, **undergone**, **undergoing**) experience or endure something; be subjected to, *The new aircraft underwent intensive tests.*

undergraduate *noun* a student at a university who has not yet taken a degree.

underground[1] *adjective & adverb* **1** under the ground. **2** done or working in secret.

underground[2] *noun* a railway that runs through tunnels under the ground.

undergrowth *noun* bushes and other plants growing closely, especially under trees.

underhand *adjective* done or doing things in a sly or secret way.

underlie *verb* (**underlay**, **underlain**, **underlying**) **1** be or lie under something. **2** be the basis or explanation of something.

underline *verb* (**underlined**, **underlining**) **1** draw a line under a word. **2** emphasise something.

underling *noun* a subordinate.

underlying *adjective* **1** lying under something, *the underlying rocks.* **2** forming the basis or explanation of something, *the underlying causes of the trouble.*

undermine *verb* (**undermined**, **undermining**) **1** make a hollow or tunnel beneath something, especially one causing weakness at the base. **2** weaken something gradually.

underneath *preposition & adverb* below; beneath; under.

underpants *plural noun* an undergarment covering the lower part of the body.

underpass *noun* (*plural* **underpasses**) a road that goes underneath another.

underpay *verb* (**underpaid**, **underpaying**) pay someone too little.

underprivileged *adjective* having less than the normal standard of living or rights in a community.

underrate *verb* (**underrated**, **underrating**) have too low an opinion of a person or thing.

undersell *verb* (**undersold**, **underselling**) sell at a lower price than another person.

underside *noun* the side or surface underneath.

undersigned *adjective* who has or have signed at the bottom of this document, *We, the undersigned, wish to protest.*

undersized *adjective* of less than the normal size.

understand *verb* (**understood, understanding**) **1** know what something means or how it works or why it exists. **2** know and tolerate a person's ways. **3** have been told. **4** take something for granted, *Your expenses will be paid, that's understood.* **understandable** *adjective*, **understandably** *adverb*

understanding[1] *noun* **1** the power to understand or think; intelligence. **2** a person's perception of a situation etc. **3** sympathy; tolerance. **4** agreement in opinion or feeling, *a better understanding between nations.* **5** an agreement.

understanding[2] *adjective* showing sympathy.

understatement *noun* an incomplete or very restrained statement of facts or truth.

understudy[1] *noun* (*plural* **understudies**) an actor who studies a part in order to be able to play it if the usual performer is absent.

understudy[2] *verb* (**understudied, understudying**) be an understudy for an actor or part.

undertake *verb* (**undertook, undertaken, undertaking**) agree or promise to do something.

undertaker *noun* a person whose job is to arrange funerals and burials or cremations.

undertaking *noun* **1** work etc. undertaken. **2** a promise or guarantee. **3** the business of an undertaker.

undertone *noun* **1** a low or quiet tone, *They spoke in undertones.* **2** an underlying quality or feeling, *His letter has a threatening undertone.*

undertow *noun* a current below that of the surface of the sea and moving in the opposite direction.

underwater *adjective & adverb* placed, used, or done beneath the surface of water.

underwear *noun* clothes worn next to the skin, under other clothing.

underweight *adjective* not heavy enough.

underwent *past tense* of **undergo**.

underworld *noun* **1** (in myths and legends) the place for the spirits of the dead, under the earth. **2** the people who are regularly engaged in crime.

underwrite *verb* (**underwrote, underwritten, underwriting**) guarantee to finance something, or to pay for any loss or damage etc. **underwriter** *noun*

undesirable *adjective* not desirable; objectionable. **undesirably** *adverb*

undies *plural noun* (*informal*) underwear.

undisciplined *adjective* lacking in discipline; uncontrolled in behaviour or manner.

undistinguished *adjective* lacking distinction; unexceptional.

undivided *adjective* **1** not divided, separated, or broken into parts. **2** devoted completely to one object.

undo *verb* (**undid, undone, undoing**) **1** unfasten; unwrap. **2** cancel the effect of something, *She has undone all our careful work.*

undoing *noun* bringing or being brought to ruin; a cause of this, *drink was his undoing.*

undoubted *adjective* certain; not regarded as doubtful. **undoubtedly** *adverb*

undress *verb* take clothes off. **undressed** *adjective*

undue *adjective* excessive; too great. **unduly** *adverb*

undulate *verb* (**undulated, undulating**) move like a wave or waves; have a wavy appearance. **undulation** *noun* [from Latin *unda* = a wave]

undying *adjective* everlasting.

unearth *verb* **1** dig something up; uncover by digging. **2** find something by searching.

unearthly *adjective* **1** not earthly; supernatural; strange and frightening. **2** (*informal*) very early or inconvenient, *We had to get up at an unearthly hour.*

uneasy *adjective* **1** uncomfortable. **2** worried; worrying about something. **uneasily** *adverb*, **uneasiness** *noun*

uneatable *adjective* not fit to be eaten.

uneconomic *adjective* not profitable.

unemployed *adjective* without a job. **unemployment** *noun*

unemployment benefit *noun* money paid by the government to unemployed people.

unending *adjective* not coming to an end.

unequal *adjective* **1** not equal. **2** not fair or balanced, *an unequal contest.* **unequally** *adverb*

unequalled *adjective* without an equal.

unerring (*say* un-**er**-ring) *adjective* making no mistake, *unerring accuracy.*

unethical *adjective* not morally correct.

uneven *adjective* **1** not level; not regular. **2** unequal. **3** of variable quality. **unevenly** *adverb*, **unevenness** *noun*

unexceptionable *adjective* not in any way objectionable.

unexceptional *adjective* not exceptional; quite ordinary.

unexciting *adjective* not exciting; dull.

unexpected *adjective* not expected. **unexpectedly** *adverb*, **unexpectedness** *noun*

unfailing *adjective* not failing; constant, reliable, *his unfailing good humour.*

unfair *adjective* not fair; not just. **unfairly** *adverb*, **unfairness** *noun*

unfaithful *adjective* not faithful; disloyal. **unfaithfulness** *noun*

unfamiliar *adjective* not familiar. **unfamiliarity** *noun*

unfashionable *adjective* not fashionable or popular at a particular time.

unfasten *verb* open the fastenings of something.

unfavourable *adjective* not favourable. **unfavourably** *adverb*

unfeeling *adjective* **1** not able to feel things. **2** not caring about other people's feelings; unsympathetic.

unfit[1] *adjective* **1** unsuitable. **2** not in perfect health.

unfit[2] *verb* (**unfitted**, **unfitting**) make a person or thing unsuitable.

unflappable *adjective* (*informal*) remaining calm in a crisis.

unfold *verb* **1** open; spread out. **2** make or become known slowly, *as the story unfolds.*

unforeseen *adjective* not foreseen; unexpected.

unforgettable *adjective* not able to be forgotten.

unforgivable *adjective* not able to be forgiven.

unforgiving *adjective* **1** not willing to forgive or excuse people's faults or wrongdoings. **2** (of a place or situation) harsh or hostile.

unfortunate *adjective* **1** unlucky. **2** unsuitable; regrettable, *an unfortunate remark.* **unfortunately** *adverb*

unfounded *adjective* not based on facts.

unfreeze *verb* (**unfroze**, **unfrozen**, **unfreezing**) thaw; cause something to thaw.

unfriend see **defriend**.

unfriendly *adjective* not friendly. **unfriendliness** *noun*

unfrock *verb* dismiss a person from being a priest.

unfurl *verb* unroll; spread out.

unfurnished *adjective* without furniture.

ungainly *adjective* awkward-looking; clumsy; ungraceful. **ungainliness** *noun* [from *un-*, + *gainly* = graceful]

ungodly *adjective* **1** not giving reverence to God; not religious. **2** (*informal*) outrageous; very inconvenient, *She woke me at an ungodly hour.* **ungodliness** *noun*

ungovernable *adjective* uncontrollable.

ungracious *adjective* not kindly; not courteous. **ungraciously** *adverb*

ungrateful *adjective* not grateful. **ungratefully** *adverb*, **ungratefulness** *noun*

unguarded *adjective* **1** not guarded. **2** without thought or caution; indiscreet, *He said this in an unguarded moment.*

unhappy *adjective* **1** not happy; sad. **2** unfortunate; unsuitable. **unhappily** *adverb*, **unhappiness** *noun*

unharmed *adjective* not harmed; uninjured.

unhealthy *adjective* **1** not in good health. **2** harmful to health. **unhealthiness** *noun*

unheard-of *adjective* never known or done before; extraordinary.

unhelpful *adjective* not helpful.

unhinge *verb* (**unhinged**, **unhinging**) cause a person's mind to become unbalanced.

uni *noun* (*informal*) a university.

uni- *prefix* one; single (as in *unicorn*). [from Latin *unus* = one]

unicorn *noun* (in legends) an animal that is like a horse with one long straight horn growing from its forehead. [from *uni-*, + Latin *cornu* = horn]

unidentified *adjective* not recognised or identified.

uniform[1] *noun* special clothes showing that the wearer is a member of a certain organisation, school, etc.

uniform[2] *adjective* always the same; not varying, *The desks are of uniform size.* **uniformity** *noun*, **uniformly** *adverb* [from *uni-* + *form*]

uniformed *adjective* wearing a uniform.

unify *verb* (**unified**, **unifying**) make into one thing; unite. **unification** *noun*

unilateral *adjective* of or done by one person or group or country. [from *uni-* + *lateral*]

unimaginative *adjective* not readily using or demonstrating the use of the imagination.

unimportant *adjective* lacking importance or significance.

uninhabitable *adjective* not suitable for habitation.

uninhabited *adjective* not inhabited.

uninhibited *adjective* not inhibited; having no inhibitions.

uninstall *verb* (also **uninstal**) remove an application or file from a computer.

unintelligible *adjective* impossible to understand.

unintentional *adjective* not done on purpose.

uninterested *adjective* not interested; showing or feeling no concern.

Usage See the note at *disinterested.*

uninteresting *adjective* not arousing curiosity or interest.

uninviting *adjective* not attractive.

union *noun* **1** the joining of things together; uniting. **2** a trade union. [from Latin *unio* = unity]

unionist *noun* **1** a member of a trade union. **2** a person who wishes to unite one country with another.

unique (*say* yoo-**neek**) *adjective* being the only one of its kind, *This vase is unique.* **uniquely** *adverb* [from Latin *unus* = one]

unison *noun* **in unison 1** with all sounding or singing the same tune etc. together, or speaking in chorus. **2** in agreement. [from *uni-*, + Latin *sonus* = sound]

unit *noun* **1** an amount used as a standard in measuring or counting things, *Centimetres are units of length; dollars are units of money.* **2** a group, device, piece of furniture, etc. regarded as a single thing but forming part of a larger group or whole, *an army unit*; *a home unit*; *a sink unit.* [from Latin *unus* = one]

unite *verb* (**united**, **uniting**) join together; make or become one thing.

unit fraction *noun* a fraction having one as its numerator.

unity *noun* **1** being united; being in agreement. **2** something whole that is made up of parts. **3** the number one.

univariate *adjective* (in statistics) involving one variate or variable quality.

universal *adjective* of or including or done by everyone or everything. **universally** *adverb*

universe *noun* everything that exists, including the earth and living things and all the heavenly bodies. [from Latin *universus* = combined into one]

university *noun* (*plural* **universities**) a place where people go to study at an advanced level after leaving school.

unjust *adjective* not fair; not just.

unkempt *adjective* looking untidy or neglected. [from *un-*, + an old word *kempt* = combed]

unkind *adjective* not kind. **unkindly** *adverb*, **unkindness** *noun*

unknown *adjective* not known.

unleash *verb* set free from a leash; let loose.

unleavened (*say* un-**lev**-uhnd) *adjective* (of bread) made without yeast or other substances that would make it rise.

unless *conjunction* except when; if not, *We cannot go unless we are invited.*

unlike[1] *preposition* not like, *Unlike me, she enjoys cricket.*

unlike[2] *adjective* not alike; different, *The two children are very unlike.*

unlikely *adjective* (**unlikelier**, **unlikeliest**) not likely to happen or be true.

unlimited *adjective* not limited; very great or very many.

unload *verb* remove the load of things carried by a ship, aircraft, vehicle, etc.

unlock *verb* open something by undoing a lock.

unlucky *adjective* not lucky; having or bringing bad luck. **unluckily** *adverb*

unmade *adjective* **1** not made. **2** (of a bed) not yet arranged ready for use. **3** (of a road) a road that has not been sealed with bitumen etc.

unmanageable *adjective* unable to be managed.

unmarried *adjective* not married.

unmask *verb* **1** remove a person's mask. **2** reveal what a person or thing really is.

unmentionable *adjective* too bad to be spoken of.

unmistakable *adjective* not able to be mistaken for another person or thing. **unmistakably** *adverb*

unmitigated *adjective* absolute, *an unmitigated disaster.*

unnatural *adjective* **1** not natural; not normal. **2** artificial; affected. **unnaturally** *adverb*

unnecessary *adjective* not necessary; more than is necessary.

unnerve *verb* (**unnerved**, **unnerving**) cause someone to lose courage or determination.

unoccupied *adjective* not occupied.

unofficial *adjective* not official. **unofficially** *adverb*

unorthodox *adjective* contrary to what is usual, traditional, or accepted; not orthodox.

unpack *verb* take things out of a suitcase, bag, box, etc.

unpaid *adjective* **1** (of a debt) not yet paid. **2** not receiving payment for work.

unparalleled *adjective* having no parallel or equal.

unparliamentary *adjective* contrary to parliamentary custom; impolite or abusive, *unparliamentary language.*

unpick *verb* undo the stitching of something.

unplanned *adjective* not planned.

unpleasant *adjective* not pleasant. **unpleasantly** *adverb*, **unpleasantness** *noun*

unpopular *adjective* not popular.

unprecedented (*say* un-**pres**-uh-den-tuhd) *adjective* that has never happened before.

unprejudiced *adjective* impartial.

unprepared *adjective* not prepared beforehand; not ready; not equipped.

unprepossessing *adjective* not attractive; not making a good impression.

unpretentious *adjective* not attempting to impress others with an appearance of greater importance, talent, or culture than is actually possessed.

unprincipled *adjective* without good moral principles; unscrupulous.

unprintable *adjective* too rude or indecent to be printed.

unproductive *adjective* **1** not producing or able to produce large amounts of goods, crops, or other commodities. **2** (of an activity or period) not achieving much.

unprofessional *adjective* **1** not professional. **2** not worthy of a member of a profession.

unprofitable *adjective* not producing a profit or advantage. **unprofitably** *adverb*

unqualified *adjective* **1** not officially qualified to do something. **2** not limited, *We gave it our unqualified approval.*

unquestionable *adjective* not able to be disputed or doubted.

unravel *verb* (**unravelled**, **unravelling**) **1** disentangle. **2** undo something that is knitted. **3** investigate and solve a mystery.

unreadable *adjective* **1** not clear enough to read. **2** too dull or difficult to be worth reading.

unreal *adjective* **1** not real, existing in the imagination only. **2** (*informal*) incredible; amazing. **unreality** *noun*

unrealistic *adjective* not realistic.

unreasonable *adjective* **1** not reasonable. **2** excessive; unjust. **unreasonably** *adverb*

unreel *verb* unwind from a reel.

unreliable *adjective* not able to be relied upon.

unrelieved *adjective* without anything to vary it, *unrelieved gloom.*

unremitting *adjective* not stopping, not relaxing; persistent.

unrepentant *adjective* showing no regret for one's wrongdoings.

unrequited (*say* un-ruh-**kwuy**-tuhd) *adjective* (of love) not returned or rewarded. [from *un-* + *requited* = paid back]

unreserved *adjective* **1** not reserved. **2** without restriction; complete, *unreserved loyalty.* **unreservedly** *adverb*

unrest *noun* restlessness; trouble caused because people are dissatisfied.

unripe *adjective* not yet ripe.

unrivalled *adjective* having no equal; better than all others.

unroll *verb* open something that has been rolled up.

unruly *adjective* difficult to control; disorderly. **unruliness** *noun* [from *un-* + *rule*]

unsafe *adjective* not safe; dangerous.

unsatisfactory *adjective* not satisfactory; not good enough.

unsaturated *adjective* (of a fat or oil) capable of further reaction by combining with hydrogen.

unsavoury *adjective* unpleasant; disgusting.

unscathed *adjective* uninjured. [from *un-*, + an old word *scathed* = harmed]

unscrew *verb* undo something that has been screwed up.

unscrupulous *adjective* having no scruples about wrongdoing.

unseat *verb* throw a person from horseback or from a seat on a bicycle etc.

unseemly *adjective* not seemly; improper.

unseen[1] *adjective* not seen; invisible.

unseen[2] *noun* a passage for translation without previous preparation.

unselfish *adjective* not selfish.

unsettled *adjective* **1** not settled; not calm. **2** likely to change.

unshakeable *adjective* not able to be shaken; firm.

unsightly *adjective* not pleasant to look at; ugly. **unsightliness** *noun*

unskilled *adjective* not having or not needing special skill or training.

unsociable *adjective* not sociable.

unsolicited *adjective* not asked for.

unsophisticated *adjective* **1** lacking refined worldly knowledge or tastes. **2** not complicated or highly developed; basic.

unsound *adjective* not sound; damaged, unhealthy, unreasonable, or unreliable. [from *un-* + *sound*[4]]

unspeakable *adjective* too bad to be described; very objectionable.

unspecified *adjective* not stated clearly or exactly, *an unspecified number of people.*

unstable *adjective* not stable; likely to change or become unbalanced.

unsteady *adjective* not steady.

unstinted *adjective* given generously.

unstuck *adjective* **come unstuck 1** cease to stick. **2** (*informal*) fail, go wrong.

unsuccessful *adjective* not successful.

unsuitable *adjective* not suitable.

unsure *adjective* not sure.

unthinkable *adjective* too bad or too unlikely to be worth considering.

unthinking *adjective* thoughtless.

untidy *adjective* (**untidier**, **untidiest**) not tidy. **untidily** *adverb*, **untidiness** *noun*

untie *verb* (**untied**, **untying**) undo something that has been tied.

until *preposition & conjunction* up to a particular time or event.

untimely *adjective* happening too soon or at an unsuitable time, *an untimely death.*

unto *preposition* (*old use*) to.

untold *adjective* **1** not told. **2** too much or too many to be counted, *untold wealth.*

untoward *adjective* inconvenient; awkward, *if nothing untoward happens.*

untraceable *adjective* unable to be traced.

untrue *adjective* **1** not true. **2** not faithful or loyal.

untruth *noun* an untrue statement; a lie. **untruthful** *adjective*, **untruthfully** *adverb*

unused *adjective* **1** (*say* un-**yoozd**) not yet used, *an unused stamp.* **2** (*say* un-**yoost**) not accustomed, *He is unused to eating meat.*

unusual *adjective* not usual; exceptional; strange. **unusually** *adverb*

unutterable *adjective* too great to be described, *unutterable joy.*

unvarnished *adjective* **1** not varnished. **2** plain and straightforward, *the unvarnished truth.*

unveil *verb* **1** remove a veil or covering from something. **2** reveal.

unwanted *adjective* not wanted.

unwarrantable *adjective* not justifiable.

unwarranted *adjective* not justified; not authorised.

unwary *adjective* not cautious. **unwarily** *adverb*, **unwariness** *noun*

unwell *adjective* not in good health.

unwholesome *adjective* not wholesome.

unwieldy *adjective* awkward to move or control because of its size, shape, or weight. **unwieldiness** *noun*

unwilling *adjective* not willing. **unwillingly** *adverb*, **unwillingness** *noun*

unwind *verb* (**unwound**, **unwinding**) **1** unroll. **2** (*informal*) relax after a time of work or strain.

unwise *adjective* not wise; foolish. **unwisely** *adverb*

unwitting *adjective* **1** unaware. **2** unintentional. **unwittingly** *adverb*

unwonted (*say* un-**wohn**-tuhd) *adjective* not customary; not usual, *She spoke with unwonted rudeness.* **unwontedly** *adverb* [from *un-* + *wont*]

unworn *adjective* not yet worn.

unworthy *adjective* not worthy.

unwrap *verb* (**unwrapped**, **unwrapping**) open something that is wrapped.

unwritten *adjective* **1** not recorded in writing. **2** (especially of a law) resting originally on custom or judicial decision rather than statute. **3** (of a convention) understood and generally accepted, although not formally established.

unyielding *adjective* **1** (of a mass or structure) not giving way to pressure; hard or solid. **2** (of a person) unlikely to be swayed.

up[1] *adverb* **1** to or in a higher place or position or level, *Prices went up.* **2** so as to be upright, *Stand up.* **3** out of bed, *It's time to get up.* **4** completely, *Eat up your peas.* **5** finished, *Your time is up.* **6** (*informal*) happening, *Something is up.*
up against 1 close to. **2** (*informal*) faced with difficulties, dangers, or challenges.
up front in advance, *pay up front.*
up to 1 until. **2** busy with or doing something, *What's he up to?* **3** capable of, *He didn't feel up to the task.* **4** needed from, *It's up to us to help her.*
up to date 1 modern; fashionable. **2** giving recent information etc.

> **Usage** Use hyphens when this is used as an adjective before a noun, e.g. *up-to-date information* (but *The information is up to date*).

up[2] *preposition* upwards through or along or into, *Water came up the pipes.*

up-and-coming *adjective* (*informal*) making good progress and likely to succeed.

upbeat *adjective* (*informal*) cheerful; optimistic.

upbraid *verb* (*formal*) reproach.

upbringing *noun* the way someone is trained during childhood.

upcoming *adjective* about to happen; imminent, *the upcoming elections.*

update *verb* (**updated**, **updating**) bring a thing up to date.

UPF *abbreviation* ultraviolet protection factor.

upfront *adjective* **1** frank, open. **2** made in advance, *upfront fees.*

upgrade *verb* raise in rank; improve equipment etc. **upgrade** *noun*

upheaval *noun* a sudden violent change or disturbance.

uphill[1] *adverb* up a slope.

uphill[2] *adjective* **1** going up a slope. **2** difficult, *It was uphill work.*

uphold *verb* (**upheld**, **upholding**) **1** support, keep something from falling. **2** support a decision or belief etc.

upholster *verb* put covers, padding, and springs etc. on furniture. **upholstery** *noun* [from *uphold* = maintain and repair]

upkeep *noun* keeping something in good condition; the cost of this.

uplift *verb* raise, *uplift their spirits.*

upload *verb* transfer data from one computer to another, typically to one that is larger or remote from the user. **upload** *noun*

upmarket *adjective & adverb* of or towards the dearer end of the market.

upon *preposition* on.

upper *adjective* higher in place or rank etc. **the upper hand** control; dominance, *He gained the upper hand.*

upper case *noun* capital letters.

uppermost[1] *adjective* highest.

uppermost[2] *adverb* on or to the top or the highest place, *Keep the painted side uppermost.*

upright[1] *adjective* **1** vertical; erect. **2** strictly honest or honourable.

upright[2] *noun* a post or rod etc. placed upright, especially as a support.

uprising *noun* a rebellion; a revolt.

uproar *noun* an outburst of noise or excitement or anger.

uproarious *adjective* very noisy.

uproot *verb* **1** remove a plant and its roots from the ground. **2** make someone leave the place where they have lived for a long time.

ups and downs *plural noun* **1** ascents and descents. **2** alternate good and bad luck.

upset[1] *verb* (**upset**, **upsetting**) **1** overturn; knock something over. **2** make a person unhappy. **3** disturb the normal working of something.

upset[2] *noun* upsetting something; being upset, *a stomach upset.*

upshot *noun* an outcome.

upside-down *adverb & adjective* **1** with the upper part underneath instead of on top. **2** in great disorder; very untidy.

upstage[1] *adverb & adjective* nearer the back of a theatre stage.

upstage[2] *verb* draw attention away from someone else.

upstairs *adverb & adjective* to or on a higher floor.

upstanding *adjective* **1** standing up. **2** honest, law-abiding.

upstart *noun* a person who has risen suddenly to a high position, especially one who then behaves arrogantly.

upstream *adjective & adverb* in the direction from which a stream flows.

uptake *noun* (*informal*) understanding, *She is quick on the uptake.*

uptight *adjective* (*informal*) tense and nervous or annoyed.

upturn[1] *verb* **1** turn upwards. **2** turn upside down.

upturn[2] *noun* an upward trend or improvement in business or fortune etc.

upward *adjective & adverb* going towards what is higher. **upwards** *adverb*

uranium *noun* a heavy radioactive grey metal used as a source of nuclear energy. [named after the planet Uranus]

Uranus *noun* one of the major planets. [named after a Greek god]

urban *adjective* of a town or city. [from Latin *urbis* = of a city]

urbane *adjective* having smoothly polite manners. **urbanely** *adverb*, **urbanity** *noun* [same origin as *urban*]

urbanise *verb* (**urbanised**, **urbanising**) change a place into a town-like area. **urbanisation** *noun*

urchin *noun* **1** a poorly dressed or mischievous boy. **2** a sea urchin. [from Latin *ericius* = hedgehog]

Urdu *noun* a language of the Indian region, spoken in Pakistan and elsewhere.

urge[1] *verb* (**urged**, **urging**) **1** try to persuade a person to do something. **2** drive people or animals onward.

urge[2] *noun* a strong desire.

urgent *adjective* needing to be done or dealt with immediately. **urgency** *noun*, **urgently** *adverb* [from Latin *urgens* = urging]

urinate (*say* **yoo**-ruh-nayt) *verb* (**urinated**, **urinating**) pass urine out of your body. **urination** *noun*

urine (*say* **yoo**-ruhn) *noun* waste liquid that collects in the bladder and is passed out of the body. **urinary** *adjective*

URL *abbreviation* uniform resource locator, an address on the World Wide Web.

urn *noun* **1** a large metal container with a tap, in which water is heated. **2** a container shaped like a vase, usually with a foot; a container for holding the ashes of a cremated person.

US *abbreviation* United States (of America).

us *pronoun* the form of *we* used when it is the object of a verb or after a preposition.

USA *abbreviation* United States of America.

usable *adjective* able to be used.

usage *noun* **1** use; the way something is used. **2** a habitual or customary practice, *modern Australian English usage.*

USB *abbreviation* (in computing) universal serial bus, a standard for connecting peripherals to a computer.

USB flash drive *noun* a small external flash drive for saving computer data.

use[1] (*say* yooz) *verb* (**used**, **using**) perform an action or job with something, *Use soap for washing.* **user** *noun*
used to 1 accustomed to; familiar with, *He is not used to the climate.* **2** was or were accustomed to, *We used to go by train.*
use up use all of something.

use[2] (*say* yoos) *noun* **1** the action of using something; being used. **2** the purpose for which something is used. **3** the quality of being useful.

used *adjective* not new; secondhand.

useful *adjective* able to be used a lot or to do something that needs doing. **usefully** *adverb*, **usefulness** *noun*

useless *adjective* not useful; producing no effect, *Their efforts were useless.* **uselessly** *adverb*, **uselessness** *noun*

user *noun* **1** a person who uses or operates something. **2** a person who takes illegal drugs.
user-friendly (of a machine or system) easy to use or understand.

username *noun* an identification used by a person with access to a computer, network, or online service.

usher[1] *noun* a person who shows people to their seats in a public hall or church etc.

usher[2] *verb* lead in or out; escort someone as an usher.

usual *adjective* such as happens or is done or used etc. always or most of the time. **usually** *adverb* [from Latin *usum* = used]

usurp (*say* yoo-**zerp**) *verb* take power or a position or right wrongfully or by force. **usurpation** *noun*, **usurper** *noun*

usury (*say* **yoo**-*zh*uh-ree) *noun* the lending of money at an excessively high rate of interest. **usurer** *noun*

ute *noun* (*Australian informal*) a utility truck.

utensil (*say* yoo-**ten**-suhl) *noun* a device or container, especially one for use in the house, *cooking utensils.*

uterus (*say* **yoo**-tuh-ruhs) another name for **womb**. [Latin, = womb]

utilise *verb* (**utilised**, **utilising**) use; find a use for something. **utilisation** *noun*

utilitarian *adjective* designed to be useful rather than decorative or luxurious; practical. [from *utility*]

utility *noun* (*plural* **utilities**) **1** usefulness. **2** a useful thing. **3** (*Australian*) (in full **utility truck**) a small truck with a cabin and a rear tray for carrying loads. **4** an organisation supplying gas, water, electricity, etc. to the community. [from Latin *utilis* = useful]

utmost *adjective* extreme; greatest, *Look after it with the utmost care.* **utmost** *noun* [from Old English, = furthest out]

utopia (*say* yoo-**toh**-pee-uh) *noun* an imaginary place where everyone is happy and everything is perfect. **utopian** *adjective* [from the title of a book by Sir Thomas More (1516), based on Greek *ou* = not, + *topos* = place]

utter[1] *verb* say or speak; make a sound with your mouth. **utterance** *noun*

utter[2] *adjective* complete; absolute, *utter misery.* **utterly** *adverb*

uttermost *adjective & noun* utmost.

U-turn *noun* **1** a U-shaped turn made in a vehicle so that it then travels in the opposite direction. **2** a complete change of policy.

UV *abbreviation* ultraviolet.

Vv

vacant *adjective* **1** empty; not filled or occupied. **2** without expression; blank, *a vacant stare.* **vacancy** *noun*, **vacantly** *adverb* [from Latin *vacans* = being empty]

vacate *verb* (**vacated**, **vacating**) leave or give up a place or position. [from Latin *vacare* = be empty or free from work]

vacation (*say* vuh-**kay**-shuhn) *noun* **1** a holiday, especially between the terms at a university. **2** vacating a place etc. [same origin as *vacate*]

vaccinate (*say* **vak**-suh-nayt) *verb* (**vaccinated**, **vaccinating**) treat with a vaccine to produce immunity against a disease; inoculate. **vaccination** *noun*

vaccine (*say* **vak**-seen) *noun* a substance used to immunise a person against a disease. [from Latin *vacca* = cow (because serum from cows was used to protect people from smallpox)]

vacillate (*say* **vas**-uh-layt) *verb* (**vacillated**, **vacillating**) keep changing your mind; waver. **vacillation** *noun* [from Latin *vacillare* = sway]

vacuous (*say* **vak**-yoo-uhs) *adjective* empty-headed; without expression, *a vacuous stare.* **vacuity** *noun*, **vacuously** *adverb*, **vacuousness** *noun* [same origin as *vacuum*]

vacuum *noun* a completely empty space; a space without any air in it. **vacuum** *verb* [from Latin *vacuus* = empty]

vacuum cleaner *noun* an electrical device that sucks up dust and dirt etc.

vacuum flask *noun* a container with double walls that have a vacuum between them, used for keeping liquids hot or cold.

vagabond *noun* a wanderer; a vagrant. [from Latin *vagari* = wander]

vagary (*say* **vay**-guh-ree) *noun* (*plural* **vagaries**) an impulsive change or whim, *the vagaries of fashion.* [from Latin *vagari* = wander]

vagina (*say* vuh-**juy**-nuh) *noun* the passage that leads from the vulva to the womb. **vaginal** *adjective* [from Latin *vagina* = sheath]

vagrant (*say* **vay**-gruhnt) *noun* a person with no settled home or regular work; a tramp. **vagrancy** *noun* [from Latin *vagans* = wandering]

vague *adjective* not definite; not clear. **vaguely** *adverb*, **vagueness** *noun* [from Latin *vagus* = wandering]

vain *adjective* **1** conceited, especially about your appearance. **2** useless, *They made vain attempts to save her.* **vainly** *adverb*
in vain with no result; uselessly. [from Latin *vanus* = empty]

Vaisakhi see **Baisakhi**.

valance *noun* a short curtain round the frame of a bed or above a window.

vale *noun* a valley. [from Latin *vallis* = valley]

valediction (*say* val-uh-**dik**-shuhn) *noun* saying farewell. **valedictory** *adjective* [from Latin *vale* = farewell, + *dicere* = say (compare *benediction*)]

valentine *noun* **1** a card sent on St Valentine's day (14 February) to the person you love. **2** the person to whom you send this card.

valet (*say* **val**-ay or **val**-uht) *noun* **1** a person who looks after the clothes and personal belongings of an employer or a guest in a hotel. **2** a person employed to clean or park cars.

valetudinarian *noun* a person who is excessively concerned about keeping healthy. [from Latin *valetudo* = health]

valiant *adjective* brave; courageous. **valiantly** *adverb* [same origin as *value*]

valid *adjective* **1** legally able to be used or accepted, *This passport is out of date and not valid.* **2** (of reasoning) sound and logical. **validity** *noun* [from Latin *validus* = strong]

validate *verb* (**validated**, **validating**) make something valid. **validation** *noun*

valley *noun* (*plural* **valleys**) **1** a long low area between hills. **2** an area through which a river flows, *the Nile valley.* [from Latin *vallis* = valley]

valour *noun* bravery. **valorous** *adjective* [from Latin *valor* = strength]

valuable *adjective* worth a lot of money; of great value. **valuably** *adverb*

valuables *plural noun* valuable things.

value[1] *noun* **1** the amount of money etc. that is considered to be the equivalent of something, or for which it can be exchanged. **2** how useful or important something is, *They learnt the value of regular exercise.* **3** a magnitude, quantity, or number.

value[2] *verb* (**valued**, **valuing**) **1** think that something is valuable. **2** estimate the value of a thing. **valuation** *noun*, **valuer** *noun* [from Latin *valere* = be strong]

valueless *adjective* having no value.

valve *noun* **1** a device for controlling the flow of gas or liquid through a pipe or tube. **2** each piece of the shell of oysters and similar animals. **valvular** *adjective* [from Latin *valva* = section of a folding door]

vamp *verb* **1** make from odds and ends, *We'll vamp something up.* **2** improvise a musical accompaniment.

vampire *noun* a ghost or revived corpse supposed to leave a grave at night and suck blood from living people.

van[1] *noun* **1** a covered vehicle for carrying goods etc. **2** a railway carriage for luggage or goods, or for the use of the guard. **3** a caravan. [short for *caravan*]

van[2] *noun* the vanguard; the forefront.

vandal *noun* a person who deliberately breaks or damages things. **vandalism** *noun* [named after the Vandals, a Germanic people who invaded the Roman Empire in the 5th century, destroying many books and works of art]

vandalise *verb* (**vandalised**, **vandalising**) damage things as a vandal.

vane *noun* **1** a weathervane. **2** the blade of a propeller, sail of a windmill, or other device that acts on or is moved by wind or water.

vanguard *noun* **1** the leading part of an army or fleet. **2** the first people to adopt a fashion or idea etc. [from French *avant* = before, + *garde* = guard]

vanilla *noun* a flavouring obtained from the pods of a tropical plant. [from Spanish *vainilla* = little pod]

vanish *verb* disappear completely.

vanity *noun* **1** conceit, especially about one's appearance. **2** futility; worthlessness; something vain. **3** a bathroom unit consisting of a washbasin and cupboard.

vanquish *verb* conquer. [from Latin *vincere* = conquer]

vantage point *noun* a place from which you have a good view of something. [from *vantage* = advantage]

vape[1] *verb* (**vaped**, **vaping**) inhale and exhale the vapour produced by an electronic cigarette or similar device. [short for *vapour* or *vaporise*]

vape[2] *noun* **1** an electronic cigarette or similar device. **2** an act or spell of vaping.

vapid *adjective* not lively; not interesting.

vaporise *verb* (**vaporised**, **vaporising**) change or be changed into vapour. **vaporisation** *noun*, **vaporiser** *noun*

vapour *noun* a visible gas to which some substances can be converted by heat; steam or mist. [from Latin *vapor* = steam]

variable[1] *adjective* **1** not consistent or having a fixed pattern; liable to change, *Local weather patterns are highly variable.* **2** (of a quantity in mathematics) able to assume different numerical values. **3** able to be changed or adapted, *The drill has variable speed.* **variability** *noun*, **variably** *adverb*

variable[2] *noun* **1** an element, feature, or factor that is liable to vary or change. **2** (in mathematics) a quantity which during calculation is assumed to vary or be capable of varying in value.

variance *noun* the amount by which things differ.
at variance differing; conflicting.

variant *adjective* differing from something, *'Gaol' is a variant spelling of 'jail'.* **variant** *noun*

variate *noun* (in statistics) **1** a quantity having a numerical value for each member of a group. **2** a variable quantity, especially one whose values occur according to a frequency distribution.

variation *noun* **1** varying; the amount by which something varies. **2** a different form of something.

varicose *adjective* (of veins) permanently swollen.

varied *adjective* of different sorts; full of variety.

variegated (*say* **vair**-ree-uh-gay-tuhd) *adjective* with patches of different colours. **variegation** *noun* [same origin as *various*]

variety *adjective* (*plural* **varieties**) **1** a quantity of different kinds of things. **2** the quality of not always being the same; variation. **3** a particular kind of something, *There are several varieties of spaniel.* **4** an entertainment that includes short performances of various kinds.

various *adjective* **1** of several kinds; unlike one another, *for various reasons.* **2** several, *We met various people.* **variously** *adverb* [from Latin *varius* = changing]

varlet *noun* (*old use*) **1** a menial servant. **2** a rascal.

varnish[1] *noun* (*plural* **varnishes**) a liquid that dries to form a hard shiny usually transparent coating.

varnish[2] *verb* coat something with varnish.

vary *verb* (**varied**, **varying**) **1** make or become different; change. **2** be different.

vascular *adjective* consisting of tubes or similar vessels for circulating blood, sap, or water in animals or plants, *the vascular system.* [from Latin *vasculum* = little vessel]

vase *noun* an open container used for holding cut flowers or as an ornament. [from Latin *vas* = vessel]

vaseline *noun* (*trademark*) a petroleum product used as an ointment. [from German *Wasser* = water, + Greek *elaion* = oil]

vassal *noun* a humble servant or subordinate.

vast *adjective* very great, especially in area, *a vast expanse of water.* **vastly** *adverb*, **vastness** *noun* [from Latin *vastus* = unoccupied, desert]

vat *noun* a very large container for holding liquid.

vaudeville (*say* **vaw**-duh-vil) *noun* a kind of variety entertainment.

vault[1] *verb* jump over something, especially while supporting yourself on your hands or with the help of a pole.

vault[2] *noun* **1** a vaulting jump. **2** an arched roof. **3** an underground room used to store things. **4** a room for storing money or valuables. **5** a burial chamber. [from Latin *volvere* = to roll]

vaulted *adjective* having an arched roof.

vaulting horse *noun* a padded structure for vaulting over in gymnastics.

vaunt *verb & noun* boast. [from Latin *vanus* = vain]

vax *noun* (*plural* **vaxes**) (*informal*) a vaccine or vaccination.

VCR *abbreviation* video cassette recorder.

VDU *abbreviation* visual display unit.

veal *noun* calf's flesh used as food. [from Latin *vitulus* = calf]

vector *noun* (in mathematics) a quantity that has size and direction (e.g. velocity = speed in a certain direction). **vectorial** *adjective*

Veda (*say* **vay**-duh or **vee**-duh) *noun* the most ancient and sacred literature of the Hindus. **Vedic** *adjective* [Sanskrit, = sacred knowledge]

veer *verb* change direction; swerve.

vegan (*say* **vee**-guhn) *noun* a vegetarian who eats no animal products (e.g. eggs) at all.

vegetable *noun* a plant that can be used as food.

vegetarian *noun* a person who does not eat meat. **vegetarianism** *noun*

vegetate *verb* (**vegetated**, **vegetating**) live a dull or inactive life.

vegetation *noun* **1** plants that are growing. **2** vegetating.

vehement (*say* **vee**-uh-muhnt) *adjective* showing strong feeling, *a vehement refusal.* **vehemence** *noun*, **vehemently** *adverb*

vehicle (*say* **vee**-uh-kuhl) *noun* a device for transporting people or goods on land or in space. **vehicular** *adjective* [from Latin *vehere* = carry]

veil[1] *noun* **1** a piece of thin material worn to cover the face or head. **2** a thing that conceals.
take the veil become a nun.

veil[2] *verb* cover with a veil or as if with a veil; conceal partially.

vein *noun* **1** any of the tubes that carry blood from all parts of the body to the heart. (Compare **artery** 1.) **2** a line or streak on a leaf, rock, insect's wing, etc. **3** a long deposit of mineral or ore in the middle of a rock. **4** a mood or manner, *She spoke in a serious vein.* [from Latin *vena* = vein]

velcro *noun* (*trademark*) a fastener consisting of two strips of fabric that cling together when pressed.

veld (*say* velt) *noun* (also **veldt**) an area of open grassland in South Africa. [Afrikaans, = field]

vellum *noun* smooth parchment or writing paper. [same origin as *veal* (because parchment was made from animals' skins)]

velocity *noun* (*plural* **velocities**) speed. [from Latin *velox* = swift]

velodrome (*say* **vel**-uh-drohm) *noun* a place or building with a track for cycle racing.

velour (*say* vuh-**loor**) *noun* a thick velvety material. [from French *velours* = velvet]

velvet *noun* a woven material with very short soft furry fibres on one side. **velvety** *adjective* [from Latin *villus* = soft fur]

venal (*say* **vee**-nuhl) *adjective* able to be bribed. **venality** *noun* [from Latin *venalis* = for sale]

vend *verb* offer something for sale. [from Latin *vendere* = sell]

vendetta *noun* a feud. [Italian, from Latin *vindicta* = vengeance]

vending machine *noun* a machine where small articles can be obtained by putting a coin in the slot.

vendor *noun* a seller. [from *vend*]

veneer *noun* **1** a thin layer of good wood covering the surface of a cheaper wood in furniture etc. **2** an outward show of some good quality, *a veneer of politeness.*

venerable *adjective* worthy of being venerated, especially because of great age.

venerate *verb* (**venerated**, **venerating**) honour with great respect or reverence. **veneration** *noun* [from Latin *venerari* = revere]

venereal (*say* vuh-**neer**-ree-uhl) *adjective* (of a disease) passed on by sexual intercourse with an infected person. [from the name of Venus, the Roman goddess of love]

venetian blind *noun* a window blind consisting of horizontal strips that can be adjusted to let light in or shut it out. [from Latin *Venetia* = Venice]

vengeance *noun* revenge.
with a vengeance very strongly or effectively. [same origin as *vindictive*]

vengeful *adjective* seeking vengeance.
vengefully *adverb*, **vengefulness** *noun*

venial (*say* **vee**-nee-uhl) *adjective* (of sins or faults) pardonable, not serious. [from Latin *venia* = forgiveness]

venison *noun* deer's flesh as food. [from Latin *venatio* = hunting]

Venn diagram *noun* a diagram of usually circular areas representing mathematical sets, the areas intersecting where they have elements in common. [named after J. Venn, English logician]

venom *noun* **1** the poisonous fluid produced by some animals such as snakes and spiders. **2** very bitter feeling towards somebody; hatred. **venomous** *adjective* [from Latin *venenum* = poison]

vent[1] *noun* an opening in something, especially to let out smoke or gas.
give vent to express your feelings etc. openly.

vent[2] *verb* **1** make a vent in something. **2** give vent to feelings. [from Latin *ventus* = wind]

ventilate *verb* (**ventilated, ventilating**) **1** let air move freely in and out of a room etc. **2** discuss or examine an opinion, issue, or complaint in public. **3** subject to artificial respiration. **ventilation** *noun* [same origin as *vent*]

ventilator *noun* **1** an appliance or aperture for ventilating a room or other space. **2** an appliance for artificial respiration; a respirator.

ventral *adjective* of or on the abdomen, *This fish has a ventral fin.* [from Latin *venter* = abdomen]

ventricle *noun* a cavity in an organ of the body, especially one of the two lower cavities of the heart.

ventriloquist *noun* a person who can make their voice appear to come from somewhere else, typically a dummy of a person or animal. **ventriloquism** *noun* [from Latin *venter* = abdomen, + *loqui* = speak]

venture[1] *noun* something you decide to do that is risky.

venture[2] *verb* (**ventured, venturing**) **1** dare to do or say something or to go somewhere, *She did not venture to stop them*; *He ventured an opinion*; *We ventured out into the snow.* **2** risk. [compare *adventure*]

Venturer *noun* a member of a senior branch of the Scout Association.

venturesome *adjective* ready to take risks; daring.

venue (*say* **ven**-yoo) *noun* the place where a meeting, sports match, etc. is held. [from French *venir* = come]

Venus *noun* one of the planets, also known as the morning and evening star. [named after the Roman goddess of love]

veracity (*say* vuh-**ras**-uh-tee) *noun* truth.
veracious *adjective* [from Latin *verus* = true]

verandah *noun* (also **veranda**) a terrace with a roof along one or more sides of a house. [from Hindi *varanda*]

verb *noun* a word that shows what a person or thing is doing, e.g. *bring*, *came*, *sing*, *were.* [from Latin *verbum* = word]

verbal *adjective* **1** of or in words. **2** spoken, not written, *a verbal statement.* **3** of verbs.
verbally *adverb* [same origin as *verb*]

verbatim (*say* ver-**bay**-tuhm) *adverb & adjective* in exactly the same words, *He copied his friend's essay verbatim.*

verbose *adjective* using more words than are needed. **verbosely** *adverb*, **verbosity** *noun*

verdant *adjective* (of grass or fields) green. [compare *verdure*]

verdict *noun* a judgement or decision made after considering something, especially that made by a jury. [from Latin *verus* = true, + *dictum* = said]

verdigris (*say* **ver**-duh-gree) *noun* green rust on copper or brass. [from French, = green (*vert*) of Greece]

verdure *noun* green vegetation; its greenness. [from Old French *verd* = green]

verge[1] *noun* **1** the extreme edge or brink of something. **2** a strip of grass along the edge of a road or path.

verge[2] *verb* (**verged, verging**) **verge on**
1 border on something. **2** be close to something.

verger *noun* a person who is caretaker and attendant in a church.

verify *verb* (**verified, verifying**) check or show that something is true or correct. **verifiable** *adjective*, **verification** *noun* [from Latin *verus* = true]

verisimilitude *noun* an appearance of being true or lifelike. [from Latin *verus* = true, + *similis* = like]

veritable *adjective* real; rightly named, *a veritable villain.* **veritably** *adverb* [same origin as *verity*]

verity *noun* (*plural* **verities**) truth. [from Latin *veritas* = truth]

vermiculture *noun* the cultivation of earthworms, especially in order to use them to convert organic waste into fertiliser.

vermilion *noun & adjective* bright red. [from Latin *vermiculus* = little worm]

vermin *plural noun* **1** pests (e.g. foxes, rats, mice) regarded as harmful to domestic animals, crops, or food. **2** unpleasant or parasitic insects, e.g. lice. **verminous** *adjective* [from Latin *vermis* = worm]

vernacular (*say* vuh-**nak**-yuh-luh) *noun* the language of a country or district, as distinct from an official or formal language. [from Latin *vernaculus* = domestic]

vernal *adjective* of the season of spring. [from Latin *ver* = spring]

verruca (*say* vuh-**roo**-kuh) *noun* a kind of wart on the sole of the foot.

versatile *adjective* able to do or be used for many different things. **versatility** *noun* [from Latin *versare* = to turn]

verse *noun* **1** writing arranged in short lines, usually with a particular rhythm and often with rhymes. **2** a group of lines forming a unit in a poem or hymn. **3** each of the short numbered sections of a chapter in the Bible. [from Latin *versus* = line of writing]

versed *adjective* **versed in** experienced or skilled in something. [from Latin *versatus* = engaged in something]

version *noun* **1** a particular person's account of something that happened. **2** a translation, *modern versions of the Bible.* **3** a special or different form of something, *the latest version of this car.* [from Latin *versum* = turned]

versus *preposition* against; competing with, *Australia versus England.* [Latin, = against]

vertebra *noun* (*plural* **vertebrae**) each of the bones that form the backbone.

vertebrate *noun* an animal that has a backbone. (The opposite is **invertebrate**.) [from *vertebra*]

vertex *noun* (*plural* **vertices**, *say* **ver**-tuh-seez) the highest point (*apex*) of a cone or triangle, or of a hill etc. [from Latin *vertex* = top of the head]

vertical *adjective* at right angles to something horizontal; upright. (The opposite is **horizontal**.) **vertically** *adverb* [from *vertex*]

vertical angles *plural noun* (in mathematics) each pair of opposite angles made by two intersecting lines.

vertigo *noun* a feeling of dizziness and loss of balance, especially when you are very high up. [Latin, = whirling (*vertere* = to turn)]

verve (*say* verv) *noun* enthusiasm; liveliness.

very[1] *adverb* **1** to a great amount or intensity; extremely, *It was very cold.* **2** (used to emphasise something), *on the very next day; the very last drop.*

very[2] *adjective* **1** exact; actual, *It's the very thing we need.* **2** extreme, *at the very end.* [from Latin *verus* = true]

Vesak *noun* (also **Wesak**) the most important Buddhist festival, commemorating the birth, enlightenment, and death of the Buddha.

vespers *plural noun* a church service held in the evening. [from Latin *vesper* = evening]

vessel *noun* **1** a ship or boat. **2** a container, especially for liquid. **3** a tube carrying blood or other liquid in the body of an animal or plant. [same origin as *vase*]

vest[1] *noun* **1** an undergarment covering the trunk of the body; a singlet. **2** a waistcoat.

vest[2] *verb* **1** confer something as a right, *The power to make laws is vested in parliament.* **2** (*old use*) to clothe. [from Latin *vestis* = garment]

vested interest *noun* a right that benefits a person or group and is securely held by them.

vestibule *noun* an entrance hall or lobby.

vestige *noun* a trace; a very small amount, especially of something that formerly existed. **vestigial** *adjective* [from Latin *vestigium* = footprint]

vestment *noun* a ceremonial garment, especially one worn by clergy or the choir at a church service. [same origin as *vest*]

vestry *noun* (*plural* **vestries**) a room in a church where vestments are kept and where clergy and the choir put these on.

vet[1] *noun* a person trained to give medical and surgical treatment to animals. [short for *veterinary surgeon*]

vet[2] *verb* (**vetted**, **vetting**) check a thing to see if it has any mistakes or faults.

vet[3] *noun* (*informal*) a veteran.

vetch *noun* a plant of the pea family.

veteran *noun* **1** a person who has had long service or experience in something. **2** an ex-serviceman or servicewoman. **veteran** *adjective* [from Latin *vetus* = old]

veteran car *noun* a car made before 1916.

veterinary (*say* **vet**-ruhn-ree) *adjective* of the medical and surgical treatment of animals, *a veterinary surgeon.* [from Latin *veterinae* = cattle]

veto[1] (*say* **vee**-toh) *noun* (*plural* **vetoes**) **1** a refusal to let something happen. **2** the right to prohibit something.

veto[2] *verb* (**vetoed**, **vetoing**) refuse or prohibit something. [Latin, = I forbid]

vex *verb* annoy; cause somebody worry. **vexation** *noun*, **vexatious** *adjective* [from Latin *vexare* = to shake]

vexed question *noun* a problem that is difficult or much discussed.

VGA *abbreviation* videographics array, a standard for defining colour display screens for computers.

VHF *abbreviation* very high frequency (between 30 and 300 megahertz).

via (*say* **vuy**-uh) *preposition* by way of; through, *The plane goes from Adelaide to Auckland via Melbourne.* [Latin, = by way]

viable *adjective* able to exist successfully; practicable. **viability** *noun* [from French *vie* = life]

viaduct *noun* a long bridge, usually with many arches, carrying a road or railway over a valley or low ground. [from Latin *via* = way, + *ducere* = to lead (compare *aqueduct*)]

vial *noun* a small glass bottle.

vibrant *adjective* **1** vibrating. **2** lively. **3** (of colours) bright and strong.

vibraphone *noun* a musical instrument like a xylophone with metal bars under which there are tiny electric fans making a vibrating effect. [from *vibrate*, + Greek *phone* = voice]

vibrate *verb* (**vibrated**, **vibrating**) **1** shake very quickly to and fro. **2** make a throbbing sound. **vibration** *noun* [from Latin *vibrare* = shake]

vibrato *noun* a vibrating effect in music, with rapid slight variation of pitch.

vicar *noun* a member of the clergy who is in charge of a parish.

vicarage *noun* the house of a vicar.

vicarious (*say* vuh-**kair**-ree-uhs) *adjective* felt by imagining you share someone else's activities, *We felt a vicarious thrill by watching people skiing.* [from Latin *vicarius* = substitute]

vice[1] *noun* **1** evil; wickedness. **2** an evil or bad habit; a bad fault. [from Latin *vitium* = fault]

vice[2] *noun* a device for gripping something and holding it firmly while you work on it. [from Latin *vitis* = vine]

vice- *prefix* **1** authorised to act as a deputy or substitute (as in *vice-captain*, *vice-president*). **2** next in rank to someone (as in *vice-admiral*). [from Latin *vice* = by a change]

viceregal *adjective* of or relating to the governor-general or a state Governor.

vice versa (*say* vuys **ver**-suh or vuy-see **ver**-suh) *adverb* the other way round.

vicinity *noun* the area near or round something.

vicious *adjective* evil; brutal; dangerously wicked or strong. **viciously** *adverb*, **viciousness** *noun* [same origin as *vice*[1]]

vicious circle *noun* a situation where a problem produces an effect which itself produces the original problem or makes it worse.

vicissitude (*say* vuh-**sis**-uh-tyood) *noun* a change of circumstances. [from Latin *vicissim* = in turn]

victim *noun* **1** someone who is injured, killed, robbed, etc. **2** someone who is tricked or deceived.

victimise *verb* (**victimised**, **victimising**) make a victim of someone; punish a person unfairly. **victimisation** *noun*

victor *noun* the winner.

victory *noun* (*plural* **victories**) success won against an opponent in a battle, contest, or game. **victorious** *adjective* [from Latin *victum* = conquered]

victuals (*say* **vit**-uhls) *plural noun* food; provisions. [from Latin *victus* = food]

vidcast *noun* (also **vodcast**) a video clip that can be downloaded to a personal computer, mobile phone, etc.

video *noun* (*plural* **videos**) **1** the recording, reproducing, or broadcasting of moving visual images. **2** a recording of moving visual images made digitally or on videotape. [Latin, = I see]

video cassette *noun* a cassette of videotape.

video game *noun* a game played by electronically manipulating images produced by a computer program on a monitor or other display.

video recorder *noun* (also **video cassette recorder**) a device for recording a television program etc. on magnetic tape for playing back later.

videotape *noun* magnetic tape for recording and reproducing visual images and sound.

vie *verb* (**vied**, **vying**) compete; carry on a rivalry, *vying with each other.*

view[1] *noun* **1** what can be seen from one place; beautiful scenery. **2** sight; range of vision, *The ship sailed into view.* **3** an opinion, *She has strong views about politics.*
in view of because of.
on view displayed for inspection.
with a view to with the hope or intention of.

view[2] *verb* **1** look at something. **2** consider. **viewer** *noun*

viewpoint *noun* a point of view.

viewscreen *noun* the screen on a television, VDU, or similar device on which images and data are displayed.

vigil (*say* **vij**-uhl) *noun* staying awake to keep watch or to pray, *a long vigil.* [from Latin *vigil* = wakeful]

vigilant (*say* **vij**-uh-luhnt) *adjective* watchful. **vigilance** *noun*, **vigilantly** *adverb* [from Latin *vigilans* = keeping watch]

vigilante (*say* vij-uh-**lan**-tee) *noun* a member of a group who organise themselves, without authority, to try to prevent crime and disorder in a small area. [Spanish, = vigilant]

vignette (*say* vee-**nyet**) *noun* a short description or character sketch.

vigoro *noun* (*Australian*) a team game with elements of baseball and cricket.

vigorous *adjective* full of vigour. **vigorously** *adverb*

vigour *noun* strength; energy; liveliness. [from Latin *vigor* = strength]

vihara (*say* vuh-**hah**-ruh) *noun* a Buddhist temple or monastery. [Sanskrit]

Viking *noun* a Scandinavian trader and pirate in the 8th–10th centuries.

vile *adjective* **1** extremely disgusting. **2** very bad or wicked. **vilely** *adverb*, **vileness** *noun* [from Latin *vilis* = cheap, unworthy]

vilify (*say* **vil**-uh-fuy) *verb* (**vilified**, **vilifying**) say unpleasant things about a person or thing. **vilification** *noun* [same origin as *vile*]

villa *noun* a house. [Latin, = country house]

village *noun* **1** a settlement smaller than a town in a country district. **2** (*Australian*) a suburban shopping centre. **villager** *noun* [from *villa*]

villain *noun* a wicked person; a criminal. **villainous** *adjective*, **villainy** *noun*

villein (*say* **vil**-uhn) *noun* a tenant in feudal times.

vim *noun* (*informal*) vigour.

vindaloo (*say* vin-duh-**loo**) *noun* a highly spiced hot Indian curry. [from Portuguese *vin d'ahalo* = wine and garlic (sauce)]

vindicate *verb* (**vindicated**, **vindicating**) **1** clear a person of blame or suspicion. **2** prove something to be true or worth while. **vindication** *noun* [from Latin *vindicare* = set free]

vindictive *adjective* showing a desire for revenge. **vindictively** *adverb*, **vindictiveness** *noun* [from Latin *vindicta* = vengeance]

vine *noun* a climbing or trailing plant whose fruit is the grape. [from Latin *vinum* = wine]

vinegar *noun* a sour liquid used to flavour food or in pickling. [from Latin *vinum* = wine, + *acer* = sour]

vineyard (*say* **vin**-yahd) *noun* a plantation of vines producing grapes for making wine.

vintage *noun* **1** the harvest of a season's grapes; the wine made from this. **2** the period from which something comes. **vintage car** a car made between 1917 and 1930.

vinyl *noun* **1** a kind of plastic. **2** vinyl used as the standard material for records, *Most of my music collection is on vinyl.*

viola[1] (*say* vee-**oh**-luh) *noun* a musical instrument like a violin but slightly larger and with a lower pitch.

viola[2] (*say* vuy-**oh**-luh) *noun* a plant of the kind that includes violets and pansies.

violate *verb* (**violated**, **violating**) **1** break a promise, law, or treaty etc. **2** break into somewhere; treat a person or place without respect. **violation** *noun*, **violator** *noun* [from Latin *violare* = treat violently]

violence *noun* force that does harm or damage. **violent** *adjective*, **violently** *adverb*

violet *noun* **1** a small plant that often has purple flowers. **2** purple.

violin *noun* a musical instrument with four strings, played with a bow. **violinist** *noun*

violoncello (*say* vuy-uh-luhn-**chel**-oh) *noun* (*plural* **violoncellos**) a cello.

VIP *abbreviation* very important person.

viper *noun* a small poisonous snake.

virago (*say* vuh-**rah**-goh) *noun* (*plural* **viragos**) a fierce or bullying woman. [Latin, = female soldier]

viral[1] (*say* **vuy**-ruhl) *adjective* **1** of or caused by a virus. **2** (of an image, video, piece of information, etc.) circulated rapidly and widely from one Internet user to another, *The video went viral and was seen by millions.*

viral[2] *noun* an image, video, advertisement, etc., that is circulated rapidly on the Internet.

viral load *noun* a measure of the number of viral particles present in an organism or environment.

virgin[1] *noun* a person who has never had sexual intercourse. **virginal** *adjective*, **virginity** *noun*

virgin[2] *adjective* **1** of a virgin. **2** spotless. **3** not yet touched, *virgin snow.*

virginals *plural noun* an instrument rather like a harpsichord, used in the 16th–17th centuries.

Virgo *noun* **1** a constellation and the sixth sign of the zodiac (the Virgin). **2** a person born when the sun is in this sign. [Latin]

virile (*say* **vi**-ruyl) *adjective* having masculine strength or vigour. **virility** *noun* [from Latin *vir* = man]

virology *noun* the study of viruses. **virological** *adjective*, **virologist** *noun* [from *virus* + *-logy*]

virtual *adjective* **1** almost or nearly as described, but not completely or according to strict definition, *His silence was a virtual admission of guilt.* **2** (in computing) not physically existing as such but made by software to appear to do so. **3** carried out, accessed, or stored by means of a computer, especially over a network.

virtually *adverb* **1** in effect; nearly; almost, *She virtually admitted it.* **2** by means of virtual reality techniques. **3** by means of a computer.

virtual reality *noun* the computer-generated simulation of a three-dimensional image or environment that can be interacted with in a seemingly real or physical way by a person using special electronic equipment.

virtue *noun* **1** moral goodness; a particular form of this, *Honesty is a virtue.* **2** a good quality; an advantage. **virtuous** *adjective*, **virtuously** *adverb*
by virtue of because of. [from Latin *virtus* = worth]

virtuoso (*say* ver-choo-**oh**-soh) *noun* (*plural* **virtuosos** or **virtuosi**) a person with outstanding skill, especially in singing or playing music. **virtuosity** *noun* [Italian, = skilful]

virulent (*say* **vi**-ruh-luhnt) *adjective* **1** strongly poisonous or harmful, *a virulent disease.* **2** bitterly hostile, *virulent criticism.* **virulence** *noun* [same origin as *virus*]

virus *noun* (*plural* **viruses**) **1** a very tiny living thing, smaller than a bacterium, that can cause disease. **2** a disease caused by a virus. **3** a hidden code in a computer program, designed to sabotage a computer system or destroy data stored in it. [Latin, = poison]

visa (*say* **vee**-zuh) *noun* an official mark put on someone's passport by officials of a foreign country to show that the holder has permission to enter that country. [Latin, = things seen]

visage (*say* **viz**-ij) *noun* a person's face. [from Latin *visus* = sight]

vis-à-vis (*say* vee-zah-**vee**) *adverb & preposition* **1** in a position facing one another; opposite to. **2** as compared with. [French, = face to face]

viscera (*say* **vis**-uh-ruh) *plural noun* the intestines and other internal organs of the body. [Latin, = soft parts]

viscid (*say* **vis**-uhd) *adjective* thick and gluey. **viscidity** *noun*

viscose (*say* **vis**-kohz) *noun* fabric made from viscous cellulose.

viscount (*say* **vuy**-kownt) *noun* a nobleman ranking below an earl and above a baron. **viscountess** *noun* [from *vice-* + *count*[3]]

viscous (*say* **vis**-kuhs) *adjective* thick and gluey, not pouring easily. **viscosity** *noun*

visible *adjective* able to be seen or noticed, *The ship was visible on the horizon.* **visibility** *noun*, **visibly** *adverb* [same origin as *vision*]

vision *noun* **1** the ability to see; sight. **2** something seen in a person's imagination or in a dream. **3** a supernatural apparition. **4** foresight and wisdom in planning things. **5** a person or thing that is beautiful to see. [from Latin *visum* = seen]

visionary[1] *adjective* imaginary; fanciful.

visionary[2] *noun* (*plural* **visionaries**) a person with visionary ideas.

visit[1] *verb* **1** go to see a person or place. **2** stay somewhere for a while. **visitor** *noun*

visit[2] *noun* the action of visiting. [from Latin *visitare* = go to see]

visitant *noun* **1** a visitor, especially a supernatural one. **2** a bird that is a visitor to an area while migrating.

visitation *noun* an official visit, especially to inspect something.

visor (*say* **vuy**-zuh) *noun* **1** the part of a helmet that covers the face. **2** a shield to protect the eyes from bright light or sunshine. [same origin as *visage*]

vista *noun* a long view. [Italian, = view]

visual *adjective* of or used in seeing; of sight. **visually** *adverb* [same origin as *vision*]

visual aids *plural noun* pictures and films etc. used as an aid in teaching.

visual display unit *noun* a device that looks like a television screen and displays data being received from a computer or fed into it.

visualise *verb* (**visualised**, **visualising**) form a mental picture of something. **visualisation** *noun*

vital *adjective* **1** connected with life; necessary for life to continue, *vital functions such as breathing.* **2** essential; very important. **vitally** *adverb* [from Latin *vita* = life]

vitalise *verb* (**vitalised**, **vitalising**) put life or vitality into something.

vitality *noun* liveliness; energy.

vitamin (*say* **vuy**-tuh-min or **vit**-uh-min) *noun* any of a number of substances that are present in various foods and are essential to keep people and animals healthy. [same origin as *vital*]

vitiate (*say* **vish**-ee-ayt) *verb* (**vitiated**, **vitiating**) spoil something by making it imperfect. **vitiation** *noun* [from Latin *vitium* = fault]

vitreous (*say* **vit**-ree-uhs) *adjective* like glass in being hard, transparent, or brittle, *vitreous enamel.* [from Latin *vitrum* = glass]

vitriol (*say* **vit**-ree-ol) *noun* **1** (*old use*) sulphuric acid or one of its compounds. **2** savage criticism. **vitriolic** *adjective*

vituperation *noun* abusive words.

vivace (*say* vuh-**vah**-chay) *adverb & adjective* (of music) in a lively brisk manner. [Italian]

vivacious (*say* vuh-**vay**-shuhs) *adjective* happy and lively. **vivaciously** *adverb*, **vivacity** *noun* [from Latin *vivere* = to live]

viva voce (*say* vuy-vuh **voh**-chay) *adjective* in a spoken test or examination. [Latin, = with the living voice]

vivid *adjective* **1** bright and strong or clear, *vivid colours; a vivid description.* **2** active and lively, *a vivid imagination.* **vividly** *adverb*, **vividness** *noun* [from Latin *vividus* = full of life]

vivisection *noun* doing surgical experiments on live animals. [from Latin *vivus* = alive, + *dissection*]

vixen *noun* a female fox.

vlog *noun* a blog with most of the content in the form of video clips.

vocabulary *noun* (*plural* **vocabularies**) **1** a list of words with their meanings. **2** the words known to a person or used in a particular book or subject etc. [from Latin *vocabulum* = name]

vocal *adjective* of or producing or using the voice. **vocally** *adverb* [from Latin *vocis* = of the voice]

vocal cords *plural noun* two strap-like membranes in the throat that can be made to vibrate and produce sounds.

vocalist *noun* a singer, especially in a pop group.

vocation *noun* **1** a person's job or occupation. **2** a strong desire to do a particular kind of work, or feeling of being called by God to do something. **vocational** *adjective* [from Latin *vocare* = to call]

vociferate (*say* vuh-**sif**-uh-rayt) *verb* (**vociferated**, **vociferating**) say something loudly or noisily. **vociferation** *noun* [from Latin *vocis* = of the voice, + *ferre* = carry]

vociferous (*say* vuh-**sif**-uh-ruhs) *adjective* making an outcry; shouting.

vodcast *noun* a vidcast.

vodka *noun* a strong alcoholic drink very popular in Russia. [from Russian *voda* = water]

vogue (*say* vohg) *noun* the current fashion.

voice[1] *noun* **1** sounds formed by the vocal cords and uttered by the mouth, especially in speaking or singing. **2** the ability to speak or sing, *She has lost her voice.* **3** an opinion expressed. **4** the right to express an opinion or desire, *I have no voice in this matter.* **5** the distinctive tone or style of a literary work or author. **6** a form or set of forms of a verb showing the relation of the subject to the action, *active voice, passive voice.* [from Latin *vox* = voice]

voice[2] *verb* (**voiced**, **voicing**) say something, *We voiced our opinions.*

voice box *noun* the larynx.

voicemail *noun* an electronic system that stores messages from telephone callers.

void[1] *adjective* **1** empty. **2** having no legal validity.

void[2] *noun* an empty space.

voile (*say* voil) *noun* a very thin almost transparent material. [French, = veil]

VOIP *abbreviation* voice over Internet protocol, a technology for making telephone calls over the Internet.

volatile (*say* **vol**-uh-tuyl) *adjective* **1** evaporating quickly, *a volatile liquid.* **2** changing quickly from one mood or interest to another. **volatility** *noun* [from Latin *volatilis* = flying]

vol-au-vent (*say* **vol**-oh-von) *noun* a small case of puff pastry with a savoury filling. [French, = flight in the wind]

volcano *noun* (*plural* **volcanoes**) a mountain with an opening at the top from which lava and hot gases etc. flow. **volcanic** *adjective* [from the name of Vulcan, the ancient Roman god of fire]

volition *noun* using your own will in choosing to do something, *She left of her own volition.* [from Latin *volo* = I wish]

volley[1] *noun* (*plural* **volleys**) **1** a number of bullets or shells etc. fired at the same time. **2** hitting back the ball in tennis before it touches the ground.

volley[2] *verb* send or hit something in a volley or volleys. [from Latin *volare* = to fly]

volleyball *noun* a game in which two teams hit a large ball to and fro over a net with their hands.

volt *noun* a unit for measuring electric force. [named after an Italian scientist, Alessandro Volta]

voltage *noun* electric force measured in volts.

volte-face (*say* volt-**fahs**) *noun* a complete change in your attitude towards something. [French]

voluble *adjective* talking very much. **volubility** *noun*, **volubly** *adverb* [from Latin *volubilis* = rolling]

volume *noun* **1** the amount of space filled by something. **2** an amount or quantity, *The volume of work has increased.* **3** the strength or power of sound. **4** a book, especially one of a set. [from Latin *volumen* = a roll (because ancient books were made in a rolled form)]

voluminous (*say* vuh-**loo**-muh-nuhs) *adjective* **1** bulky; large and full, *a voluminous skirt.* **2** numerous; filling many volumes, *a voluminous writer.*

voluntary[1] *adjective* **1** done or doing something willingly, not by being compelled. **2** unpaid, *voluntary work.* **voluntarily** *adverb*

voluntary[2] *noun* (*plural* **voluntaries**) an organ solo, often improvised, played before or after a church service. [from Latin *voluntas* = the will]

volunteer[1] *verb* give or offer something of your own accord.

volunteer[2] *noun* a person who volunteers to do something, e.g. to serve in the armed forces.

voluptuous *adjective* **1** giving a luxurious feeling, *voluptuous furnishings.* **2** (of a woman) having a full and attractive figure. [from Latin *voluptas* = pleasure]

vomit *verb* bring up food etc. from the stomach and out through the mouth; be sick. **vomit** *noun*

voodoo *noun* a form of witchcraft and magical rites.

voracious (*say* vuh-**ray**-shuhs) *adjective* **1** greedy; devouring things eagerly. **2** eager in some activity, *a voracious reader.* **voraciously** *adverb*, **voracity** *noun* [from Latin *vorare* = devour]

vortex *noun* (*plural* **vortices**) a whirlpool or whirlwind. [Latin]

vote[1] *verb* (**voted**, **voting**) show which person or thing you prefer by putting up your hand, making a mark on a paper, etc. **voter** *noun*

vote[2] *noun* **1** the action of voting. **2** the right to vote. [from Latin *votum* = a wish or vow]

votive *adjective* given in fulfilment of a vow, *votive offerings at the shrine.*

vouch *verb* **vouch for** guarantee that something is true or certain, *I will vouch for his honesty.*

voucher *noun* a piece of paper that can be exchanged for certain goods or services; a receipt.

vouchsafe *verb* (**vouchsafed**, **vouchsafing**) grant something in a gracious or condescending way, *She did not vouchsafe a reply.*

vow[1] *noun* a solemn promise, especially to God or a saint.

vow[2] *verb* make a vow.

vowel *noun* any of the letters a, e, i, o, u, and sometimes y, that represent sounds in which breath comes out freely. (Compare **consonant**.) [from Latin *vocalis littera* = vocal letter]

voyage[1] *noun* a long journey on water or in space.

voyage[2] *verb* (**voyaged**, **voyaging**) make a voyage. **voyager** *noun*

VRML *abbreviation* virtual reality modelling language.

vulcanise *verb* (**vulcanised**, **vulcanising**) treat rubber with sulphur to strengthen it. **vulcanisation** *noun* [same origin as *volcano*]

vulgar *adjective* rude; without good manners. **vulgarity** *noun*, **vulgarly** *adverb* [from Latin *vulgus* = the ordinary people]

vulgar fraction *noun* a fraction shown by numbers above and below a line (e.g. ⅔, ³⁄₁₀), not a decimal fraction.

vulnerable *adjective* able to be hurt or harmed or attacked. **vulnerability** *noun* [from Latin *vulnus* = wound]

vulture *noun* a large bird that feeds on dead animals.

vulva *noun* the outer parts of the female genitals. [Latin]

vuvuzela (*say* voo-vuh-**zel**-uh) *noun* (originally in South Africa) a long plastic instrument in the shape of a trumpet, blown by fans at soccer matches etc. [Zulu]

vying *present participle* of **vie**.

Ww

W *abbreviation* west; western.

wad[1] (*say* wod) *noun* a pad or bundle of soft material or pieces of paper.

wad[2] *verb* (**wadded**, **wadding**) pad something with soft material.

waddle *verb* (**waddled**, **waddling**) walk with short steps, swaying from side to side.
waddle *noun*

waddy *noun* (*Australian*) a club or bludgeon, used traditionally by Aboriginal people in fighting and hunting. [from Sydney language *wadi* = tree; stick; club]

wade *verb* (**waded**, **wading**) walk through water or mud etc. **wader** *noun*

wafer *noun* a kind of thin biscuit.

waffle[1] (*say* **wof**-uhl) *noun* a small cake made of batter and eaten hot.

waffle[2] (*say* **wof**-uhl) *noun* (*informal*) vague wordy talk or writing. **waffle** *verb* [from a dialect word *waff* = yelp]

waft (*say* woft) *verb* carry or float gently through the air or over water.

wag[1] *verb* (**wagged**, **wagging**) **1** move quickly to and fro. **2** (*informal*) be absent from school without permission. **wag** *noun*

wag[2] *noun* a person who makes jokes.

wage[1] *noun* (also **wages**) a regular payment to someone in return for their work.

wage[2] *verb* (**waged**, **waging**) carry on a war or campaign.

wager (*say* **way**-juh) *noun & verb* bet.

waggle *verb* (**waggled**, **waggling**) move quickly to and fro; wag. **waggle** *noun*

wagon *noun* **1** a cart with four wheels, pulled by a horse or an ox. **2** an open railway truck, e.g. for coal. **3** (*informal*) a station wagon.

wagtail *noun* **1** a small bird with a long tail that it moves up and down. **2** a willy wagtail.

waif *noun* **1** a homeless and helpless person, especially a child. **2** a person who appears thin or poorly nourished.

wail *verb* make a long sad cry. **wail** *noun*

wainscoting *noun* wooden panelling on the wall of a room.

waist *noun* the narrow part in the middle of the body.

waistcoat *noun* a short close-fitting jacket without sleeves, worn over a shirt and under a jacket.

wait[1] *verb* **1** stay somewhere or postpone an action until something happens; pause. **2** be postponed, *This question must wait until our next meeting.* **3** wait on people.
wait on 1 hand food and drink to people at a meal. **2** be an attendant to someone.

wait[2] *noun* an act or time of waiting, *We had a long wait for the train.*

waiter *noun* a person who serves people with food and drink in a restaurant etc.

waiting list *noun* a list of people waiting for something to become available.

waiting room *noun* a room provided for people who are waiting for something.

waitress *noun* a woman who serves people with food and drink in a restaurant.

waive *verb* (**waived**, **waiving**) not insist on having something, *She waived her right to compensation.* [from Old French, = abandon (compare *waif*)]

waiver *noun* the waiving of a legal right.

wake[1] *verb* (**woke**, **woken**, **waking**) **1** stop sleeping, *Wake up! I woke when I heard the bell.* **2** cause someone to stop sleeping, *You have woken the baby.*

wake[2] *noun* festivities held in connection with a funeral.

wake[3] *noun* **1** the track left on the water by a moving ship. **2** currents of air left behind a moving aircraft.
in the wake of following.

wakeboarding *noun* the sport of riding on a board and performing acrobatic manoeuvres while being towed behind a motor boat.

wakeful *adjective* unable to sleep.

waken *verb* wake.

walk[1] *verb* move along on your feet at an ordinary speed. **walker** *noun*
walk out 1 leave angrily or suddenly. **2** go on strike.
walk out on desert.

walk[2] *noun* **1** a journey on foot. **2** the manner of walking. **3** a path or route for walking.

walkabout *noun* **1** (*Australian*) a journey on foot by an Aboriginal person in order to live in the traditional way. **2** an informal stroll among a crowd by an important visitor.
go walkabout (*Australian*) **1** wander around from place to place taking your time. **2** (*informal*) be lost, missing, or stolen, *My phone has gone walkabout.*

walkie-talkie *noun* (*informal*) a small portable radio transmitter and receiver.

walking stick *noun* a stick for use as a support while walking.

walk of life *noun* a person's occupation or social level.

walkover *noun* an easy victory.

wall[1] *noun* **1** a continuous upright structure, usually made of brick or stone, forming one of the sides of a building or room or supporting something or enclosing an area. **2** the outside part of something.

wall[2] *verb* enclose or block with a wall.

wallaby *noun* (*plural* **wallabies**) a marsupial similar to but smaller than a kangaroo.
on the wallaby (*Australian*) travelling as a swagman in search of work. [from Sydney language *walabi*, *waliba*]

wallaroo *noun* a large kangaroo living in rocky or hilly areas. [from Sydney language *walaru*]

wallet *noun* a small flat folding case for holding banknotes, documents, etc.

wallflower *noun* **1** a garden plant with fragrant flowers, blooming in spring. **2** (*informal*) a socially awkward person.

wallop *verb* (**walloped**, **walloping**) (*informal*) thrash. **wallop** *noun*

wallow *verb* **1** roll about in water, mud, etc. **2** get great pleasure by being surrounded by something, *wallowing in luxury.*
wallow *noun*

wallpaper *noun* paper used to cover the inside walls of rooms.

walnut *noun* an edible nut with a wrinkled surface.

walrus *noun* (*plural* **walruses**) a large Arctic sea animal with two long tusks.

waltz[1] *noun* (*plural* **waltzes**) a dance with three beats to a bar.

waltz[2] *verb* dance a waltz. [from German *walzen* = revolve]

wan (*say* won) *adjective* pale from being ill or tired. **wanly** *adverb*, **wanness** *noun*

wand *noun* a thin rod, especially one used by a magician.

wander *verb* **1** go about without trying to reach a particular place. **2** leave the right path or direction; stray. **wander** *noun*, **wanderer** *noun*

wanderlust *noun* an eagerness for travelling.

wane *verb* (**waned**, **waning**) **1** (of the moon) show a bright area that becomes gradually smaller after being full. (The opposite is **wax**[3] 1.) **2** become less or smaller, *His popularity waned.* **wane** *noun* [from Old English *wanian* = reduce]

wangle *verb* (**wangled**, **wangling**) (*informal*) get or arrange something by using trickery, special influence, etc. **wangle** *noun*

want[1] *verb* **1** wish to have something. **2** need, *Your hair wants cutting.* **3** be without something; lack. **4** be without the necessaries of life, *Waste not, want not.*

want[2] *noun* **1** a wish to have something. **2** lack or need of something. [same origin as *wane*]

wanted *adjective* (of a suspected criminal) that the police wish to find or arrest.

wanton (*say* **won**-tuhn) *adjective* irresponsible; without a motive, *wanton damage.*

war *noun* **1** fighting between nations or groups, especially using armed forces. **2** a serious struggle or effort against crime, disease, poverty, etc.
at war engaged in a war.

waratah *noun* an Australian shrub with bright red flowers. [from Sydney language *warrada*]

warble *verb* (**warbled**, **warbling**) sing with a trilling sound, as some birds do. **warble** *noun*

warbler *noun* a kind of small bird.

war cry *noun* **1** a word or phrase shouted to rally troops or support a team. **2** a political or other slogan.

ward[1] *noun* **1** a room with beds for patients in a hospital. **2** a child looked after by a guardian. **3** an area electing a councillor to represent it.

ward[2] *verb* **ward off** keep something away. [from Old English *weard* = guard]

warden *noun* an official who is in charge of a hostel, college, etc., or who supervises something.

warder *noun* an official in charge of prisoners in a prison.

wardrobe *noun* **1** a cupboard to hang clothes in. **2** a stock of clothes or costumes. [French]

ware *noun* manufactured goods of a certain kind, *hardware*; *silverware.*

warehouse *noun* a large building where goods are stored.

wares *plural noun* goods offered for sale.

warfare *noun* war; fighting.

warhead *noun* the head of a missile or torpedo, containing explosives.

warlike *adjective* **1** fond of making war. **2** of or for war.

warlock *noun* a wizard or sorcerer.

warm[1] *adjective* **1** fairly hot; not cold or cool. **2** (of clothes) keeping the body warm. **3** loving; enthusiastic, *a warm welcome.* **warmly** *adverb*, **warmness** *noun*, **warmth** *noun*

warm[2] *verb* make or become warm.

warm-blooded *adjective* having blood that remains at a constant temperature.

warm-hearted *adjective* kind; friendly.

warmonger *noun* a person who seeks to bring about war.

warn *verb* tell someone about a danger etc. that may affect them, or about what they should do, *I warned you to take your umbrella.* **warning** *noun*

warp[1] (*say* wawp) *verb* **1** bend out of shape, e.g. by dampness. **2** distort a person's ideas etc., *Jealousy warped his mind.*

warp[2] *noun* **1** a warped condition. **2** the lengthwise threads in weaving, crossed by the weft.

warrant[1] *noun* a document that authorises a person to do something (e.g. to search a place) or to receive something.

warrant[2] *verb* **1** justify, *Nothing can warrant such rudeness.* **2** guarantee.

warranty *noun* a guarantee.

warren *noun* **1** a piece of ground where there are many burrows in which rabbits live and breed. **2** a building or place with many winding passages.

warrigal[1] *noun* (*Australian*) **1** a dingo. **2** an untamed horse. [from Sydney language]

warrigal[2] *adjective* (*Australian*) wild; untamed.

warring *adjective* occupied in war.

warrior *noun* a person who fights in battle; a soldier.

warship *noun* a ship for use in war.

wart *noun* a small hard lump on the skin, caused by a virus.

wartime *noun* a time of war.

wary (*say* **wair**-ree) *adjective* cautious; looking carefully for possible danger or difficulty. **warily** *adverb*, **wariness** *noun* [compare *aware*]

was 1st and 3rd person singular past tense of **be**, *I was very angry*; *She was a brave soldier.*

wash[1] *verb* **1** clean something with water or other liquid. **2** be washable, *Cotton washes easily.* **3** flow against or over something, *Waves washed over the deck.* **4** carry along by a moving liquid, *A wave washed him overboard.* **5** (*informal*) be accepted or believed, *That excuse won't wash.*
wash out (*informal*) cancel something, *The game was washed out.*
wash up wash dishes and cutlery etc. after use. **washing-up** *noun*

wash[2] *noun* (*plural* **washes**) **1** the action of washing. **2** clothes etc. being washed. **3** the disturbed water or air behind a moving ship or aircraft. **4** a thin coating of colour.

washable *adjective* able to be washed without becoming damaged.

washbasin *noun* a small sink for washing your hands etc.

washer *noun* **1** a small ring of rubber or metal placed between two surfaces (e.g. under a bolt or screw) to fit them tightly together. **2** a washing machine. **3** (*Australian*) a small cloth for washing yourself.

washing *noun* clothes etc. being washed.

washing machine *noun* a machine for washing clothes etc.

washout *noun* (*informal*) **1** an event or period that is spoiled by constant or heavy rain. **2** a disappointing failure.

wasn't was not, *there wasn't much time left.*

wasp *noun* a stinging insect with black and yellow stripes round its body.

wassail (*say* **wos**-ayl) *noun* (*old use*) spiced ale drunk especially at Christmas. **wassailing** *noun* [from Norse *ves heill* = be in good health]

wastage *noun* loss of something by waste.

waste[1] *verb* (**wasted**, **wasting**) **1** use something in an extravagant way or without getting enough results. **2** fail to use something, *You wasted an opportunity.* **3** make or become gradually weaker or useless.

waste[2] *adjective* **1** left over or thrown away because it is not wanted. **2** not used; not usable, *waste land.*
lay waste destroy the crops and buildings etc. of a district.

waste[3] *noun* **1** the action of wasting a thing, not using it well, *a waste of time.* **2** things that are not wanted or not used. **3** an area of waste land, *the wastes of the Sahara Desert.* **wasteful** *adjective*, **wastefully** *noun*, **wastefulness** *noun* [from Latin *vastus* = empty]

wastrel (*say* **way**-struhl) *noun* a person who wastes their time and does nothing useful.

wat (*rhymes with* hot) *noun* a Buddhist monastery or temple. [Thai from Sanskrit *vāṭa* = enclosure]

watch[1] *verb* **1** look at a person or thing for some time. **2** keep under observation. **3** be on guard or ready for something to happen, *Watch for the lights to turn green.* **4** take care of something. **watcher** *noun*

watch[2] *noun* (*plural* **watches**) **1** the action of watching. **2** a turn of being on duty on a ship. **3** a device like a small clock, usually worn on the wrist.

watchdog *noun* **1** a dog kept to guard property. **2** a person or organisation acting as a guardian of people's rights.

watchful *adjective* watching closely; alert.
watchfully *adverb*, **watchfulness** *noun*

watchman *noun* (*plural* **watchmen**) a person employed to look after an empty building etc., especially at night.

watchword *noun* a word or phrase that sums up a group's policy; a slogan, *Our watchword is 'safety first'.*

water[1] *noun* **1** a colourless odourless tasteless liquid that is a compound of hydrogen and oxygen. **2** a lake, sea, river, etc. **3** the tide, *at high water.* **4** urine; sweat; saliva.

water[2] *verb* **1** sprinkle or supply something with water. **2** produce tears or saliva, *It makes my mouth water.*
water down dilute.

waterboarding *noun* a form of torture in which a person is tied to a board and water is poured over their face to simulate drowning.

water closet *noun* a toilet with a pan that is flushed by water.

watercolour *noun* **1** paint made with pigment and water (not oil). **2** a painting done with this kind of paint.

watercress *noun* a kind of cress that grows in water.

waterfall *noun* a stream flowing over the edge of a cliff or large rock.

waterhole *noun* **1** a pond. **2** a hole in which water collects, especially in the bed of an otherwise dry river.

watering can *noun* a container with a long spout, for watering plants.

water lily *noun* a plant that grows in water, with broad floating leaves and large flowers.

waterlogged *adjective* completely soaked or swamped in water.

watermark *noun* **1** a mark showing how high a river or tide rises or how low it falls. **2** a design that can be seen in some kinds of paper when they are held up to the light.

watermelon *noun* a large melon with a smooth green skin, red pulp, and watery juice.

waterproof *adjective* that keeps out water, *waterproof boots.* **waterproof** *verb*

watershed *noun* **1** a line of high land from which streams flow down on each side. **2** a turning point in the course of events.

waterskiing *noun* (also **water skiing**) skimming over the surface of water on a pair of flat boards (**waterskis**) while being towed by a motor boat.

waterspout *noun* a column of water formed when a whirlwind draws up a whirling mass of water from the sea.

water table *noun* the level below which the ground is saturated with water.

watertight *adjective* **1** made or fastened so that water cannot get in or out. **2** that cannot be changed or set aside or proved to be untrue, *a watertight excuse.*

waterway *noun* a river or canal that ships can travel on.

waterworks *noun* a place with pumping machinery etc. for supplying water to a district.

watery *adjective* **1** of or like water. **2** full of water, *watery eyes.* **3** containing too much water.

watt *noun* a unit of electric power. [named after James Watt, a Scottish engineer]

wattage *noun* electric power measured in watts.

wattle[1] *noun* **1** sticks and twigs woven together to make fences, walls, etc. **2** an Australian tree with golden flowers.

wattle[2] *noun* a red fold of skin hanging from the throat of turkeys and some other birds.

wattlebird *noun* a large Australian honeyeater.

wave[1] *noun* **1** a ridge moving along the surface of the sea etc. or breaking on the shore. **2** a wave-like curve, e.g. in hair. **3** the wave-like movement by which heat, light, sound, or electricity etc. travels. **4** the action of waving. **5** a sudden increase of a condition, emotion, etc., *a wave of anger; a crime wave.*

wave[2] *verb* (**waved, waving**) **1** move loosely to and fro or up and down. **2** move your hand to and fro as a signal or greeting etc. **3** make a thing wavy. **4** be wavy.

waveband *noun* the wavelengths between certain limits.

wavelength *noun* the size of a sound wave or electromagnetic wave.

waver *verb* **1** be unsteady; move unsteadily. **2** hesitate; be uncertain.

wavy *adjective* full of waves or curves. **wavily** *adverb*, **waviness** *noun*

wax[1] *noun* (*plural* **waxes**) **1** a soft substance that melts easily, used to make candles, crayons, and polish. **2** beeswax.
waxy *adjective*

wax[2] *verb* coat or polish something with wax.

wax[3] *verb* **1** (of the moon) show a bright area that becomes gradually larger. (The opposite is **wane** 1.) **2** become larger, stronger or more important.

waxen *adjective* **1** made of wax. **2** like wax.

waxwork *noun* a model of a person etc. made in wax.

way[1] *noun* **1** a line of communication between places, e.g. a path or road. **2** a route or direction. **3** a distance to be travelled. **4** how something is done; a method or style. **5** a particular aspect of something; a respect, *It's a good idea in some ways.* **6** a condition or state, *Things were in a bad way.*
get or **have your own way** make people let you do what you want.
give way 1 collapse. **2** let somebody else move first. **3** yield.
in the way forming an obstacle or hindrance.
no way (*informal*) that is impossible!

way[2] *adverb* (*informal*) far, *That is way beyond what we can afford.*

wayfarer *noun* a traveller, especially someone who is walking.

waylay *verb* (**waylaid**, **waylaying**) lie in wait for a person or people, especially so as to talk to them or rob them.

wayside *noun* the land beside a road or path.

wayward *adjective* disobedient; wilfully doing what you want.

WC *abbreviation* water closet.

we *pronoun* a word used by a person to refer to himself or herself and another or others.

weak *adjective* **1** not strong; easy to break, bend, defeat, etc. **2** lacking vigour; sickly, feeble. **3** lacking in determination or strength of character. **4** not convincing, *a weak excuse.* **5** dilute; watery.

weaken *verb* make or become weaker.

weakling *noun* a weak person or animal.

weakly[1] *adverb* in a weak manner.

weakly[2] *adjective* sickly; not strong.

weakness *noun* **1** being weak. **2** a weak point; a defect. **3** an inability to resist something; a liking.

weal *noun* a ridge raised on the flesh by a cane or whip etc.

wealth *noun* **1** much money or property; riches. **2** a large quantity, *The book has a wealth of illustrations.* [from *well*[4]]

wealthy *adjective* (**wealthier**, **wealthiest**) having wealth; rich. **wealthiness** *noun*

wean *verb* make a baby take food other than its mother's milk.

weapon *noun* something used to do harm in a battle or fight. **weaponry** *noun*

wear[1] *verb* (**wore**, **worn**, **wearing**) **1** have something on your body as clothes, ornaments, etc. **2** damage something by rubbing or using it often; become damaged in this way, *The carpet has worn thin.* **3** last while in use, *It has worn well.* **wearable** *adjective*, **wearer** *noun*
wear off 1 be removed by wear or use. **2** become less intense.
wear on pass gradually, *The night wore on.*
wear out 1 use or be used until it becomes weak or useless. **2** exhaust.

wear[2] *noun* **1** clothes, *formal wear.* **2** damage resulting from ordinary use, *wear and tear.*

wearisome *adjective* causing weariness.

weary[1] *adjective* (**wearier**, **weariest**) **1** tired. **2** tiring, *It's weary work.* **wearily** *adverb*, **weariness** *noun*

weary[2] *verb* (**wearied**, **wearying**) tire.

weasel *noun* a small fierce animal with a slender body and reddish-brown fur.
weasel out default on an obligation or commitment, *He weaselled out of his promise.*

weasel word *noun* a word that is intentionally ambiguous or misleading.

weather[1] *noun* the rain, snow, wind, sunshine etc. at a particular time or place.
under the weather 1 feeling ill or depressed. **2** drunk.

weather[2] *verb* **1** expose something to the effects of the weather. **2** come through something successfully, *The ship weathered the storm.*

weatherboard[1] *noun* one of a series of horizontal boards with overlapping edges covering the outside wall of a house.

weatherboard[2] *adjective* (of a building) having outside walls of weatherboard.

weathercock *noun* (also **weathervane**) a pointer, often shaped like a cockerel, that turns in the wind and shows from which direction the wind is blowing.

weave[1] *verb* (**wove**, **woven**, **weaving**) **1** make material or baskets etc. by passing crosswise threads or strips under and over lengthwise ones. **2** put a story together, *She wove a thrilling tale.* **weaver** *noun*

weave[2] *noun* a style of weaving, *a loose weave.*

weave[3] *verb* (**weaved**, **weaving**) twist and turn, *He weaved through the traffic.*

web *noun* **1** a cobweb. **2** a network. **3** (**the Web**) the World Wide Web.

webbed *adjective* (also **web-footed**) having toes joined by pieces of skin, *Ducks have webbed feet; they are web-footed.*

web browser *noun* a computer program with a graphical user interface for displaying and navigating between webpages.

webcam *noun* a video camera that is connected to a computer connected to the

Internet, so that its images can be seen by Internet users.

webcast *noun* a video broadcast transmitted over the Internet. **webcast** *verb*

weblog *noun* see **blog**[1].

webpage *noun* a document connected to the World Wide Web.

website *noun* a location connected to the Internet that maintains one or more webpages.

webspace *noun* **1** the amount of disk storage space allowed on an Internet server. **2** the place in which communication over computer networks occurs.

wed *verb* (**wedded**, **wedding**) **1** marry. **2** unite two different things.

we'd **1** we had, *we'd lost our way home.* **2** we should; we would, *we'd like to make you an offer.*

wedding *noun* the ceremony when a man and woman get married.

wedge[1] *noun* **1** a piece of wood or metal etc. that is thick at one end and thin at the other. It is pushed between things to force them apart or prevent something from moving. **2** a wedge-shaped thing.

wedge[2] *verb* (**wedged**, **wedging**) **1** keep something in place with a wedge. **2** pack tightly together, *Ten of us were wedged in the lift.*

wedge politics *noun* the use of divisive social issues that cut across traditional political loyalties in order to gain votes.

wedlock *noun* the condition of being married; matrimony. [from Old English, = marriage vow]

Wednesday *noun* the day of the week following Tuesday. [Old English = day of Woden or Odin (the chief Norse god)]

wee *adjective* (*Scottish*) little.

weed[1] *noun* a wild plant that grows where it is not wanted.

weed[2] *verb* remove weeds from the ground. **weed out** remove unwanted items.

weeds *plural noun* the black clothes formerly worn by a widow in mourning.

weedy *adjective* (**weedier**, **weediest**) **1** full of weeds. **2** thin and weak.

week *noun* a period of seven days, especially from Sunday to the following Saturday.

weekday *noun* a day other than Saturday or Sunday.

weekend *noun* Saturday and Sunday.

weekender *noun* (*Australian*) a cottage or shack used for weekend visits.

weekly *adjective & adverb* happening or done once a week.

weeny *adjective* (*informal*) tiny.

weep *verb* (**wept**, **weeping**) **1** shed tears; cry. **2** ooze moisture in drops. **weep** *noun*, **weepy** *adjective*

weeping *adjective* (of a tree) having drooping branches, *a weeping willow.*

weevil *noun* a kind of small beetle.

weft *noun* the crosswise threads in weaving, passing through the warp.

weigh *verb* **1** measure the weight of something. **2** have a certain weight. **3** be important; have influence, *Her evidence weighed with the jury.*

weigh anchor raise the anchor and start a voyage.

weigh down **1** keep something down by its weight. **2** depress or trouble somebody.

weigh up estimate or assess something.

weight[1] *noun* **1** how heavy something is; an object's mass expressed as a number according to a scale of units. (Compare **mass**[1] 3.) **2** a piece of metal of known weight, especially one used on scales to weigh things. **3** a heavy object. **4** load; burden, *a weight off his mind.* **5** importance; influence.

weight[2] *verb* put a weight on something.

weighty *adjective* **1** heavy. **2** important, *weighty issues.* **weightiness** *noun*

weir (*say* weer) *noun* a small dam across a river or canal to control the flow of water.

weird *adjective* **1** very strange. **2** uncanny. **weirdly** *adverb*, **weirdness** *noun*

weirdo *noun* (*informal*) an odd or eccentric person.

welcome[1] *noun* a greeting or reception, especially a kindly one.

welcome[2] *adjective* **1** that you are glad to receive or see, *a welcome gift.* **2** gladly allowed, *You are welcome to come.*

welcome[3] *verb* (**welcomed**, **welcoming**) show that you are pleased when a person or thing arrives. [from *well*[3] + *come*]

welcome to country *noun* (*Australian*) a formal welcome to the traditional land of an Aboriginal people by a member or members of the local Aboriginal community.

weld *verb* **1** join pieces of metal or plastic by heating and pressing or hammering them together. **2** unite people or things into a whole.

welfare *noun* **1** people's health, happiness, and comfort. **2** financial support given by the government to those in need. [from *well*[3] + *fare*]

welfare state *noun* a country that looks after the welfare of its people by social services run by the government.

well[1] *noun* **1** a deep hole dug to bring up water or oil from underground. **2** a deep space, e.g. containing a staircase.

well[2] *verb* rise or flow up, *Tears welled up in our eyes.* [from Old English *wella* = spring of water]

well[3] *adverb* (**better, best**) **1** in a good or suitable way, *She swims well.* **2** thoroughly, *Polish it well.* **3** easily; probably, *This may well be our last chance.*
well off 1 fairly rich. **2** in a good situation.

well[4] *adjective* **1** in good health, *He is not well.* **2** satisfactory, *All is well.* [from Old English *wel* = prosperously]

we'll we shall; we will, *we'll keep an eye on things.*

well-being *noun* the state of being comfortable, healthy, or happy.

wellingtons *plural noun* (*British*) rubber or plastic waterproof boots. [named after the first Duke of Wellington]

well-known *adjective* **1** known to many people. **2** known thoroughly.

well-mannered *adjective* having good manners.

well-meaning *adjective* (also **well-meant**) having good intentions that are not always effective.

wellnigh *adverb* almost.

well-read *adjective* having read much literature.

well-to-do *adjective* fairly rich.

Welsh *noun* **1** the Celtic language of Wales. **2** (**the Welsh**) the people of Wales.

welsh *verb* cheat someone by avoiding paying what you owe them or by breaking an agreement. **welsher** *noun*

welt *noun* **1** a strip or border. **2** a weal.

welter[1] *verb* (of a ship) be tossed to and fro by waves.

welter[2] *noun* a confused mixture.

wench *noun* (*plural* **wenches**) (*old use*) a girl or young woman.

wend *verb* **wend your way** go.

went *past tense* of **go**[1].

wept *past tense & past participle* of **weep**.

were plural and 2nd person singular past tense of **be**, *My brothers were very helpful*; *You were a lovely baby.*

we're we are, *we're nearly home.*

weren't (*informal*) were not.

werewolf *noun* (*plural* **werewolves**) (in myths) a person who sometimes changes into a wolf. [from Old English *wer* = man, + *wolf*]

Wesak see **Vesak**.

west[1] *noun* **1** the direction where the sun sets, opposite east. **2** the western part of something. **3** (**the West**) Europe and North America seen in contrast to other civilisations.

west[2] *adjective* **1** situated in the west, *the west coast.* **2** coming from the west, *a west wind.*

west[3] *adverb* towards the west, *We sailed west.*

westerly *adjective* to or from the west.

western[1] *adjective* of or in the west.

western[2] *noun* a film or story about cowboys or indigenous Americans in western North America.

Westminster System *noun* a form of parliamentary democracy based on that established in the United Kingdom, in which an executive council sits within and is responsible to the legislature, the Crown does not actively participate in government, and the judiciary is independent. [from the name of an inner London borough that contains the Houses of Parliament]

westward *adjective & adverb* towards the west. **westwards** *adverb*

wet[1] *adjective* (**wetter, wettest**) **1** soaked or covered in water or other liquid. **2** not yet dry, *wet paint.* **3** rainy, *wet weather.* **wetly** *adverb*, **wetness** *noun*

wet[2] *verb* (**wetted, wetting**) make a thing wet.

wet[3] *noun* **1** moisture. **2** (**the wet**) the rainy season. [from Old English *wæt* = wet]

wet blanket *noun* (*informal*) a gloomy person who prevents others from enjoying themselves.

wet market *noun* (especially in Asia) a market for the sale of live animals, fresh meat, fish, and produce.

wet nurse *noun* a woman employed to suckle another's child.

wet season *noun* (*Australian*) a period with high rainfall. (The opposite is **dry season**.)

wetsuit *noun* a close-fitting rubber garment worn by a diver etc.

we've we have, *we've found the park.*

whack *verb* hit hard, especially with a stick. **whack** *noun*

whale *noun* a very large sea animal.
a whale of a (*informal*) very good or great, *We had a whale of a time.*

whaler *noun* a person or ship that hunts whales. **whaling** *noun*

wharf (*say* wawf) *noun* (*plural* **wharves** or **wharfs**) a quay where ships are loaded and unloaded.

wharfie *noun* (*Australian informal*) a wharf labourer.

what[1] *adjective* used to ask the amount or kind of something (*What kind of bike have you got?*) or to say how strange or great a person or thing is (*What a fool you are!*).

what[2] *pronoun* **1** what thing or things, *What did you say?* **2** the thing that, *This is what you must do.*
what's what (*informal*) which things are important or useful.

whatever[1] *pronoun* **1** anything or everything, *Do whatever you like.* **2** no matter what, *Keep calm, whatever happens.*

whatever[2] *adjective* of any kind or amount, *Take whatever books you need; There is no doubt whatever.*

wheat *noun* a cereal plant from which flour is made. **wheaten** *adjective*

wheedle *verb* (**wheedled, wheedling**) coax.

wheel[1] *noun* **1** a round device that turns on a shaft that passes through its centre. **2** a horizontal revolving disc on which clay is made into a pot.

wheel[2] *verb* **1** push a bicycle or trolley etc. along on its wheels. **2** move in a curve or circle; change direction and face another way, *He wheeled round in astonishment.*

wheelbarrow *noun* a small cart with one wheel at the front and legs at the back, pushed by handles.

wheelchair *noun* a chair on wheels for a person who cannot walk.

wheeze *verb* (**wheezed, wheezing**) make a hoarse whistling sound as you breathe.
wheeze *noun*, **wheezy** *adjective*

whelk *noun* a shellfish that looks like a snail.

whelp *noun* a young dog; a pup.

when[1] *adverb* at what time; at which time, *When can you come to tea?*

when[2] *conjunction* **1** at the time that, *The bird flew away when I moved.* **2** although; considering that, *Why do you smoke when you know it's dangerous?*

whence *adverb & conjunction* from where; from which.

whenever *conjunction* at whatever time; every time, *Whenever I see it, I smile.*

where[1] *adverb & conjunction* in or to what place or that place, *Where did you put it? Leave it where it is.*

where[2] *pronoun* what place, *Where does she come from?*

whereabouts[1] *adverb* in or near what place.

whereabouts[2] *plural noun* the place where something or somebody is, *Do you know his whereabouts?*

whereas *conjunction* but in contrast, *Some people enjoy sport, whereas others hate it.*

whereby *adverb* by which.

wherefore *adverb* (*old use*) why.

whereupon *conjunction* after which; and then.

wherever *adverb* in or to whatever place.

wherewithal *noun* (*informal*) money or other resources needed for a purpose.

wherry *noun* a light rowing boat; a large light barge.

whet *verb* (**whetted, whetting**) **1** sharpen. **2** stimulate, *whet your appetite.* [from Old English *hwettan* = sharpen]

whether *conjunction* as one possibility; if, *I don't know whether to believe her or not.*

whey (*say* way) *noun* the watery liquid left when milk forms curds.

which[1] *adjective* what particular, *Which way did he go?*

which[2] *pronoun* **1** what person or thing, *Which is your desk?* **2** the person or thing referred to, *The film, which is a musical, will be shown on Saturday.*

> **Usage** When is it correct to use *that* and when should you use *which*? The general rule is that when introducing clauses that define or identify something it is preferable to use *that*: *a book that aims to simplify scientific language. Which* should be used to introduce clauses giving additional information: *the book, which costs $30, has sold a million copies.*

whichever *pronoun & adjective* no matter which; any which, *Take whichever you like.*

whiff *noun* **1** a puff of smoke, gas, etc. **2** a smell.

while[1] *conjunction* **1** during the time that; as long as, *Whistle while you work.* **2** although; but, *She is dark, while her sister is fair.*

while[2] *noun* a period of time; the time spent on something, *a long while.*

while[3] *verb* (**whiled, whiling**)
while away pass time, *She whiled away the day reading.*

whilst *conjunction* while.

whim *noun* a sudden wish to do or have something.

whimper *verb* cry or whine softly.
whimper *noun*

whimsical *adjective* impulsive and playful.
whimsicality *noun*, **whimsically** *adverb*

whine *verb* (**whined, whining**) **1** make a long high miserable cry or a shrill sound. **2** complain in a petty or feeble way.
whine *noun*

whinge *verb* (**whinged, whinging**) (*informal*) whine; grumble persistently. **whinge** *noun*, **whinger** *noun*

whinny *verb* (**whinnied**, **whinnying**) neigh gently or happily. **whinny** *noun*

whip[1] *noun* **1** a cord or strip of leather fixed to a handle and used for hitting people or animals. **2** an official of a political party in parliament.

whip[2] *verb* (**whipped**, **whipping**) **1** hit with a whip. **2** beat cream, eggs, etc. until thick or frothy. **3** move or take suddenly, *He whipped out a gun.*
whip up 1 arouse people's feelings etc., *She whipped up support for her plans.* **2** make something quickly, *She whipped up a skirt in an evening.*

whipbird *noun* an Australian bird with a cry like the crack of a whip.

whiplash injury *noun* a neck injury caused by a sudden jerk of the head, especially in a car accident.

whippet *noun* a small dog rather like a greyhound, used for racing.

whipstick *noun* (*Australian*) a kind of eucalypt with several slim stems.

whirl *verb* turn or spin very quickly. **whirl** *noun*

whirlpool *noun* a whirling current of water.

whirlwind *noun* a strong wind that whirls round a central point.

whirr *verb* make a continuous buzzing sound. **whirr** *noun*

whisk[1] *verb* **1** move or brush away quickly and lightly. **2** beat eggs etc. until they are frothy.

whisk[2] *noun* **1** a device for whisking things. **2** a whisking movement.

whisker *noun* **1** a hair of those growing on a man's face, forming a beard or moustache if not shaved off. **2** a long bristle growing near the mouth of a cat and certain other animals. **whiskery** *adjective*

whisky *noun* (*plural* **whiskies**) a strong alcoholic drink.

whisper *verb* **1** speak very softly. **2** talk secretly. **whisper** *noun*

whist *noun* a card game usually for four people.

whistle[1] *verb* (**whistled**, **whistling**) make a shrill or musical sound, especially by blowing through your lips. **whistler** *noun*

whistle[2] *noun* **1** a whistling sound. **2** a device that makes a shrill sound when air or steam is blown through it.

whistleblower *noun* a person who exposes an irregularity or a crime, especially from within an organisation.

whit *noun* the least possible amount, *not a whit better.* [from an old word *wight* = an amount]

white[1] *noun* **1** the very lightest colour, like snow or salt. **2** (also **White**) a member of a light-skinned race. **3** the transparent substance (*albumen*) round the yolk of an egg, turning white when cooked.

white[2] *adjective* **1** of the colour white. **2** (also **White**) of the human group with light-coloured skin. **3** very pale from the effects of illness or fear etc. **4** (of tea or coffee) with milk. **whiteness** *noun*

white ant *noun* a termite.

whitebait *noun* (*plural* **whitebait**) a small silvery-white fish.

whiteboard *noun* a white plastic board that can be written on with a felt-tipped pen and wiped clean.

white-collar worker *noun* a worker who is not engaged in manual work, e.g. an office worker.

white elephant *noun* a useless possession.

white-hot *adjective* extremely hot; so hot that heated metal looks white.

whiten *verb* make or become whiter.

White Paper *noun* a government report giving information or proposals on an issue. (Compare **Green Paper**.)

whitewash *noun* a white liquid containing lime or powdered chalk, used for painting walls and ceilings etc. **whitewash** *verb*

whither *adverb & conjunction* (*old use*) to what place.

whiting *noun* (*plural* **whiting**) any of several sea or estuarine fish.

Whit Sunday *noun* the seventh Sunday after Easter; Pentecost. **Whitsun** *noun* [from Old English *hwit* = white, because people used to be baptised on that day and wore white clothes]

whittle *verb* (**whittled**, **whittling**) **1** shape wood by trimming thin slices off the surface. **2** reduce something by removing various things from it, *whittle down the cost.*

whiz *verb* (**whizzed**, **whizzing**) **1** move very quickly. **2** sound like something rushing through the air.

whizkid *noun* (*informal*) a brilliant or very successful young person.

who *pronoun* which person or people; the particular person or people, *This is the boy who stole the apples.*

> **Usage** See the entry at *whom*.

whoa *interjection* a command to a horse to stop or stand still.

whoever *pronoun* **1** any or every person who. **2** no matter who.

whole[1] *adjective* complete; not injured or broken.

whole[2] *noun* **1** the full amount. **2** a complete thing.
on the whole considering everything; mainly.

wholehearted *adjective* complete and without reservations, *wholehearted support.*

wholemeal *adjective* made from the whole grain of wheat or other cereal plants.

whole number *noun* a number without fractions.

wholesale[1] *noun* selling goods in large quantities to be resold by others. (Compare **retail**[2].) **wholesaler** *noun*

wholesale[2] *adjective & adverb* **1** on a large scale; including everybody or everything, *wholesale destruction.* **2** in the wholesale trade.

wholesome *adjective* good for health; healthy, *wholesome food.*
wholesomeness *noun*

wholly *noun* completely; entirely.

whom *pronoun* the form of *who* used when it is the object of a verb or comes after a preposition, as in *the boy whom I saw* or *to whom we spoke.*

whoop (*say* woop) *noun* a loud cry of excitement. **whoop** *verb*

whoopee *interjection* a cry of joy.

whooping cough (*say* **hoo**-ping) *noun* an infectious disease that causes spasms of coughing and gasping for breath.

whopper *noun* (*informal*) something very large.

whopping *adjective* (*informal*) very large or remarkable, *a whopping lie.*

whorl *noun* **1** a coil or curved shape. **2** a ring of leaves or petals.

who's **1** who has, *who's got the keys?* **2** who is, *who's the fastest?*

whose *pronoun* belonging to what person or persons; of whom; of which, *Whose house is that?*

why *adverb* for what reason or purpose; the particular reason on account of which, *This is why I came.*

wick *noun* **1** the string that goes through the middle of a candle and is lit. **2** the strip of material that you light in a lamp or heater etc. that uses oil.

wicked *adjective* **1** morally bad or cruel. **2** very bad; severe, *wicked weather.* **3** mischievous, *a wicked smile.* **wickedly** *adverb*, **wickedness** *noun*

wicker *noun* thin canes or twigs woven together to make baskets or furniture etc.
wickerwork *noun*

wicket *noun* **1** a set of three stumps and two bails used in cricket. **2** the part of a cricket ground between or near the wickets.

wicketkeeper *noun* the fielder in cricket who stands behind the batter's wicket.

wide[1] *adjective* **1** measuring a lot from side to side; not narrow. **2** measuring from side to side, *The cloth is one metre wide.* **3** covering a great range, *a wide knowledge of birds.* **4** fully open, *staring with wide eyes.* **5** far from the target, *The shot was wide of the mark.* **widely** *adverb*, **wideness** *noun*

wide[2] *adverb* **1** widely. **2** completely; fully, *wide awake.* **3** far from the target, *The shot went wide.*

widen *verb* make or become wider.

widespread *adjective* existing in many places or over a wide area.

widgeon *noun* a kind of wild duck.

widow *noun* a woman whose spouse has died. **widowed** *adjective*, **widowhood** *noun*

widower *noun* a man whose spouse has died.

width *noun* how wide something is; wideness.

wield *verb* hold something and use it.

wife *noun* (*plural* **wives**) a married woman considered in relation to her spouse.

Wi-Fi *noun* (*trademark*) a facility allowing computers, smartphones, or other devices to connect to the Internet or communicate with one another wirelessly within a particular area. [from *wireless*[2] + an apparently arbitrary second element, after *hi-fi*]

wig *noun* a covering made of real or artificial hair, worn on the head.

wiggle *verb* (**wiggled**, **wiggling**) move from side to side; wriggle. **wiggle** *noun*

wigwam *noun* a dome-shaped hut or tent originally used by North American indigenous people. [from an indigenous North American word, = their house]

wiki *noun* a website or database developed collaboratively by a community of users, allowing any user to add and edit content. [probably from Hawaiian *wiki* = fast, quick]

wild *adjective* **1** living or growing in its natural state, not looked after by people. **2** not cultivated, *a wild landscape.* **3** not civilised, *the Wild West.* **4** not controlled; very violent or excited. **5** stormy; tempestuous. **6** very foolish or unreasonable, *these wild ideas.* **wildly** *adverb*, **wildness** *noun*

wildebeest (*say* **wil**-duh-beest) *noun* a large ox-like antelope. Also called a *gnu.*

wilderness *noun* (*plural* **wildernesses**) a wild uncultivated area; a desert.

wildlife *noun* wild animals.

wile *noun* a piece of trickery.

wilful *adjective* **1** obstinately determined, *a wilful child.* **2** deliberate, *wilful murder.* **wilfully** *adverb*, **wilfulness** *noun* [from *will*[2] + *-ful*]

wilga *noun* a small drought-resistant Australian tree with white flowers. [from Wiradjuri and neighbouring languages *wilgarr*]

will[1] *auxiliary verb* used to express the future tense, questions, or promises.

Usage See the entry for *shall.*

will[2] *noun* **1** the mental power to decide and control what you do. **2** a desire; a chosen decision, *I went to the party against my will.* **3** determination, *They set to work with a will.* **4** a person's attitude towards others, *full of good will.* **5** a written statement of how a person's possessions are to be disposed of after their death.
at will as you like, *You can come and go at will.*

will[3] *verb* **1** use your willpower; influence something by doing this, *I was willing you to win!* **2** bequeath by a will.

willing *adjective* ready and happy to do what is wanted. **willingly** *adverb*, **willingness** *noun*

willow *noun* a tree or shrub with flexible branches, usually growing near water.

willpower *noun* strength of mind to control what you do.

willy-nilly *adverb* whether you want to or not. [from *will I, nill* (= will not) *I*]

willy wagtail *noun* a small Australian bird with a swaying tail when at rest.

willy willy *noun* (*Australian*) a whirlwind or dust storm. [from Yindjibarndi or a neighbouring language *wili-wili*]

wilt *verb* lose freshness or strength; droop.

wily (*say* **wuy**-lee) *adjective* (**wilier**, **wiliest**) cunning; crafty. **wiliness** *noun* [from *wile*]

wimp *noun* (*informal*) a feeble and cowardly person. **wimpish** *adjective*

wimple *noun* a piece of cloth folded round the head and neck, worn by women in the Middle Ages.

win[1] *verb* (**won, winning**) **1** be victorious in a battle, game or contest. **2** get or achieve something by a victory or by using effort or skill etc., *She won the prize.*

win[2] *noun* a victory.

wince *verb* (**winced, wincing**) make a slight movement because of pain or embarrassment etc.

winch[1] *noun* (*plural* **winches**) a device for lifting or pulling things, using a rope or cable etc. that winds on to a revolving drum or wheel.

winch[2] *verb* lift or pull with a winch.

wind[1] (*rhymes with* tinned) *noun* **1** a current of air. **2** gas in the stomach or intestines that makes you feel uncomfortable. **3** breath used for a purpose, e.g. for running or speaking. **4** the wind instruments of an orchestra.
get or **have the wind up** (*informal*) feel frightened.

wind[2] *verb* cause a person to be out of breath, *The climb had winded us.*

wind[3] (*rhymes with* find) *verb* (**wound, winding**) **1** go or turn something in twists, curves, or circles. **2** twist or wrap something round and round upon itself. **3** wind up a watch or clock. **winder** *noun*
wind up 1 make a clock or watch work by tightening its spring. **2** close a business. **3** (*informal*) end up in a place or condition, *He wound up in jail.*

windbag *noun* (*informal*) a person who talks at great length.

windbreak *noun* a screen or row of trees protecting something from the full force of the wind.

windcheater *noun* a windproof jacket or jumper.

winded *adjective* having difficulty breathing because of exertion or a blow to the stomach.

windfall *noun* **1** a fruit blown off a tree by the wind. **2** a piece of unexpected good luck, especially a sum of money.

wind farm *noun* a group of energy-producing wind turbines.

wind instrument *noun* a musical instrument played by blowing, e.g. a flute.

windlass *noun* (*plural* **windlasses**) a device for pulling or lifting things (e.g. a bucket from a well), with a rope or cable that is wound round an axle by turning a handle.

windmill *noun* a mill worked by the wind that turns projecting parts (*sails*).

window *noun* **1** an opening in a wall or roof etc. to let in light and often air, usually filled with glass. **2** the glass in this opening. **3** (in computing) a rectangular area on a computer screen in which information can be displayed. [from Old Norse *vindauga* = wind-eye]

windpipe *noun* the tube by which air passes from the throat to the lungs.

windscreen *noun* the window at the front of a motor vehicle.

windsurfing *noun* surfing on a board that has a sail fixed to it. **windsurfer** *noun*

wind tunnel *noun* a tunnel-like device to produce an airstream past models of aircraft etc. for the study of the wind effects upon them.

wind turbine *noun* a turbine having a large vaned wheel rotated by the wind to generate electricity.

windward *adjective* facing the wind, *the windward side of the ship.*

windy *adjective* with much wind.

wine *noun* **1** an alcoholic drink made from grapes or other plants. **2** dark red colour. [from Latin *vinum* = wine (compare *vine*)]

wing[1] *noun* **1** each of a pair of projecting parts of a bird, bat, or insect, used in flying. **2** each of a pair of long flat projecting parts that support an aircraft while it flies. **3** a projecting part at one end or side of something. **4** (**the wings**) the sides of a theatre stage out of sight of the audience. **5** the part of a motor vehicle's body above a wheel. **6** a player at either end of the forward line in football or hockey etc. **7** a section of a political party, with more extreme opinions than the others.
on the wing flying.
take wing fly away.

wing[2] *verb* **1** fly; travel by means of wings, *The bird winged its way home.* **2** wound a bird in the wing or a person in the arm.

winged *adjective* having wings.

wingless *adjective* without wings.

wink[1] *verb* **1** close and open your eye quickly, especially as a signal to someone. **2** (of a light) flicker; twinkle.

wink[2] *noun* **1** the action of winking. **2** a very short period of sleep, *I didn't sleep a wink.*

winkle[1] *noun* a kind of edible shellfish.

winkle[2] *verb* (**winkled**, **winkling**)
winkle out extract; prise a thing out.

winner *noun* **1** a person or animal etc. that wins. **2** something very successful, *Her latest book is a winner.*

winnings *plural noun* money won.

winnow *verb* toss or fan grain so that the loose dry outer part is blown away.

winsome *adjective* charming.

winter *noun* the coldest season of the year, between autumn and spring. **wintry** *adjective*

wipe *verb* (**wiped**, **wiping**) **1** dry or clean something by rubbing it. **2** spread something over a surface by rubbing. **3** remove data from a magnetic tape or disk. **wiper** *noun*
wipe out 1 cancel, *wipe out the debt.* **2** destroy something completely.

wire[1] *noun* **1** a strand or thin flexible rod of metal. **2** a fence etc. made from wire. **3** a piece of wire used to carry electric current.

wire[2] *verb* (**wired**, **wiring**) **1** fasten or strengthen with wire. **2** fit or connect with wires to carry electric current.

wireless[1] *noun* **1** broadcasting, computer networking, or other communications using radio signals, microwave, etc. **2** (*old use*) radio; a radio set.

wireless[2] *adjective* using radio, microwaves, etc. (as opposed to wires or cables) to transmit signals, *wireless broadband.*
wirelessly *adverb*

wiry *adjective* **1** like wire. **2** lean and strong.

wisdom *noun* **1** being wise. **2** wise sayings.

wisdom tooth *noun* a molar tooth that may grow at the back of the jaw of a person aged about 20 or more.

wise[1] *adjective* knowing or understanding many things; judging well. **wisely** *adverb*

wise[2] *noun* (*old use* or as a suffix) manner or direction, *It is in no wise better*; *otherwise*; *clockwise*; *crosswise.*

wish[1] *verb* **1** feel or say that you would like to have or do something or would like something to happen. **2** say that you hope someone will get something, *Wish me luck!*

wish[2] *noun* (*plural* **wishes**) **1** something you wish for; a desire. **2** the action of wishing, *Make a wish when you blow out the candles.*

wishbone *noun* a forked bone between the neck and breast of a bird (sometimes pulled apart by two people; the person who gets the bigger part can make a wish).

wishful *adjective* desiring something.

wishful thinking *noun* believing something because you want it to be true.

wisp *noun* **1** a few strands of hair or bits of straw etc. **2** a small streak of smoke or cloud etc. **wispy** *adjective*

wisteria (*say* wis-**teer**-ree-uh) *noun* a climbing plant with hanging blue, purple, or white flowers.

wistful *adjective* sadly longing for something.
wistfully *adverb*, **wistfulness** *noun*

wit *noun* **1** intelligence; cleverness, *Use your wits.* **2** a clever kind of humour. **3** a witty person.
at your wits' end not knowing what to do.

witch *noun* (*plural* **witches**) a person, especially a woman, who uses magic to do things. **witchcraft** *noun*

witchdoctor *noun* a tribal magician, credited with powers of healing, divination, and protection against the magic of others.

witchetty *noun* (in full **witchetty grub**) the edible larva of various Australian beetles and moths. [from Adnyamathanha *wityu* = hooked stick used to extract grubs, + *varti* = grub, insect]

with *preposition* used to indicate **1** being in the company or care etc. of (*Come with me*), **2** having (*a man with a beard*), **3** using (*Hit it with a hammer*), **4** because of (*shaking with laughter*), **5** feeling or showing (*We heard it with pleasure*), **6** towards, concerning (*I was*

angry with him), **7** in opposition to; against (*Don't argue with your father*), **8** being separated from (*We had to part with it*).
with it (*informal*) **1** up to date, fashionable. **2** alert.

withdraw *verb* (**withdrew**, **withdrawn**, **withdrawing**) **1** take back or away; remove, *She withdrew money from the bank.* **2** go away from a place or people, *The troops withdrew from the frontier.* **3** cancel a statement, offer, etc. **withdrawal** *noun*

withdrawn *adjective* shy and unsociable.

wither *verb* **1** shrivel; wilt. **2** cause to shrivel or wilt. [from *weather*]

withering *adjective* scornful, *a withering look.*

withers *plural noun* the ridge between a horse's shoulder blades.

withhold *verb* (**withheld**, **withholding**) refuse to give or allow something (e.g. information or permission). [from *with-* = away, + *hold*]

within *preposition & adverb* inside; not beyond something.

without[1] *preposition* **1** not having, *without food.* **2** free from, *without fear.* **3** (*old use*) outside, *without the city wall.*

without[2] *adverb* outside, *We looked at the house from within and without.*

withstand *verb* (**withstood**, **withstanding**) endure something successfully; resist.

withy *noun* (*plural* **withies**) a thin flexible branch for tying bundles etc.

witness[1] *noun* (*plural* **witnesses**) **1** a person who sees or hears something happen, *There were no witnesses to the accident.* **2** a person who gives evidence in a lawcourt.

witness[2] *verb* **1** be a witness of something. **2** sign a document to confirm that it is genuine. [from *wit*]

witted *adjective* having wits of a certain kind, *quick-witted.*

witticism *noun* a witty remark.

wittingly *adverb* intentionally. [from *wit*]

witty *adjective* (**wittier**, **wittiest**) clever and amusing; full of wit. **wittily** *adverb*, **wittiness** *noun*

wizard *noun* **1** a male witch; a magician. **2** a person with amazing abilities. **3** (in computing) a help feature of a software package that automates complex tasks by asking the user a series of easy-to-answer questions. **wizardry** *noun* [from *wise* (originally = *wise man*)]

wizened (*say* **wiz**-uhnd) *adjective* full of wrinkles, *a wizened face.*

WMD *abbreviation* weapon of mass destruction.

woad *noun* a kind of blue dye formerly made from a plant.

wobble *verb* (**wobbled**, **wobbling**) stand or move unsteadily; shake slightly. **wobble** *noun*, **wobbly** *adjective*

woe *noun* **1** sorrow. **2** misfortune. **woeful** *adjective*, **woefully** *adverb*

woebegone *adjective* looking unhappy.

wog[1] *noun* (*offensive*) a foreigner or migrant.

wog[2] *noun* (*Australian informal*) a usually minor illness or infection; the germ etc. causing this.

woggle *noun* a neckerchief ring of leather etc. used by Scouts and Guides.

wok *noun* a large bowl-shaped cooking pan used especially in Asian cookery.

woke[1] *past tense* of **wake**[1], *I woke up early this morning.*

woke[2] *adjective* (*informal*) alert to injustice in society.

woken *past participle* of **wake**[1].

wold *noun* a piece of high open uncultivated land or moor.

wolf[1] *noun* (*plural* **wolves**) a fierce wild animal of the dog family.

wolf[2] *verb* eat something greedily.

woman *noun* (*plural* **women**) a grown-up female human being. **womanhood** *noun*, **womanish** *adjective*, **womanly** *adjective*

womb (*say* woom) *noun* the hollow organ in a female's body where babies develop before they are born. Also called the *uterus.*

wombat *noun* an Australian burrowing marsupial with a thickset body and short legs. [from Darkinyung or an inland dialect of Sydney language *wambaj*]

womma *noun* (also **woma**) an Australian python of arid areas. [from Dieri and neighbouring languages *wama*]

won *past tense & past participle* of **win**[1].

wonder[1] *noun* **1** a feeling of surprise and admiration or curiosity. **2** something that causes this feeling; a marvel.
no wonder it is not surprising.

wonder[2] *verb* **1** feel that you want to know; try to form an opinion, *We are still wondering what to do next.* **2** feel wonder.

wonderful *adjective* marvellous; surprisingly good; excellent. **wonderfully** *adverb*

wonderment *noun* a feeling of wonder.

wondrous *adjective* (*old use*) wonderful.

wont[1] (*say* wohnt) *adjective* (*old use*) accustomed, *He was wont to dress in rags.*

wont[2] *noun* a habit or custom, *He was dressed in rags, as was his wont.*

won't will not, *she won't answer the phone.*

woo *verb* **1** (*old use*) court a woman. **2** seek someone's favour. **wooer** *noun*

wood *noun* **1** the substance of which trees are made. **2** many trees growing close together.

woodcut *noun* an engraving made on wood; a print made from this.

wooded *adjective* covered with growing trees.

wooden *adjective* **1** made of wood. **2** stiff and clumsy. **3** showing no expression or liveliness, *a wooden stare.* **woodenly** *adverb*

woodland *noun* wooded country.

woodpecker *noun* a bird that taps tree trunks with its beak to find insects.

woodwind *noun* wind instruments that are usually made of wood, e.g. the clarinet and oboe.

woodwork *noun* **1** making things out of wood. **2** things made out of wood.

woodworm *noun* the larva of a kind of beetle that bores into wooden furniture etc.

woody *adjective* **1** like wood; consisting of wood. **2** full of trees.

woof *noun* the gruff bark of a dog. **woof** *verb*

wool *noun* **1** the thick soft hair of sheep and goats etc. **2** thread or cloth made from this.

woollen *adjective* made of wool.

woollens *plural noun* woollen clothes.

woolly *adjective* **1** covered with wool or wool-like hair. **2** like wool; woollen. **3** not thinking clearly; vague or confused, *woolly ideas.* **woolliness** *noun*

woolshed *noun* (*Australian*) a shed for shearing and packing wool.

woomera *noun* (*Australian*) an implement traditionally used by Aboriginal people to help throw a spear. [from Sydney language *wamara*]

Woop Woop *noun* (*Australian*) an imaginary remote town or district.

word[1] *noun* **1** a set of sounds or letters that has a meaning, and when written or printed has no spaces between the letters. **2** a promise, *She kept her word.* **3** a command or spoken signal, *Run when I give the word.* **4** a message; information, *We sent word of our safe arrival.*

word for word in exactly the same words.

word[2] *verb* express something in words, *Word the question carefully.*

wording *noun* the way something is worded.

word of honour *noun* a solemn promise.

word-perfect *adjective* having memorised every word perfectly.

word processor *noun* a computer or program used for storing, editing, and printing text.

wordy *adjective* using too many words; not concise.

wore *past tense* of **wear**[1].

work[1] *noun* **1** the use of effort or energy to do something (contrasted with *play* or *recreation*). **2** something you have to do that needs effort or energy. **3** a job; employment. **4** something produced by work, *The teacher marked our work*; *literary works.*

at work working.

out of work having no work; unable to find paid employment.

work[2] *verb* **1** do work. **2** have a job; be employed, *She works in a bank.* **3** act or operate correctly or successfully, *Is the lift working?* **4** make something act; operate, *Can you work the machine?* **5** shape or press etc., *Work the mixture into a paste.* **6** make a way; pass, *The grub works its way into timber.* **7** bring about, *He works miracles.*

work out 1 find an answer by thinking or calculating. **2** have a particular result. **3** exercise.

work up make people become excited; arouse.

workable *adjective* usable; practicable.

workbook *noun* a student's book containing instruction and exercises relating to a particular subject.

worker *noun* **1** a person who works. **2** a member of the working class. **3** a bee or ant etc. that does the work in a hive or colony but does not produce eggs.

working class *noun* people who work for wages, especially in manual or industrial work.

workman *noun* (*plural* **workmen**) a man employed to do manual labour; a worker.

workmanship *noun* a person's skill in working; the result of this.

work of art *noun* a fine picture, building, etc.

workout *noun* a session of physical exercise.

workshop *noun* **1** a place where things are made or mended. **2** a meeting for discussion or group activity.

world *noun* **1** the earth with all its countries and peoples. **2** the universe. **3** the people or things belonging to a certain activity, *the world of sport.* **4** a very great amount, *It will do him a world of good.*

worldly *adjective* **1** of life on earth, not spiritual. **2** interested only in money, pleasure, etc. **worldliness** *noun*

worldwide *adjective & adverb* throughout the world.

World Wide Web *noun* (also **Web**) an extensive information system on the Internet providing facilities for documents to be linked to other documents.

worm[1] *noun* **1** an animal with a long small soft rounded or flat body and no backbone or limbs. **2** an unimportant or unpleasant person. **wormy** *adjective*

worm[2] *verb* move by wriggling or crawling.

wormwood *noun* a woody plant with a bitter taste.

worn[1] *past participle* of **wear**[1].

worn[2] *adjective* **1** damaged by use or wear. **2** looking tired and exhausted.

worried *adjective* feeling or showing worry.

worry[1] *verb* (**worried**, **worrying**) **1** be troublesome to someone; make a person feel slightly afraid. **2** feel anxious. **3** hold something in the teeth and shake it, *The dog was worrying a rat.* **worrier** *noun*

worry[2] *noun* (*plural* **worries**) **1** the condition of worrying; being uneasy. **2** something that makes a person worry. [the verb originally meant 'to strangle']

worse *adjective & adverb* more bad or more badly; less good or less well.

worsen *adjective* make or become worse.

worship[1] *verb* (**worshipped**, **worshipping**) **1** give praise or respect to God or a god. **2** love or respect a person or thing greatly. **worshipper** *noun*

worship[2] *noun* **1** worshipping; religious ceremonies. **2** a title of respect for a mayor or certain magistrates. [from *worth*]

worst *adjective & adverb* most bad or most badly; least good or least well.

worsted *noun* a kind of woollen material.

worth[1] *adjective* **1** having a certain value, *This stamp is worth $100.* **2** deserving something; good or important enough for something, *That book is worth reading.*
worth while worth the time or effort needed, *The job was not worth while.*

> **Usage** Use *worthwhile* when it comes before the noun (e.g. *a worthwhile job*).

worth[2] *noun* value; usefulness.

worthless *adjective* having no value; useless. **worthlessness** *noun*

worthwhile *adjective* important or good enough to do; useful, *a worthwhile job.*

> **Usage** See *worth*[1] for the use of *worth while.*

worthy *adjective* having great merit; deserving respect or support, *a worthy cause.* **worthiness** *noun*
worthy of deserving, *This charity is worthy of your support.*

would *auxiliary verb* used **1** as the past tense of **will**[1] (*We said we would do it*), in questions (*Would you like to come?*), and polite requests (*Would you come in, please?*), **2** with *I* and *we* and the verbs *like, prefer, be glad*, etc. (e.g. *I would like to come; we would be glad to help*), where the strictly correct use is *should*, **3** of something to be expected (*That's just what he would do!*).

would-be *adjective* wanting or pretending to be, *a would-be comedian.*

wouldn't would not, *he wouldn't go swimming.*

wound[1] (*say* woond) *noun* **1** an injury done by a cut, stab, or hit. **2** a hurt to a person's feelings.

wound[2] *verb* **1** cause a wound to a person or animal. **2** hurt a person's feelings.

wound[3] (*say* wownd) *past tense & past participle* of **wind**[3].

wove *past tense* of **weave**[1].

woven *past participle* of **weave**[1].

wow *interjection* (*informal*) a cry of astonishment or admiration, *Wow! That was a great movie.*

wowser *noun* (*Australian*) a person with very strict morals; a spoilsport.

wraith *noun* a ghost.

wrangle *verb* (**wrangled**, **wrangling**) have a noisy argument or quarrel. **wrangle** *noun*

wrap[1] *verb* (**wrapped**, **wrapping**) **1** enclose in soft or flexible material used as a covering. **2** arrange (a flexible covering or garment etc.) around a person or thing. **3** (in computing) cause (text) to be carried over to the next line automatically as the margin is reached.

wrap[2] *noun* **1** a shawl, coat, or cloak etc. **2** a tortilla wrapped around a cold filling, eaten as a sandwich.

wrapper *noun* a piece of paper or other material wrapped round something.

wrath (*rhymes with* cloth) *noun* anger. **wrathful** *adjective*, **wrathfully** *adverb*

wreak (*say* reek) *verb* inflict, *Rain wreaked havoc with the building work.* [from Old English *wrecan* = avenge]

wreath (*say* reeth) *noun* **1** flowers or leaves etc. fastened into a circle, *wreaths of holly.* **2** a curving line of mist or smoke. [compare *writhe*]

wreathe (*say* reeth) *verb* (**wreathed**, **wreathing**) **1** surround or decorate with a wreath. **2** cover, *Their faces were wreathed in smiles.* **3** move in a curve, *Smoke wreathed upwards.*

wreck[1] *verb* **1** damage something, especially a ship, so badly that it cannot be used again. **2** completely ruin chances, hopes, etc.

wreck[2] *noun* **1** a wrecked ship or building or vehicle. **2** a person who is left very weak, *a nervous wreck.* **3** the wrecking of something. [same origin as *wreak*]

wreckage *noun* the pieces of a wreck.

wren *noun* a very small bird with an erect tail.

wrench[1] *verb* twist or pull something violently.

wrench[2] *noun* (*plural* **wrenches**) **1** a wrenching movement. **2** pain caused by parting, *Leaving home was a great wrench.* **3** an adjustable tool rather like a spanner, used for gripping and turning bolts, nuts, etc.

wrest *verb* force or wrench something away, *We wrested the knife from him.*

wrestle *verb* (**wrestled**, **wrestling**) **1** fight by grasping your opponent and trying to throw them to the ground. **2** struggle with a problem etc. **wrestle** *noun*, **wrestler** *noun*

wretch *noun* (*plural* **wretches**) **1** a person who is very unfortunate. **2** a person who is disliked; a rascal.

wretched *adjective* **1** miserable; unhappy. **2** shabby. **3** not satisfactory; causing a nuisance, *This wretched car won't start.* **wretchedly** *adverb*, **wretchedness** *noun*

wriggle *verb* (**wriggled**, **wriggling**) move with short twisting movements. **wriggle** *noun*, **wriggly** *adjective*
wriggle out of avoid work or blame cunningly.

wring *verb* (**wrung**, **wringing**) **1** twist and squeeze a wet thing to get water etc. out of it. **2** squeeze firmly or forcibly. **3** get something by a great effort, *We wrung a promise out of him.* **wring** *noun*

wringer *noun* a device with a pair of rollers for squeezing water out of washed clothes etc.

wrinkle[1] *noun* a small crease; a small furrow or ridge in the skin.

wrinkle[2] *verb* (**wrinkled**, **wrinkling**) make wrinkles in something; form wrinkles.

wrist *noun* the joint that connects the hand and arm.

writ *noun* a formal written command issued by a lawcourt etc.
Holy Writ the Bible.

write *verb* (**wrote**, **written**, **writing**) **1** put letters or words on paper or another surface. **2** be the author or composer of something, *write books or music.* **3** send a letter to somebody. **writer** *noun*, **writing** *noun*
write down put into writing.
write off 1 cancel a debt etc. **2** damage a vehicle so badly that it cannot be repaired.

writhe *verb* (**writhed**, **writhing**) **1** twist your body because of pain. **2** wriggle. **3** suffer because of great shame.

wrong[1] *adjective* **1** incorrect; not true, *the wrong answer.* **2** morally bad; unfair; unjust, *It is wrong to cheat.* **3** not working properly, *There's something wrong with the engine.* **wrongly** *adverb*, **wrongness** *noun*

wrong[2] *adverb* wrongly, *You guessed wrong.*

wrong[3] *noun* something morally wrong; a wrong action; an injustice.
in the wrong having done or said something wrong.

wrong[4] *verb* do wrong to someone; treat a person unfairly.

wrongdoer *noun* a person who does wrong. **wrongdoing** *noun*

wrongful *adjective* unfair; unjust; illegal. **wrongfully** *adverb*

wrote *past tense* of **write**.

wrought *adjective* (of metal) worked by being beaten out or shaped by hammering or rolling etc., *wrought iron.*

wrung *past tense & past participle* of **wring**.

wry *adjective* (**wryer**, **wryest**) **1** twisted or bent out of shape. **2** showing disgust or disappointment or mockery, *a wry grin.* **wryly** *adverb*, **wryness** *noun*

wurley *noun* (*plural* **wurlies**) (*Australian*) (in traditional Aboriginal use) a hut or shelter. [from Kaurna and other languages *warli*]

wuss (*say* wuus) *noun* (*informal*) a feeble or inept person, a wimp. **wussy** *adjective*

WWW *abbreviation* (also **www**) World Wide Web.

x-axis *noun* the principal or horizontal axis of a system of coordinates, points along which have a value of zero for all other coordinates.

X chromosome *noun* (in humans and other mammals) a sex chromosome, two of which are normally present in female cells and only one in male cells.

xenophobia (*say* zen-uh-**foh**-bee-uh) *noun* strong dislike of foreigners. **xenophobic** *adjective* [from Greek *xenos* = foreigner, + *phobia*]

xenotransplantation *noun* the process of grafting or transplanting organs or tissue between members of different species.

X factor *noun* (*informal*) a noteworthy special talent or quality.

Xmas *noun* Christmas. [the X represents the Greek letter chi, the first letter of *Christos* = Christ]

XML *abbreviation* extensible markup language, a subset of SGML, designed for use on the World Wide Web, and compatible with SGML and HTML.

X-rated *adjective* pornographic or indecent.

X-ray[1] *noun* a photograph or examination of the inside of something, especially a part of the body, made by a kind of radiation (called **X-rays**) that can penetrate solid things.

X-ray[2] *verb* make an X-ray of something.

xylophone (*say* **zuy**-luh-fohn) *noun* a musical instrument made of wooden bars that you hit with small hammers. [from Greek *xylon* = wood, + *phone* = sound]

Yy

yabber *verb* (*Australian informal*) talk; chat. **yabber** *noun*

yabby *noun* (*plural* **yabbies**) a small Australian freshwater crayfish. [from Wemba Wemba *yabij*]

yacca *noun* a grass tree. [from Kaurna *yagu* = a kind of gum]

yacht (*say* yot) *noun* **1** a sailing boat used for racing or cruising. **2** a powered vessel used for cruising. **yachting** *noun*, **yachtsman** *noun*, **yachtswoman** *noun* [from Dutch *jaghtschip* = fast pirate ship]

yak[1] *noun* an ox with long hair, found in central Asia. [from Tibetan]

yak[2] *verb* (**yakked**, **yakking**) (*informal*) chatter. **yak** *noun*

yakka *noun* (*Australian informal*) work. [from Yagara *yaga*]

yam *noun* the edible starchy tuber of a tropical plant.

Yank *noun* (*informal*) an American.

yank *verb* (*informal*) pull something strongly and suddenly. **yank** *noun*

yap *verb* (**yapped**, **yapping**) bark shrilly. **yap** *noun*, **yappy** *adjective*

yard[1] *noun* **1** a measure of length, 36 inches or about 91 centimetres. **2** a long pole stretched out from a mast to support a sail.

yard[2] *noun* **1** an enclosed area beside a building or used for a certain kind of work, *a timber yard.* **2** (*Australian & American*) the garden of a house.

yardstick *noun* a standard by which something is measured.

yarmulke *noun* (also **yarmulka**) a small cap traditionally worn on the head by Jewish men. [Yiddish]

yarn *noun* **1** thread spun by twisting fibres together, used in knitting etc. **2** (*informal*) a tale or story; a chat.

yarraman *noun* (*Australian old use*) a horse.

yarran *noun* an Australian acacia with rough bark and an unpleasant smell and yielding a dark brown, durable wood. [from Gamilaraay and nearby languages *yarraan*]

yashmak *noun* a veil worn in public by some Muslim women.

yate *noun* a Western Australian eucalypt yielding a strong timber.

yawl *noun* a kind of sailing or fishing boat.

yawn *verb* **1** open the mouth wide and breathe in deeply when feeling sleepy or bored. **2** form a wide opening, *A pit yawned in front of us.* **yawn** *noun*

y-axis *noun* the secondary or vertical axis of a system of coordinates, points along which have a value of zero for all other coordinates.

yay *interjection* (*informal*) a cry of triumph, approval, or encouragement.

Y chromosome *noun* (in humans and other mammals) a sex chromosome that is normally present only in male cells.

ye *pronoun* (*old use*, in speaking to two or more people) you.

yea (*say* yay) *adverb* (*old use*) yes.

yeah *interjection* (*informal*) a cry of triumph, approval, or encouragement.

year *noun* **1** the time the earth takes to go right round the sun, about 365 ¼ days. **2** the time from 1 January to 31 December. **3** an academic level or grade. **yearly** *adjective & adverb*

yearling *noun* an animal between one and two years old.

yearn *verb* long for something.

yeast *noun* a substance that causes alcohol and carbon dioxide to form as it develops, used in making beer and wine and in baking bread.

yell *verb* give a loud cry; shout. **yell** *noun*

yellow[1] *noun* the colour of butter, egg yolk, or ripe lemons.

yellow[2] *adjective* **1** of yellow colour. **2** (*informal*) cowardly. **yellowness** *noun*

yellowcake *noun* impure uranium oxide obtained during processing of uranuim ore.

yellow fever *noun* a tropical disease with fever and jaundice.

yelp *verb* give a shrill bark or cry. **yelp** *noun*

yen[1] *noun* (*plural* **yen**) the unit of money in Japan. [from Chinese *yuan* = round thing]

yen[2] *noun* a longing. [probably from Chinese]

yes *adverb* used to agree to something (= the statement is correct) or as an answer (= I am here).

yesterday *noun & adverb* the day before today.

yet[1] *adverb* **1** up to this time; by this time, *The mail hasn't come yet.* **2** eventually, *I'll get even with him yet!* **3** in addition; even, *She became yet more excited.*

yet[2] *conjunction* nevertheless, *It is strange, yet it is true.*

yeti *noun* (*plural* **yetis**) a very large animal thought to live in the Himalayas, sometimes called the 'Abominable Snowman'. [from Tibetan]

yew *noun* an evergreen tree with dark green needle-like leaves and red berries.

Yiddish *noun* a language used by Jewish people in or from Europe, originally a German dialect with words from Hebrew and several modern languages.

yield[1] *verb* **1** surrender; do what is asked or ordered; give way, *He yielded to persuasion.* **2** produce as a crop or as profit etc.

yield[2] *noun* the amount yielded or produced, *What is the yield of wheat per hectare?* [from Old English, = pay]

yob *noun* (also **yobbo**) (*informal*) a lout or hooligan.

yodel *verb* (**yodelled**, **yodelling**) sing or shout with the voice continually going from a low note to a high note and back again. **yodeller** *noun*

yoga (*say* **yoh**-guh) *noun* a Hindu system of meditation and self-control.

yoghurt (*say* **yoh**-guht) *noun* milk thickened by the action of certain bacteria, giving it a sharp taste. [Turkish]

yoke[1] *noun* **1** a curved piece of wood put across the necks of animals pulling a cart or plough etc. **2** a shaped piece of wood fitted across a person's shoulders, with a pail or load hung at each end. **3** a close-fitting upper part of a garment, from which the rest hangs.

yoke[2] *verb* (**yoked**, **yoking**) harness or join by means of a yoke.

yokel (*say* **yoh**-kuhl) *noun* a simple country fellow.

yolk (*rhymes with* coke) *noun* the round yellow part inside an egg.

Yom Kippur (*say* yom ki-**poor**) *noun* the Day of Atonement, a solemn Jewish religious festival, a day of fasting and repentance. [Hebrew]

yon *adjective & adverb* (*literary*) yonder.

yonder *adjective & adverb* over there.

yore *noun* **of yore** of long ago, *in days of yore.*

you *pronoun* **1** the person or people being spoken to, *Who are you?* **2** anyone; everyone; one, *You can't tell what will happen next.*

you'd **1** you had, *you'd better not be late.* **2** you would, *I was afraid you'd ask me that.*

you'll you will, *you'll get cold outside.*

young[1] *adjective* having lived or existed for only a short time; not old.

young[2] *noun* children or young animals or birds, *The dove was feeding its young.*

youngster *noun* a young person; a child.

your *adjective* belonging to you.

you're you are, *you're going to get in trouble.*

yours *possessive pronoun* belonging to you. **Yours faithfully** or **sincerely** or **truly** ways of ending a letter before you sign it. (*Yours faithfully* and *Yours truly* are more formal than *Yours sincerely.*)

Usage It is incorrect to write *your's.*

yourself *pronoun* (*plural* **yourselves**) you and nobody else, used to refer back to the subject of a verb, *Have you hurt yourself?* **by yourself** on your own; alone, *Did you do the work all by yourself?*

youth *noun* **1** being young; the time when you are young. **2** a young man. **3** young people. **youthful** *adjective*, **youthfulness** *noun*

you've you have, *you've run out of time.*

yowie *noun* an ape-like monster supposed to inhabit parts of eastern Australia. [perhaps from Yuwaalaraay *yuwi* = dream spirit]

yowl *verb & noun* wail; howl.

yo-yo *noun* (*plural* **yo-yos**) (*trademark*) a round toy that can be made to rise and fall on a string that winds round it.

yuan (*say* yoo-**ahn**) *noun* the unit of money in China.

yuck *interjection* (*informal*) an expression of disgust.

yucky *adjective* (*informal*) disgusting, repulsive.

yule *noun* (also **yuletide**) (*old use*) the Christmas festival.

yum *interjection* (also **yum yum**) (*informal*) used to express pleasure at eating, or at the prospect of eating, a particular food.

yumcha (*say* yum-**chah**) *noun* a Chinese meal in which diners choose from a wide range of dishes served from a trolley. [from Chinese *yin ch'a* = drink tea]

yummy *adjective* (*informal*) tasty; delicious.

yuppy *noun* (also **yuppie**) (*plural* **yuppies**) (*informal*, usually *derogatory*) a young urban professional person. [from the initials of these words]

Zz

zany *adjective* crazily funny.

zap *verb* (**zapped**, **zapping**) (*informal*) **1** attack or destroy something forcefully. **2** move quickly. **3** silence a television commercial using a remote control device. **4** exhaust.

zeal *noun* enthusiasm; keenness. **zealous** (*say* **zel**-uhs) *adjective*, **zealously** *adverb*

zealot (*say* **zel**-uht) *noun* a zealous person; a fanatic.

zebra (*say* **zeb**-ruh) *noun* an African animal of the horse family, with black and white stripes all over its body.

zebra crossing *noun* a place for pedestrians to cross a road safely, marked with broad white stripes.

zebu (*say* **zee**-boo) *noun* a humped ox, found in India, eastern Asia, and Africa.

zenith *noun* **1** the part of the sky directly above you. **2** the highest point, *His power was at its zenith.* [from Arabic *samt ar-ras* = path over the head]

zephyr (*say* **zef**-uh) *noun* a soft gentle wind. [from Greek *Zephyros* = god of the west wind]

zero *noun* (*plural* **zeros**) **1** nought; the figure 0; nothing. **2** the point marked 0 on a thermometer etc. [from Arabic *sifr* = cipher]

zero hour *noun* the time when something is planned to start.

zest *noun* **1** great enjoyment or interest. **2** the peel of an orange, lemon, or other citrus fruit used as flavouring. **zestful** *adjective*, **zestfully** *adverb*

zigzag[1] *noun* a line or route that turns sharply from side to side.

zigzag[2] *verb* (**zigzagged**, **zigzagging**) move in a zigzag.

zilch *noun* (*informal*) nothing.

zillion *noun* (*informal*) an extremely large number.

zinc *noun* a white metal.

zing *noun* (*informal*) vigour; energy.

zip[1] *noun* **1** (also **zipper**) a fastener consisting of two strips of material, each with rows of small teeth that interlock when a sliding tab brings them together. **2** a sharp sound like a bullet going through the air. **3** liveliness; vigour. **zippy** *adjective*

zip[2] *verb* (**zipped**, **zipping**) **1** fasten with a zip. **2** move quickly with a sharp sound.

zit *noun* (*informal*) a pimple.

zither *noun* a musical instrument with many strings stretched over a shallow box-like body.

zodiac (*say* **zoh**-dee-ak) *noun* a strip of sky where the sun, moon, and main planets are found, divided into 12 equal parts (called **signs of the zodiac**), each named after a constellation. [from Greek *zoidion* = image of an animal]

zombie *noun* **1** (in voodoo) a corpse said to have been revived by witchcraft. **2** (*informal*) a person who seems to have no mind or will. [from West African *zumbi* = fetish]

zone *noun* an area of a special kind or for a particular purpose. [Greek, = girdle]

zoo *noun* (*plural* **zoos**) a place where wild animals are kept so that people can look at them or study them. [short for *zoological gardens*]

zoology (*say* zoh-**ol**-uh-jee) *noun* the study of animals. **zoological** *adjective*, **zoologist** *noun* [from Greek *zoion* = animal, + *-logy*]

zoom *verb* **1** move very quickly, especially with a buzzing sound. **2** rise quickly, *Prices had zoomed.* **zoom** *noun*

zoom lens *noun* a camera lens that can be adjusted continuously to focus on things that are close up or far away.

zucchini (*say* zoo-**kee**-nee) *noun* (*plural* **zucchini** or **zucchinis**) a kind of small vegetable marrow. Also called a *courgette.* [from Italian, plural of *zucchino* from *zucca* = gourd]

zygomatic bone *noun* the bone that forms the prominent part of the cheek and the outer side of the eye socket. [from Greek *zugon* = yoke]

zygote *noun* a cell formed by the union of two gametes. [from Greek *zugon* = yoke]

Appendix: Countries of the world

Country	Adjective and Noun
Afghanistan	Afghan
Albania	Albanian
Algeria	Algerian
America (see United States of America)	
Andorra	Andorran
Angola	Angolan
Antigua and Barbuda	Antiguan, Barbudan
Argentina	Argentinian
Armenia	Armenian
Australia	Australian
Austria	Austrian
Azerbaijan	Azerbaijani
Bahamas	Bahamian
Bahrain	Bahraini (pl. -is)
Bangladesh	Bangladeshi (n., pl. -is)
Barbados	Barbadian
Belarus	Belorussian or Byelorussian
Belgium	Belgian
Belize	Belizian
Benin	Beninese
Bhutan	Bhutanese
Bolivia	Bolivian
Bosnia and Herzegovina	Bosnian, Herzegovinian
Botswana	Motswana, pl. Batswana
Brazil	Brazilian
Brunei	Bruneian
Bulgaria	Bulgarian
Burkina Faso	Burkinese
Burma (see Myanmar)	Burmese
Burundi	Burundian
Cambodia	Cambodian
Cameroon	Cameroonian
Canada	Canadian
Cape Verde Islands	Cape Verdean
Central African Republic	Central African
Chad	Chadian
Chile	Chilean
China	Chinese
Colombia	Colombian
Comoros	Comoran
Congo	Congolese
Congo, Democratic Republic of (formerly Zaire)	
Costa Rica	Costa Rican
Croatia	Croat or Croatian
Cuba	Cuban
Cyprus	Cypriot
Czech Republic	Czech
Denmark	Danish (a.), Dane (n.)
Djibouti	Djiboutian
Dominica	Dominican

Country	Adjective and Noun
Dominican Republic	Dominican
East Timor	East Timorese
Ecuador	Ecuadorean
Egypt	Egyptian
El Salvador	Salvadorean
Equatorial Guinea	Equatorial Guinean
Eritrea	Eritrean
Estonia	Estonian
Eswatini	Swazi
Ethiopia	Ethiopian
Fiji	Fijian
Finland	Finnish (a.), Finn (n.)
France	French (a.), Frenchman (n.), Frenchwoman (n.)
Gabon	Gabonese
Gambia	Gambian
Georgia	Georgian
Germany	German
Ghana	Ghanaian
Greece	Greek
Grenada	Grenadian
Guatemala	Guatemalan
Guinea	Guinean
Guinea-Bissau	Guinean
Guyana	Guyanese
Haiti	Haitian
Holland (see Netherlands)	
Honduras	Honduran
Hungary	Hungarian
Iceland	Icelandic (a.), Icelander (n.)
India	Indian
Indonesia	Indonesian
Iran	Iranian
Iraq	Iraqi (pl. -is)
Ireland, Republic of	Irish (a.), Irishman (n.), Irishwoman (n.)
Israel	Israeli (pl. -is)
Italy	Italian
Ivory Coast	Ivorian
Jamaica	Jamaican
Japan	Japanese
Jordan	Jordanian
Kazakhstan	Kazakh
Kenya	Kenyan
Kiribati	I-Kiribati
Korea	Korean
Kosovo	Kosovar
Kuwait	Kuwaiti (pl. -is)
Kyrgyzstan	Kyrgyz
Laos	Laotian
Latvia	Latvian
Lebanon	Lebanese

Country	Adjective and Noun
Lesotho	Mosotho (n.; pl. Basotho)
Liberia	Liberian
Libya	Libyan
Liechtenstein	Liechtensteiner
Lithuania	Lithuanian
Luxemburg	Luxemburger (n.)
Madagascar	Malagasy or Madagascan
Malawi	Malawian
Malaysia	Malaysian
Maldives	Maldivian
Mali	Malian
Malta	Maltese
Marshall Islands	Marshallese
Mauritania	Mauritanian
Mauritius	Mauritian
Mexico	Mexican
Micronesia, Federated States of	Micronesian
Moldova	Moldovan
Monaco	Monégasque or Monacan
Mongolia	Mongolian
Montenegro	Montenegrin
Morocco	Moroccan
Mozambique	Mozambican
Myanmar	Myanmarese
Namibia	Namibian
Nauru	Nauruan
Nepal	Nepalese
Netherlands, the	Dutch (a.), Dutchman (n.), Dutchwoman (n.) or Netherlander
New Zealand	New Zealander (n.)
Nicaragua	Nicaraguan
Niger	Nigerien
Nigeria	Nigerian
North Korea	North Korean
North Macedonia	North Macedonian
Norway	Norwegian
Oman	Omani (pl. -is)
Pakistan	Pakistani (pl. -is)
Palau	Palauan
Panama	Panamanian
Papua New Guinea	Papua New Guinean
Paraguay	Paraguayan
Peru	Peruvian
Philippines	Philippine (a.), Filipino (n., pl. -os), Filipina (n.fem.)
Poland	Polish (a.), Pole (n.)
Portugal	Portuguese
Qatar	Qatari
Romania	Romanian
Russian Federation	Russian
Rwanda	Rwandan

Country	Adjective and Noun
St Kitts-Nevis	Kittitian, Nevisian
St Lucia	St Lucian
St Vincent and the Grenadines	Vincentian, Grenadian
Samoa	Samoan
San Marino	Sanmarinese
São Tomé and Príncipe	São Toméan
Saudi Arabia	Saudi Arabian or Saudi
Senegal	Senegalese
Serbia	Serb or Serbian
Seychelles	Seychellois
Sierra Leone	Sierra Leonean
Singapore	Singaporean
Slovak Republic	Slovak
Slovenia	Slovene or Slovenian
Solomon Islands	Solomon Islander (n.)
Somalia	Somali (pl. -is)
South Africa	South African
South Korea	South Korean
South Sudan	South Sudanese
Spain	Spanish (a.), Spaniard (n.)
Sri Lanka	Sri Lankan (a.)
Sudan	Sudanese
Suriname	Surinamese or Surinamer (n.)
Swaziland (see Eswatini)	
Sweden	Swedish (a.), Swede (n.)
Switzerland	Swiss
Syria	Syrian
Taiwan	Taiwanese
Tajikistan	Tajik or Tadjik
Tanzania	Tanzanian
Thailand	Thai
Togo	Togolese
Tonga	Tongan
Trinidad and Tobago	Trinidadian, Tobagonian or Tobagan
Tunisia	Tunisian
Turkey	Turkish (a.), Turk (n.)
Turkmenistan	Turkem or Turkomen
Tuvalu	Tuvaluan
Uganda	Ugandan
Ukraine	Ukranian
United Arab Emirates	Emirian
United Kingdom	British (a.), Briton (n.)
United States of America	American
Uruguay	Uruguayan
Uzbekistan	Uzbek
Vanuatu	Vanuatuan or Ni-Vanuatu
Vatican City	Vatican (a.)
Venezuela	Venezuelan
Vietnam	Vietnamese
Yemen	Yemeni (pl. -is)
Zambia	Zambian
Zimbabwe	Zimbabwean